SCARBOROUGH ■ ZIMMEREI

File   Edit   View   Go   Help   8:23 AM

Netscape: Entreprenuer and Small Business Resource Site

Back Forward Reload Home Search Guide Images Print Security Stop   N

Netsite: http://www.prenhall.com/scarbzim/

Effective Small Business Management teaches you how to use the Internet as a profitable business tool.

New to this edition, our Companion Web site provides the resources that help you use the Internet as an invaluable teaching, learning, and business tool.

◆ Over 1,250 small business management/entrepreneurship links to help harness the power of the Internet as a business and research tool.

◆ WWW activities (in addition to those that appear in every chapter in the text) get students onto the Web, a powerful business tool, teaching students to use the Web for research and learning.

◆ 569 full color PowerPoint slides bring the concepts to life. The slides can be accessed from the Internet or downloaded for use in class.

◆ An on-line study guide with multiple choice questions to ensure that students understand the content of each chapter and to help them prepare for tests. Students can submit their answers to the server for grading and receive immediate feedback, including page references to the book for reviewing questions they answered incorrectly. Students can also e-mail their results to the instructor.

◆ Overviews of each chapter complete with learning objectives, a preview of the chapter's content, and hyperlinks related to each chapter.

◆ Monthly updates focus on articles that relate to topics in the textbook.

ED TO THE WEB

SIXTH EDITION

Effective Small Business Management
An Entrepreneurial Approach

Norman M. Scarborough
Presbyterian College

Thomas W. Zimmerer
Drury College

Prentice Hall, Upper Saddle River, New Jersey 07458

Senior Editor: Stephanie Johnson
Editorial Assistant: Hersch Doby
Editor-in-Chief: Natalie Anderson
Assistant Editor: Shane Gemza
Marketing Manager: Michael Campbell
Associate Managing Editor: Judith Leale
Permissions Coordinator: Monica Stipanov
Manufacturing Buyer: Ken Clinton
Manufacturing Supervisor: Arnold Vila
Senior Manufacturing Manager: Vincent Scelta
Senior Designer: Kevin Kall
Design Manager: Patricia Smythe
Interior Design: Digitex
Illustrator (Interior):   Warren Fischbach
Cover Illustration: Adam Cotten/Photonica
Cover Design: Karen Quigley
Composition: Rainbow Graphics, LLC

Library of Congress Cataloging-in-Publication Data
Scarborough, Norman M.
    Effective small business management : an entrepreneurial approach
/ Norman M. Scarborough, Thomas W. Zimmerer. — 6th ed.
        p.   cm.
    Includes bibliographical references and index.
    ISBN 0-13-080708-7 (hardcover)
    1. Small business—Management.   2. New business enterprises—
Management.   3. Small business—United States—Management.   4. New
business enterprises—United States—Management.   I. Zimmerer,
Thomas.   II. Title.
HD62.7.S27   1999
658.02′2—dc21   98-27731
                                                                    CIP

Prentice-Hall International (UK) Limited, London
Prentice-Hall of Australia Pty. Limited, Sydney
Prentice-Hall Canada, Inc., Toronto
Prentice-Hall Hispanoamericana, S.A., Mexico
Prentice-Hall of India Private Limited, New Delhi
Prentice-Hall of Japan, Inc., Tokyo
Pearson Education Asia Pte. Ltd., Singapore
Editora Prentice-Hall do Brasil, Ltda., Rio de Janeiro

Printed in the United States of America
10 9 8 7

Brief Contents

Contents

Section II   BUILDING THE BUSINESS PLAN: BEGINNING CONSIDERATIONS   39

In the Footsteps of an Entrepreneur
Grading the Mission Statement 44

In the Footsteps of an Entrepreneur
What's the Difference? 52

Gaining the Competitive Edge
The Power of Written Goals and Objectives 54

Wired to the Web
Bookstore Wars 62

Gaining the Competitive Edge
What's in a Name? 74

Gaining the Competitive Edge
How to Avoid a Business Divorce 82

Gaining the Competitive Edge
How to Avoid Corporate Woes 88

In the Footsteps of an Entrepreneur
Which Form of Ownership Is Best? 91

Wired to the Web
A Plan for the Future 95

4. Franchising and the Entrepreneur   101

5. Buying an Existing Business   134

Section III   BUILDING THE BUSINESS PLAN: MARKETING AND FINANCIAL CONSIDERATIONS   171

8. Managing Cash FLow 245

9. Crafting a Winning Business Plan 279

Section V PUTTING THE BUSINESS PLAN TO WORK: SOURCES OF FUNDS 411

Section VI   LOCATION AND LAYOUT: KEY CRITERIA   491

Section VII CONTROLLING THE SMALL BUSINESS: TECHNIQUES FOR ENHANCING PROFITABILITY 539

In the Footsteps of an Entrepreneur
Why Certify? 546

Gaining the Competitive Edge
A Funny Thing Happened on the Way to Your Business 555

In the Footsteps of an Entrepreneur
Fewer Surprises Are a Good Thing 565

Wired to the Web
The Power of the Web 569

In the Footsteps of an Entrepreneur
A High-Tech Salvage Yard 580

In the Footsteps of an Entrepreneur
HOG Heaven 586

In the Footsteps of an Entrepreneur
The Best Hardware Store in the World 592

Preface

The field of entrepreneurship is growing at an incredible rate, not only in the United States but across the world as well. People of all ages, backgrounds, and stations of life are launching businesses of their own and, in the process, are reshaping the global economy. As the twenty-first century dawns, small companies are discovering that the natural competitive advantages resulting from their size—speed, flexibility, sensitivity to customers' needs, creativity, spirit of innovation, and many others—enable them to compete successfully with companies many times their size and with budgets to match. As large companies struggle to survive wrenching changes in competitive forces by downsizing, mergers, and restructuring, the unseen army of small businesses continues to flourish and to carry the economy on its back. Entrepreneurs willing to assume the risks of the market to gain its rewards are the heart of capitalism. We need look no further than the economies of those nations that are throwing off decades of control and central planning in favor of capitalism to see where the process begins. In every case, it is the entrepreneurs creating small companies that lead those nations out of the jungles of economic oppression to higher standards of living and hope for the future. Even in countries that stubbornly cling to the fragments of communism, entrepreneurs survive. They operate businesses in underground economies, often producing as much or more value than the "official" economy does.

In the United States, we can be thankful that the small business sector is strong and thriving. Small companies deliver the goods and services we use every day, provide jobs and training for millions of workers, and lead the way in creating the products and services that will make our lives easier and more enjoyable in the future. Small businesses were responsible for introducing to the world the elevator, the airplane, FM radio, the zipper, the personal computer, and a host of other marvelous inventions. Only the imaginations of the next generation of entrepreneurs—of which you may be a part—can see what other fantastic products and services lie in our future! Whatever those ideas may be, we can be sure of one thing: Small businesses will be there to deliver them.

The purpose of this book is to excite you about the possibilities, the challenges, and the rewards of becoming an entrepreneur and to provide the tools you will need to be successful if you choose the path of the entrepreneur. It is not an easy road to follow, but the rewards—both tangible and intangible—are well worth the risks. Not only may you be rewarded financially for your business idea, but, like entrepreneurs the world over, you will be able to work at something you love doing!

This edition of *Effective Small Business Management* provides the material you will need to launch and manage a small business successfully in the hotly competitive environment of the twenty-first century. In writing this edition, we have worked hard to provide you with plenty of practical, hands-on tools and techniques to make your business venture a success. Many people launch businesses every year, but only some succeed. This book teaches you the right way to launch and manage a small business with the staying power to succeed and grow.

Text Features

- *Thorough coverage of the World Wide Web (WWW).* One of the most important business tools in existence today is the World Wide Web. Still in its infancy as a business tool, it is already proving to be a powerful force in reshaping the face of business. *Effective Small Business Management,* sixth edition, offers the most comprehensive coverage of the WWW of any book in the market. In these pages, you will find many references to the Web, ideas for using the Web as a business tool, and examples of entrepreneurs who have discovered the power of the Web. Every chapter contains a Wired to the Web feature that is designed to get you onto the Web to research topics, gather data, solve problems, and engage in a variety of other activities that will make you a more "Web-wise" entrepreneur.

- *An impressive Web site that both professors and students will find extremely useful.* Locate the Web site <**http://prenhall.com/scarbzim**> for *Effective Small Business Management,* sixth edition. This site includes many useful features, including a Business Plan Evaluation Scale, a "Before You Start" checklist, a list of hundreds of links to useful small business sites (organized by topic and ranging from advertising and business planning to market research and taxes), and additional cases, including "Family Business Incidents": short cases giving students valuable insight into the special problems and opportunities of running a small family business. For professors, the site contains a full set of transparencies (prepared by one of the authors and professionally designed for teaching) as well as other support material for their courses.

- *Text material that is relevant, practical, and key to entrepreneurial success.* You will also find it easy and interesting to read. This edition offers streamlined coverage of the topics you will need to know about when you launch your own business without sacrificing the quality or the content of earlier editions of this book.

- *Updated coverage of important topics such as:*

  Finding sources of financing, both equity and debt

  Conducting business in global markets

- Boxed features that follow four important themes:

  Wired to the Web. Web-based activities take students to the World Wide Web, where they search for data, research relevant topics, and experience firsthand the power of the Web as a tool that will influence the way companies do business in the twenty-first century.

  In the Footsteps of an Entrepreneur. In-depth, interesting stories tell how successful entrepreneurs are using the concepts covered in the text and reinforce the learning objectives.

  Gaining the Competitive Edge. This hands-on, how-to feature offers practical advice on a particular topic that students can use to develop a competitive edge for their business.

  Small Business Across the Globe. International examples reinforce the idea that small companies are not limited to doing business within the borders of the United States. This feature shows students that many prime business opportunities lie in the global business arena.

- *Lots of examples.* Examples help people learn. The many examples in this edition are set off in italics. These illustrations tell how entrepreneurs are using the concepts covered in the text to make their businesses more successful. These examples are also a great way to stimulate creativity.

- *Emphasis on building and using a business plan.* Chapter 9 is devoted to building a business plan, and features in many other chapters reinforce the business planning process.

- *A sample business plan for a business, Nature's Oven.* Many courses in entrepreneurship and small business management require students to write business plans. Students of entrepreneurship find it helpful to have a model to guide them as they build their own plans.

- *Features in every chapter that help students master the material.* Learning objectives introduce each chapter, and they appear in the text margins at the appropriate places to keep students focused on what they are learning. Chapter summaries are organized by learning objectives as well. Experiential exercises entitled "Step into the Real World" invite students to learn about the exciting world of entrepreneurship firsthand by giving them interesting assignments that encourage them to interact with practicing entrepreneurs.

*A*cknowledgments

Behind every author team is a staff of professionals who work extremely hard to bring a book to life. They handle the thousands of details involved in transforming a rough manuscript into the finished product you see before you. Their contributions are immeasurable, and we appreciate all they did to make this book successful. We have been blessed to work with the following outstanding publishing professionals:

- Stephanie Johnson, acquisitions editor, who always performed her often-difficult job professionally, tirelessly, and cheerfully. She skillfully steered this took into a safe harbor through more than its share of treacherous shoals.

- Shane Gemza, assistant editor, who supervised all of the components of the teaching package that plays such a vital role in the success of this book.

- Judith Leale, production editor, who managed to keep this project on schedule despite many obstacles that were beyond her control.

- Margo Quinto, copy editor, whose eye for detail is truly amazing. Her eagerness for perfection played a major role in making this book fun to read.

- David Nusspickel, multimedia project manager, who is truly a Web master. He brought to life the superb World Wide Web site we originally envisioned, adding many outstanding features of his own design along the way. This team of dedicated professionals truly is the best editorial and production team with which we have ever worked. We are grateful for them and their tireless efforts.

- Dawn Marie Reisner and Hersch Doby, editorial assistants, who handled so capably the many details involved in putting together this book.

- Tami Wederbrand, marketing manager, who gave us many ideas based on her extensive contact with those who count the most: our customers.

Especially important in the development of the sixth edition were the following professors, who reviewed the manuscript and provided valuable input that improved the final product. Sol Ahiarah, Buffalo State College; John E. Butler, University of Washington; Mary Lou Lockerby, College of DuPage; and Charles N. Toftoy, George Washington University.

We also are grateful to our colleagues who support us in the sometimes grueling process of writing a book: Sam Howell, Foard Tarbert, Meredith Holder, Suzanne Smith, Jerry Slice, and Jody Lipford.

Finally, we thank Cindy Scarborough and Linda Zimmerer, for their love, support, and understanding while we worked many long hours to complete *Effective Small Business Management,* sixth edition. For them, this project represents a labor of love.

Norman M. Scarborough
Presbyterian College
Clinton, South Carolina
e-mail: nmscarb@cs1.presby.edu

Thomas W. Zimmerer
Director, Breech School of Business
Professor of Management
Drury College
Springfield, Missouri

CHAPTER

1

Entrepreneurs: The Driving Force Behind Small Business

Real success is finding your lifework in the work that you love.

—David McCullough

An entrepreneur is the kind of person who will work 16 hours a day just to avoid having to work 8 hours a day for someone else.

—Anonymous

Upon completion of this chapter, you will be able to

1. Define the role of the entrepreneur in business—in the United States and across the globe.

2. Describe the entrepreneurial profile.

3. Describe the benefits and opportunities of owning a small business.

4. Describe the potential drawbacks of owning a small business.

5. Explain the forces that are driving the growth in entrepreneurship.

6. Discuss the role of diversity in small business and entrepreneurship.

7. Describe the contributions small businesses make to the U.S. economy.

8. Describe the small business failure rate and explain why small businesses fail.

9. Put business failure into the proper perspective.

10. Analyze the major pitfalls involved in managing a small business and understand how small business owners can avoid them.

1. Define the role of the entrepreneur in business—in the United States and across the globe.

*T*his is the age of the entrepreneur! Never before have more people been realizing that Great American Dream of owning and operating their own business. A study by the Entrepreneurial Research Con-

1

sortium found that more than 35 million U.S. households—37 percent of the U.S. total—"have an intimate involvement in a new or small business." Approximately 18 million of those households include someone currently running a business, and another 6.8 million include someone trying to start a business.[1] This resurgence of the entrepreneurial spirit is the most significant economic development in recent business history. These heroes of the new economy are rekindling an intensely competitive business environment that had once disappeared from the landscape of U.S. business. With amazing vigor, their businesses have introduced innovative products and services, pushed back technological frontiers, created new jobs, opened foreign markets, and, in the process, sparked the U.S. economy into regaining its competitive edge in the world.

Scott Cook, co-founder of Intuit Inc., a highly successful publisher of personal financial software, explains the new attitude toward entrepreneurship and the vital role small businesses play:

> *Small business is cool now, and I don't mean that lightly. . . . People are seeing that the stuff that makes our lives better comes from business more often than it comes from government. It used to be that there was an exciting part of big business that attracted people. But today it's the reverse; small companies are the heroes . . . and now the entrepreneurs get the attention.*[2]

Record numbers of entrepreneurs have been launching businesses since the mid-1970s (see Figure 1.1), and there is no indication that this trend is slowing. Increasing numbers of young people are choosing entrepreneurship as a career rather than joining the ranks of the

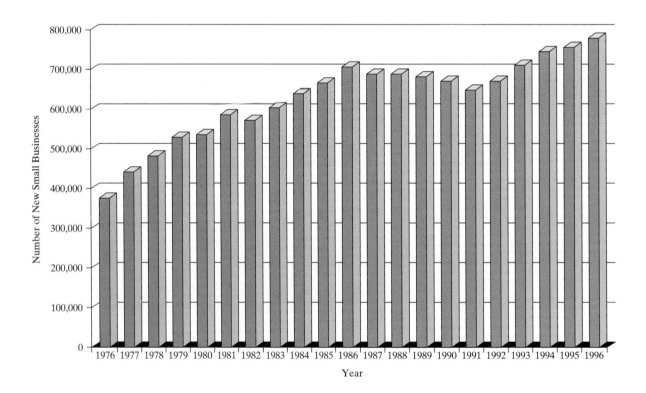

Figure 1.1 **Number of New Incorporations in the United States, 1976–1996** Source: Dun & Bradstreet.

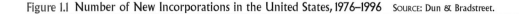

pin-striped masses in major corporations. In a recent survey of college seniors, 49 percent of the men and 31 percent of the women said they were interested in pursuing entrepreneurship when they graduate.[3] The Entrepreneurial Research Consortium reported that 10 percent of people who call themselves students are starting their own companies.[4] In short, the probability that you will become an entrepreneur at some point in your life has never been higher!

Current conditions suggest that we may be on the crest of a new wave of entrepreneurial activity—not only in the United States but across the globe as well. Technology makes it possible for companies to accomplish more with fewer people. The largest U.S. companies have engaged in massive downsizing campaigns, dramatically cutting the number of managers and workers on their payrolls. This flurry of "pink slips" has spawned a new population of entrepreneurs—"castoffs" from large corporations (many of whom thought they would be lifetime ladder climbers in their companies) with solid management experience and many productive years left before retirement. This downsizing has all but destroyed the long-standing notion of job security in large corporations. As a result, people who once saw launching a business as being too risky now see it as the ideal way to create their own job security.

This downsizing trend among large companies has created a more significant philosophical change. It has ushered in an age in which "small is beautiful." Twenty-five years ago, competitive conditions favored large companies with their hierarchies and layers of management; today, with the pace of change constantly accelerating, fleet-footed, agile small companies have the competitive advantage. These nimble competitors can dart into and out of market niches; they can quickly exploit opportunities; and they can use technology to create in weeks or months products and services that it once took years and all of the resources of a giant corporation to produce. The balance has tipped in favor of small, entrepreneurial companies. Intuit Inc.'s Scott Cook explains, "Only a few years back, small businesses were trying to act like big businesses. . . . Now big businesses are trying to act like small businesses."[5]

Another significant shift in the bedrock of our nation's economic structure is influencing this swing in favor of small companies. The nation is rapidly moving away from an industrial economy to a knowledge-based one. What matters now is not so much the factors of production but knowledge and information. The final impact of this shift will be as dramatic as the move from an agricultural economy to an industrial one that occurred 200 years ago in the United States. A knowledge-based economy favors small businesses because the cost of managing and transmitting knowledge and information is very low, and computer- and information-technology are driving these costs lower still.

The United States is not the only nation to benefit from the surge in entrepreneurship; Eastern European countries, Vietnam, Russia, and many others whose economies were state-controlled and centrally planned are now fertile ground for growing small businesses. Even in communist China, entrepreneurship is flourishing and creating jobs—about 100 million of them since economic reform began in 1978.[6] The number of small private companies, called town and village enterprises (TVEs), has grown from 1.4 million to 20.8 million, and their share of China's industrial output has climbed from just 9 percent to more than 40 percent.[7] *Pan Ning, a former Chinese government official, left the security of his government job to launch a TVE in 1983 after he had traveled around the country looking for opportunities. What he discovered was a tremendous demand for refrigerators. With $30,000 from the Rongqi township as seed capital, Ning launched Rongqi's Guangdong Kelon Electrical Holdings, which today is China's largest refrigerator manufacturer. The company recently became the first TVE to go public outside China, and its shares are traded on the Hong Kong stock exchange.*[8]

Wherever they may choose to launch their companies, these business builders continue to embark on one of the most exhilarating, and one of the most frightening, adventures ever known: launching a business. It is never easy, but it can be incredibly rewarding, both financially and emotionally. One successful business owner claims that an entrepreneur is "anyone who wants to experience the deep, dark canyons of uncertainty and ambiguity and wants to walk the breathtaking highlands of success. But I caution: Do not plan to walk the latter until you have experienced the former."[9] One writer calls it "life without a safety net—thrilling and dangerous."[10] Still, true entrepreneurs see owning a business as the real measure of success. Indeed, entrepreneurship often provides the only avenue for success to those who otherwise might have been denied the opportunity.

Who are these entrepreneurs, and what drives them to work so hard with no guarantee of success? What forces lead them to risk so much and to make so many sacrifices in an attempt to achieve an ideal? Why are they willing to give up the security of a steady paycheck working for someone else to become the last person to be paid in their own companies? This chapter will examine the entrepreneur, the driving force behind the U.S. economy.

*W*hat Is an Entrepreneur?

2 Describe the entrepreneurial profile.

An **entrepreneur** is a person who creates a new business in the face of risk and uncertainty for the purpose of achieving profit and growth by identifying opportunities and assembling the necessary resources to capitalize on them. Entrepreneurs usually start with nothing more than an idea, often a simple one, and then assemble the resources necessary to transform that idea into a sustainable business. "The entrepreneur's job is to put everything together, wearing 10 different hats, juggling 20 different balls, relying on [his or her] own knowledge and instincts and creativity to get . . . to positive cash flow," says one expert.[11]

Many people dream of owning their own business. A recent survey by KRC Research and Consulting found that 55 percent of Americans want to be their own boss.[12] Most of those dreamers will never actually launch a company. Those who do take the entrepreneurial plunge, however, will experience the thrill of creating something grand from nothing; they will also discover the challenges and the difficulties of building a business "from scratch." Researchers have invested a great deal of time and effort over the last decade studying entrepreneurs and trying to paint a clear picture of "the entrepreneurial personality." Although no study has isolated a particular set of traits required for success, we can provide a brief summary of the several characteristics entrepreneurs tend to exhibit: an entrepreneurial profile.[13]

1. *Desire for responsibility*. Entrepreneurs feel a personal responsibility for the outcome of ventures in which they are associated. They prefer to be in control of their resources, and they use those resources to achieve self-determined goals.

2. *Preference for moderate risk*. Entrepreneurs are not wild risk takers; they are calculating risk takers. Unlike "high-rolling, riverboat" gamblers, they rarely "gamble." The entrepreneur looks at a project or venture in terms of some personal level of perceived risk. The goal may be high—even impossible—in others' perceptions, but the entrepreneur has usually thought through the situation and believes that the goal is reasonable and attainable. Paul Hawken, co-founder of Smith & Hawken, a highly successful mail-order garden-tool company, explains:

   Good entrepreneurs are risk avoiders, not risk takers. They appear to be risk takers because they see the market differently than the rest of us do; they see a product or service that will converge with how the culture is changing. Once they create it, they methodically eliminate all the factors that will prevent them from getting to market. They become risk eliminators.[14]

IN THE FOOTSTEPS OF AN ENTREPRENEUR

Creativity and Opportunity: Hallmarks of the Entrepreneur

*T*wo characteristics common to entrepreneurs are creativity and an eye for opportunity. The entrepreneurs in the following stories are living proof!

Pickled Trees When Dennis Gabrick started Preserved Treescapes International, Inc. (PTI) in 1987, he had difficulty explaining to the architects and interior designers he was targeting exactly what he was selling. "People would look at me and say, 'You're trying to sell me an embalmed palm?' And I would say, 'Please, they're not embalmed; they're preserved.'" Preserved Trees International takes branches and leaves from live trees (without killing the trees) and preserves them in a special solution. Workers attach the limbs and leaves to a metal-core trunk covered with real bark. The result: a "pickled" tree that looks real but never needs watering!

Gabrick got the idea for PTI while working as a sales executive for a Swedish company after he met Per Monie, a Swede who had developed a solution that preserved plant material. "We discovered that one in every three live trees planted indoors dies or needs to be replaced each year," he says. "It becomes very costly." Using Monie's formula and Gabrick's money, the partners started preserving small plants for the floral industry. Soon they graduated to trees, and, in 1989, they convinced the Mirage hotel in Las Vegas to let PTI install 200 preserved palm trees. That proved to be the company's big break. Tree prices range from $100 to $300 a foot, but PTI has been successful by showing customers how preserved trees actually save them money. PTI has sold more than 10,000 trees, some as tall as 72 feet, and generates sales of $6.5 million a year. Gabrick and Monie have already opened offices in England, Thailand, and Australia. "We've . . . started a whole new industry," says Gabrick.

A Song of Love David Pearl had no idea that a business would spring from a special request from a good friend. His friend told him that he knew a young woman who had always wanted to be serenaded. Pearl's serenade was to be a surprise "gift" from a group of her friends. He recalls the event: "Before I knew it, I was singing Leoncavallo's "Mattinata" on the steps of an Edwardian house in north London. At the end, a sylph in a red dress ran to the door, gave me a hug and a not entirely platonic kiss. Joanna and I were married two years later." Thinking that there might be a market for serenading, the couple set up Serenading Service, a business that keeps alive a practice that started in sixteenth-century Italy and spread across Europe. Complete with guitars, mandolin, a ladder, champagne, and a dozen roses, the serenade usually brings a tear to the eye of the recipient as the singer expresses "a vocal celebration of love that can make the stiffest upper lip tremble," says Pearl. He recalls one client who hired the company to serenade her husband and warned that he was completely unsentimental. "Our soprano had hardly sung a note when the Man of Stone was awash with tears," he says. Even the serenade business has occupational hazards, however. While David serenades, Joanna sometimes must convince overzealous neighbors that the serenaders are not burglars.

A Hopping Business In 1953, Richard Fluker bought a cricket farm. In the early days of the business, the only market for crickets was for fish bait. Today, however, Fluker Farms ships boxes of live crickets, mealworms, and other insects to pet stores, zoos, and universities all over the world. So that no cricket goes unused, those insects that don't make it to market alive are freeze-dried and sold for snacks—for birds, reptiles, and humans. Customers who try a chocolate-covered cricket get an "I Ate a Bug Club" button. Now under the leadership of David Fluker, Richard's son, Fluker Farms generates more than $6 million in revenues a year.

---

1. Assume that you are a banker and each of these three entrepreneurs approaches you with a loan request to start these companies. What questions will you ask them? Would you approve the loan? Explain.

2. Using these business ventures as a source of inspiration, work in a team with two or three of your classmates to generate ideas for unusual business ventures that you could start.

3. Select one idea from those your team generated in question 2. What could you do to convince skeptical lenders or investors to put money into your company and to increase the probability of its success?

Sources: Adapted from David Carnoy "Virtual Trees," *Success*, December 1996, p. 26; David Pearl, "Confessions of a Hired Seducer," *Reader's Digest*, December 1996, pp. 48A–48B; Debra Phillips, Cynthia E. Griffin, Heather Page, Lynn Beresford, Holly Celeste Fisk, and Charlotte Mulhern, "Entrepreneurial Superstars," *Entrepreneur*, April 1997, pp. 108–139. ◆

3. *Confidence in their ability to succeed.* Entrepreneurs typically have an abundance of confidence in their ability to succeed. They tend to be optimistic about their chances for success, and usually their optimism is based on reality. One recent study by the National Federation of Independent Businesses (NFIB) found that one-third of the entrepreneurs surveyed rated their chances of success to be 100 percent![15] This high

Bill Kimberlin, president of OBJ Marketing Corporation, typifies the entrepreneurial spirit. His first business venture, which he started in college, failed, but he refused to give up. Much of Kimberlin's success today stems from his ability to spot market opportunities and to capitalize on them.

level of optimism may explain why some of the most successful entrepreneurs have failed in business, often more than once, before finally succeeding.

4. *Desire for immediate feedback.* Entrepreneurs like to know how they are doing and are constantly looking for reinforcement. Tricia Fox, founder of Fox Day Schools, Inc., claims, "I like being independent and successful. Nothing gives you feedback like your own business."[16]

5. *High level of energy.* Entrepreneurs are more energetic than the average person. That energy may be a crucial factor given the incredible effort required to launch a start-up company. Long hours—often 60 to 80 hours a week—and hard work are the rule rather than the exception.

6. *Future orientation.* Entrepreneurs have a well-defined sense of searching for opportunities. They look ahead and are less concerned with what they accomplished yesterday than with what they can do tomorrow. Ever vigilant for new business opportunities, entrepreneurs *observe* the same events other people do, but they *see* something different. *For example, Bill Kimberlin, who started his first business while in college (a real estate venture that ultimately failed), is always looking for new business opportunities in his hometown, Nashville, Tennessee. He once heard that a large clothing manufacturer was trying to get rid of 70,000 pairs of irregular jeans. He called the company and offered to sell the jeans. In three months, he had sold all 70,000 pairs to small clothing stores across the region. That success led Kimberlin to launch OBJ Marketing Corporation, a $1.5 million business that today resells irregulars for several jeans manufacturers. Kimberlin also owns a recording studio on Nashville's Music Row and a limousine service.*[17]

7. *Skill at organizing.* Building a company "from scratch" is much like piecing together a giant jigsaw puzzle. Entrepreneurs know how to put the right people and resources

together to accomplish a task. Effectively combining people and jobs enables entrepreneurs to bring their visions to reality.

8. *Value of achievement over money.* One of the most common misconceptions about entrepreneurs is that they are driven wholly by the desire to make money. To the contrary, *achievement* seems to be the primary motivating force behind entrepreneurs; money is simply a way of "keeping score" of accomplishments; it is a *symbol* of achievement. "Money is not the driving motive of most entrepreneurs," says Nick Grouf, the 28-year-old founder of a high-tech company. "It's just a very nice by-product of the process."[18]

A recent study of the entrepreneurial personality by the Hayberg Consulting Group found that entrepreneurs share 10 characteristics that set them apart from managers at Fortune 500 companies. Table 1.1 summarizes those characteristics.

Other characteristics that entrepreneurs exhibit are:

◆ *High degree of commitment.* Launching a company successfully requires total commitment from the entrepreneur. Business founders often immerse themselves in their businesses. "The commitment you have to make is tremendous; entrepreneurs usually put everything on the line," says one expert.[19] But that commitment helps overcome business-threatening mistakes and obstacles. An entrepreneur's commitment to her idea and the business it spawns determines how successful her company ultimately becomes.

◆ *Tolerance for ambiguity.* Entrepreneurs tend to have a high tolerance for ambiguous, ever-changing situations: the environment in which they most often operate. This ability to handle uncertainty is crucial because these business builders constantly make decisions using new, sometimes conflicting information gleaned from a variety of unfamiliar sources.

◆ *Flexibility.* One hallmark of true entrepreneurs is their ability to adapt to the changing demands of their customers and their businesses. In this rapidly changing world economy, rigidity often leads to failure. As our society, its people, and their tastes change, entrepreneurs must be willing to adapt their businesses to meet those changes. *When Bill Hewlett and Dave Packard founded their company in the late 1930s, they had no clear idea what to make. They knew that they wanted to create a business in the vaguely*

Table 1.1 Ten Characteristics of Entrepreneurs

1. Aggressively pursue goals, pushing themselves and others very hard.
2. Seek autonomy, independence, and freedom from boundaries; are individualistic.
3. Send consistent messages to everyone involved in the business; employ focused strategies; are undeviating in their purpose.
4. Act quickly, sometimes without careful deliberation; have a "ready-fire-aim" mentality.
5. Keep their distance and maintain objectivity; expect others to be self-sufficient and tough-minded.
6. Seek simple, practical solutions to problems; cut through complexity; search out essential and important information and discard the irrelevant.
7. Are willing to take risks; are comfortable with the ambiguity of a new or fast-growing venture.
8. Have clear opinions and values; are able to make quick judgments; are critical and have high expectations of themselves and of others.
9. Are impatient for results and with others; are poor listeners; exhibit a "just do it" attitude.
10. Are positive and upbeat; communicate optimism and hopefulness; always see the glass as half full (and want to own it).

SOURCE: Adapted from Janean Chun, "Type E Personality," *Entrepreneur*, January 1997, p. 10.

defined field of electronic engineering. Their company, Hewlett-Packard (now one of the most successful electronics companies in the world), probably survived because of the founders' flexibility. Some of their early product ideas included a clock drive for a telescope, a bowling foul-line indicator, a device to make urinals flush automatically, and a shock machine to make people lose weight![20]

◆ *Tenacity.* Obstacles, obstructions, and defeat typically do not dissuade entrepreneurs from doggedly pursuing their visions. "They have the ability to negate barriers that stand in the way of using their innate traits profitably," says one researcher of entrepreneurial behavior.[21]

What conclusion can we draw from the volumes of research conducted on the entrepreneurial personality? Entrepreneurs are not of one mold; no one set of characteristics can predict who will become entrepreneurs or whether they will succeed. Indeed, *diversity* seems to be a central characteristic of entrepreneurs. As you can see from the examples in this chapter, *anyone*—regardless of age, race, gender, color, national origin, or any other characteristic—can become an entrepreneur. There are no limitations on this form of economic expression. Entrepreneurship is not a genetic trait; it is a skill that is learned. The editors of *Inc.* magazine claim, "Entrepreneurship is more mundane than it's sometimes portrayed. . . . You don't need to be a person of mythical proportions to be very, very successful in building a company."[22]

*T*he Benefits of Owning a Small Business

3 Describe the benefits and opportunities of owning a small business.

Surveys show that owners of small businesses believe they work harder, earn more money, and are happier than if they worked for a large company. Before launching any business venture, every potential entrepreneur should consider the benefits and opportunities of small business ownership.

OPPORTUNITY TO GAIN CONTROL OVER YOUR OWN DESTINY

Owning a business provides entrepreneurs the independence and the opportunity to achieve what is important to them. Christopher Good, who at age 28 founded Good Food Systems, a maker of bar-code scanning equipment for school cafeterias, explains, "I knew I'd be OK if I did something I was happy doing and was in control of my life."[23] Like Good, entrepreneurs want to "call the shots" in their lives, and they use their businesses to bring this desire to life. They reap the intrinsic rewards of knowing they are the driving forces behind their businesses.

OPPORTUNITY TO MAKE A DIFFERENCE

Increasingly, entrepreneurs are starting businesses because they see an opportunity to make a difference in a cause that is important to them. Whether it is providing low-cost, sturdy housing for families in developing countries or establishing a recycling program to preserve the earth's limited resources, entrepreneurs are finding ways to combine their concerns for social issues and their desire to earn a good living. *Mike Riebel left his teaching job in the engineering department at Mankato University in Minnesota to start Phenix Biocomposites, Inc., a company that developed and sells an environmentally friendly composite material called Environ made from recycled newsprint and soybeans that offers an alternative to hardwoods at a comparable cost. "I grew up on a farm, so agricultural materials were in my blood—not to mention that the market trends favored renewable resources," says Riebel. The company's sales are growing rapidly as designers and manufacturers who have traditionally used wood are discovering the versatility and the benefits of Environ. The biocomposite material is sturdy and extremely dense, and it can be finished to look like wood, granite, marble, tile, and many other materials. Phenix's customer base has expanded far beyond its original market for commercial interior components such as countertops and desktops to include plaques and awards, flooring, and audio equipment. (Speakers made from Environ produce much less rattle than traditional wooden speakers.) Phenix is now building another plant that will increase its capacity 20-fold to meet the growing demand for Environ.*[24]

OPPORTUNITY TO REACH YOUR FULL POTENTIAL

Too many people find their work boring, unchallenging, and unexciting. But to most entrepreneurs, there is little difference between work and play. Richard Melman, founder of Lettuce Entertain You Enterprises, says, "I think it all adds up to having fun. When it stops being fun, I'll stop doing it."[25]

Entrepreneurs' businesses become the instrument for self-expression and self-actualization. Owning your own business will challenge all of your skills, abilities, and determination. The only barriers to your success are those you impose on yourself. An entrepreneur's creativity, determination, and enthusiasm—not limits artificially created by an organization (e.g., the "glass ceiling")—determine how high she can rise.

OPPORTUNITY TO REAP UNLIMITED PROFITS

Although money is *not* the primary force driving most entrepreneurs, the profits their businesses can earn are an important motivating factor in their decisions to launch companies. If accumulating wealth is high on your list of priorities, owning a business is usually the best way to achieve it. In fact, self-employed business owners make up two-thirds of the nation's millionaires! According to researchers Thomas Stanley and William Danko, the typical American millionaire is first-generation wealthy, owns a small business in a less-than-glamorous industry such as welding, junkyards, or auctioneering, and works between 45 and 55 hours a week.[26]

Greg Brophy typifies these entrepreneurial millionaires. Using extensive research he had conducted and $22,000 he had earned renovating and selling houses while in college and some loans, Brophy, then 24, leased a truck, mounted an industrial-grade paper shredder on it, and launched a portable shredding company. He targeted companies in the Toronto area, and "within three weeks we were so booked, I had to lease another truck," he recalls. In 1993, Brophy began franchising his company, Shred-it America. He now has 38 offices in Canada, the United States, Hong Kong, and Argentina. Today, Brophy's Shred-it America is the largest portable shredding service in North America, shredding some 1,800 tons of paper a month and bringing in $22 million a year![27]

OPPORTUNITY TO CONTRIBUTE TO SOCIETY AND TO BE RECOGNIZED FOR YOUR EFFORTS

Often, small business owners are among the most respected, and most trusted, members of their communities. Business deals based on trust and mutual respect are the hallmark of many established small companies. These owners enjoy the trust and the recognition they receive from the customers whom they have served faithfully over the years. Playing a vital role in their local business systems and knowing that the work they do has a significant impact on how smoothly our nation's economy functions is yet another reward for small business managers. Says one young entrepreneur, "I want to be a person who 20 years down the road can look back and say, 'I was instrumental in creating something. I left a mark.'"[28]

OPPORTUNITY TO DO WHAT YOU ENJOY DOING

A common sentiment among small business owners is that their work *really* is not work. Most successful entrepreneurs choose to enter their particular business fields because they have an interest in them and enjoy those lines of work. They have made their avocations (hobbies) their vocations (work) and are glad they did. These entrepreneurs are living the advice Harvey McKay offers: "Find a job doing what you love, and you'll never have to work a day in your life."

Ed Krech, owner of The Train Man, did just that and has never regretted it! Since his childhood, Krech has loved miniature trains. As an adult, Krech not only continues to run trains, but he also runs his own business selling model trains and train supplies and designing train layouts. Krech started his business as a part-time venture out of his home. During the day, he was an architect at an engineering firm, but at night, he became the Train Man, quickly carving out a niche designing and installing train layouts for homes, gardens, and businesses. "I wanted to be my own boss," he says. "I got tired of the 8-to-5 grind." One of Krech's most popular designs runs along the walls of a dentist's office (whose motto is "Get on board for good dental health"). Not only has Krech found a way to make a living, but he also is doing something he loves! "People come up to me and say, 'Gee, it must be really nice to turn your hobby into a business,'" says Krech.[29]

𝒯he Potential Drawbacks of Entrepreneurship

Describe the potential drawbacks of owning a small business.

Although owning a business has many benefits and provides many opportunities, anyone planning to enter the world of entrepreneurship should be aware of its potential drawbacks. "If you aren't 100 percent sure you want to own a business," says one business consultant, "there are plenty of demands and mishaps along the way to dissuade you."[30]

UNCERTAINTY OF INCOME

Opening and running a business provides no guarantees that an entrepreneur will earn enough money to survive. Some small businesses barely earn enough to provide the owner-manager with an adequate income. In the early days of a business, the owner often has trouble meeting financial obligations and may have to live on savings. The regularity of income that comes with working for someone else is absent. The owner is always the last one to be paid.

RISK OF LOSING YOUR ENTIRE INVESTED CAPITAL

The small business failure rate is relatively high. According to recent research, 24 percent of new businesses fail within two years, and 51 percent shut down within four years. Within six years, 63 percent of new businesses will have folded. Studies also show that when a company creates at least one job in its early years, the probability of failure plummets to 35 percent![31]

Before "reaching for the golden ring," entrepreneurs should ask themselves if they can cope psychologically with the consequences of failure. They should consider the risk–reward trade-off before putting their personal assets and their mental well-being at risk:

◆ What is the worst that could happen if I open my business and it fails?

◆ How likely is the worst to happen? (Am I truly prepared to launch a business?)

◆ What can I do to lower the risk that my business will fail?

◆ What is my contingency plan for coping if my business fails?

SECTION I THE CHALLENGE OF ENTREPRENEURSHIP

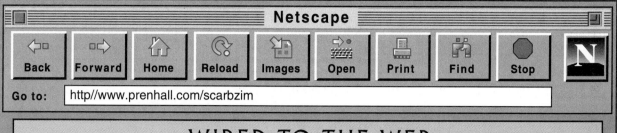

Netscape

Back | Forward | Home | Reload | Images | Open | Print | Find | Stop | N

Go to: http//www.prenhall.com/scarbzim

WIRED TO THE WEB

THE WEDDING PLANNER

*D*uring her senior year in college, the sister of Margaret Ellen Pender's boyfriend, Christian, got married. Because she was majoring in business and had taken several courses in computer applications, Margaret Ellen offered to help the family "manage" the wedding using a computer database and spreadsheets. Little did Margaret Ellen realize that the wedding would spawn an idea for a business. She spent several hours creating a database to track the 600 wedding invitations sent (including addresses), the guests' responses to the invitations, the gifts the couple received, the thank-you notes the couple sent, and other details. She also set up spreadsheets to tally the myriad expenses associated with the wedding: the flowers, the rehearsal party, the wedding cake, the reception, and many others. Margaret Ellen's wedding planner could print reports on any topic the bride, Lana, wanted in just seconds. One day, as she was showing the latest printouts to Lana and her mother, Lana's father, Jake, came in, took one glance at the expense report and laughingly said, "What a great program you've created. I have just one suggestion: Get it to tell us how to pay for this wedding!"

It was as if a bell went off in Margaret Ellen's head. "This is a great business opportunity," she thought. "I've already created the basic structure of the program and the reports. It won't take much to modify my wedding planner to fit *any* wedding of *any* size."

From that point on, Margaret Ellen watched and listened to Lana and her mother as they planned the wedding. Whenever someone said, "Wouldn't it be nice if . . . ," Margaret Ellen would jot down the idea as a way to improve her wedding planner. She also began to incorporate some of the business tools she had learned in college. Working with an experienced wedding coordinator, Margaret Ellen set up a "time line" to guide brides through "the countdown to the wedding."

Margaret Ellen had the opportunity to test the updated version of her wedding planner a few months later when one of her best friends became engaged. She offered to help manage her friend's wedding using the planner. The wedding went off without a hitch, and the couple's families raved about how much Margaret Ellen's planner had helped them. "You've got a real winner here," the bride's mother told her. "Have you considered marketing your wedding planner?"

"Actually," said Margaret Ellen, "I've been thinking about it quite a bit. I've just accepted a job as a lending officer with a major bank, but this would be an excellent way to supplement my income. I believe the World Wide Web would be a great way to market my planner, but I don't know exactly where to start."

1. How should Margaret Ellen use the World Wide Web to market her business? What other methods might she use to market her wedding planner?

2. Using one of the search engines on the WWW, find at least three sites with which Margaret Ellen should establish links. Did you find any competitors already on the Web?

3. Work with a team of your classmates to develop a design for a Web site for Margaret Ellen's business.

4. Would you recommend that Margaret Ellen operate this business from her home? Explain. If so, what pitfalls would you warn her to avoid? Use the WWW to identify the steps she should take to avoid those pitfalls.

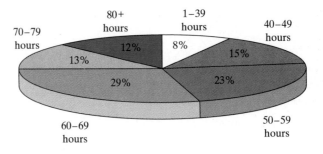

Figure 1.2 **Number of Hours New Business Owners Work (hours per week, by percentage of business owners)** SOURCE: Dun & Bradstreet.

LONG HOURS AND HARD WORK

Business start-ups often demand that owners keep nightmarish schedules. Figure 1.2 shows that most new business owners work more than 60 hours a week, and one-fourth put in more than 70 hours a week! In many start-ups, six- or seven-day workweeks with no paid vacations may be the norm. When the business closes, the revenue stops coming in and the customers go elsewhere. Many business owners start down the path of entrepreneurship thinking that they will own a business only to discover later that the business owns them!

LOWER QUALITY OF LIFE
UNTIL THE BUSINESS GETS ESTABLISHED

The long hours and hard work needed to launch a company can take their toll. Business owners often find that their roles as husbands and wives or fathers and mothers take a backseat to their roles as company founders. Part of the problem is that most entrepreneurs launch their businesses between the ages of 25 and 39, just when they start their families (see Figure 1.3). Jim Katzman, co-founder of Tandem Computers, says "It's very tough to

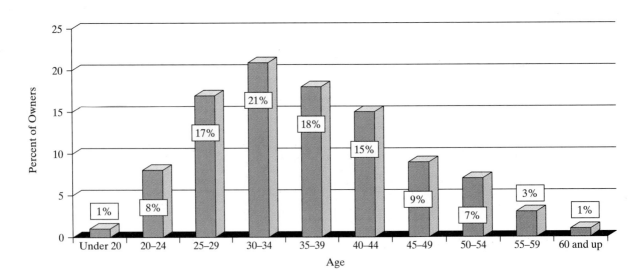

Figure 1.3 **Owner Age When Business Formed** SOURCE: National Federation of Independent Business.

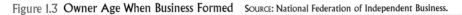

give the amount of work that's required to build a company without slighting your family."[32] As a result, marriages and friendships are too often casualties of small business ownership.

HIGH LEVELS OF STRESS

Launching and running a business can be an extremely rewarding experience, but it also can be a highly stressful one. Most entrepreneurs have made significant investments in their companies, have left behind the safety and security of a steady paycheck, and have mortgaged everything they own to get into business. Failure often means total financial ruin as well as a serious psychological blow, and that creates high levels of stress and anxiety.

COMPLETE RESPONSIBILITY

It's great to be the boss, but many entrepreneurs find that they must make decisions on issues about which they are not really knowledgeable. When there is no one to ask, the pressure can build quickly. The realization that the decisions they make are the cause of success or failure of the business has a devastating effect on some people. Small business owners realize quickly that *they* are the business.

*W*hy the Boom: The Fuel Feeding the Entrepreneurial Fire

5 Explain the forces that are driving the growth in entrepreneurship.

What forces are driving this entrepreneurial trend in our economy? Which factors have led to this age of entrepreneurship? Some of the most significant ones follow.

ENTREPRENEURS AS HEROES

An intangible but very important factor is the attitude that Americans have toward entrepreneurs. As a nation, we have raised them to hero status and have held out their accomplishments as models to follow. Business founders such as Fred Smith (Federal Express), Lillian Vernon (Lillian Vernon Catalogs), Mary Kay Ash (Mary Kay Cosmetics), and Phil Knight (Nike) are to entrepreneurship what Shaquille O'Neil and Emmit Smith are to sports.

ENTREPRENEURIAL EDUCATION

Colleges and universities have discovered that entrepreneurship is an extremely popular course of study. A rapidly growing number of students see owning a business as an attractive career option, and many of them are launching companies while in college. Today, more than 1,500 colleges and universities offer courses in entrepreneurship and small business to some 15,000 students. One study of college students found that 80 percent expressed an interest in taking one or more courses in entrepreneurship or new venture management.[33] Another study forecast that demand for such courses will outstrip resources for the immediate future.[34]

DEMOGRAPHIC AND ECONOMIC FACTORS

Most entrepreneurs start their businesses between the ages of 25 and 39, and that age group represents a large portion of our nation's population. The economic growth that lasted for most of the 1980s created many business opportunities and a significant pool of capital to launch companies to exploit them.

SHIFT TO A SERVICE ECONOMY

The service sector now accounts for about 90 percent of the jobs and 85 percent of the gross domestic product (GDP) in the United States. Because of their relatively low start-up costs, service businesses have been very popular with entrepreneurs. The booming service sector has provided entrepreneurs with many business opportunities, from hotels and health care to financial advising and computer services.

TECHNOLOGICAL ADVANCEMENTS

With the help of modern business machines—personal computers, laptop computers, fax machines, copiers, color printers, answering machines, and voice mail—even one person working at home can look like a big business. At one time, the high cost of such technological wizardry made it impossible for small businesses to compete with larger companies who could afford the hardware. Although entrepreneurs may not be able to manufacture heavy equipment in their spare bedrooms, they can run a service- or information-based company from their homes very effectively and look like any Fortune 500 company to customers and clients. *For example, Paul Wenner, creator of the highly successful Gardenburger, a meatless hamburger, spends 90 percent of his working time at his Portland, Oregon, residence. Wenner, a classic entrepreneur, started several businesses—a company that sold electric cars, one that remodeled houses with recycled materials, and a natural foods restaurant, all of which eventually failed. While concocting the lunch special at his restaurant one day, Wenner was experimenting with food he found in the refrigerator. He formed a patty from leftover rice pilaf, added some mushrooms and onions, oats, and low-fat cheeses and grilled it. After the restaurant folded, Wenner "was so broke, I couldn't afford to buy toothpaste," he recalls. He began making Gardenburgers at night and taking them to restaurants and cafeterias during the day. Sales climbed slowly, and Wholesome and Hearty Foods was born. Today, the company sells its Gardenburger and other meatless foods in more than 35,000 outlets across the United States and Canada. Wenner runs this multimillion-dollar empire from his home office, which is actually three rooms in one. A test kitchen allows Wenner to experiment with new products; a dining room with a 16-foot-long table is ideal for spreading out his work, conducting meetings, and entertaining; and a work space equipped with a computer, printer, fax machine, and scanner keeps him in touch with the world.*[35]

INDEPENDENT LIFESTYLE

Entrepreneurship fits the way Americans want to live—independently and self-sufficiently. Entrepreneurs want the freedom to choose where they live, the hours they work, and what they do. Although financial security remains an important goal for most entrepreneurs, lifestyle issues such as more time with family and friends, more leisure time, and more control over work-related stress are also important. In a recent study by Hilton Hotels, 77 percent of adults surveyed listed spending more time with family and friends as their top priority; 66 percent wanted more free time. Making money ranked a lowly fifth place, and spending money on material possessions came in last.[36]

THE WORLD WIDE WEB (WWW)

The proliferation of the **World Wide Web,** the vast network that links computers around the globe via the Internet and opens up oceans of information to its users, has spawned thousands of entrepreneurial ventures since its beginning in 1993. Experts estimate that the volume of electronic commerce transacted on the Web will have grown from $518 million in 1996 to $6.6 billion by the year 2000 (see Figure 1.4).[37] Currently, about 141,000 small businesses have Web sites. Although most of them are not yet making a profit from their Web

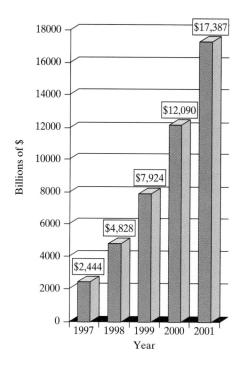

Figure 1.4 **On-Line Commerce** SOURCE: Forrester Research Inc.

sites, the entrepreneurs behind these businesses know that they must establish a presence on the Web *now* if they are to reap its benefits in the future. These "netpreneurs" are using the Web to connect with their existing customers and, eventually, to attract new ones. A few businesses, however, are already generating impressive sales from their Web sites. *In fact, the world's largest bookstore, Amazon.com <http://www.amazon.com>, has no physical location; it exists only on the Web! Founder Jeff Bezos left a lucrative Wall Street job to start Amazon.com after he became intrigued by the World Wide Web and its sales potential. On the Web, Bezos's creation has an unlimited amount of shelf space. Amazon.com lists 2.5 million titles (accessible by a search engine that allows customers to track down any book, author, or topic), 15 times as many as the largest brick-and-mortar chain bookstore. Customers not only get a much larger selection of titles than they would from a typical bookstore, but they also get low prices. Amazon discounts its 350,000 most popular books by 10 to 30 percent. The company's Web site includes book reviews by readers and offers "meet the author" sessions on the Internet. Amazon even offers an e-mail service that lets customers know when a new book by a favorite author or on a particular subject is published. Sales are growing at a rate of 34 percent per month, and Bezos' ultimate target is to become one of the nation's three largest booksellers.*[38]

INTERNATIONAL OPPORTUNITIES

Small businesses are no longer limited to pursuing customers within their own borders. The shift to a global economy has opened the door to tremendous business opportunities for entrepreneurs who are willing to reach across the globe. Although the United States is an attractive market for entrepreneurs, approximately 95 percent of the world's population lives outside its borders. Recent world events—the crumbling of the Berlin Wall, the revolt of the

Soviet Union's Baltic states, the breaking down of trade barriers as a result of the European Union's 1993 Treaty of Maastricht—have opened much of that world market to entrepreneurs. Still, only 6 percent of U.S. small businesses currently export; however, those small companies account for 30 percent of total exports.[39] International opportunities for small businesses will continue to grow rapidly into the twenty-first century.

Although "going global" can be fraught with dangers and problems, especially for small companies, many entrepreneurs are discovering that it is not really that difficult. Small companies that successfully expand into international markets tend to go slowly at first, targeting one country in which to establish a presence, rather than blanketing several foreign markets at once. Often, small companies form joint ventures with foreign partners, who guide them through the maze of local customs and help them navigate local markets.

For some small businesses, branching into global markets is a natural part of growth. *For instance, as a student at the University of West Florida, Robert Bizzell started making tie-dyed T-shirts and selling them in local stores. Soon, he and best friend, Scott Martin, were traveling around the country, selling their shirts at Grateful Dead concerts. Within three years, their company, Eye-Dye, took an order from a large retailer, and production went from 150 shirts a day to 4,000 a day. Two years later, a Japanese wholesaler saw Eye-Dye's display at a Las Vegas trade show and placed a $100,000 order.*[40]

*7*he Cultural Diversity of Entrepreneurship

⬥ Discuss the role of diversity in small business and entrepreneurship.

Diversity is one of entrepreneurship's greatest strengths. The entrepreneurial sector of the United States consists of a rich blend of women and men of all races, ages, backgrounds, and cultures.

WOMEN ENTREPRENEURS

Despite years of legislative effort, women still face discrimination in the workforce. Small business has been a leader in offering women opportunities for economic expression through employment and entrepreneurship. Increasing numbers of women are discovering that the best way to break the "glass ceiling" that prevents them from rising to the top of many organizations is to start their own companies (see Figure 1.5). In fact, women are opening businesses at a rate two times that of men, and they are launching businesses in fields that traditionally have been male-dominated. Although 72 percent of all women-owned businesses are concentrated in retailing and services, the hottest growth areas include construction, transportation, communications, wholesale trade, agribusiness, and manufacturing.[41] Women entrepreneurs have even broken through the comic strip barrier. Dagwood's wife, Blondie Bumstead, long a typical suburban housewife, now owns her own catering business with her best friend and neighbor, Tootsie Woodly.

Although the businesses women start tend to be smaller than those men start, their impact is anything but small. The 8 million women-owned companies across the United States employ 18.5 million workers, 25 percent of all company workers in the country. Women own about 37 percent of all businesses, and these companies generate approximately $2.5 trillion in sales—16 percent of the nation's total—each year.[42]

Some key differences exist between companies started by women and those started by men. Women-owned businesses typically start smaller and grow more slowly but more steadily. "They don't have the high growth spurts, but they're also less likely to decline in size," explains Sharon Hadary of the National Foundation for Women Business Owners.[43] Although they tend to grow more slowly than those owned by men, women-owned businesses have a higher survival rate than U.S. businesses overall. One recent study found that

16   SECTION I   THE CHALLENGE OF ENTREPRENEURSHIP

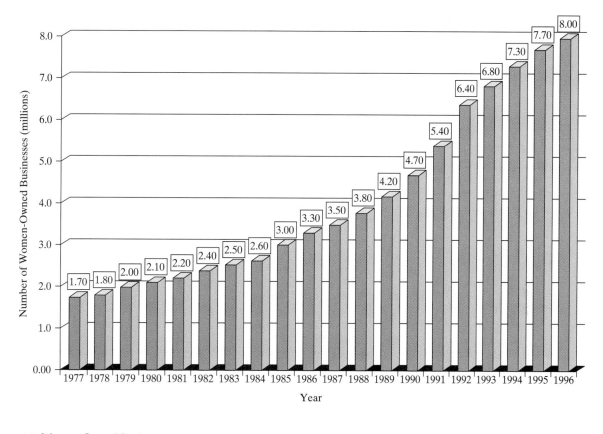

Figure 1.5 **Women-Owned Businesses**   SOURCE: National Association of Women Business Owners.

Women now own 37 percent of all businesses. Carolee Friedlander, founder of Carolee Designs, sells jewelry across the globe. She overcame many obstacles to build a successful business.

the three-year survival rate for companies owned by women was 72.2 percent, compared with 66.6 percent for all businesses.[44] Another key difference between men- and women-owned businesses is the barriers they face when starting up. One of the most persistent barriers women entrepreneurs must overcome is limited access to capital. Women are more likely to rely on personal savings, credit cards, and family loans to launch their companies than are men. Once in business, women tend to run their companies differently than men. For example, they are more likely to offer family-friendly benefits such as flextime and tuition reimbursement, and they launch profit-sharing plans much earlier in the lives of their businesses than do men.[45]

Carolee Friedlander ran headlong into the financing barrier when she launched her costume jewelry and watch business in 1972. The bank where she had applied for a business loan told her that she would have to have her husband cosign the loan before it could accept her application. Friedlander refused, choosing, instead, to borrow $5,000 from family members and to slow the growth of her company, Carolee Designs. Friedlander had become interested in designing jewelry when she was a student studying architecture at Bennington College. Working from a how-to book she taught herself how to cast pewter jewelry on her kitchen stove. As she began selling her designs to local stores, she saw a market for high-quality costume jewelry emerging. Soon, she had landed a large order from Bloomingdale's, which allowed her to get a $50,000 bank loan to expand the company. Today, Carolee Designs has 300 employees and generates annual sales of more than $50 million. In addition to retail icons such as Bloomingdale's and Saks, Friedlander's customers include department

A Rush to Entrepreneurship in Russia

*E*ntrepreneurship is not a uniquely American phenomenon. The desire to create businesses is taking root all across the globe, even in nations whose economies were, for many years, centrally planned. In Russia, for instance, small businesses are playing an important role in rebuilding an economy that collapsed in the early 1990s. Small companies account for 12 percent of all of the goods produced in Russia, and that proportion is growing rapidly. Because they make up 75 percent of Russia's unemployed, women have become a dominant force in the blossoming entrepreneurial movement. Women have received about half of the loans made by a $300 million European reconstruction and development fund. A venture capital fund in London is targeting women-owned businesses across Central and Eastern Europe, with a special emphasis on Russia. "We believe women are much lower business risks and often run very promising companies that have so far gone unnoticed," says the fund's founder.

Of course, many Russian start-ups, like those in any country, fail. Most of the problems women entrepreneurs in Russia face, however, are exactly the same ones men face. The obstacles entrepreneurs must overcome are substantial. They must battle an especially onerous bureaucracy, cope with taxes that can eat up more than 90 percent of their profits, and avoid running afoul of organized crime, whose guns speak louder than laws. In addition, the country's economic instability makes long-range planning impossible.

Tatyana Zeleranskaya and Irina Koroleva, both former reporters for Soviet state radio, were willing to brave the obstacles when they launched Moscow's Radio Nadezhda. They decided to forgo the usual political shows and popular music that are the mainstay of so many Russian radio stations, opting instead for programs on topics such as family and health. The station also features music by popular Russian bands (rather than American rock stars) and was the first station to air call-in talk shows. Radio Nadezhda is now Russia's eighth largest station, but its founders have fought hard to bring it to this point. Zeleranskaya recalls the time a private bank folded, taking the station's account with it. Taxes, she says, are oppressive.

Olga Romashko is another entrepreneur who grew tired of a grueling state job and left to start her own business. She quit her post as a researcher at a top-secret biophysics lab to launch a company selling a line of skin-care products. Her Olga line now carries 14 products, and sales are coming in at $20,000 a month. She has earned enough to build a new house and to help her daughter start a construction company. "Everything we have we earn from zero," she says. "But I also like that. I like tough conditions, where you set yourself goals and overcome obstacles."

1. How do the entrepreneurial experiences described above differ from those of the typical American enterprise? In what ways are they similar?

2. What impact do you predict the small business sector will have on the Russian economy over the next 10 to 20 years?

3. What impact do you think entrepreneurship will have on Russia's women over the next 10 to 20 years?

SOURCE: Adapted from Sophia Kishkovsky and Elizabeth Williamson, "Second-Class Comrades No More: Women Stoke Russia's Start-Up Boom," *Wall Street Journal*, January 30, 1997, p. A12.

◆

stores in Japan and London. She is now planning expansions into South America and the Far East.[46]

MINORITY ENTERPRISES

Minorities also are choosing entrepreneurship more than ever before, but minority business ownership remains low. African Americans, for example, make up 12.7 percent of the U.S. population; yet they own just 3.6 percent of the nation's businesses, and those businesses account for only 1 percent of total U.S. commercial revenues.[47] Like women, minorities cite discrimination as a principal reason for their limited access to the world of entrepreneurship. Asians, Hispanics, and blacks, in that order, are most likely to become entrepreneurs.

Minority-owned businesses have come a long way in the past decade, however. Increasingly, minorities are finding ways to overcome the barriers to business ownership. For instance, the Census Bureau's latest statistics show that the number of companies owned by African Americans grew almost twice as fast as the total number of new business formations. Hispanic-owned businesses grew at an even faster pace, expanding at almost three times the rate of all businesses.[48] The new generation of minority entrepreneurs is better educated, has more business experience, and is better prepared for business ownership than their predecessors. *For example, Yla Eason, a Harvard business school graduate and a former editor at Standard & Poor's, decided to start a business in response to her three-year-old son's statement about a popular cartoon action figure. "He said he wanted to be like He-Man," she recalls, "but he said he couldn't because He-Man was white." After searching New York unsuccessfully for an African American superhero doll, Eason decided to create her own. Within months, she was meeting with toy suppliers to bring her creations, Sun Man and his nemesis Pig Head, to life. Eason now runs Olmec Toys, a $5-million-a-year business that sells more than 30 toys and dolls designed for children of color.*[49]

IMMIGRANT ENTREPRENEURS

The United States has always been a melting pot of diverse cultures. Many immigrants have been lured to this nation by its economic freedom, but today's immigrants arrive with more education and experience than the unskilled "huddled masses" of the past had. Although many of them come to the United States with few assets, their dedication and desire to succeed enable them to achieve their entrepreneurial dreams. *Marty and Helen Shih, immigrants from Taiwan, typify this new breed of immigrant entrepreneurs. In 1979, the Shihs began selling flowers on a Los Angeles street corner from a former cigarette stand they had borrowed. Their first day's sales totaled $1.99, but the Shihs were determined to succeed. They found a better location inside the lobby of a professional building, often working 16- and 18-hour days. Every time the Shihs made a sale, they collected information about their customers and the occasions for which they were buying flowers, painstakingly writing it down in notebooks. Using their database, the Shihs began sending their customers personalized reminders of upcoming birthdays, anniversaries, and other events. They also offered speedy deliveries using mopeds, a significant advantage in car-choked Los Angeles. Soon, they opened their first florist shop in Beverly Hills, where Marty came up with the idea of offering standardized floral designs, an idea he got from McDonald's approach to hamburgers and one that slashed the labor cost of creating floral arrangements by 60 percent. In addition to the chain of florist shops they own, the Shihs also created the Asian American Association, which markets products to Asian Americans and helps other companies do the same. Today, the Shihs sit atop a conglomerate that sells more than $500 million in goods and services to the Asian American community.*[50]

PART-TIME ENTREPRENEURS

Starting a part-time business is a popular gateway to entrepreneurship. Part-timers have the best of both worlds. They can ease into a business without sacrificing the security of a steady paycheck. Some 13 million Americans are self-employed part-time.[51] A major advantage of going into business part-time is the lower risk in case the venture flops. Many part-timers are "testing the entrepreneurial waters" to see whether their business ideas will work and whether they enjoy being self-employed. As they grow, many part-time enterprises absorb more of the entrepreneur's time until they become full-time businesses.

For more than a decade, Charles Manning Jr. ran a part-time business in an unusual niche: accident investigation, a skill he learned while serving in the Air Force during the Korean War. Manning investigated the causes of everything from plane crashes and auto accidents to train derailments and medical accidents. In 1980, Manning's son, Charles III, convinced him to make Accident Reconstruction Analysis a full-time business. Their company has worked on such high-profile cases as the Challenger *space shuttle and ValuJet explosions and generates annual revenues of $3.6 million.*[52]

HOME-BASED BUSINESS OWNERS

Entrepreneurs operate 30.7 million businesses from their homes (a trend dubbed HomeComing by marketing experts), and 14.9 million of those are full-time businesses.[53] Their ranks are growing rapidly; on average, a new home-based business pops up every 11 seconds! These companies generate $383 billion in revenues and create an estimated 8,219 new jobs each day.[54] The biggest advantage home-based businesses offer entrepreneurs is the cost savings of not having to lease or buy an external location. Figure 1.6 illustrates the growth in the number of home-based entrepreneurs in recent years.

In the past, home-based businesses tended to be rather unexciting cottage industries such as crafts or sewing. Today's home-based businesses are more diverse; modern home-based entrepreneurs are likely to be running high-tech or service companies with millions of dollars in sales. *Scott Adams, creator of* Dilbert, *the daily comic strip about the hapless office worker who suffers under the hand of a half-witted boss with a band of bizarre coworkers, recently left his cubicle at giant Pacific Bell to devote himself full-time to his home-based business. Adams runs the entire* Dilbert *empire—which includes the cartoon strip, books, licenses, and other items—from his home office.*[55]

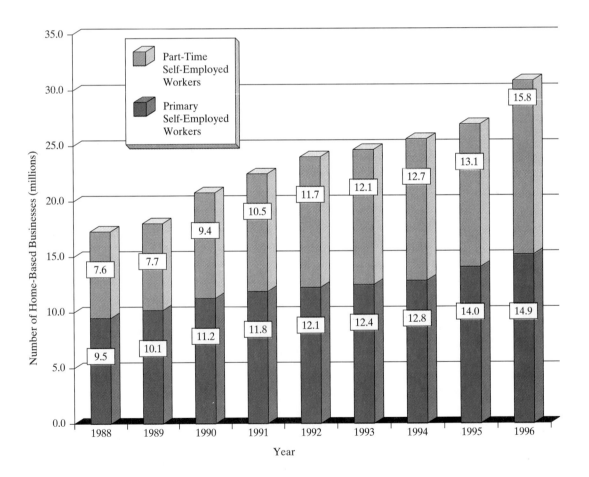

Figure 1.6 The Growth of U.S. Home-Based Businesses   SOURCE: Link Resources, Inc.

About 57 percent of home-based businesses involve white-collar work. They produce attractive incomes for their owners, who work an average of 61 hours a week. The average home-based business earns $50,250 in annual income; 33 percent earn more than $60,000 a year.[56] Home-based companies are an important entrepreneurial outlet for women, who own two-thirds of all home-based businesses. The increasing number of women entrepreneurs and part-time entrepreneurs will continue to feed the growth of these home-based businesses, as will technological advances (computers and communication devices), which are transforming many ordinary homes into "electronic cottages." Esther Schindler, who operates a computer software company out of her home, says, "Clients care about the product, the results. It's becoming less relevant whether or not your office is within 30 feet of your kitchen."[57] Studies by IDC/Link, a research and consulting firm, suggest that the success rate for home-based businesses is high: 85 percent of such businesses are still in operation after three years.[58]

Table 1.2 offers 18 guidelines home-based entrepreneurs should follow to be successful.

FAMILY BUSINESS OWNERS

A **family-owned business** is one that includes two or more members of a family with financial control of the company. They are an integral part of our economy. Of the 22 million businesses in the United States, 90 percent are family-owned and managed. These companies employ more than 50 million people and generate 55 percent of the U.S. gross domestic product (GDP). Not all of them are small; one-third of the Fortune 500 companies are family businesses.[59]

"When it works right," says one writer, "nothing succeeds like a family firm. The roots run deep, embedded in family values. The flash of the fast buck is replaced with long-term plans. Tradition counts."[60] Despite their magnitude, family businesses face a major threat—a threat from within: management succession. Only 33 percent of family businesses survive to the second generation, and just 13 percent make it to the third generation.[61] Business periodicals are full of stories describing bitter disputes among family members that have crippled or destroyed once-thriving businesses. To avoid such senseless destruction of valuable assets, founders of family businesses should develop plans for management succession long before retirement. *For example, when Jim Henson, founder of Jim Henson Productions and creator of the Muppets, died unexpectedly, his 26-year-old son, Brian, who is ten years younger than Kermit the Frog, was able to step in to run the $50 million company and to keep it moving forward. "I . . . couldn't have anticipated how the transition to second-generation leadership would be smoothed . . . by groundwork my father laid," Henson says. The creative spark within the company could have died with Jim Henson, but it did not because he had taken the time to pave the way for the next generation of family management. Brian Henson explains: "I . . . was more prepared by my father for succession than I knew. . . . I'm suddenly very aware of all the teaching my father was doing when we worked together—the conversations . . . about how to treat people, how people should work together, how you can't hold a grudge. He thought about what his philosophies were and about how people should live and talked with me a lot about those things over the last nine years. Now I use those ideas every day, and . . . they've turned out to be the main reason we've all been able to carry on here so well."[62]* We will discuss family businesses and management succession in more detail in chapter 20.

COPRENEURS

Copreneurs are entrepreneurial couples who work together as co-owners of their business. Unlike the traditional "Mom & Pop" (Pop as "boss" and Mom as "subordinate"), copreneurs "are creating a division of labor that is based on expertise as opposed to gender," says one

Table 1.2 Managing a Successful Home-Based Business

Eighty-five percent of home-based entrepreneurs are satisfied with their working arrangement. Yet working from home poses several unique challenges, including feelings of isolation and learning to separate work and home life. How do those who succeed do it? They follow these guidelines.

◆ *Do your homework.* Much of a home-based business's potential for success depends on how much preparation an entrepreneur makes before ever opening for business. The library is an excellent source for research on customers, industries, competitors, and the like.

◆ *Find out what your zoning restrictions are.* In some areas, local zoning laws make running a business from home illegal. Avoid headaches by checking these laws first. You can always request a variance from the local zoning commission.

◆ *Choose the most efficient location for your office.* About half of all home-based entrepreneurs operate out of spare bedrooms. The best way to determine the ideal office location is to examine the nature of your business and your clients. Avoid locating your business in your bedroom or your family room.

◆ *Focus your home–based business idea.* Avoid the tendency to be "all things to all people." Most successful home-based businesses focus on a particular customer group or in some specialty.

◆ *Discuss your business rules with your family.* Running a business from your home means you can spend more time with your family . . . and that your family can spend more time with you. Establish the rules for interruptions up front.

◆ *Select an appropriate business name.* Your first marketing decision is your company's name, so make it a good one! Using your own name is convenient, but it's not likely to help you sell your product or service.

◆ *Buy the right equipment.* Modern technology allows a home-based entrepreneur to give the appearance of any Fortune 500 company—but only if you buy the right equipment. A well-equipped home office should have a separate telephone line, a computer, a laser or inkjet printer, a fax machine (or board), a copier, a scanner, and an answering machine (or voice mail), but realize that you don't have to have everything from Day One.

◆ *Dress appropriately.* Being an "open-collar worker" is one of the joys of working at home. But when you need to dress up (to meet a client, make a sale, meet your banker, close a deal), do it! Resist the temptation to work in your bathrobe all day.

◆ *Learn to deal with distractions.* The best way to fend off the distractions of working at home is to create a business that truly interests you. Budget your time wisely. Avoid leaving your office except for prescheduled breaks. Your productivity determines your company's success.

◆ *Realize that your phone can be your best friend or your worst enemy.* As a home-based entrepreneur, you'll spend lots of time on the phone. Be sure you use it productively. Install a separate phone line for the exclusive use of your business.

◆ *Be firm with friends and neighbors.* Sometimes friends and neighbors get the mistaken impression that because you're at home, you're not working. If neighbors drop by to chat while you're working, tactfully ask them to come back "after work."

◆ *Take advantage of tax breaks.* Although a 1993 Supreme Court decision tightened considerably the standards for business deductions for an office at home, many home-based entrepreneurs still qualify for special tax deductions on everything from computers to cars. Check with your accountant.

◆ *Make sure you have adequate insurance coverage.* Some homeowner's policies provide adequate coverage for business-related equipment, but many home-based entrepreneurs have inadequate coverage on their business assets. Ask your agent about a business owner's policy (BOP), which may cost as little as $300 to $500 a year.

◆ *Understand the special circumstances under which you can hire outside employees.* Sometimes zoning laws allow in-home businesses, but they prohibit hiring employees. Check zoning laws carefully.

◆ *Be prepared if your business requires clients to come to your home.* Dress appropriately. Make sure your office presents a professional image.

◆ *Get a post office box.* With burglaries and robberies on the rise, you're better off using a "P.O. Box" address rather than your specific home address. Otherwise you may be inviting crime.

◆ *Network, network, network.* Isolation can be a problem for home-based entrepreneurs, and one of the best ways to combat it is to network. It's also a great way to market your business.

◆ *Be proud of your home–based business.* Merely a decade ago there was a stigma attached to working from home. Today, home-based entrepreneurs and their businesses command respect. Be proud of your company!

SOURCES: Susan Biddle Jaffe, "Balancing Your Home Business," *Nation's Business*, April 1997, pp. 56–58; Ronaleen Roha, "Home Alone," *Kiplinger's Personal Finance Magazine*, May 1997, pp. 85–89; Lynn Beresford, Janean Chun, Cynthia E. Griffin, Heather Page, and Debra Phillips, "Homeward Bound," *Entrepreneur*, September 1995, pp. 116–118; Janean Huber, "House Rules," *Entrepreneur*, March 1993, pp. 89–95; Hal Morris, "Home-Based Businesses Need Extra Insurance," *AARP Bulletin*, November 1994, p. 16; Stephanie N. Mehta, "What You Need," *Wall Street Journal*, October 14, 1994, p. R10.

expert.[63] Studies suggest that companies co-owned by spouses represent one of the fastest growing business sectors, up by 90 percent from 1980.

Managing a small business with a spouse may appear to be a recipe for divorce, but most copreneurs say not. "There is nothing more exciting than nurturing a business and watching it grow with someone you love," says Marcia Sherrill, who, with her husband, William Kleinberg, runs Kleinberg Sherrill, a leather goods and accessories business.[64] Successful copreneurs learn to build the foundation for a successful working relationship before they ever launch their companies. Here are some of the characteristics they rely on:

◆ An assessment of whether their personalities will mesh or conflict in a business setting

◆ Mutual respect for each other and one another's talents

◆ Business and life goals that are compatible: a common "vision"

◆ A view that they are full and equal partners, not a superior and a subordinate

◆ The ability to keep lines of communication open, talking and listening to each other about personal as well as business issues

◆ A clear division of roles and authority—ideally based on each partner's skills and abilities—to minimize conflict and power struggles

◆ The ability to encourage each other and to "lift up" a disillusioned partner

◆ Separate work spaces that allow them to "escape" when the need arises

◆ Boundaries between their business life and their personal life so that one does not consume the other

◆ A sense of humor

Although copreneuring is not for everyone, it works extremely well for many couples and often leads to successful businesses. "Both spouses are working for a common purpose but also focusing on their unique talents," says a family business counselor. "With all these skills put together, one plus one equals more than two."[65] *For instance, copreneurs Bob and Cindy Maynard have built and managed two successful businesses together. In 1977, they launched Vermont Country Cyclers, a company that took 6,000 people a year on bicycle trips across the world. When the company began to take more time away from their growing family than they wanted, the Maynards decided to sell it. Two years later, they launched Country Walkers, a business that offers walking vacations in the United States and more than a dozen other countries, including France, Greece, Costa Rica, and Tanzania. Each tour is led by local guides who are extremely knowledgeable about the history and culture of the area. The Maynards say that the educational component of their tours is one reason that their customer retention rate is 79 percent. Like most successful copreneurs, the Maynards split their responsibilities on the basis of their skills and abilities. Cindy manages Country Walkers' finances and books the accommodations, and Bob designs the tours and markets them.*[66]

CORPORATE CASTOFFS

Shedding the excess bulk they took on during the 1970s and 1980s, U.S. corporations have been downsizing in an attempt to remain competitive. One major corporation after another has announced layoffs. Over the last decade, major corporations have shed about 6 million jobs—and not just among blue-collar workers.[67] Companies are cutting back their executive ranks as well. "[Downsizing] is turning legions of blue- and white-collar workers into dislocated refugees, the boat people of economic upheaval. Neither they nor the survivors and witnesses are likely to put their loyalties into a corporation that deals with people as interchangeable digits," says one business article.[68]

These "corporate castoffs" have become an important source of entrepreneurial activity. The proportion of discharged corporate managers who have become entrepreneurs has doubled to 15 percent since 1994, and many of those left behind in corporate America would like to join them.[69] A recent study by Accountemps found that nearly half of the executives surveyed believed that their peers would take the entrepreneurial plunge if they had the money to do so. Four years before, just one-third of corporate executives were inclined to start their own companies.[70]

Many corporate castoffs are deciding that the best defense against future job insecurity is an entrepreneurial offense. Armed with years of experience, a tidy severance package, a working knowledge of their industries, and a network of connections, former managers are setting out to start companies of their own. *After spending 18 years as the head of worldwide research for pharmaceutical giant Burroughs Wellcome, David Barry found himself part of the company's downsizing initiative. Rather than going to work for another large company, Barry launched Triangle Pharmaceuticals, a company developing drugs to fight AIDS, hepatitis, and other serious diseases. The start-up business already has 15 employees, 12 of whom worked with Barry at Burroughs Wellcome. "Most of us—and I'll be the first to admit this—probably wouldn't have [launched a company] voluntarily," says Barry. Now, however, like many corporate castoffs, Barry finds that the entrepreneurial experience suits him well, offering more security, satisfaction, and stimulation than his corporate job ever did![71]*

CORPORATE DROPOUTS

The downsizing of corporate America has created another effect among the employees left after restructuring: a trust gap. The result of this trust gap is a growing number of "dropouts" from the corporate structure who then become entrepreneurs. Although their workdays may grow longer and their incomes may shrink, those who strike out on their own often find their work more rewarding and more satisfying because they are doing what they enjoy and they are in control. *When one dropout left his corporate post, he invited his former coworkers to a bonfire in the parking lot—fueled by a pile of his expensive business suits! He happily passed out marshmallows to everyone who came. Today, he and his wife run an artists' gallery in California's wine country.[72]*

Because they have college degrees, a working knowledge of business, and years of management experience, both corporate dropouts and castoffs may ultimately increase the small business survival rate. A recent survey by Richard O'Sullivan found that 64 percent of people starting businesses have some college education, and 16 percent have advanced degrees.[73] Better trained, more experienced entrepreneurs are less likely to fail. The National Federation of Independent Businesses reports that 77 percent of new companies formed since the mid-eighties were still in operation three years later.[74]

7he Contributions of Small Businesses

7 Describe the contributions small businesses make to the U.S. economy.

Of the 22.4 million businesses in the United States today, approximately 22.1 million, or 98.5 percent, can be considered small. They thrive in virtually every industry, although the majority of small companies are concentrated in the retail and service industries (see Figure 1.7). Their contributions to the economy are as numerous as the businesses themselves. For example, small companies employ 53 percent of the nation's private-sector workforce, even though they possess less than one-fourth of total business assets. And, because they are primarily labor-intensive, small businesses actually create more jobs than do big businesses. In the mid-1990s, for instance, small companies created 75 percent of the nation's new jobs.[75] David Birch, president of the research firm Cognetics, says that the ability to create jobs is

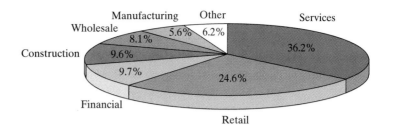

Figure 1.7 Small Business by Industry Source: Statistical Abstract of the United States, 1996.

not distributed evenly across the small business sector, however. His research shows that just 4 percent of these small companies created 70 percent of the new jobs, and they did so across all industry sectors, not just in "hot" industries. Birch calls these job-creating small companies "gazelles," those growing at 20 percent or more a year with at least $100,000 in annual sales. His research also identified "mice," small companies that never grow much and do not create many jobs. Most small companies are mice. Birch tabbed the country's largest job-shedding businesses "elephants," who continued to cut jobs through the 1990s.[76]

Not only do small companies lead the way in creating jobs, but they also bear the brunt of training workers for them. A recent study by the Small Business Administration (SBA) concluded that small businesses are the leaders in offering training and advancement opportunities to workers. Small companies offer more general skills instruction and training than large ones, and their employees receive more benefits from the training than do those in larger firms. Although their training programs tend to be informal, in-house, and on-the-job, small companies teach employees valuable skills—from written communication to computer literacy.[77]

Small businesses also produce 50 percent of the country's gross domestic product (GDP) and account for 47 percent of business sales. Overall, small firms provide directly or indirectly the livelihoods of over 100 million Americans.[78] Research conducted for the National Science Foundation concluded that small firms create four times as many innovations for each research and development (R&D) dollar as medium-sized firms do and 24 times as many as large companies. In another study of the most important technological innovations introduced into the U.S. market, researchers found that, on average, smaller companies contributed 20 percent more of these innovations per employee than did large companies.[79] Many important inventions trace their roots to an entrepreneur; for example, the zipper, FM radio, air conditioning, the escalator, the light bulb, and the automatic transmission.

*7*he Business Failure Record: Can You Beat the Odds?

8 Describe the small business failure rate and explain why small businesses fail.

Because of their limited resources, inexperienced management, and lack of financial stability, small businesses suffer a mortality rate significantly higher than that of larger established businesses. Studies by the Small Business Administration suggest that 63 percent of new businesses will have failed within six years. Exploring the causes of business failure may help you avoid it.

MANAGEMENT INCOMPETENCE

Management inexperience or poor decision-making ability is the chief problem of most failing small businesses. Sometimes the manager of the small business does not have the capacity to operate it successfully. The owner lacks the leadership ability and knowledge neces-

IN THE FOOTSTEPS OF AN ENTREPRENEUR

Never Too Young

*I*nterested in starting your own business but afraid you're too young and inexperienced? Take heart! According to the following entrepreneurs, you're never too young (or too old) to launch your own business. A recent study of 1,200 business owners found that the highest percentage of entrepreneurs starting businesses was in the 25 to 35 age group. Twenty-something entrepreneurs are not unusual, especially with more college courses in entrepreneurship and small business management available and poor job prospects in big companies. The World Wide Web has created a tremendous opportunity for young, computer-savvy entrepreneurs because it offers low financial barriers to entry. Also popular with young entrepreneurs are "knowledge-based businesses," such as public relations, telemarketing, consulting, and others. After Annette Quintana had a dispute with her employer, she decided to start a business of her own. Annette and her sister Victoria founded Excel Professional Services, a computer consulting company. First-year sales were $250,000, and within five years, their company was bringing in sales of $15 million.

Columbia University students Seth Kamil and Ed O'Donnell took an idea for a walking tour business in New York City suggested by one of their professors and built a company around it. Needing money to pay their way through school, Kamil and O'Donnell started Big Onion Walking Tours, which now employees 10 other students and conducts more than 700 walking tours each year. Some tours draw as many as 500 guests a day. Now approaching graduation, Kamil, who bought out O'Donnell when he graduated, must decide what to do with the company. "We had no idea this would take off as it has," he says. "I don't know if I can walk away from this now. We're growing so fast, and I'm not sure I can find another opportunity as exciting as this one."

Not satisfied with building just one business, many youthful entrepreneurs are creating more than one company. One study found that entrepreneurs between the ages of 18 and 35 started an average of 2.3 companies. Alan Ezier, a typical serial entrepreneur, recently launched his fifth company, FreedomStarr Communications. He started his first two businesses while still in college.

Some entrepreneurs don't wait until they're in their twenties to start their companies; they start even earlier. Before graduating from elementary school, Richie Stachowski was an entrepreneur. While on a Hawaiian vacation with his family, 10-year-old Richie was frustrated by his inability to talk to his father while they were snorkeling. Researching the problem on the Internet, Richie discovered that sound travels better underwater than through air. Using $267 of his own savings, he invented the Water Talkie, a cone-shaped device that allows users to talk underwater, patented his new product, and formed a limited liability company, Short Stack, to sell it. Major retailers such as Toys "R" Us and Sportmart have purchased more than 50,000 Water Talkies from Short Stack. Richie is busy developing other product ideas, including an underwater pogo stick. If it is successful, he plans to sell Short Stack and launch another company for his ideas.

When K-K Gregory was 10 years old, while playing in the snow outside her Bedford, Massachusetts, home, her wrists became cold from the snow that had gotten up the sleeves of her jacket. K-K went inside and sewed a piece of fleece fabric into a tubular shape; she added a thumbhole to keep it from sliding up her arm. A few weeks later, she sewed fleece tubes of the same design for her Girl Scout troop, and they were a big hit. Recognizing a business opportunity, K-K and her mother created a company named after their trademark product, Wristies. Today, 15-year-old K-K and her mother operate Wristies out of their home, and their customer list includes notables such as FedEx and McDonald's.

1. In addition to the normal obstacles of starting a business, what other barriers do young entrepreneurs face?
2. What factors do you think contribute to a young person's taking the risk of starting a business?

Sources: Adapted from Gary M. Stern, "Young Entrepreneurs Make Their Mark," *Nation's Business*, August 1996, pp. 49–51; Stephanie N. Mehta, "Young Entrepreneurs Are Starting Business After Business, Study Says," *Wall Street Journal*, March 19, 1997, p. B2; Susan Caminiti, "Teen Inc." *Your Company*, June/July 1998, p. 43; Michael Liedtke, "11-Year-Old Selling to Toys "R" Us, Not Buying from It," *Upstate Business*, March 16, 1997, pp. 3, 8; Hal Plotkin, "Student Uprising," *Inc.*, August 1996, pp. 30–38. ◆

sary to make the business work. Many managers simply do not have what it takes to run a small enterprise. *Andrew Kay was a pioneer in the earliest days of the portable computer with his Kaypro model (which in 1981 weighed in at a hefty 25 pounds and had 64 KB of RAM, hardly a laptop by modern standards). Unfortunately, he had no experience in running a high-tech start-up, and, despite the popularity of his computer, Kay made a series of managerial blunders that ultimately forced the company into bankruptcy.[80]*

LACK OF EXPERIENCE

Small business managers need to have experience in the field they want to enter. For example, a person who wants to open a retail clothing business should first work in a retail clothing store to gain practical experience and to learn the nature of the business. This type of experience can spell the difference between failure and success. *One West Coast entrepreneur had always wanted to own a restaurant, but he had no experience in the restaurant business. He later admitted that he had thought that running a restaurant consisted primarily of dressing up in black tie, greeting his regular customers at the door, and showing them to his best tables. He invested $150,000 of his own money and found a partner to put up more capital and to help manage the restaurant. They opened and immediately ran into trouble because they knew nothing about running a restaurant. In desperation, the restaurateurs came up with an idea to attract business: Why not become the first topless restaurant in the area? The gimmick worked for a while, and then business dropped off. Then they decided to become the first bottomless restaurant. Again, business picked up briefly, but the novelty soon wore off, and sales slipped. Eventually, the restaurant closed, and the partners lost their original investments, their homes, and their cars; they also spent the next several years paying off back taxes.*[81] Ideally, a prospective entrepreneur should have adequate technical ability; a working knowledge of the physical operations of the business; sufficient conceptual ability; the power to visualize, coordinate, and integrate the various operations of the business into a synergistic whole; and the skill to manage the people in the organization and motivate them to higher levels of performance.

POOR FINANCIAL CONTROL

Sound management is the key to a small company's success, and effective managers realize that any successful business venture requires proper financial control. The margin for error in managing finances is especially small for most small businesses, and neglecting to install proper financial controls is a recipe for disaster. *For instance, while working at Apple Computers, Mark Kvamme saw an opportunity to sell non-English computer keyboards to foreign computer users in the United States. Kvamme's company reached $3 million in sales but ultimately folded because of sloppy financial controls. "We were so busy plugging along that we didn't track how much money we were making or spending," says Kvamme, now head of his own advertising agency.*[82]

LACK OF STRATEGIC MANAGEMENT

Too many small business managers neglect the process of strategic management because they think it is something that benefits only large companies. "I don't have the time" or "We're too small to develop a strategic plan," they rationalize. Failure to plan, however, usually results in failure to survive. Without a clearly defined strategy, a business has no sustainable basis for creating and maintaining a competitive edge in the marketplace. *James Salter and Tim Pogue, founders of Ride, Inc., a snowboard equipment company, made this mistake, and their company barely survived. Riding the popularity of snowboarding, the company went public, and its stock price skyrocketed. The young entrepreneurs became instant millionaires, but, without a clear strategy, Ride soon ran into serious problems. Both founders resigned from the company, and the board brought in an experienced manager, Robert Hall, to try to turn the ailing company around. According to Hall, the biggest problem the company faced was a lack of strategic management. "They didn't even have a business plan when I arrived," he says.*[83]

Building a strategic plan forces an entrepreneur to assess *realistically* the proposed business's potential. Is it something customers are willing and able to purchase? Who is the target customer? How will the business attract and keep those customers? What is the company's basis for serving customers' needs better than existing companies? We will explore these and other vital issues in chapter 2.

UNCONTROLLED GROWTH

Growth is a natural, healthy, and desirable part of any business enterprise, but it must be planned and controlled. Management expert Peter Drucker says that start-up companies can expect to outgrow their capital bases each time sales increase 40 to 50 percent.[84] Ideally, expansion should be financed by retained earnings or by capital contributions from the owner, but most businesses wind up borrowing at least a portion of the capital investment.

Expansion usually requires major changes in organizational structure, business practices such as inventory and financial control procedures, personnel assignments, and other areas. But the most important change occurs in managerial expertise. As the business increases in size and complexity, problems tend to increase in proportion, and the manager must learn to deal with them. Sometimes entrepreneurs encourage rapid growth, and the business outstrips their ability to manage it. *Shortly after Maryles Casto started Casto Travel, a corporate travel agency, sales exploded. Her customers were fast-growing companies such as Intel and Apple Computer. But Casto soon saw the dark side of growth. The quality of her customer service plummeted, and she was losing clients because of it. She realized that uncontrolled growth was sending her business spinning out of control. "Business was coming in so fast I couldn't handle it," she recalls. That's when Casto made a dramatic move: She put the business in a holding pattern, taking on no new clients until she could get*

SOURCE: *The New Yorker*, August 7, 1995, p. 58.

the company in a position to handle them. It paid off. Today, Casto Travel has five offices, 155 employees, and $70 million in annual sales.[85]

INAPPROPRIATE LOCATION

For any business, choosing the right location is partly an art and partly a science. Too often, business locations are selected without proper investigation and planning. Some beginning owners choose a particular location just because they notice a vacant building. But the location question is much too critical to leave to chance. Especially for retailers, the lifeblood of the business—sales—is influenced heavily by choice of location. One small merchandiser located in a rural area was heavily dependent on the customers of a nearby restaurant for her clientele. Because of the inconvenience of this location, sales suffered and the business failed.

Another factor to consider in selecting location is the rental rate. Although it is prudent not to pay an excessive amount for rent, business owners should weigh the cost against the location's effect on sales. Location has two important features: what it costs and what it generates in sales volume.

LACK OF INVENTORY CONTROL

Normally, the largest investment the small business manager must make is in inventory; yet, inventory control is one of the most neglected of all the managerial responsibilities. Insufficient inventory levels result in shortages and stockouts that cause customers to become disillusioned and not return. A more common situation is that the manager not only has too much inventory but also has too much of the wrong type of inventory. Many small firms have an excessive amount of working capital tied up in an accumulation of needless inventory. We will discuss both purchasing and inventory control techniques in section VII.

INABILITY TO MAKE THE "ENTREPRENEURIAL TRANSITION"

If a business fails, it is most likely to do so in its first five years (see Figure 1.8). Making it over the "entrepreneurial start-up hump," however, is no guarantee of business success. After the start-up, growth usually requires a radically different style of leadership and management. Ted Waitt, founder of the highly successful direct-mail computer retailer Gateway 2000 says, "Over the last ten years, although I've been doing the same job, it has probably been six or seven completely different jobs as the company has grown."[86]

The very abilities that make an entrepreneur successful often lead to *managerial* ineffectiveness. Growth requires entrepreneurs to delegate authority and to relinquish hands-on control of daily operations—something many entrepreneurs simply cannot do. Their compa-

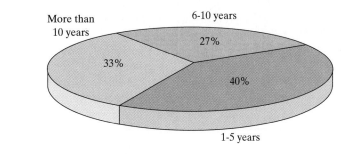

Figure 1.8 **Business Failures by Age of Company**   SOURCE: Dun & Bradstreet.

nies' success requires that they avoid micromanaging and become preservers and promoters of their companies' vision, values, and culture.

Table 1.3 offers some interesting insights into the 10 stages in a company's life cycle.

$\mathcal{P}$utting Failure into Perspective

❾ Put business failure into the proper perspective.

Because they are building businesses in an environment filled with uncertainty and shaped by rapid change, entrepreneurs recognize that failure is likely to be a part of their lives, but they are not paralyzed by that fear. "The excitement of building a new business from scratch is far greater than the fear of failure," says one entrepreneur who failed in business several times before finally succeeding.[87] Instead, they use their failures as a rallying point and as a means of defining their companies' reason for being more clearly. They see failure for what it really is: an opportunity to learn what does not work! Successful entrepreneurs have the attitude that failures are simply stepping stones along the path to success. Walt Disney was fired from a newspaper job because, according to his boss, he "lacked ideas." Disney also went bankrupt several times before he created Disneyland.

Failure is a natural part of the creative process. The only people who never fail are those who never do anything or never attempt anything new. Baseball fans know that Babe Ruth held the record for career home runs (714) for many years, but how many know that he also held the record for strikeouts (1,330)? Successful entrepreneurs realize that hitting an entrepreneurial home run requires a few strikeouts along the way, and they are willing to accept them. Lillian Vernon, who started her mail-order company with $2,000 in wedding present money, says, "Everybody stumbles. . . . The true test is how well you pick yourself up and move on, and whether you're willing to learn from that."[88] Indeed, one hallmark of successful entrepreneurs is the ability to fail *intelligently*, learning why they failed so that they can avoid making the same mistake again. They know that business success does not depend on their ability to avoid making mistakes but to be open to the lessons each mistake brings. They learn from their failures and use them as fuel to push themselves closer to their ultimate target. Entrepreneurs are less worried about what they might lose if they try something and fail than about what they will miss if they fail to try.

Entrepreneurial success requires both persistence and resilience, the ability to bounce back from failures. Thomas Edison discovered about 1,800 ways *not* to build a lightbulb before hitting upon a design that worked. Entrepreneur Bryn Kaufman explains this "never say die" attitude: "If you are truly an entrepreneur, giving up is not an option."[89] *Kaufman started Computer Market Place at age 19, selling computer accessories from his parents' home. Within five years, the company's sales had grown to $1.7 million, and Kaufman opened a retail computer store. Unfortunately, the store couldn't compete with retail giants CompUSA and Circuit City, who had gotten into the computer retail business, and Kaufman shut it down after just 10 months. Undaunted, he began supplying computers and components to two computer retail outlets, one in Russia and one in Armenia, in late 1991. Sales dried up when the Russian economy collapsed and the two stores closed, forcing Kaufman to reduce his staff from 12 to two. "I had to cut costs and do whatever it took to keep the company alive," he recalls. The turning point for Computer Market Place came when Kaufman hired a young woman who knew how to sell to government agencies. To reduce the paperwork in his dealings with the agencies, Kaufman began to use the Internet to submit bids and specifications. He quickly realized that the Internet was an ideal way to sell computers and accessories to anyone anywhere without the problems of running an actual retail store. The company's Web site now generates more than $500,000 in sales each month, about half of Computer Market Place's total sales.[90]*

Table 1.3 "Swimming" in the 10 Stages of the Corporate Life Cycle

First-time entrepreneurs about to launch businesses often wonder what sequence of start-up activities they should follow. The results of one study indicate that there is no single "correct" sequence of start-up activities; the activities depend on the individual entrepreneur and on the particular venture. Researcher Paul Reynolds compares the process of starting a business to learning to swim:

> In swimming, first you get over your fear of the water. Once you jump into the shallow end of the pool, you may start by getting your head wet, or you may try floating or exhaling underwater. Whatever the sequence, in the end, you may learn to stay afloat in the deep end and actually get from one side to the other. Some people take to swimming in no time; others take much longer. Some never quite get the hang of it and climb out of the pool. . . . Just as there is no one way to learn to swim, there is no one way to start a business. On the other hand, all swimmers must master the basics, and all the new businesses eventually got around to most of the basic [start-up] activities.

Reynolds's study suggests that entrepreneurs typically launch businesses after about one year of concentrated effort. Once they are in business, what can these entrepreneurs expect? Researcher Ichak Adizes says that companies, like living organisms, go through normal stages of development, accompanied by normal problems associated with each stage. Adizes outlines the following 10 stages in a company's life cycle and suggests that an entrepreneur's goal should be to reach *and stay* at the stage called Prime:

◆ *Stage 1: Courtship.* An entrepreneur focuses on ideas for a business venture, makes ambitious plans for the future, and talks about them enthusiastically. No business exists, yet.

◆ *Stage 2: Infancy.* The entrepreneur actually launches the business, shifting attention from imagined possibilities to actual results. The need to make sales drives this action-oriented, opportunity-driven stage. Paperwork, controls, systems, and procedures are not important to the founder, who often works 16-hour days trying to do everything herself.

◆ *Stage 3: Go–Go.* In this period of rapid growth, sales remain king. As she tastes success, the founder begins to believe she can do no wrong. Opportunities are everywhere, but the founder's tendency to reach for all of them leaves the company vulnerable to a multitude of problems. Employees wear lots of hats but are frustrated because the founder continues to make every decision.

◆ *Stage 4: Adolescence.* In this stage, the company takes on a new form. The founder hires (or promotes) top managers but usually has difficulty learning to delegate real authority and responsibility to them. Internal conflicts abound, and the company suffers from a temporary loss of focus.

◆ *Stage 5: Prime.* The entrepreneur refocuses the company and redefines her vision for it. The business achieves a balance between control and flexibility and "hits its stride." Disciplined yet innovative, the company consistently meets its customers' needs and exceeds their expectations. Creativity abounds in the organization, and new businesses sprout and grow in it as employees find new opportunities.

◆ *Stage 6: Stability.* The company remains strong but lacks the vitality and enthusiasm of its earlier stages. New ideas are welcome, but not with the same degree of enthusiasm as during the formulation and growth stages. The focus shifts to efficiency as managers impose controls for short-term results that often curtail long-term innovation.

◆ *Stage 7: Aristrocracy.* "Don't make waves" becomes the company theme. Outward symbols of respectability—dress, office decor, and titles—take on enormous importance. Rather than incubate its own new businesses, the organization looks to acquire businesses with new ideas, technology, patents, or markets. Company culture emphasizes how things are done instead of what is done and why. Management relies on what has worked in the past to carry the company into the future.

◆ *Stage 8: Recrimination.* In this stage of decay, the focus shifts to finding out who did wrong from finding out what went wrong and how to fix it. "Witch hunts" are prevalent, and creativity dries up as employees live in fear of making mistakes. Managers emphasize cost-reduction strategies over revenue-enhancing strategies. Office politics, infighting, and turf-protecting run rampant throughout the organization.

◆ *Stage 9: Bureaucracy.* If a company does not die in stage 8, it becomes a bureaucracy. Procedures, rules, and policies choke innovation and creativity. Employees are so focused on procedure that they forget about serving customers. Forgotten and forsaken, customers leave the company in droves.

◆ *Stage 10: Death.* This final stage may creep up over several years, or it may arrive in one sudden, massive blow. The company crumbles as cash flow evaporates.

SOURCES: Adapted from Paul Reynolds, "The Truth about Start-Ups," *Inc.*, February 1995, pp. 23–24; Ichak Adizes, "The 10 Stages of Corporate Life Cycles," *Inc.*, October 1996, pp. 95–98.

*H*ow to Avoid the Pitfalls

10 Analyze the major pitfalls involved in managing a small business and understand how small business owners can avoid them.

As valuable as failure can be to the entrepreneurial process, no one sets out to fail. We have seen the most common reasons behind many small business failures. Now we must examine the ways to avoid becoming another failure statistic and gain insight into what makes a start-up successful. Entrepreneurial success requires much more than just a good idea for a product or service. It also takes a solid plan of execution, adequate resources (including capital and people), the ability to assemble and manage those resources, and perseverance. The following suggestions for success follow naturally from the causes of business failures.

KNOW YOUR BUSINESS IN DEPTH

We have already emphasized the need for the right type of experience in the business. Get the best education in your business area you possibly can *before* you set out on your own. Read everything you can—trade journals, business periodicals, books, Web pages—relating to your industry. Personal contact with suppliers, customers, trade associations, and others in the same industry is another excellent way to get that knowledge. *Before she launched Executive Temporaries, Suzanne Clifton contacted other entrepreneurs in the temporary personnel services business (far enough away from her home base to avoid competitors) to find out "what it takes to operate this kind of business." She picked up many valuable tips and identified the key factors required for success. Today, her company has achieved sales exceeding $4 million.*[91] Successful entrepreneurs are like sponges, soaking up as much knowledge as they can from a variety of sources, and they continue to learn about their businesses, markets, and customers as long as they are in business.

PREPARE A BUSINESS PLAN

To the new entrepreneur, a well-written business plan is a crucial ingredient in preparing for business success. Without a sound business plan, a firm merely drifts along without any real direction. Yet entrepreneurs, who tend to be people of action, too often jump right into a business venture without taking time to prepare a written plan outlining the essence of the business. "Most entrepreneurs don't have a solid business plan," says one business owner. "But a thorough business plan and timely financial information are critical. They help you make the important decisions about your business; you constantly have to monitor what you're doing against your plan."[92]

Planning allows you to replace "I think" with "I know." In many cases, entrepreneurs attempt to build businesses on faulty assumptions such as "I think there are enough customers in town to support a health food shop." The experienced entrepreneur investigates these assumptions and replaces them with facts before making the decision to go into business. We will discuss the process of developing a business plan in chapter 9.

MANAGE FINANCIAL RESOURCES

The best defense against financial problems is developing a practical information system and then using this information to make business decisions. No entrepreneur can maintain control over a business unless he is able to judge its financial health.

The first step in managing financial resources effectively is to have adequate start-up capital. Too many entrepreneurs begin their businesses with too little capital. One experienced business owner advises, "Estimate how much capital you need to get the business going and then double that figure." His point is well taken; it almost always costs more to launch a business than *any* entrepreneur expects.

The most valuable financial resource to any small business is *cash*. Although earning a profit is essential to its long-term survival, a business must have an adequate supply of cash to pay its bills and obligations. Some entrepreneurs count on growing sales to supply their company's cash needs, but it almost never does. Growing companies usually consume more cash than they generate; and the faster they grow, the more cash they gobble up! We will discuss cash management techniques in chapter 8.

UNDERSTAND FINANCIAL STATEMENTS

Every business owner must depend on records and financial statements to know the condition of her business. All too often, these records are used only for tax purposes and not as vital control devices. To truly understand what is going on in the business, an owner must have at least a basic understanding of accounting and finance.

When analyzed and interpreted properly, these financial statements are reliable indicators of a small firm's health. They can be helpful in signaling potential problems. For example, declining sales, slipping profits, rising debt, and deteriorating working capital are all symptoms of potentially lethal problems that require immediate attention. We will discuss financial statement analysis in chapter 7.

LEARN TO MANAGE PEOPLE EFFECTIVELY

No matter what kind of business you launch, you must learn to manage people. Every business depends on a foundation of well-trained, motivated employees. No business owner can do everything alone. The people an entrepreneur hires ultimately determine the heights to which the company can climb—or the depths to which it can plunge. Attracting and retaining a corps of quality employees is no easy task, however; it remains a challenge for every small business owner. One entrepreneur destroyed his company by failing to share any information with his employees and setting up cameras inside and outside his building to monitor his employees.[93] Successful entrepreneurs value their employees and constantly find ways to show their appreciation. We will discuss the techniques of managing and motivating people effectively in chapter 19.

SET YOUR BUSINESS APART FROM THE COMPETITION

The formula for almost certain business failure involves becoming a "me-too business"—copying whatever the competition is doing. Most successful entrepreneurs find a way to convince their customers that their companies are superior to their competitors even if they sell similar products or services. It is especially important for small companies going up against larger, more powerful rivals with greater financial resources. Ideally, the basis for differentiating a company from its competitors is founded in what it does best. For small companies, that basis often is customer service, convenience, speed, quality, or whatever else is important to attracting and keeping happy customers. We will discuss the strategies for creating a unique footprint in the marketplace in chapter 6.

KEEP IN TUNE WITH YOURSELF

"Starting a business is like running a marathon. If you're not physically and mentally in shape, you'd better do something else," says one business consultant.[94] The success of a business, especially in the early days, requires *lots* of energy and enthusiasm. Therefore, good health is essential. Stress is a primary problem for many entrepreneurs, especially if it is not kept in check.

Achieving business success also requires an entrepreneur to have a positive mental attitude toward business and the discipline to stick with it. Successful entrepreneurs recognize that their most valuable resource is their time, and they learn to manage it effectively to make themselves and their companies more productive. None of this, of course, is possible without passion—passion for their businesses, their products or services, their customers, their communities. Passion is what enables a failed business owner to get back up, try again, and make it to the top.

Chapter Summary

1 Define the role of the entrepreneur in business—in the United States and across the globe.
- ◆ Record numbers of people have launched companies over the past decade. The boom in entrepreneurship is not limited solely to the United States; many nations across the globe are seeing similar growth in the small business sector. A variety of competitive, economic, and demographic shifts have created a world in which "small is beautiful."
- ◆ Society depends on entrepreneurs to provide the drive and risk taking necessary for the business system to supply people with the goods and services they need.

2 Describe the entrepreneurial profile.
- ◆ Entrepreneurs have some common characteristics, including a desire for responsibility, a preference for moderate risk, confidence in their ability to succeed, a desire for immediate feedback, a high energy level, a future orientation, skill at organizing, and a value of achievement over money. In a phrase, they are high achievers.

3 Describe the benefits and opportunities of owning a small business.
- ◆ Driven by these personal characteristics, entrepreneurs establish and manage small businesses to gain control over their lives, become self-fulfilled, reap unlimited profits, contribute to society, and do what they enjoy doing.

4 Describe the potential drawbacks of owning a small business.
- ◆ Small business ownership has some potential drawbacks. There are no guarantees that the business will make a profit or even survive. The time and energy required to manage a new business may have dire effects on the owner and family members.

5 Explain the forces that are driving the growth in entrepreneurship.
- ◆ Several factors are driving the boom in entrepreneurship, including the portrayal of entrepreneurs as heroes, better entrepreneurial education, economic and demographic factors, a shift to a service economy, technological advancements, more-independent lifestyles, and increased international opportunities.

6 Discuss the role of diversity in small business and entrepreneurship.
- ◆ Several groups are leading the nation's drive toward entrepreneurship: women, minorities, immigrants, "part-timers," home-based business owners, family business owners, copreneurs, corporate castoffs, and corporate dropouts.

7 Describe the contributions small businesses make to the U.S. economy.
- ◆ The small business sector's contributions are many. They make up 99 percent of all businesses, employ 53 percent of the private sector workforce, create most of the new jobs in the economy, produce 50 percent of the country's gross domestic product (GDP), and account for 47 percent of business sales.

8 Describe the small business failure rate and explain why small businesses fail.
- ◆ The failure rate for small businesses is higher than for big businesses, and profits fluctuate with general economic conditions. Small Business Administration statistics show that 63 percent of new businesses will have failed within six years. The primary cause of business failure is incompetent management. Other reasons include poor financial control, failure to plan, inappropriate location, lack of inventory control, improper managerial attitudes, and inability to make the "entrepreneurial transition."

9 Put business failure into the proper perspective.
- ◆ Because they are building businesses in an environment filled with uncertainty and shaped by rapid change, entrepreneurs recognize that failure is likely to be a part of their lives, but they are not paralyzed by that fear. Successful entrepreneurs have the attitude that failures are simply stepping stones along the path to success.

10 Analyze the major pitfalls involved in managing a small business and understand how the small business owner can avoid them.

◆ There are several general tactics the small business owner can use to avoid failure. The entrepreneur should know the business in depth, develop a solid business plan, manage financial resources effectively, understand financial statements, learn to manage people effectively, set the business apart from the competition, and keep in tune with himself.

Discussion Questions

1. What forces have led to the boom in entrepreneurship in the United States and across the globe?
2. What is an entrepreneur? Give a brief description of the entrepreneurial profile.
3. *Inc.* magazine claims, "Entrepreneurship is more mundane than it's sometimes portrayed. . . . You don't need to be a person of mythical proportions to be very, very successful in building a company." Do you agree? Explain.
4. What are the major benefits of business ownership?
5. Which of the potential drawbacks to business ownership are most critical?
6. Briefly describe the role of the following groups in entrepreneurship: women, minorities, immigrants, "part-timers," home-based business owners, family business owners, copreneurs, corporate castoffs, and corporate dropouts.
7. What contributions do small businesses make to our economy?
8. Describe the small business failure rate.
9. Outline the causes of business failure. Which problems cause most business failures?
10. How can the small business owner avoid the common pitfalls that often lead to business failures?
11. Why is it important to study the small business failure rate?

12. Explain the typical entrepreneur's attitude toward failure.
13. One entrepreneur says that too many people "don't see that by spending their lives afraid of failure, they *become* failures. But when you go out there and risk as I have, you'll have failures along the way, but eventually the result is great success if you are willing to keep risking. . . . For every big yes in life, there will be 199 nos." Do you agree? Explain.
14. What advice would you offer an entrepreneurial friend who has just suffered a business failure?

Step into the Real World

1. Choose an entrepreneur in your community and interview him or her. What's the "story" behind the business? What advantages and disadvantages does the owner see in owning a business? What advice would he or she offer to someone considering launching a business?
2. Search through recent business publications (especially those focusing on small companies such as *Inc.*, *Entrepreneur*, *Business Start-Ups*, *Nation's Business*, or *Your Company*) and find an example of an entrepreneur—past or present—who exhibits the entrepreneurial spirit of striving for success in the face of failure as Gail Borden did. Prepare a brief report for your class.
3. Select one of the categories under the section "The Diversity of Entrepreneurship" in this chapter and research it in more detail. Find examples of the entrepreneurial profile. Prepare a brief report for your class.
4. Interview a local banker who has experience lending to small companies. What factors does he or she believe are important to a small company's success? What factors has he or she seen to cause business failures? What does the lender want to see in a business start-up before agreeing to lend any money?

Take It to the Net

Visit the Scarborough/Zimmer home page at
www.prenhall.com/scarbzim
for updated information, on-line resources, and Web-based exercises.

Endnotes

1. Tom Richman, "Creators of the New Economy," *Inc. Special Report: The State of Small Business 1997*, p. 45; "American Way," *Entrepreneur*, March 1997, p. 11; Jerry Useem, "Start-up Chasers Track New-Biz Storm," *Inc.*, April 1997, p. 22.
2. "Small Business Is Cool Now," *Inc. Special Report: The State of Small Business 1996*, p. 17.
3. Lynn Beresford, "Dream Job," *Entrepreneur*, January 1997, p. 13.
4. Jerry Useem, "Start Me Up," *Inc.*, April 1997, p. 22.
5. "Small Business Is Cool Now," p. 17.
6. Andrew Tanzer, "Small Is Beautiful," *Forbes*, September 23, 1996, pp. 90–96.
7. John Case, "Is America Really Different?" *Inc. Special Report: The State of Small Business 1996*, pp. 108–109; Tanzer, "Small Is Beautiful."
8. Tanzer, "Small Is Beautiful."
9. Jeffry A. Timmons, "An Obsession with Opportunity," *Nation's Business*, March 1985, p. 68.
10. Charles Burck, "The Real World of the Entrepreneur," *Fortune*, April 5, 1993, p. 62.
11. Norm Brodsky, "Who Are the Real Entrepreneurs?" *Inc.*, December 1996, p. 34.
12. Amy Saltzman, "You, Inc.," *U.S. News and World Report*, October 28, 1996, pp. 66–79.
13. David McClelland, *The Achieving Society* (Princeton, N.J.: Van Nostrand, 1961), p. 16.
14. Paul Hawken, "A 'New Age' Look at Business," *U.S. News & World Report*, November 30, 1987, p. 51.
15. Martha E. Mangelsdorf, "Insider," *Inc.*, June 1988, p. 14.
16. Sabin Russell, "Being Your Own Boss in America," *Venture,* May 1984, p. 40.
17. Saltzman, "You, Inc."
18. Stephanie N. Mehta, "Young Entrepreneurs Are Starting Business after Business, Study Finds," *Wall Street Journal*, March 19, 1997, p. B2.
19. Roger Ricklefs and Udayan Gupta, "Traumas of a New Entrepreneur," *Wall Street Journal*, May 10, 1989, p. Bl.
20. James C. Collins, "Sometimes a Great Notion," *Inc.*, July 1993, pp. 90–91; Andrew E. Serwer, "Lessons from America's Fastest Growing Companies," *Fortune*, August 8, 1994, pp. 42–62.
21. Carla Goodman, "Are You or Aren't You?" *Business Start-Ups*, July 1996, p. 66.
22. John Case, "The Origins of Entrepreneurship," *Inc.*, June 1989, p. 52.
23. Michael Selz, "Young America Still Fosters Entrepreneurial Ambitions," *Wall Street Journal*, April 6, 1992, p. B2.
24. Mary Kittel, "An Idea Becomes a Best Seller," *In Business*, November/December 1996, pp.14–15.
25. Liza Leung, "Turn It On," *Entrepreneur*, May 1994, p. 94.
26. Sheryl Nance-Nance, "You Can Be a Millionaire," *Your Company*, June/July 1997, pp. 26–33; Anita Sharpe, "The Rich Aren't So Different After All," *Wall Street Journal*, November 12, 1996, pp. B1, B10.
27. Luisa Kroll, "Fear of Failing," *Forbes*, March 24, 1997, pp. 108–110; Janean Chun, Debra Phillips, Heather Page, Lynn Beresford, Holly Celeste Fisk, and Charlotte Mulhern, "Young Millionaires," *Entrepreneur*, November 1996, pp. 118–134.
28. Selz, "Young America Still Fosters Entrepreneurial Ambitions."
29. Samantha Thompson, "Riding the Railroad to Success," *Upstate Business*, December 15, 1996, pp. 6–7.
30. Gayle Sato-Stodder, "Never Say Die," *Entrepreneur*, December 1990, p. 95.
31. Roger Ricklefs and Udayan Gupta, "Traumas of a New Entrepreneur," *Wall Street Journal*, May 10, 1989, p. B1.
32. Kristen Von Kreisler-Bomben, "The Daddy Track," *Entrepreneur*, March 1990, p. 126.
33. G. E. Hills and H. P. Welsch, "Entrepreneurship Behavioral Intentions and Student Independence Characteristics and Experiences," *Frontiers of Entrepreneurship Research* (Babson College, 1986), pp.173–186.
34. A. L. Boberg and P. Kiecker, "Changing Patterns of Demand: Entrepreneurship Education for Entrepreneurs," *Frontiers of Entrepreneurship Research* (Babson College, 1986), pp. 600–661.
35. Lisa Silver, "Getting Down to Business," *Success*, December 1996, pp. 58–62.
36. Stephanie Barlow, "Making It," *Entrepreneur*, December 1992, pp. 103–106.
37. William E. Bulkeley, "How Can You Make Money from the Web?" *Wall Street Journal*, December 9, 1996, p. R18.
38. Lesley Hazleton, "Profile: Jeff Bezos," *Success*, July 1998, pp. 58–60; Gregory Spears, "Making Money on the Web," *Kiplinger's Personal Finance Magazine*, December 1996, pp. 67–74; Amazon.com at <http://www.amazon.com>.
39. James Worsham, "Markets At Risk," *Nation's Business*, August 1998, pp. 14–20.
40. Judith Valente, "You Can Start Your Own Business," *Parade Magazine*, June 23, 1996, pp. 8–11.
41. Sharon Nelton, "Women's Firms Thrive," *Nation's Business*, August 1998, p. 39.
42. Nelton, "Women's Firms Thrive," p. 38; Richard Miniter, "Enterprising Women," *Reader's Digest*, November 1996, pp. 107–111.
43. Elaine Pofeldt, "The Self-Made Woman," *Success*, June 1997, p. 44.
44. Nelton, "Women's Firms Thrive," p. 38; Janean Chun, "Hear Them Roar," *Entrepreneur*, June 1995, pp. 10–11.
45. Pofeldt, "The Self-Made Woman."
46. Luisa Kroll, "Mother of Pearls," *Forbes*, January 26, 1998, p. 64; Pofeldt, "The Self-Made Woman."
47. "Black Entrepreneurship in America," *Wall Street Journal* (Advertising Supplement), July 1994, pp. 1–4; (U.S. Census Bureau: <http://www.census.gov>.
48. Carla Goodman, "Ahead of the Pack," *Entrepreneur*, June 1996, p. 16; Sharon Nelton, "Hispanic-Owned Firms Set the Pace for Growth," *Nation's Business*, October 1996, p. 8.
49. Maria Mallory, "From the Ground Up," *U.S. News & World Report*, February 19, 1996, pp. 68–72.
50. Carol Mauro-Noon, "American Dream," *Success*, March 1997, pp. 37–42.
51. Carla Goodman, "The Big Time," *Business Start-Ups*, August 1998, pp. 26–29; Imran Husain, "After Hours," *Entrepreneur*, March 1995, pp. 230–233.
52. Debra Phillips, Cynthia E. Griffin, Heather Page, Lynn Beresford, Holly Celeste Fisk, and Charlotte Mulhern, "Entrepreneurial Superstars," *Entrepreneur*, April 1997, pp. 108–139.
53. "Home Business Motivation," *The Greenville News*, December 27, 1997, p. 5B; Robert Lewis, "All the 'Comforts' of Home," *AARP Bulletin*, October 1996, pp. 2, 13.
54. Janean Huber, "The Quiet Revolution," *Entrepreneur*, September 1993, pp. 77–81; Janean Huber, "Bright Lights, Small City," *Entrepreneur*, March 1994, pp. 102–109.
55. Andy Meisler, "Dilbert: Home Alone, Too," *Business News*, Spring 1997, pp. 20–24.

56. Ronaleen Roha, "Home Alone," *Kiplinger's Personal Finance Magazine*, May 1997, pp. 85–89; Janean Huber, "The Quiet Revolution," Entrepreneur, September 1993, pp. 77–81.

57. Huber, "The Quiet Revolution."

58. "Quickstats," *Home Business News Report*, Fall 1994, p. 1.

59. (Mass Mutual Family Business Network: www.massmutual.com/FBN); "Keeping the Firm in the Family," *Upstate Business*, May 18, 1997, p. 8; G. Scott Budge, "Family Ties," *Sky*, March 1992, pp. 16–20; John L. Ward and Craig E. Aronoff, "Just What Is a Family Business?" *Nation's Business*, February 1990, pp. 32–33; Nancy Kercheval, "Business Grows with Family Tree," *Times Picayune*, November 12, 1989, pp. Gl, G4; Erik Calonius, "Blood & Money," *Newsweek*, Special Issue, pp. 82–84.

60. Calonius, "Blood & Money," p. 82.

61. "Keeping the Firm in the Family."

62. Brian Henson, "Setting the Stage," *Inc.*, June 1994, pp. 23–24.

63. Udayan Gupta, "And Business Makes Three: Couples Working Together," *Wall Street Journal*, February 26, 1990, p. B2.

64. Bob Weinstein, "For Better or Worse," *Your Company*, Spring 1992, pp. 28–31.

65. Echo M. Garrett, "And Business Makes Three," *Small Business Reports*, September 1993, pp. 27–31.

66. Sharon Nelton, "Succeeding in a Walk," *Nation's Business*, January 1997, pp. 12–14.

67. Mary Lord, "No Deadwood Here," *U.S. News & World Report*, October 28, 1996, pp. 82–84.

68. Mark Musick, Gene Logsdon, and Jerome Goldstein, "Independent Cure for Overworked Americans," *In Business*, May/June 1992, pp. 28–30.

69. Heather Page, "Executive Decision," *Entrepreneur*, July 1996, pp. 149–153.

70. "Going Places," *Entrepreneur*, June 1994, p.14.

71. Randall Lane, "Involuntary Entrepreneurs," *Forbes*, June 3, 1996, pp. 81–82.

72. Donna Kato, "Changing Course, Burning Suits," *Greenville News*, June 6, 1993, p. 1D.

73. Brian O'Reilly, "The New Face of Small Business," *Fortune*, May 2, 1994, p. 82.

74. Kenneth Labich, "The New Low-Risk Entrepreneurs," *Fortune*, July 27, 1992, p. 84.

75. Suzie Riddle, "Small Business Facts," *Upstate Business*, June 1, 1997, p. 5.

76. Michael Hopkins, "Help Wanted," *Inc. Special Report: The State of Small Business 1997*, pp. 35–41; Janean Chun and Cynthia E. Griffin, "The Mouse That Roared," *Entrepreneur*, September 1996, pp. 118–122; Ingrid Abramovitch, "Gazelles Create Jobs," *Success*, September 1994, p. 8; Andrew F. Serwer, "Lessons from America's Fastest Growing Companies," *Fortune*, August 8, 1994, p. 44; "Business Bulletin," *Wall Street Journal*, May 4, 1993, p. Al; "Where Good Jobs Grow," *Fortune*, June 14, 1993, p. 22.

77. Erskine Bowles, "Training Ground," *Entrepreneur*, March 1994, p. 168.

78. Riddle, "Small Business Facts."

79. John LaFalce, "The Driving Force," *Entrepreneur*, February 1990, pp. 161–166.

80. David Taymond, "Famous Flops," *Forbes ASAP*, June 2, 1997, pp. 101–103.

81. Roy Hoopes, "Mind Your Own Business," *Modern Maturity*, February–March 1991, pp. 26–33.

82. Clint Willis, "Try, Try Again," *Forbes ASAP*, June 2, 1997, pp. 59–64.

83. Alex Markels, "A Snowboard Start-Up Hits Big Bumps," *Wall Street Journal*, November 27, 1996, pp. B1, B2.

84. Eugene Carlson, "Spreading Your Wings," *Wall Street Journal*, October 16, 1992, p. R2.

85. Sharon Nelton, "Ten Key Threats to Success," *Nation's Business*, June 1992, pp. 20–28.

86. Michael Barrier, "Entrepreneurs Who Excel," *Nation's Business*, August 1996, p. 28.

87. Michael Warshaw, "Great Comebacks," *Success,* July/August 1995, p. 43.

88. Barrier, "Entrepreneurs Who Excel," p. 26.

89. Willis, "Try, Try Again," p. 63.

90. Ibid., pp. 60–63.

91. Joshua Hyatt, "Should You Start a Business?" *Inc.*, February 1992, p. 50.

92. Stephanie Barlow, "Hang On!" *Entrepreneur*, September 1992, p. 156.

93. Lee Patterson, "Tanking It Five Ways," *Forbes ASAP*, June 2, 1997, pp. 75–76.

94. Kirsten Von Kriesler-Bomben, "The Obstacle Course," *Entrepreneur*, July 1990, p. 175.

Strategic Management
and the Entrepreneur

To accomplish great things, we must not only
act, but we must also dream; not only plan,
but also believe.

—*Anatole France*

You either have to be first, best, or different.

—*Loretta Lynn*

Upon completion of this chapter, you will be able to

1 Understand the importance of strategic management
to a small business.

2 Explain why and how a small business must create a
competitive advantage in the market.

3 Develop a strategic plan for a business using the 10
steps in the strategic planning process.

4 Understand the Entrepreneurial Strategy Matrix and
how to apply it.

5 Discuss the characteristics of three basic strategies:
low-cost, differentiation, and focus.

6 Understand the importance of controls such as the
balanced scorecard in the planning process.

1 Understand the impor-
tance of strategic management to a small business.

*F*ew activities in the life of a business are as vital—or as overlooked—as that of developing a strategy for success. Too often, entrepreneurs brimming with optimism and enthusiasm launch businesses
destined for failure because their founders never stop to define a workable strategy that sets them apart from their competition. Because they
tend to be people of action, entrepreneurs often find the process of developing a strategy dull and unnecessary. Their tendency is to start a
business, try several approaches, and see what works. However, entrepreneurs without a cohesive plan of action have as much chance of
building a successful business as a defense contractor without blueprints has of building a jet fighter. Companies lacking clear strategies
may achieve some success in the shortrun, but as soon as competitive

conditions stiffen or an unanticipated threat arises, they usually "hit the wall" and fold. Without a basis for differentiating itself from a pack of similar competitors, the best a company can hope for is mediocrity in the marketplace.

In today's global competitive environment, any business, large or small, that is not thinking and acting strategically is extremely vulnerable. Every business is exposed to the forces of a rapidly changing competitive environment, and in the future small business executives can expect even greater uncertainty. From sweeping political changes around the planet and rapid technological advances to more intense competition and newly emerging global markets, the business environment has become more turbulent and challenging to business owners. Entrepreneurs must develop plans to contend with these extensive changes and the challenges and opportunities they create. Perhaps the biggest change business owners face is unfolding now: the shift in the world's economy from a base of *financial* to *intellectual* capital. "Knowledge is no longer just a factor of production," says futurist Alvin Toffler. "It is the *critical* factor of production."[1] That shift will create as much change in the world's business systems as the Industrial Revolution did in the agricultural-based economies of the 1800s. This Knowledge Revolution will spell disaster for companies that are not prepared for it, but it will spawn tremendous opportunities for entrepreneurs who are equipped with the strategies to exploit them.[2]

In short, the rules of the competitive game of business have been dramatically altered. To be successful, entrepreneurs can no longer do things in the way they have always done them. Consequently, the successful small business manager needs a powerful weapon to cope with such a hostile environment: the process of strategic management. **Strategic management** involves developing a game plan to guide the company as it strives to accomplish its vision, mission, goals, and objectives and to keep it from straying off its desired course. The idea is to give the owner a blueprint for matching the company's strengths and weaknesses to the opportunities and threats in the environment.

*B*uilding a Competitive Advantage

❷ Explain why and how a small business must create a competitive advantage in the market.

The goal of developing a strategic plan is to create for the small company a **competitive advantage**—the aggregation of factors that sets the small business apart from its competitors and gives it a unique position in the market. Every small firm must establish a plan for creating a unique image in the minds of its potential customers. No business can be everything to everyone. In fact, one of the biggest pitfalls many entrepreneurs stumble into is failing to differentiate their companies from the crowd of competitors. *For instance, No Kidding!, a small toy store in Brookline, Massachusetts, has continued to thrive despite the fact that many independent toy stores have closed in the face of intense competition from superstores such as Toys 'R' Us. The company's "secret" for success: a well-defined strategy for offering customers exactly what they want and cannot get at the mass merchandising toy giants. Recognizing that trying to compete with its larger rivals on the basis of price and selection is senseless, No Kidding! doesn't carry traditional toys such as Barbie and Nintendo, but it does stock many toys that customers cannot find at large toy chains. The store courts its target customers, well-educated affluent professionals in the surrounding area, with lots of service, little extras such as free gift wrap, and plenty of advice from its sales staff (most of whom are moonlighting teachers) on selecting the right toy to stimulate a child intellectually. Because most of its product line is not advertised on television, No Kidding! sales staffers must be knowledgeable about the products they sell as well as about childhood development. As part of their mission to educate as they sell, co-owners Judy Cockerton and Carol Nelson work closely with local schools to encourage children to read more and to find joy in learning. The store recently hired a part-time liaison to assist schools with reading, writing, and storytelling.*[3]

When it comes to developing a strategic plan, small companies have a variety of natural advantages over their larger competitors. The typical small business has fewer product lines, a better-defined customer base, and a specific geographic market area. Small business owners usually are in close contact with their markets, giving them valuable knowledge on how to best serve their customers' needs and wants. Consequently, strategic management may come more naturally to small businesses than to larger companies.

Strategic management can increase a small firm's effectiveness, but owners first must have a procedure designed to meet their needs and their business's special characteristics. It is a mistake to attempt to apply a big business's strategic development techniques to a small business because a small business is not a little big business. Because of their size and their particular characteristics—resource poverty, a flexible managerial style, an informal organizational structure, and adaptability to change—small businesses need a different approach to the strategic management process. The strategic management procedure for a small business should include the following features:

◆ Use a relatively short planning horizon: two years or less for most small companies.

◆ Be informal and not overly structured; a shirt-sleeve approach is ideal.

◆ Encourage the participation of employees and outside parties to improve the reliability and creativity of the plan.

◆ Do not begin with setting objectives; extensive objective setting early on may interfere with the creative process.

◆ Focus on strategic thinking, not just on planning, by linking long-range goals to day-to-day operations.

The Strategic Management Process

③ Develop a strategic plan for a business using the 10 steps in the strategic planning process.

Strategic planning is a continuous process that consists of 10 steps:

Step 1. Develop a clear vision and translate it into a meaningful mission statement.

Step 2. Define the firm's core competences and target market segment, and position the business to compete effectively.

Step 3. Assess the company's strengths and weaknesses.

Step 4. Scan the environment for significant opportunities and threats.

Step 5. Identify the key factors for success.

Step 6. Analyze the competition.

Step 7. Create company goals and objectives.

Step 8. Formulate strategic options and select the appropriate strategies.

Step 9. Translate strategic plans into action plans.

Step 10. Establish accurate controls.

STEP 1: DEVELOP A CLEAR VISION AND TRANSLATE IT INTO A MEANINGFUL MISSION STATEMENT

Vision. Throughout history, the greatest political and business leaders have been visionaries. Whether the vision is as grand as Martin Luther King Jr.'s "I have a dream" speech or as simple as Ray Kroc's devotion to quality, service, cleanliness, and value at McDonald's, the purpose is the same: to focus everyone's attention and efforts on the same target. The vision touches everyone associated with the company—employees, investors, lenders, customers, the community. It is an expression of what the owner stands for and believes in. Highly successful entrepreneurs are able to communicate their vision and their enthusiasm to the people around them. One study of more than 500 "hidden champions"—little-known superperforming companies that hold worldwide market shares of at least 50 percent—identified having a clear vision as an important factor in the competitive edge these companies had established. The founders of these companies adhere strongly to their own fundamental vision and purpose while giving employees the freedom to handle daily activities within the context of that vision.[4]

Vision is based on an entrepreneur's values. Successful entrepreneurs build their businesses around a set of three to six core values, which might range from respect for the individual and innovation to creating satisfied customers and making the world a better place. Indeed, truly visionary entrepreneurs see their companies' primary purpose as more than just "making money." One writer explains: "Almost all workers are making decisions, not just filling out weekly sales reports or tightening screws. They will do what they think best. If you want them to do as the company thinks best too, then you must [see to it that] they have an inner gyroscope aligned with the corporate compass."[5] That gyroscope's alignment depends on the entrepreneur's values and how well she transmits them throughout the company.

The best way to put values into action is to create a written mission statement that communicates those values to everyone the company touches.

Mission. The **mission statement** addresses the first question of any business venture: What business am I in? Establishing the purpose of the business in writing must come first in order to give the company a sense of direction. "If you don't reduce [your company's purpose] to paper, it just doesn't stick," says the owner of an architecture firm. "Reducing it to paper really forces you to think about what you are doing."[6] The mission is the mechanism for making it clear to everyone the company touches "why we are here" and "where we are going." *After her company had survived two crises that nearly put her out of business, Judy Creiner recognized the importance of creating a written mission statement that would crystallize her vision for MobileFitness, which provides fitness programs and health and fitness instruction for companies. Her mission reads, in part: "To be pre-eminent in the health and wellness arena. To provide our members with unlimited opportunities to make healthy lifestyle changes in a success-oriented and supportive environment."*[7] Without a concise, meaningful mission statement, a small business risks wandering aimlessly in the marketplace, with no idea of where to go or how to get there. The mission statement essentially sets the tone for the entire company.

Elements of a Mission Statement. A sound mission statement need not be lengthy to be effective. Some of the key issues an entrepreneur and his employees should address as they develop a mission statement for the company include:

◆   What are the basic beliefs and values of the organization? What do we stand for?

◆   Who are the company's target customers?

◆   What are our basic products and services? What customer needs and wants do they satisfy?

◆   How can we better satisfy those needs and wants?

◆   Why should customers do business with us rather than with the competitor down the street (or across town, on the other coast, on the other side of the globe)?

- What constitutes value to our customers? How can we offer them better value?
- What is our competitive advantage? What is its source?
- In which markets (or market segments) will we choose to compete?
- Who are the key stakeholders in our company, and what effect do they have on it?
- What benefits should we be providing our customers five years from now?
- What business do we want to be in five years from now?

By answering such basic questions, the company will have a much clearer picture of what it is and what it wants to be.

The firm's mission statement may be the most essential and basic communication that it puts forward. If the people on the plant, shop, retail, or warehouse floor do not know what a company's mission is, then, for all practical purposes, it does not have one! The mission statement expresses the firm's character, identity, and scope of operations, but writing it is only part of the battle. The more difficult part is living that mission every day. To be effective, a mission statement must become a natural part of the organization, embodied in the minds, habits, attitudes, and decisions of everyone in the company every day. Consider the mission statement of Fetzer Vineyards, a vineyard whose own acreage is 100 percent organic with no chemical pesticides or fertilizers, and the message its sends to company stakeholders:

> We are an environmentally and socially conscious grower, producer, and marketer of wines of the highest quality and value.
>
> Working in harmony with respect for the human spirit, we are committed to sharing information about the enjoyment of food and wine in a lifestyle of moderation and responsibility.
>
> We are dedicated to the continuous growth and development of our people and our business.[8]

A company may have a powerful competitive advantage, but it is wasted unless (1) the owner has communicated that advantage to workers, who, in turn, are working hard to communicate it to customers and potential customers and (2) customers are recommending the company to their friends because they understand the benefits they are getting from it that they cannot get elsewhere. *That's* the real power of a mission statement.

STEP 2: DEFINE THE FIRM'S CORE COMPETENCES AND ITS TARGET MARKET SEGMENT, AND POSITION THE BUSINESS TO COMPETE EFFECTIVELY

Core Competences. In the long run, what sets a company apart from its competition is the ability to develop a set of core competences that enable it to serve its selected target customers better. **Core competences** are a unique set of capabilities that a company develops in key operational areas, such as quality, service, innovation, team building, flexibility, responsiveness, and others that allow it to vault past competitors. Typically, a company is likely to build core competences in no more than five or six (sometimes fewer) areas. These core competences become the nucleus of a company's competitive advantage and are usually quite enduring over time. To be effective, these competences should be difficult for competitors to duplicate, and they must provide customers with some kind of perceived benefit. Small companies' core competences often have to do with the advantages of their size: agility, speed, closeness to their customers, superior service, ability to innovate. In short, their smallness is an advantage, allowing them to do things that their larger rivals cannot.

IN THE FOOTSTEPS OF AN ENTREPRENEUR

Grading the Mission Statement

*A*lan Lewis developed a mission statement for his travel agency, Grand Circle Travel (GCT), that described the company's responsibilities to "our customers, our associates, our stakeholders, and our world." Then the company hit a huge growth spurt, going from 150 to 230 employees and making it much more difficult for Lewis to measure how well GCT was performing in regard to its mission. To gauge how well GCT measured up to the standards set forth in its mission statement, Lewis asked the people who knew best—his employees (or associates, as GTC calls them)—to grade the company's performance in each of the four major areas the mission statement covered.

Associate Responsibility *Grade: B–.* Employees said that the company's rapid growth had created confusion about how the business worked, that its compensation levels were too subjective, and that workers needed more training and development.

GTC's response: Lewis established an open-book management program called *BusinessWorks,* giving workers access to all of GTC's records and reports (operating as well as financial) and training in how to read, understand, and use them in their jobs. GTC shifted its incentive system away from overall company profitability to departmental profitability.

Responsibility to Customers *Grade: B.* Employees saw a need to improve the quality of customers' travel experiences and to coordinate customer services among departments.

GTC's response: Lewis created teams of employees to study existing processes and procedures and to come up with ideas for improving them. "We fiddled with our top 20 programs," Lewis says. "We changed hotels, got rid of some airlines, added events, and deleted some cities."

Financial Responsibility *Grade: C+.* Associates noted that loose financial controls and unnecessary expenses were cutting into the company's profits, reducing everyone's bonuses.

GTC's response: Lewis established a new financial reporting system and found ways, with associates' help, to reduce advertising and ticketing expenses. GTC also created a one-year finance and business training program for all supervisors and managers.

Social Responsibility *Grade: A.* Employees wanted to know more about which charitable organizations GTC was supporting and what volunteer opportunities were available.

GTC's response: Lewis created a monthly newsletter, written by associates, that covers all of GTC's donations and lists upcoming volunteer opportunities.

1. What benefits does GTC reap from its associate report card?

2. What impact do you think this report card will have on the company? On its mission statement?

3. Use the World Wide Web to find examples of two organizational mission statements, one you think is effective and the other ineffective. Discuss the differences between the two mission statements. Explain in your own words why it is important for a company to have a mission statement.

SOURCE: Adapted from: "Can the Boss Make the Grade?" *Inc.,* May 1996, p. 114. ◆

The key to success is building these core competences (or identifying the ones a company already has) and then concentrating on them to provide superior service and value for the company's target customers.

Developing core competences does *not* necessarily require a company to spend a great deal of money. It does, however, require an entrepreneur to use creativity, imagination, and vision to identify those things that it does best and that are most important to its target customers. Building a company's strategy around its core competences allows the business to gain a sustainable competitive edge over its rivals and to ride its strategy to victory. *For example, Thomas Ryan and John Rigos, founders of CDuctive, have set their Web-based retail music business apart from its more traditional competitors by targeting aficionados of offbeat music categories and by offering them the ability to design customized CDs with any assortment of songs that suit their individual tastes. Customers who log on the CDuctive's Web site can hear snippets of songs from the company's repertoire of 10,000 titles (organized by category), pick the titles they like, and create their own custom CDs in just minutes. Producing CDs is extremely fast because the process is automated; computers retrieve digitized songs stored in their memories and burn them onto blank CDs. By relying on several distinctive competences, including exclusive licensing agreements with more than 50 independent record labels and a low-cost structure (no retail storefront and no expensive inventory), CDuctive offers its customers the ultimate convenience: shopping any time of day for CDs containing only the songs they want to hear.[9]*

Table 2.1 provides an interesting look at defining a small company's core competences.

Successful small businesses know the market segments in which they compete and build and retain core competences that directly contribute to their long-term effectiveness. Answering the following questions will help entrepreneurs focus their resources on creating or reinforcing their companies' core competences:

◆ What are our target customers' characteristics (e.g., age, income, buying habits, location)?

◆ Why do they buy our goods or use our service?

Table 2.1 Identifying Core Competences

In the battle of strategies for success, the tide may be turning in favor of small businesses. Although outgunned by their larger competitors' checkbooks, small companies have managed to find ways to outmaneuver big companies in developing core competences in such key areas as customer service, productivity gains, and flexibility in coping with change.

Core Competence	Who Wins?	Why?
Customized products	Small companies	Require smaller runs, which are ideally suited to small firms
Better customer service	Small companies	Flexible, friendly company cultures that focus on the customer
Quick response to change	Small companies	Unencumbered by giant bureaucracies and systems laden with rigid policies and procedures
Productivity gains	Small companies	Lower levels of overhead expenses and the ability to use "off-the-shelf" technology applications creatively to solve problems and improve customer service

To gain these core competence advantages over their much bigger competitors, small companies often turn to technology; in fact, research suggests that smaller businesses have an advantage in profiting from technology. For example, one small architectural-lighting firm did not have the staff or the resources to send preliminary designs to clients (something its larger rivals routinely do), so managers set up an audio-conferencing and on-line document-sharing system that allows designers and customers anywhere in the world to discuss and modify blueprints on a computer screen. The result: improved customer service and a speed advantage over its rivals—in short, a core competence.

How can a small business owner use technology—or any other competitive tool—to create core competences? Asking these four questions about the company's products or services will help:

◆ Which characteristics that our industry takes for granted should we *eliminate?*

◆ Which ones should we *reduce well below* the current industry standard?

◆ Which ones should we *raise well above* the current industry standard?

◆ What characteristics should we *create* that the industry has never offered?

Sources: Adapted from David H. Freedman, "Through the Looking Glass," *Inc. Special Report: The State of Small Business 1996*, pp. 48–54; W. Chan Kim and Renee Mauborgne, "When 'Competitive Advantage' Is Neither," *Wall Street Journal*, April 21, 1997, p. A22.

- What unique skills, knowledge, service, or other resources do we possess that would improve our target customers' lives?
- How can we use those resources to offer value to customers that our competitors cannot?
- How loyal are they to their present suppliers?
- What factors cause them to increase or decrease purchases?
- To what extent does our market focus build on skills that we already have?
- What skills must we develop to serve our customers in the future?

Market Segmentation. Market segmentation simply means carving up the mass market into smaller, more homogeneous units and then attacking each segment with a specific marketing strategy designed to appeal to its members. This requires information: knowing who the firm's customers are, their characteristics, and their likes and dislikes. To segment a market successfully, a small business owner must first identify the characteristics of two or more groups of customers with similar needs or wants. The owner must develop a basis for segmenting the market—benefits sought, product usage, brand preference, purchase patterns, and so on—and use this basis to identify the various submarkets to enter. Then the owner must verify that the segments are large enough and have enough purchasing power to generate a profit for the firm, because segmentation is useless if the firm cannot earn a profit serving its segments. Finally, the owner must reach the market. To be profitable, a segment must be accessible. Typical market segments might be college students, retired people, young singles, ethnic groups, or high-income baby boomers.

Small companies that focus on particular target segments and take the time to learn their customers' habits, wants, and needs can market their goods and services effectively. *For example, Dennis Lambert, owner of two Tinder Box shops that sell tobacco products and collectibles, uses market segmentation to zero in on serving his customers' individual needs. When Lambert received a shipment of exquisite cigars from the Dominican Republic, he used his customer database to identify 600 cigar customers, which represent about a fourth of his total customer base. He sent each one a postcard about the cigars, explaining the characteristics of their West Indian tobacco. The mailing drew a 20 percent response rate, about 10 times the rate on a typical direct mail ad!*[10]

Positioning. Positioning the company in the market involves influencing customers' perceptions to create the desired image for the business and its goods and services. Most often, a business attempts to position its products by differentiating them from those of competitors using some characteristic important to the customer such as price, quality, service, or performance. *Bruce Wilson changed the entire focus of his company, Healthy Planet Products, when he discovered that sales of its traditional greeting cards were growing at 3 percent a year and that sales of its wildlife and environmental cards (printed on high-quality, recycled paper with stunning images of wildlife and nature) were growing at 30 percent a year. "We were trying to be everything to everyone," recalls Wilson, "but there was no way we could compete with Hallmark, American Greetings, and Gibson." Wilson decided to position Healthy Planet Products as "a marketer of cause-related greeting cards." Within three years, 90 percent of the company's cards and stationery were linked to organizations supporting environmental causes, such as the Sierra Club, and sales had climbed 80 percent to $5.8 million. Healthy Planet Products' primary target audience is baby boomers who are concerned about environmental issues and who prefer to do business with companies that support environmental causes.*[11]

Proper positioning gives the small business a foundation for developing a competitive advantage, some way of setting itself apart from the competition. Lower prices are a common method of establishing a competitive advantage, but this can be especially dangerous for small businesses, which cannot rely on the economies of scale that larger businesses can.

A smarter tactic for the small business owner is to rely on a natural advantage, such as the small firm's flexibility in reaching the market, a wider variety of customer services, or special knowledge of the good or service. For example, small independently owned drugstores cannot offer lower prices than can the chain drugstores, which can take advantage of high-volume purchases to get quantity discounts. However, local drugstores can develop a competitive advantage by offering such extras as more-convenient hours, customer credit, delivery services, or some special feature such as an old-fashioned soda fountain. In customers' eyes, these features set independent drugstores apart from their larger competitors.

STEP 3: ASSESS THE COMPANY'S STRENGTHS AND WEAKNESSES

Having identified the firm's driving force and desired position in the market, the entrepreneur can turn her attention to assessing company strengths and weaknesses. Building a successful competitive strategy demands that a business magnify its strengths and overcome or compensate for its weaknesses. **Strengths** are positive internal factors that contribute to the accomplishment of a company's mission, goals, and objectives; **weaknesses** are negative internal factors that inhibit the accomplishment of its mission, goals, and objectives.

Identifying strengths and weaknesses helps the owner understand her business as it exists (or will exist). The organization's strengths should originate in the core competences that are essential to remaining competitive in each of the market segments in which the firm competes. The key to building a successful strategy is to use the company's strengths as its foundation and to match those strengths against competitors' weaknesses.

One effective technique for taking this strategic inventory is to prepare a balance sheet of the company's strengths and weaknesses (see Table 2.2). The positive side should reflect important skills, knowledge, or resources that contribute to the firm's success. The negative side should record honestly any limitations that detract from the company's ability to compete. This balance sheet should analyze all key performance areas of the business: personnel, finance, production, marketing, product development, organization, and others. This analysis should give owners a realistic perspective of their business, pointing out foundations on which they can build strengths and obstacles they must remove. This exercise can help owners move from their current position to future actions.

STEP 4: SCAN THE ENVIRONMENT FOR SIGNIFICANT OPPORTUNITIES AND THREATS

Opportunities. Once entrepreneurs have taken an internal inventory of company strengths and weaknesses, they must turn to the external environment to identify any opportunities and

Table 2.2 Identifying Company Strengths and Weaknesses

Strengths (Positive Internal Factors)	Weaknesses (Negative Internal Factors)

threats that might have a significant impact on the business. **Opportunities** are positive external factors that the firm could employ to accomplish its objectives. The number of potential opportunities is limitless, so managers need analyze only factors significant to the business (probably two or three at most).

When identifying opportunities, a business owner must pay close attention to new potential markets. Are competitors overlooking a niche in the market? Is there a better way to reach customers? *The Indian River Fruit Company, a simple, family-owned business in Titusville, Florida, sold fresh fruit the old-fashioned way and had changed little through the years. Then president Barry Gainer saw a ripe opportunity to increase Indian River's market exposure: the World Wide Web. Gainer, a self-admitted computer novice when he started, said the rest of the family "thought he was nuts" when he told them about his idea. Gainer, however, believed that with a Web site "we could expose our business to millions and millions of customers at relatively low cost." He researched other gift sites on the Web, talked with customers, and discussed his idea with business experts on the Internet. In addition to direct sales opportunities, Indian River's Web site includes contests, recipes, and other items of interest to customers. The site <http://www.giftfruit.com> cost $2,000 to launch, and Gainer pays $50 a month to maintain it. Capitalizing on this opportunity has paid off; Web customers now account for about 25 percent of Indian River's annual revenues.*[12]

Threats. **Threats** are negative external forces that inhibit the firm's ability to achieve its objectives. Threats to the business can take a variety of forms: New competitors might enter the local market; the government might issue a new mandate regulating a business activity; there could be an economic recession; interest rates might rise; technological advances could make a company's product obsolete; and so on. *For instance, Gibson Guitar Corporation, the company that helped pioneer the electric guitar, has watched sales of its flagship products slide dramatically from the boom days of the 1960s and 70s when rock and roll bands from the Beatles to Led Zepplin inspired thousands of young people to buy their own guitars and learn to play. As musical tastes changed over the years, however, guitars fell out of favor, and Gibson's sales have fallen off dramatically. "There have been no guitar heroes for several years now," says CEO Henry Juszkiewicz, "and that's what spurs sales of guitars." To combat this serious threat to Gibson, Juszkiewicz has shifted the company's strategy and diversified its product line to include a wider array of musical instruments. Gibson has also opened several Gibson Cafes, a combination coffee shop, performance space, and guitar museum.*[13] Like Juszkiewicz, entrepreneurs must prepare plans for shielding their components from such threats.

Figure 2.1 illustrates that opportunities and threats are products of the interactions of forces, trends, and events outside the direct control of the business. These external forces will have direct impact on the behavior of the markets in which the business operates, the behavior of competitors, and the behavior of customers. Table 2.3 provides a form that enables business owners to take a strategic inventory of the opportunities and threats facing their companies.

STEP 5: IDENTIFY THE KEY SUCCESS FACTORS

In every industry there are controllable variables that determine the relative success of market participants. Identifying and manipulating these variables is how a small business gains a competitive advantage. By focusing efforts to maximize their companies' performance on these key success factors, entrepreneurs can achieve dramatic market advantages over their competitors. Companies that understand these key success factors tend to be leaders of the pack, whereas those who fail to recognize them become also-rans.

Key success factors are relationships between a controllable variable (e.g., plant size, size of sales force, advertising expenditures, product packaging) and a critical factor influencing the firm's ability to compete. Obviously, which factors will be key depends on the in-

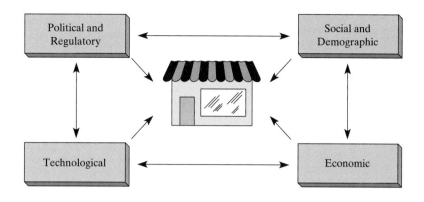

Figure 2.1 The Power of External Forces

dustry. Many are based on cost factors such as manufacturing cost per unit, distribution cost per unit, or development cost per unit. Some are less tangible and less obvious, but just as important, such as product quality, services offered, store location, customer credit. *For example, one restaurant owner identified the following key success factors:*

◆ *Tight cost control (labor: 15–18 percent of sales and food costs, 35–40 percent of sales)*
◆ *Trained, dependable, honest in-store managers*
◆ *Close monitoring of waste*
◆ *Careful site selection (the right location)*
◆ *Maintenance of food quality*
◆ *Consistency*
◆ *Cleanliness*
◆ *Friendly and attentive service from a well-trained waitstaff*

These controllable variables determine the ability of any restaurant in his market segment to compete. Restaurants lacking these key success factors are not likely to survive, whereas those who build their strategies with these factors in mind will prosper. However, before any small business owner can build a strategy on the foundation of the industry's key

Table 2.3 Identifying Opportunities and Threats

Opportunities (Positive External Factors)	Threats (Negative External Factors)

Table 2.4 Identifying Key Success Factors

List the specific skills, characteristics, and core competences that your business must possess if it is to be successful in its market segment.

Key Success Factor	How Your Company Rates
1	Low 1 2 3 4 5 6 7 8 9 10 High
2	Low 1 2 3 4 5 6 7 8 9 10 High
3	Low 1 2 3 4 5 6 7 8 9 10 High
4	Low 1 2 3 4 5 6 7 8 9 10 High
5	Low 1 2 3 4 5 6 7 8 9 10 High

Conclusions:

success factors, she must identify them. Table 2.4 presents a form to help the owner identify the most important success factors and their implications for the company.

STEP 6: ANALYZE THE COMPETITION

When a recent survey asked small business owners to identify the greatest challenge they faced in the upcoming year, the overwhelming response was *competition*.[14] Thus, keeping tabs on rivals' movements through competitive intelligence programs is a vital strategic activity. "Business is like any battlefield. If you want to win the war, you have to know who you're up against," says one small business consultant.[15] The primary goals of a competitive intelligence program include the following:

◆ Avoiding surprises from existing competitors' new strategies and tactics

◆ Identifying potential new competitors

◆ Improving reaction time to competitors' actions

◆ Anticipating rivals' next strategic moves

Unfortunately, many small companies fail to gather competitive intelligence because their owners mistakenly assume that doing so is too costly or simply unnecessary. In reality, the cost of collecting information about competitors typically is minimal, but it does require discipline.

Sizing up the competition gives a business owner a realistic view of the market and her position in it. A competitive intelligence exercise enables entrepreneurs to update their knowledge of competitors by answering the following questions:

◆ Who are your major competitors? Where are they located? (The Yellow Pages is a great place to start.)

◆ What distinctive competences have they developed?

◆ How do their cost structures compare with yours? Their financial resources?

◆ How do they market their products and services?

◆ What do customers say about them? How do customers describe their products or services; their way of doing business; the additional services they supply?

◆ What are their key strategies?

◆ What are their strengths? How can your company surpass them?

- What are their primary weaknesses? How can your company capitalize on them?
- Are new competitors entering the business?

A small business owner can collect a great deal of information about competitors through low-cost methods including the following:

- Read industry trade publications for announcements from competitors.
- Ask questions of customers and suppliers on what they hear competitors may be doing. In many cases, this information is easy to gather because some people love to gossip.
- Attend trade shows and collect the competitors' sales literature.
- If appropriate, buy the competitors' products and assess their quality and features. Benchmark their products against yours. The owner of a mail-order gourmet brownie business periodically orders from her primary rivals and compares their packaging, pricing, service, and quality with her own.[16]
- Obtain credit reports from firms such as Dun & Bradstreet on each of your major competitors to evaluate their financial condition.
- Check out the resources of your local library, including articles, computerized databases, and on-line searches. For local competitors, review back issues of the area newspaper for articles on and advertisements by competitors.
- Use the vast resources of the World Wide Web to learn more about your competitors.
- Visit competing businesses periodically to observe their operations. Tom Stemberg, CEO of Staples, a chain of office supply superstores, says, "I've never visited a store where I didn't learn something."[17]

Using the information gathered, a business owner can set up teams of managers and employees to evaluate each competitor and make recommendations on specific strategic actions that will improve the firm's competitive position against each. The owner can use the results of the competitor intelligence analysis to construct a competitive profile matrix for each market segment in which the firm operates. A **competitive profile matrix** allows the owner to evaluate her firm against major competitors on the key success factors for that market segment. The first step is to list the key success factors identified in step 5 of the strategic planning process and to attach weights to them reflecting their relative importance. (See Table 2.5. For simplicity, the weights in this matrix add up to 1.00.) In this example, notice that product quality is weighted twice as heavily (twice as important) as price competitiveness.

The next step is to identify the company's major competitors and to rate each one (and your company) on each of the key success factors:

If factor is a:	Rating is:
Major weakness	1
Minor weakness	2
Minor strength	3
Major strength	4

Once the rating is completed, the owner simply multiplies the weight by the rating for each factor to get a weighted score and then adds up each competitor's weighted scores to get a total weighted score. Table 2.5 shows a sample competitive profile matrix for a small company. The results should show which company is strongest, which is weakest, and which of the key success factors each one is best and worst at meeting. By carefully studying and

What's the Difference?

*T*he worst nightmare for many small retailers is the announcement that a large "category killer" retail store such as Home Depot, Wal-Mart, or Toys 'R' Us is opening in their local market. "How can we possibly survive?" is their immediate worry. Unfortunately, some do not. Yet many of these small companies not only survive in the shadow of the giants, they thrive! What is it that permits some companies to prosper while others whither away in the face of competition from larger, more powerful rivals that can offer lower prices? Consider the following two small companies, one a small nursery and the other a small soft drink bottler.

The Nursery Josh and Michael Bracken's Nicholson-Hardie Nursery and Garden Center operates in an industry where giant retailers now control two-thirds of the $71 billion lawn-and-garden market, up from just 50 percent a decade ago. When Wal-Mart and Home Depot began dotting the Dallas landscape with stores selling plants and garden equipment, many people predicted that the small, independent nursery would wilt like an impatiens in the summer sun. It never happened. Profits at the family-owned business are climbing steadily, and the brothers are about to expand, opening another store even though both Home Depot and Lowe's are opening retail outlets nearby. Opened in 1938 as a seed store and purchased in 1974 by the Bracken brothers' parents, Nicholson-Hardie grew until the 1980s, when the big chain stores began hurting its business. The two brothers took over the business and quickly realized that the only way their company could survive was to change its strategy. Their new strategy was to avoid taking on their larger rivals head-to-head. "If I tried to compete with Home Depot," says Josh, "they were going to kick my butt."

Taking notes from other successful independent nurseries, the Brackens began to define ways to set themselves apart from their larger, more powerful competitors. Both Josh and Michael are master-certified horticulturists (as are one-third of the company's 35 employees), but the brothers are quick to point out that they see themselves first and foremost as retailers. Because they do not buy in bulk, the Brackens do not even try to match the prices of the chain retailers. Instead, they stock more than 1,000 plant varieties, far more than the chains carry; most of their inventory consists of plants that are ideally suited for local soil and climate conditions. The Brackens also set their business apart from the chain stores by selling their extensive knowledge of plants. They even make house calls! On a recent house call, Josh advised a customer concerning the types of plants that would be best suited to the conditions in his yard.

Nicholson-Hardie targets a particular customer, those who "would buy a Land Rover vs. a Chevrolet," Josh says. Their primary target is middle-aged women. Everything about their stores is designed to appeal to this upscale customer. Gardeners can browse through animal-shaped fountains (some selling for thousands of dollars), high-quality garden tools ($35 British grass-trimming shears or $45 Swiss pruners), and imported British rosemary-scented hand cream ($20.95 per bottle). Nicholson-Hardie also sells its own private-label potting soil and private-label fertilizer.

The company's radio ads reinforce its image. Rather than tout low prices, the ads discuss gardening in terms of emotion and flowery imagery. One invites listeners to "Meander through the azaleas. Listen to the music of soothing fountains."

The Soft Drink Bottler Pierce Sears grew up helping his father and his grandfather in the family's Rockport, Massachusetts, soda-bottling business, which produced a soft drink called Twin Lights. In those days, nine workers washed, bottled, and delivered Twin Lights in a convoy of bright blue trucks. "Business was booming," recalls Sears. "We had every bar, every store, every tavern, and every restaurant."

Today, Sears runs the business alone. Thomas Wilson and Company's 7-ounce, 79-cent bottles of Twin Lights collect dust on the bottom shelves of a few local stores, outflanked by a bevy of canned sodas, tropical juice drinks, canned coffees and teas, bottled waters, and power drinks. Like so many old-fashioned bottlers of soft drinks, Sears's company is on the verge of being crushed by the rapid expansion and cutthroat competition from modern bottling companies with their massive marketing budgets and their expansive product lines. "It's definitely a dying business," laments Sears, as he operates an ancient cast-iron Dixie Bottling Machine.

In the early 1900s, approximately 2,800 independent soda bottlers operated across the United States. Then, in the mid-1980s, large numbers of bottlers began closing their operations. Critics say these mass closings stemmed from bottlers' failure to change their businesses as their customers' tastes and habits shifted. To young people, who are the heaviest soda drinkers, old-fashioned flavors are just that—old-fashioned. Traditional flavors such as cream soda, lemon—lime, or sarsaparilla pale in comparison to today's peach—mango punch or honey—kiwi juice. To the health-conscious crowd, the traditional drinks send up red flags because they are filled with "artificial" flavorings. And because their bottling volume is so small, drinks such as Twin Lights do not offer good value to bargain hunters used to purchasing Coke or Pepsi at big discounts.

1. What similarities and differences exist between these two companies' competitive situations? In their strategic positions?

2. Using the World Wide Web and other resources, develop a profile of the industries in which these two companies compete. What strategic changes would you suggest these entrepreneurs make?

SOURCE: Adapted from Louise Lee, "If You Also Want to Buy a Crock-Pot, This Isn't the Place," *Wall Street Journal*, August 26, 1997, pp. A1, A11; Paul Beckett, "Recipe for Nostalgia: Making Up Batches of Twin Lights Soda," *Wall Street Journal*, August 18, 1997, p. A1. ◆

Table 2.5 Sample Competitive Profile Matrix

Key Success Factor (from step 5)	Weight	Your Business		Competitor 1		Competitor 2	
		Rating	Weighted Score	Rating	Weighted Score	Rating	Weighted Score
Market share	0.10	3	0.30	2	0.20	3	0.30
Price competitiveness	0.20	1	0.20	3	0.60	4	0.80
Financial strength	0.10	2	0.20	3	0.30	2	0.20
Product quality	0.40	4	1.60	2	0.80	1	0.40
Customer loyalty	0.20	3	0.60	3	0.60	2	0.40
Total	1.00		2.90		2.50		2.10

interpreting the results, the small business owner can begin to envision the ideal strategy for building a competitive edge in her market segment.

By this stage of the planning, the owner has begun to compare her firm's strengths with those of her competitors and to formulate ways of magnifying her strengths and exploiting their weaknesses. In other words, the entrepreneur is looking toward the future and planning ahead.

STEP 7: CREATE COMPANY GOALS AND OBJECTIVES

Before a small business owner can build a comprehensive set of strategies, he must first establish business goals and objectives, which give him targets to aim for and provide a basis for evaluating his company's performance. Without them, the owner cannot know where the business is going or how well it is performing. Creating goals and objectives is an essential part of the strategic management process.

Goals. Goals are the broad, long-range attributes that a business seeks to accomplish; they tend to be general and sometimes even abstract. Goals are not intended to be specific enough for a manager to act on, but simply state the general level of accomplishment sought. Do you want to boost your market share? Does your cash balance need strengthening? Would you like to enter a new market or increase sales in a current one? What return on investment do you seek? Addressing these broad issues will help you focus on the next phase—developing specific, realistic objectives.

Objectives. Objectives are specific targets of performance. Common objectives concern profitability, productivity, growth, efficiency, markets, financial resources, physical facilities, organizational structure, employee welfare, and social responsibility. Because some objectives might conflict with one another, the manager must establish priorities. Which objectives are most important? Which are least important? Arranging objectives in a hierarchy according to their priority can help the small business manager resolve conflicts when they arise. Well-written objectives have the following characteristics:

They Are Specific. Objectives should be quantifiable and precise. For example, "to achieve a healthy growth in sales" is not a meaningful objective; whereas "to increase retail sales by 12 percent and wholesale by 10 percent in the next fiscal year" is precise and spells out exactly what management wants to accomplish.

They Are Measurable. Managers should be able to plot the organization's progress toward its objectives; this analysis requires a well-defined reference point from which to start and a scale for measuring progress.

They Are Assignable. Unless an entrepreneur assigns responsibility for an objective to an individual, the company is unlikely to ever achieve it. Creating objectives without giving someone responsibility for accomplishing them is futile.

GAINING THE COMPETITIVE EDGE

The Power of Written Goals and Objectives

*E*mmit Smith firmly believes in their power. So does J. J. Stupp. The various businesses that Smith, the famous Dallas Cowboy running back, owns have a record for running past their competition that is as impressive as Smith's record for running past defenders on the gridiron. Stupp, founder of TableTalk, a St. Louis–based business that sells decks of cards to inspire meaningful conversations on topics ranging from sports to the Bible, credits the success of her company to them.

What are they? Written goals and objectives.

When Smith was a football star at Escambia High School in Pensacola, Florida, his coach constantly emphasized the power of written goals and objectives. "It's a dream until you write it down," he told his players. "Then it's a goal." Smith listened and learned. Smith, holder of four rushing titles and three Super Bowl rings, still begins each football season by making a list of the goals he wants to accomplish. He also follows the same practice for his four business ventures. "One day Emmitt came in with [a plan] detailing exactly where he wants to be in six months," says a marketing manager at Smith's cellular phone business. "He wrote it all out, even projecting future job assignments for people. He knows what he wants. And nothing will stop him."

J. J. Stupp's TableTalk cards are sold in 2,500 retail outlets across the country, a result that stems directly from her focus on goals. "Goals are vital to the work plan of any small business," she says. "Writing down short-term and long-term goals for my business helps me stay focused. That's really important when I'm involved with multiple projects."

Successful goal setting requires an entrepreneur to do the following:

Dare to Dream and Then Set Your Sights Setting meaningful goals starts with deciding what you want to accomplish. Think BIG!!! While still a scrawny teenager living in Austria, Arnold Schwarzenegger set a goal of becoming a world-class bodybuilder. Despite doubts from family and friends, Schwarzenegger threw himself into weightlifting. He worked out faithfully at a nearby gym and lifted weights every night at home. He eventually went on to dominate the bodybuilding circuit for several years, winning an unprecedented 13 world titles, including Mr. Universe and Mr. Olympia. Today, that scrawny teenager has become one of the biggest box-office stars in Hollywood.

Take the Time to Write Down Your Goals and Objectives There's something almost magical about writing down

goals. They become more real, more pressing. Writing them down "helps imprint the goals in your mind and helps you stay focused," says Stephen Covey, author of *The 7 Habits of Highly Effective People.*

Make Sure Your Targets Are Measurable One secret to success with objectives is making them quantifiable so that you can measure your progress toward them. Setting an objective to "complete my business plan by March 15" gives an entrepreneur a specific target to shoot for.

Take One Step at a Time toward Your Ultimate Goal Too often, people look beyond intermediate goals and objectives focusing exclusively on their final target, which at the outset seems far away and hard to reach. As a result, they never get started because the task appears to be overwhelming. The key is to establish intermediate or short-term goals. Covey suggests asking, "What can I do this week (or today) that would have a positive impact on my long-term goals?" How do you write a business plan (or a book)? One section at a time.

Reward Yourself for Achieving Success Establishing meaningful goals and objectives is hard work, so as you accomplish each goal, reward yourself in some way. Treat yourself to a minivacation or enjoy a night out with someone special. "Celebrate as you reach each major goal," says Stupp. "You deserve it. Then you're ready to buckle down and start again."

Pause Periodically to Review Your Progress So That You Can Improve Your Future Performance Tony Gwynn, an outfielder for the San Diego Padres, has won six National League batting championships. One reason for his tremendous success is his impressive library of videotapes. Gwynn has *every one* of his at-bats on videotape, and he reviews the tape so that at the next practice he can work to overcome any flaws he has noticed.

Focus on the Golden Ring Not on the Hole inside It Make no mistake about it: Setting and then achieving challenging goals and objectives requires lots of hard work. Successful entrepreneurs see hard work as a rewarding part of the process of achieving their goals, not as punishment they must endure. Rather than become preoccupied with the sacrifices required, they focus instead on the rewards their work will produce. According to one writer, "Hard work is the way to the end of the rainbow."

1. Use the guidelines above to create a set of meaningful goals and objectives for a task you want to complete. What can you do this week (or today) that would have a positive impact on your long-term goal?

SOURCE: Adapted from "Personal Glimpses," *Reader's Digest,* January 1997, p. 152; John E. Anderson, "If You Really Want to Succeed," *Reader's Digest,* May 1996, pp. 157–160. ◆

They Are Realistic, Yet Challenging. Objectives must be within the reach of the organization or motivation will disappear. In any case, managerial expectations must remain high. In other words, the more challenging an objective is (within realistic limits), the higher the performance will be. Set objectives that will challenge your business and its employees.

They Are Timely. Objectives must specify not only what is to be accomplished but also when it is to be accomplished. A time frame for achievement is important.

They Are Written Down. This writing process does not have to be complex; in fact, the manager should make the number of objectives relatively small, from five to fifteen.

The strategic planning process works best when managers and employees are actively involved jointly in setting objectives. Developing a plan is top management's responsibility, but executing it falls to managers and employees; therefore, encouraging them to participate broadens the plan's perspective and increases the motivation to make the plan work. In addition, managers and employees know a great deal about the organization and usually are willing to share this knowledge.

STEP 8: FORMULATE STRATEGIC OPTIONS AND SELECT THE APPROPRIATE STRATEGIES

By now, the small business owner should have a clear picture of what her business does best and what its competitive advantages are. Similarly, she should know her firm's weaknesses and limitations as well as those of its competitors. The next step is to evaluate strategic options and then prepare a game plan designed to achieve the business's objectives.

4 Understand the Entrepreneurial Strategy and Matrix and how to apply it.

Strategy. A **strategy** is a road map of the actions the entrepreneur draws up to fulfill the firm's mission, goals, and objectives. In other words, the mission, goals, and objectives spell out the ends, and the strategy defines the means for reaching them. A strategy is the master plan that covers all of the major parts of the organization and ties them together into a unified whole. The plan must be action-oriented; it should breathe life into the entire planning process. An entrepreneur must build a sound strategy based on the preceding steps that uses the company's core competences as the springboard to success. Joseph Picken and Gregory Dess, authors of *Mission Critical: The Seven Strategic Traps That Derail Even the Smartest Companies,* write, "A flawed strategy—no matter how brilliant the leadership, no matter how effective the implementation—is doomed to fail. A sound strategy, implemented without error, wins every time."[18]

A successful strategy is comprehensive and well integrated. It focuses on establishing the key success factors that the manager identified in step 5. For instance, if maximum shelf space is a key success factor for a small manufacturer's product, the strategy must identify techniques for gaining more in-store shelf space (e.g., offering higher margins to distributors and brokers than competitors do, assisting retailers with in-store displays, or redesigning a wider, more attractive package).

The Entrepreneurial Strategy Matrix. Matthew C. Sonfield and Robert N. Lussier have developed a model using a four-cell matrix that outlines various strategic alternatives for entrepreneurs (see Figure 2.2).[19] The matrix is built on two independent variables: *innovation,* the creation of something new and different, and *risk,* the probability of a major financial loss. At the different combinations of innovation and risk levels (low to high), an entrepreneur will find that certain strategies will be more effective than others. The four combinations are as follows:

High Innovation, Low Risk (I-r). The top left cell of the matrix indicates a high-innovation, low-risk situation. These ventures involve a truly novel idea that carries with it very little risk for an entrepreneur, usually because they require small amounts of start-up capital. Examples might include entrepreneurs who invent low-tech products that are simple and inexpen-

	Low ← Risk → High	
High ↑ Innovation	**I-r** • Move quickly: "first-mover" advantage. • Protect innovation. • Lock in low-cost investments and operating costs.	**I-R** • Reduce risk by lowering investment and operating costs. • Maintain innovation. • Outsource high-cost, high-investment operations. • Consider joint ventures.
Low ↓	**i-r** • Defend present position. • Accept limited payback. • Accept limited growth potential.	**i-R** • Increase innovation; develop a competitive advantage. • Reduce risk by minimizing investment or franchising. • Develop a business plan.

Figure 2.2 The Entrepreneurial Strategy Matrix   Source: Matthew C. Sonfield and Robert N. Lussier, "The Entrepreneurial Strategy Matrix: A Model for New and Ongoing Ventures," *Business Horizons*, May–June 1997, pp. 73–77.

sive to manufacture and distribute or those whose inventions are more high-tech but who choose to subcontract or license production to others.

   Software producer McAfee Associates, the leader in programs that prevent, detect, and cure computer viruses, is a company that fits into the I-r quadrant of the matrix. CEO William Larson is truly an innovator in the software business. He conducts business in exactly the opposite way almost all of his competitors do. For instance, most software companies sell their software, but McAfee Associates licenses its programs to customers for two years at a time. Rather than following the long-established industry practice of selling software upgrades every 18 months, McAfee offers upgrades every quarter and gives them to customers free of charge! The result: software renewal rates that top 85 percent. Rather than mail its software to customers on disks, McAfee chose to distribute its software the low-cost way: over the Internet. McAfee, the company that pioneered software distribution over the Internet, can underprice competitors who still sell products on floppy disks or CDs, often by as much as 50 percent. "You can't achieve the kinds of results we've achieved without breaking the rules," says Larson.[20]

   Like McAfee Associates, companies in high-innovation, low-risk situations tend to have a "first-mover advantage." Because they are often pioneers in a market, they tend to capture it before competitors can move in or, in some cases, before competitors are aware that a market exists. Entrepreneurs should focus their strategic moves on keeping costs (and therefore risk) low and competitors out. Acquiring patent protection when possible, establishing brand names, and using techniques to encourage customer loyalty are effective strategies for companies in this quadrant.

High Innovation, High Risk (I-R). The top right quadrant of the matrix represents a high-innovation, high-risk environment. These businesses also market highly innovative products or services, but the risk associated with them is high, often because the initial financial requirement is high or because competition in the market is stiff.

   The strategic prescription for high-innovation, high-risk situations involves finding ways to reduce the level of risk without sacrificing the ability to innovate. Lowering risk might involve outsourcing operations with high investment requirements or operating expenses or forming a joint venture with an already established company.

In the pharmaceutical industry, for instance, the success ratio for most companies is about one potential drug candidate for every 1,000 tested, and the development costs can be staggering. Plus, because of government regulations and the extensive clinical trials required before a new drug is approved, a company may have to wait for 10 or 15 years before putting a drug on the market. Imagine having 10 to 15 years of expenses with zero revenues! Lisa Conte founded Shaman Pharmaceuticals, a company that fits the I-R profile, with a unique strategy. Recognizing the high risks involved in the pharmaceutical industry, Conte saw a better way to develop new drugs: tapping the knowledge of natural healers (known as shamans) around the world. The idea is to comb the world's tropical forests, seeking out the native men and women who use their knowledge of local plants and their by-products to heal the sick. By learning how these shamans use these plants for medication, Shaman is tapping into a rich bank of knowledge passed down from generation to generation by natural healers. The strategy is working; Shaman's success ratio for developing potentially successful drugs is 50 percent, much higher than the industry average.[21]

Low Innovation, High Risk (i-R). The most common environment in which small companies operate is represented by the lower right cell of the matrix, low innovation and high risk. Most entrepreneurs launch conventional businesses in well-established industries. Innovation is minimal. They may enter retail markets, such as restaurants and clothing stores, or commercial markets, such as machine shops or printing services, but the investment required can be substantial. In many cases, the entrepreneur has invested most of her savings in the venture and has borrowed even more, pushing the risk level higher. Also, entering markets where they are in direct competition with established businesses creates a high-risk situation.

Amy Nye's company, AltiTunes Partner, LP, fits the characteristics of the i-R cell of the matrix. During her travels as an investment banking analyst, Nye noticed that an "airport is a melting pot of different people . . . all looking for a way to pass the time." She believed that a company selling compact discs, audiocassettes, and portable electronics would thrive in an airport location. Not wanting to pay the steep rents a store in New York's LaGuardia Airport would command, Nye convinced officials to rent her space for a 220-square-foot kiosk in an airport hallway. "Selling CDs and tapes in the airport hadn't been done before," she says, "[but] I needed a way to bring my costs down; that meant a small but compact site, like a kiosk." Nye's strategy has worked so well that AltiTunes now has kiosks, each generating sales of $1,000 per day, in six airports and plans to add 14 more.[22]

Just as Amy Nye has built a competitive advantage by choosing a unique convenient location for her customers, entrepreneurs whose companies fall into the i-R cell of the ma-

A team of ethnobotanists and physicians from Shaman Pharmaceuticals works with a local shaman (natural healer) in the jungles of Nigeria to learn about the healing powers of indigenous plants and roots and their byproducts. As part of its innovative strategy, the company draws on the extensive knowledge of such shamans around the world to improve the odds of developing successful drugs to combat modern diseases.

trix should concentrate on identifying ways to build their own competitive advantages. Finding many small ways to create innovations in a traditional business can give an entrepreneur a distinct advantage over rivals. Other strategies appropriate for companies in this cell include reducing the level of risk associated with the business. Many entrepreneurs decide to lower the risk of launching a company by starting a franchise. Of course, every entrepreneur has the ability to lower the risk associated with starting a new business by preparing a solid business plan, a topic we will discuss in detail in chapter 9.

Low Innovation, Low Risk (i-r). The final cell in the matrix represents low-innovation, low-risk situations. For many modern business start-ups, the investment required is low; therefore, the risk level is also low. In other cases, the investment required may be higher, but market demand is strong or competition is weak, creating low levels of risk. Many service, part-time, and home-based businesses fall into this cell of the matrix. Although these businesses usually do not offer the potential for huge returns, their low-risk levels make them relatively safe.

4 Discuss the characteristics of three basic strategies: low-cost, differentiation, and focus.

The strategic emphasis for low-innovation, low-risk firms is on defending their present positions and searching for ways to stimulate growth, recognizing that in most cases, the potential for growth and return on investment is limited. *After Dave Wiggins bought American Wilderness Experience, a tiny $20,000-a-year operation offering Western-style horseback vacations, in 1978, he began transforming the sleepy little business. Over the years, Wiggins steadily added new and different types of excursions to his vacation packages, expanded his mailing list, and created high-quality travel brochures. Today, American Wilderness Adventures books $2.6 million in worldwide adventure travel vacations a year. "[We had] to ride out some pretty lean years," says Wiggins. "We always said the big payoff was down the road, and we were willing to wait."*[23]

Three Strategic Options. Obviously, the number of strategies from which the small business owner can choose is infinite. When all the glitter is stripped away, however, three basic strategies remain. In his classic book *Competitive Strategy*,[24] Michael Porter defines these three strategies: cost leadership, differentiation, and focus.

Patience and hard work paid off for entrepreneur Dave Wiggins, owner of American Wilderness Experience. After purchasing the company in 1978, Wiggins expanded it from horseback excursions to offering customers a wide variety of adventure travel experiences around the globe.

Cost Leadership. A company pursuing a **cost-leadership strategy** strives to be the lowest-cost producer relative to its competitors in the industry. Low-cost leaders have a competitive advantage in reaching buyers whose primary purchase criterion is price, and they have the power to set the industry's price floor. Such a strategy works well when buyers are sensitive to price changes, when competing firms sell the same commodity products, and when companies can benefit from economies of scale. Not only is a low-cost leader in the best position to defend itself in a price war, but it also can use its power to attack competitors with the lowest price in the industry.

There are many ways to build a low-cost strategy, but the most successful cost leaders know where they have cost advantages over their competitors, and they use these as the foundation for their strategies. For example, a small nonunion airline is likely to have a significant advantage in labor costs, but not in fuel costs, over its larger, unionized competitors. *At Medusa Corporation, an Ohio-based cement manufacturer, CEO Robert Evans looks for every possible opportunity to cut costs. To reduce Medusa's energy costs, two of its four plants burn waste liquid fuels rather than coal. (Waste collectors actually pay Medusa to take the waste liquids off their hands.) Given the nature of the product, one of the largest expenses a cement manufacturer incurs is transportation. Medusa delivers 40 percent of its cement to its distribution points by ship rather than using the more expensive truck or rail deliveries its competitors rely on. The company also has invested in faster, more efficient equipment at its distribution points. Using simple bucket elevators, Medusa can unload its two ships at a rate of 1,500 tons per hour; its competitors, who rely on standard pneumatic elevators, can unload just 250 to 350 tons per hour. The managers' philosophy is to invest in capital improvements that produce constant, incremental improvements. For instance, a new computerized system regulates the temperature and fuel usage in the kilns to keep production as high and as cost-effective as possible. Because the company sells a standardized commodity product, managers understand the importance of a successful cost-leadership strategy. "You just have to be the lowest-cost producer in your patch," explains Evans.*[25]

Of course, there are dangers in following a cost-leadership strategy. Sometimes, a company focuses exclusively on lower manufacturing costs without considering the impact of purchasing, distribution, or overhead costs. Another danger is misunderstanding the firm's true cost drivers. For instance, one food-processing plant drastically underestimated its overhead costs and, as a result, was selling its products at a loss. Finally, a firm may pursue a low-cost leadership strategy so zealously that it essentially locks itself out of other strategic choices.

Differentiation. A company following a **differentiation strategy** seeks to build customer loyalty by positioning its goods or services in a unique or different fashion. In other words, the firm strives to be better than its competitors at something that customers value. There are many ways to create a differentiation strategy, but the key concept is to be special at something that is important to the customer. "You'd better be on top of what it is your customers value and continually improve your offerings to better deliver that value," advises Jill Griffin, a strategic marketing consultant.[26] If a small company can improve the product's (or service's) performance, reduce the customer's cost and risk of purchasing it, or both, it has the potential to differentiate. *For example, Joanne Shaw, who founded The Coffee Beanery in 1976, saw the need to differentiate her chain of coffee shops as the specialty coffee industry caught fire in the late 1980s and competitors began to flood the market. "We looked at what we were doing," she recalls, "and said, 'OK, what's different about us [compared with] all the other coffee concepts? What can we be proud of that makes us special?'" For the Coffee Beanery, the primary point of differentiation proved to be the company's practice of flavoring its own coffees, something that few of its competitors do. Shaw also decided to differentiate her company by making its coffee products more convenient for customers to find. She expanded beyond the Coffee Beanery's traditional mall locations into street-front cafes, espresso carts, and kiosks in high-traffic locations. "What we really did was gear everything up to do it better [than the competition] and then talk about it—stressing our points of difference," she says. Shaw's differentiation strategy has succeeded; every outlet has seen steady sales increases every year.*[27]

The key to a successful differentiation strategy is to build it on a *distinctive competence*, something the small company is uniquely good at doing in comparison with its competitors. Common bases for differentiation include superior customer service, special product features, complete product lines, instantaneous parts availability, absolute product reliability, supreme product quality, and extensive product knowledge. To be successful, a differentiation strategy must create the perception of value in the customer's eyes. No customer will purchase a good or service that fails to produce its perceived value, no matter how real that value may be. One business consultant advises, "Make sure you tell your customers and prospects what it is about your business that makes you different. Make sure that difference is in the form of a true benefit to the customer."[28]

There are risks in pursuing a differentiation strategy. One danger is trying to differentiate a product or service on the basis of something that does not boost its performance or lower its cost to the buyer. Another pitfall is overdifferentiating and charging so much that the company prices its products out of the market. The final risk is focusing only on the physical characteristics of a product or service and ignoring important psychological factors: status, prestige, image, and customer service.

Focus. A **focus strategy** recognizes that not all markets are homogeneous. In fact, in any given market, there are many different customer segments, each having different needs, wants, and characteristics. The principal idea of this strategy is to select one or more segments, identify customers' special needs, wants, and interests, and approach the customers with a good or a service designed to excel in meeting those needs, wants, and interests. Focus strategies build on *differences* among market segments.

A successful focus strategy depends on a small company's ability to identify the changing needs of its targeted customer group and to develop the skills required to serve them. The owner and everyone in the organization must have a clear understanding of how to add value to the product or service for the customer. How does the product or service meet the customer's needs at each stage—from raw material to final sale?

Rather than attempting to serve the total market, the focusing firm specializes in serving a specific target segment or niche. A focus strategy is ideally suited to many small businesses, which often lack the resources to reach a national market. Their goal is to serve their narrow target markets more effectively and efficiently than do competitors that pound away at the broad market. Common bases for building a focus strategy include zeroing in on a small geographic area, targeting a group of customers with similar needs or interests (e.g., left-handed people), or specializing in a specific product or service (e.g., petite clothing). *For example, Ida Krenzin owns a business that specializes in an unusual niche: buttons! Krenzin, a skilled seamstress who enjoyed making tailored suits and blouses at home, had difficulty finding just the right buttons to complement her high-quality garments. Rather than settle for cheap, plastic buttons that break and chip easily and don't offer the polished look she wanted for her designs, Krenzin decided to open her own button shop, appropriately called The Button Shop. Her Carmichael, California, store carries an extensive (almost unbelievable!) line of buttons—thousands of them in hundreds of different shapes, sizes, designs, and textures. Her target customers design and make most of their own clothes or they want to change the look of store-bought garments. They are willing to pay anywhere from $1 to $20 for a single button because they know the Button Shop will have the designs they seek, from sterling silver stars and gold leaves to fish-shaped buttons and Raggedy Ann and Andy patterns.*[29]

The most successful focusers build a competitive edge by concentrating on specific market niches and serving them better than any other competitor can. Essentially, this strategy depends on creating value for the customer either by being the lowest-cost producer or by differentiating the product or service in a unique fashion, but doing it in a narrow target segment.

Copreneurs Tom Braun and Collette Morgan have relied on a focus strategy for success in a hotly competitive retail book market. Braun's and Morgan's children's bookstore, Wild Rumpus, is a mecca for children because everything in it is designed for them. Drawing on her experience at a small, independent bookstore that closed, Morgan knew what appealed to kids—and what didn't. The bookstore's theme and its name were inspired by scenes from one of the couple's favorite children's books, Where the Wild Things Are, *in which children live among animals. The store's front door has built into it a four-foot purple door designed for Wild Rumpus's smaller patrons. Inside, two cats roam freely to greet visitors, as does Flicka the rooster. A pet tarantula, lizards, and songbirds live in cages scattered about the 2,000-square-foot store. Under the glass floor in the scary books section lives a family of white rats that children can watch. Morgan is planning to bring in a horse for a shoeing demonstration. "That's something a chain couldn't do," she says. Past demonstrations have featured a "Mummify Your Barbie" workshop (led by an archaeologist) and a Mother's Day "Mama versus Llama" spitting contest, and both drew large numbers of potential customers. Kids, of course, aren't Wild Rumpus's only target audience. Morgan and Braun have worked to establish close ties with local schools and educators, who use the store for book fairs and field trips. The school tie-ins not only help children learn to appreci-ate reading, but they also are a powerful marketing tool. "Kids who had been here with school groups [are] coming back with their parents [on weekends] to show them the store," says Braun. Wild Rumpus's focus strategy has proved very successful; sales have increased by double digits every year since it opened in 1992, and the company has been profitable since its second year of operation.*[30]

Pursuing a focus strategy is not without risk, however. Companies sometimes must struggle to capture a large enough share of a small market to be profitable. If a small com-pany is successful in a niche, there is also the danger that larger competitors will enter the market and erode its market share. Sometimes a company with a successful niche strategy gets distracted by its success and tries to branch out into other areas. As it drifts further away from its core strategy, it loses its competitive edge and runs the risk of confusing or alienat-ing its customers. *Victoria's Secret, the mail-order company once known for its niche in lin-gerie has lost much of its appeal to its traditional customers as the business has strayed too far from its roots. In addition to its wide selection of lingerie, Victoria's Secret sells ball gowns, jeans and casual wear, and career clothing.*[31] Muddying its image with customers puts a company in danger of losing its identity.

An effective strategic plan identifies a complete set of success factors—financial, oper-ating, and marketing—that, taken together, produce a competitive advantage for the small business. The resulting action plan distinguishes the firm from its competitors by exploiting its competitive advantage. The focal point of this entire strategic plan is the customer. The customer is the nucleus of the business, so a competitive strategy will succeed only if it is aimed at serving customers better than the competitor does. An effective strategy draws out the competitive advantage in a small company by building on its strengths and by focusing on the customer. It also designates methods for overcoming the firm's weaknesses, and it identifies opportunities and threats that demand action.

Strategy in Action. The strategies a small business selects depend on its competitive advan-tages in the market segments in which it competes. In some cases, the business will be im-plementing more than one strategy. A business that has a well-defined strategic advantage can aggressively attempt to deepen its market penetration, especially if the business has achieved a "first-mover" advantage with little direct competition. A company does not have to be large to be a strong and aggressive competitor. In many cases, the old adage of being the "big frog in a small pond" allows a relatively small firm to pursue a highly aggressive strategy.

In other circumstances, a small business is best served by avoiding a high profile, seeking instead to secure a small number of highly profitable, loyal customers without ever achieving a substantial share of the market. Some firms use a "specialist" strategy in which they build a highly defensible market position through product uniqueness, or service, or knowledge that competitors cannot easily duplicate. *An example of this strategy is Red Adair, the world-famous fighter of oil well fires. His is not a large organization, but certainly it is a "specialist" in a unique service that requires years of learning the hard way.*

Small companies must learn to develop strategies that exploit all of the competitive ad-vantages of their size by:

◆ Responding quickly to customers' needs

◆ Remaining flexible and willing to change

◆ Continually searching for new emerging market segments

◆ Building and defending market niches

◆ Erecting "switching costs" through personal service and loyalty

6 Understand the impor-tance of controls such as the balanced scoreboard in the planning process.

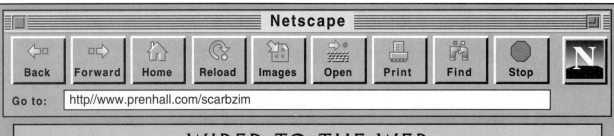

WIRED TO THE WEB

BOOKSTORE WARS

*M*any people pick up a good book, looking to escape the pressures of life for just a few hours. For the people who sell those books, however, escaping the competitive pressures of real life is a fantasy they know they are not likely to live out. Across the country, the explosion of book superstores has put intense pressure on small independent booksellers. The number of bookstore failures has increased in recent years, and the independents' share of the market has slipped. Superstores such as Books-a-Million and Barnes & Noble, already with outlets numbering in the hundreds, are adding more each year. They offer a wide selection of titles and discount prices and bill themselves as "destination stores" that customers are willing to seek out. That can make it tough for some small, independent booksellers to remain competitive.

Yet, many are doing just that—and more; they are thriving in the face of the giants. A variety of well-planned, well-executed strategies give these independent bookstores the ability to retain a base of loyal customers and to increase sales and profits. For instance, chain stores often have a more difficult time adapting their inventories to suit local tastes and culture. Because they are locally owned and operated, small bookstores are better at stocking books that are unique to a particular community or region. Other independents are settling successfully into niches, such as cookbooks, children's books, science fiction, mystery, or travel.

Virtually every small bookstore has at its disposal a powerful competitive weapon that often turns out to be a dandy giant slayer: customer service and lots of little "extras" that keep customers coming back. At The Open Book in Greenville, South Carolina, owner Tom Gower can fill an order much faster than a superstore by relying on his network of publishers and book brokers. In nearby Spartanburg, South Carolina, Jane Hughes, owner of Pic-a-Book, keeps customers coming back with in-store book signings, readings, and workshops featuring well-known local authors. "And we still gift wrap free of charge," she says.

Workshops and classes have boosted sales at Book Passage, a small shop in Corte Madera, California. Because their nearest competitor is a superstore just a few yards away, owners Bill and Elaine Petrocelli draw customers by offering short courses and workshops on everything from Italian to mystery writing. Book Passage also publishes a stylish, informative newsletter. Booksmith, a San Francisco store, recently hired science fiction writer Harlan Ellison to sit in its window at his typewriter and compose a short story.

The newest battle zone in the bookstore wars is in cyberspace. Amazon.com, billing itself as "the world's largest bookstore," exists only on the World Wide Web. Not to be outdone, retail giant Barnes & Noble recently launched what it calls "the biggest electronic book clearinghouse in the world." Customers will have access to 1.2 million titles at heavily discounted prices—lower than those in its own retail stores.

1. What advice would you offer the owner of a small bookstore located in a town where one of the book superstores has just announced it will open an outlet?
2. Visit Amazon.com's World Wide Web site at <http://www.amazon.com> and Barnes & Noble's site at <http://www.barnesandnoble.com>. What benefits do these companies' Web sites offer customers? What weaknesses do booksellers on the Web experience?
3. What advice would you offer the owner of a small bookstore about conducting business on the World Wide Web?

SOURCES: Adapted from Deirdre Donahue, "Bookstores May Be on the Upswing, But Book Sales Are Down," *USA Today,* June 31, 1997, p. 5D; Barbara Carton, "Bookstore Survival Stunts Have Scant Literary Merit," *Wall Street Journal,* June 3, 1997, pp. B1, B8; Patrick M. Reilly, "Booksellers Prepare to Do Battle in Cyberspace," *Wall Street Journal,* January 28, 1997, pp. B1, B8; Ed O'Donoghue, "Reading the Market," *Upstate Business,* July 20, 1997, pp. 1, 6–7; Betty Parker Ellis, "Finding a Niche," *GSA Business,* February 16, 1998, p. 7b.

- Remaining entrepreneurial and willing to take risks and act with lightning speed
- Constantly innovating

STEP 9: TRANSLATE STRATEGIC PLANS INTO ACTION PLANS

Small business managers must convert strategic plans into operating plans that guide the company on a daily basis and become a visible, active part of the business. No small business can benefit from a strategic plan that is sitting on a shelf collecting dust.

To make the plan workable, the business owner should divide the plan into projects, carefully defining each one by the following:

- *Purpose.* What is the project designed to accomplish?
- *Scope.* Which areas of the company will be involved in the project?
- *Contribution.* How is the project related to other projects and to the overall strategic plan?
- *Resource requirements.* What human and financial resources are needed to complete the project successfully?
- *Timing.* Which schedules and deadlines will ensure project completion?

Once managers assign priorities to these projects, they can begin to implement the strategic plan. Involving employees and delegating adequate authority to them is essential because these projects affect them most directly.

If the organization's people have been involved in the strategic management process to this point, they will have a good grasp of the steps they must take to achieve the organization's goals as well as their own professional goals. Early involvement of the total workforce in the strategic management process is a luxury that larger businesses cannot achieve. Commitment to achieve the objectives of the firm is a powerful force for success, but involvement is a prerequisite for achieving total employee commitment. It is important to remember that without committed, dedicated employees, an organization's strategies usually fail.

STEP 10: ESTABLISH ACCURATE CONTROLS

So far, the planning process has created company objectives and has developed a strategy for reaching them, but rarely, if ever, will the company's actual performance match stated objectives. The manager quickly realizes the need to control actual results that deviate from plans.

The measures created in the control-planning process become the standards against which actual performance is compared. Everyone in the organization must understand, and be involved in, the control-planning process.

To control projects and keep them on schedule, employees must identify and track key performance indicators. The source of these indicators is the operating data from the company's normal business activity; they are the guideposts for detecting deviations from established standards. Accounting, production, sales, inventory, and other operating records are primary sources of data the manager can use for controlling activities. *For example, at Colonial Mills Inc., a specialty rug manufacturer, a huge "scoreboard" stretches 30 feet across the company cafeteria, displaying Colonial Mills' performance on a dozen different operational scales. A variety of graphs and charts compare actual performance against company objectives. Colonial Mills managers say the scoreboard encourages employees to set and then achieve challenging objectives by helping them measure their progress towards them.*[32]

To evaluate the effectiveness of their strategies, some companies are developing **balanced scorecards,** a set of measurements unique to a company that includes both financial and operational measures and gives managers a quick yet comprehensive picture of the company's total performance. One writer says that a balanced scorecard

> is a sophisticated business model that helps a company understand what's really driving its success. It acts a bit like the control panel on a spaceship—the business equivalent of a flight speedometer, odometer, and temperature gauge all rolled into one. It keeps track of many things, including financial progress and softer measurements—everything from customer satisfaction to return on investment—that need to be managed to reach the final destination: profitable growth.[33]

Rather than sticking solely to the traditional financial measures of a company's performance, the balanced scorecard gives managers a comprehensive view from *both* a financial and an operational perspective. The premise behind such a scorecard is that relying on any single measure of company performance is dangerous. Just as a pilot in command of a jet cannot fly safely by focusing on a single instrument, an entrepreneur cannot manage a company by concentrating on a single measurement. The complexity of managing a business demands that an entrepreneur be able to see performance measures in several areas simultaneously.

When creating a balanced scorecard for her company, an entrepreneur should establish goals for each critical indicator of company performance and then create meaningful measures for each one. The balanced scorecard looks at a business from four important perspectives (see Figure 2.3).[34]

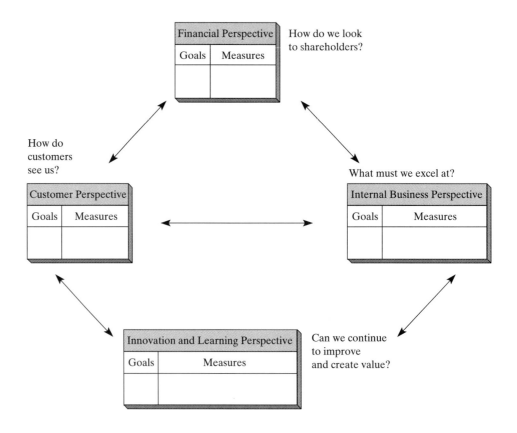

Figure 2.3 The Balanced Scorecard Links Performance Measures

Customer Perspective: How Do Customers See Us? Customers judge companies by at least four standards: time (how long it takes the company to deliver a good or service), quality (how well a company's product or service performs in terms of reliability, durability, and accuracy), performance (the extent to which a good or service performs as expected), and service (how well a company meets or exceeds customers' expectations of value). Because customer-related goals are external, managers must translate them into measures of what the company must do to meet customers' expectations.

Internal Business Perspective: What Must We Excel At? The internal factors that managers should focus on are those that have the greatest impact on customer satisfaction and retention and on company effectiveness and efficiency. Developing goals and measures for factors such as quality, cycle time, productivity, costs, and others that employees directly influence is essential.

Innovation and Learning Perspective: Can We Continue to Improve and Create Value? This view of a company recognizes that the targets required for success are constantly changing. If a company wants to continue its pattern of success, it cannot stand still; it must continuously improve. A company's ability to innovate, learn, and improve determines its future. These goals and measures emphasize the importance of continuous improvement in customer satisfaction and internal business operations.

Financial Perspective: How Do We Look to Shareholders? The most traditional performance measures, financial standards, tell how much the company's overall strategy and its execution are contributing to its bottom line. These measures focus on such factors as profitability, growth, and shareholder value. On balanced scorecards, companies often break their financial goals into three categories: survival, success, and growth.

Figure 2.4, on page 66, shows a sample balanced scorecard for a hypothetical company, Electronic Circuits Inc. (ECI). Although the balanced scorecard is a vital tool that helps managers keep their companies on track, it is also an important tool for changing behavior in an organization and for keeping everyone focused on what really matters. As conditions change, managers must make corrections in performances, policies, strategies, and objectives to get performance back on track. A practical control system is also economical to operate. Most small businesses have no need for a sophisticated, expensive control system. The system should be so practical that it becomes a natural part of the management process.

Conclusion and Beginning

The strategic planning process does *not* end with the 10 steps outlined here; it is an ongoing procedure that the small business owner must repeat. With each round, he gains experience, and the steps become much easier. The planning process outlined here is designed to be as simple as possible. No small business should be burdened with an elaborate, detailed formal planning process that it cannot easily use. Such programs require excessive amounts of time to operate, and they generate a sea of paperwork. The small business manager needs neither.

What does this strategic planning process lead to? It teaches the small business owner a degree of discipline that is important to his business's survival. It helps him in learning about his business, his competitors, and, most important, his customers. Although strategic planning cannot guarantee success, it does dramatically increase the small firm's chances of survival in a hostile business environment. Unfortunately, most business owners forgo the benefits of strategic planning. A recent survey of family businesses by Arthur Andersen Consulting and MassMutual Life Insurance Company found that just 30 percent of the companies had a written strategic plan.[35] Don't let that happen to you!

Financial Perspective	
Goals	Measures
Survive	Cash flow
Succeed	Quarterly sales growth and operating income by division
Prosper	Increased market share and return on equity

Customer Perspective	
Goals	Measures
New products	Percent of sales from new products Percent of sales from proprietary products
Responsive supply	On-time delivery (defined by customer)
Preferred supplier	Share of key accounts' purchases Ranking by key accounts
Customer partnership	Number of cooperative engineering efforts

Internal Business Perspective	
Goals	Measures
Technology capability	Manufacturing geometry versus competition
Manufacturing excellence	Cycle time Unit cost Yield
Design productivity	Silicon efficiency Engineering efficiency
New product introduction	Actual introduction schedule versus plan

Innovation and Learning Perspective	
Goals	Measures
Technology leadership	Time to develop next generation
Manufacturing learning	Process time to maturity
Product focus	Percent of products that equal 80% sales
Time to market	New product introduction versus competition

Figure 2.4 **ECI's Balanced Business Scorecard** Source: Robert S. Kaplan and David P. Norton, "The Balanced Scorecard—Measures That Drive Performance," *Harvard Business Review,* January–February 1992, p. 76.

Chapter Summary

❶ Understand the importance of strategic management to a small business.

   ◆ Strategic planning, often ignored by small companies, is a crucial ingredient in business success. The planning process forces potential entrepreneurs to subject their ideas to an objective evaluation in the competitive market.

❷ Explain why and how a small business must create a competitive advantage in the market.

   ◆ The goal of developing a strategic plan is to create for the small company a competitive advantage—the aggregation of factors that sets the small business apart from its competitors and gives it a unique position in the market. Every small firm

must establish a plan for creating a unique image in the minds of its potential customers.

❸ Develop a strategic plan for a business using the 10 steps in the strategic planning process.

   ◆ Small businesses need a strategic planning process designed to suit their particular needs. It should be relatively short, be informal and not structured, encourage the participation of employees, and not begin with extensive objective setting. Linking the purposeful action of strategic planning to an entrepreneur's little ideas can produce results that shape the future.

   ◆ **Step 1.** Develop a clear vision and translate it into a meaningful mission statement. Highly successful entrepreneurs are able to communicate their vision to those around them. The firm's mission statement answers the first question of any venture: What business am I in? The mission statement sets the tone for the entire company.

◆ **Step 2.** Define the firm's core competences and its target market segments, and position the business to compete effectively. Core competences are a unique set of capabilities that a company develops in key operational areas, such as quality, service, innovation, team building, flexibility, responsiveness, and others that allow it to vault past competitors. They are what the company does best and are the focal point of the strategy. This step must identify target market segments and determine how to position the firm in those markets. The owner must identify some way to differentiate her business from its competitors.

◆ **Step 3.** Assess the company's strengths and weaknesses. Strengths are positive internal factors; weaknesses are negative internal factors.

◆ **Step 4.** Scan the environment for significant opportunities and threats facing the business. Opportunities are positive external options; threats are negative external forces.

◆ **Step 5.** Identify the key factors for success in the business. In every business, key factors determine the success of the firms in it, so they must be an integral part of a company's strategy. Key success factors are relationships between a controllable variable (e.g., plant size, size of sales force, advertising expenditures, product packaging) and a critical factor influencing the firm's ability to compete in the market.

◆ **Step 6.** Analyze the competition. Business owners should know their competitors' businesses almost as well as they know their own. A competitive profile matrix is a helpful tool for analyzing competitors' strengths and weaknesses.

◆ **Step 7.** Create company goals and objectives. Goals are the broad, long-range attributes that the firm seeks to accomplish. Objectives are quantifiable and more precise; they should be specific, measurable, assignable, realistic, timely, and written down. The process works best when subordinate managers and employees are actively involved.

◆ **Step 8.** Formulate strategic options and select the appropriate strategies. A strategy is the game plan the firm will use to achieve its objec-

tives and mission. It must center on establishing for the firm the key success factors identified earlier.

◆ **Step 9.** Translate strategic plans into action plans. No strategic plan is complete until the owner puts it into action.

◆ **Step 10.** Establish accurate controls. Actual performance rarely, if ever, matches plans exactly. Operating data from the business serve as guideposts for detecting deviations from plans. Such information is helpful when plotting future strategies.

◆ The strategic planning process does not end with these 10 steps; rather, it is an ongoing process.

④ Understand the Entrepreneurial Strategy Matrix and how to apply it.

◆ The Entrepreneurial Strategy Matrix helps entrepreneurs develop appropriate strategies given the different levels of risk and innovation associated with their businesses.

⑤ Discuss the characteristics of three basic strategies: low-cost, differentiation, and focus.

◆ Three basic strategic options are cost leadership, differentiation, and focus. A company pursuing a cost leadership strategy strives to be the lowest-cost producer relative to its competitors in the industry.

◆ A company following a differentiation strategy seeks to build customer loyalty by positioning its goods or services in a unique or different fashion. In other words, the firm strives to be better than its competitors at something that customers value.

◆ A focus strategy recognizes that not all markets are homogeneous. The principal idea of this strategy is to select one or more segments; identify customers' special needs, wants, and interests; and approach them with a good or service designed to excel in meeting those needs, wants, and interests. Focus strategies build on *differences* among market segments.

⑥ Understand the importance of controls such as the balanced scorecard in the planning process.

◆ Just as a pilot in command of a jet cannot fly safely by focusing on a single instrument, an entrepreneur cannot manage a company by concentrating on a single measurement. The balanced scorecard is a set of measurements unique to a company that includes both financial and operational measures and gives managers a quick yet comprehensive picture of the company's total performance.

Discussion Questions

1. Why is strategic planning important to a small company?
2. What is a competitive advantage? Why is it important for a small business to establish one?
3. What are the steps in the strategic management process?
4. What are strengths, weaknesses, opportunities, and threats? Give an example of each.
5. Explain the characteristics of effective objectives. Why is setting objectives important?
6. What are business strategies?
7. Explain the concept of the Entrepreneurial Strategy Matrix and how entrepreneurs can use it to develop appropriate strategies.
8. Describe the three basic strategies available to small companies. Under what conditions is each most successful?
9. How is the controlling process related to the planning process?
10. What is a balanced scorecard? What value does it offer entrepreneurs who are evaluating the success of their current strategies?

Step into the Real World

1. Choose an entrepreneur in your community and interview him or her. Does the company have a strategic plan? A mission statement? Why or why not? What does the owner consider the company's strengths and weaknesses to be? What opportunities and threats does the owner perceive? What image is the owner trying to create for the business? Does the owner think the effort has been successful? (Do you agree?) Which of the generic competitive strategies is the company following? Who are the company's primary competitors? On a scale of 1 to 10, how does the owner rate his or her chances for success in the future?

2. Using the resources on your campus (such as magazines in the library focusing on entrepreneurship and small business or the World Wide Web) or in your community (such as your knowledge of local businesses), find an example of a company in each of the four quadrants in the Entrepreneurial Strategy Matrix. Prepare a brief report on each company explaining why it fits in a particular cell. What strategic recommendations would you make to each business owner?

3. Contact a local entrepreneur and help him or her devise a balanced scorecard for his or her company. What goals did you and the owner establish in each of the four perspectives? What measures did you use to judge progress toward those goals?

4. Contact the owner of a small business that competes directly with an industry giant (such as Home Depot, Wal-Mart, Barnes & Noble, or others). What does the owner see as his or her competitive advantage? How does the business communicate this advantage to its customers? What competitive strategy is the owner using? How successful is it? What changes would you suggest the owner make?

5. Use the strategic tools provided in this chapter to help a local small business owner discover his or her firm's strengths, weaknesses, opportunities, and threats; identify the relevant key success factors; and analyze its competitors. Help the owner devise a strategy for success for his or her business.

Take It to the Net

Visit the Scarborough/Zimmerer home page at
www.prenhall.com/scarbzim
for updated information, on-line resources, and Web-based exercises.

Endnotes

1. Alvin Toffler, "Shocking Truths about the Future," *Journal of Business Strategy*, July/August 1996, p. 6.
2. Geoffrey Colvin, "The Changing Art of Becoming Unbeatable," *Fortune*, November 24, 1997, pp. 299–300.
3. Joseph Pereira, "A Small Toy Store Manages to Level the Playing Field," *Wall Street Journal*, December 20, 1996, pp. A1, A8.
4. Hermann Simon, "The World's Best Unknown Companies," *Wall Street Journal*, May 20, 1996, p. A18.
5. Thomas A. Stewart, "Why Values Statements Don't Work," *Fortune*, June 10, 1996, p. 137.
6. Michael Barrier, "Back from the Brink," *Nation's Business*, September 1995, p. 21.
7. Barrier, "Back from the Brink."
8. Miriam Shulman, "Winery with a Mission," *Ethics*, Spring 1996, p. 14.
9. Marc Ballon, "Sale of Modern Music Keyed to Customization," *Inc.*, May 1998, pp. 23, 25.
10. Carol Steinberg, "Target Selling," *Success*, May 1995, pp. 79–83.
11. Carla Goodman, "Finding Your Niche," *Business Start-Ups*, April 1997, pp. 72–74.
12. David Noack, "Choosing the Right Path to the Net," *Nation's Business*, March 1997, pp. 16–20; Heather Page, "Fruitful Idea," *Entrepreneur*, January 1997, p. 20.
13. Joshua Rosenbaum, "Guitar Maker Looks for New Key," *Wall Street Journal*, February 11, 1998, pp. B1, B5.
14. Janean Chun, "Mighty Morphing," *Entrepreneur*, November 1996, p. 16; Stephanie Gruner, "What Worries CEOs," *Inc.*, February 1997, p. 98.
15. Carolyn Z. Lawrence, "Know Your Competition," *Business Start-Ups*, April 1997, p. 51.
16. Ibid., pp. 51–56.
17. Stephanie Gruner, "Spies Like Us," *Inc.*, August 1998, p. 45.
18. Joseph C. Picken and Gregory Dess, "The Seven Traps of Strategic Planning," *Inc.*, November 1996, p. 99.
19. Matthew C. Sonfield and Robert N. Lussier, "The Entrepreneurial Strategy Matrix: A Model for New and Ongoing Ventures," *Business Horizons*, May–June 1997, pp. 73–77.
20. Scott Wooley, "The New Distribution," *Forbes*, November 4, 1996, pp. 164–165.
21. Mary Scott, "Responsible Remedies," *Business Ethics*, July/August 1994, pp. 15–16.
22. Kristin Dunlap Godsey, "Terminal Velocity," *Success*, October 1997, p. 12; Goodman, "Finding Your Niche."
23. Goodman, "Finding Your Niche."
24. Michael Porter, *Competitive Strategy*, New York: Macmillan Publishing Company, 1980.
25. Kambiz Foroohar, "Step Ahead—and Avoid Fads," *Forbes*, November 4, 1996, pp. 172–176.
26. Debra Phillips, "Leaders of the Pack," *Entrepreneur*, September 1996, p. 127.
27. Ibid., pp. 124–128.
28. Ibid., p. 128.
29. Goodman, pp. 72–74.
30. Ronald B. Lieber, "Beating the Odds," *Fortune*, March 31, 1997, pp. 82–90; Barbara Carton, "Bookstore Survival Stunts Have Scant Literary Merit," *Wall Street Journal*, June 3, 1997, pp. B1, B8.
31. Laura Bird, "Is Overexposure a Problem at Victoria's Secret?" *Wall Street Journal*, November 22, 1996, pp. B1, B8.
32. John Case, "Keeping Score," *Inc.*, June 1998, pp. 80–86.
33. Joel Kurtzman, "Is Your Company Off Course? Now You Can Find Out Why," *Fortune*, February 17, 1997, p. 128.
34. Robert S. Kaplan and David P. Norton, "The Balanced Scorecard—Measures That Drive Performance," *Harvard Business Review*, January–February 1992, pp. 71–79.
35. Patricia Schiff Estess, "Survival Training," *Entrepreneur*, September 1997, pp. 78–81.

Choosing a Form
of Ownership

Nothing in fine print is ever good.

—*Anonymous*

There is no trap so deadly as the trap you set
for yourself.

—*Phillip Marlowe*

Upon completion of this chapter, you will be able to

1 Describe the advantages and disadvantages of the sole proprietorship.

2 Describe the advantages and disadvantages of the partnership.

3 Describe the advantages and disadvantages of the corporation.

4 Describe the features of the alternative forms of ownership such as the S corporation, the limited liability company, and the joint venture.

*O*ne of the first decisions an entrepreneur faces when starting a new business is selecting the form of ownership for the new business venture. Too often, entrepreneurs give little thought to choosing a form of ownership and simply select the form that is most popular, even though it may not suit their needs best. Although the decision is not irreversible, changing from one form of ownership to another once a business is up and running can be difficult, expensive, and complicated, so it is important for an entrepreneur to make the right choice at the outset. This seemingly mundane decision can have far-reaching consequences for almost every aspect of a business and its owners—from the taxes the company pays and how it raises money to the owner's liability for the company's debts and her ability to transfer the business to the next generation. Each form of ownership has its own unique set of advantages and disadvantages. The key to choosing the "right" form of ownership is understanding the characteristics of each one and knowing how they affect an entrepreneur's business and personal circumstances.

Although there is no best form of ownership, there may be a form of ownership that is best suited to each entrepreneur's circumstances.

The following are a few considerations that every entrepreneur should review before choosing the form of ownership:

◆ *Tax considerations.* Because of the graduated tax rates under each form of ownership, the government's constant tinkering with the tax code, and the year-to-year fluctuations in a company's income, an entrepreneur should calculate the firm's tax bill under each ownership option every year.

◆ *Liability exposure.* Certain forms of ownership offer business owners greater protection from personal liability due to financial problems, faulty products, and a host of other difficulties. Entrepreneurs must weigh the potential for legal and financial liabilities and decide the extent to which they are willing to assume personal responsibility for their companies' obligations.

◆ *Start-up and future capital requirements.* Forms of ownership differ in their ability to raise start-up capital. Depending on how much capital an entrepreneur needs and where she plans to get it, some forms are better than others. Also, as a business grows, its capital requirements increase, and some forms of ownership make it easier to attract financing from outsiders. *For instance, Mark Kalish and John Berthold, co-founders of Enviro-Tech Coating Systems, a small company that uses an electrostatic process to paint a variety of surfaces, started their business as a corporation because they were anticipating the day when they would need external financing to fuel their company's growth. "We wanted to be able to bring in stockholders as we grew," says Kalish.*[1]

◆ *Control.* By choosing certain forms of ownership, an entrepreneur automatically gives up some control over the company. Entrepreneurs must decide early on how much control they are willing to sacrifice in exchange for help from other people in building a successful business.

◆ *Managerial ability.* Entrepreneurs must assess their own ability to manage their companies. If they lack skills or experience in certain areas, they may need to select a form of ownership that allows them to bring into the company people who possess those skills and experience.

◆ *Business goals.* How big and how profitable an entrepreneur plans for the business to become will influence the form of ownership chosen. Businesses often switch forms of ownership as they grow, but moving from some formats to others can be extremely complex and expensive. For instance, business owners wanting to switch from a corporation to a limited liability company face daunting liabilities under current tax laws. "That conversion gets taxed as though the entire company was liquidated or sold off," says tax attorney Jeffrey Hart, "which entails such an exorbitant tax bill that it's not worth doing."[2]

◆ *Management succession plans.* When choosing a form of ownership, business owners must look ahead to the day when they will pass their companies on to the next generation or to a buyer. Some forms of ownership make this transition much smoother than others. In other cases, when the owner dies, so does the business.

◆ *Cost of formation.* Some forms of ownership are much more costly and involved to create than others. Entrepreneurs must weigh carefully the benefits and the costs of the particular form they choose.

Although a decision regarding the initial form of ownership is not irreversible, the cost of changing the form of ownership can be high and will create unnecessary distractions. As a business grows and changes, the founders may discover the need to modify the form of ownership they chose initially. For example, a business may begin as a sole proprietorship but become so successful that it has a real opportunity for large-scale growth. However, to achieve this level of growth requires a very large infusion of capital. Under these conditions, an entrepreneur may find it necessary to convert the business from a sole proprietorship to a corporation or an S corporation, which would allow her to attract the necessary capital more easily. In short, as their companies' needs change, the entrepreneurs behind them must reexamine the factors that determine the "best" form of ownership for them and be willing to change when necessary. *For instance, Marian Fletcher, founder of Let's Go Party, a party-planning and catering service, launched her company as a sole proprietorship primarily because that form of ownership was the simplest and least expensive choice. Also, Fletcher considered the personal liability risks associated with her business to be minimal. However, when she brought her daughter into the growing company two years later, Fletcher switched to a limited liability company. "After talking to a couple of accountants and a lawyer, we decided this was the best way for us to go," says Fletcher.*[3]

Business owners have traditionally had three major forms of ownership from which to choose: the sole proprietorship, the partnership, and the corporation (see Figure 3.1). In recent years, various hybrid forms of business ownership have emerged. This chapter will outline the key features of the forms of ownership, beginning with the three most common forms and then moving on to the hybrid forms, including the S corporation, the limited liability company, and the joint venture.

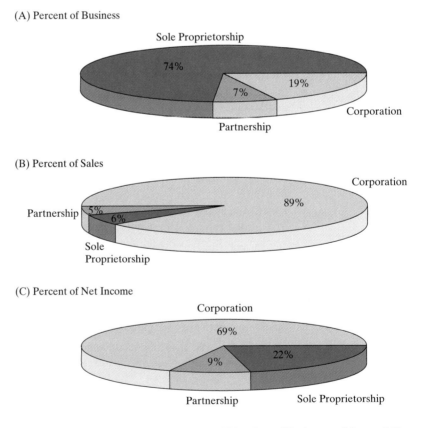

Figure 3.1 Forms of U.S. Businesses by Percentage of Number of Businesses, Sales, and Net Income, 1997 Source: Internal Revenue Service, 1997.

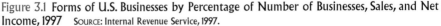

$\mathcal{T}$he Sole Proprietorship

The **sole proprietorship** is a business owned and managed by one individual. This form of ownership is by far the most popular. Approximately 74 percent of all businesses in the United States are sole proprietorships.

ADVANTAGES OF A SOLE PROPRIETORSHIP

Simple to Create. One attractive feature of a proprietorship is the ease and speed of its formation. If an entrepreneur wants to form a business under her own name (e.g., Williams Financial Consulting), she obtains the necessary business licenses from state, county, and/or local governments and begins operation! In most cases, an entrepreneur can complete all of the necessary paperwork in a single day.

Least Costly Form of Ownership to Establish. In addition to being quick and easy to establish, the proprietorship is generally the least expensive form of ownership to establish. There is no need to create and file the legal documents that are recommended for partnerships and are required for corporations. An entrepreneur simply goes to the city or county government, states the nature of the business he will start, and pays the appropriate fees and license costs. Paying these fees and license costs gives the entrepreneur the right to conduct business in that particular jurisdiction.

In many jurisdictions, entrepreneurs planning to conduct business under a trade name are usually required to acquire a Certificate of Doing Business under an Assumed Name from the secretary of state. The fee for this certificate is usually nominal. Acquiring this certificate involves conducting a search to determine that the name chosen for the business is not already registered as a trademark or service mark with the secretary of state. Filing this certificate also notifies the state of who the owner of the business is. In a proprietorship, the owner *is* the business.

Profit Incentive. One major advantage of the proprietorship is that once the owner has paid all of the company's expenses, she can keep the remaining profits (less taxes, of course). The profit incentive is a powerful one, and profits represent an excellent way of "keeping score" in the game of the business.

Total Decision-Making Authority. Because the sole proprietor is in total control of operations, she can respond quickly to changes. The ability to respond quickly is an asset in a rapidly shifting market, so the freedom to set the company's course of action is a major motivational force. For people who thrive on seeking new opportunities, the freedom of fast, flexible decision making is vital.

No Special Legal Restrictions. The proprietorship is the least regulated form of business ownership. In a time when government requests for information seem never-ending, this feature has much merit.

Easy to Discontinue. If the entrepreneur decides to discontinue operations, he can terminate the business quickly, even though he will still be liable for all of the business's outstanding debts and obligations.

Although these advantages of a proprietorship are extremely attractive to most individuals contemplating starting a new business, it is important to recognize that this form of ownership has some significant disadvantages.

GAINING THE COMPETITIVE EDGE

What's in a Name?

*I*s the name an entrepreneur gives his business *really* that important? Florist Aron Benon swears that it is. Benon recently changed his flower shop's name from The French Flower Market to Floral and Hardy, and the impact amazed him. Sales immediately picked up. "When we were the French Flower Market, people couldn't find us or phone in orders because they couldn't remember our name," says Benon. "Now, when someone wants to buy flowers, Floral and Hardy is the first name they think of."

Name consultants agree with Benon that the moniker an entrepreneur chooses for her business really *can* make a difference. The right name for a company can convey exactly what the business does, create the right image in customers' minds, and deliver a subtle message about its unique features. A poorly chosen name, on the other hand, will confuse customers and keep the company lost in a fog of obscurity among dozens of other competitors. Names that incorporate puns and clever plays on words can be especially effective because they attract potential customers' attention and encourage people to think about what the company does. For example, by the time one figures out that Thinker Toys sells educational playthings, Twice Sold Tales is a used book shop, and Mud, Sweat, and Tears is a bicycle shop, one has pondered the nature of the business. And that can translate into increased sales.

For small companies, which often lack the financial resources to embark on costly advertising campaigns, the right business name can be a powerful tool. When Michael Wyckoff started his computer consulting business, he named it after himself. He is convinced that the company's name, which did nothing to describe the company or its business, is the main reason it never got off the ground. Then one day, while talking to a client, Wyckoff described himself as a "Rent-a-Nerd." "What a great idea for a name," he thought. He decided to change the name of his company and even had business cards printed describing himself as "Head Nerd." "I couldn't believe what three little words could do," said Wyckoff when sales took off.

How can you find the perfect name for your business?

Decide what you want your business name to convey about your company. Should it create an image of quality and elegance or one of fun and whimsy? What would you like customers to think about when they hear your company's name?

Conduct a brainstorming session. Work with partners, employees, friends, and others to generate as many names as possible. Do not evaluate or criticize ideas; just let them flow. When Bart Brannon and Gary German were searching for a name for their company that would sell bare-bones computers to fearful first-time users, they conducted an informal brainstorming session while eating in a Mexican restaurant. The winning name: StupidPC, Inc. To reinforce the image their company name conjures up, the two entrepreneurs use a fleet of Vintage Volkswagen Beetles to deliver computers to customers. Employees, dressed in company "uniforms" that include pocket protectors, glasses with tape on them, and slicked-back hair, set up customers' computers and offer one hour of free instruction to get customers up and running on their new systems. Brannon says that, thanks largely to the company's name, StupidPC is selling hundreds of computers each week!

Pick a name that will be an effective marketing tool. A good name is short, attention-getting, and memorable. The name should also be easy to spell and pronounce. Ideally, it should tell customers what your company does and the products or services it offers, but it should not be so limiting that it does not accommodate your company's growth. A good name has both ear and eye appeal.

Test the name on people before you commit to it. Survey a wide variety of people to get their reactions and feedback. You may discover connotations and meanings that you never thought of.

Once you find a suitable name, conduct a fictitious name search to make sure that no one else in your jurisdiction has already claimed it. In most states, all that is required is a call or a visit to the secretary of state's office or the state department of commerce. If the name you have chosen is free, register it with the appropriate office so that it is protected. Entrepreneur Vic Brounsuzian wanted to name his roasted nut shop Nuts to You, but when he conducted a name search, he found that someone else was already using that name. Brounsuzian went back to brainstorming. One day, while he was working on his computer, the word *mega* jumped out at him, and Brounsuzian decided to name the company Meg-A-Nut, Inc.

Review the following company names to see if you can figure out what businesses they are in:

Name	Business
Salvador Deli	_____
Bait and Tackle	_____
Tender Lubing Care	_____
Wok and Roll	_____
Hair It Is	_____
The Filling Station	_____
Blazing Salads	_____
Hannah and Her Scissors	_____
The Ferret and Firkin	_____

Answers: delicatessen; lingerie shop; auto service center; Chinese takeout restaurant; hairstyling salon; dental center; vegetarian restaurant; hairstyling salon; British pub.

Sources: Adapted from Rodney Ho, "These Guys May Be Smart Indeed for Calling Their Company Stupid," *Wall Street Journal*, July 8, 1997, p. B2; Carlienne A. Frisch, "Personalize Your Plates," *Business Start-Ups*, December 1996, pp. 28–30; Dennis Whittington, "Naming Your Business," *Business Start-Ups*, December 1995, pp. 52–53; Joan Delaney, "What's in a Name?" *Your Company*, Winter 1994, p. 4; "What's in a Name? Plenty, If It's a New Company," *Greenville News*, October 8, 1994, p. C3; Gayle Sato Stodder, "Word Games," *Entrepreneur*, April 1994, p. 48; "Business Directory," *Reader's Digest*, June 1993, p. 145; "Enterprising Names," *Reader's Digest*, December 1993, p. 73; "Business Directory," *Reader's Digest*, June 1995, p. 142; Kylo-Patrick Hart, "Select Your Name," *Business Start-Ups*, July 1996, pp. 70–72; Sue Clayton, "Name That Business," *Business Start-Ups*, April 1996, pp. 18–20. ◆

Can a catchy name increase a company's sales? Bart Brannon and Gary German, co-founders of StupidPC, Inc., a company that sells bare-bones computers to first-time users, believe that it can. Brannon and German pose in front of their fleet of delivery vehicles, vintage Volkswagen Beetles.

DISADVANTAGES OF A SOLE PROPRIETORSHIP

Unlimited Personal Liability. Probably the greatest disadvantage of a sole proprietorship is the unlimited personal liability of the owner; the sole proprietor is personally liable for all of the business's debts. Remember, in a proprietorship, the owner *is* the business. The proprietor owns all of the business's assets, and if the business fails, creditors can force the sale of those assets to cover its debts. If unpaid business debts remain, creditors can also force the sale of the proprietor's *personal* assets to recover payment. In short, the company's debts are the owner's debts. Laws vary from one state to another, but most states require creditors to leave the failed business owner a minimum amount of equity in a home, a car, and some personal items. The reality: *Failure of the business can ruin the sole proprietor financially.*

Limited Access to Capital. If the business is to grow and expand, a sole proprietor often needs additional financial resources. However, many proprietors have already put all they have into their businesses and have used their personal resources as collateral on existing loans, so it is difficult for them to borrow additional funds. A sole proprietorship is limited to whatever capital the owner can contribute and whatever money he can borrow. In short, proprietors, unless they have great personal wealth, find it difficult to raise additional money while maintaining sole ownership. Most banks and other lending institutions have well-defined formulas for determining borrowers' eligibility. Unfortunately, many sole proprietorships cannot meet those borrowing requirements, especially in the early days of business.

Limited Skills and Abilities. A sole proprietor may not have the wide range of skills running a successful business requires. Each of us has areas in which our education, training, and work experiences have taught us a great deal; yet there are other areas in which our decision-

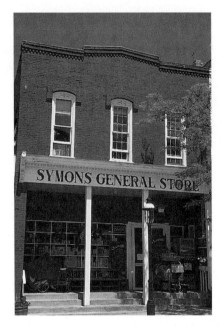

Because of their simplicity and low cost, sole proprietorships are the most common form of ownership. The primary disadvantage is the unlimited liability the proprietor assumes for the company's debts.

making ability is weak. Many business failures occur because owners lack skills, knowledge, and experience in areas that are vital to business success. Owners tend to push aside problems they do not understand or do not feel comfortable with in favor of those they can solve more easily. Unfortunately, the problems they set aside seldom solve themselves. By the time an owner decides to ask for help in addressing these problems, it may be too late to save the company.

Feelings of Isolation. Running a business alone allows an entrepreneur maximum flexibility, but it also creates feelings of isolation; there is no one to turn to for help in solving problems or getting feedback on a new idea. Most small business owners report that they sometimes feel alone and frightened when they must make decisions knowing that they have nowhere to turn for advice or guidance. The weight of each critical decision rests solely on the proprietor's shoulders. Lee Gardner, the sole proprietor of a company that arranges sponsorships for sporting events, says, "After I set up my company, I realized I was all by myself and responsible for everything. Building a business brick by brick, alone, is not easy."[4]

Lack of Continuity for the Business. Lack of continuity is inherent in a sole proprietorship. If the proprietor dies, retires, or becomes incapacitated, the business automatically terminates. Unless a family member or employee can take over, the business could be in jeopardy. Because people look for secure employment and an opportunity for advancement, proprietorships, being small, often have trouble recruiting and retaining good employees. If no one is trained to run the business, creditors can petition the court to liquidate the assets of the dissolved business to pay outstanding debts.

For founders who have no intention of ultimately creating a large, complex business, a sole proprietorship may be ideal. Some entrepreneurs, however, find that forming partnerships is one way to overcome the disadvantages of the sole proprietorship. For instance, a person who lacks specific managerial skills or has insufficient access to needed capital can compensate for those weaknesses by forming a partnership with someone who has complementary management skills or money to invest.

The Partnership

A **partnership** is an association of two or more people who co-own a business for the purpose of making a profit. In a partnership the co-owners (partners) share the business's assets, liabilities, and profits according to the terms of a previously established partnership agreement.

The law does not require a written partnership agreement (also known as the articles of partnership), but it is wise to work with an attorney to develop one that spells out the exact status and responsibility of each partner. All too often the parties think they know what they are agreeing to, only to find later that no real meeting of the minds took place. The **partnership agreement** is a document that states in writing all of the terms of operating the partnership for the protection of each partner involved. Every partnership should be based on a written agreement. "When two entrepreneurial personalities are combined, there is a tremendous amount of strength and energy, but it must be focused in the same direction, or it will tear the relationship apart," explains one business writer. "A good partnership agreement will guide you through the good times, provide you with a method for handling problems, and serve as the infrastructure for a successful operation."[5]

When no partnership agreement exists, the Uniform Partnership Act (discussed below) governs the partnership, but its provisions may not be as favorable as a specific agreement hammered out among the partners. Creating a partnership agreement is not costly. In most cases, the partners can discuss each of the provisions in advance. Once they have reached an agreement, an attorney can draft the formal document. Banks will often want to see a copy of the partnership agreement before lending the business money. Probably the most important feature of the partnership agreement is that it addresses in advance sources of conflict that could result in partnership battles and the dissolution of a business that could have been successful. Spelling out details—especially sticky ones such as profit splits, contributions, workloads, decision-making authority, dispute resolution, and others—at the outset will help avoid tension in a partnership that could lead to a business "divorce." Business divorces, like marital ones, are almost always costly and unpleasant for everyone involved.

Unfortunately, the tendency for partners just starting out is to ignore writing a partnership agreement as they ride the emotional high of launching a company together. According to one writer, "In the eager, hectic days of start-up, when two people come together with a 'brilliant idea,' they never imagine that some day they may not want to be partners anymore. Instead, their thoughts race to marketing strategies, product development, sales pitches, and customer service."[6] The result? Every year, thousands of partners find themselves mired in irreconcilable disputes that damage their businesses because they failed to establish a partnership agreement. In general, a partnership agreement can include any terms the partners want (unless they are illegal). The standard partnership agreement will likely include the following:

1. Name of the partnership.
2. Purpose of the business. What is the reason the partners created the business?
3. Domicile of the business. Where will the principle business be located?
4. Duration of the partnership. How long will the partnership last?
5. Names of the partners and their legal addresses.
6. Contributions of each partner to the business, at the creation of the partnership and later. This would include each partner's investment in the business. In some situations a partner may contribute assets that are not likely to appear on a balance sheet.

Experience, sales contracts, or a good reputation in the community may be reason for asking a person to join in a partnership.

7. Agreement on how the profits or losses will be distributed.

8. Agreement on salaries or drawing rights against profits for each partner.

9. Procedure for expansion through the addition of new partners.

10. Distribution of the partnership's assets if the partners voluntarily dissolve the partnership.

11. Sale of partnership interest. How can partners sell their interests in the business?

12. Absence or disability of one of the partners. If a partner is absent or disabled for an extended period of time, should the partnership continue? Will the absent or disabled partner receive the same share of profits as she did before her absence or disability? Should the absent or disabled partner be held responsible for debts incurred while unable to participate?

13. Voting rights. In many partnerships, partners have unequal voting power. The partners may base their voting rights on their financial or managerial contributions to the business.

14. Decision-making authority. When can partners make decisions on their own, and when must other partners be involved?

15. Financial authority. Which partners are authorized to sign checks, and how many signatures are required to authorize bank transactions?

16. Handling tax matters. The Internal Revenue Service requires partnerships to designate one person to be responsible for handling the partnership's tax matters.

17. Alterations or modifications of the partnership agreement. No document is written to last forever. Partnership agreements should contain provisions for alterations or modifications. As a business grows and changes, partners often find it necessary to update their original agreement.

THE UNIFORM PARTNERSHIP ACT

The Uniform Partnership Act (UPA) codifies the body of law dealing with partnerships in the United States. Under the UPA, the three key elements of any partnership are common ownership interest in a business, sharing the business's profits and losses, and the right to participate in managing the operation of the partnership. Under the act, each partner has the right to:

1. Share in the management and operations of the business.

2. Share in any profits the business might earn from operations.

3. Receive interest on additional advances made to the business.

4. Be compensated for expenses incurred in the name of the partnership.

5. Have access to the business's books and records.

6. Receive a formal accounting of the partnership's business affairs.

The UPA also sets forth the partners' general obligation. Each partner is obligated to:

1. Share in any losses sustained by the business.

2. Work for the partnership without salary.

3. Submit differences that may arise in the conduct of the business to majority vote or arbitration.

4. Give the other partner complete information about all business affairs.

5. Give a formal accounting of the partnership's business affairs.

Beyond what the law prescribes, a partnership is based above all else on mutual trust and respect. Any partnership missing those elements is destined to fail. Like sole proprietorships, partnerships have advantages and disadvantages.

ADVANTAGES OF THE PARTNERSHIP

Easy to Establish. Like the proprietorship, the partnership is easy and inexpensive to establish. The owners must obtain the necessary business license and submit a minimal number of forms. In most states, partners must file a Certificate for Conducting Business As Partners if the business is run under a trade name.

Complementary Skills. In a sole proprietorship, the owner must wear lots of different hats, and not all of them fit well. In successful partnerships, the parties' skills and abilities complement one another, strengthening the company's managerial foundation. *When architects Deborah Verderame and Tobias Arianna formed a partnership, they knew that their complementary skills could be the basis for a successful architectural business. They also realized that they had to manage their differences to avoid tearing the company apart. In the early days, the partners' heated arguments over management styles, spending, and other important issues created problems, but Verderame and Arianna quickly found ways to compromise. They began focusing on communicating with one another frequently, putting their disagreements behind them, and maintaining a sense of humor in the office. The partners say that the synthesis of their drastically different styles has resulted in some of their best work for clients. "Professionally, we need each other," says Arianna. "Combined, we're much stronger than we are apart."*[7]

Division of Profits. There are no restrictions on how partners distribute the company's profits as long as they are consistent with the partnership agreement and do not violate the rights of any partner. The partnership agreement should articulate the nature of each partner's contribution and proportional share of the profits. If the partners fail to create an agreement, the UPA says that the partners share equally in the partnership's profits, even if their original capital contributions are unequal.

Larger Pool of Capital. The partnership form of ownership can significantly broaden the pool of capital available to a business. Each partner's asset base improves the business's ability to borrow needed funds; together the partners' personal assets will support a larger borrowing capacity than either partner would have had alone. Undercapitalization is a common cause of business failures.

Ability to Attract Limited Partners. Not every partner takes an active role in the operation of a business. Partners who take an active role in managing a company and who share in its rewards, liabilities, and responsibilities are **general partners.** Every partnership must have at least one general partner (although there is no limit on the number of general partners a business can have). General partners have unlimited personal liability for the company's debts and obligations and are expected to take an active role in managing the business.

    Limited partners, on the other hand, cannot take an active role in the operation of the company. They have limited personal liability for the company's debts and obligations. If the business fails, they lose only what they have invested in it and no more. Essentially, limited partners are financial investors who do not participate in the day-to-day affairs of the partnership. If limited partners are "materially and actively" involved in a business (defined as spending more than 500 hours a year in the company), they will be treated as general partners and will lose their limited liability protection. Silent partners and dormant partners are special types of limited partners. **Silent partners** are not active in a business but generally are known to be members of the partnership. **Dormant partners** are neither active nor generally known to be associated with the business.

A limited partnership can attract investors by offering them limited liability and the potential to realize a substantial return on their investments if the business is successful. Many individuals find it very profitable to invest in high-potential small businesses, but only if they avoid the disadvantages of unlimited liability while doing so.

Little Governmental Regulation. Like the proprietorship, the partnership form of operation is not burdened with red tape.

Flexibility. Although not as flexible as sole proprietorships, partnerships can generally react quickly to changing market conditions because no giant organization stifles quick and creative responses to new opportunities. In large partnerships, however, getting all partners' approval on key decisions can slow down a company's strategic actions.

Taxation. The partnership itself is not subject to federal taxation. It serves as a conduit for the profit or losses it earns or incurs; its net income or losses are passed through to the individual partners as personal income, and the partners, not the business, pay income tax on their distributive shares. The partnership, like the proprietorship, avoids the "double taxation" disadvantage associated with the corporate form of ownership.

DISADVANTAGES OF THE PARTNERSHIP

Unlimited Liability of at Least One Partner. At least one member of every partnership must be a general partner. The general partner has unlimited personal liability, even though he is often the partner with the least personal resources. In most states, certain property belonging to a proprietor or a general partner is exempt from attachment by creditors of a failed business. The most common is the homestead exemption, which allows the debtor's home to be sold to satisfy the debt but stipulates that a certain dollar amount be reserved to allow the debtor to find other shelter. Some states require that the debtor have a family before the homestead exemption is allowed. Also, state laws normally exempt certain personal property items from attachment by creditors. For example, household furniture (up to a specified amount), clothing and personal possessions, government or military pensions, and bonuses are protected and cannot be taken to satisfy an outstanding business debt.

Capital Accumulation. Although the partnership form of ownership is superior to the proprietorship in its ability to attract capital, it is generally not as effective as the corporate form of ownership, which can raise capital by selling shares of ownership to outside investors.

Difficulty in Disposing of Partnership Interest without Dissolving the Partnership. Most partnership agreements restrict how partners can dispose of their shares of the business. Often, a partner is required to sell his interest to the remaining partner. Even if the original agreement contains such a requirement and clearly delineates how the value of each partner's ownership will be determined, there is no guarantee that the other partners will have the financial resources to buy the seller's interest. When the money is not available to purchase a partner's interest, the other partners may be forced either to accept a new partner or to dissolve the partnership, distribute the remaining assets, and begin again. When a partner withdraws from the partnership, the partnership ceases to exist unless there are specific provisions in the partnership agreement for a smooth transition. When a general partner dies, becomes incompetent, or withdraws from the business, the partnership automatically dissolves, although it may not terminate (the difference is discussed below). Even when there are numerous partners, if one wishes to disassociate her name from the business, the remaining partners will probably form a new partnership.

Lack of Continuity. If one partner dies, complications arise. Partnership interest is often nontransferable through inheritance because the remaining partners may not want to be in a partnership with the person who inherits the deceased partner's interest. Partners can make provisions in the partnership agreement to avoid dissolution due to death if all parties agree to accept as partners those who inherit the deceased's interest.

Potential for Personality and Authority Conflicts. Being in a partnership is much like being married. Making sure partners' work habits, goals, ethics, and general business philosophy are compatible is an important step in avoiding a nasty business divorce. Still, as in a marriage, friction among partners is inevitable and can be difficult to control. The key is having a mechanism such as a partnership agreement and open lines of communication for controlling it. The demise of many partnerships can often be traced to interpersonal conflicts and the lack of a partnership agreement for resolving those conflicts. *For instance, one lawyer and his partner split because they could not agree on either major or minor issues affecting their practice. "We were fighting about everything from what kind of work we should be going after to what kind of paper we should put in the copy machine," he says. "It was almost comical." When they split, each partner agreed to take the clients he had been responsible for. One partner took over the office space, and the other hired the paralegal who had worked in the partnership. Their business split wasn't pleasant for either partner, but it was amiable.*[8] The accompanying Gaining the Competitive Edge feature describes how to avoid business divorces.

Partners Are Bound by the Law of Agency. A partner is like a spouse in that decisions made by one, in the name of the partnership, bind all. Each partner is an agent for the business and can legally bind the other partners to a business agreement. Because of this agency power, all partners must exercise good faith and reasonable care in performing their responsibilities.

Some partnerships survive a lifetime; others experience the difficulties described above. In a general partnership, the continued exposure to personal liability for partners' actions can wear an entrepreneur down. Knowing that they could lose their personal assets because of a partner's bad business decision is a fact of life in partnerships. Conflicts between or among partners could force a successful business to close. Few partnerships ever put into place a mutually agreed upon means for conflict resolution. The result is that disagreements can escalate to the point where the partnership is dissolved and the business ceases to operate.

DISSOLUTION AND TERMINATION OF PARTNERSHIP

Partnership dissolution is not the same as partnership termination. **Dissolution** occurs when a general partner ceases to be associated with the business. **Termination** is the final act of winding up the partnership as a business. Termination occurs after the partners have expressed their intent to cease operations and all affairs of the partnership have been concluded. In other words, dissolution ends the partnership as a business; termination winds up its affairs.

GAINING THE COMPETITIVE EDGE

How to Avoid a Business Divorce

*C*o-owners of businesses are very much like marriage partners. Together they experience ups and downs, happiness and heartbreak, success and failure. Some co-owners spend more time with each other than they do with their spouses. Unfortunately, like some marriages, business relationships can end in divorce. Even when a business is succeeding, the relationship that built it may be failing.

Although every business dispute is unique, most have one common element: no written agreement spelling out the rights, duties, privileges, and obligations of the owners. In a start-up's early phases, co-founders are immersed in details and are too busy to prepare a document defining the major components of their business relationship. They believe that they can work out any disputes that arise; after all, that's what friends do, right? Stressing the importance of a written agreement, one expert advises, "Don't be [deluded] by the fact that you and your partners are best friends. As a practical matter, partners have fallings out that need to be handled in a practical way."

How can co-owners avoid such disputes? The following tips will help:

Make sure that you and your business partners have common business objectives. One entrepreneur who was too insecure to launch a telecommunications company alone persuaded three friends to join him. Looking back, he realizes his mistake. "I didn't screen our business goals," he admits. "They wanted the company to pay for their cars and to conduct meetings in the Bahamas. I wanted to plow the money back into the business." Outvoted by his partners, this entrepreneur could only watch as they drained the company's capital to the point that the business collapsed.

Divide responsibilities on the basis of ability and interest and stick to the agreement. When the four Sasson brothers created Scorpus Technology, they acknowledged the potential problems their strong egos might cause in their business relationship. To minimize conflicts, each committed to a particular function—one to sales and marketing, another to operations, a third to technology, and the fourth to finance. Their strategy worked, and within three years, the company had 70 employees and sales of $8 million.

Share and share alike. Make sure that everyone involved understands the hard work, commitment, and risk required to launch a company. Clarify beforehand the roles and expectations of each owner involved in the business. The philosophy that "some of us are more equal than others" does not make for a lasting business.

Don't lie. Resist the temptation to "protect" the other owners from bad news. News, both good and bad, provides useful feedback to owners, who must adjust their company to shifting market conditions.

Get it in writing. Once owners agree to their responsibilities, duties, and expectations, they should put them in writing. Avoid the tendency to go into business with nothing more than high hopes and a handshake. It's a recipe for disaster.

Realize that conflict will occur. Conflict is a natural part of any business relationship; co-owners will never agree on everything. The key to avoiding a business divorce is to manage that conflict and not merely cover it up. That requires *communication.* One consultant says, "Partners are afraid that bringing up disagreements will ruin the relationship. So they ruin the relationship anyway by not talking."

Cultivating a business relationship with other co-owners requires time, energy, and hard work—just as cultivating a lasting marriage does. Sometimes, however, things just don't work out, and business owners decide to go their separate ways. How do you know when it's time to leave? One counselor suggests asking yourself the following questions:

◆ Do you and your co-owners still share the goals that brought you together?
◆ Have you resolved difficult problems before?
◆ Do you still basically respect and trust each other?
◆ When you imagine the future, does it seem brighter if you see yourself working with your partners than without them?

If the answer to at least three of these questions is yes, the co-owners can probably salvage their relationship. Bringing in a mediator to help resolve the problem may not be necessary, but it is worth a try.

Sources: Adapted from Tom McGrath, "How to Fire Your Partner," *Success,* February 1998, pp. 30–31; Robert A. Mamis, "Partner Wars," *Inc.,* June 1994, pp. 36–40; Robert A. Mamis, "Two Who Made Good," *Inc.,* June 1994, pp. 40–44; Richard J. Maturi, "Firing Squad," *Entrepreneur,* May 1993, pp. 152–155; Eric L. Chase, "Owner vs. Owner," *Small Business Reports,* September 1990, pp. 69–76; Stephen Davis, "Why Partnerships Break Up," *Inc.,* July 1981, pp. 67–70; Frances Huffman, "Irreconcilable Differences," *Entrepreneur,* February 1992, pp. 108–113; Jerry Useem, "Partners on the Edge," *Inc.,* August 1998, pp. 52–64. ◆

Dissolution occurs as a result of one or more of the following events:

- Expiration of a time period or completion of the project undertaken as delineated in the partnership agreement.
- Expressed wish of any general partner to cease operation.
- Expulsion of a partner under the provisions of the agreement.
- Withdrawal, retirement, insanity, or death of a general partner (except when the partnership agreement provides for a method of continuation).
- Bankruptcy of the partnership or of any general partner.
- Admission of a new partner resulting in the dissolution of the old partnership and establishment of a new partnership.
- Any event that makes it unlawful for the partnership to continue operations or for any general partner to participate in the partnership.
- A judicial decree that a general partner is insane or permanently incapacitated, making performance or responsibility under the partnership agreement impossible.
- Mounting losses that make it impractical for the business to continue.
- Impropriety or improper behavior of any general partner that reflects negatively on the business.

LIMITED PARTNERSHIPS

A **limited partnership,** which is a modification of a general partnership, is composed of at least one general partner and at least one limited partner. In a limited partnership the general partner is treated, under the law, exactly as in a general partnership. Limited partners are treated as investors in the business venture, and they have limited liability. They can lose only the amount they have invested in the business.

Most states have ratified the Revised Uniform Limited Partnership Act. To form a limited partnership, the partners must file a Certificate of Limited Partnership in the state in which the limited partnership plans to conduct business. The Certificate of Limited Partnership should include the following information.

- The name of the limited partnership.
- The general character of its business.
- The address of the office of the firm's agent authorized to receive summonses or other legal notices.
- The name and business address of each partner, specifying which ones are general partners and which are limited partners.
- The amount of cash contributions actually made, and agreed to be made in the future, by each partner.
- A description of the value of noncash contributions made or to be made by each partner.
- The times at which additional contributions are to be made by any of the partners.
- Whether and under what conditions a limited partner has the right to grant limited partner status to an assignee of his or her interest in the partnership.
- If agreed upon, the time or the circumstances when a partner may withdraw from the firm (unlike the withdrawal of a general partner, the withdrawal of a limited partner does not automatically dissolve a limited partnership).

- If agreed upon, the amount of, or the method of determining, the funds to be received by a withdrawing partner.
- Any right of a partner to receive distributions of cash or other property from the firm, and the times and circumstances for such distributions.
- The time or circumstances when the limited partnership is to be dissolved.
- The rights of the remaining general partners to continue the business after withdrawal of a general partner.
- Any other matters the partners want to include.

Although limited partners do not have the right to take an active role in managing the business they can make management suggestions to the general partners, inspect the business, and make copies of business records. A limited partner is, of course, entitled to a share of the business's profits as agreed on and specified in the Certificate of Limited Partnership. The primary disadvantage of limited partnerships is the complexity and the cost of establishing them.

MASTER LIMITED PARTNERSHIPS

A relatively new form of business structure, **master limited partnerships (MLPs),** are just like regular limited partnerships, except their shares are traded on stock exchanges. They provide most of the same advantages to investors as a corporation—including limited liability. One analyst says that a master limited partnership "looks like a corporation, acts like a corporation, and trades on major stock exchanges like a corporation."[9] Congress originally allowed MLPs to be taxed as partnerships. However, in 1987 it ruled that any MLP not involved in natural resources or real estate would be taxed as a corporation, eliminating their ability to avoid the double taxation disadvantage. Master limited partnership profits typically must be divided among thousands of partners.

LIMITED LIABILITY PARTNERSHIPS

Many states now recognize **limited liability partnerships (LLPs)** in which *all* partners in the business are limited partners, having only limited liability for the debts and obligations of the partnership. Most states restrict LLPs to certain types of professionals such as attorneys, physicians, dentists, accountants, and others. Just as with any limited partnership, the partners must file a Certificate of Limited Partnership in the state in which the partnership plans to conduct business. Also, like every partnership, an LLP does not pay taxes; its income is passed through to the limited partners, who pay taxes on their shares of the company's net income.

7he Corporation

3 Describe the advantages and disadvantages of the corporation.

The corporation is the most complex of the three major forms of business ownership. It is a separate entity apart from its owners and may engage in business, make contracts, sue and be sued, and pay taxes. The Supreme Court has defined a **corporation** as "an artificial being, invisible, intangible, and existing only in contemplation of the law."[10] Because the life of the corporation is independent of its owners, the shareholders can sell their interest in the business without affecting its continuation. "When you incorporate, you're setting up a legal entity that has a life separate and apart from the shareholders, directors or officers, and that has the ability to conduct business and to insulate the owners from personal liability," says one attorney.[11]

Corporations (also known as C corporations) are creations of the state. When a corporation is founded, it accepts the regulations and restrictions of the state in which it is incorporated and any other state in which it chooses to do business. A corporation doing business in the state in which it is incorporated is a **domestic corporation.** When a corporation conducts business in another state, that state considers it to be a **foreign corporation.** Corporations that are formed in other countries but do business in the United States are **alien corporations.**

Corporations have the power to raise large amounts of capital by selling shares of ownership to outside investors, but many corporations have only a handful of shareholders. **Publicly held corporations** are those that have a large number of shareholders, and their stock is usually traded on one of the large stock exchanges. **Closely held corporations** are those whose shares are in the control of a relatively small number of people, often family members, relatives, or friends. Their stock is not traded on any stock exchange but instead is passed from one generation to the next. Many small corporations are closely held.

In general, a corporation must report annually its financial operations to its home state's attorney general. These financial reports become public record. If the corporation's stock is sold in more than one state, the corporation must comply with federal regulations governing the sale of corporate securities. There are substantially more reporting requirements for a corporation than for the other forms of ownership.

REQUIREMENTS FOR INCORPORATION

Most states allow entrepreneurs to incorporate without the assistance of an attorney. Some states even provide incorporation kits to help in the incorporation process. Although it is cheaper for entrepreneurs to complete the process themselves, it is not always the best idea. In some states, the application process is complex, and the required forms are confusing. The price for filing incorrectly can be high. "If you [complete the incorporation process] yourself and you do it improperly, it's generally invalid," explains one attorney.[12]

Once the owners decide to form a corporation, they must choose the state in which to incorporate. If the business will operate within a single state, it usually makes sense to incorporate in that state. States differ—sometimes dramatically—in the requirements they place on the corporations they charter and in how they treat corporations chartered in other states. They also differ in the tax rate imposed on corporations, the restrictions placed on their activities, the capital required to incorporate, and the fees or organization tax charged to incorporate.

Every state requires a Certificate of Incorporation or charter to be filed with the secretary of state. The following information is generally required to be in the Certificate of Incorporation:

◆ The corporation's name. The corporation must choose a name that is not so similar to that of another firm in that state that it causes confusion or lends itself to deception. It must also include a term such as *corporation, incorporated, company,* or *limited* to notify the public that they are dealing with a corporation.

◆ The corporation's statement of purpose. The incorporators must state in general terms the intended nature of the business. The purpose must, of course, be lawful. An illustration might be "to engage in the sale of office furniture and fixtures." The purpose should be broad enough to allow for some expansion in the activities of the business as it develops.

◆ The corporation's time horizon. Most corporations are formed with no specific termination date; they are formed "for perpetuity." However, it is possible to incorporate for a specific duration (e.g., 50 years).

- Names and addresses of the incorporators. The incorporators must be identified in the articles of incorporation and are liable under the law to attest that all information in the articles of incorporation is correct. In some states, one or more of the incorporators must reside in the state in which the corporation is being created.
- Place of business. The post office address of the corporation's principal office must be listed. This address, for a domestic corporation, must be in the state in which incorporation takes place.
- Capital stock authorization. The articles of incorporation must include the amount and class (or type) of capital stock the corporation wants to be authorized to issue. This is not the number of shares it must issue; a corporation can issue any number of shares up to the amount authorized. This section must also define the different classification of stock and any special rights, preferences, or limits each class has.
- Capital required at the time of incorporation. Some states require a newly formed corporation to deposit in a bank a specific percentage of the stock's par value before incorporating.
- Provisions for preemptive rights, if any, that are granted to stockholders.
- Restrictions on transferring share. Many closely held corporations—those owned by a few shareholders, often family members—require shareholders interested in selling their stock to offer it first to the corporation. (Shares the corporation itself owns are called **treasury stock.**) To maintain control over their ownership, many closely held corporations exercise this right, known as the **right of first refusal.**
- Names and addresses of the officers and directors of the corporation.
- Rules under which the corporation will operate. **Bylaws** are the rules and regulations the officers and directors establish for the corporation's internal management and operation.

Once the attorney general of the incorporating state has approved a request for incorporation and the corporation pays its fees, the approved articles of incorporation become its charter. With the charter in hand, the next order of business is to hold an organizational meeting for the stockholders to formally elect directors, who, in turn, will appoint the corporate officers.

Corporations may dominate sales and profitability in our economy, but, like the preceding forms of ownership, they have advantages and disadvantages.

ADVANTAGES OF THE CORPORATION

Limited Liability of Stockholders. The primary reason most entrepreneurs choose to incorporate is to gain the benefit of limited liability, which means that investors can limit their liability to the total amount of their investment. This legal protection of personal assets beyond the business is of critical concern to many potential investors. The shield of limited liability may not be impenetrable, however. Because start-up companies are so risky, lenders and other creditors require the owners to *personally* guarantee loans made to the corporation. Robert Morris Associates, a national organization of bank loan officers, estimates that 95 percent of small business owners have to sign personal guarantees to get the financing they need. By making these guarantees, owners are putting their personal assets at risk (just as in a proprietorship) despite choosing the corporate form of ownership. Recent court decisions have extended the personal liability of small corporation owners beyond the financial guarantees that banks and other lenders require, "piercing the corporate veil" much more than ever before. Courts are increasingly holding entrepreneurs personally liable for environmental, pension, and legal claims against their corporations—much to the surprise of the owners, who chose the corporate form of ownership to shield themselves from such liability.[13]

Courts will pierce the corporate veil and hold owners liable for the company's debts and obligations if the owners deliberately commit criminal or negligent acts when handling corporate business. Corporate shareholders most commonly lose their liability protection, however, because owners and officers have commingled corporate funds with their personal funds. Failing to keep corporate and personal funds separate is most often a problem in closely held corporations. *For instance, Lincoln Polan formed a corporation, Industrial Realty Company, in West Virginia and was the sole shareholder. Although he filed the Certificate of Incorporation properly, Polan never paid any capital into the corporation, never held an organizational meeting, and elected no officers. When Industrial Realty entered into a contract to sublease a commercial site from the Kinney Shoe Corporation, Polan paid the first rental payment with a personal check. When Industrial Realty breached the contract by failing to make any further rental payments on the property, Kinney filed suit against Polan individually, asking the court to pierce the corporate veil that Polan had established. Because Polan had failed to observe the necessary "corporate formalities," had failed to finance the corporation properly, and had commingled his personal funds with those of the corporation, the court held him personally liable for Industrial Realty's debts of $66,400.*[14] The accompanying Gaining the Competitive Edge feature offers some helpful tips for avoiding such problems.

Ability to Attract Capital. Because of the protection of limited liability, corporations have proved to be the most effective form of ownership for accumulating large amounts of capital. Limited only by the number of shares authorized in its charter (which can be amended), the corporation can raise money to begin business and expand as opportunity dictates by selling shares of its stock to investors. A corporation can sell its stock to a limited number of private investors (a private placement) or to the public (a public offering).

Ability to Continue Indefinitely. Unless limited by its charter, a corporation is a separate legal entity and can continue indefinitely. Unlike a proprietorship or partnership, in which the death of a founder ends the business, the corporation lives beyond the lives of those who gave it life. This perpetual life gives rise to the next major advantage, transferable ownership.

Transferable Ownership. If stockholders in a corporation are displeased with the business's progress, they can sell their shares to someone else. Millions of shares of stock representing ownership in companies are traded daily on the world's stock exchanges. Shareholders can also transfer their stock through inheritance to a new generation of owners. During all of these transfers of ownership, the corporation continues to conduct business as usual.

Unlike that of large corporations, whose shares are traded on organized stock exchanges, the stock of many small corporations is held by a small number of people ("closely held"), often company founders, family members, or employees. Because only a small number of people hold the stock the resale market for shares is limited, so the transfer of ownership might be difficult.

DISADVANTAGES OF THE CORPORATION

Cost and Time Involved in the Incorporation Process. Corporations can be costly and time-consuming to establish. The owners are giving birth to an artificial legal entity, and the gestation period can be prolonged for the novice. In some states, an attorney must handle incorporation, but in most states entrepreneurs can complete all of the required forms alone. However, an owner must exercise great caution when incorporating without the help of an attorney. Also, incorporating a business requires fees that are not applicable to proprietorships or partnerships. Creating a corporation can cost between $500 and $2,500, typically averaging around $1,000.

Double Taxation. Because a corporation is a separate legal entity, it must pay taxes on its net income to the federal, most state, and some local governments. Before stockholders re-

How to Avoid Corporate Woes

The main reason entrepreneurs choose the corporate form of ownership is to avoid having unlimited personal liability for their companies' debts. Some entrepreneurs, however, have discovered that their limited liability protection crumbles if they fail to maintain certain standards of behavior. Courts call it "piercing the corporate veil" and will hold shareholders personally responsible for the debts and obligations of the corporation. For instance, if an individual forms a corporation for fraudulent purposes, he cannot hide behind the structure of the company, avoiding personal liability for the corporation's fraudulent acts. The courts would allow persons damaged by the fraudulent acts to make claims not only against the corporation's assets but also against the individual owner's personal assets. However, most cases in which corporate owners are held personally liable for the business's obligations involve careless behavior rather than deliberately fraudulent behavior. Traditionally, courts will pierce the corporate veil and hold a corporation's owners liable if they form the corporation without sufficient capital to operate it, if they fail to observe corporate formalities, or if they fail to keep separate the corporation's assets and their personal assets. To avoid problems such as these, entrepreneurs who form corporations should use the following procedures.

File all of the reports and pay all of the necessary fees required by the state in a timely manner. Most states require corporations to file reports with the secretary of state on an annual basis. Failing to do so will jeopardize the validity of your corporation and will open the door for personal liability problems for its shareholders.

Hold annual meetings to elect officers and directors. In a closely held corporation, the officers elected may *be* the shareholders, but that does not matter. Corporations formed by an individual are not required to hold meetings, but the sole shareholder must file a written consent form.

Keep minutes of every meeting of the officers and directors, even if it takes place in the living room of the founders. It is a good idea to elect a secretary who is responsible for recording the minutes.

Make sure that the corporation's board of directors makes all major decisions. Problems arise in closely held corporations when one owner makes key decisions alone without consulting the elected board.

Make it clear that the business is a corporation by having all officers sign contracts, loan agreements, purchase orders, and other legal documents in the corporation's name rather than in their own names. Failing to designate their status as agents of the corporation can result in the officers' being held personally liable for agreements they think they are signing on the corporation's behalf. The proper way for a corporate officer to sign is:

MicroTech, Inc.
by: *Julian Rembert*
Julian Rembert, President

By signing a document simply as "Julian Rembert," the owner of this corporation would make himself personally liable for that obligation.

Keep corporate assets and the personal assets of the owners separate. Few things make courts more willing to hold shareholders personally liable for a corporation's debts than commingling corporate and personal assets. In some closely held corporations, owners have been known to use corporate assets to pay their personal expenses (or vice versa) or to mix their personal funds and corporate funds into a single bank account. Don't do it! Protect the corporation's identity by keeping it completely separate from the owners' personal identities. "Draw a salary and pay your personal expenses through your own personal checking account," advises one attorney.

SOURCES: Adapted from Jacquelyn Lynn, "Your Business Inc.," *Business Start-Ups,* July 1996, pp. 52–59; Steven C. Bahls and Jane Easter Bahls, "Best Defense," *Entrepreneur,* January 1997, pp. 72–74. ◆

ceive a penny of its net income as dividends, a corporation must pay these taxes at the *corporate* tax rate. Then, stockholders must pay taxes on the dividends they receive from these same profits at the *individual* tax rate. Thus, a corporation's profits are taxed twice—once at the corporate level and again at the individual level. This **double taxation** is a distinct disadvantage of the corporate form of ownership.

Potential for Diminished Managerial Incentives. As corporations grow, they often require additional managerial expertise beyond that which the founder can provide. Because they created their companies and often have most of their personal wealth tied up in them, entrepreneurs have an intense interest in ensuring their success and are willing to make sacrifices for their businesses. Professional managers an entrepreneur brings in to help run the business as it grows do not always have the same degree of interest in or loyalty to the company. As a result, the business may suffer without the founder's energy, care, and devotion. One way to minimize this potential problem is to link managers' (and even employees') compensation to the company's financial performance through a profit-sharing or bonus plan. Corporations can also stimulate managers' and employees' incentive on the job by creating an employee stock ownership plan (ESOP) in which managers and employees become part or whole owners in the company.

Legal Requirements and Regulatory Red Tape. Corporations are subject to more legal and financial requirements than other forms of ownership. Entrepreneurs must resist the temptation to commingle their personal funds with those of the corporation and must meet more-stringent requirements for recording and reporting business transactions. They must also hold annual meetings and consult the board of directors about major decisions that are beyond day-to-day operations. Managers may be required to submit some major decisions to the stockholders for approval. Corporations that are publicly held must file quarterly and annual reports with the Securities and Exchange Commission (SEC).

Potential Loss of Control by the Founders. When entrepreneurs sell shares of ownership in their companies, they relinquish some control. Especially when they need large capital infusions for start-up or growth, entrepreneurs may have to give up significant amounts of control, so much, in fact, that they become minority shareholders. Losing majority ownership—and therefore control—in their companies leaves founders in a precarious position. They no longer have the power to determine the company's direction; "outsiders" do. In some cases, founders' shares have been so diluted that majority shareholders actually vote them out of their jobs! *Steven Jobs, chairman of Apple Computers, once owned the majority of stock in the company he co-founded with Steve Wozniak. Over the years, however, his ownership was diluted as he sold stock in the company to raise the capital needed to fuel Apple Computer's growth. When a dispute arose over the company's direction, the majority shareholders ousted him from his job as chairman. Only when the company's performance faltered several years later did the shareholders reinstate the inspirational founder to his position as chairman of the company.*

THE PROFESSIONAL CORPORATION

A **professional corporation** is designed to offer professionals such as lawyers, doctors, dentists, accountants, and others the advantage of the corporate form of ownership. Corporate ownership is ideally suited for licensed professionals, who must always be concerned about malpractice lawsuits, because it offers limited liability. For example, if three doctors form a professional corporation, none of them would be liable for the malpractice of the other. (Of course, each would be liable for his or her own actions.) Professional corporations are created in the same way as regular corporations. They often are identified by the abbreviation P.C. (professional corporation), P.A. (professional association), or S.C. (service corporation).

*A*lternative Forms of Ownership

4 Describe the features of the alternative forms of ownership such as the S corporation, the limited liability company, and the joint venture.

In addition to the sole proprietorship, the partnership, and the corporation, entrepreneurs can choose from other forms of ownership, including the S corporation, the limited liabilty company, and the joint venture.

THE S CORPORATION

In 1954 the Internal Revenue Service Code created the Subchapter S corporation. In recent years the IRS has changed the title to S corporation and has made a few modifications in its qualifications. An **S corporation** is a distinction that is made only for federal income tax purposes and is, in terms of legal characteristics, no different from any other corporation. In 1996, Congress passed legislation to simplify or eliminate some of the restrictive rules and requirements for S corporation so that businesses seeking "S" status must meet the following criteria:

1. It must be a domestic (U.S.) corporation.
2. It cannot have a nonresident alien as a shareholder.
3. It can issue only one class of common stock, which means that all shares must carry the same rights (e.g., the right to dividends or liquidation rights). The exception is voting rights, which may differ. In other words, an S corporation can issue voting and nonvoting common stock.
4. It cannot have more than 75 shareholders (increased from 35).

By increasing the number of shareholders allowed in S corporations to 75, the new law makes succession planning easier for business owners. Aging founders now can pass their stock on to their children and grandchildren without worrying about exceeding the maximum allowable number of owners. The larger number of shareholders allowed also increases S corporations' ability to raise capital by attracting more investors. The new law includes another provision that enables S corporations to raise money more readily. It permits them to sell shares of their stock to certain tax-exempt organizations such as pension funds. (Previous rules limited ownership strictly to individuals, estates, and certain trusts.) "This should provide even greater access to capital because there are pension plans willing to invest in closely held small business stock," says one accountant.[15] The new law also allows S corporations to own subsidiary companies. Previously, the owners of S corporations had to establish separate businesses if they wanted to launch new ventures, even those closely related to the S corporation. This change is especially beneficial to entrepreneurs with several businesses in related fields. They can establish an S corporation as the "parent" company and then set up multiple subsidiaries as either C or S corporations as "offspring" under it. Because they are separate corporations, the liabilities of one business cannot spill over and destroy the assets of another.

Violating any of the requirements for an S corporation automatically terminates a company's S status. If a corporation satisfies the definition for an S corporation, the owners must actually elect to be treated as one. The election is made by filing IRS Form 2553 (within the first 75 days of the tax year), and all shareholders must consent to have the corporation treated as an S corporation.

Advantages of an S Corporation. S corporations retain all of the advantages of a regular corporation, such as continuity of existence, transferability of ownership, and limited personal liability for its owners. The most notable provision of the S corporation is that it passes all of its profits or losses through to the individual shareholders and its income is taxed only once at the individual tax rate. Thus, electing S corporation status avoids a primary disadvantage of the regular (or C) corporation—double taxation. In essence, the tax treatment of an S corporation is exactly like that of a partnership; its owners report their proportional shares of the company's profits on their individual income tax returns and pay taxes on those profits at the individual rate (even if they never take the money out of the business). *Before Vic and Suzette Brounsuzian launched Meg-A-Nut, their small shop selling dry-roasted nuts, chocolates, and other items, they studied the advantages and the disadvantages of all of the forms of ownership and how each form would affect them. After weighing their options, the Brounsuzians decided that an S corporation would be the best choice for them, primarily because of the limited liability and favorable tax treatment it offered. "We put everything we have into this business," says Vic. "After talking with our accountant and with others, we figured that going with the S corporation was the best way of organizing the business."[16]*

IN THE FOOTSTEPS OF AN ENTREPRENEUR

Which Form of Ownership Is Best?

*W*hen Deborah Williams started Black Cat Computer Wholesale as a home-based business, she had no idea that her company would grow so fast. Because she was the only worker in the company at the outset and because she had little business experience, she selected the simplest form of ownership available: the sole proprietorship. "I hadn't started a company before, and I was ignorant about how much all this mattered," she recalls. Williams's wholesale computer operation soon outgrew its home-based location and its form of ownership. Selecting the right form of ownership, says Williams, "has been a nightmare, mainly because we grew so quickly that it was tough to figure out just what structure made sense for us." Black Cat, now with annual sales of $7 million, went through three forms of ownership in its first five years of operation! Williams has spent the last two years trying to undo the mistakes that resulted from selecting the wrong forms of ownership in the past. Looking back, she realizes that she could have avoided most of those mistakes by choosing a form of ownership that suited her needs as well as those of her fast-growing company.

One business consultant says he sees the same story played out all the time. "Clients come in and don't even want to think about [choosing a form of ownership]. All they want is for me to tell them quickly what's the best form for them. But there's no quick answer to that question. We absolutely need to discuss their goals for the company and all kinds of other issues." Many business owners do not realize the far-reaching consequences the choice of a form of ownership has on a business and its owners.

As soon as she saw Black Cat's sales climb rapidly, Williams knew that she needed to make some changes in her business. "The big thing I was worried about was limiting my personal liability," she recalls. "After a year of operation, I switched to S corporation status to give myself the limited liability." For Williams and Black Cat, the switch from a sole proprietorship to an S corporation was relatively easy and inexpensive.

The company continued to experience rapid growth, and Williams soon discovered the need for external financing. Although she has no immediate plans to take her company public, Williams is not ruling out that option in the future. Such a move would be impossible for an S corporation, and that's why Williams recently switched to a C corporation. "My real goal was to create a broader base of financing for the company, which I'm convinced is easier with C corporation structure," she says. With that switch, Williams loses the tax advantages of an S corporation. Now, Black Cat pays taxes on its profits at the corporate rate, and Williams pays taxes on any dividends distributed to her from those profits. That doesn't bother Williams, however. "I am leaving most of my money in the company, anyhow, to fund growth. So the double taxation really didn't matter." Williams believes the C corporation is the form of ownership that is best suited for her company. "With the right structure and financing now in place, I'm in great shape to do what I want to do, which is go after new market opportunities."

---

1. In the early stages of her business, what benefits did a sole proprietorship offer Williams? What disadvantages did she face?

2. What factors prompted Williams to switch to an S corporation? What benefits did she give up, and what advantages did she gain by switching to a C corporation?

SOURCE: Adapted from Jill Andresky Fraser, "Perfect Form," *Inc.,* December 1997, pp. 155–158. ◆

Another advantage of the S corporation is that it avoids the tax C corporations pay on assets that have appreciated in value and are sold. Also, owners of S corporations enjoy the ability to make year-end payouts to themselves if profits are high. In a C corporation, owners have no such luxury because the IRS watches for excessive compensation to owners and managers.

Disadvantages of an S Corporation. When the Tax Reform Act (TRA) of 1986 restructured individual and corporate tax rates, many business owners switched to S corporations to lower their tax bills. For the first time since Congress enacted the federal income tax in 1913, the maximum individual rate was lower than the maximum corporate rate. However, in 1993, Congress realigned the tax structure by raising the maximum personal tax rate to 39.6 percent from 31 percent. This new rate is 4.6 percent *higher* than the maximum corporate tax rate of 35 percent. Although these changes make S corporation status much less attractive than before, entrepreneurs considering switching to C corporation status must consider the total impact of such a change on their companies, especially if they pay out a significant amount of earnings to owners. In addition to the tax implications of making the switch from an S corporation, owners should consider the size of the company's net profits, the tax rates of its shareholders, plans (and their timing) to sell the company, and the impact of the C corporation's double taxation penalty on income distributed as dividends.

Consider the following example offered by one tax adviser:

> *Take $1 of net income. If you are a C corporation, after you pay the 34 percent [corporate] income tax, you have 66 cents left. Then you distribute that 66 cents to the shareholder/owner, and it gets taxed again—say at the top [personal tax] rate of 39.6 percent. That's another 26 cents, leaving 40 cents in your pocket.*[17]

If the same owner had chosen to form an S corporation, that same $1 of net income would have been subject to 40 cents in tax, and the owner would have kept the remaining 60 cents. Sixty cents versus 40 cents per dollar: The choice is clear.

Another disadvantage of the S corporation is that the costs of many fringe benefits—insurance, meals, lodging—paid to shareholders who have 2 percent or more of stock cannot be deducted as business expenses for tax purposes; these benefits are then considered to be taxable income. In addition, S corporations offer shareholders only a limited range of retirement benefits, whereas regular corporations make a wide range of retirement plans available.

When Is an S Corporation a Wise Choice? Choosing S corporation status is usually beneficial to start-up companies anticipating net losses and to highly profitable firms with substantial dividends to pay out to shareholders. In these cases the owner can use the loss to offset other income or is in a lower tax bracket than the corporation, thus saving money in the long run. Companies that plan to reinvest most of their earnings to finance growth also find S corporation status favorable. Small business owners who intend to sell their companies in the near future will prefer S over C status because the taxable gains on the sale of an S corporation are generally lower than those on the sale of a C corporation.

On the other hand, small companies with the following characteristics are *not* likely to benefit from S corporation status:

◆ Highly profitable personal-service companies with large numbers of shareholders, in which most of the profits are passed on to shareholders as compensation or retirement benefits.

◆ Fast-growing companies that must retain most of their earnings to finance growth and capital spending.

◆ Corporations in which the loss of fringe benefits to shareholders exceeds tax savings.

◆ Corporations in which the income before any compensation to shareholders is less than $100,000 a year.

◆ Corporations with sizable net operating losses that cannot be used against S corporation earnings.

THE LIMITED LIABILITY COMPANY (LLC)

A relatively new creation, the **limited liability company (LLC)** is, like an S corporation, a cross between a partnership and a corporation. Originating in Wyoming in 1977, LLCs are gaining in popularity because, like S corporations, they combine many of the benefits of the partnership and the corporate forms of ownership but are not subject to many of the restrictions imposed on S corporations. For example, S corporations cannot have more than 75 shareholders, and they are limited to only one class of stock. Those restrictions do not apply to LLCs. Although an LLC can have one owner, most have multiple owners (called members). An LLC offers its owners limited liability without imposing any requirements on their characteristics or any ceiling on their numbers. Unlike a limited partnership, which prohibits limited partners from participating in the day-to-day management of the business, an LLC does not restrict its members' ability to become involved in managing the company.

In addition to offering its members the advantage of limited liability, LLCs also avoid the double taxation imposed on C corporations. Like an S corporation, an LLC does not pay income taxes; its income flows through to the members, who are responsible for paying income taxes on their shares of the LLC's net income. Because they are not subject to the many restrictions imposed on other forms of ownership, LLCs offer entrepreneurs another significant advantage: flexibility. Like a partnership, an LLC permits its members to divide income (and thus tax liability) as they see fit.

These advantages make the LLC an ideal form of ownership for small companies in virtually any industry—retail, wholesale, manufacturing, real estate, or service. *For instance, when movie director Steven Spielberg, former Disney executive Jeffrey Katzenberg, and recording entrepreneur David Geffen decided to launch their own movie and recording production company, they formed DreamWorks SKG as a limited liability company.* Because LLCs offer the tax advantages of a partnership, the legal protection of a corporation, and maximum flexibility, they have become an extremely popular form of ownership among entrepreneurs. Of all the forms of ownership, "limited liability companies remain 'the fairest of them all,'" says one expert.[18] They are becoming especially popular among family-owned businesses because of the benefits they offer. "LLCs provide most family businesses with continuity of life, limited liability for participants, and advantages in handling estate and gift taxes," says one tax attorney.[19]

When Robert Crane created Octagon Communications L.L.C. as a holding company for a rural cellular telephone business, he chose to form the company as an LLC. The company has eight members, each of whom made a small capital contribution. The primary attraction of the LLC, says Crane, was the limited liability protection it offered the members in a risky business venture.[20]

Creating an LLC is much like creating a corporation. Forming an LLC requires an entrepreneur to file two documents with the secretary of state: the articles of organization and the operating agreement. The LLCs **articles of organization,** similar to the corporation's articles of incorporation, establish the company's name, its method of management (board-managed or member-managed), its duration, and the names and addresses of each organizer. In most states, the company's name must contain the words *limited liability company*, *limited company*, or the letters *L.L.C.* or *L.C.* Unlike a corporation, an LLC does not have perpetual life; in most states, an LLC's charter may not exceed 30 years. However, the same factors that would cause a partnership to dissolve would also cause an LLC to dissolve before its charter expired.

The **operating agreement,** similar to a corporation's bylaws, outlines the provisions governing the way the LLC will conduct business. To ensure that their LLCs are classified as a partnership for tax purposes, entrepreneurs must draft the operating agreement carefully. The operating agreement must create an LLC that has more characteristics of a partnership than of a corporation to maintain this favorable tax treatment. Specifically, an LLC cannot have any more than two of the following four corporate characteristics:

1. *Limited liability.* Limited liability exists if no member of the LLC is personally liable for the debts or claims against the company. Because entrepreneurs choosing this form of ownership usually do so to get limited liability protection, the operating agreement almost always contains this characteristic.

2. *Continuity of life.* Continuity of life exists if the company continues to exist despite changes in stock ownership. To avoid continuity of life, any LLC member must have the power to dissolve the company. Most entrepreneurs choose to omit this characteristic from their LLC's operating agreements. Thus, if one member of an LLC resigns, dies, or declares bankruptcy, the LLC automatically dissolves and all remaining members must vote to keep the company going.

3. *Free transferability of interest.* Free transferability of interest exists if each LLC member has the power to transfer his ownership to another person without the consent of other members. To avoid this characteristic, the operating agreement must state that a recipient of a member's LLC stock cannot become a substitute member without the consent of the remaining members.

4. *Centralized management.* Centralized management exists if a group that does not include all LLC members has the authority to make management decisions and to conduct company business. To avoid this characteristic, the operating agreement must state that the company elects to be "member-managed."

Despite their universal appeal to entrepreneurs, LLCs suffer some disadvantages. They can be expensive to create, often costing between $1,500 and $5,000. Although an LLC may be ideally suited for an entrepreneur launching a new company, it may pose problems for business owners who are considering converting an existing business to an LLC. Switching to an LLC from a general partnership, a limited partnership, or a sole proprietorship reorganizing to bring in new owners is usually not a problem. However, owners of corporations and S corporations would incur large tax obligations if they converted their companies to LLCs.

To date, the biggest disadvantage of the LLC stems from its newness. As yet, no uniform legislation for LLCs exists (although a Uniform Limited Liability Act is pending at the federal level). Two states (Vermont and Hawaii) still do not recognize LLCs as a legal form of ownership.

THE JOINT VENTURE

A **joint venture** is very much like a partnership, except that it is formed for a specific, limited purpose. For instance, suppose that you have a 500-acre tract of land 60 miles from Chicago. This land has been cleared and is normally used for farming. One of your friends has solid contacts among major musical groups and would like to put on a concert. You expect prices for your agricultural products to be low this summer, so you and your friend form a joint venture for the specific purpose of staging a three-day concert. Your contribution will be the exclusive use of the land for one month, and your friend will provide all the performers as well as technicians, facilities, and equipment. All costs will be paid out of receipts, and the net profits will be split, with you receiving 20 percent for the use of your land. When the concert is over, the facilities removed, and the accounting for all costs completed, you and your friend will split the profits 20-80, and the joint venture will terminate. The "partners" form a new joint venture for each new project they undertake. The income derived from a joint venture is taxed as if it had arisen from a partnership.

In any endeavor in which neither party can effectively achieve the purpose alone, a joint venture becomes a common form of ownership. That's why joint ventures have become increasingly popular in global business dealings. For instance, a small business in the United States may manufacture a product that would be in demand in Brazil, but the U.S. firm has no knowledge of how to do business in Brazil. Forming a joint venture with a Brazilian firm that knows the customs and laws of the country, has an established distribution network, and can promote the product effectively could result in a mutually beneficial joint venture.

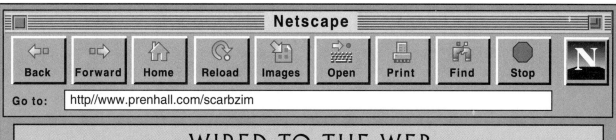

WIRED TO THE WEB

A PLAN FOR THE FUTURE

*W*hen he was just five years old, Kirk Sweeney began ice-skating with a pair of skates his older brother had outgrown. Soon, Kirk's parents bought him his own pair of skates, and Kirk put them to good use. He loved skating because it gave him a sense of freedom, speed, and control.

As Kirk grew older, his love for skating did not fade. He became an accomplished hockey player and was a key member of every team he joined. His consistently stellar performances on the ice attracted the attention of several college hockey programs, and Kirk earned a four-year scholarship to a large state school. While in college, Kirk became interested in owning his own business and decided to major in entrepreneurship.

During his senior year, Kirk went home to attend a special ceremony at his high school alma mater. While he was at home, Kirk learned that the couple who had run the skating rink for as long as he could remember, were going to retire next year and wanted to sell the rink. Kirk couldn't believe the opportunity unfolding before him! He began to explore the possibility of buying the skating rink and transforming it into a complete sports complex.

When he returned to school for his final semester, Kirk threw himself into developing the business plan for what he hoped would become his skating complex with as much enthusiasm as he had for skating. He researched the local market, studied competitors, and spent hours developing marketing strategies and financial forecasts. He took his second draft of the plan home one weekend to talk to his father about helping him make his dream come true.

Kirk's plan was to operate the rink for two years after making only moderate improvements to the facility. Then he planned to initiate a major expansion that would transform the skating rink into a serious sports complex that would draw customers from a much larger trading area. The expansion would require *serious* cash—more than he could get from his family and more than the business could generate in just two years. Kirk believed that his market and financial forecasts were accurate. He knew that the expansion would transform the business from a small skating rink that generated a healthy profit into a thriving business that could produce significant profits.

On Friday night, Kirk handed his plan to his father and asked him to read it.

"Dad, I want you to be my partner in this venture," Kirk said. "I'll run the business, and you can be the investor. Of course, you can offer me advice any time you think I might need it."

"Son, you know I'll help you buy that skating rink. I think you're going to make a tremendous success of it, and this plan is a good indication of why. I think we need to be very careful how we set up this business, though. I'm at the stage in my life where I've accumulated some pretty valuable assets, and I don't want to put them at risk. Plus, if things go according to your plan, in a couple of years, you're going to need more money than I have access to. We've got to think about these things as we choose a form of ownership."

1. Use the resources in this chapter and on the World Wide Web to help Kirk and his father decide which form of ownership would be best suited for them. Use the WWW to find out how much it would cost to create the form of ownership you recommend in your state.
2. What factors should Kirk and his father consider in their choice of a form of ownership? Explain.

Summary of the Major Forms of Ownership

Figure 3.2 shows the liability features of the major forms of ownership discussed in this chapter. Table 3.1 summarizes of the key features of the sole proprietorship, the partnership, the C corporation, the S corporation, and the limited liability company.

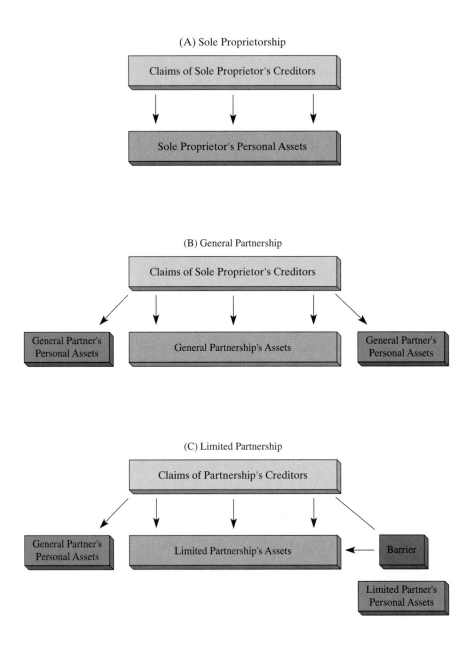

Figure 3.2 **Liability Features of the Basic Forms of Ownership** Source: Adapted from A. James Barnes, Terry M. Dworkin, and Eric L. Richards, *Law for Business*, 5th ed. (Burr Ridge, IL: Irwin Publishing, 1994), p. 400.

(continues)

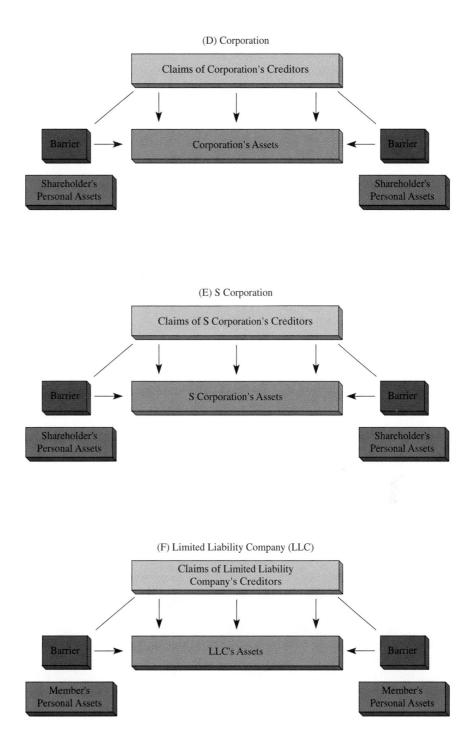

Figure 3.2 **Liability Features of the Basic Forms of Ownership** *(continued).*

Table 3.1 Characteristics of the Major Forms of Ownership

Feature	Sole Proprietorship	Partnership	C Corporation	S Corporation	Limited Liability Company
Owner's personal liability	Unlimited	Unlimited for general partners Limited for limited partners	Limited	Limited	Limited
Number of owners	1	2 or more (at least 1 general partner required)	Any number	Maximum of 75 (with restriction on who they are)	2 or more
Tax liability	Single tax: proprietor pays at individual rate	Single tax: partners pay on their proportional shares at individual rate	Double tax: corporation pays tax and shareholders pay tax on dividends distributed	Single tax: owners pay on their proportional shares at individual rate	Single tax: members pay on their proportional shares at individual rate
Maximum tax rate	39.6%	39.6%	35% (39.6% on dividends distributed)	39.6%	39.6%
Transferability of ownership	Fully transferable through sale or transfer of company assets	May require consent of all partners	Fully transferable	Transferable (but transfer may affect S status)	Usually requires consent of all members
Continuity of business	Ends on death or insanity of proprietor or upon termination by proprietor	Dissolves upon death, insanity, or retirement of a general partner (business may continue)	Perpetual life	Perpetual life	Perpetual life
Cost of formation	Low	Moderate	High	High	High
Liquidity of owner's investment in business	Poor to average	Poor to average	High	High	High
Complexity of formation	Extremely low	Moderate	High	High	High
Ability to raise capital	Low	Moderate	Very high	Moderate to high	High
Formation procedure	No special steps required other than buying necessary licenses	No written partnership agreements required (but highly advisable)	Must meet formal requirements specified by state law	Must follow same procedures as C corporation, then elect S status with IRS	Must meet formal requirements specified by state law

Chapter Summary

◆ Describe the advantages and the disadvantages of the sole proprietorship.

- ◆ A sole proprietorship is a business owned and managed by one individual and is the most popular form of ownership.
- ◆ Sole proprietorships offer these *advantages*: They are simple to create; they are the least costly form to begin; the owner has total decision-making authority; there are no special legal restrictions; and they are easy to discontinue.
- ◆ They also suffer from these *disadvantages*: unlimited personal liability of owner; limited managerial skills and capabilities; limited access to capital; lack of continuity.

◆ Describe the advantages and the disadvantages of the partnership.

- ◆ A partnership is an association of two or more people who co-own a business for the purpose of making a profit. Partnerships offer these *advantages*: ease of establishing; complementary skills of partners; division of profits; larger pool of capital available; ability to attract limited partners; little government regulation; flexibility; and tax advantages.
- ◆ Partnerships suffer from these *disadvantages*: unlimited liability of at least one partner; difficulty in disposing of partnership interest; lack of continuity; potential for personality and authority conflicts; and partners bound by the law of agency.
- ◆ A limited partnership operates like any other partnership except that it allows limited partners (who are primarily investors and cannot take an active role in managing the business) to become owners without subjecting themselves to unlimited personal liability for the company's debts.

◆ Describe the advantages and disadvantages of the corporation.

- ◆ A corporation, the most complex of the three basic forms of ownership, is a separate legal entity. To form a corporation, an entrepreneur must file the articles of incorporation with the state in which the company will incorporate.
- ◆ Corporations offer these *advantages*: limited liability of stockholders; ability to attract capital; ability to continue indefinitely; and transferable ownership.
- ◆ Corporations suffer from these *disadvantages*: cost and time involved in incorporating; double taxation; potential for diminished managerial incentives; legal requirements and regulatory red tape; and potential loss of control by the founders.

◆ Describe the advantages and the disadvantages of the alternative forms of ownership such as the S corporation, the limited liability company, and the joint venture.

- ◆ An S corporation offers its owners limited liability protection but avoids the double taxation of C corporations.
- ◆ A limited liability company, like an S corporation, is a cross between a partnership and a corporation, yet it operates without the restrictions imposed on an S corporation. To create an LLC, an entrepreneur must file the articles of organization and the operating agreement with the secretary of state.
- ◆ A joint venture is like a partnership, except that it is formed for a specific purpose.

Discussion Questions

1. What factors should an entrepreneur consider before choosing a form of ownership?
2. Why are sole proprietorships so popular as a form of ownership?
3. How does personal conflict affect partnerships? How can co-owners avoid becoming sparring partners?
4. What issues should the articles of partnership address? Why are the articles important to a successful partnership?
5. Can one partner commit another to a business deal without the other's consent? Why?
6. Explain the differences between a domestic corporation, a foreign corporation, and an alien corporation.
7. What issues should the Certificate of Incorporation cover?
8. How does an S corporation differ from a regular corporation?
9. How does a joint venture differ from a partnership?
10. What role do limited partners play in a partnership? What will happen if a limited partner takes an active role in managing the business?
11. What advantages does a limited liability company offer over an S corporation? Over a partnership?
12. How is an LLC created?
13. What criteria must an LLC meet to avoid double taxation?
14. Briefly outline the advantages and disadvantages of the major forms of ownership.

Step into the Real World

1. Interview five local small business owners. What form of ownership did they choose? Why? Prepare a brief report summarizing your findings, and explain advantages and disadvantages those owners face because of their choices.
2. Contact the secretary of state to determine the status of limited liability companies in your state. Are they recognized? How does an entrepreneur create one? What requirements must an LLC meet? Report your findings to the class.
3. Invite entrepreneurs who operate as partners to your classroom. Do they have a written partnership agreement? Are their skills complementary? How do they divide responsibility for running their company? How do they handle decision making? What do they do when disputes and disagreements arise?
4. Find in the Yellow Pages of your local telephone book the names of four businesses that you think are effective marketing tools. Also find four companies whose names do little or nothing to help market their products or services. Explain the reasons for your choices. Select a business with the "wrong" name and work with a team of your classmates to brainstorm a better name.

Take It to the Net

Visit the Scarborough/Zimmerer home page at
www.prenhall.com/scarbzim
for updated information, on-line resources, and Web-based exercises.

Endnotes

1. Lin Grensing-Pophal, "Choose Your Vehicle," *Business Start-Ups*, December 1996, pp. 24–27.
2. Jill Andresky Fraser, "Perfect Form," *Inc.*, December 1997, pp. 155–158.
3. Kylo-Patrick Hart, "Step 4: Decide Your Legal Structure," *Business Start-Ups*, August 1996, p. 64.
4. Barbara Bucholz and Margaret Crane, "One-Man Bands," *Your Company*, Summer 1993, p. 24.
5. Jacquelyn Lynn, "Partnership Procedures," *Business Start-Ups*, June 1996, p. 73.
6. Frances Huffman, "Irreconcilable Differences," *Entrepreneur*, February 1992, p. 108.
7. Roberta Maynard, "Opposites Attract—With Time and Effort," *Nation's Business*, July 1996, p. 9.
8. Tom McGrath, "How to Fire Your Partner," *Success*, February 1998, pp. 30–31.
9. Manuel Schiffres, "Partnerships with a Plus," *Changing Times*, October 1989, p. 49.
10. Chief Justice John Marshall, cited by Henry R. Cheeseman, *Contemporary Business Law* (Upper Saddle River, N.J.: Prentice Hall, 1997), p. 596.
11. Jacquelyn Lynn, "Your Business Inc.," *Business Start-Ups*, July 1996, p. 52.
12. Ibid., p. 59.
13. Jane Easter Bahls, "Rethinking Inc." *Entrepreneur*, August 1994, pp. 60–63; Barbara Marsh, "Suits Go After Personal Assets of Firms' Owners," *Wall Street Journal*, August 13, 1993, pp. B1, B2.
14. Kinney Shoe Corporation v. Polan, 939 F. 2d 209 (4th Cir. 1991).
15. Joan Szabo, "Good News," *Entrepreneur*, January 1997, pp. 60–62.
16. Hart, "Step 4," p. 64.
17. David R. Evanson, "Now You C It, Now You Don't," *Entrepreneur*, February 1993, p. 29.
18. Szabo, "Good News," p. 62.
19. Jerry A. Kasner, "Does Check-the-Box Spell Doom for Family Limited Partnerships?" *Tax Notes 27*, no. 4 (January 27, 1997), p. 474.
20. Deborah L. Jacobs, "Choosing a Business Structure," *Your Company*, Winter 1993, pp. 36–41.

Franchising and the Entrepreneur

Experience is a hard teacher because she gives the test first, the lesson afterward.

—Vernon Law

The big print giveth, the fine print taketh away.

—Bishop Fulton J. Sheen

Upon completion of this chapter, you will be able to

1 Explain the importance of franchising in the U.S. economy.

2 Define the concept of franchising.

3 Describe the different types of franchises.

4 Explain the forces behind franchising's popularity.

5 Describe the benefits of franchising for the franchisor.

6 Describe the benefits and limitations of franchising for the franchisee.

7 Discuss what franchisors look for in a franchisee.

8 Describe the legal aspects of franchising, including the protection offered by the FTC's Trade Regulation Rule.

9 Explain the *right* way to buy a franchise.

10 Describe a typical franchise contract and some of its provisions.

11 Understand current trends shaping modern franchising.

1 Explain the importance of franchising in the U.S. economy.

*S*ince 1990, sales by franchised businesses have grown 10 times as fast as the U.S. economy as a whole.[1] Much of franchising's popularity arises from its ability to offer persons who lack business experience the chance to own and operate a business with a high probability of success. Franchising has grown in recent years far beyond the traditional auto dealerships and fast-food outlets. Through franchised businesses, consumers can buy nearly every good or service imaginable—from singing telegrams and computer training to tax services and waste-eating microbes. "Franchising is the most successful marketing concept ever created," says trend tracker John Naisbitt.[2]

Today, some 4,500 franchisors operate more than 600,000 franchise outlets throughout the world, and more are opening at an incredibly fast pace. A new franchise opens somewhere in the United States every eight minutes and somewhere in the world every six-and-a-half minutes![3] Franchises account for 43 percent of all retail sales, totaling more than $810 billion, and they employ more than 8 million people in more than 70 major industries.[4]

Franchising's impressive growth will continue into the new millennium. Experts predict that, by 2004, franchises will be ringing up sales of $2.5 trillion worldwide.[5] By then, franchising will account for 50 percent of all retail sales. One International Franchise Association (IFA) spokesperson says that franchising "will become the dominant form of retailing in most of the developed countries around the world."[6]

*W*hat Is Franchising?

2 Define the concept of franchising.

Franchising can be traced to Civil War times, when Isaac M. Singer devised a more efficient, less expensive way to sell his Singer sewing machines through franchised outlets. From this modest beginning as a distribution system, franchising has become a major force in the U.S. economy, expanding into a broad range of retail and service businesses. The concept has reached beyond the traditional fast-food enterprises (which still account for about 40 percent of all the goods sold by franchisees) into businesses as diverse as diamond jewelry, on-site furniture repair, in-home pet care, and management training for executives. Retail outlets dominate franchising, accounting for about 85 percent of all franchise sales, but increasing demand for consumer and business services is producing a boom among service-oriented franchises.

In **franchising,** semi-independent business owners (franchisees) pay fees and royalties to a parent company (franchisor) in return for the right to sell its products or services and often to use its business format and system. Franchisees do not establish their own autonomous businesses; instead, they buy a "success package" from the franchisor, who shows them how to use it. *Ulf Schaefer, who operates a highly successful Play It Again Sports franchise with partner T. J. Western, says, "Buying a franchise is like buying a cookbook: The recipe is there, but you have to do the cooking yourself. But a good franchisor gives you a system— advertising support, group buying power, continuing training, market research, and so on. That support . . . is like a little insurance policy."*[7]

Franchisees, unlike independent business owners, do not have the freedom to change the way they run their businesses—for example, shifting advertising strategies or adjusting product lines—but they do have a formula for success that the franchisor has worked out. "In fact," says one writer, "the secret to success in franchising is following the formula precisely. . . . Successful franchisors claim that neglecting to follow the formula is one of the chief reasons that franchisees fail."[8] *Steve Gaffney, a highly successful MAACO (automotive services) franchisee, is convinced that the system the franchisor taught him was the key to his company's progress and growth. "You have to follow the plan every day," he says. "The [franchisor's] operations manuals are my road map. They explain the business in terms anyone can understand. And I follow every detail to make the system work."*[9]

Because franchisors develop the business systems their franchisees use and direct their distribution methods, they maintain substantial control over their franchisees. This standardization lies at the core of franchising's success as a method of distribution. One writer explains:

The science of franchising is an exacting one; products and services are delivered according to tightly wrapped operating formulas. There is no variance. A product is developed and honed under the watchful eye of the franchisor, then offered by franchisees under strict quality standards. The result: a democratization of products and services. Hamburgers that taste as good in Boston as in Beijing. Quick lubes available to everyone, whether they drive a Toyota or a Treblinka.[10]

Types of Franchising

3 Describe the different types of franchises.

There are three basic types of franchising: tradename franchising, product distribution franchising, and pure franchising. **Trade-name franchising** involves a brand name such as True Value Hardware or Western Auto. The franchisee buys the right to become identified with the franchisor's trade name without distributing particular products exclusively under the manufacturer's name. **Product distribution franchising** involves licensing the franchisee to sell specific products under the manufacturer's brand name and trademark through a selective, limited distribution network. This system is commonly used to market automobiles (Chevrolet, Oldsmobile, Chrysler), gasoline products (Exxon, Sunoco, Texaco), soft drinks (Pepsi Cola, CocaCola), bicycles (Schwinn), appliances, cosmetics, and other products. Both of these forms of franchising allow franchisees to acquire some of the parent company's identity.

Pure (or **comprehensive** or **business format**) **franchising** involves providing the franchisee with a complete business format, including a license for a trade name, the products or services to be sold, the physical plant, the methods of operation, a marketing strategy plan, a quality control process, a two-way communications system, and the necessary business services. The franchisee purchases the right to use all the elements of a fully integrated business operation. Pure franchising is the most rapidly growing of all types of franchising and is common among fast-food restaurants, hotels, business service firms, car rental agencies, educational institutions, beauty aid retailers, and many others. Although product and trade name franchises annually ring up more sales than pure franchises, pure franchising outlets' sales are growing much faster.

What's Behind Franchising's Popularity?

4 Explain the forces behind franchising's popularity.

Franchising's popularity stems from several underlying trends. The rekindling of the entrepreneurial spirit in the United States is encouraging more individuals to launch businesses, and, for many, franchising is the ideal path. Opening franchises allows them to be in control of their own destinies while retaining the security of a support structure from the franchisor.

Demographic factors and shifting lifestyles, such as the baby boom and the proliferation of the dual-career couple, have put a premium on convenience and service—two of franchising's specialties. Many franchises, such as those offering maid services, meal deliveries, and other services, are targeting dual-career couples. *As its name implies, Pressed4Time Inc. is a franchise built on saving time for its target customers. Franchisees of this small but growing company pick up and deliver dry cleaning for busy clients, primarily people who work at corporate offices. Customers merely take their laundry with them to the office, where a Pressed4Time franchisee picks it up and then returns it, usually the next day.*[11]

Other factors leading to the impressive growth rate of franchising include the rapidly growing number of women entering the workforce. Career women, tired of bumping against the glass ceiling in large corporations, are choosing to open their own businesses in record numbers, and many take the franchise route to entrepreneurship. Although one study found that 11 percent of franchise outlets were owned by women (and 22 percent were owned by male–female partnerships), the number of women involved in franchising is growing rapidly.[12] Some franchisors, such as Mr. Build Handi-Man Services (home repair services), Kinderdance International (child-care centers), and Decorating Den Systems (custom home-decorating services) have targeted working women with children as franchise owners.

Executives who are jumping off the corporate ladder in search of job security and control over their careers and lives represent another important factor in the popularity of franchising. These executives have earned a wealth of experience during their corporate careers and are looking for franchises where they can apply it. *At The Maids, a franchise offering in-home cleaning services, more than 50 percent of prospective franchisees are former corporate executives, up from just 20 percent in the early 1990s. Harry Edgar, now an owner of four of The Maids outlets, was a 50-year-old senior vice president with Lerner's Stores in charge of 100 stores across a nine-state area. When the retail chain underwent a change of ownership, Edgar decided to leave his corporate position and began researching franchises. He ultimately chose The Maids because he felt comfortable with the concept and he liked the way the franchise was positioned in a growing market. He has no regrets. "I would do it again in a minute," he says.*[13]

Downsizing at major companies is also feeding the growth of franchising. As companies reorganize and downsize their operations, more former "pinstripers" are becoming franchisees. One franchisor, who gets more than 150 calls a week from downsized individuals, says, "They would like to be in a certain corporate setting and follow some corporate guidelines, yet control their own destiny."[14]

Franchisors are also seeing young, well-educated people take greater interest in franchising. Rather than risk joining a large corporation only to become victims of downsizing, recent college graduates are building their careers around franchising. Many of the lower-cost, service-oriented franchises appeal to this group.

Perhaps the most important reason franchising has been so successful is the mutual benefits it offers franchisors and franchisees. In a franchising relationship, each party depends on the other for support. The ideal franchising relationship is a partnership based on trust and a willingness to work together for mutual success. One franchisor explains, "A golden rule is that the franchisor should treat the franchisee as a working partner and never like someone they look down on. The franchisor has to understand the equation of franchising and that the franchisee is the most important part of that equation."[15]

*7*he Franchisor

◆ Describe the benefits of franchising for the franchisor.

Franchising offers franchisors a relatively quick way to expand a distribution system with minimum capital. The franchisor sells the rights to her goods or service and the accompanying business system to prospective entrepreneurs, who use their own capital to expand the franchise.

Another attraction for the franchisor is the ability to grow without the cost and inconvenience of locating and developing key managers internally. Of course, the franchisor must screen out potential franchisees who are unqualified, but the task generally is much simpler and faster than developing management talent internally. The chairman of the Program Store, a software franchise, explains, "Franchising is the best way to find entrepreneurs who are willing to run stores while we concentrate on organization and expansion."[16]

Franchisors also receive income from franchisees through franchise fees and ongoing royalties. For example, fast-food champion McDonald's collects a royalty fee of 4 percent of sales (plus a rental rate of 8.5 percent and an advertising fee of 4 percent) from its 23,000 franchisees for a total of more than $1.3 *billion* a year. (Rental fees total more than $2.7 billion.)

The King's Global Market

*D*uring the next 24 hours, McDonald's, the king of franchising, will open three more shiny new restaurants. Chances are good that two of them will be outside the United States. As same-store sales at outlets in the United States have climbed only slightly over the past several years, McDonald's has increasingly looked to foreign markets to fuel its growth. In fact, McDonald's has taken its standardized food, quality, value, and cleanliness on a global jaunt with a vengeance. The company serves customers on every continent except Antarctica!

If more than 23,000 restaurants in more than 100 countries already sounds like plenty, just wait. Cantalupo uses the following formula to guesstimate how many stores a particular country can support.

$$\frac{\text{Population of}}{\text{No. of people per McDonald's in the U.S. (25,000)}} \times \frac{\text{Per capita income of country A}}{\text{Per capita income of U.S. (\$23,120)}} = \begin{array}{c}\text{No. of McDonald's} \\ \text{stores country} \\ \text{A can support}\end{array}$$

Using "Cantalupo's theorem" to compute the number of franchises McDonald's could build worldwide produces an estimate of about 42,000, twice as many as it currently has!

Just how does McDonald's export the key to its success—service—around the globe? By following several simple strategies:

- ◆ Gather people together often for face-to-face meetings to learn from each other.
- ◆ Put employees through arduous and repetitive management training.
- ◆ Develop long-term relationships with the best suppliers.
- ◆ Understand a country's culture before locating there.
- ◆ Hire local employees whenever possible.
- ◆ Maximize workers' autonomy.
- ◆ Tweak the standard menu only slightly to adapt it to local tastes.
- ◆ Keep prices low to build market share; profits will follow.

McDonald's also adds to its global success by blanketing the world with advertising and promotion. The McDonald's name is the single most advertised brand in the world, with a

$1.4 billion annual global advertising budget behind it. That explains how the company's signature character, Ronald McDonald, has become the most recognized figure in the world, surpassing even Santa Claus! "The company is an army with one objective that has never strayed," says one board member of McDonald's incredible focus.

CEO Mike Quinlan (known as "Q") knows that sustaining the company's phenomenal growth record forever will be no easy task, so he has placed a premium on innovation and is scouring the globe for new ideas. Many are coming from McDonald's foreign franchisees. The Dutch have developed a prefab modular store that can be moved over a weekend. The Swedes came up with an improved meat freezer. High-rent Singapore invented the concept of satellite "mini-McDonald's" stores.

Much of McDonald's success in global markets comes from its intense preparation for entering a foreign market. For instance, before opening its first store in Poland, McDonald's planned for 18 months, working out in advance locations, real estate, construction, legal issues, and government regulation. (One official told managers they would have to change "that silly logo with those arches." They convinced him to change his mind.) Bureaucracy and foot-dragging officials often create barriers, but McDonald's officials somehow manage to negotiate what they need. One of his first problems in Poland was convincing local customers not to bring in vodka to drink with their Big Macs since McDonald's is a family restaurant.

Finding reliable, high-quality suppliers in some countries where free enterprise is a new concept has proved to be a challenge. When McDonald's first enters a country, it often has to import its supplies. Then it tries to shift as quickly as possible to local sources, which it often plays a key role in developing to ensure that supplies meet McDonald's rigid quality standards. Before it opened its first store in Russia, McDonald's brought in potatoes from Idaho to be transplanted in Russian fields and even imported bull semen to upgrade the quality of the local cattle herds. "To some it seems insane what we do," says one international manager. "But we realize our product isn't just meat; it's service."

Going global can pose risks for any company, especially those stepping into foreign markets for the first time. However, in this global economy, failing to expand into foreign markets is an even greater risk. So far, McDonald's plans to serve the world have paid off richly, and there's no indication of that changing soon. "The world is becoming a service society," says the head of McDonald's German unit. "People are hungry for service, but in many countries they don't get it except at McDonald's. That's why we're ahead."

1. What advantages does McDonald's global strategy provide for the company?

2. What risks does the company's global expansion entail?

SOURCE: Adapted from Andrew E. Serwer, "McDonald's Conquers the World," *Fortune*, October 17, 1994, pp. 103–116; <http://www.mcdonalds.com>. ◆

A franchisor gains the opportunity to grab a share of a regional or national market relatively quickly without having to invest huge amounts of her own money, and she gets paid while she does it. Growth is not always explosive, however. In fact, most franchisors are small. Approximately 70 percent of all franchisors have fewer than 50 locations.[17] The average franchise company sells only three franchises in its first year, four in the second year, and four in the third year. The growth rate accelerates after that, but it still averages fewer than 10 franchises a year for the first decade.[18]

*7*he Franchisee

6 Describe the benefits and limitations of franchising for the franchisee.

BENEFITS

A franchisee gets the opportunity to own a small business relatively quickly, and, because of the identification with an established product and brand name, a franchise often reaches the break-even point faster than an independent business would. Still, most new franchise outlets don't break even for at least 6 to 18 months.

Franchisees also benefit from the franchisor's business experience. In fact, *experience* is the essence of what a franchisee is buying from a franchisor. Entrepreneurs who go into business by themselves often come to decisions by trial-and-error. Given the thin margin for error in the typical start-up, the new business owner who makes too many costly mistakes will soon be out of business. In a franchising arrangement, the franchisor already has worked out the kinks in the system, and franchisees benefit from that experience. Tony Melvin, who retired from the military after 23 years and purchased a United Check Cashing franchise, says, "What I liked about franchising is the idea that they offered a proven system and that I didn't have to start from scratch."[19]

Franchisees also earn a great deal of satisfaction from their work. According to a Gallup survey of franchise owners, 82 percent of franchisees said they were "somewhat satisfied," to "very satisfied" with their work. Plus, 75 percent said they would purchase their franchises again if given the opportunity (compared with just 39 percent of Americans who say they would choose the same job or business again).[20]

Before jumping at a franchise opportunity, an entrepreneur should consider carefully the question "What can a franchise do for me that I cannot do for myself?" The answer to the question will depend on the particular situation and is just as important as a systematic evaluation of any franchise opportunity. After careful deliberation, the franchisee may conclude that the franchise offers nothing that she could not do on her own; on the other hand, it may turn out that the franchise is the key to success as a business owner. "You don't make a decision by examining businesses first," says one franchise consultant. "You start out by examining yourself."[21]

Let us investigate the specific advantages of franchising to the franchisee.

Management Training and Support. Recall from chapter 1 that the leading cause of business failure is incompetent management. Franchisors are well aware of this fact, and, in an attempt to reduce the number of franchise casualties, they offer managerial training programs to franchisees before they open a new outlet. Many franchisors, especially the well-established ones, also provide follow-up training and counseling services. This service is vital because most franchisors do not require a franchisee to have experience in the business. "Just putting a person in business, giving him a trademark, patting him on the [back], and saying, 'Good luck,' is not sufficient," says a franchise consultant.[22] Another franchise expert contends, "The franchisor's training program and ongoing support should keep the franchisee from making costly or disastrous business mistakes."[23]

Training programs often involve both classroom and on-site instruction to teach franchisees the basic operations of the business—from producing and selling the good or service to purchasing raw materials and completing paperwork. Before beginning operations, McDonald's franchisees spend 14 days in Illinois at Hamburger University, where they learn everything from how to scrape the grill correctly to how to handle the accounting system. MAACO franchisees spend four weeks at the company's headquarters delving into a five-volume set of operations manuals and learning to run an auto services shop. H & R Block teaches its franchisees to unravel the mysteries of tax preparation, while Dunkin' Donuts trains franchisees for as long as five weeks in everything from accounting to dough making. Although such training programs are beneficial, franchisees should not expect that a two- to five-week program will make them management experts. Management is much too complex to learn in any single crash course.

To ensure franchisees' continued success, many franchisors supplement their start-up training programs with on-going instruction and support. Franchisors commonly provide field support in customer service, quality control, inventory management, and general management. Some franchisors assign field consultants to guide new franchisees through the first week or two of operation after the grand opening. Franchisors offer this support because they realize that their ultimate success depends on the franchisee's success. Because the level of field support provided is one of the most common causes of franchisee–franchisor lawsuits, prospective franchisees should know exactly what the franchise contract says about the nature, extent, and frequency of field support they can expect.

Despite the positive features of training, inherent dangers exist in the trainer–trainee relationship. Every would-be franchisee should be aware that, in some cases, "assistance" from the franchisor tends to drift into "control" over the franchisee's business. Also, some franchisors charge fees for their training services, so the franchisee should know exactly what she is agreeing to, and what it costs.

Brand Name Appeal. A licensed franchisee purchases the right to use a nationally known and advertised brand name for a product or service. Thus, the franchisee has the advantage of identifying his business with a widely recognized name, which usually provides a great deal of drawing power. Customers recognize the identifying trademark, the standard symbols, the store design, and the products of an established franchise. Indeed, one of franchising's basic tenets is cloning the franchisor's success. "You buy a franchise because it's successful," says Max Cooper, owner of 47 McDonald's restaurants. "You're buying the [franchisor's] reputation."[24] Nearly everyone is familiar with the golden arches of McDonald's or the red roof of the Red Roof Inn, and the standard products and quality offered at each. A customer is confident that the quality and content of a meal at McDonald's in Fort Lauderdale will be consistent with a meal at a San Francisco McDonald's. One franchising expert explains, "The day you open a McDonald's franchise, you have instant customers. If you chose to open [an independent] hamburger restaurant, . . . you'd have to spend a fortune on advertising and promotion before you'd attract customers."[25]

Standardized Quality of Goods and Services. Because a franchisee purchases a license to sell the franchisor's product or service and the privilege of using the associated brand name, the quality of the goods or service sold determines the franchisor's reputation. Building a sound reputation in business is not achieved quickly, although destroying a good reputation takes no time at all. If some franchisees were allowed to operate at substandard levels, the image of the entire chain would suffer irreparable damage; therefore, franchisors normally demand compliance with uniform standards of quality and service throughout the entire chain. In many cases, the franchisor conducts periodic inspections of local facilities to help maintain acceptable levels of performance. Maintaining quality is so important that most franchisors retain the right to terminate the franchise contract and to repurchase the outlet if the franchisee fails to comply with established standards.

National Advertising Programs. An effective advertising program is essential to the success of virtually all franchise operations. Marketing a brand-name product or service over a wide geographic area requires a far-reaching advertising campaign. A regional or national advertising program benefits all franchisees. Normally, such an advertising campaign is organized and controlled by the franchisor. It is financed by each franchisee's contribution of a percentage of monthly sales, usually 1 to 5 percent or a flat monthly fee, into an advertising pool. For example, Kentucky Fried Chicken franchisees must pay 1.5 percent of gross revenues to the KFC national advertising program. The franchisor uses this pool of funds to create a cooperative advertising program, which has more impact than if the franchisees had spent the same amount of money separately.

Most franchisors also require franchisees to spend a minimum amount on local advertising. To supplement their national advertising efforts, both Wendy's and Burger King require franchisees to spend at least 3 percent of gross sales on local advertising. Some franchisors help each franchise outlet design and produce its local ads. Many companies help franchisees create promotional plans and provide press releases, advertisements, and special materials such as signs and banners for grand openings.

Financial Assistance. Because they rely on their franchisees' money to grow their businesses, franchisors typically do not provide any extensive financial help for franchisees. Franchisors rarely make loans to enable franchisees to pay the initial franchise fee. However, once a franchisor locates a suitable prospective franchisee, he may offer the qualified candidate direct financial assistance in specific areas, such as purchasing equipment, inventory, or even the franchise fee. In fact, equipment leasing is one of the most common financing methods among franchisors. *ServiceMaster Acceptance Corporation, a franchisor of commercial cleaning services, offers its franchisees a financing package that covers up to 70 percent of the cost of the equipment package and the franchise fee.*[26]

Because the total start-up costs of some franchises are already at breathtaking levels, some franchisors find that they must offer direct financial assistance. *For example, Valvoline Instant Oil Change Franchising Inc., with more than 500 outlets across the United States, offers 100 percent financing to franchisees who lease their land and buildings. Valvoline also offers a mortgage-based financing program for franchisees who choose to purchase rather than lease their franchises' fixed assets, which cost an average of $500,000. The company-sponsored financing programs translate into much lower up-front costs for franchisees. "We've found that financing is a big motivator because it gives our franchisees more options. Financing allows them to expand at the pace they want."*[27]

Nearly half of the International Franchise Association's members indicate that they offer some type of financial assistance to their franchisees; however, only one-fourth offer direct financial assistance. In most instances, financial assistance takes a form other than direct loans, leases, or short-term credit. Many franchisors offer to help franchisees prepare a business plan or apply for a loan from a bank or from the Small Business Administration. Franchisors usually are willing to help qualified franchisees establish relationships with banks, private investors, and other sources of funds. *For instance, Dunkin' Donuts has created an arrangement with two national small business lending programs in which its franchisees can qualify for up to 75 percent of the cost of a franchise. Through this preferred lender relationship, Dunkin' Donuts franchisees can obtain loans to cover the initial franchise fee, fixtures, vehicles, working capital, and equipment purchases.*[28] Such support from the franchisor enhances the franchisees' chances of getting the financing they seek because most lenders recognize the lower failure rate among reputable franchises. "A franchisee has a more bankable loan than the independent business person because the franchisee has a track record," says the president of the International Franchise Association.[29]

Proven Products and Business Formats. What a franchisee essentially is purchasing is the franchisor's experience, expertise, and products. A franchise owner does not have to build the business from scratch. Instead of being forced to rely solely on personal ability to establish a business and attract a clientele, the franchisee can depend on the methods and techniques of an established business. These standardized procedures and operations greatly enhance the franchisee's chances of success and avoid the most inefficient type of learning—trial and error. "When we say 'Do things our way,'" says an executive at Subway Sandwiches & Salads, "it's not just an ego thing on the part of the franchisor. We've proven it works."[30]

A franchisee does not have to struggle for recognition in the local marketplace as much as an independent owner might. *Kenneth Gabler's independent video rental store had the largest share of the local market when his landlord leased space in the same shopping center to a nationally known video franchise, West Coast Video. When he discovered that the unit was company-owned, Gabler offered to buy it. "I figured that if I stayed an independent and tried to compete, West Coast would take away 30 percent of my business anyway. So it was cheaper for me to pay the $15,000 initial fee and a 7 percent royalty every month," he says. West Coast Video's broader tape selection, marketing techniques, and recognized name "have helped tremendously," according to Gabler. Since he converted his business to a franchise, Gabler's sales have tripled.*[31]

Reputable franchisors also invest resources in researching and developing new products and services (or improvements on existing ones) and in tracking market trends that influence the success of their product line. In fact, many franchisees cite this as one of the primary benefits of the franchising arrangement.

Centralized Buying Power. A significant advantage a franchisee has over the independent small business owner is participation in the franchisor's centralized and large-volume buying power. If franchisors sell goods and materials to franchisees, they may pass on to franchisees any cost savings from quantity discounts they earn by buying in volume. For example, it is unlikely that a small, independent ice cream parlor could match the buying power of Baskin-Robbins, with its 3,000 retail ice cream stores. In many instances, economies of scale simply preclude the independent owner from competing head-to-head with a franchise operation.

Site Selection and Territorial Protection. A proper location is critical to the success of any small business, and franchises are no exception. In fact, franchise experts consider the three most important factors in franchising to be *location*, *location*, and *location*. Becoming affiliated with a franchisor may be the best way to get into prime locations. McDonald's, for example, is well known for its ability to obtain prime locations in high-traffic areas. Although choosing a location is the franchisee's responsibility, the franchisor usually reserves the right to approve the final site. Many franchisors will make an extensive location analysis for each new outlet (for a fee), including studies of traffic patterns, zoning ordinances, accessibility, and population density. Even if the franchisor does not conduct a site analysis, the franchisee must. A thorough demographic and statistical analysis of potential locations is essential to selecting the site that offers the greatest potential for success. We will discuss these topics in more detail in chapters 6 and 15.

Franchisors also may offer a franchisee territorial protection, which gives the franchisee the right to exclusive distribution of brand-name goods or services within a particular geographic area. Under such an agreement, the franchisor agrees not to sell another franchise outlet or to open a company-owned unit within the franchisee's assigned territory. The size of a franchisee's territory varies from company to company. For example, one fast-food restaurant agrees not to license another franchisee within a mile-and-a-half of existing locations. But one softserve ice cream and yogurt franchisor defines its franchisees' territories on the basis of ZIP code designations. The purpose of such protection is to prevent an invasion of existing franchisees' territories and the accompanying dilution of sales.

As the competition for top locations has escalated over the past decade, the placement of new franchise outlets has become a source of friction between franchisors and franchisees. Existing franchisees charge that franchisors are encroaching on their territories by granting new franchises so close to them that their sales are diluted. According to Susan Kezios, president of the American Franchisee Association, territorial encroachment is "the number one problem" for the organization's 7,000 members.[32] Although the new outlets that franchisors grant lie outside the boundaries of existing franchisees' territories, their market coverage and reach overlap those of existing territories, causing sales and profits to decline. *A recent ruling by a court of appeals in California gives franchisees greater protection from encroachment. When Naugles Inc., a Mexican restaurant chain, opened a company-owned outlet within 1.5 miles of an existing franchisee's location, the franchisee, Vylene Enterprises, charged that Naugles' opening of the new restaurant breached the franchise agreement and violated the implied requirement of fair dealing. Vylene testified that the new outlet caused a 35 percent sales decline at its store. Even though the franchise agreement did not grant Vylene an exclusive territory, the court ruled in Vylene's favor, stating that "Naugles' construction of a competing restaurant within a mile and a half of Vylene's restaurant was a breach of the covenant of good faith and fair dealing."*[33] Because of such disputes over territories, many franchisors no longer offer exclusive territories to franchisees.

Greater Chance for Success. Investing in a franchise is not risk-free. Between 200 and 300 new franchise companies enter the market each year, and not all of them survive. But available statistics suggest that franchising is less risky than building a business from the ground up. One expert says that "becoming a franchisee can be the safest way to scratch the entrepreneurial itch."[34] Approximately 24 percent of new businesses fail by the second year of operation; in contrast, only about 7 to 10 percent of all franchises will fail by the second year. After five years, about 85 percent of franchises are still in business compared with less than 50 percent of independent businesses.[35] This impressive success rate for franchises is attributed to the broad range of services, assistance, and guidelines the franchisor provides. These statistics must be interpreted carefully, however, because when a franchise is in danger of failing, the franchisor often repurchases or relocates the outlet and does not report it as a failure. As a result, some franchisors boast of never experiencing a failure. According to the American Bar Association's Franchise Committee, one-third of the franchisees in a typical franchise system are making a decent profit, one-third are breaking even, and one-third are losing money.[36]

The risk of purchasing a franchise is two-pronged: Success depends on the entrepreneur's managerial skills and motivation and on the franchisor's business experience and system. "Don't think that because you become a franchisee you'll automatically be successful," warns one franchise consultant. "The franchisor is only providing the tools; the rest is up to you."[37] Many owners are convinced that franchising has been a crucial part of their success. "With a franchise, you get a business system and the opportunity to go into business not only for yourself but with the franchise system behind you. You're going into business *for* yourself but not *by* yourself."[38]

LIMITATIONS

Obviously, the benefits of franchising can mean the difference between success and failure for a small business. However, franchisees must sacrifice some freedom to the franchisor. The prospective franchisee must explore other limitations of franchising before undertaking this form of ownership. Thoroughly researching potential franchise opportunities is the only way an entrepreneur can find a franchise that is a good match with her personality, likes, and

IN THE FOOTSTEPS OF AN ENTREPRENEUR

Choosing the Right Franchise

A Costly Lesson Wayne Flesjer discovered that the fast-food business wasn't for him. Unfortunately, he didn't make that discovery until *after* he had invested $135,000 in a Subway sandwich franchise. It was an expensive lesson. Flesjer began to have doubts about his choice in franchises after he got to know the owners of an American Fastsigns franchise located next door to his Subway franchise. He was amazed to learn that they were making more money than he was, and they were working fewer hours and no nights or weekends. Not only did the hours the sandwich shop demanded not suit Flesjer, but the relationships with his customers weren't what he was looking for either. Flesjer never got a chance to build long-term relationships with his customers; customers simply dashed in, ordered their food, and ran out the door.

Looking back on his decision to open a fast-food franchise, Flesjer realizes that he made a mistake that is all too common in franchising: buying a franchise without really understanding what the day-to-day business is like. "Anybody looking for a franchise today had better understand the business he's looking into, and he'd better understand whether he likes it or not," says a top manager at McDonald's. Flesjer's story does have a happy ending, however. He still owns the Subway franchise, but he and partner Laura Dressler purchased their own American Fastsigns franchise. To make sure that they would enjoy owning the franchise, both Dressler and Flesjer worked in an outlet for several months to learn what operating a sign business is like. "I highly recommend [working in a franchise before buying an outlet]," says Dressler. "It gives you a chance to see if it's a good match. And if you buy the franchise, it gives you a leg up on operating your own store."

A Good Fit Manuel Morales Jr. didn't work for an HQ Business Center franchise before he bought one, but he did analyze the franchise thoroughly before he made the purchase. HQ Business Centers provide offices, conference room facilities, personalized telephone answering, and complete administrative support services for executives in more than 150 locations worldwide. "I visited 22 HQ Centers and talked with seven owners before I bought one," says Morales, whose center is located in San Juan, Puerto Rico. During his visits,

Morales was impressed with the caliber of the HQ franchisees he interviewed; many were former executives at high-profile companies. He questioned franchisees extensively about their operations, the system, the support from the franchisor, and what made them successful. Today, Morales is on track to reach his target of opening 57 HQ Business Centers in his territories.

Finding the right franchise is no easy task, but the results are well worth the effort. Franchisees who have made both wise and ill-advised franchise purchases offer the following advice:

- ◆ Start by evaluating your own personal and business interests. What activities do you enjoy? Which ones do you dislike?
- ◆ Establish a budget. Know how much you can afford to spend *before* you ever go shopping for a franchise.
- ◆ Do your research. Study broad trends to determine which franchise concepts are likely to be most successful in the future.
- ◆ Identify potential franchise candidates and narrow your search to the top five or six. Create a profile of the most promising franchises that best fit both your interests and market trends.
- ◆ Get these companies' UFOCs (Uniform Franchise Offering Circular, discussed in the section "Franchising and the Law") and review them thoroughly. Get an experienced attorney to review the fine print in each UFOC.
- ◆ Study your local market. Use what you learned from existing franchisees to determine whether the concept would be successful in the area you are considering. Don't forget to evaluate the level of competition.
- ◆ Meet with company officials to discuss the details of buying a franchise.

1. Develop a list of the mistakes franchisees commonly make when selecting and purchasing their outlets.

2. What can a franchisee do to avoid making those mistakes?

3. Use the World Wide Web and your local library to compile a list of resources that would help potential franchisees as they evaluate franchise opportunities.

SOURCE: Adapted from Katherine Callan, "Do Your Due Diligence," *Success*, November 1996, pp. 112–117; Andrew A. Caffey, "The Buying Game," *Entrepreneur*, January 1997, pp. 174–177; Roberta Maynard, "Choosing a Franchise," *Nation's Business*, October 1996, pp. 56–63; Carol Steinberg, "Franchises of the Future," *Success*, November 1996, pp. 88–95. ◆

way an entrepreneur can find a franchise that is a good match with her personality, likes, and dislikes.

Franchise Fees and Profit Sharing. Virtually all franchisors impose some type of fees and demand a share of the franchisee's sales revenues in return for the use of the franchisor's name, products or services, and business system. Franchise fees and initial capital requirements vary. The Commerce Department reports that total investments for franchises range from $1,000 for business services up to $10 million for hotel and motel franchises. For example, The Sports Section, a home-based franchise, sells franchises for $9,900 to $29,500, depending on the territory's population size; I Can't Believe It's Yogurt requires $55,000 to $60,000 in equity capital; and McDonald's requires an investment of $408,600 to $647,000 (but McDonald's owns the land and the building). The average start-up cost for a franchise is between $150,000 and $200,000.[39]

Start-up costs for franchises sometimes include numerous additional fees not included in the franchise fee. Most franchises impose a franchise fee ranging from $5,000 to $50,000 up front for the right to use the company name. Wendy's International, for example, charges a $20,000 "technical assistance fee" for each restaurant a franchisee opens, and McDonald's up-front franchise fee is $45,000. Additional start-up costs might include site purchase and preparation, construction, signs, fixtures, equipment, management assistance, and training. Before signing any contract, a prospective franchisee should determine the total cost of a franchise. For example, Holiday Inns, Inc., provides prospective franchisees with estimates of start-up costs for a 100-room, two-story hotel. The estimates list a range of costs for the initial franchise application fee plus building; furniture, fixtures, and equipment; opening inventory; working capital; free-standing sign; training expenses; property management and multimedia; and Holidex reservation system. Total estimates range from $4,076,000 to $6,088,800 plus real estate, licenses, permits, and professional fees.[40]

Franchisors also impose continuing royalty fees as profit-sharing devices. The royalty usually involves a percentage of gross sales with a required minimum or a flat fee levied on the franchise. Royalty fees typically range from 1 percent to 15 percent of sales (the average royalty fee is between 5 and 7 percent) and can increase the franchisee's overhead expenses significantly. Because franchisors' royalties and fees are calculated as a percentage of a franchisee's sales, they get paid even if the franchisee fails to earn a profit. Sometimes unprepared franchisees discover (too late) that the franchisor's royalties and fees are about what the normal profit margin is for a franchise. To avoid such problems, a prospective franchisee should find out which fees are required (some are merely recommended) and then determine what services and benefits the fees cover. One of the best ways to do this is to itemize what you are getting for your money, and then determine whether the cost corresponds to the benefits provided. Be sure to get the details on all expenses: amount, time of payment, and financing arrangements. Find out which items are included in the initial franchise fee and which ones are "extra."

Strict Adherence to Standardized Operations. Although the franchisee owns the business, she does not have the autonomy of an independent owner. The terms of the franchise agreement govern the franchisor–franchisee relationship. That agreement requires franchisees to operate their outlets according to the principles spelled out in the franchisor's operations manual. Typical topics covered in the manual include operating hours, dress standards, operating policies and procedures, product or service specifications, and confidentiality requirements.

To protect its public image, the franchisor requires that the franchisee maintain certain operating standards. If a franchise constantly fails to meet the minimum standards established for the business, the franchisor can terminate its license. Compliance with standards is usually determined by periodic inspections. At times, strict adherence to franchise standards may become a burden to the franchisee. The owner may believe that the written reports the franchisor demands require an excessive amount of time. In other instances, the owner may be required to enforce specific rules she believes are inappropriate or unfair.

Restrictions on Purchasing. In the interest of maintaining quality standards, franchisees may be required to purchase products or special equipment from the franchisor, and perhaps other items from an "approved" supplier. For example, Kentucky Fried Chicken requires that franchisees use only seasonings blended by a particular company. A poor image for the entire franchise could result from some franchisee's using inferior products to cut costs. Under some conditions, these purchase arrangements may be challenged in court as a violation of antitrust laws, but generally the franchisor has a legal right to see that franchisees maintain acceptable quality standards. Franchisees at several chains have filed antitrust suits alleging that franchisors overcharge their outlets for supplies and equipment and eliminate competition by failing to approve alternative suppliers.[41] A franchisor can legally set the prices paid for such products but cannot establish the retail prices to be charged on products sold by the franchisee. A franchisor legally can suggest retail prices but cannot force the franchisee to abide by them.

Limited Product Line. In most cases, the franchise agreement stipulates that the franchise can sell only those products approved by the franchisor. Unless willing to risk license cancellation, a franchisee must avoid selling any unapproved products through the franchise. Franchisors strive for standardization in their product lines so that customers, wherever they may be, know what to expect. Some companies allow franchisees to modify their product or service offerings to suit regional or local tastes, but only with the franchisor's approval.

A franchisee may be required to carry an unpopular product or be prevented from introducing a desirable one by the franchise agreement. A franchisee's freedom to adapt a product line to local market conditions is restricted. But some franchisors solicit product suggestions from their franchisees. *In fact, a McDonald's franchisee, Herb Peterson, created the highly successful Egg McMuffin while experimenting with a Teflon-coated egg ring that gave fried eggs rounded corners and a poached appearance. Peterson put his round eggs on English muffins, adorned them with Canadian bacon and melted cheese, and showed his creation to McDonald's chief, Ray Kroc. Kroc devoured two of them and was sold on the idea when Peterson's wife suggested the catchy name. In 1975, McDonald's became the first fast-food franchise to open its doors for breakfast, and the Egg McMuffin became a staple on the breakfast menu.*[42]

Unsatisfactory Training Programs. Every would-be franchisee must be wary of the unscrupulous franchisor who promises extensive services, advice, and assistance but delivers nothing. For example, one owner relied on the franchisor to provide what had been described as an "extensive, rigorous training program" after paying a handsome technical assistance fee. The program was nothing but a set of pamphlets and do-it-yourself study guides. Other examples include those impatient entrepreneurs who paid initial franchise fees without investigating the business and never heard from the franchisor again. Although disclosure rules have reduced the severity of the problem, dishonest characters still thrive on unprepared prospective franchisees.

Market Saturation. As the owners of many fast-food and yogurt and ice cream franchises have discovered, market saturation is a very real danger. Although some franchisors offer franchisees territorial protection, others do not. Territorial encroachment has become a hotly contested issue in franchising as growth-seeking franchisors have exhausted most of the prime locations and are now setting up new franchises close to existing ones. The biggest challenge to the growth potential of franchising is the lack of satisfactory locations. In some areas of the country, franchisees are upset, claiming that their markets are oversaturated and

Table 4.1 A Franchise Evaluation Quiz

Taking the emotion out of buying a franchise is the goal of this self-test developed by Franchise Solutions, Inc., a franchise consulting company in Portsmouth, New Hampshire. Circle the number that reflects your degree of certainty or postive feelings for each of the following 12 statements: 1 is low, 5 is high.

	Low				High
1. I would really enjoy being in this kind of business.	1	2	3	4	5
2. This franchise will meet or exceed my income goals.	1	2	3	4	5
3. My people-handling skills are sufficient for this franchise.	1	2	3	4	5
4. I understand fully my greatest challenge in this franchise, and I feel comfortable with my abilities.	1	2	3	4	5
5. I have met with the company management and feel compatible.	1	2	3	4	5
6. I understand the risks with this business and am prepared to accept them.	1	2	3	4	5
7. I have researched the competition in my area and feel comfortable with the potential market.	1	2	3	4	5
8. My family and friends think this is a great opportunity for me.	1	2	3	4	5
9. I have had an adviser review the disclosure documents and the franchise agreement.	1	2	3	4	5
10. I have contacted a representative number of the existing franchisees; they were overwhelmingly positive.	1	2	3	4	5
11. I have researched this industry and feel comfortable about the long-term growth potential.	1	2	3	4	5
12. My background and experience make franchise an ideal choice.	1	2	3	4	5

The maximum score on the quiz is 60. A score of 45 or below means that either the franchise opportunity is unsuitable or that you need to do more research on the franchise you are considering.

SOURCE: Roberta Maynard, "Choosing a Franchise," *Nation's Business*, October 1996, p. 57.

their sales are suffering. "No reputable franchisor will place units in a market that can't sustain them," says a franchise attorney. "It doesn't make sense. There's too much expenditure of time and capital by the franchisor and the franchisee if oversaturation results."[43]

Less Freedom. When a franchisee signs a contract, he agrees to sell the franchisor's product or service by following its prescribed formula. When McDonald's rolls out a new national product, for instance, all franchisees put it on their menus. Franchisors want to ensure success, and most monitor their franchisees' performances closely. Strict uniformity is the rule rather than the exception. "There is no independence. Successful franchisees are happy prisoners," says one writer.[44] Entrepreneurs who want to be their own bosses and to avoid being subject to the control of others will most likely be frustrated as franchisees. Highly independent, "go-my-own-way" individuals probably should not choose the franchise route to business ownership. Table 4.1 offers a Franchise Evaluation Quiz designed to help potential franchisees decide whether a franchise is right for them.

*W*hat Do Franchisors Look for in a Franchisee?

7 Discuss what franchisors look for in a franchisee.

What kind of person does the typical franchisor look for? To most franchisors, a "good franchisee" is willing to follow the franchisor's business system, has adequate financing to make the business work, and understands the importance of quality and superior customer service.

The portrait of the typical franchisee has changed over the years to become more professional, more experienced, and more diverse. Studies show that the average franchisee is 40 years old with a net worth of $329,704 (before investing in a franchise). Some 90 percent are college-educated, 20 percent are women, 11 percent are minorities, and more than 33 percent are corporate castoffs or dropouts.[45]

Will a franchisor look for someone who has the following characteristics?

Experienced? Not necessarily. In fact, "no experience necessary" is a key selling point of franchising. Most franchisors do not require franchisees to have experience because experience is what they are selling through their franchises. A person does not have to be a skilled mechanic to run an automotive repair franchise successfully; however, it does help to have basic business skills and some management experience. Most franchisees find that a certain level of business know-how and savvy is crucial to a successful franchise operation. A basic understanding of business law, finance, marketing, and general management is useful.

Hard Working? Definitely. Most franchisees work long hours. There are no eight-hour days or five-day weeks. A franchisee must be willing to do any job that needs to be done: preparing paperwork, reconciling the bank statement, sweeping the floor, and selling merchandise. "A franchise will help you, but it won't start shoveling money through your door," says a franchisee who bought his first outlet at age 23. "You have to be willing to grow your business."[46] A franchisee cannot be allergic to hard work because that is what is required to get a franchise established.

Team Player? Yes. Franchisors are looking for people who are willing to work hard not only for their own success but for the success of the entire franchise. Although franchisors expect franchise owners to be loyal to the franchise and to follow the format, many encourage franchisees to use their creativity to generate new ideas for improving the system. *For instance, Ron Schupp, owner of a Surface Doctor outlet, a franchise that refurbishes appliances, countertops, bathtubs, and other household items, developed a method for converting standard bathtubs into whirlpool tubs. He shared his idea with the franchisor, who spent a year refining the technique before making it available to every franchisee in the system.*[47]

Leadership and Management Skills? No doubt. Managing people is a significant part of every successful business operation. A franchisee must be able to lead, motivate, and work with other people. Franchisees must realize that they are in the people business and that their workforce is often unskilled and transitory. Successful franchisees must be able to train and coach subordinates to perform their jobs properly.

Risk-Averse? Definitely not. Although franchises have a much lower failure rate than do independent businesses, they are not without risks. There is no guarantee of success in a franchise package. "A franchise is relatively safe, but not *every* franchise is safe," cautions one expert.[48]

Educated? Yes, but a franchisee does not have to have an MBA and a Ph.D. in management to run a franchise successfully. Mike Bloom of Orange Julius says his company prefers someone who "has a good basic education, either scholastically or experientially."[49]

Financially Stable? Certainly. Some franchises have breathtakingly high capital requirements; others, especially the new growth-oriented service franchises, are much more affordable. Still, every franchisor requires each applicant to submit a personal financial statement proving that he is financially sound. Orange Julius's Mike Bloom says, "We scrutinize every financial statement a potential franchisee submits to us because we don't want to give someone a franchise and then see that person get into trouble."[50]

A Desire to Succeed? Absolutely. A burning desire to succeed and a healthy dose of enthusiasm can carry a franchisee through many difficult situations. One franchisor says his company looks for someone with "the ability to overcome hardships. A stick-to-itiveness that allows a franchisee to continue through good times and bad."[51]

One business writer summarizes what franchisors look for in a franchisee: "[Franchisors] want franchisees who think for themselves and aggressively seek new ways to improve business. At the same time, they want someone who's willing to follow the franchisor's format. In other words, the ideal franchisee is a creative, outgoing person who's eager to succeed, but not so independent that he resents other people's advice."[52]

Franchising and the Law

8 Describe the legal aspects of franchising, including the protection offered by the FTC's Trade Regulation Rule.

The franchising boom spearheaded by McDonald's in the late 1950s brought with it many prime investment opportunities. However, the explosion of legitimate franchises also ushered in with it several fly-by-night franchisors who defrauded their franchisees. In response to these specific incidents and to the potential for deception inherent in a franchise relationship, California, in 1971, enacted the first Franchise Investment Law. The law (and similar laws subsequently passed by 16 other states) requires franchisors to register a **Uniform Franchise Offering Circular (UFOC)** and deliver a copy to prospective franchisees *before* any offer or sale of a franchise. The UFOC establishes full disclosure guidelines for the franchising company. According to franchise expert Andrew Kostecka, "The full disclosure document helped clean out the fly-by-nighters who operated from a public telephone. This was the turning point in upgrading the system of franchising."[53]

In October 1979, the Federal Trade Commission (FTC) enacted the **Trade Regulation Rule,** requiring all franchisors to disclose detailed information on their operations at the first personal meeting or at least 10 days before a franchise contract is signed or any money is paid. The FTC rule covers all franchisors, even those in the 33 states lacking franchise disclosure laws. The purpose of the regulation is to assist the potential franchisee's investigation of the franchise deal and to introduce consistency into the franchisor's disclosure statements. In 1994, the FTC modified the requirements for the UFOC, making more information available to prospective franchisees and making the document easier to read and understand. The FTC's philosophy is not so much to prosecute abusers as to provide information to prospective franchisees and help them make intelligent decisions. Although the FTC requires each franchisor to provide a potential franchisee with this information, it does not verify its accuracy. Prospective franchisees should use these data only as a starting point for the investigation. The Trade Regulation Rule requires a franchisor to include 23 major topics in its disclosure statement:

1. Information identifying the franchisor and its affiliates and describing their business experience and the franchises being sold.
2. Information identifying and describing the business experience of each of the franchisor's officers, directors, and management personnel responsible for the franchise program.
3. A description of the lawsuits in which the franchisor and its officers, directors, and managers have been involved.
4. Information about any bankruptcies in which the franchisor and its officers, directors, and managers have been involved.
5. Information about the initial franchise fee and other payments required to obtain the franchise, including the intended use of the fees.

6. A description of any other continuing payments franchisees are required to make after start-up, including royalties, service fees, training fees, lease payments, advertising charges, and others.

7. A detailed description of the payments a franchisee must make to fulfill the initial investment requirement and how and to whom they are made. The categories covered are initial franchise fee, equipment, opening inventory, initial advertising fee, signs, training, real estate, working capital, legal, accounting, and utilities.

8. Information about quality restrictions on goods and services used in the franchise and where they may be purchased, including restricted purchases from the franchises.

9. Information covering requirements to purchase goods, services, equipment, supplies, inventory, and other items from approved suppliers (including the franchisor).

10. A description of any financial assistance available from the franchisor in the purchase of the franchise.

11. A description of all obligations the franchisor must fulfill in helping a franchisee prepare to open, open, and operate a unit. Plus, information covering location selection methods and the training program provided to franchisees.

12. A description of any territorial protection that will be granted to the franchise and a statement as to whether the franchisor may locate a company-owned store or other outlet in that territory.

13. All relevant information about the franchisor's trademarks, service marks, trade names, logos, and commercial symbols, including where they are registered.

14. Similar information on any patents and copyrights the franchisor owns and the rights to these transferred to franchisees.

15. A description of the extent to which franchisees must participate personally in the operation of the franchise.

16. A description of any restrictions on the goods or services franchises are permitted to sell and with whom franchisees may deal.

17. A description of the conditions under which the franchise may be repurchased or refused renewal by the franchisor, transferred to a third party by the franchisee, and terminated or modified by either party.

18. A description of the involvement of celebrities and public figures in the franchise.

19. A complete statement of the basis for any earnings claims made to the franchisee, including the percentage of existing franchises that have actually achieved the results that are claimed. New rules put two requirements on franchisors making earnings claims: (1) Any earnings claim must be included in the UFOC, and (2) the claim must "have a reasonable basis at the time it is made." However, franchisors are not required to make any earnings claims at all; in fact, 80 percent of franchisors don't make earnings claims in their circulars, primarily because of liability concerns about committing such numbers to paper.[54]

20. Statistical information about the present number of franchises; the number of franchises projected for the future; the number of franchises terminated; the number the franchisor has not renewed; the number repurchased in the past; and a list of the names and addresses of other franchises.

21. The financial statements of the franchisors.

22. A copy of all franchise and other contracts (leases, purchase agreements, etc.) the franchisee will be required to sign.

23. A standardized, detachable "receipt" to prove that the prospective franchisee received a copy of the UFOC.

The typical UFOC is about 100 pages long, but every potential franchisee should take the time to read and understand it. Unfortunately, most do not, and often those uninformed franchisees are faced with unpleasant surprises.[55] The information contained in the UFOC does not fully protect a potential franchise from deception, nor does it guarantee success. It does, however, provide enough information to begin a thorough investigation of the franchisor and the franchise deal. Many experts recommend that potential franchisees have an experienced franchise attorney or consultant review a company's UFOC before they invest. "Considering the investment at stake, not spending the $1,000 to $2,000 to have the circular reviewed and negotiated is penny-wise and pound-foolish," says one franchise attorney.[56] In a recent FTC study, more than half of all franchisors said it would be difficult for a prospective franchisee to obtain on his own and at a reasonable cost and effort, all of the information contained in the UFOC. Another survey of franchisees found that 88 percent of franchisees believed the UFOC was useful in making their investment decisions, saving them time and giving them more complete information.[57]

How to Buy a Franchise

⬧9 Explain the *right* way to buy a franchise.

The UFOC is a powerful tool designed to help potential franchisees avoid dishonest franchisors. The best defenses a prospective entrepreneur has against unscrupulous franchisors are preparation, common sense, and patience. By investigating thoroughly before investing in a franchise, a potential franchisee eliminates the risk of being hoodwinked into a nonexistent business.

The president of a franchise consulting firm estimates that 5 to 10 percent of franchisors are dishonest: "the rogue elephants of franchising." Potential franchisees must beware. Franchise fraud has become a major growth market in the United States in recent years. Because dishonest franchisors tend to follow certain patterns, well-prepared franchisees can avoid getting burned. The following clues should arouse the suspicion of an entrepreneur about to invest in a franchise:

◆ Claims that the franchise contract is a standard one and that "you don't need to read it."

◆ A franchisor who fails to give you a copy of the required disclosure document at your first face-to-face meeting.

◆ A marginally successful prototype store or no prototype at all.

◆ A poorly prepared operations manual outlining the franchise system or no manual (or system) at all.

◆ Oral promises of future earnings without written documentation.

◆ A high franchisee turnover rate or a high termination rate.

◆ An unusual amount of litigation brought against the franchisor.

◆ Attempts to discourage you from allowing an attorney to evaluate the franchise contract before you sign it.

◆ No written documentation to support claims and promises.

◆ A high-pressure sale: sign the contract now or lose the opportunity.

- Claiming to be exempt from federal laws requiring complete disclosure of franchise details.
- "Get-rich-quick schemes," promises of huge profits with only minimum effort.
- Reluctance to provide a list of present franchisees for you to interview.
- Evasive, vague answers to your questions about the franchise and its operation.

Not every franchise "horror story" is the result of dishonest franchisors. More often than not, the problems that arise in franchising have more to do with franchisees who buy legitimate franchises without proper research and analysis. They end up in businesses they do not enjoy and that they are not well-suited to operate. The following steps will help any franchisee make the right choice.

EVALUATE YOURSELF

Henry David Thoreau's advice to "Know thyself" is excellent advice for prospective franchisees. Before looking at any franchise, an entrepreneur should study her own personality, experiences, likes, dislikes, goals, and expectations. Will you be comfortable working in a structured environment? What kinds of franchises fit your desired lifestyle? Do you want to sell a product or a service? Do you want to work with the public? Do you enjoy selling? What hours do you expect to work? Do you mind getting dirty? Do you want to work with people, or do you prefer to work alone? Which franchise concepts mesh best with your past work experience? What activities and hobbies do you enjoy? What income do you expect a franchise to generate? How much can you afford to invest in a franchise? According to the president of the International Franchise Association (IFA), potential franchisees should "not only do thorough research of the prospective franchise opportunity, but more importantly, they [should] take a complete inventory of themselves and their capabilities."[58]

RESEARCH THE MARKET

Before shopping for a franchise, an entrepreneur should research the market in the area she plans to serve. How fast is the overall area growing? In which areas is that growth occurring fastest? Investing some time in the library or on the World Wide Web developing a profile of the customers in the target area is essential; otherwise the potential franchisee is flying blind. Who are your potential customers? What are their characteristics, income, and education levels? What kinds of products and services do they buy? What gaps exist in the market? These gaps represent potential franchise opportunities for you.

Solid market research should tell a prospective franchisee whether a particular franchise is merely a passing fad. Steering clear of fads and into long-term trends is a key to sustained success in franchising. The president of the IFA advises franchisees to "go with a product [or a service] that [is] established in the marketplace and is going to fit with the demographic trends and basic American tastes for the next 15 or 20 years."[59] Following that advice requires sound market research that focuses not only on local market opportunities but also on "the big picture."

CONSIDER YOUR FRANCHISE OPTIONS

The International Franchise Association publishes the *Franchise Opportunities Guide*, which lists its members and some basic information about them. Many cities host franchise trade shows throughout the year, where hundreds of franchisors gather to sell their franchises. Many business magazines such as *Entrepreneur*, *Inc.*, *Business Start-Ups*, *Success*, and others devote at least one issue to franchising, where they often list hundreds of franchises. Plus, many franchisors now publish information about their systems on the World Wide Web. These listings can help potential franchisees find a suitable franchise within their price range.

GET A COPY OF THE FRANCHISOR'S UFOC AND STUDY IT

Once you narrow down your franchise choices, you should contact each franchise and get a copy of its UFOC. Then read it! This document is an important tool in your search for the right franchise, and you should make the most of it. Not only does the UFOC cover the 23 items discussed in the previous section, but it also includes a copy of the company's franchise agreement and any contracts accompanying it (item 22). It is best to have an attorney experienced in franchising review the UFOC and discuss it with you. The franchise contract summarizes the details that will govern the franchisor–franchisee relationship over its life. It outlines *exactly* the rights and the obligations of each party and sets the guidelines that govern the franchise relationship. Franchise contracts typically are long-term; 50 percent run for 15 years or more, so it is extremely important for prospective franchisees to understand their terms before they sign them.

Particular items in the UFOC that entrepreneurs should focus on include the franchisor's experience (items 1 and 2), fees and total investment (items 5, 6, and 7), the franchisee turnover rate for the past three years (item 20), and the current and past litigation against the franchisor (item 3). The **franchisee turnover rate** is the rate at which franchisees leave the system. If the turnover rate is less than 5 percent, the franchise is probably sound. However, a rate approaching 20 percent is a sign of some serious, underlying problems in a franchise. Although virtually every franchisor has been involved in lawsuits, an excessive amount of litigation against a franchisor should alert a prospective franchisee to potential problems. Determining what the cases were about and whether they have been resolved is important.

TALK TO EXISTING FRANCHISEES

Perhaps the best way to evaluate the reputation of a franchisor is to interview (in person) several franchise owners who have been in business at least one year about the positive and the negative features of the agreement and whether the franchisor delivered what it promised. Knowing what they know now, would they buy the franchise again? *Val Gomez, a happy and successful Merry Maids, Inc., franchisee, says, "My wisest move was calling about 10 other franchisees—at random, a couple in my area and the rest all over the country—to ask them about the franchisor and the business." Gomez had already spent two months researching the franchise and his local market and was pleased with what existing franchisees told him about Merry Maids, so he bought the franchise. A year later, he won the Rookie of the Year award. "There will be some disgruntled franchisees no matter what," says Gomez, now owner of three Merry Maids territories, "but watch out if you turn up many unhappy franchisees or a lot of litigation."*[60] Item 20 of the UFOC lists all of a company's franchisees and their addresses by state, making it easy for potential franchisees to contact them.

It is also wise to interview past franchisees to get their perspectives on the franchisor–franchisee relationship. (UFOC item 20 also lists franchisees who have left the system within the past fiscal year.) Why did they leave? Franchisees of some companies have formed associations, which might provide prospective franchisees with valuable information. Other sources of information include the American Association of Franchisees and Dealers, the American Franchise Association, and the International Franchise Association. Table 4.2 offers some important questions to ask existing franchisees.

ASK THE FRANCHISOR SOME TOUGH QUESTIONS

Take the time to vist the franchisor's headquarters and ask plenty of questions about the company and its relationship with its franchisees. You will be in this relationship a long time, and you need to know as much about it as you possibly can beforehand. What is its philosophy con-

Table 4.2 Questions to Ask Existing Franchisees

The following questions will reveal how well the franchisor supports its franchisees and the nature of the franchisor–franchisee relationship.

- How much did it cost to start your franchise?
- How much training did you receive at the outset? How helpful was it? Did it prepare you to run your franchise?
- Does the franchisor provide you with adequate ongoing support? How much? Are you pleased with the level of support you receive? What is the nature of this support?
- Is the company available to answer your questions? How often do you contact the company? What is the typical response?
- How much marketing assistance does the franchisor provide? Is it effective? How can you tell?
- Which of your expectations has the franchisor met? Failed to meet?
- How often does someone from the franchise check on your operation? What is the purpose of those visits?
- What is a "typical day" like for you? How do you spend most of your time?
- Which day-to-day tasks do you enjoy performing most? Least?
- How much did your franchise gross last year? How much do you expect to gross this year? What has been the pattern of your outlet's sales since you started?
- Is your franchise making a profit? If so, how much? What is your net profit margin?
- How long did you operate before your outlet began to earn a profit? Is your outlet consistently profitable?
- What is your franchise's break-even point?
- Has your franchise met your expectations for return on investment (ROI)?
- Is this business seasonal? If so, how do you get through the off-season?
- Is there a franchisee association? Do you belong to it? What is its primary function?
- Does the franchisor sponsor systemwide meetings? Do you attend? Why?
- What changes would you recommend the franchisor make in its business system?
- Where do you purchase supplies, equipment, and products for your franchise?
- How much freedom do you have to run your business?
- Does the franchisor encourage franchisees to apply their creativity to running their businesses, or does it frown upon innovation in the system?
- Has the franchisor given you the tools you need to compete effectively?
- How much are your royalty payments and franchise fees? What do you get in exchange for your royalty payments? Do you consider it to be a good value?
- Are you planning to purchase additional territories or franchises? Why?
- Has the franchisor lived up to its promises?
- Looking back, what portions of the franchise contract would you change?
- Are most franchisees happy with the franchise system? With the franchisor?
- What advice would you give to someone considering purchasing a franchise from this franchisor?
- Knowing what you know now, would you buy this franchise again?

SOURCES: Adapted from Roger Brown, "Ask More Questions of More People before Deciding, Then Plan to Work Very Hard," *Small Business Forum*, Winter 1996/1997, pp. 91–93; Roberta Maynard, "Choosing a Franchise," *Nation's Business*, October 1996, pp. 56–63; Andrew A. Caffey, "The Buying Game," *Entrepreneur*, January 1997, pp. 174–177; Julie Bawden Davis, "A Perfect Match," *Business Start-Ups*, July 1997, pp. 44–49; Andrew A. Caffey, "Check It Out," *Entrepreneur*, January 1998, pp. 180–183.

Franchises such as Merry Maids, Inc., are growing fast because they give customers service and convenience. They also offer franchisees the opportunity to be in business for themselves but not by themselves. What should people considering buying a franchise do to make sure the business suits their needs and interests?

cerning the relationship? What is the company culture like? How much input do franchisee's have into the system? What are the franchise's future expansion plans? How will they affect your franchise? What kind of profits can you expect? (If the franchisor made no earnings claims in item 19 of the UFOC, why not?) Does the franchisor have a well-formulated strategic plan? Are you allowed to sell the franchise to a third party? If so, will you receive the proceeds?

MAKE YOUR CHOICE

The first lesson in franchising is "Do your homework *before* you get out your checkbook." Once you have done your research, you can make an informed choice about which franchise is right for you. Then it is time to put together a solid business plan that will serve as your road map to success in the franchise you have selected. The plan is also a valuable tool to use as you arrange the financing for your franchise. We will discuss the components of a business plan in chapter 9.

*F*ranchise Contracts

The amount of franchisor–franchisee litigation has risen steadily since the 1980s. A common source of much of this litigation is the interpretation of the franchise contract's terms. Most often, difficulties arise after the agreement is in operation. Typically, because the franchisor's attorney prepares franchise contracts, the provisions favor the franchisor. Courts have relatively little statutory law and few precedents on which to base decisions in franchise disputes, so there is minimal protection for franchisees. The problem stems from the tremendous growth of franchising, which has outstripped the growth of franchise law.

The contract summarizes the details that will govern the franchisor–franchisee relationship over its life. It outlines *exactly* the rights and the obligations of each party and sets the guidelines that govern the franchise relationship. To protect potential franchisees from having to rush into a contract without clearly understanding it, the Federal Trade Commission requires that the franchisee be allowed to hold the completed contract with all revisions for at least five business days before having to sign it. Despite such protection, one study by the FTC suggests that 40 percent of new franchisees sign contracts *without reading them!*[61]

Every potential franchisee should have an attorney evaluate the franchise contract and review it with him *before* he signs anything. Franchise contracts typically are long-term, so it is extremely important for prospective franchisees to understand their terms before they sign them. Too many franchisors don't discover unfavorable terms in their contracts until after they have invested in a franchise. By then, however, it's too late to negotiate changes. Although most large, established franchisors are not willing to negotiate the franchise contract's terms, many smaller franchises will, especially for highly qualified candidates. Although franchise contracts cover everything from initial fees and continuing payments to training programs and territorial protection, three items are responsible for most franchisor–franchisee disputes: termination of the contract, contract renewal, and transfer and buy-back provisions.

TERMINATION

Probably the most litigated subject of a franchise agreement is the termination of the contract by either party. Most contracts prohibit termination "without just cause." However, prospective franchisees must be sure they know exactly when and under what conditions they—and the franchisor—can terminate the contract. In general, the franchisor has the right to cancel a contract if a franchisee declares bankruptcy, fails to make required payments on time, or fails to maintain quality standards. For example, one franchisor reserves the right to terminate within 30 days of a franchisee's bankruptcy, within seven days of default on the continuing franchise royalties, or "if the franchise owner fails to comply with any of the requirements imposed . . . by the franchise agreement." Note that the scope of this last clause leaves room for interpretation.

Terminations usually are costly to both parties and are seldom conducted in an atmosphere of goodwill. Most attorneys encourage franchisees to avoid conditions for termination or to use alternative routes, such as formal complaints through franchise associations, arbitration, or selling the franchise.

RENEWAL

Franchisors usually retain the right to renew or refuse to renew franchisees' contracts. If a franchisee fails to make payments on schedule or does not maintain quality standards, the franchisor has the right to refuse renewal. In some cases, the franchisor has no obligation to offer contract renewal to the franchisee when the contract expires.

A recent dispute over a franchisor's refusal to renew a franchisee's contract led to a nasty lawsuit between General Aviation Inc. (the franchisee) and Cessna Aircraft Company (the franchisor). General Aviation, a Cessna franchisee for six years, charged the franchisor with discrimination and claimed that it unfairly ended their business relationship when the contract came up for renewal. General Aviation, citing that it was one of the top two best-selling Cessna franchises in the world, argued that the franchisor had no legitimate reason to refuse to renew its contract. (Cessna had renewed contracts with other franchisees whose performances were similar to or below General Aviation's.) General Aviation claimed that the real reason for nonrenewal was Cessna's anger over General Aviation's complaints about the quality of the aircraft it sold. In its ruling for General Aviation, a Michigan court of appeals held that a franchisor "cannot discriminate between franchisees—renewing one while refusing to renew another who has a similar record of performance."[62]

When a franchisor grants renewal, the two parties must draw up a new contract. Frequently, the franchisee must pay a renewal fee and may be required to fix any deficiencies of the outlet or to modernize and upgrade it. The FTC's Trade Regulation Rule requires the franchisor to disclose these terms before any contracts are signed.

TRANSFER AND BUYBACKS

At any given time, about 10 percent of the franchisees in a system have their outlets up for sale.[63] Franchisees typically are not free to sell their businesses to just anyone, however. Under most franchise contracts, a franchisee cannot sell his franchise to a third party or will it to a relative without the franchisor's approval. Most franchisors, however, do approve a franchisee's request to sell an outlet to another person. *American Leak Detection, a system with more than 300 franchisees, lists the company's resale opportunities on its World Wide Web site. That's where Jim Dickson found the two Florida-based territories he purchased when*

The franchisees of American Leak Detection take great pride in "pooling" their experience to help one another succeed.

he decided to leave his corporate job to operate a business of his own. After finding the franchises listed for sale on the Web, Dickson began his research in earnest, poring over the company's financial records and operating history. "I . . . knew there was no way the [previous owner] was tapping the potential of the franchise," he says.[64]

Most franchisors retain the right of first refusal in franchise transfers; the franchisee must offer the franchise to the franchisor first. For example, McDonald's Corporation repurchased 13 restaurants under its first refusal clause from a franchisee who wanted to retire.[65] If the franchisor refuses to buy the outlet, the franchisee may sell the outlet to a third party who meets the franchisor's approval (essentially the same standards buyers of new franchisees must meet).

*T*rends in Franchising

◀▶ Understand current trends shaping modern franchising.

Franchising has experienced three major growth waves since its beginning. The first wave occurred in the early 1970s when fast-food restaurants used the concept to grow rapidly. The fast-food industry was one of the first to discover the power of franchising, but other businesses soon took notice and adapted the franchising concept to their industries. The second wave took place in the mid-1980s as our nation's economy shifted heavily toward the service sector. Franchises followed suit, springing up in every service business imaginable—from maid services and copy centers to mailing services and real estate. The third wave began in the early 1990s and continues today. It is characterized by new, low-cost franchises that focus on specific market niches. In the wake of major corporate downsizing and the burgeoning costs of traditional franchises, these new franchises allow would-be entrepreneurs to get into proven businesses quickly and at lower costs than traditional franchises. These companies feature start-up costs in the $2,000 to $250,000 range and span a variety of industries, from leak detection in homes to auto detailing to day care to tile glazing. Other significant trends affecting franchising include international opportunities, nontraditional ways of locating and creating a franchise, and changing demographics.

INTERNATIONAL OPPORTUNITIES

Currently, the biggest trend in franchising is the globalization of U.S. franchise systems. Increasingly, franchising is becoming a major export industry for the United States because markets outside U.S. borders offer most franchisors the greatest potential for growth. Faced with extremely competitive conditions in domestic markets that are already saturated, a rapidly rising number of franchises are moving into international markets to boost sales and profits. Others are taking their franchise systems abroad simply because they see tremendous growth potential there. *For instance, Realty Executives International, a real estate brokerage franchise, has seven franchisees in South Africa and 26 outlets in Thailand. When the company first started franchising in 1988, executives had no immediate plans to branch out beyond the borders of the United States. Their initial focus was setting up franchisees in North America. Yet, when executives saw the undeveloped market potential in South Africa and Thailand, they decided to move before the opportunity passed. "I don't have an office in Austin, Texas, and yet I have an office in Bangkok," says president Rich Rector.*[66]

Canada is the primary market for U.S. franchisors, with Mexico, Japan, and Europe following. These markets are most attractive to franchisors because they have features similar to the U.S. market: rising personal incomes, strong demand for consumer goods, growing service economies, and spreading urbanization. For franchisors moving into foreign markets, adaptation is one key to success. Although they keep their basic systems intact, franchises that are successful in foreign markets quickly learn how to change their concepts to appeal to local tastes. "Today's [franchises] must adjust their domestic businesses to meet the interna-

The Battle of the Menu Boards: Seaweed Soup, Anyone?

*W*hen McDonald's opened its first store in Japan in 1971, it not only launched a campaign to bring the traditional American hamburger and french fries to the Far East but it also sparked the imagination of a local entrepreneur, Satoshi Sakurai. Inspired by the fast-food king's instant success in Tokyo, Sakurai launched his own version of a hamburger franchise, Mos Burger, the next year. Although its annual sales are less than half of McDonald's Japanese stores, Mos Burger is rapidly gaining a reputation for serving tastier burgers. In a recent survey of Japanese consumers, Mos Burger ranked first as the chain serving "good food" and "using fresh ingredients." McDonald's finished a distant third in both of those categories.

Mos Burger also has outpaced its competitors, including KFC (Japan's second-largest fast-food chain behind McDonald's), Wendy's, McDonald's, and others in adapting its menu to the particular taste of its Japanese customers. Rather than merely imitate McDonald's menus as other less successful Japanese fast-food chains attempted to do, Mos Burger modified its menu to suit the Japanese idea of a tasty hamburger. For instance, Mos Burger patties are not 100 percent beef but a Japanese-style combination of minced beef and pork mixed with chopped onions. Mos Burger also spends more money on its ingredients than its rivals do, but that makes its products more expensive. McDonald's "is such a big establishment," says a Mos Burger official. "We had to think of something different to survive." Not only is Mos Burger's menu different from McDonald's, but it also has more outlets, although smaller ones.

For years, Mos Burger posed little threat to its much larger competitors from the United States. Thanks to its exotic, localized menu, however, the company grew quietly but rapidly. Now McDonald's and other fast-food chains are having to fight back, launching new menu items to please locals' palates. "Consumers are now looking for the homemade touch, the Japanese taste," says Toshio Hayashi, a McDonald's spokesman. In 1989, McDonald's launched the Teriyaki Burger, and other fast-food franchises quickly followed with their own versions of teriyaki beef, pork, and chicken burgers. Then the fast-food giant introduced a rice burger (shredded beef sandwiched between grilled rice shaped like a bun), but that was four years after Mos Burger had put rice burgers on its menu. In 1988, Mos Burger added the highly successful Roast Katsu Burger (cheese wrapped in a roast pork cutlet, drenched in katsu sauce and topped with shredded cabbage). Three years later, McDonald's brought out its own Cheese Katsu Burger. Meanwhile, KFC introduced a deep-fried chicken cutlet topped with cabbage and splashed with teriyaki sauce. Other menu additions from American chains include fried rice balls, steamed Chinese dumplings, seaweed soup, curry with rice, and fried salmon sandwiches. So far, though, no one has copied Mos Burger's sweet drink based on a vegetable called konnyaku or its milky drink made with liquefied cheese.

What's driving this battle of the menu boards? Experts point to Japan's maturing fast-food market, which makes impressive sales gains hard to come by. "We are now entering an era of aggressive competition," says a KFC official. The heated competition among fast-food chains in Japan guarantees two things: increased innovation by competing companies and more menu choices for Japanese customers.

Seaweed soup, anyone?

1. How might a franchise agreement with a Japanese franchisee differ from such an agreement with a U.S.-based franchise?

2. Use the World Wide Web to conduct research on fast-food companies operating in other parts of the world (Eastern Europe and Australia, for example).

3. McDonald's is locating franchised restaurants in India. Use the World Wide Web to develop some specific recommendations for modifications McDonald's should make in its locations there.

SOURCE: Adapted from Yumiko Ono, "Japan's Fast-Food Companies Cook Up Local Platters to Tempt Local Palates," *Wall Street Journal*, May 29, 1992, pp. B2, B16; Steven Butler, "The Whopper Killed the Salmon Burger," *U.S. News & World Report*, January 20, 1997, p. 57. ◆

tional cultures," says one international franchise expert. "They must be firm and command quality while remaining flexible."[67]

SMALLER, NONTRADITIONAL LOCATIONS

As the high cost of building full-scale locations continues to climb, more franchisors are searching out nontraditional locations in which to build smaller, less expensive outlets. Based on the principle of **intercept marketing,** the idea is to put a franchise's products or services directly in the paths of potential customers, wherever they may be. Franchises are putting scaled-down outlets on college campuses, in high school cafeterias, in sports arenas, in hospitals, on airline flights, and in zoos. Today, customers are likely to find a mini-McDonald's inside the convenience store at a Mobil gas station, a Dunkin' Donuts outlet in the airport, or a Mail Boxes Etc. store on a college campus.[68] Many franchisees have discovered that smaller outlets in these nontraditional locations generate nearly the same sales volume as full-sized outlets at just a fraction of the cost. Such locations will be a key to continued franchise growth in the domestic market. One franchise expert explains, "Years ago, we never dreamed you could purchase pizza over the Internet or be served a McDonald's hamburger on an airplane. There are so many ways of franchising now, there's no telling what the future might bring."[69]

CONVERSION FRANCHISING

The trend toward **conversion franchising,** whereby owners of independent businesses become franchisees to gain the advantage of name recognition, will continue. In a franchise conversion, the franchisor gets immediate entry into new markets and experienced operators; franchisees get increased visibility and often a big sales boost. In fact, the average sales gain in the first year for converted franchisees is 20 percent.[70] *Michael Lawrence, with his wife Dee, launched the Cafe Manhattan Bagel Shop in New York City in 1988. When the Manhattan Bagel Company approached him about becoming one of their franchisees, he studied the opportunity and decided to take it. He knew his two locations would benefit from the franchise's name recognition and that the franchisor's system would improve the efficiency of his operation. Manhattan Bagel waived the usual franchise fee for Lawrence, but he still invested a total of $100,000 to upgrade his stores to franchise standards. The conversion has been extremely successful. Sales are up 20 percent in one location and 50 percent in the other. Profit margins (after paying the franchise royalty) have climbed from zero at one store and 14 percent at the other to an impressive 18 percent in both stores.*[71]

MULTIPLE-UNIT FRANCHISING

Multiple-unit franchising (MUF) became extremely popular in the early 1990s, and the trend has accelerated rapidly since then. In multiple-unit franchising, a franchisee opens more than one unit in a broad territory within a specific time period. In recent years, franchising has attracted more-professional, experienced, and sophisticated entrepreneurs who have access to more capital—and who have their sights set on big goals that owning a single outlet cannot meet. "Multiple ownership of units by franchisees has exploded," says one franchise expert. "Twenty or 30 years ago, it would have been rare for any one franchisee to own 10 or 20 units. Now it's not uncommon . . . for one franchisee to own 60, 70, or even 200 units. . . . It's far more efficient in the long run to have one well-trained franchisee operate a number of units than to train many franchises."[72] The typical multi-unit franchisee owns between three and six outlets, but some franchisees own many more. For instance, a recent study by the Restaurant Finance Monitor found that the top 100 franchisees operate some 9,100 restaurants.[73]

For franchisors, multiple-unit franchising is an efficient way to expand into either domestic or international markets quickly. Multiple-unit franchising is an extremely effective strategy for franchisors targeting foreign markets, where having a local representative who knows the territory is essential. For franchisees, multiple-unit franchising offers the opportunity for rapid growth without leaving the safety net of the franchise. Also, because franchisors usually offer discounts of about 25 percent off their standard fees on multiple units, franchisees can get fast-growing companies for a bargain. *Daniel Del Prete bought his first Dunkin' Donuts franchise as a way to make a living; then he saw the potential that owning multiple units offered. Nearly three decades later, Del Prete owns 18 Dunkin' Donuts units and three Blimpie franchises.*[74]

MASTER FRANCHISING

A **master franchise** (or **subfranchise**) gives a franchisee the right to create a semi-independent organization in a particular territory to recruit, sell, and support other franchisees. A master franchisee buys the right to develop subfranchises within a broad geographic area or, sometimes, an entire country. Subfranchising "turbocharges" a franchisor's growth. It enables franchisors to open outlets in international markets quickly and efficiently because the master franchisees understand local laws and the nuances of selling in local markets. The head of one international franchise who licenses master franchisees in foreign countries says, "It's good to have someone there who knows not only the language but also the laws, and, beyond the laws, the traditions. They can tell you the things you need to know that can save you from embarrassment."[75] *One master franchisee with TCBY International, a yogurt franchise, has opened 21 stores in China and Hong Kong. On the basis of his success in those markets, the company has sold him the master franchise in India.*[76]

PIGGYBACKING

Some franchisors are discovering new ways to reach customers by teaming up with other franchisors selling complementary products or services. A growing number of companies are **piggybacking** (or **co-branding** or **combination franchising**) outlets: combining two or more distinct franchises under one roof. This "buddy system" approach works best when the two franchise ideas are compatible and appeal to similar customers. For example, ActionFax, a franchise that sells completely equipped fax booths, has found its way into many existing franchises, including print shops, drugstores, and convenience stores. "We fit in with many other preexisting franchises where the facility and manpower are already in place, and we offer an added-value service to customers," says one ActionFax executive.[77] McDonald's operates minirestaurants in 600 Wal-Mart stores across the country.[78] At one location, a Texaco gasoline station, a Pizza Hut restaurant, and a Dunkin' Donuts—all owned by the same franchisee—work together in a piggyback arrangement to draw customers.[79] Doughnut franchisor Dunkin' Donuts and ice cream franchisor Baskin-Robbins are working together to build hundreds of combination outlets, a concept that has proved to be highly successful.[80] Properly planned, piggybacked franchises can magnify many times over the sales and profits of individual, self-standing outlets.

SERVING AGING BABY BOOMERS

Now that dual-career couples have become the norm, especially among baby boomers, the market for franchises offering convenience and time-saving services is booming. Customers are willing to pay for products and services that will save them time or trouble, and franchises are ready to provide them. Franchisees of Around Your Neck go into the homes and offices of busy male executives to sell men's apparel and accessories ranging from shirts and ties to custom-made suits. To better serve their customers, franchisees of Pinnacle Brew Thru convenience stores have taken the idea of the drive-through window a step further: Each outlet has a driveway that runs through the entire store. Employees fill orders for customers, who never have to leave their cars.[81] Other areas in which franchising is experiencing rapid growth include home delivery of meals, house-cleaning services, continuing education and training (especially computer and business training), leisure activities (such as crafts, hobbies, health spas, and travel-related activities), products and services aimed at home-based businesses, and health care (ranging from fitness and diet products and services to in-home elder care and medical services).[82]

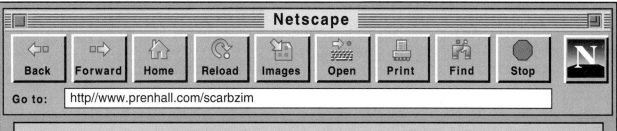

WIRED TO THE WEB

THE POWER OF THE WEB

*T*he World Wide Web is reshaping the franchise industry, allowing franchisors to locate potential franchisees more efficiently, improving communications between franchisors and their franchisees, and giving franchisees the ability to sell their products and services across the globe. For entrepreneurs considering investing in franchises, the World Wide Web makes the process of gathering information much easier and faster. With just a few mouse clicks, would-be franchisees can find out about the investment requirements of a particular franchise or search databases for existing franchises that are for sale.

Since launching its Web site, Molly Maid <http://www.mollymaid.com>, a home cleaning service franchise, has sold 12 franchises to prospects who discovered the franchise opportunity while surfing the World Wide Web. MAACO <http://www.maaco.com>, an automotive repair franchise, recently sold its first franchise to a Web prospect. "The franchisee was able to read through the [information on the] site and determine right away that he could qualify," says MAACO's franchise development manager.

The World Wide Web also helps franchisors to keep in close contact with their franchisees and to provide them with better support services. Molly Maid franchisees e-mail their operating information to headquarters, where experienced field advisers analyze it. Then, the field advisers e-mail the data back to franchisees with specific recommendations on how to improve their daily operations in a variety of areas. Under Molly Maid's system, franchisees also can e-mail questions, comments, and suggestions to top managers at headquarters, including McKinnon, who receives an average of 10 messages a day.

The Tinderbox, a tobacco and gift shop franchise, sees the Web as a powerful marketing tool. In addition to using its own Web site <http://www.tinderbox.com> as

an important part of its marketing strategy, the Tinderbox encourages its franchisees to develop their own Web sites. Many franchisees have responded and are reaching both national and international customers with their Web sites.

Although franchising experts differ in their opinions about the direction in which the World Wide Web will take franchising, they do agree that both franchisors and franchisees have only begun to explore the possibilities the Web offers.

1. What possibilities do you see for franchising on the World Wide Web? Work with a team of your classmates to brainstorm ways in which franchisors and franchisees could use the Web to improve their businesses.
2. Investigate several franchisors' Web sites (such as McDonald's at <http://www.mcdonalds.com>, Ben & Jerry's Homemade at <http://benjerry.com>, Wendy's at <http:wendys.com>, and others you locate with a Web search engine). Select two franchises and prepare a one-page report comparing the Web sites and how the franchisors use them. How would you score each site on the following factors (1 is low; 10 is high)?

Design	1	2	3	4	5	6	7	8	9	10
Interactivity	1	2	3	4	5	6	7	8	9	10
Ease of navigation	1	2	3	4	5	6	7	8	9	10
Appeal	1	2	3	4	5	6	7	8	9	10
Interest	1	2	3	4	5	6	7	8	9	10
Quality of information	1	2	3	4	5	6	7	8	9	10

3. Is each site effective? Why? What recommendations would you make for improving each site?

SOURCES: Adapted from Heather Page, "Net Rewards," *Entrepreneurs*, March 1997, pp. 144–146; Janean Chun, "Franchise Frenzy," *Entrepreneur*, January 1997, pp. 160–163; Roberta Maynard, "Rejuvenated Sales," *Nation's Business*, July 1997, pp. 49–54.

*C*onclusion

Franchising has proved its viability in the U.S. economy and has become a key part of the small business sector because it offers many would-be entrepreneurs the opportunity to own and operate a business with a greater chance for success. Despite its impressive growth rate to date, the franchising industry still has a great deal of room left to grow, especially globally. Describing the future of franchising, one expert says, "Franchising has not yet come close to reaching its full potential in the American marketplace."[83]

Chapter Summary

1. Explain the importance of franchising in the U.S. economy.
   - Since 1990, sales by franchised businesses have grown l0 times as fast as the U.S. economy as a whole. Through franchised businesses, consumers can buy nearly every good or service imaginable.
   - A new franchise opens somewhere in the United States every eight minutes and somewhere in the world every six-and-a-half minutes. Franchises account for 43 percent of all retail sales, totaling more than $810 billion, and they employ more than 8 million people in more than 70 major industries.

2. Define the concept of franchising.
   - Franchising is a method of doing business involving a continuous relationship between a franchisor and a franchisee. The franchisor retains control of the distribution system, while the franchisee assumes all of the normal daily operating functions of the business.

3. Describe the different types of franchises.
   - There are three types of franchising: trade-name franchising, where the franchisee purchases only the right to use a brand name; product distribution franchising, which involves a license to sell specific products under a brand name; and pure franchising, which provides a franchisee with a complete business system.

4. Explain the forces behind franchising's popularity.
   - Franchising has been a successful business format, in part, because of the mutual benefits it provides to franchisors and franchisees.

5. Describe the benefits of franchising for the franchisor.
   - The franchisor has the benefits of expanding his business on limited capital and growing without developing key managers internally.

6. Describe the benefits and limitations of franchising for the franchisee.
   - The franchisee receives many key *benefits*: management training and counseling, customer appeal of a brand name, standardized quality of goods and services, national advertising programs, financial assistance, proven products and business formats, centralized buying power, territorial protection, and greater chances for success.
   - The limitations involved in buying a franchise include franchise fees and profit sharing, strict adherence to standardized operations, restrictions on purchasing, limited product lines, possible ineffective training programs, and less freedom than independent owners have.

7. Discuss what franchisors look for in a franchisee.
   - Franchisors look for franchisees who are hardworking team players with leadership and management skills, are educated and financially stable, and have a strong desire to succeed.

8. Describe the legal aspects of franchising, including the protection offered by the FTC's Trade Regulation Rule.
   - The FTC's Trade Regulation Rule is designed to help the franchisee evaluate a franchising package. It requires each franchisor to disclose information covering 23 topics at least 10 days before accepting payment from a potential franchisee. This document, the Uniform Franchise Offering Circular (UFOC) is a valuable source of information for anyone considering investing in a franchise.

9. Explain the *right* way to buy a franchise.
   - Evaluate yourself; research your market; consider your franchise options; get a copy of the franchisor's UFOC and study it; talk to existing franchisees; ask the franchisor some tough questions; and make your choice.

10. Describe a typical franchise contract and some of its provisions.

♦ The amount of franchisor–franchisee litigation has risen steadily over the past decade. Three items are responsible for most franchisor–franchisee disputes: termination of the contract, contract renewal, and transfer and buy-back provisions.

11. Understand current trends shaping modern franchising.

♦ Trends influencing franchising include low-cost franchises that target specific market niches, international opportunities, the emergence of smaller nontraditional locations, conversion franchising, multiple-unit franchising, master franchising, piggyback (or combination) franchising, and products and services targeting aging baby boomers.

Discussion Questions

1. What is franchising?
2. Describe the three types of franchising and give an example of each.
3. How does franchising benefit the franchisor?
4. Discuss the advantages and the disadvantages of franchising for the franchisee.
5. How beneficial to the franchisee is a quality training program? Why?
6. Compare the failure rates for franchises with those of independent businesses.
7. Why might an independent entrepreneur be dissatisfied with a franchising arrangement?
8. What do franchisors look for in a franchisee?
9. What are the clues in detecting an unreliable franchisor?
10. How and in what areas should a prospective franchisee investigate before investing in a franchise?
11. What is the function of the FTC's Trade Regulation Rule?
12. Outline the rights given all prospective franchisees by the Trade Regulation Rule.
13. What are the causes of most franchisor–franchisee litigation? Whom does the standard franchise contract favor?
14. Describe the current trends of franchises.
15. What areas of franchising offer the greatest growth potential in the near future? Why?
16. One franchisee says, "Franchising is helpful because it gives you somebody [the franchisor] to get you going, nurture you, and shove you along a little. But, the franchisor won't make you successful. That depends on what you bring to the business, how hard you are prepared to work, and how committed you are to finding the right franchise for you." Do you agree? Explain.

Step into the Real World

1. Visit a local franchise operation. Is it a trade name, product distribution, or pure franchise? To what extent did the franchisee investigate before investing? What assistance does the franchisor provide?
2. Consult a copy of the International Franchise Association publication *Franchise Opportunities Handbook* (the library should have a copy). Write several franchisors in a particular business category and ask for their franchise packages. Write a report comparing their treatment of the topics covered by the Trade Regulation Rule.
3. Analyze the terms of the franchise contracts of the franchisors found in exercise 2. What are the major differences? Are some terms more favorable than others? If you were about to invest in the franchise, which terms would you want to change?
4. Ask a local franchisee to ask his or her regional franchise representative to lead a class discussion on franchising.
5. Contact the International Franchise Association (1350 New York Avenue, N.W., Suite 900, Washington, D.C., 20005-4709 [202] 628-8000) for a copy of *Investigate before Investing*. Also search the resources on the World Wide Web for information on franchising. Prepare a report outlining what a prospective franchisee should do before buying a franchise.
6. Working with several of your classmates, select a franchise concept with which you are familiar. Conduct a brainstorming session in which your goal is to identify as many nontraditional locations for franchised outlets as possible. Prepare a short report on your ideas and the justification for them.

Take It to the Net

Visit the Scarborough/Zimmerer home page at
www.prenhall.com/scarbzim
for updated information, on-line resources, and Web-based exercises.

Endnotes

1. Barbara Rudolph, "Franchising Is BIG Business for Small Business," *Your Company*, Spring 1992, p. 44.
2. Janean Huber, "Franchise Forecast," *Entrepreneur*, January 1993, p. 72.
3. International Franchise Association, <http://www.franchise.org/resources/buying/success.html>; Echo M. Garrett, "Job Creation," *Inc.*, December 1993, p. 151.
4. Lynn Beresford, "New Horizons," *Franchise and Business Opportunities 1996*, p. 4; Huber, "Franchise Forecast," p. 72.
5. Dan Fost and Susan Mitchell, "Small Stores with Big Names," *American Demographics*, November 1992, p. 52.
6. Meg Whittemore, "Changes Ahead for Franchising," *Nation's Business*, June 1990, p. 29.
7. Ronaleen R. Roha, "Making It, Franchise Style," *Kiplinger's Personal Finance Magazine*, July 1996, pp. 71–72.
8. Rudolph, "Franchising Is BIG Business for Small Business," p. 46.
9. Gregory Matusky, "What Every Business Can Learn from Franchising," *Inc.*, January 1994, p. 91.
10. Gregory Matusky, "The Franchise Hall of Fame," *Inc.*, April 1994, pp. 86–89.
11. "Do You Have What It Takes to Be a Franchisee?" *Business Start-Ups*, May 1997, pp. 55–69.
12. Barbara Presley Noble, "Many McDonald's Franchises Owned by Women," *Spartanburg Herald Journal*, April 3, 1994, p. B10.
13. Roberta Maynard, "Prospecting for Gold," *Nation's Business*, June 1996, pp. 69–74.
14. Carol Steinberg, "Venture's Guide to Franchising," *Venture*, July 1988, p. 56.
15. Julie Bawden Davis, "A Perfect Match," *Business Start-Ups*, July 1997, p. 48.
16. Kevin Farrell, "Franchising Hits a Snag," *Venture*, February 1982, p. 69.
17. Janean Huber, "Early Birds," *Entrepreneur*, April 1994, p. 105.
18. Buck Brown, "Enterprise," *Wall Street Journal*, November 14, 1988, p. B1.
19. Maynard, "Prospecting for Gold," p. 70.
20. Echo M. Garrett, "Reengineering the Franchise," *Inc.*, December 1993, p. 148.
21. Davis, "A Perfect Match," p. 44.
22. Janean Huber, "The Buddy System," *Entrepreneur*, January 1993, p. 96.
23. Irwin W. Fisk, "Attention, Franchise Shoppers," *Entrepreneur*, January 1991, p. 96.
24. Kristin Dunlap Godsey, "Market Like Mad," *Success*, January/February 1997, p. 83.
25. Janean Huber, "Franchise Forecast," p. 73.
26. Julie Bawden Davis, "Financing Your Franchise," *Business Start-Ups*, September 1997, pp. 106–110.
27. Ibid.
28. Ibid.
29. Ibid., p. 106.
30. Stephanie Barlow, "Sub-stantial Success," *Entrepreneur*, January 1993, p. 126.
31. Nancy Croft Baker, "Independents Try Franchising," *Nation's Business*, June 1989, pp. 31–32.
32. Richard Gibson, "Court Decides Franchisees Get Elbow Room," *Wall Street Journal*, August 14, 1996, pp. B1, B4.
33. Gibson, "Court Decides Franchisees Get Elbow Room"; *Franchise Law Update*, A Publication of Luce, Forward, Hamilton & Scripps LLP, vol. 1, no. 6 (October 1996), <http://www.luce.com/publicat/flu1_6-3.html>.
34. Meg Whittemore, "The Franchise Search," *Nation's Business*, April 1993, p. 27.
35. Glen Weisman, "The Choice Is Yours," *Business Start-Ups*, May 1997, pp. 24–30; Dan Morse & Jeffrey Tannenbaum, "Poll on High Success Rate for Franchises Raises Eyebrows," *Wall Street Journal*, March 17, 1998, p. B2.
36. Kirk Shivell and Kent Banning, "What Every Prospective Franchisee Should Know," *Small Business Forum*, Winter 1996/1997, pp. 33–42.
37. Davis, "A Perfect Match," p. 45.
38. Weisman, "The Choice Is Yours," p. 25.
39. Ibid., pp. 24–30; Anne P. Thrower, "Beneath the Golden Arches," *Upstate Business*, June 14, 1998, pp. 1, 10–11.
40. UFOC disclosure document, Holiday Inns, Inc.
41. Jeffrey A. Tannenbaum, "Franchisees Balk at High Prices for Supplies from Franchisers," *Wall Street Journal*, July 5, 1995, pp. B1–B2.
42. Matusky, "The Franchise Hall of Fame."
43. Janean Huber, "What's Next?" *Entrepreneur*, September 1994, p. 150.
44. Matusky, "What Every Business Can Learn from Franchising," p. 90.
45. Huber, "Franchise Forecast," pp. 72–75.
46. "Do You Have What It Takes to Be a Franchisee?" p. 60.
47. Ibid., pp. 55–69.
48. Weisman, "The Choice Is Yours," p. 25.
49. J. A. Dunnigan, "Two Veterans Discuss the Evolution of Franchising," *Entrepreneur*, January 1985, p. 50.
50. Ibid.
51. John P. Hayes and Gregory Matusky, "Franchising," *Inc.*, April 1989, p. 153.
52. "Franchising: The Strings Attached to Being Your Own Boss," *Changing Times*, September 1984, p. 70.
53. Erika Kotite, "Franchise 500: A Salute to 10 Years." *Entrepreneur*, January 1989, p. 116.
54. Catherine Siskos, "Franchises May Have to Tell All," *Kiplinger's Personal Finance Magazine*, March 1997, p. 16.

55. Andrew A. Caffey, "Check It Out," *Entrepreneur*, January 1998, pp. 180–183.
56. Roberta Maynard, "Choosing a Franchise," *Nation's Business*, October 1996, p. 62R.
57. David J. Kaufman, "The First Step," *Entrepreneur*, January 1992, p. 97.
58. "Do You Have What It Takes to Be a Franchisee?" p. 56.
59. Carla Goodman, "Fast-Growing Trends," *Business Start-Ups*, February 1997, p. 46.
60. Roha, "Making It, Franchise Style," p. 74.
61. Jeannie Ralston, "Before You Bet Your Buns," *Venture*, March 1988, p. 57.
62. Janean Huber, "Renewed Interest," *Entrepreneur*, May 1994, pp. 192–193; Jeffrey A. Tannenbaum, "New Rulings Clonk Franchisees with Sturdier Armor," *Wall Street Journal*, December 30, 1993, p. B2.
63. Roberta Maynard, "Rejuvenated Sales," *Nation's Business*, July 1997, pp. 49–54.
64. Ibid.
65. Fred Monk, "McDonald's Franchise Changes Hands," *The State*, March 1, 1985, p. C1.
66. Janean Chun, "Global Warming," *Entrepreneur*, April 1997, p. 156.
67. Ibid., p. 158.
68. Goodman, "Fast-Growing Trends," pp. 42–46; Dan Morse, "School Cafeterias Are Enrolling as Fast-Food Franchises," *Wall Street Journal*, July 28, 1998, p. B2.
69. Janean Chun, "Franchise Frenzy," *Entrepreneur*, January 1997, p. 162.
70. Carol Steinberg, "Instant Growth," *Success*, July/August 1996, pp. 77–83.
71. Ibid.
72. Janean Huber, "What's Next?" *Entrepreneur*, September 1994, p. 149.
73. Janean Chun, "Power of One," *Entrepreneur*, December 1996, pp. 166–168.
74. Ibid.
75. Chun, "Global Warming," p. 159.
76. Roberta Maynard, "Why Franchisers Look Abroad," *Nation's Business*, October 1995, pp. 65–72.
77. Kevin McLaughlin, "A Welcome Addition," *Entrepreneur*, January 1990, p. 211.
78. David Fischer, "The New Meal Deals," *U.S. News & World Report*, October 30, 1995, p. 66.
79. Meg Whittemore, "Teaching Franchise Success," *Kiplinger's Personal Finance Magazine*, February 1996, pp. 82–84; Christina Grace Peterson, "Q & A," *Business Start-Ups*, November 1997, p. 6.
80. Lynn Beresford, "Seeing Double," Entrepreneur, October 1995, pp. 164–167; Gordon Williams, "Roadside Attraction," Financial World, October 21, 1996, pp. 96–98; Roberta Maynard, "The Hit Parade for 2000," *Nation's Business,* April 1997, pp. 68–74.
81. Jeffrey A. Tannenbaum, "Franchisers Court Fat Cats, Especially Those Overseas," *Wall Street Journal*, April 28, 1997, p. B2.
82. Maynard, "The Hit Parade for 2000."
83. Huber, "What's Next?" p. 151.

CHAPTER 5

Buying an Existing Business

Don't ask the barber whether you need a hair-cut.

—*Daniel Greenberg*

I had rather have a fool to make me merry than experience to make me sad.

—*William Shakespeare,* As You Like It

Upon completion of this chapter, you will be able to

1 Understand the advantages and disadvantages of buying an existing business.

2 Define the steps involved in the *right* way to buy a business.

3 Explain the process of evaluating an existing business.

4 Describe the various ways of determining the value of a business.

5 Understand the seller's side of the buyout decision and how to structure the deal.

6 Understand how the negotiation process works and identify the factors that affect it.

*G*rowing numbers of people are becoming secondhand entrepreneurs, buying existing businesses rather than starting them "from scratch." Experts estimate that the market for U.S. small businesses is about $200 billion a year. Each year, more than 500,000 companies are sold, and 90 percent of those are valued at less than $5 million.[1] The average sale price of these companies is less than $200,000.[2] Buying an established company has become a popular way to get into business, but it is not something an entrepreneur should do quickly. "It could take two to three years to find the right company," says Richard Joseph, co-author of *How to Buy a Business*. "It takes some time looking at and reviewing deals before you recognize the difference between a good deal and a bad one."[3] Problems often arise when entrepreneurs are in a hurry to close a deal. In almost every situation, it takes many months to analyze and evaluate the positives and negatives of a particular business opportunity. It may take even longer to negotiate the final deal. The cardinal rule is this: Be patient, and do the necessary homework. Be sure that you have answers to all of the following questions.

- Is the right type of business for sale in the market in which you want to operate?
- What experience do you have in a particular business and the industry in which it operates?
- How critical is experience in the business to your ultimate success?
- What price and payment methods are reasonable for you and acceptable to the seller?
- Should you start a business and build it from the ground up, or should you shop around to buy an existing company?
- What is each purchase candidate's potential for success?
- Are you willing to consider a business in decline with the intention of turning it around?
- What kinds of changes will you have to make—and how extensive will they be—to realize the business's full potential?

Buying an Existing Business

① Understand the advantages and disadvantages of buying an existing business.

ADVANTAGES OF BUYING AN EXISTING BUSINESS

A Successful Business May Continue to Be Successful. Purchasing a thriving business at an acceptable price increases the likelihood of success. The previous management already has established a customer base, built supplier relationships, and set up a business system. The new owner's objective should be to make modifications that will attract new customers while retaining the firm's existing customers. Maintaining the proper balance of old and new is not an easy task. The customer base that you inherit through the purchase can carry you while you study how the business has become successful and why customers want to buy from you. The time you spend learning about the business and its customers before introducing changes will increase the probability that the changes you do make will be successful.

An Existing Business May Already Have the Best Location. When the location of the business is critical to its success, it may be wise to purchase a business that is already in the right place. Opening in a second-choice location and hoping to draw customers often proves fruitless. In fact, the existing business's biggest asset may be its location. If this advantage cannot be matched by other locations, an entrepreneur may have little choice but to buy instead of build.

Employees and Suppliers Are in Place. An existing business already has experienced employees who can help the company earn money while a new owner learns the business. In addition, an existing business has an established set of suppliers with a history of business dealings. Those vendors can continue to supply the business while the new owner investigates the products and services of other suppliers. Thus, the new owner is not pressured to choose a supplier quickly without thorough investigation.

Equipment Is Installed and Productive Capacity Is Known. Acquiring and installing new equipment exerts a tremendous strain on a fledgling company's financial resources. In an existing business, a potential buyer can determine the condition of the plant and equipment and its capacity before he buys. The previous owner may have established an efficient production operation through trial and error, although the new owner may need to make modifications to improve it. In many cases, the entrepreneur can purchase physical facilities and equipment at prices significantly below replacement costs.

Inventories Are in Place and Trade Credit Has Been Established. The proper amount of inventory is essential to both cost control and sales volume. If the business has too little inventory, it will not have the quantity and variety of products to satisfy customer demand. But if the business has too much inventory, it is tying up excessive capital, increasing costs, reducing profitability, and increasing the danger of cash flow problems. Many successful established businesses have learned a balance between these extremes. Previous owners also have established trade credit relationships of which the new owner can take advantage. The business's proven track record gives the new owner leverage in negotiating favorable trade credit terms. No supplier wants to lose a good customer.

The New Business Owner Hits the Ground Running. Buying a business is one of the fastest pathways to entrepreneurship. The entrepreneur who purchases an existing business saves the time, costs, and energy required to plan and launch a new business. The buyer gets a business that is already generating cash and sometimes profits. The day he takes over the ongoing business is the day his revenues begin. In this way, he earns while he learns.

When Roland Reems and Mike Nofsinger decided to go into business for themselves, they knew that the best route for them was to buy an existing company. Both Reems and Nofsinger had spent the bulk of their careers in the printing industry, so it was natural for them to buy a printing business. They knew the local printing market and the tremendous opportunities it offered, but they also saw the need to move into the market quickly before competitors they knew were coming. Reems estimates that it would have taken at least a year to start a printing business from scratch, which would have put them at a distinct competitive disadvantage. "We needed to be immediate producers and providers without losing momentum," he says. Reems and Nofsinger contacted the owner of a family-run printing company who was nearing retirement and wanted out. Within months, they were the proud owners of the printing business.[4]

The New Owner Can Use the Experience of the Previous Owner. In many business sales, the previous owner spends time in an orientation period with the new owner, which gives the new manager the opportunity to question him about the policies and procedures he developed and the reasons for them. Previous owners also can be extremely helpful in unmasking the unwritten rules of business in the area: what types of behavior are acceptable, whom to trust, and other important intangibles. After all, most owners who sell out want to see the buyer succeed in carrying on the business. Hiring the previous owner as a consultant is the best move many business buyers can make. Even if the previous owner is not around after the sale, the new owner will have access to all of the business's records, which can guide him until he becomes acclimated to the business and the local market. He can trace the impact on costs and revenues of the major decisions the previous owner made and can learn from his mistakes and profit from his achievements.

It's a Bargain. Some existing businesses may be real bargains. If the current owners want to sell quickly, they may sell the business at a low price. The more specialized the business is, the greater the likelihood is that a buyer will find a bargain. Any special skills or training required to operate the business limit the number of potential buyers. If the owner wants a substantial down payment or the entire selling price in cash, there may be few qualified buyers; those who do qualify may be able to negotiate a good deal.

Finding Financing Usually Is Easier. Because the risk associated with buying an existing business is lower than that of a start-up, financing for the purchase is easier. A buyer can point to the existing company's track record and to the plans she has for improving it to convince potential lenders to finance the purchase. Also, in many buy–sell agreements, the buyer uses a "built-in" source of financing: the seller!

DISADVANTAGES OF BUYING AN EXISTING BUSINESS

It's a Loser. A business may be for sale because it has never been profitable. Such a situation may be disguised; owners can use various creative accounting techniques that make the firm's financial picture appear much brighter than it really is. The reason that a business is for sale will seldom be stated honestly as "It's losing money." If there is an area of business in which the maxim "let the buyer beware" still prevails, it is in the sale of a business. Any buyer unprepared to do a thorough analysis of the business may be stuck with a real loser.

Although buying a money-losing business is risky, it is not necessarily taboo. If your analysis of a company indicates that it is poorly managed or suffering from neglect, you may be able to turn it around. However, buying a struggling business without a well-defined plan for solving the problems it faces is an invitation to disaster.

The Previous Owner May Have Created Ill Will. Just as proper business dealings create goodwill, improper business behavior creates ill will. The business may look great on the surface, but customers, suppliers, creditors, or employees may have extremely negative feelings about it. Too many business buyers discover (after the sale) that they have inherited undisclosed credit problems, poor supplier relationships, soon-to-expire leases, lawsuits, building code violations, and other problems caused by the previous owner. Vital business relationships may have begun to deteriorate, but their long-term effects may not yet be reflected in the business's financial statements. Ill will can permeate a business for years. The best way to avoid these problems is to investigate a prospective purchase target thoroughly *before* closing a deal.

Employees Inherited with the Business May Not Be Suitable. If the new owner plans to make changes in a business, the present employees may not suit her needs. Some workers may have a difficult time adapting to the new owner's management style and vision for the company. Previous managers may have kept marginal employees because they were close friends or because they started off with the company. The new owner, therefore, may have to make some very unpopular termination decisions. For this reason, employees often do not welcome a new owner because they feel threatened. Further, employees who may have wanted to buy the business themselves but could not afford it are likely to see the new owner as the person who stole their opportunity. Bitter employees are not likely to be productive workers.

The Business Location May Have Become Unsatisfactory. What was once or is currently an ideal location may become obsolete as market and demographic trends change. Large shopping malls, new competitors, or highway reroutings can spell disaster for a small retail shop. Prospective buyers should always evaluate the existing market in the area surrounding an existing business as well as its potential for expansion.

Equipment and Facilities May Be Obsolete or Inefficient. Potential buyers sometimes neglect to have an expert evaluate a companies' building and equipment before they purchase it. Only after it's too late do they discover that the equipment is obsolete and inefficient, pushing operating expenses to excessively high levels. Modernizing equipment and facilities is seldom inexpensive.

Change and Innovation Are Difficult to Implement. It is easier to plan for change than it is to implement it. Methods and procedures the previous owner used created precedents that can be difficult or awkward for a new owner to change. For example, if the previous owner granted a 10 percent discount to customers purchasing 100 or more units in a single order, it may be impossible to eliminate that discount without losing some of those customers. The previous owner's policies, even those that are unwise, can influence the changes the new owner can make. Implementing changes to reverse a downward sales trend in a turnaround business can be just as difficult as eliminating unprofitable procedures. Convincing alienated customers to return can be an expensive and laborious process and may take years.

Inventory May Be Obsolete. Inventory is valuable only if it is salable. Too many owners make the mistake of trusting a company's balance sheet to provide them with the value of its inventory. The inventory value reported on a company's balance sheet is seldom an accurate refection of its real market value. In some cases, a company's inventory may actually appreciate during periods of rapid inflation, but more likely it has depreciated in value. The value reported on the balance sheet reflects the original cost of the inventory, not its actual market value. Most businesses for sale include inventory and other assets that are absolutely worthless because they are outdated and obsolete! It is the buyer's responsibility to discover the real value of the assets included in the sale.

After Hendrix Neimann had already agreed in principle to purchase Automatic Door Specialists, a security company, from its founder, he and his team of advisers discovered that much of the inventory reported on the company's books was useless. After taking into account the worthless inventory and past-due accounts receivable, Neimann ultimately offered the owner 50 percent of the amount in the original preliminary agreement.[5]

Accounts Receivable May Be Worth Less Than Face Value. Like inventory, accounts receivable rarely are worth their face value. The prospective buyer should age the accounts receivable to determine their collectibility. The older the receivables are, the less likely they are to be collected, and, consequently, the lower their value is. Table 5.1 shows a simple but effective method of evaluating accounts receivable once the buyer ages them.

The Business May Be Overpriced. Most business sales are asset purchases rather than stock purchases, and a buyer must be sure that he knows which assets are included in the deal and what their real value is. Each year, many people purchase businesses at prices far in excess of their value. A buyer who correctly values a business's accounts receivable, inventories, and other assets will be in a good position to negotiate a price that will allow the business to be profitable. Making payments on a business that was overpriced is a millstone around the new owner's neck; it will be difficult to carry this excess weight and keep the business afloat.

Table 5.1 Valuing Accounts Receivable

A prospective buyer asked the current owner of a business about the value of her accounts receivable. The owner's business records showed $101,000 in receivables. But when the prospective buyer aged them and then multiplied the resulting totals by his estimated probabilities of collection, he discovered their *real* value.

Age of Accounts (days)	Amount	Probability of Collection	Value
0–30	$ 40,000	.95	$38,000
31–60	25,000	.88	22,000
61–90	14,000	.70	9,800
91–120	10,000	.40	4,000
121–150	7,000	.25	1,750
151+	5,000	.10	500
Total	$101,000		$76,050

Had he blindly accepted the "book value" of these accounts receivable, this prospective buyer would have overpaid by nearly $25,000 for them!

$\mathcal{H}$ow to Buy a Business

2 Define the steps involved in the *right* way to buy a business.

Buying an existing business can be risky if approached haphazardly. Studies show that more than 50 percent of all business acquisitions fail to meet the buyer's expectations. To avoid costly mistakes, an entrepreneur-to-be should follow a logical, methodical approach:

◆ Analyze your skills, abilities, and interests to determine what kinds of businesses you should consider.

◆ Develop a list of criteria that defines the "ideal business" for you.

◆ Prepare a list of potential candidates.

◆ Investigate those candidates and evaluate the best ones.

◆ Negotiate the deal.

◆ Explore financing options.

◆ Ensure a smooth transition.[6]

ANALYZE YOUR SKILLS, ABILITIES, AND INTERESTS

The first step in buying a business is conducting a self-audit to determine the ideal business for you. Consider, for example, the following:

◆ What business activities do you enjoy most? Least?

◆ Which industries interest you most? Least? Why?

◆ What kind of business do you want to buy?

◆ What kinds of businesses do you want to *avoid*?

◆ In what geographic area do you want to live and work?

◆ What do you expect to get out of the business?

◆ How much can you put into the business—in both time and money?

◆ What business skills and experience do you have? Which ones do you lack?

◆ How easily can you transfer your existing skills and experience to other types of businesses? In what kinds of businesses would that transfer be easiest?

◆ How much risk are you willing to take?

◆ What size company do you want to buy?

Answering those and other questions *beforehand* will allow you to develop a list of criteria that a company must meet before you will consider it to be a purchase candidate.

DEVELOP A LIST OF CRITERIA

The next step is to develop a list of criteria that a potential business acquisition must meet. Looking at every company you find up for sale is a terrific waste of time. The goal is to identify the characteristics of the "ideal business" for you. Addressing these issues early in your search will save a great deal of time and trouble as you wade through a multitude of business opportunities. *For example, before Mitchell Mondry, a former electronics retailer, began searching for a business to purchase with his brother and his cousin, the three partners developed a set of criteria they used to narrow their search. To increase their chances for success, they wanted a business in which they could utilize their past business experience. "We wanted service- or retail-oriented businesses," says Mondry. "Those were things we have ex-*

perience and skills to manage. We don't know manufacturing or finance or high tech, and it's too steep a learning curve, too difficult and time-consuming to tackle. We wanted a business we could understand at first blush." Mondry and his partners also ruled out troubled companies in need of turning around.[7] Taking the time to develop these criteria gives a buyer specific parameters with which to begin her search for acquisition candidates.

PREPARE A LIST OF POTENTIAL CANDIDATES

Once you know what your goals are for acquiring a business, you can begin your search. One technique is to start at the macro level and work down. Drawing on the resources in the library, the World Wide Web, government publications, and industry trade associations and reports, buyers can discover which industries are growing fastest and offer the greatest potential in the future. For entrepreneurs with a well-defined idea of what they are looking for, another effective approach is to begin searching in an industry in which they have experience or one they understand well. *To narrow the field of businesses he and his partners would consider, Mitchell Mondy conducted extensive research on a variety of industries that met the criteria they had established. He discovered that many of the fastest-growing industries were in high-tech areas (something the group was not interested in), but his research also showed that the staffing industry was growing rapidly and had very bright projections. Focusing on the staffing industry, Mondy and his partners soon found four companies that met their purchase criteria. They purchased all four businesses and merged them into one. Their staffing company, Teamplayers, based in Birmingham, Michigan, generates $9 million in annual revenues.*[8]

Typical sources for identifying potential acquisition candidates include the following:

◆ Business brokers

◆ Bankers

◆ Accountants

◆ Investment bankers

◆ Industry contacts: suppliers, distributors, customers, and others

◆ Knocking on the doors of businesses you would like to buy (even if they're not advertised "for sale")

◆ Newspaper and trade journal listings of businesses for sale: e.g., the Business Opportunities section of the *Wall Street Journal*

◆ Trade associations

◆ The World Wide Web, where several sites include listings of companies for sale

◆ "Networking": social and business contact with friends and relatives

Buyers should consider every business that meets their criteria, even those that may not be listed for sale. Just because a business does not have a "for sale" sign in the window does not mean it is not for sale. In fact, the **hidden market** of companies that might be for sale but are not advertised as such is one of the richest sources of top-quality businesses. "About 85 percent of [purchase] opportunities are tucked away in the unadvertised hidden market," says one business broker.[9]

Finding the right business often takes months. Avoid the temptation to rush into a decision or to buy the first business that looks acceptable. Doing so usually results in buying the wrong business. Buying a business is one of the biggest transactions you will ever undertake in your life, and you should study the opportunity carefully to make sure that it is the best one for you.

INVESTIGATE AND EVALUATE CANDIDATE BUSINESSES AND DETERMINE THE VALUE OF THE BEST ONES

The next step is to investigate the candidates in more detail through a process known as due diligence. **Due diligence** involves studying, reviewing, and verifying all of the relevant information concerning your top acquisition candidates. The goal is to discover exactly what you will be buying and to avoid any unpleasant surprises after the deal is closed. Thoroughly exploring a company's character and condition through the Better Business Bureau, credit-reporting agencies, the company's banker, its vendors and suppliers, your accountant, your attorney, and other resources is a vital part of making sure you get a good deal on a business with the capacity to succeed. Other important questions to investigate include:

♦ What are the company's strengths? Weaknesses?

♦ What major threats is the company facing? Are there hidden threats you don't yet know about?

♦ Is the company profitable? What is its overall financial condition?

♦ What growth rate can you expect from the company in the near future?

♦ What is its cash flow cycle?

♦ Who are its major competitors?

♦ How large is the company's customer base? Is it growing or shrinking?

♦ Are the current employees suitable? Will they stay?

♦ Will the seller stay on as a consultant to help you make a smooth transition?

♦ What is the physical condition of the business, its equipment, and its inventory?

♦ What is the company's reputation in the community and among customers and vendors?

Determining the answers to these (and other questions addressed in this chapter) will make the task of valuing the business much easier.

Conducting a thorough analysis of a potential acquisition candidate usually requires an entrepreneur to assemble a team of advisers. Finding a suitable business, structuring a deal, and negotiating the final bargain involves many complex legal, financial, tax, and business issues, and good advice can be a valuable tool. Many entrepreneurs bring in an accountant, an attorney, an insurance agent, a banker, and a business broker to serve as consultants during the due-diligence process.

NEGOTIATE THE DEAL

Placing a value on an existing business represents a major hurdle for many would-be entrepreneurs. (We will discuss valuation techniques later in this chapter.) Once an entrepreneur has a realistic value for the business, the next challenge in making a successful purchase is negotiating a suitable deal. Although most buyers do not realize it, the price they pay for a company typically is not as crucial to its continued success as the terms on which they make the purchase. In other words, *the structure of the deal is more important than the actual price the seller agrees to pay*. Of course, wise business buyers will try to negotiate a reasonable price, but they are much more focused on negotiating favorable terms: how much cash they must pay out and when, how much of the price the seller is willing to finance and for how long, the interest rate at which the deal is financed, which liabilities they will assume, and other such terms. The buyer's primary concern should be to make sure that the deal does not endanger the company's financial future and that it preserves the company's cash flow.

Before purchasing Rational Technology Inc., Larry Hammons took the time to conduct a thorough evaluation of the company to make sure the fit was a good one. His due diligence paid off; the company's sales and profits have grown rapidly under Hammons's leadership.

After an extensive three-year search for the right company, Larry Hammons, with the help of a business broker, discovered Rational Technology Inc., a human resources staffing firm for computer engineers. Looking back at his experience in managing engineering project teams, Hammons knew that Rational Technology was a perfect fit. After his initial evaluation of the company turned up positive, Hammons signed a letter of intent to purchase it, assuming that the due-diligence process uncovered no serious problems. Hammons and his team of advisers spent weeks evaluating the company and its assets, studying its operations, and interviewing employees. The total cost of the entire process was $20,000, but Hammons considers the money well spent. Hammons then entered into serious negotiations with the seller; the two settled on a price of just over $1 million. Even though the price stretched Hammons's financial resources, he knew from his due diligence that Rational Technology was profitable and had several important "hidden resources." The deal was successful. Within three years after the purchase, Hammons had doubled the company's sales, and its profits were growing by more than 30 percent a year.[10]

EXPLORE FINANCING OPTIONS

Ideally, a buyer has already begun to explore the options available for financing the purchase. (Recall that many entrepreneurs include bankers on their teams of advisers.) Traditional lenders often shy away from deals involving the purchase of an existing business. Those that are willing to finance business purchases normally lend only a portion of the value of the assets, so buyers often find themselves searching for alternative sources of funds. Fortunately, most business buyers discover an important source of financing built into the deal: the seller. Typically, a deal is structured so that the buyer makes a down payment to the seller, who then finances a note for the balance. The buyer makes regular principal and interest payments over time, perhaps with a larger balloon payment at the end, until the note is paid off. In most business sales, the seller is willing to finance 40 percent to 70 percent of the purchase price over time, usually 3 to 10 years. The terms and conditions of such a loan are vital to both buyer and seller. They cannot be so burdensome that they threaten the company's continued existence; that is, the buyer must be able to make the payments to the seller out of the company's cash flow. Defining reasonable terms is the result of the negotiation process between the buyer and the seller.

ENSURE A SMOOTH TRANSITION

Once the parties have negotiated a deal, the challenge of making a smooth transition immediately arises. No matter how well planned the sale is, there are always surprises. For instance, the new owner may have ideas for changing the business—perhaps radically—that cause a great deal of stress and anxiety among employees and the previous owner. Charged with such emotion and uncertainty, the transition phase is always difficult and frustrating—and sometimes painful. To avoid a bumpy transition, a business buyer should do the following:

◆ Concentrate on communicating with employees. Business sales are fraught with uncertainty and anxiety, and employees need reassurance. Take the time to explain your plans for the company.

◆ Be honest with employees. Avoid telling them only what they want to hear.

◆ Listen to employees. They have intimate knowledge of the business and its strengths and weaknesses and usually can offer valuable suggestions. "Keep your door and your ears open," advises an entrepreneur with experience in purchasing an existing business. "Don't let people see you as a threat. Come in as somebody who's going to be good for the entire organization."[11]

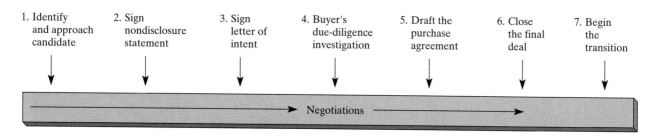

| 1. Identify and approach candidate | 2. Sign nondisclosure statement | 3. Sign letter of intent | 4. Buyer's due-diligence investigation | 5. Draft the purchase agreement | 6. Close the final deal | 7. Begin the transition |

Negotiations

Step 1: Approach the candidate company. If a business is advertised for sale, the proper approach is through the channel defined in the ad. Sometimes, buyers will contact business brokers to help them locate potential target companies. If you have targeted a company in the "hidden market," an introduction from a banker, accountant, or lawyer often is the best approach. During this phase, the seller checks out the buyer's qualifications, and the buyer begins to judge the quality of the company.

Step 2: Sign a nondisclosure document. If the buyer and the seller are satisfied with the results of their preliminary research, they are ready to begin serious negotiations. Throughout the negotiation process, the seller expects the buyer to maintain strict confidentiality of all of the records, documents, and information he receives during the investigation and negotiation process. The nondisclosure document is a legally binding contract that ensures the secrecy of the parties' negotiations.

Step 3: Sign a letter of intent. Before a buyer makes a legal offer to buy the company, he typically will ask the seller to sign a letter of intent. The letter of intent is a nonbinding document that says that the buyer and the seller have reached a sufficient "meeting of the minds" to justify the time and expense of negotiating a final agreement. The letter should state clearly that it is nonbinding, giving either party the right to walk away from the deal. It should also contain a clause calling for "good-faith negotiations" between the parties. A typical letter of intent addresses terms such as price, payment terms, categories of assets to be sold, and a deadline for closing the final deal. Typically, a letter of intent includes a "no-shop" clause. This clause states that the seller cannot use the deal that you are negotiating as leverage to raise the offer from other potential buyers for a given time frame, usually 90 days.

Step 4: Conduct buyer's due diligence. While negotiations are continuing, the buyer is busy studying the business and evaluating its strengths and weaknesses. In short, the buyer must do his homework to make sure that the business is a good value. He should obtain an independent valuation of the business and conduct a detailed review of all company records, employment agreements, leases, pending litigation, and even current or past compliance with federal, state, and local regulations.

Step 5: Draft the purchase agreement. The purchase agreement spells out the parties' final deal. It sets forth all of the details of the agreement and is the final product of the negotiation process. Typical purchase agreement provisions include:

- Definitions for terms in the agreement.
- Description of assets (including liabilities assumed) or stock to be sold, selling price, form of payment (e.g., cash, stock, property) and timing of payment.
- Purchase price.
- Special conditions that the parties must satisfy to close the deal.
- Allocation of purchase price to specific assets.
- Whether the purchaser assumes any liabilities, and, if so, which ones.
- Lease transfers and their terms.
- Warranties, representations, and agreements.
- A clause addressing bulk transfer provisions, if appropriate.
- Conduct of the business between the date of the purchase agreement and the closing date.
- Conditions necessary to close the deal.
- Provisions specifying procedures for resolving postclosing disputes and breaches of seller's warranties and representations.
- Covenants restricting competition (i.e., a noncompete clause).
- Miscellaneous matters regarding escrows, payment of broker commissions, and various legal and regulatory provisions.
- Time and place of closing.

Step 6: Close the final deal. Once the parties have drafted the purchase agreement, all that remains to make the deal "official" is the closing. Both buyer and seller sign the necessary documents to make the sale final. The buyer delivers the required money, and the seller turns the company over to the buyer.

Step 7: Begin the transition. For the buyer, the real challenge now begins: Making the transition to a successful business owner!

Figure 5.1 **The Steps in the Acquisition Process** SOURCE: Adapted from *The Buying and Selling a Company Handbook* (New York: Price Waterhouse, 1993), pp. 38–42; "Small Business Practices: How to . . . Buy a Business," Edgeonline, <http://www.edgeonline.com/main/bizbuilders/BIZ/Sm_business/buybus.shtml>; "Buying a Business," <http://www.ptbo.igs.net/~lbk/bab.htm>; Ronaleen R. Roha, "Don't Start It, Buy It," *Kiplinger's Personal Finance Magazine*, July 1997, pp. 74–78.

- Devote time to selling your vision for the company to its key stakeholders, including major customers, suppliers, bankers, and others.
- Consider asking the seller to serve as a consultant until the transition is complete. The previous owner can be a valuable resource.

Figure 5.1 illustrates the sequence of events leading up to a successful negotiation with a seller.

*E*valuating an Existing Business

3 Explain the process of evaluating an existing business.

The best protection entrepreneurs have against buying a business ill-suited for them is performing the due diligence on potential candidates. That requires time, effort, and the support of the advisory team described earlier. With his advisory team assembled, the potential buyer is ready to explore the business opportunity by examining five critical areas:

1. Why does the owner want to sell?
2. What is the physical condition of the business?
3. What is the potential for the company's products or services?
4. What legal aspects are important?
5. Is the business financially sound?

WHY DOES THE OWNER WANT TO SELL?

Every prospective business owner should investigate the *real* reason the business owner wants to sell. A recent study by the Geneva Corporation found that the most common reasons that owners of small and medium-sized businesses gave for selling were boredom and burnout.[12] Others decided to cash in their business investments and diversify into other types of assets.

Other less obvious reasons that a business owner might have for selling his venture include a major competitor's moving into the market, highway rerouting, frequent burglaries and robberies, expiring lease agreements, cash flow problems, and a declining customer base. Every prospective buyer should investigate *thoroughly* any reason the seller gives for selling the business.

Businesses do not last forever, and most owners know when the time has come to sell. Some owners think ethical behavior requires only not making false or misleading statements, but they may not disclose the whole story. In most business sales, the buyer bears the responsibility of determining whether the business is a good value. Visiting local business owners may reveal general patterns about the area and its overall vitality. The local chamber of commerce also may have useful information. Suppliers and competitors may be able to shed light on why the business is up for sale. By combining this information with an analysis of the company's financial records, a potential buyer should be able to develop a clear picture of the business and its real value.

WHAT IS THE PHYSICAL CONDITION OF THE BUSINESS?

A prospective buyer should evaluate the business's assets to determine their value. Are they reasonably priced? Are they obsolete? Will they need to be replaced soon? Do they operate efficiently? The potential buyer should check the condition of both the equipment and the building. It may be necessary to hire a professional to evaluate the major components of the building: its structure and its plumbing, electrical, and heating and cooling systems. Renova-

SECTION II BUILDING THE BUSINESS PLAN: BEGINNING CONSIDERATIONS

tions are rarely inexpensive or simple. Unexpected renovations can punch a gaping hole in a buyer's budget.

How fresh is the firm's inventory? Is it consistent with the image the new owner wants to project? How much of it would the buyer have to sell at a loss? A potential buyer may need to get an independent appraisal to determine the value of the firm's inventory and other assets because the current owner may have priced them far above their actual value. These items typically constitute the largest portion of a business's value, and a potential buyer should not accept the seller's asking price blindly. Remember: *Book value is not the same as market value*. Usually, a buyer can purchase equipment and fixtures at substantially lower prices than book value. Value is determined in the market, not on a balance sheet.

Other important factors that the potential buyer should investigate include the following.

Accounts Receivable. If the sale includes accounts receivable, the buyer should check their quality before purchasing them. How creditworthy are the accounts? What portion of them are past due? By aging the accounts receivable, the buyer can judge their quality and determine their value. (Refer to Table 5.1.)

Lease Arrangements. Is the lease included in the sale? When does it expire? What restrictions does it have on renovation or expansion? The buyer should determine *beforehand* what restrictions the landlord has placed on the lease and should negotiate any change before purchasing the business.

Business Records. Well-kept business records can be a valuable source of information and can tell a prospective buyer a lot about the company's pattern of success (or lack of it). Unfortunately, many business owners are sloppy record keepers. Consequently, the potential buyer and his team may have to reconstruct some critical records. It is important to verify as much information about the business as possible. For instance, does the owner have customer or mailing lists? These can be a valuable marketing tool for a new business owner.

Intangible Assets. Does the sale include any intangible assets such as trademarks, patents, copyrights, or goodwill? Determining the value of such intangibles is much more difficult than computing the value of the tangible assets, yet intangible assets can be one of the most valuable parts of a business acquisition.

Location and Appearance. The location and the overall appearance of the building are important. What had been an outstanding location in the past may be totally unacceptable today. Even if the building and equipment are in good condition and are fairly priced, the business may be located in a declining area. What kinds of businesses are in the area? Every buyer should consider the location's suitability several years into the future.

The potential buyer should also check local zoning laws to ensure that any changes he wants to make are legal. In some areas, zoning laws are very difficult to change and, as a result, can restrict the business's growth.

WHAT IS THE POTENTIAL FOR THE COMPANY'S PRODUCTS OR SERVICES?

No one wants to buy a business with a dying market. A thorough market analysis can lead to an accurate and realistic sales forecast. This research should tell a buyer whether he should consider a particular business and help define the trend in the business's sales and customer base.

Customer Characteristics and Composition. Before purchasing an existing business, a business owner should analyze both the existing and potential customers. Discovering why customers buy from the business and developing a profile of the entire customer base can

IN THE FOOTSTEPS OF AN ENTREPRENEUR

In Search of the Perfect Business: Part 1

*A*fter becoming a victim of corporate downsizing, Hendrix Neimann decided to buy an existing business rather than start one from scratch. At the time, his wife, Judi, was expecting their third child, and Neimann did not want to risk all of the family's personal assets or to commit to the time and emotional demands of a start-up company. He had no idea what kind of business he was looking for, but he believed he would know the right company when he found it. "When I started looking for a company," he says, "I decided that I'd be very clever and find one to buy *before* anyone knew it was on the market."

For months, Neimann found nothing, so he began calling business brokers. As the weeks slipped by and the end of his severance pay approached, Neimann became discouraged and nervous. "Is this what I should be doing?" he asked himself. Then he found a promising company through a blind ad in the *Wall Street Journal*: an access control and security company with sales of nearly $2 million whose owner was retiring. He met with the owner, Peter Klosky, and the broker, Lauren Finberg. In their initial meeting, Klosky told Neimann that there was nothing wrong with the company that a little salesmanship and marketing muscle wouldn't cure. He thought his employees would stay on if he asked them to, and he promised to tell Neimann everything he wanted to know.

On his first visit to Automatic Door Specialists (ADS), Neimann was shocked. "I had never seen such a dirty building," he recalls. "The walls were filthy, and inventory, files, and notebooks were stacked everywhere." His first thought: "This is a mistake." Still, the business intrigued him. The price was affordable, and Neimann's severance pay was about to run out.

Klosky sent Neimann a proposal showing how he could buy ADS with 100 percent financing, while keeping the debt service at manageable levels and taking out 75 percent of what his previous salary was. The deal appealed to Neimann, and he and Klosky signed a letter of intent, that, although not legally binding, indicated that they had a serious deal in the works.

The next step was for Neimann to meet with ADS employees. What they told him was unsettling: The company was going downhill *fast*. Neimann asked the employees if they thought he should go ahead with the deal. Their response: "Yes, but only if the price is rock-bottom." Neimann's accountant brought more bad news: ADS was losing money, and there were scads of bad accounts receivable on the books; nearly half were more than 90 days old. Also, the accountant told him, after paying the debts from the purchase, there would be *nothing* left for Neimann's salary! "I was despondent," says Neimann. "And furious. And scared."

Despite his reservations, Neimann went ahead with the purchase, but only after offering Klosky just 50 percent of the amount stated in the letter of intent. Klosky accepted the offer the next day. The final step was the actual closing, which was scheduled to occur three days after Neimann's severance pay ended. Neimann was astonished when Klosky and his attorney suddenly wanted to rewrite the entire deal at the closing. Both Neimann and Klosky came close to walking out, but seven hours—and more negotiations—later, they signed the deal. Hendrix Neimann had bought himself a business.

---

1. Critique the way in which Neimann went about buying Automatic Door Specialists.

2. Suppose that Neimann is a friend of yours and that he has come to you for advice about whether to purchase ADS. What will you tell him? Explain.

SOURCE: Adapted from Hendrix F. C. Neimann, "Buying a Business," *Inc.*, February 1990, pp. 28–38. ◆

help the buyer identify a company's strengths and weaknesses. The entrepreneur should determine the answers to the following questions:

◆ Who are my customers in terms of race, age, gender, and income level?

◆ What do the customers want the business to do for them? What needs are they satisfying?

◆ How often do customers buy? Do they buy in seasonal patterns?

◆ How loyal are present customers?

◆ Will it be practical to attract new customers? If so, will the new customers be significantly different from existing customers?

◆ Does the business have a well-defined customer base? Is it growing or shrinking? Do these customers come from a large geographic area, or do they all live near the business?

Analyzing the answers to those questions can help the potential owner implement a marketing plan. He will most likely try to keep the business attractive to existing customers but also change some features of its advertising plan to attract new customers.

Competitor Analysis. A potential buyer must identify the company's direct competition: the businesses in the immediate area that sell the same or similar products or services. The potential profitability and survival of the business may well depend on the behavior of these competitors.

In addition to analyzing direct competitors, the buyer should identify businesses that compete indirectly. For example, supermarkets and chain retail stores often carry a basic product line of automobile supplies (oil, spark plugs, and tune-up kits), competing with full-line auto parts stores. These chains often purchase bulk quantities at significant price reductions and do not incur the expense of carrying a full line of parts and supplies. As a result, they may be able to sell such basic products at lower prices. Even though these chains are not direct competitors, they may have a significant impact on local auto parts stores. Indirect competitors frequently limit their product lines to the most profitable segments of the market, and, by concentrating on high-volume or high-profit items, they can pose a serious threat to other businesses.

A potential buyer should also evaluate the trend in the competition. How many similar businesses have entered the market in the past five years? How many similar businesses have closed in the past five years? What caused these failures? Has the market already reached the saturation point? Being a late comer in an already saturated market is not the path to long-term success.

When evaluating the competitive environment, the prospective buyer should answer other questions:

◆ Which competitors have survived, and what characteristics have led to the success of each?

◆ How do the competitors' sales volumes compare with those of the business the entrepreneur is considering?

◆ What unique services do the competitors offer?

◆ How well organized and coordinated are the marketing efforts of competitors?

◆ What are the competitors' reputations?

◆ What are the strengths and weaknesses of the competitors?

◆ How can you gain market share in this competitive environment?

WHAT LEGAL ASPECTS ARE IMPORTANT?

Business buyers face myriad legal pitfalls. The most significant legal issues involve liens, bulk transfers, contract assignments, covenants not to compete, and ongoing legal liabilities.

Liens. The key legal issue in the sale of any asset is typically the proper transfer of good title from seller to buyer. However, because most business sales involve a collection of assorted assets, the transfer of a good title is complex. Some business assets may have **liens** (creditors' claims) against them, and unless those liens are satisfied before the sale, the buyer must assume them and become financially responsible for them. One way to reduce this potential problem is to include a clause in the sales contract stating that any liability not shown on the balance sheet at the time of sale remains the responsibility of the seller. A prospective buyer should have an attorney thoroughly investigate all of the assets for sale and their lien status before buying any business.

Bulk Transfers. A **bulk transfer** is a transaction in which a buyer purchases all or most of a business's inventory (as in a business sale). To protect against surprise claims from the seller's creditors after purchasing a business, the buyer should meet the requirements of a bulk transfer under Section 6 of the Uniform Commercial Code. Suppose that an owner owing many creditors sells his business to a buyer. The seller, however, does not use the proceeds of the sale to pay his debts to business creditors. Instead, he "skips town," leaving his creditors unpaid. Without the protection of a bulk transfer, those creditors could make claim (within six months) to the assets that the buyer purchased in order to satisfy the previous owner's debts.

To be effective, a bulk transfer must meet the following criteria:

◆ The seller must give the buyer a sworn list of existing creditors.

◆ The buyer and the seller must prepare a list of the property included in the sale.

◆ The buyer must keep the list of creditors and the list of property for six months.

◆ The buyer must give notice of the sale to each creditor at least 10 days before he takes possession of the goods or pays for them (whichever is first).

By meeting these criteria, a buyer acquires free and clear title to the assets purchased. Because Section 6 can create quite a burden on a business buyer, 16 states have repealed it, and more may follow. About half a dozen states have adopted a new, revised Section 6 that makes it easier for buyers to notify creditors. Under the revised Section 6, if a business has more than 200 creditors, the buyer may notify them by public notice rather than by contacting them individually.

Contract Assignments. A buyer must investigate the rights and the obligations he would assume under existing contracts with suppliers, customers, employees, lessors, and others. To continue the smooth operation of the business, the buyer must assume the rights of the seller under existing contracts. For example, the current owner may have four years left on a 10-year lease and so will need to assign this contract to the buyer. In general, the seller can assign any contractual right, unless the contract specifically prohibits the assignment or the contract is personal in nature. For instance, loan contracts sometimes prohibit assignments with **due-on-sale clauses.** These clauses require the buyer to pay the full amount of the remaining loan balance or to finance the balance at prevailing interest rates. Thus, the buyer cannot assume the seller's loan at a lower interest rate. Also, a seller usually cannot assign his credit arrangements with suppliers to the buyer because they are based on the seller's business reputation and are personal in nature. If such contracts are crucial to the business operation and cannot be assigned, the buyer must negotiate new contracts.

The prospective buyer also should evaluate the terms of any other contracts the seller has, including the following:

◆ Patent, trademark, or copyright registrations

◆ Exclusive agent or distributor contracts

◆ Real estate leases

◆ Insurance contracts

◆ Financing and loan arrangements

◆ Union contracts

Covenants Not to Compete. One of the most important and most often overlooked legal considerations for a prospective buyer is negotiating a **covenant not to compete** (or a **restrictive covenant**) with the seller. Under a restrictive covenant, the seller agrees not to open a new competing store within a specific time period and geographic area of the existing one. (The covenant should be negotiated with the owner, not the corporation, because if the corporation signs the agreement, the owner may not be bound.) However, the covenant must be a part of a business sale and must be reasonable in scope in order to be enforceable. Without such protection, a buyer may find his new business eroding beneath his feet. For example, Bob purchases a tire business from Alexandra, whose reputation in town for selling tires is unequaled. If Bob fails to negotiate a restrictive covenant, nothing can stop Alexandra from opening a new shop next to her old one and keeping all of her customers, thereby driving Bob out of business. A reasonable covenant in this case may restrict Alexandra from opening a tire store within a three-mile radius for three years. Every business buyer should negotiate a covenant not to compete with the seller.

Ongoing Legal Liabilities. Finally, the potential buyer must look for any potential legal liabilities the purchase might expose. These typically arise from three sources: (1) physical premises, (2) product liability claims, and (3) labor relations. First, the buyer must examine the physical premises for safety. Is the employees' health at risk because of asbestos or some other hazardous material? If a manufacturing environment is involved, does it meet Occupational Safety and Health Administration (OSHA) and other regulatory agency requirements?

Second, the buyer must consider whether the product contains defects that could result in **product liability lawsuits,** which claim that a company is liable for damages and injuries caused by the products or services it sells. Existing lawsuits might be an omen of more to follow. In addition, the buyer must explore products that the company has discontinued, for he might be liable for them if they prove to be defective. The final bargain between the parties should require the seller to guarantee that the company is not involved in any product liability lawsuits.

Third, what is the relationship between management and employees? Does a union represent employees in a collective bargaining agreement? The time to discover sour management–labor relations is before the purchase, not after.

The existence of such liabilities does not necessarily eliminate the business from consideration. Insurance coverage can shift such risks from the potential buyer, but the buyer should check to see whether the insurance covers lawsuits resulting from actions taken before the purchase. Despite conducting a thorough search, a buyer may purchase a business only to discover later the presence of hidden liabilities such as unpaid back taxes or delinquent bills, unpaid pension fund contributions, undisclosed lawsuits, or others. Including a clause in the purchase agreement that imposes the responsibility for such hidden liabilities on the seller can protect a buyer from unpleasant surprises after the sale.

IS THE BUSINESS FINANCIALLY SOUND?

The prospective buyer must analyze the financial records of the business to determine its health. He shouldn't be afraid to ask an accountant for help. Accounting systems and methods can vary tremendously from one type of business to another and can be quite confusing to a novice. Current profits can be inflated by changes in the accounting procedure or in the method for recording sales. For the buyer, the most dependable financial records are audited statements, those prepared by a certified public accountant in accordance with generally accepted accounting principles (GAAP). Any investment in a company should produce a reasonable salary for the owner and a healthy return on the money invested. Otherwise, it makes no sense to purchase the business.

A buyer also must remember that he is purchasing the future profit potential of an existing business. To evaluate the firm's profit potential, a buyer should review past sales, operating expenses, and profits as well as the assets used to generate those profits. He must compare current balance sheets and income statements with previous ones and then develop pro forma statements for the next two or three years. Sales tax records, income tax returns, and financial statements are valuable sources of information.

Are profits consistent over the years, or are they erratic? Is this pattern typical in the industry, or is it a result of unique circumstances or poor management? Can the business survive with such a serious fluctuation in revenues, costs, and profits? If these fluctuations are caused by poor management, can a new manager turn the business around? Some of the financial records that a potential buyer should examine include the following.

Income Statements and Balance Sheets for the Past Three to Five Years. It is important to review data from several years because creative accounting techniques can distort financial data in any single year. Even though buyers are purchasing the future profits of a business, they must remember that many businesses intentionally show low profits in order to minimize the owners' tax bills. Low profits should prompt a buyer to investigate their causes.

Income Tax Returns for the Past Three to Five Years. Comparing basic financial statements with tax returns can reveal discrepancies of which the buyer should be aware. Some small business owners "skim" from their businesses; that is, they take money from sales without reporting it as income. Owners who skim will claim their businesses are more profitable than their tax returns show. However, buyers should not pay for "phantom profits."

Owner's Compensation (and That of Relatives). The owner's compensation is especially important in small companies; and the smaller the company is, the more important it will be. Although many companies do not pay their owners what they are worth, others compensate their owners lavishly. Buyers must consider the impact of fringe benefits—company cars, insurance contracts, country club memberships, and the like. It is important to adjust the company's income statements for the salary and fringe benefits that the seller has paid himself and others.

Cash Flow. Most buyers understand the importance of evaluating a company's profit history, but few recognize the need to analyze its cash flow. They assume that if profits are adequate, there will be sufficient cash to pay all of the bills and to fund an adequate salary for themselves. *That is not necessarily the case!* Before closing any deal, a buyer should sit down with an accountant and convert the target company's financial statements into a cash flow forecast. This forecast must take into account not only existing debts and obligations but also any modifications or additional debts the buyer plans to make in the business. It should reflect the repayment of financing the buyer arranges to purchase the company. The telling question is: Can the company generate sufficient cash to be self-supporting? How much cash will it generate for the buyer?

A potential buyer must look for suspicious deviations from the average (in either direction) for sales, expenses, profits, assets, and liabilities. Have sales been increasing or decreasing? Is the equipment really as valuable as it is listed on the balance sheet? Is advertising expense unusually high? How is depreciation reflected in the financial statements?

This financial information gives the buyer the opportunity to verify the seller's claims about the business's performance. Sometimes, however, an owner will take short-term actions that produce a healthy financial statement but weaken the firm's long-term health and profit potential. For example, a seller might lower costs by gradually eliminating equipment maintenance or might boost sales by selling to marginal businesses that will never pay their bills. Such techniques can artificially inflate assets and profits, but a well-prepared buyer should be able to see through them.

Table 5.2 The Records a Business Buyer Should Review before Committing to a Deal

1. Balance sheets and income statements from the previous three to five years
2. Income tax returns for the previous three to five years
3. Cash flow analysis and forecasts
4. Records of accounts receivable (preferably aged)
5. Records of accounts payable
6. Loan agreements with banks and other lenders
7. Existing contracts with major suppliers and customers
8. Contracts or leases on real estate
9. Repair and maintenance records on equipment, machinery, and fixtures
10. Insurance policies, including workers' compensation coverage
11. Documentation on existing patents, trademarks, or copyrights
12. Individual employees' labor contracts or union (collective bargaining) contracts
13. Copies of business licenses
14. Articles of incorporation (if incorporated) or articles of organization and operating agreement (if a limited liability company)
15. Details of any lawsuits the company is currently involved in

SOURCE: Adapted from Joseph Anthony, "Maybe You Should Buy a Business," *Kiplinger's Personal Finance Magazine*, May 1993, p. 84.

Finally, a potential buyer should always be wary of purchasing a business if the present owner refuses to disclose his financial records.

Table 5.2 lists the records that a potential buyer should review before making a final decision about buying a business.

*M*ethods for Determining the Value of a Business

4 Describe the various ways of determining the value of a business.

Business valuation is partly an art and partly a science. What makes establishing a reasonable price for a privately owned business so difficult is the wide variety of factors that influence its value: the nature of the business itself, its position in the market or industry, the outlook for the market or industry, the company's financial status and stability, its earning capacity, any intangible assets it may own (e.g., patents, trademarks, and copyrights), the value of other similar companies that are publicly owned, and many other factors.

Computing the value of the company's tangible assets normally poses no major problem, but assigning a price to the intangibles, such as goodwill, almost always creates controversy. The seller expects goodwill to reflect the hard work and long hours invested in building the business. The buyer, however, is willing to pay extra only for those intangible assets that produce exceptional income. So how can the buyer and the seller arrive at a fair price? There are few hard-and-fast rules in establishing the value of a business, but the following guidelines can help.

◆ There is no single best method for determining a business's worth, because each business sale is unique. The wisest approach is to compute a company's value using several techniques and then to choose the one that makes the most sense.

◆ The deal must be financially feasible for both parties. The seller must be satisfied with the price received for the business, but the buyer cannot pay an excessively high price that would require heavy borrowing and would strain her cash flows from the outset.

◆ Both the buyer and the seller should have access to the business records.

- Valuations should be based on facts, not fiction.

- No surprise is the best surprise. The two parties should deal with one another honestly and in good faith.[13]

The main reason that buyers purchase existing businesses is to get their future earnings potential. The second most common reason is to obtain an established asset base. It is often much easier to buy assets than to build them. Although evaluation methods should take these characteristics into consideration, too many business sellers and buyers depend on rules of thumb that ignore the unique features of many small companies. For example, one rule of thumb says that a typical pizza restaurant is worth 30 to 40 percent of its gross sales; another claims that a motel is worth 4.5 times its annual revenues.[14] Often, these rules of thumb are based on multiples of a company's earnings and vary from industry to industry. A recent study of small business sales across the country conducted by Bizcomps found that average sales price was 2.7 times a company's earnings.[15] The problem is that such "one-size-fits-all" approaches seldom work because no two companies are alike. The best rule of thumb to use when valuing businesses is "Don't use rules of thumb to value businesses."

IN THE FOOTSTEPS OF AN ENTREPRENEUR

In Search of the Perfect Business: Part 2

*T*wo years after purchasing Automatic Door Specialists (ADS), Hendrix Neimann was well aware of the dark side of buying a business. "Never, but never, had an owner known so little about his business," he says, "or been so totally at the mercy of his employees. What's more, I barely even knew what business we were in. I had always thought we were in the security/access control industry. It turned out we were a subset of the construction industry. I had never had any desire to be in construction or anything remotely resembling construction," he says.

Neimann discovered that a substantial portion of ADS sales came from government contracts, where the lowest bidder got the job. Under Neimann, however, ADS was focusing on quality product lines and full installation and service practices. Unfortunately, Neimann also discovered that potential customers saw ADS's products as commodities and made their purchase decisions on the basis of price, not quality and service. "I couldn't, or wouldn't, do business that way," says Neimann. As government jobs became more scarce, competition became more intense. Sales slumped, and ADS lost $53,000 in Neimann's first year.

Neimann's attempts to change the company's culture met with no more success than did his marketing strategies. He tried all of the latest management philosophies, but they never seemed to work. "The staff nodded, smiled, asked a few ques-

tions—and then proceeded to ignore everything I had said and go about their business," he says. Several long-time employees decided to leave what they saw as a sinking ship.

As in many small companies, cash flow was a constant problem. On two occasions, Neimann barely made payroll—with $37 to spare one week and $95 the other. "We just couldn't seem to develop any momentum," Neimann says. Slipping into panic, he took virtually all decision-making authority away from his workers, further alienating them. Paying creditors soon became a problem, and Neimann was forced to juggle the company's bills. Unpaid telephone bills, vendor invoices, even the payments to former owner Peter Klosky were piling up.

Looking back on his purchase of ADS, Neimann says, "Before I bought the business, I never really, truly assembled enough information to tell if I was actually going to like what I was doing. I got so caught up in the details of negotiating the deal and in checking out all the facts that I didn't take enough time to figure out if I'd be happy. It took a year for me to admit that I didn't like the industry I had joined or what I had to do to be successful in it." Neimann felt trapped. "Here I was," he says, "not having any fun, in fact hating a lot of what I was doing, with every personal asset on the line, and unable to get out. That's as trapped as you get."

1. Review the sections in this chapter entitled "How to Buy a Business" and "In Search of the Perfect Business: Part 1." Which steps did Neimann violate?

2. What could Neimann have done to avoid the problems at ADS?

3. What is your forecast for ADS and Hendrix's future?

Source: Adapted from Hendrix F. C. Neimann, "How to Buy a Business," *Inc.*, October 1991, pp. 38–46. ◆

This section describes three basic techniques—the balance sheet method, the earnings approach, and the market approach—and several variations on them for determining the value of a hypothetical business, Lewis Electronics.

BALANCE SHEET METHOD: NET WORTH = ASSETS − LIABILITIES

Balance Sheet Technique. The **balance sheet technique** is one of the most commonly used methods of evaluating a business, although it is not highly recommended because it oversimplifies the valuation process. This method computes the book value of company's net worth, or **owner's equity** (net worth = assets − liabilities) and uses this figure as the value. The problem with this technique is that it fails to recognize reality: Most small businesses have market values that exceed their reported book values.

The first step is to determine which assets are included in the sale. In most cases, the owner has some personal assets that he does not want to sell. Professional business brokers can help the buyer and the seller arrive at a reasonable value for the collection of assets included in the deal. Remember that net worth on a financial statement will likely differ significantly from actual net worth in the market. Figure 5.2 shows the balance sheet for Lewis Electronics. Based on this balance sheet, the company's net worth is $266,091 − $114,325 = $151,766.

Variation: Adjusted Balance Sheet Technique. A more realistic method for determining a company's value is to adjust the book value of net worth to reflect the actual market value. The values reported on a company's books may either overstate or understate the true value of assets and liabilities. Typical assets in a business sale include notes and accounts receivable, inventories, supplies, and fixtures. If a buyer purchases notes and accounts receivable, he should estimate the likelihood of their collection and adjust their value accordingly (refer to Table 5.1).

In manufacturing, wholesale, and retail businesses, inventory is usually the largest single asset in the sale. Taking a physical inventory count is the best way to determine accurately the quantity of goods to be transferred. The sale may include three types of inventory, each having its own method of valuation: raw materials, work-in-process, and finished goods.

The buyer and the seller must arrive at a method for evaluating the inventory. First-in–first-out (FIFO), last-in–first-out (LIFO), and average costing are three frequently used techniques, but the most common methods use the cost of last purchase and the replacement value of the inventory. Before accepting any inventory value, the buyer should evaluate the condition of the goods. *One young couple purchased a lumber yard without sufficiently examining the inventory. After completing the sale, they discovered that most of the lumber in a warehouse they had neglected to inspect was warped and was of little value as building material. The bargain price they paid for the business turned out not to be the good deal they had expected.*

To avoid such problems, some buyers insist on having a knowledgeable representative on an inventory team to count the inventory and check its condition. Nearly every sale involves merchandise that cannot be sold, but by taking this precaution, a buyer minimizes the chance of being stuck with worthless inventory. Fixed assets transferred in a sale might include land, buildings, equipment, and fixtures. Business owners frequently carry real estate and buildings on their books at prices well below their actual market value. Equipment and fixtures, depending on their condition and usefulness, may increase or decrease the true value of the business. Appraisals of these assets on insurance policies are helpful guidelines for establishing market value. Also, business brokers can be useful in determining the current value of fixed assets. Some brokers use an estimate of what it would cost to replace a

Figure 5.2 Balance Sheet for Lewis Electronics, June 30, 199X

Assets

Current Assets

Cash	$11,655	
Accounts receivable	15,876	
Inventory	56,523	
Supplies	8,574	
Prepaid insurance	5,587	
Total current assets		$98,215

Fixed Assets

Land		$24,000	
Buildings	$141,000		
less accumulated depreciation	51,500	89,500	
Office equipment	$ 12,760		
less accumulated depreciation	7,159	5,601	
Factory equipment	$ 59,085		
less accumulated depreciation	27,850	31,235	
Trucks and autos	$ 28,730		
less accumulated depreciation	11,190	17,540	
Total fixed assets			$167,876
Total Assets			$266,091

Liabilities

Current Liabilities

Accounts payable	$19,497	
Mortgage payable (current portion)	5,215	
Salaries payable	3,671	
Not payable	10,000	
Total current liabilities		$38,383

Long-Term Liabilities

Mortgage payable	$54,542	
Note payable	21,400	
Total long-term liabilities		$ 75,942
Total Liabilities		$114,325

Owner's Equity

Owner's Equity (net worth)	$151,766
Total Liabilities + Owner's Equity	$266,091

company's physical assets (less a reasonable allowance for depreciation) to determine value. For Lewis Electronics, the adjusted net worth is $274,638 − $114,325 = $160,313 (see the adjusted balance sheet in Figure 5.3), indicating that some of the entries on its books did not accurately reflect market value.

Business evaluations based on balance sheet methods suffer one major drawback: They do not consider the future earnings potential of the business. These techniques value assets at current prices and do not consider them as tools for creating future profits. The next method for computing the value of a business is based on its expected future earnings.

EARNINGS APPROACH

The buyer of an existing business is essentially purchasing its future income. The **earnings approach** is more refined than the balance sheet method because it considers the future income potential of the business.

Variation 1: Excess Earnings Method. This method combines both the value of the firm's existing assets (over its liabilities) and an estimate of its future earnings potential to determine a business's selling price. One advantage of the **excess earnings method** is that it offers an estimate of goodwill. Goodwill is an intangible asset that often creates problems in a business sale. In fact, the most common method of valuing a business is to compute its tangible net worth and then to add an often arbitrary adjustment for goodwill. In essence, goodwill is the difference between an established, successful business and one that has yet to prove itself. It is based on the company's reputation and its ability to attract customers. A buyer should not accept blindly the seller's arbitrary adjustment for goodwill because it is likely to be inflated.

The excess earnings method provides a fairly consistent and realistic approach for determining the value of goodwill. It measures goodwill by the amount of profit the business earns above that of the average firm in the same industry. It also assumes that the owner is entitled to a reasonable return on the firm's adjusted tangible net worth.

Step 1: Compute Adjusted Tangible Net Worth. Using the previous method of valuation, the buyer should compute the firm's adjusted tangible net worth. Total tangible assets (adjusted for market value) minus total liabilities yields adjusted tangible net worth. In the Lewis Electronics example, adjusted tangible net worth is $274,638 − $114,325 = $160,313 (refer to Figure 5.3).

Step 2: Calculate the Opportunity Costs of Investing in the Business. **Opportunity costs** represent the cost of forgoing a choice. If the buyer chooses to purchase the assets of a business, he cannot invest his money elsewhere. Therefore, the opportunity cost of the purchase would be the amount that the buyer could have earned by investing the same amount in a similar risk investment.

There are three components in the rate of return used to value a business: (1) the basic, risk-free return, (2) an inflation premium, and (3) the risk allowance for investing in the particular business. The basic, risk-free return and the inflation premium are reflected in investments such as U.S. Treasury bonds. To determine the appropriate rate of return for investing in a business, the buyer must add to this base rate a factor reflecting the risk of purchasing the company. The greater the risk is, the higher the rate of return will be. A normal-risk business typically indicates a 25 percent rate of return. In the Lewis Electronics example, the opportunity cost of the investment is $160,313 × 25% − $40,078.

The second part of the buyer's opportunity cost is the salary that she could have earned working for someone else. For the Lewis Electronics example, if the buyer purchases the business, she must forgo the $25,000 that she could have earned working elsewhere. Adding these amounts yields a total opportunity cost of $65,078.

Figure 5.3 Balance Sheet for Lewis Electronics Adjusted to Reflect Market Value, June 30, 199X

Assets

Current Assets

Cash	$11,655	
Accounts receivable	10,051	
Inventory	39,261	
Supplies	7,492	
Prepaid insurance	5,587	
Total current assets		$74,046

Fixed Assets

Land		$36,900	
Buildings	$177,000		
less accumulated depreciation	51,500	125,500	
Office equipment	$ 11,645		
less accumulated depreciation	7,159	4,486	
Factory equipment	$ 50,196		
less accumulated depreciation	27,850	22,346	
Trucks and autos	$ 22,550		
less accumulated depreciation	11,190	11,360	
Total fixed assets			$200,592
Total Assets			$274,638

Liabilities

Current Liabilities

Accounts payable	$19,497	
Mortgage payable (current portion)	5,215	
Salaries payable	3,671	
Note payable	10,000	
Total current liabilities		$38,383

Long-Term Liabilities

Mortgage payable	$54,542	
Note payable	21,400	
Total long-term liabilities		$ 75,942
Total Liabilities		$114,325

Owner's Equity

Owner's Equity (adjusted net worth)	$160,313
Total Liabilities + Owner's Equity	$274,638

Step 3: Project Net Earnings. The buyer must estimate the company's net earnings for the upcoming year before subtracting the owner's salary. Averages can be misleading, so the buyer must be sure to investigate the trend of net earnings. Have they risen steadily over the past five years, dropped significantly, remained relatively constant, or fluctuated wildly? Past income statements provide useful guidelines for estimating earnings. In the Lewis Electronics example, the buyer and an accountant project net earnings to be $74,000.

Step 4: Compute Extra Earning Power. A company's extra earning power is the difference between forecasted earnings (step 3) and total opportunity costs (step 2). Many small businesses that are for sale do not have extra earning power (i.e., excess earnings) and they show marginal or no profits. The extra earning power of Lewis Electronics is $74,000 − $65,078 = $8,922.

Step 5: Estimate the Value of Intangibles. The owner can use the business's extra earning power to estimate the value of its intangible assets: that is, its goodwill. Multiplying the extra earning power by a years-of-profit figure yields an estimate of the intangible assets' value. The years-of-profit figure for a normal-risk business ranges from three to four. A very high-risk business may have a years-of-profit figure of one, whereas a well-established firm might use a figure of seven. For Lewis Electronics, the value of intangibles (assuming normal risk) would be $8,922 × 3 = $26,766.

Step 6: Determine the Value of the Business. To determine the value of the business, the buyer simply adds together the adjusted tangible net worth (step 1) and the value of the intangibles (step 5). Using this method, the value of Lewis Electronics is $160,313 + $26,766 = $187,079.

Both the buyer and seller should consider the tax implications of transferring goodwill. The amount that the seller receives for goodwill is taxed as ordinary income. The buyer cannot count this amount as a deduction because goodwill is a capital asset that cannot be depreciated or amortized for tax purposes. Instead, the buyer would be better off paying the seller for signing a covenant not to compete because its value is fully tax deductible. The success of this approach depends on the accuracy of the buyer's estimates of net earnings and risk, but it does offer a systematic method for assigning a value to goodwill.

Variation 2: Capitalized Earnings Approach. Another earnings approach capitalizes expected net profits to determine the value of a business. The buyer should prepare his own pro forma income statement and should ask the seller to prepare one also. Many appraisers use a five-year weighted average of past sales (with the greatest weights assigned to the most recent years) to estimate sales for the upcoming year.

Once again, the buyer must evaluate the risk of purchasing the business to determine the appropriate rate of return on the investment. The greater the perceived risk, the higher the return the buyer will require. Risk determination is always somewhat subjective, but it is necessary for proper evaluation.

The **capitalized earnings approach** divides estimated net earnings (after subtracting the owner's reasonable salary) by the rate of return that reflects the risk level. For Lewis Electronics, the capitalized value (assuming a reasonable salary of $25,000) is:

$$\frac{\text{Net earnings (after deducting owner's salary)}}{\text{Rate of return}} = \frac{\$74,000 - \$25,000}{25\%} = \$196,000$$

Clearly, firms with lower risk factors are more valuable (a 10 percent rate of return would have yielded a value of $499,000) than are those with higher risk factors (a 50 percent rate of return would have yielded a value of $99,800). Most normal-risk businesses use a rate-of-return factor ranging from 25 to 33 percent. The lowest risk factor that most buyers would accept for any business ranges from 15 to 20 percent.

Variation 3: Discounted Future Earnings Approach. This variation of the earnings approach assumes that a dollar earned in the future will be worth less than that same dollar today. Therefore, using the **discounted future earnings approach,** the buyer estimates the company's net income for several years into the future and then discounts these future earnings back to their present value. The resulting present value is an estimate of the company's worth.

The reduced value of future dollars has nothing to do with inflation. Instead, present value represents the cost of the buyers' giving up the opportunity to earn a reasonable rate of return by receiving income in the future instead of today. To visualize the importance of the time value of money, consider two $1 million sweepstakes winners. Rob wins $1 million in a sweepstakes, and he receives it in $50,000 installments over 20 years. If Rob invests every installment at 15 percent interest, he will have accumulated $5,890,505.98 at the end of 20 years. Lisa wins $1 million in another sweepstakes, but she collects her winnings in one lump sum. If Lisa invests her $1 million today at 15 percent, she will have accumulated $16,366,537.39 at the end of 20 years. The difference in their wealth is the result of the time value of money.

The discounted future earnings approach has five steps:

Step 1: Project Earnings for Five Years into the Future. One way is to assume that earnings will grow by a constant amount over the next five years. Perhaps a better method is to develop three forecasts—an optimistic, a pessimistic, and a most likely—for each year and then find a weighted average using the following formula:

$$\text{Forecasted earnings for year } i = \frac{\text{Optimistic earnings for year } i + (\text{Most likely earnings for year } i \times 4) + \text{Pessimistic earnings for year } i}{6}$$

For Lewis Electronics, the buyer's forecasts are:

Year	Pessimistic	Most Likely	Optimistic	Weighted Average
XXX1	$65,000	$ 74,000	$ 92,000	$ 75,500
XXX2	74,000	90,000	101,000	89,167
XXX3	82,000	100,000	112,000	99,000
XXX4	88,000	109,000	120,000	107,333
XXX5	88,000	115,000	122,000	111,667

The buyer must remember that the further into the future he forecasts, the less reliable the estimates will be.

Step 2: Discount These Future Earnings Using the Appropriate Present Value Factor. The appropriate present value factor can be found by looking in published present value tables, by using modern calculators or computers, or by solving the equation $1/(1 + k)^t$, where $k =$ rate of return and $t =$ time (year 1, 2, 3, . . ., n). The rate that the buyer selects should reflect the rate he could earn on a similar risk investment. Because Lewis Electronics is a normal-risk business, the buyer chooses 25 percent.

Year	Income Forecast (Weighted Average)	Present Value Factor (at 25 percent)	Net Present Value
XXX1	$75,500	0.8000	$60,400
XXX2	$89,167	0.6400	57,067
XXX3	$99,000	0.5120	50,688
XXX4	$107,333	0.4096	43,964
XXX5	$111,667	0.3277	36,593
Total			$248,712

Step 3: Estimate the Income Stream beyond Five Years. One technique suggests multiplying the fifth-year income by 1/(rate of return). For Lewis Electronics, the estimate is:

$$\text{Income beyond year 5} = \$111,667 \times \frac{1}{25\%} = \$446,668$$

Step 4: Discount the Income Estimate beyond Five Years Using the Present Value Factor for the Sixth Year. For Lewis Electronics:

$$\text{Present value of income beyond year 5} = \$446,668 \times 0.2622 = \$117,116$$

Step 5: Compute the Total Value of the Business.

$$\text{Total value} = \$248,712 + \$117,116 = \$365,828$$

The primary advantage of this technique is that it evaluates a business solely on the basis of its future earnings potential, but its reliability depends on making forecasts of future earnings and on choosing a realistic present value factor. The discounted future earnings approach is especially well-suited for valuing service businesses (whose asset bases are often small) and for companies experiencing high growth rates.

MARKET APPROACH

The **market** (or **price/earnings**) **approach** uses the price/earnings ratios of similar businesses to establish the value of a company. The buyer must use businesses whose stocks are publicly traded in order to get a meaningful comparison. A company's **price/earnings ratio** (or **P/E ratio**) is the price of one share of its common stock in the market divided by its earnings per share (after deducting preferred stock dividends). To get a representative P/E ratio, the buyer should average the P/Es of as many similar businesses as possible.

To compute the company's value, the buyer multiplies the average price/earnings ratio by the private company's estimated earnings. For example, suppose that the buyer found four companies comparable to Lewis Electronics but whose stock is publicly traded. Their price/earnings ratios are:

Company 1	3.3
Company 2	3.8
Company 3	4.7
Company 4	4.1
Average	3.975

Using this average P/E ratio produces a value of $294,150:

$$\text{Value} = \text{Average P/E ratio} \times \text{Estimated net earnings}$$
$$= 3.975 \times \$74,000 = \$294,150$$

The biggest advantage of the market approach is its simplicity. But this method does have several disadvantages, including the following:

Necessary comparisons between publicly traded and privately owned companies. The stock of privately owned companies is illiquid, and, therefore, the P/E ratio used is often subjective and lower than that of publicly held companies.

Unrepresentative earnings estimates. The private company's net earnings may not realistically reflect its true earnings potential. To minimize taxes, owners usually attempt to keep profits low and rely on fringe benefits to make up the difference.

Finding similar companies for comparison. Often, it is extremely difficult for a buyer to find comparable publicly held companies when estimating the appropriate P/E ratio.

Applying the after-tax earnings of a private company to determine its value. If a prospective buyer is using an after-tax P/E ratio from a public company, he also must use the after-tax earnings from the private company.[16]

Despite its drawbacks, the market approach is useful as a general guideline to establishing a company's value.

THE BEST METHOD

Which of these methods is best for determining the value of a small business? Simply stated, there is no single best method. These techniques will yield a range of values. Buyers should look for values that might cluster together and then use their best judgment to determine their offering price.

$\mathcal{U}$nderstanding the Seller's Side

◆5 Understand the seller's side of the buyout decision and how to structure the deal.

Few events are more anticipated—and emotional—than selling your business. For many entrepreneurs, it has produced vast personal wealth and a completely new lifestyle, and in turn, freedom and the opportunity to catch up on all the things the owners missed out on while building the business. Yet, many entrepreneurs who sell out experience a tremendous void in their lives. After they sell, they discover that their businesses were not only the focal point of their lives for many years but also an essential element in their identities. Letting go is not easy, and putting a price on what they have worked most of their lives to build is even more difficult. "The owner of a business—especially if he built it up himself—*always, always, always* thinks it's worth more than it is," says one business valuation specialist.[17]

PICK THE RIGHT TIME

Selling a business is no simple task. Done properly, it takes time, patience, and preparation to locate a suitable buyer, strike a deal, and make the transition. Too often, business owners put off the selling process until the last minute: at retirement age or when a business crisis looms. Such a "fire sale" approach rarely yields the maximum price for a business. Advance planning and maintaining accurate financial records are keys to a successful sale.

Before selling a business, an entrepreneur must address some important questions: Do I want to walk away from the business completely, or do I plan to stay on after the sale? If I

WIRED TO THE WEB

PLANNING FOR A PURCHASE

*T*ony Kurtz and Randa Alexander wanted to purchase the Bettendorf, Iowa, branch of the wholesale heating, air-conditioning, and refrigeration supply chain where Kurtz had worked for the past 11 years. Although the branch was currently losing money, Kurtz and Alexander had confidence that they could turn the business around. Besides, said Alexander, "It would take a lot more money to start a new place."

When the entrepreneurs approached the owner about buying the business and got a positive response, they immediately jumped into action. They attended a seminar sponsored by the Small Business Association's Service Corps of Retired Executives program on how to write a business plan. As they developed their plan, Kurtz and Alexander assembled a team of professionals, including attorneys and accountants, to help them with the transaction.

Kurtz and Alexander signed a letter of intent and began analyzing the company's records and market potential as part of their due diligence. The biggest obstacle occurred when the owner revealed his asking price of $350,000, about *twice* what the pair was hoping to pay. Believing that the owner's asking price was negotiable, Kurtz and Alexander began looking at their financing options. Between the two of them, they could come up with almost $58,000 in cash. Alexander suggested that they apply for a Small Business Administration loan guarantee, and Kurtz thought that the present owner might be willing to finance part of the sale by accepting a note for part of the purchase price. "What we *don't* want to do is get the business into too much debt at the outset," said Kurtz. "We have to make sure that the company's cash flow will be sufficient to repay the loans we'll need to make the purchase and to keep the business operating smoothly."

"Let's take the initiative," said Alexander. "We should make him a counteroffer that we think is realistic and that establishes terms that are fair to him and practical for us."

1. Use the resources on the World Wide Web to assemble a plan for Kurtz and Alexander as they prepare to purchase this business. What specific pitfalls should they watch for?
2. Search the World Wide Web for negotiating tips that will help Kurtz and Alexander as they work to strike a bargain with the current owner.
3. How should Kurtz and Alexander go about determining the value of the business?

SOURCE: Adapted from Ronaleen R. Roha, "They Got a Cool Price and Creative Financing," *Kiplinger's Personal Finance Magazine*, July 1997, p. 6.

decide to stay on, how involved do I want to be in running the company? How much can I realistically expect to get for the business? Is this amount of money sufficient to maintain my desired lifestyle? Rather than sell the business to an outsider, should I be transferring ownership to my children or to my employees? Who are the professionals (business brokers, accountants, attorneys, tax advisers, and others) I will need to help me close the sale successfully? How do I expect the buyer to pay for the company? Am I willing to finance at least part of the purchase price? If so, on what terms?[18]

One hundred eighty years after James Hart Stark had first grafted shoots onto crab apple seedlings, his company, Stark Brothers Nurseries, had grown into a $10 million-plus business. Stark's descendants, John Logan and his sons Clay and Walter, were running the closely

Walter and Clay Logan, descendants of the founder of Stark Brothers Nurseries, recognized the opportunity to accelerate their company's growth by selling it to one of their largest customers, Foster & Gallagher.

held nursery business when a customer offered to buy the business. Foster & Gallagher Inc., a $220-million business, owned 18 direct-marketing horticultural and gift companies, was growing rapidly, and had become one of Stark Brothers' largest accounts. Having seen their company's nursery stock barely survive the terrible floods along the Mississippi River in 1993, the Logans considered Foster & Gallagher's offer, although they originally had had no intentions of selling the business. They hired an investment adviser and soon signed a letter of intent. Within three months, they had closed the deal, which offered many benefits for the company, its stockholders, and its employees. Not only did the two companies mesh well, but their management teams already knew one another and had trust and confidence in one another. Less than two years after the sale, Stark Brothers has boosted sales, hired 50 new workers, and sees a bright future. Looking back on the sale, Clay Logan advises, "Be ready to sell when the right moment—and the right offer—arrives."[19]

PLOT AN EXIT STRATEGY AND STRUCTURE THE DEAL

Once a business owner decides to sell the business, the focus shifts to structuring the most beneficial deal. Next to picking the right buyer, planning the structure of the deal is the most important decision a seller can make. Entrepreneurs who sell their companies without considering the tax implications of the deal can wind up paying as much as 70 percent of the proceeds in the form of capital gains and other taxes![20] A skilled tax adviser or financial planner can help business sellers legally minimize the bite various taxes take out of the proceeds of a sale.

Straight Business Sale. A straight business sale may be best for entrepreneurs who want to step down and turn over the reins of the company to someone else. A recent study of small business sales in 60 categories found that 94 percent were asset sales; the remaining 6 percent involved the sale of stock. About 22 percent were for cash, and 75 percent included a down payment with a note carried by the seller. The remaining 3 percent relied on a note from the seller with no down payment. When the deal included a down payment, it averaged 33 percent of the purchase price. Only 40 percent of the business sales studied included covenants not to compete.[21]

Although selling a business outright is often the safest exit path for an entrepreneur, it is usually the most expensive one. Sellers who want cash and take the money up front face an oppressive tax burden. They must pay a capital gains tax on the sale price less their investments in the company. Nor is a straight sale an attractive exit strategy for those who want to stay on with the company or for those who want to surrender control of the company gradually rather than all at once.

Form a Family Limited Partnership. Entrepreneurs who want to pass their businesses on to their children should consider forming a family limited partnership. Using this exit strategy, an entrepreneur can transfer her business to her children without sacrificing control over it. The owner takes the role of general partner while her children become limited partners. The general partner keeps just 1 percent of the company, but the partnership agreement gives her total control over the business. The children own 99 percent of the company but have little or no say over how to run the business. Until the founder decides to step down and turn the reins of the company over to the next generation, she continues to run the business and sets up significant tax savings for the ultimate transfer of power.

Sell Controlling Interest. Sometimes, business owners sell the majority interest in their companies to investors, competitors, suppliers, or large companies with an agreement that they will stay on after the sale. *For example, Leon and Pam Seidman sold 55 percent of Cosmic Pet Products, a catnip business Leon had started while in college, to Four Paws Pet Products, a much larger company. Four Paws gives the Seidmans the autonomy to run the business as they did before the sale, although the Seidmans do work with Four Paws on strategic planning and pricing issues. For both the Seidmans and Four Paws, the sale has produced positive outcomes. The Seidmans still get to run the day-to-day operations of the business they love without having to worry about the financial struggles of keeping a small company going. With the Seidman's help, Four Paws has improved Cosmic Pet Products' distribution and pricing and built it into the largest catnip company in the country, commanding 60 percent of the market![22]*

Restructure the Company. Another way for business owners to cash out gradually is to replace the existing corporation with a new one, formed with other investors. The owner essentially is performing a leveraged buyout of his own company. For example, assume that you own a company worth $15 million. You form a new corporation with $12 million borrowed from a bank and $3 million in equity: $1.5 million of your own equity and $1.5 million in equity from an investor who wants you to stay on with the business. The new company buys your company for $15 million. You net $13.5 in cash ($15 million − your $1.5 million equity investment) and still own 50 percent of the new leveraged business (see Figure 5.4).[23]

Sell to an International Buyer. In an increasingly global marketplace, small U.S. businesses have become attractive buyout targets for foreign companies. Foreign buyers—mostly European—buy more than 1,000 U.S. businesses each year. Despite the publicity that Japanese buyouts get, England leads the list of nations acquiring U.S. companies. Small business owners are receptive to international offers. According to one survey, of the entrepreneurs considering selling their businesses, 69 percent said they would sell to a foreign investor.[24]

In most instances, foreign companies buy U.S. businesses to gain access to a lucrative, growing market. They look for a team of capable managers, whom they typically retain for a given time period. They also want companies that are profitable, stable, and growing.

Selling to foreign buyers can have disadvantages, however. They typically purchase 100 percent of a company, thereby making the previous owner merely an employee. Relationships with foreign owners also can be difficult to manage. In a recent survey, executives at foreign-owned small businesses stated that they didn't understand what motivated their bosses and that their relationships generally got worse over time.[25]

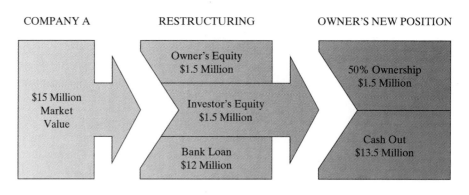

COMPANY A	RESTRUCTURING	OWNER'S NEW POSITION

Figure 5.4 **Corporate Restructuring**   SOURCE: Peter Collins, "Cashing Out and Maintaining Control," *Small Business Reports*, December 1989, p. 28.

Use a Two-Step Sale. For owners wanting the security of a sales contract now but not wanting to step down from the company's helm for several years, a two-step sale may be ideal. The buyer purchases the business in two phases, getting 20 to 70 percent today and agreeing to buy the remainder within a specific time period. Until the final transaction takes place, the entrepreneur retains at least partial control of the company.

Establish an Employee Stock Ownership Plan (ESOP). Some owners cash out by selling to their employees through an **employee stock ownership plan (ESOP).** An ESOP is a form of employee benefit plan in which a trust created for employees purchases their employers' stock. Here's how an ESOP works: The company transfers shares of its stock to the ESOP trust, and the trust uses the stock as collateral to borrow enough money to purchase the shares from the company. The company guarantees payment of the loan principal and interest and makes tax-deductible contributions to the trust to repay the loan (see Figure 5.5). The company then distributes the stock to employees' accounts on the basis of a predetermined formula. In addition to the tax benefits an ESOP offers, the plan permits the owner to transfer all or part of the company to employees as gradually or as suddenly as preferred.

To use an ESOP successfully, a small business should be profitable (with pretax profits exceeding $100,000) and should have a payroll of more than $500,000 a year. In general,

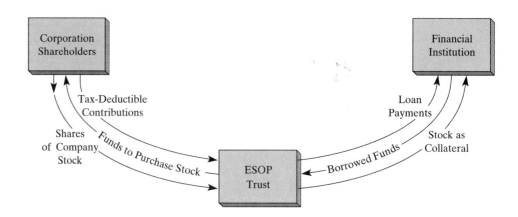

Figure 5.5 **A Typical Employee Stock Ownership Plan (ESOP)**   SOURCE: Corey Rosen, "Sharing Ownership with Employees," *Small Business Reports*, December 1990, p. 63.

companies with fewer than 15 to 20 employees do not find ESOPs beneficial. For companies that prepare properly, however, ESOPs offer significant financial and managerial benefits. "The owner gets to sell off his stock at whatever annual pace appeals to him. There's no cost to the employees, who eventually get to take over the company. And for the company the cost of the buyout is fully deductible," says one consultant.[26]

*N*egotiating the Deal

6 Understand how the negotiation process works and identify the factors that affect it.

Although determining the value of a business for sale is an important step in buying a business, it is not the final one. The buyer and the seller must sit down to negotiate the actual selling price for the business, and, more important, the terms of the deal. The final deal the parties strike depends, in large part, on their negotiating skills. In a business sale, the party who is the better bargainer usually comes out on top. In a business sale, the seller is looking to:

◆ Get the highest price possible for the company.

◆ Sever all responsibility for the company's liabilities.

◆ Avoid unreasonable contract terms that might limit her future opportunities.

◆ Maximize the cash she gets from the deal.

◆ Minimize the tax burden from the sale.

◆ Make sure the buyer will make all future payments.

The buyer seeks to:

◆ Get the business at the lowest price possible.

◆ Negotiate favorable payment terms, preferably over time.

◆ Get assurances that he is buying the business he thinks he is getting.

◆ Avoid enabling the seller to open a competing business.

◆ Minimize the amount of cash paid up front.

FACTORS AFFECTING THE NEGOTIATION PROCESS

Before beginning negotiations, a buyer should take stock of some basic issues. How strong is the seller's desire to sell? Is the seller willing to finance part of the purchase price? What terms does the buyer suggest? Which ones are most important to him? Is it urgent that the seller close the deal quickly? What deal structure best suits your needs? What are the tax consequences for both parties? Will the seller sign a restrictive covenant? Is the seller willing to stay on with the company for a time as a consultant? What general economic conditions exist in the industry at the time of the sale? Sellers tend to have the upper hand in good economic times, and buyers will have an advantage during recessionary periods in an industry.

THE NEGOTIATION PROCESS

On the surface, the negotiation process appears to be strictly adversarial. Although each party may be trying to accomplish objectives that are at odds with those of the opposing party, the negotiation process does not have to turn into a nasty battle with overtones of "If you win, then I lose." The negotiation process will go much more smoothly and much faster if the two parties work to establish a cooperative relationship based on honesty and trust

In Search of the Perfect Business: Part 3

"*How* could I possibly have been so foolish?" asks Hendrix Neimann. "I thought I had done a decent job of checking out [Automatic Door Specialists] during the summer-long due-diligence process." After Neimann and his accountant discovered the unpaid bills, inflated inventory values, and past-due accounts receivable, they discounted heavily the price they offered Peter Klosky for the company. "The good news is that I didn't pay much," says Neimann. "The bad news is that I didn't get much."

Yet he went ahead with the deal, and, in the process, put all of his family's personal assets at risk. Looking back, Neimann says, "I really thought I was a smart, talented, hard-working guy and that I could fix whatever was wrong with the company. Never mind that I didn't have a technical bone in my body and that this was a technical business in a technical industry. Never mind that the company turned out to be struggling and, in fact, losing money when I bought it. I, Neimann the Great, could do it."

But he couldn't. On February 12, 1997, Neimann closed the company, now called ADS Systems, that he had purchased nearly eight years before. He contacted the company's banker and its creditors and told them that he was ceasing operations. Preparing a summary of the company's financial position shone a spotlight on just how bleak the situation was. ADS had $473,000 in debt and accounts payable and only $142,000 in assets and receivables. Neimann explained to his creditors that he did not want to declare bankruptcy and that he intended to pay everything he owed, even if it took years. The bank stood first in line and had the right to claim all of the company's assets and, if those were insufficient (and they were), to claim the Neimanns' personal assets (including their home and personal bank accounts) as well.

For Neimann, the next few months were a nightmare. "[The banker] called me daily (sometimes twice daily) for no particular reason other than to let me know he was there and, unlike a bad dream, was not going to go away. Creditors called every day by the dozen." Concerned customers called wanting to know who would finish their jobs and who would service the equipment ADS had already installed. The landlord served notice that ADS would be evicted on March 24. The telephone and electric bills were more than two months past due, and the utility companies were threatening to shut off service.

From the time Neimann had bought ADS, the company was struggling financially and was never able to recover. The company was constantly in a cash flow bind, was usually behind in paying its bills, and rarely had a payables-to-receivables ratio of less than 2.5 to 1. When the company fell behind on employee withholding taxes, the Internal Revenue Services swept its bank account, taking out the $7,200 it owed.

To raise as much cash as possible to pay off some of the company's debts, Neimann advertised a business liquidation sale in the local newspaper. As friends and family pitched in to organize the sale, Neimann reflected on the path that had brought him to this point. Looking around at the condition he had allowed his company to degenerate into, Neimann was embarrassed. "Like the former owner, I no longer had noticed the dirt, the grease, the grime, the disorganization. I had allowed the men's offices, their desks, their vans to become no better than the inside of garbage cans. I had let the shop remain in a state of chaos since we had moved in there. The technicians and I never connected—ever. My lack of technical experience and knowledge grated on them—and rightly so. But the worst part of the seven and a half years was the overwhelming sense of hopelessness, of fearing that I would never, ever be able to dig out of the hole. I hated the business, hated the industry, hated the job. Yet I would not, could not, give up or in. My house was the ultimate collateral for the loan I'd taken out to buy the business. Therefore, lose the business, lose the house. I was trapped."

Finally, on March 24, 1997, with the building completely cleared out and all of ADS's assets sold off, Neimann's wife Judi, unplugged the office clock at exactly 5 P.M. and took it off the wall. "We were finished." says Neimann.

---

1. Using Hendrix Neimann's experience with ADS, develop a list of "red flags" that should alert a buyer that a particular business is not for him or her.

2. Looking back at Neimann's experience, what advice would you give to someone who is considering buying a business?

SOURCE: Adapted from Hendrix F. C. Neimann, "The End of the Story," *Inc.,* October 1997, pp. 68–77. ◆

from the outset. A successful deal requires both parties to examine and articulate their respective positions while trying to understand the other party's position. Recognizing that neither of them will benefit without a deal, both parties must work to achieve their objectives while making certain concessions to keep the negotiations alive. To avoid a stalled deal, both buyer and seller should go into the negotiation with a list of objectives ranked in order of priority. Prioritizing increases the likelihood that both parties will get most of what they want from the bargain. Knowing which terms are most important (and which are least important) to them enables the parties to make concessions without "giving away the farm" and without getting bogged down in nit-picking. If, for instance, the seller insists on a term that the buyer cannot agree to, he can explain why he cannot concede on that term and then offer to give up something in exchange. The following negotiating tips can help parties reach a mutually satisfying deal:[27]

- ◆ Know what you want to have when you walk away from the table. What will it take to reach your business objectives? What would the perfect deal be? Although it may not be possible to achieve the perfect deal, defining it helps you identify which issues are most important to you.

- ◆ Develop a negotiation strategy. Once you know where you want to finish, decide where you will start . . . and remember to leave some room to give. Try not to be the first one to mention price. Let the other party do that; then negotiate from there.

- ◆ Recognize the other party's needs. For a bargain to result, both parties must believe that they have met at least some of their goals. Asking open-ended questions can clue you in to the other side's position and why it's important.

- ◆ Be an empathetic listener. To truly understand what the other party's position is, you must listen attentively.

- ◆ Focus on the problem, not on the person. If the negotiation reaches an impasse, a natural tendency is to attack the other party. Resist! Instead, focus on developing a workable solution.

- ◆ Avoid seeing the other side as "the enemy." Such an attitude reduces the negotiation to an "I win, you lose" mentality that only hinders the process.

- ◆ Educate; don't intimidate. Rather than trying to bully the other party into accepting your point of view, try explaining your reasoning and the logic behind your proposal.

- ◆ Be patient. Resist the tendency to become angry and insulted at the proposals the other party makes. Similarly, don't be in such a hurry to close the deal that you give in on crucial points.

- ◆ Remember that "no deal" is an option. What would happen if the negotiations failed to produce a deal? In most negotiations, walking away from the table is an option. In some cases, it may be the best option.

- ◆ Be flexible and creative. Always have a fall-back position: an alternative that, although not ideal, satisfies you and is acceptable to the other party.

Chapter Summary

◆ Understand the advantages and disadvantages of buying an existing business.
  - ◆ The *advantages* of buying an existing business include: A successful business may continue to be successful; the business may already have the best location; employees and suppliers are already established; equipment is installed and its productive capacity known; inventory is in place and trade credit established; the owner hits the ground running; the buyer can use the expertise of the previous owner; the business may be a bargain.

- ◆ The *disadvantages* of buying an existing business include: An existing business may be for sale because it is deteriorating; the previous owner may have created ill will; employees inherited with the business may not be suitable; its location may have become unsuitable; equipment and facilities may be obsolete; change and innovation are hard to implement; inventory may be outdated; accounts receivable may be worth less than face value; the business may be overpriced.

2. Define the steps involved in the *right* way to buy a business.

   ◆ Buying a business can be a treacherous experience unless the buyer is well-prepared. The right way to buy a business is: analyze your skills, abilities, and interests to determine the ideal business for you; prepare a list of potential candidates, including those that might be in the "hidden market"; investigate and evaluate candidate businesses and evaluate the best one; explore financing options before you actually need the money; and, finally, ensure a smooth transition.

3. Explain the process of evaluating an existing business.

   ◆ Rushing into a deal can be the biggest mistake a business buyer can make. Before closing a deal, every business buyer should investigate five critical areas: (1) Why does the owner wish to sell? Look for the *real* reason. (2) Determine the physical condition of the business. Consider both the building and its location. (3) Conduct a thorough analysis of the market for your products or services. Who are the present and potential customers? Conduct an equally thorough analysis of competitors, both direct and indirect. How do they operate and why do customers prefer them? (4) Consider all of the legal aspects that might constrain the expansion and growth of the business. Did you comply with the provisions of a bulk transfer? Negotiate a restrictive covenant? Consider ongoing legal liabilities? (5) Analyze the financial condition of the business, looking at financial statements, income tax returns, and especially cash flow.

4. Describe the various ways of determining the value of a business.

   ◆ Placing a value on a business is partly an art and partly a science. There is no single best method for determining the value of a business. The following techniques (with several variations) are useful: the balance sheet technique (adjusted balance sheet technique); the earnings approach (excess earnings method, capitalized earnings approach, and discounted future earnings approach); and the market approach.

5. Understand the seller's side of the buyout decision and how to structure the deal.

   ◆ Selling a business takes time, patience, and preparation to locate a suitable buyer, strike a deal, and make the transition. Sellers must always structure the deal with tax consequences in mind. Common exit strategies include a straight business sale, forming a family limited partnership, selling a controlling interest in the business, restructuring the company, selling to an international buyer, using a two-step sale, and establishing an employee stock ownership plan (ESOP).

6. Understand how the negotiation process works and identify the factors that affect it.

   ◆ The first rule of negotiating is never confuse price with value. In a business sale, the party who is the better negotiator usually comes out on top. Before beginning negotiations, a buyer should identify the factors that are affecting the negotiations and then develop a negotiating strategy. The best deals are the result of a cooperative relationship based on trust.

Discussion Questions

1. What advantages can an entrepreneur who buys a business gain over one who starts a business from scratch?
2. How would you go about determining the value of the assets of a business if you were unfamiliar with them?
3. Why do so many entrepreneurs run into trouble when they buy an existing business? Outline the steps involved in the *right* way to buy a business.
4. When evaluating an existing business that is for sale, what areas should an entrepreneur consider? Briefly summarize the key elements of each area.
5. How should a buyer evaluate a business's goodwill?
6. What is a restrictive covenant? Is it fair to ask the seller of a travel agency located in a small town to sign a restrictive covenant for one year covering a 20-square-mile area? Explain.
7. How much negative information can you expect the seller to give you about the business? How can a prospective buyer find out such information?
8. Why is it so difficult for buyers and sellers to agree on a price for a business?
9. Which method of valuing a business is best? Why?
10. Outline the different exit strategies available to a seller.
11. Explain the buyer's position in a typical negotiation for a business. Explain the seller's position. What tips would you offer a buyer about to begin negotiating the purchase of a business?

Step into the Real World

1. Ask several new owners who purchased existing businesses the following questions.
   a. How did you determine the value of the business?
   b. How close was the price paid for the business to the value assessed before purchase?
   c. What percentage of the accounts receivable was collectible?
   d. How accurate were the projections concerning customers (sales volume and number of customers, especially)?
   e. Did you encounter any surprises after buying the business?
   f. If you were negotiating the deal again, what would you do differently?
2. Visit a business broker and ask him how he brings a buyer and seller together. What does he do to facilitate the sale? What methods does he use to determine the value of a business?
3. Ask a local attorney about the legal aspects of buying a business. What recommendations does she have for someone considering the purchase of an existing business? What negotiating tips can she offer? Prepare a brief report on what you learned for your class.
4. Use some of the following resources on the World Wide Web (or conduct your own search) to locate two businesses for sale that interest you:

BizQuest	http://www.bizQuest.com/
BizBuySell	http://www.bizbuysell.com/
Be The Boss	http://www.betheboss.com/
Internet Business Multiple Listing Site	http://www.bbn-net.com/

Write a brief synopsis of these businesses and explain why they interest you. Create a plan outlining the steps you would take to actually evaluate and purchase one of these companies.

Take It to the Net

Visit the Scarborough/Zimmerer home page at
www.prenhall.com/scarbzim
for updated information, on-line resources, and Web-based exercises.

Endnotes

1. Gianna Jacobson, "Mission: Acquisition," *Success*, October 1997, pp. 62–66.
2. Ronaleen R. Roha, "Don't Start It, Buy It," *Kiplinger's Personal Finance Magazine*, July 1997, pp. 74–76.
3. Jacobson, "Mission," p. 66.
4. Jacquelyn Lynn, "Unlocking the Door to Success," *Business Start-Ups*, September 1997, pp. 27–30.
5. Hendrix F. C. Neimann, "Buying a Business," *Inc.*, February 1990, pp. 28–38.
6. Thomas Owens, "Growth through Acquisition," *Small Business Reports*, August 1990, p. 63.
7. Jacobson, "Mission," p. 62.
8. Ibid., pp. 62–66.
9. Steven B. Kaufman, "Before You Buy, Be Careful," *Nation's Business*, March 1996, p. 45.
10. Jacobson, "Mission," pp. 62–66.
11. Lynn, "Unlocking the Door to Success," p. 30.
12. John Case, "Buy Now—Avoid the Rush," *Inc.*, February 1991, p. 38.
13. Richard M. Rodnick, "Getting the Right Price for Your Firm," *Nation's Business*, March 1984, pp. 70–71.
14. Stephen Blakely, "Figuring Your Company's Worth," *Nation's Business*, April 1997, p. 78; Jill Andresky Fraser, "What's Your Company Worth?" *Inc.*, November 1997, pp. 111–112.
15. Christopher Caggiano, "The 8 Dumbest Ways to Try to Sell Your Company," *Inc.*, November 1994, pp. 73–79.
16. "Selling Your Business," *The Business Owner*, no. 4 (Special Report, November 1991), p. 8.
17. Blakely, "Figuring Your Company's Worth," p. 78.
18. Dennis Rodkin, "For Sale by Owner," *Entrepreneur*, January 1998, pp. 148–153.
19. M. John Storey, "Pick Your Moment," *Success*, November 1996, p. 14.
20. Peter Nulty, "Smart Ways to Sell Your Business," *Fortune*, March 17, 1996, pp. 97–98.
21. Shannon P. Pratt, "Business Buyer's Valuation Guide," *In Business*, March–April 1987, p. 59.
22. Laura M. Litvan, "Selling Off, Staying On," *Nation's Business*, August 1995, pp. 29–30.
23. Peter Collins, "Cashing Out and Maintaining Control," *Small Business Reports*, December 1989, p. 28.
24. "More Business Owners May Be Selling Out," *Small Business Reports*, May 1990, p. 26.

25. "Problems with Foreign Owners," *Small Business Reports*, May 1991, p. 11.
26. "The Time Honored ESOP," *Inc.*, June 1991, p. 139.
27. Bruce A. Blitman, "Tips for Negotiation," *Business Start-Ups*, April 1997, p. 75; Jacquelyn Lynn, "Unlocking the Door to Success," *Business Start-Ups*, September 1997, pp. 27–30.

Creating the Marketing Plan

There is only one boss—the customer. Customers can fire everybody in the company from the chairman on down, simply by spending their money somewhere else.

—*Sam Walton*

There is less to fear from outside competition than from inside inefficiency, discourtesy, and bad service.

—*Anonymous*

Upon completion of this chapter, you will be able to

1. Describe the components of a marketing plan and explain the benefits of preparing one.

2. Discuss the role of market research.

3. Outline the market research process.

4. Explain how small businesses can pinpoint their target markets.

5. Describe the factors on which a small business can build a competitive edge.

6. Discuss the marketing opportunities the World Wide Web offers entrepreneurs and how to best take advantage of them.

7. Discuss the "four Ps" of marketing—product, place, price, and promotion—and their role in building a successful marketing strategy.

This and the next three chapters cover the creation of a valuable business tool: the *business plan*. This document is a statement of what the entrepreneur plans to accomplish in both quantitative and qualitative terms and of how she plans to accomplish it. The business plan consolidates many of the topics we have discussed in preceding chapters with those of the next three chapters to produce a concise statement of how the entrepreneur plans to achieve success.

Too often, entrepreneurs create business plans that describe in great detail what the entrepreneur intends to accomplish (e.g., "the financials") and pay little, if any, attention to the strategies to achieve those targets. Other entrepreneurs fail miserably because they are not willing to invest the time and energy to identify and research their target markets or to assemble any business plan at all. These entrepreneurs squander enormous effort pulling together capital, staff, products, and services because they neglect to determine what it will take to attract and retain a profitable customer base. To be effective, a business plan must contain both a financial plan and a marketing plan. Like the financial plan, an effective marketing plan projects numbers and analyzes them, but from a different perspective. Rather than focus on cash flow, net profits, and owner's equity, the marketing plan concentrates on the *customer*.

This chapter is devoted to creating an effective marketing plan, which is an integral part of a total business plan. Before producing reams of computer-generated spreadsheets of financial projections, an entrepreneur must determine what to sell, to whom and how often, on what terms and at what price, and how to get the product or service to the customer. In short, a marketing plan identifies a company's target customers and describes how that business will attract and keep them.

*M*arket-Driven Companies and the Marketing Plan

◆ Describe the components of a marketing plan and explain the benefits of preparing one.

Marketing is the process of creating and delivering goods and services to customers and involves all of the activities associated with winning and retaining loyal customers. The "secret" to successful marketing is to understand the company's target customers' needs, demands, and wants before competitors can; to offer them the products and services that will satisfy those needs, demands, and wants; and to provide those customers with quality, service, convenience, and value so that they will keep coming back. The marketing function cuts across the entire organization, affecting every aspect of its operation—from finance and production to hiring and purchasing. As the global business environment becomes more turbulent, small business owners must understand the importance of developing relevant marketing strategies; they are *not* just for megacorporations competing in international markets. Though they may be small in size and cannot match their larger rivals' marketing budgets, entrepreneurial companies are not powerless when it comes to developing effective marketing strategies. By using "guerrilla marketing strategies"—unconventional, low-cost, creative techniques—small companies can wring as much or more "bang" from their marketing bucks. For instance, facing discount giants such as Wal-Mart and Kmart and sports superstores determined to increase their market shares, small retailers are turning to guerrilla marketing tactics to lure new customers and to keep existing ones. *Although his Just Books bookstore in Greenwich, Connecticut, is very small (just 650 square feet of store space with one-and-a-half employees), Warren Cassell says he competes "very effectively" with the giant chain bookstores. Cassell uses a variety of guerrilla marketing techniques and doting customer service to differentiate his store and to keep his customers coming back. Cassell knows his customers so well that he is able to call them when Just Books gets a title by a favorite author. He also offers special orders at no extra charge, provides free gift wrapping, a toll-free number with multiple lines, a newsletter devoted to books, worldwide "no-hassle" shipping, autographed copies of books, out-of-print book searches, and many other extras customers cannot get at large chain stores. Using relationships he has developed over the years in the publishing industry, Cassell has hosted many "Meet the Author" breakfasts, which have included authors Margaret Thatcher and Henry Kissinger, among others. The result of Cassell's marketing strategy: an impressive mailing list of 6,000-plus loyal customers who don't mind paying full price for the books they buy and $1,500 in sales per square foot—a number most big chains can only envy.*[1]

Developing a winning marketing strategy requires a business to master three vital resources: people, information, and technology. People are the most important ingredient in formulating a successful marketing strategy. Hiring and retaining creative, talented, well-trained people to develop and implement a marketing strategy is the first step. Just as in sports, implementing a successful marketing strategy relies on an entrepreneur's ability to recruit people with the talent to do the job and to teach them to work together as a team.

In today's sophisticated and competitive markets, successful marketing relies on a company's ability to capture data and transform them into useful, meaningful information. Information is the fuel that feeds the marketing engine. Without it, a marketing strategy soon sputters and stops. Collecting more data than competitors, putting them into a meaningful form faster, and disseminating the information to everyone in the business, especially those who deal with customers, can give a company a huge competitive edge. Unfortunately, many small business owners fail to see the importance of capturing the information needed to drive a successful marketing strategy.

Technology has proved to be a powerful marketing weapon. (Consider what potent marketing tools portable computers and the World Wide Web have become already.) Yet, technology alone is not the key to marketing success. Competitors may duplicate or exceed the investment a small business makes in technology, but that may not guarantee their marketing success. The way a company integrates the use of technology into its overall marketing strategy is what matters most. *For instance, Craig Heard, president of Gateway Outdoor Advertising, was among the first companies in the outdoor advertising business to use geographic information systems (GISs) to select the ideal location for specific outdoor ads. (A GIS is a sophisticated computer program that combines the power of an extensive database with the graphical ability of a mapping program to allow a user to display an almost endless variety of characteristics on a map. The system is like a series of plastic overlays, with each layer displaying a different database feature, enabling the user to detect patterns and profiles that otherwise would go unnoticed.) Today, all of the company's 7,000-plus billboards are coded in a GIS, giving the company the ability to coordinate clients' outdoor ad campaigns so that they reach the greatest number of target customers. When a Gateway customer wants to advertise an athletic shoe aimed at children, for example, Heard uses the system to find the billboards that are near playgrounds, schools, and sports fields. Heard credits his GIS system with helping his company generate record revenues despite increased competition in his market.*[2]

The marketing plan focuses the company's attention on the *customer* and recognizes that satisfying the customer is the foundation of every business. Its purpose is to build a strategy of success for a business—but *from the customer's point of view.* Indeed, the customer is the central player in the cast of every business venture. According to marketing expert Theodore Levitt, the primary purpose of a business is not to earn a profit; instead, it is "to create and keep a customer. The rest, given reasonable good sense, will take care of itself."[3] Every area of the business must practice putting the customer first in planning and actions. Tom Melohn, retired CEO of the highly successful North American Tool & Die Inc., explains his company's customer focus, "You know why we're such an enormously customer-driven company? 'Cause we like to eat, that's why. If the customer wants the product packed in a paper bag and shipped at midnight during a full moon, then baby, that's the way we deliver it."[4]

A marketing plan should accomplish four objectives:

1. It should determine customer needs and wants through market research.
2. It should pinpoint the specific target markets the small company will serve.
3. It should analyze the firm's competitive advantages and build a marketing strategy around them.
4. It should help create a marketing mix that meets customer needs and wants.

This chapter will focus on building a customer orientation into these four objectives of the small company's marketing plan.

*7*he Value of Market Research

2 Discuss the role of market research.

The changing nature of the U.S. population is a potent force altering the landscape of business. Shifting patterns in age, income, education, race, and other population characteristics (which are the subject of demographics) will have a major impact on companies, their customers, and the way they do business with those customers. Businesses that ignore demographic trends and fail to adjust their strategies accordingly run the risk of becoming competitively obsolete.

A demographic trend is like a train; a business owner must find out early on where it's going and decide whether to get on board. Once the train is roaring down the tracks and gaining speed, it's too late to get on board. However, by checking the schedule early and planning ahead, an entrepreneur may find himself at the train's controls wearing the engineer's hat! Similarly, small companies that spot demographic trends early and act on them can gain a distinctive edge in the market. "A company has to . . . know what it's about, and it has to have a vision of the future to match what it's about with where the world is going," says one trend tracker.[5]

One of the most significant demographic trends creating opportunities for alert entrepreneurs is the aging of America. More than 40 percent of the U.S. population is over 50 years of age. Over the next 25 years, the under-50 population will grow by just 3 percent, but the over-50 population will increase by a whopping 73 percent! Businesses that adapt to the changing needs of these mature citizens will tap into a customer base that is very affluent and willing to spend. In 1995, the Valley View Fitness and Racquet Club in Lacrosse, Wisconsin, created a "Fit Over Fifty" program targeted directly at these customers. The club created exercise programs—from water aerobics and tennis to weight training and walking—designed to appeal to adults over 50, and it has seen its customer base grow. When managers noticed that their mature customers lingered after their workouts to visit with one another, they started a social program for the over-50 group. Thanks to these changes in its marketing strategy, the club now has a large and growing segment of loyal customers over 50, a market that many fitness clubs overlook.[6]

By performing some basic market research, small business owners can detect key demographic trends. Indeed, *every* business can benefit from a better understanding of its market, customers, and competitors. **Market research** is the vehicle for gathering the information that serves as the foundation for the marketing plan. It involves systematically collecting, analyzing, and interpreting data pertaining to the small company's market, customers, and competitors. Describing how market research can help entrepreneurs reach the highly fragmented markets they face today, one entrepreneur says, "The imperative for the marketer is to really understand who your customers are on a number of levels: what their motivation is, how a particular product or service fits into their lives, what they're looking for, what options are available."[7] Such information is an integral part of developing a productive marketing plan.

When marketing its goods and services, a small company must avoid marketing mistakes because there is no margin for error when funds are scarce and budgets are tight. Avoiding mistakes usually requires conducting market research *before* an entrepreneur launches a company. *For example, when Larry Work and Michael Sternberg decided to open a restaurant in Washington, D.C., their goal was to attract celebrities as regular customers, something they knew would set their eatery apart from others. Before they opened Sam and Harry's (they named the restaurant after their grandfathers), the partners developed a mail-*

Pluggers are eternal optimists.

ing list of 600 celebrities from Beverly Hills to Capitol Hill and sent them a survey on their dining preferences. They promised survey respondents a free bottle of champagne on their first visit. Analyzing the results of their market research (525 customers returned surveys), Work and Sternberg were able to learn exactly what their target customers wanted—and didn't want—in a restaurant. Not only did the survey help the restaurateurs design their establishment to suit their target customers' preferences, but it also generated future business for them. Since its opening in 1990, Sam and Harry's has won numerous awards for its food and its impeccable service and has become a magnet for celebrities from around the world.[8]

Market research often uncovers unmet needs in the market that owners can take advantage of. *For example, after Karen Scott launched her mail-order baby-products company, Chelsea and Scott, she decided to conduct some market research on her own. For months, she clipped birth announcements from the local newspaper and then contacted the new mothers. She sent them surveys and conducted telephone interviews to learn what products they were looking for but could not find. On the basis of her market research, Scott added more baby travel products to her product line. Today, those travel products remain the top-selling items in the $28 million a year catalog company.[9]*

As Karen Scott's experience proves, market research does *not* have to be formal, time-consuming, complex, or expensive to be useful. One retailer discovered the most common traffic pattern and most popular displays and items with a very simple, inexpensive, and creative form of market research. He offered shoppers free roasted peanuts, and by the end of the promotion, he had peanut hull trails showing the most heavily traveled areas. Mounds of hulls piled up in front of the most popular items. This store owner learned a great deal about his customers' behavior "for peanuts."[10]

Faith Popcorn, a marketing consultant, encourages small business owners to be their own "trend-tracking sleuths." Merely by observing their customers' attitudes and actions, small business owners can shift their product lines and services to meet changing tastes in the market. Popcorn claims that signs of these trends are all around us, but we must learn to recognize them. To spot significant trends, Popcorn suggests:

◆ Read as many current publications as possible.
◆ Watch the top 10 TV shows. ("They're indicators of consumers' attitudes and values and what they're going to be buying.")
◆ See the top 10 movies. They also influence consumer behavior.
◆ Talk to at least 150 customers a year about what they're buying and why.
◆ Talk with the 10 smartest people you know. They can offer valuable insights and fresh perspectives.
◆ Listen to your children. ("They can be tremendous guides for you.")
◆ Sensitize yourself to trend tracking. Be on the lookout for new trends emerging every day by stepping outside your usual pattern of activities and noticing what's happening around you.
◆ Periodically engage in brainstorming activities with employees, customers, industry observers, and outsiders.[11]

Next, the owner should list the major trends spotted and should briefly describe how well his products or services match the trends. "If you see your product falling away from too many trends, you've got to either change your product or dump it, because you know you're going to have a failure," Popcorn says.[12] The ultimate goal of such trend watching is to enable entrepreneurs to change their businesses to fit emerging trends, a process Popcorn calls "clicking." "You click when you're in the right place, at the right time, doing the right things."[13] Staying on trend means staying in synchronization with the market as it shifts and changes over time. Table 6.1 summarizes the 16 trends that Faith Popcorn says will shape the business environment for the next decade. The more trends a business clicks with, the more likely it is to be successful. According to Popcorn, a business built on fewer than four trends is out of sync with the way the market is moving or is picking up on a quickly passing fad and is likely to fail.

Trends are powerful forces and can be a business owner's greatest friend or greatest enemy. *Arthur Landry purchased the Dydee Diaper Company in 1960 and ran it as a family business for the next 28 years before turning it over to his son Steven. Founded in 1933, Dydee Diapers was one of the country's oldest diaper services. For each of its customers, Dydee kept about 200 diapers in cycle—half with the customer, half being laundered by its four industrial washing machines. The company's 20 trucks delivered diapers to customers' doorsteps on a regular schedule. The business grew steadily until 1990, when the major disposable diaper makers began an advertising blitz touting the convenience and the health benefits of their products. Busy baby boomers switched their babies to disposables, and Dydee Diapers' business fell by 20 percent (as did sales for diaper services nationwide). The slide continued as diaper services continued to fall out of favor with a new generation of parents until Dydee Diapers was forced to file for bankruptcy in January 1997.*[14]

Table 6.1 Sixteen Trends Shaping the Business Environment for the Next Decade

1. *Cocooning.* Nesting; staying at home; building safe harbors to protect against the uncertain and dangerous outside world.
2. *Clanning.* Connecting with people who hold similar interests, ideas, and values. The Internet allows people to cocoon and clan simultaneously.
3. *Fantasy adventure.* Thrill seeking in small, "safe," palatable doses; risk-free adventures that allow us to break out of the routine (travel, virtual reality, amusement rides).
4. *Pleasure revenge.* A backlash against the austerity of the 1990s, without all of the flashiness of the 1980s (steaks, cigars, martinis).
5. *Small indulgences.* Splurging on inexpensive luxuries as rewards and refreshers (gourmet chocolates and coffees).
6. *Anchoring.* The search for spiritual roots and meanings; revisiting the spiritual foundation from childhood to prepare for the future.
7. *Egonomics.* Consumers' craving for recognition for their individuality; a rebellion against uniformity and sterility ("personal" everything!).
8. *FemaleThink.* A new set of values that is shifting away from a traditional goal- and achievement-oriented focus to a more caring and sharing, relationship-based one.
9. *Mancipation.* A new way of thinking for men; breaking out of traditional "macho" roles into more individual lifestyles.
10. *99 lives.* Customers' overscheduled, overcommitted lives.
11. *Cashing out.* Leaving high-powered conventional careers to assume simpler, more fulfilling ways of life, often in small towns or in the country.
12. *Being alive.* Seeking a better quality of life and longevity; "wellness" and healthy living are dominant concerns.
13. *Down–aging.* A "retro" movement, especially among baby boomers; people engaging in fashions and activities typically reserved for the youth culture (resurgence of Mickey Mouse and Rocky and Bullwinkle).
14. *Vigilante consumption.* Shunning environmentally harmful products, companies that violate ethical standards, and businesses that are totally profit-focused.
15. *Icon toppling.* Attitude: If it's big, established, and traditional, it must be bad. Belief: Small is beautiful. Revolt against many traditional pillars of society (e.g., government and major corporations).
16. *SOS (Save Our Society).* A growing sense of living on a fragile and endangered planet, spawning a new sense of environmental consciousness and compassion for nature.

SOURCES: Adapted from Constance Gustke, "Trend-Bending," *Industry Week*, May 5, 1997, p. 51; Robert McGarvey, "Top Picks," *Entrepreneur*, December 1996, p. 148.

How to Conduct Market Research

3 Outline the market research process.

The goal of market research is to reduce the risks associated with making business decisions. It can replace misinformation and assumptions with facts. Opinion and hearsay are not viable foundations on which to build a solid marketing strategy. Successful market research consists of four steps.

STEP 1: DEFINE THE PROBLEM

The first, and most crucial, step in market research is defining the research problem clearly and concisely. A common flaw at this stage is to confuse a symptom with the true problem. For example, dwindling sales is not a problem; it is a symptom. To get to the heart of the matter, the owner must consider all the possible factors that could have caused it. Is there new competition? Are the firm's sales representatives impolite or unknowledgeable? Have customer tastes changed? Is the product line too narrow? Do customers have trouble finding what they want? In other cases, an owner may be interested in researching a specific type of question. What are the characteristics of my customers? What are their income levels? What radio stations do they listen to? Why do they shop here? What factors are most important to their buying decisions? What impact do in-store displays have on their purchasing patterns? Do they enjoy their shopping experience? If so, why? If not, why not? What would they like to see the store do differently?

Business owners also can use market research to uncover new market opportunities. For example, when the owner of a fitness center surveyed his customers, he discovered that many had an interest in aerobic exercises. He added an aerobics program, and within a year his revenues had grown by 25 percent.

STEP 2: COLLECT THE DATA

The marketing approach that has emerged in the 1990s is **individualized** (or **one-to-one**) **marketing,** gathering data on individual customers and then developing a marketing program designed specifically to appeal to their needs and tastes. Its goal is not only to attract customers but also to keep them and to increase their purchases. In a society where people feel isolated and transactions are impersonal, one-to-one marketing gives a business a competitive advantage. Rather than try to blanket an entire geographic area with mass-marketing techniques (which are out of many small companies' price ranges), businesses using individualized marketing rely on now-affordable technology to create computerized databases and to develop close, one-to-one relationships with their customers. Building a database requires business owners to gather and assimilate detailed information about their target customers. Indeed, building and using databases effectively is the key to developing successful one-to-one relationships with customers. Fortunately, even owners of the smallest businesses can collect and use such information relatively easily with the help of a little creativity and a computerized database.

For an individualized marketing campaign to be successful, business owners must collect three types of information:

1. *Geographic*. Where are my customers located? Do they tend to be concentrated in one geographic region?

2. *Demographic*. What are the characteristics of my customers (age, education level, income, gender, marital status)?

3. *Psychographic*. What drives my customers' buying behavior? Are they receptive to new products, or are they among the last to accept them? What values are most important to them?

For most business owners, collecting valuable information about their target customers is simply a matter of noting and organizing data that are already floating around somewhere in their companies. "Most companies are data-rich and information-poor," claims one marketing expert.[15] The key is to mine those data and turn them into useful information that allows the company to "court" its customers with special products, services, and attention. *For example, at the seed company Pioneer Hi-Bred International, Inc., a database contains extensive information on the company's commercial farming customers. Pioneer's database tracks the usual demographics (names, addresses, farm size) as well as other useful data such as the crops planted, the farm's yield, any livestock holdings, and what, when, and how much the farmer purchased in the past. Sales representatives have instant access to the database from the field via portable computers. This extensive database has changed the way the company and its sales force do business with customers. "By knowing ahead of time what a farmer has purchased in the past, says Pioneer's marketing manager, the salespeople can make suggestions on new products or provide comparative information on competitive products. They can also bring relevant literature to the sales presentation and immediately an-*

swer the question 'What did I order last year?' The database helps us tailor messages—both in person and through direct mail—specifically to the needs of a particular farmer."[16]

      Figure 6.1 explains how to become an effective individualized marketer, and Table 6.2 offers suggestions for building and using a database of customer information.

STEP 3: ANALYZE AND INTERPRET THE DATA

The results of market research alone do not provide a solution to the problem; the owner must attach some meaning to them. What do the facts mean? Is there a common thread running through the responses? Do the results suggest any changes needed in the way the business is run? Are there new opportunities the owner can take advantage of? There are no hard-and-fast rules for interpreting market research results; the owner must use judgment and common sense to determine what the numbers mean.

STEP 4: ACT ON THE DATA

The market research process is not complete until the business owner acts on the information collected. In many cases, the action needed is obvious once an entrepreneur has interpreted the results of her market research. On the basis of her understanding of the facts, the owner

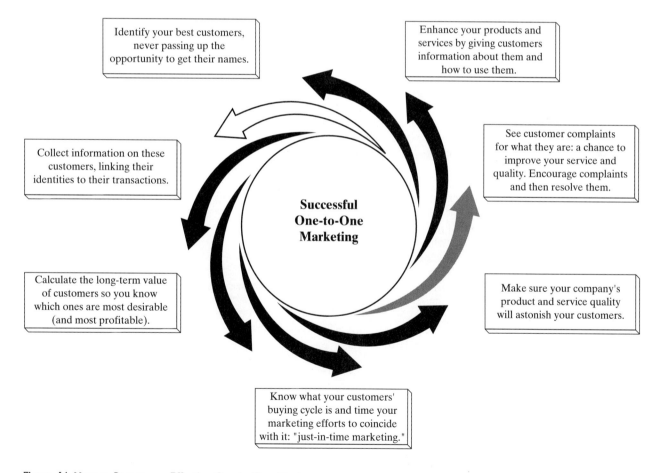

Identify your best customers, never passing up the opportunity to get their names.

Enhance your products and services by giving customers information about them and how to use them.

Collect information on these customers, linking their identities to their transactions.

See customer complaints for what they are: a chance to improve your service and quality. Encourage complaints and then resolve them.

Successful One-to-One Marketing

Calculate the long-term value of customers so you know which ones are most desirable (and most profitable).

Make sure your company's product and service quality will astonish your customers.

Know what your customers' buying cycle is and time your marketing efforts to coincide with it: "just-in-time marketing."

Figure 6.1 How to Become an Effective One-to-One Marketer   Source: Adapted from Susan Greco, "The Road to One-to-One Marketing," *Inc.*, October 1995, pp. 56–66.

Table 6.2 Building and Using a Customer Database

The first step in building a useful database is determining what information to collect. The typical database includes at a minimum the following for each customer.

♦ Customer's name, address, job title, company, age, telephone number, fax number, e-mail address, and whatever other information is relevant to your product or service.
♦ What products or services the customer has purchased from you in the past and when.
♦ How much the customer has spent with your company.
♦ Information on when and where the customer makes purchases of the products or services you sell.
♦ Sales strategies that have been successful in making sales to the customer (e.g., telephone calls, direct mail, visit from a sales representative).
♦ A record of all of your companies interactions with a customer or a prospect.
♦ A score or rating that measures the value or potential value of the customer to your company.

The next step is collecting and organizing the data. Here are some suggestions.

♦ Organize the information your company has on customers from its accounts receivable records.
♦ Collect information from warranty cards that customers complete.
♦ Pull information from checks customers write when they pay for goods and services.
♦ Conduct a drawing for a special prize and use the entry form to gather the information you need.
♦ Start a frequent buyer club that offers loyal customers benefits and use it to collect data.
♦ Talk to sales and customer service representatives and others in your company who deal directly with customers about the information they have on customers. Make it a habit to routinely "debrief" these employees on what they are learning about their customers.
♦ Learn to share information within the company. Information sales representatives collect is of no value as a marketing tool if no one else in the company knows about it.

The final step is to determine how you will use the data to market to your customers and prospects more effectively. Consider the following applications.

♦ Develop demographic and geographic profiles of your customers so that you can look for underlying trends and patterns that otherwise would go unnoticed.
♦ Use these profiles of your existing customer base to identify new markets with similar characteristics.
♦ Scan the database over time to look for changes in its composition and customers' buying habits.
♦ Make sure that everyone who deals with customers has access to the most current information in the database. For example, giving sales representatives the ability to tap into the database from the field using notebook computers can be a powerful selling tool.
♦ Use your database to coordinate and personalize sales and promotional campaigns.
♦ Use your database to build long-term one-to-one relationships with customers.

SOURCES: Adapted from Shari Caudron, "Database Checklist," *Industry Week*, September 2, 1996, p. 48; Tim McCollum, "Making the Most of Information," *Nation's Business*, June 1997, p. 42.

must decide how to use the information in her business. For example, the owner of a retail shop discovered from a survey that her customers preferred evening shopping hours over early morning hours. She made the schedule adjustment, and sales began to climb.

*M*arket Diversity: Pinpointing the Target Market

One of the primary objectives of conducting market research is to identify the small company's **target market,** the group of customers at whom the company aims its products or services. The more a business learns from market research about its local markets, its customers, and their buying habits and preferences, the more precisely it can focus its marketing efforts on the groups of prospective and existing customers who are most likely to buy its products or services. Unfortunately, most marketing experts contend that the greatest marketing mistake small businesses make is failing to define clearly the target market to be served. In other words, most small businesses follow a "shotgun approach" to marketing, firing marketing blasts at every customer they see, hoping to capture just some of them. Most small companies simply cannot use shotgun marketing to compete successfully with larger rivals and their deep pockets. Many small businesses develop new products that do not sell because they failed to target them at a specific audience's needs: They broadcast ads that attempt to reach everyone and end up reaching no one; they spend precious resources trying to reach customer who are not the most profitable; and many of the customers they manage to attract leave because they don't know what the company stands for. "You have limited resources to deliver 100 percent [customer] satisfaction, so you have to target customers and aim your service better than ever," explains one marketing consultant.[17]

Failing to pinpoint their target markets is especially ironic because small firms are ideally suited to reaching market segments that their larger rivals overlook or consider too small to be profitable. Why, then, is the shotgun approach so popular? Because it is easy and does not require market research or a marketing plan! The problem is that the shotgun approach is a sales-driven rather than a customer-driven strategy. To be customer-driven, a marketing program must be based on a clear, concise definition of the firm's targeted customers. *Before she launched her custom footwear company, Suzanne George spent months in the business library in San Francisco conducting research to refine her definition of her company's target market for her business plan. Her focus was on building a geographic, demographic, and psychographic profile of her potential customer base. "I was trying to define who my customer was [in terms of] socioeconomic status and lifestyle preferences," says George. She found volumes of useful information in market studies conducted by researchers, in industry publications, and in other secondary sources. She supplemented her library research with information she collected on her own from focus groups she conducted with potential customers from her target market. In the focus group sessions, participants completed questionnaires and gave George valuable feedback about their preferences, purchasing habits, and perceptions of custom-made footwear. On the basis of her extensive market research, George identified three primary target customers for her company: upscale customers who already purchase custom-made items; people looking for "special event" shoes, such as shoes for a wedding or a black-tie affair; and customers with moderate incomes who are looking for the quality and value that handmade products offer. With her target customers clearly in focus, George was able to coordinate the successful launch of her company, Suzanne George Shoes.*[18]

A "one-size-fits-all" approach to business no longer works because the mass market is rapidly disappearing. The population of the United States, like that of many countries, is becoming increasingly diverse. The mass market that dominated the business world of 25 years ago has been replaced by an increasingly fragmented market of multicultural customers including the Hispanic, African American, Asian Pacific, Native American, and many other populations. To be successful, businesses must understand the multicultural nature of the modern marketplace. Small businesses that take the time to recognize, understand, and cater to the unique needs of these multicultural markets (and their submarkets) will reap immense rewards. *For instance, a decade ago, Vons, a 180-store supermarket chain in California, took note of the large Hispanic population in its territory. When managers discovered that only a handful of small, independent grocery stores were targeting this underserved market, they decided to open Tianguis (a Spanish adaptation of the Aztec word for "marketplace"), a chain that the company advertised as "100% Hispanic supermarkets." Research showed that Hispanic customers view shopping as a gala social event. They enjoy browsing, like to eat when they go shopping, and enjoy hearing music that reminds them of home. In short, they want a shopping trip to be a fiesta! Tianguis set up stands that serve Mexican foods and patios for dining. Designers used bright, festive colors inside and hung dozens of piñatas from the ceiling. Live mariachi bands play happy songs that Tianguis customers all know. Employees speak Spanish, and the stores' selection of products is geared specifically toward Hispanic households. The chain became an immediate success with its target audience, and sales have climbed steadily with the opening of each new Tianguis store.*[19]

Like Tianguis, the most successful businesses have well-defined portraits of the customers they are seeking to attract. From market research, they know their customers' income levels, lifestyles, buying patterns, likes and dislikes, and even their psychological profiles. The target customer permeates the entire business—from the merchandise purchased to the layout and decor of the store. These businesses have an advantage over their rivals because the images they have created for their companies appeal to their target customers, and that's why they prosper. *Lori Granger Leveen and Steve Leveen have taken their mail-order business from just $10,000 to more than $60 million in sales in just 10 years by serving the needs of a specific target market: people who are serious readers and writers. Their catalog company, Levenger <http://www.levenger.com>, sells a variety of "tools for the serious reader," including desk and floor lamps designed for reading, custom-designed 100 percent cotton stationery, pens, dictionaries, attaché cases, reading chairs, reading desks, and many other items designed just for their target customers. Not only is Levenger's product mix unparalleled, but the company is also known for its impeccable customer service, something the Leveens have learned is vitally important to their customers. They have become experts in reading and writing supplies and how to use them, and in their catalogs they pass along that knowledge to their customers.*[20]

The nation's increasingly diverse population offers businesses of all sizes tremendous marketing opportunities if they target specific customers, learn how to reach them, and offer goods and services designed specifically for them. The key to success is understanding those target customers' unique needs, wants, and preferences. For instance, one market research firm says that the $120 billion Asian American market encompasses some 22 distinct subcultures, all with their own traditions and habits and many with their own languages.[21] *Through market research, one California real estate developer discovered that the state's Asian American population had doubled during the previous decade and that its purchasing power had climbed dramatically. Seeing an opportunity to market homes to this target audience, he began studying Asian culture. He discovered that making a handful of low-cost design alterations in the homes he built would attract Asian buyers to whom the concept of feng shui was important. Feng shui (which translates into "the wind and the water") is the art of designing a physical environment so that it promotes harmony and well-being. Because many Asians believe that a home loaded with right angles will bring bad luck, the developer minimized the number of "T-intersections" in his designs. He also avoided locating houses at the end of cul-de-sacs, into which the negative energy of the entire street would flow; homes in such a location would have an ample share of bad luck. Other modifications he made to create a good feng shui environment for his Asian target audience included rejecting rectangular lawns in favor of kidney-shaped ones, planting live trees and shrubs native to Asia, and adding rounded rocks to the landscape. Home sales to the Asian target market skyrocketed— and all because the builder had taken the time to do what none of his competitors had done:*

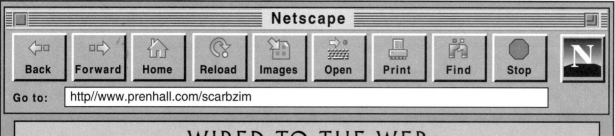

WIRED TO THE WEB

COFFEE + COMPUTERS = A CYBERCAFE

*W*hile studying for a semester abroad a few years ago, Larissa Janus was sitting at a quaint cafe visiting with her friends. As she looked around the crowded room, she saw other groups of college students and young professional workers reading their mail and chatting with friends. She mentioned her observation to one of her friends, who was from France. "Oh yes!" the friend commented, "the tradition of stopping by a cafe to read your mail started in Europe in the last century. The mail service is only slightly faster now, but it's still the continental thing to do."

Now, sitting at her computer "surfing the Net," Larissa thought back to the days in the cafe. That's when the idea came to her: "Why not set up a cybercafe in the European tradition where people could come to check their e-mail rather than read their 'snail mail'? I could serve gourmet coffees and teas along with a few pastries and have computers set up all around the cafe."

Larissa began to list the questions she would have to answer as she developed a business plan for her idea. How many computers would I need? How must they be equipped? What kind of network connection would I need? Would used computers do the job, or will I have to buy top-of-the-line models equipped with all of the "bells and whistles"? What kind of software will I need? Does it matter which Web browser I use? How much will all of this equipment cost? How much should I charge customers? Do I charge an hourly rate for the computer time they use, or do I give customers free computer access if they make purchases from the cafe? Are there cybercafes already in existence? If so, how do they operate? How important is choosing the right location?

As her list of questions grew, Larissa said to herself, "Surely I can find some information on the World Wide Web."

1. What other questions must Larissa address as she begins to plan to launch her cybercafe? Help her by adding to her list of questions.
2. Use the resources of the World Wide Web to locate some Web sites that would help Larissa. On the basis of what you learn from your Web search, outline the issues Larissa should address in her marketing plan. What types of customers should she target?

SOURCE: Adapted from Nora Carrera, "Cybercafe.com," *Business Start-Ups*, March 1997, pp. 62–66.

RESEARCH.[22] Reading publications such as *Marketing News*, *Hispanic Market Handbook*, *Hispanic Business News*, *TransPacific*, *Native Peoples*, *Black Enterprise*, and others will help entrepreneurs learn more about the various multicultural markets they are targeting.

Sometimes new target markets emerge on their own, even within already small niches. *Bill O'Gara, CEO of O'Gara Corporation, has carved out a small but lucrative niche in an unusual business: fabricating armored vehicles. The company takes standard passenger vehicles from virtually any auto manufacturer—Volkswagen and Hyundai to Jeep and Chevrolet—strips them down to their skeletons, and rebuilds them with features such as armor plates, bullet-resistant glass, "run-flat" tires, underbody grenade protection, and gun ports. For most of its 50-year history, the majority of O'Gara's customers were foreign governments who purchased armored cars for their leaders. In the 1990s, however, the company saw its market begin to shift to businesses trying to protect their managers from terrorists and organized crime. O'Gara sells all but about 15 or 20 of the cars it produces each year to businesses outside the United States. Another recent change in O'Gara's market is the type of cars customers want rebuilt. Abandoning the ostentatious cars that were so popular in the past, O'Gara's customers now favor those that blend in, such as Jeep Grand Cherokees and the Chevrolet Suburban, the company's best seller.*[23]

Plotting a Marketing Strategy: Building a Competitive Edge

5 Describe the factors on which a small business can build a competitive edge.

A competitive edge is crucial for business success. A small company has a competitive edge when customers perceive that its products or services are superior to those of its competitors. A business owner can create this perception in a variety of ways. Small companies sometimes try to create a competitive edge by offering the lowest prices. That approach may work for many products and services—especially those that customers see as being commodities—but price can be a dangerous criterion upon which to build a competitive edge. Independent bookstores have discovered that large chains can use their buying power to get volume discounts and undercut the independents' prices. Individual shop owners are finding new ways, such as special ordering, adult reading groups, children's story hours, newsletters, and autograph parties, to differentiate themselves and to retain customer loyalty. These entrepreneurs are finding that the best way to gain a competitive advantage is to create value by giving customers want they really want that they cannot get elsewhere.

Recreational Equipment Inc. (REI), a retailer of outdoor gear and clothing, uses its new two-story flagship store in Seattle, Washington, as a powerful tool to gain a competitive advantage over rival stores. One customer gushes, "The new $30 million, 80,000-square-foot store . . . is apt to fit almost any outdoor enthusiast's idea of at least a lower rung of heaven." The store, with its rustic, natural look is environmentally friendly, with countertops made of recycled paper and logs culled from normal tree-thinning processes rather than cut from old-growth forests. Both levels offer weary shoppers cozy benches arranged around fireplaces. REI also features an incredible selection of outdoor gear and clothing, and most of it is sold through interactive displays. There is a darkroom for testing bicycle headlamps, a sloping gravel path for trying out hiking boots, and places to test water filters and camp stoves. A shower chamber gives customers the opportunity to put raingear to the test before making their purchases, and bikers can test mountain bikes on the store's 470-foot bicycle trail. As part of its "hands-on" philosophy of retailing, REI also boasts the world's largest free-standing indoor climbing rock, a 105-ton monolith that can take on 15 customers at a time. REI has become a shopping destination; some 15,000 customers attended the store's grand-opening celebration.[24]

Like REI, successful businesses often use the special advantages they have to build a competitive edge over their larger rivals. Their close contact with the customer, personal attention, focus on service, and organizational and managerial flexibility provide a solid foundation from which to build a towering competitive edge in the market. Small companies are more effective than their larger rivals at **relationship marketing**—developing and maintaining long-term relationships with customers so that they will want to keep coming back. "We try to create a circle of friends, with the customer at the center," says one marketing consultant.[25]

To make relationship marketing work, a small business must achieve the highest of the following four levels of customer involvement:

Level 1: Customer awareness. The prevailing attitude in the company is "There's a customer out there." Managers and employees know little about the company's customers

At Recreational Equipment Inc., part of the market strategy is to get the customer involved. Several interactive displays such as an on-site bicycle trail and an in-store shower chamber allow customers to "test drive" products before they make their purchases.

and view them only in the most general terms. No one understands the benefits of a close customer-supplier relationship.

Level 2: Customer sensitivity. A wall stands between the company and its customers. Employees know something about their customers' characteristics, but they have not begun to share much information with them. Similarly, the company doesn't solicit feedback from its customers.

Level 3: Customer alignment. Managers and employees understand the customer's central role in the business. They spend considerable time talking with, and about, customers. They also seek out customer feedback through surveys, focus groups, customer interviews, and visits.

Level 4: Customer partnership. The company has refined its customer-service attitude from mere techniques to an all-encompassing part of its culture. Customers are part of all major issues. Employees at every level of the organization receive intelligence reports on customers and interact with them whenever possible. Customers play an important role in product development and in other aspects of the business. Managers and employees focus on building lasting relationships with customers.[26]

To achieve the highest level of customer satisfaction, many small businesses rely on six important sources to develop a competitive edge: a focus on the customer; devotion to quality; attention to convenience; concentration on innovation; dedication to service; and emphasis on speed.

FOCUS ON THE CUSTOMER

Too many companies have lost sight of the most important component of every business: *the customer*. Studies show that the average U.S. company loses about half of its customer base every five years, and many of those defections are the result of companies' failing to take care of their customers.[27] Wooing these disillusioned customers back will require businesses to focus on them as never before. Businesses must realize that *everything* in the business—even the business itself—depends on the satisfied customer. One consultant says, "No matter how good the product or how brilliant the marketing plan, it all comes to naught if there is a breakdown at the most critical interface in all of business—the point at which the customer comes in contact with the company."[28]

Businesses are just beginning to discover the true costs of poor customer relations. For instance:

◆ Sixty-seven percent of customers who stop patronizing a particular store do so because an indifferent employee treated them poorly.[29]

◆ Ninety-six percent of dissatisfied customers never complain about rude or discourteous service, *but*

◆ Ninety-one percent of those dissatisfied customers will not buy from the business again.

◆ One hundred percent of those unhappy customers will tell their "horror stories" to at least nine other people.

◆ Thirteen percent of those unhappy customers will tell their stories to at least 20 other people.[30]

According to the authors of "Keeping Customers for Life," "The nasty result of this customer indifference costs the average company from 15 to 30 percent of gross sales."[31] Because 70 percent of the average company's sales come from present customers, few can afford to alienate any shoppers. In fact, the typical business loses 20 percent of its customers each year. But a recent study by the consulting firm Bain & Co. shows that companies that increase their customer retention rate by just 5 percent experience profit increases of at least 25 percent! Studies by the Boston Consulting Group also show that companies with high customer retention rates produce above-average profits and superior growth in market share.[32] In short, customer loyalty translates into increased profitability because long-term customers are likely to be willing to pay above-average prices and to tell others about the company. "Companies that are successful in customer retention are those that understand that their most important assets are not their products or their services, but their customers," says one marketing consultant. "They understand the need to manage their 'customer portfolio' as closely as they would manage any other asset."[33]

Because about 20 to 30 percent of a typical companies' customers account for about 70 to 80 percent of its sales, it makes more sense to focus resources on keeping the best (and most profitable) customers than to spend them trying to chase "fair weather" customers who will defect to any better deal that comes along. Suppose that a company increases its customer base by 20 percent each year but retains only 85 percent of its existing customers. Its effective growth rate is just 5 percent per year [20% − (100% − 85%) = 5%]. If this same company can raise its customer retention rate to 95 percent, its net growth rate *triples* to 15 percent [20% − (100% − 95%) = 15%].[34] *When Ted Butler, president of Taylor & Fenn Com-*

pany, a foundry that makes metal parts for specialized machinery, analyzed his company's customer base, he was surprised. Of Taylor & Fenn's 450 customers, 67 of them (15 percent) accounted for 85 percent of its total sales. "The greatest opportunity for new business is with existing customers," says Butler.[35]

Although winning new customers keeps a company growing, keeping existing ones is essential to success. Attracting a new customer actually costs *five times* as much as keeping an existing one. Table 6.3 shows the high cost of lost customers. Given these statistics, small business owners would be better off asking "How can we improve customer value and service to encourage our existing customers to do more business with us?" rather than "How can we increase our market share by 10 percent?" *Todd Burns, owner of six Time-It Lube locations in Shreveport, Louisiana, understands the value of customer retention. When a customer comes in for an oil change, an employee punches the car's license tag number into a computer, which gives a complete repair history for the vehicle. The computer also tracks the time between customers' visits; customers who haven't brought their cars in for service after 113 days automatically receive a reminder notice. To keep his customers coming back, Burns also counts on a frequent-user card. On their third visit within a year, customers can use the card to get $3 off of the normal service price of $24.95; a fourth visit within a year entitles them to a $5 discount. With his simple customer-retention plan, Burns says that 90 percent of his customers return for repeat business.*[36]

The most successful small businesses have developed a customer orientation and have instilled a customer satisfaction attitude *throughout* the company. Companies with world-class customer attitudes set themselves apart by paying attention to little things. For example, when McDonald's opened stores in the financial districts of Los Angeles and New York, it installed stock "ticker boards" and telephones on the tables.[37] As a special service for customers who forget a special event, one small flower shop will insert a card reading, "Please forgive us! Being short-handed this week, we were unable to deliver this gift on time. We hope the sender's thoughtfulness will not be less appreciated because of our error. Again, we apologize."[38]

How do these companies focus so intently on their customers? They follow basic principles:

◆ When you create a dissatisfied customer, fix the problem *fast*. One study found that, given the chance to complain, 95 percent of customers will buy again if a business handles their complaints promptly and effectively.[39] The worst way to handle a complaint is to ignore it, to pass it off to a subordinate, or to let a lot of time slip by before dealing with it.

Table 6.3 The High Cost of Lost Customers (per year, based on a 7-day week)

If you lose . . .	Spending $5 weekly	Spending $10 weekly	Spending $50 weekly	Spending $100 weekly	Spending $200 weekly	Spending $300 weekly
1 customer a day	$ 94,900	$ 189,800	$ 949,000	$ 1,898,000	$ 3,796,000	$ 5,694,000
2 customers a day	189,800	379,600	1,898,000	3,796,000	7,592,000	11,388,000
5 customers a day	474,500	949,000	4,745,000	9,490,000	18,980,000	28,470,000
10 customers a day	949,000	1,898,000	9,490,000	18,980,000	37,960,000	56,940,000
20 customers a day	1,898,000	3,796,000	18,980,000	37,960,000	75,920,000	113,880,000
50 customers a day	4,745,000	9,490,000	47,450,000	94,900,000	189,800,000	284,700,000
100 customers a day	9,490,000	18,980,000	94,900,000	189,800,000	379,600,000	569,400,000

SOURCE: Copyright 1989, Customer Service Institute. Reprinted by permission of Customer Service Institute, 1010 Wayne Avenue, Silver Spring, Md.

- *Encourage* customer complaints. You can't fix something if you don't know it's broken. Table 6.4 describes seven ways to turn complaints into satisfied customers.

- Ask employees for feedback on improving customer service. A study by Technical Assistance Research Programs (TARP), a customer service research firm, found that front-line service workers can predict nearly 90 percent of the cases that produce customer complaints.[40] Emphasize that *everyone* is part of the customer satisfaction team.

- Get total commitment to superior customer service from top managers—and allocate resources appropriately.

- Allow managers to wait on customers occasionally. It's a great dose of reality. The founder of a small robot manufacturer credits such a strategy with saving his company. "We now require every officer of this company—including myself—to meet with customers at least four times a month," he says.[41]

- Carefully select and train *everyone* who will deal with customers. *Never* let rude employees work with customers.

- Develop a service theme that communicates your attitude toward customers. Customers want to feel they are getting something special.

- Reward employees "caught" providing exceptional service to the customer.

Remember: The customer pays the bills. Special treatment wins customers and keeps them coming back. For example, one mail-order customer was delighted when she received a $0.01 refund on merchandise she had ordered from L.L. Bean. The customer couldn't believe it, but such policies are part of Bean's customer orientation.

DEVOTION TO QUALITY

In this intensely competitive global business environment, quality goods and services are a prerequisite for success—and even survival. According to one marketing axiom, the worst of all marketing catastrophes is to have great advertising and a poor-quality product. Customers have come to expect and demand quality goods and services, and the businesses that provide them consistently have a distinct competitive advantage.

Today, quality is more than just a slogan posted on the company bulletin board; world-class companies treat quality as a strategic objective—an integral part of the company culture. "The real difference comes when you decide [quality is] no longer a program; it's a business strategy," says one top manager.[42] This philosophy is called **total quality manage-**

Table 6.4 Ways to Turn Complaints into Satisfied Customers

When faced with a complaining customer, business owners naturally defend their companies. Don't do it! Here are seven ways to turn disgruntled buyers into loyal customers.

1. Let unhappy customers vent their feelings; *don't interrupt*; maintain eye contact and listen to them.
2. Remain objective; avoid labeling customers' emotions or passing judgment on them.
3. Promptly appologize and accept responsibility for the problem.
4. See the complaint for what it is. The customer is upset about something; zero in on what it is.
5. Wait until the customer finishes expressing a complaint and then respond with a solution.
6. Thank the customer; let him or her know you appreciate being told about the situation. Try to win a friend, not an argument.
7. Follow up with the customer. Tell him or her what you're doing about the problem.

SOURCES: "Five Ways to Turn Complaints into Satisfied Customers," *Personal Selling Power*, April 1991, p. 53; © 1991 by PERSONAL SELLING POWER. Reprinted by permission of the publisher, "Handling Disgruntled Customers," *Your Company*, Spring 1993, p. 5.

ment (TQM): quality not just in the product or service itself but in every aspect of the business and its relationship with the customer and *continuous improvement* in the quality delivered to customers.

Companies on the cutting edge of the quality movement are developing new ways to measure quality. Manufacturers were the first to apply TQM techniques, but retail, wholesale, and service organizations have seen the benefits of becoming champions of quality. They are tracking customer complaints, contacting "lost" customers, and finding new ways to track the cost of quality and their return on quality (ROQ). The ROQ measure recognizes that although any improvement in quality may improve a company's competitive ability, only the improvements that produce a reasonable rate of return are worthwhile. In essence, ROQ requires managers to ensure that the quality improvements they implement will more than pay for themselves.

Dean Dunaway, president of Capweld Inc., a small gas distributor in Jackson, Mississippi, turned to a TQM philosophy known as poka-yoke *(which comes from two Japanese words meaning "avoid errors") when the cost of lost gas tanks began to cause the company's profits to decline. When Capweld sells $20 worth of oxygen, it is delivered in a $200 tank. Although all of Capwell's tanks are numbered, keeping up with 15,000 to 20,000 transactions each month was difficult and inevitably led to missing tanks. Losing just one tank erased the profits on a huge number of sales. Putting together a team of employees to study the causes of the problem revealed that employee errors were the source of many lost tanks. The quality team suggested a computerized solution to solve the lost tank problem. Capweld now uses a computerized database to track the location of every one of its 40,000 tanks and has attached scannable microchips to them to avoid employee input errors. The company's poka-yoke efforts have more than paid for themselves by significantly lowering the number of lost tanks. "It's helped a lot," says Dunaway, who hopes to keep whittling away at the small errors that have a big impact at Capweld. "It's just hundreds of little bitty things," he says.*[43]

The key to developing a successful TQM philosophy is seeing the world from the customer's point of view. In other words, quality must reflect the needs and wants of the customer. How do customers define quality? According to a recent poll, Americans rank quality components in this order: reliability (average time between failures), durability (how long it lasts), ease of use, a known or trusted brand name, and, last, a low price.[44] In services, customers are likely to look for similar characteristics: tangibles (equipment, facilities, and people), reliability (doing what you say you will do), responsiveness (promptness in helping customers), assurance and empathy (conveying a caring attitude). *For example, the owner of a very successful pest-control company offered his customers a unique unconditional guarantee: If the company fails to eliminate all roach and rodent breeding and nesting areas on the client's premises, it will refund the customer's last 12 monthly payments and will pay for one full year's service by another exterminator. The company has had to honor its guarantee only once in 17 years.*

Companies successful in capturing a reputation for top-quality products and services follow certain guidelines to "get it right the first time":

♦ Build quality into the process; don't rely on inspection to obtain quality.

♦ Foster teamwork and dismantle the barriers that divide disparate departments.

♦ Establish long-term ties with select suppliers; don't award contracts on low price alone.

♦ Provide managers and employees the training needed to participate fully in the quality improvement program.

♦ Empower workers at all levels of the organization; give them authority and responsibility for making decisions that determine quality.

- Get managers' commitment to the quality philosophy. Otherwise, the program is doomed. Describing his role in his company's TQM philosophy, one CEO says, "People look to see if you just talk about it or actually do it."[45]

- Rethink the processes the company uses now to get its products or services to its customers. *Employees at Analog Devices redesigned its production process and significantly lowered the defect rate on its silicon chips and saved $1.2 million a year.*[46]

- Reward employees for quality work. Ideally, workers' compensation is linked clearly and directly to key measures of quality and customer satisfaction.

- Develop a companywide strategy for constant improvement of product and service quality.

The goal of these procedures is to achieve 100 percent quality. Most entrepreneurs would love for their companies to operate at even the 99.9 percent level of quality. However, unless business leaders and their companies continuously strive for 100 percent quality, there is little chance that they will ever achieve 99.9 percent quality. Table 6.5 offers insight into why 99.9 percent quality simply isn't good enough.

ATTENTION TO CONVENIENCE

In this busy, fast-paced world of dual-career couples and lengthy commutes to and from work, customers increasingly are looking for convenience. Today, 65 percent of American women work outside the home, compared with just 20 percent in 1950.[47] In an attempt to balance their home and work lives, families demand convenience. Several studies have found that customers rank easy access to goods and services at the top of their purchase criteria. Unfortunately, too few businesses deliver adequate levels of convenience, and they fail to attract and retain customers. One print and framing shop, for instance, alienated many potential customers with its abbreviated business hours: 9 to 5 daily, except for Wednesday afternoons, Saturday, and Sunday, when the shop was closed. Other companies make it a chore to do business with them. In an effort to defend themselves against unscrupulous customers, these businesses have created elaborate procedures for exchanges, refunds, writing checks, and other basic transactions. One researcher claims, "What they're doing is treating the 98 percent of honest customers like crooks to catch the 2 percent who are crooks."[48]

Table 6.5 Is 99.9% Quality Good Enough?

Isn't 99.9 percent defect-free good enough? Consider the following consequences of 99.9 percent quality and then decide:

- 1 hour of unsafe drinking water every month
- 730 unsafe landings at Chicago's O'Hare Airport each year
- 16,000 pieces of mail lost by the U.S. Postal Service every hour
- 20,000 incorrect drug prescriptions processed each year
- 500 incorrect surgical procedures each week
- 22,000 checks deducted from the wrong bank accounts each hour
- 2 million documents lost by the IRS in a typical year
- 12 babies delivered to the wrong parents each day
- 1,314 telephone calls misrouted every minute
- 2,488,200 magazines published with the wrong covers each year
- 5,517,200 cases of soft drinks produced without any snap, sparkle, or fizz each year

SOURCES: Adapted from Sal Marino, "Is 'Good Enough' Good Enough?" *Industry Week*, February 3, 1997, p. 22; "Why 99.9% Just Won't Do," *Inc.*, April 1989, p. 276.

Successful companies go out of their way to make sure that it is easy for customers to do business with them. *Once a lowly truck stop, the GiantTravel Center in Jamestown, New Mexico, has transformed itself into a full-service travel center specializing in offering its customers the ultimate in convenience. In addition to the usual gas pumps, Giant has a full-service post office, a movie theater that doubles as a chapel on Sundays, a laundromat, clothing and craft stores, a Baker's Hearth Restaurant, and other shops, all located in an airy two-story atrium.* Picking up on the trend, other travel centers around the country have added fax machines, computer booths with Web access, professional masseuses, museums, dentist offices, gyms, and pet-grooming facilities in makeovers that more closely resemble malls than truck stops. The focus on offering weary travelers on-the-road convenience has extended travel centers' customer bases well beyond their traditional target market of professional truck drivers. Centers are swarming with tourists and others traveling in passenger cars, a phenomenon that has pushed industry revenue to a record $35 billion a year, a 30 percent increase in just five years.[49]

How can a business owner boost the convenience level of her business? By conducting a "convenience audit" from the customer's point of view to get an idea of its ETDBW ("Easy To Do Business With") index:

◆ Is your business located near your customers? Does it provide easy access?

◆ Are your business hours suitable to your customers? Should you be open evenings and weekends to serve them better?

◆ Would customers appreciate pickup and delivery service? *The owner of a restaurant located near a major office complex installed a fax machine to receive orders from busy workers; a crew of workers would deliver lunches to office workers at their desks!*

◆ Does your company make it easy for customers to purchase on credit or with credit cards?

◆ Are your employees trained to handle business transactions quickly, efficiently, and politely? Waiting while rude, incompetent employees fumble through routine transactions destroys customer goodwill.

◆ Does your company handle telephone calls quickly and efficiently? Long waits "on hold," transfers from one office to another, and too many rings before answering signal customers that they are not important.

Many small companies have had success by finding simple ways to make it easier for customers to do business with them. *Raley's, a supermarket chain based in Sacramento, California, offers customers a free baby-sitting service at its in-store Play Care centers for up to 90 minutes while they shop. Workers in the centers are trained in child care, and parents receive beepers in case workers need to summon them for some reason. Matching hand stamps improve security, and television monitors located around the store allow parents to keep an eye on their children while they shop. Not only do parents appreciate the convenience of an in-store child-care service, but they can take longer to shop knowing that their children are safe and happy. In fact, store managers have discovered that parents who are free to shop alone actually do spend more time—and more money—than those who are busy catering to children.*[50]

CONCENTRATION ON INNOVATION

Innovation is the key to future success. Markets change too quickly and competitors move too fast for a small company to stand still and remain competitive. Because of their organizational and managerial flexibility, small businesses often can detect and act on new opportunities faster than large companies. Innovation is one of the greatest strengths of the entrepreneur, and it shows up in the new products, unique techniques, and unusual approaches they introduce. A recent Coopers and Lybrand study of companies with revenues of less than $50 million showed that nearly two-thirds of their CEOs believe their ability to develop new products represents a major competitive advantage.[51]

Despite financial constraints, small businesses frequently are leaders in innovation. For instance, small companies accounted for every breakthrough in the computer industry, including microcomputers (Apple Computer), minicomputers (Digital), and supercomputers (Cray Research). Start-up businesses also led the way in developing each generation of computer disk drive. Even in the hotly competitive pharmaceutical industry, the dominant drugs in most markets were discovered by small companies rather than the industry giants like Merck or Glaxos with their multimillion-dollar R&D budgets.

Although product and service innovation has never been more important to small companies' success, it has never been more challenging. Companies of all sizes are feeling the pressure to develop new products and get them to market faster than ever before. More intense competition, often from across the globe, as well as rapid changes in technology and improvements in communication have made innovation crucial to business success. According to Robert Cooper, a professor of marketing and technology management at McMaster University in Ontario, Canada, the percentage of sales coming from new products "has been increasing over the past few years—across all industries and sizes of businesses."[52] One survey of U.S. companies found that executives expected new products to account for 39 percent of profits in the next five years compared with just 25 percent in the previous five.[53] *Ely Callaway, the founder of Callaway Golf, the company that makes the famous Big Bertha club, says that innovation is his "No. 1 priority and a core value outlined in the company's mission statement. That's because Callaway Golf's long-term success depends on satisfying our customers with a constant stream of innovative new products."*[54]

There is more to innovation than spending megadollars on research and development. How do small businesses manage to maintain their leadership role in innovating new products and services? They use their size to their advantage, maintaining their speed and flexibility much as a martial arts expert does against a larger opponent. Their closeness to their customers enables them to read subtle shifts in the market and to anticipate trends as they unfold. Their ability to concentrate their efforts and attention in one area also gives small businesses an edge in innovation. "The small companies have an advantage: a dedicated management team totally focused on a new product or market," says one venture capitalist.[55] *Although Millie Thomas, president of RGT Enterprises, had little money to invest in developing and testing an idea she had for a new children's toothbrush, she did not quit. She molded a prototype of her design in clay and took it to pediatric dentists for feedback. She also convinced day-care centers to allow her to interview parents on their opinions of the triangular safety handle. "There was an overwhelmingly positive response," says Thomas, whose company now has more than $1 million in sales annually.*[56]

To be an effective innovator, an entrepreneur should:

◆ Make innovation a priority in the company by devoting management time and energy to it.

◆ Measure the company's innovative ability. The number of new products or services introduced and the proportion of sales generated by products less than five years old can be useful measures of a company's ability to innovate.

◆ Set goals and objectives for innovation. Establishing targets and rewarding employees for achieving them can produce amazing results.

◆ Encourage new product and service ideas among employees. Workers have many incredible ideas, but they will lead to new products or services only if someone takes the time to listen to them.

◆ Always be on the lookout for new product and service ideas. They can come to you (or to anyone in the company) when you least expect it.

◆ Keep a steady stream of new products and services coming. *Even before sales of her safety-handle children's toothbrush took off, Millie Thomas had developed other children's products using the same triangular handle, including a crayon holder, paintbrushes, and fingernail brushes.*[57]

Table 6.6 describes a screening device for testing the viability of new product ideas.

DEDICATION TO SERVICE AND CUSTOMER SATISFACTION

In the new economy, companies are discovering that unexpected innovative, customized service can be a powerful strategic weapon. Small companies that lack the financial resources of their larger rivals have discovered that offering exceptional customer service is one of the most effective ways to differentiate themselves and to attract and maintain a growing customer base. Unfortunately, the level of service in most companies is poor. John Tschol, head of the Service Quality Institute says, "Ironically, we've moved into a service economy where the only thing lacking is service."[58] Companies that do not provide quality service to customers will fail, while those that do will excel.

Chocolates á la Carte, a small specialty chocolate service in Sylmar, California, uses a customized service strategy to differentiate itself from competitors and to avoid the need to compete on the basis of price. Every day, Rick and Rena Pocrass and their staff of 100 chocolate artists face the stiff challenge of pleasing the nation's most demanding customers: the top echelon of the hospitality industry and their specialized, often last-minute orders for chocolates. To satisfy their customers' exacting needs, the Pocrasses created a separate "E.R. team" of their most capable workers to handle emergency orders. One long-time customer says, "Chocolates á la Carte may not be the cheapest, but they make up for it in quality of product, personal attention, involvement, and commitment."[59]

Table 6.6 Testing the Viability of a New Product Idea

Testing the viability of new product ideas in their early stages of development can help entrepreneurs avoid expensive product failures later. The Chester Marketing Group, Inc. of Washington Crossing, Pennsylvania, has developed the following test to determine the viability of a new product idea at each stage in the product development process. To calculate a new product idea's score, simply multiply the score for each criterion by its weight and then add up the resulting weighted scores. For a product to advance to the next stage in the development process, its score should be at least 16.

Criterion	Score			Weight	Weighted Score
	Below Average	Average	Above Average		
Extent of target market need	1	2	3	2	
Potential profitability	1	2	3	2	
Likely emergence of competition	1	2	3	1	
Service life cycle	1	2	3	1	
Compatibility with company strengths	1	2	3	2	
Total weighted score					

SOURCE: Roberta Maynard, "Test Your Product Idea," *Nation's Business*, October 1997, p. 23.

Successful businesses recognize that superior customer service is only an intermediate step toward the goal of *customer satisfaction*. These companies seek to go beyond customer satisfaction, striving for *customer astonishment*! They concentrate on providing customers with quality, convenience, and service *as their customers define those terms*. Certainly the least expensive, and the most effective, way to achieve customer satisfaction is through friendly, personal service. Numerous surveys of customers in a wide diversity of industries—from manufacturing and services to banking and high tech—conclude that the most important element of service is "the personal touch." Calling customers by name, making attentive, friendly contact, and truly caring about customers' needs and wants are more essential than any other factor—even convenience, quality, and speed! One manager explains, "Customers have come to expect high-quality products and services, but not personalized attention when problems occur. And that's exactly where a company's opportunity to impress them lies."[60] How can a company achieve stellar customer service and satisfaction?

Listen to Customers. The best companies constantly listen to their customers and respond to what they hear. Listening enables them to keep up with customers' changing needs and expectations. The only way to find out what customers really want and value is to *ask them*. Businesses rely on several techniques, including surveys, focus groups, telephone interviews, comment cards, suggestion boxes, toll-free "hot lines," and regular one-on-one conversations (perhaps the best technique). *When business slowed at Price's Market, a Richmond, Virginia, convenience store, owners Bob and Candy Kocher started asking their neighborhood customers, "What are you always looking for but can't get?" The overwhelming answer surprised them: imported beer. They began stocking it, and now their small convenience store is the hottest spot in town. Not only has neighborhood traffic picked up, but the store also attracts customers from all over town to buy its imported brews.*[61]

Define Superior Service. On the basis of what customers say, managers and employees must decide exactly what "superior service" means in the company. Such a statement should (1) be a strong statement of intent, (2) differentiate the company from others, and (3) have value to customers. Deluxe Corporation, a printer of personal checks, defines superior service quite simply: "Forty-eight-hour turnaround; zero defects."[62]

Set Standards and Measure Performance. To be able to deliver on its promise of superior service, a business must establish specific standards and measure overall performance against them. Satisfied customers should exhibit at least one of three behaviors: loyalty (evidenced by high customer retention rate), increased purchases (climbing sales and sales per customer), and resistance to rivals' attempts to lure them away with lower prices (market share and price tolerance).[63] Companies must track performance on these and other service standards and reward employees accordingly.

Examine Your Company's Service Cycle. What steps must a customer go through to get your product or service? Business owners often are surprised at the complexity that has seeped into their customer service systems as they have evolved over time. One of the most effective techniques is to work with employees to map on a flowchart each component in the company's service cycle, including *everything* a customer has to do to get your product or service. The goal is to find steps and procedures that are unnecessary, redundant, or unreasonable and then to eliminate them.

Hire the Right Employees. The key ingredient in the superior service equation is *people*. There is no substitute for friendly, courteous sales and service representatives. The new service attitude "demands a new breed of service worker, folks who are empathetic, flexible, informed, articulate, inventive, and able to work with minimal levels of supervision," says one writer.[64]

Train Employees to Deliver Superior Service. Successful businesses train *every* employee who deals directly with customers; they don't leave customer service to chance. Superior service companies devote 1 to 5 percent of their employees' work hours to training, concentrating on how to meet, greet, and serve customers. Leading mail-order companies such as Lands' End and L.L. Bean spend 80 hours training the employees who handle telephone orders before they deal with their first customer.[65]

Empower Employees to Offer Superior Service. One of the biggest single variables determining whether employees deliver superior service is whether they perceive they have permission to do so. The goal is to push decision making down the organization to the employees who have contact with customers. This includes giving them the freedom to circumvent company policy if it means improving customer satisfaction.

Use Technology to Provide Improved Service. The role of technology is not to create a rigid bureaucracy but to free employees from routine clerical tasks, giving them time, information, and tools to serve customers effectively. *Emerald Dunes, a top-ranked public golf course in Palm Beach, California, relies heavily on technology to solve the problems that have plagued low-tech golf courses for decades and to deliver premier service to its customers. A computerized reservation system allows golfers to book rounds 24 hours a day from any telephone up to six days in advance and to receive accurate tee times. Space-age "electronic caddies" installed in every golf cart constantly communicate with satellites orbiting 11,800 miles in space and give golfers an overhead view of the hole they're playing, a diagram of the upcoming putting green, the length of their last shot, and the distance re-*

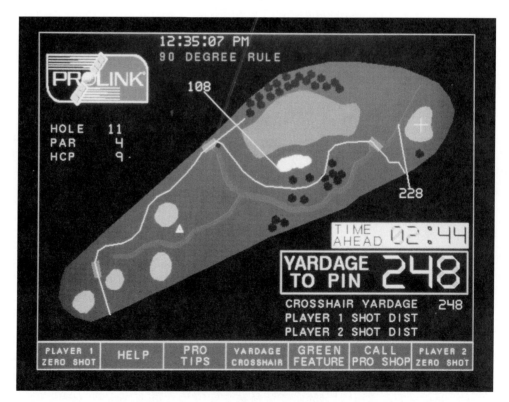

At Emerald Dunes golf course, many players manage to shave a few strokes off their games with the help of a high-tech solution: an "electric caddy" installed in every cart. The ProLink system also reduces the problem of slow play for schedulers and gives the course a competitive advantage.

maining to the pin. The system, called Prolink, not only improves players' scores (a distinct competitive advantage in itself), but it also reduces slow play, a problem that wreaks havoc with otherwise neatly planned tee times. Since installing Prolink, president Ray Finch says that the average time for a round of golf has shrunk by 20 minutes, allowing course managers to schedule two more tee times a day. Emerald Dunes' high-tech solutions to decidedly low-tech problems gives the course a distinct edge over other courses, public or private. That edge shows up in both revenues and profits, which run more than five times those of the typical public golf course.[66]

Reward Superior Service. What gets rewarded gets done. Companies that want employees to provide stellar service must offer rewards for doing so. A recent National Science Foundation study concluded that when pay is linked to performance, employees' motivation and productivity climb by as much as 63 percent.[67] *When MasterCare auto centers discovered that its customer service system was failing, it revamped its compensation system, linking it more closely with customer service measures. Employees—including mechanics—who keep loyal customers earn salary bonuses. The new system has raised customer retention 25 percent and has lowered employee turnover 40 percent.*[68]

Get Top Managers' Support. The drive toward superior customer service will fall far short of its target unless top managers support it fully. Success requires more than just a verbal commitment; it calls for managers' involvement and dedication. Achieving customer satisfaction must become part of the strategic planning process and work its way into every nook and cranny of the organization.

EMPHASIS ON SPEED

We live in a world of instantaneous expectations. Technology that produces immediate results at the click of a mouse and allows for real-time communication has altered our sense of time and space. Customers now expect an immediate response from companies, whatever products or services they may be buying. In such a world, speed has become a major competitive weapon. World-class companies recognize that reducing the time it takes to develop, design, manufacture, and distribute a product reduces costs, increases quality, and boosts market share. One study by McKinsey and Company found that high-tech products that come to market on budget but six months late will earn 33 percent less profit over five years than products that are on schedule. Bringing the product out on time but 50 percent over budget cuts profits just 4 percent![69] Service companies also know that they must build speed into their business systems if they are to satisfy their impatient, time-sensitive customers.

This philosophy of speed is called **time compression management (TCM),** and it involves three aspects: (1) speeding new products to market, (2) shortening customer response time in manufacturing and delivery, and (3) reducing the administrative time required to fill an order. Studies show plenty of room for improvement; most businesses waste 85 to 99 percent of the time it takes to produce products or services without ever realizing it![70] *For example, when managers and employees at United Electric Controls, a family-owned maker of temperature and pressure controls and sensors, studied their production process, they were amazed at what they found. In their 50,000-square-foot factory, "We had one product that traveled 12 miles just in our plant," says one manager. Rearranging the plant's layout around products rather than processes solved the problem. "The product that once traveled 12 miles now travels 40 feet," he says "The outcome was a reduction in lead time from 10 or 12 weeks to just a couple of days."*[71]

Although speeding up the manufacturing process is a common goal, companies using TCM have learned that manufacturing takes only 5 percent to 10 percent of the total time between an order and getting the product into the customer's hands. The rest is consumed by clerical and administrative tasks. The primary opportunity for TCM lies in its application to the administrative process.

Companies relying on TCM to help them turn speed into a competitive edge should:

◆ Reengineer the entire production and delivery process rather than attempt to do the same things in the same way only faster.

◆ Create cross-functional teams of workers and give them the power to attack and solve problems. In world-class companies, product teams include engineers, manufacturers, salespeople, quality experts, and even customers.

◆ Set aggressive goals for time reduction and stick to the schedule. Some companies using TCM have been able to reduce cycle time from several weeks to just a few hours.

◆ Instill speed in the culture. At Domino's Pizza, kitchen workers watch videos of the fastest pizza makers in the country.

◆ Use technology to find shortcuts wherever possible. Rather than build costly, time-consuming prototypes, many time-sensitive businesses use computer-aided design and computer-assisted manufacturing (CAD/CAM) to speed product design and testing.

*M*arketing on the World Wide Web

◆ Discuss the marketing opportunities the World Wide Web offers entrepreneurs and how to best take advantage of them.

Much like the telephone, the fax machine, and home shopping networks, the World Wide Web (WWW, or the Web) promises to become a revolutionary business tool. With more than 50 million people now on line, electronic commerce has soared from $518 million in 1996 to $6.6 billion in 2000.[72] Sales volume on the Web will accelerate even faster once experts resolve consumers' fears about the security of their transactions. The management consulting firm Booz, Allen, and Hamilton estimates that by 2007 as much as 20 percent of all household expenditures will occur in cyberspace.[73] Although most entrepreneurs have heard about the World Wide Web, most of them are still struggling to understand what it is, how it can work for them, and how they can establish a presence on it. Businesses get on the Web by using one of thousands of "electronic gateways" to set up an address (called a universal resource locator, or URL) there. By establishing a creative, attractive **Web site,** the "electronic storefront" for a company on the Web, even the smallest companies can market their products and services to customers across the globe. With its ability to display colorful graphics, sound, animation, and video as well as text, the Web allows small companies to equal—even surpass—their larger rivals' Web presence. Although small companies cannot match the marketing efforts of their larger competitors, a creative Web page can be "the Great Equalizer" in a small company's marketing program, giving it access to markets all across the globe. The Web gives small businesses the power to broaden their scope to unbelievable proportions.

Well-designed Web sites, commonly called "home pages," include interactive features that allow customers to access information about a company, its products and services, its history, and other features such as question-and-answer sessions with experts or the ability to conduct electronic conversations with company officials. The Web also allows business owners to link their companies' home pages to other related Web sites, something advertisements in other media cannot offer. For instance, the home page of a company selling cookware might include hypertext links to Web pages containing recipes, cookbooks, foods, and other cooking resources. This feature enables small business owners to cross-market with companies on the Web that are selling complementary products or services.

Currently about 141,000 small businesses have Web sites.[74] Companies are selling everything from wine and vacations to jewelry and electronics on the Web. So far, the top-selling items on the Web are computers and accessories, software, travel and financial services, and consumer electronics.[75] Although most of them are not yet making a profit from their Web sites, the entrepreneurs behind these businesses know that they must establish a presence on the Web now if they are to reap its benefits in the future. They are using the Web to connect with their existing customers and, eventually, to attract new ones. *Ann Giard-Chase and her sister, Joan, founded Joan & Annie's Brownies in 1988 in their kitchens and marketed their brownies from pushcarts at fairs and festivals. Joan (Annie left the company in 1991) saw the potential to transform the small company doing business only locally into one conducting business globally with the help of the Web. For just $500 and a reasonable monthly fee, Joan & Annie's Brownies launched a Web site <http://www.mmink.com/brownies.html> that generated immediate attention. Inquiries and orders began rolling in through e-mail and by telephone, and soon customers were ordering Brownie-Grams (personalized brownie gift packages) straight off the Web site. Within a year of opening the Web site, the company's annual electronic sales doubled to $100,000, and they have continued to climb. Thanks to her Web site, says Joan, "My company's eight varieties of brownies and its Brownie-Grams were building an international reputation virtually overnight," something she would not have been able to do without the power of the World Wide Web.[76]*

Small companies have plenty of incentive to set up shop on the World Wide Web. The number of cybershoppers is growing rapidly, and the demographic profile of the typical Web user is very attractive to plenty of entrepreneurs: young (see Figure 6.2), educated, and wealthy. According to a recent study of Web users:

◆ The average age is 35.

◆ Sixty-four percent have college degrees.

◆ Average annual household income is $69,000, and 25 percent earn more than $80,000 per year.

◆ Sixty percent are male.

◆ Seventy-seven percent browse the Web at least once a day.[77]

Although the current profile of Web customers is decidedly slanted toward affluent, well-educated males, the fact is that the Web is rapidly becoming a mainstream marketing medium, one that small business owners cannot afford to ignore.

Just as in any marketing venture, the key to successful marketing on the World Wide Web is selling the right product or service at the right price to the right target audience. Entrepreneurs on the Web, however, also have two additional challenges: attracting Web users to their Web sites and converting them into paying customers. They have to set up an electronic storefront that is inviting, easy to navigate, interactive, and offers more than a monotonous laundry list of items. The accompanying Gaining the Competitive Edge feature offers advice on designing an effective Web site.

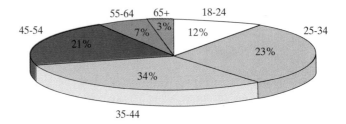

Figure 6.2 **World Wide Web Users by Age** SOURCE: e-land, http://www.e-land.com/e-stat_pages/net_user_demo_finance.html

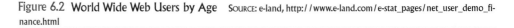

GAINING THE COMPETITIVE EDGE

Designing a Killer Web Site

*W*orld Wide Web users are not a patient lot. They sit before their computers, surfing the Net, their fingers poised on their mouse buttons, daring any Web site to delay them with files that take a long time (to many, that's anything more than 5 seconds) to load. Slow-loading sites or sites that don't deliver on their promises will cause a Web user to move on faster than a bolt of lightning can strike. Research shows that most users visit no more than 10 Web sites on a regular basis. How can an entrepreneur design a Web site that will capture and hold potential customers' attention long enough to make a sale? There's no sure-fire formula for stopping surfers in their tracks but the following suggestions will help.

Be Easy to Find With millions of pages already on the Web and more coming on every day, making your site easy for people to find is the first challenge. Smart Web site designers embed codes into their home pages that will move their sites to the top of search engines such as Yahoo!, AltaVista, Infoseek, and others.

Give Customers What They Want Although Web shoppers are price-conscious, they rank fast delivery as the most important criterion in their purchase decisions. Studies also show that surfers look for a large selection of merchandise available to them immediately.

Promote Your Web Site in Other Media Ads in other media such as direct mail or newspapers that mention your site's URL will bring customers to it. Be sure to put your Web address on everything your company publishes, from its letterhead to its business cards.

Establish "Hot Links" with Other Businesses, Preferably Those Selling Products or Services That Complement Yours Listing their Web addresses on your site and having them list your address on theirs offers customers more value and can bring traffic to your site that you otherwise would have missed.

Include an E-Mail Option in Your Site Customers will appreciate the opportunity to communicate with your company. Note: If you include e-mail access on your site, be sure to respond to it. Nothing alienates cybercustomers faster than a company that is nonresponsive to e-mail messages.

Offer Web Shoppers a Special All Their Own Give Web customers a special deal that you don't offer in any other advertising piece. Change your specials often (weekly, if possible) and use clever "teasers" to draw attention to your offer.

Use a Simple Design Catchy graphics and photographs are important to snaring customers, but designers must choose

them carefully. Designs that are overly complex take too long to load.

Specific design tips include:

- ◆ Avoid clutter. The best designs are simple and elegant with a balance of text and graphics.
- ◆ Include a menu bar at the top of the page that makes it easy for customers to find their way around your site.
- ◆ Include navigation buttons at the bottom of pages that enable customers to return to the top of the page or to the menu bar. Otherwise, you run the risk of customers' getting lost in your site and leaving.
- ◆ Avoid fancy typefaces and small fonts because they are too hard to read.
- ◆ Don't put small fonts on "busy" backgrounds; no one will read them!
- ◆ Use contrasting colors of text and graphics. For instance, blue text on a green background is nearly impossible to read.
- ◆ Be careful with frames. Don't use frames that are so heavy that they crowd out text.
- ◆ Avoid automated music that plays continuously and cannot be cut off.
- ◆ Make sure the overall look of the page is appealing. "The number one problem with most Web pages is that people have mastered, or are playing with, all new features and have forgotten about the importance of good design," says one expert.
- ◆ Remember: Simpler usually is better.

Assure Customers That Their On-Line Transactions Are Secure If you are serious about doing business on the Web, make sure that your site includes the proper security software and encryption devices. Computer-savvy customers are not willing to divulge their credit card numbers on sites that are not secure.

Keep Your Site Updated Customers want to see something new when they visit stores, and they expect the same when they visit virtual stores as well. Delete any hot links that have disappeared, and keep the information on your Web site current. You're sure to run off customers on the Web if you're advertising your company's Christmas Special in August!

Small business owners must remember that on the World Wide Web every company, no matter how big or small, has the exact same screen size for its site. What matters most is not the size of your company but how you put that screen size to use.

SOURCES: Adapted from Sandra E. Eddy, "Make Money While You Sleep," *Business Start-Ups,* July 1997, pp. 14–16; Sandra E. Eddy, "A Lasting Impression," *Business Start-Ups,* May 1997, pp. 14–16; Jennifer Sucov, "Me and My Website!" *Your Company,* June/July 1997, pp. 36–41; "Q&A," *Business Start-Ups,* March 1997, p. 5; Elyse Mall, "Talkin' about the Webolution," *Your Company,* April/May 1997, p. 23; David Carnoy, "Virtual Start-Up," *Success,* January 1998, pp. 38–41; Lisa Chadderdon, "How Dell Sells on the Web," *Fast Company,* September 1998, pp. 58–60. ◆

*T*he Marketing Mix

7 Discuss the "four Ps" of marketing—product, place, price, and promotion—and their role in building a successful marketing strategy.

The major elements of a marketing strategy are the **four Ps of marketing:** product, place, price, and promotion. These four elements are self-reinforcing and, when coordinated, increase the sales appeal of a product or service. Small business managers must integrate these elements to maximize the impact their product or service will have on the consumer. All four Ps must reinforce the image of the product or service the company presents to the potential customer. One long-time retailer claims, "None of the modern marvels of computerized inventory control and point-of-sale telecommunications have replaced the need for the entrepreneur who understands the customer and can translate that into the appropriate merchandise mix."[78]

PRODUCT

The product itself is an essential element in marketing. A **product** is any item or service that satisfies the need of a consumer. Products can have form and shape, or they can be services with no physical form. Products travel through various stages of development. The **product life cycle** (see Figure 6.3) measures these stages of growth, and these measurements enable the company's management to make decisions about whether to continue selling the product and when to introduce new follow-up products.

In the *introductory stage*, the marketers present their product to the potential consumers. Initial high levels of acceptance are rare. In general, new products must break into existing markets and compete with established products. Advertising and promotion help the new product gain recognition. Potential customers must get information about the product and the needs it can satisfy. The cost of marketing a product at this level of the life cycle is usually high. The small company must overcome customer resistance and inertia. Thus profits are generally low, or even negative, at the introductory stage.

After the introductory stage, the product enters the *growth and acceptance stage*. In the growth stage, consumers begin to purchase the product: Sales rise and profits increase. Products that reach this stage, however, do not necessarily become successful. If in the intro-

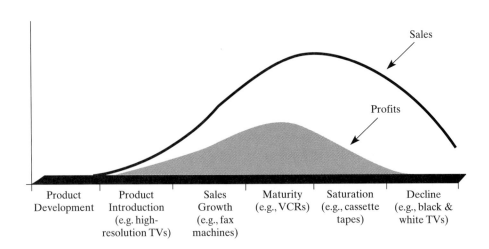

Figure 6.3 Product Life Cycle

Are We Making the Grade?

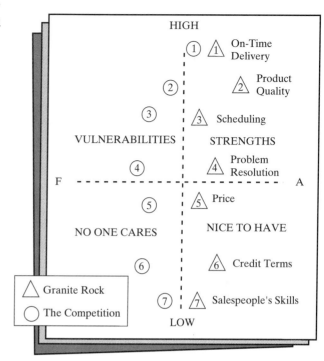

*O*n the surface, Granite Rock Company looks like any other small, family-owned construction material supplier. But a closer examination reveals a highly sophisticated, quality-conscious, customer-oriented industry leader in what is ordinarily considered a "commodity business." Granite Rock quarries granite; produces concrete, asphalt, sand, and gravel; and sells brick, drywall, cinder block, and masonry tools. On average, Granite Rock customers pay a 6 percent premium over competitors' prices. How, then, does Granite Rock maintain its leadership position in such a cutthroat industry? "Our competitors tend to see price as the main wedge," says general manager Wes Clark. "We are not low price, but we are high value."

Selling "value" can be a successful marketing strategy, but only if customers recognize and are willing to pay for it. Granite Rock concentrates on understanding *exactly* how its customers define such nebulous terms as *value*, *quality*, and *service*. The company also monitors its performance (from customers' perspective) regularly and feeds all of this information directly to its workforce. "If you set goals and lofty ideals without means of measuring, you're just kidding yourself," says Val Verutti, quality-support manager.

Granite Rock does measure its progress toward achieving specific customer satisfaction goals. Here's how the system works: Every three or four years, the company conducts an extensive survey of its customers to determine their needs and wants and what factors are most important to them when choosing a supplier.

Every year, Granite Rock sends a "report card" to customers, asking them to "grade" their top three suppliers on these factors. The factors include various measures of product quality and customer service, and the grades range from A ("The Best") to F ("Terrible") with a "No Opinion" option. "If you work hard at it, you can eventually come up with a customer survey that tells you how your customers place you versus your competitors," says CEO Bruce Woolpert.

Granite Rock then combines the results of the survey with those from the report cards to generate a Customer Service Graph (see sample). The graph has two axes: the vertical importance axis and the horizontal performance axis. The importance axis depends upon the results of the extensive customer survey. In its most recent survey, Granite Rock found that on-time delivery and product quality were most important to customers and credit terms and salespeople's skills were least important. The performance axis plots the results of the report card. The company's grade is determined by adding the number of As and Bs it gets.

The resulting four quadrants give Granite Rock valuable information. If the company scores in the Strengths quadrant,

it is performing well in an area important to its customers. If it scores in the Vulnerabilities sector, it is performing poorly in an area important to customers. The No One Cares area means Granite Rock is performing poorly in an area that customers do not really consider important. The Nice to Have area shows the company performing well in an area that is unimportant to customers. "We have a strong belief that if something is worth doing, it's probably worth measuring," says quality planning head Dave Franceschi.

Granite Rock's customer surveys led the company to create its "automatic loadout system" at its crushed rock quarry. The system works like a bank's ATM machine: The customer drives up, inserts a card, and tells the machine how much of what material he wants. The system, called Granite Xpress, automatically loads the truck, and a bill follows later. With Granite Xpress, Granite Rock is open 24 hours a day, seven days a week—the ultimate in customer convenience. The company's attitudes toward customer satisfaction and its system for measuring it have helped Granite Rock maintain its profitability and nearly double its marketshare, even through a severe recession.

1. What benefits does Granite Rock's customer satisfaction system offer customers? What are its benefits to the company itself?

2. Which areas of the Customer Service Graph would be most important to Granite Rock? Least important? Why?

SOURCES: Adapted from Edward O. Welles, "How're We Doing?" *Inc.*, May 1991, pp. 80–83; Michael Barrier, "Learning the Meaning of Measurement," *Nation's Business*, June 1994, pp. 72–74. ◆

ductory or the growth stage the product fails to meet consumer needs, sales will decline and eventually the product will disappear from the marketplace. For successful products, sales and profit margins continue to rise through the growth stage.

In the *maturity and competition stage*, sales volume continues to rise, but profit margins peak and then begin to fall as competitors enter the market. Normally, the product's selling price must be lowered to meet competition and to hold its share of the market.

Sales peak in the *market saturation stage* and give the marketer fair warning that it is time to begin product innovation.

The final stage is the *product decline stage*. Sales continue to drop, and profit margins fall drastically. However, reaching this stage of the cycle does not mean that a product is doomed to failure. Products that have remained popular are always being revised. No firm can maintain its market position without product innovation and change. Even the maker of Silly Putty, first introduced at the 1950 International Toy Fair (with lifetime sales of more than 200 million "eggs") recently introduced new Day-Glo and glow-in-the-dark colors. These innovations have caused the classic toy's sales to surge by more than 60 percent.[79]

The time span of the stages in the product life cycle depends on the type of products involved. High-fashion and fad clothing have a short product life cycle, lasting for only four to six weeks. Products that are more stable may take years to complete a life cycle. Research conducted by MIT suggests that the typical product's life cycle lasts 10 to 14 years. For example, the standard household refrigerator went through a long product life cycle. Profit margins and sales began to decline, but the cycle began again with the introduction of product variations such as the freezer; frost-free operation; automatic ice makers; water, juice, and ice dispensers; and a variety of door locations. The latest models include motors that drastically reduce energy consumption. The introduction of such models sent the sales and profit margins of less-sophisticated models into severe decline.

Understanding the product life cycle can help a business owner plan the introduction of new products to the company's product line. Often, companies wait too late into the life cycle of one product to introduce another. The result is that they are totally unprepared when a competitor produces "a better mousetrap" and their sales decline. The ideal time to develop new products is early on in the life cycle of the current product (see Figure 6.4). Waiting until the current product is in the saturation or decline stage is like living on borrowed time.

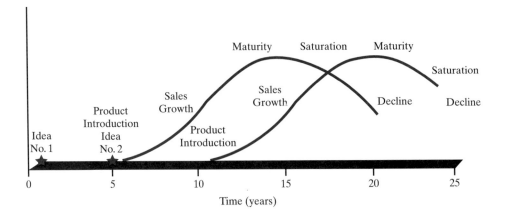

Figure 6.4 Time between Introduction of Products

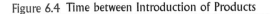

Launching successful new products is no easy task. The head of a new-product consulting firm estimates that out of every 3,000 new product ideas, only about two products are actually launched, and only one of those succeeds.[80] The most commonly cited reasons for product failures are:

♦ Too little differentiation from existing products

♦ Inadequate knowledge of the market

♦ Poor planning and execution of the introduction

♦ Failure to adjust product strategy when changes dictate

♦ Inadequate funding for or lack of commitment to the new product[81]

PLACE

Place (or method of distribution) has grown in importance as customers expect greater service and more convenience from businesses. Because of this trend, mail-order houses, home shopping channels, and the World Wide Web have experienced booming sales in the last decade. In addition, many businesses have added wheels, becoming mobile animal clinics, computer shops, and dentist offices.

Any activity involving movement of goods to the point of consumer purchase provides place utility. Place utility is directly affected by the marketing **channel of distribution,** the path that goods or services take in moving from producer to consumer. Channels typically involve intermediaries who perform specialized functions that add valuable utility to the good or service. Specifically, these intermediaries provide **time utility** (making the product available when customers want to buy it) and **place utility** (making the product available where customers want to buy it).

For consumer goods, there are four common channels of distribution (see Figure 6.5).

1. *Manufacturer to consumer.* In some markets, producers sell their goods or services directly to consumers. Services, by nature, follow this channel of distribution. Dental care and haircuts, for example, go directly from creator to consumer.

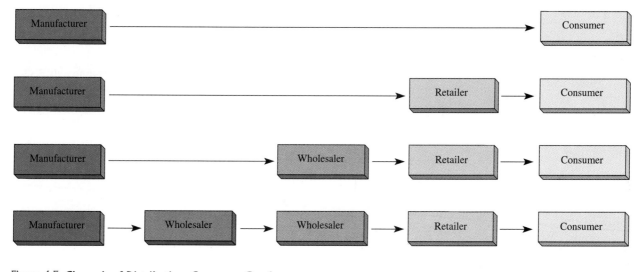

Figure 6.5 **Channels of Distribution: Consumer Goods**

2. *Manufacturer to retailer to consumer.* Another common channel involves a retailer as an intermediary. Many clothing items, books, shoes, and other consumer products are distributed in this manner.

3. *Manufacturer to wholesaler to retailer to consumer.* This is the most common channel of distribution. Prepackaged food products, hardware, toys, and other items are commonly distributed through this channel.

4. *Manufacturer to wholesaler to wholesaler to retailer to consumer.* A few consumer goods (e.g., agricultural goods and electrical components) follow this pattern of distribution.

Two channels of distribution are common for industrial goods (see Figure 6.6).

1. *Manufacturer to industrial user.* Most industrial goods are distributed directly from manufacturers to users. In some cases, the goods or services are designed to meet the user's specifications.

2. *Manufacturer to wholesaler to industrial user.* Most expense items (paper clips, paper, rubber bands, cleaning fluids) that firms commonly use are distributed through wholesalers. For most small manufacturers, distributing goods through established wholesalers and agents is often the most effective route.

With their limited resources, entrepreneurs sometimes have to rely on nontraditional distribution channels and use their creativity to get their products into customers' hands. *For instance, when Paul Iams founded the Iams Pet Food Company in 1946, the large pet food manufacturers sold their products strictly through supermarkets and the occasional feed store. Knowing that his products would never receive enough attention in this traditional distribution channel, Iams began selling his premium pet foods through veterinarians, breeders, and pet stores. Even though its markets are now international, Iams still relies on this same distribution channel.*[82]

PRICE

Almost everyone agrees that the price of the product or service is a key factor in the decision to buy. Price affects both sales volume and profits, and without the right price, both sales and profits will suffer. As we will see in chapter 10, the right price for a product or service depends on three factors: (1) a small company's cost structure, (2) an assessment of what the market will bear, and (3) the desired image the company wants to create in its customers' minds.

For many small businesses, nonprice competition—focusing on factors other than price—is a more effective strategy than trying to beat larger competitors in a price war. Non-

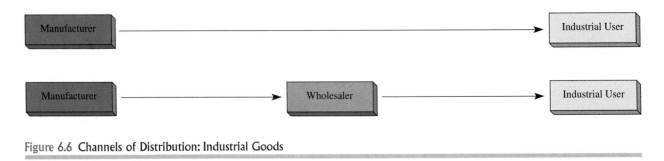

Figure 6.6 Channels of Distribution: Industrial Goods

price competition, such as free trial offers, free delivery, lengthy warranties, and money-back guarantees, plays down the product's price and stresses its durability, quality, reputation, or special features.

PROMOTION

Promotion involves both advertising and personal selling. Advertising communicates to potential customers through some mass medium the benefits of a good or service. Personal selling involves the art of persuasive sales on a one-to-one basis.

The goals of a small company's promotional efforts are to create a brand image, to persuade customers to buy, and to develop brand loyalty. Promotion can take many forms and is put before the public through a variety of media. Entrepreneurs often must find ways to use low-cost guerrilla tactics to create promotions that get their companies noticed by both local and national media. *For instance, Richard Thompson, owner of Thompson's Pet Products, a very small player in the $10 billion pet food industry, gained national attention for his tiny company by sponsoring a nationwide "Teach Your Dog to Say 'Pasta' Contest." (Melbourne, a dog from Buffalo, New York was the winner.) Thompson also runs promotional events in grocery store "barking lots" in key cities across the country every year to encourage pet owners to buy his company's pasta for dogs.*[83] Chapter 11 is devoted to creating an effective advertising and promotion campaign for a small company.

Chapter Summary

1 Describe the components of a marketing plan and explain the benefits of preparing one.
- ◆ A major part of the entrepreneur's business plan is the marketing plan, which focuses on a company's target customers and how best to satisfy their needs and wants. A solid marketing plan should:
  - ◆ Determine customer needs and wants through market research.
  - ◆ Pinpoint the specific target markets the company will serve.
  - ◆ Analyze the firm's competitive advantages and build a marketing strategy around them.
  - ◆ Create a marketing mix that meets customer needs and wants.

2 Discuss the role of market research.
- ◆ Market research is the vehicle for gathering the information that serves as the foundation of the marketing plan. Good research does *not* have to be complex and expensive to be useful.

3 Outline the market research process.
- ◆ The steps in conducting market research include:
  - ◆ Defining the problem: "What do you want to know?"
  - ◆ Collecting the data from either primary or secondary sources.
  - ◆ Analyzing and interpreting the data.
  - ◆ Acting on the data.

4 Explain how small businesses can pinpoint their target markets.
- ◆ Sound market research helps the owner pinpoint his target market. The most successful businesses have well-defined portraits of the customers they are seeking to attract.

5 Describe the factors on which a small business can build a competitive edge.
- ◆ When plotting a marketing strategy, owners must strive to achieve a competitive advantage: some way to make their companies different from and better than the competition. Successful small businesses rely on six sources to develop a competitive edge:
  - ◆ Focus on the customer
  - ◆ Devotion to quality
  - ◆ Attention to convenience
  - ◆ Concentration on innovation
  - ◆ Dedication to service
  - ◆ Emphasis on speed

6 Discuss the marketing opportunities the World Wide Web offers entrepreneurs and how to best take advantage of them.
- ◆ The Web offers small business owners tremendous marketing potential on a par with their larger rivals. Entrepreneurs are just beginning to uncover the Web's profit potential, which is growing rapidly. Establishing a presence on the Web is important for companies targeting educated, wealthy,

young customers. Successful Web sites are attractive, easy to navigate, and interactive, and they offer users something of value.

7 Discuss the "four Ps" of marketing—product, place, price, and promotion—and their role in building a successful marketing strategy.

◆ *Product.* Entrepreneurs should understand where in the product life cycle their products are.

◆ *Place.* The focus is on choosing the appropriate channel of distribution and using it most efficiently.

◆ *Price.* The right price depends on the company's cost structure and image and what the market will bear.

◆ *Promotion.* Promotion helps create a company image, persuades customers to buy, and develops customer loyalty.

Discussion Questions

1. Define the marketing plan. What lies at its center?
2. What objectives should a marketing plan accomplish?
3. How can market research benefit a small business owner? List some possible sources of market information.
4. Does market research have to be expensive and sophisticated to be valuable? Explain.
5. Describe several market trends that are driving markets in the 1990s and their impact on small businesses.
6. Why is it important for small business owners to define their target markets as part of their marketing strategies?
7. What is a competitive edge? How might a small company gain a competitive edge?
8. Describe how a small business owner could use each of the following to gain a competitive advantage:
   ◆ Focus on the customer
   ◆ Devotion to quality
   ◆ Attention to convenience
   ◆ Concentration on innovation
   ◆ Dedication to service
   ◆ Emphasis on speed
9. What is the World Wide Web? Describe its marketing potential for small businesses.
10. Explain the concept of the marketing mix. What are the four Ps?
11. List and explain the stages in the product life cycle. How can a small firm extend its product's life?
12. With a 70 percent customer retention rate (average for most U.S. firms according to the American Manage-

ment Association), every $1 million of 1995 business will have grown to more than $4 million by the year 2005. If you retain 80 percent of your customers, the $1 million will grow to a little over $6 million. If you can keep 90 percent of your customers, that $1 million will grow to more than $9.5 million. What can the typical small business do to increase its customer retention rate?

Step into the Real World

1. Interview the owner of a local restaurant about its marketing strategy. From how large a geographic region does the restaurant draw its clientele? What is the firm's target market? What are the restaurant's characteristics? Does the restaurant have a competitive edge?
2. Select a local small manufacturing operation and evaluate its primary product. What stage of the product life cycle is it in? What channels of distribution does the product follow after leaving the manufacturer?
3. Research current business periodicals such as *Inc., Inc. Technology, Nation's Business, Your Company, Fortune, Forbes,* and others to determine how small companies are using the World Wide Web to market their products and services more effectively. Find at least one example of a company effectively using the Web as a marketing tool. Visit its Web site and evaluate it using the criteria described in the Gaining the Competitive Advantage feature in this chapter.
4. Using one of the search engines on the World Wide Web, research the current demographic profile of Web users. What is the growth rate for Web users? Prepare a brief report on your findings. What implications do your conclusions have for entrepreneurs considering setting up Web sites?
5. Contact three local small business owners and ask them about their marketing strategies. How have they achieved a competitive edge? Develop a series of questions to determine the sources of their competitive edge: a focus on the customer, devotion to quality, attention to convenience, concentration on innovation, dedication to service, emphasis on speed. How do the businesses compare?
6. Select a local small business owner and work with him or her to develop a "report card" like the one Granite Rock uses. On the basis of this customer feedback, make specific recommendations to improve the business's ability to serve its customers effectively.

Take It to the Net

Visit the Scarborough/Zimmerer home page at
www.prenhall.com/scarbzim
for updated information, on-line resources, and Web-based exercises.

Endnotes

1. Dale D. Buss, "The Little Guys Strike Back," *Nation's Business*, July 1996, p. 19.
2. Kazumi Tanaka, "Putting Your Business on the Map," *Inc. Technology*, no. 2 (1996), pp. 94–99.
3. Howard Dana Shaw, "Customer Care Checklist," *In Business*, September/October 1987, p. 28.
4. David Altany, "Call Me Tom," *Industry Week*, January 22, 1990, p. 22.
5. Frances Huffman, "Search for Tomorrow," *Entrepreneur*, December 1993, pp. 94–95.
6. Peter Weaver, "How to Reach Older Consumers," *Nation's Business*, June 1997, pp. 35–36; Dan Marin, "Si, Senior," *Business News*, Spring 1997, pp. 61–62; Carter Henderson, "Make Way for the Woopie Market," *In Business*, January/February 1998, pp. 30–32.
7. Janean Chun, "Direct Hit," *Entrepreneur*, October 1996, pp. 142–143.
8. Roberta Maynard, "Dining Styles of the Rich and Famous," *Nation's Business*, May 1997, p. 12.
9. Stephanie Gruner, "I Can't Afford Formal Market Research," *Inc.*, July 1997, p. 105.
10. J. Ford Laumer, James R. Harris, and Hugh J. Guffey, *Learning about Your Market*, Management Aid No. 4.019 (Washington, D.C.: U.S. Small Business Administration, 1982), p. 2.
11. Constance Gustke, "Previewing the 21st Century," *Industry Week*, May 5, 1997, pp. 48–55; see also Debra Phillips, "Trend Tracking," *Entrepreneur*, August 1996, p. 21; and Nancy L. Croft, "Smart Selling," *Nation's Business*, March 1988, pp. 51–52.
12. Gustke, "Previewing the 21st Century," p. 51.
13. Robert McGarvey, "Trend Spotting," *Entrepreneur*, December 1996, p. 144.
14. Phaedra Hise, "Industry Bottoms Out, Disposes of Diaper Service," *Inc.*, June 1997, p. 32.
15. Shari Caudron, "Right on Target," *Industry Week*, September 2, 1996, p. 45.
16. Ibid., pp. 45–50.
17. Patricia Sellers, "Companies That Serve You Best," *Fortune*, May 31, 1993, p. 76.
18. Kylo-Patrick Hart, "Who Are Your Customers?" *Business Start-Ups*, August 1997, pp. 78–80.
19. Rhonda Albey, "Multicultural Marketing," *Business Start-Ups*, March 1997, pp. 44–48.
20. Gayle Sato Stodder, "Read All about It," *Entrepreneur*, January 1997, pp. 144–150.
21. Gayle Sato Stodder, "Consumer Report," *Entrepreneur*, May 1997, pp. 125–130.
22. Albey, "Multicultural Marketing"; Dan Fost, "Asian Homebuyers Seek Wind and Water," *American Demographics*, June 1993, pp. 23–25.
23. Timothy Aeppel, "O'Gara Co.'s Cars Aren't Just for Presidents Anymore," *Wall Street Journal*, October 1, 1997, p. B2.
24. Douglas Gantenbein, "REI: Enjoying the Great Outdoors Indoors," *Wall Street Journal*, October 15, 1996, p. A20.
25. Joshua Levine, "Relationship Marketing," *Forbes*, December 20, 1993, p. 232.
26. Bradford McKee, "How Much Do You Really Value Your Customers?" *Nation's Business*, August 1993, p. 8.
27. Joseph R. Garber, "Know Your Customer," *Forbes*, February 10, 1997, p. 128.
28. Howard Upton, "Don't Let Bad Company Manners Hurt Good Products," *Wall Street Journal*, April 11, 1988, p. 31.
29. "Deadly Game of Losing Customers," *In Business*, May 1988, p. 189.
30. Jim Campbell, "Good Customer Service Pays Off," *UP*, November 1988, pp. 12–13.
31. "Keeping Customers for Life," *Communication Briefings*, September 1990, p. 3.
32. Mark Henricks, "Staying Power," *Entrepreneur*, July 1997, pp. 70–72; Joan Koob Cannie, "Turning Customers into Lost Gold," *Small Business Reports*, May 1994, p. 58; Sellers, "Companies That Serve You Best," p. 75.
33. Michael Barrier, "Building Your 'Customer Portfolio,'" *Nation's Business*, December 1996, p. 45; Elyse Mall, "Reward Your Best Clients with Tailor-Made Service," *Your Company*, Forecast 1998, pp. 33–40.
34. Henricks, "Staying Power"; William A. Sherden, "The Tools of Retention," *Small Business Reports*, November 1994, pp. 43–47.
35. Barrier, "Building Your 'Customer Portfolio,'" pp. 45–46.
36. Ibid.
37. "Be on the Lookout for Changes," *Communication Briefings*, October 1993, p. 4.
38. "Ways & Means," *Reader's Digest*, January 1993, p. 56.
39. "Encourage Customers to Complain," *Small Business Reports*, June 1990, p. 7.
40. Dave Zielinski, "Improving Service Doesn't Require a Big Investment," *Small Business Reports*, February 1991, p. 20.
41. John H. Sheridan, "Out of the Isolation Booth," *Industry Week*, June 19, 1989, pp. 18–19.
42. Frank Rose, "Now Quality Means Service Too," *Fortune*, April 22, 1991, p. 100.
43. Mark Henricks, "Make No Mistake," *Entrepreneur*, October 1996, pp. 86–89.
44. Faye Rice, "How to Deal with Tougher Customers," *Fortune*, December 3, 1990, pp. 39–40.
45. Rahul Jacob, "TQM: More Than a Dying Fad," *Fortune*, October 18, 1993, p. 67.

46. Ibid.

47. Bob Weinstein, "Consider It Done," *Business Start-Ups*, October 1997, pp. 40–47.

48. Zielinski, "Improving Service Doesn't Require a Big Investment."

49. Anna Wilde Matthews, "Truck Stops Now Offer Massages, Movies, and Marriages," *Wall Street Journal*, July 22, 1997, pp. B1, B6.

50. Jerry Nachtigal, "Supermarkets Offer Free Child Care As Parents Wander Aisles, Spend Money," *Upstate Business*, January 19, 1997, p. 4; Catherine Siskos, "Peace in the Cereal Aisle," *Kiplinger's Personal Finance Magazine*, December 1996, p. 10.

51. Roberta Maynard, "The Heat Is On," *Nation's Business*, October 1997, pp. 14–23.

52. Ibid., p. 16.

53. Ibid.

54. Joseph R. Mancuso, "How Callaway Runs His Idea Factory," *Your Company*, April/May 1997, p. 72.

55. Alan Deutschman, "America's Fastest Risers," *Fortune*, October 7, 1991, p. 58.

56. Maynard, "The Heat Is On."

57. Ibid.

58. Robert McGarvey, "Full Service," *Entrepreneur*, January 1997, p. 129.

59. Elyse Mall, "Make Sure That Your Customers Love You," *Your Company*, Forecast 1997, pp. 23–29.

60. David Altany, "One Step *Beyond* Customer Satisfaction," *Industry Week*, September 3, 1990, p. 13.

61. Joan Koob Cannie, "We Are the Champions," *Small Business Reports*, January 1993, pp. 31–41.

62. Ron Zemke and Dick Schaaf, "The Service Edge," *Small Business Reports*, July 1990, pp. 57–60.

63. Thomas A. Stewart, "After All You've Done for Your Customers, Why Are They Still NOT HAPPY?" *Fortune*, December 11, 1995, pp. 178–182; Gil Gerretsen, "Special Tools Are Used by Super Markets," *Upstate Business*, June 14, 1998, p. 4.

64. Ronald Henkoff, "Service Is Everybody's Business," *Fortune*, June 27, 1994, p. 49.

65. Carla Goodman, "Satisfaction Guaranteed," *Business Start-Ups*, December 1997, pp. 54–58.

66. John Grossman, "The Wiring of the Green," *Inc. Technology*, no. 4 (1996), pp. 55–58.

67. Ron Zemke and Dick Schaaf, "The Service Edge," *Small Business Reports*, July 1990, p. 60.

68. Patricia Sellers, "What Customers Really Want," *Fortune*, June 4, 1990, p. 60.

69. Brian Dumaine, "How Managers Can Succeed through Speed," *Fortune*, February 13, 1989, pp. 54–59.

70. Mark Henricks, "Time Is Money," *Entrepreneur*, February 1993, p. 44.

71. Ibid.

72. David Stipp, "The Birth of Digital Commerce," *Fortune*, December 9, 1996, pp. 159–164; <http://www.e-land.com/e-stat_pages/electronic_com_frames.html>.

73. Stipp, "The Birth of Digital Commerce."

74. Jennifer Sucov, "Me and My Website!" *Your Company*, June/July 1997, pp. 36–41.

75. Veronica Byrd and Brian L. Clark, "Increasing Your Net Profits," *Your Company*, June/July 1996, pp. 22–28; <http://www.e-land.com/e-stat_pages/electronic_com_frames.html>.

76. Ann Giard-Chase, "Untangling the Web for Retail Sales," *Nation's Business*, March 1997, p. 21.

77. <http://www.e-land.com/e-stat_pages/electronic_com_frames.html>; <http://www.cyberatlas.com/>.

78. Stanley J. Winkelman, "Why Big-Name Stores Are Losing Out," *Fortune*, May 8, 1989, pp. 14–15.

79. Deanna Hodgin, "A War Baby Bounces Back in Trendy Style, *Insight*, April 1, 1991, p. 44.

80. Jeannie Mandelker, "Crush Rivals by Launching Great Products," *Your Company*, October/November 1997, pp. 54–61.

81. Maynard, "The Heat Is On"; "Business Bulletins," *Small Business Reports*, February 1988, p. 15.

82. Erin Davies, "Selling Sex and Cat Food," *Fortune*, June 9, 1997, p. 36.

83. Dyan Machan, "Ziti for Dogs," *Forbes*, February 24, 1997, pp. 94–95; Roberta Maynard, "The Lighter Side of Promotions," *Nation's Business*, July 1996, p. 48.

Creating the Financial Plan

You can't tell who's swimming naked until after the tide goes out.

—*David Darst*

To know is to control.

—*Scott Reed*

Upon completion of this chapter, you will be able to

1. Understand the importance of preparing a financial plan.

2. Describe how to prepare financial statements and use them to manage the small business.

3. Create pro forma financial statements.

4. Understand the basic financial statements through ratio analysis.

5. Explain how to interpret financial ratios.

6. Conduct a breakeven analysis for a small company.

1. Understand the importance of preparing a financial plan.

*O*ne of the most important steps in launching a new business venture is fashioning a well-designed, logical financial plan. Potential lenders and investors demand such a plan before putting their money into a start-up company. More important, this financial plan can be a vital tool that helps entrepreneurs manage their businesses effectively, steering their way around the pitfalls that cause failures. Entrepreneurs who ignore the financial aspects of their business run the risk of watching their company sink into failure. One financial expert says of small companies, "Those that don't establish sound controls at the start are setting themselves up to fail."[1] Still, according to one recent survey, more than one-third of all entrepreneurs admitted that they were not spending sufficient time tracking key financial indicators such as sales, accounts receivable, and cash flow.[2] Another study found that only 11 percent of small business owners analyzed their financial statements as part of the managerial planning and decision-making process.[3] To reach profit objectives, small business managers must be aware of their firm's overall financial position and the changes in financial status that occur over time.

This chapter focuses on some practical tools that will help entrepreneurs develop workable financial plans, keep them focused on their company's financial plan, and enable them to plan for profit. They can use these tools to anticipate changes and to plot an appropriate profit strategy to meet them head on. These profit planning techniques are not difficult to master, nor are they overly time-consuming. We will discuss the techniques involved in preparing projected (pro forma) financial statements, conducting ratio analysis, and performing breakeven analysis.

*B*asic Financial Reports

Before we begin building projected financial statements, it will be helpful to review the basic financial reports that measure a company's financial position: the balance sheet, the income statement, and the statement of cash flows. Studies show that the level of financial reporting among small businesses is high; some 81 percent of the companies in one survey regularly produced summary financial information, almost all of it in the form of these traditional financial statements.[4]

THE BALANCE SHEET

The **balance sheet** takes a "snapshot" of a business, providing owners with an estimate of the firm's worth on a given date. Its two major sections show the assets a business owns and the claims creditors and owners have against those assets. The balance sheet is usually prepared on the last day of the month. Figure 7.1 shows the balance sheet for Sam's Appliance Shop for the year ended December 31, 200X.

The balance sheet is built on the fundamental accounting equation: assets = liabilities + owner's equity. Any increase or decrease on one side of the equation must be offset by an equal increase or decrease on the other side; hence, the name *balance sheet*. It provides a baseline from which to measure future changes in assets, liabilities, and equity (or net worth). The first section of the balance sheet lists the firm's assets (valued at cost, not actual market value) and shows the total value of everything the business owns. **Current assets** consist of cash and items to be converted into cash within one year or within the normal operating cycle of the company, whichever is longer, such as accounts receivable and inventory, and **fixed assets** are those acquired for long-term use in the business. Intangible assets include items that, although valuable, do not have tangible value, such as goodwill, copyrights, and patents.

The second section shows the business's **liabilities:** creditors' claims against the firm's assets. **Current liabilities** are those debts that must be paid within one year or within the normal operating cycle of the company, whichever is longer, and **long-term liabilities** are those that come due after one year.

The final section of the balance sheet shows the owner's equity, the value of the owner's investment in the business. It is the balancing factor on the balance sheet, representing all of the owner's capital contributions to the business plus all accumulated earnings not distributed to the owners.

THE INCOME STATEMENT

The **income statement** (or **profit and loss statement** or "**P&L**") compares expenses against revenue over a certain period of time to show the firm's net profit or loss. The income statement is a "moving picture" of the firm's profitability over time. The annual P&L statement

Figure 7.1 Balance Sheet, Sam's Appliance Shop, for the Year Ended December 31, 200X

Assets

Current Assets

Cash		$ 49,855
Accounts receivable	$179,225	
Less allowance for doubtful accounts	$ 6,000	$173,225
Inventory		$455,455
Prepaid expenses		$ 8,450
Total Current Assets			$686,985

Fixed Assets

Land		$59,150
Buildings	$74,650	
Less accumulated depreciation	$ 7,050	$67,600
Equipment	$22,375	
Less accumulated depreciation	$ 1,250	$21,125
Furniture and fixtures	$10,295	
Less accumulated depreciation	$ 1,000	$ 9,295
Total Fixed Assets			$ 157,70
Intangibles (goodwill)			$ 3,500
Total Assets			$847,655

Liabilities

Current Liabilities

Accounts payable	$152,580
Notes payable	$ 83,920
Accrued wages and salaries payable	$ 38,150
Accrued interest payable	$ 42,380
Accrued taxes payable	$ 50,820
Total Current Liabilities	$367,850

Long-Term Liabilities

Mortgage	$127,150
Note payable	$ 85,000
Total Long-Term Liabilities	$212,150

Owner's Equity

Sam Lloyd, capital	$267,655
Total Liabilities + Owner's Equity	$847,655

reports the bottom line of the business over the fiscal or calendar year. Figure 7.2 shows the income statement for Sam's Appliance Shop for the year ended December 31, 200X.

To calculate net profit or loss, the owner records sales revenues for the year, which includes all income that flows into the business from sales of goods and services. Income from other sources (rent, investments, interest) also must be included in the revenue section of the income statement. To determine net sales revenue, owners subtract the value of returned items and refunds from gross revenue. **Cost of goods sold** represents the total cost, including shipping, of the merchandise sold during the year. Most wholesalers and retailers calculate cost of goods sold by adding purchases to beginning inventory and subtracting ending inventory. Service companies typically have no cost of goods sold. Subtracting the cost of goods sold from net sales revenue yields a company's **gross profit,** an important number that many

Figure 7.2 Income Statement, Sam's Appliance Shop, for the Year Ended December 31, 200X

Net Sales Revenue		$1,870,841
Cost of Goods Sold		
Beginning Inventory, 1/1/XX	$ 805,745	
+ Purchases	$ 939,827	
Goods Available for Sale	$1,745,572	
– Ending Inventory, 12/31/XX	$ 455,455	
Total Cost of Goods Sold		$1,290,117
Gross Profit		$ 580,724
Operating Expenses		
Advertising	$139,670	
Insurance	$ 46,125	
Depreciation		
Building	$ 18,700	
Equipment	$ 9,000	
Salaries	$224,500	
Travel	$ 4,000	
Entertainment	$ 2,500	
Total Operating Expenses		$ 444,495
General Expenses		
Utilities	$ 5,300	
Telephone	$ 2,500	
Postage	$ 1,200	
Payroll Taxes	$25,000	
Total General Expenses		$ 34,000
Other Expenses		
Interest Expense	$39,850	
Bad Check Expense	$ 1,750	
Total Other Expenses		$ 41,600
Total Expenses		$ 520,095
Net Income		$ 60,629

business owners overlook. Allowing the cost of goods sold to get out of control will whittle away a company's gross profit, virtually guaranteeing a net loss on the income statement. "You don't make money on what you sell," declares Richard Yobs, owner of Painten' Place Inc., a retail paint and wall-covering store. "You make it on how you buy."[5] **Operating expenses** include those costs that contribute directly to the manufacture and distribution of goods. **General expenses** are indirect costs incurred in operating the business. "Other expenses" is a catch-all category covering all expenses that don't fit into the other two categories. Total revenue minus total expenses yields the company's net profit (or loss). *Cary Vaughn, owner of Vaughn's Inc., which operates two Popeye's Famous Fried Chicken restaurants, relies on his company's income statement for important management information. He uses the numbers to help him make key decisions about the future of his business. "I don't let too much time go by before I figure out where we are," he says. "A one percent difference (on our income statement) is worth about $20,000 at the end of a year."[6]* Figure 7.3 shows the results of a recent study by TEC, an international organization of CEOs, concerning the financial reporting patterns of fast-growing companies.

THE STATEMENT OF CASH FLOWS

The **statement of cash flows** shows the changes in the firm's working capital since the beginning of the year by listing the sources of funds and the uses of those funds. Many small businesses never need such a statement; instead, they rely on a cash budget, a less formal managerial tool that tracks the flow of cash into and out of a company over time. (We will discuss cash budgets in chapter 8.) Sometimes, however, creditors, lenders, investors, or new owners may require this information.

To prepare the statement, the owner must assemble the balance sheets and the income statements summarizing the present year's operations. She begins with the company's net income for the accounting period (from the income statement). Then she adds the sources of funds: borrowed funds, owner contributions, decreases in accounts payable, decreases in inventory, depreciation, and any others. Depreciation is listed as a source of funds because it is a non-cash expense that is deducted as a cost of doing business. Because the owner has already paid for the item being depreciated, its depreciation is a source of funds. Next the owner subtracts the uses of these funds: plant and equipment purchases, dividends to owners, repayment of debt, increases in accounts receivable, decreases in accounts payable, increases in inventory, and so on. The difference between the total sources and the total uses of funds is the increase or decrease in working capital. By investigating the changes in the firm's working capital and the reasons for them, owners can create a practical financial plan of action for the future of the enterprise.

These statements are more than just complex documents used only by accountants and financial officers. When used in conjunction with the analytical tools described in the follow-

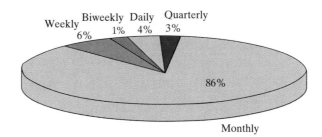

Figure 7.3 **How Often Small Business Owners Prepare a Profit-and-Loss Statement**
SOURCE: TEC, San Diego, California.

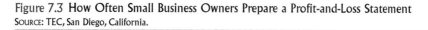

ing sections, they can help small business managers map their firm's financial future and actively plan for profit. Mere preparation of these statements is not enough, however; owners and employees must *understand and use* the information contained in them to make the business more effective and efficient. Delegating the financial task to someone else and then forgetting about it is another invitation to disaster. "Keep your fingers on everything financial," advises the owner of a successful day-care center. "No one looks after your business like you do."[7]

$\mathcal{C}$reating Projected (Pro Forma) Financial Statements

3 Create pro forma financial statements.

Creating projected financial statements via the budgeting process helps the small business owner transform business goals into reality. Once developed, a budget will answer such questions as: What profit can the business expect to obtain? If the owner's profit objective is *X* dollars, what sales level must she achieve? What fixed and variable expenses can she expect at that level of sales? The answers to those and other questions are critical in formulating a successful financial plan for the small business.

This section will focus on creating projected income statements and balance sheets for the small business. These projected (or pro forma) statements estimate the profitability and the overall financial condition of the business for future months. They are an integral part of convincing potential lenders and investors to provide the financing needed to get the company off the ground. Also, because these statements project the firm's financial position through the end of the forecasted period, they help the owner plan the route to improved financial strength and healthy business growth.

Because the established business has a history of operating data from which to construct pro forma financial statements, the task is not nearly as difficult as it is for the beginning business. When creating pro forma financial statements for a brand new business, an entrepreneur typically relies on published statistics summarizing the operation of similar-sized companies in the same industry. These statistics are available from a number of sources (described later), but this section draws on information found in *Robert Morris Associates Annual Statement Studies*, a compilation of financial data on thousands of companies across hundreds of industries (organized by Standard Industrial Classification [SIC] Code).

One of the most important tasks confronting the entrepreneur launching a new enterprise is to determine the funds needed to begin operation as well as those required to keep going through the initial growth period. The amount of money needed to begin a business depends on the type of operation, its location, inventory requirements, sales volume, and other factors. But every new firm must have enough capital to cover all start-up costs, including funds to rent or buy plant, equipment, and tools as well as to pay for advertising, licenses, utilities, and other expenses. *In addition, the owner must maintain a reserve of capital to carry the company until it begins to make a profit.* Too often entrepreneurs are overly optimistic in their financial plans and fail to recognize that expenses initially exceed income for most small firms. This period of net losses is normal and may last from just a few months to several years. Owners must be able to meet payrolls, maintain adequate inventory, take advantage of cash discounts, grant customer credit, and meet personal obligations during this time.

THE PRO FORMA INCOME STATEMENT

When creating a projected income statement, an entrepreneur has two options: develop a sales forecast and work down, or set a profit target and work up. Most businesses use the latter method; the owner targets a profit figure and then determines what sales level he must achieve to reach it. Of course, it is important to compare this sales target against the results of the marketing plan to determine whether it is realistic. Although they are projections, financial forecasts must be based in reality; otherwise, they are nothing more than a hopeless dream. The next step is to estimate the expenses the business will incur in securing those sales. In any small business, the annual profit must be large enough to produce a return for time the owners spend operating the business plus a return on their investment in the business.

An entrepreneur who earns less in his own business than he could earn working for someone else must weigh carefully the advantages and disadvantages of choosing the path of entrepreneurship. Why be exposed to all of the risks, sacrifices, and hard work of beginning and operating a small business if the rewards are less than those of remaining in the secure employment of another? Ideally, the firm's net profit after taxes should be at least as much as the owner could earn by working for someone else.

An adequate profit must also include a reasonable return on the owner's total investment in the business. The owner's total investment is the amount contributed to the company at its inception plus any retained earnings (profits from previous years funneled back into the operation). If a would-be owner has $70,000 to invest and can invest it in securities and earn 10 percent, she should not consider investing it in a small business that would yield only 3 percent.

So, the owner's target income is the sum of a reasonable salary for the time spent running the business and a normal return on the amount invested in the firm. Determining how much this should be is the first step in creating the pro forma income statement.

The owner then must translate this target profit into a net sales figure for the forecasted period. To calculate net sales from a target profit, the owner needs published statistics for this type of business. Suppose an entrepreneur wants to launch a small retail bookstore and has determined that his target income is $29,000 annually. Statistics gathered from *Robert Morris Associates (RMA) Annual Statement Studies* show that the typical bookstore's net profit margin (net profit ÷ net sales) is 9.3 percent. Using this information, he can compute the sales level required to produce a net profit of $29,000:

$$\text{Net profit margin} = \frac{\text{Net profit}}{\text{Net sales (annual)}}$$

$$9.3\% = \frac{\$29,000}{\text{Net sales (annual)}}$$

$$\text{Net sales} = \frac{\$29,000}{0.093}$$

$$= \$311,828$$

Now the entrepreneur knows that to make a net profit of $29,000 (before taxes), he must achieve annual sales of $311,828. To complete the projected income statement, the owner simply applies the appropriate statistics from *RMA Annual Statement Studies* to the annual sales figure. Because the statistics for each income statement item are expressed as percentages of net sales, he merely multiplies the proper statistic by the annual sales figure to obtain the desired value. For example, cost of goods sold usually constitutes 61.4 percent of net sales for the typical small bookstore. So the owner of this new bookstore expects his cost of goods sold to be the following:

$$\text{Cost of goods sold} = \$311,828 \times 0.614 = \$191,462$$

The bookstore's complete projected income statement is shown as follows:

Net sales	(100%)	$311,828
−Cost of goods sold	(61.4%)	191,462
Gross profit margin	(38.6%)	$120,366
−Operating expenses	(29.3%)	91,366
Net profit (before taxes)	(9.3%)	$ 29,000

At this point, the business appears to be a lucrative venture. But remember: This income statement represents a goal that the entrepreneur may not be able to attain. The next step is to determine whether this required sales volume is reasonable. One useful technique is to break down the required annual sales volume into daily sales figures. If the store will be open six days a week for 52 weeks (312 days), the owner must average $999 a day in sales:

$$\text{Average daily sales} = \frac{\$311,828}{312 \text{ days}}$$

$$= \$999/\text{day}$$

This calculation gives the owner a better perspective of the sales required to yield an annual profit of $29,000.

To determine whether the profit expected from the business will meet or exceed the entrepreneur's target income, the prospective owner should create an income statement based on a realistic sales estimate. The previous analysis showed the owner what sales level is needed to reach his desired profit. But what will happen if sales are lower or higher? The entrepreneur requires a reliable sales forecast using the market research techniques described in chapter 6.

Suppose, for example, that after conducting a marketing survey of local customers and talking with nearby business owners, the prospective bookstore operator projects annual sales for the proposed business to be only $285,000. The entrepreneur must take this expected sales figure and develop a pro forma income statement.

Net sales	(100%)	$285,000
−Cost of goods sold	(61.4%)	174,990
Gross profit margin	(38.6%)	110,010
−Operating expenses	(29.3%)	83,505
Net profit (before taxes)	(9.3%)	$26,505

On the basis of sales of $285,000, this entrepreneur should expect a net profit (before taxes) of $26,505. If this amount is acceptable as a return on the investment of time and money in the business, he should proceed with his planning.

At this stage in developing the financial plan, the owner should create a more detailed picture of the firm's expected operating expenses. One common method is to use the operating statistics data found in Dun & Bradstreet's *Cost of Doing Business* reports. These booklets document typical selected operating expenses (expressed as a percentage of net sales) for 190 lines of business.

To ensure that they have overlooked no business expenses in preparing their business plans, entrepreneurs should list all of the initial expenses they will incur and have an accountant review the list. Figures 7.4 and 7.5 show two useful forms designed to help assign dollar

Worksheet No. 2

Estimated Monthly Expenses Item	Your estimate of monthly expenses based on sales of $_____ per year	Your estimate of how much cash you need to start your business (See column 3.)	What to put in column 2 (These figures are typical for one kind of business. You will have to decide how many months to allow for in your business.)
	Column 1	Column 2	Column 3
Salary of owner-manager	$	$	2 times column 1
All other salaries and wages			3 times column 1
Rent			3 times column 1
Advertising			3 times column 1
Delivery expense			3 times column 1
Supplies			3 times column 1
Telephone and telegraph			3 times column 1
Other utilities			3 times column 1
Insurance			Payment required by insurance company
Taxes, including Social Security			4 times column 1
Interest			3 times column 1
Maintenance			3 times column 1
Legal and other professional fees			3 times column 1
Miscellaneous			3 times column 1
Starting Costs You Have to Pay Only Once			Leave column 2 blank
Fixtures and equipment			Fill in worksheet 3 and put the total here
Decorating and remodeling			Talk it over with a contractor
Installation of fixtures and equipment			Talk to suppliers from whom you buy these
Starting inventory			Suppliers will probably help you estimate this
Deposits with public utilities			Find out from utilities companies
Legal and professional fees			Lawyer, accountant, and so on
Licenses and permits			Find out from city offices what you have to have
Advertising and promotion for opening			Estimate what you'll use
Accounts receivable			What you need to buy more stock until credit customers pay
Cash			For unexpected expenses or losses, special purchases, etc.
Other			Make a separate list and enter total
Total Estimated Cash You Need to Start		$	Add up all the numbers in column 2

Figure 7.4 **Anticipated Expenses**   Source: U.S. Small Business Administration, *Checklist for Going into Business,* Small Marketers Aid No. 71 (Washington, D.C.: GPO, 1982), pp. 6–7.

Worksheet No. 3
List of Furniture, Fixtures, and Equipment

Leave out or add items to suit your business. Use separate sheets to list exactly what you need for each of the items below.	If you plan to pay cash in full, enter the full amount below and in the last column.	If you are going to pay by installments, fill out the columns below. Enter in the last column your down payment plus at least one installment.			Estimate of the cash you need for furniture, fixtures, and equipment.
		Price	Down payment	Amount of each installment	
Counters	$	$	$	$	$
Storage shelves and cabinets					
Display stands, shelves, tables					
Cash register					
Safe					
Window display fixtures					
Special lighting					
Outside sign					
Delivery equipment if needed					
Total Furniture, Fixtures, and Equipment (Enter this figure also in worksheet 2 under "Starting Costs You Have to Pay Only Once.")					$

Figure 7.5 **Anticipated Expenditures for Fixtures and Equipment** Source: U.S. Small Business Administration, *Checklist for Going into Business*, Small Marketers Aid No. 7I (Washington, D.C.: GPO, 1982), p. 12.

values to anticipated expenses. Totals derived from this list of expenses should approximate the total expense figures calculated from published statistics. Naturally, an entrepreneur should be more confident of the total from his own list of expenses because it reflects his particular set of circumstances.

Entrepreneurs who follow the other approach to building an income statement—developing a sales forecast and working down to net income—must be careful to avoid falling into the trap of excessive optimism. Many entrepreneurs using this method overestimate their future revenues and underestimate their actual expenses, and the result is disastrous. To avoid this problem, one expert advises entrepreneurs to use the rule that many venture capitalists apply when they evaluate business start-ups: Divide revenues by two, multiply expenses by two, and if the business can still make it, it's a winner![8]

THE PRO FORMA BALANCE SHEET

In addition to projecting the small firm's net profit or loss, the entrepreneur must develop a pro forma balance sheet outlining the fledgling firm's assets and liabilities. Most entrepreneurs' primary focus is on the potential profitability of their businesses, but the assets their businesses use to generate profits are no less important. In many cases, small companies begin life on weak financial footing because their owners fail to determine their firms' total asset requirements. To prevent this major oversight, the owner should prepare a projected balance sheet listing every asset the business will need and all the claims against those assets.

Assets. *Cash* is one of the most useful assets the business owns; it is highly liquid and can quickly be converted into other tangible assets. But how much cash should a small business have at its inception? Obviously, there is no single dollar figure that fits the needs of every small firm. One practical rule of thumb, however, suggests that the company's cash balance should cover its operating expenses (less depreciation, a noncash expense) for one inventory turnover period. Using this rule, we can calculate the cash balance for the small bookstore as follows:

Operating expenses = $83,250 (from projected income statement) – Depreciation (0.9% of annual sales) of $2,565 (a noncash expense) = Cash expenses (annual) = $80,940

$$\text{Cash requirement} = \frac{\text{Cash expenses}}{\text{Average inventory turnover}}$$

$$= \frac{80,940}{3.5} \quad \text{(from \textit{RMA Annual Statement Studies})}$$

$$= \$23,126$$

Notice the inverse relationship between the small firm's average inventory turnover ratio and its cash requirements.

Another decision facing the entrepreneur is how much *inventory* the business should carry. A rough estimate of the inventory requirement can be calculated from the information found on the projected income statement and from published statistics:

Cost of goods sold = $174,990 (from projected income statement)

$$\text{Average inventory turnover} = \frac{\text{Cost of goods sold}}{\text{Inventory level}}$$

$$= 3.5 \text{ times/year}$$

Substituting,

$$3.5 \text{ times/year} = \frac{\$153,500}{\text{Inventory level}}$$

Solving algebraically,

$$\text{Inventory level} = \$49,997$$

The owner can use the planning forms shown in Figures 7.4 and 7.5 to estimate fixed assets (land, building, equipment, and fixtures). Suppose the estimate of fixed assets is as follows:

Fixtures	$ 7,500
Office equipment	1,100
Cash register	1,200
Signs	300
Total	$10,100

Figure 7.6 Projected Balance Sheet for a Small Bookstore

ASSETS

Current Assets:

Cash	$23,126.00
Inventory	49,997.00
Miscellaneous	1,800.00
TOTAL CURRENT ASSETS	$74,923.00

Fixed Assets:

Fixtures	$ 7,500.00
Office Equipment	1,100.00
Cash Register	1,200.00
Signs	300.00
TOTAL FIXED ASSETS	$10,100.00
TOTAL ASSETS	$85,023.00

LIABILITIES

Current Liabilities:

Accounts Payable	$24,998.00
Notes Payable	3,750.00
TOTAL CURRENT LIABILITIES	$28,748.00

Long-Term Liabilities:

Notes Payable	$20,000.00
Owner's Equity	$36,275.00
TOTAL LIABILITIES AND OWNER'S EQUITY	$85,023.00

Liabilities. To complete the projected balance sheet, the owner must record all of the small firm's liabilities: the claims against the assets. The bookstore owner was able to finance 50 percent of inventory and fixtures through suppliers. The only other major claim against the firm's assets is a note payable to the entrepreneur's father-in-law for $20,000.

The final step is to compile all of these items into a projected balance sheet, as shown in Figure 7.6.

*R*atio Analysis

❹ Understand the basic financial statements through ratio analysis.

Would you be willing to drive a car on an extended trip without being able to see the dashboard displays showing fuel level, engine temperature, oil pressure, battery status, or the speed at which you were traveling? Not many people would! Yet, many small business owners run their companies exactly that way. They never take the time to check the vital signs of their businesses using their "financial dashboards." The result: Their companies develop engine trouble, fail, and leave them stranded along the road to successful entrepreneurship.

Smart entrepreneurs know that once they have their businesses up and running with the help of a solid financial plan, the next step is to keep the company moving in the right

GAINING THE COMPETITIVE EDGE

Between the Lines of Financial Statements

*W*hen he was president and owner of a small medical equipment firm, Dan Cronin knew how important it was to stay focused on the basics of business success. Every day, he would stop by the order desk and ask, "How are our orders today?" Later in the day, he would check with the accounts receivable department, asking, "How are our checks coming in?" Toward the end of the day he would wander out to the loading dock to check with the shippers on what was going out the door and whether it was on schedule.

Cronin's simple system allowed him to maintain control over the most important aspects of his business. But how does an entrepreneur establish timely, relevant financial controls for a rapidly growing small business? Turnaround specialist Raleigh Minor offers five rules for setting up proper financial controls.

1. *Generate numbers quickly and accurately.* For financial statements to be of any value to managers, growing businesses must compile them no more than 10 days after the end of each month.
2. *Establish different timetables for different numbers.* All companies must establish priorities concerning which numbers to monitor monthly and which to watch weekly. Minor offers these guidelines:

Monthly updates on:
◆ inventory
◆ accounts receivable (aging of accounts and average collection period)
◆ accounts payable (aging of accounts and average payable period)

Weekly updates on:
◆ current cash position
◆ cash disbursements by major category
◆ cash receipts
◆ new sales
◆ order backlogs

◆ number of employees (with productivity measures such as sales per employee ratio)

3. *Compare results with projections.* "To make actual numbers really useful," says Minor, "you've got to know what expectations the company had and how those compare with actual results." Such comparisons allow managers to make proper adjustments in company strategy.
4. *Prioritize.* Once managers decide which numbers are most important to the company's success, they should develop a "Weekly Condition Report" summarizing them. The report should show the most recent projections as well as actual results.
5. *Circulate financial reports to responsible managers.* Tracking these numbers does no good unless managers and key employees have access to them and use them in their daily decision making.

Although analyzing financial data intimidates some business owners, it is an integral part of running a business successfully. "If the owners don't understand the numbers or have the time to understand them, they can hire an accountant . . . to monitor and manage them," says Bob Porreca, a financial analyst. "Eventually, however, they should learn how to read a financial statement. It's ultimately their responsibility to protect themselves and their businesses."

Analyzing the numbers over time and comparing them with industry standards is one of the most practical ways of putting them to work to make a business better. Porreca recommends using ratio analysis to measure a company's performance. "By analyzing these ratios," he says, "we know how well a company is doing year to year and how it's performing against others in the same industry." And, as many business owners have found, that is the best way to read between the lines of financial statements.

1. Which financial summaries should small business owners prepare to improve control over their companies?
2. Why do some business owners fail to prepare adequate financial summaries and reports?
3. What are the benefits of conducting the type of financial analysis described here?

SOURCES: Adapted from Jack Falvey, "Strong Sales Focus Keeps Your Eye on the Ball," *Wall Street Journal*, May 3, 1993, p. A16; "The Five Cardinal Rules of Financial Controls," *Inc.*, May 1992, p. 156; William Bak, "The Numbers Game," *Entrepreneur*, April 1993, pp. 54–57. ◆

direction with the help of proper financial controls. Establishing these controls—and using them consistently—is one of the keys to keeping a business vibrant and healthy. "If you don't keep a finger on the pulse of your company's finances, you risk making bad decisions," explains one business writer. "You could be in serious financial trouble and not even realize it."[9]

A smoothly functioning system of financial controls can serve as an early warning device for underlying problems that could destroy a young business. They allow an entrepreneur to step back and see the big picture and to make adjustments in the company's direction when necessary. According to one writer:

A company's financial accounting and reporting system will provide signals, through comparative analysis, of impending trouble, such as:

◆ *Decreasing sales and falling profit bargains.*

◆ *Increasing corporate overheads.*

◆ *Growing inventories and accounts receivable.*

These are all signals of declining cash flows from operations, the lifeblood of every business. As cash flows decrease, the squeeze begins:

◆ *Payments to vendors become slower.*

◆ *Maintenance on production equipment lags.*

◆ *Raw material shortages appear.*

◆ *Equipment breakdowns occur.*

All of these begin to have a negative impact on productivity. Now the downward spiral has begun in earnest. The key is hearing and focusing on the signals.[10]

What are these signals, and how does an entrepreneur go about hearing and focusing on them? One extremely helpful tool is ratio analysis. **Ratio analysis,** a method of expressing the relationship between any two accounting elements, provides a convenient technique for performing financial analysis. When analyzed properly, ratios serve as barometers of a company's financial health. These comparisons allow the small business manager to determine if the firm is carrying excessive inventory, experiencing heavy operating expenses, overextending credit, and paying its debts on time and to answer other questions relating to the efficient operation of the firm. Unfortunately, few business owners actually use ratio analysis; one study discovered that just 2 percent of all entrepreneurs compute financial ratios and use them in managing their businesses![11]

Clever business owners use financial ratio analysis to identify problems in their businesses while they are still problems, not business-threatening crises. Tracking these ratios over time permits an owner to spot a variety of "red flags" that are indications of problem areas. Spotting problems is critical to business success because a business owner cannot solve problems he does not know exist. *At Atkinson-Baker & Associates, a Los Angeles court reporting service, every one of the firm's 50 employees is responsible for tracking every day a key financial statistic relating to his or her job. CEO Alan Atkinson-Baker believes that waiting until the month's end to compile financial ratios takes away a company's ability to respond to events as they happen. "Employees have statistics for their job, and it helps them see how well they are producing," he says. Because the statistics are linked directly to their jobs, employees quickly learn which numbers to track and how to compile or to calculate them. "Each day everybody reports their statistics," explains Atkinson-Baker. A spreadsheet summarizes the calculations and generates 27 graphs so managers can analyze trends in a meeting the following morning. One rule the company developed from its financial analysis is "Don't spend more today than you brought in yesterday." Atkinson-Baker explains, "You can never run into trouble as long as you stick to that rule." He also notes that effective financial planning would be impossible without timely data. "When we have bad problem areas, the statistics have helped us catch them before they become a bigger problem," he says.*[12]

Business owners also can use ratio analysis to increase the likelihood of obtaining bank loans. By analyzing his financial statements with ratios, an owner can identify weaknesses and strengths in advance. One bank loan officer explains, "We look closely at debt to net worth, debt to net income, and the quick ratio. . . . We are primarily interested in trends."[13] But how many ratios should a small business manager monitor to maintain adequate financial control over the firm? The number of ratios that could be calculated is limited only by the number of accounts recorded on the firm's financial statements. However, tracking too many ratios only creates confusion and saps the meaning from an entrepreneur's financial analysis. The secret to successful ratio analysis is simplicity, focusing on just enough ratios to provide a clear picture of a company's financial standing.

TWELVE KEY RATIOS

In keeping with the idea of simplicity, we will describe 12 key ratios that will enable most business owners to monitor their firms' financial position without becoming bogged down in financial details. This chapter presents explanations of these ratios and examples based on the balance sheet and the income statement for Sam's Appliance Shop shown in Figures 7.1 and 7.2. We will group them into four categories: liquidity ratios, leverage ratios, operating ratios, and profitability ratios.

LIQUIDITY RATIOS

Liquidity ratios tell whether the small business will be able to meet its maturing obligations as they come due. A small company with solid liquidity not only is able to pay its bills on time, but it also is in a position to take advantage of attractive business opportunities as they arise. The primary measures of liquidity are the current ratio and the quick ratio.

1. Current Ratio. The **current ratio** measures the small firm's solvency by indicating its ability to pay current liabilities from current assets. It is calculated in the following manner:

$$\text{Current ratio} = \frac{\text{Current assets}}{\text{Current liabilities}}$$

$$= \frac{\$686,985}{\$367,850}$$

$$= 1.87{:}1$$

THE WALL STREET JOURNAL

"In the future, Clayton, always make sure you have correctly placed your decimal points."

SOURCE: Dave Carpenter. *Wall Street Journal*, October 8, 1997, p. A23.

Sam's Appliance Shop has $1.87 in current assets for every $1 it has in current liabilities. Current assets normally include cash, notes and accounts receivable, inventory, and any other short-term marketable securities. Current liabilities include notes and accounts payable, taxes payable, and accruals.

The current ratio, sometimes called the *working capital ratio*, is the most commonly used measure of short-term solvency. Typically, financial analysts suggest that a small business maintain a current ratio of at least 2:1 (i.e., $2 of current assets for every $1 of current liabilities) to maintain a comfortable cushion of working capital. In general, the higher the firm's current ratio, the stronger its financial position; but a high current ratio does not guarantee that the firm's assets are being used in the most profitable manner. For example, a business maintaining excessive balances of idle cash or overinvesting in inventory would likely have a high current ratio.

With its current ratio of 1.87:1, Sam's Appliance Shop could liquidate its current assets at 53.5% (1 ÷ 1.87 = 0.535) of book value and still manage to pay its current creditors in full.

2. Quick Ratio. The current ratio can sometimes be misleading because it does not show the quality of a company's current assets. The **quick ratio** (or the **acid test ratio**) is a more conservative measure of a firm's liquidity because it shows the extent to which its most liquid assets cover its current liabilities. It is calculated as follows:

$$\text{Quick ratio} = \frac{\text{Quick assets}}{\text{Current liabilities}}$$

$$= \frac{\$686,985 - \$455,455}{\$367,850}$$

$$= 0.63{:}1$$

Quick assets include cash, readily marketable securities, and notes and accounts receivables—assets that can be converted into cash immediately if needed. Most small firms determine quick assets by subtracting inventory from current assets because inventory cannot be converted into cash quickly. Also, inventories are the assets on which losses are most likely to occur in case of liquidation.

The quick ratio is a more specific measure of a firm's ability to meet its short-term obligations and is a more rigorous test of its liquidity than the current ratio. It expresses capacity to repay current debts if all sales income ceased immediately. In general, a quick ratio of 1:1 is considered satisfactory. A ratio of less than 1:1 indicates that the small firm is overly dependent on inventory and on future sales to satisfy short-term debt. A quick ratio of more than 1:1 indicates a greater degree of financial security.

LEVERAGE RATIOS

Leverage ratios measure the financing supplied by the firm's owners against that supplied by its creditors; they are a gauge of the depth of a company's debt. These ratios show the extent to which an entrepreneur relies on debt capital (rather than equity capital) to finance operating expenses, capital expenditures, and expansion costs. As such, it is a measure of the degree of financial risk in a company. In general, small businesses with low leverage ratios are not dramatically affected by economic downturns, but the returns for these firms are not great during economic booms. Conversely, small firms with high leverage ratios are vulnerable to economic slides because their debt loads demolish cash flow; however, they have greater potential for large profits.

3. Debt Ratio. The small firm's **debt ratio** measures the percentage of total assets financed by creditors. The debt ratio is calculated as follows:

$$\text{Debt ratio} = \frac{\text{Total debt (or liabilities)}}{\text{Total assets}}$$

$$= \frac{\$367,850 + \$212,150}{\$847,655}$$

$$= 0.68:1$$

Total debt includes all current liabilities and any outstanding long-term notes and bonds. Total assets represent the sum of the firm's current assets, fixed assets, and intangible assets. Clearly, a high debt ratio means that creditors provide a large percentage of the firm's total financing. Owners generally prefer a high leverage ratio; otherwise, business funds must come either from the owners' personal assets or from taking on new owners, which means giving up more control over the business. Also, with a greater portion of the firm's assets financed by creditors, the owner is able to generate profits with a smaller personal investment. However, creditors typically prefer moderate debt ratios because a lower debt ratio indicates a smaller chance of creditor losses in case of liquidation. To lenders and creditors, high debt ratios mean a high risk of default.

According to a senior analyst at Dun & Bradstreet's Analytical Services, "If managed properly, debt can be beneficial because it's a great way to have money working for you. You're leveraging your assets, so you're making more money than you're paying out in interest." However, excessive debt can be the downfall of a business. "As we pile up debt on our personal credit cards our lifestyles are squeezed," he says. "The same thing happens to a business. Overpowering debt sinks thousands of businesses each year."[14]

4. Debt to Net Worth Ratio. The small firm's **debt to net worth ratio** also expresses the relationship between the capital contributions from creditors and those from owners. This ratio compares what the business "owes" with "what it owns." It is a measure of the small firm's ability to meet both its creditor and owner obligations in case of liquidation. The debt to net worth ratio is calculated as follows:

$$\text{Debt to net worth ratio} = \frac{\text{Total debt (or liabilities)}}{\text{Tangible net worth}}$$

$$= \frac{\$367,850 + \$212,150}{\$267,655 - \$3,500}$$

$$= 2.20:1$$

Total debt is the sum of current liabilities and long-term liabilities, and tangible net worth represents the owners' investment in the business (capital + capital stock + earned surplus + retained earnings) less any intangible assets (e.g., goodwill) the firm owns.

The higher this ratio, the lower the degree of protection afforded creditors if the business should fail. Also, a higher debt to net worth ratio means that the firm has less capacity to borrow; lenders and creditors see the firm as being "borrowed up." Conversely, a low ratio typically is associated with a higher level of financial security, giving the business greater borrowing potential. As a firm's debt to net worth ratio approaches 1:1, the creditors' interest in the business approaches that of the owners. If the ratio is greater than 1:1, the creditors' claims exceed those of the owners, and the business may be undercapitalized. In other words, the owner has not supplied an adequate amount of capital, forcing the business to be overextended in terms of debt.

5. Times Interest Earned Ratio. The **times interest earned ratio** earned is a measure of the small firm's ability to make the interest payments on its debt. It tells how many times the company's earnings cover the interest payments on the debt it is carrying. The times interest earned ratio is calculated as follows:

$$\text{Times interest earned} = \frac{\text{Earnings before interest and taxes (EBIT)}}{\text{Total interest expense}}$$

$$= \frac{\$60,629 + 39,850}{\$39,850}$$

$$= 2.52:1$$

EBIT is the firm's profit *before* deducting interest expense and taxes; the denominator measures the amount the business paid in interest over the accounting period.

A high ratio suggests that the company would have little difficulty meeting the interest payments on its loans; creditors would see this as a sign of safety for future loans. Conversely, a low ratio is an indication that the company is overextended in its debts; earnings will not be able to cover its debt service if this ratio is less than 1:1. "I look for a [times interest earned] ratio of higher than three-to-one," says one financial analyst, "which indicates that management has considerable breathing room to make its debt payments. When the ratio drops below one-to-one, it clearly indicates management is under tremendous pressure to raise cash. The risk of default or bankruptcy is very high."[15] Many creditors look for a times interest earned ratio of at least 4:1 to 6:1 before pronouncing a company a good credit risk.

Trouble looms on the horizon for companies whose debt loads are so heavy that they must starve critical operations such as research and development, customer service, and others just to pay interest on the debt. Because their interest payments are so large, highly leveraged companies find that they are restricted when it comes to spending cash, whether on normal operations, an acquisition, or capital expenditures.

Debt is a powerful financial tool, but companies must handle it carefully, just as a demolitionist handles dynamite; like too much dynamite, too much debt can be dangerous. Apparently, many business owners understand the danger of debt. A recent survey by the American Institute of Certified Public Accountants asked business owners what they would do with a significant increase in profits. The owners' most common response: Pay down their companies' debt.[16] Unfortunately, some companies have gone on borrowing binges, pushing their debt loads beyond the optimal zone (see Figure 7.7) and are struggling to survive. Managed carefully, however, debt can boost a company's performance and improve its productivity. Its treatment in the tax code also makes debt a much cheaper means of financial growth than equity. When companies with AA financial ratings borrow at 10 percent, the after-tax cost is just 7.2 percent (because interest payments to lenders are tax-deductible); equity financing costs more than twice that.

OPERATING RATIOS

Operating ratios help the owner evaluate the small firm's performance and indicate how effectively the business uses its resources. The more effectively its resources are used, the less capital a small business will require. These five operating ratios help entrepreneurs spot areas they must improve if their businesses are to remain competitive.

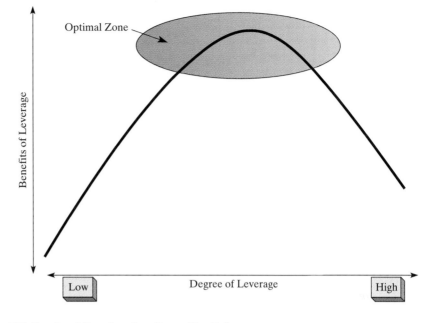

Figure 7.7 Keeping Afloat Requires Controlling Debt

6. Average Inventory Turnover Ratio. The small firm's **average inventory turnover ratio** measures the number of times its average inventory is sold out, or turned over, during the accounting period. This ratio tells the owner whether the firm's inventory is being managed properly. It apprises the owner of whether the business inventory is understocked, overstocked, or obsolete. The average inventory turnover ratio is calculated as follows:

$$\text{Average inventory turnover ratio} = \frac{\text{Cost of goods sold}}{\text{Average inventory}}$$

$$= \frac{\$1,290,117}{(\$805,745 + \$455,455)/2}$$

$$= 2.05 \text{ times/year}$$

Average inventory is found by adding the firm's inventory at the beginning of the accounting period to the ending inventory and dividing the result by 2.

This ratio tells the owner how fast the merchandise is moving through the business and helps to balance the company on the fine line between oversupply and undersupply. To determine the average number of days units remain in inventory, the owner can divide the average inventory turnover ratio into the number of days in the accounting period (e.g., 365 ÷ average inventory turnover ratio). The result is called *days' inventory*. An above-average inventory turnover indicates that the small business has a healthy, salable, and liquid inventory and a supply of quality merchandise supported by sound pricing policies. A below-average inventory turnover suggests an illiquid inventory characterized by obsolescence, overstocking, and stale merchandise.

Businesses that turn their inventories rapidly require a relatively small inventory investment to produce a particular sales volume. These companies do not tie up cash in inventory that sits on shelves. For instance, if Sam's could turn its inventory *four* times each year instead of just *two*, the company would require an average inventory of just $322,529 instead of the current level of $630,600 to generate sales of $1,870,841. Increasing the number of inventory turns would free up more than $308,000 currently tied up in excess inventory. Sam's would benefit from improved cash flow and higher profits (see Figure 7.8).

The inventory turnover ratio can be misleading, however. For example, an excessively high ratio could mean the firm has a shortage of inventory and is experiencing stockouts. Similarly, a low ratio could be the result of planned inventory stockpiling to meet seasonal peak demand. Another problem is that, because the ratio is based on an inventory balance calculated from only two days out of the entire accounting period, inventory fluctuations due to seasonal demand patterns are ignored; thus, the resulting ratio may be biased. There is no universal, ideal inventory turnover ratio. Financial analysts suggest that a favorable turnover ratio depends on the type of business, its size, its profitability, its method of inventory valuation, and other relevant factors.

7. Average Collection Period Ratio. The small firm's **average collection period ratio** (or **days' sales outstanding, DSO**) tells the average number of days it takes to collect accounts

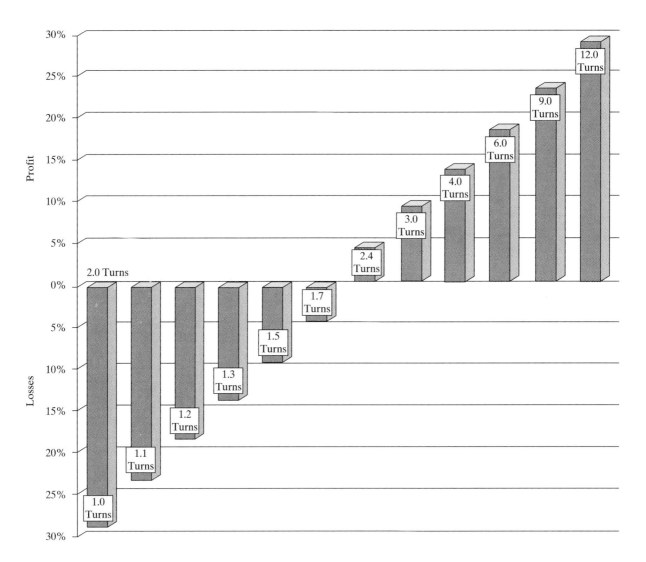

Figure 7.8 **The Effect of Turnover on Profits**   SOURCE: Retail Merchandising Service Information, Inc.

receivable. To compute the average collection period ratio, you must first calculate the firm's receivables turnover. If Sam's *credit* sales for the year were $1,309,589, then the **receivables turnover ratio** would be as follows:

$$\text{Receivables turnover ratio} = \frac{\text{Credit sales (or net sales)}}{\text{Accounts receivable}}$$

$$= \frac{\$1,309,589}{\$179,225}$$

$$= 7.31 \text{ times/year}$$

This ratio measures the number of times the firm's accounts receivable turn over during the accounting period. Sam's Appliance Shop turns over its receivables 7.31 times per year. The higher the firm's receivables turnover ratio, the shorter the time lag between making a sale and collecting the cash from it.

Use the following equation to calculate the firm's average collection period ratio:

$$\text{Average collection period ratio} = \frac{\text{Number of days in accounting period}}{\text{Receivables turnover ratio}}$$

$$= \frac{365 \text{ days}}{7.31}$$

$$= 50.0 \text{ days}$$

Sam's Appliance Shop's accounts and notes receivable are outstanding for an average of 50 days. Typically, the higher the firm's average collection period ratio, the greater the chance of bad debt losses.

One of the most useful applications of the collection period ratio is to compare it with the industry average and with the firm's credit terms. Such a comparison will indicate the degree of the small company's control over its credit sales and collection techniques. One rule of thumb suggests that the firm's collection period ratio should be no more than one-third greater than its credit terms. For example, if a small company's credit terms are "net 30," its average collection period ratio should be no more than 40 days. A ratio greater than 60 days would indicate poor collection procedure.

Slow payers represent great risk to many small businesses. Many entrepreneurs proudly point to rapidly rising sales only to find that they must borrow money to keep their companies going because credit customers are paying their bills in 45, 60, or even 90 days instead of 30. Slow receivables often lead to a cash crisis that can cripple a business.

8. Average Payable Period Ratio. The converse of the average collection period ratio, the **average payable period ratio,** tells the average number of days it takes a company to pay its accounts payable. Like the average collection period, it is measured in days. To compute this ratio, first calculate the **payables turnover ratio.** Sam's payables turnover ratio is as follows:

$$\text{Payables turnover ratio} = \frac{\text{Cost of purchases}}{\text{Accounts payable}}$$

$$= \frac{\$939,827}{\$152,580}$$

$$= 6.16 \text{ times/year}$$

To find the average payable period, use the following computation:

$$\text{Average payable period ratio} = \frac{\text{Number of days in accounting period}}{\text{Payables turnover ratio}}$$

$$= \frac{365 \text{ days}}{6.16}$$

$$= 59.3 \text{ days}$$

Sam's Appliance Shop takes an average of 59 days to pay its accounts with suppliers.

An excessively high average payable period ratio indicates the presence of a significant amount of past-due accounts payable. Although sound cash management calls for business owners to keep their cash as long as possible, slowing payables too drastically can severely damage a company's credit rating. Ideally, the average payable period would match (or exceed) the time it takes to convert inventory into sales and ultimately into cash. In this case, the company's vendors would be financing its inventory and its credit sales.

One of the most meaningful comparisons for this ratio is against the credit terms offered by suppliers (or an average of the credit terms offered). If the average payable ratio slips beyond vendors' credit terms, it is an indication that the company is suffering from cash shortages or a sloppy accounts payable procedure and its credit rating is in danger. If this ratio is significantly lower than vendors' credit terms, it may be a sign that the firm is not using its cash most effectively.

9. Net Sales to Total Assets. The small company's **net sales to total assets ratio** (also called the **total assets turnover ratio**) is a general measure of its ability to generate sales in relation to its assets. It describes how productively the firm uses its assets to produce sales revenue. The total assets turnover ratio is calculated as follows:

$$\text{Total assets turnover ratio} = \frac{\text{Net sales}}{\text{Net total assets}}$$

$$= \frac{\$1,870,841}{\$847,655}$$

$$= 2.21:1$$

The denominator of this ratio, net total assets, is the sum of all of the firm's assets (cash, inventory, land, buildings, equipment, tools, everything owned) less depreciation. This ratio is meaningful only when compared with that of similar firms in the same industry category. A total assets turnover ratio below the industry average may indicate that the small firm is not generating an adequate sales volume for its asset size.

10. Net Sales to Working Capital. The **net sales to working capital ratio** measures how many dollars in sales the business generates for every dollar of **working capital** (working capital = current assets − current liabilities). Also called the **turnover of working capital ratio,** this proportion tells the owner how efficiently working capital is being used to generate sales. It is calculated as follows:

$$\text{Net sales to working capital ratio} = \frac{\text{Net sales}}{\text{Current assets} - \text{current liabilities}}$$

$$= \frac{\$1,870,841}{\$686,985 - \$367,850}$$

$$= 5.86:1$$

An excessively low net sales to working capital ratio indicates that the small firm is not using its working capital efficiently or profitably. On the other hand, an extremely high ratio points to an inadequate level of working capital to maintain a suitable level of sales, which puts creditors in a vulnerable position. This ratio is very helpful in maintaining sufficient working capital as the small business grows. It is critical for the small firm to keep a satisfactory level of working capital to nourish its expansion, and the net sales to working capital ratio helps define the level of working capital required to support higher sales volume.

PROFITABILITY RATIOS

Profitability ratios indicate how efficiently the small firm is being managed and how successfully it is conducting business. In other words, they provide information about the company's bottom line.

11. Net Profit on Sales Ratio. The **net profit on sales ratio** (also called the **profit margin on sales**) measures the firm's profit per dollar of sales. The computed percentage shows the number of cents of each sales dollar remaining after deducting all expenses and income taxes. The profit margin on sales is calculated as follows:

$$\text{Net profit on sales ratio} = \frac{\text{Net profit}}{\text{Net sales}}$$

$$= \frac{\$60,629}{\$1,870,841}$$

$$= 3.24\%$$

Most small business owners believe that a high profit margin on sales is necessary for a successful business operation, but this is a misconception. To evaluate this ratio properly, the owner must consider the firm's asset value, its inventory and receivables turnover ratios, and its total capitalization. For example, the typical small supermarket earns an average net profit of only one or two cents on each dollar of sales, but its inventory may turn over as many as 20 times a year. If the firm's profit margin on sales is below the industry average, it may be a sign that its prices are relatively low or that its costs are excessively high, or both.

If a company's net profit on sales ratio is excessively low, the owner should check the gross profit margin (net sales minus cost of goods sold expressed as a percentage of net sales). Of course, a reasonable gross profit margin varies from industry to industry. For instance, a service company may have a gross profit margin of 75 percent, whereas a manufacturer's may be 35 percent. If this margin slips too low, the company's future will be in immediate jeopardy.

12. Net Profit to Equity. The **net profit to equity ratio** (or the **return on net worth ratio**) measures the owners' rate of return on investment. Because it reports the percentage of the owners' investment in the business that is being returned through profits annually, it is one of the most important indicators of the firm's profitability or a management's efficiency. The net profit to equity ratio is computed as follows:

$$\text{Net profit to equity ratio} = \frac{\text{Net profit}}{\text{Owners' equity (or net worth)}}$$

$$= \frac{\$60,629}{\$267,655}$$

$$= 22.65\%$$

This ratio compares profits earned during the accounting period with the amount the owner has invested in the business during that time. If this interest rate on the owners' investment is excessively low, some of this capital might be better employed elsewhere.

$\mathcal{I}$nterpreting Business Ratios

5 Explain how to interpret financial ratios.

Key performance ratios vary dramatically among industries and even within different segments of the same industry. Every manager must know and understand which ratios are most crucial to his company's success and focus on monitoring and controlling those. Sometimes, business owners develop ratios that are unique to their own operations to help them achieve success. One entrepreneur calls them "critical numbers."[17] *For instance, Steve Simon, CEO of AutoLend Group Inc., a used-car financing company, focuses on just a few critical numbers to determine his company's exact financial position every day. He uses several ratios that describe the relationships among his company's cash balance, its total loans outstanding, and its loans in delinquency. Simon and his top financial staffers developed a spreadsheet to monitor the "key numbers we really needed to keep closest track of," he says. The result is AutoLend's "Daily Flash Report," which is available to everyone by 7 A.M. each day. "The relationship between numbers is just as important as the results themselves," says Simon. "We've got very clear goals about how these numbers need to relate for us to achieve profitable growth."[18]*

Another valuable way to utilize ratios is to compare them with those of similar businesses in the same industry. "By themselves, these numbers are not that meaningful," says one financial expert of ratios, "but when you compare them [with those of] other businesses in your industry, they suddenly come alive because they put your operation in perspective."[19]

The principle behind calculating these ratios and comparing them with industry norms is the same as that of most medical tests. Just as a healthy person's blood pressure and cholesterol levels should fall within a range of normal values, so should a financially healthy company's ratios. A company cannot deviate too far from these normal values and remain successful for long. When deviations from "normal" do occur (and they will), a business owner should focus on determining the cause of the deviations. In some cases, deviations are the result of sound business decisions, such as taking on inventory in preparation for the busy season, investing heavily in new technology, and others. In other instances, however, ratios that are out of the normal range for a particular type of business are indicators of what could become serious problems for a company.

Several organizations regularly compile and publish operating statistics, including key ratios, summarizing the financial performance of many businesses across a wide range of industries. The local library should subscribe to most of these publications:

Robert Morris Associates. Established in 1914, Robert Morris Associates publishes its *Annual Statement Studies*, showing ratios and other financial data for more than 350 industrial, wholesale, retail, and service categories.

Dun & Bradstreet, Inc. Since 1932, Dun & Bradstreet has published *Key Business Ratios*, which covers 22 retail, 32 wholesale, and 71 industrial business categories. Dun &

Norman Mayne, president of the grocery chain Dorothy Lane Market, encourages his employees to help the company run more efficiently by teaching them the details of its financial statements.

IN THE FOOTSTEPS OF AN ENTREPRENEUR

Good News in the Grocery Business

*A*s part of a training program for new employees in his supermarket business, Norman Mayne gives a quiz: How much profit does a $25 grocery order yield? Mayne displays his answers on little wooden cutouts shaped like grocery bags: $12.50, $10, $2.50, or 25 cents. Most new workers miss the question, guessing either $2.50 or $10. The correct answer is 25 cents. Designed to demonstrate the razor-thin 1 percent profit margins supermarkets typically have operated on, the exercise is an effective part of Mayne's presentation.

Recently, however, Mayne has updated his quiz and has happily made another wooden cutout displaying "50 cents." For the first time, Mayne's company, Dorothy Lane Market <http://www.dorothylane.com>, based in Dayton, Ohio, is operating at a 2 percent profit margin. For many years, supermarket owners have lived with profit margins of just 1 percent of sales, but thanks to improved management techniques and the application of technology, industry profits have never looked better. With annual sales of $36 million, Dorothy Lane Market's improvements yield a net profit of just over $720,000, up from just $360,000.

Mayne explains that the chain has come a long way in its management techniques since his father rang up total sales of $35 on his first day in business in 1948. Taking a cue from the major discounters such as Wal-Mart, Target, and Kmart (all of whom are encroaching on the grocery business), supermarkets have learned how to increase the number of times they turn their inventory, have streamlined their distribution systems, and have adopted serious cost-cutting strategies to become more efficient. Combining technology such as checkout scanners with new marketing techniques, including frequent-shopper cards, has reduced the need for constant sales, which cut into profit margins. The results are going straight to the bottom line.

Like airlines with their frequent-flier clubs, grocery stores are creating frequent-shopper cards that allow them to track exactly what and when their best customers are buying. Through their frequent-shopper program, supermarkets can offer sales just to their best customers and can customize promotional materials to individual shoppers. For instance, Mayne decided to eliminate the huge storewide sales Dorothy Lane Market had relied on for so many years and created the Club DLM, the company's frequent-shopper program. When cus-

tomers signed up for a card, they provided some basic demographic data about themselves, which the company uses to track buying habits (using customers' cards and the checkout scanner). Marrying customers' demographic profiles with their purchasing patterns has enabled Dorothy Lane Market to discontinue much of its sale-price newspaper ads and to focus more on direct mail ads to its best customers, the 60,000 members of the Club DLM. Most of the $250,000 the chain used to spend on newspaper advertising now goes into the club. Price discounts go only to club members. The company's direct mail ads are customized with coupons tied specifically to each customer's buying habits. A customer who buys lots of bread gets discount coupons for bread and related items. The store sends its monthly newsletter to the top 30 percent of its cardholders, who account for 83 percent of the company's sales. At Thanksgiving, Dorothy Lane Market gives these loyal customers free turkeys.

The card program has helped Dorothy Lane Market reduce its investment in inventory, increase the number of items it turns in inventory, and speed up distribution. Using the card system, store managers can tell exactly which items are selling fast and which ones are not. Rather than storing large amounts of inventory, the company now times its orders to arrive when needed, and the goods go straight onto store shelves. Once on the shelves, the merchandise doesn't sit as long as it used to, so spoilage costs also are down. Dorothy Lane Market has been able to reduce its inventory investment by about 35 percent, freeing up valuable cash for use elsewhere in the business. Some supermarkets have gone a step further, ordering from their vendors by computer to reduce the amount of costly paperwork they must handle.

Employees at Dorothy Lane Market are happy about the brighter profit picture because they share in the gains. The company routinely pays out bonuses equal to 20 percent of its profits. Even the company mission statement reflects the focus on profitability. When he joined the company several years ago, Calvin Mayne, Norman's son, pushed to include a reference to profits in the mission statement. It says, in part, "the Mission of Dorothy Lane Market is to create a satisfied customer, resulting in profitable growth."

1. How successfully can small supermarkets use the techniques that Dorothy Lane Market is using to boost profitability? Explain. What benefits can stores that use these techniques expect?

2. Work with a team of your classmates to brainstorm other profit-boosting techniques for grocers.

Source: Adapted from Calmetta Y. Coleman, "Finally Supermarkets Find Ways to Increase Their Profit Margins," *Wall Street Journal*, May 29, 1997, pp. A1, A6. ◆

Bradstreet also publishes *Cost of Doing Business*, a series of operating ratios compiled from the IRS's *Statistics of Income*.

Vest Pocket Guide to Financial Ratios. This handy guide, published by Prentice Hall, gives key ratios and financial data for a wide variety of industries.

Bank of America. Periodically, the Bank of America publishes many documents relating to small business management, including the *Small Business Reporter*, which details costs of doing business ratios.

Trade associations. Virtually every type of business is represented by a national trade association, which publishes detailed financial data compiled from its membership. For example, the owner of a small supermarket could contact the National Association of Retail Grocers or the *Progressive Grocer*, its trade publication, for financial statistics relevant to his operation.

Government agencies. Several government agencies (the Federal Trade Commission, Interstate Commerce Commission, Department of Commerce, Department of Agriculture, and Securities and Exchange Commission) offer a great deal of financial operating data on a variety of industries, although the categories are more general than those used by other organizations. In addition, the IRS annually publishes *Statistics of Income*, which includes income statement and balance sheet statistics compiled from income tax returns. The IRS also publishes the *Census of Business*, which gives a limited amount of ratio information.

WHAT DO ALL OF THESE NUMBERS MEAN?

Learning to interpret financial ratios just takes a little practice. This section will show you how it's done by comparing the ratios from the operating data already computed for Sam's Appliance Shop with those taken from Robert Morris Associates' *Annual Statement Studies*. (The industry median is the ratio falling exactly in the middle when sample elements are arranged in ascending or descending order.)

1. *Current ratio.* Sam's: 1.87:1   Industry median 1.50:1

   Sam's Appliance Shop falls short of the rule of thumb of 2:1, but its current ratio is above the industry median by a significant amount. Sam's should have no problem meeting its short-term debts as they come due. By this measure, the company's liquidity is solid.

2. *Quick ratio.* Sam's 0.63:1   Industry median 0.50:1

   Again, Sam's is below the rule of thumb of 1:1, but the company passes this test of liquidity when measured against industry standards. Sam's relies on selling inventory to satisfy short-term debt (as do most appliance shops). A sales slump could cause liquidity problems for Sam's.

3. *Debt ratio.* Sam's 0.68:1   Industry median 0.64:1

   Creditors provide 68 percent of Sam's total assets, very close to the industry median of 64 percent. Although Sam's does not appear to be overburdened with debt, the company might have difficulty borrowing additional money, especially from conservative lenders.

4. *Debt to net worth ratio.* Sam's 2.20:1   Industry median 1.90:1

   Sam's Appliance Shop owes $2.20 to creditors for every $1.00 the owners have invested in the business (compared with $1.90 in debt to every $1.00 in equity for the typical business). Although this is not an exorbitant amount of debt, many lenders and creditors will see Sam's as "borrowed up." Borrowing capacity is somewhat limited because creditors' claims against the business are more than twice what the owners have invested.

5. *Times interest earned ratio.* Sam's 2.52:1   Industry median 2.0:1

Sam's earnings are high enough to cover the interest payments on its debt by a factor of 2.52, slightly better than the typical firm in the industry, whose earnings cover its interest payments just two times. Sam's Appliance Shop has a cushion (although a small one) in meeting its interest payments.

6. *Average inventory turnover ratio.*   Industry median 4.0 times/year
Sam's 2.05 times/year

Inventory is moving through Sam's at a very slow pace, half that of the industry median. The company has a problem with slow-moving items in its inventory and, perhaps, too much inventory. Which items are they, and why are they moving so slowly? Does Sam's need to drop some product lines?

7. *Average collection period ratio.*   Industry median 19.3 days
Sam's 50.0 days

Sam's Appliance Shop collects the average accounts receivable after 50 days (compared with the industry median of 19 days): more than two-and-a-half times as long. A more meaningful comparison is against Sam's credit terms; if credit terms are net 30 (or anywhere close to that), Sam's has a dangerous collection problem, one that drains cash and profits and demands *immediate* attention!

8. *Average payable period ratio.*   Industry median 43 days
Sam's 59.3 days

Sam's payables are nearly 40 percent slower than those of the typical firm in the industry. Stretching payables too far could seriously damage the company's credit rating, causing suppliers to cut off future trade credit. This could be a sign of cash flow problems or a sloppy accounts payable procedure. This problem also demands *immediate* attention.

9. *Net sales to total assets ratio.*   Industry median 2.7:1
Sam's 2.21:1

Sam's Appliance Shop is not generating enough sales, given the size of its asset base. This could be the result of a number of factors: improper inventory, inappropriate pricing, poor location, poorly trained sales personnel, and many others. The key is to find the cause . . . *Fast!*

10. *Net sales to working capital ratio.*   Industry median 10.8:1
Sam's 5.86:1

Sam's generates just $5.86 in sales for every $1 in working capital, just over half of what the typical firm in the industry does. Given the previous ratio, the message is clear: Sam's simply is not producing an adequate level of sales. Improving the number of inventory turns will boost this ratio; otherwise, Sam's is likely to experience a working capital shortage soon.

11. *Net profit on sales ratio.* Sam's 3.24%   Industry median 7.6%

After deducting all expenses, 3.24 cents of each sales dollar remains as profit for Sam's: less than half the industry median. Sam's should check its gross profit margin and investigate its operating expenses, checking them against industry standards and looking for those that are out of balance.

12. *Net profit to equity ratio.* Sam's 22.65%   Industry median 12.6%

Sam's Appliance Shop's owners are earning 22.65 percent on the money they have invested in the business. This yield is nearly twice that of the industry median. Given the previous ratio, it is more a result of the owners' relatively low investment than an indication of the business's superior profitability. The owners are using O.P.M. (other people's money) to generate a profit.

When comparing ratios for their individual businesses with published statistics, small business owners must remember that the comparison is made against averages. The owner must strive to achieve ratios that are at least as good as these average figures. The goal should be to manage the business so that its financial performance is above average. As the owner compares financial performance with measures covered in the published statistics, he inevitably will discern differences between them. He should note those items that are substantially out of line from the industry average. However, a ratio that varies from the average does not *necessarily* mean that the small business is in financial jeopardy. Instead of making drastic changes in financial policy, the owner must explore *why* the figures are out of line. *Steve Cowan, co-owner of Professional Salon Concepts, a wholesale beauty products distributor, routinely performs such an analysis on his company's financial statements. "I need to know whether the variances for expenses and revenues for a certain period are similar,"* he says. *"If they're not, are the differences explainable? Is an expense category up just because of a decision to spend more, or were we just sloppy?"*[20]

In addition to comparing ratios with industry averages, owners should analyze their firms' financial ratios over time. By themselves, these ratios are "snapshots" of the firm's finances at a single instant; by examining these trends over time, the owner can detect gradual shifts that otherwise might go unnoticed until a financial crisis is looming (see Figure 7.9).

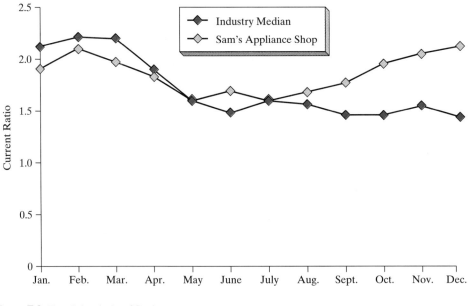

Figure 7.9 **Trend Analysis of Ratios**

*B*reak-even Analysis

◆ Conduct a break-even analysis for a small company.

Another key component of every sound financial plan is the breakeven analysis. The small firm's **break-even point** is the level of operation (sales dollars or production quantity) at which it neither earns a profit nor incurs a loss. At this level of activity, sales revenue equals expenses; that is, the firm "breaks even." By analyzing costs and expenses, the owner can calculate the minimum level of activity required to keep the firm in operation. These techniques can then be refined to project the sales needed to generate the desired profit. Most potential lenders and investors will require the potential owner to prepare a break-even analysis to assist them in evaluating the earning potential of the new business. In addition to its being a simple, useful screening device for financial institutions, break-even analysis can also serve as a planning device for the small business owner. It occasionally will show a poorly prepared entrepreneur just how unprofitable a proposed business venture is likely to be.

CALCULATING THE BREAK-EVEN POINT

A small business owner can calculate a firm's break-even point by using a simple mathematical formula. To begin the analysis, the owner must determine fixed expenses and variable expenses. **Fixed expenses** are those that do not vary with changes in the volume of sales or production (e.g., rent, depreciation expense, interest payments). **Variable expenses,** on the other hand, vary directly with changes in the volume of sales or production (e.g., raw materials costs, sales commissions).

Some expenses cannot be neatly categorized as fixed or variable because they contain elements of both. These semivariable expenses change, although not proportionately, with changes in the level of sales or production (electricity would be one example). These costs remain constant up to a particular production or sales volume and then climb as that volume is exceeded. To calculate the break-even point, the owner must separate these expenses into their fixed and variable components. A number of techniques can be used (which are beyond the scope of this text), but a good cost accounting system can provide the desired results.

Here are the steps an entrepreneur must take to compute the breakeven point using an example of a typical small business, The Magic Shop:

Step 1. *Determine the expenses the business can expect to incur.* With the help of a budget, an entrepreneur can develop estimates of sales revenue, cost of goods sold, and expenses for the upcoming accounting period. The Magic Shop expects net sales of $950,000 in the upcoming year, with a cost of goods sold of $646,000 and total expenses of $236,500.

Step 2. *Categorize the expenses estimated in step 1 into fixed expenses and variable expenses.* Separate semivariable expenses into their component parts. From the budget, the owner anticipates variable expenses (including the cost of goods sold) of $705,125 and fixed expenses of $177,375.

Step 3. *Calculate the ratio of variable expenses to net sales.* For the Magic Shop, this percentage is $705,125 ÷ $950,000 = 74 percent. So the Magic Shop uses $0.74 out of every sales dollar to cover variable expenses, leaving $0.26 as a contribution margin to cover fixed costs and make a profit.

Step 4. *Compute the break-even point by inserting this information into the following formula.*

$$\text{Break-even sales (\$)} = \frac{\text{Total fixed cost}}{\text{Contribution margin expressed as a percentage of sales}}$$

WIRED TO THE WEB

A RECIPE FOR FINANCIAL CONTROL

*I*lene Polansky owns two trendy restaurants in Montreal, Canada. When her business, Maestro S.V.P., got a bill for $1,000 for a six-month supply of dishwashing soap, she knew she had to do something. "I know it was an oversight," she says of the bill. "I just wasn't watching." That's understandable for an entrepreneur who routinely puts in 60- to 70-hour weeks managing her busy eateries. Since starting with her first restaurant, Polansky has been juggling the roles of owner, maitre d', chief financial officer, human resources manager, and, when necessary, dishwasher. In her attempt to keep tight control over every aspect of her restaurants, whose revenues exceed $1.5 million, Polansky believes she may be shortchanging their profitability. Because she refuses to allow anyone else—even her father, who is an accountant (and an investor in the business)—to help her with Maestro S.V.P.'s financial management, Polansky is often too busy to negotiate lower prices with vendors. And then there's the occasional fiasco like the dishwashing soap. "All this juggling is keeping me awake nights," she admits.

Although her restaurants' net profit margin of 10 to 15 percent is within the industry average and loyal patrons pack both locations virtually every night, Polansky continues to experience periodic financial problems. "I know what I have to make each week," she says. "If I have money left over, then I buy what I need. If not, I don't."

Polansky counts on what she learned in a 10-week bookkeeping course to manage her company's finances. Her secretary writes all the checks, but she does not track the restaurants' expenses over time. Once a month, the secretary goes to Polansky's father's accounting firm to use his computer to input invoices. Polansky compiles all of the company's financial statements from hand-prepared ledger sheets. She does outsource Maestro's payroll for its 40 employees to Comcheq, a human resources firm, for $140 a month. "She has her own financial system," says Polansky's father, "but it isn't sufficient to properly assess how the restaurants are really doing right now or over the year to date."

Polansky is planning to open a third location within a year, but she knows she has to get her financial "plate" in order first. Maestro's currently operates without a budget, and Polansky needs to know how her food and labor costs (the two biggest expenses for most restaurants) stack up against industry averages. She also thinks it would be helpful to conduct some kind of analysis on the restaurants' financial statements. "Knowing these numbers will help me get the financing I need to open my third Maestro's," says Polansky.

1. Critique the existing financial control system Polansky has in place for her restaurants. What recommendations can you make for improving it? Which financial reports would you advise Polansky to prepare? How should she use them to manage her restaurants?
2. Would you recommend that Polansky computerize her financial records? If so, use the resources of the World Wide Web and your library to provide her with suggestions for accounting packages designed for small businesses such as Maestro's.
3. Search the World Wide Web for sources of information that could help Polansky gain better financial control over her business. (Hint: Check out sites such as the National Restaurant Association, Dun & Bradstreet, and Robert Morris Associates).

Source: Adapted from Sheryl Nance-Nash, "Finding the Right Financial Recipe for Growth," *Your Company*, August/September 1997, pp. 40–46.

For the Magic Shop,

$$\text{Breakeven sales} = \frac{\$177,375}{0.26}$$

$$= \$682,212$$

The same break-even point will result from solving the following equation algebraically:

Break-even sales (S) = Fixed expense + Variable expenses expressed as a percentage of sales
$$S = \$\ 177,375 + 0.74S$$
$$100S = 17,737,500 + 74S$$
$$26S = 17,737,500$$
$$S = \$682,212$$

Thus, the Magic Shop will break even with sales of $682,212. At this point, sales revenue generated will just cover total fixed and variable expense. The Magic Shop will earn no profit and will incur no loss. To verify this result, make the following calculations:

Sales at break-even point	$ 682,212
−Variable expenses (74% of sales)	−504,837
Contribution margin	177,375
−Fixed expenses	−177,375
Net profit (or net loss)	$ 0

ADDING IN A PROFIT

What if the Magic Shop's owner wants to do better than just breakeven? His analysis can be adjusted to consider such a possibility. Suppose the owner expects a reasonable profit (before taxes) of $80,000. What level of sales must the Magic Shop achieve to generate this amount? He can calculate this by treating the desired profit as if it were a fixed cost. In other words, he modifies the formula to include the desired net income:

$$\text{Break-even sales (\$)} = \frac{\text{Total fixed expenses} + \text{Desired net income}}{\text{Contribution margin expressed as a percentage of sales}}$$

$$= \frac{\$177,375 + \$80,000}{0.26}$$

$$= \$989,904$$

To achieve a net profit of $80,000 (before taxes), the Magic Shop must generate net sales of $989,904.

BREAK-EVEN POINT IN UNITS

Some small businesses may prefer to express the break-even point in units produced or sold instead of in dollars. Manufacturers often find this approach particularly useful. The following formula computes the break-even point in units:

$$\text{Break-even volume} = \frac{\text{Total fixed costs}}{\text{Sales price per unit} - \text{Variable cost per unit}}$$

For example, suppose that Trilex Manufacturing Company estimates its fixed costs for producing its line of small appliances at $390,000. The variable costs (including materials, direct labor, and factory overhead) amount to $12.10 per unit, and the selling price per unit is $17.50. Trilex computes its contribution margin this way:

$$\text{Contribution margin} = \text{Price per unit} - \text{Variable cost per unit}$$
$$= \$17.50 \text{ per unit} - \$12.10 \text{ per unit}$$
$$= \$5.40 \text{ per unit}$$

So Trilex's break-even volume is as follows:

$$\text{Break-even volume (units)} = \frac{\text{Total fixed costs}}{\text{Per unit contribution margin}}$$
$$= \frac{\$390,000}{\$5.40}$$
$$= 72,222 \text{ units}$$

To convert this number of units to break-even sales dollars, Trilex simply multiplies it by the selling price per unit:

$$\text{Break-even sales (\$)} = 72,222 \text{ units} \times \$17.50 = \$1,263,889$$

Trilex could compute the sales required to produce a desired profit by treating the profit as if it were a fixed cost:

$$\text{Sales (units)} = \frac{\text{Total fixed costs} + \text{Desired net income}}{\text{Per unit contribution margin}}$$

For example, if Trilex wanted to earn a $60,000 profit, its required sales would be:

$$\text{Sales (units)} = \frac{390,000 + 60,000}{5.40} = 83,333 \text{ units}$$

CONSTRUCTING A BREAK-EVEN CHART

The following outlines the procedure for constructing a graph that visually portrays the firm's break-even point (the point at which revenues equal expenses):

Step 1. *On the horizontal axis, mark a scale measuring sales volume in dollars* (or in units sold or some other measure of volume). The break-even chart for the Magic Shop shown in Figure 7.10 uses sales volume in dollars because it applies to all types of businesses, departments, and products.

Step 2. *On the vertical axis, mark a scale measuring income and expenses in dollars.*

Step 3. *Draw a fixed expense line intersecting the vertical axis at the proper dollar level parallel to the horizontal axis.* The area between this line and the horizontal axis represents the firm's fixed expenses. On the break-even chart for the Magic Shop shown in Figure 7.10, the fixed expense line is drawn horizontally beginning at $177,375 (point A). Because this

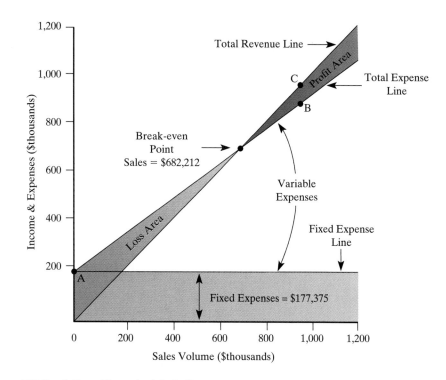

Figure 7.10 **Break-Even Chart, the Magic Shop**

line is parallel to the horizontal axis, it indicates that fixed expenses remain constant at all levels of activity.

Step 4. *Draw a total expense line that slopes upward beginning at the point where the fixed cost line intersects the vertical axis.* The precise location of the total expense line is determined by plotting the total cost incurred at a particular sales volume. The total cost for a given sales level is found by the following formula:

Total cost for a given sales level = Fixed expenses + (Variable expenses expressed as a percentage of sales × sales level)

Arbitrarily choosing a sales level of $950,000, the Magic Shop's total costs would be as follows:

$$\text{Total expenses} = \$177{,}375 + (0.74 \times \$950{,}000)$$
$$= \$880{,}375$$

Thus, the Magic Shop's total cost is $880,375 at a net sales level of $950,000 (point B). The variable cost line is drawn by connecting points A and B. The area between the total cost line and the horizontal axis measures the total costs the Magic Shop incurs at various levels of sales. For example, if the Magic Shop's sales are $850,000, its total costs will be $806,375.

Step 5. *Beginning at the graph's origin, draw a 45 degree revenue line showing where total sales volume equals total income.* For the Magic Shop, point C shows that sales equals income at $950,000.

Step 6. *Locate the break-even point by finding the intersection of the total expense line and the revenue line.* If the Magic Shop operates at a sales volume to the left of the break-even point, it will incur a loss because the expense line is higher than the revenue line over this range. This is shown by the triangular section labeled Loss Area. On the other hand, if the firm operates at a sales volume to the right of the break-even point, it will earn a profit because the revenue line lies above the expense line over this range. This is shown by the triangular section labeled Profit Area.

USING BREAK-EVEN ANALYSIS

Break-even analysis is a useful planning tool for the potential small business owner, especially when approaching potential lenders and investors for funds. It provides an opportunity for integrated analysis of sales volume, expenses, income, and other relevant factors. Break-even analysis is a simple, preliminary screening device for the entrepreneur faced with the business start-up decision. It is easy to understand and use. With just a few calculations, the small business owner can determine the effects of various financial strategies on the business operation. It is a helpful tool for evaluating the impact of changes in investments and expenditures. For instance, before Donald Trump opened the billion dollar Trump Taj Mahal, an opulent casino-hotel complex in Atlantic City, a cost-revenue analysis showed that the complex needed revenues of $400 million a year—*$1.1 million a day*—just to break even![21]

Break-even analysis does have certain limitations. It is too simple to use as a final screening device because it ignores the importance of cash flows. Also, the accuracy of the analysis depends on the accuracy of the revenue and expense estimates. Finally, the assumptions pertaining to break-even analysis may not be realistic for some businesses. Break-even calculations assume the following: fixed expenses remain constant for all levels of sales volume; variable expenses change in direct proportion to changes in sales volume; and changes in sales volume have no effect on unit sales price. Relaxing those assumptions does not render this tool useless, however. For example, the owner could employ nonlinear break-even analysis using a graphical approach.

Chapter Summary

1. Understand the importance of preparing a financial plan.
   - Launching a successful business requires an entrepreneur to create a solid financial plan. Not only is such a plan an important tool in raising the capital needed to get a company off the ground, but it also is an essential ingredient in managing a growing business.
   - Earning a profit does not occur by accident; it takes planning.
2. Describe how to prepare the basic financial statements and use them to manage the small business.
   - *The balance sheet.* Built on the accounting equation Assets = Liabilities + Owner's equity (capital). It provides an estimate of the company's value on a particular date.
   - *The income statement.* Compares the firm's revenues against its expenses to determine its net profit (or loss). It provides information about the company's bottom line.

   - *The statement of cash flows.* Shows the change in the company's working capital over the accounting period by listing the sources and the uses of funds.
3. Create pro forma financial statements.
   - Projected (pro forma) financial statements are a basic component of a sound financial plan. They help the manager plot the company's financial future by setting operating objectives and by analyzing the reasons for variations from targeted results. Also, the small business in search of start-up funds will need these pro forma statements to present to prospective lenders and investors. They also assist in determining the amount of cash, inventory, fixtures, and other assets the business will need to begin operation.
4. Understand the basic financial statements through ratio analysis.
   - The 12 key ratios described in this chapter are divided into four major categories: *liquidity ratios*, which show the small firm's ability to meet its current obligations; *leverage ratios*, which tell how much of the company's financing is provided by owners and how much by creditors; *operating ra-*

tios, which show how effectively the firm uses its resources; and *profitability ratios*, which disclose the company's profitability.

◆ Many agencies and organizations regularly publish such statistics. If there is a discrepancy between the small firm's ratios and those of the typical business, the owner should investigate the reason for the difference. A below-average ratio does not necessarily mean that the business is in trouble.

5 Explain how to interpret financial ratios.

◆ To benefit from ratio analysis, the small company should compare its ratios with those of other companies in the same line of business and look for trends over time.

◆ When business owners detect deviations in their companies' ratios from industry standards, they should determine the cause of the deviations. In some cases, such deviations are the result of sound business decisions; in other instances, however, ratios that are out of the normal range for a particular type of business are indicators of what could become serious problems for a company.

6 Conduct a break-even analysis for a small company.

◆ Business owners should know their firm's break-even point, the level of operations at which total revenues equal total costs; it is the point at which companies neither earn a profit nor incur a loss. Although just a simple screening device, break-even analysis is a useful planning and decision-making tool.

Discussion Questions

1. Why is it important for entrepreneurs to develop financial plans for their companies?

2. How should a small business manager use the ratios discussed in this chapter?

3. Outline the key points of the 12 ratios discussed in this chapter. What signals does each give a business owner?

4. Describe the method for building a projected income statement and a projected balance sheet for a beginning business.

5. Why are pro forma financial statements important to the financial planning process?

6. How can break-even analysis help an entrepreneur planning to launch a business?

Step into the Real World

1. Ask the owner of a small business to provide your class with copies of the firm's financial statements (current or past) or go to the SEC's Edgar file at <http://www.sec.gov/edgarhp.htm> to find the financial statements of a publicly held company that interests you.
   a. Using these statements, compute the 12 key ratios described in this chapter.
   b. Compare the firm's ratios with those of the typical firm in this line of business.
   c. Interpret the ratios and make suggestions for operating improvements.
   d. Prepare a break-even analysis for the owner.

2. Use In the Footsteps of an Entrepreneur: Good News in the Grocery Business as a guide to develop a set of interview questions for the owner or manager of a local grocery store. What is the store's net profit margin? Is the local store using any of the techniques Dorothy Lane Market is using to boost its profitability? Is the store using any other strategies to enhance its profits? Prepare a brief report on your findings for your class.

Take It to the Net

Visit the Scarborough/Zimmerer home page at
www.prenhall.com/scarbzim
for updated information, on-line resources, and Web-based exercises.

Endnotes

1. Eileen Davis, "Dodging the Bullet," *Venture*, December 1988, p. 78.
2. Heather Page, "Code Red," *Entrepreneur*, August 1997, p. 11.
3. Richard G. P. McMahon and Scott Holmes, "Small Business Financial Managment Practices in North America: A Literature Review," *Journal of Small Business Management*, April 1991, p. 21.
4. Daniel Kehrer, "Big Ideas for Your Small Business," *Changing Times*, November 1989, p. 57.
5. Ronaleen R. Roha, "How Small Businesses Control Costs," *Kiplinger's Personal Finance Magazine*, February 1997, p. 81.
6. Ibid., p.78.
7. Ibid., p. 80.
8. Grace W. Weinstein, "Order from Chaos," *Business Start-Ups*, June 1997, pp. 18–20.
9. William Bak, "The Numbers Game," *Entrepreneur*, April 1993, p. 54.
10. Diedrich Von Soosten, "The Roots of Financial Destruction," *Industry Week*, April 5, 1993, pp. 33–34.
11. McMahon and Holmes, "Small Business Financial Management Practices in North America," p. 21.
12. Jill Andresky Fraser, "When Staffers Track Results," *Inc.*, October 1993, p. 42; Dan Callahan, "Everybody's an Accountant," *Business Ethics*, January/February 1994, p. 37.
13. "Putting Ratios to Work," *In Business*, December 1988, pp. 14–15.
14. Bak, "The Numbers Game," p. 57.
15. "Analyzing Creditworthiness," *Inc.*, November 1991, p. 196.
16. Michael Selz, "Entrepreneurs Would Use Boost in Profit to Cut Debt," *Wall Street Journal*, October 31, 1996, p. B2.
17. Jack Stack, "The Logic of Profit," *Inc.*, March 1996, p. 17.
18. Jill Andresky Fraser, "The No-Surprises Daily Money Watcher," *Inc.*, August 1995, pp. 73–74.
19. William Doescher, "Taking Stock," *Entrepreneur*, November 1994, p. 64.
20. Jeannie Mandelker, "Put Numbers on Your Side," *Your Company*, Winter 1994, p. 32.
21. Jack Egan, "Trump Plays His Biggest Ace," *U.S. News & World Report*, April 9, 1990, p. 41.

Managing Cash Flow

A deficit is what you have when you haven't got as much as when you had nothing.

—*Gerald F. Lieberman*

In a perfect world, the mail would be early, the check would always be in the mail, and it would be written for more than you expected.

—*John Gratton*

Upon completion of this chapter, you will be able to

1. Explain the importance of cash management to the success of the small business.

2. Differentiate between cash and profits.

3. Understand the five steps in creating a cash budget and use them to create a cash budget.

4. Describe fundamental principles involved in managing the "Big Three" of cash management: accounts receivable, accounts payable, and inventory.

5. Explain the techniques for avoiding a cash crunch in a small company.

---

*C*ash: a four-letter word that has become a curse for many small businesses. Lack of this valuable asset has driven countless small companies into bankruptcy. Unfortunately, many more firms will become failure statistics because their owners have neglected the principles of cash management that can spell the difference between success and failure. One small business owner compares a small company's cash to oxygen on a space trip:

> *Astronauts who take off on a long space flight must take along plenty of food and water (their "healthy balance sheet"). But if they happen to run out of oxygen any time between takeoff and landing, all that food and water is of no use to them; they will perish. Cash is like oxygen to a business. When it's there, it's easily taken for granted. When it's not, death can come quickly.*[1]

Developing a cash forecast is essential for new businesses because in the early stages businesses usually do not generate sufficient cash to keep afloat. Too often, entrepreneurs launch their companies with insufficient cash to cover their start-up costs, and a cash flow gap results as expenses outstrip revenues. The result is business failure. "The most common reason small businesses fail is running out of cash," says Andy Bangs Jr., an entrepreneur and small business expert.[2]

Controlling the financial aspects of a business with the techniques described in the previous chapter is immensely important; however, by themselves, those techniques are insufficient to achieve business success. Entrepreneurs are prone to focus on their companies' income statements—particularly sales and profits. The balance sheet and the income statement, of course, show an important part of a company's financial picture, but it is just that: only *part* of the total picture. It is entirely possible for a business to have a solid balance sheet and to make a profit and still go out of business *by running out of cash*. Managing cash effectively requires an entrepreneur to look beyond the "bottom line" and focus on what it takes to keep a company going: cash. *For example, when Paul Lyon and a partner decided to launch a company that manufactured framed desk toys made of sand and an oily liquid, they knew nothing about the dangers of cash flow. After investing several thousand dollars, the two built prototypes and took them to local trade shows, where they landed orders for more than 3,000 units. Sales began to climb, and by the third year, the company, Exotic Sands, was generating $2.5 million in revenues. "It was heady stuff," Lyon recalls. "We thought we were millionaires." Lyon and his partner spent like millionaires, too, purchasing expensive houses, cars, boats, and other symbols of success. The partners never took the time to create a cash plan for Exotic Sands. "True entrepreneurs never sit down to do a cash flow plan," Lyon remembers rationalizing. Soon, however, they discovered that in the gift business, products that are red hot one season may languish on shelves the next. Sales slipped, and cash flow became a serious problem. Their returned check charges alone were running more than $1,000 a month, and they were constantly overdrawing their bank line of credit. Lyon and his partner turned to the bank when they would run out of cash only to have "the banker laugh at us," recalls Lyon. Problems stemming from the constant cash flow shortage began to snowball, and Lyon knew the company was in trouble. He soon left to start his own business, and this time he is using cash flow forecasts![3]*

*C*ash Management

◆ Explain the importance of cash managment to the success of the small business.

Cash is the most important yet least productive asset that a small business owns. A business must have enough cash to meet its obligations or it will be declared bankrupt. Creditors, employees, and lenders expect to be paid on time, and cash is the required medium of exchange. But some firms retain an excessive amount of cash to meet any unexpected circumstances that might arise. These dormant dollars have an income-earning potential that the owners are ignoring, and dormant dollars restrict the firm's growth and lower its profitability. Proper cash management enables the owner to adequately meet the cash demands of the business, to avoid retaining unnecessarily large cash balances, and to stretch the profit-generating power of each dollar the business owns.

One survey asking small business owners to identify their "greatest financial obstacle" found that the most common response was "uneven cash flow" (see Figure 8.1). Managing cash flow is an acute problem, especially for rapidly growing businesses. In fact, fast-track companies are the ones most likely to suffer cash shortages. Many successful, growing, and profitable businesses fail because they become insolvent; they do not have adequate cash to meet the needs of a growing business with a booming sales volume. If a company's sales are up, the owner also must hire more employees, expand plant capacity, increase the sales

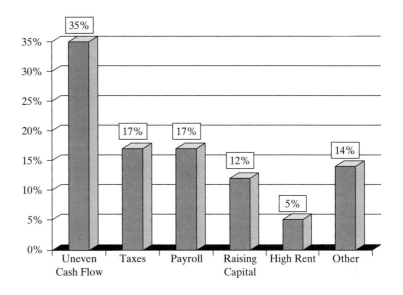

Figure 8.1 What Is Your Greatest Financial Obstacle? SOURCE: *Inc.,* September 1990, p. 130.

force, build inventory, and incur other drains on the firm's cash supply. The head of the National Federation of Independent Businesses says that many small business owners "wake up one day to find that the price of success is no cash on hand. They don't understand that if they're successful, inventory and receivables will increase faster than profits can fund them."[4] The resulting cash crisis may force the owner to lose equity control of the business or, ultimately, declare bankruptcy and close. Table 8.1 describes the five key cash management roles every entrepreneur must fill.

Table 8.1. Five Cash Management Roles of the Entrepreneur

Role 1: Cash finder. This is the entrepreneur's first and foremost responsibility. You must make sure there is enough capital to pay all present (and future) bills. This is *not* a one-time task; it is an ongoing job.

Role 2: Cash planner. As cash planner, an entrepreneur makes sure the company's cash is used properly and efficiently. You must keep track of its cash, make sure it is available to pay bills, and plan for its future use. Planning requires you to forecast the company's cash inflows and outflows for the months ahead with the help of a cash budget (discussed later in this chapter).

Role 3: Cash distributor. This role requires you to control the cash needed to pay the company's bills and the priority and the timing of those payments. Forecasting cash disbursements accurately and making sure the cash is available when payments come due is essential to keeping the business solvent.

Role 4: Cash collector. As cash collector, your job is to make sure your customers pay their bills on time. Too often, entrepreneurs focus on pumping up sales, while neglecting to collect the cash from those sales. Having someone in your company responsible for collecting accounts receivable is essential. Uncollected accounts drain a small company's pool of cash very quickly.

Role 5: Cash conserver. This role requires you to make sure your company gets maximum value for the dollars it spends. Whether you are buying inventory to resell or computers to keep track of what you sell, it is important to get the most for your money. Avoiding unnecessary expenditures is an important part of this task. The goal is to spend cash so it will produce a return for the company.

SOURCE: Adapted from Bruce J. Blechman, "Quick Change Artist," *Entrepreneur,* January 1994, pp. 18–21.

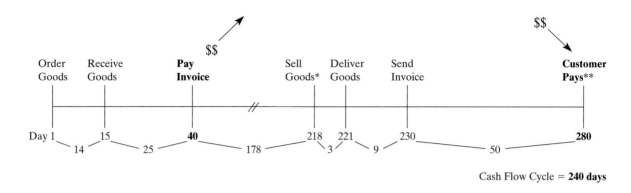

Figure 8.2 **The Cash Flow Cycle**
 * Based on average inventory turnover: 365 days/2.05 times/year = 178 days
** Based on average collection period: 365 days/7.31 times/year = 50 days

The first step in managing cash effectively is to understand the company's **cash flow cycle:** the time lag between paying suppliers for merchandise and receiving payment from customers (see Figure 8.2). The longer this cash flow cycle, the more likely the business owner is to encounter a cash crisis. Preparing a cash forecast that recognizes this cycle, however, will help avoid a crisis. "To develop a cash management strategy," says one small business owner, "you must understand [the] cash flow patterns [of your business]."[5]

The next step in effective cash management is to begin cutting down the length of the cash flow cycle. Reducing the cycle from 240 days to, say, 150 days would free up incredible amounts of cash that this company could use to finance growth and dramatically reduce its borrowing costs. What steps would you suggest the owner of the business whose cash flow cycle is illustrated in Figure 8.2 take to reduce the cycle's length?

Cash and Profits Are Not the Same

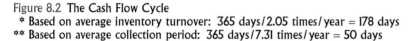

 Differentiate between cash and profits.

When analyzing cash flow, a small business manager must understand that cash and profits are *not* the same. "Profit is not cash flow, and cash flow is not profit," says one entrepreneur. "Anyone who tries to glean something about one from looking at the other may be easily misled."[6] **Profit** (or net income) is the difference between a company's total revenue and its total expenses. It measures how efficiently the business is running. As important as earning a profit is, no business owner can pay creditors, employees, and lenders in profits; those payments require cash! Profits are tied up in many forms, such as inventory, computers, or machinery; **cash** is the money that flows through a business in a continuous cycle without being tied up in any other asset. "When you show a negative profit but maintain a positive cash flow, life goes on—at least for a while," explains one expert. "Run out of cash, and trouble brews really fast. Payrolls cannot be met. Suppliers cannot be paid. New products cannot be launched."[7] In short, the business is headed for extinction.

Figure 8.3 shows the flow of cash through a typical small business. **Cash flow** is the volume of cash that comes into and goes out of the business during an accounting period. Decreases in cash occur when a business purchases, on credit or for cash, goods for inventory or materials for use in production. The resulting inventory is sold either for cash or on credit. When cash is taken in or when accounts receivable are collected, the firm's cash balance increases. Notice that purchases for inventory and production lead sales; that is, these

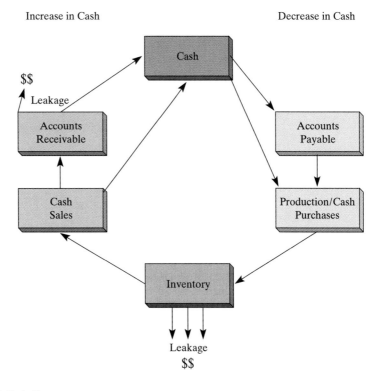

Increase in Cash   Decrease in Cash

Figure 8.3 **Cash Flow**

bills typically must be paid before sales are generated. But collection of accounts receivable lags behind sales; that is, customers who purchase goods on credit may not pay until the next month.

*T*he Cash Budget

Every small business manager should track the flow of cash through her business so she can project the cash balance available throughout the year. One recent study of 230 fast-growing companies by TEC, an international organization of CEOs, found that 73 percent tracked cash flow either daily or weekly.[8] Still, too many business owners operate their businesses without knowing the pattern of their cash flows, believing that the process is too complex or time-consuming. In reality, the small business manager simply cannot afford to disregard the process of cash management. The owner must ensure that an adequate, but not excessive, supply of cash is on hand to meet her operating needs. "The aim of prudent cash-flow management," says one business writer, "is to make sure there'll be enough cash in the till to meet given demands for that cash at any given time."[9]

How much cash is enough? What is suitable for one business may be totally inadequate for another, depending on each firm's size, nature, and particular situation. The small business manager should prepare a **cash budget,** which is nothing more than a "cash map," showing the amount and timing of cash receipts and cash disbursements day by day, week by week, or month by month. It is used to predict the amount of cash the firm will need to operate smoothly over a specific period of time, and it is a valuable tool in managing a company successfully.

The Price of Success

*R*ochelle Zabarkes is a classic entrepreneur. Before she opened her specialty food store in Manhattan in 1991, she put together a detailed business plan, lined up financing, and rented space on one of New York City's busiest streets. With its universal mix of gourmet foods and spices from around the world, ethnic takeout food, and exotic gift items, Adriana's Bazaar was an instant hit with customers. The *New Yorker* magazine featured the store in an article, and *Gourmet* magazine frequently mentions it as a source of ingredients for its recipes. This year daily sales revenues averaged $1,100, up 40 percent from last year. A newly installed coffee bar is drawing new customers, and Zabarkes has even started a mail-order business. She plans to open two more stores in New York City before going national. "My dream is to be as big as Body Shop," says the entrepreneur.

What more could Zabarkes ask for?

C-A-S-H!!!

Despite her company's success, its rapid growth has devoured all of her start-up capital and then some. When she launched Adriana's Bazaar, Zabarkes raised $245,000 through loans from a local bank and the National Association of Female Executives and in contributions from friends. She has since raised another $40,000 to keep the business going. Unfortunately, the rapid growth of the company pushed cash requirements closer to $350,000.

Failing to forecast cash requirements accurately during the volatile start-up period almost cost Zabarkes her business. She defaulted on a $145,000 bank loan, which the Small Business Administration has taken over. She had to give up her 4,300-square-foot loft apartment because she couldn't keep up the mortgage payments. Her desk is in a perpetual state of overflow—mostly past-due bills from suppliers and other creditors. The owner of the building housing her business is threatening eviction unless she comes up with the back rent—totaling nearly $20,000—pronto! Recently, she sent a check for $8,500 to a creditor by bicycle messenger to meet a court-ordered deadline.

At one point, Zabarkes was so desperate for cash that she used the proceeds of a check a state agency had made out to her for work a consultant did for her. Although the agency was furious at her for snagging the money, the consultant for whom the check was intended was not. "I don't hold it against her," he says. "I admire her for being aggressive." Zabarkes promises she will repay the money, but she claims she had no choice.

So far, her efforts to rescue her store from the cash crisis have been successful. Zabarkes has mollified most of her creditors with repeated phone calls and letters explaining her situation, asking for their patience, and promising eventual payment. She also has convinced the Small Business Administration into being flexible about her loan repayment schedule. "I called the SBA and asked: 'What is the worst that could happen?'" she recalls. "The SBA official said he could get a court order, auction off my assets, and close me down. I said, 'Are you crazy? I owe you $145,000, and you wouldn't get $2,500 in an auction.'" Zabarkes even threw a Depression-era "rent party" at her store to raise cash. "I'm absolutely dedicated to this store," she admits. "I'll do anything—beg, borrow, or steal—to keep it alive." And, she adds, "I will save it."

1. What factors caused the cash crises affecting Adriana's Bazaar?

2. Evaluate the manner in which Zabarkes has handled the cash crisis in her business.

3. What ethical dilemmas does Zabarkes face as a result of her company's cash crisis? How should she handle them?

SOURCE: Adapted from Brent Bowers, "This Store Is a Hit But Somehow Cash Flow Is Missing," *Wall Street Journal*, April 13, 1993, p. B2. ◆

> *One consultant recalls how a cash budget helped salvage a once-successful service firm that had fallen on hard times. The five-year-old firm, with $20 million in annual billings, began to lose money and was having trouble paying its bills. After working with the consultant, the company began sending customer invoices much faster and implemented a much stricter collection policy. The new collection system involved employees in collecting overdue payments and took immediate action when an account became overdue. Managers set up a receivables report and reviewed it at weekly staff meetings. They also beefed up the company's financial reports, added a cash budget, and used it to make managerial decisions. Within six months, the company's cash balance had improved dramatically (a turnaround of $1.5 million); managers were able to pay down a line of credit at the bank, and the business was back on track again!*

$\mathcal{P}$reparing the Cash Budget

3 Understand the five steps in creating a cash budget and use them to create a cash budget.

Typically, a small business should prepare a projected monthly cash budget for at least one year into the future and a quarterly estimate several years in advance. It must cover all seasonal sales fluctuations. The more variable the firm's sales pattern, the shorter its planning horizon should be. For example, a firm whose sales fluctuate widely over a relatively short time frame might require a weekly cash budget. The key is to track cash flows *over time*. One entrepreneur says, "As of today, I have $329.72 in the bank. This Thursday I have to pay 50 employees a total of $250,000. Our problem is, a big check was on its way, but one major customer just pulled out. We are still running at a $4 million to $5 million annual [sales] rate, but we're eating cash like baked beans."[10] Managing cash flow successfully requires an entrepreneur to monitor not only the amount of cash flowing into and out of the company but also the timing of those cash flows. "An alert cash flow manager keeps an eye not on cash receipts or on cash demands as average quantities but on cash as a function of the *calendar*."[11]

Regardless of the time frame selected, the cash budget must be in writing for the small business owner to properly visualize the firm's cash position. Creating a written cash plan is not an excessively time-consuming task and can help the owner avoid unexpected cash shortages. One financial consultant describes "a client who won't be able to make the payroll this month. His bank agreed to meet the payroll for him—but banks don't like to be surprised like that," he adds.[12]

The cash budget is based on the cash method of accounting, which means that cash receipts and cash disbursements are recorded in the forecast only when the cash transaction is expected to take place. For example, credit sales to customers are not reported until the company expects to receive the cash from them. Similarly, purchases made on credit are not recorded until the owner expects to pay them. Because depreciation, bad debt expense, and other noncash items involve no cash transfers, they are omitted entirely from the cash budget.

The cash budget is nothing more than a forecast of the firm's cash inflows and outflows for a specific time period, and it will never be completely accurate. But it does give the small business manager a clear picture of the firm's estimated cash balance for the period, pointing out where external cash infusions may be required or where surplus cash balances may be available for investing. Also, by comparing actual cash flows with projections, the owner can revise his forecast so that future cash budgets will be more accurate. *Michael Koss, president and CEO of Koss Corporation, a manufacturer of stereo headphones, now emphasizes cash flow management after his company's brush with failure. In the 1980s, Koss Corporation expanded rapidly—so rapidly, in fact, that its cash flow couldn't keep pace. Debt climbed, and the company filed for reorganization under Chapter 11 bankruptcy. Emergency actions saved the business, and today Koss manages with the determination never to repeat the same mistakes. "I look at cash every single day," he says. "Every single day. That is absolutely critical."*[13]

Formats for preparing a cash budget vary depending on the pattern of a company's cash flow. Table 8.2 shows a monthly cash budget for a small department store over a four-month period. Each monthly column should be divided into two sections—estimated and actual (not shown)—so that each succeeding cash forecast can be updated according to actual cash transactions. There are five basic steps in completing a cash budget:

1. Determine an adequate minimum cash balance.
2. Forecast sales.

Table 8.2 Cash Budget for Small Department Store

Assumptions:

Cash balance on December 31 = $12,000

Minimum cash balance desired = $10,000

Sales are 75% credit and 25% cash.

Credit sales are collected in the following manner:

◆ 60% collected in the first month after the sale

◆ 30% collected in the second month after the sale

◆ 5% collected in the third month after the sale

◆ 5% are never collected

Sales forecasts are as follows:	Pessimistic	Most Likely	Optimistic
October [actual]		$300,000	
November [actual]		350,000	
December [actual]		400,000	
January	$120,000	150,000	$175,000
February	160,000	200,000	250,000
March	160,000	200,000	250,000
April	250,000	300,000	340,000
May	190,000	250,000	310,000

The store pays 70% of sales price for merchandise purchased and pays for each month's anticipated sales in the preceding month.

Rent is $2,000 per month.

An interest payment of $7,500 is due in March.

A tax prepayment of $50,000 must be made in March.

A capital addition payment of $130,000 is due in February.

Utilities expenses amount to $850 per month.

Miscellaneous expenses are $70 per month.

Interest income of $200 will be received in February.

Wages and salaries are estimated to be

January—$30,000

February—$40,000

March—$45,000

April—$50,000

Cash Budget
Pessimistic Sales Forecast

	OCT.	NOV.	DEC.	JAN.	FEB.	MAR.	APR.	MAY
Cash Receipts:								
Sales	$300,000	$350,000	$400,000	$120,000	$160,000	$ 160,000	$250,000	$190,000
Credit Sales	225,000	262,500	300,000	90,000	120,000	120,000	187,500	142,500
Collections:								
60%—1st month after sale				$180,000	$ 54,000	$ 72,000	$ 72,000	$112,500
30%—2nd month after sale				78,750	90,000	27,000	36,000	36,000
5%—3rd month after sale				11,250	13,125	15,000	4,500	6,000
Cash Sales				30,000	40,000	40,000	62,500	47,500
Interest				0	200	0	0	0
Total Cash Receipts				$300,000	$197,325	$ 154,000	$175,000	$202,000
Cash Disbursements:								
Purchases				$112,000	$112,000	$ 175,000	$133,000	—
Rent				2,000	2,000	2,000	2,000	
Utilities				850	850	850	850	
Interest				0	0	7,500	0	
Tax Prepayment				0	0	50,000	0	
Capital Addition				0	130,000	0	0	
Miscellaneous				70	70	70	70	
Wages/Salaries				30,000	40,000	45,000	50,000	
Total Cash Disbursements				$144,920	$284,920	$ 280,420	$185,920	
End of Month Balance:								
Cash (beginning of month)				$ 12,000	$167,080	$ 79,485	$ 10,000	
+ Cash Receipts				300,000	197,325	154,000	175,000	
– Cash Disbursements				144,920	284,920	280,420	185,920	
Cash (end of month)				167,080	79,485	(46,935)	(920)	
Borrowing/Repayment				0	0	56,935	10,920	
Cash (end of month [after borrowing])				$167,080	$ 79,485	$ 10,000	$ 10,000	

[continued]

Table 8.2 Cash Budget for Small Department Store *(continued)*

Cash Budget
Most Likely Sales Forcast

	OCT.	NOV.	DEC.	JAN.	FEB.	MAR.	APR.	MAY
Cash Receipts:								
Sales	$300,000	$350,000	$400,000	$150,000	$200,000	$200,000	$300,000	$250,000
Credit Sales	225,000	262,500	300,000	112,000	150,000	150,000	225,000	187,500
Collections:								
60%—1st month after sale				$180,000	$67,500	$90,000	$90,000	$135,000
30%—2nd month after sale				78,750	90,000	33,750	45,000	45,000
5%—3rd month after sale				11,250	13,125	15,000	5,625	7,500
Cash Sales				37,500	50,000	50,000	75,000	62,500
Interest				0	200	0	0	0
Total Cash Receipts				$307,500	$220,825	$188,750	$215,625	$250,000
Cash Disbursements:								
Purchases				$140,000	$140,000	$210,000	$175,000	—
Rent				2,000	2,000	2,000	2,000	
Utilities				850	850	850	850	
Interest				0	0	7,500	0	
Tax Prepayment				0	0	50,000	0	
Capital Addition				0	130,000	0	0	
Miscellaneous				70	70	70	70	
Wages/Salaries				30,000	40,000	45,000	50,000	
Total Cash Disbursements				$172,920	$312,920	$315,420	$227,920	
End of Month Balance:								
Cash (beginning of month)				$12,000	$146,580	$54,485	$10,000	
+ Cash Receipts				307,500	220,825	188,750	215,625	
– Cash Disbursements				172,920	312,920	315,420	227,920	
Cash (end of month)				146,580	54,485	(72,185)	(2,295)	
Borrowing/Repayment				0	0	82,185	12,295	
Cash (end of month [after borrowing])				$146,580	$54,485	$10,000	$10,000	

Cash Budget
Optimistic Sales Forcast

	OCT.	NOV.	DEC.	JAN.	FEB.	MAR.	APR.	MAY
Cash Receipts:								
Sales	$300,000	$350,000	$400,000	$175,000	$250,000	$250,000	$340,000	$310,000
Credit Sales	225,000	262,500	300,000	131,250	187,500	187,500	255,000	232,500
Collections:								
60%—1st month after sale				$180,000	$ 78,750	$112,500	$112,500	$153,000
30%—2nd month after sale				78,750	90,000	39,375	56,250	56,250
5%—3rd month after sale				11,250	13,125	15,000	6,563	9,375
Cash Sales				43,750	62,500	62,500	85,000	77,500
Interest				0	200	0	0	0
Total Cash Receipts				$313,750	$244,575	$229,375	$260,313	$296,125
Cash Disbursements:								
Purchases				$175,000	$175,000	$238,000	$217,000	—
Rent				2,000	2,000	2,000	2,000	
Utilities				850	850	850	850	
Interest				0	0	7,500	0	
Tax Prepayment				0	0	50,000	0	
Capital Addition				0	130,000	0	0	
Miscellaneous				70	70	70	70	
Wages/Salaries				30,000	40,000	45,000	50,000	
Total Cash Disbursements				$207,920	$347,920	$343,420	$269,920	
End of Month Balance:								
Cash [Beginning of month]				$ 12,000	$117,830	$ 14,485	$ 10,000	
+ Cash Receipts				313,750	244,575	229,375	296,125	
− Cash Disbursements				207,920	317,920	343,120	269,920	
Cash [end of month]				117,830	14,485	(99,560)	36,205	
Borrowing/Repayment				0	0	109,560	0	
Cash [end of month [after borrowing]]				$117,830	$ 14,485	$ 10,000	$ 36,205	

3. Forecast cash receipts.

4. Forecast cash disbursements.

5. Determine the end-of-month cash balance.

STEP 1: DETERMINE AN ADEQUATE MINIMUM CASH BALANCE

What is considered an excessive cash balance for one small business may be inadequate for another, even though the two firms are in the same trade. Some financial analysts suggest that a firm's cash balance should equal at least one-fourth of its current debts, but this clearly will not work for all small businesses. The most reliable method of deciding cash balance is based on experience. Past operating records should indicate the cash cushion needed to cover any unexpected expenses after all normal cash outlays are deducted from the month's cash receipts. For example, past records may indicate that it is desirable to maintain a cash balance equal to five days' sales. Seasonal fluctuations may cause the firm's minimum cash balance to change. For example, the desired cash balance for a retailer in December may be greater than in June.

STEP 2: FORECAST SALES

The heart of the cash budget is the sales forecast. It is the central factor in creating an accurate picture of the firm's cash position because sales ultimately are transformed into cash receipts and cash disbursements. For most businesses, sales constitute the major source of the cash flowing into the business. Similarly, sales of merchandise require that cash be used to replenish inventory. As a result, the cash budget is only as accurate as the sales forecast from which it is derived.

For the established business, the sales forecast can be based on past sales, but the owner must be careful not to be excessively optimistic in projecting sales. Economic swings, increased competition, fluctuations in demand, and other factors can drastically alter sales patterns.

Several quantitative techniques, which are beyond the scope of this text (e.g., linear regression, multiple regression, time series analysis, exponential smoothing), are available to the owner of an existing business with an established sales pattern for forecasting sales. These methods enable the small business owner to extrapolate past and present sales trends to arrive at a fairly accurate sales forecast.

The task of forecasting sales for a new firm is difficult but not impossible. For example, an entrepreneur might conduct research on similar firms and their sales patterns in the first year of operation to come up with a forecast. The local chamber of commerce and trade associations in the various industries also collect such information. Marketing research is another source of information that may be used to estimate annual sales for the fledgling firm. Other sources that may help predict sales include census reports, newspapers, radio and television customer profiles, polls and surveys, and local government statistics. Table 8.3 gives an example of how one entrepreneur used such marketing information to derive a sales forecast for his first year of operation.

No matter what techniques the small business manager employs, he must recognize even the best sales estimate will be wrong. Many financial analysts suggest that the owner create *three* estimates—an optimistic, a pessimistic, and a most likely sales estimate—and then make a separate cash budget for each forecast (a very simple task with a computer spreadsheet), as was done on Table 8.2. "You should have a 'pie-in-the-sky' plan, a realistic plan, and a worst-case plan," says one financial adviser.[14] This dynamic forecast enables the owner to determine the range within which his sales and cash flows will likely be as the year progresses.

Table 8.3 Forecasting Sales for a Business Start-Up

Robert Adler wants to open a repair shop for imported cars. The trade association for automotive garages estimates that the owner of an imported car spends an average of $485 per year on repairs and maintenance. The typical garage attracts its clientele from a trading zone (the area from which a business draws its customers) within a 20-mile radius. Census reports show that the families within a 20-mile radius of Robert's proposed location own 84,000 cars, of which 24 percent are imports. On the basis of a local market consultant's research, Robert believes he can capture 9.9 percent of the market this year. Robert's estimate of his company's first year's sales are as follows:

Number of cars in trading zone	84,000 autos
× Percent of imports	× 24%
= Number of imported cars in trading zone	20,160 imports
Number of imports in trading zone	20,160
× Average expenditure on repairs and maintenance	× $485
= Total import repair potential	$9,777,600
Total import repair sales potential	$9,777,600
× Estimated share of market	× 9.9%
= Sales estimate	$ 967,982

Now Robert Adler can convert this annual sales estimate of $967,982 into monthly sales estimates for use in his company's cash budget.

STEP 3: FORECAST CASH RECEIPTS

As noted earlier, sales constitute the major source of cash receipts. When a firm sells goods and services on credit, the cash budget must count for the delay between the sale and the actual collection of the proceeds. Remember: You cannot spend cash you haven't collected yet! For instance, proceeds for appliances sold in February might not be collected until March or April, and the cash budget must reflect this delay. To project accurately the firm's cash receipts, the owner must analyze the accounts receivable to determine the collection pattern. For example, past records may indicate that 20 percent of sales are for cash, 50 percent are paid in the month following the sale, 20 percent are paid two months after the sale, 5 percent after three months, and 5 percent are never collected. In addition to cash and credit sales, the small business may receive cash in a number of forms: interest income, rental income, dividends, and others.

Some small business owners never discover the hidden danger in accounts receivable until it is too late for their companies. Receivables act as cash sponges, tying up valuable dollars until the entrepreneur collects them. *For example, when Mary and Phil Baechler started Baby Jogger Company in 1983 to make strollers that would enable parents to take their babies along on their daily runs, Mary was in charge of the financial aspects of the business and watched its cash flow closely. As the company grew, the couple created an accounting department to handle its financial affairs. Unfortunately, the financial management system could not keep up with the company's rapid growth and failed to provide the necessary information to keep its finances under control. As inventory and accounts receivable ballooned, the company headed for a cash crisis. To ensure Baby Jogger's survival, the Baechlers were forced to reduce their workforce by half. Then they turned their attention to the accounts receivable and discovered that customers owed the business almost $700,000! In addition, most of the accounts were past due. Focusing on collecting the money owed their company, the Baechlers were able to steer clear of a cash crisis and get Baby Jogger back on track.[15]*

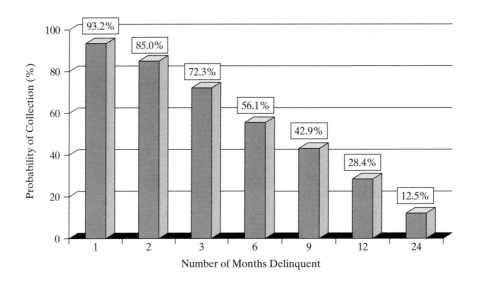

Figure 8.4 **Collecting Delinquent Accounts** SOURCE: Commercial Collection Agency Section of the Commercial Law League of America.

Figure 8.4 demonstrates how vital it is to act promptly once an account becomes past due. Notice how the probability of collecting an outstanding account diminishes the longer the account is delinquent. Table 8.4 illustrates the high cost of failing to collect accounts receivable on time.

Table 8.4 Managing Accounts Receivable

Are your customers who purchase on credit paying late? If so, these outstanding accounts receivable probably represent a significant leak in your company's profits. Regaining control of these late payers will likely improve your company's profits and cash flow.

Slow-paying customers, in effect, are borrowing money from your business interest-free! They are using your money without penalty while you forgo opportunities to place it in interest-bearing investments. Exactly how much are poor credit practices costing you? The answer may surprise you.

The first step is to compute the company's average collection period ratio (see chapter 7), which tells the number of days required to collect the typical account receivable. Then you compare this number with your company's credit terms. The following example shows how to calculate the cost of past-due receivables for a company whose credit terms are "net 30":

Average collection period	65 days
Less: credit terms	−30 days
Excess in accounts receivable	35 days
Average daily sales* of $21,500 × 35 days excess	$752,500
Normal rate of return on investment	10%
Annual cost of excess	$75,250

If your business is highly seasonal, quarterly or monthly figures may be more meaningful than annual ones.

* Average daily sales $= \dfrac{\text{Annual sales}}{365} = \dfrac{\$7,487,500}{365} = \$21,500$

STEP 4: FORECAST CASH DISBURSEMENTS

Most owners of established businesses have a clear picture of the firm's pattern of cash disbursements. In fact, many cash payments, such as rent, loan repayment, and interest, are fixed amounts due on specified dates. The key factor in forecasting disbursements for a cash budget is to record them *in the month in which they will be paid*, not when the obligation is incurred. Of course, the number of cash disbursements varies with each particular business, but the following disbursement categories are standard: purchases of inventory or raw materials; wages and salaries; rent, taxes, loans, and interest; selling expenses; overhead expenses; and miscellaneous expenses.

Usually, an owner's tendency is to underestimate cash disbursements, which can result in a cash crisis. To prevent underestimation, the wise entrepreneur cushions each cash disbursement account, assuming it will be higher than expected. A cushion is particularly important for entrepreneurs opening new businesses. In fact, some financial analysts recommend that a new owner estimate cash disbursements as best he can and then add on another 25 to 50 percent of the total. Whatever forecasting technique is used, the small business manager must avoid underestimating cash disbursements, which may lead to severe cash shortages and possibly bankruptcy.

Sometimes, business owners have difficulty developing initial forecasts of cash receipts and cash disbursements. One of the most effective techniques for overcoming the "I don't know where to begin" hurdle is to make a daily list of the items that generated cash (receipts) and those that consumed it (disbursements). *For example, Susan Bowen, CEO of Champion Awards, a $9 million T-shirt screen printer, monitors cash flow by tracking the cash that flows into and out of her company every day. Focusing on keeping the process simple, Bowen sets aside a few minutes each morning to track updates from the previous day on four key numbers:*

Accounts receivable: (1) *What was billed yesterday?* (2) *How much was actually collected?*

Accounts payable: (3) *What invoices were received yesterday?* (4) *How much in total was paid out?*

If Bowen observes the wrong trend—more new bills than new sales or more money going out than coming in—she makes immediate adjustments to protect her cash flow. The benefits produced (not the least of which is the peace of mind of knowing no cash crisis is looming) more than outweigh the 10 minutes she invests in the process every day. "I've tried to balance my books every single day since I started my company in 1970," says Bowen.[16]

STEP 5: DETERMINE THE END-OF-MONTH CASH BALANCE

To estimate the firm's cash balance for each month, the small business manager first must determine the cash balance at the beginning of each month. The beginning cash balance includes cash on hand as well as cash in checking and savings accounts. As development of the cash budget progresses, the cash balance at the end of a month becomes the beginning balance for the succeeding month. Next, the owner simply adds total cash receipts and subtracts total cash disbursements to obtain the end-of-month balance before any borrowing takes place. A positive amount indicates that the firm has a cash surplus for the month; a negative amount shows that a cash shortage will occur unless the manager is able to collect or borrow additional funds.

A firm's cash balance might fluctuate from month to month, reflecting seasonal sales patterns. Such fluctuations are normal, but the small business owner must watch closely any increases and decreases in the cash balance over time. A trend of increases indicates that the small firm has ample cash that could be placed in some income-earning investment. On the other hand, a pattern of cash decreases should alert the owner that the business is approaching a cash crisis.

A cash budget not only illustrates the flow of cash into and out of the small business, but it also allows the owner to anticipate cash shortages and cash surpluses. "Then," explains a small business consultant, "you can go to the bank and get a 'seasonal' line of credit for six months instead of twelve. Right there you can cut your borrowing costs in half."[17] By planning cash needs ahead of time, the small business is able to do the following:

- Take advantage of money-saving opportunities, such as economic order quantities and cash discounts.

- Make the most efficient use of cash.

- Finance seasonal business needs.

- Develop a sound borrowing program.

- Develop a workable program of debt repayment.

- Provide funds for expansion.

- Plan for the investment of surplus cash.

"Cash flow spells survival for every business," claims one expert. Manage cash flow effectively, and your business works. If your cash flow is not well managed, then sooner or later your business goes under. It's that simple."[18]

Unfortunately, most small business owners forego these rewards because they fail to manage their cash properly. One recent study reported that just 26 percent of all small businesses used formal techniques for tracking the level of their cash balances. Improper cash management often proves to be a costly—and fatal—mistake.

*7*he "Big Three" of Cash Management

4 Describe fundamental principles involved in managing the "Big Three" of cash management: accounts receivable, accounts payable, and inventory.

It is unrealistic for business owners to expect to trace the flow of every dollar through their businesses. However, by concentrating on the three primary causes of cash flow problems, they can dramatically lower the likelihood of experiencing a devastating cash crisis. The "Big Three" of cash management are accounts receivable, accounts payable, and inventory. A firm should always try to accelerate its receivables and to stretch out its payables. As one company's chief financial officer states, the idea is to "get the cash in the door as fast as you can, cut costs, and pay people as late as possible."[19] Business owners also must monitor inventory carefully to avoid tying up valuable cash in an excessive stock of inventory.

ACCOUNTS RECEIVABLE

Selling merchandise and services on credit is a necessary evil for most small businesses. Many customers expect to buy on credit, so business owners extend it to avoid losing customers to competitors. However, selling to customers on credit is more expensive than cash sales; it requires more paperwork, more staff, and more cash to service accounts receivable. Also, because extending credit is, in essence, lending money, the risk involved is higher. Every business owner who sells on credit will encounter customers who pay late or, worst of all, never pay at all.

Selling on credit is a common practice in business. One recent survey of small businesses in a variety of industries reported that 77 percent extend credit to their customers.[20] Because credit sales are so prevalent, an assertive collection program is essential to managing a company's cash flow. A credit policy that is too lenient can destroy a business's cash flow, attracting nothing but slow-paying and "deadbeat" customers. On the other hand, a carefully designed policy can be a powerful selling tool, attracting customers and boosting cash flow. "A sale is not a sale until you collect the money," warns the head of the National

IN THE FOOTSTEPS OF AN ENTREPRENEUR

Coping with the Ups and Downs of Business

$\mathcal{M}$anaging cash flow is no easy task in any small business, but the challenge becomes even greater when the business is highly seasonal. The dramatic swings in revenue make the peaks and the valleys of highly seasonal businesses all the more pronounced, often plunging these companies into a cash crisis. Consider the plights of the following entrepreneurs.

Wintertime Blues Joe Sergio, co-owner of Sergio's Pools and Spas in South Bend, Indiana, says, "Managing cash flow is my number one stress." To survive in business, Sergio and his partners knew that they had to find a way to increase sales during the winter months, when pool construction and maintenance in Indiana come to a screeching halt. Although the pool business boomed in the warmer months and produced a healthy cash flow, it simply wasn't enough to keep the business afloat throughout the long winters. In an attempt to come up with a solution to their vexing cash flow difficulties, Sergio and his two partners came up with the idea of starting First Response Construction, a business that repairs fire damage. "Pools are obviously seasonal," says Sergio, "and most of the fires happen in winter." Together, the two companies employ 50 workers year-round. A few employees specialize in pool construction and maintenance, others work to restore fire-damaged buildings, and most constitute a "swing force" that does both. "We've never had a layoff," says Sergio proudly.

Because both businesses are growing rapidly, he and his partners know that they must monitor their cash balance constantly. To make that task easier, Sergio generates weekly and monthly cash flow forecasts on a computer. "Growth means having to hire new employees, buy new trucks, and keep higher inventories," he explains. "You also end up with bigger receivables," all of which devour cash quickly. "Projecting cash flow is never easy," Sergio admits, but he and his partners know that if their businesses are to succeed, it is something they must do and do well.

Avoiding "Gorillas" For Chris Batalis, a significant part of cash management is maintaining a balance between the size of his workforce and the volume of work his advertising agency attracts from clients. Since starting his agency, Heptagon, in 1979, Batalis has seen revenues grow steadily at rates between 4 and 9 percent a year. However, he also knows that the advertising business is prone to large swings in revenues and, hence, cash flow. When managing Heptagon's cash, Batalis relies heavily on the experience he gained early in his career as a bank loan officer. "I've built a career and a business in marketing," he says, "but when it comes to cash, I still think like a loan officer."

Batalis has 17 employees, and payroll is, by far, his largest cash outflow. Rather than burden his full-time staff with excessive overtime during peak periods and then lay off workers during slack times, Batalis relies on part-time workers to handle overloads when they inevitably occur. "It works great," he says. "There are a lot of creative people out there who, for one reason or another, want a part-time schedule."

Batalis also is careful to keep his company's growth rate reined in to a steady rate because he knows the cash flow dangers of growing too fast. He saw uncontrolled growth destroy more than one business when he was a loan officer, and he's determined not to let it demolish Heptagon. To the amazement of some of his competitors, Batalis also has turned away business from major companies, those he calls "gorilla accounts." "A gorilla account is any account that's simply too big for your business," he explains. "I've seen too many companies hire staff and buy equipment to handle one big customer and then have the client leave. That's part of being a gorilla. You pretty much go when and where you please." Batalis defines a gorilla account as one that would make up at least 20 percent of the company's total revenues.

Batalis also sees that Heptagon collects its accounts receivable on time because he recognizes the danger in letting receivables spiral out of control. "Our philosophy of business is to deal only with people who pay their bills on time," says Batalis.

---

1. Contact the owner of a highly seasonal business in your community and interview him or her about the problems of managing cash flow. What similarities do you see to the stories told here? What strategies is the owner using to cope with the problems of uneven cash flow?

2. Work with a team of your classmates to brainstorm other strategies for helping the business owner cope with the seasonal swings in cash flow. Prepare a short report of your recommendations and present them to the business owner.

SOURCE: Adapted from Gloria Gibbs Marullo, "Case Studies in Cash Management," *Nation's Business*, September 1996, pp. 62–63. ◆

Association of Credit Management. "Receivables are the second most important item on the balance sheet. The first is cash. If you don't turn those receivables into cash, you're not going to be in business very long."[21]

When Thomas Re's company, Earthly Elements Inc., a maker of dried floral gifts and accessories, landed a $10,000 order from a home-shopping service, he threw a party for his

The highly seasonal nature of pool and spa sales created cash flow problems for Joe Sergio (center). To balance the lack of cash from Sergio's Pools and Spas during the winter months, Sergio created First Response Construction, a company that repairs fire-damaged buildings.

employees. The order represented 20 percent of the start-up company's sales for the year. Four months later, the bill was still outstanding, and Re was no longer celebrating. Without that cash, Earthly Elements could not pay its bills, and Re had to lay off some of his workers. Six months after the sale, he finally collected the $10,000, but by then, it was too late to revive the company. Re folded his business for lack of cash.[22]

How to Establish a Credit and Collection Policy. The first step in establishing a workable credit policy is to screen customers carefully *before* granting credit. Unfortunately, few small businesses conduct any kind of credit investigation before selling to a new customer. According to one survey, nearly 95 percent of small firms that sell on credit sell to *anyone* who wants to buy; most have no credit-checking procedure.[23] "One of the big problems we have had with . . . debt collection is that businesses open accounts without knowing whom they're dealing with," says an attorney specializing in debt collection. "It is a sad day when a business owner comes to me with a $10,000 bad debt claim and he doesn't have any information on the people he has been dealing with."[24]

The first line of defense against bad-debt losses is a detailed credit application. Before selling to any customer on credit, a business owner should have the customer fill out a customized application designed to provide the information needed to judge his creditworthiness. At a minimum, this credit profile should include the following information about customers:

◆   Name, address, Social Security number, and telephone number

◆   Form of ownership (proprietorship, S corporation, limited liability company, corporation, etc.) and number of years in business

◆   Credit references (e.g., other suppliers) including contact names, addresses, and telephone numbers

◆   Bank and credit card references

After collecting this information, the business owner should use it by checking the potential customer's credit references! The World Wide Web is an excellent place to start. On the Web, entrepreneurs can gain access to potential customers' credit information at many sites including the Securities and Exchange Commission's EDGAR database of corporate information <http://www.sec.gov/edgarhp.htm>, the NASDAQ stock market <http://www.nasdaq.com>, the New York Stock Exchange <http://www.nyse.com>, Dun and Bradstreet <http://www.dnb.com>, Equifax <http://www.equifax.com>, and Trans Union <http://www.tuc.com>.[25] The savings from lower bad-debt expenses can more than offset the cost of using a credit reporting service such as Trans Union or Dun & Bradstreet. The National Association of Credit Management (NACM) is another important source of credit information because it collects information on many small businesses that other reporting services ignore. The cost to check a potential customer's credit at reporting services such as these ranges from $10 to $35, a small price to pay when considering selling thousands of dollars worth of goods or services to a new customer. Unfortunately, few small businesses take the time to conduct a credit check; in one study, just one-third of the businesses protected themselves by checking potential customers' credit.[26] One retailer of large appliances advertised, "Good credit, bad credit, no credit at all! Come see us!" His sales volume was high, but his extremely low collection rate forced him out of business.

The next step involves establishing a firm written credit policy and letting every customer know in advance the company's credit terms. The credit agreement should specify each customer's credit limit (limits usually vary among customers, depending on their credit ratings) and any deposits required (often stated as a percentage of the purchase price). It should state clearly all the terms the business will enforce if the account goes bad, including interest, late charges, attorney's fees, and others. If these terms are not specified in the contract, they cannot be added later after problems arise. When will you invoice? How soon is payment due: immediately, 30 days, 60 days? Will you offer early-payment discounts? Will you add a late charge? If so, how much? The credit policies should be as tight as possible and within federal and state credit laws. According to the American Collectors Association, if a business is writing off more than 5 percent of sales as bad debts, the owner should tighten its credit and collection policy.[27]

The third step in an effective credit policy is to send invoices promptly because customers rarely pay *before* they receive their bills. "The cornerstone of collecting accounts receivable on time is making sure you invoice your customers or send them their periodic billing statements promptly. The sooner you mail your invoice, the sooner the check will be in the mail," says one writer. "In the manufacturing environment, get the invoice en route to the customer as soon as the shipment goes out the door," he advises. "Likewise, service industries with billable hours should keep track of hours daily or weekly and bill as often as the contract or agreement with the client permits."[28]

Small business owners can take several steps to encourage prompt payment of invoices:

◆ Ensure that all invoices are clear, accurate, and timely.

◆ State clearly a description of the goods or services purchased and an account number, if possible.

◆ Make sure that prices on invoices agree with the price quotations on purchase orders or contracts.

◆ Highlight the terms of sale (e.g., "net 30") on all invoices and reinforce them, if necessary.

◆ Include a telephone number and a contact person in your organization in case the customer has a question or a dispute.

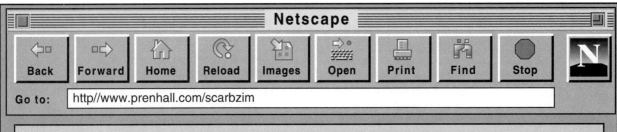

WIRED TO THE WEB

A BLESSING OR A CURSE?

*D*ona McKenzie, owner of a graphics design company, thought she had it made when she landed a contract with a major bank to design some marketing brochures. She saw the contract as a doorway to other lucrative jobs with the bank and to work with other large corporate clients. "Once you prove that you can do quality work for one big client, it makes it much easier to land other big clients," she says. She launched into the design job, determined to make it one of her best efforts.

Four months after completing the job to the bank's satisfaction, however, McKenzie was not as enthusiastic. The problem? The bank had just gotten around to paying the $11,302 it owed her for the work! "I had to incur all of the time and expense of designing the brochures, putting them together, and having them printed up front," she sighs. "That took a significant amount of cash, not to mention time I could have spent on other jobs. Now, I've fallen behind on payments to some of my suppliers and vendors. This was a huge job to my little company. I've had to lay off all four of my employees because I didn't have the cash to pay them. Because of this con-

tract, I now own a one-person business. This job turned out to be more of a curse than the blessing I first thought it would be."

The bank's slow payment devastated McKenzie's business, but what really annoyed her was the bank's attitude toward the past-due bill. After two months of "the check's in the mail" excuses, McKenzie complained to one of the bank's attorneys. "Their corporate lawyer said, 'You're little. We're big. You lose,'" she says. "What kind of attitude is that?" Enraged, McKenzie threatened to sue. Settlement talks dragged on for months before she finally got a check from the bank. "It took more energy to get the money than it did to do the work," says McKenzie glumly.

1. Use the resources of the World Wide Web to research ideas that will help small business owners such as Dona McKenzie collect their accounts payable promptly. (Hint: In addition to conducting your own searches, visit some of the sites listed on the Scarborough/Zimmerer Web site at <http://www.prenhall.com/scarbzim>.

2. What other cash management techniques would you suggest business owners use to avoid the problems that Dona McKenzie encountered?

SOURCE: Adapted from Joann S. Lublin, "Waiting for Payment Vexes Self-Employed," *Wall Street Journal,* September 3, 1997, pp. B1, B2.

Invoices that are well-organized, easy to read, and allow customers to identify what is being billed are much more likely to get paid than those that are not. The key to creating "user-friendly" invoices is to design them from the customer's perspective.

Bob Dempster, co-founder of American Imaging Inc., a distributor of x-ray tubes, once handled receivables the same way most entrepreneurs do: When customers ignored the "net 30" terms on invoices, he would call them around the forty-fifth day to ask what the problem was. Payments usually would trickle in within the next two weeks, but by then 60 days had elapsed, and American Imaging's cash flow was always strained. Then, Dempster decided to try a different approach. Today, he makes a "customer relations call" on the twentieth day of the billing period to determine if the customer is satisfied with the company's performance on the order. Before closing, he reminds the customer of the invoice due date and asks if there will be any problems meeting it. Dempster's proactive approach to collect-

ing receivables has cut his company's average collection period by at least 15 days, has improved cash flow, and has increased customer satisfaction![29]

When an account becomes overdue, small business owners must take immediate action. The longer an account is past due, the lower is the probability of collecting it. As soon as an account becomes overdue, many business owners send a "second notice" letter requesting immediate payment. If that fails to produce results, the next step is a telephone call. "When you get on the phone, ask for payment in full," advises one expert who claims that a personal phone call "is ten times more productive than a letter."[30] If the customer still refuses to pay the bill after 30 days, collection experts recommend the following:

- Send a letter from the company's attorney.
- Turn the account over to a collection agency.
- Hire a collection attorney.

Although collection agencies and attorneys will take a portion of any accounts they collect, they are often worth the price paid. According to the American Collectors Association, only 5 percent of accounts over 90 days delinquent will be paid voluntarily.[31]

Business owners must be sure to abide by the provisions of the federal Fair Debt Collection Practices Act, which prohibits any kind of harassment when collecting debts (e.g., telephoning repeatedly, issuing threats of violence, telling third parties about the debt, or using abusive language). The primary rule in dealing with past-due accounts is "Never lose your cool." Even if the debtor launches into an X-rated tirade when questioned about an overdue bill, the worst thing a collector can do is respond out of anger. One collection expert suggests allowing the debtor to vent his frustrations and then say "I understand how you feel. Let's talk about how we can solve the problem."[32]

Table 8.5 offers practical insights into building a successful collection system.

Other Techniques for Accelerating Accounts Receivable. Small business owners can rely on a variety of other techniques to speed cash inflow from accounts receivable:

- Speed up orders by having customers fax them to you.
- Send invoices when goods are shipped rather than a day or a week later; consider faxing invoices to reduce "in transit" time to a minimum.
- Indicate in conspicuous print the invoice due date and any late payment penalties. (Check with an attorney to be sure all finance charges comply with state laws.)
- Restrict the customer's credit until past-due bills are paid.
- Deposit customer checks and credit card receipts *daily*.
- Identify the top 20 percent of your customers (by sales volume), create a separate file system for them, and monitor them closely. Twenty percent of the typical company's customers generate 80 percent of all accounts receivable.
- Ask customers to pay a portion of the purchase price up front.
- Watch for signs that a customer may be about to declare bankruptcy. If that happens, creditors typically collect only a small fraction, if any, of the debt owed. If a customer does file for bankruptcy, the bankruptcy court notifies all creditors with a "Notice of Filing" document. Upon receipt of this notice, the wise creditor creates a file to track the events surrounding the bankruptcy and takes action immediately. To have a valid claim against the debtor's assets, a creditor must file a proof-of-claim form with the bankruptcy court within a specified time, often 90 days. (The actual time depends on which form of bankruptcy the debtor declares.) If, after paying the debtor's secured creditors,

Table 8.5 Designing a Collection System That *Really* Works

A collection system that meets the business owner's cash flow requirements and deals fairly with customers can make collecting accounts receivable on time much easier. The best approach is a proactive one that seeks to avoid past-due accounts. Review your collection system and consider these questions:

◆ Do you perform credit checks on new customers by contacting credit-rating services, analyzing their financial statements, or checking their credit references?

◆ Have you established a credit policy that spells out your company's expected payment terms and internal procedures for dealing with slow- or non-paying customers?

◆ Have you circulated that policy to all employees, especially salespeople?

◆ Do you routinely send a copy of your credit policy to new cusotmers? Do you ask them to sign and return a copy of the policy?

◆ Have you segmented your customer base into high- and low-risk customers? Do employees know which customers fall into which categories?

◆ Does your policy include a mechanism for handling high- and low-risk customers differently?

◆ Do you and other managers in the company receive a weekly accounts receivable update that shows an aging of the company's accounts receivable?

◆ Do your sales and financial management staffs work together to collect past-due payments from customers?

◆ Do sales representatives earn commissions on sales whether or not the company actually receives payment?

◆ Does your credit policy establish clear trigger points that tell you when to turn an account over to a collection agency or attorney and when to stop doing business with delinquent customers?

Even the best collection system produces some past-due accounts. One collection expert describes four stages in the past-due debt collection process: the notification or polite reminder, the discussion, the "push" or firm demand, and the bitter end.

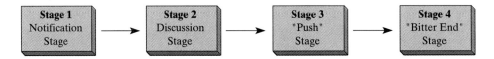

In the *notification or polite reminder stage*, the best approach is an upbeat, positive one. It should begin immediately after an invoice is past due. "Our records show that this bill is still unpaid. Can you check on it?"

During the *discussion stage*, the goal is to motivate the customer to pay the past-due account. Generally, it is not productive to explore the reasons behind the late payment; instead, the focus should be on the business at hand: getting the customer to make a firm commitment to pay by a specific deadline.

If the debt reaches the *push stage*, a business must take a stronger approach to collecting the outstanding debt. Experts recommend limiting this stage to no more than 10 days.

Once a debt reaches *the bitter end stage*, the company usually has few options but to turn the account over to a collection agency or attorney or to file suit in small claims court. By this stage, the relationship with the customer has soured, and the company is no longer willing to do business with that customer.

One expert recommends persistence when dealing with past-due accounts. "Remember," she says, "it's your money, and you don't make money until you're paid."

Sources: Adapted from Jill Adresky Fraser, "Get Paid Promptly," *Inc.*, November 1996, p. 87; Jacquelyn Lynn, "You Owe It to Yourself," *Business Start-Ups*, October 1996, pp. 54–60.

any assets remain, the court will distribute the proceeds to unsecured creditors who have legitimate proof-of-claim.

◆ Consider using a bank's lockbox collection service (located near customers) to reduce mail time on collections. In a **lockbox arrangement,** customers send payments to a post office box the bank maintains. The bank collects the payments several times each day and deposits them immediately into the company account. The procedure sharply reduces processing and clearing times from the usual two to three days to just hours, especially if the lockboxes are close to the firm's biggest customers' business addresses. The system can be expensive to operate (typically $55 to $100 per month plus a 30 to 40 cents charge for each check) and is most economical for companies with a high volume of large checks (at least 200 checks each month).

Combining a lockbox with other cash management services from banks—such as zero balance accounts (ZBAs) and sweep accounts—can dramatically improve a small firm's ability to get the most out of its available cash. A **zero balance account** is a checking account that technically never has funds in it but is tied to a master account such as payroll. The company keeps the funds in the master account (where they earn interest), but it writes checks on the ZBA. At the end of each day, checks drawn on the ZBA are funded; then, all activity is posted against the master account. The ZBA allows the company to keep more cash working during the float period, the time between a check's being issued and its being cashed. By combining the zero balance account with a **sweep account,** which automatically "sweeps" all funds above a predetermined minimum into an interest-bearing account, the company keeps otherwise idle cash invested until it is needed to cover checks.

ACCOUNTS PAYABLE

The second element of the Big Three of cash management is accounts payable. The timing of payables is just as crucial to proper cash management as the timing of receivables, but the objective is exactly the opposite. An entrepreneur should strive to stretch out payables as long as possible *without damaging the company's credit rating.* If the entrepreneur waits too long to pay, suppliers may begin demanding prepayment or C.O.D. terms, which severely impair the company's cash flow. One cash management consultant claims, "Some companies pay too early and wind up forgoing the interest they could have earned on their cash. Others pay too late and either wind up with late penalties or being forced to buy on a C.O.D. basis."[33] It is entirely reasonable for small business owners to regulate payments to their company's advantage. Efficient cash managers set up a payment calendar each month that allows them to pay their bills on time and to take advantage of cash discounts for early payment.

Nancy Dunis, CEO of Dunis & Associates, a Portland, Oregon, marketing firm, recognizes the importance of controlling accounts payable. "Our payables must be functioning just right to keep our cash flow running smoothly," says Dunis. She has set up a simple five-point accounts payable system:[34]

1. Set scheduling goals. *Dunis strives to pay her company's bills 45 days after receiving them and to collect all her receivables within 30 days. Even though "it doesn't always work that way," her goal is to make the most of her cash flow.*

2. Keep paperwork organized. *Dunis dates every invoice she receives and carefully files it according to her payment plan. "This helps us remember when to cut the check," she says, and, "it helps us stagger our payments over days or weeks," significantly improving the company's cash flow.*

3. Prioritize. *Dunis cannot stretch out all of her company's creditors for 45 days; some demand payment sooner. Those suppliers are at the top of the accounts payable list.*

4. Be consistent. *"Companies want consistent customers," says Dunis. "With a few exceptions," she explains, "most businesses will be happy to accept 45-day payments, so long as they know you'll always pay your full obligation at that point."*

5. Look for warning signs. *Dunis sees her accounts payable as an early warning system for cash flow problems. "The first indication I get that cash flow is in trouble is when I see I'm getting low on cash and could have trouble paying my bills according to my staggered filing system," she says.*

Business owners should verify all invoices before paying them. Some unscrupulous vendors will send out invoices for goods they never shipped, knowing that many business owners will simply pay the bill without checking its authenticity.[35] Someone in the company—for instance, the accounts payable clerk—should have the responsibility of verifying *every* invoice received.

In general, it is a good idea for owners to take advantage of cash discounts that vendors offer. A cash discount (e.g., "2/10, net 30": take a 2 percent discount if you pay the invoice within 10 days; otherwise, total payment is due in 30 days) offers a price reduction if the owner pays an invoice early. A clever cash manager also will negotiate the best possible credit terms with his suppliers. Almost all vendors grant their customers trade credit, and the small business owner should take advantage of it. However, because trade credit is so easy to get, the owner must be careful not to abuse it, putting the business in a precarious financial position.

Favorable credit terms can make a tremendous difference in a firm's cash flow. Table 8.6 shows the same most likely cash budget as that shown in Table 8.2, with one exception: Instead of purchasing on C.O.D. terms (Table 8.2), the owner has negotiated "net 30" payment terms (Table 8.6). Notice the drastic improvement in the company's cash flow resulting from improved credit terms.

Owners who do find themselves financially strapped when payment to a vendor is due should avoid making empty promises that "the check is in the mail." Instead, they should discuss openly the situation with the vendor. Most suppliers will work out payment terms for extended credit. One small business owner who was experiencing a cash crisis claims:

> *One day things got so bad I just called up a supplier and said, "I need your stuff, but I'm going through a tough period and simply can't pay you right now." They said they wanted to keep me as a customer, and they asked if it was okay to bill me in three months. I was dumbfounded: They didn't even charge me interest.*[36]

SOURCE: © Cathy Guisewite. September 13, 1997.

SMALL BUSINESS ACROSS THE GLOBE

Collecting International Accounts

$\mathscr{S}$elling globally is an excellent strategy for boosting sales and profits, but only if you get paid for what you sell! Collecting accounts receivable from U.S. companies takes an average of 42 days; collecting from foreign customers usually takes a good deal longer. For example, the countries with the worst payment records are Iran (310 days), Syria (175 days), Chile (109 days), and Ecuador (107 days).

The head of one European debt-collection operation says, "On average, all payments [in Europe] are made 15 days late for domestic trade and 16 days late for exports." A recent study of European companies reported that these late payments result in higher interest costs for 80 percent of the businesses. In addition, 60 percent reported liquidity problems.

Uniform laws giving businesses the right to pursue late payers and to add interest charges to their accounts do not exist across Europe. "U.S. companies make a big mistake when they assume that they can deal with problem foreign accounts the same way they do [in the United States]," says the head of an international collection agency. In countries like Mexico, for example, the legal process involved in chasing after a problem payer is very, very complicated." As a result, some companies have developed some rather unusual strategies for encouraging their customers to pay their bills on time. One Spanish company has its staff members dress up in Pink Panther outfits and follow debtors and their employees around 24 hours a day until they pay up! Another innovative company uses a similar tactic—with bright yellow scuba-diving suits.

Before they send thousands of dollars of merchandise halfway around the world, U.S. entrepreneurs must take some basic precautions to make sure their foreign customers will pay their bills. The following techniques have worked for many small businesses:

Require cash in advance. To eliminate the risk of not getting paid, Jean-Luc Berne, president of Plein Air Inc., an exporter of automotive parts, required his foreign customers to pay cash in advance. Such terms can make it hard to sell in the global market, however. "Not every buyer is ready to pay in advance," says Berne.

Purchase export credit insurance. After his company's sales began to slip, Berne changed tactics. Now, he buys credit insurance from Eximbank, a government agency

that provides export assistance, to protect his receivables. "Having the insurance allows us to extend our terms of credit up to 90 days," says Berne.

Secure a letter of credit. For some small companies, the cost of export credit insurance is prohibitive. Perhaps the easiest and safest way to guarantee payment from a foreign customer is to secure a letter of credit from its bank. If the customer defaults, then the bank issuing the letter of credit must make the payment. Because letters of credit have expiration dates, business owners must process their paperwork promptly.

Research a company's payment norms and creditor protection laws before shipping goods. The International Trade Association <http://www.ita.doc.gov> and the Export-Import Bank <http://www.exim.gov> are excellent sources of this information. It is also a good idea to keep abreast of the political and economic conditions in countries where major customers are located. The U.S. Department of Commerce offers a variety of publications and several "country desks" that track such information.

Conduct thorough credit checks on all prospective foreign customers. Many of the credit-checking services mentioned in this chapter also offer international evaluations. Some services specialize in international credit reports, which range in price from $47 to $275, depending on the level of detail:

Justitia International Inc.: (860) 589-1698
Owens OnLine: (800) 745-4656
Piquet International: (302) 778-0457
Graydon America: (212) 633-1434 or (212) 620-9797
Veritas: (800) 929-8374 or (203) 328-7918

In addition, for $100, the International Trade Administration at the U.S. Department of Commerce will prepare World Traders Data Reports that provide information on the reliability and the financial status of overseas companies.

Bill only in U.S. dollars and insist on payment in U.S. dollars. This practice will shield against losses due to fluctuations in currency exchange rates. "A lot of exporters are shocked to learn that they could lose 25 percent of the value of their receivables overnight" to currency fluctuations, says one expert.

SOURCES: Adapted from "Risky Business," *Small Business Reports,* January 1994, p. 7; "Risky Business," *Small Business Reports,* November 1992, p. 8; Heidi Jacobs, "Payments from Afar," *Small Business Reports,* May 1993, pp. 21–25; Nigel Dudley, "Creative Debt Collecting," *Profiles,* August 1994, p. 19; <http://www.ita.doc.gov/how_to_export/finance.html>; Vivian Pospisil, "Cross-Border Collections," *Industry Week,* January 20, 1997, p. 6; Jill Andresky Fraser, "Around the World in 180 Days," *Inc.,* April 1997, pp. 107–108.

Table 8.6 Cash Budget,* Most Likely Sales Forecast

	JAN.	FEB.	MAR.	APR.
Cash Receipts:				
Sales	$150,000	$200,000	$200,000	$300,000
Credit Sales	112,500	150,000	150,000	225,000
Collections:				
60%—lst month after sale	$180,000	$ 67,500	$ 90,000	$ 90,000
30%—2nd month after sale	78,750	90,000	33,750	45,000
5%—3rd month after sale	11,250	13,125	15,000	5,625
Cash Sales	37,500	50,000	50,000	75,000
Interest	0	200	0	0
Total Cash Receipts	$307,500	$220,825	$188,750	$215,625
Cash Disbursements:				
*Purchases	$105,000	$140,000	$140,000	$210,000
Rent	2,000	2,000	2,000	2,000
Utilities	850	850	850	850
Interest	0	0	7,500	0
Tax Prepayment	0	0	50,000	0
Capital Addition	0	130,000	0	0
Miscellaneous	70	70	70	70
Wages/Salaries	30,000	40,000	45,000	50,000
*Total Cash Disbursements	$137,920	$312,920	$245,420	$262,920
End-of-Month Balance:				
*Cash (Beginning of Month)	$ 12,000	$181,580	$ 89,485	$ 32,815
+ Cash Receipts	307,500	220,825	188,750	215,625
*− Cash Disbursements	137,920	312,920	245,420	262,920
*Cash (end of month)	181,580	89,485	32,815	(14,480)
*Borrowing	0	0	0	24,480
*Cash (end of month [after borrowing])	$181,580	$ 89,485	$ 32,815	$ 10,000

*After negotiating "net 30" trade credit terms.

Small business owners also can improve their firms' cash flow by scheduling controllable cash disbursements so that they do not come due at the same time. For example, paying employees every two weeks (or every month) rather than every week reduces administrative costs and gives the business more time to use its cash. Owners of fledgling businesses may be able to conserve cash by hiring part-time employees or by using freelance workers rather than full-time, permanent workers. Scheduling insurance premiums monthly or quarterly rather than annually also improves cash flow.

Wise use of business credit cards is another way to stretch the firm's cash balance. However, owners should avoid cards that charge transaction fees. Credit cards differ in their interest-charging policies; many begin charging interest from the date of purchase, but some charge interest only from the invoice date.

INVENTORY

Inventory is a significant investment for many small businesses and can create a severe strain on cash flow. Although inventory represents the largest capital investment for most businesses, few owners use any formal methods for managing it. As a result, the typical small business not only has too much inventory but also has too much of the wrong kind of inventory! Because inventory is illiquid, it can quickly siphon off a company's pool of available cash. "Small companies need cash to grow," says one consultant. "They've got to be able to turn [cash] over quickly. That's difficult to do if a lot of money is tied up in excess inventory."[37]

Surplus inventory yields a zero rate of return and unnecessarily ties up the firm's cash. "Carrying inventory is expensive," says one small business consultant. "A typical manufacturing company pays 25 percent to 30 percent of the value of the inventory for the cost of borrowed money, warehouse space, materials handling, staff, lift-truck expenses, and fixed costs. This shocks a lot of people. Once they realize it, they look at inventory differently."[38] Marking down items that don't sell will keep inventory lean and allow it to turn over frequently. Even though volume discounts lower inventory costs, large purchases may tie up the company's valuable cash. In fact, only 20 percent of a typical business's inventory turns over quickly, so the owner must watch constantly for stale items.[39]

Carrying too much inventory increases the chances that a business will run out of cash. *For example, when Tom Meredith joined Dell Computer Corporation as its chief financial officer, he quickly discovered that excessive inventory was a major source of the cash crisis the company was experiencing then. Because the company was focusing on growth, it held large inventories of costly computer components to make sure it could meet every sales opportunity. Meredith's top priority in his first few months at Dell was to cut inventory levels. "Low inventory equals high profit; high inventory equals low profit," he declares. Because the inventory that Dell carries becomes technologically obsolete rapidly (in as little as four months), high inventory levels increase the likelihood of wasted cash. Plus, the activities required to purchase, store, and control inventory are themselves costly.*[40] "The cash that pays for goods is channeled into inventory," says one business writer, "where its flow is deadended until the inventory is sold and the cash is set free again. The cash flow trick is to commit just enough cash to inventory to meet demand."[41] Scheduling inventory deliveries at the latest possible date will prevent premature payment of invoices. Finally, given goods of comparable quality and price, an entrepreneur should purchase goods from the fastest supplier to keep inventory levels low.

*A*voiding the Cash Crunch

💲 Explain the techniques for avoiding a cash crunch in a small company.

Nearly every small business has the potential to improve its cash position with little or no investment. The key is to make an objective evaluation of the company's financial policies, searching for inefficiency in its cash flow. Young firms cannot afford to waste resources, especially one as vital as cash. By utilizing these tools, the small business manager can get maximum benefit from the company's pool of cash.

BARTERING

Bartering, the exchange of goods and services for other goods and services, is an effective way to conserve cash. An ancient concept, bartering began to regain popularity during recent recessions. Over the last decade, nearly 700 barter exchanges have cropped up, catering primarily to small and medium-sized businesses. More than 400,000 companies—most of them small—engage in more than $9.1 billion worth of barter each year (see Figure 8.5).[42] Every

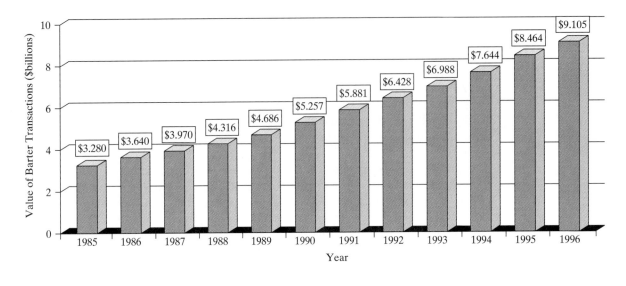

Figure 8.5 Dollar Value of Bartering in North America, 1985 to 1996 SOURCE: International Reciprocal Trade Association.

day, entrepreneurs across the nation use bartering to buy materials, equipment, and supplies *without using cash.* "Bartering is a great way to get the things your business needs without spending cash on them," says Sheri Smith, owner of Gourmet Catering, Inc. The president of one barter exchange estimates that business owners can save "between $5,000 and $150,000 in yearly business costs."[43] In addition to conserving cash, companies using bartering can transform slow-moving inventory into much-needed goods and services. Often, business owners who join barter exchanges find new customers for the products and services they sell.

Of course, there is a cost associated with bartering, but the real benefit is that entrepreneurs "pay" for products and services at their wholesale cost of doing business and get credit in the barter exchange for the retail price. In a typical arrangement, businesses accumulate trade credits when they offer goods or services through the exchange. Then, they can use their trade credits to purchase other goods and services from other members of the exchange. The typical exchange charges a $500 membership fee and a 10 percent transaction fee (5 percent from the buyer and 5 percent from the seller) on every deal. The exchange tracks the balance in each member's account and typically sends a monthly statement summarizing account activity.

Rather than join a barter exchange, many enterprising entrepreneurs choose to barter on an individual basis. The place to start is with the people the company normally does business with. *Sheri Smith, owner of Gourmet Catering, has relied on bartering since the start-up phase of her business. She traded for everything from T-shirts (her employees' uniforms) to paper goods and printing. Contacting her suppliers on an individual basis, Smith was tightfisted in her approach. "Basically, I just said, 'This is what I do. Can we trade?'" she recalls. Today, Smith trades $10,000 to $15,000 worth of goods and services a year.*[44]

TRIMMING OVERHEAD COSTS

High overhead expenses can strain a small firm's cash supply to the breaking point. Frugal small business owners can trim their overhead in a number of ways.

When Practical, Lease Instead of Buy. By leasing automobiles, computers, office equipment, machinery, and other assets rather than buying them, an entrepreneur can conserve valuable cash. The value of such assets is not in owning them but in using them. Leasing is "a better use of cash flow versus putting out the full purchase price," says one business owner. "Lessees can use that money to invest in their businesses without investing valuable capital in an asset that's depreciating and is not going to make any money for them."[45] Approximately 80 percent of U.S. companies use leasing as a cash management strategy.[46] *PWS Foods, Inc., a 75-employee supplier of ice cream and frozen desserts for restaurants, recently gave up the battle to keep its fleet of trucks updated and in good repair and began leasing trucks. "We were able to get a whole new fleet," says Arnold O. Felner, a top manager at PWS. Keeping a modern fleet of trucks in good condition is crucial to the company's ability to deliver frozen desserts in the warm climate of Texas. "There's no way that a company our size could invest in vehicles and have enough capital [left] to run a business," says Felner.[47]*

Although total lease payments typically are greater than those for a conventional loan, most leases offer 100 percent financing, which means the owner avoids the large capital outlays required as down payments on most loans. Also, leasing is an "off-the-balance-sheet" method of financing; the lease is considered an operating expense on the income statement, not a liability on the balance sheet. Thus, leasing conserves a company's borrowing capacity. Leasing companies typically allow businesses to stretch payments over a longer period than is allowed in a conventional loan. Lease agreements also are flexible. "There are so many ways to tailor a lease agreement to a company's individual equipment and financial needs that you might call it a personalized rental agreement," says the owner of a small construction firm.[48] Leasing gives entrepreneurs access to equipment even when they can't borrow the money to buy it. *After his bank rejected his loan request for a $4,000 machine to straighten car frames, Roger Wolfanger decided to lease the equipment. He filled out a simple one-page application, and within two days the machine was in place.[49]*

Avoid Nonessential Outlays. By forgoing costly indulgences such as ostentatious office equipment, first-class travel, and flashy company cars, business owners can make efficient use of the company's cash. Before putting scarce cash into an asset, every business owner should put the decision to the acid test: What will this purchase add to the company's ability to compete and to become more successful? Making across-the-board spending cuts to conserve cash is dangerous, however, because the owner runs the risk of cutting expenditures that literally drive the business. One common mistake during business slowdowns is cutting marketing and advertising expenditures. "As competitors pull back," says one adviser, "smart marketers will keep their ad budgets on an even keel, which is sufficient to bring increased attention to their products."[50] The secret to success is cutting *nonessential* expenditures. "If the lifeblood of your company is marketing, cut it less," advises one advertising executive. "If it is customer service, that is the last thing you want to cut back on. Cut from areas that are not essential to business growth."[51]

Negotiate Fixed Loan Payments to Coincide with Your Company's Cash Flow Cycle. Many banks allow businesses to structure loans so that they can skip specific payments when their cash flow ebbs to its lowest point. Negotiating such terms gives businesses the opportunity to customize their loan repayments to their cash flow cycles. *For example, Ted Zoli, president of Torrington Industries, a construction-materials supplier and contracting business, consistently uses "skipped-payment loans" in his highly seasonal business. "Every time we buy a piece of construction machinery," he says, "we set it up so that we're making payments for eight or nine months, and then skipping three or four months during the winter."[52]*

Buy Used or Reconditioned Equipment, Especially If It Is "Behind-the-Scenes" Machinery. One restaurateur saved significant amounts of cash in the start-up phase of his business by purchasing used equipment from a restaurant equipment broker.

Hire Part-Time Employees and Freelance Specialists Whenever Possible. Hiring part-timers and freelancers rather than full-time workers saves on the cost of both salaries and benefits. *Robert Ross, president of Xante Corporation, a maker of laser printer products, hires local college students for telemarketing and customer support positions. "They are smart, and it keeps hiring, overhead, and insurance costs down," he says.*[53]

Control Employee Advances and Loans. A manager should grant only those advances and loans that are necessary and should keep accurate records on payments and balances.

Establish an Internal Security and Control System. Too many owners encourage employee theft by failing to establish a system of controls. Reconciling the bank statement monthly and requiring special approval for checks over a specific amount, say $1,000, will help minimize losses. Separating recordkeeping and check-writing responsibilities, rather than assigning them to a single employee also offers protection.

Develop a System to Battle Check Fraud. Merchants take in more than $13 billion in bad checks each year, and a study by *American Banker* estimates that losses from check fraud will grow by 25 percent annually in the coming years.[54] About 70 percent of all "bounced" checks occur because nine out of ten customers fail to keep their checkbooks balanced; the remaining 30 percent of bad checks are the result of fraud.[55] The most effective way to battle bad checks is to subscribe to an electronic check-approval service. The service works at the cash register, and approval takes about a minute. The fee a small business pays to use the service depends on the volume of checks. For most small companies, charges range from a base of $25 to $100 plus a percentage of the cleared checks' value.

Change Your Shipping Terms. Changing the firm's shipping terms from "F.O.B (free on board) buyer," in which the seller pays the cost of freight, to "F.O.B seller," in which the *buyer* absorbs all shipping costs, will improve cash flow.

Switch to Zero-Based Budgeting. **Zero-based budgeting (ZBB)** primarily is a shift in the philosophy of budgeting. Rather than build the current year budget on increases from the previous year's budget, ZBB starts from a budget of zero and evaluates the necessity of every item. "Start with zero and review all expenses, asking yourself whether each one is necessary," says one business consultant.[56]

Keep Your Business Plan Current. Before approaching any potential lender or investor, a business owner must prepare a solid business plan. Smart owners keep their plans up to date in case an unexpected cash crisis forces them to seek emergency financing. Revising the plan annually also forces the owner to focus on managing the business more effectively.

INVESTING SURPLUS CASH

Because of the uneven flow of receipts and disbursements, a company will often temporarily have more cash than it needs—for a week, a month, a quarter, or longer. When this happens, most small business owners simply ignore the surplus because they are not sure how soon they will need it. They believe that relatively small amounts of cash sitting around for just a few days or weeks are not worth investing. But entrepreneurs who put surplus cash to work *immediately* rather than allowing it to sit idle soon discover that the yield adds up to a significant amount over time. This money can help ease the daily cash crunch during business troughs. "Your goal should be to identify every dollar you don't need to pay today's bills and to keep that money invested to improve your cash flow," explains a consultant.[57] However, when investing surplus cash, the owner's primary objective should *not* be to earn the maximum yield (which usually carries with it maximum risk); instead, the focus should be on the safety and the liquidity of the investments. The need to minimize risk and to have ready access to the cash restricts the small business owner's investment options to just a few.

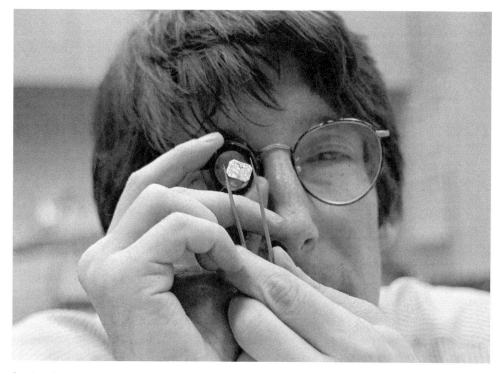

Stanley Grossbard, president of RCDC Corporation, a New York City diamond-cutting and wholesale business, relies on an asset-management account at a brokerage firm to manage his company's cash.

Asset-management accounts, which integrate checking, borrowing, and investing services under one umbrella and were once available only to large businesses, now help small companies conserve cash. *Stanley Grossbard, president of RCDC Corporation, a diamond-cutting and wholesale business in New York City, estimates that opening an asset-management account through a brokerage firm has earned his company several thousand dollars in interest and has saved $7,000 in interest paid. RCDC, with annual sales of $10 million, has a $1 million line of credit, which means the company borrows only what it needs exactly when it needs it, eliminating unnecessary interest expense. The account automatically moves the company's cash where it will earn—or save—the most money by either sweeping excess cash into interest-bearing accounts or applying it to the company's outstanding loan balance.*[58]

$\mathcal{C}$onclusion

Successful owners run their businesses "lean and mean." Trimming wasteful expenditures, investing surplus funds, and carefully planning and managing the company's cash flow enables them to compete effectively in a hostile market. The simple but effective techniques covered in this chapter can improve every small company's cash position. One business writer says, "In the day-to-day course of running a company, other people's capital flows past an imaginative CEO as opportunity. By looking forward and keeping an analytical eye on your cash account as events unfold (remembering that if there's no real cash there when you need it, you're history), you can generate leverage as surely as if that capital were yours to keep."[59]

Chapter Summary

1. Explain the importance of cash management to the success of the small business.

- Cash is the most important but least productive asset the small business has. The manager must maintain enough cash to meet the firm's normal requirements (plus a reserve for emergencies) without retaining excessively large, unproductive cash balances.
- Without adequate cash, a small business will fail.

2. Differentiate between cash and profits.

- Cash and profits are *not* the same. More businesses fail for lack of cash than for lack of profits.
- Profits, the difference between total revenue and total expenses, are an accounting concept. Cash flow represents the flow of actual cash (the only thing businesses can use to pay bills) through a business in a continuous cycle. A business can be earning a profit and be forced out of business because it runs out of cash.

3. Understand the five steps in creating a cash budget and use them to create a cash budget.

- The cash budgeting procedure tracks the flow of cash through the business and enables the owner to project cash surpluses and cash deficits at specific intervals.
- The five steps in creating a cash budget are determining an adequate minimum cash balance, forecasting sales, forecasting cash receipts, forecasting cash disbursements, and determining the end-of-month cash balance.

4. Describe fundamental principles involved in managing the "Big Three" of cash management: accounts receivable, accounts payable, and inventory.

- Controlling accounts receivable requires business owners to establish clear, firm credit and collection policies and to screen customers *before* granting them credit. Sending invoices promptly and acting on past-due accounts quickly also improve cash flow. The goal is to collect cash from receivables as quickly as possible.
- When managing accounts payable, a manager's goal is to stretch out payables as long as possible without damaging the company's credit rating. Other techniques include verifying invoices before paying them, taking advantage of cash discounts, and negotiating the best possible credit terms.
- Excess inventory earns a zero rate of return and ties up a company's cash unnecessarily. Owners must watch for stale merchandise.

5. Explain the techniques for avoiding a cash crunch in a small company.

- Trimming overhead costs by bartering, leasing assets, avoiding nonessential outlays, using zero-based budgeting, and implementing an internal control system boost a firm's cash flow position.
- Investing surplus cash maximizes the firm's earning power. The primary criteria for investing surplus cash are security and liquidity.

Discussion Questions

1. Why must small business owners concentrate on effective cash flow management?
2. Explain the difference between cash and profit.
3. Outline the steps involved in developing a cash budget.
4. How can an entrepreneur launching a new business forecast sales?
5. Outline the basic principles of managing a small firm's receivables, payables, and inventory.
6. How can bartering improve a company's cash position?
7. What steps should business owners take to conserve cash in their companies?
8. What should be a small business owner's primary concerns when investing surplus cash?

Step into the Real World

1. Ask several local small business owners about their cash management policies. Do they know how much cash their businesses have during the month? How do they track their cash flows? Do they use some type of cash budget? If not, ask if you can help the owner develop one. Does the owner invest surplus cash?
2. Volunteer to help a small business owner develop a cash budget for his or her company. What patterns do you detect? What recommendations can you make for improving the company's cash management system?
4. Use the resources available in your local library and on the World Wide Web to prepare a brief report on bartering. What benefits does barter offer business owners? How does the typical barter exchange operate? What fees are involved? How are barter transactions taxed? A useful source of information is the International Reciprocal Trade Association's Web site at <http://www.irta.com>.
5. Interview several local business owners about their policies on accepting payments by check. How much do they typically lose each year to bad checks? What safe-

guards do they use to combat check fraud? Contact the American Collectors Association at P.O. Box 39106, Minneapolis, MN. 55439-0106 or access the ACA's Web site at <http://www.collector.com/>. How prevalent is check fraud? What can business owners do to prevent it? Using these resources and those in your local library, develop a set of recommendations for the owners you interviewed to reduce their losses to check fraud.

Take It to the Net

Visit the Scarborough/Zimmerer home page at
www.prenhall.com/scarbzim
for updated information, on-line resources, and Web-based exercises.

Endnotes

1. John Mariotti, "Cash Is Like Oxygen," *Industry Week*, April 21, 1997, p. 42.
2. Carla Goodman, "Fueling Up," *Business Start-Ups*, December 1996, pp. 46–48.
3. Robert A. Mamis, "Second-Time Smart," *Inc. 500 1995*, pp. 47–48.
4. Daniel Kehrer, "Big Ideas for Your Small Business," *Changing Times*, November 1989, p. 58.
5. William Bak, "I Owe, I Owe," *Entrepreneur*, October 1993, p. 56.
6. Jeannie Mandelker, "Put Numbers on Your Side," *Your Company*, Winter 1994, p. 33.
7. Mariotti, "Cash Is Like Oxygen," p. 42.
8. Jill Andresky Fraser, "How Often Do You Monitor Key Financial Indicators?" *Inc.*, August 1997, p. 92.
9. Robert A. Mamis, "Money In, Money Out," *Inc.*, March 1993, p. 98.
10. Mo Schumpeter, "Step 4: Fast Cash," *Forbes ASAP*, October 7, 1996, p. 22.
11. Mamis, "Money In, Money Out."
12. Douglas Bartholomew, "4 Common Financial Management Mistakes . . . And How to Avoid Them," *Your Company*, Fall 1991, p. 9.
13. Karen M. Kroll, "Ca$h Wears the Crown," *Industry Week*, May 6, 1996, pp. 16–18.
14. Jan Norman, "How to Manage Your Cash Flow," *Business Start-Ups*, June 1998, pp. 42–45.
15. Kroll, "4 Common Financial Management Mistakes . . . And How to Avoid Them," p. 9.
16. Jill Andresky Fraser, "Monitoring Daily Cash Trends," *Inc.*, October 1992, p. 49.
17. William G. Shepherd Jr., "Internal Financial Strategies," *Venture*, September 1985, p. 66.
18. David H. Bangs, *Financial Troubleshooting: An Action Plan for Money Management in the Small Business* (Dover, NH: Upstart Publishing Company, 1992), p. 61.
19. George Anders, "Truckers Trials: How One Firm Fights to Save Every Penny As Its Profits Plummet," *Wall Street Journal*, April 13, 1982, pp. 1, 22.
20. William Bak, "Make 'Em Pay," *Entrepreneur*, November 1992, p. 64.
21. Michael Selz, "Big Customers' Late Bills Choke Small Suppliers," *Wall Street Journal*, June 22, 1994, p. Bl.
22. Ibid.
23. Richard G. P. McMahon and Scott Holmes, "Small Business Financial Management Practices in North America: A Literature Review," *Journal of Small Business Management*, April 1991, p. 21.
24. Roger Thompson, "Business Copes with the Recession," *Nation's Business*, January 1991, p. 21.
25. Dave Miller, "Netting Crucial Credit Records," *GSA Business*, May 25, 1998, p. 9A.
26. "The Check Isn't in the Mail," *Small Business Reports*, October 1991, p. 6.
27. Howard Muson, "Collecting Overdue Accounts," *Your Company*, Spring 1993, p. 4.
28. Richard J. Maturi, "Collection Dues and Don'ts," *Entrepreneur*, January 1992, p. 326.
29. Frances Huffman, "Calling to Collect," *Entrepreneur*, September 1993, p. 50.
30. Thompson, "Business Copes with the Recession."
31. "Time Shrinks Value of Debts," *Collection*, Winter 1992, p. 1.
32. Brent Bowers, "Bill Collectors Thrive Using Kinder, Gentler Approach," *Wall Street Journal*, March 2, 1992, p. B2.
33. Jill Andresky Fraser, "A Confidence Game," *Inc.*, December 1989, p. 178.
34. Jill Andresky Fraser, "How to Get Paid," *Inc.*, March 1992, p. 105.
35. Paul DeCeglie, "Bogus Bills," *Business Start-Ups*, January 1998, p. 19.
36. William G. Shepherd Jr., "Internal Financial Strategies," *Venture*, September 1985, p. 68.
37. Stephanie Barlow, "Frozen Assets," *Entrepreneur*, September 1993, p. 53.
38. Roberta Maynard, "Can You Benefit from Barter?" *Nation's Business*, July 1994, p. 6.
39. "33 Ways to Increase Your Cash Flow and Manage Cash Balances," *The Business Owner*, February 1988, p. 8.
40. Kroll, "Ca$h Wears the Crown."
41. Mamis, "Money In, Money Out," p. 102.
42. Eleena De Lisser and Rodney Ho, "Barter Exchanges Say Future Looks Promising," *Wall Street Journal*, November 12, 1997, p. B2; <http://www.irta.net/barterstatistics.html>; Blakely Dickson Griggs, "Bartering Is Back with a Vengeance," *GSA Business*, June 8, 1998, p. 8B.
43. Maturi, "Collection Dues and Don'ts," p. 328.
44. Stephanie Barlow, "Trading Up," *Entrepreneur*, November 1991, pp. 167–172.

45. Julie Candler, "Leasing Passes the Road Test," *Nation's Business*, May 1997, p. 56.
46. Jack Wynn, "To Use But Not to Own," *Nation's Business*, January 1991, p. 38; David R. Evanson and Art Beroff, "Lease Is More," *Entrepreneur*, August 1998, pp. 58–61.
47. Candler, "Leasing Passes the Road Test," p. 54.
48. Wynn, "To Use But Not to Own."
49. Michael Selz, "Many Small Businesses Are Sold on Leasing Equipment," *Wall Street Journal*, October 27, 1993, p. B2.
50. Thompson, "Business Copes with the Recession," p. 20.
51. Ibid.
52. Bruce G. Posner, "Skipped-Payment Loans," *Inc.*, September 1992, p. 40.
53. Ronaleen R. Roha, "How Small Businesses Control Costs," *Kiplinger's Personal Finance Magazine*, February 1997, pp. 77–81.
54. <http://www.collector.com/>.
55. "How to Win the Battle of Bad Checks," *Collection*, Fall 1990, p. 3.
56. Thompson, "Business Copes with the Recession," p. 21.
57. Jill Andresky Fraser, "Better Cash Management," *Inc.*, May 1993, p. 42.
58. Randy Myers, "Asset Accounts Keep Cash Working," *Nation's Business*, July 1997, pp. 30–32.
59. Mamis, "Money In, Money Out," p. 103.

Crafting a Winning Business Plan

It is the set of the sails, not the strength of the gales, which determines the course of the ship.

—*Old English seafaring saying*

Anyone who says businessmen deal only in facts, not fiction, has never read old five-year projections.

—*Malcolm Forbes*

> **Upon completion of this chapter, you will be able to**
>
> ① Explain the two essential functions and the value of a business plan.
>
> ② Describe the elements of a solid business plan.
>
> ③ Explain the three tests that a business plan must pass.
>
> ④ Understand the keys to making an effective business plan presentation.
>
> ⑤ Explain the five Cs of credit and why they are important to potential lenders and investors reading business plans.

*S*tarting a business requires lots of planning, and one of the most important activities an entrepreneur should undertake before launching a company is building a solid business plan. It is the best insurance against becoming just another business failure statistic. For entrepreneurs, a business plan is:

♦ A systematic, realistic evaluation of a venture's chances for success in the market

♦ A way to determine the principal risks facing the venture

♦ A game plan for managing the business successfully

♦ A tool for comparing actual results against targeted performance

♦ An important tool for attracting capital in the challenging hunt for money

Dave King learned the importance of a business plan the hard way. After participating in a poorly organized softball tournament, King and his wife, Annette, decided to launch a business that would offer participants the perfect amateur weekend tournament. They sketched out some rough financial estimates and saw that, to make the business viable, they would have to sponsor three tournaments, giving rise to their company's name, Triple Crown Sports. For the next five years, the Kings ran Triple Crown with no business plan and no long-term goals. Then a near-catastrophe forced them to sit down and get serious about developing a plan. As part of their planning process, the Kings created a seven-point plan for the company's survival, reorganizing the entire company and establishing a model for running tournaments. Participant entry fees, which typically were a few hundred dollars, would generate 50 to 60 percent of revenues, and corporate sponsorships would produce another 20 to 25 percent. The remainder of the company's revenues would come from sales of T-shirts and hats.

The plan saved Triple Crown Sports from failure. "With that little plan, we were able to swing $900,000 on the bottom line, [from a $500,000 loss] to a $400,000 profit," says Dave. Triple Crown now runs more than 400 tournaments a year, not only in softball but also in baseball, hockey, soccer, and basketball. With the help of their plan, the Kings have also expanded into the youth market. The Kings have hit a home run and are beginning to franchise Triple Crown Sports, which now generates $9 million in annual revenues![1]

This chapter describes how to build and use this vital business document. It will help entrepreneurs build a business plan on the foundation laid in the previous chapters of this book.

*W*hy Develop a Business Plan?

◆ Explain the two essential functions and the value of a business plan.

A **business plan** is a written summary of an entrepreneur's proposed business venture, its operational and financial details, its marketing opportunities and strategy, and its managers' skills and abilities. There is no substitute for a well-prepared business plan, and there are no shortcuts to creating one. The plan serves as an entrepreneur's road map on the journey toward building a successful business. It describes the direction the company is taking, what its goals are, where it wants to be, and how it's going to get there. The plan is written proof that the entrepreneur has performed the necessary research and has studied the business opportunity adequately. In short, the business plan is the entrepreneur's best insurance against launching a business destined to fail or mismanaging a potentially successful company.

The business plan serves two essential functions. First and most important, it *guides the company's operations* by charting its future course and devising a strategy for following it. The plan provides a battery of tools—a mission statement, goals, objectives, budgets, financial forecasts, target markets, strategies—to help managers lead the company successfully. It gives managers and employees a sense of direction, but only if everyone is involved in creating, updating, or altering it. As more team members become committed to making the plan work, it takes on special meaning. It gives everyone targets to shoot for, and it provides a yardstick for measuring actual performance against those targets, especially in the crucial and chaotic start-up phase.

The greatest waste of a completed business plan is to let it sit unused on a shelf. When properly done, a plan becomes an integral and natural part of a company. In other words, successful entrepreneurs actually use their business plans to help them build strong companies. "A business plan is . . . only a valuable tool if [entrepreneurs] use it," says one expert.[2] *For instance, Judy Proudfoot, owner of Proudfoot Wearable Art, a home-based business that sells unique hand-painted clothing, uses the business plan she wrote to keep her company focused and competitive. "I refer to it monthly," says Proudfoot. "It lets me compare projections to reality and discover what works well and what needs to be changed."[3]*

Play Ball! With the help of a solid business plan, Dave and Annette King created Triple Crown Sports, a company that runs more than 400 tournaments a year in a variety of sports, including softball, baseball, soccer, hockey, and basketball.

The second function of the business plan is to *attract lenders and investors*. Too often small business owners approach potential lenders and investors without having prepared to sell themselves and their business concept. Simply scribbling a few rough figures on a note pad to support a loan application is not enough. A plan is a reflection of its creator. It should demonstrate that the entrepreneur has thought seriously about the venture and what will make it succeed. Preparing a solid plan demonstrates that the entrepreneur has taken the time to commit the idea to paper. Building a plan also forces the entrepreneur to consider both the positive and the negative aspects of the business. A detailed and thoughtfully developed business plan makes a positive first impression on those who read it. In most cases, potential lenders and investors read a business plan before they ever meet with the entrepreneur behind it. Sophisticated investors will not take the time to meet with an entrepreneur whose business plan fails to reflect a serious investment of time and energy. They know that an entrepreneur who lacks the discipline to develop a good business plan likely lacks the discipline to run a business.

An entrepreneur should not allow others to prepare a business plan for him because outsiders cannot understand the business or envision the proposed company as well as he can. The entrepreneur is the driving force behind the business idea and is the one who can best convey the vision and the enthusiasm he has for transforming that idea into a successful business. Also, because the entrepreneur will make the presentation to potential lenders and investors, he must understand every detail of the business plan. Otherwise, an entrepreneur cannot present it convincingly, and in most cases the financial institution or investor will reject it. *Alice Medrich, co-founder of Cocolat, a manufacturer of specialty candies and desserts, recalls her first attempt at presenting her business plan:*

First of all, I went to the bank, and I was so ill-prepared and so insecure about what I was asking about. . . . I didn't know how to describe what I was doing with any confidence. I did not know how to present a business plan. And he was condescending to me. Looking back on it, I can understand why: I wasn't prepared. . . . We didn't get the loan.[4]

Investors want to feel confident that an entrepreneur has realistically evaluated the risk involved in the new venture and has a strategy for addressing it. They also want to see proof that a business will become profitable and produce a reasonable return on their investment.

Perhaps the best way to understand the need for a business plan is to recognize the validity of the "two-thirds rule," which says that only two-thirds of the entrepreneurs with a sound and viable new business venture will find financial backing. Those who do find financial backing will get only two-thirds of what they initially requested, and it will take them two-thirds as long to get the financing as they anticipated.[5] The most effective strategy for avoiding the two-thirds rule is to build a business plan!

Sometimes the greatest service a business plan provides an entrepreneur is the realization that "it just won't work." The time to find out that a potential business idea won't succeed is in the planning stages, *before* the entrepreneur commits significant resources to the venture. In other cases, the business plan reveals important problems to overcome before launching a company. According to one business consultant, "If you do a really good job of writing your business plan, it's more than just putting words on paper. You do a lot of research, and you expose a lot of flaws. [With] each one that you expose and treat, you enhance the chances of your success."[6]

The real value in preparing a business plan is not so much in the plan itself as it is in the process the entrepreneur goes through to create the plan. Although the finished product is useful, the process of building a plan requires an entrepreneur to subject his data to an objective, critical evaluation. What the entrepreneur learns about his company, its target market, its financial requirements, and other factors can be essential to making the venture a success. During the process, the entrepreneur replaces "I thinks" with "I knows" and makes mistakes on paper, which is much cheaper than making them in reality. Simply put, building a business plan reduces the risk and uncertainty in launching a company by teaching the entrepreneur to do it the right way! Table 9.1 describes the four bases every business plan should cover.

*7*he Elements of a Business Plan

② Describe the elements of a solid business plan.

The elements of a business plan may be standard, but how the entrepreneur tells her story should be unique and reflect her personal excitement about the new venture. If this is a first attempt at writing a business plan, it may be very helpful to seek the advice of individuals with experience in this process. Consultants with small business development centers, accountants, business professors, and attorneys can be excellent sources of advice in refining a business plan. Remember, however, not to allow someone else to write *your* plan!

Initially, the prospect of writing a business plan may appear to be overwhelming. Many entrepreneurs would rather launch their companies and "see what happens" than invest the necessary time and energy defining and researching their target markets, defining their strategies, and mapping out their finances. After all, building a plan is hard work! However, it is hard work that pays many dividends—not all of them immediately apparent. Entrepreneurs who invest their time and energy building plans are better prepared to face the hostile environment in which their companies will compete than those who do not. Earlier, we said that a business plan is like a road map that guides an entrepreneur on the journey to building a successful business. If you were making a journey to a particular destination through unfamiliar, harsh, and dangerous territory, would you rather ride with someone equipped with a road map and a trip itinerary or with someone who didn't believe in road

Table 9.1 Covering the Bases in a Business Plan

What do potential lenders and investors look for in a business plan? Although there's no sure-fire method for satisfying every lender or investor, entrepreneurs who emphasize the following four points will cover their bases:

Key people. Potential lenders and investors want to see proof of the experience, skills, and abilities of a venture's key players. Even though the company may be new, it helps for potential lenders and investors to see that it's not being run by a bunch of amateurs.

Promising opportunity. A basic ingredient in the success of any business venture is the presence of a real market opportunity. The best way to show that such an opportunity exists is with facts. Smart entrepreneurs use the results of market research and an industry analysis to prove that the market for a business is rapidly expanding or that it is already large enough to support a niche profitably. It is also important to show how a venture will gain a competitive advantage in its market segement.

Business context. A business plan should also demonstrate that an entrepreneur understands how macroeconomic factors such as inflation and interest rates affect the business. Another important issue for many businesses is the role that government regulation plays.

Risks and rewards. A business plan should cover the risks a venture faces without dwelling on them. Investors and lenders like to see plans that describe the most serious threats to a venture and how entrepreneurs will deal with them. A plan should address the rewards investors can expect from the company's success. That means defining lenders' and investors' exit paths. How will the company repay lenders and "cash out" investors? Is an initial public offering in the future? A sale to a larger company?

Source: Adapted from Brent Pollock, "Remember the Investor," *Success*, October 1997, p. 24.

maps or in planning trips, destinations, and layovers? Although building a business plan *does not* guarantee success, it *does* raise an entrepreneur's chances of succeeding in business.

A business plan typically ranges from 25 to 55 pages in length. Shorter plans usually are too sketchy to be of any value, and a longer plan might never get used or read! One business plan consultant who has helped assemble nearly 400 plans says, "It should take less than an hour to read your plan, and in that time, readers should be able to understand the entire concept—where you're going and how you're going to get there."[7]

This section explains the most common elements of a business plan. However, entrepreneurs must recognize that, like every business venture, every business plan is unique. An entrepreneur should view the following elements as a starting point for building a plan and should modify them as needed to better tell the story of his new venture.

THE EXECUTIVE SUMMARY

The executive summary presents the essence of the plan in a capsulized form. It should be concise—a maximum of two pages—and should summarize all of the relevant points of the proposed deal. It should explain the dollar amount requested, how the funds will be used, and how (and when) any loans will be repaid. It is designed to capture the reader's attention. If it doesn't, the chances that the remainder of the plan will be read are minimal. A well-developed, coherent summary introducing the financial proposal establishes a favorable first impression of the entrepreneur and the business and can go a long way toward obtaining financing. Although the executive summary is the first part of the business plan, it should be the last section written.

MISSION STATEMENT

As you learned in chapter 2, a mission statement expresses in words the entrepreneur's vision for what her company is and what it is to become. It is the broadest expression of a company's purpose and defines the direction in which it will move. It serves as the thesis statement for the entire business plan.

COMPANY HISTORY

The manager of an existing small business should prepare a brief history of the operation, highlighting the significant financial and operational events in the company's life. This section should describe when and why the company was formed, how it has evolved over time, and what the owner envisions for the future. It should highlight the successful accomplishment of past objectives and should convey the firm's image in the marketplace.

BUSINESS AND INDUSTRY PROFILE

To acquaint lenders and investors with the nature of the business, the owner should describe it in the business plan. This section should begin with a statement of the company's general business goals and a narrower definition of its immediate objectives. Together they should spell out what the business plans to accomplish, how, when, and who will do it. **Goals** are broad, long-range statements of what a company plans to do in the distant future that guide its overall direction and express its *raison d'être*. In other words, they answer the question "Why am I in business?" The answer to such a basic question appears to be obvious, but, in fact, many entrepreneurs cannot define the basis of their businesses. "Composing a business plan makes you really focus on your goals and plan ahead," says Judy Proudfoot. "It's a challenging thing to do when you first start out, but it gives you a clearer picture of what it's going to take to accomplish what you want to accomplish."[8]

Objectives are short-term, specific performance targets that are attainable, measurable, and controllable. Every objective should reflect some general business goal and include a technique for measuring progress toward its accomplishment. To be meaningful, an objective must have a time frame for achievement. Both goals and objectives should be related to the company's basic mission. In other words, accomplishing each objective should move a business closer to achieving its goals, which, in turn, should move it closer to its mission.

When summarizing the small company's background, an owner should describe the present state of the art in the industry and what she will need to succeed in the market segment in which her business will compete. She should then identify the current applications of the product or service in the market and include projections for future applications.

This section should provide the reader with an overview of the industry or market segment in which the new venture will operate. Industry data such as market size, growth trends, and the relative economic and competitive strength of the major firms in the industry all set the stage for a better understanding of the viability of the new product or service. Strategic issues such as ease of market entry and exit, the ability to achieve economies of scale or scope, and the existence of cyclical or seasonal economic trends further help the reader evaluate the new venture. This part of the plan also should describe significant industry trends and an overall outlook for its future. The *U.S. Industrial Outlook Handbook* is an excellent reference that profiles a variety of industries and offers projections for future trends in them. Information about the evolution of the industry helps the reader comprehend its competitive dynamics.

The industry analysis should also focus on the existing and anticipated profitability of the firms in the targeted market segment. Any significant entry or exit of firms or consolidations and mergers should be discussed in terms of their impact on the competitive behavior of the market. The entrepreneur also should mention any events that have significantly altered the industry in the past 10 years.

BUSINESS STRATEGY

An even more important part of the business plan is the owner's view of the strategy needed to meet, and beat, the competition. In the previous section, the entrepreneur defined *where* he wants to take his business by establishing goals and objectives. This section addresses the

GAINING THE COMPETITIVE EDGE

The *Right* Way to Build a Business Plan

*B*uilding a plan forces entrepreneurs to ask—and to answer—questions that are vitally important to their company's ultimate success. Building a solid plan is an essential part of launching a business *whether or not an entrepreneur is seeking outside financing.* How can you create a plan that will help your business become more successful? By integrating the following 10 characteristics into your plan.

1. *Detailed market research.* Prove that you know your target customers and the problems your product or service solves for them. At whom are you aiming your product or service? How can you best reach your target audience? How big is the potential market? How fast is it growing? What competitive advantage does your product or service offer? "The 'better mousetrap' idea, where the public beats a path to your door is passé," says one investor. We're more cynical than that. It's the marketing that counts. It doesn't matter how great the product is."
2. *Clear and realistic financial projections.* Potential lenders and investors often start and end their investigation of a business here. They want to see summaries of a company's financial performance to date (if it is an existing business) and realistic forecasts for the future. Every business plan should contain forecasted balance sheets, income statements, and cash flow statements. Plus, it helps to include the assumptions on which the entrepreneur has built those forecasts and notes explaining all significant line items.
3. *A detailed competitor analysis.* A business plan that omits an analysis of competitors immediately raises a red flag to potential lenders and investors. Every business has competitors, and a plan should show that an entrepreneur understands the competition and its strengths and weaknesses.
4. *A description of the management team.* If there is one universal factor that potential lenders and investors look for, it is a sound management team. Lenders and investors know that poor management will kill even the best product or service idea. At "the top of the list for a successful business plan is management experience in the field," says one small business adviser. Use the plan to show your management team's breadth and depth of experience and how that will translate into success for the business.
5. *A distinct vision.* Entrepreneurs who have a clear vision of what they want their companies to stand for and to accomplish create a sense of excitement among investors. Your plan should demonstrate a detailed knowledge of the industry, your customers, your products or services, and how your company's offering is different from (and superior to) the competition's. It must paint a clear picture of where the company is going and how it intends to get there.
6. *An understanding of financial options.* A plan should explain why a company needs financing, how much money it needs, how it will use the money, and how it will repay lenders or investors. That means entrepreneurs must understand which types of financing best suit their companies. Those seeking loans need rock-solid cash flows to prove their ability to repay their debts. Companies in search of equity investments must prove their growth potential and show investors how they can "cash out."
7. *Proper format and a flowing writing style.* "The first requisite of a business plan is that it be interesting to read, well-written, and smooth-flowing," says one investor. "The second is that it be well organized, so I can look at the table of contents and find what I need." No one is going to read a plan that is boring, unorganized, or riddled with spelling, grammatical, or typographical errors.
8. *Conciseness.* Business plans must include enough detail to answer potential lenders' and investors' questions without overloading them with unneccessary clutter. It's a fine line for an entrepreneur to walk. Plans that are too short beg to be rejected, and those that are too long never get read. One investor recalls a single business plan that arrived in 12 notebooks accompanied by a bottle of champagne. "I drank the champagne and never read the plan," he says.
9. *A killer summary.* The executive summary may be the toughest part of a business plan to write. It's the section almost every potential lender or investor reads first. If the executive summary fails to capture their interest or attention, the odds are that they will not bother to read the rest of the plan. A good executive summary captures the essence of the plan and piques the reader's interest—all in no more than two pages.
10. *Customization.* The hundreds of books on how to write a business plan and software packages such as Business Plan Pro designed to create plans can be valuable sources of help for entrepreneurs facing the challenge of writing a business plan. Be careful, however, to avoid the cookie cutter look. Use those guides and resources as a starting point for your plan. After all, no two business ventures are exactly alike, so no two business plans should be exactly alike. Make sure your plan presents your company in the most favorable way. Don't hire someone to write the plan for you, either. Getting help and feedback from others is an excellent idea, but you should always create the plan yourself first. You are the driving force behind the business, and the plan must reflect your vision of the company.

SOURCE: Adapted from Linda Elkins, "Tips for Preparing a Business Plan," *Nation's Business,* June 1996, pp. 60R–61R; Robert Schmidt, "Planning Ahead," *Business Start-Ups,* January 1998, p. 12. ◆

question of *how* to get there: the business strategy. It should explain how the entrepreneur plans to gain a competitive edge in the market. He should comment on how he plans to achieve business goals and objectives in the face of competition and government regulation, and he should identify the image that the business will try to project. An important theme in this section is what makes the company unique in the eyes of its customers. One of the quickest routes to business failure is trying to sell "me-too" products or services that offer customers nothing new, better, bigger, faster, or different. The foundation for this part of the business plan comes from the material in chapter 2.

This segment of the business plan should outline the methods the company can use to meet the key success factors cited earlier. If, for example, a strong, well-trained sales force is considered critical to success, the owner must devise a plan of action for assembling one.

DESCRIPTION OF FIRM'S PRODUCT/SERVICE

The business owner should describe the company's overall product line, giving an overview of how customers use its goods or services. Drawings, diagrams, and illustrations may be required if the product is highly technical. It is best to write product and service descriptions so that laypeople can understand them. A statement of a product's position in the product life cycle might also be helpful. An entrepreneur should include a summary of any patents, trademarks, or copyrights protecting the product or service from infringement by competitors. Finally, the owner should honestly compare the company's product or service with those of competitors, citing specific advantages or improvements that make his goods or services unique and indicating plans for creating the next generation of goods and services that will evolve from the present product line. What competitive advantage does the venture's product or service offer?

One danger entrepreneurs must avoid in this part of the plan is the tendency to dwell excessively on the features of their products or services. This problem is the result of the "fall-in-love-with-your-product" syndrome, which often afflicts inventors. Customers, lenders, and investors care less about how much work, genius, and creativity went into a product or service than about what it will do for them. The emphasis of this section should be on defining the *benefits* customers get by purchasing the company's products or services rather than on just a "nuts and bolts" description of the features of those products or services. A **feature** is a descriptive fact about a product or service ("An ergonomically designed, more comfortable handle"). A **benefit** is what the customer gains from the product or service feature ("Fewer problems with carpal tunnel syndrome and increased productivity"). Advertising legend Leo Burnett once said, "Don't tell the people how good you make the goods; tell them how good your goods make them."[9] This part of the plan must describe how a business will transform tangible product or service *features* into important, but often intangible, customer *benefits*: e.g., lower energy bills, faster access to the Internet, less time writing checks to pay monthly bills, greater flexibility in building floating structures, or shorter time required to learn a foreign language. Remember: Customers buy benefits, *not* product or service features. Table 9.2 offers an easy exercise designed to help entrepreneurs translate their product's or service's features into meaningful customer benefits.

Jonathan Milchman is one entrepreneur not suffering from the "fall-in-love-with-your-product" syndrome. After inventing a do-it-yourself house-selling kit, Milchman was convinced that major retailers would be as excited about his idea as he was. They weren't, but Milchman wasn't so enamored of his product that he let a business opportunity pass by. When a buyer for a major retail chain suggested that he create a do-it-yourself kit for garage sales (something Milchman had planned to do later), he decided to try it. Changing his business idea to reflect his target customers' preferences resulted in a successful business. The same major retailers that had turned down his house-selling kit have made Milchman's garage sale kit a huge success.[10]

Table 9.2 Transforming Features into Meaningful Benefits

For many entrepreneurs, there's a big gap between what a business is selling and what its customers are buying. The worksheet below is designed to eliminate that gap.

First, develop a list of the features your company's product or service offers. List as many as you can think of, which may be 25 or more. Consider features that are related to price, performance, convenience, location, customer service, delivery, reputation, reliability, quality, and other aspects.

Next, group features with similar themes together by circling them with the same color ink. Then, translate those groups of features into specific benefits to your customers by addressing the question "What's in it for me?" *from the customer's perspective.* Note: It usually is a good idea to ask actual customers why they buy from you. They will give reasons that you never thought of. As many as six or eight product or service (or even company) features may translate into a single customer benefit, such as saving money or time or making life safer. Don't ignore intangible benefits such as increased status; they can be more important than tangible benefits.

Finally, combine all of the benefits you identify into a single sentence or paragraph. Use this statement as a key point in your business plan and to guide your company's marketing strategy.

Features	Benefits

Benefit Statement:

Manufacturers should describe their production process, strategic raw materials required, sources of supply they will use, and their costs. They should also summarize the production method and illustrate the plant layout. If the product is based on a patented or proprietary process, a description (including diagrams, if necessary) of its unique market advantages is helpful. It is also helpful to explain the company's environmental impact and how the entrepreneur plans to mitigate any negative environmental consequences the process may produce.

MARKETING STRATEGY

One crucial concern of entrepreneurs and the potential lenders and investors who finance their companies is whether there is a real market for the proposed good or service. Every entrepreneur must therefore describe the company's target market and its characteristics. Defining the target market and its potential is one of the most important, and most difficult, parts of building a business plan. Building a successful business depends on an entrepreneur's ability to attract real customers who are willing and able to spend real money to buy its products or services. Perhaps the worst marketing error an entrepreneur can commit is failing to define her target market and trying to make her business "everything to everybody." Small companies usually are much more successful focusing on a specific market niche where they can excel at meeting customers' special needs or wants.

Annette Zientek knows that one key to her company's success is focusing on the unique needs of her target market, upscale women who travel frequently. Zientek's company, Christine Columbus, is a mail-order company that sells women-oriented travel products. After two years of extensive market research, much of it with real customers, Zientek was able to determine what to sell and how to sell it to her target customers. With her target audience's profile in place, Zientek was able to purchase mailing lists to reach them. "It is so important to know who your market is," Zientek says. "A good idea is not enough. You need to know what your demographics are and how to find those people." Wanting to expand her catalog and to eventually create her own product line, Zientek has revised her original business plan into a constantly updated five-year plan for success.[11]

Defining a company's target market involves using the techniques described in chapter 6. Questions in this part of the business plan should address market issues such as target market, market size and trends, location, advertising and promotion, pricing, and distribution. Successful entrepreneurs know that a solid understanding of their target markets is the first step in building an effective marketing strategy. Indeed, every other aspect of marketing depends on their having a clear picture of their customers and their unique needs and wants. Proving that a profitable market exists involves two steps: showing customer interest and documenting market claims.

Showing Customer Interest. The entrepreneur must be able to prove that her target customers need or want her good or service and are willing to pay for it. This phase is relatively straightforward for a company with an existing product or service but can be quite difficult for one with only an idea or a prototype. In this case the entrepreneur might offer the prototype to several potential customers in order to get written testimonials and evaluations to show to investors. Or the owner could sell the product to several customers at a discount. Either approach would prove that there are potential customers for the product and would allow demonstrations of the product in operation. Getting a product into customers' hands is also an excellent way to get valuable feedback that can lead to significant design improvements and increased sales down the road.

Documenting Market Claims. Too many business plans rely on vague generalizations such as, "This market is so huge that if we get just 1 percent of it, we will break even in eight months." Such statements are not backed by facts and usually reflect an entrepreneur's unbridled optimism. In most cases, they are also unrealistic!

Entrepreneurs must support claims of market size and growth rates with *facts*, and that requires market research. Results of market surveys, customer questionnaires, and demographic studies lend credibility to an entrepreneur's optimistic sales projections. (Refer to the market research techniques and resources in chapter 6.) *Bob Black, inventor of a product called Clean Shower that competes with products from giant corporations such as Procter & Gamble and Clorox, relied on simple market research techniques to test the response to his product before manufacturing the cleanser on a large scale. Black spent months researching existing products to determine how they work and then used his extensive knowledge to develop a superior product: a work-free shower cleaner. For a year-and-a-half, Black mixed small batches of his cleaner and gave them to friends and neighbors to use. His test was simple: If enough of them came back for more, he could be confident that Clean Shower would sell. Those early "customers" came back in such numbers that Black was convinced of his product's marketability. Today, more than 50,000 retail outlets in 8 countries sell Clean Shower, which generates more than $85 million in annual sales.[12]*

Quantitative market data are important because they form the basis for all of the company's financial projections in the business plan. *To get such data before incurring the ex-*

Bob Black, inventor of Clean Shower, a product designed to make customers' lives easier, relied on simple market research techniques to test the response to his product before launching into full-scale production.

pense of launching a full-blown barbecue restaurant, entrepreneur Ronald Byrd decided to test the local taste for barbecue by selling his product from a street cart. "This is a marketing research project," he says, pointing to his cart. "I didn't want to invest a lot of money into moving into a restaurant [and have no market] so, I started with a cart." Sales that outpaced his expectations proved to him (and to bankers) that the demand for his creative barbecue dishes was sufficient to support a restaurant. This aspiring restaurateur also used feedback and suggestions from customers to fine-tune his menu offerings—all before ever opening the doors to his "official" restaurant, Baby Byrd's Q.[13]

One of the essential goals of this section of the plan is to identify the basics for financial forecasts that follow. Sales, profit, and cash forecasts must be founded on more than wishful thinking. An effective market analysis should identify the following:

◆ *Target market.* Who are the most promising customers or prospects (demographics)? Where do they live and shop? What are their characteristics? What do they buy? Why do they buy? When do they buy? What expectations do they have about the product or service? Will the business focus on a niche? How does the company seek to position itself in its markets?

◆ *Advertising and promotion.* Once an entrepreneur defines her company's target market, she can design a promotion and advertising campaign to reach those customers most effectively and efficiently. Which media are most effective in reaching the target market? How will they be used? How much will the promotional campaign cost? How will the promotional campaign position your company's products or services? How can the company benefit from publicity? How large is the company's promotional budget?

◆ *Market size and trends.* How large is the potential market? Is it growing or shrinking? Why? Are the customers' needs changing? Are sales seasonal? Is demand tied to another product or service?

◆ *Location.* For many businesses, choosing the right location is a key success factor. For retailers, wholesalers, and service companies, the best location usually is one that is most convenient to their target customers. Using census data and other market research, entrepreneurs can determine the sites with the greatest concentrations of their customers and locate there. Which specific sites put the company in the path of its target customers? Do zoning regulations restrict the use of the site? For manufacturers, the location issue often centers on finding a site near its key raw materials or near its major customers. Using demographic reports and market research to screen potential sites takes the guesswork out of choosing the right location for a business.

◆ *Pricing.* What does the product or service cost to produce or deliver? What is the company's overall pricing strategy? What image is the company trying to create in the market? Will the planned price support the company's strategy and desired image? (See Figure 9.1.) Can it produce a profit? How does the planned price compare with the prices of similar products or services? Are customers willing to pay it? What price tiers exist in the market? How sensitive are customers to price changes? Will the business sell to customers on credit? Will it accept credit cards? Will the company offer discounts? If so, what kinds and how much?

◆ *Distribution.* How will the product or service be distributed? Will distribution be extensive, selective, or exclusive? What is the average sale? How large will the sales staff be? How will the company compensate its sales force? What are the incentives for salespeople? How many sales calls does it take to close a sale? What can the company do to make it as easy as possible for customers to buy?

This portion of the plan also should describe the channels of distribution that the business will use (mail, in-house sales force, sales agent, retailers). The owner should summarize the firm's overall pricing and promotion strategies, including the advertising budget, media used, and publicity efforts. The company's warranties and guarantees for its products and services should be addressed as well.

COMPETITOR ANALYSIS

An entrepreneur should discuss the new venture's competition. Failing to assess competitors realistically makes entrepreneurs appear to be poorly prepared, naive, or dishonest. Gathering information on competitors' market shares, products, and strategies is usually not difficult. Trade associations, customers, industry journals, marketing representatives, and sales literature are valuable sources of data. This section of the plan should focus on demonstrating that the entrepreneur's company has an advantage over its competitors. Who are the

	Low Perceived Quality	High Perceived Quality
High Price	Contradictory image. Target: Unknown; this is a dangerous position to be in.	Upscale image. Target: Those who want the best and are able to pay for it.
Low Price	Bargain image. Target: Those to whom low prices are more important than quality.	Value image. Target: Those who are looking for the best value for what they spend.

Figure 9.1 The Links Between Pricing, Perceived Quality, and Company Image

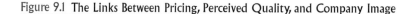

company's key competitors? What are their strengths and weaknesses? What are their strategies? What images do they have in the marketplace? How successful are they? What distinguishes the entrepreneur's product or service from others already on the market, and how will these differences produce a competitive edge? This section of the plan should demonstrate that the firm's strategies are clearly customer-focused.

OFFICERS' AND OWNERS' RÉSUMÉS

The most important factor in the success of a business venture is its management, so financial officers and investors weight heavily the ability and experience of the firm's managers in financing decisions. Thus, the plan should include the résumés of business officers, key directors, and any person with at least 20 percent ownership in the company. Remember: Lenders and investors prefer experienced managers.

A résumé should summarize the individual's education, work history (emphasizing managerial responsibilities and duties), and relevant business experience. When compiling a personal profile, an entrepreneur should review the primary reasons for small business failure (refer to chapter 1) and show how her team will use its skills and experience to avoid them. Lenders and investors look for the experience, talent, and integrity of the people who will breathe life into the plan. This portion of the plan should show that the company has the right people organized in the right fashion for success. One experienced private investor advises entrepreneurs to remember the following:

◆ Ideas and products don't succeed; people do. Show the strength of your management team. A top-notch management team with a variety of proven skills is crucial.

◆ Show the strength of key employees and how you will retain them. A board of directors or advisers consisting of industry experts lends credibility and can enhance the value of the management team.[14]

PLAN OF OPERATION

To complete the description of the business, the owner should construct an organizational chart identifying the business's key positions and the personnel occupying them. Assembling a management team with the right stuff is difficult, but keeping it together until the company is established may be harder. Thus, the entrepreneur should describe briefly the steps taken to encourage important officers to remain with the company. Employment contracts, shares of ownership, and perks are commonly used to keep and motivate such employees. Finally, a description of the form of ownership (partnership, joint venture, S corporation, limited liability company) and of any leases, contracts, and other relevant agreements pertaining to the operation is helpful.

FINANCIAL DATA

One of the most important sections of the business plan is a detailed outline of the loan or investment package—the "dollars and cents" of the proposed deal. Lenders and investors use past financial statements to judge the health of an existing small company and its ability to repay loans or to generate adequate returns. The owner should supply copies of the firm's major financial statements from the past three years. Ideally, these statements should be audited by a certified public accountant, because most financial institutions prefer that extra reliability, although a financial review of the statements by an accountant sometimes may be acceptable.

Whether assembling a plan for an existing business or for a start-up, an entrepreneur should carefully prepare monthly projected (or pro forma) financial statements for the operation for the next two to three years (and possibly for two more years by quarters) using past operating data, published statistics, and judgment to derive three sets of forecasts of the income statement, balance sheet, cash budget, and schedule of planned capital expenditures. There should be forecasts under pessimistic, most likely, and optimistic conditions to reflect the uncertainty of the future. Preparing an extensive set of financial forecasts can be a daunting task for an inexperienced entrepreneur, but spreadsheets can make the job much easier. *"I found the financial forecasting hard," admits Steve Sibulsky, who developed a business plan that landed a $15,000 loan for his company, which produces message-on-hold telephone announcements. "But spreadsheets were invaluable. I could plug in different numbers and see the results instantly."*[15] Entrepreneurs who lack financial aptitude should not hesitate to get help from accountants or consultants when preparing their financial analysis.

It is essential that all three sets of forecasts be realistic. Entrepreneurs must avoid the tendency to fudge the numbers in order to look good. Financial officers compare these projections against published industry standards and can detect unreasonable forecasts. In fact, some venture capitalists automatically discount an entrepreneur's financial projections by as much as 50 percent. Upon completing the forecasts, the owner can perform a breakeven analysis and a ratio analysis on the projected figures.

It is also important to include a statement of the assumptions on which these financial projections are based. Potential lenders and investors want to know how the entrepreneur derived forecasts for sales, cost of goods sold, operating expenses, accounts receivable, collections, inventory, and other such items. Spelling out such assumptions gives a plan credibility.[16]

THE REQUEST FOR FUNDS

The loan proposal section of the business plan should state the purpose of the loan, the amount requested, and the plans for repayment. One important by-product of preparing a business plan is discovering how much money it will take to launch the business. When describing the purpose of the loan, the owner must specify the planned use of the funds. "You'd be surprised how many people request a loan for a specific amount but can't articulate what they would use the money for," says one banker.[17] General requests for funds using terms such as "for modernization," "working capital," or "for expansion" are unlikely to win approval. Instead, descriptions such as "to modernize production facilities by purchasing five new, more-efficient looms that will boost productivity by 12 percent" or "to rebuild merchandise inventory for fall sales peak, beginning in early summer" are much more likely to win approval. Entrepreneurs should state the precise amount of money they are requesting and include relevant backup data, such as vendor estimates of costs or past production levels. They should not hesitate to request the amount of money needed; however, inflating the amount of a loan request in anticipation of the financial officer's trying to "talk them down" is a mistake. Remember: Lenders and investors are familiar with industry cost structures.

Another important element of the loan or investment proposal is the repayment schedule and exit strategy. A lender's main consideration in granting a loan is the reassurance that the applicant will repay, whereas an investor's major concern is earning a satisfactory rate of return. Financial projections must reflect the firm's ability to repay loans and to produce adequate yields. Without this proof, a request for additional funds stands little chance of being accepted. "Plan an exit for the investor," says the owner of a financial consulting company. "Generally, the equity investor's objective with early-stage funding is to earn a 30 percent to 50 percent annual return over the life of the investment. To enhance the investors' interest in your enterprise, show how they can cash out, perhaps through a public offering or acquisition."[18]

Finally, the owner should have a timetable for implementing the proposed plan. He should present a schedule showing the estimated start-up date for the project and noting any

IN THE FOOTSTEPS OF AN ENTREPRENEUR

Turning a Dream into Reality

*D*avid Cupp, a professional photographer with credits in high-profile magazines such as *National Geographic*, wanted to launch his own stock photography house, but he needed outside cash to do it. An experienced computer and Internet user, Cupp says he "saw an opportunity to put together an electronic photography stock house in a way that hadn't been done before." Photo stock houses purchase the rights to photographs from photographers and then resell them to magazines, book publishers, and a host of other media. Traditional stock houses market their photos by sending customers catalogs (which are very expensive to print) or low-resolution compact disks (which don't provide the highest quality images). Customers typically order photographs by phone and receive prints of them by mail, a slow and tedious process.

Cupp, who already owned hundreds of thousands of photographs from hundreds of freelance photographers around the world, saw a better way to provide photographs to customers: the Internet! Cupp's proposed company, Photos Online, would allow customers to use the World Wide Web to browse through his extensive collection of photographs by topic. Once they had selected the photos they wanted, they could order them through the Web site and receive them by downloading them on-line—all in a single transaction! Quick, easy, and convenient, just what Cupp knew his customers wanted.

The only problem was that he needed $25,000 to finance the computers, the software, and the start-up expenses to launch the company. Cupp's first stop was the Small Business Administration's office in Columbus, Ohio. Officials there asked to see a copy of his business plan. "A what?" Cupp recalls saying. "I didn't even know what a business plan was," he admits. Cupp quickly enrolled in an SBA-sponsored seminar on writing a business plan. Afterward, he began working with Harry Long, a retired CEO of a small lumber company, through another SBA program, the Service Corps of Retired Executives (SCORE). Long agreed to help Cupp develop a business plan to raise the money he needed to launch Photos Online. Cupp found that getting started was the hard part. "I told him to write a clear and succinct statement of purpose as

well as an opening balance sheet and at least two years' of profit and loss projections," says Long.

"This was unlike anything I'd ever done," recalls Cupp. "I don't know how many times Harry made me rewrite my business plan, but it was a lot." For help with his financial projections, Cubb began working with accountant Wayne Logan. In addition to helping Cupp develop realistic financial projections, Logan peppered him with questions his plan had to address: What is your business idea, in one sentence? How much revenue does the sale of a photograph generate? How many photographs can you supply? How long will it take you to sell the first photo? "The goal is to translate your ideas into dollars," explains Logan. "Once your figures are complete, it's a matter of organizing them into a recognizable financial statement."

Finally, Cupp had a business plan he could take to potential lenders and investors. Given the amount of money he needed, Cupp decided to focus on banks. His first four calls resulted in four rejections, but with each rejection, Cupp went back and revised his plan on the basis of what the lender had told him. He added material until he had a polished, professional-looking 35-page plan.

The extra work paid off. On his next visit, this time to James Grant, a vice president at Bank One, Cupp was successful; and he didn't even need the loan guarantee from the Small Business Administration the bank usually required on loans to small start-up companies. Grant was impressed with the business idea and with Cupp's business plan. "We thought David Cupp had the background to make it happen," says Grant.

Bank One not only approved a $26,000 term loan but also extended Photos Online a $24,000 line of credit for short-term needs. Photos Online is the only electronic photography stock house in the region and has surged ahead of competitors who lack the Internet technology. David Cupp's dream is coming true—all because he took the time to develop a business plan to transform his dream into a reality.

---

1. Would David Cupp have been able to attract the money he needed to launch Photos Online without a business plan?

2. Assume that you were a private investor whom Cupp approached for the start-up capital he needed. Would you have considered investing in Cupp's business if he had had no business plan? Explain.

3. Which parts of Cupp's business plan would interest you most? Why?

SOURCE: Adapted from Susan Hodges, "One Giant Step toward a Loan," *Nation's Business*, August 1997, pp. 34–36. ◆

milestones along the way. Entrepreneurs tend to be optimistic, so the owner must be sure that his timetable of events is realistic.

It is beneficial to include an evaluation of the risks of a new venture. Evaluating risk in a business plan requires an entrepreneur to walk a fine line. Dwelling too much on everything that can go wrong will discourage potential lenders and investors from financing the venture. Ignoring the project's risks makes those who evaluate the plan tend to believe that the entrepreneur is either naive, dishonest, or unprepared. The best strategy is to identify the most significant risks the venture faces and then to describe what plans have been developed to avoid them altogether or to overcome the negative outcome if the event does occur. "A good plan will provide some contingencies and show that [the entrepreneur] has reviewed both the best- and worst-case situations," says one banker specializing in small business loans.[19]

APPEARANCE

There is a difference between a working business plan—the one the entrepreneur is using to guide her business—and the presentation business plan—the one she is using to attract capital. Coffee rings and penciled-in changes in a working plan don't matter (in fact, they're a good sign that the entrepreneur is actually *using* the plan), but they have no place on a plan going to someone outside the company. A plan is usually the tool that an entrepreneur uses to make a first impression on potential lenders and investors. To make sure that impression is a favorable one, an entrepreneur should follow these tips:

- Make sure the plan is free of spelling and grammatical errors and typos. It is a professional document and should look like one.
- Make it visually appealing. Use color charts, figures, and diagrams to illustrate key points. Don't get carried away, however, and end up with a "comic book" plan.
- Leave ample white space in margins.
- Create an attractive (but not extravagant) cover that includes the company's name and logo.
- Include a table of contents to allow readers to navigate the plan easily.
- Write in a flowing, conversational style and use "bullets" to itemize points in lists.
- Support claims with facts and avoid generalizations.
- Avoid overusing industry jargon and abbreviations with which readers may not be familiar.
- Make it interesting. Boring plans seldom get read.
- Use computer spreadsheets to generate financial forecasts. They allow entrepreneurs to perform valuable "what if" (sensitivity) analysis in just seconds.
- *Always* include cash flow projections. Entrepreneurs sometimes focus excessively on their proposed venture's profit forecasts and ignore cash flow projections. Although profitability is important, lenders and investors are much more interested in cash flow because they know that's where the money to pay them back or to cash them out comes from.
- The ideal plan is crisp: long enough to say what it should but not so long that it is a chore to read.
- Tell the truth. Absolute honesty is critical in a business plan.

*T*esting the Plan

❸ Explain the three tests that a business plan must pass.

A well-assembled plan helps prove to outsiders that a business idea can be successful. To get external financing, an entrepreneur's plan must pass three tests with potential lenders and investors: the reality test, the competitive test, and the value test.[20] The first two tests have both an external and an internal component.

REALITY TEST

The external component of the reality test revolves around proving that a market for the product or service really does exist. It focuses on industry attractiveness, market niches, potential customers, market size, degree of competition, and similar factors. Entrepreneurs who pass this part of the reality test prove in the marketing portion of their business plans that there is strong demand for their business idea.

The internal component of the reality test focuses on the product or service itself. Can the company really build it for the cost estimates in the business plan? Is it truly different from what competitors are already selling? Does it offer customers something of value?

COMPETITIVE TEST

The external part of the competitive test evaluates the company's position relative to its key competitors. How do the company's strengths and weaknesses match up with those of the competition? How are existing competitors likely to react when the new business enters the market? Will their reactions threaten the new company's success and survival?

The internal competitive test focuses on management's ability to create a company that will gain an edge over existing rivals. To pass this part of the competitive test, a plan must prove the quality of the venture's management team. What resources does the company have that can give it a competitive edge in the market?

VALUE TEST

To convince lenders and investors to put their money into the venture, a business plan must prove to them that the business offers a high probability of repayment or an attractive rate of return. Entrepreneurs usually see their businesses as good investments because they consider the intangibles of owning a business—gaining control over their own destinies, freedom to do what they enjoy, and others; lenders and investors, however, look at a venture in colder terms: dollar-for-dollar returns. A plan must convince lenders and investors that they will earn an attractive return on their money.

*M*aking the Business Plan Presentation

4 Understand the keys to making an effective business plan presentation.

Lenders and investors are favorably impressed by entrepreneurs who are informed and prepared when requesting a loan or investment. When entrepreneurs try to secure funding from lenders or investors, the written business plan almost always precedes the opportunity to meet face to face. If the written plan does pass muster, the time allotted for the personal meeting usually is quite limited. (The time allotted for presenting a plan to a venture capital forum is usually 15 to 20 minutes, 30 minutes at the maximum.) When that time comes, an entrepreneur must be well prepared. It is important to rehearse, rehearse, and then rehearse more. It is a mistake to begin by leading the audience into a long-winded explanation about the technology on which the product or service is based. Within minutes, most of the audience will be lost; and so will be any chance of obtaining financing for the venture. A business plan presentation should cover five basic areas:[21]

◆ The company's background and its products or services
◆ A market analysis and a description of the opportunities it presents
◆ Marketing strategies and tactics
◆ The management team and its members' qualifications
◆ A financial analysis that shows lenders and investors an attractive payback or payoff

(Boot) Camp Entrepreneur

*E*ntrepreneur Rob Ryan learned two valuable lessons after starting his first company, Softcom, which he sold to a larger competitor when he ran out of money. "First, never start a company without a great team," he says. "Second, raise a lot of money." He put those lessons into practice with his second company, Ascend, which he co-founded with three partners in 1989 and $2.5 million in venture capital financing. Ascend, a maker of remote networking equipment, was successful and went public in 1994. After undergoing extensive back surgery, Ryan stepped down as Ascend's CEO and chairman and, at age 46, found himself a very rich man with not much to do.

Rather than "retire," Ryan decided to devote his life to helping other entrepreneurs become successful. He established Entrepreneur America, a bootcamp for budding entrepreneurs housed on his 1,200-acre Roaring Lion Ranch on the outskirts of Hamilton, Montana. His guests must pay their own fare to Montana, but once there, Ryan houses them, feeds them, and puts them through the ringer as he helps them refine their ideas and hone their business plans. Occasionally, he even saddles up some of his horses and takes them out into the breathtakingly beautiful Bitterroot Mountains. "If I could grow one great company a year, a really great company, that would be a great contribution to mankind," reflects Ryan. His goal is to expand the program and get other successful founders to mentor entrepreneurial wanna-bes.

As tactful as a drill sergeant, Ryan challenges the entrepreneurs under his tutelage, questioning the assumptions underlying their plans and cajoling them into improving the quality of their business plans. "I see them all make the same mistakes," he says. "They put an incoherent business plan together, run around and talk to whoever they can in the venture capital community, burn all their bridges, and wonder why nobody returns their calls."

Working with Randy Thomae, a 25-year-old M.I.T. graduate who has no job and no company (yet), Ryan demonstrates his technique. Since 5 A.M. (his choice: getting up that early is *not* a camp requirement), Thomae has been working on his business plan for an Internet company called Agent Audio, which will sell a package of software and services that will enable radio stations to customize music for their listeners. As Thomae shows Ryan the latest version of his business plan, Ryan repeatedly interrupts him with questions or to challenge the assumptions the young entrepreneur is making about his product and services. Thomae's plan has changed a great deal since he first met Ryan in Boston. Thomae recalls that Ryan told him to trash his first draft of a slide presentation on Agent Audio he had planned to show to venture capitalists. "This is garbage. No one will sit through this," he recalls Ryan's saying.

Although it sounds harsh to outsiders, entrepreneurs love Ryan's tough, straightforward style. In response to one of Ryan's blistering assaults, one entrepreneur practicing his business plan presentation exclaimed, "This is good. It's making my head hurt, which is why I came here." Ryan's entrepreneurial students sense that Ryan's tough talk is designed to help them, and they don't resent it. "Once you realize he's being intimidating because you're up to the challenge, it's very motivating," says one.

Thomae has been trying to convince Ryan that he should promote Agent Audio as a media business not as an Internet company. "I'm putting everything in terms of radio," he tells Ryan. "The Internet raises a lot of alarms (among potential investors)." Ryan dismisses that logic as he sketches out a chart to illustrate the rapidly growing market for Internet advertising. "This is the hot, sexy part," he tells Thomae.

"But it's risky and unproven," counters Thomae.

"Yes, it's risky, but as an entrepreneur, that's where you put your bet," says Ryan before launching into a discourse on the finer points of presenting a business plan to potential investors.

Another of Ryan's students who has launched a highly successful technology company says, "There is a saying, 'There is no progress without the unreasonable man.' Unless you're absolutely unreasonable, things become the status quo. That's really the definition of Rob. You have to ask for the impossible. Certainly, Rob challenges people to do that."

---

1. What benefits does Rob Ryan's entrepreneurial boot camp offer aspiring entrepreneurs?
2. Critique the confrontational style that Ryan uses with his entrepreneurial students. What benefits does it give them?
3. Use the resources in the library and on the World Wide Web to develop a list of suggestions and advice for entrepreneurs presenting their business plans to lenders and investors.

SOURCE: Adapted from Susan Beck, "Out of Business," *Inc.*, May 1997, pp. 73–80. ◆

No matter how good a written business plan is, entrepreneurs who muff the presentation to potential lenders and investors will blow the deal. *For example, the founder of a hot Internet company wanted to show a group of potential investors how cutting-edge his business was by conducting a live demonstration of his company's product on a portable computer and a projection system. Initially, the presentation went well; then the computer failed to make the con-*

nection to the Internet. The presentation program was locked up, and the entrepreneur had to reboot the entire system while trying to hold the audience's attention and get the presentation back on track. The technological glitch occurred at the most crucial part of the entrepreneur's presentation, making his company look like a minor league player in a major league industry. His company's prospects for an initial public offer crashed the second his computer did![22]

At a similar gathering of investment bankers considering companies' bids for an initial public offering, Dean Suposs, founder of Avert Inc., a company that conducts employee background checks, realized that his presentation was the last in a series of what had proved to be rather boring presentations by a dozen other entrepreneurs. The room was darkened from the previous presenter's slide show. Looking around at the bored faces of the audience, Suposs knew he had to do something to change the energy level in the room. "I turned the lights all the way up, asked for a roving microphone, and started moving around the room," he recalls. "I had to get their attention." Apparently, he did, because one month after his presentation, Avert Inc. had raised the $5.25 million Suposs was seeking.[23]

Dean Suposs succeeded in raising the capital his company needed to grow because he had a solid business plan and he made a convincing presentation of it. Here are some tips for making a business plan presentation to potential lenders and investors.

- ◆ Demonstrate enthusiasm about the venture, but don't be overemotional.
- ◆ Fight the temptation to launch immediately into a lengthy discourse about the details of your product or service or how much work it took to develop it. Focus instead on communicating the dynamic opportunity your idea offers and how you plan to capitalize on it. Otherwise, you'll never have the chance to describe the details to lenders and investors.
- ◆ "Hook" investors quickly with an up-front explanation of the new venture, its opportunities, and the anticipated benefits to them.
- ◆ Use visual aids. They make it easier for people to follow your presentation. But don't make the mistake of relying on visuals to communicate the entire message. Visual aids should punctuate your spoken message and focus the audience's attention on what you are saying.
- ◆ Hit the highlights; specific questions will bring out the details later. Don't get caught up in too much detail in early meetings with lenders and investors.
- ◆ Keep the presentation crisp. Otherwise, says one experienced investor, "information that might have caused an investor to bite gets lost in the endless drone."[24]
- ◆ Avoid the use of technological terms that will likely be above most of the audience. Do at least one rehearsal before someone who has no special technical training. Tell him to stop you anytime he does not understand what you are talking about. Rewrite any portion of your presentation that made him stop you.
- ◆ Remember that every potential lender and investor you talk to is thinking "What's in it for me?" Be sure to answer that question in your presentation.
- ◆ Close by reinforcing the nature of the opportunity. Be sure you have sold the benefits the investors will realize when the business is a success.
- ◆ Be prepared for questions. In many cases, there is seldom time for a long "Q&A" session, but interested investors may want to get you aside to discuss the details of the plan.
- ◆ Anticipate and prepare for the questions the audience is most likely to ask.
- ◆ Be sensitive to the issues that are most important to lenders and investors by "reading" the pattern of their questions. Focus your answers accordingly. For instance, some investors may be interested in the quality of the management team while others are more interested in marketing strategies. Be prepared to offer details on either.

◆ Follow up with every investor you make a presentation to. Don't sit back and wait; be proactive. They have what you need—investment capital. Demonstrate that you have confidence in your plan and have the initiative necessary to run a business successfully.

ℒenders, and What They Look for in a Loan Application

$ Explain the five Cs of credit and why they are important to potential lenders and investors reading business plans.

Banks and other lenders will rarely be a new venture's sole source of capital because a bank's return is limited by the interest rate it negotiates, but its risk could be the entire amount of the loan if the new business fails. Once the business is operational and has established a financial track record, the bank becomes the traditional source of financing. For this reason the small business owner needs to be aware of the criteria bankers use in evaluating the creditworthiness of loan applicants. Most bankers refer to these criteria as the **five Cs of credit:** capital, capacity, collateral, character, and conditions. The higher a small business scores on these five Cs, the greater its chance will be of receiving a loan. The wise entrepreneur keeps the five Cs in mind when preparing a business plan and presentation.

CAPITAL

A small business must have a stable capital base before a bank will grant a loan. Otherwise the bank would be making, in effect, a capital investment in the business. Most banks refuse to make loans that are capital investments because the potential for return on the investment is limited strictly to the interest on the loan, and the potential loss would probably exceed the reward. In fact, the most common reasons that banks give for rejecting small business loan applications are undercapitalization or too much debt. The bank expects the small business to have an equity base of investment by the owners that will help support the venture during times of financial strain.

CAPACITY

A synonym for capacity is *cash flow*. The bank must be convinced of the firm's ability to meet its regular financial obligations and to repay the bank loan, and that takes cash. In chapter 8 we saw that more small businesses fail from lack of cash than from lack of profit. It is possible for a company to be showing a profit and still have no cash: that is, to be technically bankrupt. Bankers expect the small business loan applicant to pass the test of liquidity, especially for short-term loans. The bank studies closely the small company's cash flow position to decide whether it meets the capacity requirement.

COLLATERAL

Collateral includes any assets the owner pledges to the bank as security for repayment of the loan. If the company defaults on the loan, the bank has the right to sell the collateral and use the proceeds to satisfy the loan. Typically, banks make very few unsecured loans (those not backed by collateral) to business start-ups. Bankers view the owner's willingness to pledge collateral (personal or business assets) as an indication of dedication to making the venture a success.

CHARACTER

Before approving a loan to a small business, the banker must be satisfied with the owner's character. The evaluation of character frequently is based on intangible factors such as honesty, competence, polish, determination, and intelligence. Although the judgments are sub-

WIRED TO THE WEB

A LITTLE HELP FROM MY FRIENDS AND THE WEB

*K*osha Batel couldn't help but smile smugly as she climbed into her sport utility vehicle. "I can't believe I finally have the money to launch my business," she thought after the family reunion. She had been waiting for months to speak with her Uncle Cal again about her business. Uncle Cal, himself a successful business owner, had seemed intrigued when she had first pitched her business idea to him five months earlier. He told Kosha then that he liked her idea and her enthusiasm for becoming an entrepreneur and that he would consider bankrolling her business idea.

She had arranged to meet with her uncle a few hours before the reunion. She answered the few questions he asked her about her idea to launch a Web site design company.

"I don't know much about all of those high-tech businesses," Uncle Cal told her. "I'm of the old school, but it certainly sounds like a great business idea. Anyway, you are my favorite niece and $25,000 isn't a lot of money."

"Not a lot of money?" Kosha thought. "Maybe not to him, but it's a lot of money to me. With the $20,000 I've saved, I can buy the computer hardware and software I need to start designing Web sites."

Several days later, Kosha ran into Liz, an old friend from college. As they caught up on what had happened in each others' lives since graduation, Liz mentioned that she was now working for a consulting firm that specialized in small and medium-sized businesses.

"How about that!" Kosha said. "I'm about to launch a business of my own. I'm going to design Web sites."

"That's great," said Liz. "I'd be glad to look over your business plan—at no charge, of course. Perhaps I could give you some tips or put you in touch with some potential funding sources."

"Business plan?" Kosha said with a hint of disdain in her voice. "I don't need a business plan. I'm not going out to bankers or professional investors for any money. My Uncle Cal is putting $25,000 into my company. That, plus my investment, is all I need to get my business up and running."

Liz couldn't disguise her shock. She didn't want to hurt Kosha's feelings, but she *had* to say something. "Kosha, whether you search for capital from lenders or investors or not, you need a business plan. How else are you going to guide your company through all of the crises you'll encounter, especially in the early months of your business venture? How do you know who your target customers are or how you'll reach them? What about cash flow and earnings forecasts? How much can you expect to generate in sales? How will you know when, or if, you can repay your uncle? A business plan is your best insurance against becoming another business failure statistic."

Kosha couldn't say a word. She just stood there, realizing that her friend was right. Finally, she said, "I can't believe I was about to launch a business so poorly prepared. But I don't know a thing about writing a business plan. Where do I start?"

Liz reached into her purse, grabbed a business card, and handed it to Kosha. "Give me a call, and we'll get together. In the meantime, go to the World Wide Web and search for information on business plans. There are lots of sites out there with good information. Some even have sample plans you can look at. Once you've had a chance to learn a little about business plans on your own, give me a call and we'll talk about putting together a plan for your company."

1. Use the search engines on the World Wide Web to help Kosha learn more about writing a business plan.
2. On the basis of what you learned in this chapter and your Web search, write a two-page report outlining for Kosha some practical advice on assembling a business plan.
3. Locate a sample business plan on the WWW that you believe would serve as a good model for Kosha to follow. Record its URL (Web address) and explain why it is a good model.

jective, this evaluation plays a critical role in the banker's decision. Loan officers know that most small businesses fail because of incompetent management, so they try to avoid extending loans to high-risk managers. The business plan and a polished presentation can go far in convincing the banker of the owner's character.

CONDITIONS

The conditions surrounding a loan request also affect the owner's chance of receiving funds. Banks consider factors relating to the business operation, such as potential growth in the market, competition, location, form of ownership, and loan purpose. Again, the owner should provide this relevant information in an organized format in the business plan. Another important condition influencing the banker's decision is the shape of the overall economy, including interest rate levels, inflation rate, and demand for money. Although these factors are beyond an entrepreneur's control, they still are an important component in a banker's decision.

*B*usiness Plan Format

Although every company's business plan will be unique, reflecting its individual circumstances, certain elements are universal. The following outline summarizes these components and the appendix at the end of this book contains a sample business plan for a company, Nature's Oven.

I. Executive Summary (not to exceed two typewritten pages)
   A. Company name, address, and phone number
   B. Names, addresses, and phone numbers of all key people
   C. Brief description of the business
   D. Brief overview of the market for your product
   E. Brief overview of the strategic actions you plan to take to make your firm a success
   F. Brief description of the managerial and technical experience of your key people
   G. Brief statement of what the financial needs are, what the money would be used for, and when any loans will be repaid
   H. Income statements, cash flow statements, and balance sheets for the last 3 years of operation

II. Detailed Business Plan
   A. Industry Analysis
      1. Industry background and overview
      2. Trends
      3. Growth rate
      4. Outlook for the future
   B. Background of Your Business
      1. Brief history of the business
      2. Current situation
      3. Your company's mission statement
      4. What makes your business unique: sources of competitive advantage
      5. How your company creates value for customers
      6. The key factors that will dictate the success of your business (e.g., price competitiveness, quality, durability, dependability, technical features)

D. Market Analysis
  1. Who are the potential buyers for your products? (Be specific.)
  2. What is their motivation to buy?
  3. How many customers does the market contain? (How large is the market?)
  4. What are their potential annual purchases?
  5. What is the nature of the buying cycle?
     a. Is this product a durable good that lasts for years or a product that is repurchased on a regular basis?
     b. Is the product likely to be purchased at only seasonal periods during the year?
  6. Specific target market: What do you know about the potential customer you are likely to sell to in your geographic area?
     a. What are the product features that influence the customer's buying decision?
     b. What, if any, research supports your conclusions?
     c. Do the customers have a preference in where they purchase comparable products? How strong is this preference?
  7. Pricing strategies
     a. Cost structure: fixed and variable
     b. Desired image in market (see Figure 9.1)
     c. Your prices versus competitors' prices
  8. Advertising and promotion strategies
     a. Most effective media in reaching your target audience
     b. Media costs
     c. Frequency of usage
     d. Means of generating publicity for your business
  9. Distribution strategy
     a. Channels of distribution
     b. Sales techniques and incentives
  10. External market influences
     a. Economic factors
        (1) Inflation
        (2) Recession
        (3) High or low unemployment
        (4) Interest rates
     b. Social factors
        (1) Age of customers
        (2) Locational demographics
        (3) Income levels
        (4) Size of household
        (5) Social attitudes
     c. Technological factors
D. Competitor Analysis
  1. Existing competitors
     a. Who are they? List major known competitors.
     b. Why do you believe the potential customers in your target market buy from them now?
     c. How will they affect your business?
  2. Potential competitors
     a. Who are they, and when and why might they enter the market?
     b. What would be the impact in your target market segment if they entered?
  3. The strengths and weaknesses of each key competitor's business and how they will affect your business

E. Strategic Analysis
  1. Core competences
  2. Market position and image
  3. SWOT analysis
     a. Strengths
     b. Weaknesses
     c. Opportunities
     d. Threats
  4. Business strategy
     a. Cost leadership
     b. Differentiation
     c. Focus
F. Strategic Action Plan
  1. Specific performance goals and objectives and their link to your company's mission
  2. Summary of your production and marketing strategies
  3. How will you convert these marketing strategies into action
  4. The control procedures you plan to establish to keep the business on track, including measures of performance
G. Specifics of Your Organization and Management
  1. Business organization
     a. Legal (corporation, S corporation, limited liability company, partnership, sole proprietorship)
     b. Functional (division of authority and chair of command)
     c. Organization chart
  2. Key people
     a. Their backgrounds and what they bring to the business that will enhance the chance of success
     b. Résumés of key managers and employees
H. Financial Plans
  1. How much money do you need to make this product and your business a long-term success? Be realistic and specific.
  2. Create a budget. Show the banker or investor how much money you need, why you need it, when you need it, and how and when you plan to generate revenues from operations and sales.
     a. Materials
     b. Labor
     c. Equipment
     d. Marketing
     e. Overhead
     f. Other (e.g., unique start-up costs)
  4. Present actual and projected balance sheets and income statements.
  5. Prepare a breakeven analysis.
  6. Prepare a ratio analysis; compare with industry standards.
  7. Create cash flow projections.
I. Loan Proposal
  1. Loan purpose
  2. Amount requested
  3. Repayment or "cash out" schedule (exit strategy)
  4. Timetable for implementation

Chapter Summary

① Explain the two essential functions and the value of a business plan.
- The business plan guides the company's operations by charting its future course and devising a strategy for following it.
- The business plan attracts lenders and investors.
- The *real* value in preparing a business plan is not so much in the plan itself as it is in the process the entrepreneur goes through to create the plan. Although the finished product is useful, the process of building a plan requires an entrepreneur to subject his idea to an objective, critical evaluation. What the entrepreneur learns about his company, its target market, its financial requirements, and other factors can be essential to making the venture a success.

② Describe the elements of a solid business plan.
- Although a business plan should be unique and tailor-made to suit the particular needs of a small company, it should cover these basic elements: an executive summary, a mission statement, a company history, a business and industry profile, a description of the company's business strategy, a profile of its products or services, a statement explaining its marketing strategy, a competitor analysis, owners' and officers' résumés, a plan of operation, financial data, and the loan or investment proposal.

③ Explain the three tests that a business plan must pass.
- The *reality test*, externally, proves that a market for the product or service exists. Internally, it proves that the cost estimates in the plan are accurate.
- The *competitive test*, externally, proves that the product or service will be able to successfully compete in its market. Internally, it proves that the company's management is competent and that the company has resources to give it a competitive advantage.
- The *value test* proves that the business offers a high probability of repayment of a loan or an attractive rate of return on an investment.

④ Understand the keys to making an effective business plan presentation.
- Demonstrate enthusiasm about the venture, but don't be overemotional; "hook investors quickly with an up-front explanation of the new venture, its opportunities, and the anticipated benefits to them; use visual aids; hit the highlights of your venture; don't get caught up in too much detail in early meetings with lenders and investors; avoid the use of technological terms that will likely be above most of the audience; rehearse your presentation before giving it; close by reinforcing the nature of the opportunity; and be prepared for questions.

⑤ Explain the five Cs of credit and why they are important to potential lenders and investors reading business plans.
- *Capital.* Lenders expect small businesses to have an equity base of investment by the owners that will help support the venture during times of financial strain.
- *Capacity.* A synonym for capacity is *cash flow*. The bank must be convinced of the firm's ability to meet its regular financial obligations and to repay the bank loan, and that takes cash.
- *Collateral.* Collateral includes any assets the owner pledges to the bank as security for repayment of the loan.
- *Character.* Bankers judge the owner's honesty, competence, polish, determination, and intelligence.
- *Conditions.* Bankers consider interest rates, the health of the nation's economy, industry growth rates, form of ownership, location, and other external and internal factors that might affect the business.

Discussion Questions

1. Why should an entrepreneur develop a business plan?
2. Why do entrepreneurs who are not seeking external financing need to prepare business plans?
3. Describe the major components of a business plan.
4. How can an entrepreneur seeking funds to launch a business convince potential lenders and investors that a market for the product or service really does exist?
5. How would you prepare to make a formal presentation of your business plan to a venture capital forum?
6. What are the five Cs of credit? How does a banker use them when evaluating a loan request?

Step into the Real World

1. Interview a local banker or investor who has experience in making loans to or investments in small businesses. Ask him or her the following questions.

a. How important is a well-prepared business plan?
b. How important is a smooth presentation?
c. How do you evaluate the owner's character?
d. How heavily do you weigh the five Cs of credit?
e. What percentage of small business owners are well prepared to request loan or investment?
f. What mistakes do entrepreneurs most commonly make when creating their business plans? When presenting them?
g. What are the major reasons for rejecting a business plan?

2. Interview a small business owner who has requested a bank loan or an equity investment from external sources. Ask him or her these questions:
a. Did you prepare a written business plan before approaching the financial officer?
b. (If the answer is yes), Did you have outside or professional help in preparing it?
c. How many times have your requests for additional funds been rejected? What reasons were given for the rejections?

Take It to the Net

Visit the Scarborough/Zimmerer home page at
www.prenhall.com/scarbzim
for updated information, on-line resources, and Web-based exercises.

Endnotes

1. Roberta Maynard, "Sliding into Home," *Nation's Business*, January 1998, p. 52.
2. Lynn H. Colwell, "Mapping Your Route," *Business Start-Ups*, December 1996, p. 44.
3. Kylo-Patrick Hart, "Step 6: Compose a Winning Business Plan," *Business Start-Ups*, October 1996, p. 70.
4. Paul Hawken, "Money," *Growing a Business*, KQED, San Francisco, 1988.
5. Steve Marshall Cohen, "Money Rules," *Business Start-Ups*, July 1995, p. 79.
6. Roger Thompson, "Business Plans: Myth and Reality," *Nation's Business*, August 1988, p. 16.
7. Colwell, "Mapping Your Route," p. 40.
8. Hart, "Step 6," p. 70.
9. "Advice from the Great Ones," *Communication Briefings*, January 1992, p. 5.
10. Lynn Beresford, "Try, Try Again," *Entrepreneur*, April 1997, p. 32.
11. Sandra Mardenfeld, "New World Order," *Business Start-Ups*, July 1996, pp. 60–64.
12. Don Debelak, "Testing the Waters," *Business Start-Ups*, February 1998, pp. 64–67.
13. "Sales and Marketing," *Venturing*, Vermont Public Television, 1991.
14. Conversation with Charles Burke, CEO, Burke Financial Associates.
15. Colwell, "Mapping Your Route," p. 42.
16. Norm Brodsky, "Due Diligence," *Inc.*, February 1998, pp. 25–26.
17. "Prepping Yourself for Credit," *Your Company*, April/May 1997, p. 9.
18. Ibid.
19. Alana Odom, "Good Plan Is Vital When Starting Business," *Money Wise*, May 4, 1998, p. 5.
20. Steve Marshall Cohen, "Reality Check," *Business Start-Ups*, October 1995, pp. 74–75.
21. David R. Evanson, "Capital Pitches That Succeed," *Nation's Business*, May 1997, pp. 40–41.
22. Ibid.
23. Gianna Jacobson, "Crowd Control," *Success*, October 1997, p. 39.
24. Evanson, "Capital Pitches That Succeed."

Pricing for Profit

The price is what you pay; the value is what you receive.

—*Anonymous*

If your price isn't right, you can't sell it regardless of fit, quality, or style.

—*Bud Kowheim*

Upon completion of this chapter, you will be able to

1. Describe effective pricing techniques for both new and existing products and services.

2. Discuss the links among pricing, image, and competition.

3. Explain the pricing techniques used by retailers.

4. Explain the pricing techniques used by manufacturers.

5. Explain the pricing techniques used by service firms.

6. Describe the impact of credit on pricing.

---

*S*etting prices is not only one of the toughest decisions small business owners face, but it is also one of the most important. Pricing errors can destroy an otherwise promising business. Prices that are too high will hurt a company's sales, and the company will not be able to build a sufficient customer base. Pricing products or services too low, a common tendency among start-up businesses, will rob a company of profits, threaten its long-term success, and leave customers with the impression that its products or services are of inferior quality. Customers' increasing demand for value-priced goods and services, the rising cost of raw materials, and intense competition only complicate the pricing decision for business owners.

Improper pricing has destroyed countless businesses. Unfortunately, many small business owners set prices on the basis of hunches, educated guesses, or overly simplistic and highly questionable formulas. Others simply charge what competitors are charging and hope that they make a profit. Setting appropriate prices requires information, facts, and analysis. The factors that small business owners must consider when determining the final price for goods and services include the following:

◆ Product or service costs

◆ Market factors: supply and demand

◆ Sales volume

◆ Competitors' prices

◆ The company's competitive advantage

◆ Economic conditions

◆ Business location

◆ Seasonal fluctuations

◆ Psychological factors

◆ Credit terms and purchase discounts

◆ Customers' price sensitivity

◆ Desired image

Price is the monetary value of a product or service. It is a measure of what customers must give up to get goods and services. Price also is an indication of a product's or service's value to an individual customer, so different customers assign different values to the same products and services. From a business owner's perspective, prices must be compatible with customers' definitions of value. "Without an understanding of how customers perceive the value of your product or service, it's almost impossible to set a price they'll be willing—and able—to pay," says one business writer.[1] At another level, prices send clear signals to customers about a company's image and position in the market.

Setting prices with a customer orientation is more important than trying to choose the ideal price for a product. In fact, for most products there is an acceptable price range, not a single ideal price. This **price range** is the area between the **price ceiling** defined by customers and the **price floor** established by the firm's cost structure (see Figure 10.1). Identifying the price ceiling requires entrepreneurs to understand their customers' characteristics and buying behavior. "The first thing any pricing planner needs to do is gain a thorough understanding of who the customer is demographically," says one successful business owner. "If you don't know that, you can't understand who they are economically."[2] Business owners must conduct research to learn as much as they can about their target audience. Small companies with effective pricing policies tend to have a clear picture of who their customers are and how their companies' products or services fit into their customers' perception of value.

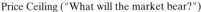

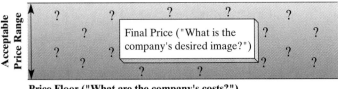

Price Ceiling ("What will the market bear?")

Final Price ("What is the company's desired image?")

Price Floor ("What are the company's costs?")

Figure 10.1 What Determines Price?

The price floor depends on a company's cost structure, which can vary considerably from one business to another. Still, many small business owners merely play follow-the-leader with their prices, charging what their competitors do on similar or identical products and services. The assumption these owners make is that their cost structures are the same as their competitors, which is rarely the case! Determining a product's or service's price floor requires business owners to have accurate, timely cost information. Unfortunately, many business owners do not have sound accounting systems in place that can give them reliable cost information, so it is virtually impossible for them to set prices accurately. Entrepreneurs should strive to put into place an accounting system that will provide the accurate information they need on a timely basis. The system should tell managers their total cost per unit, including such obvious costs as materials and labor as well as less visible costs such as delivery, employee benefits, and general overhead.

The entrepreneur's goal should be to position the firm's prices within this acceptable price range. The final price that business owners set depends on the desired image they want to create for their products or services: discount (bargain), middle-of-the-road (value), or prestige (upscale). "There is a direct and strong relationship between the prices you charge and the image of your company," says one expert.[3] A prestige pricing strategy is not necessarily better or more effective than a no-frills, value pricing strategy. What matters most is that the company's pricing strategy enhances the image the owner wants to create for it.

For instance, one career consultant was having trouble attracting clients, even though he had considerable experience in the field. After more than a year of networking and advertising, his consulting business was stagnant. At an industry conference, he discussed his problem with several very successful career consultants, all of whom advised him to raise his prices. *Figuring he had nothing to lose, he took their advice. To his delight, his sales rose dramatically. "I finally realized that what I was selling was knowledge, experience, and information," he says. "Most of my clients are well-paid professionals who want quality in everything they purchase. When my consulting services were priced so low, potential clients perceived them as being of low value. As my prices went up, so did potential clients' perceived value of my services. Sales soon went in the same direction."[4]* Not every business has the good fortune of raising prices and experiencing a sales increase; however, this consultant's experience proves the powerful link between price and perception.

Business owners must walk a fine line when pricing their products and services, setting their prices high enough to cover costs and earn a reasonable profit but low enough to attract customers and generate an adequate sales volume. Furthermore, the right price today may be completely inappropriate tomorrow because of changing market and competitive conditions. For instance, companies often find themselves in a pricing dilemma because of rapidly rising raw materials costs. If they raise their prices to cover the increased materials cost, they run the risk of losing customers, perhaps forever. If they absorb the additional costs themselves, their profits shrink, which can threaten the long-term viability of the company.

That's the situation Danny O'Neill, owner of The Roasterie, a wholesale coffee business that sells to upscale restaurants, coffee houses, and supermarkets, found himself in when coffee prices nearly doubled in just three months.[5] Similarly, Jim Park, president of Paarlo Plastics, a small manufacturer of plastic parts, saw the price of his company's raw materials climb 23 percent in just months.[6] Businesses faced with rapidly rising raw materials costs should consider the following strategies:

◆ *Communicate with customers.* Let your customers know what's happening. *The Roasterie's O'Neill was able to pass along the rising costs of his company's raw material to customers without losing a single one. He sent his customers a six-page letter and copies of newspaper articles about the increases in coffee prices. The approach gave the Roasterie credibility and helped show customers that the necessary price increases were beyond his control.*

◆ *Focus on improving efficiency everywhere in the company.* Although raw materials costs may be beyond a business owner's control, other costs within the company are not. One way to dampen the effects of a rapid increase in costs is to find ways to cut costs and to improve efficiency in other areas. These improvements may not totally offset higher raw materials costs, but they can dampen their impact.

◆ *Consider absorbing cost increases to save accounts with long-term importance to the company.* Saving a large account might be more important than keeping pace with rising costs. *When one of Paarlo Plastics' biggest customers demanded a 5 percent price cut, Jim Park agreed to it because he couldn't afford to lose a customer of that magnitude. "I could [cut our prices] because I was able to lower costs in other ways," he says.*[7]

◆ *Emphasize the value your company provides to customers.* Unless a company reminds them, customers can forget the benefits and value its products offer. *When some casinos balked at paying premium prices ($2,000 to $2,600) for his company's portable carts that dispense change to slot machine players, Russell Pike, owner of Advanced Cart Technology, emphasized to casino managers the value his carts offer. He showed them how the convenient carts would pay for themselves in a single weekend by letting casinos use them for two weeks free of charge. He then showed them how his prices compared with their increased profits. "Even though our prices are high," says Pike, "they are not high for what we are doing for them."*[8]

◆ *Anticipate rising materials costs and try to lock in prices early.* It pays to keep tabs on raw materials prices and to be able to predict cycles of inflation. *Linda Smithers, president of Susan's Coffee and Tea, routinely tracks the prices for coffee and tea on the New York Coffee, Sugar, and Cocoa Exchange to help her forecast significant price movements. Using her computer, she checks the prices of her raw materials every night. Recently, she noticed coffee prices moving upward and decided to commit early on to pur-*

Thanks to a strategy that used newsletters to keep his customers informed when the price of his raw materials nearly doubled in just three months, Danny O'Neill, owner of the Roasterie, passed along the rising costs to his customers without losing a single one. Here, Danny stands ankle-deep in coffee beans in Costa Rica.

chase 125,000 pounds of coffee over the course of the year. Whei coffee prices more than doubled, Smithers was able to save $80,000 in raw materials cost.[9]

$\mathcal{P}$ricing Strategies and Tactics

◆Describe effective pricing techniques for both new and existing products and services.

There is no limit to the number of variations in pricing strategies and tactics. The wide variety of options is exactly what allows entrepreneurs to be so creative with their pricing. This section will examine some of the more commonly used tactics under a variety of conditions. Pricing always plays a critical role in a firm's overall strategy; pricing policies must be compatible with a company's total marketing plan.

NEW PRODUCTS: PENETRATION, SKIMMING, OR SLIDING

Most entrepreneurs approach setting the price of a new product with a great deal of apprehension because they have no precedent on which to base their decision. If the new product's price is excessively high, it is in danger of failing because of low sales volume. However, if its price is too low, the product's sales revenue might not cover costs. When pricing any new product, the owner should try to satisfy three objectives:

1. *Get the product accepted.* No matter how unusual a product is, its price must be acceptable to the firm's potential customers.

2. *Maintain market share as competition grows.* If a new product is successful, competitors will enter the market, and the small company must work to expand or at least maintain its market share. Continuously reappraising the product's price in conjunction with special advertising and promotion techniques helps the firm acquire and retain a satisfactory market share.

3. *Earn a profit.* Obviously, a small firm must establish a price for the new product that is higher than its cost. Managers should not introduce a new product at a price below cost because it is much easier to lower the price than to increase it once the product is on the market. Pricing their products too low is a common and often fatal mistake for new businesses; entrepreneurs are tempted to underprice their products and services when they enter a new market to ensure its acceptance. *When Judy Proudfoot, founder of Proudfoot Wearable Art, launched her company, she made the mistake of underpricing the hand-painted clothing she designs and sells. To determine her prices, Proudfoot says she "figured out how much I would pay for each type of clothing item. Then, I simply added $15 for my design and painting time and another $3 to cover [shipping costs]. What I soon found out, however, was that I significantly underpriced my offerings by following this approach." Only after several customers expressed amazement at her low prices did Proudfoot begin to compare her prices with competitors'. After visiting numerous stores selling similar merchandise, Proudfoot raised her prices to be more in line with those at other specialty clothing businesses. "The funny thing about this whole experience," she says, "is that my clothing items have actually sold better since I significantly raised my prices."*[10]

Entrepreneurs have three basic strategies to choose from in establishing a new product's price: penetration, skimming, and sliding down the demand curve.

Penetration. If a small business introduces a product into a highly competitive market in which a large number of similar products are competing for acceptance, the product must penetrate the market to be successful. To gain quick acceptance and extensive distribution in the mass market, a company introduces the product at a low price. In other words, it sets the price just above total unit cost to develop a wedge in the market and quickly achieve a high volume of sales. The resulting low profit margins may discourage other competitors from entering the market with similar products.

In most cases, a penetration pricing strategy is used to introduce relatively low-priced goods into a market where no elite segment and little opportunity for differentiation exist. The introduction is usually accompanied by heavy advertising and promotional techniques, special sales, and discounts. Entrepreneurs must recognize that penetration pricing is a long-range strategy; until a company achieves customer acceptance for the product, profits are likely to be small. Another danger of a penetration pricing strategy is that it attracts customers who know no brand loyalty. Companies that attract customers by offering low introductory prices must wonder what will become of their customer bases if they increase their prices or if a competitor undercuts them. "Customers who come to you strictly for price will leave you for a better price," warns one marketing expert.[11] If a penetration pricing strategy works, however, and the product achieves mass market penetration, sales volume will increase, and the company will earn adequate profits. The objective of the penetration strategy is to achieve quick access to the market in order to realize high sales volume as soon as possible.

Skimming. A skimming pricing strategy often is used when a company introduces a new product into a market with little or no competition. Sometimes a company uses this tactic when introducing a product into a competitive market that contains an elite group that is able to pay a premium price. The firm uses a higher-than-normal price in an effort to quickly recover the initial developmental and promotional costs of the product. Product development or start-up costs usually are substantial owing to intensive promotional expenses and high initial costs. The idea is to set a price well above the total unit cost and to promote the product heavily to appeal to the segment of the market that is not sensitive to price. This pricing tactic often reinforces the unique, prestigious image of a store and projects a quality picture of the product. *For instance, Cartier, the famous upscale jeweler, offers its Pasha Golf watch, which keeps both time and up to four golfers' scores for $79,300 (the watch does come with 342 diamonds, and each scorekeeping button is adorned with a different gemstone)!*[12] Another advantage of a skimming pricing strategy is that business owners can correct pricing mistakes quickly and easily. If a company sets a price that is too low under a penetration strategy, raising the price can be very difficult. But if a business using a skimming strategy sets a price too high to generate sufficient volume, it can always lower the price.

Sliding Down the Demand Curve. One variation of the skimming pricing strategy is called sliding down the demand curve. Using this tactic, the small company introduces a product at a high price. Then, technological advancements enable the firm to lower its costs quickly and to reduce the product's price sooner than its competition can. By beating other businesses in a price decline, the small company discourages competitors and, over time, becomes a high-volume producer. Computers are a prime example of a product introduced at a high price that quickly cascaded downward as companies forged important technological advances.

Sliding is a short-term pricing strategy that assumes that competition will eventually emerge. But even if no competition arises, the small business almost always lowers the product's price to attract a larger segment of the market. Yet, the initial high price contributes to a rapid return of start-up costs and generates a pool of funds to finance expansion and technological advances.

ESTABLISHED GOODS AND SERVICES

Each of the following pricing techniques can become part of the toolbox of pricing tactics entrepreneurs can use to set prices of established goods and services.

SOURCE: *The New Yorker*, July 29, 1996, p. 40.

Odd Pricing. Although studies of consumer reactions to prices are mixed and generally inconclusive, many small business managers use the technique known as **odd pricing.** They set prices that end in odd numbers (frequently 5,7,9) because they believe that an item selling for $12.95 appears to be much cheaper than an item selling for $13.00. Psychological techniques such as odd pricing are designed to appeal to certain customer interests, but their effectiveness remains to be proved.

Price Lining. Price lining is a technique that greatly simplifies the pricing function. Under this system, the manager stocks merchandise in several different price ranges or price lines. Each category of merchandise contains items that are similar in appearance, quality, cost, performance, or other features. For example, most music stores use price lines for their tapes and CDs to make it easier for customers to select items and to simplify stock planning. Most lined products appear in sets of three—good, better, and best—at prices designed to satisfy different market segment needs and incomes.

Leader Pricing. Leader pricing is a technique in which the small retailer marks down the customary price (i.e., the price consumers are accustomed to paying) of a popular item in an attempt to attract more customers. The company earns a much smaller profit on each unit because the markup is lower, but purchases of other merchandise by customers seeking the leader item often boost sales and profits. In other words, the incidental purchases that consumers make when shopping for the leader item boost sales revenue enough to offset a lower profit margin on the leader. Grocery stores frequently use leader pricing.

Another application of leader pricing that has had a powerful effect throughout the entire business is in the music industry. *Just a few years ago, megachains such as Best Buy and Circuit City began using leader pricing on CDs as bait to draw customers into their stores. The chains' primary profit centers are the big-ticket electronics items they sell, but to entice customers to come into their stores, Best Buy and Circuit City sell CDs at miniscule markups. They often sell CDs for as little as $9.99, about what most small, independent music stores pay for them at wholesale, and $2 to $3 below the average music store's prices! The electronics chains make virtually nothing on their CDs, but that is not their primary goal to begin with. The impact on music stores has been devastating. In less than two years, seven music store chains, including Camelot and Wherehouse Entertainment, have filed for bankruptcy protection. Small, independent stores are feeling the pressure too, but those that are successful are carving out niches in which to operate, such as used CDs or large collections of a particular type of music (e.g., jazz, blues, rap, bluegrass). Jack Campbell, owner of Poindexter Records in Raleigh, North Carolina, specializes in used CDs and music from offbeat, independent artists and says his store is thriving. By refusing to compete on the basis of price with a larger, more powerful rival, and emphasizing nonprice competition, Campbell believes he has found the key to success. "A store like mine flies below the corporate radar," he says. "They can open all the Best Buys they want."*[13]

Geographic Pricing. Small businesses whose pricing decisions are greatly affected by the costs of shipping merchandise to customers across a wide range of geographic regions frequently employ one of the **geographic pricing** techniques. For these companies, freight expenses constitute a substantial portion of the cost of doing business and often cut deeply into already narrow profit margins. One type of geographic pricing is **zone pricing,** in which a small company sells its merchandise at different prices to customers located in different territories. For example, a manufacturer might sell at one price to customers east of the Mississippi and at another to those west of the Mississippi. The U.S. Postal Service's parcel post charges are a good example of zone pricing. The small business must be able to show a legitimate basis (e.g., difference in selling or transportation costs) for the price discrimination or risk violating Section 2 of the Clayton Act.

Another variation of geographic pricing is the **uniform delivered pricing,** a technique in which the firm charges all of its customers the same price regardless of their location, even though the cost of selling or transporting merchandise varies. The firm calculates the proper freight charges for each region and combines them into a uniform fee. The result is that local customers subsidize the firm's charge for shipping merchandise to distant customers.

A final variation of geographic pricing is **F.O.B. factory,** in which the small company sells its merchandise to customers on the condition that they pay all shipping costs. In this way, the company can set a uniform price for its product and let each customer cover the freight costs.

Opportunistic Pricing. When products or services are in short supply, customers are willing to pay more for products they need. Some businesses use such circumstances to maximize short-term profits by engaging in price gouging. Many customers have little choice but to pay the higher prices. Opportunistic pricing may backfire, however, because customers know that a company that charges unreasonably high prices is exploiting them. *For instance, after a recent hurricane, one convenience store jacked up prices on virtually every item, selling packs of batteries for $10 each. Neighborhood residents had little choice but to pay the higher prices. After the incident, customers remembered the store's price gouging and began to shop elsewhere. The convenience store's sales never recovered.*

Discounts. Many small businesses use **discounts,** or **markdowns,** reductions from normal list prices, to move stale, outdated, damaged, or slow-moving merchandise. A seasonal dis-

IN THE FOOTSTEPS OF AN ENTREPRENEUR

What Price Success?

*A*fter she was fired from her sales job at a downtown Philadelphia bicycle courier firm, Claudia Post started her own courier service, determined to outperform her former company. Using every sales tool she knew, Post took Diamond Courier Service to the $1 million sales level in just 17 months. In Diamond's third year of operation, the company reached sales of $3.1 million. By then, Post employed 40 bike messengers and an office staff of 25 and had a large and growing base of loyal and satisfied customers. Along the way, she saw opportunities in related areas and created a total of six enterprises. In addition to the bicycle courier business, Post also owned companies that specialized in driver deliveries, truck deliveries, parts distribution, airfreight services, and a legal service that delivered subpoenas and court papers. Each business had

its own employees, manager, customer base, and pricing strategy.

Just when things seemed to be taking off, however, Post's businesses began to experience serious difficulties, careening from one cash crisis to another. "I was busy having a great time selling," she recalls. "Cash flow? Profit before taxes? I didn't know how to figure out any of that stuff." Ultimately, cash shortages became constant. By the end of the company's third year, Post was shuffling accounts payable, trying to decide which creditor to pay and when. Her response was the typical entrepreneur's solution: SELL MORE! Finally, Post knew she had to do something when the company's financial situation became so desperate that she had to resort to selling her jewelry and her personal investments to meet payroll.

Knowing she needed help—and fast—Post turned to her friend Al Sloman, a veteran consultant in the courier industry. After carefully examining the company's financial records, Sloman delivered his prognosis. "Claudia," he said, "you're headed for the rocks." Post couldn't believe it! Sales were climbing, the customer base was growing, and customers were satisfied. Outwardly, Post's businesses showed all the indications of a successful company—except there was no cash. Post remembers thinking, "Here I am with a company that's doing $3 mil-

What Post Assumed		What She Discovered	
Revenue	$4.69	Revenue	$4.69
Messenger's pay	2.35	Messenger's pay	4.23
Overhead	2.11	Overhead	5.01
Profit	$0.23	Profit (loss)	($4.55)

The items she had failed to consider in overhead and messenger's pay were:

Overhead

Dispatcher's pay (monitoring deliveries)	$0.54
Telephone charges (Bicycle messengers' calls to office)	0.14
Overhead (to cover insurance, administrative salaries, rent, insurance, and so on)	3.60
Customer service	0.57
Worker's compensation	0.09
Miscellaneous	0.07
	$5.01

Messenger's pay

Wages and commissions	$3.87
Payroll taxes	0.36
	$4.23

Post had failed to take into account details such as the disproportionate amount of time bicycle deliveries required of the dispatcher, messengers' commissions and payroll taxes, messengers' T-shirts, the costs of customer service and record keeping, and a host of other costs.

How Much Does a Bicycle Delivery Cost?

lion-plus, and I have no money. I'm working a gazillion hours a week. There's something terribly wrong here."

Sloman knew that Post understood the sales side of the courier business, but his goal was to teach her the "business" side of the business. He saw that she was operating her business from a set of reasonable but untested assumptions. One of the most basic assumptions involved pricing. Post assumed that because her prices were equivalent to her competitors' prices, the more she sold, the more money she would make. From his review of the company's financial records, Sloman suspected that Diamond was losing money on most of the deliveries it made because its prices were too low. But he needed accurate information to verify his suspicion.

The first thing Sloman and Post did was to pore over the company's work records, computer files, and financial data. They isolated each of Post's six businesses as a separate profit center and began to allocate labor, operating, and administrative costs to each one. Their goal was to build a separate income statement for each profit center. The biggest challenge they faced was allocating the indirect (i.e., overhead) cost accurately to each profit center. Sloman turned to activity-based costing to do the job because it allowed them to assign overhead costs to each center on the basis of the proportion of total company resources each used (rather than on the more conventional basis of using each center's contribution to total revenue).

As the weeks went by, Post began to see her business from a different perspective and to realize that many of the assumptions on which she had been running her company were not valid. Nowhere had her assumptions been more invalid than in her original bicycle courier business. Post had assumed that if she kept her delivery prices in line with competitors (in fact, her prices were above those of some competitors), she would have to earn a profit. She had never calculated what it actually cost her to make a delivery! "Most entrepreneurs have no idea what it really costs them to produce a product or service," says Sloman. Post figured that because her bicycle customers were some of her oldest and largest accounts, the courier business contributed handsomely to Diamond's bottom line.

She was wrong. What Post thought of as Diamond's core business actually contributed only 10 percent of the company's total revenues and was not even generating enough to cover its costs! The accompanying figure compares what Post originally thought the bicycle courier division's income statement was and what it actually was.

Post thought each delivery was generating a profit of $.23, when in reality, her delivery prices were so low that each delivery produced a *loss* of $4.55! When she saw that she would have to triple her courier prices just to earn a reasonable profit in a market where competitors' prices were as low as $3, Post decided that she had to close that business. Her decision to close the bicycle courier business became easier after she discovered that her driver- and truck-delivery divisions were highly profitable, generating an average of $6.37 per delivery in profit.

On the basis of a similar analysis of the other divisions' prices and costs, Post decided to shut them down and focus on her true profit centers. Today, Diamond is a healthy company. Post has money in the bank to weather any unexpected cash crisis. More important, Post knows *exactly* what Diamond's costs are and that its prices are appropriate. She has learned her lesson well, even though it took a brush with disaster for her to learn. "[If] you own a business, [proper financial management] is your responsibility," she says.

1. Describe the pricing mistakes that Post made with her courier service. What caused these mistakes?

2. How common are these mistakes among small business owners? Explain.

SOURCE: Adapted from Susan Greco, "Are We Making Any Money Yet?" *Inc.*, July 1996, pp. 53–61. ◆

count is a price reduction designed to encourage shoppers to purchase merchandise before an upcoming season. For instance, many retail clothiers offer special sales on winter coats in midsummer. Some firms grant purchase discounts to special groups of customers, such as senior citizens or students, to establish a faithful clientele and to generate repeat business. *For example, one small drugstore located near a state university offered a 10 percent student discount on all purchases and was quite successful in developing a large volume of student business.*

Multiple Pricing. Multiple pricing is a promotional technique that offers customers discounts if they purchase in quantity. Many products, especially those with relatively low unit value, are sold using multiple pricing. For example, instead of selling an item for 50 cents, a small company might offer 5 for $2.

Bundling. Many small businesses have discovered the marketing benefits of **bundling,** grouping together several products or services, or both, into a package that offers customers extra value at a special price. For instance, many software manufacturers bundle several computer programs (such as a word processor, spreadsheet, database, presentation graphics, and Web browser) into "suites" that offer customers a discount over purchasing the same packages separately. *One small bed and breakfast was able to boost sales significantly by offering bundles of packages with special themes to its guests. For instance, the owners offered a romance package, which included special dinners, flowers, champagne, hot-air balloon rides, massages by professional masseurs, and other special services all for one price. Another package focused on guests with outdoor interests and included guided hikes, a tour of a nearby nature conservancy, a canoeing or kayaking trip, and presentations by a local nature expert on a variety of topics.*

Suggested Retail Prices. Many manufacturers print suggested retail prices on their products or include them on invoices or in wholesale catalogs. Small business owners frequently follow these suggested retail prices because doing so eliminates the need to make a pricing decision. Nonetheless, following prices established by a distant manufacturer may create problems for the small firm. For example, a haberdasher may try to create a high-quality, exclusive image through a prestige pricing policy, but manufacturers may suggest discount outlet prices that are incompatible with the small firm's image. Another danger of accepting the manufacturer's suggested price is that it does not take into consideration the small firm's cost structure or competitive situation. A manufacturer cannot force a business to accept a suggested retail price or require a business to agree not to resell merchandise below a stated price because such practices violate the Sherman Antitrust Act and other legislation.

*7*wo Potent Pricing Forces: Image and Competition

❷ Discuss the links among pricing, image, and competition.

PRICE CONVEYS IMAGE

A company's pricing policies offer potential customers important information about its overall image (see Figure 9.1). For example, the prices charged by a posh men's clothing store reflect a completely different image from those charged by a factory outlet. Customers look at prices to determine what type of store they are dealing with. High prices frequently convey the idea of quality, prestige, and uniqueness. Accordingly, when developing a marketing approach to pricing, business owners must establish prices that are compatible with what their customers expect and are willing to pay. Too often, small business owners *underprice* their goods and services, believing that low prices are the only way they can achieve a competitive advantage. They fail to identify the extra value, convenience, service, and quality they give their customers—all things many customers are willing to pay for. These companies fall into the trap of trying to compete solely on the basis of price when they lack the sales volume—and hence, the lower costs—of their larger rivals. It is a recipe for failure.

Business owners must recognize that the prices they set for their company's goods and services send clear signals to customers about quality and value. "Customers judge the value of a product by the price when they don't have anything else to go by," says one consultant.[14] The secret to setting prices properly is based on understanding a company's target market, the customer groups at which the small company is aiming its goods or services. Target market, business image, and price are closely related. *For instance, as beers made by microbreweries have gained popularity, many of these tiny breweries now target upscale beer connoisseurs with brews at prices reminiscent of those of fine wines. For years, microbreweries have been selling all the beer they can produce at $4 to $7 per bottle, but now makers of "luxury beers" are selling their brews at 6 to 12 times that! Boon Marriage Parfait Gueze goes for $21.50 a bottle, and a three-liter bottle of Duvel goes for $75 (and is fermented three times and sold in corked, oversized bottles like champagne). Although they account for a small part of the total beer market, these microbreweries' sales are growing rapidly in an otherwise flat market.*[15]

COMPETITION AND PRICES

An important part of setting appropriate prices is tracking competitors' prices regularly; however, what the competition is charging is just one variable in the pricing mix. When setting prices, business owners should take into account their competitors' prices, but they should not automatically match or beat them. Businesses that offer customers extra quality, value, service, or convenience can charge higher prices *as long as customers recognize the "extras" they are getting. For instance, when an upscale maker of wooden jigsaw puzzles retired, Steve Richardson, CEO of Stave Puzzles, saw an opportunity to enter the puzzle business. Richardson has positioned his company to appeal to the segment of serious puzzle collectors who appreciate quality and customer service and are willing to pay for them. He offers his upscale target customers high quality puzzles made from exotic woods, customized puzzles ranging from just 44 pieces in complex puzzles with multiple solutions to 1,000 pieces in a traditional landscape scene, and lots of individual attention. Stave Puzzles' satisfied customers don't think twice about paying prices that range from $75 to $10,000 per puzzle. At those prices, these puzzles are not made for kids!*[16]

Steve Richardson, CEO of Stave Puzzles, targets upscale customers with his company's unique, high-quality jigsaw puzzles made from exotic woods. Stave's puzzles sell at prices ranging from $75 to $10,000.

Two factors are vital to studying the effects of competition on the small firm's pricing policies: the location of the competitors and the nature of the competing goods. In most cases, unless a company can differentiate the quality and the quantity of extras it provides, it must match the prices charged by nearby competitors for identical items. For example, if a self-service station charges a nickel more for a gallon of gasoline than the self-service station across the street charges, customers will simply go across the street to buy. Without the advantage of a unique business image—quality of goods sold, value of service provided, convenient location, favorable credit terms—a small company must match local competitors' prices or lose sales. Although the prices that distant competitors charge are not nearly as critical to the small business as are those of local competitors, it can be helpful to know them and to use them as reference points. Before matching any competitor's price change, however, the small business owner should consider the rival's motives. The competition may be establishing its price structure on the basis of a unique set of criteria and a totally different strategy.

The nature of competitors' goods also influences the small firm's pricing policies. The manager must recognize which products are substitutes for those he sells and then strive to keep prices in line with them. For example, the local sandwich shop should consider the hamburger restaurant, the taco shop, and the roast beef shop as competitors because they all serve fast foods. Although none of them offer the identical menu of the sandwich shop, they're all competing for the same quick-meal dollar. Of course, if a company can differentiate its product by creating a distinctive image in the consumer's mind, it may be able to set higher prices for its food. "Your price differential should not be more than 5 percent higher or lower than competitors, unless you are offering a value-added service," advises the head of a management consulting firm.[17]

In general, the small business manager should avoid head-to-head price competition with other firms that can more easily achieve lower prices through lower cost structures. Most locally owned drugstores cannot compete with the prices of large national drug chains. However, many local drugstores operate successfully by using nonprice competition; these stores offer more personal service, free delivery, credit sales, and other extras that the chains have eliminated. Nonprice competition can be an effective strategy for a small business in the face of larger, more powerful enterprises, especially because there are many dangers in experimenting with prices. For instance, price shifts cause fluctuations in sales volume that the small firm many not be able to tolerate. Also, frequent price changes may damage the company's image and its customer relations.

One of the deadliest games a small business can get into with competitors is a price war. Price wars can eradicate companies' profit margins and scar an entire industry for years.

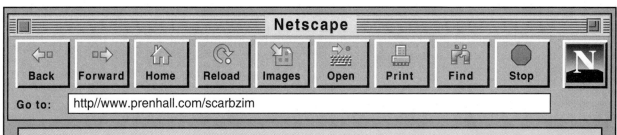

Go to: http//www.prenhall.com/scarbzim

WIRED TO THE WEB

(HOME) MADE FOR THE WEB

*F*or years, people had been telling Sasha and Seth Dowager that they should package and sell their brownies. Based on a recipe their grandmother had developed, the brownies were the hit of every party and social event in their small Midwestern town. After both Sasha and Seth had graduated from college and had gotten established in their careers, they opened a brownie business. Sasha and Seth baked brownies in Sasha's kitchen in the evenings and on weekends to supply local demand for their product. They sold their brownies at fairs, festivals, and other events that attracted customers from the surrounding area. As a result, their business began to earn greater notoriety and name recognition across the region. Their orders skyrocketed after a local television celebrity did a story on their brownies.

Within a year of the television program, Sasha and Seth had quit their jobs to devote their time and energy to developing their brownie business. They renamed the company Grandma's Brownies and moved into a new location where they set up all of the equipment they needed to turn out their brownies in greater quantities. The site they chose was strategically situated in a refurbished historic district with a good mix of retail and service businesses and professional offices. The volume of traffic in their store was enough to generate a solid profit in the first year of business.

Nearing the end of their second year of operation, Sasha and Seth see the potential to expand their business. Their product has a following of loyal customers in local communities, and the Dowagers have employees set up booths at fairs and festivals. The primary issue they face is how to expand the market for their product. Seth and Sasha have considered developing a mail-order catalog, but they have no mailing list.

They know that they can rent or buy lists, but as Sasha points out, "The risks there are just too big. Based on what I've read, a *successful* mail-order campaign is one that pulls orders in from just 2 percent of its target. There's got to be a better way."

Seth and Sasha are seriously considering building a page on the World Wide Web from which to sell their brownies. "Before we build a Web site, we've got to develop our Web marketing strategy," says Seth.

"That's true," agrees Sasha. "For instance, how much should we charge? We know it costs us 21 cents to make a brownie that we sell in our store, but what about shipping costs? Plus, customers on the Web aren't likely to order just *one* brownie. What kind of packages should we offer?"

"What price will best support our high-quality, home-made image?" adds Seth.

"What do other companies that sell brownies on the Web do?" Sasha wonders aloud. "Before we launch into this venture, we need to do our homework, Seth."

1. Use the resources of the World Wide Web to help Sasha and Seth conduct some basic market research on competitors who are selling brownies over the Web. (You may find it helpful to review the "Gaining the Competitive Edge," feature titled "Designing a Killer Website" in chapter 6 first.) Develop a chart that shows all the competitors you find, their prices, their competitive edge, and any other relevant marketing information you discover. Include a column in your chart that rates the quality of each company's Web site on a 1 (low) to 10 (high) scale.
2. Use the information gathered in question 1 to recommend a pricing strategy to the Dowagers. What factors should they consider when establishing prices for their brownies?
3. On the basis of the characteristics of the Web sites you discovered, write a one-page memo to Sasha and Seth with your recommendations for designing an effective Web site.

CHAPTER 10 PRICING FOR PROFIT 317

"Many entrepreneurs cut prices to the point of unprofitability just to compete," says one business writer. "In doing so, they open the door to catastrophe. Less revenue often translates into lower quality, poorer service, sloppier salesmanship, weaker customer loyalty, and financial disaster."[18] Price wars usually begin when one competitor thinks it can achieve higher volume instantaneously by lowering prices. Rather than sticking to their strategic guns, competitors believe they must follow suit.

For instance, when a large national office supply chain opened a store only a block away from The King Group, a small office-product store in New York City, CEO Robert Gillon Jr. wisely decided not to get into a price war with the larger, more powerful rival. Instead, Gillon focused on retaining his company's customers by dramatically improving the company's efficiency and offering products and services customers could not get at the chain store. By working in partnership with a supplier, the King Group restructured its distribution system, making it much faster and more efficient and enabling the store to offer same- and next-day delivery service. The King Group also introduced a complete line of products such as executive gifts and stationery that its larger rival did not sell. Finally, Gillon and his team established a set of 12 daily measurements to track the level of quality and customer service the company provides. Rather than try to sell strictly on the basis of price, the King Group focused on serving its customers' needs more effectively. The result: competitive prices, more satisfied customers, and climbing sales and profits![19]

Entrepreneurs usually overestimate the power of price cuts. Sales volume rarely rises enough to offset the lower profit margins of a lower price. *In an attempt to jump-start sales, McDonald's rolled out with much fanfare "Campaign 55," in which it planned to lower to 55 cents the price of a different sandwich each month. The 55 cent price was a throwback to the prices in 1955, the year McDonald's was founded. The company kicked off the campaign by selling Big Macs (which cost around 40 cents to make) for 55 cents and hoped to increase store traffic and boost sales on other menu items enough to offset the lower margin on the sandwich. Unfortunately, the increased traffic never materialized and same-store sales fell 6 percent from the year before. In less than two months, McDonald's abandoned the promotion.[20]*

In a price war, a company may cut its prices so severely that it is impossible to achieve the volume necessary to offset the lower profit margins. "If you have a 25 percent gross [profit] margin, and . . . you cut your price 10 percent, you have to roughly triple your sales volume just to break even," says one management consultant.[21] Even when price cuts work, their effects often are temporary. Customers lured by the lowest price usually have almost no loyalty to a business. The lesson: The best way to survive a price war is to stay out of it by emphasizing the unique features, benefits, and value your company offers its customers!

The underlying forces that dictate how a business prices its goods or services vary greatly among industries. In many instances, the nature of the business itself has unique factors that determine a firm's pricing strategy. The next three sections will investigate pricing techniques used in retailing, manufacturing, and service firms.

*P*ricing Techniques for Retailers

3 Explain the pricing techniques used by retailers.

As retail customers have become more price conscious, retailers have changed their pricing strategies to emphasize value. This value-price relationship allows for a wide variety of highly creative pricing and marketing practices. Delivering high levels of recognized value in products and services is one key to retail customer loyalty. To justify paying a higher price than those charged by competitors, customers must perceive a company's products or services as giving them greater value.

MARKUP

The basic premise of a successful business operation is selling a good or service for more than it costs to produce it. The difference between the cost of a product or service and its selling price is called **markup** (or **markon**). Markup can be expressed in dollars or as a percentage of either cost or selling price:

$$\text{Dollar markup} = \text{Retail price} - \text{Cost of the merchandise}$$

$$\text{Percentage (of retail price) markup} = \frac{\text{Dollar markup}}{\text{Retail price}}$$

$$\text{Percentage (of cost) markup} = \frac{\text{Dollar markup}}{\text{Cost of unit}}$$

For example, if a man's shirt costs $15, and the manager plans to sell it for $25, markup would be as follows:

$$\text{Dollar markup} = \$25 - \$15 = \$10$$

$$\text{Percentage (of retail price) markup} = \frac{\$10}{\$25}$$

$$= 0.40 = 40\%$$

$$\text{Percentage (of cost) markup} = \frac{\$10}{\$15}$$

$$= 0.6667 = 66.67\%$$

The cost of merchandise used in computing markup includes not only the wholesale price of the merchandise but also any incidental costs (e.g., selling or transportation charges) that the retailer incurs and a profit minus any discounts (quantity, cash) that the wholesaler offers.

Once business owners have a financial plan in place, including sales estimates and anticipated expenses, they can compute the firm's initial markup. The **initial markup** is the *average* markup required on all merchandise to cover the cost of the items, all incidental expenses, and a reasonable profit:

$$\text{Initial dollar markup} = \frac{\text{Operating expenses} + \text{Reductions} + \text{Profits}}{\text{Net sales} + \text{Reductions}}$$

Operating expenses are the cost of doing business, such as rent, utilities, and depreciation; reductions include employee and customer discounts, markdowns, special sales, and the cost of stockouts. For example, if a small retailer forecasts sales of $380,000, expenses of $140,000, and $24,000 in reductions, and she expects a profit of $38,000, the initial markup percentage will be:

$$\text{Initial markup percentage} = \frac{\$140,000 + \$24,000 + \$38,000}{\$380,000 + \$24,000}$$

$$= 50\%$$

This retailer thus knows that an average markup of 50 percent is required to cover costs and generate an adequate profit.

Some businesses use a standard markup on all of their merchandise. This technique, which is usually used in retail stores carrying related products, applies a standard percentage markup to all merchandise. Most stores find it much more practical to use a flexible markup, which assigns various markup percentages to different types of products. Because of the wide range of prices and types of merchandise they sell, department stores frequently rely on a flexible markup. It would be impractical for them to use a standard markup on all items because they have such a divergent cost and volume range. For instance, the markup percentage for socks is not likely to be suitable as a markup for washing machines.

Once owners determine the desired markup percentage, they can compute the appropriate retail price. Knowing that the markup of a particular item represents 40 percent of the retail price:

$$\text{Cost} = \text{Retail price} - \text{Markup}$$

$$= 100\% - 40\%$$

$$= 60\% \text{ of retail price}$$

and assuming that the cost of the item is $18.00, the retailer can rearrange the percentage (of retail price) markup formula:

$$\text{Retail price} = \frac{\text{Dollar cost}}{\text{Percentage cost}}$$

Solving for retail price, the retailer computes a price of the following:

$$\text{Retail price} = \frac{\$18.00}{0.60} = \$30.00$$

Thus, the owner establishes a retail price of $30.00 for the item using a 40 percent markup.

Finally, retailers must verify that the computed retail price is consistent with their planned initial markup percentage. Will it cover costs and generate the desired profit? Is it congruent with the firm's overall price image? Is the final price in line with the company's strategy? Is it within an acceptable price range? How does it compare with the prices charged by competitors? And, perhaps most important, are the customers willing and able to pay this price? Figure 10.2 illustrates the concept of markup by showing the price breakdown on a common item, a concert T-shirt.

FOLLOW-THE-LEADER PRICING

Some small companies make no effort to be price leaders in their immediate geographic areas and simply follow the prices that their competitors establish. Managers wisely monitor their competitors' pricing policies and individual prices by reviewing their advertisements or by hiring part-time or full-time comparison shoppers. But then these retailers use this information to establish a "me too" pricing policy, which eradicates any opportunity to create a special price image for their businesses. Although many retailers must match competitors' prices on identical items, maintaining a follow-the-leader pricing policy may not be healthy for a small business because it robs the company of the opportunity to create a distinctive image in its customers' eyes.

BELOW-MARKET PRICING

Some small businesses choose to create a discount image in the market by offering goods at below-market prices. By setting prices below those of their competitors, these firms hope to attract a sufficient level of volume to offset the lower profit margins. Many retailers using a

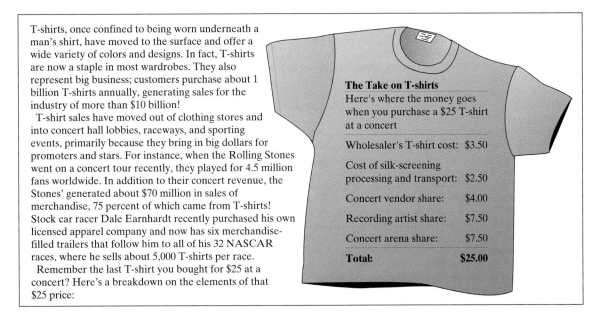

T-shirts, once confined to being worn underneath a man's shirt, have moved to the surface and offer a wide variety of colors and designs. In fact, T-shirts are now a staple in most wardrobes. They also represent big business; customers purchase about 1 billion T-shirts annually, generating sales for the industry of more than $10 billion!

T-shirt sales have moved out of clothing stores and into concert hall lobbies, raceways, and sporting events, primarily because they bring in big dollars for promoters and stars. For instance, when the Rolling Stones went on a concert tour recently, they played for 4.5 million fans worldwide. In addition to their concert revenue, the Stones' generated about $70 million in sales of merchandise, 75 percent of which came from T-shirts! Stock car racer Dale Earnhardt recently purchased his own licensed apparel company and now has six merchandise-filled trailers that follow him to all of his 32 NASCAR races, where he sells about 5,000 T-shirts per race.

Remember the last T-shirt you bought for $25 at a concert? Here's a breakdown on the elements of that $25 price:

The Take on T-shirts

Here's where the money goes when you purchase a $25 T-shirt at a concert

Wholesaler's T-shirt cost:	$3.50
Cost of silk-screening processing and transport:	$2.50
Concert vendor share:	$4.00
Recording artist share:	$7.50
Concert arena share:	$7.50
Total:	**$25.00**

Figure 10.2 Price Breakdown of a $25 Concert T-shirt SOURCE: Dan McGraw, "Dressing Down for Dollars," *U.S. News & World Report*, May 13, 1996, pp. 64–65.

below-market pricing strategy eliminate most of the extra services that their above-market-pricing competitors offer. For instance, these businesses trim operating costs by cutting out services such as delivery, installation, credit granting, and sales assistance. Below-market pricing strategies can be risky for small companies because they require them to constantly achieve high sales volume to remain competitive.

Pricing Techniques for Manufacturers

4 Explain the pricing techniques used by manufacturers.

For manufacturers, the pricing decision requires the support of accurate, timely accounting records. The most commonly used pricing technique for manufacturers is cost-plus pricing. Using this method, manufacturers establish a price composed of direct materials, direct labor, factory overhead, selling and administrative costs, plus the desired profit margin.

The main advantage of the cost-plus pricing method is its simplicity. Given the proper cost accounting data, computing a product's final selling price is relatively easy. Also, because it adds a profit onto the top of the firm's costs, the manufacturer is guaranteed the desired profit margin. This process, however, does not encourage the manufacturer to use its resources efficiently. Even if the company fails to use its resources in the most effective manner, it will still earn a reasonable profit, and thus, there is no motivation to conserve resources in the manufacturing process. Finally, because manufacturers' cost structures vary so greatly, cost-plus pricing fails to consider the competition sufficiently. But, despite its drawbacks, the cost-plus method of establishing prices remains prominent in many industries such as construction and printing.

DIRECT COSTING AND PRICE FORMULATION

One requisite for a successful pricing policy in manufacturing is a reliable cost accounting system that can generate timely reports to determine the costs of processing raw materials into finished goods. The traditional method of product costing is called **absorption costing** because all manufacturing and overhead costs are absorbed into the finished product's total cost. Absorption costing includes direct materials and direct labor, plus a portion of fixed and variable factory overhead costs, in each unit manufactured. Full-absorption financial statements, used in published annual reports and in tax reports, are very useful in performing financial analysis. But full-absorption statements are of little help to a manufacturer when determining prices or the impact of price changes.

A more useful technique for managerial decision making is **variable** (or **direct**) **costing,** in which the cost of the products manufactured includes only those costs that vary directly with the quantity produced. In other words, variable costing encompasses direct materials, direct labor, and factory overhead costs that vary with the level of the firm's output of finished goods. Factory overhead costs that are fixed (for instance rent, depreciation, insurance) are *not* included in the costs of finished items. Instead, they are considered to be expenses of the period.

A manufacturer's goal in establishing prices is to discover the cost combination of selling price and sales volume that exceeds the variable costs of producing a product and contributes enough to cover fixed costs and earn a profit. The problem with using full-absorption costing is that it clouds the true relationships among price, volume, and costs by including fixed expenses in unit cost. Using a direct-costing basis yields a constant unit cost of the product no matter what the volume of production is. The result is a clearer picture of the price-volume-costs relationship.

The starting point for establishing product prices is the direct-cost income statement. As Table 10.1 indicates, the direct-cost statement yields the same net profit as does the full-absorption income statement. The only difference between the two statements is the format. The full-absorption statement allocates costs such as advertising, rent, and utilities according to the activity that caused them, but the direct-cost income statement separates expenses into fixed and variable costs. Fixed expenses remain constant regardless of the production level, but variable expenses fluctuate according to production volume.

When variable costs are subtracted from total revenues, the result is the manufacturer's **contribution margin,** the amount remaining that contributes to covering fixed expenses and earning a profit. Expressing this contribution margin as a percentage of total revenue yields the firm's contribution percentage. Computing the contribution percentage is a critical step in establishing prices through the direct-costing method. This manufacturer's contribution percentage is 36.5 percent, which is calculated as:

$$\text{Contribution percentage} = 1 - \frac{\text{Variable expenses}}{\text{Revenues}}$$

$$= 1 - \frac{\$502,000}{\$790,000} = 36.5\%$$

COMPUTING A BREAK-EVEN SELLING PRICE

A manufacturer's contribution percentage tells what portion of total revenues remains after covering variable costs to contribute toward meeting fixed expenses and earning a profit. This manufacturer's contribution percentage is 36.5 percent, which means that variable costs absorb 63.5 percent of total revenues. In other words, variable costs represent 63.5 percent $(1.00 - 0.365 = 0.635)$ of the product's selling price. Suppose that this manufacturer's variable costs include the following:

Material	$2.08/unit
Direct labor	$4.12/unit
Variable factory overhead	$0.78/unit
Total variable cost	$6.98/unit

Table 10.1 A Full-Absorption versus a Direct Cost Income Statement

Full-Absorption Income Statement

Revenues		$790,000
Cost of goods sold:		
Materials	250,500	
Direct labor	190,200	
Factory overhead	120,200	560,900
Gross Profit		229,100
Operating expenses:		
General & administrative	66,100	
Selling	112,000	
Other	11,000	
Total Expenses		189,100
Net Profit (before taxes)		$ 40,000

Direct Cost Income Statement

Revenues (100%)		$790,000
Variable costs:		
Materials	250,500	
Direct labor	190,200	
Variable factory overhead	13,200	
Variable selling expenses	48,100	
Total Variable Costs (63.54%)		502,000
Contribution Margin (36.46%)		288,000
Fixed Costs		
Fixed factory overhead	107,000	
Fixed selling expenses	63,900	
General & administrative	66,100	
Other	11,000	
Total Fixed Costs		248,000
Net Profit (before taxes)		$ 40,000

The minimum price at which the manufacturer would sell the item is $6.98. Any price below that would *not* cover variable costs. To compute the break-even selling price for this product, find the selling price using the following equation:

$$\text{Profit} = \frac{\left(\begin{array}{c}\text{Selling} \\ \text{price}\end{array} \times \begin{array}{c}\text{Quantity} \\ \text{produced}\end{array}\right) + \left(\begin{array}{c}\text{Variable cost} \\ \text{per unit}\end{array} \times \begin{array}{c}\text{Quantity} \\ \text{produced}\end{array}\right) + \begin{array}{c}\text{Total} \\ \text{fixed cost}\end{array}}{\text{Quantity produced}}$$

which becomes:

$$\text{Break-even selling price} = \frac{\text{Profit} + \left(\begin{array}{c}\text{Variable cost} \\ \text{per unit}\end{array} \times \begin{array}{c}\text{Quantity} \\ \text{produced}\end{array}\right) + \begin{array}{c}\text{Total} \\ \text{fixed cost}\end{array}}{\text{Quantity produced}}$$

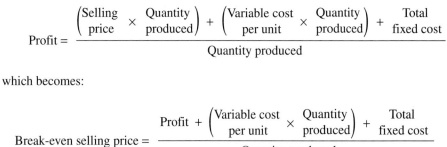

A Different Perspective on Pricing

*F*or many years, U.S. companies have sought to emulate the Japanese approach to quality. Now, from across the Pacific comes Japan's unique approach to pricing, and with it, a cost management system that stands conventional thinking on its head. The methods are simple and very effective, encouraging companies to design and build new products in the shortest time possible and at the lowest possible cost.

The typical U.S. company researching and developing a new product designs the product first and then estimates the cost to determine the final price. If the cost and the resulting price are too high, the product goes back to the drawing board for revisions, delaying the introduction of the new product. The Japanese approach, however, is to start with a target cost for the product based on the price most customers

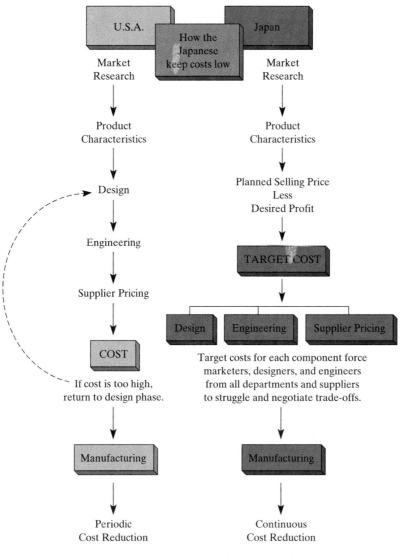

The target cost is the key, and it's based on the price that is most likely to appeal to buyers minus the desired profit. "Cost engineers" make sure the product meets that target. Western companies more often design the product, calculate the cost, and then try to figure out whether it will sell.

are likely to accept; then, designers and manufacturers engineer the product to meet that target price.

The Japanese system focuses on pinning down the key cost elements of the product in the planning and design stage. This concept is central to the entire process because that's the point at which practically all subsequent costs of the product are built in, from manufacturing to service. Careful planning and coordination in this phase mean lower costs and better cost control further down the manufacturing pipeline.

Rather than depending on the disjointed efforts in various departments, the Japanese approach relies on a team of workers from a wide variety of disciplines to bring a new product idea to market. The team researches the market to come up with the product's target price. From this crucial decision, all else follows. After deducting the desired profit from the target sales price, the team of planners develops cost estimates for each element of the product: design and engineering, raw materials, manufacturing, sales, and marketing. The team treats every part or function as a component and assigns each one a part of the total cost. "This is where the battle begins," says one Japanese manager. The Japanese use the word *tataku*, which means "to beat down," to describe the battle over costs with their suppliers. The battle is an intense negotiation process between the company and outside suppliers to push down costs to meet the overall target cost. Initially, the sum of the components' cost estimates may exceed the overall target price, but by the time the battle is over, the team usually is within striking distance of the original target.

The accompanying figure summarizes the dramatic differences between the pricing approaches used by Japan and the United States (and other Western nations). The contrast is striking. "U.S. companies design a product by throwing it over the wall from one department to another—from engineering, to marketing, and so on," says one manufacturing expert. "At the end of the design phase, after something like 85 percent of the product's costs have been built in, the specifications are given to the accountants, who tell you what the product will cost." The system makes no allowance for what the product should cost. One Harvard business professor says, "We tend to build up a model of the product, determine what it's going to cost, and then ask whether we can sell it for that. The Japanese turn it around. They say, 'It's got to sell for X. Let's work backwards to make sure we can achieve it.'" The resulting difference is that the Western pricing model tends to maintain the status quo; the Japanese approach, however, strives for continuous improvement, pushing costs and prices down. Their system encourages managers to view a product's price from a broad, strategic perspective and always with an eye on the customer.

---

1. What are the key differences between the U.S. and Japanese companies' approaches to pricing new products?

2. What advantages does the Japanese system offer? Disadvantages?

3. What kinds of changes in their management systems would U.S. companies have to make to implement the Japanese pricing approach successfully?

SOURCE: Adapted from Ford S. Worthy, "Japan's Smart New Secret Weapon," *Fortune*, August 12, 1990, pp. 72–75. ◆

To break even, the manufacturer assumes $0 profit. Suppose that its plans are to produce 50,000 units of the product and that fixed costs will be $110,000. The break-even selling price is as follows:

$$\text{Break-even selling price} = \frac{\$0 + (\$6.98/\text{unit} \times 50,000 \text{ units}) + \$110,000}{50,000 \text{ units}}$$

$$= \frac{\$459,000}{50,000 \text{ units}}$$

$$= \$9.18/\text{unit}$$

Thus, $2.20 ($9.18/unit − $6.98/unit) of the $9.18 break-even price goes toward meeting fixed production costs. But suppose the manufacturer wants to earn a $50,000 profit. Then the required selling price is:

$$\text{Selling price} = \frac{\$50,000 + (\$6.98/\text{unit} \times 50,000 \text{ units}) + \$110,000}{50,000 \text{ units}}$$

$$= \frac{\$509,000}{50,000 \text{ units}}$$

$$= \$10.18/\text{unit}$$

Now the manufacturer must decide whether customers will purchase 50,000 units at $10.18. If it thinks they won't, it must decide either to produce a different, more profitable product or to lower the selling price by lowering either its cost or its profit target. Any price above $9.18 will generate some profit, although less than that desired. In the short run, the manufacturer could sell the product for less than $9.18 if competitive factors so dictate, but not below $6.98 because a price below $6.98 would not cover the variable costs of production.

Because the manufacturer's capacity in the short run is fixed, pricing decisions should be aimed at using its resources most efficiently. The fixed cost of operating the plant cannot be avoided, and the variable costs can be eliminated only if the firm ceases to offer the product. Therefore, the selling price must be at least equal to the variable costs (per unit) of making the product. Any price above that amount contributes to covering fixed costs and providing a reasonable profit.

Of course, over the long run, the manufacturer cannot sell below total costs and continue to survive. So selling price must cover total product costs—both fixed and variable—and generate a reasonable profit.

5. Explain the pricing techniques used by service firms.

$\mathcal{P}$ricing Techniques for Service Firms

Service businesses must establish their prices on the basis of the materials used to provide the service, the labor employed, an allowance for overhead, and a profit. As in a manufacturing operation, a service firm must have a reliable, accurate accounting system to keep a tally of the total costs of providing the service. Most service firms base their prices on an hourly rate, usually the actual number of hours required to perform the service. Some companies, however, base their fees on a standard number of hours, determined by the average number of hours needed to perform the service. For most firms, labor and materials constitute the largest portion of the cost of the service. To establish a reasonable, profitable price for service, the small business owner must know the cost of materials, direct labor, and overhead for each unit of service. Using these basic cost data and a desired profit margin, the owner of the small service firm can determine the appropriate price for the service.

Consider a simple example for pricing a common service—television repair. Ned's TV Repair Shop uses the direct-costing method to prepare an income statement for exercising managerial control (see Table 10.2). Ned estimates that he and his employees spend about 12,800 hours in the actual production of television repair service. So total cost per productive hour for Ned's TV Repair Shop comes to the following:

$$\text{Total cost per hour} = \frac{\$172,000}{12,800 \text{ hours}} = \$13.44/\text{hour}$$

Now Ned must add in an amount for his desired profit. He expects a net operating profit margin of 18 percent on sales. To compute the final price he uses this equation:

$$\text{Price per hour} = \text{Total cost per productive hour} \times \frac{1.00}{(1.00 - \text{Net profit target as \% of sales})}$$

$$= \$13.44 \times 1.219$$

$$= \$16.38/\text{hour}$$

Table 10.2 Direct Cost Income Statement, Ned's TV Repair Shop

Sales Revenue		$199,000
Variable Expenses:		
Labor	52,000	
Materials	40,500	
Variable factor overhead	11,500	
Total	104,000	
Fixed Expenses:		
Rent	2,500	
Salaries	38,500	
Fixed overhead	27,000	
Total	68,000	
Total Costs		172,000
Net Income		$ 27,000

A price of $16.38 per hour will cover Ned's costs and generate the desired profit. Smart service shop owners compute the cost per production hour at regular intervals throughout the year because they know that rising costs can eat into their profit margins very quickly. Rapidly rising labor costs and materials prices dictate that the service firm's price per hour be computed even more frequently. As in the case of the retailer and the manufacturer, Ned must evaluate the pricing policies of competitors and decide whether his price is consistent with his firm's image.

Of course, the price of $16.38 per hour assumes that all jobs require the same amount of materials. If this is not a valid assumption, Ned must recompute the price per hour without including the cost of materials:

$$\text{Cost per productive hour} = \frac{172,000 - 40,500}{12,800 \text{ hours}}$$

$$= \$10.27/\text{hour}$$

Adding in the desired 18 percent net operating profit on sales yields:

$$\text{Price per hour} = \$10.27/\text{hour} \times \frac{1.00}{(1.00 - 0.18)}$$

$$= \$10.27/\text{hour} \times 1.219$$

$$= \$12.52/\text{hour}$$

Under these conditions Ned would charge $12.52 per hour plus the actual cost of materials used and any markup on the cost of materials. For instance, a repair job that takes four hours to complete would have the following price:

Cost of service (4 hours × 12.52/hour)	$50.08
Cost of materials	$21.00
Markup on materials	$ 2.10
Total price	$73.18

*T*he Impact of Credit on Pricing

The pricing of goods and services must take into account how the business will be paid. The straight exchange of cash for goods or services is becoming a thing of the past.

Modern consumers crave convenience when they shop, and one of the most common conveniences they demand is the ability to purchase goods and services on credit. Small businesses that fail to offer customers credit will lose sales to their competitors who do. Yet companies that do sell on credit incur additional expenses for offering this convenience. Most merchants, however, believe that the benefits far outweigh the added costs. Small companies have three options for selling to customers on credit: credit cards, installment credit, and trade credit.

CREDIT CARDS

Credit cards are a popular method of payment among customers. Approximately 70 percent of the U.S. adult population uses credit cards to make purchases, and 36 percent of consumer debt is credit-card debt.[22] There are more than 1 billion credit cards in circulation in the United States, an average of about four cards per person! Customers use credit cards to pay for $28 out of every $100 spent on consumable goods and services.[23] One recent study found that accepting credit cards increases the probability, speed, and magnitude of customer spending. In addition, surveys show that customers rate businesses offering credit options higher on key performance measures such as reputation, reliability, and service.[24] In short, accepting credit cards broadens a small company's customer base and closes sales it would normally lose if customers had to pay in cash.

Business owners cite the following advantages of accepting credit cards:

◆ Customers prefer to carry credit cards instead of cash for the sake of both convenience and safety.

◆ Credit card users are more likely to spend and to spend in higher amounts than nonusers.

◆ Accepting credit cards enhances a business's image.

◆ Businesses that fail to display that they accept credit cards (even when they might) lose revenues because customers are too embarrassed to ask and simply leave without buying.

◆ Customers rate businesses offering credit higher on key performance measures than those that do not (see Table 10.3).

Table 10.3 Customer Credit and Perceptions of Businesses

Customers' Perceptions	Cash-Only Stores ($)	Cash-and-Credit Stores (%)	No Difference (%)
Better overall reputation	8.0	62.8	36.4
Better merchandise variety	3.8	35.8	60.4
Generally more reliable	1.4	59.7	38.9
Easier to return merchandise	3.1	75.7	21.2
Easier to resolve complaints	3.1	76.5	20.4

Source: Richard J. Maturi, "Charging Ahead," *Entrepreneur*, July 1990, p. 56. Reprinted with permission from *Entrepreneur* magazine.

The convenience of credit cards is not free to business owners, however. Companies must pay to use the system, typically 1 to 6 percent of the company's total credit card charges, which they must factor into the prices of their products or services. They also pay a transaction fee of 5 to 50 cents per charge and must purchase or lease equipment to process transactions. Given customer expectations, small businesses find it difficult to refuse major cards, even when the big card companies raise the fees that merchants must pay. Fees operate on a multistep process. On a $100 Visa or MasterCard purchase at a typical business, a processing bank buys the credit card slip from the retailer for $97.44. Then, that bank sells the slip to the bank that issued the card for about $98.80. The remaining $1.20 discount is called the interchange fee, which is what the processing bank passes along to the issuing bank. Before it can accept credit cards, a business must obtain merchant status from either a bank or an independent sales organization (ISO). The accompanying Gaining the Competitive Edge feature describes how a small company can obtain merchant status.

More small businesses also are equipping their stores to handle debit-card transactions, which act as electronic checks, automatically deducting the purchase amount from a customer's checking account. The equipment is easy to install and to set up, and the cost to the company is negligible. The payoff can be big, however, in the form of increased sales. "How can you possibly lose when you're offering customers another avenue for purchasing merchandise?" asks Mark Knauff, who recently installed a debit-card terminal in his guitar shop.[25]

INSTALLMENT CREDIT

Small companies that sell big-ticket consumer durables—major appliances, cars, and boats—frequently rely on installment credit. Because very few customers can purchase such items in a single lump-sum payment, small businesses finance them over an extended time. The time horizon may range from just a few months up to 30 or more years. Most companies require the customer to make an initial down payment for the merchandise and then finance the balance for the life of the loan. The customer repays the loan principal plus interest on the loan. One advantage of installment loans for a small business is that the owner retains a security interest as collateral on the loan. If the customer defaults on the loan, the owner still holds the title to the merchandise. Because installment credit absorbs a small company's cash, many rely on financial institutions such as banks and credit unions to provide the installment credit. When a business has the financial strength to "carry its own paper," the interest income from the installment loan contract often yields more than the initial profit on the sale of the product. For some businesses, such as furniture stores, this has traditionally been a major source of income.

TRADE CREDIT

Companies that sell small-ticket items frequently offer their customers trade credit; that is, they create customer charge accounts. The typical small business bills its credit customers each month. To speed collections, some offer cash discounts if customers pay their balances early; others impose penalties on late payers. Before deciding to use credit as a competitive weapon, the small business owner must make sure that the firm's cash position is strong enough to support that additional pressure.

For manufacturers and wholesalers, trade credit is traditional. Chapter 8 showed how the potential problems of being unable to adequately control the amount of accounts payable outstanding is a major cause of lost profitability and even total failure. In reality, trade credit is a two-edged sword. Small businesses must be willing to grant credit to purchasers in order to get, and keep, their business; they must work extremely hard, and often be very tough, with debtors who do not pay as they agreed to.

GAINING THE COMPETITIVE EDGE

How to Obtain Merchant Status

*A*cquiring merchant status enables a small business to accept credit-card payments for goods and services. Offering customers the convenience of paying with credit cards enhances a company's reputation and translates directly into higher sales. Qualifying for merchant status is not easy for many small companies, however, because banks view it in the same manner as making a loan to a business. "When we give you the ability to accept credit cards," explains one banker, "we are giving you the use of funds before we get them." Although small storefront businesses with short operating histories may have difficulty qualifying for merchant status, home-based businesses and mail-order companies or entrepreneurs doing business over the World Wide Web typically have the greatest difficulty convincing banks to set them up with credit-card accounts. For instance, when Steve and Shelly Bloom, owners of Crystal Collection, a small glass art importer, applied for merchant status, their bank denied their request because their company is home-based. The Blooms turned to an independent sales organization (ISO) the bank recommended, and the ISO helped them get merchant status through another bank. Because their business represents a higher-than-normal risk to credit-card-issuing banks, the Blooms pay higher fees than small storefront companies. Their fees include either 2.5 percent of their monthly credit-card transactions or $25 (whichever is higher), a 20 cent per transaction handling fee, a $15 monthly fee, and $32 per month to rent the point-of-sale terminal to process credit-card transactions.

What can business owners do to increase their chances of gaining merchant status so that they can accept customers' credit cards without driving their costs sky high? Try these tips:

◆ *Recognize that business start-ups and companies that have been in business less than three years face the greatest obstacles to getting merchant status.* Entrepreneurs just starting out in business should consider applying for merchant status when they approach a bank for start-up capital. Existing companies can boost their chances of success by preparing a package to present to the bank—credit references, financial statements, business description, and an overview of the company's marketing plan, including a detailed customer profile.

◆ *Apply with your own bank first.* The best place to begin the application process is with your own bank. "When we look at an application," says one banker, "we consider three critical things: the principal, the product, and the process. In other words, we need to know about you, what you are selling, and how you are selling it." If your banker cannot set up a credit-card account for your business, ask for a referral to an ISO that might be interested.

◆ *Know what information the bank or ISO is looking for and be prepared to provide it.* Before granting merchant status, banks and ISOs want to make sure that a business is a good credit risk. Treat the application process in the same way you would an application for a loan—because, in essence, it *is.* In addition to the package mentioned above, business owners should be able to estimate their companies' credit-card volume and their average transaction size.

◆ *Make sure you understand the costs involved.* When merchants accept credit cards, they do not receive the total amount of the sale; they must pay a transaction charge to the bank. Costs typically include start-up fees ranging from $50 to $200; transaction fees of 5 cents to 50 cents per purchase; the discount rate, which is a percentage of the actual sales amount and usually ranges from 1 to 6 percent; monthly statement fees of $4 to $20; equipment rental or purchase costs, which can range from $250 to $1,500 or more; and miscellaneous fees. Because the cost of accepting credit cards can be substantial, business owners must be sure that accepting them will produce valuable benefits.

◆ *Shop around.* Too often, business owners take the first deal offered them, only to regret it later. "One of the problems is that merchants are forced by society to give people credit, and they get panicky if they can't take credit cards," says one expert. "So they make a pact with the devil and don't do their due diligence before signing [the merchant status agreement]."

◆ *Have a knowledgeable attorney look over your contract before you sign it.* Otherwise, you may not discover clauses that work a hardship on your business until it's too late.

Accepting credit cards is not important for every business, but for those whose customers expect that convenience, acquiring merchant status can spell the difference between making a sale and losing it.

1. Use the World Wide Web to research how businesses on the Web conduct credit-card transactions. How do they secure the privacy of these transactions?

SOURCES: Adapted from Johanna S. Billings, "Taking Charge," *Business Start-Ups*, November 1997, pp. 16–18; Lin Grensing-Pophal, "Let Them Use Plastic," *Business Start-Ups*, May 1996, pp. 16–18; Cynthia E. Griffin, "Charging Ahead," *Entrepreneur*, April 1997, pp. 54–57; Frances Cerra Whittelsey, "The Minefield of Merchant Status," *Nation's Business*, January 1997, pp. 38–40.

Chapter Summary

❶ Describe effective pricing techniques for both new and existing products and services.

- Pricing a new product is often difficult for the small business manager, but it should accomplish three objectives: getting the product accepted; maintaining market share as the competition grows; and earning a profit.
- There are three major pricing strategies generally used to introduce new products into the market: penetration, skimming, and sliding down the demand curve.
- Pricing techniques for existing products and services include odd pricing, price lining, leader pricing, geographic pricing, opportunistic pricing, discounts, multiple pricing, bundling, and suggested retail pricing.

❷ Discuss the links among pricing, image, and competition.

- A company's pricing policies offer potential customers important information about its overall image. Accordingly, when developing a marketing approach to pricing, business owners must establish prices that are compatible with what their customers expect and are willing to pay. Too often, small business owners *underprice* their goods and services, believing that low prices are the only way they can achieve a competitive advantage. They fail to identify the extra value, convenience, service, and quality they give their customers—all things many customers are willing to pay for.
- An important part of setting appropriate prices is tracking competitors' prices regularly; however, what the competition is charging is just one variable in the pricing mix. When setting prices, business owners should take into account their competitors' prices, but they should not automatically match or beat them. Businesses that offer customers extra quality, value, service, or convenience can charge higher prices as long as customers recognize the "extras" they are getting. Two factors are vital to studying the effects of competition on the small firm's pricing policies: the location of the competitors and the nature of the competing goods.

❸ Explain the pricing techniques used by retailers.

- Pricing for the retailer means pricing to move merchandise. Markup is the difference between the cost of a product or service and its selling price.

Most retailers compute their markup as a percentage of retail price, but some retailers put a standard markup on all their merchandise; more frequently, they use a flexible markup.

❹ Explain the pricing techniques used by manufacturers.

- A manufacturer's pricing decision depends on the support of accurate cost accounting records. The most common technique is cost-plus pricing, in which the manufacturer charges a price that covers the cost of producing a product plus a reasonable profit. Every manufacturer should calculate a product's breakeven price, the price that produces neither a profit nor a loss.

❺ Explain the pricing techniques used by service firms.

- Service firms often suffer from the effects of vague, unfounded pricing procedures and frequently charge the going rate without any idea of their costs. A service firm must set a price based on the cost of materials used, labor involved, overhead, and a profit. The proper price reflects the total cost of providing a unit of service.

❻ Describe the impact of credit on pricing.

- Offering consumer credit enhances a small company's reputation and increases the probability, speed, and magnitude of customers' purchases. Small firms offer three types of consumer credit: credit cards, installment credit, and trade credit (charge accounts).

Discussion Questions

1. What does a price represent to the customer? Why is a customer orientation to pricing important?
2. How does pricing affect a small firm's image?
3. What competitive factors must the small firm consider when establishing prices?
4. Describe the strategies a small business could use in setting the price of a new product. What objectives should the strategy seek to achieve?
5. Define the following pricing techniques: odd pricing, price lining, leader pricing, geographic pricing, and discounts.
6. Why do many small businesses use the manufacturer's suggested retail price? What are the disadvantages of this technique?
7. What is a markup? How is it used to determine prices?

8. What is a standard markup? A flexible markup?
9. What is follow-the-leader pricing? Why is it risky?
10. What is cost-plus pricing? Why do so many manufacturers use it? What are the disadvantages of using it?
11. Explain the difference between full-absorption costing and direct costing. How does absorption costing help a manufacturer determine a reasonable price?
12. Explain the techniques for a small service firm setting an hourly price.
13. What is the relevant price range for a product or service?
14. What advantages and disadvantages does offering trade credit provide to a small business?
15. What advantages does accepting credit cards provide a small business? What costs are involved?
16. What steps should a small business owner take to earn merchant status?

Step into the Real World

1. Interview two successful small retailers in your area and ask the following questions: Do you seek a specific image through your prices? What role do your competitors play in pricing? Do you use specific pricing techniques such as odd pricing, price lining, leader pricing, or geographic pricing? How are discounts calculated? What markup percentage does the firm use? What is your cost structure?

2. Select an industry that has several competing small firms in your area. Contact these firms and compare their approaches to determining prices. Do prices on identical or similar items differ? Why?

3. Contact two local small businesses: one that does accept credit cards and one that doesn't. Ask the owner of the business that does accept credit cards why he or she does. What role do customers' expectations play? Does the owner believe that accepting credit cards leads to increased sales? What does it cost the owner to accept credit cards? How difficult was it to gain merchant status? Ask the owner of the business that does not accept credit cards why he or she does not. Has the business lost sales because it does not accept credit cards? What would it take and how much would it cost for the owner to be able to accept credit cards?

Take It to the Net

Visit the Scarborough/Zimmerer home page at
www.prenhall.com/scarbzim
for updated information, on-line resources, and Web-based exercises.

Endnotes

1. Carolyn Z. Lawrence, "The Price Is Right," *Business Start-Ups*, February 1996, p. 64.
2. Jacquelyn Lynn, "The Middle of the Road," *Business Start-Ups*, December 1996, p. 33.
3. Ibid.
4. Susan Greco, "Are Your Prices Right?" *Inc.*, January 1998, pp. 88–89.
5. Roberta Maynard, "Take Guesswork Out of Pricing," *Nation's Business*, December 1997, pp. 27–30.
6. Rick Bruns, "Tips for Coping with Rising Costs of Key Commodities," *Your Company*, August/September 1997, p. 14.
7. Ibid.
8. Jeannie Mandelker, "Pricing Right from the Start," *Profit*, September/October 1996, p. 20.
9. Bruns, "Tips for Coping with Rising Costs of Key Commodities."
10. Kylo-Patrick Hart, "Step 10: Set Your Price," *Business Start-Ups*, March 1997, pp. 72–74.
11. Lynn, "The Middle of the Road."
12. Ed Brown, "$79K—And It Keeps Score!" *Fortune*, March 3, 1997, p. 42.
13. Tim Carvell, "These Prices Really Are Insane," *Fortune*, August 4, 1997, pp. 109–116; Su-Jin Yim, "Big Stores Force CD Change," *News and Observer*, August 27, 1996 <http://www3.nando.net/newsroom/nao/biz/082796/bizt_16077.html>.
14. Maynard, "Take Guesswork Out of Pricing," p. 28.
15. Bob Ortega, "When These Drinkers Crack Open a Cold One, It Can Cost $75," *Wall Street Journal*, August 18, 1995, pp. B1, B10.

16. Peter Nulty, "Make Certain That Your Price Is Right," *Your Company*, *Forecast* 1997, pp. 15–16.

17. Ibid., p. 15.

18. Gayle Sato Stodder, "Paying the Price," *Entrepreneur*, October 1994, p. 54.

19. "Improving Efficiency in a Price War," *Nation's Business*, July 1997, p. 10.

20. Richard Gibson, "Big Price Cut at McDonald's Seems a McFlop," *Wall Street Journal*, May 9, 1997, pp. B1, B2; Richard Gibson, "Prices Tumble on Big Macs, But Fries Rise," April 25, 1997, *Wall Street Journal*, pp. B1, B2; Cliff Edwards, "Some McDonalds Franchisees Quietly Boosting Some Prices to Offset Cost of Promotion," *Greenville News*, April 26, 1997, p. 8D.

21. Mark Henricks, "War & Price," *Entrepreneur*, June 1995, p. 156.

22. Bob Weinstein, "Getting Carded," *Entrepreneur*, September 1995, pp. 76–80; Jeff Bennett, "Holiday Hangover," *Upstate Business*, December 28, 1997, pp. 1, 8–9.

23. "Business Bulletin," *Wall Street Journal*, July 26, 1990, p. A1.

24. Richard J. Maturi, "Charging Ahead," *Entrepreneur*, July 1990, p. 56.

25. Weinstein, "Getting Carded," p. 56.

Creative Use of Advertising and Promotion

Advertising is salesmanship mass produced. No one would bother to use advertising if he could talk to all his prospects face to face. But he can't.

—*Morris Hite*

It ain't braggin' if you can do it.

—*Dizzy Dean*

Upon completion of this chapter, you will be able to

1. Describe the steps in developing an advertising strategy.

2. Explain the differences among promotion, publicity, personal selling, and advertising.

3. Describe the advantages and disadvantages of the various advertising media.

4. Identify four basic methods for preparing an advertising budget.

5. Explain practical methods for stretching a small business's advertising budget.

Some small business owners believe that because of limited budgets they cannot afford the "luxury" of advertising. In their view, advertising is a leftover expense, something to spend money on only if there's something left after the other bills have been paid. These owners discover, often after it's too late, that advertising is not just an expense; it is an *investment* in a company's future. Without a steady advertising and promotional campaign, a small business's customer base will soon vanish. Advertising can be an effective means of increasing sales by informing customers of the business and its goods or services; by improving the image of the firm and its products; or by persuading customers to purchase the firm's goods or services. A megabudget is *not* a prerequisite for building an effective advertising campaign. With a little creativity and ingenuity, a small company can make its voice heard above the clamor of its larger competitors and still stay within a limited budget. *For example,* *when Vic and Suzette Brounsuzian opened Meg-A-Nut Inc., a small shop selling nuts and snacks, they knew they had to find creative, low-cost ways to reach potential customers. The entrepreneurial couple convinced their bank (which was across the street from their shop) to hand out free samples of their products to customers at teller windows. "We made up small packets containing a mixture of our nuts, labeled them with our store name and information, and left a huge basket of them [at the bank]," says Vic. That single promotion generated a large volume of business for Meg-A-Nut. The Brounsuzians also brought in a lot of customers with a gala grand opening celebration and convinced the local newspaper to do a feature story on the event. "I also placed a newspaper advertisement promoting the grand opening celebration," says Vic. Today, the Brounsuzians continue their pattern of creative, economical promotions. In addition to the ads they run regularly in several local media, they place coupons in a bimonthly direct-mail pack and set up a booth at special events around town. Perhaps most important, the Brounsuzians emphasize friendly service and a quality product, knowing that satisfied customers can be a powerful, yet inexpensive, source of advertising. "Advertising is important," says Vic, "but the best promotion of all is word-of-mouth referrals."[1]*

Developing an effective advertising program has become more of a challenge for business owners in recent years. Because of media overflow, overwhelming ad clutter, increasingly fragmented audiences, and more-skeptical consumers, companies have had to become more innovative and creative in their promotional campaigns. Rather than merely turning up the advertising volume on their campaigns, companies are learning to change their frequencies, trying out new approaches in different advertising media.

Developing an Advertising Strategy

◆ Describe the steps in developing an advertising strategy.

Every small business needs an advertising strategy to ensure that it does not waste the money it spends on advertising. A well-developed strategy does not guarantee advertising success, but it does increase the likelihood of good results. "Without a decisive ad strategy, you may simply wind up reacting to the moves of the competition," says one advertising expert. "For advertising to work, it must fit into your company's overall marketing strategy."[2]

The first step is to define the purpose of the company's advertising program by creating specific, measurable objectives. In other words, entrepreneurs must decide, "What do I want to accomplish with my advertising?" Some ads are designed to stimulate immediate responses by encouraging customers to purchase a particular product in the immediate future. The object is to trigger a purchase decision. Other ads seek to build name recognition among potential customers and the general public. These ads try to create goodwill by keeping the firm's name in the public's memory so that customers will recall the small firm's name when they decide to purchase a product or service. Although measuring the success of name-recognition ads is more difficult than measuring purchasing results, successful campaigns should produce increased sales within six to nine months. Still other ads strive to draw new customers, build mailing lists, increase foot traffic in a store, or introduce a company or a product into a new territory.

The next step in developing an advertising strategy is to identify the company's target customers. Entrepreneurs who do not know who their advertising targets are cannot reach them! Before considering either the advertising message or the media by which to send it, business owners must understand their target customers. The idea is to match both the message and the media to the target audience. Business owners should address the following questions:

◆ What business are we in?

◆ What image do we want to project?

- Who are our target customers and what are their characteristics?
- Where can we best reach them?
- What do my customers *really* purchase from us?
- What benefits can the customer derive from our goods or services?
- How do I want to position our company in the market?
- What advertising approach do our competitors take?

Answering those questions will help business owners define their business, profile their customers, and focus their advertising messages on their specific target market to get more for their advertising dollars. *Jackie Lent's Inward Bound Adventures, a travel tour service, targets one of the nation's fastest-growing markets: the elderly. By the year 2030, the already sizable population of people over 65 will nearly double, and their spending power will extend into the hundreds of billions of dollars. Recognizing the market potential of this growing market and its abundance of leisure time led Lent to begin designing travel tours for senior citizens looking for unique destinations and activities catering to their needs and interests. Inward Bound tours avoid the typical "tourist destinations," favoring instead quaint, out-of-the-way spots that let visitors see what life in that location is really like. "My goal was to have my customers experience the place rather than just see it," says Lent. All of Inward Bound Adventures' promotions are aimed specifically at Lent's target audience and emphasize the details that elderly leisure travelers want.*[3]

Once the small business owner has defined her target audience, she can design an advertising message and choose the media for transmitting it. At this stage, the owner decides what to say and how to say it. One advertising expert claims, "You won't win customers by boring them into buying. You've got to create a desire."[4]

Owners should build their ads around a **unique selling proposition (USP),** a key customer benefit of a product or service that sets it apart from its competition. To be effective, a USP must be unique—something the competition does not (or cannot) provide—and strong enough to encourage the customer to buy. A successful USP answers the critical question every customer asks: "What's in it for me?" It should express in 10 words or less exactly what a business can do for its customers. The USP becomes the heart of the advertising message. *For instance, the owner of a quaint New England bed and breakfast came up with a four-word USP that captures the essence of the escape her business offers guests from their busy lives: "Delicious beds; delicious breakfasts." Sheila Paterson, co-founder of Macro International, a marketing consulting firm, says her company's USP is "Creative solutions for impossible marketing problems."*[5]

Sometimes, the most powerful USPs are the *intangible* or *psychological* benefits a product or service offers customers: e.g., safety, security, acceptance, or status. An advertiser must be careful, however, to avoid stressing minuscule differences that are irrelevant to customers. Table 11.1 describes a six-sentence advertising strategy designed to create powerful ads that focus on a USP.

The best way to identify a meaningful USP is to describe the primary benefit your product or service offers customers and then to list secondary benefits it provides. "You are not likely to have more than three top benefits you can give someone," says one advertising expert.[6] It is also important to develop a brief list of the facts that support your company's USP: e.g., 24-hour service, a fully trained staff, or awards won. By focusing ads on these top benefits and the facts supporting them, business owners can communicate their USPs to their target audiences in a meaningful, attention-getting way. Building an ad around a USP spells out for customers the specific benefit they will get if they buy that product or service. "If your audience has to study your ad to figure out what you're trying to say, forget it!" says

Table 11.1 A Six-Sentence Advertising Strategy

Does your advertising deliver the message you want to the audience you are targeting? If not, try stating your strategy in six sentences:

◆ **Primary purpose.** What is the primary purpose of this ad? "The purpose of Rainbow Tours' ads is to get people to call or write for a free video brochure."

◆ **Primary benefit.** What USP can you offer customers? "We will stress the unique and exciting places our customers can visit."

◆ **Secondary benefits.** What other key benefits support your USP? "We will also stress the convenience and value of our tours and the skill of our tour guides."

◆ **Target audience.** At whom are we aiming the ad? "We will aim our ads at adventurous male and female singles and couples, 21 to 34, who can afford our tours."

◆ **Audience reaction.** What response do you want from your target audience? "We expect our audience to call or write to request our video brochure."

◆ **Company personality.** What image do we want to convey in our ads? "Our ads will reflect our innovation, excitement, and conscientiousness and our warm, caring attitude toward our customers."

SOURCE: Adapted from Jay Conrad Levinson, "The Six-Sentence Strategy," *Communication Briefings*, December 1994, p. 4.

one expert.[7] *For example Dale Kesel, owner of a small photography studio, targets families with children and offers his customers enduring family memories in the form of high-quality family portraits that capture the personalities of the children he photographs. His ads appeal to customers at an emotional level.*[8]

A company's target audience and the nature of its message determine the advertising media it will use. Some messages are much more powerful in some media than in others. *For instance, because Kesel uses samples of portraits in his ads, he relies heavily on ads in the community newspapers nearest his location, although he does supplement his campaign with radio spots.*[9]

The process does not end with creating and broadcasting an ad. The final step involves evaluating the ad campaign's effectiveness. Did it accomplish the objectives it was designed to accomplish? One advertising executive claims that a successful ad for a special sale should generate at least two to three times the amount invested in the campaign.[10] Immediate-response ads can be evaluated in a number of ways. For instance, managers can include coupons that customers redeem to get price reductions on products and services. Dated coupons identify customer responses over certain time periods. Some firms use hidden offers, statements hidden somewhere in an ad that offer customers special deals if they make a special request. *For example, one small firm offered a price reduction to any customer who mentioned that he had heard the advertisement for the product on the radio.*[11]

A businesss owner can also gauge an ad's effectiveness by measuring the volume of store traffic generated. Effective advertising should increase store traffic; higher traffic boosts sales of both advertised and nonadvertised items. Of course, if an advertisement promotes a particular bargain item, the manager can judge its effectiveness by comparing sales of that item with preadvertising sales. Remember: The ultimate test of an ad is whether it increases sales!

Ad tests can help determine the most effective methods of reaching potential customers. Owners can design two different ads (or use two different media or broadcast times) that are coded for identification and see which one produces more responses. For example, the manager can use a split run of two different ads in a local newspaper. That is, he can place one ad in part of the paper's press run and another ad in the remainder of the run. Then he can measure the response level to each ad.

Table 11.2 offers 12 tips for creating an effective advertising campaign.

Table 11.2 Twelve Tips for Effective Advertising

1. *Plan more than one advertisement at a time.* An advertising campaign is likely to be more effective if it is developed from a comprehensive plan for a specific time period. A piecemeal approach produces ads that lack continuity and a unified theme.

2. *Set long–run advertising objectives.* One cause of inadequate planning is the failure to establish specific objectives for the advertising program. If what is expected from advertising hasn't been defined, the program is likely to lack a sense of direction.

3. *Use advertisements, themes, and vehicles that appeal to diverse groups of people.* Although personal judgment influences every business decision, you cannot afford to let bias interfere with advertising decisions. For example, you should not use a particular radio station just because you like it.

4. *View advertising expenditures as investments not as expenses.* In an accounting sense, advertising is a business expense, but money spent on ads tends to produce sales and profits over time that might not be possible without advertising. An effective advertising program generates more sales than it costs. You must ask, "Can I afford *not* to advertise?"

5. *Use advertising that is different from your competitors' advertising.* Some managers tend to "follow the advertising crowd" because they fear being different from their competitors. "Me-too" advertising frequently is ineffective because it fails to create a unique image for the firm. Don't be afraid to be different!

6. *Choose the media vehicle that is best for your business even if it's not number one.* It is not uncommon for several media within the same geographic region to claim to be "number one." Different media offer certain advantages and disadvantages. The manager should evaluate each according to its ability to reach his target audience effectively.

7. *Consider using someone else as the spokesperson on your TV and radio commercials.* Although being your own spokesperson may lend a personal touch to your ads, the commercial may be seen as nonprofessional or "homemade." The ad may detract from the firm's image rather than improve it.

8. *Limit the content of each ad.* Some small business owners think that to get the most for their advertising dollar, they must pack their ads full of facts and illustrations. But overcrowded ads confuse customers and are often ignored. Simple, well-designed ads that focus on your USP are much more effective.

9. *Devise ways of measuring your ads' effectiveness that don't depend on just two or three customers' responses.* Measuring the effectiveness of advertising is an elusive art at best. But the opinions of a small sample of customers, whose opinions may be biased, is not a reliable gauge of an ad's effectiveness. The techniques described earlier offer a more objective measurement of an ad's ability to produce results.

10. *Stop the ad if something does not happen immediately.* Some ads are designed to produce immediate results, but many ads require more time because of the lag effect they experience. One of advertising's rules is: It's not the size; it's the frequency. The head of one advertising agency claims, "The biggest waste of money is stop-and-start advertising."

11. *Emphasize the benefits that the product or service provides to the customer.* Too often, ads emphasize only the features of the products or services a company offers without mentioning the benefits they provide customers. Customers really don't care about a product's or service's "bells and whistles"; they are much more interested in the *benefits* those features can give them! Their primary concern is "How can this solve my problem?"

12. *Evaluate the cost of different advertising medium.* Remember the difference between the absolute and relative cost of an ad. The medium that has a low absolute cost may actually offer a high relative cost if it does not reach your intended target audience. Evaluate the cost of different media by looking at the cost per thousand customers reached. Remember: No medium is a bargain if it fails to connect you with your intended customers.

You must be patient, giving the advertising campaign a reasonable time to produce results. One recent study concluded that sales increases are most noticeable four to six months after an advertising campaign begins. One advertising expert claims that successful advertisers "are not capricious ad-by-ad makers; they're consistent ad campaigners."

SOURCES: Adapted from Sue Clayton, "Advertising," *Business Start-Ups*, December 1995, pp. 6–7; *Marketing for Small Business*, The University of Georgia Small Business Development Center: Athens, Georgia, 1992, p. 69; "Advertising Leads to Sales," *Small Business Reports*, April 1988, p. 14; Shelly Meinhardt, "Put It in Print," *Entrepreneur*, January 1989, p. 54; Danny R. Arnold and Robert H. Solomon, "Ten, 'Don'ts' in Bank Advertising," *Burroughs Clearing House*, vol. 16, no. 12, September 1980, pp. 20–24, 42–43; Howard Dana Shaw, "Success with Ads," *In Business*, November/December 1991, pp. 48–49; Jan Alexander and Aimee L. Stern, "Avoid the Deadly Sins in Advertising," *Your Company*, August/September 1997, p. 22.

$\mathcal{A}$dvertising versus Promotion

❷ Explain the differences among promotion, publicity, personal selling, and advertising.

The terms *advertising* and *promotion* are often confused. **Promotion** is any form of persuasive communication designed to inform consumers about a product or service and to influence them to purchase these goods or services. It includes publicity, personal selling, and advertising.

PUBLICITY

Publicity is any commercial news covered by the media that boosts sales but for which the small business does not pay. "[Publicity] is telling your story to the people you want to reach—namely, the news media, potential customers, and community leaders," says the head of a public relations firm. "It is not . . . haphazard. . . . It requires regular and steady attention."[12] Publicity has power; a national survey found that a news feature about a company or a product appearing in a newspaper or magazine would have more impact on people's buying decisions than an advertisement would.[13] The following tactics can help any small business owner stimulate publicity for her firm:

Write an article that will interest your customers or potential customers. One investment adviser writes a monthly column for the local newspaper on timely topics such as "retirement planning," "minimizing your tax bill," and "investing strategies for the next century." Not only do the articles help build her credibility as an expert; they also have attracted new customers to her business.

Contact local TV and radio stations and offer to be interviewed. Many local news or talk shows are looking for guests to talk about topics of interest to their audiences (especially in January and February). Even local shows can reach new customers.

Publish a newsletter. With a personal computer and desktop publishing software, any entrepreneur can publish a professional-looking newsletter. Freelancers can offer design and editing advice. Use the newsletter to reach present and potential customers.

Contact local business and civic organizations and offer to speak to them. A powerful, informative presentation can win new business. (Be sure your public speaking skills are up to par first! If they aren't, consider joining Toastmasters.)

Offer or sponsor a seminar. Teaching people about a subject you know a great deal about builds confidence and goodwill among potential customers. *The owner of a landscaping service and nursery offers a short course in landscape architecture and always sees sales climb afterward.*

Write news releases and fax them to the media. The key to having a news release picked up and printed is finding a unique angle on your business or industry that would interest an editor. Keep it short, simple, and interesting.

Volunteer to serve on community and industry boards and committees. You can make your town a better place to live and work and raise your company's visibility at the same time.

Sponsor a community project or support a nonprofit organization or charity. Not only will you be giving something back to the community, but you will also gain recognition, goodwill, and, perhaps, customers for your business. *Each year, Martha Morgan, owner of Morgan's of Delaware Avenue, a women's apparel store, sponsors a clothing drive for low-income working women with the local YWCA. Morgan offers customers who donate secondhand clothing to the YWCA a receipt for their donations (for tax purposes) and a $25 gift certificate on their next purchase of $125 or more in her store. Morgan* *says that the drive not only has provided needed clothing for deserving women, but it also has boosted her company's sales by more than $40,000.*[14]

Promote a cause. What started out as a socially responsible act has turned into a successful public relations campaign for one entrepreneur. *Joseph Crilley, owner of Crilley's Circle Tavern, was concerned about the dangers of drinking and driving, so he renovated an old school bus and began offering his customers a free shuttle service. Not only has his service made the roads safer, but it also has boosted his business. During off-peak hours, Crilley uses the bus to shuttle school kids on field trips and senior citizens around town to run errands.*[15]

Sometimes publicity is a matter of knowing a celebrity or, as in the case of Drake Bakeries, having a celebrity who knows and loves your product. *Drake Bakeries, founded in Brooklyn, New York, in 1900 by two brothers, makes a variety of snack cakes that native New Yorkers, including talk-show star Rosie O'Donnell, have loved for decades. O'Donnell, who describes Drake's products as "heaven in a foil wrapper," has promoted the snack cakes on her television show. She has interviewed the company's president, Jack Gallagher, and has even managed to convince supermodel Cindy Crawford to eat a Ring Ding (a cream-filled chocolate cake) on the air! With the help of O'Donnell's publicity, Drake Bakeries' sales climbed 11 percent.*[16]

PERSONAL SELLING

Personal selling is the personal contact between salespeople and potential customers resulting from sales efforts. Effective personal selling can give the small company a definite advantage over its larger competitors by creating a feeling of personal attention. Personal selling deals with the salesperson's ability to match customer needs to the firm's goods and services. Recent studies of top salespeople found that they:[17]

- Are enthusiastic and are alert to opportunities. Star sales representatives demonstrate deep concentration, high energy, and drive.
- Concentrate on select accounts. They focus on customers with the greatest sales potential, bypassing lukewarm prospects.
- Plan thoroughly. On every sales call, the best representatives act with a purpose to close the sale.
- Use a direct approach. They get right to the point with customers.
- Work from the customer's perspective. They know their customers' businesses and their needs.
- Spend 60 to 70 percent of a sales call letting the customer talk while they *listen*. They know that the best way to solve customers' problems and overcome their objections is to learn what they are.
- See customers' objections for what they really are—a source of valuable information. Objections give salespeople the chance to hear what customers are worried about. Once they know that, they can develop a strategy for overcoming the objections. "Sales objections are not a negative, but positive and necessary parts of a successful sale," says one expert.[18]
- Focus on building a rapport with prospects before attempting to sell them anything.
- Don't offer product or service recommendations until 40 percent or more of the time in the sales call has elapsed.

◆ Emphasize customer benefits, not product or service features, when selling (see chapter 9).

◆ Use "past success stories." They encourage customers to express their problems and then present solutions using examples of past successes.

◆ Leave sales material with clients. The material gives the customer the opportunity to study company and product literature in more detail.

◆ See themselves as problem solvers, not just vendors.

◆ Measure their success not just by sales volume but also by customer satisfaction.

One extensive study of salespeople found that just 20 percent of all salespeople have the ability to sell and are selling the "right" product or service. That 20 percent makes 80 percent of all sales. The study also concluded that 55 percent of sales representatives have "absolutely no ability to sell"; the remaining 25 percent have sales ability but are selling the wrong product or service.[19]

A study by Dartnell Corporation found that it takes an average of 3.9 sales calls to close a deal.[20] Common causes of sales rejections include the representative's failure to determine customers' needs, talking too much, and neglecting to ask for the order. (Studies show that 60 percent of the time, salespeople never ask the customer to buy!)[21] Unfortunately, the cost of making a sales call exceeds $225, making those "missed opportunities" quite costly.[22] Figure 11.1 shows how sales representatives spend their time in an average 45.5-hour workweek.

Small business owners can improve their sales representatives' "batting averages" by following some basic guidelines:

Develop a Selling System. One sales consultant recommends a six-step process to increase the likelihood of closing a sale:

1. *Approach.* Establish rapport with the prospect. Customers seldom buy from salespeople they dislike or distrust.

2. *Interview.* Get the prospect to do most of the talking; the goal is to identify his needs, preferences, and problems.

3. *Demonstrate, explain, and show* the features and benefits of your product or service and point out how they meet the prospect's needs or solve his problems.

4. *Validate.* Prove the claims about your product or service. If possible, offer the prospect names and numbers of other satisfied customers (with their permission, of course). Testimonials really work.

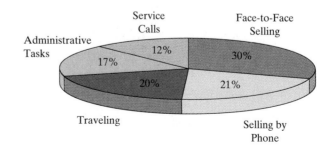

Figure 11.1 **How Salespeople Spend Their Time (based on an average 45.5-hour workweek)** Source: Dartnell Corporation, Chicago, Illinois, 1997.

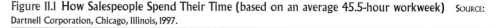

5. *Negotiate*. Listen for objections from the prospect. Try to determine the *real* objection and confront it. Work to overcome it. Objections can be the salesperson's best friend; they tell her what must be "fixed" before the prospect will commit to an order.

6. *Close*. Ask for a decision. Good sales representatives know when the prospect flashes the green light on a sale. They stop talking and ask for the order.[23]

Be Empathetic. The best salespeople look at the sale from the customer's viewpoint, not their own! Doing so encourages the sales representative to stress *value* to the customer. *Mary Kay Ash, founder of Mary Kay Cosmetics, advises, "Pretend that every single person you meet has a sign around his or her neck that says, 'Make me feel important.'"*[24]

Set Multiple Objectives. Before making a sales call, salespeople should set three objectives:

1. *The primary objective.* The most reasonable outcome expected from the meeting. It may be to get an order or to learn more about a prospect's needs.

2. *The minimum objective.* The very least the salesperson will leave with. It may be to set another meeting or to identify the prospect's primary objections.

3. *The visionary objective.* The most optimistic outcome of the meeting. This objective forces the salesperson to be open-minded and to shoot for the top.

Monitor Sales Efforts and Results. Selling is just like any other business activity and must be controlled. At a minimum, small business managers should know:

1. Actual sales versus projected sales
2. Sales generated per call made
3. Total sales costs
4. Sales by product, salesperson, territory, customer, etc.
5. Profit contribution by product, salesperson, territory, customer, etc.[25]

ADVERTISING

Advertising is any sales presentation that is nonpersonal in nature and is paid for by an identified sponsor. One recent study on the effectiveness of advertising concluded that ads influence purchases of some products for six to nine months. "Advertising can develop long-term brand equity," says the study's author.[26] The remainder of this chapter will focus on selecting advertising media, developing an advertising plan, and creating an advertising budget.

Selecting Advertising Media

3 Describe the advantages and disadvantages of the various advertising media.

One of the most important decisions a small business manager must make is which media to use in disseminating the advertising message. The medium used to transmit the message influences the consumer's perception—and reception—of it. By choosing the proper advertising means, a small business owner can reach his target audience effectively at minimum cost. One promotion expert says, "There are literally thousands of conduits for reaching your potential customer. And there's not a person managing a business who can afford not to be concerned with reaching, precisely, his or her target audience."[27] Although no single formula

Wanted: Dedicated Sales Force

$\mathscr{F}$raternal twin sisters Karen Hilderbrand and Kim Thompson started Twin Sisters, a company that produces educational products for children, in 1987. Their tapes, activity books, and CD-ROM-book sets use original music and songs to teach children from ages one to 11 the alphabet, colors and shapes, math, foreign languages, social studies, and science. Hilderbrand and Thompson write all of their own material, but they rely on input from educators and professionals in a variety of fields to produce their instructional books, cassettes, and CDs. Their products have won 21 coveted national awards, including the Parents' Choice Award and a spot on Dr. Toy's 100 Best Children's Products list. In its first year of operation, Twin Sisters tallied a measly $11,000 on sales, but, building on their record of success, Hilderbrand and Thompson have pushed sales to more than $1 million.

What more could Twin Sisters hope for?

A sales force!

Although the company's products are now sold in more than 21,500 stores, Hilderbrand and Thompson know they are missing out on a large volume of sales. Sales of children's educational products in the United States are growing by 5 percent a year, and the sisters believe their company could generate revenue of more than $2 million—if only they had a top-notch sales force. Nearly half of Twin Sisters' employees are in sales; unfortunately, that means just five in-house sales representatives (the company has 12 employees). With such a small sales force, Twin Sisters is having difficulty getting its products onto store shelves. To Hilderbrand and Thompson, this situation is extremely frustrating because they know that their products really do help children learn.

To supplement their small sales force, the sisters have hired 350 independent sales representatives who earn 10 to 15 percent sales commissions to cover the country and selected foreign markets. The approach has been only marginally successful. "It's really hard to get reps to care about your product," says Hilderbrand. That lack of concern has shown up in stagnant sales for the past two years.

When they first started Twin Sisters, Hilderbrand and Thompson ran the business as a part-time venture out of their homes, selling strictly through mail-order. Within five years,

they had hired a national team of six sales representatives to cover school-supply stores. That attempt proved to be unsuccessful. "Customers complained that they rarely saw the reps," says Hilderbrand. Unfortunately, Twin Sisters' experience with independent sales representatives is not uncommon. High turnover and handling large numbers of products from different companies make selling through independent reps a risky venture for many small companies. In 1994, Twin Sisters hired a sales management group, hoping to overcome many of the problems of using an independent sales force. Unfortunately, that experiment failed too. Within two years, the company had run through about 100 sales reps with little to show for it; sales were still stagnant.

By 1995, Hilderbrand and Thompson had come up with a new sales strategy: hiring a sales manager to coordinate selling activities. They brought in Liz Mullen, who had more than 20 years of experience as a national sales manager. Shortly afterward, they hired a second sales manager, Julie Post. Mullen and Post have the responsibility of managing most of the company's selling efforts. Post concentrates on toy stores, school-supply chains, and distributors while Mullen takes care of museums, hobby shops, and bookstores. Hilderbrand and Thompson direct international sales and take care of all of the large accounts themselves. Since taking over the sales function, the sisters, Mullen, and Post have hired more than 100 independent sales representatives, and they have installed a new computer system that "helps us track and manage the productivity of individual sales reps," says Mullen. The new sales strategy is starting to pay off, but battling the problems inherent in an independent sales force remains a concern for Hilderbrand and Thompson. Their goals include doubling sales within a year, continuing their expansion into England and Mexico, and exploring the video game and CD-ROM markets, where they see market potential.

---

1. What advice would you give Hilderbrand and Thompson about the following issues?
   - Hiring sales representatives
   - Retaining sales representatives
   - Motivating the sales force
   - Compensating the sales force
   - Controlling the sales force
   (Hint: Try searching the World Wide Web for ideas.)
2. What advice would you offer the sisters about promoting their products and increasing customers' awareness of them? What kind of unique selling proposition would you suggest for Twin Sisters?

SOURCE: Adapted from Sheryl Nance-Nash, "Rebuilding a Teeter-Totter Sales Team," *Your Company*, April/May 1997, pp. 46–50. ◆

exists for determining the ideal medium to use, there are several important characteristics that make some media better suited than others. *Gary Coxe, owner of Coxe's Enterprises, a sales and personal development training company, knew the importance of advertising when he launched his company. However, he didn't know which media would best reach his target customers. In the early years of his business, Coxe spent as much as $10,000 a year on local newspaper ads without much impact on company sales. Frustrated with the lack of results that that advertising medium was producing, Coxe switched to telemarketing. Soon, he saw sales climb from just $30,000 a year to $250,000 a year. In hopes of attracting international customers, Coxe recently launched a Web site, where he sells his seminars and training videos.*[28]

Understanding the qualities of the various media available can simplify an owner's decision. Before selecting the vehicle for the message, the owner should consider several questions:

How large is my firm's trading area? How big is the geographic region from which the firm will draw its customers? The size of this area clearly influences the choice of media.

Who are my target customers, and what are their characteristics? A customer profile often points to the appropriate medium to get the message across most effectively.

Which media are my target customers most likely to watch, listen to, or read? Until he knows who his target audience is, a business owner cannot select the proper advertising media to reach it.[29]

What budget limitations do I face? Every business owner must direct the firm's advertising program within the restrictions of its operating budget. Certain advertising media cost more than others.

What media do my competitors use? It is helpful for the small business manager to know the media his competitors use, although he should not automatically assume that they are the best. An approach that differs from the traditional one may produce better results.

How important are repetition and continuity of my advertising message? In general, an ad becomes effective only after it is repeated several times, and many ads must be continued for some time before they produce results. Some experts suggest that an ad must be run at least six times in most mass media before it becomes effective; other studies suggest the number of runs is as high as 15.[30]

What does the advertising medium cost? Business owners must consider two types of advertising costs: absolute cost and relative cost. **Absolute cost** is the actual dollar outlay a business owner must make to place an ad in a particular medium for a specific time period. An even more important measure is an ad's **relative cost,** the ad's cost per potential customer reached.

Suppose a manager decides to advertise his product in one of two newspapers in town. The *Sentinel* has a circulation of 21,000 and charges $1,200 for a quarter-page ad. The *Democrat* has a circulation of 18,000 and charges $1,300 for the same space. Reader profiles of the two papers suggest that 25 percent of *Sentinel* readers and 37 percent of the *Democrat* readers are potential customers. Using this information, the manager computes the following relative costs:

	Sentinel	*Democrat*
Circulation	21,000	18,000
Percent of readers that are potential customers	×25%	×37%
Potential customers reached	5,250	6,660
Absolute cost of ad	$1,200	$1,300

Relative cost of ad (per potential customer reached)

$$\frac{\$1,200}{5,250} = 22.86 \text{ cents per potential customer} \qquad \frac{\$1,300}{6,660} = 19.52 \text{ cents per potential customer}$$

Although the *Sentinel* has a larger circulation and a lower absolute cost for running the ad, the *Democrat* will serve the small business owner better because it offers a lower cost per potential customer reached. It is important to note that this technique does not give a reliable comparison across media; it is a meaningful comparison only within a single medium. Differences in the format, presentation, and coverage of ads in different media are so vast that such comparisons are not meaningful.

MEDIA OPTIONS

Figure 11.2 gives a breakdown of U.S. business advertising expenditures by medium. Although newspapers and television are the most popular advertising media, many small business owners use other media to reach their target customers successfully. Choosing advertising media is no easy task; each medium has distinctive advantages, disadvantages, and costs. The "right" message in the "wrong" medium will miss its mark.

Newspapers. Traditionally, the local newspaper has been the medium that most advertisers rely on to get their messages across to customers. Although the number of newspapers in the United States has declined 19 percent since 1960, this medium attracts 22.7 percent of all advertising dollars nationwide, establishing it as a leader among all media.

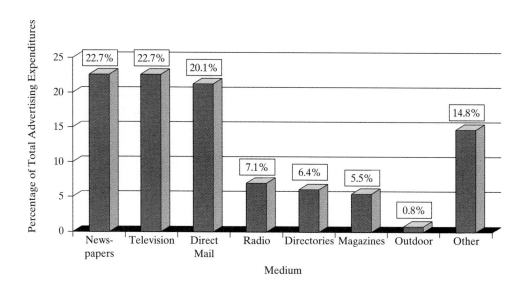

Figure 11.2 Advertising Expenditures by Medium, 1997   SOURCE: Statistical Abstract of the United States, 1997.

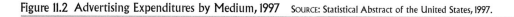

Newspapers provide several *advantages* to the small business advertiser:

Selected geographic coverage. Newspapers are geared to a specific geographic region, and they reach potential customers in all demographic classes. In general, they provide extensive coverage in a firm's immediate trading area.

Flexibility. Newspaper advertisements can be changed readily on very short notice. The owner can select the size of the ad, its location in the paper, and the days on which it runs. For instance, garages often advertise their tune-up specials in the sports section on weekends; party shops display their ads in the entertainment section.

Timeliness. Papers almost always have very short closing times, or publication deadlines. Many papers permit advertisers to submit their copy as late as 24 hours before the ad runs.

Communication potential. Newspaper ads can convey a great deal of information by employing attractive graphics and copy. Properly designed, they can be very effective in attracting attention and persuading readers to buy.

Low costs. Newspapers normally offer advertising space at a low absolute cost and, because of their blanket coverage of a geographic area, at a low relative cost as well.

Prompt responses. Newspaper ads typically produce relatively quick customer responses. A newspaper ad is likely to generate sales the very next day. This advantage makes newspapers an ideal medium for promoting special events such as sales, grand openings, or the arrival of a new product.

Of course, newspaper advertisements also have *disadvantages*:

Wasted readership. Because newspapers reach such a variety of people, at least a portion of an ad's coverage will be wasted on those who are not potential customers. This nonselective coverage makes it more difficult for newspapers to reach specific target markets than ads in other media.

Reproduction limitations. The quality of reproduction in newspapers is limited, especially when it is compared with that of magazines and direct mail. Recent technological advances, however, are improving the quality of reproduction in newspaper ads.

Lack of prominence. One frequently cited drawback of newspapers is that they carry so many ads that a small company's message might be lost in the crowd. The typical newspaper is 65 percent advertising. This disadvantage can be overcome by increasing the size of the ad or by adding color to it. Color can increase the reading of ads by as much as 80 percent over black-and-white ads. Studies show that two-color ads do "pull" better than black-and-white ones but only by a small margin. The *real* increase in ad recall and response comes from using full four-color ads. In fact, a small full-color ad usually produces a better response than a larger two-color ad.[31] Bold headlines, illustrations, and photographs also increase an ad's prominence.

Proper ad placement in the newspaper can increase an ad's effectiveness. The best locations are on a right-hand page, near the right margin, above the half-page mark, or next to editorial articles. The most-read sections in the typical newspaper are the main news section and the comics!

Declining readership. Newspaper circulation as a percentage of U.S. households has dropped from 98 percent in 1970 to 70 percent today. Newspaper ads would be least effective for small businesses targeting young people, who are least likely to read newspapers. Older adults and high-income households (above $60,000) of college graduates have the highest newspaper readership rates.[32]

Short ad life. The typical newspaper is soon discarded and, as a result, an ad's life is extremely short. Business owners can increase the effectiveness of their ads by giving them greater continuity. Spot ads can produce results, but maintaining a steady flow of business requires some degree of continuity in advertising.

Buying Newspaper Space. Newspapers typically sell ad space by lines and columns or inches and columns. For instance, a 4-column by 100-line ad occupies four columns and 100 lines of space (14 lines are equal to 1 column-inch). For this ad, the small business owner would pay the rate for 400 lines. Most papers offer discounts for bulk, long-term, and frequency contracts and for full-page ads. Advertising rates vary from one paper to another, depending on such factors as circulation and focus. A small business owner would do well to investigate the circulation statements, advertising rates, and reader profiles of the various newspapers available before selecting one.

Radio. Newspapers offer blanket advertising coverage of a region, but radio permits advertisers to appeal to specific audiences over large geographic areas. By choosing the appropriate station, program, and time for an ad, a small company can reach virtually any target market.

Radio advertising offers several advantages:

Universal infiltration. The radio's nearly universal presence gives advertisements in this medium a major advantage. Virtually every home and car in the United States is equipped with a radio, which means that radio ads receive a tremendous amount of exposure in the target market. According to the Radio Advertising Bureau, radio reaches 77 percent of all customers each day and 95 percent of customers each week![33]

Market segmentation. Radio advertising is flexible and efficient because advertisers can choose stations directed toward a specific market within a broad geographic region. Radio stations design their formats to appeal to specific types of audiences. (Ever notice how the stations you listen to are not the same ones your parents listen to?) AM stations, which once ruled the airways, now specialize mainly in "talk formats" such as call-in, news, religion, sports, and automotive shows. On the FM dial, country, top 40, rap, easy listening, modern rock, rhythm and blues, Spanish, and "golden oldies" stations have listener profiles that give entrepreneurs the ability to pinpoint virtually any advertising target.

Flexibility and timeliness. Radio commercials have short closing times and can be changed quickly. Small firms dealing in seasonal merchandise or advertising special sales or events can change their ads on short notice to match changing market conditions. *For example, Steve Braunstein, owner of a men's clothing store, frequently changes his radio ads to match current weather conditions. "If the weather gets cold suddenly," he says, "I can call on Tuesday, have a new commercial recorded promoting our down coats, and have it on the air Wednesday."*[34]

Friendliness. Radio ads are more "active" than ads in printed media because they use the spoken word to influence customers. Vocal subtleties used in radio ads are impossible to convey through printed media. Spoken ads can suggest emotions and urgency, and they lend a personalized tone to the message. Table 11.3 offers a guide to producing effective radio copy.

Radio advertisements also have some *disadvantages*:

Poor listening. Radio's intrusiveness into the public life almost guarantees that customers will hear ads, but they may not listen to them. Listeners are often engaged in other activities while the radio is on and may ignore the message.

Table 11.3 Guidelines for Effective Radio Copy

◆ *Mention the business often.* This is the single most important and inflexible rule in radio advertising. Also make sure listeners know how to find your business. If the address is complicated, use landmarks.

◆ *Stress the benefit to the listener.* Don't say "Bryson's has new fall fashions"; say "Bryson's fall fashions make you look fabulous."

◆ *Use attention-getters.* Radio has a whole battery of attention-getters: music, sound effects, unusual voices. Crack the customer-resistance barrier with sound.

◆ *Zero in on your audience.* Know who you're selling to. Radio's selectivity attracts the right audience. It's up to you to communicate in the right language.

◆ *Keep the copy simple and to the point.* Don't try to impress listeners with vocabulary. "To be or not to be" may be the best-known phrase in the language, and the longest word has just three letters.

◆ *Sell early and often.* Don't back into the selling message. At most, you've got 60 seconds. Make the most of them. Don't be subtle.

◆ *Write for the ear.* Write conversationally.

◆ *Prepare your copy.* Underline words you want to emphasize.

◆ *Triple-space.* Type clean, legible copy. Make the announcer rehearse.

◆ *Convey a sense of urgency.* Use words such as *now* and *today*, particularly when you're writing copy for a sale. Radio has qualities of urgency and immediacy. Take advantage of them by including a time limit or the date the sale ends.

◆ *Put the listener in the picture.* Radio's "theater of the mind" enables you to put the listener behind the wheel of a new car with sounds and music.

◆ *Focus the spot on getting a response.* Make it clear what you want the listener to do. Don't try to get a mail response. Use phone numbers only, and repeat the number three times. End the spot with the phone number.

◆ *Don't stay with a loser.* Direct response ads produce results right away or not at all. Don't stick with a radio spot that is not generating sales. Change it.

SOURCE: *Radio Basics,* Radio Advertising Bureau, <http://www.rab.com>.

Need for repetition. Listeners usually do not respond to radio ads after a single exposure to them. Radio ads must be broadcast repeatedly to be effective. Consistency in radio ads is the key to success.

Limited message. Radio ads are limited to one minute or less, so small business owners must keep their messages simple, covering only one or two points. Also, radio spots do not allow advertisers to demonstrate their products or services. Although listeners can hear the engine purr, they can't see the car; spoken messages can only describe the product or service.

Buying Radio Time. The small business owner can zero in on a specific advertising target by using the appropriate radio station. Stations follow various formats—from rap to rhapsodies—to appeal to specific audiences. Radio advertising time usually sells in 10-second, 20-second, 30-second, and 60-second increments, with the last being the most common. *Fixed spots* are guaranteed to be broadcast at the times specified in the owner's contract with the station. *Preemptible spots* are cheaper than fixed spots, but the advertiser risks being preempted by an advertiser willing to pay the fixed rate for a time slot. *Floating spots* are the least expensive, but the advertiser has no control over broadcast times. Many stations offer package plans, using flexible combinations of fixed, preemptible, and floating spots.

Radio rates vary depending on the time of day they are broadcast, and, like television, there are prime time slots known as drive-time spots. Although exact hours may differ from station to station, the following classifications are common:

Class AA: Morning drive time—6 A.M. to 10 A.M.

Class A: Evening drive time—4 P.M. to 7 P.M.

Class B: Home worker time—10 A.M. to 4 P.M.

Class C: Evening time—7 P.M. to midnight

Class D: Nighttime—midnight to 6 A.M.

Some stations may also have different rates for weekend time slots.

Television. In advertising dollars spent, television is tied with newspapers in popularity. Although the cost of national TV ads precludes their use by most small businesses, local spots on cable stations can be an extremely effective means of broadcasting a small company's message. A 30-second commercial on network television may cost well over $500,000 (30-second spots during the Super Bowl now go for more than $1.3 million), but a 30-second spot on a local cable station may go for $200 or less.

Television advertising has some distinct *advantages*.

Broad coverage. Television ads provide extensive coverage of a sizable region, and they reach a significant portion of the population. About 97 percent of the homes in any area will have a television, and those sets are on an average of 7 hours and 8 minutes each day. Therefore, television ads can reach a large number of people in a short amount of time.

The nation's 200-plus cable channels now draw 50 percent of television viewership, up from just 20 percent in 1990.[35] As the number of cable channels continues to increase, television exposure time will also rise. Because many channels focus their broadcasting in topical areas—from home and garden or food to science or cartoons—cable television offers advertisers the ability to reach specific target markets much as radio ads do. Because there is an inverse relationship between time spent in television viewing and education level, television ads overall are more likely to reach people with lower educational levels.

Visual advantage. The primary benefit of television is its capacity to present the advertiser's product or service visually. Research shows that 46 percent of television ads result in long-term sales increases and that 70 percent of campaigns boost sales immediately.[36] With TV ads, entrepreneurs are not limited to mere descriptions of a product or service; instead, they can demonstrate their uses and show firsthand their advantages. For instance, a specialty shop selling a hydraulic log splitter can design a television commercial to show how easily the machine works. The ability to use sight, sound, and motion makes TV ads a powerful selling tool.

Flexibility. Television ads can be modified quickly to meet the rapidly changing conditions in the marketplace. Advertising on TV is a close substitute for personal selling. Like a sales representative's call, television commercials can use "hard sell" techniques, attempt to convince through logic, appeal to viewers' emotions, persuade through subtle influence, or use any number of other strategies. In addition, advertisers can choose the length of the spot (30-second ads are most common), its time slot, and even the program during which to broadcast the ad.

Design assistance. Few small business owners have the skills to prepare an effective television commercial. Although professional production firms might easily charge $50,000 to produce a commercial, the television station from which a manager purchases the air time often is willing to help design and produce the ad very inexpensively.

Television advertising also has several *disadvantages*:

Brief exposure. Most television ads are on the screen for only a short time and require substantial repetition to achieve the desired effect. One study found that nearly half of all adults engage in other activities during television commercials and are likely to miss them. The group of advertisers' most popular subjects—mothers with young children—are the ones most likely to miss TV ads.[37]

Clutter. The typical person sees 1,500 advertising messages a day, and more ads are on the way! With so many ads beaming across the airwaves, a small business's advertising message could easily become lost in the shuffle.

"Zapping." **"Zappers,"** television viewers who flash from one channel to another, especially during commercials, pose a real threat to TV advertisers. Remote controls invite zapping, which can cut deeply into an ad's target audience. Zapping prevents TV advertisers from reaching the audiences they hope to reach.

Cost. TV commercials can be expensive to create. A 30-second ad can cost several thousand dollars to develop, even before the owner purchases air time.[38] Advertising agencies and professional design firms offer design assistance—sometimes at hefty prices—so many small business owners hire less expensive freelance ad designers or turn to the stations on which they buy air time for help with their ads. Table 11.4 offers some suggestions for developing creative television commercials.

The World Wide Web. The newest medium business owners have in their advertising arsenal is the World Wide Web. The Web not only draws customers with attractive demographic profiles—young, educated, and wealthy—but it also gives small companies the ability to reach growing numbers of customers outside the United States very inexpensively; nearly 27 percent of Web surfers are located outside U.S. borders.[39] Those impressive numbers explain why more than three-fourths of all registered Internet addresses, called domain names, are commercial sites.[40] Experts estimate that about 141,000 of those Web sites belong to small businesses. Companies that normally advertise through direct mail can bring the two-

Table 11.4 Guidelines for Creative TV Ads

◆ *Keep it simple.* Avoid confusing the viewer. Stick to a simple concept.

◆ *Have one basic idea.* The message should focus on a single, important benefit to the customer. Why should people buy from your business?

◆ *Make your point clear.* The customer benefit should be obvious and easy to understand.

◆ *Make your ad unique to get viewer attention.* To be effective, a television ad must grab the viewer's attention. Unless viewers watch the ad, its effect is lost.

◆ *Involve the viewer.* To be most effective, an ad should portray a situation the viewer can relate to. Common, everyday experiences are easiest for people to identify with.

◆ *Use emotion.* The most effective ads evoke an emotion from the viewer: a laugh, a tear, or a pleasant memory.

◆ *Consider production values.* Television offers vivid sights, colors, motions, and sounds. Use them!

◆ *Prove the benefit.* Television enables an advertiser to prove a product's or service's customer benefit by actually demonstrating it.

◆ *Identify your company clearly and often.* Make sure your store's name, location, and product line stand out. The ad should reflect your company's image.

Source: Adapted from *How to Make a Creative Television Commercial*, Television Bureau of Advertising, Inc.

dimensional photos and product descriptions in their print catalogs to life and avoid the expense of mailing them at the same time.

The Internet's explosive growth and the time that Net surfers spend on the World Wide Web make it a natural tool for advertising. One study shows that 80 percent of Web users log on at least once a day and that 36 percent of them go on line instead of watching television![41] Another reports that 20 million Americans consider the Internet "indispensable."[42] With its capacity for sound, color, full-motion video, and visual appeal, the Web offers advertisers many of the same advantages as television ads but at a lower cost. For instance, a restaurant might place on its Web site reviews from local publications, comments from patrons, its menu, photographs of popular dishes, a map showing its location, and video clips of its chef at work—in short, everything but the aroma! *Michael Monti, owner of Monti's La Casa Vieja, a restaurant in Tempe, Arizona, calls his company's Web site "the greatest marketing bang for the buck around anywhere these days."*[43]

When Dan Sullivan, owner of the Faucet Outlet, a retailer of discount plumbing fixtures, opened for business in 1991, he advertised his products through a catalog that cost $2 each to print and mail. The company took orders from the catalog by telephone. Four years later, seeing the Web's potential as a potent advertising medium for the Faucet Outlet, Sullivan launched a Web site <http://www.faucet.com/faucet/>. He saw the Web site as a way to display his merchandise to a larger audience while simultaneously reducing costs. Once on line, the Faucet Outlet's site drew a few thousand "hits" (visits) each month. Within a year, traffic volume on the site had grown to 17,000 visitors a month. The Faucet Outlet now gets several orders every day from the site, which accounts for 5 percent of the company's sales. "The results have been fantastic," says Sullivan. "It costs just pennies for me to get leads on the Internet, and I can show so much more with an Internet catalog [than with] my paper catalog."[44]

Advertisements on the Web take four basic forms: banner ads, cookies, full-page ads, and "push" technology ads. **Banner ads** are small, rectangular ads that reside on Web sites, much like roadside billboards, touting a company's product or service. Their primary disadvantage is that Web users can easily ignore them. **Cookies** are small programs that attach to users' computers when they visit a Web site. They track the locations users visit while in the site and use this electronic footprint to send pop-up ads that would be of interest to the user. **Full-page ads** are those that download to Web users' screens before they can access certain Web sites. They are common on popular game sites that sustain high volumes of Web traffic. **Push technology ads** appear on users' screens when they download information such as news, sports, or entertainment from another site. For instance, a Web user downloading sports information might receive an ad for athletic shoes or T-shirts with the information. Table 11.5 offers guidelines for Internet ad campaigns.

Magazines. Another advertising medium available to the small business owner is magazines. Some 1,800 nontrade magazines are in circulation across the United States. Magazines have a wide reach; today, nearly 9 out of 10 adults read an average of seven magazines each month. The average magazine attracts 6 hours and 3 minutes of total adult reading time, and studies show that the reader is exposed to 89 percent of the ads in the average issue.[45]

Magazines offer several *advantages* for advertisers:

Long life spans. Magazines have a long reading life because readers tend to keep them longer than other printed media. Few people read an entire magazine at one sitting. Instead, most pick it up, read it at intervals, and come back to it later. The result is that each magazine ad has a good chance of being seen several times.

Multiple readership. The average magazine has a readership of 3.9 adult readers, and each reader spends about one hour and 33 minutes with each copy. Many magazines

Table 11.5 Guidelines for Internet Ad Campaigns

Use active messages and techniques. There's another site just a mouse click away. You must grab visitors' attention *immediately.*

Avoid slow download. Although a site or an ad must capture Web surfers' attention instantly, it cannot be so complex that it requires a long time to download. Otherwise, the audience will never see it! A recent study discovered that speed—or lack of it—was Web users' most common complaint. Slow download will kill even the most captivating Web site or most brilliant ad.

Change content often. Visitors get bored if a Web site looks exactly the same every time they visit. If you cannot revise your site or ad at least monthly, include a section that you can change more frequently such as a quotation of the day or a photograph.

Run ads about your company's Web site in ads in other advertising media. To draw traffic to your Web site, you have to let people know it's there. Include your Web site's address in print ads, in broadcast commercials, on your product packaging, and anywhere else customers will see it!

Offer visitors something of interest and of value. Let cutomers know up front what benefits your site or ad will offer them. Otherwise, they may not stick around long enough to find it. Establishing links to other sites of interest gives Web surfers more reason to visit your site.

Go for the hard sell. Use your Web site or ad to actually sell something. If you are making a special offer, discount, or sale to Web customers, highlight it on the opening page and make it highly visible. "Soft-sell" techniques do not work on the Web!

Assure customers that paying on line is secure. One concern customers have about doing business on line is making sure that their credit-card information is safe from hackers and thieves. Entrepreneurs serious about doing business on the Web will install the necessary security software to ensure the safety of their customers' credit-card information.

Respond to customers' requests and inquiries quickly. The fastest way to lose Web customers is to ignore them or to provide them with poor service. Companies that fill orders or respond to requests the same day have an edge over those that do not.

SOURCES: Adapted from "Rules for Internet Selling," *Communication Briefings,* December 1997, p. 6; Jennifer Sucov, "Me and My Website," *Your Company,* June/July 1997, pp. 36–41; Sandra E. Eddy, "A Lasting Impression, *Business Start-Ups,* May 1997, pp. 14–16.

have a high "passalong" rate; they are handed down from reader to reader. For instance, the in-flight magazines on jets reach many readers in their lifetimes.

Target marketing. By selecting the appropriate special-interest periodical, small business owners can reach those customers with a high degree of interest in their goods or service. Once business owners define their target markets, they can select magazines whose readers most closely match their customer profiles. For instance, *Modern Bride* magazine reaches a very different audience than *Rolling Stone.*

Ad quality. Magazine ads usually are of high quality. Photographs and drawings can be reproduced very effectively, and color ads are readily available. Advertisers can also choose the location of their ads in a magazine and can design creative ads that capture readers' attention.

Magazines also have several *disadvantages:*

Costs. Magazine advertising rates vary according to their circulation rates; the higher the circulation, the higher the rate. Thus, local magazines, whose rates are often comparable to newspaper rates, may be the best bargain for small businesses.

Long closing times. Another disadvantage of magazines is the relatively long closing times they require. For a weekly periodical, the closing date for an ad may be several weeks before the actual publication date. Long lead times and the time needed to plan and design magazine ads reduce the timeliness of this medium.

Lack of prominence. Another disadvantage of magazine ads arises from their popularity as an advertising vehicle. The effectiveness of a single ad may be reduced because of a lack of prominence. Proper ad positioning, therefore, is critical to an ad's success. Research shows that readers "tune out" right-hand pages and look mainly at left-hand pages.

Direct Mail. Direct mail has long been a popular method of small business advertising and includes such tools as letters, postcards, catalogs, discount coupons, brochures, computer disks, and videotapes mailed to homes or businesses. The earliest known catalogs were printed by fifteenth-century printers. Today, direct mail marketers sell virtually every kind of product imaginable, from Christmas trees and lobsters to furniture and clothing (the most popular mail-order purchase). Responding to the convenience of shopping at home, customers purchase more than $420 billion worth of goods and services through mail order each year.[46] Direct mail offers a number of distinct *advantages* to small business owners:

Selectivity. The greatest strength of direct mail advertising is its ability to target a specific audience to receive the message. Depending on mailing list quality, an owner can select an audience with virtually any set of characteristics. Small business owners can develop, rent, or purchase a mailing list of prospective residential, commercial, or industrial customers. *When Sandy and Tom Callahan launched their mail-order company, Grand River Toy Company, which markets toys made from environmentally safe materials, they placed newspaper ads and mailed their brief catalog to those who responded. Their list grew, albeit slowly, by word of mouth. In their third year of business, the Callahans purchased mailing lists of upscale, educated buyers concerned about the environment and education from list brokers. Their home-based company has doubled its sales every year since.[47]*

Flexibility. Another advantage of direct mail is its capacity to tailor the message to the target. The advertiser's presentation to the customer can be as simple or as elaborate as necessary. *For instance, one custom tailor shop achieved a great deal of success with fliers it mailed to customers on its mailing list when it included a swatch of material from the fabric for the upcoming season's suits.* With direct mail, the tone of the message can be personal, creating a positive psychological effect. In addition, the advertiser controls the timing of the campaign; she can send the ad when it is most appropriate.

Reader attention. With direct mail, an advertiser's message does not have to compete with other ads for the reader's attention. People enjoy getting mail, and one study found that recipients opened and read 48 percent of their direct mail.[48] For at least a moment, direct mail gets the recipient's undivided attention. If the message is on the mark and sent to the right audience, direct mail ads can be a powerful advertising tool. Table 11. 6 describes common categories of direct mail campaigns with examples of each.

Rapid feedback. Direct mail advertisements produce quick results. In most cases, the ad will generate sales within three or four days after customers receive it. Business owners should know whether a mailing has produced results within a relatively short time period.

Measurable results and testable strategies. Because they control their mailing lists, direct marketers can readily measure the results their ads produce. Also, direct mail allows advertisers to test different ad layouts, designs, and strategies (often within the same "run") to see which one "pulls" the greatest response. The best direct marketers are always fine-tuning their ads to make them more effective. Table 11.7 offers guidelines for creating direct mail ads that really work.

Direct mail ads also suffer from several *disadvantages*:

Inaccurate mailing lists. The key to the success of the entire mailing is the accuracy of the customer list. The Direct Marketing Association estimates that 60 percent of the suc-

Table 11.6 Categories of Direct Mail Campaigns

Category	Definition	Examples
Package insert programs	Inserts ride along in merchandise shipments.	Spiegel Fingerhut Lillian Vernon Hanover House
Statement insert programs	Inserts ride along in customer invoices or statements.	Visa MasterCard U.S. Cable Network *Family Circle Books*
Billing or renewal insert programs	Inserts accompany magazines' billing or renewal efforts mailed to active prospective subscribers.	*McCall's* *Hachette* *Parenting*
Ride-along programs	Inserts are carried in "other" direct mail marketers' own prospecting or negative option mailings.	BMG Music/Video Columbia House Doubleday
National co-op mailings	Direct mail packages contain a mix of direct response inserts and customer product coupons.	Carol Wright Jane Tucker Select & Save
Local co-op mailings	Direct mail packages contain a mix of direct response inserts and local retail coupons.	Money Mailer On Target Trimark
On the pack invoices	Inserts ride along in invoices affixed to the outside of merchandise book shipments.	Field Publications Weekly Reader Books McCalls Cooking School
Premium insert programs	Inserts are carried in free gift shipments sent to new and renewing magazine subscribers.	*Money Magazine* *Yankee Magazine* *Organic Gardening*
Card packs	Inserts or postcards are commingled in polywraps and mailed to targeted audiences.	*Business Week* Direct Response Deck WG&L Real Estate Action Cards Exec-Cards
Catalog bind-ins	Postcards or inserts are bound into catalogs mailed to customers and targeted prospects.	Gardener's Choice Gander Mountain Gurney Seed
Take-one displays	Inserts or brochures are placed on racks in high-visibility locations.	Good Neighbor College Take-Ones Tourist/Business Traveler Take-Ones

SOURCE: Reprinted with permission of *Sales & Marketing Strategies & News,* January 1992, p. 27. © by Hughes Communications, Inc.

cess of direct marketing is based on the quality of the mailing list.[49] If mailing lists are inaccurate or incomplete, advertisers will be addressing the wrong audiences and risk alienating their customers with misspelled names.

High relative costs. Direct mail has a higher cost per thousand (cpm) than any other advertising medium. Relative to the size of the audience reached, the cost of designing, producing, and mailing a direct mail advertisement is high. A typical direct mailing

Table 11.7 Guidelines for Creating Direct Mail Ads That *Really* Work

Successful direct mail advertisements require copy that catches readers' attention. Try these proven techniques:

◆ Promise readers your most important benefits in the headline or first paragraph.

◆ Use a postscript (P.S.) *always,* they are the most often read part of a printed page.

◆ Use short "action" words and paragraphs.

◆ Make the copy look easy to read; leave lots of white space.

◆ Use eye-catching words such as *free, you, save, guarantee, new, profit, benefit, improve,* and others.

◆ Write as if you were speaking to the reader.

◆ Repeat the offer three or more times in various ways.

◆ Back up claims and statements with proof and endorsements whenever possible.

◆ Get right to the point. Make it easy for readers to see why they should respond to your offer.

◆ Ask for the order or a response.

◆ Ask questions such as "Would you like to lower your home's energy costs?" in the copy.

◆ Use high-quality paper and envelopes (those with windows are best; envelopes that resemble bills always get opened) because they stand a better chance of being opened and read. One entrepreneur who relies heavily on direct mail says, "Your envelope and its contents have [only] seconds to make an effective first impression."

◆ Address the envelope to an individual, not "Occupant."

◆ Include a separate order form that passes the following "easy" test:

Easy to find. Consider using brightly colored paper or a form with a unique shape.

Easy to understand. Make sure the offer is easy for readers to understand. As direct marketing expert Paul Goldberg says, "Confuse 'em, and ya lose 'em."

Easy to complete. Keep the order form simple and unconfusing.

Easy to pay. Direct mail ads should give customers the option to pay by whatever means is most convenient.

Easy to return. Including a postage-paid return envelope (or at a minimum a return envelope) will increase a direct mail ad's response rate.

◆ Build and maintain a quality mailing list over time. The right mailing list is the key to a successful direct mail campaign. You may have to rent lists to get started, but once you are in business, use every opportunity to capture information about your customers. Constantly focus on improving the quality of your mailing list.

SOURCES: Adapted from "Five Easy Order Form Rules," *Communication Briefings,* November 1997, p. 3; Howard Scott, "Targeting Prospects with Direct Mail," *Nation's Business,* September 1997, p. 52; Paul Hughes, "Profits Due," *Entrepreneur,* February 1994, pp. 74–78; "Why They Open Direct Mail," *Communication Briefings,* December 1993, p. 5; Teri Lammers, "The Elements of Perfect Pitch," *Inc.,* March 1992, pp. 53–55; "Special Delivery," *Small Business Reports,* February 1993, p. 6; Gloria Green and James W. Peltier, "How to Develop a Direct Mail Program," *Small Business Forum,* Winter 1993/1994, pp. 30–45; Carolyn Campbell, "A Direct Hit," *Business Start-Ups,* August 1997, pp. 8–10.

costs $400 or more per thousand customers reached.[50] Figure 11.3 shows the breakdown of costs for a typical 3,000-piece mailing. But if the mailing is well planned and properly executed, it can produce a high percentage of returns, making direct mail one of the least expensive advertising methods in terms of results.

Rising postal rates. One of the primary causes of the high costs of direct mail ads is postage costs, which continue to rise. According to the Direct Marketing Association, postal rates have risen 75 percent since 1987.[51]

High throwaway rate. The average family receives 10 pieces of direct mail each week, and much of that ends up in the trash.[52] Often called junk mail, direct mail ads become "junk" when an advertiser selects the wrong audience or broadcasts the wrong message.

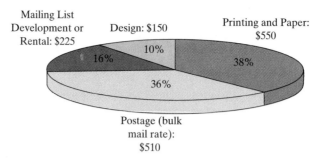

Mailing List Development or Rental: $225

Design: $150

Printing and Paper: $550

10%

16%

38%

36%

Postage (bulk mail rate): $510

Figure II.3 Cost Breakdown of a 3,000-Piece Direct Mailing SOURCE: John Horton, Horton Associates, Providence, RI.

To boost returns, small business owners can supplement their traditional direct mail pieces with toll-free (800) numbers (an increase of 1 to 2 percent) and carefully timed follow-up phone calls (an increase of 2 to 14 percent).[53] *For instance, Marc Kaner, owner of Fitness Connection, a retailer of vitamin supplements, estimates that his 800 number has increased his sales by 15 percent.*[54]

Creative entrepreneurs have found other ways to boost their direct mail response rates, including three-dimensional mailers, computer diskettes, and compact disks. *When one cruise line wanted to introduce a new ship, it mailed travel agents invitations to a cruise inside wine bottles filled with sand and miniature palm trees. The campaign was a huge success.*[55] *Mike Friedman, owner of three pizza restaurants, found a way to make the coupons he mailed to customers stand out by switching from standard coupons to self-adhesive ones that look like Post-It notes. The initial mailing generated a 30 percent response. "It was phenomenal," says Friedman. "In this business, a 1 to 3 percent response is considered good. A year later the Post-It coupons were still drawing a 20 percent response rate.*[56]

"High-Tech" Direct Mail. Sending out ads on computer diskettes is an excellent way to reach upscale households and businesses. Not only do computer-based ads give advertisers the power to create flashy, attention-grabbing designs, but they also hold the audience's attention. "Customized diskettes are rarely thrown away," says the founder of one diskette advertising firm. "Human curiosity practically guarantees they will be reviewed." Studies show that recipients of a computer diskette ad spend an average of 26 to 30 minutes interacting with it and that their retention rate is twice that of other ads. "Disks accomplish what every salesperson hopes for," says one ad designer. "They get the prospect involved."[57]

Compact discs (CDs) offer advertisers the same benefits as computer disks with one extra—more space to do it in. Companies are using CDs with interactive ads to sell everything from cars to computers. The ads usually contain videos, computer games, quizzes, animation, music, graphics, and other features to engage more of their audiences' senses. In a world where U.S. households receive *3.7 million tons* of paper each year in the form of direct mail ads, multimedia ads can offer a distinct advantage: They get noticed. One expert explains the appeal of multimedia ads, "You remember 20 percent of what you see, 30 percent of what you see and hear, and 60 percent of what you interact with."[58]

How to Use Direct Mail. The key to a direct mailing's success is the right mailing list. Even the best direct mail ad will fail if sent to the "wrong" customers. Owners can develop lists themselves, using customer accounts, telephone books, city and trade directories, and other sources. Other sources for mailing lists include companies selling complementary, but not

IN THE FOOTSTEPS OF AN ENTREPRENEUR

A Tough Market to Reach

*A*bout 33 percent of American men and 36 percent of American women are considered overweight. For years, marketers ignored this plus-sized segment of the population, acting as if the typical customer were shaped like models selling *haute couture* on the runways of the world's greatest fashion houses. That left larger customers with little choice but to try to squeeze into clothing styles and designs made for smaller people. More recently, however, businesses have begun to realize the potential for catering to this growing market. In fact, since 1980, there has been a 9 percent increase in the number of overweight people in this country. Increasingly, companies of all sizes have been providing products and services aimed at this target audience. In 1989, Jan Herrick began publishing Royal Resources, a directory of companies offering plus-sized products and services. The first edition contained just 137 entries. Today, Royal Resources lists in more than 50 categories more than 1,200 companies selling everything from dating services and toilet seats to wigs and motorcycle gear.

One small company focusing on the plus-sized market is Anne Kelly's Junonia Ltd., a maker of active-wear that sells its products through a mail-order catalog. Kelly, herself a full-figured person, says that she got the idea for her business when she had difficulty finding active wear for her workouts at the gym. Kelly's direct mail catalog carries items such as bike shorts, swimsuits, sports bras, ski jackets, leggings, and many others. Within three years, Junonia's mailing list topped 350,000, and sales surged past $2 million.

Like Kelly, many companies targeting the plus-sized market have discovered that direct mail is an excellent avenue for reaching their customers. For many large people, shopping in retail stores can be frustrating, embarrassing, and painful. "Who wants to schlep around to stores looking for [clothes] when you know they don't carry your size?" says Bill Fabrey. "And big people get really insensitive treatment from salespeople." Fabrey launched his own mail-order catalog, Amplestuff, featuring home furnishings, closet and bath items, and other gadgets for large people in 1988.

Companies selling to the plus-sized market must exercise caution, however. The problem stems from America's obsession with thinness: No one, not even an overweight person, likes to think of himself as "fat." "Do you know how people react when they receive a mailing for large-sized people?" asks Fabrey. "They're insulted and annoyed." Few advertisements succeed by insulting the very people they are targeting, so advertisers must find other ways to reach this target market. One way many have found to work well is by placing ads in magazines such as *BBW*, *Radiance*, and *Dimension* and other media that invite customers to write, fax, call, or e-mail for a catalog. Magazines, however, reach only a portion of the total market, leaving advertisers searching for creative ways to reach their target audience. "We're really pioneers in this market," says Fabrey. "It's like the Wild West used to be."

1. Working with a team of your classmates, develop at least five methods small companies targeting the plus-sized market could use to reach their customers.

2. What kinds of unique selling propositions should they consider?

SOURCE: Adapted from Frances Huffman, "Living Large," *Entrepreneur*, October 1997, pp. 156–159. ◆

---

competing products; professional organizations' membership lists; business or professional magazine's subscription lists; and mailing list brokers who sell lists for practically any need.

Outdoor Advertising. National advertisers have long used outdoor ads, and small firms (especially retailers) are now using this medium. Very few small businesses rely solely on outdoor advertising; instead, they supplement other advertising media with billboards. With a creative outdoor campaign, a small company can make a big impact, even on a small budget. *South of the Border, a unique tourist complex with a Mexican theme sitting on 350 acres near tiny Dillon, South Carolina, uses more than 200 billboards along Interstate 95 from Philadelphia to Daytona Beach, Florida, to lure visitors. During the busy summer travel season, as many as 50,000 people a day stop to satisfy the curiosity that the company's billboards create. As they pull into the main gate, visitors are greeted by a 97-foot sign featuring Pedro, the official mascot of South of the Border. Once inside, guests can stay in the complex's hotels or campgrounds and enjoy amusement rides, miniature golf, poker arcades, and restaurants. Owners credit much of their company's success to their creative outdoor advertising campaign.*[59]

"You've got to admire their truth-in-advertising."

SOURCE: *Forbes*, February 24, 1997, p. 30.

Outdoor advertising offers certain *advantages* to the small business:

High exposure. Outdoor advertising offers a high-frequency exposure; studies suggest that the typical billboard reaches an adult 29 to 31 times each month. Most people tend to follow the same routes in their daily traveling, and billboards are there waiting for them when they pass by. Also, when located near the advertiser's business, billboards can be effective as last-minute reminders.

Broad reach. The nature of outdoor ads makes them effective devices for reaching a large number of potential customers within a specific area. The people outdoor ads reach tend to be younger, wealthier, and better-educated than the average person.

Attention-getting. The introduction of new technology such as 3-D, fiber optics, and other creative special effects to outdoor advertising has transformed billboards from flat, passive signs to innovative, attention-grabbing promotions that passers-by cannot help but notice.

Flexibility. Advertisers can buy outdoor advertising units separately or in a number of packages. Through its variety of graphics, design, and unique features, outdoor advertising enables the small advertiser to match his message to the particular audience. Modern computer and printing technology have given outdoor ads a design facelift. A decade ago, only 5 percent of billboards actually used such technology; today, about 80 percent of billboards rely on some kind of computer technology. Not only does this technology make billboards look better, but its speed allows advertisers to change boards more frequently at lower costs.[60]

Cost efficiency. Outdoor advertising offers one of the lowest costs per thousand customers reached of all the advertising media.

Outdoor ads also have several *disadvantages*:

Brief exposure. Because billboards are immobile, the reader is exposed to the advertiser's message for only a short time, typically no more than five seconds. As a result, the message must be short and to the point. Outdoor advertisers must consider the type of traffic passing a billboard location as well as the volume of traffic going by (slower is better). Outdoor advertising copy cannot be as detailed or as informative as ads in other media.

Legal restrictions. Outdoor billboards are subject to strict regulations and to a high degree of standardization. At the federal level, the Highway Beautification Act of 1965 requires signs and billboards to be a standard size and to be attractive. At the local level, many cities place limitations on the number and type of signs and billboards allowed along the roadside. Recently, several major cities have severely restricted or banned the construction of new outdoor signs. Supporting such a ban, one opponent of outdoor advertising calls billboards "litter on a stick."[60]

Lack of prominence. More than 450,000 billboards now line the nation's highways, up from 330,000 in 1965.[62] This clutter of billboards and signs tends to reduce the effectiveness of a single ad, which loses its prominence in the crowd of billboards.

Using Outdoor Ads. Because the outdoor ad is stationary and the viewer is in motion, the small business owner must pay special attention to its design. An outdoor ad should:

◆ Identify the product and the company clearly and quickly.

◆ Use a simple background. The background should not compete with the message.

◆ Rely on large illustrations that jump out at the viewer.

◆ Include clear, legible type. All lower case or a combination of upper and lower case letters is best. Very bold or very thin type faces become illegible at a distance.

◆ Use black-and-white designs. Research shows that black-and-white outdoor ads are more effective than color ads. If color is important to the message, pick color combinations that contrast in both hue and brightness: e.g., black on yellow.

◆ Emphasize simplicity; short copy and short words are best. Don't try to cram too much onto a billboard. One study found that ads with fewer than eight words were most effective, and those containing more than 10 words were least effective.

◆ Use sharp, eye-catching graphics. Many billboards now use three-dimensional features or extensions that capture viewers' attention.

◆ Be located on the right-hand side of the highway. Studies show that ads located there draw higher recall scores than those located on the left-hand side.

◆ Use billboards as a reinforcement for other methods of advertising and to remind prospects of where you are and what you do.[63]

A spinoff of the billboard is the cold-air balloon—those giant balloons shaped like King Kong or Godzilla that sit atop businesses holding signs that promote a special sale or event. *One car dealer says that placing a giant balloon on the roof of his business is a sure-fire way to boost business. The owner of a child-care center rented a 30-foot-tall panda bear to attract attention to his business. The center's walk-in traffic tripled, and the entrepreneur says the $1,200 per week rental was more effective than his past attempts with radio or newspaper ads.*[64]

Transit Advertising. Transit advertising includes advertising signs inside and outside some 70,000 public transportation vehicles throughout the country's urban areas. The medium is

Cold-air balloons, such as this one of King Kong, add a new dimension to outdoor advertising. They offer one important benefit to advertisers: Customers notice them!

likely to grow as more cities look to public transit systems to relieve transportation problems. Transit ads offer a number of *advantages*:

Wide coverage. Transit advertising offers advertisers mass exposure to a variety of customers. The message literally goes to where the people are. This medium also reaches people with a wide variety of demographic characteristics. *Kathy Ruff and Martha Olson, owners of Tablescapes Party Rental decided to transform their company's two delivery trucks into rolling billboards. Working with a professional photographer and a graphics company, the two outfitted their trucks with 18-foot photographs of attractive table settings—one formal and the other informal. The rolling ads, which cost $3,500 per truck, have generated incredible amounts of attention for Tablescapes. "The response has been amazing," says Ruff. "Over 80 percent of the phone inquiries we get come from people who have seen the trucks." The transit ads have been so successful that the entrepreneurs have purchased a third truck that they will decorate in a similar fashion.*[65]

Repeat exposure. Transit ads provide repeated exposure to a message. The typical transit rider averages 24 rides per month and spends 61 minutes per day riding.[66] This gives advertisers ample opportunity to present their messages to transit riders.

Low cost. Even small business owners with limited budgets can afford transit advertising. One study shows that transit advertising costs on average only 30 cents per thousand.[67] Many transit systems offer discounts for long-term contracts.

Flexibility. Transit ads come in a wide range of sizes, numbers, and durations. With transit ads, an owner can select an individual market or any combination of markets across the country.

Transit ads also have several *disadvantages*:

Generality. Even though a small business can choose the specific transit routes on which to advertise, it cannot target a particular segment of the market through transit advertising. The effectiveness of transit ads depends on the routes that public vehicles travel and on the people they reach. Unfortunately, the advertiser cannot control either of those factors.

Limited appeal. Unlike many media, transit ads are not beamed into the potential customer's residence or business. The result is that customers cannot keep them for future reference. Also, these ads do not reach with great frequency the upper income, highly educated portion of the market.

Brief message. Transit ads do not permit the small advertiser to present a detailed description or a demonstration of the product or service for sale. Although inside ads have a relatively long exposure (the average ride lasts 22.5 minutes), outside ads must be brief and to the point.

Directories. Directories are an important advertising medium for reaching customers who have already made purchase decisions. The directory simply helps these customers locate the specific product or service they have decided to buy. Directories include telephone books, industrial or trade guides, buyer's guides, annuals, catalog files, and yearbooks that list various businesses and the products they sell. Directories offer several *advantages* to advertisers:

Prime prospects. Directory listings reach customers who are prime prospects, since they have already decided to purchase an item. The directory just helps them find what they are looking for.

Long life. Directory listings usually have long lives. A typical directory may be published annually.

However, there are certain *disadvantages* to using directories:

Lack of flexibility. Listings and ads in many directories offer only a limited variety of design features. Business owners may not be as free to create unique ads as in other printed media.

Obsolescence. Because directories are commonly updated only annually, some of their listings become obsolete. This is a problem for a small firm that changes its name, location, or phone number.

Using Directories. When choosing a directory, the small business owner should evaluate several criteria:

◆ *Completeness.* Does the directory include enough listings that customers will use it?

◆ *Convenience.* Are the listings well organized and convenient? Are they cross-referenced?

◆ *Evidence of use.* To what extent do customers actually use the directory? What evidence of use does the publisher offer?

◆ *Age.* Is the directory well established, and does it have a good reputation?

◆ *Circulation.* Do users pay for the directory, or do they receive complimentary copies? Is there an audited circulation statement?

Trade shows. Trade shows provide manufacturers and distributors with a unique opportunity to advertise to a preselected audience of potential customers who are inclined to buy.

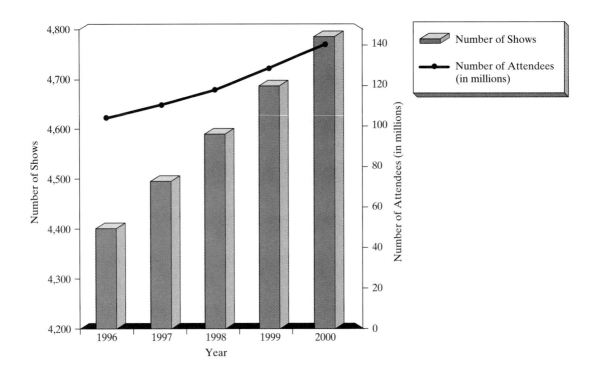

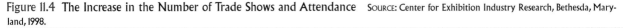

Figure 11.4 The Increase in the Number of Trade Shows and Attendance Source: Center for Exhibition Industry Research, Bethesda, Maryland, 1998.

Nearly 5,000 thousand trade shows are sponsored each year (see Figure 11.4), and carefully evaluating and selecting a few shows can produce profitable results for a small business owner. *Jonathan King and Jim Stott, co-founders of Stonewall Kitchens Ltd., a maker of specialty foods, saw an opportunity to attract new business at the International Fancy Food and Confection Show. When the company, based in York, Maine, won an award for the "most outstanding product line" at the show, King and Stott parlayed the interest the award generated into sales meetings with representatives from retailers across the country. During the show, Stonewall wrote up more than $85,000 in new orders, many of them from large national retailers. "Attending that show helped us reach markets that were just impossible for us to reach from here in York, Maine," says King. "We couldn't possibly see that many people or send out that many samples."*[68]

Trade shows offer the following *advantages*:

A natural market. Trade shows bring together buyers and sellers in a setting where products can be explained, demonstrated, and handled. Comparative shopping is easy, and the buying process is efficient. After displaying his company's line of bicycle pumps and locks at the National Sporting Goods Association trade show, the marketing manager for Paradigm Products says, "It's great to come here and talk with independent bike dealers where they're bunched up like bananas—600 to 800 of them come through here."[69]

Preselected audience. Trade exhibits attract potential customers with a specific interest in the goods or services being displayed. There is a high probability that these prospects

Jonathan King and Jim Stott, co-founders of Stonewall Kitchens, a maker of specialty foods, attracted attention for their small company by winning several awards at the International Fancy Food and Confection Show. Their trade show awards translated into increased sales for their company.

will make a purchase. One recent study by Exhibit Surveys found that 87 percent of those attending trade shows either make the purchase decisions in their companies or influence those decisions for the goods exhibited at the show.[70]

New customer market. Trade shows offer exhibitors a prime opportunity to reach new customers and to contact people who are not accessible to sales representatives. Plus, there is no better place to introduce new products (or a new company) than at a trade show, where all of the people there are interested in what's new and exciting.

Industry information. Trade shows provide excellent opportunities for entrepreneurs to find out what is happening in their industries and to size up their competitors—all in one place. Observant entrepreneurs can spot key trends in the industry and find out which products or services will be the next hot sellers.

International contacts. Many small companies make their first international sales at trade shows, which are extremely popular with foreign businesses. *Journey International, a small manufacturer of hand exercisers, made its first export sale to a Japanese company at the National Association of Sporting Goods show. "I can't imagine the incredible expense it would be for us to travel to Japan to try to find the right people to talk with," says Marc Mauseth, co-founder.*[71]

Cost advantage. As the cost of making a field sales call continues to escalate, more companies are realizing that trade shows are an economical method for making sales contacts and presentations. Studies show that the cost per visitor reached at trade shows is still well below the average cost of a personal sales call. For making a connection with the best sales prospects, trade shows provide good value for every dollar spent.

There are, however, certain *disadvantages* associated with trade shows:

Increasing costs. The cost of exhibiting at trade shows is rising quickly. Registration fees, travel and setup costs, sales salaries, and other expenditures may be a barrier to some small firms. The largest expenses at most trade shows are the cost of the display and booth rental.

Wasted effort. A poorly planned exhibit ultimately costs the small business more than its benefits are worth. Too many firms enter exhibits in trade shows without proper preparation, and they end up wasting their time, energy, and money on unproductive activities.

To avoid these disadvantages, business owners should:

◆ Study the profile of trade show guests and compare it with their target customers before committing to a show.

◆ Consider less-expensive local or regional trade shows.

◆ Communicate with key potential customers *before* the show; send them invitations. Many businesses have success with "half-premiums." They send out half of a premium or gift to prospects before a show and give away the other half at the booth at the trade show.

◆ Have knowledgeable salespeople staffing the booth.

◆ Demonstrate the product or service; let customers see it in action.

◆ Learn to distinguish between serious customers and "tirekickers." Ask probing questions to weed out those who are not good prospects.

◆ Distribute literature that clearly communicates the product or service sold.

◆ Project a professional image at all times.

◆ Follow up promptly on sales leads.

Specialty Advertising. As advertisers have shifted their focus to "narrow casting" their messages to target audiences and away from "broadcasting," specialty advertising has grown in popularity. Advertisers now spend more than $3 billion annually on specialty items. This category includes all customer gift items imprinted with the company's name, address, telephone number, and slogan. Specialty items are best used as reminder ads to supplement other forms of advertising and to help create goodwill with existing and potential customers.

Specialty advertising offers several *advantages*:

Reaching select audiences. Advertisers can reach specific audiences with well-planned specialty items.

Personalized nature. By carefully choosing a specialty item, business owners can personalize their advertisements. A small business owner should choose items that are unusual, related to the nature of the business, and meaningful to customers.

Versatility. The rich versatility of specialty advertising is limited only by the business owner's imagination. Advertisers print their logos on everything from pens and scarves to wallets and caps. When choosing advertising specialties, entrepreneurs should use items that are unusual and related to the nature of the business.

There are *disadvantages* to specialty advertising:

Potential for waste. Unless the owner chooses the appropriate specialty item, he will be wasting his time and money. The options are virtually infinite.

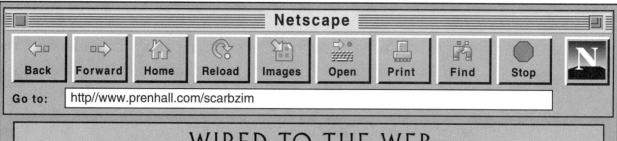

WIRED TO THE WEB

THE ADVERTISING PUZZLE

*F*our years ago, Lisa and Isaac Sineath launched The Chef's Companion, a small retail shop selling an up-scale line of condiments, kitchen accessories, and food-related gift items on Hilton Head Island, South Carolina. Although quite small, Hilton Head Island is known as a playground for the rich and famous. With its multi-million-dollar developments, luxury hotels, beautiful beaches, tennis tournaments, and world-class golf courses, the island draws wealthy visitors from around the world. Although their business took off slowly in the beginning, the Chef's Companion was rapidly gaining a reputation as the place to go on Hilton Head for gourmet foods and gifts with an unusual flare. "When we first started in business, we underestimated the amount of money it would take to run a company like this," says Lisa. "As a result, we didn't have enough money to spend on advertising and promotion in the early days. That really hurt, and we almost went out of business before our shop finally caught on with customers."

In those days, the Sineaths advertised occasionally in the local newspaper, the *Island Packet*, and in the tourism magazines available at hotels and restaurants around the island. Business picked up during the spring and summer tourist season, when the island's population swells to more than eight times its normal size. "And not a moment too soon," says Lisa.

"One of the best decisions we made was to rent a booth at a celebration during the Heritage," says Lisa, referring to the golf tournament held every spring on the island's famous Harbor Town golf course. "The booth fee and setup expenses represented a lot of money in those days," she recalls, "but we really believed that exposure would help our sales take off. Fortunately, we were right."

Although business is good and the company is successful, the Sineaths suspect that they are missing out on opportunities to sell their products and services. "There's plenty of purchasing power on this island, but I'm sure we're not tapping as much of it as we could be," says Isaac. "Last week, this young couple in their thirties climbed out of their Porsche, came in, and bought more than $500 worth of merchandise. As they were leaving, they said that this was their first visit to the island, but that they would definitely be back. They were pleased to find a store like ours, and the young woman even asked if we had a Web site! She was hoping to order some of our products from home."

"What did you tell her?" asked Lisa.

"I told her that you were working on building a Web site!" Isaac said, winking at her.

"Our problem is that we really don't have an integrated advertising and promotion strategy for the Chef's Companion," says Lisa. "Every month, we get calls and visits from sales representatives from lots of different media—from cable television and radio stations to newspapers and directories. We buy some ads, but we're really not sure which ones work and which ones don't. We've even thought about launching a catalog, but we're not sure where we could get a mailing list."

"That's true," echoes Isaac. "We haven't yet solved the advertising puzzle."

1. Use the resources of the World Wide Web and the resources in the library to research the demographics of the population of Hilton Head Island, South Carolina, and to learn about the island's tourist trade. Prepare a brief summary of your findings.

2. On the basis of your summary, help the Sineaths develop an advertising and promotion strategy for the Chef's Companion. Which advertising media would you suggest they use to advertise? Why? Use the Web to learn more about the media you suggest.

3. Would the Chef's Companion benefit from a mail-order catalog? If it would, how could the Sineaths get a mailing list?

Costs. Some specialty items can be quite expensive. Plus, some owners have a tendency to give advertising materials to anyone—even people who are not potential customers.

Special Events and Promotions. A growing number of small companies are finding that special events and promotions attract a great deal of interest and provide a lasting impression of the company. As customers become increasingly harder to reach through any single advertising medium, companies of all sizes are finding that sponsoring special events and promotions—from wine tastings and beach volleyball tournaments to fitness walks and rock climbs—is an excellent way to reach their target audiences. *In Japan, one maker of pork products generates millions of dollars of publicity and recognition by sponsoring a baseball team—the Nippon Ham Fighters!*[72]

Creativity and uniqueness are essential ingredients in any special event promotion, and most entrepreneurs excel at those. *For example, the owner of For Paws, a California pet boutique, sponsors free "doggy brunches" each week, complete with "kibble quiche" and "wheat-germ woofies." The shop also caters birthday parties, beach parties (picture a dog with a whistle around his neck, a muscle T-shirt, and a dab of Noxzema on his nose), and other gala events for its four-legged customers and their owners.*[73]

Point-of-Purchase Ads. In the last several years, in-store advertising has become more popular as a way of reaching the customer at a crucial moment—the point of purchase. Research suggests that consumers make two-thirds of all buying decisions at the point of sale. Self-service stores are especially well suited for in-store ads as they remind people of the products as they walk the aisles. These in-store ads are not just bland signs or glossy photographs of the product in use. Some businesses use in-store music interspersed with household hints and, of course, ads. Another ploy involves tiny devices that sense when a customer passes by and triggers a prerecorded sales message. Other machines emit scents—chocolate chip cookies or piña coladas—to appeal to passing customers' sense of smell.[74]

In sum, small business owners have an endless array of advertising tools, techniques, and media available to them. Even postage stamps, bathroom walls, sides of cows, and parking meters offer advertising space!

*P*reparing an Advertising Budget

4 Identify four basic methods for preparing an advertising budget.

One of the most challenging decisions confronting a small business owner is how much money to invest in advertising. The amount the owner wants to spend and the amount the firm can afford to spend on advertising usually differ significantly. There are four methods of determining an advertising budget: what is affordable, matching competitors, percentage of sales, and objective-and-task.

Under the *what-is-affordable method*, the owner sees advertising as a luxury. She views advertising completely as an expense, not as an investment that produces sales and profits in the future. Therefore, as the name implies, management spends whatever it can afford on advertising. Too often, the advertising budget is allocated funds only after all other budget items have been financed. The result is an inadequate advertising budget. This method also fails to relate the advertising budget to the advertising objective.

Another approach is to *match* the advertising expenditures of the firm's competitors, either in a flat dollar amount or as a percentage of sales. This method assumes that a firm's advertising needs and strategies are the same as those of its competitors. Competitors' actions can be helpful in establishing a floor for advertising expenditures, but relying on this technique can lead to blind imitation instead of a budget suited to the small firm's circumstances.

The most commonly used method of establishing an advertising budget is the simple *percentage-of-sales approach.* This method relates advertising expenditures to actual sales

October						
Sun	Mon	Tue	Wed	Thu	Fri	Sat
Advertising Budget for October: 9% of Sales = $2,275 Co-op Ads = $ 550 Total = $2,825		October Advertising Expenditures: $2,845 Under/(Over) Budget: $20 Remaining Balance: $6,400		**1** WPCC Radio 5 spots, $125 Billboard, $350	**2** The Chronicle 140 lines, $100	**3**
4	**5**	**6**	**7**	**8**	**9** The Chronicle 140 lines, $100	**10**
11	**12**	**13** Meet w/ Leslie re: November ad campaigns, 2 p.m.	**14**	**15** Envelope "Stuffer" in invoices: Halloween Sale, $175	**16** The Chronicle 140 lines, $100	**17** WPCC Radio, 5 spots, $100
18	**19**	**20** WPCC Radio, 5 spots, $125	**21**	**22** Direct Mail, Halloween Sale Promo "Preferred Customers," $120	**23** The Chronicle 140 lines, $100	**24** WPCC Radio, 5 spots, $100
25	**26** WPCC Radio, 5 spots, $125	**27** WPCC Radio, 5 spots, $125	**28** WPCC Radio, 5 spots, $125	**29** WPCC Radio, 5 spots, $125	**30** The Chronicle Half-page spread, Sale, $300	**31** Halloween Sale WPCC Radio, Live remote broadcast, $425

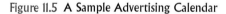

Figure 11.5 **A Sample Advertising Calendar**

results. Tying advertising expenditures to sales is generally preferred to relating them to profits because sales tend to fluctuate less than profits. One expert suggests a useful rule of thumb when establishing an advertising budget: 10 percent of projected sales the first year in business; 7 percent the second year; and at least 5 percent each year after that.[75] Relying totally on such broad rules can be dangerous, however. They may not be representative of a small company's advertising needs.

The *objective-and-task method* is the most difficult and least used technique for establishing an advertising budget. It also is the method most often recommended by advertising experts. With this method, an owner links advertising expenditures to specific objectives. Whereas the other three methods break down the total amount of funds allocated to advertising, the task method builds up the advertising funds by analyzing what it will cost to accomplish the specific objectives. For example, suppose that a manager wants to boost sales of a particular product 10 percent by attracting local college students. He may determine that a nearby rock radio station would be the best medium to use. Then he must decide on the number and frequency of the ads and estimate their costs. Entrepreneurs simply follow this same process for each advertising objective. A common problem with the method is that managers tend to be overly ambitious in setting advertising objectives, and, consequently, they set unrealistically high advertising expenditures. The manager may be forced to alter objectives, or the plans to reach them, to bring the advertising budget back to a reasonable level. However, the plan can still be effective.

Most small companies find it useful to plan in advance their advertising expenditures on a weekly basis. This short-term planning ensures a consistent advertising effort throughout the year. A calendar like the one pictured in Figure 11.5 can be one of the most valuable tools in planning a small company's advertising program. The calendar enables owners to prepare for holidays and special events, to monitor actual and budgeted expenditures, and to ensure that ads are scheduled on the appropriate media at the proper times.

$\mathscr{H}$ow to Advertise Big on a Small Budget

◆ Explain practical methods for stretching a small business's advertising budget.

The typical small business does not have the luxury of an unlimited advertising budget. Most cannot afford to hire a professional ad agency. This does not mean, however, that the small company should assume a second-class advertising posture. Most advertising experts say that, unless a small company spends more than $10,000 a year on advertising, it probably doesn't need an ad agency. For most, hiring freelance copywriters and artists on a per-project basis is a much better bargain. With a little creativity and a dose of ingenuity, small business owners can stretch their advertising dollars and make the most of what they spend. Three useful techniques to do this are cooperative advertising, shared advertising, and publicity.

COOPERATIVE ADVERTISING

In **cooperative advertising,** a manufacturing company shares the cost of advertising with a small retailer if the retailer features its products in those ads. Both the manufacturer and the retailer get more advertising per dollar by sharing expenses. *David Lang, owner of a small lawn equipment store, purchases his inventory from 10 different manufacturers, nine of whom offer cooperative advertising programs. "Without [the manufacturers' help], we could only spend $20,000 a year [on advertising]," says Lang. "But now we can spend $40,000 because we're getting $20,000 back."*[76]

Unlike Lang, who uses every dollar of cooperative advertising available to him, most small business owners fail to take advantage of manufacturers' cooperative advertising programs. Manufacturers, whose products cover the entire retail spectrum, make an estimated $30 billion of co-op ad dollars available each year; yet, more than half of it goes unused![77] You're missing the boat if you're not taking [advantage of] co-op advertising," says the owner of an office products company who used co-op funds to put a new sign on his building.[78] *Barbara Malki, co-owner of Cahaba Cycles, is now a believer in the power of cooperative advertising, although she admits that she had not always been. "Two years ago," she says, "I was leaving co-op money on the table. I'm more aggressive about that now. [Now] I . . . use every co-op dollar." Cahaba Cycles recoups about 10 percent of its annual advertising budget through cooperative advertising.*[79]

Manufacturers offer cooperative advertising programs in almost every medium. *For example, when a steep sales decline hit Bromby's Sport & Ski, Inc., owner Susan Fabbiano was forced to cut her advertising budget. Recognizing the importance of advertising to her business, Fabbiano was determined to maintain quality advertising despite a reduced budget. So she began to pursue co-op ads with the manufacturers of her product line. One company split the costs of radio and outdoor ads with Fabbiano 50-50. She claims, "Co-op advertising has allowed the store to keep its name before the public without increasing expenditures."*[80]

The "Scoop" on Successful Promotions

*I*t all started with $12,000 and a complete disregard for business rules in a converted gas station in Burlington, Vermont. Entrepreneurs Ben Cohen and Jerry Greenfield, founders of the world-famous Ben & Jerry's Homemade Inc., mixed a dash of irreverence with a pinch of optimism and a dollop of social activism to produce a business that scoops more than $167 million a year in ice cream. Cohen and Greenfield's attitude that business should be fun has led them to develop a host of fun—and very successful—promotions. After their first successful summer in business, Ben and Jerry decided to throw a party for their customers to celebrate the upcoming fall season. At the first annual "Fall Down," they worked with other Burlington business owners to create a street fair featuring a stilts-walking contest, an apple-peeling contest, and *lots* of ice cream. Fall Down was the company's first promotion and marked the birth of Ben and Jerry's unique brand of event marketing.

Even if your business doesn't have a promotional budget anywhere near the size of Ben and Jerry's, you can learn from them. Remember, they started out *very* small! The fact that they had almost no money for promotion and advertising in the early days of their business forced Ben and Jerry to come up with clever, creative ways to promote their company. Here are some lessons from these pundits of promotion.

Offer special off-season promotions. Their first winter in business (given the winter temperatures in Vermont, it seemed longer than it was), Ben and Jerry created several special promotions to keep customers interested. One was the POPCDBZWE sale, the "pennies of per Celsius degree below zero winter extravaganza." Inspired by major department stores' January bedding sales, they also ran "white sales" with specially priced vanilla ice cream and whipped cream treats.

Give away product samples. Product sampling is one of the promotions Ben and Jerry have relied on most often. They even took their sampling techniques out of their stores and put them on the road with the Cowmobile, a converted recreational vehicle, which they drove across the country doling out free scoops of ice cream.

Encourage your customers to take part in your business. Periodically, Ben and Jerry run contests, allowing cus-

tomers to come up with a name for one of their new flavors. Customers named Chunky Monkey, Cherry Garcia, and Chubby Hubby. The promotions generated tons of publicity from the town.

Throw a party. Today, Ben and Jerry sponsor the One World/One Heart festival, which offers not only family fun, entertainment, and, of course, free ice cream but also the opportunity to learn about and to get involved in a variety of social and environmental causes at "social action tents."

Build a relationship with your customers. Ben and Jerry go to great extremes to portray themselves as "those friendly hippies next door." Customers feels a close connection to this zany pair of entrepreneurs because they are so approachable and friendly.

Run your business in a socially responsible fashion and let customers know you're doing it. Part of Ben and Jerry's charm is that they run their business in a socially responsible and ethical manner (see the company's three-part mission statement at the Web site below), openly support a variety of social causes, and create products to benefit those causes. With its Rainforest Crunch ice cream, the company promotes awareness of the problem of deforestation of the world's fragile rain forests.

Business owners who want to take a lesson from Ben & Jerry's Homemade should consider the following tips:

Create an event that is related to your business. Promotions should not only attract customers but should also remind them of your business.

Consider a nontraditional "holiday" to run a promotion. Chase's Calendar of Events lists a variety of unusual events for every day of the year around which you can build a unique promotion.

Choose a local charity or nonprofit organization with which your company can get involved. Develop a unique promotion that will benefit both the charity and your company.

Find ways to get your customers involved in and excited about your business. Parties, celebrations, and contests are just some ways to keep your business in customers' minds.

Offer a scholarship. It doesn't have to be a large one, but it shows your concern for education and your commitment to the local community.

Sponsor a contest. A pet store owner might have a contest for the "Best-Dressed Pet," or the owner of a men's clothing store could hold a "Tackiest Tie" contest.

(*continued*)

Conduct a seminar. The owner of a small flower shop can generate lots of new business by sponsoring a short course on the basics of flower arranging.

Create a "Frequent Buyer" program. Remember how valuable existing customers are. Work hard to keep the customers you have!

Create an award for your community. For example, a landscape company might present a "best lawn" award each spring.

1. Visit Ben and Jerry's Homemade Web site at <http://www.benjerry.com>. Write a one-page paper summarizing some of the company's current promotional campaigns.

2. Working with a team of your classmates, select a local business, and develop ideas for special promotions that would benefit that company.

SOURCE: Adapted from Laura Tiffany, "Here's the Scoop," *Business Start-Ups,* December 1997, pp. 30–36. ◆

Cooperative advertising not only helps small businesses stretch their advertising budgets; it also offers another source of savings: the free advertising packages that many manufacturers supply to retailers. These packages usually include photographs and illustrations of the product as well as professionally prepared ads to use in different media. *Once, when Fabbiano was preparing an outdoor ad featuring Solomon products, she requested "a good photograph," from a sales representative. The supplier sent her, free of charge, the artwork for a billboard that would have cost $700 to produce. On another occasion, Fabbiano found and used two 30-second radio spots that had been "professionally written by the manufacturer's agency." Her cost: only the air time.*[81]

SHARED ADVERTISING

In **shared advertising,** a group of similar businesses forms a syndicate to produce generic ads that allow the individual businesses to dub in local information. The technique is especially useful for small businesses that sell relatively standardized products or services such as legal assistance, autos, and furniture. Because the small firms in the syndicate pool their funds, the result usually is higher-quality ads and significantly lower production costs.

PUBLICITY

The press can be either a valuable friend or a fearsome foe to a small business, depending on how well the owner handles her firm's publicity. Too often, entrepreneurs take the attitude, "My business is too small to be concerned about public relations." However, wise small business managers recognize that investing time and money in public relations (publicity) benefits both the community and the company. The community gains the support of a good business citizen, and the company earns a positive image in the marketplace.

Many small businesses rely on media attention to get noticed, and getting that attention takes a coordinated effort. Publicity doesn't just happen; business owners must work at getting their companies noticed by the media. Although such publicity may not be free, it definitely can lower the company's advertising expenditures and still keep its name before the public.[82] Because small companies' advertising budgets are limited, publicity takes on significant importance. *Bob Mayberry, a car dealer in Monroe, North Carolina, recently bought a 1961 Ford squad car like the one used on the 1960s hit TV series* The Andy Griffith Show. *Not only does the car lure potential customers onto his lot, but it also has gotten the dealership into several newspaper articles. "We have sold a lot of cars from it," says Mayberry.*[83]

One successful publicity technique is **cause marketing,** in which a small business sponsors and promotes fund-raising activities of nonprofit groups and charities while raising its own visibility in the community. *For example, Leon Bitelman, president of Shenoa and Company, a New York City jewelry store, offered a specially designed gold pin to the local PBS television station as a promotional gift for its annual fund-raising auction. The station* *featured the $1,500 pin (as well as the name, address, and telephone number for Shenoa and Company) in its direct mail catalog, which it sent to 750,000 viewers in the New York metropolitan area. The pin generated a large sum for the station and $500,000 in additional sales for Shenoa and Company. "I never dreamed a charity auction catalog would trigger 2,000 calls about a pin," says Bitelman.*[84]

OTHER WAYS TO SAVE

Other cost-saving suggestions for advertising expenditures include the following:

◆ *Repeat ads that have been successful.* In addition to reducing the cost of ad preparation, repetition may create a consistent image in a small firm's advertising program.

◆ *Use identical ads in different media.* If a billboard has been an effective advertising tool, an owner should consider converting it to a newspaper or magazine ad or a direct mail flier.

◆ *Hire independent copywriters, graphic designers, photographers, and other media specialists.* Many small businesses that cannot afford a full-time advertising staff buy their advertising services à la carte. They work directly with independent specialists and usually receive high-quality work that compares favorably with that of advertising agencies without paying a fee for overhead.

◆ *Concentrate advertising during times when customers are most likely to buy.* Some small business owners make the mistake of spreading an already small advertising budget evenly—and thinly—over a 12-month period. A better strategy is to match advertising expenditures to customers' buying habits.

Chapter Summary

❶ Describe the steps in developing an advertising strategy.
  ◆ Define the purpose of the company's advertising program by creating specific, measurable objectives.
  ◆ Analyze the firm and its target audience.
  ◆ Decide what to say and how to say it, making sure to build the message around the company's unique selling proposition (USP).
  ◆ Evaluate the ad campaign's effectiveness.

❷ Explain the differences among promotion, publicity, personal selling, and advertising.
  ◆ Promotion is any form of persuasive communication designed to inform consumers about a product or service and to influence them to purchase those goods or services.
  ◆ Publicity is any commercial news covered by the media that boosts sales but for which the small business does not pay.
  ◆ Personal selling is the personal contact between salespeople and potential customers resulting from sales efforts.
  ◆ Advertising is any sales presentation that is nonpersonal in nature and is paid for by an identified sponsor.

❸ Describe the advantages and disadvantages of the various advertising media.
  ◆ The medium used to transmit an advertising message influences the consumer's perception—and reception—of it.
  ◆ Media options include newspapers, radio, television, magazines, direct mail, the World Wide Web, outdoor advertising, transit advertising, directories, trade shows, special events and promotions, and point-of-purchase ads.

❹ Identify four basic methods for preparing an advertising budget.
  ◆ Establishing an advertising budget presents a real challenge to the small business owner. There are four basic methods: what is affordable; matching competitors; percentage of sales; objective-and-task.

❺ Explain practical methods for stretching a small business's advertising budget.
  ◆ Despite their limited advertising budgets, small businesses do not have to take a second-class approach to advertising. Three techniques that can stretch a small company's advertising dollars are cooperative advertising, shared advertising, and publicity.

Discussion Questions

1. What are the three elements of promotion? How do they support one another?
2. What factors should a small business manager consider when selecting advertising media?
3. What is a unique selling proposition? What role should it play in a company's advertising strategy?
4. Create a table to summarize the advantages and disadvantages of the following advertising media:

   Newspapers   Direct mail
   Radio   Outdoor advertising
   Television   Transit advertising
   Magazines   Directories
   Specialty advertising   Trade shows

5. What are fixed spots, preemptible spots, and floating spots in radio advertising?
6. Describe the characteristics of an effective outdoor advertisement.
7. Briefly outline the steps in creating an advertising plan. What principles should the small business owner follow when creating an effective advertisement?
8. Describe the common methods of establishing an advertising budget. Which method is most often used? Which technique is most often recommended? Why?
9. What techniques can small businesses use to stretch their advertising budgets?

Step into the Real World

1. Contact a small retailer, a manufacturer, and a service firm and interview each one about his or her advertising program.
   a. Are there specific advertising objectives?
   b. What media does the owner employ? Why?
   c. How does the manager evaluate an ad's effectiveness?
   d. What assistance does the manager receive in designing ads?
2. Contact several small business owners and determine how they establish their advertising budgets. Why do they use the method they do?
3. Collect two or three advertisements for local small businesses and evaluate them on a scale of 1 (low) to 10 (high) using the following criteria: attention-getting, distinctive, interesting, concise, appealing, credible, USP-focused, convincing, motivating, and effective. How would you change the ads to make them more effective?
4. Browse through a magazine and find two ads that use sex to sell a good or service—one that you consider effective and one that you consider offensive. Compare your ads and reasoning with those of your classmates. What implications does your discussion have for advertisers?

Take It to the Net

Visit the Scarborough/Zimmerer home page at
www.prenhall.com/scarbzim
for updated information, on-line resources, and Web-based exercises.

Endnotes

1. Kylo-Patrick Hart, "Step 11: Promote Your Business," *Business Start-Ups*, April 1997, pp. 64–66; Mark Henricks, "Spread the Word," *Entrepreneur*, February 1998, pp. 120–125.
2. Jan Alexander and Aimee L. Stern, "Avoid the Deadly Sins in Advertising," *Your Company*, August/September 1997, p. 22.
3. Bob Weinstein, "A Golden Opportunity," *Business Start-Ups*, November 1997, pp. 63–65.
4. Shelby Meinhardt, "Put It in Print," *Entrepreneur*, January 1989, p. 54.
5. Lin Grensing-Pophal, "Who Are You?" *Business Start-Ups*, September 1997, pp. 38–44.
6. Sue Clayton, "Handsome Prints," *Business Start-Ups*, October 1995, p. 30.
7. Ibid.
8. Ibid.
9. Ibid.
10. Jan Alexander and Aimee L. Stern, "Avoid the Deadly Sins in Advertising," p. 22.
11. Lynn H. Colwell, "What's the Score?" *Business Start-Ups*, January 1998, pp. 56–58.
12. Meg Whittemore, "PR on a Shoestring," *Nation's Business*, January 1991, p. 31.
13. "Publicity Scores over Ads," *Communication Briefings*, December 1994, p. 5.
14. Meg Whittemore, "Partner with a Charity for Profits," *Your Company*, August/September 1997, p. 24.
15. Lynn Beresford, "Going My Way?" *Entrepreneur*, February 1996, p. 32.

16. Elizabeth Jensen, "Rosie and 'Friends' Make Drake's Cakes a Star," *Wall Street Journal*, February 10, 1997, pp. B1, B7.

17. "Nine Habits of Highly Effective Salespeople," *Inc.*, June 1997, p. 96; "Traits of Top Salespeople," *Small Business Reports*, December 1990, pp. 7–8; Jaclyn Fierman, "The Death and Rebirth of the Salesman," *Fortune*, July 25, 1994, pp. 80–91; Robert McGarvey, "Hard Sell," *Entrepreneur*, August 1997, pp. 98–109; Carla Goodman, "25 Super Sales Secrets," *Business Start-Ups*, April 1997, pp. 20–25.

18. Carla Goodman, "Closing the Deal," *Business Start-Ups*, July 1997, p. 62.

19. "Most Salespeople Can't Sell," *Small Business Reports*, September 1990, p. 10.

20. "Prepare for Sales Calls," *Success*, May 1996, p. 25.

21. "Those Who Ask, Get," *The Competitive Advantage* (Sample Issue 19), p. 7.

22. "The Cost of a Sales Call," *Inc.*, May 1991, p. 86.

23. "Meeting Customer Needs," *In Business*, May/June 1989, p. 14.

24. "An Invisible Sign," *Reader's Digest*, December 1993, p. 26.

25. Barry Trailer, "Driving By the Seat of Their Pants," *Sales & Field Force Automation*, May 1998, pp. 22–26.

26. "Business News," *Wall Street Journal*, July 13, 1995, p. A1.

27. Tom L. Brown, "Honesty Is the Best (PR) Policy," *Industry Week*, November 7, 1988, p. 13.

28. Alexander and Stern, "Avoid the Deadly Sins in Advertising," pp. 22–24.

29. Bill Reynolds, "The Eye of the Beholder," *GSA Business*, February 2, 1998, p. 3B.

30. "What Makes Products Sell?" *Communication Briefings*, July 1997, p. 6.

31. Ibid.

32. "Which Media?" *Communication Briefings*, January 1994, p. 4.

33. <http://www.rab.com/station/radfact/fact1.html>.

34. Phil Hall, "Make Listeners Your Customers," *Nation's Business*, June 1994, p. 53R.

35. Kyle Pope, "Why TV Ad Proceeds Are Rising Even As Viewership Is Falling," *Wall Street Journal*, May 12, 1997, pp. B1, B6.

36. "Ad Suggestion from New Study," *Communication Briefings*, June 1995, p. 2.

37. Judith Waldrop, "And Now a Break from Our Sponsor," *American Demographics*, August 1993, pp. 16–17.

38. Sally Beatty, "Some Great Ads You'll Probably Never See," *Wall Street Journal*, June 2, 1998, p. B8.

39. Robert McGarvey, "Surf Watch," *Entrepreneur*, September 1996, p. 28.

40. Jill H. Ellsworth, "Staking a Claim on the Internet," *Nation's Business*, January 1996, pp. 29–31.

41. McGarvey, "Surf Watch."

42. "CyberStats," *Computing Today*, March/April 1998, p. 16.

43. Ellsworth, "Staking a Claim on the Internet."

44. Ibid., p. 29.

45. *The Dynamics of Change in Markets and Media*, from a Magazine Publishers Association seminar, New York.

46. Glen Weisman and Karin Moeller, "Pushing the Envelope," *Business Start-Ups*, October 1997, pp. 26–30.

47. Paul Hughes, "Winning Ways," *Entrepreneur*, February 1994, pp. 80–88.

48. "Why They Open Direct Mail," *Communication Briefings*, December 1993, p. 5.

49. Ernan Roman, "More for Your Money," *Inc.*, September 1992, p. 116.

50. Charlotte Mulhern, "Direct Hit," *Entrepreneur*, April 1997, p. 192.

51. Weisman and Moeller, "Pushing the Envelope."

52. Carolyn Campbell, "A Direct Hit," *Business Start-Ups*, August 1997, pp. 8–10.

53. Roman, "More for Your Money."

54. Nancy Bader, "1-800-4-MO'BIZ," *Your Company*, Summer 1994, p. 4.

55. Gewn Sublette, "Eye Catchers," *Entrepreneur*, August 1992, p. 156.

56. Gayle Sato Stodder, "Getting Noticed," *Entrepreneur*, October 1997, p. 33.

57. Ed Nanas, "Computer Diskettes," *Your Company*, Spring 1993, pp. 8–9.

58. Gillian Newson, "Interactive Marketing Is Driven to Succeed," *NewMedia*, June 1993, pp. 73–77; Kristin Davis, "Junk Mail Worthy of the Name," *Kiplinger's Personal Finance Magazine*, March 1993, pp. 56–61.

59. Anna Kelly, "Doing Business South of the Border," *Region Focus*, Spring 1998, p. 8.

60. <http://www.signweb.com/buy-guides/july97/outdoor1b.html>.

61. "South Carolina Singled Out by Billboard Critics As Example of 'Litter on a Stick,'" *Greenville News*, April 26, 1997, p. 3D.

62. Ibid.

63. *The Big Outdoor* (New York: Institute of Outdoor Advertising), p. 15; "Outdoor Ads That Work Best," *Communication Briefings*, October 1993, p. 6; Lynn Beresford, "The Big Picture," *Entrepreneur*, July 1996, p. 38.

64. Rodney Ho, "Retailers Love Big Balloons, But Others Try to Pop Them," *Wall Street Journal*, October 7, 1997, pp. B1, B2.

65. Roberta Maynard, "Ads on Wheels Send a Message in Traffic," *Nation's Business*, August 1997, p. 10.

66. *TAA Rate Directory of Transit Advertising* (New York: Transit Advertising Association), p. 2.

67. Ibid.

68. Dale D. Buss, "Cashing In on Trade Shows," *Nation's Business*, November 1996, p. 22.

69. Ibid., p. 23.

70. Buss, "Cashing In on Trade Shows," p. 23; <http://www.edgeon-line.com/main/edgemag/archives/mau3.shtm>.

71. Buss, "Cashing In on Trade Shows," p. 23.

72. Randall Lane, "The Ultimate Sponsorship," *Forbes*, March 14, 1994, p. 106.

73. Carrie Dolan, "Putting on the Dog Just Comes Naturally in Fey Marin County," *Wall Street Journal*, September 20, 1985, p. 1.

74. Ronald Alsop, "To Snare Shoppers, Companies Test Talking, Scented Displays," *Wall Street Journal*, June 12, 1986, p. 31.

75. Meinhardt, "Put It in Print."

76. Denise Osburn and Dawn Kopecki, "A Way to Stretch Ad Dollars," *Nation's Business*, May 1994, p. 68.

77. Richard Breen, "Small Businesses Run with the Big Dogs," *GSA Business*, February 16, 1998, p. 3B.

78. Ibid.

79. Jane Easter Bahls, "Ad It Up," *Entrepreneur*, December 1994, pp. 47–49.

80. Carol Rose Carey, "Cut Ad Costs without Cutting Quality," *Inc.*, April 1982, pp. 108–110.

81. Ibid., p. 108.

82. Frederick Ingram, "Who Do You Turn To?" *GSA Business*, February 2, 1998, p. 5B.

83. "Advertising Vehicles: Businesses Discover New Use for Old Cars," *Greenville News*, June 19, 1993, p. 1D.

84. Whittemore, "Partner with a Charity for Profits."

International Opportunities for Small Business

It is easier to go to the moon than it is to enter the world of another civilization. Culture—not space—is the greatest distance between two people.

—*Jamake Highwater*

Knowledge, learning, information, and skilled intelligence are the raw materials of international commerce and are today spreading throughout the world as vigorously as miracle drugs, synthetic fertilizers, and blue jeans did earlier.

—*From* A Nation at Risk

Upon completion of this chapter, you will be able to

1. Explain why "going global" has become an integral part of many small companies' strategies.

2. Describe the eight principal strategies small businesses have for going global.

3. Explain how to build a thriving export program.

4. Discuss the major barriers to international trade and their impact on the global economy.

5. Describe the trade agreements that will have the greatest influence on foreign trade into the twenty-first century.

*U*ntil recently, the world of international business was much like the world of astronomy before Copernicus, who revolutionized the study of the planets and the stars with his theory of planetary motion. In the sixteenth century, his Copernican system replaced the Ptolemaic system, which held that the earth was the center of the universe, with the sun and all the other planets revolving around it. The Copernican system, however, placed the sun at the center of the solar system with all of the planets, including the earth, revolving around it. Astronomy would never be the same.

In the same sense, business owners across the globe have had a Ptolemaic perspective when it came to viewing international business opportunities. Owners have thought in terms of an economy that revolved around their national home base and have believed that market opportunities stopped at their homeland's borders. Global trade was only for giant corporations who had the money and the management to tap foreign markets and enough resources to survive if the venture flopped.

Today, the global marketplace is as much the territory of small, upstart companies as it is that of giant multinational corporations. *For instance, Original Log Cabin Homes, Ltd., a manufacturer of log homes, based in tiny Rocky Mount, North Carolina, started its foray into international markets quite innocently. The company received an inquiry from a person in Japan and made the sale. That single sale sparked the company's interest in international markets, and a small resort project in South Korea soon followed. Original Log Cabin Homes now sells its prefabricated log homes in more than 50 countries and has just signed a $6.4 million contract with a distributor in Thailand. International sales account for 70 percent of the company's sales.*[1]

Just a few years ago, military might governed world relationships; today, commercial trade has become the force that drives global interaction. Since World War II, the proportion of trade as a share of global income has climbed from 7 percent to 21 percent. In that same time period, world trade has increased 15-fold, compared with a six-fold increase in production. Countries at every stage of development are reaping the benefits of increased global trade. Developing countries now account for about 25 percent of world trade, up from 20 percent a decade ago. In the United States alone, international trade now accounts for 25 percent of gross domestic product. The future of international business appears to be bright. The Organization for Economic Cooperation and Development (OECD) projects the growth rate of global business at 3.5 to 4 percent per year over the next two decades. At that rate of growth, global trade will double by the year 2020.[2]

Political, social, cultural, and economic changes are sweeping the world, creating a new world order—and a legion of both problems and opportunities for businesses of all sizes. These changes are creating instability for businesses of *any* size going global, but they also are creating tremendous opportunities for small companies ready to capitalize on them. *For instance, Sheila Brady, president of Brady Associates Inc., a small landscape architecture firm in California, observed the rapid pace at which many Asian economies were expanding and decided that her company could benefit from that growth. A trip to Vietnam and several visits to China opened the door to international markets for Brady's 23-person business. Eventually, meetings with government officials in those countries produced contracts for urban design and environmental planning services across the Pacific Rim, where rapid, often uncontrolled growth has created a huge need for Brady's services. International business has been so good at her $2 million a year company that Brady ultimately plans to establish a small office in Asia.*[3]

Expanding a business beyond its domestic borders may actually enhance a small company's performance. A recent study by Coopers and Lybrand found that small companies that export grow at an average rate of 31.2 percent a year compared with just 24.9 percent for companies that operate domestically.[4] Another study, by the Conference Board, concluded that U.S. manufacturers with global operations earn more and grow faster than do those that remain purely domestic (see Figure 12.1). In addition, multinational firms were 50 percent more likely to survive the decade than were those who limited their businesses to the United States.[5] Another study, from the Commerce Department, found that companies that export create better, higher-paying jobs for their workers than do their purely domestic counterparts.[6]

*W*hy Go Global?

◆ Explain why "going global" has become an integral part of many small companies' strategies.

Businesses can no longer consider themselves to be domestic companies in this hotly competitive, global environment. "In the global economy, the competitor six time zones away is potentially as serious a threat as the competitor six blocks away," says one expert.[7] For com-

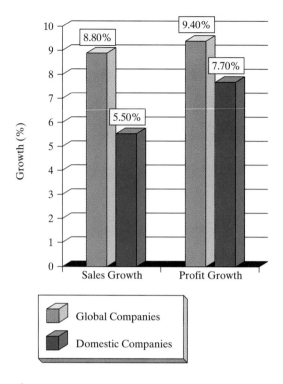

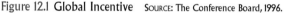

Figure 12.1 Global Incentive SOURCE: The Conference Board, 1996.

panies across the world, going global is a matter of survival, not preference. No matter where a company's home base is, competitors are forcing it to think globally. *For example, the executives of a small Oregon company manufacturing robotic-vision systems to cut french fries discovered that a Belgian company had developed a similar, competing device. "There are an awful lot of people in the rest of the world who think they are pretty good at doing your business," warns Lester Thurow.*[8] In the 1950s, just 5 percent of the goods made in the United States faced foreign competition; by the year 2000, 80 percent will go up against foreign goods. "If you ultimately are going to succeed in a global world, you need to go global," says one foreign trade specialist.[9]

Failure to cultivate global markets can be a lethal mistake for modern businesses, whatever their size. Increasingly, small businesses will be under pressure to expand into international markets, to consider themselves businesses without borders. "If a company really is a global competitor, it is going to be shipping all over the place from all over the place," says one executive.[10]

Going global can put tremendous strain on a small company, but entrepreneurs who take the plunge into global business can reap the following benefits:

◆ **Offset sales declines in the domestic market.** Markets in foreign countries may be booming when those in the United States are sagging. *When Bicknell Manufacturing Company, a manufacturer of drill bits for construction equipment, saw its sales falter because of a severe recession in the construction industry, manager John Purcell began scrambling for new business. The 102-year-old company saw little hope of a fast recovery in its traditional domestic market, so managers began exploring market opportunities abroad. Through their research, they discovered building booms in several foreign* countries, including Brazil, Mexico, and Colombia. Today, international sales account for 20 percent of Bicknell's total revenue.[11]

◆ **Increase sales and profits.** As income levels rise in many developing nations, demand for imported goods increases accordingly, and many consumers across the world have an affinity for anything American. "Companies are realizing that [by] relying only on the domestic market, they have been ignoring 4 billion other [potential] customers," says one export consultant.[12] Indeed, 96 percent of the world's consumers live *outside* the United States![13]

◆ **Extend their products' life cycle.** Some companies have been able to take products that had reached the maturity stage of the product life cycle in the United States and sell them successfully in foreign markets.

◆ **Lower manufacturing costs.** In industries characterized by high levels of fixed costs, businesses who expand into global markets can lower their manufacturing costs by spreading those fixed costs over a larger number of units.

◆ **Improve competitive position and enhance reputation.** Going up against some of the toughest competition in the world forces a company to hone its competitive skills. *Avid Technology, a small manufacturer of computerized video editing systems, has taken the bold step of selling its systems in the heart of the world's base for consumer electronics: Japan. Avid's owners believe its presence in Japan is an important component in the company's ability to stay ahead of its competitors. "We gain more credibility in the United States as well," says Avid's Asia-Pacific sales manager.*[14]

◆ **Raise quality levels.** Customers in many global markets are much tougher to satisfy than those in the United States. One reason Japanese products have done so well worldwide is that Japanese companies must build products to satisfy their customers at home, who demand extremely high quality and are sticklers for detail. Businesses who compete in global markets learn very quickly how to boost their quality levels to world-class standards.

◆ **Become more customer-oriented.** Delving into global markets teaches business owners about the unique tastes, customs, preferences, and habits of customers in many different cultures. Responding to these differences imbues businesses with a degree of sensitivity toward their customers, both domestic and foreign.

Unfortunately, not enough entrepreneurs have learned to see their companies from a global perspective. The Competitiveness Policy Council's report warns that "an absence of global thinking" is one of the elements that permeates our society and most directly hurts its competitive position."[15] Indeed, learning to *think globally* may be the first—and most difficult—goal an entrepreneur must achieve on the way to creating a truly global business. One British manager explains:

> If you are operating in South America, you'd better know how to operate in conditions of hyper-inflation. If you're operating in Africa, you'd better know a lot about government relations and the use of local partners. If you're operating in Germany, you'd better understand the mechanics of codetermination and some of the special tax systems that one finds in that country. If you're operating in China, it's quite useful in trademark matters to know how the People's Court of Shanghai works. . . . If you're operating in Japan, you'd better understand the different trade structure.[16]

David Montague, owner of Montague Corporation, a small maker of unique folding bikes, operates his business from a global perspective. Montague designs its bikes in Cambridge, Massachusetts, manufactures them in Taiwan, and sells most of them in Europe. Coordinating his business across three continents requires Montague to use the latest information and communication technology available. (He often gets up at 5 A.M. to talk to workers

Montague Corporation, a small maker of unique folding bikes, is a global company. Montague designs its bikes in the United States, manufactures them in Taiwan, and sells most of them in Europe.

in Germany.) However, his global diversification offers a measure of security: Montague is not dependent on any single economy for his company's success.[17]

Gaining a foothold in newly opened foreign markets or maintaining a position in an existing one is no easy task, however. "The key to the problem of how to truly become global can be summarized in one word: *attitude*," says one U.S. manager. "Until you have the attitude that you are truly an international company, not just a U.S. company also doing business abroad, you cannot achieve your goals."[18] Success in the global economy also requires constant innovation; staying nimble enough to use speed as a competitive weapon; maintaining a high level of quality and constantly improving it; being sensitive to foreign customers' unique requirements; adopting a more respectful attitude toward foreign habits and customs; hiring motivated, multilingual employees; and retaining a desire to learn constantly about global markets. In short, the path to success requires businesses to become "insiders" rather than just "exporters."

Before venturing into the global marketplace, a small business owner should consider five questions:[19]

1. Are we willing to commit adequate resources of time, people, and capital to our international campaign?
2. Can we make money there?
3. If so, can we get it out? (i.e., Is the currency convertible?)
4. Will we feel comfortable doing business there? (i.e., Are we sensitive to the cultural differences of conducting international business?)
5. Can we afford not to go global?

The accompanying Gaining the Competitive Edge feature describes a matrix that can help small businesses assess their level of global readiness.

*G*oing Global: Strategies for Small Businesses

2 Describe the eight principal strategies small businesses have for going global.

A growing number of small businesses are recognizing that going global is not a strategy reserved solely for industry giants such as General Motors, IBM, and Boeing. In fact, John Naisbitt, trend-spotting author of *The Global Paradox*, says that the increasing globalization

GAINING THE COMPETITIVE EDGE

Assessing Your Company's Global Potential

A.T. Kearney Inc., a Chicago-based management consulting firm, recently developed a matrix to help businesses assess the level of their global business competitiveness. The matrix describes the characteristics of companies at each of four stages of global development (see accompanying figure). "The stages are a reflection of management's leadership and ability to advance its [international] capabilities," says William Best, director of A.T. Kearney International. "As a company develops from the lower stages to the more advanced stages of global development, its chances for prospering [internationally] are increased."

Stages of Global Development

	I Domestic	II International	III Multinational	IV Global
Management Orientation	Domestic orientation	Select international experience	Localization of management	Country-neutral
Product/Service/Quality Approach	U.S. standards and products only	Minor modification from U.S. standard	Major adaptation of U.S. product/service	Global design, Local adaptation
Financial Perspective	Cost/margins	Short-term return on investment (ROI)	Long-term ROI and penetration	Strategically adjusted ROI
Perceived Constraints	Export focus	Local marketing, service, and assembly	Full-line manufacturing, Local R&D	Global integration and feedback
Functional	Tariffs Quotas Culture Language	Distribution and market penetration	Resource and partnership concerns	Information and control linkages

Stage I These are firms whose main focus is the domestic market. Any exporting is likely to be an attempt to increase revenues at low cost; products designed for domestic consumption are marketed through international distribution channels. As a result, these companies have little or no presence in overseas markets. These firms tend to have a top-down, autocratic decision-making style and a very short-term, cost- and margin-oriented financial perspective. Many of their managers see tariffs, quotas, culture, or language as major constraints on foreign market entry or expansion.

Stage II These international companies recognize the need to adapt products to local markets but are slow to do so—or to manufacture or make major investments overseas. Senior management is conversant with, but not fluent in, the ways of international business. Short-term return on investment likely determines their financial perspective. Foreign frustrations are related to market penetration and product distribution.

Stage III These multinational firms are experienced in tailoring products to overseas markets and in offshore research, development, and production. Service needs are likely to be fulfilled locally. A majority of managers are hired locally. Their financial perspective is much longer-term than that of stage II firms.

Stage IV These global companies, operating with worldwide strategies, are at home in every market. There's so much foreign presence at the senior management and board levels that the companies could be dubbed country-neutral. Financial targets are tied to strategic plans, which means operations often are linked to five- to ten-year planning cycles. "Stage IV company operations are truly global in scope and scale; [they feature] global design with local adaptation, global functional integration, and global information and control linkages," says Best.

A.T. Kearney designed this matrix to help businesses assess their capacity for global competitiveness. Best suggests using it to help companies answer five key questions:

1. How worldly is management's orientation?
2. What is the firm's approach to products, service, and quality?
3. Is the company's financial perspective short- or long-term?
4. How is the company organized for foreign business?
5. What foreign constraints on business exist?

---

1. At what level in the matrix do most U.S. small businesses fall? Why?

2. What steps can a small business take to advance to higher levels on the matrix?

Source: John S. McClenahen, "This Matrix Was Made for You." Reprinted with permission from *Industry Week*, September 2, 1991, pp. 91–92. Copyright, Penton Publishing, Inc., Cleveland, Ohio. ◆

of business actually favors smaller companies. "In the huge global economy, there will be smaller and smaller market niches," says Naisbitt. "In this global economy, . . . the competitive edge is swiftness to market and innovation. Small units are much better at speed to market and innovation. . . . As a result, they can innovate faster, not just in products but in internal operations, to take advantage of the new technologies."[20] Their agility and adaptability give small firms the edge in today's highly interactive, fast-paced global economy. "The bigger the world economy, the more powerful its smallest players," concludes Naisbitt.[21]

Small companies go global for a variety of reasons. Some move into foreign markets because their domestic sales have sagged. *For example, Sally Corporation, a small company that makes audio-animatronic robots for theme parks, casinos, museums, and retailers, began in the 1970s when an entrepreneurial dentist saw an opportunity to provide such creations to then-booming pizza restaurant chains in the United States. When that market faltered, a new team of owners purchased Sally and broadened the company's customer base to include its current mix of global customers. "What really turned the company around," says president Howard Kelley, "was becoming an international company. Now we do about 70 percent of our business abroad." For a large Hong Kong retail and office complex, Sally recently completed work on its most sophisticated project to date, The Maestro, a $120,000 robot that will conduct the jets of a fountain to the accompaniment of a musical symphony.*[22]

Other small businesses have discovered soaring demand for their products and services among foreign customers. *For instance, when Rostilav Ordovsky-Tanaevsky traveled for the first time to the former Soviet Union, he stumbled upon his father's relatives, many of whom had been missing since the 1917 Bolshevik Revolution. When he went to buy film for his camera to record the event, "I couldn't find a single roll," he recalls. On another trip, Ordovsky-Tanaevsky tried to have lunch but couldn't find an open restaurant! Sensing the business opportunities before him, Ordovsky-Tanaevsky spent the next five years building his business, Rostik International. Today, he owns more than 200 Fokus photo retail stores and is Moscow's leading restaurateur. His restaurants include a string of hamburger stands, pizzerias, New York–style delicatessens, and theme restaurants. "Growth is here for the next 20 years," Ordovsky-Tanaevsky says.*[23]

Still other entrepreneurs realize that their future success depends on their ability to go global. *Copreneurs Edward Wierzbowski and Pamela Roberts saw global markets as the key to success for their small television production company, Global American Television. Although small in size (annual revenues of less than $500,000), Global American Television has big aspirations: to help create a successful commercial television industry in Russia. Because it has been working with Russian television companies since the early 1980s, the company has a head start on its much larger competitors and does plenty of high-profile business in Russia. Global American has coproduced several projects with Russian companies and was the first to persuade Russian television companies to sell commercial air time to Western companies. "We compete as a small company by being willing to take risks and always looking for a new niche," says Wierzbowski, who is interested in developing other foreign markets as well.*[24]

Becoming a global business depends on instilling a global culture throughout the organization that permeates *everything* the company does. Entrepreneurs who routinely conduct international business have developed a global mind-set for themselves and their companies. As one business writer explains:

> *The global [business] . . . looks at the whole world as one market. It manufactures, conducts research, raises capital, and buys supplies wherever it can do the job best. It keeps in touch with technology and market trends around the world. National boundaries and regulations tend to be irrelevant, or a mere hindrance. [Company] headquarters might be anywhere.*[25]

Sally Corporation, a small company that manufactures animatronic robots, started by selling its unique products only in the United States but quickly saw the potential for growth in foreign markets. Today, the company's robots perform around the world. Here, one of the company's creations, The Maestro, conducts dancing fountains in the six-story Grand Century Place, a shopping mall in Kowloon, Hong Kong.

As cultures from around the globe become increasingly interwoven, the ability to "go global" will determine the relative degree of success for more and more small businesses.

Small companies pursuing a global presence have eight principal strategies available: the World Wide Web, relying on trade intermediaries, joint ventures, foreign licensing, franchising, countertrading and bartering, exporting, and establishing international locations (see Figure 12.2).

THE WORLD WIDE WEB

Perhaps the simplest and least expensive way for a small business to begin conducting business globally is to establish a site on the World Wide Web (WWW). As we have seen in earlier chapters, the Web gives small businesses tremendous marketing potential all across the globe. With a well-designed Web site, a small company can extend its reach to customers anywhere in the world—and without breaking the budget! A Web site is available to anyone, anywhere in the world and provides 24-hour exposure to a company's products or services, so time differences become meaningless. "Every business I've talked to says they're seeing exponential growth in the numbers of visitors they're receiving [on their Web sites] from overseas," says Lisa Kjaer, a director of a Commerce Department Export Assistance Center. When it comes to conducting international business, "[the World Wide Web] soon will become as necessary a tool as the phone and the fax," she says.[26]

Most small companies follow a four-step evolutionary process to conducting global business on the Web:

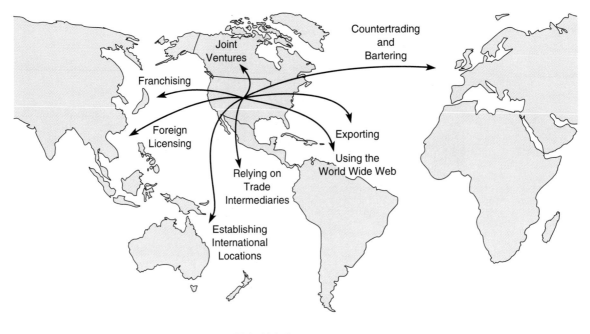

Figure 12.2 **Eight Principal Strategies for Pursuing Global Markets**

Step 1. Connecting to e-mail. Even though it lacks the ability to provide the wealth of visual images and sounds available on the WWW, e-mail gives entrepreneurs the ability to communicate with customers anywhere in the world quickly and easily. E-mail correspondence is often the first step to establishing lasting relationships with international customers. *Rod J. Gutierrez, president of Modulex Inc., a small maker of aluminum door frames, began its export efforts with e-mail. "E-mail cuts down on the phone expenses, and, with the time differences, eliminates a lot of wasted effort trying to communicate internationally," says Gutierrez.*[27]

Step 2. Building an informational Web site. Companies soon see the need to educate their international customers about the features and the benefits of their products and services and set up Web sites. Designed properly, a Web site can be an engaging marketing tool. *Kris Olson, owner of Beater Wear in Bellevue, Washington, says his company's Web site <http://www.beater.com> has been an important part of its marketing plan. Beater Wear manufactures ski apparel and accessories, and its Web site promotions have generated both sales and leads on potential distributors. At first, Beater Wear's Web site, which Olson designed himself, received about 100 hits a day; now it averages about 2,700 hits a day, which Olson expects to climb as a result of cross-promotional arrangements with several ski magazines. Olson's ultimate goal for Beater Wear's Web site is to smooth out the company's highly seasonal sales by sparking export sales to the Southern Hemisphere, where seasons are reversed from those in the Northern Hemisphere.*[28]

Step 3. Conducting international market research electronically. Once business owners begin to see the power of the Web and its ability to attract customers across the globe, they become interested in using it as a more proactive tool to generate sales, researching markets in other countries. *After experiencing initial success with her company's Web site <http://www.vellus.com>, Sharon Doherty, owner of Vellus Products Inc., a maker of pet-grooming products in Columbus, Ohio, began using the Web to explore potential* *markets abroad. She spends an average of two hours a day researching markets, studying competitors, and scouting out potential customers in foreign countries. International sales now account for more than half of Vellus Products' revenues.*[29] As Doherty's experience shows, entrepreneurs have a wealth of marketing information at their fingertips from sources on the Web.

Step 4. Establishing a secure ordering and payment system for on-line customers. Currently, the most common purchase pattern on the WWW is for customers to tap a company's Web site for product or service information and then to use the fax or phone to place orders. Their primary concerns involve on-line security. Increasingly, companies are offering secure on-line ordering procedures, and customers are beginning to view electronic transactions as being as safe as telephone orders. *Kris Olson of Beater Wear recently set up a secure on-line ordering system for his customers, which he expects will increase his WWW sales to global customers.*[30]

TRADE INTERMEDIARIES

Another relatively easy way to break into international markets is by using a trade intermediary. **Trade intermediaries** are domestic agencies that serve as distributors in foreign countries for domestic companies of all sizes. They rely on their networks of contacts, their extensive knowledge of local customs and markets, and their experience in international trade to market products effectively and efficiently all across the globe. Trade intermediaries account for about 10 percent of all U.S. exports.[31] Although a broad array of trade intermediaries is available, the following are ideally suited for small businesses.

Export Management Companies. **Export management companies (EMCs)** are an important channel of foreign distribution for small companies just getting started in international trade or for those lacking the resources to assign their own people to foreign markets. Most EMCs are merchant intermediaries, working on a buy-and-sell arrangement with domestic small companies. They provide small businesses with a low-cost, efficient, independent, international marketing department, offering services ranging from market research and advice on patent protection to arranging financing and handling shipping. More than 1,000 EMCs operate across the United States, and many of them specialize in particular products or product lines.

Hamilton Manufacturing Corporation, a small maker of machines that exchange coins for paper currency, used an export management company to break into foreign markets. James Nesmith, president of the small concern, turned to International Projects Inc., a Toledo-based EMC, for help in selling Hamilton's newly developed machines designed to exchange foreign currency. Going global alone "was a lot more than I could handle," says Nesmith. So Hamilton signed a five-year agreement with International Projects to sell the machines abroad, and its foreign sales are climbing rapidly.[32]

Export Trading Companies. Another tactic for getting into international markets with a minimum of cost and effort is through export trading companies (ETCs), which have been an important vehicle in international trade throughout history. The Hudson's Bay Company and the East India Company were ETCs that were dominant powers in world trade in the sixteenth, seventeenth, and eighteenth centuries.[33] **Export trading companies** are businesses that buy and sell products in a number of countries, and they typically offer a wide range of services such as exporting, importing, shipping, storing, distributing, and others to their clients. Unlike EMCs, which tend to focus on exporting, ETCs usually perform both import and export trades across many countries' borders. However, like EMCs, ETCs lower the risk of exporting for small businesses. Some of the largest ETCs in the world are based

IN THE FOOTSTEPS OF AN ENTREPRENEUR

Blasting Their Way into International Markets

*A*nna Chong and her husband, Eric Kelly, are co-owners of Engineered Demolition, a family business with 20 employees that operates in a unique niche market that spans the globe: explosive demolition. The Minneapolis-based company is one of just a handful of businesses worldwide that uses implosion to destroy old buildings in metropolitan areas to make way for new ones. Implosion destroys a building by causing it to burst inward (compared with an explosion, which causes things to burst outward) as a result of carefully planned and precisely timed explosives placed at strategic points in the structure.

Imploding a building costs about 20 percent less than tearing it down the old-fashioned way. Still, Chong and Kelly spend a great deal of time educating clients about the implosion process, dispelling the misconceived images people have of debris shooting out for hundreds of yards from the work site. To emphasize the safety of Engineered Demolition's work, Chong often shows videotapes of demolitions from the company's portfolio. One of the company's most challenging jobs was to implode a building that was actually touching another building that had to be saved! Chong and Kelly also successfully imploded an old refrigeration plant in Montreal that left a 236-year-old home just 15 feet away untouched.

Imploding a typical 10-story building requires about 300 pounds of explosives and costs about $250,000. After studying the blueprints of the target building, Engineered Demolition workers plan the blast, emphasizing four key elements: the direction of the fall, how straight the fall is, the material structure of the building, and the proximity and location of adjoining buildings. Taking these factors into account, demolition experts develop a schematic of the number, placement, and size of the explosives needed to do the job. After a contractor "preps" the building by gutting as much of it as possible, the team of demolitionists go inside to insert the explosives, a process called loading. The team attaches blasting caps to touch off the explosions and wires the whole network together with miles of wire connected to a plunger on a detonating device located several hundred feet away.

As one might imagine, implosion is a highly specialized field that requires extensive training. Both Kelly and Chong hold blaster's licenses valid in the United States and internationally. In fact, Chong is one of the few women to hold such a license. Engineered Demolition currently averages about 75 jobs a year, but business is doubling about every four years. Chong says that the number of jobs from international cus-

tomers is increasing rapidly. Currently, about one-third of the company's contracts come from international clients, but Chong expects that number to accelerate. "What we are seeing is an increased worldwide demand to make more efficient use of costly and limited land space by removing old structures," she says. As nations around the globe upgrade their infrastructure to spur economic growth, Engineered Demolition is discovering new opportunities to market its unique service. "In Asia, it's very common for the land costs to be higher than the value of the structures [currently sitting on the land], and the buildings are so close together that it's impossible to use a wrecking ball without damaging adjoining structures," says Chong. The only alternative is implosion.

Although used for years in the United States and Canada, demolition by implosion has caught on in Asia, Europe, and Latin America only recently. "Canada is our largest and most accessible market outside of the United States because of its proximity, similarity of culture, and ways of doing business," says Chong. Implosion jobs in congested cities in Asia, Europe, and Latin America are on the rise, however. Performing an implosion in these countries is more difficult because of the time required to get the necessary permits. "We tend to rely on local labor as much as possible when doing our work internationally because it's more cost-effective for both parties in arranging handling, sales, transportation, and simple things like getting a local permit. They understand the culture and have the right connections to get the job done."

As their international clientele increases, Chong and Kelly have learned to be more sensitive to their customers' cultural preferences and customs. "In countries like Japan and Korea," says Chong, "the number 4 means death. We won't demolish a structure on the fourth of the month, and we often avoid loading explosives on the fourth floor of a building." Chong also steps into the background in many jobs in Asia because "clients don't always feel comfortable about a woman pushing down the plunger on the detonating device because they believe it might bring bad luck."

Engineered Demolition is actively pursuing business in European markets. Chong was one of 22 women who participated in a recent Women in Trade mission to Europe led by the U.S. Commerce Department. "These missions are great for establishing contacts for the long term because you can't get that kind of exposure on your own," says Chong. The exposure has already paid off. Not long after Chong returned from the trip, Engineered Demolition landed one of its most unusual jobs in Europe. "We found an old power plant they wanted destroyed," she recalls, "but officials did not want us to use explosives even though it was the best way to go. So we actually had our people go in and hand-cut all the key supporting beams, a lengthy and involved process." The last person out of the building? Chong's husband, Eric, who made the final cut that began the building's collapse.

Not only are Chong and Kelly successful, but they also love their work. "It's something beautiful to start and complete a project to the finish," she says. "You have to be gutsy and a risk taker, but how many people can say their work is a real blast?" she asks with a smile.

2. Work with a team of your classmates to brainstorm ways that Engineered Demolition can locate international customers.

1. What factors are contributing to the growth of Engineered Demolition's international business? Which countries should the company target? Why?

SOURCE: Adapted from Curtice K. Cultice, "Blasting a Path to World Markets: U.S. Demolition Exporter "Levels Playing Field," *Business America Magazine,* January–February 1997, pp. 21–26.   ◆

in the United States and Japan. In fact, many businesses that have navigated successfully Japan's complex system of distribution have done so with the help of ETCs.

In 1982, Congress passed the Export Trading Company Act to allow producers of similar products to form ETC cooperatives without the fear of violating antitrust laws. The goal was to encourage U.S. companies to export more goods by allowing businesses in the same industry to band together to form export trading companies.

Manufacturer's Export Agents. Manufacturer's export agents (MEAs) act as international sales representatives in a limited number of markets for various noncompeting domestic companies. Unlike the close, partnering relationship formed with most EMCs, the relationship between an MEA and a small company is a short-term one, and the MEA typically operates on a commission basis.

Export Merchants. Export merchants are domestic wholesalers who do business in foreign markets. They buy goods from many domestic manufacturers and then market them in foreign markets. Unlike MEAs, export merchants often carry competing lines, which means they have little loyalty to suppliers. Most export merchants specialize in particular industries: office equipment, computers, industrial supplies, and others.

Resident Buying Offices. Another approach to exporting is to sell to a **resident buying office,** a government-owned or privately owned operation of one country established in another country for the purpose of buying goods made there. Many foreign governments and businesses have set up buying offices in the United States. Selling to them is just like selling to domestic customers because the buying office handles all the details of exporting.

Foreign Distributors. Some small businesses work through foreign distributors to reach international markets. Domestic small companies export their products to these distributors, who handle all of the marketing, distribution, and service functions in the foreign country. *Ed Anderson, founder of Lil' Orbits, a Minnesota-based company that makes doughnut machines, sold his machinery only in the United States for nearly 15 years with great success. Then he began to wonder why his doughnut-making hardware wouldn't sell in international markets as well. In 1987, he placed a $40 ad in a U.S. Department of Commerce publication and was flooded with inquiries from foreign distributors. Today, Lil' Orbits has 42 long-time foreign distributors who sell the company's line of seven machines around the world. The company collects more than 60 percent of its $10 million annual revenue from abroad.*[34]

The Value of Using Trade Intermediaries. Trade intermediaries such as these are becoming increasingly popular among businesses attempting to branch out into world markets because they make that transition much faster and easier. Most small businesses simply do not have the knowledge, resources, or confidence to go global alone. Intermediaries' global networks of buyers and sellers allow their small business customers to build their international sales much faster and with fewer hassles and mistakes.

The key to establishing a successful relationship with a trade intermediary is conducting a thorough screening to determine what type of intermediary—and which one in particular—will best serve a small company's needs. A company looking for an intermediary should compile a list of potential candidates using some of the sources listed in Table 12.1. The 50 World Trade Centers (most of which are affiliated with the U.S. government) and the 15 Export Assistance Centers located across the United States offer valuable advice and assistance to small companies wanting to get started in conducting global business. In addition, entrepreneurs can find reliable intermediaries by using their network of contacts in foreign countries and by attending international trade shows while keeping an eye out for potential candidates.

JOINT VENTURES

Joint ventures, both domestic and foreign, lower the risk of entering global markets for small businesses. They also give small companies more clout in foreign lands. In a **domestic joint venture,** two or more U.S. small businesses form an alliance for the purpose of exporting their goods and services. For export ventures, participating companies get antitrust immunity, allowing them to cooperate freely. The businesses share the responsibility and the costs of getting export licenses and permits, and they split the venture's profits. Establishing a joint venture with the right partner has become an essential part of maintaining a competitive position in global markets for a growing number of industries. *Yamas Controls Inc., a small California maker of environmental control systems, formed a joint venture with Bechtel Group Inc., a giant construction and engineering company, to provide its systems to the Chinese government. Without the joint venture, Yamas most likely would not have been able to break into the Chinese market. With it, the company's annual sales have grown from $4 million to $40 million in just eight years. Not only did the joint venture lower Yamas's risk of selling in foreign markets, but it also opened the door for similar projects with several American, European, and Chinese firms.*[35]

In a **foreign joint venture,** a domestic small business forms an alliance with a company in the target nation. The host partner brings to the joint venture valuable knowledge of the local market and its method of operation as well as of the customs and the tastes of local customers, making it much easier to conduct business in the foreign country. Sometimes foreign countries place certain limitations on joint ventures. Some nations, for example, require host companies to own at least 51 percent of the venture. "The only way to be German in Germany, Canadian in Canada, and Japanese in Japan is through alliances," says one international manager.[36] *Gerard Compain, managing director of Ignecio, one of the world's leading makers of smart-card readers, relies heavily on foreign joint ventures to sell its product line in foreign lands. (A smart card looks like a standard credit card but is embedded with a computer chip that can store volumes of both money and information. Used in Europe for more than 20 years, smart cards only recently have begun to catch on in other parts of the world.) Compain, whose company is based in Paris, has established successful joint ventures with entrepreneurs in Australia, China, Singapore, Germany, Russia, and the United States. Citing the major benefits Ignecio receives by using foreign joint ventures, Compain says, "These people know their countries better than we do. And they know how to design and sell products for those markets."*[37]

The most important ingredient in the recipe for a successful joint venture is choosing the right partner. A productive joint venture is much like a marriage, requiring commitment and understanding. In addition to picking the right partners, a second key to creating a successful alliance is to establish common objectives. Defining *exactly* what each party in the joint venture hopes to accomplish at the outset will minimize the opportunity for misunderstandings and disagreements later on. One important objective should always be to use the joint venture as a learning experience, which requires a long-term view of the business relationship.

Unfortunately, most joint ventures fail. According to a recent study, the average success rate is just 43 percent; the average life of a joint venture is only 3.5 years.[38] That makes it essential for the companies in an alliance to establish a contingency plan for getting out in

Table 12.1 Resources for Locating a Trade Intermediary

Trade intermediaries make doing business around the world much easier for small companies, but finding the right one can be a challenge. Fortunately, several government agencies offer a wealth of information to businesses interested in reaching into global markets with the help of trade intermediaries. Entrepreneurs looking for help in breaking into global markets should contact the International Trade Administration, the U.S. Commerce Department, and the Small Business Administration first to take advantage of the following services:

◆ *Agent/Distributor Service (ADS).* Provides customized searches to locate interested and qualified foreign distributors for a product or service. (Search cost, $250 per country.)

◆ *Commercial Service International Contacts (CSIC) List.* Provides contact and product information for more than 82,000 foreign agents, distributors, and importers interested in doing business with U.S. companies.

◆ *Country Directories of International Contacts (CDIC) List.* Provides the same kind of information as the CSIC List but is organized by country.

◆ *Industry Sector Analyses (ISAs).* Offer in-depth reports on industries in foreign countries, including information on distribution practices, end-users, and top sales prospects.

◆ *International Market Insights (IMIs).* Include reports on specific foreign market conditions, upcoming opportunities for U.S. companies, trade contacts, trade show schedules, and other information.

◆ *Trade Opportunity Program (TOP).* Provides up-to-the-minute, prescreened sales leads around the world for U.S. businesses, including joint venture and licensing partners, direct sales leads, and representation offers.

◆ *International Company Profiles (ICPs).* Commercial specialists will investigate potential partners, agents, distributors, or customers for U.S. companies and will issue profiles on them.

◆ *Commercial News USA.* A government-published magazine (10 issues a year) that promotes U.S. companies' products and services to 259,000 business readers in 152 countries at a fraction of the cost of commercial advertising. Small companies can use *Commercial News USA* to reach new customers around the world for as little as $395.

◆ *Gold Key Service.* For a small fee, business owners wanting to target a specific country can use the Department of Commerce's Gold Key Service, in which experienced trade professionals arrange meetings with prescreened contacts whose interests match their own.

◆ *Matchmaker Trade Delegations Program.* Helps small U.S. companies establish business relationships in major markets abroad by introducing them to the right contacts.

◆ *Multi–State/Catalog Exhibition Program.* Working with state economic development offices, the Department of Commerce presents companies' product and sales literature to hundreds of interested business prospects in foreign countries.

◆ *International Fair Certification Program.* Promotes U.S. companies' participation in foreign trade shows that represent the best marketing opportunities for them.

◆ *National Trade Data Bank (NTDB).* Most of the information listed above is available on the NTDB, the U.S. government's most comprehensive database of world trade data. With the NTDB, small companies have access to information that only Fortune 500 companies could afford.

◆ *Economic Bulletin Board (EBB).* Provides on-line trade leads and valuable market research on foreign countries compiled from a variety of federal agencies.

◆ *U.S Export Assistance Centers.* The Department of Commerce has established 19 export centers (USEACs) around the country to serve as one-stop shops for entrepreneurs needing export help. Call (800) 872-8723.

◆ *Trade Information Center.* Helps locate federal export assistance, provides export assistance, and offers a 24-hour automated fax retrieval system that gives entrepreneurs free information on export promotion programs, regional market information, and international trade agreements. Call (800) USA-TRADE.

◆ *Office of International Trade.* The Small Business Administration provides a variety of export development assistance, how-to publications, and information on foreign markets.

◆ *Export Hotline.* Provides no-cost trade information on more than 50 industries in 80 countries. Call (800) 872-9767.

◆ *Export Opportunity Hotline.* Trade specialists have access to on-line databases and reports from government and private agencies concerning foreign markets. Call (202) 628-8389.

case the joint venture doesn't work. Common problems leading to failure include improper selection of partners, incompatible management style, failure to establish common goals, inability to be flexible, and failure to trust one another. "The usual problem," says one recent study of joint ventures, "is growing discontent between the partners as they discover how differently they view the world, how hard it is to keep their relationship in balance, and how easy it is . . . to forget what [they have] learned about making alliances work."[39]

What can entrepreneurs do to avoid these pitfalls in joint ventures?

◆ Define at the outset important issues such as each party's contributions and responsibilities, the distribution of earnings, the expected life of the relationship, and the circumstances under which the parties can terminate the relationship.

◆ Understand in depth their partner's reasons and objectives for joining the venture.

◆ Select a partner who shares their company's values and standards of conduct.

◆ Spell out in writing exactly how the venture will work and where decision-making authority lies.

◆ Select a partner whose skills are different from but compatible with those of their own companies.

◆ Prepare a "prenuptial agreement" that spells out what will happen in case of a business "divorce."

FOREIGN LICENSING

Rather than sell their products or services directly to customers overseas, some small companies enter foreign markets by licensing businesses in other nations to use their patents, trademarks, copyrights, technology, processes, or products. In return for licensing such assets, the small company collects royalties from the sales of its foreign licenses. Licensing is a relatively simple way for even the most inexperienced business owner to extend his reach into global markets. Eugene M. Lang, a foreign licensing expert, says, "Many small companies can't afford to invest capital in foreign facilities, and they don't have the personnel to send over there. Often, small company owners don't even have the time to acquaint themselves with foreign markets. The alternative is to license—to find someone who can capture the market for you who is already at home in that market."[40] Licensing is ideal for companies whose value lies in unique products or services, a recognized name, or proprietary technology or processes. "You have this little treasure-trove of value," says one intellectual property attorney, "and licensing is the key to unlocking it."[41] *For example, Joe Boxer Corporation, the widely known and highly successful maker of underwear, activewear, lingerie, sleepwear, bedding, towels, tablecloths, and placemats, licenses its uniquely designed collections (picture boxer shorts adorned with pink pigs or glow-in-the-dark lips) to companies across the globe. Because of Joe Boxer's licensing arrangements, even the most conservative dressers in Canada, Australia, New Zealand, the United Kingdom, Mexico, Belgium, and the Netherlands can add a splash of excitement to their wardrobes—even if it is underneath![42]*

Although many business owners consider licensing only their products to foreign companies, the licensing potential for intangibles such as processes, technology, copyrights, and trademarks often is greater. "You often make more money from licensing your know-how for production or product control than you could from actually selling your finished product in a highly competitive market," explains Lang.[43] *Disney often licenses its famous cartoon characters, including Mickey and Minnie Mouse, Goofy, Roger Rabbit, and others, to manufacturers in countries across the world. Catesby Jones, president of Peace Frogs, a small retailer, explains why his company used a foreign licensing arrangement for its copyrighted designs in Spain. "We export our Peace Frogs T-shirts directly to Japan, but in Spain per capita income is lower, competition from domestic producers is stronger, and tariffs are high, so we licensed a Barcelona-based company the rights to manufacture our product.*"[44] Foreign licensing enables a small business to enter foreign markets quickly, easily, and with virtually no capital investment. Risks to the company include the potential of losing control over its manufacturing and marketing and creating a competitor if the licensee gains too much knowledge and control. Securing proper patent, trademark, and copyright protection beforehand can minimize those risks, however.

INTERNATIONAL FRANCHISING

Franchising has become a major export industry for the United States. The International Franchise Association estimates that more than 20 percent of the nation's 4,000-plus franchisors have outlets in foreign countries.[45] Over the past decade, a growing number of franchises have been attracted to international markets to boost sales and profits as the domestic market has become increasingly saturated with outlets and much tougher to wring growth from. International franchisors sell virtually every kind of product or service imaginable—from fast food to child day care—in international markets. In some cases, the products and services sold in international markets are identical to those sold in the United States. However, most franchisors have learned that they must modify their products and services to suit local tastes and customs. *For instance, Domino's Pizza operates 1,160 restaurants in 46 countries, where local managers have developed new pizza flavors such as mayonnaise and potato (Japan), pickled ginger (India), and reindeer sausage (Iceland) to cater to customers' palates.*[46] *Although McDonald's builds its foreign menus around the same items and standardized assembly-line approach that have made it such a success in the United States, it makes changes to accommodate local tastes. In Switzerland, McDonald's reaches hungry commuters in transit. The company has commissioned two railroad dining cars, each seating about 40 people, that run on two routes: from Geneva to Basel and Geneva to Brig. In addition to Big Macs, diners have a choice of red or white wine and beer. And because Egg McMuffins don't appeal to Swiss palates, the rolling restaurants offer the more traditional Swiss breakfast of croissant, marmalade, butter, and hard cheese.*[47] *In Germany, McDonald's restaurants sell beer, and in Great Britain they offer British Cadbury chocolate sticks.*[48]

Although franchise outlets span the globe, Canada is the primary market for U.S. franchisors, with Japan and Europe following. These markets are most attractive to franchisors because they are similar to the U.S. market: rising personal incomes, strong demand for consumer goods, growing service economies, and spreading urbanization. *For instance, after Danny Benususan, owner of the trendy Blue Note jazz club in Manhattan, noticed that the stars who drew crowds in New York also toured Japan, he conducted some market research and discovered that after World War II, Japan had evolved into a major jazz capital. Sensing an opportunity for international growth, Benususan soon found two businesses that were interested in establishing Blue Note franchises in Japan. Two Blue Note franchises now draw full houses in Tokyo and Osaka, featuring international jazz stars such as Herbie Hancock, Branford Marsalis, and B. B. King. The Japanese clubs display the same details and quality standards as the original club and are so successful that Benususan has signed a franchise agreement with a Korean entrepreneur.*[49]

Europe also holds special interest for many U.S. franchises as trade barriers there continue to topple, opening up the largest—and one of the most affluent—markets in the world. Although large franchisors are already well established in many European nations, a new wave of smaller franchisors is seeking to establish a foothold there. Growth potential is the primary attraction. Eastern European countries that recently have thrown off the chains of communism are turning to franchising to help them move toward a market economy. "Nothing better suits the start-up of a free-market economy than franchising," says a franchising attorney.[50] Some countries of Eastern Europe, including Hungary and Poland, are attracting franchises. Southeast Asian countries such as Indonesia, Malaysia, and Vietnam hold promise for franchising in the future, as do India and Russia, with their large populations and blooming economies. For franchisors entering these emerging nations, many of which are still in the volatile stages of formation, patience is the key. Profits may be years in coming, but franchisors see the long-term benefits of establishing a presence in these markets early on. Future growth is likely to occur in other countries as well. Because of its growing middle class and recent free-trade agreement with the United States, Mexico is becoming a popular target for franchises.

COUNTERTRADING AND BARTERING

As business becomes increasingly global, companies are discovering that attracting customers is just one part of the battle. Another problem global businesses face when selling to some countries is that their currencies are virtually worthless outside their borders, so getting paid in a valuable currency is a real challenge! In fact, 70 percent of all countries do not have either convertible currencies or sufficient cash flow to pay for imported goods.[51] Companies wanting to reach these markets must countertrade or barter. A **countertrade** is a transaction in which a company selling goods or services in a foreign country agrees to help promote investment and trade in that country. The goal of the transaction is to help offset the capital drain from the foreign country's purchases. Experts estimate that countertrading accounts for 20 to 30 percent of all global trade, and its use will continue to escalate.[52]

Big businesses are accustomed to countertrading to reach certain markets, but small and medium-sized companies usually lack the skills and the resources needed to conduct countertrades on their own. However, they can tie into deals made by large corporations. *For instance, when export giant McDonnell Douglas sold $1.5 billion worth of jets to Spain recently, it agreed to a countertrade. As part of the deal, Cornnuts, Inc., a small maker of snack foods, agreed to open an office in Spain and to introduce hybrid corn technology there. Cornnuts had been eyeing Spain as an export market but didn't know how to get started. McDonnell Douglas arranged key meetings with Spanish officials and even helped the small company write its presentation and translate it into Spanish. The countertrade has proved to be a winner for Spain, McDonnell Douglas, and Cornnuts.[53]*

Countertrading does suffer from numerous drawbacks. Countertrade transactions can be complicated, cumbersome, and time-consuming. They also increase the chances that a company will get stuck with merchandise that it cannot move. They can lead to unpleasant surprises concerning the quantity and quality of products required in the countertrade. Still, countertrading offers one major advantage: Sometimes it's the only way to make a sale!

Entrepreneurs must weigh the advantages against the disadvantages for their company before committing to a countertrade deal. Because of its complexity and the risks involved, countertrading is not the best choice for a novice entrepreneur looking to break into the global marketplace.

Bartering, the exchange of goods and services for other goods and services, is another way of trading with countries lacking convertible currency. In a barter exchange, a company that manufactures electronics components might trade its products for the coffee that a business in a foreign country processes, which it then sells to a third company for cash. Barter transactions require finding a business with complementary needs, but they are much simpler than countertrade transactions.

3 Explain how to build a thriving export program.

EXPORTING

Small companies increasingly are looking toward exporting as a global business strategy. Large companies still dominate exporting. Although small companies account for 97 percent of the companies involved in exporting, they generate only one-third of the dollar value of the nation's exports.[54] However, small companies, realizing the incredible profit potential it offers, are making exporting an ever-expanding part of their marketing plans. Nearly half of U.S. companies with annual revenues under $100 million export goods, up from only 36 percent in 1990.[55] A recent study by Grant Thornton LLP reported that the percentage of small and medium-sized exporters that generate at least 10 percent of their revenue from exports doubled to 51 percent in just two years.[56] "Exporting is one of the best ways for a small business to expand its markets and increase sales," says the director of the Small Business Administration's Office of International Trade.[57]

Colleen and Keith Austin, founders of Lilliput LLC, a Wyoming-based small company that makes products designed to stimulate learning in visually impaired children, discovered that exporting is not meant only for giants such as Boeing and General Motors. Shortly after launching their company, the Austins received an order from Canada, which made them realize their company's export potential. They began working with a trade specialist at the U.S. Export Assistance Center in Denver, Colorado, and soon found themselves mastering the intricacies of producing, financing, shipping, and collecting foreign orders. By just its second year of business, one-third of Lilliput's sales originated in foreign countries, primarily Canada.[58]

Approximately 100,000 U.S. companies currently export; however, experts estimate that at least twice as many are capable of exporting but are not doing so.[59] The biggest barrier facing companies that have never exported is not knowing where or how to start. Paul Hsu, whose company sells ginseng across the globe, explains, "Exporting . . . starts with a global mind-set, which unfortunately, is not all that common among owners of small and medium-sized businesses in the United States. . . . Most entrepreneurs in the United States envision markets only within domestic and sometimes even state borders, while Japanese and other foreign entrepreneurs look at export markets first."[60] Breaking the psychological barrier to exporting is the first, and most difficult, step in setting up a successful program. What other steps must an entrepreneur take to get an export program under way?

1. Recognize that even the tiniest companies and least experienced entrepreneurs have the potential to export. *Richie Harral, owner of Windchimes by Russco III, started making windchimes with his brother at age 10 in 1978 in the cellar of his home. Their company started really small—two kids selling windchimes to neighbors door to door. Their big break came seven years later when Wal-Mart ordered 30,000 chimes. In 1992, Windchimes experienced another stroke of luck when a British distributor, whose parents had bought a chime in a Missouri Wal-Mart, placed a $2,500 order. Today, the United Kingdom accounts for 6 percent of the company's $2 million in sales, and Harral predicts that exports soon will rise to 30 percent of sales.*[61]

   Exporting not only can boost a small company's sales, but it also can accelerate its growth rate. One study found that small companies that export grow markedly faster than those that do not. The study also concluded that the growth gap is widening as business becomes increasingly global in scope.[62]

2. *Analyze your product or service.* Is it special? New? Unique? High-quality? Priced favorably because of lower costs or exchange rates? In which countries would there be sufficient demand for it? In many foreign countries, products from America are in demand because they have an air of mystery about them! Exporters quickly learn the value foreign customers place on quality. *Ron Schutte, president of Creative Bakers of Brooklyn, a company that makes presliced cheesecakes for restaurants, saw an opportunity to sell in Japan. The only modification Schutte made to his high-quality cheesecakes was reducing the portion size from 4.5 ounces to 2.25 ounces. "The Japanese aren't as gluttonous as we are," he explains.*[63]

3. *Analyze your commitment.* Are you willing to devote the time and the energy to develop export markets? Does your company have the necessary resources? Few business owners realize "the amount of management resources it will suck up at the top levels of the company," says one export consultant.[64] Export start-ups can take from six to eight months (or longer), but entering foreign markets isn't as tough as most entrepreneurs think. "One of the biggest misconceptions people have is that they can't market overseas unless they have a big team of lawyers and specialists," says one export specialist. "That just isn't true."[65] Table 12.2 summarizes key issues managers must address in the export decision.

4. *Research markets and pick your target.* Before investing in a costly sales trip abroad, entrepreneurs should make a trip to the local library or the nearest branch of the Department of Commerce. Exporters can choose from a multitude of guides, manuals, books, newsletters, videos, and other resources to help them research potential markets. Armed with research, small business owners can avoid wasting a lot of time and money on markets with limited potential for their products and can concentrate on those with the greatest promise. The World Bank projects that, by 2020, the world's largest economies will be China, the United States, Japan, India, Indonesia, Germany, and Korea. It predicts that other "hot" export markets will include France, Taiwan, Brazil, Italy, Russia, Great Britain, and Mexico.[66]

Managers at Ekkwill Tropical Fish Farm, a wholesale fish supplier, discovered through research that collecting fish is an even more popular hobby in Japan than in the United States. Ekkwill now flies one-third of its production—some 4 million fish— to Japan as well as to Latin America, Asia, Canada, and the West Indies. Its best-selling fishes in international markets are Florida gars, red swordtails, and New World cichlids, all common species in North America but considered exotic in other lands.[67]

Research shows export entrepreneurs whether they need to modify their existing products and services to suit the tastes and preferences of their foreign target customers. Sometimes foreign customers' lifestyles, housing needs, body sizes, and cultures require exporters to make alterations in their product lines. *For instance, when Rodney Robbins, CEO of Robbins Industries, a measuring-cup-and-spoon maker, was negotiating with a distributor before entering the Swedish and British markets, he learned that he would have to modify his products slightly. The British use measuring utensils labeled in milliliters, and the Swedes prefer deciliters.*[68] Such modifications can sometimes spell the difference between success and failure in the global market.

In other cases, products destined for export need little or no modification. *For example, for more than 40 years Richland Beverage Corporation has been exporting its Texas brand of nonalcoholic beer and soft drinks to Asia, Canada, and Mexico in exactly the same form used in the United States.* Experts estimate that one-half of exported products require little modification; one-third require moderate modification; only a few require major changes.[69] Table 12.3 on page 394 offers questions to guide entrepreneurs conducting export research.

5. *Develop a distribution strategy.* Should you use an export middleperson or sell directly to foreign customers? Small companies just entering international markets may prefer to rely on export middlepeople to break new ground. *Lynn Cooper, president of BFW, a 25-year-old medical lighting supplier, uses wholesale distributors to sell her company's products in 25 countries. Exports account for 30 percent of BFW's sales, and Cooper is happy with her method of distribution. "With distribu-*

Table 12.2 Management Issues in the Export Decision

I. Experience

1. With what countries has your company already conducted business (or from what countries have you received inquiries about your product or service)?
2. What product lines do foreign customers ask about most often?
3. Prepare a list of sale inquiries for each buyer by product and by country.
4. Is the trend of inquiries or sales increasing or decreasing?
5. Who are your primary domestic and foreign competitors?
6. What lessons has your company learned from past export experiences?

II. Management and Personnel

1. Who will be responsible for the export entity's organization and staff? (Do you have an export "champion"?)
2. How much top management time
   a. should you allocate to exporting?
   b. can you afford to allocate to exporting?
3. What does management expect from its exporting efforts? What are your company's export goals and objectives?
4. What organization structure will your company require to ensure that it can service export sales properly? (Note the political implications, if any.)
5. Who will implement the plan?

III. Production Capacity

1. To what extent is your company using its existing production capacity? Is there any excess? If so, how much?
2. Will filling export orders hurt your company's ability to make and service domestic sales?
3. What will additional production for export markets cost your company?
4. Are there seasonal or cyclical fluctuations in your company's workload? When? Why?
5. Is there a minimum quantity foreign customers must order for a sale to be profitable?
6. To what extent would your company need to modify its products, packaging, and design specifically for its export targets? Is your product quality adequate for foreign customers?
7. What pricing structure will your company use? Will prices be competitive?
8. How will your company collect payment on its export sales?

IV. Financial Capacity

1. How much capital will your company need to begin exporting? Where will it come from?
2. How will you allocate the initial costs of your company's export effort?
3. Does your company have other expansion plans that would compete with an exporting effort?
4. By what date do you expect your company's export program to pay for itself?
5. How important is establishing a global presence to your company's future success?

SOURCE: Adapted from *A Basic Guide to Exporting* (Washington, D.C.: U.S. Department of Commerce, 1986), p. 3.

tors, the risk to us is minimal, but we still know just where the products are going," she says.[70]

6. *Find your customer.* Small businesses can rely on a host of export specialists to help them track down foreign customers. (Refer to Table 12.1 for a list of some of the resources available from the government.) The U.S. Department of Commerce and the

Table 12.3 Questions to Guide International Market Research

◆ Is there an overseas market for your company's products or services?

◆ Are there specific target markets that look most promising?

◆ Which new markets abroad are most likely to open up or expand?

◆ How big is the market your company is targeting, and how fast is it growing?

◆ What are the major economic, political, legal, social, technological, and other environmental factors affecting this market?

◆ What are the demographic and cultural factors affecting this market: e.g., disposable income, occupation, age, gender, opinions, activities, interests, tastes, and values?

◆ Who are your company's present and potential customers abroad?

◆ What are their needs and desires? What factors influence their buying decisions: price, credit terms, delivery terms, quality, brand name, etc.?

◆ How would they use your company's product or service? What modifications, if any, would be necessary to sell to your target customers?

◆ Who are your primary competitors in the foreign market?

◆ How do competitors distribute, sell, and promote their products? What are their prices?

◆ What are the best channels of distribution for your product?

◆ What is the best way for your company to gain exposure in this market?

◆ Are there any barriers such as tariffs, quotas, duties, or regulations to selling your product in this market? Are there any incentives?

◆ Are there any potential licensing or joint venture partners already in this market?

SOURCE: Adapted from *A Basic Guide to Exporting* (Washington, D.C.: U.S. Department of Commerce, 1986), p. 11.

International Trade Administration should be the first stops on an entrepreneur's agenda for going global. These agencies have the market research available for locating the best target markets for a particular company and specific customers in those markets. Industry Sector Analyses (ISAs), International Market Insights (IMIs), and Customized Market Analyses (CMAs) are just some of the reports and services global entrepreneurs find most useful. They also have knowledgeable staff specialists experienced in the details of global trade and in the intricacies of foreign cultures. *Jimmy Kaplanges, head of GP66 Chemical Corporation, a small producer of industrial degreasers, had led his company into exporting its products to Brazil, Spain, France, and Greece. He also saw plenty of opportunity for the company's products in China, but Kaplanges knew that cracking that market was more than GP66 Chemical could accomplish on its own. That's when Kaplanges turned to the Export Assistance Center in the company's hometown of Baltimore, Maryland. Kaplanges credits the trade specialist there, Nasir Abbasi, with helping his company enter the Chinese market successfully. Sales to Chinese customers have climbed from $3 million to more than $12 million.*[71]

Other entrepreneurs search out customers on their own. *For instance, Jeff Ake, co-owner of Electronic Liquid Fillers, Inc., a small packaging equipment company, spent seven weeks calling on potential customers in the Pacific Rim. He identified his target customers with the help of foreign-based English-language industry trade magazines. During his travels, Ake used the local English-language equivalent of the Yellow Pages to find others.*[72]

7. *Find financing.* One of the biggest barriers to small business exports is lack of financing. Access to adequate financing is a crucial ingredient in a successful export program because the cost of generating foreign sales often is higher and collection cycles are longer than in domestic markets. The trouble is that bankers and other

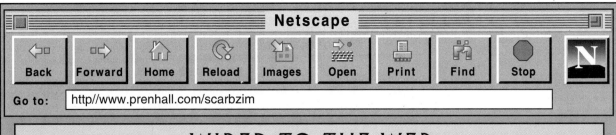

WIRED TO THE WEB

WHERE DO WE START?

*S*pecialty Building Supplies is a small company with $6.4 million in annual sales that manufactures and sells a line of building products such as foundation vents, insulation materials, and fireplace blowers to building supply stores in the Northeastern United States. The eight-year-old company, founded by Tad Meyers, has won several awards for its unique and innovative products and has earned a solid reputation among its supply store customers and the builders and homeowners who ultimately buy its products. Before launching the company, Meyers had been a home builder. As he watched the price of home heating fuels climb dramatically over time, Meyers began to incorporate into the houses he built simple, inexpensive ways to help homeowners save energy. He began tinkering with existing products, looking for ways to improve them. The first product he designed (and the product that ultimately led him to launch Specialty Building Supplies) was an automatic foundation vent that was thermostatically controlled (no electricity needed). The vent would automatically open and close as the outside temperature changed, keeping cold drafts from blowing under a house. Simple and inexpensive in its design, the Autovent was a big hit in newly constructed homes in the Northeast because it not only saved energy but also avoided a major headache for homeowners in cold climates: water pipes that would freeze and burst. Before long, Meyers stopped building houses and focused on selling the Autovent. Its success prompted him to add other products to the company's line.

Specialty's sales have been lackluster for more than a year now, primarily because of a slump in new home construction in its primary market. Tad Meyers recently met with the company's top marketing managers and sales-people to talk about their options for getting Specialty's sales and profit growth back on track. "What about selling our products in international markets?" asked Dee Rada, the company's marketing manager. "I read an article just last week about small companies doing good business in other countries, and many of them were smaller than we are."

"Interesting idea," Meyers said, pondering the concept. "I've never really thought about selling anything overseas. In fact, other than my years in the military, I've never traveled overseas and don't know anything about doing business there."

"It's a big world out there. Where should we sell our products?" said Hal Milam, Specialty's sales manager. "How do we find out what the building codes are for in foreign countries? Would we have to modify our designs to meet foreign standards?"

"I don't know," shrugged Meyers. "Those are some good questions."

"How would we distribute our products?" asked Rada. "We have an established network of distributors here in the United States, but how do we find *foreign* distributors?"

"I wonder if exporting is our only option," said Meyers. "There must be other ways to get into the global market besides exporting. What do you think? Where do we start?"

1. What advice would you offer Meyers and the other managers at Specialty Building Supplies about their prospects of going global?
2. How would you suggest these managers go about finding the answers to the questions they have posed? What other questions would you advise them to answer?
3. Using the resources of the World Wide Web, develop an outline of the steps these managers should take to assemble an international marketing plan.

sources of capital don't always understand the intricacies of international sales and view financing them as excessively risky. Also, among major industrialized nations, the U.S. government spends the least per capita to promote exports.

Several federal, state, and private programs are operating to fill this export financing void, however. Programs such as the Small Business Administration's Export Working Capital Program (90 percent loan guarantees up to $750,000), the Export-Import Bank <http://www.exim.gov>, the Overseas Private Investment Corporation, and a variety of state-sponsored programs offer export-minded entrepreneurs both direct loans and loan guarantees. (A list of all state foreign trade assistance offices is available in the Commerce Department's National Export Directory.) In recent years, the Export-Import Bank has emphasized loans and loan guarantees for small exporters; 81 percent of its lending volume has gone to small companies.[73] The Bankers Association for Foreign Trade (telephone number 1-800 49-AXCAP) is an association of 450 banks that matches exporters needing foreign trade financing with interested banks. *When Robert Cavallarin was traveling in Europe in 1989, he realized that he and partner Steve Macri, co-owners of S&S Seafood, could export Maine lobsters to Europe. Unfortunately, Cavallarin and Macri could not get the $100,000 in financing necessary to start their export venture, despite the fact that they had orders from seafood importers in hand. Macri turned to a trade consultant for help, and soon S&S Seafood had a business plan for its proposed export business and a contact at the Export-Import Bank. With a 90 percent loan guarantee from the Export-Import Bank, S&S Seafood was able to secure a $100,000 bank loan and begin exporting. Today, the company has eight employees and generates annual sales of $12 million, 95 percent of which comes from exports to Europe and Asia.*[74]

8. *Ship your goods.* Export novices usually rely on international freight forwarders and custom-house agents—experienced specialists in overseas shipping—for help in navigating the bureaucratic morass of packaging requirements and paperwork demanded by customs. These specialists, also known as transport architects, are to exporters what travel agents are to passengers and normally charge relatively small fees for a valuable service. They move shipments of all sizes to destinations all over the world efficiently, saving entrepreneurs many headaches. "[A freight forwarder] is going to be sure that his client conforms with all the government regulations that apply to export cargo," explains the owner of an international freight-forwarding business. "He acts as an agent of the exporter, and, in most circumstances, is like an extension of that exporter's traffic department." *The Johnston Sweeper Company, a manufacturer of street sweepers, ships its 20,000-pound pieces of equipment worldwide with the help of an international freight forwarder.*[75]

9. *Collect your money.* Collecting foreign accounts can be more complex than collecting domestic ones, but by picking their customers carefully and checking their credit references closely, entrepreneurs can minimize bad-debt losses. Financing foreign sales often involves special credit arrangements such as letters of credit and bank (or documentary) drafts. A **letter of credit** is an agreement between an exporter's bank and the foreign buyer's bank that guarantees payment to the exporter for a specific shipment of goods. In essence, a letter of credit reduces the financial risk for the exporter by substituting a bank's creditworthiness for that of the purchaser. A **bank draft** is a document the seller draws on the buyer, requiring the buyer to pay the face amount (the purchase price of the goods) either on sight (a sight draft) or on a specified date (a time draft) once the goods have been shipped. Rather than use letters of credit or drafts, some exporters simply require cash in advance or cash on delivery (C.O.D.). Insisting on cash payments up front, however, may cause some foreign

buyers to reject a deal. The parties to an international deal should always come to an agreement in advance on an acceptable method of payment.

Planned carefully and taken one step at a time, exporting can be a highly profitable route for small businesses. "When properly structured, [exporting] can be more safe and profitable than domestic trade," says one trade consultant.[76] Many small companies are forming **foreign sales corporations** (**FSCs**, pronounced "fisks") to take advantage of a tax benefit that is designed to stimulate exports. Although large companies have used the tax advantages of FSCs for many years, a rapidly growing number of small exporters is beginning to catch on. More than 5,000 U.S. corporations have created FSCs in the past decade, and the number is growing by 25 percent a year. By forming an FSC, a company can shelter about 15 percent of its profits on foreign sales from federal—and in some cases state—income taxes. Setting up an FSC requires a company to establish a shell corporation in the Virgin Islands, Barbados, or one of another 40 tax-friendly offshore locations that have tax treaties with the United States. The company also must have fewer than 25 shareholders and one non-U.S.-resident board member. Because it costs about $2,500 to establish an FSC and about $1,500 a year to maintain one, a business should earn at least $50,000 a year to make the savings from an FSC worthwhile. (For help on setting up an FSC, contact the FSC/DISC Tax Association at (914) 642-8924.) *Harry and Linde Martin, owners of Products for Research, created an FSC 10 years ago and estimate that they have saved $15,000 in that time. The company, with $2 million a year in sales, generates 40 percent of its revenue from exporting protective cooling enclosures for high-tech light sensors used in research labs around the world.*[77]

ESTABLISHING INTERNATIONAL LOCATIONS

Once established in international markets, some small businesses set up permanent locations there. Establishing an office or a factory in a foreign land can require a substantial investment reaching beyond the budgets of many small companies. Plus, setting up an international office can be an incredibly frustrating experience in some countries. Business infrastructures are in disrepair or are nonexistent. Getting a telephone line installed can take months in some places, and finding reliable equipment to move goods to customers is nearly impossible. Securing necessary licenses and permits from bureaucrats often takes more than filing the necessary paperwork; in some nations, bureaucrats expect payments to "grease the wheels." Finding the right person to manage an international office is crucial to success; it also is a major challenge, especially for small businesses. Small companies usually have lean management staffs and cannot afford to send key people abroad without running the risk of losing their focus.

Few small businesses begin their global ventures by establishing international locations, preferring, instead, to build a customer base through some of the strategies already covered. *For example, in 1984, managers at Santec Inc., a U.S.-based manufacturer of electronic connectors, saw the tremendous potential the European market offered. Rather than plunge into the market by establishing a location on the continent, however, they decided to begin by exporting. "We have worked our way up to full-scale manufacturing," says Santec's president, John Shine. The sales channels the company established in Europe in 1984 have evolved into a full-fledged manufacturing facility at Cumbernauld, Scotland. The move was a natural extension of Santec's globalization strategy. To ensure its long-term success, "it's just a necessity" to have operations for sales, service, and manufacturing in North America, Europe, and Asia, which is Santec's next stop on its global agenda, according to Shine.*[78]

Small companies that do establish international locations can reap significant benefits. Start-up costs are lower in some foreign countries, and lower labor costs can produce signifi-

Businesses large and small can no longer view a single country as their sole market. Today, successful businesses see the entire world as their potential market.

cant savings as well. Robert Brooker and Adam Haven-Weiss launched their New York Bagel Company in Budapest, Hungary, with just $40,000 in seed money, a fraction of what it would have cost in the United States.[79]

*B*arriers to International Trade

4 Discuss the major barriers to international trade and their impact on the global economy.

Governments have always used a variety of barriers to block free trade among nations in an attempt to protect businesses within their own borders. The benefit of protecting their own companies, however, comes at the expense of foreign businesses, which face limited access to global markets. Numerous trade barriers—domestic and international—restrict the freedom of businesses in global trading. Even with these barriers, international trade has grown 26-fold to more than $6.6 *trillion* over the past 30 years.[80]

DOMESTIC BARRIERS

Sometimes the biggest barriers potential exporters face are right here at home. Three major domestic roadblocks are common: attitude, information, and financing. Perhaps the biggest barrier to small businesses exporting is the attitude "I'm too small to export. That's just for big corporations." The first lesson of exporting is "Take nothing for granted about who can export and what you can and cannot export." The first step to building an export program is recognizing that the opportunity to export exists.

Another reason entrepreneurs neglect international markets is a lack of information about how to get started. The key to success in international markets is choosing the correct target market and designing the appropriate strategy to reach it. That requires access to information and research. Although a variety of government and private organizations make volumes of exporting and international marketing information available, many small business owners never use it. A successful global marketing strategy also recognizes that not all international markets are the same. Companies must be flexible, willing to make adjustments to their products and services, promotional campaigns, packaging, and sales techniques.

Another significant obstacle is the lack of export financing available. A recent survey of exporters found that 53 percent said they had lost export business because they couldn't get financing.[81] "There is no such thing as export financing for small companies in this country," says one trade consultant, exaggerating only slightly.[82] *For example, N & N Contact Lens International, Inc. recently got an order from a Brazilian customer for $247,000 worth of contact lenses. The buyer had good credit with its Brazilian bank, and a credit check produced a favorable report. But N & N's bank refused to finance the deal. "We just don't finance foreign receivables," explained one bank official. N & N's president laments, "[Yet] I can get an order from Atlanta from a guy who went bankrupt and the bank will finance it, without question."*[83]

INTERNATIONAL BARRIERS

Domestic barriers aren't the only ones export-minded entrepreneurs must overcome. Trading nations also erect obstacles to free trade. Two types of international barriers are common: tariff and nontariff.

Tariff Barriers. A **tariff** is a tax, or duty, that a government imposes on goods and services imported into that country. Imposing tariffs raises the price of the imported goods—making them less attractive to consumers—and protects the makers of comparable domestic products and services. Established in the United States in 1790 by Alexander Hamilton, the tariff system generated the majority of federal revenues for about 100 years. Today, the U.S. tariff code lists duties on 8,862 items—from brooms and olives to flashlights and teacups.[84]

Nontariff Barriers. Many nations have lowered the tariffs they impose on products and services brought into their borders, but they rely on other nontariff structures as protectionist trade barriers.

Quotas. Rather than impose a direct tariff on certain imported products, nations often use quotas to protect their industries. A **quota** is a limit on the amount of a product imported into a country. Worried about the Japanese economic juggernaut, the European Union has limited Japanese automakers' share of the European market to just 16 percent. In the U.S. auto market, the Japanese have agreed to "voluntary quotas," limiting the number of autos shipped here.

Japan, often criticized for its protectionist attitude toward imports, traditionally used tariffs and quotas to keep foreign competitors out. Japan's tariffs are now among the world's lowest—averaging just 2 percent—but quotas still exist on many products. *The Dexter Shoe Company faces a formidable trade barrier in its attempt to sell its leather shoes in Japanese markets. Because leather working is a traditional craft of a Japanese social underclass called the burakumin, the shoe industry is protected by a strong quota-tariff system. Every year, Dexter must fight for even a modest expansion in its quota allotment, which now stands at a measly 50,000 pairs.*[85]

Embargoes. An **embargo** is a total ban on imports of certain products. The motivation for embargoes is not always economic. For instance, because of South Africa's history of apartheid policies, many nations have embargoed imports of Krugerrands (gold coins). Traditionally, Taiwan, South Korea, and Israel have banned imports of Japanese autos.

Dumping. In an effort to grab market share quickly, some companies have been guilty of **dumping** products: selling large quantities of them in foreign countries below cost. The United States has been a dumping target for steel, televisions, shoes, and computer chips in the past. Under the U.S. Antidumping Act, a company must prove that the foreign com-

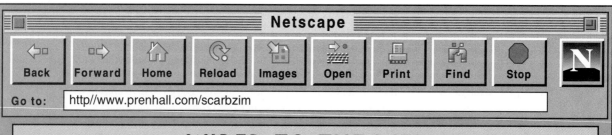

WIRED TO THE WEB

ON TO JAPAN

"*I*t's hard to believe how far we've come in just 14 months," said Tad Meyers, president of Specialty Building Supplies.

"That's true," chimed in Dee Rada, the company's marketing manager. "When we started this whole international business idea, we had no notion of how complicated and time-consuming it would be. We were total rookies! Which one of us would have thought we'd be trying to sell our products in Japan?"

"True. But now it looks like the big payoff is just around the corner," said Hal Milam, the company's sales manager.

As the three celebrated their success in taking their company into the exciting world of international business, each was proud of what they had accomplished and how much they had learned in just a short time. Yet their excitement was tinged with anxiety because Meyers and Rada were about to travel abroad to meet with several potential distributors for the company's building supplies. In one week, they would be in Japan, negotiating deals with businesspeople whom they had never met and whose native language neither spoke.

"I do know how to say 'Thank you' in Japanese," said Rada. "It's pronounced *Du-omo ah-ree-gha-toe.*"

"You should probably find out how to say, 'Where's the bathroom?' and 'We're lost. Will you take us home?' in Japanese too," joked Milam.

"You know, we probably should find out as much as possible about how the Japanese do business," said Meyers. "I understand their way is very different from what we're used to."

"Such as?" said Milam.

"You know, little things," said Rada. "I do know that they make a big deal out of exchanging business cards. They call it *meishi.* In fact, I've had cards printed for Tad and me with English on one side and Japanese on the other. When you take their cards, don't just stick them in your pocket or scribble notes on the backs of them. That's an insult."

"I thought we'd take some gifts along to give to our guests," said Rada. "I've had them wrapped in pure white paper with these big red ribbons."

"What are you going to give them?" asked Milam.

"I had some nice golf shirts printed up with our logo, and then I had them add the U.S. and Japanese flags crossing one another."

"We're taking along some brochures detailing our product line, emphasizing its unique nature and superb quality," said Rada. "I had them printed in Japanese just for this trip. Full color, lots of pictures. They cost a few bucks, but I thought it would be a wise investment."

"We will be on a tight schedule while we're there," said Meyers. "We'll have to get right down to business, close the deal, and then get on to the next appointment. There won't be a lot of time for sight-seeing or small talk. I hope we can have some of these deals done by the time we get back on the plane for home. I just hope they don't try to impress us with authentic Japanese meals while we're there. I'm pretty much a meat-and-potatoes kind of guy. I *don't* do sushi. "

"Where's your sense of adventure?" teased Rada. "Remember: We can't afford to offend our guests. We need to be sensitive to their culture, habits, and tastes. I just hope we don't do something unintentional that upsets somebody."

1. Evaluate the preparations Meyers and Rada have made for their upcoming trip to Japan.
2. Using the library* and the WWW as resources, read about Japanese culture and Japanese business practices. On the basis of what you learn, would you advise them to change any of their plans? Explain.

*The Do's and Taboos of International Trade (1994); Gestures: The Do's and Taboos of Body Language around the World (1998); and Do's and Taboos around the world: A Guide to International Behavior (1985), all by Roger Axtell and published by John Wiley and Sons are excellent resources.

pany's prices are lower here than in the home country and that U.S. companies are directly harmed.

POLITICAL BARRIERS

Entrepreneurs who go global quickly discover a labyrinth of political tangles. Although many U.S. business owners complain of excessive government regulation in the United States, they are often astounded by the complex web of governmental and legal regulations and barriers they encounter in foreign countries.

Companies doing business in politically risky lands face the very real dangers of government takeovers of private property; attempts at coups to overthrow ruling parties; kidnappings, bombings, and other violent acts against businesses and their employees; and other threatening events. Their investments of millions of dollars may evaporate overnight in the wake of a government coup or the passage of a law nationalizing an industry (giving control of an entire industry to the government).

Some nations welcome foreign business investment; others do everything they can to discourage competition from foreign companies. *For example, the Japanese recently used a web of regulations to stall a California company that had developed a system for electronically mapping cities to improve ambulance, police, and fire services until Japanese companies could catch up. The government decided that the company, Etak, needed a license before it could proceed. By the time the license materialized, a Japanese competitor had erased Etak's head start and captured most of the market.*[86]

BUSINESS BARRIERS

American companies doing business internationally quickly learn that business practices and regulations in foreign lands can be quite different from those in the United States. Simply duplicating the practices they have adopted (and have used successfully) in the domestic market and using them in foreign markets is not always a good idea. Perhaps the biggest shock comes in the area of human resources management, where international managers discover that practices common in the United States, such as overtime, women workers, and employee benefits are restricted, disfavored, or forbidden in other cultures. Business owners new to international business sometimes are shocked at the wide range of labor costs they encounter and the accompanying wide range of skilled labor available. In some countries, what appear to be "bargain" labor rates turn out to be excessively high after accounting for the quality of the labor force and the benefits their governments mandate: from company-sponsored housing, meals, and clothing to profit-sharing and extended vacations. In many nations, labor unions are present in almost every company, yet they play a very different role from the unions in the United States. Although management-union relations are not as hostile as in the United States and strikes are not as common, unions can greatly complicate a company's ability to compete effectively.

For example, five years after opening for business in Russia, Ben & Jerry's Homemade Inc., decided to get out of the market, citing the many difficulties of doing business in such a challenging environment. Although the company's financial losses on the Russian venture had little impact on the company, the huge time commitments it required of key personnel were beginning to show. "We're a small company," says the manager of the Russian operation. "You tie up two or three senior managers and you end up having a measurable effect on the company's performance." Ben & Jerry's constantly experienced quality control problems due to inadequate infrastructure and equipment, which meant that ice cream often arrived having been thawed and refrozen numerous times. Also, an unexpected change in tax laws sent the company's tax liability soaring.[87]

CULTURAL BARRIERS

The culture of a nation includes the beliefs, values, views, and mores that its inhabitants share. Differences in cultures among nations create another barrier to international trade. The diversity of languages, business philosophies, practices, and traditions make international trade more complex than selling to the business down the street. "It's essential for anyone wanting to do business in an international market to have a clear understanding and appreciation of the culture in which they plan to do business," says one international consultant.[88] Consider the following examples:

◆ A U.S. entrepreneur, eager to expand into the European Union, arrives at his company's potential business partner's headquarters in France. Confidently, he strides into the meeting room, enthusiastically pumps his host's hand, slaps him on the back, and says "Tony, I've heard a great deal about you; please, call me Bill." Eager to explain the benefits of his product, he opens his briefcase and gets right down to business. The French executive politely excuses himself and leaves the room before negotiations ever begin, shocked by the American's rudeness and ill manners. Rudeness and ill manners? Yes— from the French executive's perspective.

◆ Another American business owner flies to Tokyo to close a deal with a Japanese executive. He is pleased when his host invites him to play a round of golf shortly after he arrives. He plays well and manages to win by a few strokes. The Japanese executive invites him to play again the next day, and again he wins by a few strokes. Invited to play another round the following day, the American asks, "But when are we going to start doing business?" His host, surprised by the question, says, "But we have been doing business."

When American businesspeople enter international markets for the first time, they often are amazed at the differences in foreign cultures' habits and customs. In the first scenario above, for instance, had the entrepreneur done his homework, he would have known that the French are very formal (backslapping is *definitely* taboo!) and do not typically use first names in business relationships (even among long-time colleagues). In the second scenario, a global manager would have known that the Japanese place a tremendous importance on developing personal relationships before committing to any business deals. Thus, he would have seen the golf games for what they really were: an integral part of building a business relationship.

Understanding and heeding these often subtle cultural differences is one of the most important keys to international business success. "There's more to business than just business," says one writer, "particularly when confronting the subtleties of deeply ingrained cultural customs, conventions, and protocols that abound in today's global marketplace."[89] Conducting a business meeting with a foreign executive in the same manner as one with an American business person could doom the deal from the outset. Business customs and behaviors that are acceptable, even expected, in this country may be taboo in others.

Entrepreneurs who fail to learn the differences in the habits and customs of the cultures in which they hope to do business are at a distinct disadvantage. "In the business arena . . . a lack of understanding of cultures and business practices can be as great an impediment to structuring and implementing a business transaction as an error in the basic assumptions of the deal," says one international expert.[90] Consider, for instance, the American who was in the final stages of contract negotiations with an Indonesian company. Given the size of the contract and his distance from home, the American business executive was nervous. Sitting across from his Indonesian counterpart, the American propped his feet up. Obviously angered, the Indonesian business owner stormed out of the room, refusing to sign the contract and leaving the American executive totally bewildered. Only later did he discover that exposing the soles of one's shoes to an Indonesian is an insult. Profuse apologies and some delicate negotiations salvaged the deal. In another incident, an American went to Malaysia to close a sizable contract. In an elaborate ceremony, he was introduced to a man he thought was named Roger. Throughout the negotiations, he called the man "Rog," not realizing that his potential client was a *rajah*—a title of nobility, not a name.[91]

On his first trip to the Middle East, an American executive was touring the city with his Arab business contact. As they strolled along the dusty streets, the host reached over, took the executive's hand in his, and the two continued to walk, the host's hand holding the executive's. Totally stunned, the American didn't even have the presence of mind to jerk his hand away—much to his good fortune. He learned later that in his host's country, taking his hand was a sign of great respect and friendship. Jerking his hand away from his host would have been considered a major insult![92]

An American businesswoman in London was invited to a party hosted by an advertising agency. Unsure of her ability to navigate the streets and subways of London alone, she approached a British colleague who was driving to the party and asked him, "Could I get a ride with you?" After he turned bright red from embarrassment, he regained his composure and politely said, "Lucky for you I know what you meant." Unknowingly, the young woman had requested a sexual encounter with her colleague, not a lift to the party![93]

The accompanying Gaining the Competitive Edge feature shows the importance of learning about a nation's culture before conducting business there.

*I*nternational Trade Agreements

5 Describe the trade agreements that will have the greatest influence on foreign trade into the twenty-first century.

In an attempt to boost world trade, nations have created a variety of trade agreements over the years. While hundreds of agreements are paving the way for freer trade across the world, two stand out with particular significance: the General Agreement on Tariffs and Trade (GATT) and the North American Free Trade Agreement (NAFTA).

GATT

Created in 1947, the General Agreement on Tariffs and Trade (GATT) became the first global tariff agreement. It was designed to reduce tariffs among member nations and to facilitate trade across the globe. Originally signed by the United States and 22 other nations, GATT has grown to include 124 member countries today. Together, they account for nearly 90 percent of world trade. The latest round of GATT negotiations, called the Uruguay Round, was completed in December 1993 and took effect on July 1, 1995. Before the Uruguay Round, the trade agreement had been successful in reducing trade barriers around the world by 90 percent since its inception. Average tariffs in industrial countries had fallen to just 4.7 percent, down from an average of 40 percent in 1947.

The Uruguay Round continues this trend. Negotiators reduced the remaining industrial tariffs by 40 percent, established new rules governing dumping goods at unfairly low prices, strengthened the global protection of patents, and cut the level of government subsidies on agricultural products. In addition, negotiators agreed to form a World Trade Organization (WTO) with more power to settle trade disputes among member nations than GATT had. Experts estimate that GATT will expand the U.S. economy by approximately $1 trillion over the next decade and create as many as 2 million jobs.[94]

Although the agreement failed to topple trade barriers for services as much as managers had hoped, GATT will benefit a wide variety of businesses: from makers of textiles and agricultural equipment to construction firms and restaurants. *For example, when Jeff*

GAINING THE COMPETITIVE EDGE

The Secret Language of International Business

*W*hen U.S. businesspeople enter international markets for the first time, they often are amazed at the differences in foreign cultures' habits and customs. Understanding and heeding these often subtle cultural differences is one of the most important keys to international business success. The maze of cultural variables from one country to another can be confusing, but with proper preparation and a little common sense, any manager can handle international transactions successfully. In short, before packing your bags, do your homework. In most cases, conducting international business successfully requires managers to have unlimited patience, a long-term commitment, and a thorough knowledge of the local market, business practices, and culture. The key for entrepreneurs is learning to be sensitive to the business cultures in which they operate. Consider these pointers.

◆ Patience is a must for doing business in Spain. Like the French, Spaniards want to get to know business associates before working with them. In the United States, business comes before pleasure, but in Spain business is conducted after dinner, when the drinks and cigars are served. "I've known American businessmen who have shocked their Spanish hosts by pulling out their portfolios and charts before dinner is even served," says one expert. In Spain, women should avoid crossing their legs; it is considered unladylike. Men usually cross their legs at the knees.

◆ Appearance and style are important to Italian businesspeople; they judge the polish and the expertise of the company's executives as well as the quality of its products and services. Italians expect presentations to be organized, clear, and exact. A stylish business wardrobe also is an asset in Italy. Physical contact is an accepted part of Italian society. Don't be surprised if an Italian businessperson uses a lingering handshake or touches you occasionally when doing business.

◆ In Great Britain, businesspeople consider it extremely important to conduct business "properly"—with formality and reserve. Boisterous behavior such as backslapping or overindulging in alcohol and ostentatious displays of wealth are considered ill-mannered. The British do not respond to hard-sell tactics but do appreciate well-mannered executives. Politeness and impeccable manners are useful tools for conducting business successfully here.

◆ In China, entrepreneurs will need an ample dose of the "three Ps": patience, patience, patience. *Nothing* in China—especially business—happens fast! In conversations and negotiations, periods of silence are common; they are a sign of politeness and contemplation. The Chinese view personal space much differently than Americans; in normal conversation, they will stand much closer to their partners.

◆ In the Pacific Rim, entrepreneurs must remember that each country has its own unique culture and business etiquette. Starting business relationships with customers in the Pacific Rim usually requires a third-party contact because Asian executives prefer to do business with people they know. Also, building personal relationships is important. Many business deals take place over informal activities in this part of the world.

◆ American entrepreneurs doing business in the Pacific Rim should avoid hard-sell techniques, which are an immediate turnoff to Asian businesspeople. Harmony, patience, and consensus make good business companions in this region. It is also a good idea to minimize the importance of legal documents in negotiations. Although getting deals and trade agreements down in writing always is advisable, attempting to negotiate detailed contracts (as most American businesses tend to do) would insult most Asians, who base their deals on mutual trust and benefits.

◆ Japanese executives conduct business much like the British: with an emphasis on formality, thoughtfulness, and respect. Don't expect to hear Japanese executives say no, even during a negotiation; they don't want to offend or to appear confrontational. Instead of no, the Japanese negotiator will say, "It is very difficult," "Let us think about that," or "Let us get back to you on that." Similarly, yes from a Japanese executive doesn't necessarily mean that. It could mean "I understand," "I hear you," or "I don't understand what you mean, but I don't want to embarrass you."

◆ In Japan and South Korea, exchanging business cards, known in Japan as *meishi*, is an important business function (unlike Great Britain, where exchanging business cards is less popular). A Western executive who accepts a Japanese companion's card and then slips it into his pocket or scribbles notes on it has committed a major blunder. Tradition there says a business card must be treated just as its owner would be—with respect. Travelers should present their own cards using both hands with the card positioned so the recipient can read it. (The flip side should be printed in Japanese, an expected courtesy.)

◆ Greeting a Japanese executive properly includes a bow and a handshake—showing respect for both cultures. In many traditional Japanese businesses, exchanging gifts at the first meeting is appropriate. Also, a love of golf (the Japanese are crazy about the game) is a real plus for winning business in Japan.

- In Mexico, making business appointments through a well-connected Mexican national will go a long way to assuring successful business deals. "People in Mexico do business with somebody they know, they like, or they're related to," says one expert. Because family and tradition are top priorities for Mexicans, entrepreneurs who discuss their family heritages and can talk knowledgeably about Mexican history are a step ahead. In business meetings, making extended eye contact is considered impolite.

---

1. What can an entrepreneur do to avoid committing cultural blunders when conducting global business?

SOURCE: Adapted from Laura Fortunato, "Japan: Making It in the USA," *Region Focus*, Fall 1997, p. 15; David Stamps, "Welcome to America," *Training*, November 1996, p. 30; Barbara Pachter, "When in Japan, Don't Cross Your Legs," *Business Ethics*, March/April 1996, p. 50; Tom Dunkel, "A New Breed of People Gazers," *Insight*, January 13, 1992, pp. 10–14; M. Katherine Glover, "Do's and Taboos," *Business America*, August 13, 1990, pp. 2–6; Deidre Sullivan, "An American Businesswoman's Guide to Japan," *Overseas Business*, Winter 1990, pp. 50–55; Stephanie Barlow, "Let's Make a Deal," *Entrepreneur*, May 1991, p. 40; "Worldly Wise," *Entrepreneur*, March 1991, p. 40; David Altany, "Culture Clash," *Industry Week*, October 2, 1989, pp. 13–20; Edward T. Hall, "The Silent Language of Overseas Business," *Harvard Business Review*, May–June 1960, pp. 5–14; John S. McClenahen, Andrew Rosenbaum, and Michael Williams, "As Others See U.S.," *Industry Week*, January 8, 1990, pp. 80–82; James Bredin, "Japan Needs to Be Understood," *Industry Week*, April 20, 1992, pp. 24–26; David L. James, "Don't Think about Winning," *Across the Board*, April 1992, pp. 49–51; "When in Japan," *Small Business Reports*, January 1992, p. 8; Bernie Ward, "Other Climates, Other Cultures," *Sky*, March 1992, pp. 72–86; Roger E. Axtell, *Gestures: The Do's and Taboos of Body Language around the World*, John Wiley and Sons, New York: 1991; Suzanne Kreiter, "Customs Differ Widely from Those in the U.S.," *Greenville News*, September 26, 1993, p. 15D; Bradford W. Ketchum, "Going Global: East Asia-Pacific Rim," *Inc.* (Special Advertising Section), May 20, 1997; Valerie Frazee, "Getting Started in Mexico," *Global Workforce*, January 1997, pp. 16–17.

Ware, owner of Dock Street Brewing Company, a popular Philadelphia microbrewery, tried to sell his beer in Europe before GATT, the deal flopped. The problem wasn't with the beer, which had already won two gold medals for taste from a Belgian organization. The venture failed because Europe imposed a stiff 24 percent tariff on all imported beer (compared with the U.S. tariff on imported beer of less than 2 percent). "There was a good public response," recalls Ware, "but the prices were too high." Now that the tariff has been reduced drastically, Ware is selling beer in Europe once again.[95]

NAFTA

The North American Free Trade Agreement (NAFTA) created a free trade area among Canada, Mexico, and the United States. A **free trade area** is an association of countries that have agreed to knock down trade barriers, both tariff and nontariff, among partner nations. Under the provisions of NAFTA, these barriers were eliminated for trade among the three countries, but each remained free to set its own tariffs on imports from nonmember nations.

NAFTA forged a unified United States–Canada–Mexico market of 380 million people with a total annual output of more than $6.5 trillion dollars of goods and services. This important trade agreement binds together the three nations on the North American continent into a single trading unit stretching from the Yukon to the Yucatan. Because Canada and the United States already had a free-trade agreement in effect, the businesses that will benefit most from NAFTA are those already doing business, or those wanting to do business, with Mexico. Before NAFTA took effect on January 1, 1994, the average tariff on U.S. goods entering Mexico was 10 percent. Under NAFTA, these tariffs will be reduced to zero on most goods over the next 10 to 15 years.[96]

NAFTA's provisions will encourage trade among the three nations, make that trade more profitable and less cumbersome, and open up new opportunities for a wide assortment of companies. *For instance, Jeff Victor, manager of Treatment Products Limited, a manufacturer of car cleaners and waxes, says that the trade agreement is the primary force behind his company's boom in exports to Mexico. Treatment Products had tried to enter the Mexican market years earlier but met with limited success, primarily because of stiff Mexican tariffs that ran as high as 20 percent. Within months of NAFTA's passage, the tariffs began dropping, and the company's export sales to Mexico began climbing, ultimately totaling 20 percent of its sales. Today, Treatment Products has landed contracts with every major retail chain in Mexico.*[97]

Among NAFTA's provisions are:

◆ *Tariff reductions.* Immediate reduction, then gradual phasing out, of most tariffs on goods traded among the three countries.

◆ *Elimination of nontariff barriers.* Most nontariff barriers to free trade are to be eliminated by 2008.

◆ *Simplified border processing.* Mexico, in particular, opens its border and interior to U.S. truckers and simplifies border processing.

◆ *Tougher health and safety standards.* Industrial standards involving worker health and safety are to become more stringent and more uniform.

*C*onclusion

To remain competitive, businesses must assume a global posture. Global effectiveness requires managers to be able to leverage workers' skills, company resources, and customer know-how across borders and throughout cultures across the world. Managers also must concentrate on maintaining competitive cost structures and a focus on the core of every business: the *customer*! Robert G. Shaw, CEO of International Jensen Inc., a global maker of home and automobile stereo speakers, explains the importance of retaining that customer focus as his company pursues its global strategy: "We want [our customers] to have the attitude of [our] being across the street. If we're going to have a global company, we have to behave in that mode, whether [the customer is] across the street or seven miles, seven minutes, or 7,000 miles away."[98] The manager of one global business discourages the use of the word *domestic* among his employees, asking, "Where's *domestic* when the world is your market?"[99] Although there are no sure-fire rules for going global, small businesses wanting to become successful international competitors should observe these guidelines:[100]

◆ Make yourself at home in all three of the world's key markets: North America, Europe, and Asia. This triad of regions is forging a new world order in trade that will dominate global markets for years to come.

◆ Appeal to the similarities within the various regions in which you operate but recognize the differences in their specific cultures. Although the European Union is a single trading bloc composed of 15 countries, smart entrepreneurs know that each country has its own cultural uniqueness and do not treat them as a unified market.

◆ Develop new products for the world market. Make sure your products and services measure up to world-class quality standards.

◆ Familiarize yourself with foreign customs and languages; constantly scan, clip, and build a file on other cultures: their lifestyles, values, customs, and business practices.

◆ Learn to understand your customers from the perspective of *their* culture, not your own. Bridge cultural gaps by being willing to adapt your business practices to suit their preferences and customs.

◆ "Glocalize": make global decisions about products, markets, and management but allow local employees to make tactical decisions about packaging, advertising, and service.

◆ Train employees to think globally, send them on international trips, and equip them with state-of-the-art communications technology.

◆ Hire local managers to staff foreign offices and branches.

◆ Do whatever seems best wherever it seems best, even if people at home lose jobs or responsibilities.

◆ Consider using partners and joint ventures to break into foreign markets you cannot penetrate on your own.

By its very nature, going global can be a frightening experience. Most entrepreneurs who have already made the jump, however, have found that the benefits outweigh the risks and that their companies are much stronger because of it.

Chapter Summary

❶ Explain why "going global" has become an integral part of many small companies' strategies.
- ◆ Companies that move into international business can reap many benefits, including offsetting sales declines in the domestic market; increasing sales and profits; extending their products' life cycles; lowering manufacturing costs; improving competitive position; raising quality levels; and becoming more customer-oriented.

❷ Describe the eight principal strategies small businesses have for going global.
- ◆ Perhaps the simplest and least expensive way for a small business to begin conducting business globally is to establish a site on the World Wide Web (WWW). Companies wanting to sell goods on the Web should establish a secure ordering and payment system for on-line customers.
- ◆ Trade intermediaries such as export management companies, export trading companies, manufacturer's export agents, export merchants, resident buying offices, and foreign distributors can serve as a small company's "export department."
- ◆ In a domestic joint venture, two or more U.S. small companies form an alliance for the purpose of exporting their goods and services abroad. In a foreign joint venture, a domestic small business forms an alliance with a company in the target nation.
- ◆ Some small businesses enter foreign markets by licensing businesses in other nations to use their patents, trademarks, copyrights, technology, processes, or products.
- ◆ Franchising has become a major export industry for the United States. The International Franchise Association estimates that more than 20 percent of the nation's 4,000 franchisors have outlets in foreign countries.
- ◆ Some countries lack a hard currency that is convertible into other currencies, so companies doing business there must rely on countertrading or bartering. A countertrade is a transaction in which a

business selling its goods in a foreign country agrees to promote investment and trade in that country. Bartering involves trading goods and services for other goods and services.
- ◆ Although small companies account for 97 percent of the companies involved in exporting, they generate only 33 percent of the dollar value of the nation's exports. However, small companies, realizing the incredible profit potential it offers, are making exporting an ever-expanding part of their marketing plans. Nearly half of U.S. companies with annual revenues under $100 million export goods.
- ◆ Once established in international markets, some small businesses set up permanent locations there. Although they can be very expensive to establish and maintain, international locations give businesses the opportunity to stay in close contact with their international customers.

❸ Explain how to build a thriving export program.
- ◆ Building a successful export program takes patience and research. Steps include: realize that even the tiniest firms have the potential to export; analyze your product or service; analyze your commitment to exporting; research markets and pick your target; develop a distribution strategy; find your customer; find financing; ship your goods; and collect your money.

❹ Discuss the major barriers to international trade and their impact on the global economy.
- ◆ Three domestic barriers to international trade are common: the attitude that "we're too small to export," lack of information on how to get started in global trade, and a lack of available financing.
- ◆ International barriers include tariffs, quotas, embargoes, dumping, and political business, and cultural barriers.

❺ Describe the trade agreements that will have the greatest influence on foreign trade into the twenty-first century.
- ◆ Created in 1947, the General Agreement on Tariffs and Trade (GATT), the first global tariff agree-

ment, was designed to reduce tariffs among member nations and to facilitate trade across the globe.

◆ The North American Free Trade Agreement (NAFTA) created a free trade area among Canada, Mexico, and the United States. The agreement created an association that knocked down trade barriers, both tariff and nontariff, among these partner nations.

Discussion Questions

1. Why must entrepreneurs learn to think globally?
2. What forces are driving small businesses into international markets?
3. What advantages does going global offer a small business owner? Risks?
4. Outline the eight strategies that small businesses can use to go global.
5. Describe the various types of trade intermediaries small business owners can use. What functions do they perform?
6. What is a domestic joint venture? A foreign joint venture? What advantages does taking on an international partner through a joint venture offer? Disadvantages?
7. What mistakes are first-time exporters most likely to make? Outline the steps a small company should take to establish a successful export program.
8. What are the benefits of establishing international locations? Disadvantages?

9. Describe the barriers businesses face when trying to conduct business internationally. How can a small business owner overcome these obstacles?
10. What is a tariff? A quota? What impact do they have on international trade?
11. What impact have the GATT and NAFTA trade agreements had on small companies wanting to go global? What provisions are included in these trade agreements?
12. What advice would you offer an entrepreneur interested in launching a global business effort?

Step into the Real World

1. Go to lunch with a student from a foreign country. What products and services are most needed? How does the business system there differ from ours? How much government regulation affects business? What cultural differences exist? What trade barriers has the government erected?
2. Review several current business publications and prepare a brief report on which nations seem to be the most promising for U.S. entrepreneurs. What steps should a small business owner take to break into those markets? Which nations are the least promising? Why?
3. Select a nation that interests you and prepare a report on its business customs and practices. How are they different from those in the United States? How are they similar?

Take It to the Net

Visit the Scarborough/Zimmerer home page at
www.prenhall.com/scarbzim
for updated information, on-line resources, and Web-based exercises.

Endnotes

1. Bradford W. Ketchum, "Going Global: East Asia-Pacific Rim," *Inc.* (Special Advertising Section), May 20, 1997.
2. Renato Ruggiero, "The High Stakes of World Trade," *Wall Street Journal*, April 28, 1997, p. A21.
3. Roberta Maynard, "Trade Tide Rises across the Pacific," *Nation's Business*, November 1995, pp. 52–56.
4. Hugh Menzies, "Export Your Way to Double-Digit Growth," *Your Company* (Forecast 1997), pp. 56–57.
5. "International Incentive," *Small Business Reports*, June 1992, p. 5.

6. Rob Norton, "Strategies for the New Export Boom," *Fortune*, August 22, 1994, p. 130.
7. Ted Miller, "Can America Compete in the Global Economy?" *Kiplinger's Personal Finance Magazine*, November 1991, p. 8.
8. Bernard Wysocki Jr., "Going Global in the New World," *Wall Street Journal*, September 21, 1990, p. R3.
8. Preston Townley, "Global Business in the Next Decade," *Across the Board*, January/February 1990, p. 16.
9. James Worsham, "Markets At Risk," *Nation's Business*, August 1998, p. 15.
10. Monci Jo Williams, "Rewriting the Export Rules," *Fortune*, April 23, 1990, p. 90.

11. Amy Barrett, "It's a Small (Business) World," *Business Week*, April 17, 1995, pp. 96–101.

12. Steven Taper, "From Main Street to Mexico City," *Cross Sections*, Fall 1995, p. 22.

13. Worsham, "Markets At Risk," p. 15.

14. Christopher J. Chipelo, "Small U.S. Companies Take the Plunge into Japan's Market," *Wall Street Journal*, July 7, 1992, p. B1.

15. "To Protect or Not Protect," *FW*, June 1992, p. 56.

16. "Globesmanship," *Across the Board*, January/February 1990, p. 26.

17. Ann Farnham, "Global—Or Just Globaloney?" *Fortune*, June 27, 1994, pp. 97–100.

18. "Globesmanship," p. 27.

19. "The Best Places to Do Business," *FW*, October 15, 1991, p. 26; *Breaking into the Trade Game: A Small Business Guide to Exporting* (Washington, D.C.: U.S. Small Business Administration and AT&T, 1994), p. 11.

20. Michael Barrier, "Why Small Looms Large in the Global Economy," *Nation's Business*, February 1994, p. 9; Vivian Pospisil, "Global Paradox: Small Is Powerful," *Industry Week*, July 18, 1994, p. 29.

21. Michael Barrier, "A Global Reach for Small Firms," *Nation's Business*, April 1994, p. 66.

22. Michael Barrier, "Creating Some Serious Fun," *Nation's Business*, December 1997, p. 54.

23. Niklas von Daehne, "Ears to the Ground," *Success*, December 1995, p. 14.

24. Stephen J. Simurda, "Trade Secrets," *Entrepreneur*, May 1994, p. 99.

25. Jeremy Main, "How to Go Global—And Why," *Fortune*, August 28, 1989, p. 70.

26. Roberta Maynard, "Trade Links via the Internet," *Nation's Business*, December 1997, p. 53.

27. Ibid., pp. 51–53.

28. Ibid.

29. Ibid.

30. Ibid.

31. Michael Self, "More Small Firms Are Turning to Trade Intermediaries," *Wall Street Journal*, February 2, 1993, p. B2.

32. Self, "More Small Firms Are Turning to Trade Intermediaries."

33. Larry M. Greenberg, "Besieged Hudson's Bay Company Starts to Blaze New Trails," *Wall Street Journal*, February 13, 1998, pp. B1, B9.

34. John R. Engen, "Rolling in Dough," *Success*, June 1997, p. 29.

35. "Reducing the Risk of Doing Business in China," *Nation's Business*, November 1994, p. 12.

36. Joseph E. Pattison, "Global Joint Ventures," *Overseas Business*, Winter 1990, p. 25.

37. David Carnoy, "Teaming Up," *Success*, April 1997, p. 20.

38. Donald L. Boroughs, "Lifting Off with Exports," *U.S. News & World Report*, June 3, 1991, p. 65.

39. "Global Alliances," *Fortune* insert, pp. 67–82.

40. Jeffrey A. Tannenbaum, "Licensing May Be Quickest Route to Foreign Markets," *Wall Street Journal*, September 14, 1990, p. B2.

41. Stephanie Hainsfurther, "Licensing Your Product," *Business Start-Ups*, January 1997, p. 50.

42. Gayle Sato Stodder, "Boxer Rebellion," *Entrepreneur*, August 1993, pp. 88–92.

43. Tannenbaum, "Licensing May Be Quickest Route to Foreign Markets."

44. *Breaking into the Trade Game*, p. 105.

45. Mary E. Tomzack, "Ripe New Markets," *Success*, April 1995, pp. 73–77.

46. Tara Parker-Pope, "Custom-Made," *Wall Street Journal*, September 26, 1996, p. R22.

47. Carla Rappaport, "Big Mac Attacks Swiss Tracks," *Fortune*, June 1, 1992, p. 13.

48. Parker-Pope, "Custom-Made."

49. Leslie Gourse, "Speed Kills," *Success*, October 1997, pp. 98–101.

50. Jeffrey A. Tannenbaum, "Franchisers See a Future in East Bloc," *Wall Street Journal*, June 5, 1990, p. Bl.

51. Nathaniel Gilbert, "The Case for Countertrade," *Across the Board*, May 1992, pp. 43–45.

52. Roger E. Axtell, *The Do's and Taboos of International Trade* (New York: John Wiley and Sons, 1994), p. 256.

53. Lourdes Lee Valeriano, "How Small Firms Can Get Free Help from Big Ones," *Wall Street Journal*, July 30, 1991, p. B2.

54. Carla Goodman, "Going Global," *Business Start-Ups*, November 1996, pp. 52–57; Gordon Fairclough and Matt Murray, "Small Banks Expand Their Trade Financing for Exports," *Wall Street Journal*, February 24, 1998, p. B2.

55. Stephanie N. Mehta, "Small Companies Look to Cultivate Foreign Business," *Wall Street Journal*, July 7, 1994, p. B2.

56. Robert L. Rose and Carl Quintanilla, "More Small U.S. Firms Take Up Exporting, with Much Success," *Wall Street Journal*, December 20, 1996, pp. A1, A8.

57. Goodman, "Going Global," p. 52.

58. Roberta Maynard, "A Simplified Route to Markets Abroad," *Nation's Business*, November 1997, pp. 46–48.

59. Axtell, *The Do's and Taboos of International Trade*, p. 10; Worsham, "Markets At Risk," p. 20.

60. Hsu, "Profiting from a Global Mind-Set."

61. Patricia M. Carey, "Growing through Exports," *Your Company*, Fall 1994, p. 14.

62. Jeffrey A. Tannenbaum, "Among Fast-Growing Small Concerns, Exporters Expand the Most, Study Says," *Wall Street Journal*, June 19, 1996, p. B2; Charlotte Mulhern, "Going the Distance," *Entrepreneur*, May 1998, pp. 129–133.

63. Jan Alexander, "To Sell Well Overseas, Customize," *Your Company*, Fall 1995, p. 15.

64. Mehta, "Small Companies Look to Cultivate Foreign Business."

65. Frances Huffman, "Hello, World!" *Entrepreneur*, August 1990, p. 108.

66. Carter Henderson. "U.S. Small Business Heads Overseas," *In Business*, November/December 1995, pp. 18–21.

67. Christopher Knowlton, "The New Export Entrepreneurs," *Fortune*, June 6, 1988, p. 98.

68. Alexander, "To Sell Well Overseas, Customize."

69. Becky Mann, "Making Worldly Decisions," *GSA Business*, March 2, 1998, p. 11B; Charlotte Mulhern, "Make No Mistake," *Entrepreneur*, February 1998, p. 38.

70. Jan Alexander, "How to Find an Overseas Distributor," *Your Company*, April/May 1996, pp. 52–54.

71. Maynard, "A Simplified Route to Markets Abroad."

72. "The Pacific Rim on a Shoestring," *Inc.*, June 1991, pp. 122–123.

73. J. Russell Boner, "Tap America's Top Export Lender to Expand Abroad," *Your Company*, October/November 1997, p. 28.

74. Ibid.

75. Charlotte Mulhern, "Fast Forward," *Entrepreneur*, October 1997, p. 34.

76. "A New Life Abroad for Small Firms," *Nation's Business*, November 1991, p. 10.

77. Kerry Pechter, "Take the Sting Out of the Tax Bite on Overseas Sales," *Your Company*, August/September 1996, p. 20.

78. John S. McClenahan, "Santec's European Connection," *Industry Week*, October 4, 1993, p. 30.

79. William Echikson, "Young Americans Go Abroad to Strike It Rich," *Fortune*, October 17, 1994, p. 190.

80. World Trade Organization, <http://www.wto.org/wto/intltrad/internat.htm>.

81. Martha E. Mangelsdorf, "Unfair Trade," *Inc.*, April 1991, pp. 28–37.

82. Mark Robichaux, "Exporters Face Big Roadblocks at Home," *Wall Street Journal*, November 7, 1990, p. Bl.

83. Ibid.

84. Walker Williams, "What Trade Laws Cost You," *Reader's Digest*, June 1993, pp. 197–202.

85. Chipelo, "Small U.S. Companies Take the Plunge into Japan's Market," p. B2.

86. Edmund Faltermayer, "Does Japan Play Fair?" *Fortune*, September 7, 1992, pp. 38–52.

87. Betsy McKay, "Ben & Jerry's Post-Cold War Venture Ends in Russia with Ice Cream Melting," *Wall Street Journal*, February 7, 1997, p. A14.

88. Simurda, "Trade Secrets," p. 120.

89. Ibid.

90. Stephanie Barlow, "Let's Make a Deal," *Entrepreneur*, May 1991, p. 40.

91. Edward T. Hall, "The Silent Language of Overseas Business," *Harvard Business Review*, May–June 1960, pp. 5–14.

92. Roger E. Axtell, *Gestures: The Do's and Taboos of Body Language around the World* (New York: John Wiley and Sons, 1991).

93. Lawrence Van Gelder, "It Pays to Watch Words, Gestures While Abroad," *Greenville News*, April 7, 1996, p. 8E.

94. Michael J. Boskin, "Pass GATT Now," *Fortune*, December 12, 1994, p. 137; Louis S. Richman, "What's Next after GATT's Victory," *Fortune*, January 10, 1994, p. 66.

95. Lawrence Ingrassia and Asra Q. Nomani, "Trading Up," *Wall Street Journal*, December 7, 1993, pp. Al, A10.

96. William Bak, "Triple Play," *Entrepreneur*, March 1994, p. 60.

97. Barrett, "It's a (Small) Business World."

98. John S. McClenahan, "Sound Thinking," *Industry Week*, May 3, 1993, p. 28.

99. Jeremy Main, "How to Go Global—And Why," *Fortune*, August 28, 1989, p. 70.

100. Frank Beeman, "Selling around the World," *Selling Power*, November/December 1996, pp. 82–83; "Going Global: Focus on Western Europe," *Inc.* (Special Advertising Section) March 1997; Main, "How to Go Global," pp. 70–76.

Sources of Equity Financing

Always try to rub up against money, for if you rub up against money long enough, some of it may rub off on you.

— *Damon Runyon, Guys and Dolls*

It's like having someone go through your panty drawer. You have to explain why you wear cotton on Monday and lace on Wednesday.

— *Lannie Bernhard, describing what it's like to take her company, Nursing Management, public*

Upon completion of this chapter, you will be able to

1 Explain what seed capital is and why it is so important to the entrepreneurial process.

2 Explain the differences in the three types of capital small businesses require: fixed, working, and growth.

3 Describe the various sources of equity financing available to entrepreneurs.

4 Explain the various simplified registrations, exemptions from registration, and other alternatives available to small businesses wanting to sell securities to investors.

*R*aising the money to launch a new business venture has always been a challenge for entrepreneurs. Although money has been flowing rather freely to businesses because of the nation's expanding economy throughout most of the 1990s, many potential lenders and investors still consider small business to be (too) risky business. Yet, business's need for capital is greater than ever before. Financing experts say that the entrepreneurial segment of our nation's economy needs *$60 billion* a year in seed capital to fuel its growth.[1] When searching for the capital to launch their companies, entrepreneurs must remember four "secrets" to successful business financing for 2000 and beyond:

◆ Choosing the right sources of capital for a business can be just as important as choosing the right form of ownership or the right location. It is a decision that will influence a company for a lifetime, so entrepreneurs must weigh their options carefully before committing to a particular funding source. "It is important that companies in need of capital align themselves with sources that best fit their needs," says one financial consultant. "The success of a company often depends on the success of that relationship."[2]

◆ The money is out there; the key is knowing where to look. "The problem is not a lack of funding sources but a lack of knowledge of how to find them," says Bruce Blechman, coauthor of *Guerilla Financing*.[3] Understanding which sources of funding are best for the various stages of a company's growth and becoming familiar with those sources are essential to success. In short, entrepreneurs must do their homework *before* embarking on their search for capital.

◆ Creativity counts. Although many popular sources of funds in the 1980s—from venture capital funds to federal loan programs—now play a smaller role in financing business start-ups, entrepreneurs have discovered new sources—from large corporations and customers to international venture capitalists and state or local programs—to take up the slack. Entrepreneurs must use as much ingenuity in financing their businesses as they do in generating their product and service ideas.

◆ Entrepreneurs cannot overestimate the importance of making sure the "chemistry" between themselves, their companies, and their funding sources is a good one. Too many entrepreneurs get into financial deals because they need the money to keep their businesses growing only to discover that their plans do not match those of their financial partners.

Rather than relying primarily on a single source of funds as they have in the past, entrepreneurs have to piece their capital together from multiple sources, a method known as **layered financing.**[4] *Entrepreneur Terry Mocherniak demonstrates the "patchwork" of start-up financing that has become so common. Over the five years it took him to build Lumion Corporation, a maker of energy efficient lighting technology, Mocherniak raised $3.2 million from several sources. Mocherniak, his brother, and his father invested $150,000 to launch the business; then, as the company grew, Mocherniak raised $600,000 through two government grants and another $1.7 million from a venture capital company. Needing another capital infusion to complete development of Lumion's product line, Mocherniak raised $750,000 in a Regulation D public offering, a special type of public offering that is exempt from federal securities laws.*[5]

This chapter and the next one will guide you through the myriad of financing options available to the entrepreneur. This chapter focuses on sources of equity (ownership) funds, and the next one is devoted to debt (borrowed) financing sources.

*T*he Importance of Seed Capital

❶ Explain what seed captial is and why it is so important to the entrepreneurial process.

Becoming a successful entrepreneur requires one to become a skilled fund-raiser, a job that usually requires more time and energy than most business founders think. In start-up companies, raising capital can easily consume as much as half of an entrepreneur's time. The process can drag on for months, exhausting the founder's energy, distracting her from the job of managing the business, and adding inordinate amounts of stress in the process. In some cases, the prospective entrepreneur has the creativity and skills required to start and manage an enterprise but lacks the knowledge and the ability to sell himself and his idea to potential lenders and investors.

Without adequate financing, a small business never gets off the ground, and the entrepreneur is trapped in a vicious cycle: Undercapitalization is a contributing factor to many business failures, but, because of the high mortality rate of new small businesses, financial institutions are unwilling to lend to or invest in new ventures. Lack of start-up capital leaves a small business on a weak financial foundation, vulnerable to the causes of business failure. Experts recommend that start-up companies have a capital base large enough to cover one year's expenses before they launch. The idea is to be able to cover the company's first-year expenses under the worst case scenario of zero revenue. "This financial cushion will help you survive the time from when you open your doors to when your first revenue check arrives," says one financing expert.[6]

The money an entrepreneur needs to begin a business is called seed money, adventure capital, or injection capital. It truly is risk capital because entrepreneurs and investors in new businesses must be prepared for the possibility of losing everything in exchange for the chance to earn significant rewards. The reward for investing in a successful start-up usually does not come in the form of dividends or interest, the traditional rewards for debt capital. Instead, it comes in the appreciation of the company's value, which can be astounding. *For example, when Ted Waitt started Gateway 2000, the highly successful direct seller of personal computers, he "was living like a bum." Using a certificate of deposit from his grandmother as collateral, Waitt convinced a bank to lend him $10,000. For the first five years in business, he drew a very modest salary of $200 a week. Then, in 1993, Gateway 2000 made an initial public offering. Today, Waitt and his brother own Gateway stock worth about $1.4 billion!*[7]

*T*ypes of Capital

2 Explain the differences in the three types of capital small businesses require: fixed, working, and growth.

Most entrepreneurs are seeking less than $1 million (indeed most need less than $100,000; see Figure 13.1), which may be the toughest money to secure. Where to find this seed money depends, in part, on the nature of the proposed business and on the amount of money required. For example, the originator of a computer software firm would have different capital

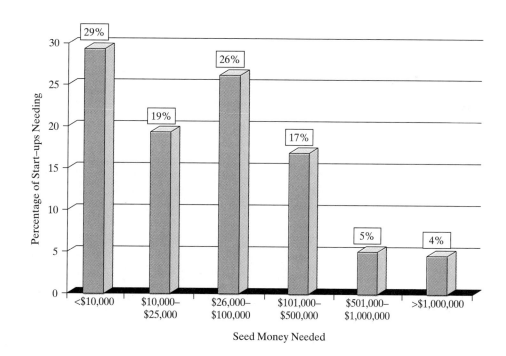

Figure 13.1 **Start-Up Requirements: Seed Money Needed by U.S. Start-Ups (by percentage of businesses)** Source: BBDO Seidman, New York, 1997.

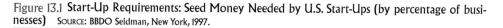

requirements than the founder of a coal-mining operation. Although the two entrepreneurs would probably approach some of the same types of lenders and investors, each would likely be more successful aiming at a few particular sources of funds suited to each industry's characteristics and needs. Thus, it is important to understand the nature of the capital requirement to determine the appropriate sources of capital.

Capital is any form of wealth used to produce more wealth for the firm. It exists in many forms in a typical business, including cash, inventory, plant, and equipment. For example, a textile manufacturer employs its plant and equipment to create an inventory used to fill customer orders. The revenue generated from sales goes to purchase more raw materials and to expand the plant or to buy more equipment. This cycle continues, increasing the capacity (and, ideally, the profitability) of the firm until it reaches the point of diminishing marginal returns. Thus, the owners' and lenders' original capital has helped create more wealth for the business and for society in general. Entrepreneurs need three different types of capital:

Fixed capital. **Fixed capital** is needed to purchase the business's permanent, or fixed, assets, such as buildings, land, computers, and equipment. Money invested in these fixed assets tends to be frozen because it cannot be used for any other purpose. Typically, large sums of money are involved in purchasing fixed assets, and credit terms are frequently lengthy. Lenders of fixed capital will expect the assets purchased to improve the efficiency and, thus, the profitability of the business and to increase its cash flow to ensure repayment.

Working capital. **Working capital** represents the business's temporary funds; it is the capital used to support the business's normal short-term operation. Accountants define working capital as current assets minus current liabilities. The need for working capital is created by the uneven flow of cash into and out of the business due to normal seasonal fluctuations. Just as an individual's income does not exactly match expenditures, a company's revenue does not match its cash outflow. Credit sales, seasonal sales swings, or unforeseeable changes in demand will create fluctuations in *any* small company's cash flow. Working capital normally is used to buy inventory, pay bills, finance credit sales, pay wages and salaries, and take care of any unexpected emergencies. Lenders of working capital expect it to produce higher cash flows to ensure repayment at the end of the production or sales cycle.

Growth capital. **Growth capital,** unlike working capital, is not related to the seasonal fluctuations in a business. Instead, growth capital requirements surface when an existing business is expanding or changing its primary direction. *For example, David Pitassi and Wally Klemp, former college buddies, launched Drypers Corporation in 1997 with the aim of wresting part of the $3 billion a year disposable diaper market from giants Procter & Gamble and Kimberly-Clark. They succeeded, and, with Dryper's growing at a five-year rate of nearly 50,000 percent, Pitassi and Klemp decided to take the company public to get the massive capital infusion needed to keep it on track. Today, Drypers is the fourth largest diaper maker in the United States.*[8] During times of such rapid expansion a growing company's capital requirements are similar to those of a business start-up. Like lenders of fixed capital, growth capital lenders expect the funds to improve a company's profitability and cash flow position, thus ensuring repayment.

Although these three types of capital are interdependent, each has certain sources, characteristics, and effects on the business and its long-term growth that entrepreneurs must recognize. Table 13.1 lists the various sources of capital for companies in the various stages of the business life cycle and their likelihood of use.

Table 13.1 The Source of Capital Matrix

Source	Business Life Cycle*			
	Start-Up	Operation	Growth	Initial Maturity
Equity Financing				
Individual investors	H	H	P	U
Corporations	U	U	P	H
Employee stock option plan	U	U	P	H
Venture capital	H	M	P	U
Small business				
Investment corporation	P	P/H	P/H	H
Public offering	U	U/P	H	H
Personal and business associates	P	H	P	U
Private limited partnership	H	P	P	U
Debt Financing				
Commercial banks	P	H	H	H
Savings and loan association	U	P	U	U
Life insurance company	U	U	P	H
Commercial credit company	P	P	H	P
Factors	U	P	H	P
Government programs				
Small Business Administration	P	H	H	U
Community Development Corporation	U	U	H	H
Economic Development Commission	U	U	H	H
Small Business Investment Corporation	P	H	U	U
Other				
Research & development grants	P/H	H	P	U
Tax shelters	P/H	P	P	P
Private foundations	P	H	P	U
Corporate annuities	U	U	P	H
Joint ventures	P	H	P	U
Licensing ventures	U	U	P	H
Vendor financing	U	U	P	H
Mezzanine financing	U	P	H	H
Pension funds	U	P	P	P

*H = Highly likely source; P = possible source; U = unlikely source.

Sources: EMCO Financial Ltd., Los Angeles; Thomas Owens, "Getting Financing in 1990," *Small Business Reports*, June 1990, p. 71.

*S*ources of Equity Financing

3 Describe the various sources of equity financing available to entrepreneurs.

Equity financing is the personal investment of the owner (or owners) in the business and is sometimes called *risk capital* or *equity capital* because these investors assume the primary risk of losing their funds if the business fails. However, if the venture succeeds, they also share in the benefits, which can be substantial. The founders of Federal Express, Intel, and Compaq Computers became multimillionaires when their equity investments finally paid off. The primary advantage of equity capital is that it does not have to be repaid as does a loan. Equity investors are entitled to share in the company's earnings and usually to have a voice in the company's future direction. The primary disadvantage of equity financing is that the entrepreneur is giving up some, perhaps most, of the ownership in the business to others. Although 50 percent of something *is* better than 100 percent of nothing, giving up control of your company can be disconcerting and dangerous. Entrepreneurs are most likely to give up more equity in their businesses in the start-up phase than in any other (see Figure 13.2).

We now turn our attention to seven common sources of equity financing.

PERSONAL SAVINGS

The first place an entrepreneur should look for start-up money is in his own pockets. It's the least expensive source of funds available. "The sooner you take outside money, the more ownership in your company you'll have to surrender," warns one small business expert.[9] Entrepreneurs apparently see the benefits of self-sufficiency; the most common source of equity funds used to start a small business is the entrepreneur's pool of personal savings. One recent study of business start-ups found that three-fourths of the entrepreneurs got at least part of their initial capital from their own pockets.[10] Figure 13.3 shows that the founders of the fastest-growing small companies in the United States tapped their personal savings more often than any other source for their start-up financing.

Entrepreneur Lenny Lipton tapped his own pool of savings to get his company, Stereo-Graphics, which builds 3-D television sets, off the ground. When Lipton was a student at

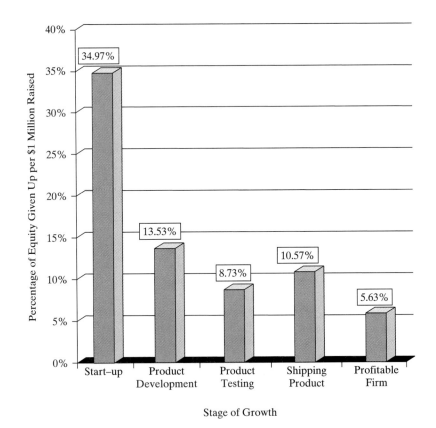

Figure 13.2 **Average Equity Given Up by Entrepreneurs Seeking Capital (%).** Total does not equal 100% because percentages indicate percentage of equity given up at various stages of growth.   SOURCE: VentureOne.

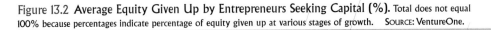

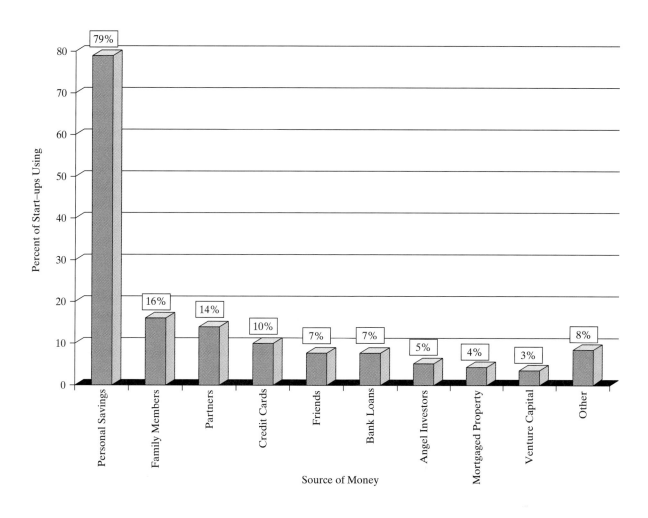

Figure 13.3 **The Inc. 500: Where Their Start-Up Money Came From.** The total comes to more than 100 percent because some businesses obtained funds from more than one source. SOURCE: Susan Greco, "The Startup Years," *Inc. 500*, October 17, 1997, p. 28.

Cornell University in 1963, he wrote a song about a toy dragon named Puff and the little boy who owned him. Fellow student Peter Yarrow set the words to music and Yarrow's folk trio, Peter, Paul, & Mary, recorded it. "Puff, The Magic Dragon" became a number one hit, and Lipton's royalties poured in.

In 1973, Lipton thought he had found a way to build inexpensive 3-D television systems. Using the money he had received in royalties, he launched StereoGraphics. By 1988, the company was still searching for the secret to an inexpensive 3-D TV, but it had produced several interesting high-tech systems for the defense industry using the same technology. That same year, StereoGraphics formed a partnership with Kaiser Aerospace and Electronics.

With a renewed focus on the consumer applications of their combined electronic technology, the partners made a significant breakthrough and shipped their first 3-D imaging system, CrystalEyes, in 1989. The system's 3-D images are astonishingly realistic. Early applications of CrystalEyes included flight simulators, mapping software, and computer-aided design. StereoGraphics' next move was into the operating room, where its imaging systems help surgeons see better during operations. StereoGraphics' CrystalEyes 3-D television system is still too expensive to have mass-market appeal, but managers are confident that the company will have a low-cost version in operation very soon.[11]

As a general rule, an entrepreneur should expect to provide at least half of the start-up funds in the form of equity capital. If an entrepreneur is not willing to risk his own money, potential investors are not likely to risk their money in the business either. Further, if an owner contributes less than half of the initial capital requirement, he must borrow an excessive amount of capital to fund the business properly, and the high repayment schedule puts intense pressure on cash flows. In some cases, however, a creative entrepreneur is able to invest as little as 10 percent of the initial capital requirement. The important point is that an entrepreneur should not surrender all hope of going into business just because he is unable to provide half of the starting funds.

FRIENDS AND RELATIVES

After emptying her own pockets, the entrepreneur should turn to friends and relatives who might be willing to invest in her business venture. Because of their relationships with the founder, these people are most likely to invest. *Leslie Wexner learned all about the retail clothing business as he grew up working in his father's clothing store in Columbus, Ohio. In 1963, at age 26, he had a disagreement with his father and left to open a small retail store in a strip mall in Columbus selling women's casual clothes. Wexner decided to focus on casual clothing because he had discovered that it sold faster than the formal and business wear that his father's store carried. Wexner opened his store with a $5,000 loan from his aunt, and it succeeded. Today, Wexner's The Limited operates more than 5,600 stores across the United States (including Abercrombie and Fitch, Lane Bryant, Structure, Victoria's Secret, and others).*[12] Often, they are more patient than other outside investors. "Most of our relatives just told us to pay them back when we could," says an entrepreneur who used $30,000 from family members to launch a gourmet coffee business."[13]

Inherent dangers lurk in family business investments, however. Unrealistic expectations or misunderstood risks have destroyed many friendships and have ruined many family reunions. To avoid such problems, an entrepreneur must honestly present the investment opportunity and the nature of the risks involved to avoid alienating friends and family members if the business fails.

- ◆ *Keep the arrangement strictly business.* The parties should treat all loans and investments in a businesslike manner, no matter how close the friendship or family relationship, to avoid problems down the line. If the transaction is a loan exceeding $10,000, it must carry a rate of interest at least as high as the market rate; otherwise the IRS may consider the loan a gift and penalize the lender.

- ◆ *Settle the details up front.* Before any money changes hands, both parties must agree on the details of the deal. How much money is involved? Is it a loan or an investment? How will the investor cash out? How will the loan be paid off? What will happen if the business fails?

- ◆ *Create a written contract.* Don't make the mistake of closing a financial deal with just a handshake. The probability of misunderstandings skyrockets! Putting an agreement in writing demonstrates both parties' commitment to the deal and minimizes the chances of disputes from faulty memories and misunderstandings. Plus, if the deal involves a loan, it is very difficult to justify interest deductions to the IRS on loans that have no documentation. In fact, most experts recommend avoiding family loans and instead using equity investments, which make family members and friends investors in the business.

How to Get the Financing You Need

*A*lmost every entrepreneur has a start-up financing horror story: how the banker giggled while reviewing the business plan or when the venture capitalist said, "Our interest in your business is lower than whale dung." Because of experiences such as these, entrepreneurs assume that lenders and investors lack either the money to put up or the sense to know a good deal when they see it. But the real reason most entrepreneurs can't get financing for their new business is they're just not ready for the money! In other words, if they got the money today, most entrepreneurs would spend it *without producing any long-term positive results.* Being ready for start-up financing means having a plan for spending the money wisely and being able to prove to others that you will follow it. Failing to convince potential lenders and investors that you can add value to your business with their money is a sure-fire way to get rejected. The following mistakes will guarantee that your plan is rejected:

Poor communications. Potential lenders and investors are amazed at the number of requests for financing they get without any description of what the business is! If you won't take the time to prepare a professional, concise business plan that explains your business concept in detail, don't expect to see much interest from outside investors and lenders. Neatness counts, too. Remember: The plan is a reflection of its creator.

Insufficient sales and marketing strategies. Too often, entrepreneurs pay insufficient attention to the marketing strategies they intend to employ. Remember the old adage: "Nothing in business happens until someone sells something." Investors like to see about 30 percent of a business plan devoted to marketing and selling.

Ignoring the negatives. Every business venture faces threats and problems. Investors get nervous if an entrepreneur cannot explain them or, worse, tries to cover them up.

Overuse of technical jargon. The safest route to use when presenting your idea is to assume the listener knows nothing about your industry or business and explain it accordingly. Don't turn off potential investors by spouting off tons of technical jargon.

Overemphasis on the product or service. A common tendency of entrepreneurs is to fall in love with their goods or services. You know why yours is a better mousetrap but will your target customers see the benefits it offers them? Initially, spend time selling the entire business concept—not just a product or a service—to potential lenders and investors.

No basis for financial projections. Entrepreneurs who cannot explain where they got the numbers for their financial projections stand little chance of attracting financing. Making financial projections involves more than just pulling numbers out of the blue. Investors usually are more interested in the assumptions behind the projections than in the projections themselves.

Insufficient evidence of a market. If you say there is a market for your good or service, prove it! Offer evidence of market research, endorsements from prototype users, purchase orders, or other signs of interest from real, live customers. Statements such as "This market is so huge that if we can get just 1 percent of it, we'll all be rich" don't carry much clout with potential investors.

Failing to know how much money you need. The correct answer to the question "How much money will you need?" is *not* "How much can I get?" This is a dead giveaway that an entrepreneur is not ready for financing.

Failing to set yourself and your business apart from the rest. Lenders and investors see thousands of entrepreneurs and business plans each year. Why should they invest in you? If you fail to show them how and why you and your business concept are superior, you'll never get the financing you need.

What can you do to prove you are ready for the financing you're seeking? Satisfy these criteria:

◆ Your business plan must explain the business—not just the product or service—and its competitive advantage.
◆ Your business plan must show you understand the power of the bottom line, providing a way to pay back loans or produce an attractive return on the investment.
◆ Your financial projections must be realistic and must make sense.
◆ You must grab your readers' attention in the executive summary; otherwise you've lost them forever.
◆ You must have a clear strategy for marketing your product or service and know what it will cost to make or provide.
◆ You must show *exactly* how you will use the money to meet your company's goals.
◆ You must prove that the business concept will work—that customers will buy your good or service.

In short, before starting your search for financing, be sure you're really ready for it!

1. What mistakes do entrepreneurs searching for financing most often make?
2. What advice would you give an entrepreneur about to begin her search for start-up capital?

SOURCES: Adapted from George Hunter, "Entrepreneurs in Search of Financial Angels," *Upstate Business,* July 13, 1997, pp. 2–3; Bruce J. Blechman, "Make No Mistake," *Entrepreneur,* August 1993, pp. 20–23; Bruce J. Blechman, "Make No Mistake," *Entrepreneur,* December 1991, pp. 28–31; Bruce J. Blechman, "Ready or Not," *Entrepreneur,* August 1991, pp. 20–22. ◆

- *Treat the money as "bridge financing."* Although family and friends can help you launch your business, it is unlikely that they can provide enough capital to sustain it over the long term. Sooner or later, you will need to establish a relationship with other sources of credit if your company is to survive and thrive. Consider money from family and friends as a bridge to take your company to the next level of financing.

- *Develop a payment schedule that suits both the entrepreneur and the lender or investor.* Although lenders and investors may want to get their money back as quickly as possible, a rapid repayment or cash-out schedule can jeopardize a fledgling company's survival. Establish a realistic repayment plan that works for both parties without putting excessive strain on the young company's cash flow.[14]

After tapping their own funds, raising capital from friends and relatives is a popular solution for cash-strapped entrepreneurs. A recent study of fast-growing manufacturing and service companies by Coopers and Lybrand discovered that 70 percent of the founders used their own money and that of relatives and friends to launch their companies.[15]

ANGELS

After dipping into their own pockets and convincing friends and relatives to invest in their business ventures, many entrepreneurs still find themselves short of the seed capital they need. Frequently, the next stop on the road to business financing is private investors. **Private investors** (or **angels***) are wealthy individuals, often entrepreneurs themselves, who invest in business start-ups in exchange for equity stakes in the companies.

Angels are a primary source of start-up capital for companies in the embryonic stage through the growth stage, and their role in financing small businesses is significant. Some experts conservatively estimate that some 250,000 angels invest more than $20 billion a year in 30,000 to 40,000 small companies. Others contend that private investors may put as much as $30 billion a year into 500,000 small businesses.[16] Because the angel market is so fragmented and disorganized, we may never get a completely accurate estimate of its investment in business start-ups. Although they may disagree on the exact amount of angel investments, experts concur on one fact: Angels are the largest single source of *external equity capital* for small businesses. Their investments in young companies dwarf those of professional venture capitalists, providing at least five times more capital to 20 to 30 times as many companies.[17]

Angels fill a significant gap in the seed capital market. They are most likely to finance start-ups with capital requirements in the $250,000 to $1,000,000 range, well below the $3 million minimum investments most professional venture capitalists prefer. One study of technology firms in New England found that more businesses raised equity capital from private investors than from any other source and that when the financing required was less than $1 million, angels were the primary source of capital.[18]

Scot Lund, founder of Midwest Process Equipment, a manufacturer of food-processing equipment, was having difficulty finding the capital he needed to launch the company. Then his father introduced him to a longtime friend, a retired banker. Lund made a pitch to the former banker, who "saw the potential in our company and decided to invest in us," says Lund. The investor put up $10,000 in cash and the collateral to support a $30,000 loan from a bank. Lund soon discovered that his angel brought a great deal more to the table than just money. "He introduced me to a lot of business contacts and met with us once a month to offer advice on how to run our company," says Lund. Since that initial investment, Midwest's sales have grown from $400,000 to more than $2 million, and the angel's original $10,000

---

*Originally used to describe investors who put up high-risk, early-stage seed capital for Broadway shows, the term now refers to private investors who back emerging entrepreneurial companies with their own money.

investment has turned into more than $30,000. "It's worked out great for everybody," says Lund.[19]

Like Lund's angel, most private investors have substantial business experience, which they are willing to invest in the businesses where they put their money. In many cases, an angel's advice can be just as valuable as his money! Putting an investor on the board of directors or encouraging him to assume the role of informal consultant can make the difference between a moderately successful company and an extremely successful one. Smart entrepreneurs will take advantage of their investors' experience and willingness to help.

The challenge, of course, is *finding* these angels. The typical angel is a 47-year-old white male with a college education earning $100,000 a year and having a net worth (excluding a home) of $1 million. Most have substantial business and financial experience and prefer to invest in companies at the start-up or infant growth stage. The typical angel accepts 30 percent of the investment opportunities presented; makes an average of two investments every three years; and has invested an average of $131,000 of equity in 3.5 firms (although investments may range from as little as $5,000 to as much as $1 million or more). Ninety percent say they're satisfied with their investment decisions.[20] Locating angels boils down to making the most of networking. Asking friends, attorneys, bankers, stockbrokers, accountants, consultants, and other business owners for suggestions and introductions is a good way to start. "Angels are . . . like trolls," says Bill Wetzel, who has studied angels extensively. "You have to look under every rock and every bridge and hope one will crawl out from under. [But] angels do exist. They are an invisible reality. They are not easy to find, but . . . they are really the bright spot for obtaining outside equity capital."[21]

Douglas Pihl and Duane Carlson used angel financing to launch NetStar, a company that manufactures gigarouters, a high-performance computer add-on that links electronic workstations to give them the power of a supercomputer at just a fraction of the cost. Pihl and Carlson spent a year and a half developing a detailed business plan for NetStar and scraping together $500,000 in seed capital from friends, relatives, and colleagues around Minneapolis, their home base. To make NetStar a success, however, the entrepreneurs knew they would need at least 10 times the capital they had already raised. They approached a local stockbroker, who, within three months, had assembled a team of private investors willing to put up $1.35 million in exchange for equity stakes in the fledgling firm. Two years later and two more rounds of angel financing produced more than $10 million in seed capital.[22]

Like NetStar's private investors, angels almost always invest their money locally, so entrepreneurs should look close to home for them—typically within a 50- to 100-mile radius. Angels also look for businesses they know something about, and most expect to invest their knowledge, experience, and energy as well as their money in a company. Angels tend to invest in clusters as well. With the right approach, an entrepreneur can attract an angel who might share the deal with some of his cronies. *For instance, the Investors' Circle is an informal organization of angels who specialize in financing socially responsible businesses. Every month, the Circle sends its 130 members two-page summaries on anywhere from four to 20 business ventures. Interested members, who often team up with one another, contact company founders directly. Cyclean Inc., a company that recycles asphalt, recently raised part of its start-up capital from Investors' Circle members.*[23]

Angels are an excellent source of "patient money," often willing to wait seven years or longer to cash out their investments. They earn their returns through the increased value of the business, not through dividends and interest. For example, more than 1,000 early investors in Microsoft Inc. (today a giant in the computer software industry) are now millionaires. The original investors in Genentech Inc. (a genetic engineering company) have seen their investments increase more than 500 times![24] Angels' return-on-investment targets tend to be lower than those of professional venture capitalists. Whereas venture capitalists shoot for 60 to 75 percent returns annually, private investors usually settle for 35 to 50 percent (depending on the level of risk involved in the venture). Private investors typically take less than 50 percent ownership, leaving the majority ownership to the entrepreneur. Venture capitalists, on the other hand, usually own 80 percent of a company by the time it goes public.[25] Sixty percent of angel investments are in seed capital (financing for businesses in the start-up phase), and 82 percent involve less than $500,000.[26] The lesson: If an entrepreneur needs relatively small amounts of money to launch a company, angels are a primary source.

Negotiating deals with private investors is not a risk-free proposition for either the angel or the entrepreneur. Although the risks to the angel are fairly obvious, those facing the entrepreneur often are hidden beneath the surface of the deal, only to be discovered after it's too late. When dealing with angels, an entrepreneur should take these steps to avoid potential problems:

Investigate the investors and their past deals. Jerry Feigen, a venture capital consultant, advises, "Know your investor well. Do a lot of homework."[27] Never get involved in a deal with an angel you don't know or trust. Be sure you and your investors have a common vision of the business and the deal.

Summarize the details of the deal in a letter of intent. Although a letter of intent is not a legal document, Feigen says, "It outlines what the deal will look like and discusses the most sensitive areas being negotiated so that there are no surprises."[28] What role, if any, will the angel play in running the business? Angels can be a source of valuable help, but some entrepreneurs complain of angels' meddling.

Keep the deal simple. The simpler the deal is, the easier it will be to sell to potential investors. "It's best to give up straight equity—a percentage of ownership of your business, represented by common stock—rather than, say, a loan that can be converted into stock," advises Bill Wetzel.[29]

Nail down the angel's exit path. Angels make their money when they sell their ownership interests. Ideally, the exit path should be part of structuring the deal. Will the company buy back the angels' shares? Will the company go public so the angels can sell their shares on the market? Will the owners sell out to a larger company? What is the time frame for doing so?

Avoid intimidating potential investors. Most angels are turned off by entrepreneurs with an attitude of "I have someone else who will do the deal if you don't." In the face of such coercion, many private investors simply walk away from the deal.

Always be truthful. Overpromising and underdelivering will kill a deal and spoil future financing arrangements.

Develop alternative financing arrangements. Never back an angel into a corner with "take this deal or leave it." Have alternative plans prepared in case the investor balks at the outset.

Don't take the money and run. Investors appreciate entrepreneurs who keep them informed about how their money is being spent and the results it shows. Prepare periodic reports for them. One entrepreneur who raised $1 million by selling stock in his company to more than 20 private investors says, "I keep my investors informed by sending them informational letters once a month and holding stockholders' meetings."[30]

Stick to the deal. It's tempting to spend the money where it's most needed once it is in hand. Resist! If you promised to use the funds for specific purposes, do it. Nothing undermines an angel's trust as quickly as violating the original plan.

Angels among Us

*A*lthough they are an important source of small business financing, angels can be extremely difficult to locate. You won't find them listed under "Angels" in the Yellow Pages. This important source of small business financing often remains invisible to all but the most patient and persistent entrepreneurs. Patience and persistence—and connections—pay off in the search for angel financing, however. How does an entrepreneur needing financing find an angel to help launch or expand a company?

- ◆ *Start early.* Finding private investors takes a lot longer than most entrepreneurs think.
- ◆ *Have a business plan ready.* Once you find a potential private investor, don't risk losing their interest while you put together a business plan. Have the plan ready to go *before* you begin your search.
- ◆ *Look close to home.* Most angels prefer to invest their money locally, so conduct a thorough search for potential angels within a 50- to 100-mile radius of your business.
- ◆ *Canvass your industry.* Angels tend to specialize in particular industries, usually ones they know a lot about. "Keep in close touch with industry contacts," advises one investment banker.
- ◆ *Recognize that, in addition to the money they invest, angels also want to provide their knowledge and expertise.* Indeed, angels' experience and knowledge can be just as valuable as their money if entrepreneurs are willing to accept it.
- ◆ *Remember that angels invest for more than just financial reasons.* Angels want to earn a good return on the money they invest in businesses, but there's usually more to it than that. "Angels tend to look at things more spiritually than [other investors do]," says one expert, often investing in companies for personal reasons.
- ◆ *Join local philanthropic organizations, chambers of commerce, nonprofit organizations, and advisory boards.* Potential investors often are involved in such organizations.
- ◆ *Ask business professionals such as bankers, lawyers, stockbrokers, accountants, and others for names of potential angels.* They know people who have the money and the desire to invest in business ventures.
- ◆ *Network, network, network.* Finding angel financing initially is a game of contacts: getting an introduction to the right person from the right person.

Networking was the key to finding angel financing for Patrick Lammert and Mark Weber, co-founders of Wisconsin Technology, a color-separation company that serves the printing business. At age 25, they were shocked when three banks rejected their loan proposal. The entrepreneurial pair had invested $50,000 of their own money to get the company running but needed another $50,000 to lease equipment, buy furniture, and cover short-term expenses. Lammert and Weber approached Jack Schumann, the son of a friend of Weber's grandmother, who was willing to put up the remaining $50,000. In return, Schumann, who also was in the print business would get 51 percent ownership in the start-up in the early years, would have a voice in major decisions, and would serve as a consultant to the young entrepreneurs. The deal also included a mandatory buyback of Schumann's equity at the end of five years: he would cash out, selling back his ownership in the company to Lammert and Weber. Right on schedule, the young entrepreneurs purchased Schumann's stock. All around it was a good deal. Wisconsin Technology got the financing it needed, Lammert and Weber ended up owning 100 percent of their company, and Schumann's $50,000 investment turned into $280,000 in just five years!

Some angels are going on-line through computer networks, making it easier for entrepreneurs to hook up with them. When Ken Hamilton's Western Call & Decoy, a small firm that makes decoys and game calls, ran into a cash crisis, he tried, unsuccessfully, for months to get financing through traditional sources. Then he subscribed to American Venture Capital Exchange, an on-line computer service that links potential investors with cash-hungry small businesses. Within months, Hamilton had found a private investor who pumped $110,000 into his company. "I couldn't get the money I needed until I tried that," says Hamilton.

The Small Business Administration (SBA) is trying to make it easier for angels and entrepreneurs to find one another with its Angel Capital Electronic Network (ACE-Net), a nationwide listing service identifying small, fast-growing companies that angels would be interested in reviewing. ACE-Net, which is accessible from the SBA's Web site <http://www.sba.gov/ADVO/acenet.htm>, helps match the estimated 250,000 angels across the country and the $20 billion they have to invest with entrepreneurs seeking between $250,000 and $5 million for their growing businesses. The computerized matchmaking service collects business plans (and a fee) from entrepreneurs in search of financing and then issues potential angels a password that allows them to review the records of the small companies listed in the database. Investors can search through ACE-Net, looking for particular types of businesses on the basis of industry, size, geographic area, and other criteria. Other organizations run networks similar to ACE-Net, but all are designed to help angels avoid a Catch 22 situation. They

(continued)

want to invest money in the "right" business ventures, but they don't want to become public figures. "It's difficult to track these people," says one angel. "They know what happens if they get identified: They get so many calls that that's all they would do all day long."

---

1. What advantages does angel financing offer an entrepreneur?

2. What advice would you offer an entrepreneur about locating an angel?

3. How would you go about finding an angel to finance a business in your local area?

Sources: Adapted from Jan Norman, "How to: Finance Your Business," *Business Start-Ups*, January 1998, pp. 46–49; Stephen Blakely, "Finding Angels on the Internet," *Nation's Business*, April 1997, p. 78; Timothy L. O'Brien, "Entrepreneurs Raise Funds through On-Line Computer Services," *Wall Street Journal*, June 2, 1994, pp. B1, B2; Leslie Brokaw, "How to Start an Inc. 500 Company: Where Do You Go for Capital?" *Inc. 500*, 1994, pp. 63–65; Udayan Gupta, "A Capital Idea: Entrepreneur Sets Up On-Line Database," *Wall Street Journal*, March 1, 1994, p. B2; Richard J. Maturi, "Calling All Angels," *Your Company*, Summer 1992, pp. 16–17; Frances Huffman, "Where Angels Tread," *Entrepreneur*, April 1993, p. 98; Dale G. Buss, "Heaven Help Us," *Nation's Business*, November 1993, pp. 29–34; Stephanie N. Mehta, "New Breed of Investor Brings More Than Cash to Hopeful Start-Ups," *Wall Street Journal*, August 25, 1997, pp. A1, A11. ◆

PARTNERS

As we saw in chapter 3, an entrepreneur can choose to take on a partner to expand the capital base of the proposed business. *Neil Swartz, CEO of Microleague Multimedia, created a partnership to raise the money he needed to develop two computer sports simulations, Sports Illustrated Presents Microleague Baseball and Hooves of Thunder. In the fast-paced business of multimedia entertainment, getting products to market while they are still hot is crucial. Swartz needed about $200,000 to complete work on the games, so he formed a limited partnership in which his new partners put up $212,500 in exchange for a 10 percent royalty on the sale of the games and a deferred interest payment. Swartz got the fast money he needed for his business, and the investors earned a handsome return on their money when Microleague Multimedia brought the games onto the market successfully.*[31]

Before entering into any partnership arrangement, however, the owner must consider the impact of giving up some personal control over operations and of sharing profits with one or more partners. Whenever an entrepreneur gives up equity in her business (through whatever mechanism), she runs the risk of losing control over it. As the founder's ownership in a company becomes increasingly diluted, the probability of losing control of its future direction and the entire decision-making process increases. *At age 19, Scott Olson started a company that manufactured in-line skates, a company that he had big dreams for. Rollerblades Inc. grew quickly and soon ran into the problem that plagues so many fast-growing companies: insufficient cash flow. Through a series of unfortunate incidents, Olson ended up trading equity in the company for the money he desperately needed to bring his innovative skate designs to market. Ultimately, his investors ended up with 95 percent of the company, leaving Olson with the remaining scant 5 percent. Frustrated at not being able to determine the company's direction, Olson soon left to start another company. "It's tough to keep control," he says. "For every penny you get in the door, you have to give something up."*[32]

CORPORATE VENTURE CAPITAL

Large corporations recently have gotten into the business of financing small companies. Today, more than 100 large corporations across the globe—from Johnson & Johnson to Genetech—maintain their own venture capital funds to finance projects with small businesses. *For example, two fast-growing small companies in multimedia technology, Kaleida Labs and General Magic, were financed almost entirely by large Japanese electronics companies.*[33] Often, the large companies providing the financing are the customers of those receiving it. Recognizing how interwoven their success is with that of their suppliers, corporate giants such as AT&T, JCPenney, and Ford now offer financial support to many of the small businesses they buy from. *When Finis Conner was launching Conner Peripherals Inc., a small maker of hard disk drives for personal computers, he set out with a prototype disk* *drive in search of customers and investors. He found both in Compaq Computers. Managers at Compaq were so impressed with Conner's product that they not only decided to buy it, but they also bankrolled the company. Compaq put up $12 million for 40 percent of Conner Peripherals' stock and bought its entire first year's production of disk drives. Conner Peripherals went on to become a Fortune 500 company in just three years.*[34]

Foreign corporations are also interested in investing in small U.S. businesses. Often, these corporations are seeking strategic partnerships to gain access to new technology, new products, or lucrative U.S. markets. Companies in the United Kingdom, Germany, Japan, and Malaysia are prime candidates for investments in small U.S. firms. *Larry E. Fondren, founder of Intervest Financial Services, Inc., had been very successful selling computer networks that allowed insurance companies to transfer data easily and in specialized formats when he saw an opportunity to provide a similar product for brokers of fixed-income securities. Fondren's electronic exchange system would enable institutional investors and brokers to trade bonds with one another without having to go through an intermediary. Fondren plowed $3.5 million of his own money and another $1.5 million from friends and family into developing the network, but he needed more. With the help of an investment banker, Fondren was able to convince a British merchant bank to put up the balance of the investment. The British corporation, Dawnay, Day, and Company, traded bonds across Europe and saw Fondren's company not only as a good investment but also as a way to purchase technology that would give them a distinct edge over their competitors in Europe.*[35]

VENTURE CAPITAL COMPANIES

Venture capital companies are private, for-profit organizations that purchase equity positions in young businesses they believe have high growth and profit potential, producing annual returns of 300 to 500 percent over five to seven years. Over the years, venture capitalists have invested billions of dollars in high-potential companies, including such notable businesses as Apple Computer, Microsoft, Intel, and Data General. More than 800 U.S. venture capital companies have active portfolios into which they have plowed nearly $80 billion in the last 20 years.[36] Although companies in high-tech industries such as computer software, medical care equipment, biotechnology, and communications are popular targets of venture capital, any company with extraordinary growth prospects has the potential to attract venture capital, whatever its industry.

Venture capital companies raise money from mutual funds, pension funds, and other institutional investors and buy shares of ownership in promising new businesses. They seek to add value to the businesses in which they invest by taking a role in managing them. "Venture capital firms want to put their own experts on the board, and they want a major leadership and management role," says one expert.[37] Entrepreneurs seeking venture capital must be willing to give up some ownership and control in their companies in exchange for the money. *For instance, David Edelberg founded American WholeHealth Inc. in 1993, hoping to build the company into a national chain of clinics that would offer not only traditional medicine but also acupuncture, massage therapy, psychotherapy, and other holistic medical treatments. After opening two clinics in three years, Edelberg met with representatives of two venture capital firms specializing in the health care industry. The two venture capital companies invested $6 million in WholeHealth, purchasing just over 50 percent of the company's stock. A representative from each firm took a seat on WholeHealth's board of directors, which soon brought in a new, professional management team to run the company. Since getting its capital boost, the company has opened four new clinics and is on schedule for reaching its goals of opening 10 new offices over the next several years. A second round of venture capital financing has the company well on its way to its goal of becoming a national chain. Managers at WholeHealth hoped to raise $7 million to $8 million, but venture capitalists* *were so optimistic about the company's prospects that they put in $15 million, putting about two-thirds of the company's stock in their hands.*[38]

Like all financiers, venture capitalists are interested in reviewing the small firm's financial history, but venture capital companies are more concerned with the future profit potential the business investment offers. As a result, they invest funds in return for a share of the ownership (instead of loaning funds as a bank or other credit would) and try to develop long-term capital gains. Venture capital companies are *not* charitable organizations; they invest in small companies and hope to make an attractive profit when they sell their equity. Table 13.2 offers a humorous look at deciphering the language of venture capitalists.

Policies and Investment Strategies. Venture capital firms usually establish stringent policies to implement their overall investment strategies.

Investment Size and Screening. Depending on the size of the venture capital corporation and its cost structure, minimum investments range from $10,000 to $3 million. Investment ceilings, in effect, do not exist. Most firms seek investments in the $1 million to $5 million range to justify the cost of investigating the large number of proposals they receive.

The venture capital screening process is *extremely* rigorous. The typical venture capital company invests in just one-tenth of 1 percent of the applications it receives! For example, an average venture capital firm screens in excess of 1,000 proposals a year but will reject more than 90 percent because they do not meet the firm's standards. The remaining 10 percent are investigated more thoroughly at a cost ranging from $2,000 to $3,000 for each proposal. At this time, approximately 10 to 15 proposals will have passed the screening process, and these are subjected to comprehensive review. Of the three to five proposals finally remaining, the venture capital firm will invest in one or two. A partner in one large venture capital firm says his company receives about 3,000 business plans a year and ultimately makes just 14 investments.[39]

Ownership. Most venture capitalists prefer to purchase ownership in a small business through common stock or convertible preferred stock. The share of ownership a venture capital company purchases may be as low as 1 percent for a profitable company to possibly 100 percent for a financially unstable firm. Although there is no limit on the amount of stock it can buy, a typical venture capital company seeks to purchase 30 to 40 percent of the business. Anything more incurs the risk of draining the entrepreneur's dedication and enthusiasm for managing the firm. Still, the entrepreneur must weigh the positive aspects of receiving the invested funds against the negative features of owning a smaller share of the business.

Control. Although the entrepreneur must sacrifice a portion of the business to the venture capitalist, he usually can maintain a majority interest and control of its operations. In most cases, venture capitalists prefer to let the founding team of managers use its skills to operate the business. However, many venture capitalists join the boards of directors of the companies they invest in or send in new managers or a new management team to protect their investments. Most venture capitalists serve as financial and managerial advisers, but some take an active role in managing the company; they recruit employees, provide sales leads, choose attorneys and advertising agencies, and make daily decisions. One survey found that 90 percent of venture capitalists eventually either become directly involved in managing or select outside managers for the companies they invest in. Seventy-five percent of these active venture capitalists say they were forced to step in because the existing management team lacked the talent to achieve growth targets.[40] One cautionary note for *every* entrepreneur seeking venture capital is to find out *before* the deal is done exactly how much control and "hands-on" management investors plan to assume.

Investment Preferences. The venture capital industry has undergone important changes over the past decade. Venture capital funds are larger, more numerous, and more specialized. As

Table 13.2 Deciphering the Language of the Venture Capital Industry

By nature, entrepreneurs tend to be optimistic. When screening business plans, venture capitalists must make an allowance for entrepreneurial enthusiasm. Here's a sample of phrases commonly found in business plans and their accompanying venture capital translations.

Acquisition strategy. The current products have no market.

Basically on plan. We're expecting a revenue shortfall of 25 percent.

A challenging year. Competitors are eating our lunch.

Company's underlying strength and resilience. We still lost money, but look how we cut our losses.

Considerably ahead of plan. Hit our plan in one of the last three months.

Core business. Our product line is obsolete.

Currently revising budget. The financial plan is in total chaos.

Cyclical industry. We posted a huge loss last year.

Entrepreneurial CEO. Totally uncontrollable, bordering on maniacal.

Facing unprecedented economic, political, and structural shifts. It's a tough world out there, but we're coping the best we can.

Ingredients are there. Given two years, we might find a workable strategy.

Investing heavily in R&D. We're trying desperately to catch the competition.

Limited downside. Things can't get much worse.

Long sales cycle. Yet to find a customer who likes the product enough to buy it.

Major opportunity. It's our last chance.

Niche strategy. A small-time player.

On a manufacturing learning curve. We can't make the product with positive margins.

Passive investor. Phones once a year to see if we're still in business.

Positive results. Our losses were less than last year.

Selective investment strategy. The board is spending more time on yachts than on planes.

Solid operating performance in a difficult year. Yes, we lost money and market share, but look how hard we tried.

Somewhat below plan. We expect a revenue shortfall of 75 percent.

Strategic investor. One who will pay a preposterous price for an equity share in the business.

Strongest fourth quarter ever. Don't quibble over the losses in the first three quarters.

Sufficient opportunity to market this product no longer exists. Nobody will buy the thing.

A team of skilled, motivated, and dedicated people. We've laid off most of our staff, and those who are left should be glad they still have jobs.

Too early to tell. Results to date have been grim.

Turnaround opportunity. It's a lost cause.

Unique. We have no more than six strong competitors.

Volume-sensitive. Our company has massive fixed costs.

Window of opportunity. Without more opportunity fast, this company is dead.

A year in which we confronted challenges. At least we know the questions even if we haven't got the answers.

We are well positioned for future growth. By virtually every measure of corporate performance, the company ranks at or near the bottom of the industry.

Management is pleased with the company's performance to date. We're constantly teetering on the verge of a major cash crisis, but the founder of the company raked in a compensation package worth several million more than last year's.

This bold initiative anticipates the competitive realities that await all companies in the twenty-first century. The new product that was supposed to be the company's next big thing fell flat on its face.

The adverse affects of these fundamental shifts in the market are rippling throughout the nation's economy. We misread the needs of our customers and sent our market share plummeting.

SOURCES: Adapted from John F. Budd Jr., "Cracking the CEO's Code," *Wall Street Journal,* March 27, 1995, p. A20; "Venture-Speak Defined," *Teleconnect,* October 1990, p. 42; David Stauffer, "What Annual Reports Won't Say, "*Wall Street Journal,* April 7, 1997, p. A14.

One Step at a Time

*P*hil Garfinkle, Yaacov Ben-Yaacov, and Elliot Jaffe peered into the future and saw the power of blending the Internet and photographic technology. In late 1995, the partners launched PictureVision, a company whose products allow users to share, manipulate, and store photographs on the World Wide Web. After launching PictureVision with their own money, Garfinkle and his co-founders knew that they were going to need lots more money to enable their company to reach its potential. They also knew that attracting that capital would be no easy task, so they decided to take it one step at a time.

Attracting capital from angel investors would be an ideal way to start feeding their company's growth. Their first move was to contact Michael Eisenberg, a consultant who specializes in tracking down angel investors. Almost immediately, Eisenberg had interest in PictureVision's business plan from several potential investors. Within two months, nine angels put up $300,000 in exchange for a 10 percent stake in the company. That was enough to take PictureVision to the next level of growth. "The money helped us become a viable company," says Garfinkle, enabling PictureVision to commercialize its technology and giving it enough credibility to move to the next level of financing.

For the next round of financing, the entrepreneurs knew that PictureVision would need larger amounts of capital. Almost immediately, the entrepreneurs began working with venture capital companies that specialized in high-tech industries. In a little more than a year, PictureVision had raised $9 million in two rounds of equity financing from venture capital companies such as Oak Investment Partners and Benchmark Capital.

Knowing that they still have a hungry company to feed, Garfinkle and his co-founders are planning to attempt an initial public offering (IPO). "An IPO is the only way we can access the volume of capital we need," explains Garfinkle. The entrepreneurs recognize that they must begin a makeover of their company to get it ready and to make it attractive for the IPO. The steps they are taking include:

◆ *Building a stronger, more professional management team.* Investors want to see a company headed by experienced, capable managers before buying into an IPO.
◆ *Creating benefit plans.* Attracting and retaining quality managers and employees is difficult for small companies because they cannot offer salaries comparable to those at major corporations. However, by providing benefits such as employee stock ownership plans, "you can bridge the gap by offering potential employees to cash in on the future," says Garfinkle.
◆ *Enlisting the help of a Big Six accounting firm.* Going public requires a company to provide audited financial statements, and hiring a Big Six firm to prepare them instills confidence in investors.
◆ *Building an active board of directors.* Investors want to see a competent board of directors that will help managers make sound decisions.
◆ *Building bridges to the financial community.* As PictureVision has grown, Garfinkle has spent more time working with members of the financial community, forging important relationships and raising the company's visibility there.

1. Evaluate the step-by-step method these entrepreneurs used to finance their business at each stage of its growth. What are the implications of planning a company's financing in stages?

2. Evaluate the steps these entrepreneurs are taking to prepare their company for an IPO. Do you predict that they will be successful in their attempted IPO? Explain.

SOURCE: Adapted from David R. Evanson, "Public School," *Entrepreneur*, October 1997, pp. 62–65; Jeff Wuorio, "Go on an Equity Hunt to Fund Expansion," *Your Company*, Forecast 1998, pp. 42–48. ◆

the industry grows, more venture capital funds are focusing their investments in niches: everything from low-calorie custards to consumer electronics. Some will invest only in particular industries; others will invest in almost any industry but prefer companies in particular stages. Although some specialize in financing start-up companies, most prefer to invest in companies in the later stages of growth and development.

Motion Technology Inc., a small manufacturer of a unique self-contained system for deep-frying foods without needing any ventilation, got the financing it needed to grow from The Food Fund, a venture capital company specializing in food and food service companies. After raising capital from family and friends, Arthur Harrison, Motion Technology's president, still needed $600,000 to expand its product line and to begin national advertising. The Food Fund studied the company's business plan, its management, and its product and liked what it saw: a unique product with a competitive edge that appealed to a broad base of cus-

tomers. Motion Technology benefited not only from the $800,000 capital injection but also from the expertise and connections of the principals of the Food Fund, all of whom had decades of experience in the food industry. Within one year of the investment, Motion Technology's sales tripled.[41]

What Venture Capitalists Look For. The small business owner must realize that it is *very* difficult for any small business, especially fledgling or struggling firms, to pass the rigorous screening process of a venture capital company and qualify for an investment. Venture capital firms finance fewer than 1,000 deals each year.[42] Two factors make a deal attractive to venture capitalists: high returns and a convenient (and profitable) exit strategy. When evaluating potential investments, venture capitalists look for the following features:

Competent management. The most important ingredient in the success of any business is the ability of the manager or the management team, and venture capitalists recognize this fact. One financing expert explains, "Venture capitalists are really buying into the management of your company. If the light isn't on at the top, it's dim all the way down."[43]

Competitive edge. Investors are searching for some factor that will enable a small business to set itself apart from its competitors. This distinctive competence may range from an innovative product or service to a unique marketing or R&D approach. It must be something with the potential to make the business a leader in its field.

Growth industry. Profits are not a must for companies seeking venture capital (although they help), but the potential for rapid growth is. Venture capitalists know that companies in rapidly growing industries are likely to produce high profits. Hot industries attract profits—and venture capital. Because of its high growth potential, the infertility industry, with its products and services aimed at couples trying to conceive babies, has become a target of large amounts of venture capital.[44] Venture capital firms are most interested in young companies that have enough growth potential to become $50 million (or more) businesses in five to seven years. "If you're not high growth, you can't even get through our door," says a manager at one large venture capital firm.[45]

Intangible factors. Some other important factors considered in the screening process are not easily measured; they are the intuitive, intangible factors the venture capitalist detects by gut feeling. This feeling might be the result of the small firm's solid sense of direction, its strategic planning process, the chemistry of its management team, or a number of other factors.

Table 13.3 presents questions entrepreneurs should answer to determine whether they can qualify for venture capital financing.

PUBLIC STOCK SALE ("GOING PUBLIC")

In some cases, an entrepreneur can "go public" by selling shares of stock in the corporation to investors. This is an effective method of raising needed capital, but it can be an expensive and time-consuming process filled with regulatory nightmares. Once a company makes an **initial public offering (IPO),** nothing will ever be the same again. Managers must consider the impact of their decisions not only on the company and its employees but also on its shareholders and the value of their stock. "When you're a private company, you only have to deal with yourself and your management team. When you're public, you have to deal with the world," says Ann Spector Lieff, who took her chain of retail music stores public.[46]

Going public is not for every small business. In fact, few entrepreneurs are able to take their start-up companies public. Only about 20,000 companies in the United States—less

Table 13.3 Do You Stand a Chance of Getting Venture Capital?

For most small businesses, the prospects of getting financing from a venture capital company are weak. However, for those companies that can pass venture capitalists' stringent standards, venture capitalists are quite willing to "show them the money." John H. Martinson, managing partner of the Edison Venture Fund, a $200 million venture capital company, offers the following litmus test to determine whether a business will catch venture capitalists' attention.

1. *Is yours a technology company?* Although venture capital companies make investments in many different industries, Martinson says that approximately 80 percent of the typical venture capital company's investment portfolio is in technology companies. Why? The next question reveals at least part of the answer.

2. *Is your company capable of becoming a market leader?* "We rarely finance a company that is going up against a[n established] market leader with a similar product," says Martinson. Why? "It's too difficult and expensive to succeed." Creative applications of technology can create vast new markets or reshape existing ones, catapulting the company that created that technology to the top.

3. *Can you build the company inexpensively?* For most venture capital companies, that means about $10 million or less. "Venture capital companies like to build companies on the cheap to limit the downside risk and because they don't want to rely on other sources of capital to pitch in to help the company reach its goal," says Martinson.

4. *Is there a clear distribution channel?* Not only do venture capital companies look for star products or services, but they also want to see easy access to low-cost, established channels of distribution. In keeping with their interest in minimizing cost, venture capitalists are leery of products or services that require building a channel of distribution from the ground up. Companies that have access to existing channels of distribution are more attractive than those that must develop their own distribution systems.

5. *Does this product require significant support?* Complex products or services usually require customer service and support structures that are expensive and difficult to establish and maintain. Martinson cites the example of a low-tech home alarm system sold through traditional mass-market outlets. Although the product would appeal to customers' rising concerns about security, the appeal to venture capitalists would be diminished if the product required a third party to install and service it. When it comes to products, simpler is better.

6. *Can the product or service generate gross profit margins of 50 percent or more?* To meet venture capital investors' aggressive rate-of-return targets, a company must have a plump gross profit margin. Thin margins leave little room for error when building a business, a situation venture capitalists want to avoid.

7. *Can the company grow to $25 million in sales within five years, with the prospect of growing into a $50 million to $100 million company?* When a company hits the $25 million mark in sales, says Martinson, it is just the beginning to earn the profits venture capital companies must have to justify their investments. "If there's no possibility you're going to hit the $25 million benchmark within five years, it's simply a waste of time to pursue institutional venture capital," he says.

SOURCE: Adapted from David R. Evanson, "Capital Questions," *Entrepreneur*, March 1997, pp. 62–65.

---

than 1 percent—are publicly held, and fewer than 1,000 companies make initial public offerings each year.[47] Few companies with less than $5 million in annual sales manage to go public successfully. It is almost impossible for a start-up company with no track record of success to raise money with a public offering. Instead, the investment bankers who underwrite public stock offerings typically look for established companies with the following characteristics:

- Consistently high growth rates
- Strong record of earnings
- Three to five years of audited financial statements
- A solid position in a rapidly growing market
- A sound management team and a strong board of directors

Figure 13.4 shows the number of U.S. IPOs from 1981 to 1996, along with the amount of capital raised during that time.

Before choosing to take a company public, an entrepreneur should consider carefully both the advantages and disadvantages of making a public offering. The *advantages* include the following:

Ability to raise large amounts of capital. The biggest benefit of a public offering is the capital infusion the company receives. After going public, the corporation has the cash to fund R&D projects, expand plant and facilities, repay debt, or boost working capital balances. *For example, FPA Medical Management, a company that assembles networks of doctors, raised $11.5 million in its IPO and $26 million in a follow-up offering. FPA used the money to hire staff, acquire existing medical practices, and open new offices. Fueled by its capital injection, FPA went from a 40-employee company with $18 million in sales and zero profits to a profitable $170 million business with 700 employees. "We owe that growth to public capital," says CEO Sol Lizerbram. Already operating in seven Western states, FPA has its sights set on more growth.*[48] As FPA's experience proves, companies can attract equity capital from the public market to get the fuel they need to

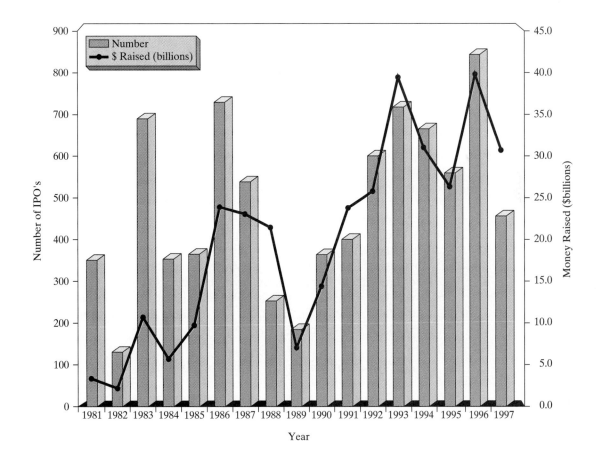

Figure 13.4 **U.S. Initial Public Offerings** SOURCE: Hale and Dorr, *The New England IPO Report,* <http://www.haledorr.com/publications/ipo/IPO_1997/pages/07_National.html>.

grow quickly without incurring the interest expense and the obligation to repay associated with debt financing.

Improved access for future financing. Going public boosts a company's net worth and broadens its equity base. Its improved financial strength makes it easier for the firm to attract more capital, both debt and equity, and to grow. *For example, Jim Hindman, president and CEO of Jiffy Lube International, claims that going public "was absolutely the key element" in growing from seven outlets in 1979 to more than 800 today. Without its public offering, the company "would have stopped growing and would have been a regional firm," he says.*[49]

Improved corporate image. All of the media attention a company receives during the registration process makes it more visible. Plus, becoming a public company in some industries improves its prestige and enhances its competitive position, one of the most widely recognized, intangible benefits of going public. Public companies typically receive more coverage and attention from the media than private companies.

Attracting and retaining key employees. Public companies often use stock-based compensation plans to attract and retain quality employees. Stock options and bonuses are excellent methods for winning employees' loyalty and for instilling a healthy ownership attitude among them. Employee stock ownership plans (ESOPs) and stock purchase plans are popular recruiting and motivational tools in many small corporations, enabling them to hire top-flight talent they otherwise would not be able to afford.

Using stock for acquisitions. A company whose stock is publicly traded can acquire other businesses by offering its own shares (rather than cash). Acquiring other companies with shares of stock eliminates the need to incur additional debt. *For example, going public gave Ringer Corporation, a national manufacturer of lawn care products, the opportunity to expand without adding any debt to its balance sheet. The company recently acquired Safer Inc., a maker of natural pesticides, with $10 million of its stock and a small amount of cash.*

Listing on a stock exchange. Being listed on an organized stock exchange, even a small regional one, improves the marketability of a company's shares and enhances its image. Most publicly held companies' stocks do not qualify for listing on the nation's largest exchanges: the New York Stock Exchange (NYSE) and the American Stock Exchange (AMEX). However, the AMEX recently created a new market for small company stocks, The Emerging Company Marketplace. Most small companies' stocks are traded either on the National Association of Securities Dealers Automated Quotation (NASDAQ) system's National Market System (NMS) and its emerging small capitalization exchange (SmallCap Market) or on one of the nation's regional stock exchanges. The most popular regional exchanges include the Midwest (MSE), Philadelphia (PHLX), Boston (ESE), and Pacific (PSE). Table 13.4 describes the requirements of each of the major markets for listing initial public offerings.

The disadvantages of going public include the following:

Dilution of founder's ownership. Whenever entrepreneurs sell stock to the public, they automatically dilute their ownership in their businesses. Most owners retain a majority interest in the business, but they may still run the risk of unfriendly takeovers years later after selling more stock.

Loss of control. If enough shares are sold in the public offering, the founder risks losing control of the company. If a large block of shares falls into the hands of dissident stockholders, they could vote the existing management team (including the founder) out.

Table 13.4 Requirements for Initial Public Offerings

	NYSE	AMEX Regular	AMEX Alternative	Nasdaq National Market Alternative 1	Nasdaq National Market Alternative 2	Nasdaq SmallCap Market
Net tangible assets	$40 million	—	—	$4 million	$12 million	$4 million
Stockholders' equity	—	$4 million	$4 million	—	—	$2 million
Revenues	—	—	—	—	—	—
Net income	—	—	—	$400,000	—	—
Pretax income	$2.5 million	$750,000	—	$750,000	—	—
Public float (shares)	1.1 million	$500,000 or 1 million	$500,000 or 1 million	$500,000	1 million	100,000
Market value of public float	$40 million	$3 million	$15 million	$3 million	$15 million	$1 million
Market capitalization	—	—	—	—	—	—
Operating history	—	—	3 years	—	3 years	—
Minimum bid price	—	$3	$3	$5	$3	$3
Number of shareholders	2,000	800 or 400	800 or 400	800 or 400	400	300
Market makers	—	—	—	2	2	2

Note. — indicates no requirement.

SOURCE: Stephen D. Solomon, "So You Want to Go Public," *Inc.*, June 1997, p. 77.

Loss of privacy. Taking a company public can be a big ego boost for an owner, but he must realize that it is no longer solely his company. Information that was once private must be available for public scrutiny. The initial prospectus and the continuous reports filed with the Securities and Exchange Commission (SEC) disclose information about the company and its operations—from financial data and raw materials sources to legal matters and patents—to *anyone*, including competitors. A recent study found that loss of privacy and loss of control were the most commonly cited reasons for CEOs' choosing not to attempt an IPO.[51] *Michael Hackworth, CEO of Cirrus Logic Inc., says that the public disclosure required of his company made the decision to go public a tough one because it gave competitors access to information "we consider proprietary."*[52]

Reporting to the SEC. Publicly held companies must file periodic reports with the SEC, which often requires a more powerful accounting system, a larger accounting staff and greater use of attorneys and other professionals.

Filing expenses. A public stock offering usually is an expensive way to generate funds for start-up or expansion. For the typical small company, the cost of a public offering is around 12 percent of the capital raised. On small offerings, costs can eat up as much as 40 percent of the capital raised, whereas on offerings above $20 million, a mere 5 percent will go to cover expenses.[53] Research suggests that once an offering exceeds $10 million, its relative issuing costs drop.[54] The largest cost is the underwriter's commission, which is typically 7 to 10 percent of the offering's proceeds. One entrepreneur who took his company public claims, "When the costs start building—accountants, lawyers, printers—you begin to have second thoughts. 'I'm supposed to be doing this to *raise* more money, not to *spend* more money.' "[55] Figure 13.5 shows a breakdown of the costs incurred by an actual company, Multicom Publishing Inc., when it raised $7.2 million in an initial public offering.

Accountability to shareholders. The capital that the entrepreneur manages and risks is no longer just her own. Managers of publicly held firms must be accountable to their

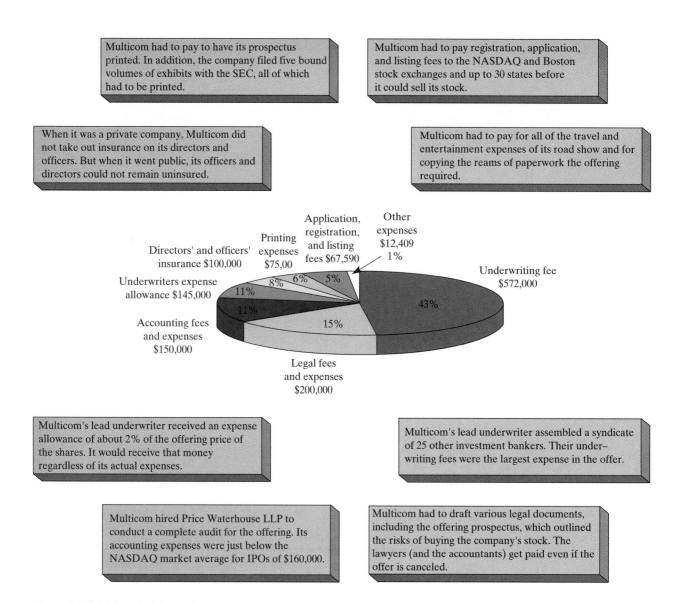

Multicom had to pay to have its prospectus printed. In addition, the company filed five bound volumes of exhibits with the SEC, all of which had to be printed.

Multicom had to pay registration, application, and listing fees to the NASDAQ and Boston stock exchanges and up to 30 states before it could sell its stock.

When it was a private company, Multicom did not take out insurance on its directors and officers. But when it went public, its officers and directors could not remain uninsured.

Multicom had to pay for all of the travel and entertainment expenses of its road show and for copying the reams of paperwork the offering required.

Directors' and officers' insurance $100,000

Printing expenses $75,00

Application, registration, and listing fees $67,590

Other expenses $12,409 1%

Underwriting fee $572,000

Underwriters expense allowance $145,000

8% 6% 5%

11%

43%

11%

15%

Accounting fees and expenses $150,000

Legal fees and expenses $200,000

Multicom's lead underwriter received an expense allowance of about 2% of the offering price of the shares. It would receive that money regardless of its actual expenses.

Multicom's lead underwriter assembled a syndicate of 25 other investment bankers. Their under-writing fees were the largest expense in the offer.

Multicom hired Price Waterhouse LLP to conduct a complete audit for the offering. Its accounting expenses were just below the NASDAQ market average for IPOs of $160,000.

Multicom had to draft various legal documents, including the offering prospectus, which outlined the risks of buying the company's stock. The lawyers (and the accountants) get paid even if the offer is canceled.

Figure 13.5 Multicom Publishing Inc. raised the capital it needed to develop its line of CD-ROMs with an initial public offering on the Nasdaq SmallCap Market. The IPO generated $7.2 million, but Multicom incurred these offering expenses.
Source: Stephen D. Solomon, "Follow the Money," *Inc.*, June 1997, pp. 80–81.

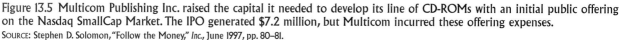

shareholders. Indeed, the law requires that they recognize and abide by a relationship built on trust. Profit and return on investment become the primary concerns for investors. *The chief financial officer at Ringer Corporation says that the company once cut prices on its lawn fertilizer in response to shareholder concerns.* "Such decisions might once have been the private concerns of company management, [but] they are now made in the public eye—in the face of public impatience, mirrored each day in the rising or falling price of the company stock," explains one observer.[56] If the stock price of a new public company falls, shareholder lawsuits are inevitable. Investors whose shares decline in value may sue the company's managers for fraud and the failure to disclose the risks to which their investment exposed them.

Loss of focus. As impatient as they can be, entrepreneurs often find the time demands of an initial public offering frustrating and distracting. Jeffrey Hollander, CEO of Seventh Generation, a mail-order company selling environmentally friendly products, says, "Doing this public offering was the most intense, complicated process I've ever been involved with. From start to finish, after completion of the business plan, the process took 11 months. During this period it took 50 to 75 percent of my time, including some very long hours."[57] Managing the public offering can cause CEOs to lose their focus on their first responsibility—managing the company—and it can drain a management team's energy. "Going public was truly a grueling process," recalls one CEO, exhausted from the intense schedule he had to keep during his company's IPO.[58]

Timing. While putting its offering together, a company runs the risk that the market for IPOs or for a particular issue may go sour. (Remember the stock market crash in October of 1997.) *For example, the IPO from A Pea in the Pod, an upscale maternity-wear retailer, suffered from poor timing caused by something completely beyond its control: the stock price of a similar new stock took a nosedive. After watching another maternity-wear company, Mothers Work, issue a highly successful IPO, managers at A Pea in the Pod decided the time was right for their company to make a public offering. They planned to issue 1,560,000 shares at a premium price. Then, Mothers Work stock plummeted 23 percent in just one day, dampening the IPO prospects for A Pea in the Pod's premium IPO.*[59]

The Registration Process. Taking a company public is a complicated bureaucratic process that usually takes several months to complete. The typical entrepreneur cannot take his company public alone. It requires a coordinated effort from a team of professionals, including company executives, accountants, attorneys, and underwriters. This section outlines the key steps in taking a company public.

Choose the Underwriter. Probably the single most important ingredient in making a successful IPO is selecting a capable **underwriter** (or **investment banker**). The underwriter's primary role is to sell the company's stock through an underwriting syndicate it develops. Depending on the size of the offering, this syndicate can consist of 10 to 120 investment bankers. The underwriter also serves as a consultant and adviser in preparing the registration statement, promoting the issue, pricing the stock, and providing aftermarket support.

Negotiate a Letter of Intent. To begin an offering, the entrepreneur and the underwriter must negotiate a **letter of intent,** which outlines the details of the deal. "The letter [of intent] spells out what each party will do and also acts as a blueprint or 'constitution' for the deal," says the president of one investment banking firm.[60] The letter of intent almost always states that the underwriter is not bound to the offering until it has been executed, usually the day before or the day of the actual offering. Until that time, the underwriter may decide that market conditions are not right or that the company's prospects have dimmed and can withdraw the offer (although withdrawals are rare). However, the letter usually creates a binding obligation for the company to pay any direct expenses the underwriter incurs in connection with the offer.

The letter of intent covers a variety of important issues, including the type of underwriting, its size and price range, the underwriter's commission, and any warrants and options included. There are two types of underwriting agreements: firm commitment and best efforts. In a **firm commitment agreement,** the underwriter agrees to purchase all of the shares in the offering and then resell them to investors. This agreement *guarantees* that the company will receive the required funds, and most large underwriters use it. In a **best-efforts agreement,** the underwriter merely agrees to use its best efforts to sell the company's shares and does not guarantee that the company will receive the needed financing. The managing underwriter acts as an agent, selling as many shares as possible through the syndicate. Some best-efforts contracts are all or nothing; if the underwriter cannot sell all of the shares, the of-

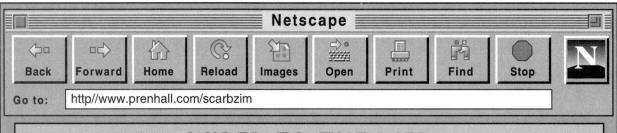

WIRED TO THE WEB

GOING . . . GOING . . . GONE . . . PUBLIC?

Too Small? Joe Falsetti, founder of ROM Tech, a publisher of multimedia CD-ROM software, knew his company was riding the crest of a wave that was pushing the popularity of CD-ROMs to record levels. From his experience in strategic planning at a large technology company, Falsetti also knew that successfully cracking a market driven by new technology requires large amounts of capital. In his conversations about financing with venture capitalists and private investors, Falsetti noticed a common theme: They all wanted to know about an exit strategy: "How do we cash out and win?" The answer they were looking for was for ROM Tech to go public so they could sell their equity positions in the company at a handsome profit.

Falsetti set up a meeting with a New York City investment banker to explore the possibility of a public offering. ROM Tech was profitable with annual sales of $1.2 million, but the investment banker was afraid that ROM Tech was too small to make a successful IPO. To raise $5 million, the minimum deal size for most underwriters, the broker estimated that Falsetti would have to sell nearly 100 percent of the company rather than the usual 25 to 33 percent. At $1.2 million in sales, "the company didn't have enough meat on its bones to get them excited," says Falsetti.

Growth Spiral Kwik Goal, a sports-equipment manufacturer, is constantly experiencing cash shortages because of its tremendous appetite for capital that resulted from the growing popularity of soccer in the United States. "We are in a growth spiral," says company founder Vincent Caruso. "Our debt is getting bigger each year by the difference between what we are making (total revenue) and what we need to keep growing." Like many fast-growing companies, Kwik Goal's cash demands are simply outstripping its ability to generate cash. With the company approaching the $4 million sales mark, Caruso figures he needs $6 million to take Kwik Goal to the next level of growth. Caruso has met with several investment bankers, but because he lacks a strong background in financial management, he does not feel comfortable selling the benefits of his company to strangers who happen to be financial experts.

Go or No Go? Best Programs Inc., a company that develops accounting and human resources software, is flush with cash but is in an industry full of competitors. To establish a stronger position in the industry, managers at Best Programs see the need to buy out some existing companies whose product lines complement their own. To make these acquisitions, however, requires big money. Best Programs has decided to file for a $23 million IPO. The company has more than $20 million in annual revenues, attractive pretax profit margins of 14 percent, and an annual growth rate of 30 percent. Because of its impressive record of success, Best has been able to interest two regional underwriters in making its public offering. In their letter of intent, the underwriters have recommended selling 2.1 million shares at $9 to $11 per share.

1. Which of these companies do you think has the greatest chance of making a successful public offering? Why?
2. Would you advise any of these companies *not* to make a public offering? Explain.
3. Use the material in this chapter and the resources of the World Wide Web to draft a memo to each of these entrepreneurs, offering them advice about taking their companies public and about any other options they might have.

SOURCE: Adapted from David R. Evanson, "Tales of Caution in Going Public," *Nation's Business*, June 1996, pp. 57–59.

fering is withdrawn. Another version of the best-efforts agreement is to set a minimum number of shares that must be sold for the issue to be completed. These methods are risky because the company has no guarantee of raising the required capital.

The company and the underwriter must decide on the size of the offering and the price of the shares. To keep the stock active in the aftermarket, most underwriters prefer to offer a *minimum* of 400,000 to 500,000 shares. A smaller number of shares inhibits sufficiently broad distribution. Most underwriters recommend selling 25 percent to 40 percent of the company in the IPO. They also strive to price the issue so that the total value of the offering is at least $8 million to $15 million. (There are exceptions: some underwriters, especially regional ones, are interested in doing IPOs in the $2 million to $5 million range.) To meet these criteria and to keep interest in the issue high, the underwriter usually recommends an initial price between $10 and $20 per share.

The number of shares offered and prevailing market conditions have a direct impact on the price of the shares. Underwriters typically do not guarantee an offering price and total proceeds amount because the final offering price is not set until shortly before the registration statement becomes effective. But the underwriter should estimate a range for the stock offering price based on current market conditions. Of course, changing market conditions could lead to changes, positive or negative, in the terms of the offering. *For instance, Shaman (which means "medicine man") Pharmaceuticals Inc. increased the size of its IPO from 2.5 to 3.0 million shares and boosted the price from the originally planned $14 per share to $15 when its underwriters found demand for its shares far greater than expected. Shaman is developing drugs from tropical plants that appear to be medically effective among the native people of Latin America, Africa, and Southeast Asia.*[61]

Most letters of intent include a **lock-up agreement** that prevents the sale of insider shares—those owned by directors, managers, founders, employees, and other insiders—for 12 to 36 months. The sale of these shares early in a company's public life could send negative signals to investors, eroding their confidence in the stock and pushing its price downward. "It's very difficult to place an issue when it looks like all of the founders are bailing out," says one underwriter.[62]

Prepare the Registration Statement. Once the company negotiates a letter of intent with an underwriter, the registration process begins. The key product of the registration process is the **registration statement,** which the company must file with the SEC before proceeding with the public offering. The statement consists of two parts: the prospectus, which is distributed to underwriters and prospective investors as a selling tool, and a section containing information for the SEC. The SEC has established a standard format for the registration statement, but the regulations are complex and change constantly.

To prepare the statement, the owner must rely on her team of professionals. At an initial meeting, company managers, underwriters, accountants, and attorneys assign responsibility for each portion of the registration statement and set a deadline for completion. The statement is extremely comprehensive and may take months to prepare. It includes information on the use of the proceeds, the company's history, its financial position, its capital structure, any risk factors it faces, the managers, and many other details.

When the registration statement is completed, the company can ask for a prefiling conference with the SEC to present the statement informally. This meeting uncovers errors and inadequacies in the statement and can help minimize the number of costly revisions required in the review process.

File with the SEC. When the statement is finished (with the exception of pricing the shares, proceeds, and commissions, which cannot be determined until just before the issue goes on the market), the company officially files the statement with the SEC and awaits the review of the division of Corporate Finance. The division sends notice of any deficiencies in the registration statement to the company's attorney in a comment letter (typically set at 20 to 60 days after the initial filing). Very few first-time registrations escape the review process with no SEC comments. The company and its team of professionals must cure all of the deficiencies in the statement noted by the comment letter. Finally, the company files the revised registration statement, along with a pricing amendment (giving the price of the shares, the proceeds, and the commissions).

Wait to Go Effective. While waiting for the SEC's approval, the managers and the underwriters are busy. The underwriters are building a syndicate of other underwriters who will market the company's stock and are approaching investors who might be interested in purchasing shares in the issue. (No sales can be made before the effective date of the offering, however.) The SEC also limits the publicity and information a company may release during this quiet period (which officially starts when the company reaches a preliminary agreement with the managing underwriter and ends 90 days after the effective date).

Securities laws do permit a **road show,** a gathering of potential syndicate members sponsored by the managing underwriter. Its purpose is to promote interest in the IPO by featuring the company, its management, and the proposed deal. *Dennis Nelson, president of The Buckle, a chain of moderately priced casual-clothing stores, describes his management team's experience: "We did road shows in San Francisco, Los Angeles, New York, Boston, Minneapolis, Denver, and London. The purpose was to inform institutional investors about our company."*[63] The managing underwriter and key company officials barnstorm major financial centers at a grueling pace. The president of one company engaged in a road show remembers, "We'd end a breakfast meeting in Chicago and rush out to be in Minneapolis at noon for lunch. Then back to the airport to make dinner that night in New York."[64]

On the last day before the registration statement becomes effective, the company signs the formal underwriting agreement. The final settlement, or closing, takes place within seven business days of the effective date for a firm commitment IPO and within 60 to 120 days after the effective date for a best-efforts issue. At this meeting the underwriters receive their shares to sell and the company receives the proceeds of the offering. Typically, the entire process of going public takes from 60 to 180 days, but it can take much longer if the issuing company fails to do its homework.

Figure 13.6 shows a typical timetable for a public offering.

Meet State Requirements. In addition to satisfying the SEC's requirements, the company also must meet the securities laws in all states in which the issue is sold. These state laws (or "blue-sky" laws) vary drastically from one state to another, and the company must ensure compliance with them.

*S*implified Registrations and Exemptions

4 Explain the various simplified registrations, exemptions from registration, and other alternatives available to small businesses wanting to sell securities to investors.

The IPO process described above requires maximum disclosure in the initial filing and discourages most small businesses from using it because of its cost and complexity. Fortunately, the SEC allows several exemptions from this full-disclosure process for small businesses. Many small businesses that go public choose one of these simplified options the SEC has designed for small companies. The SEC has established the following simplified registration statements and exemptions from the registration process.

SIMPLIFIED REGISTRATION: REGULATION S-B

In August 1992, the SEC approved Regulation S-B, which created a simplified registration process for small companies seeking to make initial or subsequent public offerings. Not only does this regulation simplify the initial filing requirements with the SEC, but it also reduces

The IPO process is a team activity, for which you need the right team, a definitive timetable, and a clear delineation of responsibilities, as shown in the timetable below.

Day	Activity	Responsibility
<0	Select underwriter, sign letter of intent, quiet period begins	Management
1	Hold board of directors' meeting to authorize: • Issuing additional shares • Preparing registration statement for filing with SEC • Negotiating underwriting agreement • Engaging professionals	Management
2	Hold initial organizational meeting of the going public team to determine: • Type and structure of the offering • Offering timetable and responsibilities • Form and format of registration statement	Team
3	Commence due-diligence review	Underwriter and its counsel
4	Begin drafting registration statement: • Textual information • Financial statements and pro forma information	Management and its counsel Management and independent accountant
5	Assign responsibilities and complete timetable; distribute to all team members	Team
12	Prepare draft of underwriting agreement, agreement among underwriters, power of attorney and blue sky survey	Management, underwriter, and respective counsel
15	Distribute questionnaires to directors, officers, and selling shareholders related to registration statement	Management and its counsel; underwriter's counsel
20	Complete corporate "cleanup"	Management and its counsel
25	Review first draft textual portion of registration statement	Team
30	Complete and submit draft of financial statements for inclusion in registration statement	Management and independent accountants
40	Review draft of registration statement, including financial statements	Team
45	Send first draft of registration statement to printer Appoint stock transfer agent and registrar and arrange for preparation of stock certificates Discuss comfort letter requirements and procedures	Management Management, underwriter, and independent accountant

Figure 13.6 Illustrative Going Public Timetable Source: *Financing Source Guide* (New York: Coopers and Lybrand, 1993), pp. 53–56.

Day	Activity	Responsibility
65	Hold board of directors' meeting to approve and sign registration statement	Management and its counsel
66	File registration statement with the SEC, NASD, and states	Management and its counsel
	Distribute preliminary prospects ("red herring") to the proposed underwriters' syndicate	Underwriter
70	Begin road show	Management, PR firm, and underwriter
90	Receive comment letter from SEC regarding registration statement	Management and its counsel
91	Hold meeting to review and discuss SEC comment letter	Team
92–94	Prepare amendments to registration statement resulting from the SEC's comment letter and send draft to printer	Team
96	Review printer's proof of amendments to registration statement	Team
98	File amendments to registration statement covering SEC comments and reflecting any material developments since date previous registration statement was filed with the SEC	Management and its counsel
	Notify SEC in writing that a final (price) amendment will be filed on day 106 and that the company requests acceleration, so that the registration statement may become effective as of the close of business on that date	
103	Resolve any final comments and changes with SEC by telephone	Management, and its counsel; independent accountants
104	Hold due-diligence meeting to determine if events have taken place that should be disclosed in the registration statement and if all parties are satisfied that the registration statement is not misleading	Team
105	Finalize offering price	Management and underwriter
106	Deliver first comfort letter to underwriter	Independent accountant
	Sign underwriting agreement	Management, underwriter, and respective counsel
	File price amendment to registration statement	Management and counsel
	Notify stock exchange and NASD of effectiveness	Management counsel
110	Deliver second comfort letter to underwriter	Independent accountants
	Complete settlement with underwriter, issue stock, collect proceeds from offering, and sign all final documents	Management, underwriter, and respective counsel
	Issue press release and tombstone ad	Management, PR firm, and underwriter

Figure 13.6 Illustrative Going Public Timetable (*continued*)

the ongoing disclosure and filings required of companies. Its primary goal is to open the doors to capital markets to smaller companies by cutting the paperwork and the costs of raising capital. Companies using the simplified registration process have two options: Form SB-1, a "transitional" registration statement for companies issuing less than $10 million worth of securities over a 12-month period; and Form SB-2 reserved for small companies seeking more than $10 million in a 12-month period.

To be eligible for the simplified registration process under Regulation S-B, a company must:

◆ Be based in the United States or Canada

◆ Have revenues of less than $25 million

◆ Have outstanding securities of less than $25 million

◆ Not be an investment company

Regulation S-B's simplified registration requirements are intended to enable small companies to go public without incurring the expense of a full-blown registration. *Pierre de Champfleury used Form SB-2 to sell 1.75 million shares of stock in his fragrance firm, Erox Corporation, at $4 per share. De Champfleury had launched Erox through private investors and venture capitalists, but he had used that money for product development. Now he needed to finance the launch of the company's newest fragrance, Realm. Before Regulation S-B, de Champfleury would have had to spend tens of thousands of dollars and many months wading through reams of paperwork to go public. Under the new rules, however, Erox spent just $2,275 and filed only 126 pages of documents with the SEC. De Champfleury says that the registration process was quite easy, and, best of all, Erox got the money it needed for a successful product launch, and its stock is now traded on the NASDAQ SmallCap Market.*[65]

EXEMPTIONS

Every securities offering must be registered unless the law allows a specific exemption from registration. Small businesses can choose from four exemptions from the tedious and expensive registration process: Regulation D (Rule 504); private placements (Regulation D, Rules 505 and 506 and Section 4(6)); intrastate offerings (Rule 147); and Regulation A.

Regulation D (Rule 504): the Small Company Offering Registration (SCOR). Created in the late 1980s, the Small Company Offering Registration (SCOR; also known as the Uniform Limited Offering Registration, ULOR) now is available in 46 states. A little-known tool, SCOR is designed to make it easier and less expensive for small companies to sell their stock to the public. The whole process typically costs less than half of what a traditional public offering costs and is possible for companies seeking as little as $200,000.[66] Entrepreneurs using SCOR will need an attorney and an accountant to help them with the issue, but many can get by without a securities lawyer, and not needing a securities lawyer can save tens of thousands of dollars. Some entrepreneurs even choose to market their company's securities themselves (for example, to customers), saving the expense of hiring a broker. However, selling an issue is both time- and energy-consuming, and most SCOR experts recommend hiring a professional securities or brokerage firm to sell the company's shares. The SEC's objective in creating SCOR was to give small companies the same access to equity financing that large companies have through the stock market without burdening them with the same costs and filing requirements. The idea is to make the process of selling securities as simple and as easy as possible.

The capital ceiling on a SCOR issue is $1 million, and the price of each share must be at least $5. That means that a company can sell no more than 200,000 shares (making the stock relatively unattractive to stock manipulators). A SCOR offering requires only minimal notification to the SEC. The company must file a standardized disclosure statement, the U-7, which consists of 50 fill-in-the-blank questions. The form, which asks for information such as how much money the company needs, what the money will be used for, what an investor receives, how the investor can sell the investment, and other pertinent questions, also serves as a business plan, a state securities offering registration, a disclosure document, and a prospectus. Entrepreneurs using SCOR may advertise their companies' offerings and can sell them to any investor with no restrictions and no minimums. An entrepreneur can sell practically any kind of security through a SCOR, including common stock, preferred stock, convertible preferred stock, stock options, stock warrants, and others.

A SCOR offering offers entrepreneurs needing equity financing several *advantages*:

◆ Access to a huge pool of equity funds without the expense of full registration with the SEC

◆ Few restrictions on the securities to be sold and on the investors to whom they can be sold

◆ The ability to market the offering through advertisements

◆ The ability of new or start-up companies to qualify

◆ No requirement of audited financial statements for offerings of less than $500,000

◆ Faster approval of the issue from regulatory agencies

◆ The ability to make the offering in several states at once

There are, of course some *disadvantages* to using SCOR to raise needed funds:

◆ Not every state recognizes SCOR offerings. (Four states, Alabama, Delaware, Hawaii, and Nebraska, have not yet authorized SCOR offerings.)

◆ Partnerships cannot make SCOR offerings.

◆ A company can raise no more than $1 million in a 12-month period.

◆ Every state in which the offering is to be made must approve it.

◆ The process can be time-consuming, distracting the entrepreneur from the daily routine of running the company.

◆ A limited secondary market for the securities may limit investors' interest. Currently, SCOR shares must be traded through brokerage firms that make small markets in specific stocks. However, the Pacific Stock Exchange and the NASDAQ's electronic bulletin board recently began listing SCOR stocks, so the secondary market for them has broadened.

The Electric Car Battery Company used a SCOR to raise the money it needed to complete development on a new battery that would greatly improve the performance of golf carts and to finance a commercial rollout of the new product. The company sold 100,000 shares of common stock and stock warrants and generated $200,000, notifying securities officials only in the states in which it would make the offer: Colorado, Florida, New York, and Washington, D.C. Don Hutton, Electric Car Battery's financial officer says the company chose to make the SCOR offering because it was "the most straightforward path to the capital we needed."[67] Despite the relative simplicity of SCOR offerings, experts estimate that only 30 to 35 percent of the companies that start a SCOR offering actually complete it.[68] The majority get bogged down in the time-consuming paperwork and never manage to work their way through the process.

Regulation D (Rules 505 and 506): Private Placements. Rules 505 and 506 are exemptions that give emerging companies the opportunity to sell stock through "private placements" without actually "going public." In a private placement, the company sells its shares directly to private investors without having to register them with the SEC. A *Rule 505* offering has a higher capital ceiling ($5 million) than a SCOR offering but imposes more restrictions (no more than 35 "nonaccredited" investors, limits on advertising, and others). Its disclosure requirements also are more stringent, requiring a company to publish information on the company, its operating history, its financial performance, its managers and directors, and the nature of the offering itself.

Rule 506 imposes no ceiling on the amount that can be raised, but it does limit the issue to 35 "nonaccredited" investors. There is no limit on the number of accredited investors, however. Rule 506 also requires detailed disclosure of information, but the extent depends on the dollar size of the offering. Private deals typically are in the $8 million to $25 million range, with investors usually buying between 10 percent and 30 percent of a company's stock. *When John Cook's company, The Profit Recovery Group, a financial services firm, needed outside capital to fuel its rapid growth, Cook raised the money through a private placement. Cook, who sees the private placement as "bridge financing" until the company makes a public stock offering, says, "I raised $12.5 million and had to give up only 15 percent of my company and one board seat to do it."*[69]

These Regulation D rules minimize the expense and the time required to raise equity capital for small businesses. They do impose limitations and demand some disclosure, but they only require a company to file a simple form (Form D) with the SEC within 15 days of the first sale of stock.

Section 4(6): Private Placements. Section 4(6) covers private placements and is similar to Regulation D, Rule 505 and Rule 506. Like Regulation D Rule 505, its ceiling is $5 million. Unlike Rules 505 and 506, however, Section 4(6) does not place a limit on the number of investors. A company does not have to register with the SEC on those offerings made only to accredited investors.

Entrepreneur Jennifer Barclay, founder of Blue Fish Clothing, a company that sells a unique line of hand block-printed clothing, started the business in her parents' garage with less than $100. To finance growth, the company made a direct public stock offering under Regulation A.

Rule 147: Intrastate Offerings. Rule 147 governs intrastate offerings: those sold only to investors in a single state by a company doing business in that state. To qualify, a company must be incorporated in the state, maintain its executive offices there, have 80 percent of its assets there, derive 80 percent of its revenues from the state, and use 80 percent of the offering proceeds for business in the state. There is no ceiling on the amount of the offering. *Gary Hoover put up just $5,000 of his own money and convinced several private investors to purchase $850,000 worth of preferred stock to launch TravelFest, a retail store that caters to travelers. As the company grew, Hoover decided to make an intrastate offering under Rule 147 to raise the money he needed for expansion. He registered the offering in TravelFest's home state of Texas, where resident investors purchased $5.6 million in convertible preferred stock.*[70]

Regulation A. Regulation A, although currently not used often, allows an exemption for offerings up to $5 million over a 12-month period. Regulation A imposes few restrictions, but it is more costly than the other types of exempted offerings, usually running between $80,000 and $120,000. The primary difference between a SCOR offering and a Regulation A offering is that a company must register its SCOR offering only in the states where it will sell its stock; in a Regulation A offering, the company also must file those documents with the SEC. Like a SCOR offering, a Regulation A offering allows a company to sell its shares directly to investors. *For instance, Blue Fish Clothing Inc., a company selling a unique line of all-natural women's clothing, made a direct public offering under Regulation A, selling 800,000 shares at $5 each. It publicized the $4 million offering through fish-shaped hanging tags on its garments* *and word of mouth from loyal customers and supporters. Blue Fish, whose shares are traded on the Chicago Stock Exchange, used the offering's proceeds to build new retail stores, to move into a larger headquarters, to install a computerized information system, and to fund the company's growth. With annual sales exceeding $13 million, the company now employs 200 people and sells its unique clothing at more than 600 boutiques and department stores across the country. Founder Jennifer Barclay says that Blue Fish was "hungry for cash, but we only wanted to offer shares to people who understood what our company was all about."[70]*

Table 13.5 provides a summary of the major types of simplified registrations and exemptions. Of these, the limited offerings and private placements are most commonly used.

ALTERNATIVES TO THE IPO PROCESS

Direct Public Offerings (DPOs). Many of the simplified registrations and exemptions discussed above give entrepreneurs the power to sidestep investment bankers and to sell their company's stock offerings directly to investors and, in the process, to save themselves thousands of dollars in underwriting fees. Selling shares of their company's stock directly to in-

Table 13.5 Simplified Registration and Exemptions: Comparative Table

Private and Limited Offerings: Regulation D

	Rule 504	Rule 505	Rule 506
Dollar limit	$1 million in any 12-month period	$5 million in any 12-month period	None
Limit on number of purchasers	No	35 nonaccredited, unlimited accredited	35 nonaccredited, unlimited accredited
Qualification for purchasers	No	No	Nonaccredited must be sophisticated
Qualification of issuers	Not available for investment companies, blank check companies, or reporting companies	Not available for investment companies or those disqualified by "bad boy" provisions	No
Disclosure requirements	Not specified	Only if one or more nonaccredited purchasers	Only if one or more nonaccredited purchasers
Financial statement requirements	Not specified	Period varies for audited statements	Period varies for audited statements
General solicitation and advertising prohibited	No	Yes	Yes
Resale restrictions	No	Yes	Yes

SOURCE: *Deciding to Go Public* (New York: Ernst & Young), 1993, pp. 70–71.

vestors in a **direct public offering (DPO)** is becoming an increasingly popular financing strategy for entrepreneurs. A recent study found that 31 percent of all of the companies seeking to raise money through initial public offerings used DPOs, going straight to Main Street instead of going through underwriters on Wall Street.[72] By cutting out the underwriter's commission and many legal and most registration fees, entrepreneurs willing to handle the paperwork requirements and to market their own shares can make DPOs for about 6 percent of the total amount of the issue, compared with 13 percent for a traditional underwritten stock offering. *For example, six years after Ann Withey founded Annie's Homegrown Inc., a small maker of macaroni and cheese, her products were sold in 6,000 health food stores and 5,700 supermarkets. To move to the next level, she knew the company needed to expand its distribution network, but that would take money Annie's Homegrown didn't have. To get its products on more grocers' shelves, the company would have to pay one-time stocking fees, which often ran as much as $25,000 for each product. Deciding to sidestep Wall Street, Withey chose to raise the money to fund the company's expansion by making a direct public offering. The most crucial step was to attract investors, so Annie's Homegrown promoted its DPO by stuffing 1 mil-*

Private Placements: Section 4(6)	Intrastate Offerings: Rule 147	Unregistered Public Offerings: Regulation A	Small Business Issuers Registration Form SB-I	Small Business Issuers Registration Form SB-2
$5 million	None	$5 million in any 12-month period	$10 million in any 12-month period	None
No	No	No	No	No
All must be accredited	All must be registrants of a single state	No	No	No
No	Must be resident and do business in same state as purchasers	Available for U.S. and Canadian companies only; not available for reporting companies, blank check companies, investment companies, sale of oil and gas or mineral rights, or those disqualified by "bad boy" provisions	Available for U.S. and Canadian companies with revenue and public float of less than $25 million; not available for investment companies or subsidiaries whose parent is not qualified to use the form	Available for U.S. and Canadian companies with revenue and public float of less than $25 million; not available for investment companies or subsidiaries whose parent is not qualified to use the form
Not specified	Not specified	Yes	Yes	Yes
Not specified	Not specified	2 years of unaudited statements	2 years of audited statements	2 years of audited statements
Yes	No	No	No	No
Yes	Yes	Yes	No	No

lion coupons in its pasta packages, sending letters to the 40,000 people on its mailing list, advertising the offer in Mother Jones *magazine, and posting a notice on its Web site. Within a year, 2,435 investors (affectionately known as "Annie's Army") had paid $6 per share for 600,000 shares of stock in Annie's Homegrown, giving the company $3.6 million it needed to get into more stores across the country. The offering stimulated the company's sales and generated enough cash internally to add another 2,000 stores to its list of retail distributors.*[73]

Like Annie's Homegrown and Blue Fish Clothing, companies that make good DPO candidates are those with annual sales between $3 million and $25 million, high name recognition, and a loyal customer base. Experts also say that, because of their simplicity, one-product companies find it easier to sell their shares directly to investors than multiproduct businesses would. Most DPOs generate between $300,000 and $4 million.[74]

Direct public offerings do have a downside. The time, energy, and attention that making a successful DPO requires can detract from an entrepreneur's ability to manage his company. Attracting investors can be challenging because the small number of shares usually issued makes trading difficult, and investors know that it may take years before the value of their thinly traded shares rises. Because many companies making DPOs are too small to have their shares listed on any stock exchange, they must make arrangements for shareholders to trade their shares. Some companies maintain in-house matching services for buyers and sellers; others hire a broker to match buy and sell orders. One company, Direct Stock Market Inc., lists securities information on about 200 small companies on its Web site, SCOR-Net <http://www.direct-stock-market.com> and receives more than 1,000 hits each day. Also, after making a DPO, a company must keep its investors informed about the company's progress and financial status. For most DPO companies with small offerings, mailing copies of the company's annual report is sufficient.

Table 13.6 provides a 10-question quiz to help entrepreneurs determine whether their company would be a good candidate for a DPO.

Direct Stock Offerings on the World Wide Web (WWW). The World Wide Web (WWW) is one of the fastest-growing sources of capital for small businesses. Much of the Web's appeal as a fund-raising tool stems from its ability to reach large numbers of prospective investors very

Table 13.6 Is a Direct Public Offering for You?

Drew Field, an expert in direct public offerings, has developed the following 10-question quiz to help entrepreneurs decide whether their company is good candidates for a DPO.

1. Does your company have a history of consistently profitable operations under the present management?
2. Is your company's present management team honest, socially responsible, and competent?
3. In 10 words or fewer, can you explain the nature of your business to laypeople new to investing?
4. Would your company excite prospective investors, making them want to share in its future?
5. Does your company have natural affinity groups, such as customers with strong emotional loyalty?
6. Do members of your natural affinity groups have discretionary cash to risk for long-term gains?
7. Would your company's natural affinity groups recognize your company's name and consider your offering materials?
8. Can you get the names, addresses, and telephone numbers of affinity group members, as well as some demographic information about them?
9. Can a high-level company employee spend half-time for six months as a DPO project manager?
10. Does your company have, or can you obtain, audited financial statements for at least the last two fiscal years?

Source: Stephanie Gruner, "Could You Do a DPO?" *Inc.,* December 1996, p. 70.

quickly and at a low cost. "This is the only form of instantaneous international contact with an enormous population," says one Web expert. "You can put your prospectus out to the world."[75] *Spring Street Brewery* <http://plaza.interport.net/witbeer/>, a New York City–based microbrewery, was the first company to use the Web to make a Regulation A direct public stock offering, which raised $1.6 million. Company founder Andrew Klein spent just $600 to develop Spring Street's home page and another $150 a month to maintain it: a fraction of what it would have cost to do a traditional IPO. More than 3,500 investors purchased 900,000 shares in Spring Street at $1.85 each. "Dollar for dollar, it was the most effective method for getting information to potential investors," says Klein. The SEC has given the microbrewery clearance to operate a permanent trading site for its stock on its Web page, where buyers and sellers can bargain without going through a broker. Spring Street's first on-line DPO was so successful that Klein is following it up with a second offering to raise $3.3 million.[76] Even though Klein made his company's offering electronically, he had to file the necessary legal documents with the SEC and the state of New York. Experts caution Web-based fund-seekers to make sure their electronic prospectuses meet SEC and state requirements. Figure 13.7 shows the number of U.S. DPOs from 1989 to 1997.

Foreign Stock Markets. Sometimes, foreign stock markets offer entrepreneurs access to equity funds more readily than U.S. markets. For instance, in 1995 the London Stock Exchange established the Alternative Investment Market (AIM <http://www.stockex.co.uk/o_market/1_1_2.htm> as a stock market for business start-ups and young, growing companies. More than 260 companies (18 of them from outside Great Britain) have raised more than $2.5 billion in financing through AIM. Most offerings through AIM raise between $1.6 million and $16 million for their companies.[77]

Another British stock exchange geared toward small companies is OFEX <http://www.ofex.co.uk/ofex/home.html>, designed for companies seeking between $800,000 and $2.5 million in their public offerings. OFEX, which is unregulated, has less stringent rules for offerings than AIM, and offerings there cost less. *Thomas Burnham,*

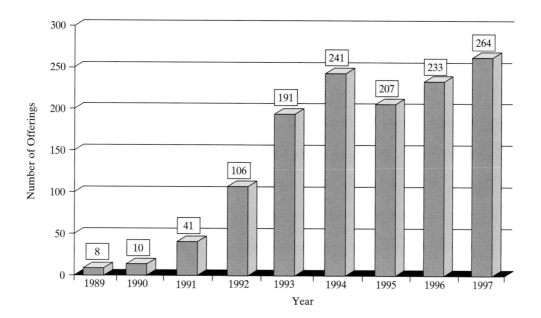

Figure 13.7 **Companies Making Direct Public Offerings** Source: Tom Stewart-Gordon, *The SCOR Report*, Dallas, Texas.

"I'll Do It Myself"

*A*fter 10 years in business, Michael Quinn wanted to transform Hahnemann Laboratories, a manufacturer of homeopathic (all natural) medicines, into a national company. Not only would Quinn need money for expansion, marketing, and distribution, but he would also have to win approval from the Food and Drug Administration as a licensed pharmaceutical manufacturer. Quinn turned first to a commercial bank, "but they said 'No way,'" he recalls. Quinn was searching for about $500,000, and investment bankers simply weren't interested in making a small initial public offering for Hahnemann Laboratories.

So Quinn decided to make his own direct public offering using Regulation A. He realized that if just 200 of his company's 28,000 customers invested about $2,000 each, he could get the equity capital he needed. He reasoned that, as customers of Hahnemann Laboratories, these people would already be enthusiasts of homeopathy and would be most likely to invest in the company. The first obstacle was to track them down. Quinn began by posting ads for the offer in the pharmacy he ran, packed announcements into every mail-order shipment, and told every customer with whom he spoke. "I had to explain to half of them what stocks are," he says.

If his offering was to be successful, Quinn realized that he would have to reach beyond his customer base for potential investors. He swapped mailing lists with a homeopathic bookseller and a homeopathic software company and mailed announcements about the offer to their customers. He also took out ads in homeopathic newsletters and magazines. All told, he sent out more than 35,000 announcements, which netted about 1,700 requests for the company's prospectus. Another 400 requests came from people whom Quinn had contacted personally or who knew him and his business. Of those 2,100 "hot prospects," 242 ultimately became investors, putting up $467,000 in exchange for one-third of Hahnemann Laboratories. Only about 15 percent of the investors sent their money in after receiving the prospectus; Quinn had to call the rest. (In all, he estimates that he talked with between 700 and 800 potential investors by phone.) Nor did raising the money come cheap. Legal, auditing, printing, and marketing costs for the offer totaled $103,000. "I ended up with $364,000, which no bank was going to lend me," says Quinn. "It was worth it."

1. What benefits did Quinn realize by choosing to make a direct public offering of his company's stock? What costs (monetary and otherwise) did he incur?

2. What other options besides Regulation A were available to Quinn to raise the capital he needed? Review the features, advantages, and disadvantages of each option you listed. Do you think Quinn made the right choice? Explain.

SOURCE: Adapted from David R. Evanson, "Direct Hit," *Entrepreneur*, June 1997, pp. 68–71. ◆

founder of South Beach Cafe, turned to OFEX to raise the $700,000 he needed to open his third cafe in London. After opening two successful locations in Michigan, Burnham decided to take his gourmet cafe concept international and to use foreign capital to finance the expansion. In about three months, after submitting a business plan and a fairly simple prospectus, he had made a successful public offering on OFEX, raising $750,000. Five months after the offering, the first South Beach Cafe in London opened its doors. Burnham's first foray into AIM proved so successful that he returned a year later and raised $3 million to fuel the company's expansion into Europe.[78]

United Kingdom offerings have several advantages:

◆ Smaller offerings are very common, are readily accepted by investors, and can be completed relatively quickly.

◆ The costs of U.K. offerings are lower than those in the United States. Underwriting fees there are usually 2 percent of the offering, whereas in the United States 3 to 10 percent of the offering is more common.

◆ U.K. offering prices may be higher than those in the United States because underwriters there use forecasted results, not historical ones, to set prices.

◆ U.K. offerings require less disclosure of information as part of the registration process.

◆ Ongoing reporting requirements are less stringent in the United Kingdom.[79]

Closer to home, Canada's Vancouver Stock Exchange <http://www.vse.com/> is becoming a popular source of equity capital for U.S. entrepreneurs. It also encourages listings of small companies, and the costs of offerings are lower than those in the United States. *Kim Jones raised $2.5 million for his software devvelopment company with an initial public offering made through the Vancouver Stock Exchange. Jones, who had explored the possibility of a U.S. IPO, found that he could get a better price for his company's stock on the Vancouver market.*[80]

Chapter Summary

◆ Explain what seed capital is and why it is so important to the entrepreneurial process.
- ◆ The money an entrepreneur needs to begin a business is called seed money, adventure capital, or injection capital. It truly is risk capital because entrepreneurs and investors in new businesses must be prepared for the possibility of losing *everything* in exchange for the chance to earn significant rewards.
- ◆ Becoming a successful entrepreneur requires one to become a skilled fund-raiser, a job that usually requires more time and energy than most business founders think.
- ◆ Without the ability to raise capital, many entrepreneurs never get their businesses off the ground.

◆ Explain the differences in the three types of capital small businesses require: fixed, working, and growth.
- ◆ Capital is any form of wealth employed to produce more wealth.
- ◆ Fixed capital is used to purchase a company's permanent, or fixed, assets; working capital represents the business's temporary funds and is used to support the business's normal short-term operations; growth capital requirements surface when an existing business is expanding or changing its primary direction.

◆ Describe the various sources of equity financing available to entrepreneurs.
- ◆ The most common source of financing a business is the owner's personal savings. After emptying their own pockets, the next place entrepreneurs turn for capital is family members and friends. Angels are private investors who not only invest their money in small companies but also offer valuable advice and counsel to them. Some business owners have success financing their companies by taking on limited partners as investors or by forming an alliance with a corporation, often a customer or a supplier. Venture capital companies are for-profit, professional investors looking for fast-growing companies in hot industries. When screening prospects, venture capital firms look for competent management, a competitive edge, a growth industry, and important intangibles that will make a business successful.

- ◆ Some owners choose to attract capital by taking their companies public, which requires registering the public offering with the SEC. Going public involves choosing the underwriter, negotiating a letter of intent, preparing the registration statement, filing with the SEC, and meeting state requirements.
- ◆ Going public offers the advantages of raising large amounts of capital, improved access to future financing, improved corporate image, and gaining a listing on a stock exchange. The disadvantages include dilution of the founder's ownership, loss of privacy, reporting to the SEC, filing expenses, and accountability to shareholders.

◆ Explain the various simplified registrations, exemptions from registration, and other alternatives available to small businesses wanting to sell securities to investors.
- ◆ Rather than go through the complete registration process, some companies use one of the simplified registration options and exemptions available to small companies: Regulation S-B, Regulation D (Rule 504, Small Company Offering Registration (SCOR); Rule 505; and Rule 506), Section 4(6), Rule 147, and Regulation A.
- ◆ Rather than make a public offering using investment bankers, some entrepreneurs sell shares of stock in their companies directly to investors in a direct public offering. The World Wide Web, with its ability to reach larger numbers of potential investors quickly and at low cost, is making direct public offerings feasible for more entrepreneurs.
- ◆ Many foreign stock markets have relaxed requirements for small companies making public stock offerings and offer lower registration and filing expenses than those in the United States.

Discussion Questions

1. Why is it so difficult for most small business owners to raise the capital needed to start, operate, or expand their ventures?
2. What is capital? List and describe the three types of capital a small business needs for its operations.
3. Define equity financing. What advantage does it offer over debt financing?
4. What is the most common source of equity funds in a typical small business? If an owner lacks sufficient equity capital to invest in the firm, what options are available for raising it?
5. What guidelines should an entrepreneur follow if friends and relatives choose to invest in her business?
6. What is an angel? Put together a brief profile of the typical private investor. How can entrepreneurs locate potential angels to invest in their business?
7. What advice would you offer an entrepreneur about to strike a deal with a private investor to avoid problems?
8. What types of businesses are most likely to attract venture capital? What investment criteria do venture capitalists use when screening potential businesses? How do these compare with the typical angel's criteria?
9. How do venture capital firms operate? Describe their procedure for screening investment proposals.
10. What characteristics make a company an attractive candidate to investment bankers for an initial public offering?
11. Briefly explain the advantages and disadvantages to a company of making a public stock offering.
12. Outline the registration process entrepreneurs must go through to take their companies public.
13. Summarize the simplified registrations and exemptions small businesses can use to raise funds through public and private markets. What is the goal of these simplified registrations and exemptions?
14. What benefits do foreign stock exchanges offer entrepreneurs in search of capital?

Step into the Real World

1. Interview several local business owners about how they financed their businesses. Where did their initial capital come from? How much money did they need to launch their business? Where did their subsequent capital come from? What advice do they offer others seeking capital?
2. Contact a local private investor and ask him or her to address your class. (You may have to search to locate one.) What kinds of businesses does this angel prefer to invest in? What screening criteria does he or she use? How are the deals typically structured?
3. Contact a local venture capitalist and ask him or her to address your class. What kinds of businesses does his or her company invest in? What screening criteria does the company use? How are deals typically structured?
4. Invite an investment banker or a financing expert from a local accounting firm to address your class about the process of taking a company public. What does the firm look for in a potential IPO candidate? What is the process, and how long does it usually take?

Take It to the Net

Visit the Scarborough/Zimmerer home page at
www.prenhall.com/scarbzim
for updated information, on-line resources, and Web-based exercises.

Endnotes

1. David R. Evanson, "Capital Questions," *Entrepreneur*, March 1997, pp. 62–65; William Wetzel, "Needed: An Economic Policy for Angels," *In Business*, March/April 1993, p. 54.
2. Udayan Gupta, "The Right Fit," *Wall Street Journal*, May 22, 1995, p. R8.
3. Elizabeth Fenner, "How to Raise the Cash You Need," *Money Guide*, Summer 1991, p. 45.
4. Jill Andresky Fraser, "How to Finance Anything," *Inc.*, February 1998, pp. 34–42; Jill Andresky Fraser, "Some Assembly Required," *Inc.*, April 1998, pp. 123–124.
5. David R. Evanson and Art Beroff, "An Offer You Can't Refuse," *Entrepreneur*, April 1998, pp. 66–71.
6. Carolyn Campbell, "Hidden Treasures," *Business Start-Ups*, October 1997, p. 8.
7. Brian Dumaine, "America's Smart Young Entrepreneurs," *Fortune*, March 21, 1994, pp. 34–48; Alessandra Bianchi, "Where Are They Now?" *Inc. 500*, October 15, 1997, pp. 46–47; Mike Hofman, "Desperation Capital: A Bootstrappers Hall of Fame," *Inc.*, August 1997, pp. 54–57.
8. Alessandra Bianchi, "My Name Is Dave, and I'm a Growthaholic," *Inc. 500*, October 1997, pp. 90–97.
9. Fenner, "How to Raise the Cash You Need."
10. Jan Norman, "How to: Finance Your Business," *Business Start-Ups*, January 1998, pp. 46–49.
11. Joseph R. Garber, "Puff, the Venture Capitalist," *Forbes*, April 11, 1994, p. 128.
12. Hofman, "Desperation Capital."
13. Fenner, "How to Raise the Cash You Need."
14. Alex Markels, "A Little Help from Their Friends," *Wall Street Journal*, May 22, 1995, p. R10.
15. Gianna Jacobson, "Money Hunt," *Success*, December 1997, pp. 45–49.
16. George Hunter, "Entrepreneurs in Search for Financial Angels," *Upstate Business*, July 13, 1997, pp. 2–3; William Wetzel, "Creating New Capital Markets for Emerging Ventures," *In Business*, July/August 1996, pp. 22–24; Stephanie Gruner, "The Trouble with Angels," *Inc.*, February 1998, pp. 47–49.
17. Gianna Jacobson, "Capture an Angel," *Success*, November 1995, p. 46.
18. William Wetzel, "Creating New Capital Markets for Emerging Ventures."
19. Hunter, "Entrepreneurs in Search for Financial Angels."
20. "Digging for Dollars," *Wall Street Journal*, February 24, 1989, p. R25.
21. Wetzel, "Creating New Capital Markets for Emerging Ventures," pp. 23–24.
22. Anne B. Fisher, "Raising Capital for a New Venture," *Fortune*, June 13, 1994, pp. 99–101.
23. Bruce G. Posner, "Talking to the Money Club," *Inc.*, June 1993, p. 39; Gianna Jacobson, "Do or Die!" *Success*, April 1997, p. 18.
24. Bruce J. Blechman, "Step Right Up," *Entrepreneur*, June 1993, pp. 20–25; Michelle Jeffers, "None of Your Business," *Forbes ASAP*, October 6, 1997, p. 87.
25. Stephanie N. Mehta, "New Breed of Investor Brings More Than Cash to Hopeful Start-Ups," *Wall Street Journal*, August 25, 1997, pp. A1, A11.
26. Ellie Winninghoff, "Guardian Angels?" *Small Business Reports*, April 1993, pp. 30–39; Bruce G. Posner, "How to Finance Anything," *Inc.*, February 1993, pp. 54–68.
27. Let's Make a Deal," *In Business*, July/August 1987, pp. 22–23.
28. Ibid.
29. "Angling for An Angel," *Money Guide*, Summer 1991, p. 46.
30. Frances Huffman, "Pennies from Heaven," *Entrepreneur*, April 1993, p. 101.
31. David R. Evanson, "Hidden Assets," *Entrepreneur*, January 1997, pp. 57–59.
32. Mark Henricks, "Stand Your Ground," *Entrepreneur*, January 1993, p. 264.
33. Richard Florida, "What Start-Ups Don't Need Is Money," *Inc.*, April 1994, pp. 27–28.
34. Andrew Kruger, "America's Fastest Growing Company," *Fortune*, August 13, 1990, pp. 48–52.
35. David R. Evanson, "Foreign Power," *Entrepreneur*, February 1997, pp. 68–71.
36. Jeffrey R. Houle, "Into the Great Unknown: The Ins and Outs of Wooing Venture Capital," *South Carolina Business Journal*, June 1997, pp. 1, 8.
37. Jacobson, "Money Hunt," p. 49.
38. Roberta Reynes, "Venturing Out for Rapid Growth," *Nation's Business*, November 1997, pp. 54–55.
39. Ibid.
40. "Venture Capitalists Take the Reins," *Small Business Reports*, April 1990, p. 23.
41. Erika Kotite, "Spreading the Wealth," *Entrepreneur*, November 1993, p. 106.
42. Price Waterhouse Coopers MoneyTree Survey Report, <http://209.67.194.61/highlights.asp>.
43. Fisher, "Raising Capital for a New Venture"; David R. Evanson and Art Beroff, "Ready, Set . . ." *Entrepreneur*, February 1998, pp. 58–61.
44. Michael Selz, "Birth Business: Industry Races to Aid Infertile," *Wall Street Journal*, November 26, 1997, pp. B1, B12.
45. Lynn Miller, "Tap into Venture Capital (Not a Bank) to Grow," *Your Company* (Forecast 1997), p. 30.
46. Rosalind Resnick, "Going Public for Growth," *Nation's Business*, May 1994, pp. 63–64.
47. Wetzel, "Creating New Capital Markets for Emerging Ventures"; Hale and Dorr LLP New England IPO Report, <http://www.hale-dorr.com/publications/ipo/IPO_9096/contents.html>.
48. John Wyatt, "America's Amazing IPO Bonanza," *Fortune*, May 27, 1996, pp. 76–79.
49. James Grieff, "Going Public Means Baring All," *Nation's Business*, June 1988, p. 28.
50. Rhonda Hillbery, "Going Public without Selling Your Soul," *Business Ethics*, September/October 1992, pp. 24–26.
51. Roberta Maynard, "Are You Ready to Go Public?" *Nation's Business*, January 1995, pp. 30–32.
52. Leslie Brokaw, "The First Day of the Rest of Your Life," *Inc.*, May 1993, p. 114.
53. Philip W. Taggart, Roy Alexander, and Robert M. Arnold, "Deciding Whether to Go Public," *Nation's Business*, May 1991, p. 52; James Morrow, "Private Eyes," *Success*, April 1998, pp. 64–67, 86.
54. Reena Aggarwal and Pietra Rivoli, "Evaluating the Costs of Raising Capital through an Initial Public Offering," *Journal of Business Venturing* 6 (1991), pp. 351–361.
55. Robert A. Mamis, "Going Public," *Inc.*, October 1988, p. 52.
56. Hillbery, "Going Public without Selling Your Soul."
57. Jack Brill and Hall Brill, "How Well Do IPOs Work?" *Wall Street Journal*, September 14, 1993, p. Cl.
58. Al Agby, "Numb and Number: Public Offering, Private Turmoil," *Inc.*, August 1997, p. 22.

59. Sara Calian, "Maternity-Wear IPO Has Pricing Problem," *Wall Street Journal,* September 14, 1993, p. C1.

60. David R. Evanson, "To the Letter," *Entrepreneur*, January 1996, p. 60.

61. Anne Newman, "Shaman's IPO Success Sets Example for Biotech Firms," *Wall Street Journal,* January 28, 1993, p. B2.

62. Ibid.

63. "Taking a Company Public," *In Focus* (Edward D. Jones & Co.), Fall 1992, p. 8.

64. Mamis, "Going Public."

65. John R. Emswiller, "SCOR Funding Provides Short Form for Going Public," *Wall Street Journal,* January 21, 1992, p. B2.

66. Roberta Reynes, "Financing for Do-It-Yourselfers," *Nation's Business*, May 1998, pp. 38–40.

67. David R. Evanson, "Easier Avenues to Equity Capital," *Nation's Business*, January 1998, pp. 44–46.

68. Ibid.

69. "A Pitch for Private Equities," *Inc.*, December 1995, p. 126.

70. Toni Mack, "They Stole My Baby," *Forbes*, February 12, 1996, pp. 90–91.

71. "Small Green Firms Use Direct Public Offerings," *In Business,* May/June 1996, p. 10; "A Fishy Success," *Business Ethics,* July/August 1996, p. 6; Kerry Hannon, "Going Public to the Public," *U.S. News & World Report,* June 17, 1996, pp. 74–75; Kerry Hannon, "Blue Fish Reels in Stylish Customers," *U.S. News &*

World Report, June 18, 1997, p. 74; Drew Field Direct Public Offerings, <http://www.dfdpo.com/clientsvm9.htm>.

72. Stephanie Gruner, "When Mom & Pop Go Public," *Inc.*, December 1996, pp. 66–73.

73. Carol Steinberg, "The DPO Revolution," *Success*, March 1997, p. 14; Hannon, "Going Public to the Public"; Steven E. Levingston, "Tiny Firms Offer Stock 'Direct' to Public," *Wall Street Journal*, May 20, 1996, pp. C1, C7.

74. Gruner, "When Mom & Pop Go Public."

75. Gianna Jacobson, "Find Your Fortune on the Internet," *Success*, November 1995, p. 50.

76. Hannon, "Going Public to the Public"; Jenny C. McCune, "Raise Money on the Internet," *Success*, July/August 1995, p. 1; Gruner, "When Mom & Pop Go Public"; Ronaleen R. Roha, "What's Brewing Online," *Kiplinger's Personal Finance Magazine*, September 1996, p. 154; Sharon Nelton, "Using the Internet to Find Funds," *Nation's Business*, August 1998, pp. 35–36.

77. "Go Public Overseas," *Success*, September 1997, pp. 89–96; <http://www.netpro.co.uk/aim-newsletter/>; <http://www.stockex.co.uk/o_market/1_1_2.htm>.

78. "Go Public Overseas."

79. *Financing Source Guide* (Coopers and Lybrand), 1993, p. 21.

80. Debra Phillips, "Northern Exposure," *Entrepreneur*, February 1996, p. 15.

CHAPTER 14

Sources of Debt Financing

It used to be that you'd get a good loan officer, establish a relationship, and then he'd disappear. Nowadays you get a good bank, establish a relationship, and the bank disappears.

—Jeffrey McKeever, MicroAge Inc.

Don't ever borrow a little bit of money because when you borrow a little bit of money, you have a serious creditor if you run short. And, if you borrow a lot of money, you have a partner when you get into trouble.

—Fred Smith, founder, Federal Express

Upon completion of this chapter, you will be able to

1. Describe the vital role that banks play in providing small business financing and the types of business loans banks make.

2. Explain the types of financing available from nonbank sources of credit.

3. Identify the sources of government financial assistance and the loan programs these agencies offer.

4. Explain the various loan programs the Small Business Administration offers.

5. Discuss state and local development programs.

6. Discuss valuable methods of financing growth and expansion internally with bootstrap financing.

7. Describe how to avoid becoming a victim of a loan scam.

*D*ebt financing involves the funds that the small business owner has borrowed and must repay with interest. Very few entrepreneurs have adequate personal savings to finance the complete start-up costs of a small business; many of them must rely on some form of debt capital to launch their companies. "Borrowing money is necessary for most growing companies," says Tom Kellogg, president of Business Lenders Inc., which lends money to small companies. "That's the way small businesses break out and become larger." Kellogg identifies nine instances in which small business owners should consider borrowing money:[1]

◆ *Increasing the company's workforce or inventory to boost sales.* Sufficient working capital is the fuel that feeds a company's growth.

◆ *Gaining market share.* Businesses often need extra capital as their customer bases expand and they incur the added expense of extending credit to customers.

◆ *Purchasing new equipment.* Financing new equipment that can improve productivity, increase quality, and lower operating expenses often takes more capital than a growing company can generate internally.

◆ *Refinancing existing debt.* As companies become more established, they can negotiate more-favorable borrowing terms than in their start-up days, when entrepreneurs take whatever money they can get at whatever rate they can get. Replacing high-interest loans with loans carrying lower interest rates can improve cash flow significantly.

◆ *Taking advantage of cash discounts.* Suppliers sometimes offer discounts to customers who pay their invoices early. As you will see in chapter 16, business owners should take advantage of those discounts in most cases.

◆ *Buying the building in which the business is located.* Many entrepreneurs start out renting; however, if location is crucial to success, it may be wise to purchase the building.

◆ *Establishing a relationship with a lender.* If a business has never borrowed money, taking out a loan and developing a good repayment and credit history can pave the way for future financing. Smart business owners know that bankers who understand their business play an integral role in their company's ultimate success.

◆ *Retiring debt held by a "nonrelationship" creditor.* Entrepreneurs find that lenders who have no real interest in their company's long-term success or do not understand their business can be extremely difficult to work with. They prefer to borrow money from lenders who are willing to help them achieve their business mission and goals.

◆ *Foreseeing a downturn in business.* Establishing access to financing before a business slowdown hits insulates a company from a serious cash crisis and protects it from failure.

Lenders of capital are more numerous than investors, although small business loans can be just as difficult (if not more difficult) to obtain. Although entrepreneurs who use borrowed capital can maintain complete ownership of their businesses, they must carry it as a liability on the balance sheet as well as repay it with interest at some point in the future. In addition, because small businesses are considered to be greater risks than bigger corporate customers, they must pay higher interest rates because of the risk-return trade-off: the higher the risk, the greater the return demanded. Most small firms pay the prime rate—the interest rate banks charge their most creditworthy customers—plus a few percentage points. Still, the cost of debt financing often is lower than that of equity financing. Because of the higher risks associated with providing equity capital to small companies, investors demand greater returns than lenders. Also, unlike equity financing, debt financing does not require entrepreneurs to dilute their ownership interest in their companies.

Entrepreneurs seeking debt capital are quickly confronted with an astounding range of credit options varying greatly in complexity, availability, and flexibility. These sources of debt capital are not equally favorable, however. By understanding the various sources of debt capital and their characteristics, entrepreneurs can enhance their chances of obtaining a loan.

*C*ommercial Banks

◆ Describe the vital role that banks play in providing small business financing and the types of business loans banks make.

Commercial banks are the very heart of the financial market, providing the greatest number and variety of loans to small businesses. Business owners consider banks to be lenders of *first* resort (see Figure 14.1). A recent study by the Federal Reserve concluded that commercial banks provide almost half the financing available to small businesses. The same study found that 80 percent of all loans to existing small businesses come from banks, and bank loans are second only to entrepreneurs' personal funds as a source of capital for launching businesses.[2]

Banks tend to be conservative in their lending practices and prefer to make loans to established small businesses rather than to high-risk start-ups. One expert estimates that only 5 to 8 percent of business start-ups get bank financing.[3] Bankers want to see evidence of a company's successful track record before committing to a loan. They are concerned with a firm's operating past and will scrutinize its records to project its position in the immediate future. They also want proof of the stability of the firm's sales and about the ability of the product or service to generate adequate cash flows to ensure repayment of the loan. If they do make loans to a start-up venture, banks like to see sufficient cash flows to repay the loan, ample collateral to secure it, or a Small Business Administration (SBA) guarantee to insure it. Studies suggest that small banks (those with less than $300 million in assets) are most likely to lend money to small businesses.[4]

Banks also focus on a company's capacity to create positive cash flow because they know that's where the money to repay their loans will come from. The first question in most bankers' minds when reviewing an entrepreneur's business plan is "Can this business gener-

> Commercial banks are one of the most important suppliers of credit to small firms. As companies grow, their reliance on the commercial banking system increases. Of the small firms that borrow, these percentages obtain their financing from commercial banks.

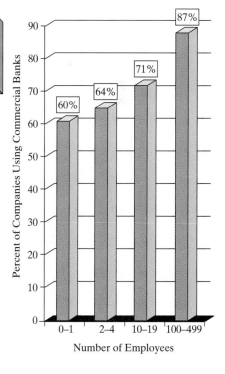

Figure 14.1 **Financing from U.S. Commercial Banks by Company Size** SOURCE: U.S. Small Business Administration.

ate sufficient cash to repay the loan?" Even though they rely on collateral to secure their loans, the last thing banks want is for a borrower to default, forcing them to sell the collateral (often at "fire sale" prices) and use the proceeds to pay off the loan. That's why bankers stress cash flow when analyzing a loan request, especially for a business start-up. "Cash is more important than your mother," jokes one experienced borrower.[5] *Jefferson Shreve, president of Shreve & Co. Inc., a company that acquires and manages ministorage facilities for residential and commercial customers, knows the importance of cash flow to his bankers. Fortunately, his storage warehouses typically generate positive cash flows within six months of opening, a fact that he emphasizes in every business plan and loan proposal he submits to a bank. Shreve, who manages 26 miniwarehouses, has never had significant problems getting bank loans because of his company's ability to generate cash quickly and because of the collateral he pledges (the warehouses themselves). Over the years, he has negotiated more than 35 loans ranging from $60,000 to $1.8 million at 20 banks for a total of $8.5 million.*[6]

SHORT-TERM LOANS

Banks primarily are lenders of short-term capital to small businesses, but they will make certain intermediate- and long-term loans. Short-term loans extend for less than one year. These funds typically are used to replenish the working capital account to finance the purchase of more inventory, boost output, finance credit sales to customers, or take advantage of cash discounts. As a result, the owner repays the loan after converting inventory and receivables into cash. There are several types of short-term loans.

Commercial Loans (or "Traditional Bank Loans"). The basic short-term loan is the commercial bank's specialty. It is usually repaid as a lump sum within three to six months and is unsecured because secured loans are much more expensive to administer and maintain. In other words, the bank grants a loan to the small business owner without requiring him to pledge any specific collateral to support the loan in case of default. The owner is expected to repay the total amount of the loan at maturity. Sometimes the interest due on the loan is prepaid by being deducted from the total amount borrowed. Until a small business is able to prove its financial strength to the bank's satisfaction, it will probably not qualify for this kind of commercial loan.

If the commercial loan exceeds a particular amount, usually about $100,000, the bank may require the entrepreneur to maintain a compensating balance in a bank account as a form of security for the loan. The size of this reserve varies from bank to bank, but it often is 10 percent of the total amount approved plus 10 percent of the credit actually used. Some banks, however, will accept flat fees or higher interest rates in place of compensating balances.

Lines of Credit. One of the most common requests entrepreneurs make of banks is for a **line of credit,** a short-term loan that provides much-needed cash flow for day-to-day operations. With an approved line of credit, a small company can borrow up to a predetermined amount at any time during the year quickly and conveniently by writing itself a loan. *A bank line of credit was essential to Joe Renosky when his small fishing lure manufacturing company landed some major orders from giant retailers Wal-Mart and Kmart. His business, Renosky Lure Company, is now recognized as a leading innovator in the fishing lure industry, but things weren't always that way. "We really started out small," recalls Renosky. "My family members and I were hand-making lures one at a time." Then came the big orders from the national retail chains, and Renosky's little company had to grow up fast. The most pressing need he faced was capital to finance the expansion required to produce the orders. Renosky's first big order doubled his business overnight. He went straight to the bank, which loaned him the money he needed on the basis of sales projections. He repaid the loan quickly, and when he got a second big order, the bank readily extended the money. "When I started to turn what*

Joe Renosky, founder of Renosky Lure Company, relies on a bank line of credit to finance growth of his fishing lure business, which is recognized as a leading innovator in the industry. What advantages does a line of credit offer a business owner?

had been a hobby of tying fishing lures into a real business, I got a $10,000 bank loan that was backed with collateral my aunt put up," says Renosky. *"Since then I've asked for lines of credit I would pay off by the end of the year. That's how you establish yourself with a bank."*[7]

Banks usually limit the open line of credit to 40 to 50 percent of the firm's present working capital, although they will lend more for highly seasonal businesses. It is usually extended for one year (or more) and is secured by collateral, although some banks offer unsecured lines of credit to small companies with solid financial track records. A business typically pays a small handling fee (1 to 2 percent of the maximum amount of credit) plus interest on the amount borrowed. A recent study of small businesses with lines of credit found that 76 percent used them; the remaining 24 percent have established their lines as a safety net but have not activated them.[8]

Two types of lines of credit are available: seasonal and sustained growth. *Seasonal lines of credit* are more common and are used to finance a company's seasonal cash needs such as financing inventory or accounts receivable. Banks allow borrowers to draw on seasonal lines as needed; however, once a year they require business owners to pay them down to zero for a short time (usually 30 to 60 days). This annual cleanup is scheduled for when a firm's cash balance is at its highest level, usually at the end of the busy season, when inventories and receivables have been converted into cash. This standard repayment protects the bank against default by forcing the firm to prove its creditworthiness before continuing the line of credit for another year. "Think of your credit line as a yo-yo," advises one bank president. "Your borrowing will go up and down—bankers expect that—but your borrowing should match your business cycles." That means paying off ("resting") the company's line of credit when its cash flow peaks. "If you can rest your credit line for 30 consecutive days, your banker won't worry about your misusing the line to hide losses," she says.[9] *Chuck Randa, owner of Whiteface Chalet, a Swiss-style inn in Wilmington, New York, has negotiated a repayment schedule for his company's loans that reflects the seasonal nature of his business. "The bank allows us to skip payments in our two slowest months, May and June," he explains. Flexible loan terms allow Whiteface Chalet to get the capital it needs and to repay its bank loans without putting undue pressure on the inn when its cash flow is at its ebb.*[10]

Sustained growth lines of credit are designed to finance rapidly growing companies' cash flow needs over a longer time period. Because they cover a longer time horizon and are designed to finance growth, sustained growth lines usually do not call for a 30-day annual cleanup.

Table 14.1 asks seven questions every entrepreneur should be able to answer before approaching a banker.

Floor Planning. Floor planning is a form of financing frequently used by retailers of big-ticket items that are easily distinguishable from one another (usually by serial number), such as automobiles, boats, and major appliances. For example, the commercial bank finances Auto City's purchase of its inventory of automobiles and maintains a security interest in each car in the order by holding its title as collateral. Auto City pays interest on the loan monthly and repays the principal as the cars are sold. The longer a floor-planned item sits in inventory, the more it costs the business owner in interest expense. Banks and other floor planners often discourage retailers from using their money without authorization by performing spot checks to verify prompt repayment of the principal as items are sold.

INTERMEDIATE- AND LONG-TERM LOANS

Intermediate and long-term loans are extended for one year or longer and are normally used to increase fixed- and growth-capital balances. Commercial banks grant these loans for starting a business, constructing a plant, purchasing real estate and equipment, and other long-

---

Table 14.1 Seven Questions to Ask Yourself *Before* Approaching a Banker

1. *How much money do I need?* The correct answer to this question is *not* "How much can I get?" Know exactly how much money you need, and be sure to include a little extra for oversights, emergencies, and "Murphy's Law" ("If anything can go wrong, it will.")

2. *Why do I need the money?* The banker might put the question this way: "Why don't you use your own money?" The banker is trying to find out whether you're looking for a loan to cover up poor management practices or whether your company needs money to fuel its growth.

3. *What will I do with the money?* The quickest way to have your loan request rejected is to offer a broad-based answer such as "For working capital." Specify a use—to buy new assets (computers, equipment, etc.), to pay for expenses (wages, salaries, ESOP contributions, etc.), to substitute new debt for equity, or to pay off old debts—and give the details of where the money will go.

4. *How will the money help my company?* Closely related to question 3, this question is designed to make sure that the money you get will go to some productive use. Banks have seen too many entrepreneurs take their money without showing any long-term benefits from it. You should be able to show that the plans you have for the money you request will produce growth, profits, and cash flow.

5. *When will I repay the loan?* This is where the cash flow projections in your business plan stand out. Bankers know that they'll be repaid only if your company generates sufficient cash flow. Your plan's cash flow projections should show that your company will be able to repay the loan in a timely fashion.

6. *How will I repay the loan?* Once again, the financial projections in your business plan will be invaluable. Your cash budget should show where the cash to repay the loan will come from. This is no time to be vague. Offering proof of your company's ability to repay is the best way to secure a loan.

7. *What will happen if my plans don't work out?* Bankers usually are skeptical as they read business plans, and they will want to know what will happen if your company fails to meet its projections and the cash flow to repay the loan never materializes. This is where bankers expect you to provide either collateral or personal guarantees to secure the loan.

Entrepreneur Jean Kristenson, owner of Armrest Security Patrol, a company that provides security guards and fire-prevention workers to other businesses, has borrowed hundreds of thousands of dollars over the years to finance Armrest's growth. Explaining her company's success in borrowing from bankers, she says, "You need to answer their questions. The bank will want to know what you'll do with the money and how you'll repay it."

SOURCES: Adapted from Jane Easter Bahls, "Borrower Beware," *Entrepreneur*, April 1994, pp. 90–97; Stephanie Barlow, "Breaking the Bank," *Entrepreneur*, May 1993, pp. 78–82; Elaine Pofeldt, "Sell Yourself to a Banker," *Success*, May 1997, p. 16.

---

term investments. Loan repayments are normally made monthly or quarterly. Four categories of intermediate and long-term loans exist: unsecured term loans, installment loans, discounted installment contracts, and character loans.

Unsecured Term Loans. Unsecured term loans are granted primarily to businesses whose past operating experience indicates a high probability of repayment. If an entrepreneur is successful in obtaining a term loan to begin a business, the bank will likely require him to provide roughly half of the start-up cost. Term loans normally involve very specific terms that may place restrictions and limitations on the firm's financial decisions. For example, a term loan agreement may set limits on owners' salaries or stipulate what percentage of profits will be used to repay the loan. The owner must investigate and understand thoroughly the conditions of the loan agreement before accepting it. Some banks will make only secured term loans.

Installment Loans. These loans are made to small firms for purchasing equipment, facilities, real estate, and other fixed assets. In financing equipment, a bank usually lends the small business from 60 to 80 percent of the equipment's value in return for a security interest in the equipment. The loan's amortization schedule typically coincides with the length of the equipment's usable life. When financing real estate (commercial mortgages), banks typically will lend up to 75 to 80 percent of the property's value and will allow a lengthier repayment schedule of 10 to 30 years.

Larry Carpenter uses installment loans to purchase the property for the sign locations for his billboard business. His company, Carpenter Outdoor Advertising in St. Louis, Missouri, owns 100 billboards in Missouri and Texas and generates more than $1 million in revenues each year. "I borrow only $40,000 to $50,000 at a time," he says, but he recently completed a $160,000 loan to finance a five-sign package. Carpenter also has a line of credit at the same bank to fund purchases of supplies and billboard construction. Having proved his company's creditworthiness, Carpenter says his loans "are around the prime [interest] rate now."[11]

Discounted Installment Contracts. Banks will also extend loans to small businesses when the owner pledges installment contracts as collateral. The process operates in the same manner as discounting accounts receivable (discussed later). For example, Acme Equipment Company sells several pieces of heavy equipment to General Contractors Inc. on an installment basis. To obtain a loan, Acme pledges the installment contract as collateral and receives a percentage of the contract's value from the bank. As Acme receives installment payments from General Contractors, it transfers the proceeds to the bank to satisfy the loan. If the installment contract is with a reliable business, the bank may lend the small firm 100 percent of the contract's value.

Character Loans. Banking regulatory changes made by the Clinton administration and intended to create jobs by increasing the credit available to small and medium-sized companies now allow banks to make **character loans.** Rather than requiring entrepreneurs to prove their creditworthiness with financial statements, evaluations, appraisals, and tax returns, banks making character loans base their lending decisions on the borrower's reputation and reliability (i.e., "character"). Approximately 80 percent of the nation's 12,000-plus banks are certified to make character loans. To qualify, a loan must be less than $900,000 and cannot exceed 3 percent of the bank's total capital.[12] *Two entrepreneurs who co-founded a river touring business received a character loan from a small local bank. Because of their solid reputations in the community and their overall business experience, they were able to borrow $20,000 to purchase canoes, supplies, and safety equipment and to hire guides without pledging any collateral. "We simply signed our names on the loan agreement and got the money to launch the company," says one of the partners.*

Maintaining a Positive Relationship with Your Banker

*T*oo often, entrepreneurs communicate with their bankers only when they find themselves in a tight spot needing money. Unfortunately, that's not the best way to manage a working relationship with a bank. "Businesspeople have a responsibility to train their bankers in their businesses," says one lending adviser. "A good banker will stay close to the business, and a good business will stay close to the banker."

How can business owners develop and maintain a positive relationship with their bankers? The first step is picking the right bank and the right banker. Some banks are not terribly enthusiastic about making small business loans, and others target small businesses as their primary customers. It's a good idea to visit several banks—both small community banks and large national banks—and talk with a commercial loan officer about your banking needs and the bank's products and services. After finding the right banker, an entrepreneur must focus on maintaining effective *communication*. The best strategy is to keep bankers informed—*of both good news and bad*. "Bankers armed with a thorough understanding of your company's operations are in a better position to structure financial arrangements capable of satisfying your needs," says one banker. "Conversely, bankers unfamiliar with your business operations have a tendency to become fair-weather lenders." If you are going to be late with a payment or will miss one altogether, alert your banker *beforehand*. Also, don't forget to keep your banker informed of the *good* things that are happening in your business.

What else can business owners do to manage their banking relationships?

Invite the banker to visit your company. An on-site visit gives the banker the chance to see exactly what a company does and how it does it. It's also a great opportunity to show the bank where and how its money is put to use.

Send customer mailings to the banker as well. "Besides the numbers, we try to give our bankers a sense of our vision for the business," says Mitchell Goldstone, president of Thirty-Minute Photos Etc. Goldstone sends customer mailings to his bankers "so they know we're thinking about opportunities to generate money."

Send the banker samples of new products. "I try to make my banker feel as if he's a partner," says Drew Santin, president of a product-development company. "Whenever we get a new machine, I go out of my way to show the banker what it does."

Show off your employees. Bankers know that one of the most important components of building a successful company is a dedicated team of capable employees. Giving bankers the opportunity to visit with employees and ask them questions while touring a company can help alleviate fears that they are pumping their money into a high-risk "one-person show."

Know your company's assets. Almost always interested in collateral, bankers will want to judge the quality of your company's assets: property, equipment, inventory, accounts receivable, and others. Be sure to point them out. "As you walk the lender through your business," says one experienced banker, "it's always a good idea to identify assets the banker might not think of."

Be prepared to personally guarantee any loans the bank makes to your business. Even though many business owners choose the corporate form of ownership for its limited liability benefits, some are surprised when a banker asks them to make personal guarantees on business loans. It's a common practice, especially on small business loans.

Keep your business plan up-to-date, and make sure your banker gets a copy of it. Bankers lend money to companies that can demonstrate that they will use the money wisely and productively. They also want to make sure that the company offers a high probability of repayment. The best way to provide bankers with that assurance is with a solid business plan. "The number one thing is that you've got to have a business plan; you've got to have something concrete before anyone will talk to you," says a former banker who now owns a successful franchise operation.

Address safety and environmental concerns. A company's physical appearance can go a long way toward making an impression on a banker. Lenders appreciate clean, safe, orderly work environments and view sloppily maintained facilities (such as spills, leaks, and unnecessary clutter) as negatives.

Consider alternative ways of showing the banker why your company needs money. Arlene DeCardia, founder of Riverwood Metro Business Resort, a business conference center, not only presents her banker with spreadsheet forecasts to justify her loan request, but she also includes a spreadsheet tracking the volume of business she's had to turn away. "We track the business we don't do as closely as the business we actually do," she says. Recently, she proved to her banker that she needed money to expand by showing that she turned down $1.3 million worth of business!

(continued)

1. What advantages do entrepreneurs gain by communicating openly with their bankers?

2. Why do so few entrepreneurs follow Tim Chen's example when dealing with their bankers?

3. What might be some consequences of an entrepreneur's failing to communicate effectively with a banker?

Sources: Adapted from Joan Pryde, "Lending a Hand with Financing," *Nation's Business*, January 1998, pp. 53–59; Joseph W. May, "Be Frank with Your Bank," *Profit*, November/December 1996, pp. 54–55; "They'll Up Your Credit If . . ." *Inc.*, April 1994, p. 99; Jane Easter Bahls, "Borrower Beware," *Entrepreneur*, April 1994, p. 97; Bruce G. Posner, "The Best Small-Business Banks in America," *Inc.*, July 1992, pp. 87–93; Jacquelyn Lynn, "You Can Bank on It," *Business Start-Ups*, August 1996, pp. 56–61; Stephanie Barlow, "Buddy System," *Entrepreneur*, March 1997, pp. 121–125. ◆

The accompanying Gaining the Competitive Edge feature describes how small business owners can maintain positive relationships with their bankers.

*N*onbank Sources of Debt Financing

2 Explain the types of financing available from nonbank sources of credit.

Although they are usually the first stop for entrepreneurs in search of debt capital, banks are not the only lending game in town. We now turn our attention to other sources of debt capital that entrepreneurs can tap to feed their cash-hungry companies.

ASSET-BASED LENDERS

Asset-based lenders, which are usually small commercial banks, commercial finance companies, or specialty lenders, allow small businesses to borrow money by pledging idle assets as collateral. Even unprofitable companies whose financial statements could not convince loan officers to make traditional loans can get asset-based loans. These cash-poor but asset-rich companies can use normally unproductive assets—accounts receivable, inventory, fixtures, and purchase orders—to finance rapid growth and the cash crises that often accompany it. *For example, after Pam Piper started a consulting business, Modern Technology Systems Inc., in her home, she had a chance to win a five-year government contract worth $400,000 a year. "It was the kind of contract you can start to build a business from," says Piper. Unfortunately, if Piper's company won the job, she wouldn't have the money to hire the staff or to purchase the equipment it would require. Without a track record of success or sufficient collateral, Modern Technology Systems could not qualify for a bank loan. So Piper approached Princeton Capital Finance Company, an asset-based lender specializing in government and commercial contracts. Princeton agreed to write a letter to the government agency, promising to finance the project, and Piper pledged the contract itself as collateral. Piper got the contract, borrowed the money from Princeton at prime plus 3 percent, and completed the job successfully. Using that job as a stepping stone, Modern Technology Systems began bidding on bigger contracts. Today, Piper's company has 195 employees and $15 million in revenues. My relationship with Princeton allowed us to grow at a rate that we hadn't even thought about before," says Piper.*[13]

The amount a small business can borrow through asset-based lending depends on the **advance rate,** the percentage of an asset's value that a lender will lend. For example, a company pledging $100,000 of accounts receivable might negotiate a 70 percent advance rate and qualify for a $70,000 asset-based loan. Advance rates can vary dramatically depending on the quality of the assets pledged and the lender. Because inventory is an illiquid asset (i.e., hard to sell), the advance rate on inventory-based loans is quite low, usually 10 percent to 50 percent. A business pledging high-quality accounts receivable as collateral, however, may be able to negotiate up to an 85 percent advance rate. The most common types of asset-based financing are discounting accounts receivable and inventory financing.

Discounting Accounts Receivable. The most common form of secured credit is accounts receivable financing. Under this arrangement, a small business pledges its accounts receivable as collateral; in return, the commercial bank advances the owner a loan against the value of approved accounts receivable. The amount of the loan tendered is not equal to the face value of the accounts receivable, however. Even though the bank screens the firm's accounts and accepts only qualified receivables, it makes an allowance for the risk involved because some will be written off as uncollectible. A small business usually can borrow an amount equal to 55 to 80 percent of its receivables, depending on their quality. In general, banks hesitate to finance receivables that are past due, and no bank will accept accounts that are as much as 90 days past due. Many commercial finance companies also engage in accounts receivable financing.

As the firm receives payment from customers on its accounts receivable, it transfers them to the bank. The bank subtracts an agreed-upon percentage of the proceeds, applies it to the loan balance, and then deposits the remainder in the firm's account. If an unusual number of accounts are uncollectible, the firm must make up the deficit to satisfy the loan.

Inventory Financing. Here, the small business loan is secured by the firm's inventory—raw materials, work in process, and finished goods. If the owner defaults on the loan, the bank can claim the firm's inventory, sell it, and use the proceeds to satisfy the loan (if the bank's claim is superior to the claims of other creditors). Because inventory is not a highly liquid asset in most cases, banks are willing to lend only a portion of its worth—usually no more than 50 percent of the inventory's value, often less. Most asset-based lenders avoid inventory-only deals; they prefer to make loans backed by inventory and more secure accounts receivable. One veteran lender explains, "The hardest asset [to evaluate] is inventory; you're guessing on its resale value."[14]

Asset-based financing is a powerful tool. A small business that could obtain a $1 million line of credit with a bank would be able to borrow as much as $3 million by using accounts receivable as collateral.[15] It is also an efficient method of borrowing because a small business owner has the money he needs when he needs it. In other words, a business pays only for the capital it actually needs and uses it when it needs it.

Sometimes, entrepreneurs have no other choice but asset-based borrowing because their young, fast-growing companies cannot qualify for loans from traditional lenders. *That's just the position John Childers, president of Classic Oak, a furniture-making start-up, found his company in: order-rich but cash-poor. He had just received $800,000 worth of orders but couldn't afford to purchase the raw materials to fill them, and no traditional lenders would consider loaning money to a start-up with no track record. A financial adviser referred Childers to Transcap Associates, an asset-based lender that targets manufacturers and distributors. Transcap, funded by private investors and unregulated, is aggressive in its lending policies and isn't afraid to assume more risk than traditional lenders. Every time Classic Oak gets an order, it borrows the money to purchase the lumber and other materials to produce it, pledging as collateral the raw materials inventory and, sometimes, the purchase orders. Childers recognizes that the finance rates Classic Oak pays are higher than those of conventional lenders, "but," he says, "if you can't get cash from other sources, it makes a lot of sense.*[16]

Asset-based loans are more expensive than traditional bank loans because of the cost of originating and maintaining them and the higher risk involved. Rates usually run from 2 to 7 percentage points above the prime rate, but for some businesses, the cost of an asset-based loan can be twice that of a typical bank loan. Because of this rate differential, small business owners should not use asset-based loans over the long term. The asset-based borrower's goal should be to move to a line of credit as soon as possible.

TRADE CREDIT

Because of its ready availability, trade credit is an extremely important source of financing to most entrepreneurs. When banks refuse to lend money to a newly formed business because it is judged a bad credit risk, the owner usually is able to turn to trade credit as a viable source of capital. Getting vendors to extend credit in the form of delayed payments (e.g., "net 30" credit terms) usually is much easier for small businesses than obtaining bank financing.

It is no surprise that businesses receive three dollars of credit from suppliers for every two dollars they receive from banks as loans.[17] Vendors and suppliers usually are willing to finance a small business owner's purchase of goods from 30 to 90 or more days, interest free. *For instance, when Jim McCann, operator of a chain of florist shops in New York State, acquired 1-800-FLOWERS in 1987, the company was generating sales of almost $1 million a year but was carrying debt of almost $6 million. "We didn't have to worry about acquiring new debt because we couldn't get any," laughs McCann. To turn 1-800-FLOWERS around, McCann desperately needed financing. In addition to mortgaging his house (several times) and selling off some stores to raise capital, McCann relied heavily on trade credit to get the company going again. "I got suppliers to advance us inventory for long periods of time," he recalls, "which is a backhanded form of financing. McCann managed to convince some suppliers to extend the usual 30-day terms to 180 days or more. "In return we learned always to exceed expectations. For example, if a $1,000 payment was due on a given date, we made sure to pay back $1,500 of the total amount owed. As long as you don't abuse creditors, they have an interest in your success."*[18]

EQUIPMENT SUPPLIERS

Most equipment vendors encourage business owners to purchase their equipment by offering to finance the purchase. This method of financing is similar to trade credit, but with slightly different terms. Usually, equipment vendors offer reasonable credit terms: only a modest down payment with the balance financed over the life of the equipment (usually several years). In some cases, the vendor will repurchase equipment for salvage value at the end of its useful life and offer the business owner another credit agreement on new equipment. Start-up companies often use trade credit to purchase equipment and fixtures: counters, display cases, refrigeration units, machinery, and the like. It pays to scrutinize vendors' credit terms, however; they may be less attractive than those of other lenders.

COMMERCIAL FINANCE COMPANIES

When denied a bank loan, a small business owner often is able to look to a commercial finance company for the same type of loan. Finance companies are second only to banks in making loans to small businesses, and they often specialize in lending to companies in particular industries.[19] Some 135 large commercial finance companies, such as The Money Store, AT&T Small Business Lending, GE Capital Small Business Finance, and others, operate across the nation, specializing in small business loans ranging from $50,000 to $2 million.[20] In fact, two of the top three lenders under the Small Business Administration's 7(a) loan guarantee program (discussed later in this chapter) are commercial finance companies.[21] Commercial finance companies are usually willing to tolerate more risk than conservative counterparts. They also are less interested in a borrower's financial position than they are in the quality of the assets the company can pledge as collateral. Of course, their primary consideration is collecting their loans, but they tend to rely on obtaining a security interest in some type of collateral, given the higher-risk loans that make up their portfolios. However, this does not mean that commercial finance companies do not carefully evaluate a company's financial position before making a loan.

At their core, commercial finance companies are fundamentally asset-based lenders. Their most common methods of providing credit to small businesses are accounts receivable financing and inventory loans, and they operate exactly as commercial banks do. "We always like to have collateral, [such as] equipment, inventory, or real estate," says an executive of one finance company.[22] In addition to such short-term financing, finance companies also extend intermediate- and long-term loans for real estate and fixed assets. *For instance, when Steve Kline decided to purchase a Primrose School franchise, he turned to a finance company, AT&T Capital, for the $1 million-plus he would need to purchase land and to build the school. Kline chose the finance company because his franchisor, Primrose School Franchising Company, had formed a partnership with AT&T Capital, one of the nation's largest lenders to franchises, that allowed qualified franchisees to get financing relatively quickly and easily.*[23]

Commercial finance companies usually offer many of the same credit options as commercial banks do. However, because their loans are subject to more risks, finance companies charge a higher interest rate than commercial banks (usually at least prime plus 4 percent). In many cases, an entrepreneur whose loan requests were denied by the banks is able to obtain financing through a commercial finance company. Before taking on higher cost debt from a finance company, an entrepreneur should consider these three questions:

1. *Can my company qualify for a bank loan instead?* For many young start-up companies without an established track record, the answer is no.

2. *Can my company afford the extra cost of this source of financing?* Although the total cost of a loan from a finance company can be as high as 20 or 30 percent for high-risk businesses (including fees), companies with high-quality assets (receivables, inventory, or equipment) can borrow at lower rates. Plus, some commercial finance companies will agree to more favorable loan terms, such as longer repayment schedules, than banks.

3. *Am I willing to allow lenders to audit my financial statements, and can my company afford to pay for those audits?* Commercial finance companies keep close tabs on the businesses they lend money to, monitoring the status of the assets pledged as collateral. That means they will want to examine a company's financial records. Most commercial finance companies also expect periodic full-scale audits, for which the borrowing company pays. These audits can cost anywhere from $1,200 to $2,000 or more.[24]

With proper planning and stringent management, business owners can afford the higher finance charge without putting undue pressure on the financial health of their businesses. *Entrepreneur Lauren Mosely knew that her retail start-up, Health & Fitness Resource, was not the type of business that commercial banks favored. Not only was her business in the high-risk retail industry, but it also was positioned on the leading edge of the newly emerging wellness movement. "The banks were not even willing to look at my business plan," says Mosely. To raise the money she needed to launch Health & Fitness Resource, Mosely approached GE Capital Small Business Finance. She put up the $45,000 in equity GE asked her to contribute, and the finance company agreed to lend her the remaining $90,000. Although GE's interest rates were about 3 points higher than a bank's on a comparable loan, its terms suited Mosely better. GE offered her a seven-year amortization schedule, much longer than she could have gotten from a bank.*[25]

SAVINGS AND LOAN ASSOCIATIONS

Savings and loan (S&L) associations specialize in loans for real property. In addition to their traditional role of providing mortgages for personal residences, savings and loan associations offer financing on commercial and industrial property. In the typical commercial or industrial loan, the S&L will lend up to 80 percent of the property's value, with a repayment schedule of up to 30 years. Minimum loan amounts are typically $50,000, but most S&Ls hesitate to lend money for specially designed buildings for a particular customer's needs. Savings and loan associations expect the mortgage to be repaid from the firm's profits.

STOCK BROKERAGE HOUSES

Stock brokers are getting into the lending business, too, and many of them offer loans to their customers at lower interest rates than banks. These "margin loans" carry lower rates because the collateral supporting them, the stocks and bonds in the customer's portfolio, is of high quality and is highly liquid. "There isn't a bank in the country that can lend more cheaply than you can borrow on margin," claims one stock broker.[26] Moreover, brokerage firms make it easy to borrow. Usually, brokers set up a line of credit for their customers when they open a brokerage account. To tap that line of credit, the customer simply writes a check or uses a debit card. Typically, there is no fixed repayment schedule for a margin loan; the debt can remain outstanding indefinitely, as long as the market value of the borrower's portfolio of collateral meets minimum requirements.

Aspiring entrepreneurs can borrow up to 70 to 80 percent of the value of their portfolios. *For example, one woman borrowed $60,000 to buy equipment for her New York City health club, and a St. Louis doctor borrowed $1 million against his brokerage account to help finance a clinic.*[27] Brokers typically lend a maximum of 50 percent of the value of stocks and bonds in a portfolio, 70 percent for corporate bonds, and 85 to 90 percent for government securities.[28]

There is risk involved in using stocks and bonds as collateral on a loan. Brokers typically require a 30 percent cushion on the loan. If the value of the borrower's portfolio drops, the broker can make a **margin call;** that is, the broker can call the loan in and require the borrower to provide more cash and securities as collateral. Such a margin call could require an entrepreneur to repay a significant portion of the loan within a matter of days—or hours. If the account lacks adequate collateral, the broker can sell off the customer's portfolio to pay off the loan. The interest rate the borrower pays depends on the broker's cost of capital. Although there is no limit on the loan term, the interest rate changes from month to month. The longer the loan is outstanding, the greater is the chance that the rate will fluctuate. To avoid high risk levels from fluctuating rates, an entrepreneur should plan to repay the loan within a year.

INSURANCE COMPANIES

For many small businesses, life insurance companies can be an important source of business capital. Insurance companies offer two basic types of loans: policy loans and mortgage loans. **Policy loans** are extended on the basis of the amount of money paid through premiums into the insurance policy. It usually takes about two years for an insurance policy to accumulate enough cash surrender value to justify a loan against it. Once cash value is accumulated in the policy, the entrepreneur may borrow up to 95 percent of the value for any length of time. Interest is levied annually, but repayment may be deferred indefinitely. However, the amount of insurance coverage is reduced by the amount of the loan. Policy loans typically offer very favorable interest rates, often around 8 percent or less. Only insurance policies that build a cash value—that is, combine a savings plan with insurance coverage—offer the option of borrowing. These include whole life (permanent insurance), variable life, universal life, and many corporate-owned life insurance policies. Term life insurance, which offers only pure insurance coverage, has no borrowing capacity.

Insurance companies make **mortgage loans** on a long-term basis on real property worth a minimum of $500,000. They are based primarily on the value of the real property being purchased. The insurance company will extend a loan of up to 75 or 80 percent of the real estate's value and will allow a lengthy repayment schedule over 25 or 30 years so that payments do not strain the firm's cash flows excessively.

Insurance companies also make intermediate-term loans in addition to the long-term loans in which they specialize. *For example, when the C. E. Niehoff Company, a manufac-*

turer of heavy-duty alternators, needed to refinance a five-year loan on one of its plants, the bank agreed, but only for $750,000, $200,000 less than the original amount. Ralph Hermann, vice president of finance, began the frustrating search for other lenders. He eventually found the corporate lending division of Metropolitan Life Insurance Company, where he negotiated a new loan for $1.2 million (which allowed Niehoff to pay down its variable-rate line of credit at the bank) at a fixed rate of 10.25 percent. Total fees came to just 2 percent of the loan.[29]

CREDIT UNIONS

Credit unions, nonprofit financial institutions that are owned by their members, are best known for making consumer and car loans. However, many are now willing to lend money to their members to launch businesses, especially since many banks shy away from loans to high-risk start-ups. Of the 11,887 state and federally insured credit unions operating in the United States, approximately 1,000 are actively making member business loans, those of more than $25,000 granted without personal collateral for the purpose of starting a business. Most credit union officials believe that business lending makes up a significant part of their loan portfolios, but the majority of loans are personal loans to entrepreneurs who use the proceeds to launch companies.

With credit union membership totaling 71.4 million people and total deposited savings of $295 billion, these financial institutions have plenty of lending power.[30] Credit unions don't make loans to just anyone, however; to qualify for a loan, an entrepreneur must be a member. Lending practices at credit unions are very much like those at banks, but credit unions usually are willing to make smaller loans. *For instance, when Michael Webb, president of U Fuel, needed $50,000 for his young automated-fueling-systems business, he turned to a local credit union, of which he was a member. The credit union approved his application and established a $50,000 line of credit for U Fuel, enabling the company to grow.*[31]

BONDS

Bonds, which are corporate IOUs, have always been a popular source of debt financing for large companies. Few small business owners realize that they too can tap this valuable source of capital. Although the smallest businesses are not viable candidates for issuing bonds, a growing number of small companies are finding the funding they need through bonds when banks and other lenders say no. Many companies raising money through bond issues use zero coupon bonds (or junk bonds) because of their attractiveness to both the investor and the issuing company. Investors earn a high yield for the duration of the bond. The issuing company gets the capital it needed but does not have to make periodic interest payments as it would if it had issued regular bonds. Instead, it sells the bond at a discount from its par value and then repays the investor the full par value at maturity. The difference between the bond's discounted price and the par value represents the missing interest. *Iridium LLC <http://www.iridium.com/>, a telecommunications company in Washington, D.C., raised $4.4 billion in a series of staggered junk bond issues to put into orbit 66 wireless satellites designed to offer full global coverage for a variety of communications services, including voice, data, fax, and paging. In its start-up days, with no satellites in orbit, the company had no revenues and could not qualify for bank loans. Iridium sold two series of junk bonds, one at 14 percent and the other at 13 percent. Hoping to become the first global wireless telephone company, Iridum recently completed an initial public offering of approximately $240 million to provide the additional capital needed to sustain its rapid growth.*[32]

Although they can help small companies raise much-needed capital, junk bonds have certain disadvantages. Unless a company makes its issue under the Securities and Exchange Commission's Rule 144A exemption, it must follow the same regulations that govern businesses selling stock to public investors follow and register the offering with the SEC. Even if the bond issue is private, the company must register the offering and file periodic reports with the SEC. The Rule 144A exemption allows companies to sell bonds without registering the issue with the SEC; however, it permits sales only to institutional investors, not to individuals. Also, because of the large cash payments they require at maturity, junk bonds can create problems for companies whose actual performances fall behind their financial projections. Given the costs involved in issuing bonds, selling zero coupon bonds may not be practical for companies with small capital requirements. One investment banker suggests that the minimum issue is $12 million; anything less and investors lack confidence that the secondary market for the bonds will be large enough to justify buying them. To be able to service the debt on a $12 million issue, a company should have about $2 million in net after-tax earnings.[33]

Small manufacturers have access to an attractive, relatively inexpensive source of funds in industrial revenue bonds (IRBs). A company wanting to issue IRBs must get authorization from the appropriate municipality and the state before proceeding. Typically, the amount of money small companies issuing IRBs seek to raise is at least $1 million, but some small manufacturers have raised as little as $500,000 using IRBs. Even though the paperwork and legal costs associated with making an IRB issue can run up to 2 or 3 percent of the financing amount, that is a relative bargain for borrowing long-term money at a fixed interest rate.

To open IRBs up to even smaller companies, some states pool the industrial bonds of several small companies too small to make an issue. By joining together to issue composite industrial bonds, companies can reduce their issuing fees and attract a greater number of investors. The issuing companies typically pay lower interest rates than they would on conventional bank loans, often below the prime interest rate.[34]

PRIVATE PLACEMENTS

In chapter 13, we saw how companies can raise money by making private placements of their stock (equity). Private placements are also available for debt instruments. A private placement involves selling debt to one or a few investors, usually insurance companies or pension funds. Private placement debt is a hybrid between a conventional loan and a bond. At its heart, it is a bond, but its terms are tailored to the borrower's individual needs, as a loan would be.

Privately placed securities offer several advantages over standard bank loans. First, they usually carry fixed interest rates rather than the variable rates banks often charge. Second, the maturity of private placements is longer than most bank loans: 15 years, rather than five. Private placements do not require complex filings with the SEC or hiring expensive investment bankers. Finally, because private investors can afford to take greater risks than banks, they are willing to finance deals for small companies. *For example, Longview Fibre, a timber company and paper-products maker, has tapped the private placement market repeatedly in recent years, borrowing to buy everything from timberland to pulp machines. The company cites the speed and ease of getting the financing it needs as major advantages.*[35]

SMALL BUSINESS INVESTMENT COMPANIES

The small business investment company program was started after Russia's successful launch of the first space satellite, *Sputnik,* in 1958. Its goal was to accelerate the United States' position in the space race by funding high-technology start-ups. Created by the 1958 Small Business Investment Act, SBICs are privately owned financial institutions that are licensed and regulated by the Small Business Administration (SBA). Their function is to use a combination of private capital and federally guaranteed debt to provide long-term capital to small businesses. There are two types of SBICs: regular SBICs and specialized SBICs (SSBICs). Approximately 88 SSBICs provide credit and capital to small businesses that are at least 51 percent owned by minorities and socially or economically disadvantaged people. Since their inception in 1969, SSBICs have helped finance more than 19,000 minority-owned companies, with investments totaling $1.86 billion. Some 194 SBICs are in operation across the United States, and they have invested more than $13 billion in nearly 80,000 small businesses since 1960 (see Figure 14.2).[36] Most SBICs prefer later-round financing (mezzanine financing) and leveraged buyouts (LBOs) over funding raw start-ups. Still, SBICs invest twice as much in start-up companies as do private venture capitalists. *Funding from SBICs helped launch companies such as America OnLine, Apple Computer, Federal Express, Intel*

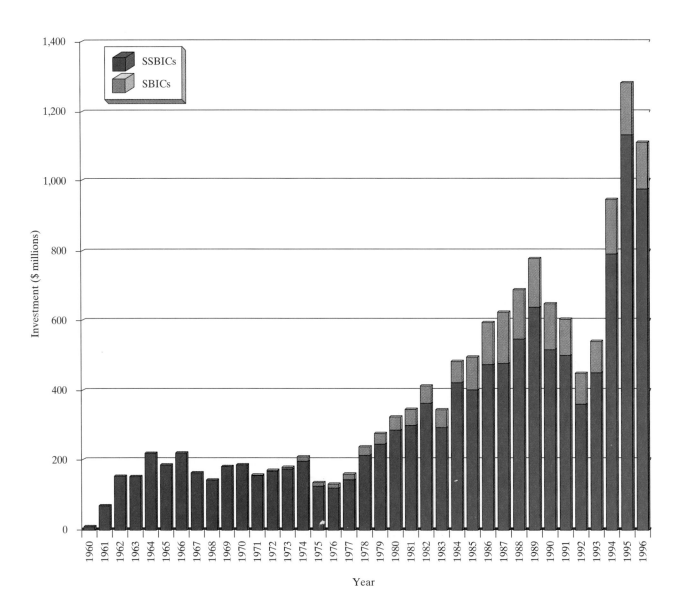

Figure 14.2 SBIC and SSBIC Financing Source: Small Business Administration.

Corporation, Outback Steakhouse, and PetSmart and have added many thousands of jobs to the U.S. economy.

Both SBICs and SSBICs must be capitalized privately with a minimum of $5 million, at which point they qualify for up to four dollars in low-rate, long-term SBA loans for every dollar of private capital invested in small businesses. As a general rule, both SBICs and SSBICs may provide financial assistance only to small businesses with a net worth of under $18 million and average after-tax earnings of $6 million during the past two years. However, employment and total annual sales standards vary from industry to industry. SBICs are limited to a maximum investment or loan amount of 20 percent of their private capital to a single client, and SSBICs may lend or invest up to 30 percent of their private capital in a single small business.

When Lucinda Heekin launched The Last Best Place Catalog Company, a catalog that sells jewelry, apparel, and accessories made by American West artists, she raised $100,000 from family members and friends. Recognizing that the initial capital investment would not be enough to sustain her fast-growing company, Heekin began planning for another capital injection. She managed to get a line of credit from a bank, which provided The Last Best Place Catalog Company with the short-term financing it needed to operate. Still, the company needed a long-term source of capital to finance its growth. "Creating a catalogue is delayed gratification," says Heekin. "It can take five or six years before you have a large enough list of established customers to become profitable." Three traditional venture capital companies showed some interest in the small catalogue company, but Heekin found that RiverCities Capital Fund, an SBIC in Cincinnati, offered the most attractive combination of financing and management experience. After eight months of negotiating, RiverCities put $1.5 million into Last Best Place and began offering valuable management assistance the company could not have afforded to go out and hire. Today, Heekin's 15-employee company generates annual sales of $10 million, and she credits much of its success to the money and management advice from the SBIC.[37]

SBICs operate as government-backed venture capitalists, providing long-term loans, equity capital, and management assistance to both start-up and existing businesses. An analysis of five-year trends in SBIC financing reveals that 19.4 percent used debt-only financing, 30.6 percent used a combination of debt and equity, and 50 percent made equity-only investments. By combining their own private capital with government funds, SBICs can provide the equivalent of venture capital to low-tech or no-tech companies that private venture capitalists would never consider. SBICs also accept deals that venture capital companies consider too small. The average SBIC investment is around $583,200; the average venture capital deal is $6.3 million.[38] Although the interest rates they charge on the loans they make are no lower than those of banks, SBICs tend to extend financing for longer time periods, a real advantage for entrepreneurs. In fact, regulations require SBICs to extend loans for at least five years. In addition, SBICs are prohibited from obtaining a controlling interest in the companies in which they make equity investments.

Lucinda Heekin, founder of The Last Best Place Catalog Company, raised the capital to start her business from friends and relatives before turning to a Small Business Investment Company (SBIC). Today, her company generates more than $10 million in annual sales.

SMALL BUSINESS LENDING COMPANIES

Small business lending companies (SBLCs) make only intermediate- and long-term SBA-guaranteed loans. They specialize in loans that many banks would not consider and operate on a nationwide basis. Most SBLC loans have terms extending for at least 10 years. The maximum interest rate for loans of seven years or longer is 2.75 percent above the prime rate; for shorter-term loans, the ceiling is 2.25 percent above prime. Another feature of SBLC loans is the expertise the SBLC offers borrowing companies.

SBLCs screen potential investors carefully, and most of them specialize in particular industries. The result is a low loan default rate at roughly 4 percent. Corporations own most of the nation's SBLCs, giving them a solid capital base. *For instance, the city of Port Jervis,*

New York, recently launched its Business Loan Program, a cooperative venture with an SBLC, the Grow America Fund, to make available $375,000 of SBA-guaranteed loan funds to small businesses in need of financial assistance for real property acquisition and improvements, purchase of machinery and equipment, and working capital. The city's goal in forming the partnership with the SBLC is to stimulate economic development in its small business sector by making capital more readily available to those companies.[39]

*F*ederally Sponsored Programs

3 Identify the sources of government financial assistance and the loan programs these agencies offer.

Federally sponsored lending programs have suffered from budget reductions in the past several years. Current trends suggest that the federal government is reducing its involvement in the lending business, but many programs are still quite active and some are actually growing.

ECONOMIC DEVELOPMENT ADMINISTRATION

The Economic Development Administration (EDA), a branch of the Commerce Department, offers loan guarantees to create new businesses and to expand existing businesses in areas with below-average income and high unemployment. Focusing on economically distressed communities, the EDA finances long-term investment projects needed to diversify local economies and to create jobs through loan guarantees. Entrepreneurs apply for loans through private lenders, who view applicants with loan guarantees much more favorably than those without such guarantees. The EDA guarantee reduces the lender's risk dramatically because the guarantee means that the government agency would pay off the loan balance (up to the ceiling) if the entrepreneur defaults on the loan. The EDA guarantees up to 80 percent of business loans between $750,000 and $10 million. Start-up businesses must contribute at least 25 percent of the guaranteed amount in the form of equity, and existing businesses must make equity investments of at least 15 percent of the guaranteed amount. Small companies can use loan proceeds for a variety of applications, including acquiring land; buying, constructing, or renovating buildings; purchasing equipment and machinery; or supplementing working capital. Terms range from no more than five years for working capital loans to 20 years for real estate loans and usually carry interest rates of prime plus 1.5 percent.[40] Loan guarantee activity is subject to federal budget cuts and therefore is uncertain.

To qualify for an EDA loan, the business must be located in a disadvantaged area, and its presence must directly benefit local residents. Applicants must prove that their business will create at least one job for every $20,000 in EDA loan guarantees. Most loan guarantee recipients are manufacturing companies, but other kinds of businesses can also qualify. Because the application process is lengthy and detailed, entrepreneurs should seek assistance from EDA personnel before filing an application.

DEPARTMENT OF HOUSING AND URBAN DEVELOPMENT

The Department of Housing and Urban Development (HUD) sponsors several loan programs to help qualified entrepreneurs raise needed capital. The Urban Development Action Grants (UDAGs) are extended to cities and towns that, in turn, lend or grant money to entrepreneurs to start small businesses that will strengthen the local economy. Grants are aimed at cities and towns that HUD considers economically distressed. Funds are normally used to construct buildings and plants to be leased to entrepreneurs, sometimes with an option to buy. No ceilings or geographic limitations are placed on UDAG loans and grants.

Urban Development Action Grant loan and grant terms are negotiated individually between the town and the entrepreneur. One entrepreneur might negotiate a low-interest, long-term loan; another might arrange for a grant in return for a promise to share a portion of the company's profits for several years with the town. *For example, Barry Lebost, founder of Lebost Turbines, Inc., needed $3 million to build and equip a plant to manufacture a wind turbine that would generate electricity and heat water. Lebost raised $300,000 in equity capital from individuals and received a grant for $150,000 from the New York State Energy Research and Development Authority to build a prototype. Then he received a UDAG of $1 million. The remaining $1.55 million of the capital was supplied by an Economic Development Administration loan. Lebost determined that he raised the necessary capital at a cost well below the existing prime rate.*[41]

FARMER'S HOME ADMINISTRATION

The U.S. Department of Agriculture provides financial assistance to certain small businesses through the Farmer's Home Administration (FmHA). The FmHA loan program is open to all types of businesses and is designed to create nonfarm employment opportunities in rural areas: those with populations below 50,000 and not adjacent to a city where densities exceed 100 persons per square mile. Entrepreneurs in many small towns, especially those with populations below 25,000, are eligible to apply for loans through the FmHA program, which makes about $100 million in loan guarantees each year.

The FmHA does not make direct loans to small businesses, but it will guarantee as much as 90 percent of a bank's loan up to $10 million (although actual guarantee amounts are almost always far less) for qualified applicants. To make a loan guarantee, the FmHA requires much of the same documentation as most banks and most other loan guarantee programs. Because of its emphasis on developing employment in rural areas, the FmHA requires an environmental impact statement describing the jobs created and the effect the business has on the area.

When Dorene Miller launched Black Tie Affair, Inc., in Wooster, Ohio, in 1980 as a catering service, she had a dream of expanding her company to include a full-service conference and party center. The opportunity to realize her dream came in 1993, when a partially finished conference center in Wooster came up for sale. Miller convinced an adventurous banker to assemble a consortium of five banks to lend Miller $2 million to buy and to finish the building. However, she still needed $450,000 for furnishings and equipment before the banks would approve the $2 million loan. After some searching, Miller discovered the FmHA's loan guarantee program, and the agency approved her $450,000 loan.[42]

RURAL ECONOMIC AND COMMUNITY DEVELOPMENT AGENCY

The Rural Economic and Community Development (RECD) Agency guarantees up to 80 percent of loans up to $10 million to businesses that will stimulate economic growth in economically depressed areas. The RECD also provides grants (with no dollar ceiling) to finance emerging and growing companies with less than $1 million in annual revenues and no more than 50 employees that are located in economically challenged areas.

LOCAL DEVELOPMENT COMPANIES

The federal government encourages local residents to organize and fund **local development companies (LDCs)** on either a profit or nonprofit basis. After raising initial capital by selling stock to at least 25 residents, the company seeks loans from banks and from the SBA. Each LDC can qualify for up to $1 million a year in loans and guarantees from the SBA to assist in starting small businesses in the community. Most LDCs are certified to operate locally, but each state may have one LDC that can operate *anywhere* within its boundaries. Local development companies enable towns to maintain a solid foundation of small businesses even when other attractive benefits such as trade zones and tax breaks are not available. *In Greenville, South Carolina, the Greenville Local Development Corporation (GLDC) operates a $535,000 loan pool from 12 local banks that makes loans ranging from $10,000 to $50,000 to new or existing small companies within the city limits. Loan terms run for 10 years, and the interest rate is prime plus 2 percent. The GLDC recently made a $50,000 loan to brothers John and Stephen Jeter, who used the money to launch The Handlebar, a restaurant that books musical acts such as Arlo Guthrie and Leon Redbone. "The loan plus $40,000 in private investments helped us pay for furniture, fixtures, advertising, inventory, and a great sound system," says John. In less than three years, the brothers had paid off two-thirds of the loan and were seeing sales increase by 40 percent!*[43]

Three parties are involved in providing the typical LDC loan: the LDC, the SBA, and a participating bank. An LDC normally requires the small business owner to assist by supplying about 10 percent of a project's cost and then arranges for the remaining capital through SBA guarantees and bank loans. Local development companies finance only the fixed assets of a small business; funds can be used to acquire land or buildings or to modernize, renovate, or restore existing facilities and sites. Funds cannot be used as working capital to supply inventory, supplies, or equipment, but LDCs can help arrange loans from banks for working capital. They usually purchase real estate, refurbish or construct buildings and plants, equip them, and then lease the entire facility to the small business. The lessee's payments extend for 20 to 25 years to allow repayment of SBA, bank, and LDC loans. When the lease expires, the LDC normally gives the small business owners an option to purchase the facility, sometimes at prices well below market value.

THE SMALL BUSINESS INNOVATION RESEARCH PROGRAM

Started as a pilot program by the National Science Foundation in the 1970s, the Small Business Innovation Research (SBIR) program has expanded to 10 federal agencies and has an annual budget in excess of $100 million. These agencies award cash grants or long-term contracts to small companies wanting to initiate or to expand their research and development (R&D) efforts. The goal is to encourage advanced research and development in science and engineering and to transform the results of that research into commercial products and services. More than 30,000 SBIR awards totaling in excess of $4.5 billion have gone to small companies, who traditionally have had difficulty competing with big corporations for federal R&D dollars.[44]

The SBIR program operates in three phases. In Phase I, small companies can receive up to $75,000 to perform basic research that establishes the technical merit and feasibility of ideas that have commercial potential. Businesses have six months to complete Phase I research. Companies that complete Phase I successfully may qualify for up to $300,000 in Phase II to continue their research, with the goal of developing it into a commercial product or service. Businesses have up to two years to complete Phase II research. In Phase III, companies no longer qualify for federal funds; by this stage, they should be far enough along in the development of their products and services that they can attract private financing. *Airborne Research Associates, a recent recipient of a Phase I grant, is developing an instrument capable of detecting and locating tornadoes. On the basis of its research, Airborne hopes to bring to market a device that will lengthen the warning time for tornadoes.*[45]

The government's dollars have been well invested. About one out of four small businesses receiving SBIR awards has achieved commercial success for its products. In addition to the financial grant a small business receives for R&D, another major benefit of an SBIR award is its potential as a powerful leveraging tool to attract other sources of funding. Many entrepreneurs tout their SBIR awards to potential lenders and investors as a sign of their company's credibility, creativity, and potential.

Several states also have developed their own versions of the federal SBIR program. For example, Iowa has earmarked a portion of state lottery funds for underwriting up to 50 percent of the cost of preparing a federal SBIR proposal. New York, the first state to establish an SBIR program, provides matching research funds for up to $50,000 to companies receiving Phase I awards from the federal SBIR program. Other states offer small companies with job-growth potential a variety of loans or grants.

THE SMALL BUSINESS TECHNOLOGY TRANSFER ACT OF 1992

The Small Business Technology Transfer (STTR) program <http://sttr.er.doe.gov/sttr/> complements the existing Small Business Innovation Research (SBIR) program. Whereas SBIR exploits commercially promising ideas that originate in small businesses, STTR uses companies to exploit a vast new reservoir of commercially promising ideas that originate in universities, federally funded R&D centers, and nonprofit research institutions. Researchers at these institutions can join forces with small businesses and can spin off commercially promising ideas while remaining employed at their research institutions. Five federal agencies award grants of up to $500,000 in three phases to these research partnerships.

*S*mall Business Administration

◆ Explain the various loan programs the Small Business Administration offers.

The Small Business Administration (SBA) has several programs designed to help finance both start-up and existing small companies that cannot qualify for traditional loans because of their thin asset base and their high risk of failure. In its 40-plus years of operation, the SBA has helped some 14 million companies get the financing they need for start-up or for growth.[46] To be eligible for SBA funds, a business must meet the SBA's criteria for a small business. Also, some types of businesses, such as those engaged in gambling, pyramid sales schemes, real estate speculation, or illegal activities, are ineligible for SBA loans. To qualify for a loan, businesses must show that they are unable to obtain private financing without the SBA's help.

The loan application process can take from three days to many months, depending on how well prepared the entrepreneur is and which bank is involved. To speed up processing times, the SBA has established a Certified Lender Program (CLP) and a Preferred Lender Program (PLP). Both are designed to encourage banks to become frequent SBA lenders. When a bank makes enough good loans to qualify as a **certified lender,** the SBA promises a fast turnaround time for the loan decision: typically three to 10 business days. Certified lenders account for nearly a third of all SBA business loan guarantees. When a bank becomes a **preferred lender,** it makes the final lending decision itself, subject to SBA review. In essence, the SBA delegates the application process, the lending decision, and other details to the preferred lender. The SBA guarantees up to 75 percent of PLP loans in case the borrower fails and defaults on the loan. The minimum PLP loan guarantee is $100,000, and the maximum is $500,000. Preferred loans account for more than 10 percent of SBA loan guarantees. Using certified or preferred lenders can reduce the processing time for an SBA loan considerably.

To further reduce the paperwork requirements involved in its loans, the SBA recently instituted the LowDoc (for "low documentation") Loan Program, which allows small businesses to use a simple one-page application for loans up to $50,000; loans between $50,000 and $100,000 require the one-page application plus personal tax returns for three years and a personal financial statement from the entrepreneur. Before the LowDoc program, a typical SBA loan application required an entrepreneur to complete at least 10 forms, and the SBA often took 45 to 90 days to decide on an application. Under the LowDoc Program, response time is just a few days. To qualify for a LowDoc loan, a company must have average sales below $5 million during the previous three years and employ fewer than 100 people. The LowDoc program focuses on applicants' character and credit history to identify qualified borrowers. Businesses can use LowDoc loans for working capital, machinery, equipment, and real estate. Since its inception, the LowDoc program has made nearly 30,000 loan guarantees totaling more than $1.5 billion. The average loan amount is about $55,500, and the program has become so popular that LowDoc loans account for about half of all SBA loan activity.[47]

Chris Baumgartner and Scott Zide used a LowDoc loan to help finance the launch of their Mr. Goodcents Subs and Pasta franchise in Ellisville, Missouri. Baumgartner and Zide, both 23 at the time, had no business experience and little capital to contribute to the venture, but their franchisor coached the two would-be franchisees in the development of a solid business plan and helped them complete the LowDoc loan application. The first bank they approached rejected their loan request, but they struck paydirt at the second, Mercantile Bank of St. Louis. Mercantile Bank previously had made a loan to another Mr. Goodcents franchisee who had been successful. Baumgartner and Zide each put up $18,000, and Mercantile Bank approved a LowDoc loan of just under $100,000 in a matter of days. Their franchise began earning a profit in its second month of operation and tallied sales increases of 10 percent per month for the first year.[48]

Another program designed to streamline the application process for SBA loan guarantees is the FA$TRAK Program, in which participating banks use their own loan procedures and applications to make loans of up to $100,000 to small businesses *without* the SBA's reviewing the loan applications. Because the SBA guarantees up to 50 percent of the loan, banks are often willing to make small loans to entrepreneurs who might otherwise have difficulty meeting lenders' standards. Eighteen SBA lenders across the United States, including many large banks, are authorized to make FA$TRAK loans.

SBA LOAN PROGRAMS

The SBA offers three basic types of loans in administering its programs: direct, immediate participation, and guaranteed. **Direct loans** are made by the SBA directly to the small business with public funds and no bank participation. In general, a direct loan cannot exceed $150,000. (A lower ceiling, $100,000, applies to a direct Economic Opportunity loan.) The interest rate charged on direct loans depends on the cost of money to the government, and it changes as general interest rates fluctuate. Activity in direct loans is very limited; they account for less than one-half of 1 percent of the SBA's total loan activity.

Immediate participation loans are made from a pool of public and private funds. The SBA provides a portion of the total loan, and a private lender supplies the remaining portion. The SBA's general policy is to fund no more than 75 percent of a participation loan, but there are exceptions. The SBA's portion of an immediate participation loan may not exceed $150,000 (except that Economic Opportunity loans are limited to $100,000). The interest rate the SBA charges on its share of the loan is usually the same as that charged on direct loans.

Guaranteed 7(a) Loans. By far, the most popular type of SBA loan is the **guaranteed loan** (or **7(a) loan**), and its popularity has increased steadily over the past 20 years (see Figure 14.3). Guaranteed loans are extended to small businesses by a private lender (usually a commercial bank) but are guaranteed by the SBA (80 percent of loans up to $100,000 and 75 percent of loans above $100,001 and up to $750,000, the loan guarantee ceiling). In other words, the SBA does not actually lend any money; it merely guarantees the bank this much repayment in case the borrower defaults on the loan. Because the SBA assumes most of the credit risk, banks are willing to consider risky deals that they normally would refuse. Figure

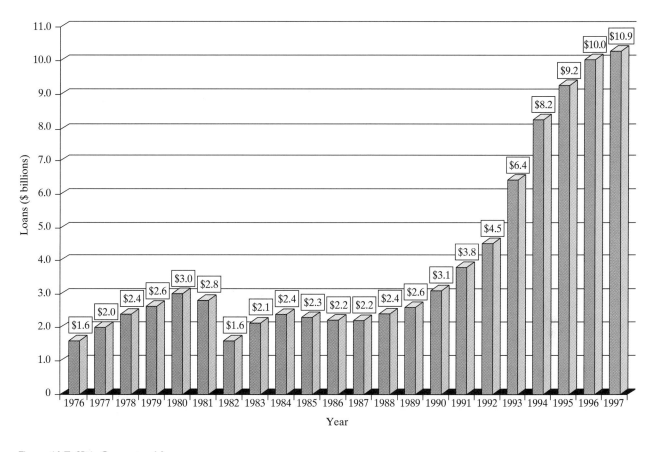

Figure 14.3 **SBA Guaranteed Loans** SOURCE: Small Business Administration.

14.4 on page 476 illustrates the path an entrepreneur's loan application takes from the local bank to the SBA guarantee program. *For instance, when Jennifer Norrid, president of PC Support Inc., a computer consulting company, needed capital to expand her business, four banks rejected her loan application. Even though her company already had an impressive list of loyal clients and was growing, the banks saw the loan as too risky. Finally, Norrid found a bank that was a certified SBA lender. She worked with a loan officer there on an application for an SBA loan guarantee. With the guarantee approval in hand, the bank loaned Norrid $48,000, of which the SBA guaranteed $36,000. "Without the SBA program, I wouldn't have been able to develop my business," says Norrid.*[49] Approximately 30 percent of SBA-guaranteed loans go to business start-ups; the remainder goes to cash-hungry ongoing small companies such as Norrid's PC Support Inc. The SBA expects entrepreneurs looking to finance start-ups to provide 30 percent of the cost in the form of equity.

Qualifying for an SBA loan guarantee requires cooperation among the entrepreneur, the participating bank, and the SBA. The participating bank determines the loan's terms and sets the interest rate within SBA limits. Contrary to popular belief, SBA-guaranteed loans do *not* carry special deals on interest rates. Typically, borrowers negotiate rates with the participating bank, with a ceiling of prime plus 2.25 percent on loans of less than seven years and prime plus 2.75 percent on loans of seven to 25 years. Interest rates on loans of less than $25,000 can run up to prime plus 4.75 percent. The average interest rate on SBA-guaranteed loans is prime plus 2 percent (compared with prime plus 1 percent on conventional bank

The Bank Branch
- You fill out the loan application.
- The relationship manager makes sure you have provided all necessary materials.
- Most banks rely on personal and business tax forms as their primary source of information.

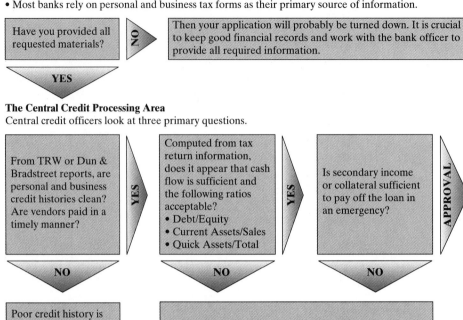

The Central Credit Processing Area
Central credit officers look at three primary questions.

Figure 14.4 **Where Does Your Loan Application Go?** SOURCE: *Small Business Success* 7, p. 30.

loans). The SBA also assesses a one-time guaranty fee of up to 3.75 percent for all loan guarantees.

The median loan through the guarantee program is $175,000, and the average duration of an SBA loan is 12 years—longer than the average commercial small business loan. In fact, longer loan terms are a distinct advantage of SBA loans. At least half of all bank business loans are for less than one year. By contrast, SBA real estate loans can extend for up to 25 years (compared with just 10–15 years for a conventional loan), and working capital loans have maturities of seven years (compared with two to five years at most banks). These longer terms translate into lower payments, which are better suited for young, fast-growing, cash-strapped companies. "Lower payments mean that you can borrow more," says one entrepreneur with an SBA loan guarantee.[50]

Entrepreneurs such as Douglas Myron prove that the SBA's loan guarantee program accomplishes its primary goals: stimulating small business growth, creating jobs, and driving economic growth. After Myron patented an energy-saving electronic device to turn office lights on when people enter and off when they leave, his employer, who was trying to launch the product, went bankrupt. Myron was left with an idea but no capital. Today, with the help *of four separate bank loans backed by SBA guarantees, Myron is the president of MyTech, which has become the largest domestic maker of "occupancy sensor" devices. The loans—which ranged from $60,000 to $235,000—have enabled MyTech to grow by a remarkable 850 percent over five years. The company, now employing 25 workers, has plans to hire 20 more to handle the growing sales volume, which exceeds $1.5 million.*[51]

The CAPline Program. In addition to its basic 7(a) loan guarantee program, the SBA provides guarantees to small businesses for start-up, real estate, machinery and equipment, fixtures, working capital, exporting, and restructuring debt through several other methods. About two-thirds of the SBA's loan guarantees are for machinery and equipment or working capital. The CAPline program offers short-term capital to growing companies needing to finance seasonal buildups in inventory or accounts receivable under five separate programs: seasonal line of credit (provides advances against inventory and accounts receivable to help businesses weather seasonal sales fluctuations), contract line of credit (finances the direct labor and materials costs associated with performing contracts), builder's line of credit (helps small general contractors or builders finance direct-labor and materials costs), standard asset-based line of credit (an asset-based revolving line of credit that provides financing for cyclical growth and recurring and/or short-term needs), and small asset-based line of credit (an asset-based revolving line of credit of up to $200,000). CAPline is aimed at helping cash-hungry small businesses by giving them a credit line to draw on when they need the money. Loans built around lines of credit are just what small businesses need most because they are so flexible, efficient, and, unfortunately, so hard to get from traditional lenders because of the cost of maintaining them.

Loans Involving International Trade. For small businesses going global, the SBA has the *Export Working Capital Program* (EWCP). Under this program, the SBA will guarantee 90 percent of a bank credit line up to $750,000. The EWCP is a combined effort of the SBA and the Export-Import Bank designed to increase small companies' access to export financing. The EWCP uses a one-page application form and streamlined documentation, with turnaround usually within 10 days. Loan proceeds must be used to finance small business exports. The *International Trade Program* is for small businesses that are engaged in international trade or adversely affected by competition from imports. It offers loans for facilities or equipment, with maturities of up to 25 years.

Section 504 Certified Development Company (CDC) Program. The SBA's Section 504 program is designed to encourage small businesses to expand their facilities and to create jobs. Section 504 deals provide long-term, fixed-asset financing to small companies to purchase land, buildings, or equipment. Three lenders play a role in every 504 loan: a bank, the SBA, and a **certified development company (CDC).** A CDC is a nonprofit organization designed to promote economic growth in a community. Some 290 CDCs operate across the United States. The entrepreneur generally is required to make a down payment of 10 percent of the total project cost. The CDC puts up 40 percent at a long-term fixed rate, supported by an SBA loan guarantee in case the entrepreneur defaults. The bank provides long-term financing for the remaining 50 percent, also supported by an SBA guarantee.

When Jerry and Loretta Schutten's manufacturing company, Commercial Lighting, outgrew the location it was renting, the Schuttens worked with their bank, the Evergreen Community Development Association (a CDC), and the SBA to finance the purchase of a new location. The Evergreen CDC provided a $148,400 loan, which the SBA guaranteed, and the Schuttens' bank made a $192,000 loan. The Schuttens put up the remaining 10 percent of the cost of the new building.[52]

As attractive as they are, 504 loans are not for every business owner. The SBA imposes several restrictions on 504 loans:

- For every $35,000 the CDC loans, the project must create at least one new job.
- Machinery and equipment financed must have a useful life of at least 10 years.
- The borrower must occupy at least two-thirds of a building constructed with the loan.
- The borrower must occupy at least half of a building purchased or remodeled with the loan.
- The borrower must qualify as a small business under the SBA's definition, must not have a tangible net worth in excess of $6 million, and must not have had an average net income in excess of $2 million after taxes for the preceding two years.

Because of strict equity requirements, existing small businesses usually find it easier to qualify for 504 loans than do start-ups.

Microloans. Recall from Figure 13.1 that about three-fourths of all entrepreneurs needed less than $100,000 to launch their businesses. Indeed, research suggests that most entrepreneurs require less than $50,000 to start their companies. Unfortunately, loans of that amount can be the most difficult to get. Lending these relatively small amounts to entrepreneurs starting businesses is the purpose of the SBA's microloan program. Called microloans because they range from just a few hundred dollars to as much as $25,000, these loans have helped thousands of people take their first steps toward entrepreneurship. Banks typically have shunned loans in such small amounts because they considered them to be unprofitable. So, in 1992, the SBA began funding microloan programs at 96 private, nonprofit lenders in 44 states in an attempt to fill the void in small loans to start-up companies. Today, more than 500 lenders provide microloans in 49 states. The average microloan is for $9,916 over four years (the maximum term is six years), and interest rates are no more than prime plus 4 percent. Lenders' standards on microloans are less demanding than those on conventional loans. Although microloans are available to anyone, the SBA hopes to target those entrepreneurs who have the greatest difficulty getting start-up capital: women, minorities, and persons with a low income. More than 39 percent of microloans go to minority entrepreneurs, and nearly 42 percent go to women.[53]

Minority and Women's Prequalified Loan Program. As its name implies, the Minority and Women's Prequalified Loan Program, started in 1994, is designed to help minority and women entrepreneurs prepare loan applications and "prequalify" for SBA loan guarantees before approaching banks and lending institutions for loans. Because lenders are much more likely to approve loans that the SBA has prequalified, these entrepreneurs have greater access to the capital they need. To be eligible for the program, a business must be at least 51 percent owned, operated, and managed by women or minorities; its annual sales cannot exceed $5 million; and it must employ 100 or fewer workers. The maximum loan amount is $250,000 (of which the SBA will guarantee up to 80 percent), and the money can be used for everything from supplementing working capital and purchasing equipment or machinery to buying inventory and real estate. Loan terms range from seven to 25 years, depending on the purpose of the loan. Since its beginning, the program has guaranteed nearly 700 loans, totaling more than $71.6 million.[54]

Despite her whirlpool tub company's rapid growth, Rhonda Cline could not find a bank to lend her the capital she needed for expansion. Kline had started her business, Aqua Life Industries, on a shoestring, and within four years sales had climbed to more than $400,000. She needed capital to move into a larger manufacturing facility, buy more equipment, and hire more employees. The lack of capital was particularly frustrating for Cline because she knew that customers wanted to purchase her company's whirlpool baths. Yet, she couldn't capitalize on that demand without sufficient money. To make matters worse, some customers were growing tired of waiting for Aqua Life to make their tubs and were canceling

Big Results from Small Loans

*M*icroloans are producing phenomenal results all around the globe. From less-developed countries such as Bangladesh and Malawi to industrialized giants such as the United States, microloans—loans as small as $25—are giving global entrepreneurship a tremendous boost. ACCION International, the Trickle Up program, and other organizations have been making microloans to entrepreneurs in developing nations for years in an effort to boost local economies and to create jobs. The money goes to entrepreneurs to start or to expand their businesses: selling vegetables, repairing shoes, sewing, making furniture, and the like. These microlending programs, which charge the local prevailing commercial loan rate, free entrepreneurs in developing nations from the clutches of loan sharks.

Rather than merely offering people a handout, these organizations are providing people with a "hand up." Although their methods of operation vary somewhat, most microloan programs are modeled after the one offered by Bangladesh's Grameen Bank. Muhammed Yunus, tired of seeing the wasted entrepreneurial potential in his homeland, realized that the poor people of Bangladesh did not need massive amounts of capital to build successful businesses. What they needed were small amounts of money. Using his own money, Yunus started the Grameen Bank in the early 1970s, lending amounts of $25 or less to peasant women to buy sewing machines or to farmers to buy a tool. Traditional development "experts" dismissed Yunus's idea as an exercise in failure, predicting that the bank would fold when the borrowers could not repay their loans. They were wrong. Today, the Grameen Bank is one of the largest and most successful in Bangladesh, providing more than $6 million each month in microloans to people in 18,000 villages.

In Monterrey, Mexico, Aaron Aguilar, an unemployed factory worker, and his wife wanted to start a business making and selling decorative figurines. The couple had no money of their own to invest in their idea, and without a collateral, they

had no hope of getting a bank loan. ACCION International, a nonprofit international development group, loaned the Aguilars the $100 start-up capital they needed to buy clay and glazes to make the figurines. Over the next six years, the Aguilars took out and repaid five loans and built their business to the point where it now employs 18 full-time workers.

In tiny Black Mountain, North Carolina, the Mountain Microenterprise Fund offers loans ranging from $500 to $8,000 to entrepreneurs who cannot qualify for traditional bank loans and other sources of capital. So far, the fund has financed a variety of innovative businesses, including a maker of miniature clay flower jewelry and a door-to-door recycling service. The Mountain Microenterprise Fund has 22 "lending circles," groups of entrepreneurs who band together to learn more about running small businesses successfully. In a recent meeting of the Candler group, for example, six entrepreneurs met outside Rick Steingress's Candlertown Chairworks Inc. to brainstorm ideas and to swap advice. Their focus was on Vicki Weiss and her husband, Howard, who had just borrowed $1,000 from the Mountain Fund for their T-shirt business. The couple designs and sells T-shirts bearing designs of Seneca Native Americans. The group asked how the Weiss's shirts were selling. "Any new accounts? Do you have a sales representative yet? Can you sell at wholesale prices?" "They've shed light in areas where, if we hadn't joined the group, we'd have learned the hard way," says Vicki. "They really make you aware of what your business is about."

---

1. What types of entrepreneurs are most likely to benefit from microloan programs?

2. Would a microloan program be useful as a tool for economic development in your area? Explain. What advantages and disadvantages do you see in setting up such programs?

3. Working with a team of your classmates, use the resources of the World Wide Web and your local library to research microloans. On the basis of your research, develop a plan for launching a microloan program in your area.

SOURCES: Adapted from Susan Hodges, "SBA Microloans Fuel Big Ideas," *Nation's Business*, February 1997, pp. 34–35; "Asians Live American Dream through Entrepreneurial Plan," *Greenville-Piedmont*, March 24, 1993, p. 6C; Brent Bowers, "Third-World Debt That Is Almost Always Paid in Full," *Wall Street Journal*, June 7, 1991, p. B2; Paul Brown Johnson and David Riggle, "Cooperative Loans for Small Businesses," *In Business*, May/June 1993, pp. 54–55; Bradford McKee, "Seed Funds for the Smallest Start-ups," *Nation's Business*, October 1992, pp. 29–30. ◆

---

their orders. "I had been turned down several times by banks due to a lack of collateral, even though my business was profitable," she says. Then Cline read about the SBA's Minority and Women's Prequalified Loan Program. She applied, received a prequalification letter from the SBA, and got the bank loan she needed for expansion. Within a year, Aqua Life's sales had climbed 25 percent.[55]

The 8(a) Program. The SBA's 8(a) program is designed to help minority-owned businesses get a fair share of federal government contracts. Through this program, the SBA directs about $4 million each year to small businesses with "socially and economically disadvantaged" owners. Once a small business convinces the SBA that it meets the program's criteria, the SBA finds a federal agency needing work done. The SBA then approaches the federal agency that needs the work done and arranges for a contract to go to the SBA. The agency then subcontracts the work to the small business. Government agencies cooperate with the SBA in its 8(a) program because the law requires them to set aside a portion of their work for minority-owned firms.

Disaster Loans. As their name implies, disaster loans are made to small businesses devastated by some kind of financial or physical loss. The maximum disaster loan usually is $500,000, but Congress often raises that ceiling when circumstances warrant. For instance, in response to the tremendous flooding in the Midwest during the summer of 1993 and again in the wake of the Los Angeles earthquake in early 1994, the SBA tripled the ceiling on disaster loans for physical damage to $1.5 million. Disaster loans carry below-market interest rates: for example, 4 percent on the loans to small companies after the L.A. earthquakes. Loans for physical damage above $10,000 and financial damage of more than $5,000 require the entrepreneur to pledge some kind of collateral, usually a lien on the business property. Over the last decade, the SBA's coffers have been stretched thin by a string of disasters, ranging from Hurricane Hugo on the Southeastern coast to a big San Francisco earthquake in 1989 to the Los Angeles riots in 1992 and the Midwest floods in 1993.

Economic Injury Disaster Loans offer companies affected by disasters working capital until they can reopen for business. *Business Physical Disaster Loans are earmarked for repairing and replacing damaged business property. For instance, Capital Sanitary Supply Company of Des Moines, Iowa, was a victim of the 1993 floods. Managers bailed its offices out of six feet of water. "It was my worst nightmare," says owner Doug Ireland. "There was no [running] water and no electricity. But the important thing was to get back in business quickly to service our customers." Ireland and his workers had to haul all of the company's office furniture to a landfill, peel away soaked drywall, and shovel mud from the building. Capital moved to temporary quarters, ordered new supplies and inventory, and was back in business in three days. With the help of a $500,000 SBA disaster loan, Capital moved back into its original—now remodeled—office. The loan also helped stabilize the company's long-term future as demand for its industrial pressure washers, floor scrubbers, and other cleaning products surged.*[56]

Other SBA Loan Programs. The Small Business Administration also offers several other loan programs for specialized purposes, such as providing financial assistance to companies with employee stock ownership plans, those installing pollution-control equipment, and those adversely affected by defense cutbacks. For an overview of these programs, go to <http://www.sbaonline.sba.gov/financing/indexloans.html> on the World Wide Web.

*S*tate and Local Development Programs

5 Discuss state and local development programs.

Just when many federally funded programs are facing cutbacks, state-sponsored loan and development programs are becoming more active in providing funds for business start-ups and expansions. Many states have decided that their funds are better spent encouraging small business growth rather than "chasing smokestacks" (trying to entice large businesses to locate in their boundaries). These programs come in a wide variety of forms, but they all tend to focus on developing small businesses that create jobs and economic benefits. For example, South Carolina's Jobs Economic Development Authority (JEDA) is a direct lending arm of the state, offering low-interest loans to manufacturing, industrial, and service businesses. It also provides financial and technical assistance to small companies seeking to develop export markets.

Although each state's approach to economic development is somewhat special, one common element is some kind of small business financing program: loans, loan guarantees, development grants, venture capital pools, and others. *Averill Cook got the idea for the Catamount Pellet Fuel Corporation, a company that manufactures clean-burning, cheap fuel pellets from sawdust, after he started his first company, a firewood business. After spending four years researching the project and building a business plan, he concluded that it would take about $1 million to launch the company. Several family members agreed to guarantee $500,000 of the loans Cook negotiated with a bank. Then he pitched his idea to industrial development organizations in Massachusetts, who offered him a package of low-cost grants and loans. In the end, Catamount's start-up capital totaled $1.3 million.*[57]

Even cities and small towns have joined in the effort to develop small businesses and help them grow. *For example, when a group of entrepreneurs wanted to open a specialty-food store in tiny Carrboro, North Carolina, they convinced a nonprofit funding organization, the Center for Community Self-Help, in nearby Durham to put up $100,000. But there was a catch: The entrepreneurs had to find $100,000 in matching funds. Carrboro quickly came up with $100,000 from its own revolving loan fund, and the town's 8,000 residents pitched in another $100,000 in loans to help launch Weaver Street Market. Today, the company has annual sales of more than $4 million and employs more than 50 workers.*[58]

*I*nternal Methods of Financing

◆ Discuss valuable methods of financing growth and expansion internally in bootstrap financing.

Small business owners do not have to rely solely on external financial institutions and government agencies for capital. Instead, the business itself has the capacity to generate capital. This type of financing, called **bootstrap financing,** is available to virtually every small business and encompasses factoring, leasing rather than purchasing equipment, using credit cards, and managing the business frugally.

FACTORING ACCOUNTS RECEIVABLE

Instead of carrying credit sales on its own books (some of which may never be collected), a small business can sell outright its accounts receivable to a factor. A **factor** buys a company's accounts receivable but pays for them in two parts. The first payment, which the factor makes immediately, usually is for 75 to 80 percent of the accounts' agreed-upon value. The factor makes the second payment, which makes up the balance less the factor's service fee, when the original customer pays the invoice. Factoring is more expensive than bank and commercial finance company loans because factors normally charge a factoring fee ranging from 0.75 percent to 7 percent of the full amount of the receivables. For businesses that cannot qualify for bank loans, however, factoring may be the only choice!

Begun by American colonists to finance their cotton trade with England, factoring has become an important source of capital for many small businesses. Factoring arrangements are either with recourse or without recourse. Under deals arranged with recourse, the small business owner retains the responsibility for customers who fail to pay their accounts. The business owner must take back these uncollectible invoices. Under deals arranged without recourse, however, the owner is relieved of the responsibility for collecting them. If some accounts are not collected, the factor bears the loss. Because the factoring company assumes the risk of collecting the accounts, it normally screens the firm's credit customers, accepts those judged to be creditworthy, and pays the small business owner the value of the accounts receivable. Factors will pay anywhere from 60 to 95 percent of the face value of a company's accounts receivable, depending on the small company's:

- Customers' financial strength and credit ratings

- Industry and its customers' industries (Some industries have a reputation for slow payments.)

- Financial strength, especially in deals arranged with recourse

- Credit policies[59]

Factoring is ideally suited for fast-growing companies, especially start-ups that cannot qualify for bank loans. "Most of the businesses we deal with are very much in an upward cycle, going through extremely rapid growth," says a manager at Altres Financial, a national factoring company.[60] Because factoring is a more expensive method of financing, a small business should have an adequate volume of accounts receivable before turning to this source of funds. Most factors prefer to work with companies billing at least $8,000 to $10,000 a month. Entrepreneurs should use factoring as a short-term financial strategy as they make the transition to more traditional financing. Most entrepreneurs use factoring for no more than two years—just long enough to enable them to qualify for more traditional financing sources. Some small business owners use factoring to take advantage of vendors' cash discounts (for early payment of invoices) because the discount often exceeds the cost of factoring.

Mac Qurashi, owner of ITI Technical Services, a Florida-based contractor that installs fiber-optic cable for cable television systems, relies on factors to provide financing for his fast-growing business. In just two years, sales shot from $250,000 to $7 million. "If I had to wait for collections to come in, I couldn't grow as fast as I need to or pay the expenses for my 22 employees, equipment, and subcontractors," says Qurashi. "To get cash right away, I sell my invoices to [a factor]," which now owns more than $1 million of ITI's accounts receivable.[61]

LEASING

Leasing is another common bootstrap financing technique. Today, small businesses can lease virtually any kind of asset: from office space and telephones to computers and heavy equipment. By leasing expensive assets, small business owners are able to use them without locking up valuable capital for an extended period of time. In other words, entrepreneurs can reduce the long-term capital requirements of their businesses by leasing equipment and facilities and avoid investing their capital in depreciating assets. Also, because no down payment is required and because the cost of the asset is spread over a longer time (lowering monthly payments), the firm's cash flow improves.

CREDIT CARDS

Unable to find financing elsewhere, some entrepreneurs have launched their companies using the most convenient source of debt capital available: credit cards! A recent study of entrepreneurs by Arthur Andersen and National Small Business United found that one-third of those with fewer than 20 employees said they use credit cards as a source of financing, up from 17.3 percent in 1993.[62] The rapid growth of entrepreneurship and the proliferation of credit cards with low introductory rates are contributing to the increased use of credit cards as a source of financing. Putting business start-up costs on credit cards, which can charge 21 percent or more in annual interest, is expensive and risky, but some entrepreneurs have no other choice. *Vincent Castelluccio, owner of T&V Printing, has used credit cards to get his business through cash squeezes since opening it in 1988. He began using credit cards as a source of capital because, as the owner of a business start-up, he could not qualify for any other kind of loan. T&V's credit-card balance hovers consistently between $25,000 and*

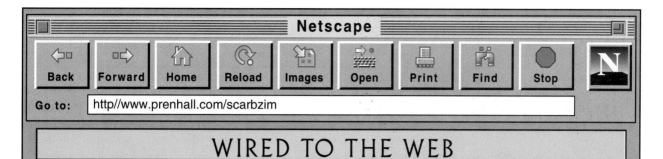

WIRED TO THE WEB

PAVING THE WAY FOR FINANCING

*J*erry Turner and Michael Clarke met while working for a road-paving company that was constantly experiencing cash flow problems and failing to meet its payroll. That's when they decided to start their own paving company, Emerald Asphalt and Concrete Inc. "We weren't getting paid," says Turner. "We figured we had nothing to lose."

They began drumming up business in Santa Ana, California, and every time they got a job, the pair would rent all of the equipment they needed to complete it. Turner and Clarke rented dump trucks, paving machines, and asphalt rollers for an average of $600 each week. They used the revenue from the jobs to pay the rental fees, but the machines were in such bad condition that they broke down often, forcing employees to stop working. Still, Turner and Clarke managed to earn $400,000 in their first year ("not much for a paving business," according to Clarke).

As they entered their second year of business, the partners knew that they had to buy their own equipment—and soon. Unfortunately, road-paving equipment is not cheap. Turner and Clarke set their sights on purchasing a used dump truck first. They found one in good shape for just under $30,000 at a local heavy-equipment dealership that advertised an attractive financing program. Unfortunately, because Emerald was a start-up company, the vendor would not approve a loan on the truck. After all, Emerald was a new company in a highly competitive business with no assets to speak of.

"What can we do?" sighed Turner. "We *really* need that truck and some other equipment, too. They say we're risky because we're a start-up business and we don't have any assets. How can we get assets if no one is willing to lend us the money to buy them?"

"I called a banker friend of mine," said Clarke. "She said that even if we could get approved for a conventional loan, we'd have to make a down payment of nearly $3,000. I'm not sure we could afford that right now."

"All I know is we can't go on much longer renting that same old broken-down equipment," said Turner. "Lately it seems we've been spending more time fixing it or waiting for a mechanic to fix it than we have actually paving roads with it. There's got to be more than one way for us to get the money we need to buy that dump truck and some of the other heavy equipment we'll need."

"You might be right," Clarke said. "We'll need somewhere in the ballpark of $150,000 to buy a good set of used equipment. Let's make a plan for getting that money. Any ideas?"

1. Use the information in this chapter and the resources of the World Wide Web to help Turner and Clarke identify potential sources of financing for their business.
2. Develop a plan for attracting the $150,000 they need to purchase the equipment for Emerald Asphalt and Concrete. What can they do to make their loan proposal attractive to potential lenders?
3. Is Turner and Clarke's dilemma common to owners of small start-up companies? Explain.

SOURCE: Adapted from Susan Hodges, "Vendors Can Pave the Way to Growth," *Nation's Business*, June 1997, pp. 46–47.

$35,000, with an average annual interest rate around 12 percent, a rate comparable to those on several bank loans the company has. Castelluccio says that to keep the rates on his credit card balance that low he does have to juggle balances among cards, shifting from one to another to take advantage of the lowest rates. "It does get complicated," he admits. "If I were to give someone advice, I'd tell them to avoid [using credit cards as a source of business fi-

nancing]," says Castelluccio. *"But sometimes you get in situations where you don't have a choice."*[63]

In the past, women entrepreneurs had difficulty convincing traditional lenders to grant them loans and were forced to rely on credit cards more often than men. Recent studies, however, show that that trend has reversed. A study by the National Foundation of Women Business Owners (NFWBO) concluded that women entrepreneurs today are almost as likely to have bank loans or lines of credit as are male entrepreneurs. From 1992 to 1996, women business owners were able to rely more on their company's retained earnings and less on credit cards to finance their company's growth. During that time period, the proportion of women entrepreneurs using credit cards as a source of capital dropped from 52 percent to 23 percent (see Figure 14.5). The study also found that gender makes a difference in the way entrepreneurs use capital. Women business owners use credit primarily for growth and expansion; men are more likely to use it to smooth out cash flow and to consolidate debt.[64]

OTHER CREATIVE SOLUTIONS

Some business owners needing cash to finance growth have found a simple solution: *print their own!* This not-so-funny money is legal. *Frank Tortoriello, owner of The Deli, a Massachusetts delicatessen, printed his own currency called "Deli Dollars." He sold $10 worth of Deli Dollars to his customers for $9. They could use the money six months after they bought it to buy anything in the store. Tortoriello's Deli Dollars were just six-month loans from his customers. They worked so well that other local merchants began to print their own currencies. Some merged their currencies so that their customers could spend their dollars at various locations around town.*[65]

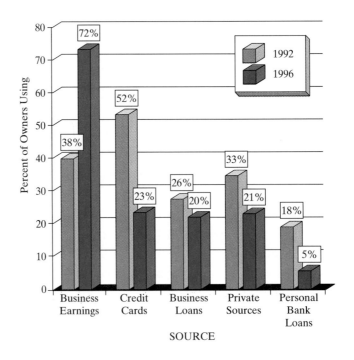

Figure 14.5 Sources of Financing for Women Entrepreneurs Note: Chart includes 5 of 13 possible responses. Multiple responses allowed. Source: National Foundation of Women Business Owners.

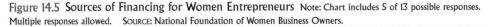

$\mathscr{W}$here *Not* to Seek Funds

7 Describe how to avoid becoming a victim of a loan scam.

Entrepreneurs searching for capital must be wary of con artists, whose targets frequently include financially strapped small businesses. The swindle usually begins when the con artist scours an area for "DEs" (Desperate Entrepreneurs) in search of quick cash injections to keep their businesses going. Usually, the small business scheme follows one of two patterns (although variations exist). Under one scheme, the small business owner is guaranteed a loan for whatever amount he needs from a nonexistent bank with false credentials. The con artist tells the owner that loan processing will take time and that, in the meantime, he must pay a percentage of the loan amount as an "advance fee." Of course, the loan never materializes, and the small business owner loses his deposit, sometimes several hundred thousand dollars. *Richard Gould, owner of a small chain of drive-through restaurants, believed that his business was an ideal candidate for franchising, but he needed the money to finance the expansion. He answered an ad in an industry trade journal from a company claiming to have capital to invest in growing businesses. When the company officials told Gould that he would have to pay a $60,000 fee up front, he refused. Ultimately, however, he paid the company $18,000 for the promise of attracting as much as $3 million from investors it supposedly represented. Gould never received a dime in investments from the company. "Once I paid that $18,000," he says. "I could never get anybody on the phone; or, if I did, it was a secretary, who told me that my contact was traveling on business out of the continental United States or that he would call me back later, which he never did."*[66]

Another common scam begins with a con artist who claims to be a representative of the Small Business Administration. He promises the cash-hungry small business owner an SBA loan if he pays a small processing fee. Again, the loan never appears, and the small business owner loses his deposit.

Unfortunately, scams by con artists who prey on unsuspecting business owners in need of capital are more common than ever. The World Wide Web has made crooks' jobs easier. On the Web, they can establish a legitimate-looking presence, approach their targets anonymously, and vanish instantly—all while avoiding mail fraud charges if they happen to get caught. These con artists move fast, cover their trails well, and are extremely smooth. The best protection against such scams is common sense and remembering that if it sounds too good to be true, it probably is. Experts offer the following advice to business owners:

◆ Be suspicious of anyone who approaches you—unsolicited—with an offer for "guaranteed financing."

◆ Watch out for red flags that indicate a scam: "guaranteed" loans, credit, or investments; up-front fees; pitches over the World Wide Web; Nigerian-letter scams (promises to cut you in for a share if you help transfer large amounts of money from distant locations, such as Nigeria. Of course, the con artists will need the number of your bank account, which they promptly clean out.).

◆ Conduct a thorough background check on any lenders, brokers, or financiers you intend to do business with. Does the company have a listing in the telephone book? Does the Better Business Bureau have a record of complaints against the company? Does the company have a physical location? If it does, visit it.

◆ Ask the lender or broker about specific sources of financing. Then call them to verify the information.

◆ Make sure you have an attorney review all loan agreements before you sign them.

◆ Never pay advance fees for financing, especially on the World Wide Web, unless you have verified the lender's authenticity.

Chapter Summary

1. Describe the vital role that banks play in providing small business financing and the types of business loans banks make.
   - Commercial banks offer the greatest variety of loans, although they are conservative lenders.
   - Typical short-term bank loans include commercial loans, lines of credit, and floor planning.
   - Intermediate- and long-term loans include discounted installment contracts and character loans.

2. Explain the types of financing available from non-bank sources of credit.
   - Asset-based financing includes discounting accounts receivable and inventory financing.
   - Trade credit is used extensively by small businesses as a source of financing. Vendors and suppliers commonly finance sales to businesses for 30, 60, or even 90 days.
   - Equipment suppliers offer small businesses financing similar to trade credit, but with slightly different terms.
   - Commercial finance companies offer many of the same types of loans that banks do, but they are more risk-oriented in their lending practices. They emphasize accounts receivable financing and inventory loans.
   - Savings and loan associations specialize in loans to purchase real property—commercial and industrial mortgages—for up to 30 years.
   - Stock brokerage houses offer loans to prospective entrepreneurs at lower interest rates than banks because they have high-quality, liquid collateral—stocks and bonds in the borrower's portfolio.
   - Insurance companies provide financing through policy loans and mortgage loans. Policy loans are extended to the owner against the cash surrender value of insurance policies. Mortgage loans are made for large amounts and are based on the value of the land being purchased.
   - Credit unions are nonprofit financial institutions that make loans to their members, many of whom use the proceeds to launch businesses.
   - Zero coupon bonds allow a company to borrow the funds it needs without having to make periodic loan payments. But a public bond issue does require the company to make public certain financial information.
   - Entrepreneurs can finance their businesses by making private placement of debt instruments with a select group of investors.

   - Small business investment companies are privately owned companies licensed and regulated by the SBA. Once they are privately capitalized, SBICs may qualify for SBA loans to be invested in or loaned to small firms.
   - Small business lending companies make only intermediate- and long-term loans that are guaranteed by the SBA.

3. Identify the sources of government financial assistance and the loan programs these agencies offer.
   - The Economic Development Administration, a branch of the Commerce Department, makes loan guarantees to create and expand small businesses in economically depressed areas.
   - The Department of Housing and Urban Development extends loans to cities that, in turn, lend and grant money to small businesses in an attempt to strengthen the local economy.
   - The Farmer's Home Administration's loan program is designed to create nonfarm employment opportunities in rural areas through loans and loan guarantees.
   - The Rural Economic Community and Development (RECD) Agency guarantees loans to businesses that will stimulate economic growth in economically depressed areas.
   - Local development companies, financed privately, seek loans from banks and from the SBA. They lend this money to small businesses to develop a sound economic base in the local community.

4. Explain the various loan programs the Small Business Administration offers.
   - The Small Business Administration has three types of loans: direct, immediate participation, and guaranteed. Most SBA loans are not really loans at all but loan guarantees.
   - SBA loan programs include the LowDoc (for "low documentation") Loan Program, the FA$TRAK program, the CAPline program, the Export Working Capital Program, the International Trade Program, the Section 504 Certified Development Company (CDC) program, microloans, the Minority and Women's Prequalified Loan program, the 8(a) program and disaster loans, the Small Business Innovation Research (SBIR) program, and the Small Business Technology Transfer (STTR) program.

5. Discuss state and local development programs.
   - In an attempt to develop businesses that create jobs and economic growth, most states offer small business financing programs, usually in the form

of loans, loan guarantees, and venture capital funds.

6 Discuss valuable methods of financing growth and expansion internally with bootstrap financing.

◆ Small business owners can find important sources of capital inside their firms. By factoring accounts receivable, leasing equipment instead of buying it, and minimizing costs, business owners can stretch their supplies of capital.

7 Describe how to avoid becoming a victim of a loan scam.

◆ Business owners hungry for capital for their growing businesses can be easy targets for con artists running loan scams. Entrepreneurs should watch out for promises of "guaranteed" loans, credit, or investments; up-front fees, pitches over the World Wide Web; and Nigerian-letter scams.

Discussion Questions

1. Define debt financing. What role do commercial banks play in providing debt financing to small businesses?
2. Outline and briefly describe the major types of short-, intermediate-, and long-term loans offered by commercial banks.
3. Explain how asset-based financing works. What is the most common method of asset-based financing? What are the advantages and the disadvantages of using this method of financing?
4. What is trade credit? How important is it as a source of debt financing to small firms?
5. What types of loans do savings and loan associations specialize in? Describe the two types of loans extended by insurance companies.
6. How do zero coupon bonds differ from standard bonds?
7. What function do SBICs serve? How does an SBIC operate?
8. Briefly describe the loan programs offered by the following:
   a. The Economic Development Administration
   b. The Farmer's Home Administration
   c. The Department of Housing and Urban Development
   d. Local development companies
9. Explain the three basic types of loans the Small Business Administration offers. Which type is most popular?
10. Outline the basic programs available to entrepreneurs from the Small Business Administration.

11. How can a firm employ bootstrap financing to stretch its capital supply?
12. How does a factor operate? What are the advantages and disadvantages of using a factor? What kinds of businesses typically use factors?

Step Into the Real World

1. Visit a local small business owner and ask the following questions:
   a. How did you raise your starting capital? What percent did you supply on your own? What percent was debt capital and what percent was equity capital?
   b. Which of the sources of funds described in this chapter does the owner use? Are the funds used to finance fixed, working, or growth capital needs?
2. After a personal visit, prepare a short report on a nearby factor's operation. How is the value of the accounts receivable purchased determined? Who bears the loss on uncollected accounts?
3. Interview the administrator of a financial institution program that offers a method of financing with which you are unfamiliar, and prepare a short report on its method of operation.
4. Go to the Small Business Adminstration's World Wide Web site at <http://www.sba/gov>. Choose one of the loan programs the SBA offers and prepare a one-page report on its purpose and method of operation.
5. Contact your state's business development board and prepare a report on the financial assistance programs it offers.
6. Develop a plan for establishing a microloan enterprise in your community. Which community groups, banks, and individuals would you approach for help? How would you establish lending criteria? For more information, contact:
   ◆ The Association for Enterprise Opportunity, 304 N. Michigan Avenue, Suite 804, Chicago, IL 60601 (312) 357-0177
   ◆ The Self-Employment Learning Project, the Aspen Institute, P.O. Box 222, Queenstown, MD 21658 <http://www.aspeninst.org/dir/polpro/SELP/SELP1.html>
   ◆ The U.S. Small Business Administration, Washington, D.C. (SBA Answer Desk 1-800-827-5722) <http://www.sbaonline.sba.gov/financing/indexloans.html>
   ◆ Trickle Up, 54 Riverside Drive, New York, N.Y. 10024 (212) 362-7958 <http://www.igc.apc.org/ia/mb/trickle.html>

- ◆ ACCION International, 235 Havemeyer Street, Brooklyn, N.Y. 11211 (718) 599-5170 <http://www.accion.org/>
7. Contact a woman entrepreneur and interview her about how she raised the capital to launch her business. Where did she find the capital? What special problems did she encounter? Was she denied financing from some sources? If so, for what reasons? Did she see evidence of discrimination in her search for capital simply because she is a woman? Prepare a brief summary of your interview.

Take It to the Net

Visit the Scarborough/Zimmerer home page at
www.prenhall.com/scarbzim
for updated information, on-line resources, and Web-based exercises.

Endnotes

1. Cynthia E. Griffin, "Something Borrowed," *Entrepreneur*, February 1997, p. 26; Business Lenders, Inc. <http://www.businesslenders.com/q&a.htm>.
2. Michelle L. Kezar, "Big Lending to Small Business," *Cross Sections*, Spring 1995, p. 28.
3. Karen Axelton, "Don't Bank on It," *Business Start-Ups*, May 1998, p. 116.
4. Rick Brooks, "Small Banks Lead the Way," *Wall Street Journal*, February 28, 1996, p. S3.
5. Daniel M. Clark, "Banks and Bankability," *Venture*, September 1989, p. 29.
6. Wirt M. Cook, "The Buddy System," *Entrepreneur*, November 1992, p. 53.
7. Rollene Saal, "Hooking the Big One," *Your Company*, Spring 1994, pp. 18–21.
8. Cook, "The Buddy System."
9. Jill Andresky Fraser, "Rest Them (or Be Told to)," *Inc.*, May 1994, p. 153.
10. Carolyn Campbell, "Hidden Treasures," *Business Start-Ups*, October 1997, pp. 8–10.
11. Gianna Jacobson, "The Money Hunter Mindset," *Success*, November 1996, pp. 34–42.
12. Marcia Bradford, "Easy Money," *Entrepreneur*, July 1993, pp. 188–191.
13. Jacobson, "The Money Hunter Mindset."
14. Robert A. Mamis, "Lender of Last Resort," *Inc.*, May 1987, pp. 149–150.
15. Teri Agins, "Asset-Based Lending to Firms Has Found Favor with Banks," *Wall Street Journal*, November 5, 1984, p. 35.
16. Bruce G. Posner, "Money for Raw Materials," *Inc.*, October 1993, p. 39.
17. "Financing Small Business," *Small Business Reporter*, c3, p. 9.
18. Timothy Middleton, "When the Bank Says No," *Your Company*, Fall 1993, p. 33.
19. Sharon Nelton, "Niche Lenders Hit the Target," *Nation's Business*, April 1998, pp. 44–45.
20. Jeannie Mandelker, "When a Commercial Finance Firm Makes Sense," *Your Company*, February/March 1997, pp. 14–15.
21. Cynthia E. Griffin, "Breaking the Bank," *Entrepreneur*, March 1998, pp. 110–115.
22. Joan C. Szabo, "A Capital Option: Finance Companies," *Nation's Business*, July 1992, p. 42.
23. Joan Pryde, "Lending a Hand with Financing," *Nation's Business*, January 1998, pp. 53–59.
24. Mandelker, "When a Commercial Finance Firm Makes Sense," pp. 14–15.
25. Jacobson, "The Money Hunter Mindset."
26. Georgette Jasen, "Pros and Cons of Borrowing from Your Broker," *Wall Street Journal*, April 21, 1993, p. Cl.
27. Scott McMurray, "Personal Loans from Brokers Offer Low Rates," *Wall Street Journal*, January 7, 1986, p. 31.
28. Jill Bettner, "Brokers Begin Pushing Margin Loans—But Critics Say Borrowers Should Beware," *Wall Street Journal*, August 26, 1987, p. 19.
29. Bruce G. Posner, "Insurance Companies Move into Smaller Deals," *Inc.*, October 1991, pp. 165–166.
30. The Center for Credit Union Research <http://www.wisc.edu/bschool/cu/cufaq.html>.
31. Bruce G. Posner, "Tapping a Credit Union," *Inc.*, December 1992, p. 35.
32. Janice Fioravante, "Find Freedom with Bondage," *Success*, January 1998, pp. 26–27, 88; Iridium LLC <http://www.iridium.com/>.
33. Bruce G. Posner, "A Bond by Any Other Name," *Inc.*, November 1983, p. 74.
34. Udayan Gupta, "Small Firms Turn to Composite Bonds," *Wall Street Journal*, May 25, 1991, p. B2; Bruce G. Posner, "Industrial Revenue Bonds," *Inc.*, August 1992, p. 85.
35. Robert McGough, "Money to Burn," *FW*, June 26, 1990, p. 18.
36. Small Business Administration <http://www.sba.gov>; Joan Pryde, "A Lending Niche Helps Small Firms," *Nation's Business*, February 1998, pp. 52–53; David R. Evanson, "Bucking the System," *Entrepreneur*, June 1998, pp. 77–81.
37. Jeff Wuorio, "Go on an Equity Hunt to Fund Expansion," *Your Company* (Forecast 1998), pp. 42–48.
38. Wuorio, "Go on an Equity Hunt to Fund Expansion"; Small Business Administration <http://www.sba.gov>.
39. Port Jervis, N.Y. <http://www.portjervisny.org//stateofc.htm>.
40. University of Minnesota, Duluth <http://www.d.umn.edu/~jjacobs/fr1a.html>.
41. "Places That Give Money Away," *Venture*, June 1980, pp. 22–23.
42. Sharon Nelton, "Capital Ideas for Financing," *Nation's Business*, September 1996, pp. 18–27.

43. Marsha Gilbert, "Small Loans Are Big Business," *Upstate Business*, January 26, 1997, pp. 1, 4–5.

44. Philip Lader, "Techin' It to the Streets," *Entrepreneur*, June 1995, p. 176; National Institute of Standards and Technology <http://www.nist.gov>.

45. National Institute of Standards of Technology <http://ts.nist.gov/ts/htdocs/200/204/97abst.htm>.

46. Joseph R. Mancuso, "The ABCs of Getting Money from the SBA," *Your Company*, June/July 1996, pp. 54–59.

47. Pryde, "Lending a Hand with Financing"; Cynthia E. Griffin, "SBA Treasure Chest," *Business Start-Ups*, January 1996, pp. 38–41; Joseph R. Mancuso, "The ABCs of Getting Money from the SBA," *Your Company*, June/July 1996, pp. 54–59; Meg Whittemore, "The Lowdown on LowDoc," *Nation's Business*, June 1995, p. 70; Kathleen Upton Finch, "Making Fast (Paper) Work of Business-Loan Applications, *Success*, December 1998, p. 77; Small Business Administration <http://www.sba.gov>; University of Minnesota, Duluth <http://www.d.umn.edu/~jjacobs/fr1a.html>; Karen Roy, "SBA Loans from A to Z," *Business Start-Ups*, August 1997, pp. 52–55.

48. Pryde, "Lending a Hand with Financing."

49. Erika Kotite, "Fed Funds," *Entrepreneur*, February 1993, p. 122.

50. Ibid.

51. Jesse H. Sweet, "A Potential Crunch in SBA Loans," *Nation's Business*, August 1993, p. 28.

52. Sharon Nelton, "Capital Ideas for Financing," *Nation's Business*, September 1996, pp. 18–27.

53. Susan Hodges, "SBA Microloans Fuel Big Ideas," *Nation's Business*, February 1997, pp. 34–35; Fraser, "How to Finance Anything," p. 40.

54. J. Tol Broome, "SBA Gives Women a Foot in the Door," *Nation's Business*, December 1997, pp. 44–45; Janean Chun, "Opportunity Knocks," *Entrepreneur*, February 1997, pp. 46–47; Small Business Administration, <http://www.sba.gov/financing/frprequal.html>.

55. Broome, "SBA Gives Women a Foot in the Door."

56. Jeanne Saddler, "Flood-Hit Businesses May Get More Government Help," *Wall Street Journal*, August 17, 1994, p. B2.

57. M. John Storey, "Triple Your Growth Power," *Success*, June 1996, p. 14.

58. Udayan Gupta and Brent Bowers, "States and Localities Help Small Firms Get New Capital," *Wall Street Journal*, April 23, 1992, p. B2.

59. Bruce J. Blechman, "The High Cost of Credit," *Entrepreneur*, January 1993, pp. 22–25.

60. Janean Chun, "Passing the Buck," *Entrepreneur*, May 1997, p. 44.

61. Donald J. Korn, "Factoring for Financial Success," *Your Company*, August/September 1996, pp. 14–15.

62. Karin Moeller, "Where Credit's Due," *Business Start-Ups*, January 1998, p. 4; Rodney Ho, "Banking on Plastic," *Wall Street Journal*, March 9, 1998, pp. A1, A10.

63. Rodney Ho, "Credit-Card Use to Finance Business Is Soaring, Says Survey of Small Firms," *Wall Street Journal*, September 25, 1997, p. B2.

64. Sharon Nelton, "Women Entrepreneurs Make Capital Gains," *Nation's Business*, January 1997, p. 8; "Banks Are Friendlier to Women," *Kiplinger's Personal Finance Magazine*, July 1997, p. 14.

65. Bruce J. Blechman, "Yankee Ingenuity," *Entrepreneur*, November 1991, pp. 26–31.

66. Jill Andresky Fraser, "Business Owners, Beware!" *Inc.*, January 1997, pp. 86–87.

Location, Layout, and Physical Facilities

We've moved our company so many times that we consider relocation one of our core competencies.

—*The president of a small medical services company*

There's no place like home. There's no place like home. There's no place like home.

—*Dorothy, in* The Wizard of Oz

Upon completion of this chapter, you will be able to

1 Explain the stages in the location decision.

2 Describe the location criteria for retail and service businesses.

3 Outline the basic location options for retail and service businesses.

4 Explain the site selection process for manufacturers.

5 Discuss the benefits of locating a start-up company in a business incubator.

6 Describe the criteria used to analyze the layout and design considerations of a building, including the Americans with Disabilities Act.

7 Explain the principles of effective layouts for retailers, service businesses, and manufacturers.

8 Evaluate the advantages and disadvantages of building, buying, and leasing a building.

---

*F*ew decisions have as big and as lasting an impact on a business as the entrepreneur's choice of location. The location decision plays a major role in many aspects of a company's life—from its cost structure and the quality of its workforce to the size of its customer base. Therefore, choosing a location is not a decision that entrepreneurs should take lightly. It requires a substantial amount of research and analysis. Investing time and resources before deciding where to locate will produce benefits many times over.

491

Unfortunately, many entrepreneurs never consider locations beyond their own hometowns. Failing to look beyond their "comfort zone" prevents them from discovering locations that might be better suited to their business and that would improve their chances for success. The "secret" to selecting the ideal location goes back to knowing who a company's target customers are (recall chapter 6) and then finding a site that makes it most convenient for those customers to do business with the company. That requires research. *For instance, before former science teacher Myron Michaels opened a retail optical store in New York City, he invested time researching potential locations and matching them against his target audience. "I went down to the Bureau of Records and worked on the computer, calling up demographic data, foot-traffic patterns, and that sort of thing," he says. One site stood out above the others. It offered easy access to a large number of middle-class customers who were young but had significant levels of disposable income—just the type of customer to whom Michaels was looking to sell his fashionable eyewear. Plus, he saw the potential spillover benefits from the cluster of nearby clothing retailers that attracted customers who were looking for quality, stylish merchandise. His research also proved that as the U.S. population ages its need for corrective lenses will increase. And, he discovered that young people consider eyewear to be an extension of their wardrobes and are spending money on it as a fashion accessory. Although a competitor had a store two blocks down the street, Michaels considered it to be far enough away that it would not reduce his customer traffic flow enough to matter. The location offered one more major benefit: a large office building across the street filled with employees whose insurance coverage would pay for glasses and contact lenses at Michaels's store, Sight on Seventh.*[1]

7he Logic of Location: From Region to State to City to Site

◆ Explain the stages in the location decision.

An entrepreneur's ultimate location goal is to locate the company at a site that will maximize the likelihood of success. The more entrepreneurs invest in researching potential locations, the higher is the probability that they will find the spot that is best suited for their company. The trick is to keep an open mind about where the best location might be. Just as with most decisions affecting a business, the customer drives the choice of the "best" location for a business. Choosing an appropriate location is essentially a matter of selecting the site that best serves the needs of the business's target market. Is there a location where the new business will have the greatest number of customers that need, want, and can afford the products or services your business provides? The better entrepreneurs know and understand their target customers' characteristics, demographic profiles, and buying behavior, the greater are their chances of identifying the right location from which to serve them.

The search for the ideal location involves research that entrepreneurs can conduct in libraries, by telephone, in person, and on the World Wide Web. The logic of location selection is to begin with a broad regional search and then to systematically narrow the focus of the site selection process (see Figure 15.1).

SELECTING THE REGION

The first step in selecting the best location is to focus at the regional level. Which region of the country has the characteristics necessary for a new business to succeed? Common requirements include rapid growth in the population of a certain age group, rising disposable incomes, the existence of specific infrastructure, a nonunion environment, and low operating costs.

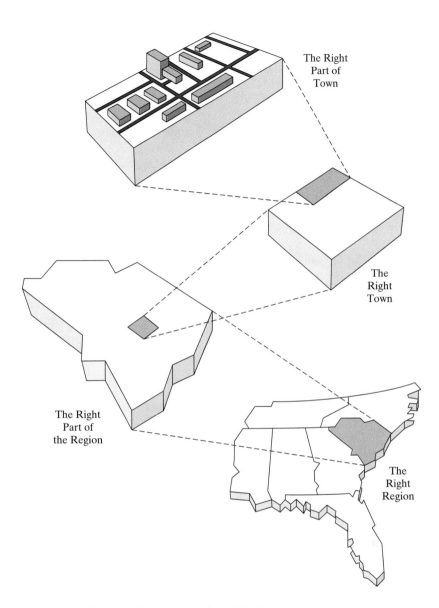

Figure 15.1 The Identification of Regional and Local Market Areas SOURCE: From Dale M. Lewison and M. Wayne DeLozier, *Retailing* (Columbus, OH: Merrill/Macmillan Publishing, 1984), p. 341. Used with permission.

At the broadest level of the location decision, entrepreneurs usually identify regions of the country that are experiencing substantial growth. Every year, many popular business publications prepare reports on which regions of the nation are growing, which are stagnant, and which are declining. Studying shifts in population and industrial growth will give an entrepreneur an idea of where the action is—and isn't. For example, how large is the population? How fast is it growing? What is the demographic makeup of the overall population? Which segments are growing fastest? Slowest? What is the population's income? Is it increasing or decreasing? Are other businesses moving into the region? If so, what kind of businesses? In general, owners want to avoid dying regions; these regions simply cannot provide a broad base of potential customers. A firm's customers will be people, businesses, and industry, and if it is to be successful, the business must locate in a place that is convenient to them.

One of the first stops entrepreneurs should make when conducting a regional evaluation is the U.S. Census Bureau. The Census Bureau produces many publications to aid entrepreneurs in their search for the best location. The Census Bureau publishes a monthly newsletter, *Census and You*, which is especially helpful to business owners. In addition, the Census Bureau makes most of the information contained in its valuable data banks available to entrepreneurs through its easy-to-use World Wide Web site <http:/www.census.gov/>. At this site, entrepreneurs can find vital demographic information for specific locations. Sorting through each report's 92 fields, entrepreneurs can prepare customized profiles of the sites they are considering. Oregon State University also has compiled much of the data from the Census Bureau, the Bureau of Economic Analysis, the National Center for Education Statistics, and the Mesa Group into the World Wide Web's Government Information Sharing Project <http:/govinfo.kerr.orst.edu/>. This Web site gives users an easy and powerful system for mining information from the vast and valuable resources the U.S. government has collected and compiled. These WWW resources give entrepreneurs instant access to important site location information that only a few years ago would have taken many hours of intense research to compile.

The Small Business Administration also has valuable aids to help you throughout your location search. Some of these are *Practical Use of Government Statistics, Using Census Data to Select a Store Site*, and *Using Census Data in Small Plant Marketing. American Demographics* magazine has two valuable booklets also: *The 1990 Census: The Counting of America* and *A Researcher's Guide to the 1990 Census.*

Four other helpful publications merit mention as well. *Sales and Marketing Management's Survey of Buying Power,* published annually, provides a detailed breakdown of population, retail sales, spendable income, and other characteristics for census regions, states, metropolitan areas, countries, and cities. The survey includes highlights and summary sections, analyses of changes in metro markets, and summaries of sales of certain merchandise. The *Editor and Publisher Market Guide* is similar to the *Survey of Buying Power*, but provides additional information on markets. The guide includes detailed information on key cities. *Rand McNally's Commercial Atlas and Marketing Guide* reports on more than 128,000 places in the United States, many of which are not available through census reports. It includes 11 economic indicators for every major geographic market; tables showing population trends, income, buying power, trade, and manufacturing activity; and large, cross-reference maps. Its format makes it easy to collect large amounts of valuable data on any region in the country (and specific areas within that region). The *Zip Code Atlas and Market Planner* is an extremely useful location and market-planning tool. It combines a breakdown of zip codes (often the basis of psychographic customer profiles) with maps featuring physical features such as mountains, rivers, and major highways. The planner contains loose-leaf, full-color maps, each with a reusable acetate overlay showing five-digit zip code boundaries. It includes detailed maps of all 50 states, plus 85 specific inset maps and 11 vicinity maps.

The Small Business Administration's Small Business Development Center (SBDC) program also offers location analysis assistance to entrepreneurs. Some 600 centers nationwide provide training, counseling, research, and other specialized assistance to entrepreneurs and existing business owners on a wide variety of subjects—all at no charge! They are an important resource, especially for entrepreneurs who may not have access to a computer. (To locate the SBDC nearest you, contact the SBA office in your state or go to the SBA's home page at <http://www.sba.gov/>.

A region's population characteristics and growth rates are important factors in the location decision, but they are not the only factors entrepreneurs must consider. For many businesses, especially manufacturers, cost considerations are driving factors in the location decision. One location consultant says that selecting the proper location for a manufacturing plant can yield a 5 percent to 10 percent increase in its profitability! "Yet," he says, "location is a strategic tool employed only marginally by CEOs. They fail to capitalize on a unique competitive advantage: enhanced operational positions and dramatically improved market accessibility."[2]

In other cases, a company's location decision stems from the availability of particular raw materials or natural resources. Locating near those materials or resources is a requirement if a company is to avoid incurring high transportation costs of raw materials. *For instance, when a maker of photographic plates used in the printing industry was looking for a location for its new plant, company managers focused their analysis on regions offering two crucial features: a large lake that would offer the plentiful supply of water necessary for its manufacturing process and a highly skilled, nonunion workforce to keep costs low and productivity high.*

The task of analyzing potential locations—gathering and synthesizing data on a wide variety of demographic and geographic variables—is one ideally suited for a computer. In fact, a growing number of entrepreneurs are relying on **geographic information systems (GISs),** powerful software programs that combine map drawing with database management capability, to pinpoint the ideal location for their business. These programs enable users to search through virtually *any* database and plot the relevant findings on a detailed map of the country, an individual state, a specific city, or even a single city block. The visual display highlights what otherwise would be indiscernible business trends. "The most significant benefit of GIS may be its ability to take the results of an analysis and display them in a visually powerful way," says the head of one GIS consulting firm.[3] The days when managers stuck colored pins into maps taped on a wall to analyze population characteristics are gone!

Using a GIS program, an entrepreneur could plot her existing customer base on a map, with various colors representing the different population densities. Then she could zoom in on the areas with the greatest concentration of customers, mapping a detailed view of Zip Code borders or even city streets. Geographic information system street files originate in the U.S. Census Department's TIGER (Topological Integrated Geographic Encoding Referencing) file, which contains map information broken down for every street in the country and detailed block statistics for the 345 largest urban areas. In essence, TIGER is a computerized map of the entire United States, and, when linked with a database, gives small business owners incredible power to pinpoint existing and potential customers. The accompanying In the Footsteps of an Entrepreneur feature describes how one entrepreneur uses a GIS program to determine the best locations for his company's franchised restaurants.

SELECTING THE STATE

Every state has a business development office to recruit new businesses to that state. Even though the publications produced by these offices will be biased in favor of locating in that state, they still are an excellent source of facts and can help entrepreneurs assess the business climate in each state. Some of the key issues to explore include the laws, regulations, and taxes that govern businesses and any incentives or investment credits the state may offer to businesses locating there. Other factors to consider include proximity to markets, proximity to raw materials, quantity and quality of the labor supply, general business climate, and wage rates.

Proximity to Markets. Locating close to markets that manufacturing firms plan to serve is extremely critical when the cost of transportation of finished goods is high relative to their value. Locating near customers is necessary to remain competitive. Service firms often find that proximity to their clients is essential. If a business is involved in repairing equipment used in a specific industry, it should be located where that industry is concentrated. The more specialized the business or the greater the relative cost of transporting the product to the customer, the more likely it is that proximity to the market will be of critical importance in the location decision. *After German automaker BMW chose upstate South Carolina as the site for its first assembly plant in North America, the counties near the plant immediately became the locations of choice for many BMW suppliers. Because BMW wanted quick deliveries with minimal inventory investment, many of its suppliers decided to set up plants close to the assembly operation.*

Proximity to Needed Raw Materials. A business that requires raw materials that are difficult or expensive to transport may need a location near the source of those raw materials. For example, fish-processing plants are almost always located close to ports. Some companies locate close to the source of raw materials because of the cost of transporting heavy low-value materials over long distances. *For instance, the owner of a small company making kitty litter chose a location near a large vein of kaolin, a highly absorbent clay and the basic raw material in his finished product. Transporting the heavy, low-value material over long distances would be impractical—and unprofitable.*

In situations in which bulk or weight is not a factor, locating close to suppliers can facilitate quick deliveries and reduce inventory holding costs. The value of products and materials, their cost of transportation, and their unique functions all interact in determining how close a business needs to be to its sources of supply.

Labor Supply. Two distinct factors are important for entrepreneurs analyzing the labor supply in a potential location: the number of workers available in the area and their level of education, training, and experience. Business owners want to know how many qualified people are available in the area to do the work required in the business. The size of the local labor pool determines a company's ability to fill jobs at reasonable wages. However, employment and labor cost statistics can be misleading if a company needs people with specific qualifications. Some states have attempted to attract industry with the promise of cheap labor. Unfortunately, businesses locating in those states found exactly what the term implied: unskilled, low-wage labor. Unskilled laborers can be difficult to train.

Knowing the exact nature of the labor needed and preparing job descriptions and job specifications in advance will help business owners determine whether there is a good match between their company and the available labor pool. Checking educational statistics in the state to determine the number of graduates in relevant fields of study will provide an idea of the local supply of qualified workers. Such planning will result in choosing a location with a steady source of quality workers.

For instance, North Carolina's Research Triangle, an area defined by the surrounding communities of Raleigh, Durham, and Chapel Hill, has become a mecca for companies in high-tech industries such as computer software, semiconductors, communications, drugs, and biotech because of the area's pool of highly skilled labor. Major colleges such as Duke University, the University of North Carolina, and North Carolina State University funnel talented graduates trained in fields such as virtual reality and market research into local companies. *Bill Stealey, founder of Interactive Management, a company making electronic games, chose the Research Triangle from which to launch his business because he found there just what his company needed: a computer-literate workforce and a pool of 3-D computer graphics experts. He was also impressed with the area's climate and the large number of golf courses it offered. "I looked at California, and it was congested," he recalls. "I flew to Route 128 (another hub of high-tech activity near Boston), and it snowed."*[4]

Business Climate. What is the state's overall attitude toward your kind of business? Has it passed laws that impose restrictions on the way a company can operate? Does the state impose a corporate income tax? Is there an inventory tax? Are there "blue laws" that prohibit certain business activity on Sundays? Does the state offer small business support programs or financial assistance to entrepreneurs? Some states are more "small business friendly" than

IN THE FOOTSTEPS OF AN ENTREPRENEUR

Mapping the Way to Success

Sonny Tillman opened his first barbecue restaurant in Gainesville, Florida, in 1968, offering customers a hearty meal for an average of about $3.50, compared with as much as $10 for some of his competitors. The business grew, and soon Tillman was selling Sonny's Bar-B-Q franchises across the Southeast. The company now has more than 1,100 franchisees, but selling franchises isn't always easy. Franchisees pay a $25,000 franchise fee and 2.5 percent of their gross revenues to Sonny's in exchange for the restaurant's name and business system. Franchisees paying that much expect their businesses to be successful and profitable, and that means that Sonny's has to define its territories properly and put restaurants in the right locations. Giving franchisees territories that lack the customer bases or the demographic traits to make their barbecue restaurants a success means setting them up for failure—something no franchisor can afford to do. Franchisors such as Sonny's also have to be extremely careful about locating restaurants too close to avoid having one cannibalize the other's sales. Oversaturating a market with franchises is a sure-fire ticket to a franchisee lawsuit. "If you put one restaurant in the wrong place, it doesn't just disrupt one," says Michael Turner, Sonny's director of franchise services. "It can kill off two."

Because defining the right territories and selecting the right locations for restaurants within those territories is crucial to Sonny's Bar-B-Q's success, the company is not willing to leave those decisions to chance. Several years ago, Sonny's began using geographic information systems (GISs) to guide territory and location decisions. Using GISs, Sonny's can superimpose on a map a color-coded representation of virtually any characteristic of the area's population—from income levels and age breakdowns to traffic counts and eating habits. The ability to display complex combinations of data in a simple, visual way makes GIS the perfect tool for selecting and evaluating potential sites for new restaurants. "Combining maps and data makes it easy for people to quickly understand a lot of information," says the head of one marketing research company.

Managers look for regions where people already are familiar with barbecue (primarily the South) but that do not have a high concentration of competing barbecue restaurants. They also cull specific data from the Census Bureau's database and then combine it with census maps to get a picture (literally!) of a site's potential for a new restaurant. The company's analysis includes a traffic count at the site, the area's total population, its population distribution and density, and the median

age and household incomes of its residents. The GIS compiles all of the data and superimposes them graphically onto a map of a site. With just a few mouse clicks, Turner can display a map showing each of the population characteristics separately, or he can show them in any combination. Turner can set the minimum criteria for each characteristic and let the GIS display the areas that meet those criteria, or he can outline a geographic area the company is interested in developing and the system will display the traits of the population in it.

Turner establishes strict criteria for locations. "We try not to have restaurants closer than seven miles from each other," he says. "In each new area we open, we like to have . . . territories with populations of 70,000 that match the characteristics we look for." Once Turner finds an area that meets the basic criteria, he then analyzes specific sites within that area to determine whether it will be able to support a franchise.

Putting together a smoothly functioning GIS was neither easy nor inexpensive for a small company such as Sonny's Bar-B-Q. Says Turner, "We developed the whole system, including the database, for $30,000." Although some of the money went for hardware, the majority of it paid for GIS software and the database of information that drives the entire system. For what the company gets, however, its GIS is a bargain at that price. "Five years ago, it was impossible to do this," says Turner, referring to the fact that only the largest companies with the most powerful computers could handle such a large volume of information. "If you did this work the traditional way, with a large computer, it would cost from $200,000 to $500,000." Sonny's uses a desktop computer that costs about $2,500 and a basic GIS package from MapInfo selling for about $1,300.

In just a short period of time, the system has paid for itself many times over. "We [recently] franchised a county in Florida," says Turner, "and the original projection was that it would hold four restaurants. After we ran the mapping program, we found out it would hold eight. We ended up franchising on the basis of seven. Just that one [application] has paid back everything we've put in over this year, and it's an ongoing payoff." Although many companies for whom finding the right location is a key to success might consider GIS a luxury, others disagree. One location consultant explains, "It can be absolutely essential. You can't afford to make major investments that deal with extensive populations without having that kind of information or being able to do that kind of analysis."

---

1. What advantages does GIS give Sonny's in franchising?

2. What other types of businesses would benefit from using a GIS program? What other business applications can you think of for GIS? Explain.

SOURCE: Adapted from Tony Seidman, "You Gotta Know the Territory," *Profit*, October 1996, pp. 21–24. ◆

others. *For instance, Entrepreneur magazine recently named Minnesota's Minneapolis/St. Paul as one of the best cities for small businesses, citing its positive attitude toward growing and developing small companies as a major asset. Many factors make the Twin Cities a desirable location: its diversified industrial base, a strong base of private investors anxious to invest in promising small companies, one of the nation's highest SBA loan rates, and several state and local government support systems offering entrepreneurial assistance and advice. The area also boasts the Mall of America, the country's largest retail mall, and an innovative plan known as "Block E" for revitalizing the city's downtown riverfront areas will create new opportunities for small businesses in the future.*[5] Table 15.1 illustrates a matrix designed to help entrepreneurs score potential locations they are considering. A matrix such as this helps entrepreneurs compare states "head-to-head" to determine the most suitable location for their company.

Wage Rates. Wage rates provide another measure for comparison among states. Entrepreneurs should determine the wage rates for jobs that are related to their particular industry or company. In addition to published government surveys, local newspapers will give entrepreneurs an idea of the wages local companies must pay to attract workers. What trends have emerged in wage rates over time? How does the rate of increase in wage rates compare among states? Another factor influencing wage rates is the level of union activity in a state. How much union organizing activity has the state seen within the past two years? Is it increasing or decreasing? Which industries have unions targeted in the recent past?

Gateway 2000, a mail-order personal computer manufacturer offering high-performance hardware at bargain-basement prices, uses its location to gain a competitive edge in a hotly competitive industry. With constant downward pressure on computer prices, Gateway must keep its costs low. The company's location, North Sioux City, South Dakota (not exactly the heart of Silicon Valley) is one variable in its low-cost formula. South Dakota has no state corporate or personal income taxes, and the low cost of living appeals to employees. Gateway's starting wage for assembly workers—a bargain by national standards—is quite attractive in the local market. Most of the company's workers come from Iowa, known for the quality of its schools. The company's midcontinent location also keeps shipping costs low for

Table 15.1 State Evaluation Matrix

Location Criterion	Weight	Score	State Weighted Score (weight × score)		
			California	Oregon	Washington
Quality of labor force		1 2 3 4 5			
Wage rates		1 2 3 4 5			
Union activity		1 2 3 4 5			
Energy costs		1 2 3 4 5			
Tax burden		1 2 3 4 5			
Educational and training assistance		1 2 3 4 5			
Start-up incentives		1 2 3 4 5			
Quality of life		1 2 3 4 5			
Availability of raw materials		1 2 3 4 5			
Other		1 2 3 4 5			
Other		1 2 3 4 5			
Total score					

Assign to each location criterion a weight that reflects its relative importance. Then score each state on a scale of 1 (low) to 5 (high). Calculate the weighted score (weight × score) for each state. Finally, add up the total weighted score for each state. The state with the highest total weighted score is the best location for your business.

a company selling computers nationwide, and managers are pleased with their employees' Midwestern work ethic.[6]

SELECTING THE CITY

Population Trends and Density. An entrepreneur should know more about a city and its various neighborhoods than do the people who live there. By analyzing population and other demographic data, an entrepreneur can examine a city in detail, and the location decision becomes more than "a shot in the dark." Studying the characteristics of a city's residents, including population sizes and density, growth trends, family size, age breakdowns, education, income levels, job categories, gender, religion, race, and nationality gives an entrepreneur the facts she needs to make an informed location decision. In fact, using only basic census data, entrepreneurs can determine the value of the homes in an area, how many rooms they contain, how many bedrooms they contain, what percentage of the population own their homes, and how much residents' monthly rental or mortgage payments are. Imagine how useful such information would be to someone about to launch a bed and bath shop!

A company's location should match the market for its products or services, and assembling a demographic profile will tell an entrepreneur how well a particular site measures up to her target market's profile. For instance, an entrepreneur planning to open a fine china shop would likely want specific information on family income, size, age, and education. Such a shop would need to be in an area where people appreciate the product and have the discretionary income to purchase it.

Trends or shifts in population components may have more meaning than total population trends. For example, if a city's population is aging, its disposable income may be decreasing and the city may be gradually dying. On the other hand, a city may be experiencing rapid growth in the population of high-income, professional young people. For example, Atlanta, where the average age of inhabitants is 29, has seen an explosion of businesses aimed at young people with rising incomes and hearty appetites for consumption.

Population density is another important factor for many small businesses. Nearly two-thirds of Americans live in high-density, urbanized areas, although these areas make up just 1.7 percent of the nation's land area.[7] For owners of businesses that depend on high traffic for their success such as restaurants, convenience stores, and retail shops, determining a city's **population density** (the number of people per square mile) can be crucial. Knowing the population density within a few miles of a potential location can give entrepreneurs a clear picture of whether the city can support their business and can even help them develop the appropriate marketing strategies to draw customers. Fitness club owners have discovered that population density is one of the most important factors in selecting a suitable location. Experience has taught them that customers are willing to drive only so far to visit a fitness club. "If you don't have enough population [density] to support your facility within an eight- to ten-minute driving radius, it doesn't matter how good your services are," says one consultant.[8] Information on population density and other important demographic characteristics is available from magazines such as *American Demographics* <http://www.demographics.com/Publications/AD/index.htm> and from market research companies.

Competition. For some retailers, locating near competitors makes sense because having similar businesses located near one another may increase traffic flow. **Clustering,** as this location strategy is known, works well for products for which customers are most likely to comparison shop. For instance, in many cities, auto dealers locate next to one another in a "motor mile," trying to create a shopping magnet for customers. The convenience of being able to shop for dozens of brands of cars all within a few hundred yards of one another draws customers from a sizable trading area. Of course, this strategy has limits. Overcrowding of businesses of the same type in an area can create an undesirable impact on the profitability of all competing firms. Consider the specific nature of the competing businesses in the area. Do they offer the same quality merchandise or comparable services? The products or services of a business may be superior to those that competitors presently offer, giving it the potential to create a competitive edge.

Entrepreneur Kevin Stamper knew that he wanted to launch a new airline that targeted business travelers—those frequent fliers who are the core of every airline's business—but he knew he would have to find exactly the right location if his company was to succeed. After scouring the entire country, Stamper set his sights on Detroit as the home of Pro Air Inc. because it gave his company the ability to create a competitive edge in several ways. First, the airline market there was dominated by Northwest Airlines, whose fares in Detroit were among the highest charged by any airline in the country. His research revealed that passengers there were displeased with the air fares they were paying and with the level of service they received. Second, Northwest operated out of Detroit Metro Airport, which is 20 minutes out of town. However, Detroit offered Stamper an alternative, Detroit City Airport, which is 14 miles closer to the downtown area and to the offices of business travelers working for companies such as General Motors, Chrysler, and Stroh Brewery. Shortly after Pro Air opened, Chrysler shifted its air travel business from Northwest to Pro Air. So far, Stamper's strategy of low fares, cost control, and aggressively targeting business travelers has worked in an industry marked by companies that often fail—largely because he selected the right location.[9]

Studying the size of the market for a product or service and the number of existing competitors will help entrepreneurs determine whether they can capture a sufficiently large market share to earn a profit. Again, Census Bureau reports can be a valuable source of information. The bureau's *County Business Patterns Economic Profile* shows the breakdown of businesses in manufacturing, wholesale, retail, and service categories and estimates companies' annual payrolls and number of employees. The *Economic Census*, which covers 15 million businesses and is published in years that end in 2 and 7, gives an overview of the businesses in an area, including their sales (or other measure of output), employment, payroll, and form of organization. It covers eight industry categories including retail, wholesale, service, manufacturing, and construction and gives statistics at not only the national level but also by state, MSA (metropolitan statistical area; the 255 MSAs are subdivided into census tracts), county, places with 2,500 or more inhabitants, and Zip Code. The *Economic Census* is a useful tool for helping entrepreneurs determine whether the areas they are considering as a location are already saturated with competitors.

The Index of Retail Saturation. For retailers, the number of customers in the trading area and the intensity of the competition are essential factors in predicting success. One traditional way to analyze potential sites is to compare them on the basis of the index of retail saturation (IRS), a measure that combines the number of customers in an area, their purchasing power, and the level of competition.[10] The **index of retail saturation (IRS)** is a measure of the potential sales per square foot of store space for a given product within a specific trading area. The index is the ratio of a trading area's sales potential for a particular product or service to its sales capacity:

$$IRS = \frac{C \times RE}{RF}$$

where:

  C = Number of customers in the trading area

  RE = Retail expenditures (the average expenditure per person [$] for the product in the trading area)

  RF = Retail facilities (the total square feet of selling space allocated to the product in the trading area)

This computation is an important one for any retailer to make. Locating in an area already saturated with competitors results in dismal sales volume and often leads to failure.

To illustrate the index of retail saturation, let's suppose that an entrepreneur looking at two sites for a shoe store finds that he needs sales of $175 per square foot to be profitable. Site 1 has a trading area with 25,875 potential customers, each of whom spends an average of $42 on shoes annually; the only competitor in the trading area has 6,000 square feet of selling space. Site 2 has 27,750 potential customers spending an average of $43.50 on shoes annually; two competitors occupy 8,400 square feet of space. The *IRS* of site 1 is:

$$IRS = \frac{25,875 \times 42}{6,000}$$

$$= \$181.12 \text{ sales potential per square foot}$$

The *IRS* of site 2 is:

$$IRS = \frac{27,750 \times 43.50}{8,400}$$

$$= \$143.71 \text{ sales potential per square foot}$$

Although site 2 appears to be more favorable on the surface, site 1 is supported by the index; site 2 fails to meet the minimum standard of $175 per square foot.

The amount of available data on the population of any city or town is staggering. These statistics allow a potential business owner to compare a wide variety of cities or towns and to narrow the choices to those few that warrant further investigation. The mass of data may make it possible to screen out undesirable locations, but it does not make a decision for an entrepreneur. The owner needs to see the locations firsthand. Only by personal investigation will the owner be able to add that intangible factor of intuition into the decision-making process.

Costs. For many businesses, especially manufacturers, the primary force driving site selection is cost. Businesses blossom in areas where costs are low. A study by Patrick Howie of Regional Financial Associates found a link between costs and business and job growth in cities. Using a cost index that incorporates labor and energy costs, local taxes, and office rents, the study found that cities offering the lowest costs experienced the greatest growth in business formations and job creation.[11]

Because they offer a lower cost of doing business, many small cities are attracting companies that are willing to look beyond the perimeters of major metropolitan areas for locations. *Joe Charles, founder of Charles Industries, a small manufacturer of telecommunications and electronics components, has located all seven of his company's manufacturing plants in small towns, where, he says, "we can build a factory for about $15 per square foot as opposed to $80 or $90 [per square foot] in a major metropolitan area."*[12]

A growing number of small cities are establishing special technology zones that offer tax exemptions and reduced fees and licensing costs in an attempt to attract high-tech businesses. *For instance, Winchester, Virginia, a town of 23,000 residents recently established a technology zone in the heart of its 100-acre downtown district that drew in TeleGrafix Communications, an Internet multimedia company.* The cities that have been most successful in transforming Main Street into Cyberstreet are those that offer other amenities that start-up and growing companies need, such as capable workforces, management consulting services, and access to capital. "Tax breaks provide a good field [for a company] to take root in, but you need capital for fertilizer," says Pat Clawson, CEO of TeleGrafix.[13]

Local Laws and Regulations. Before selecting a particular site within a city, small business owners must explore the local zoning laws to determine if there are any ordinances that would place restrictions on business activity or that would prohibit establishing a business altogether. **Zoning** is a system that divides a city or county into small cells or districts to control the use of land, buildings, and sites. Its purpose is to contain similar activities in suitable locations. For instance, one section of a city may be zoned industrial to house manufacturing operations. Before choosing a site, an entrepreneur must explore the zoning regulations governing it to make sure it is not out of bounds. In some cases, an entrepreneur may appeal to the local zoning commission to rezone a site or to grant a **variance** (a special exception to a zoning ordinance), but this tactic is risky and could be devastating if the board disallows the variance.

Compatibility with the Community. One of the intangibles that an entrepreneur can determine only by visiting a particular city is the degree of compatibility a business has with the surrounding community. In other words, a company's image must fit in with the character of the town and the needs and wants of its residents. Consider the costs associated with opening a retail business in an upscale, high-income community. To succeed, the business would have to match the flavor of the surrounding businesses and create an image that would appeal to upscale customers. Rents, along with fixtures and other decor items, would likely be expensive. Is there an adequate markup in your merchandise to justify such costs?

Charles Industries has grown into a $100 million company with more than 1,000 workers by locating its plants in small Midwestern towns that were compatible with its business and with its business philosophy. "When we opened our facilities in these towns," says Joe Charles, "we found a community atmosphere that helped us increase overall productivity, product quality, and customer service while allowing us to meet our financial objectives."[14]

Quality of Life. One of the most important, yet most difficult to measure, criteria for a city is the quality of life it offers. Entrepreneurs have the freedom and the flexibility to locate their companies in cities that suit not only their business needs but also their personal preferences. When choosing locations for their companies, entrepreneurs often consider factors such as cultural events, outdoor activities, entertainment opportunities, safety, and the city's "personality." *Software retailer Egghead Inc. recently moved its corporate headquarters to Spokane, Washington, primarily because of the area's quality of life. A key factor in the company's decision was the desire to locate in an area that gave employees a chance to enjoy the family values that sometimes get lost in larger urban areas.*[15]

Transportation Networks. Manufacturers and wholesalers in particular must investigate the quality of local transportation systems. If a company receives raw materials or ships finished goods by rail, is a location with railroad access available in the city under consideration? What kind of highway access is available? Does the city have smoothly flowing highways that will make transporting materials and products efficient? Will transportation costs be reasonable? In some situations, double or triple handling of merchandise and inventory causes transportation costs to skyrocket. For retailers, the availability of loading and unloading zones is an important feature of a suitable location. Some downtown locations suffer from a lack of space for carriers to unload deliveries of merchandise.

Police and Fire Protection. Does the community in which you plan to locate offer adequate police and fire protection? Inadequate police and fire services will be reflected in the cost of the company's business insurance.

Public Services. The location should be served by some governmental unit that provides water and sewer services, trash and garbage collection, and other necessary utilities. The

Small Is Beautiful—and Profitable

*I*t's an undisputed fact that Ed Deitrick makes the best pizza in West Fairview, Pennsylvania. In fact, Deitrick makes the *only* pizza in West Fairview! Not only is his Uni-Mart store the only place to buy pizza, it is the only *store* in the tiny town (population 1,532).

Deitrick's store in West Fairview embodies the strategy that Uni-Mart founder Henry Sahakian has followed to take his chain of convenience stores to the $330 million level of annual sales. His 416 stores are scattered throughout the mid-Atlantic states, and all of them are located in small (often *really* small) towns. "We're not afraid to go into small towns," says Sahakian, munching on a sandwich in the mini-Arby's franchise operating from the Uni-Mart in Dillsburg, Pennsylvania (population 1,920). "We are their gas station, their restaurant, their newspaper stand."

The typical Uni-Mart carries more than 3,500 items, but local owners and managers can add up to 100 items that are unique to their particular locations. For instance, at a store just outside Harrisburg, Pennsylvania, manager David Snyder carries work gloves for the primarily blue-collar population in the area. At another store located next to the Susquehanna River, the owner carries live bait for local fishermen. Night crawlers cost $2.19 a dozen.

Originally a franchisee of another convenience store chain, Sahakian decided to branch out on his own. As he looked for new locations for his expanding business, he realized that most of the cities and suburban areas he was considering were already saturated with convenience store competitors. The only competition he faced in small towns were the local "mom-and-pop stores" that could not match the lower costs generated by his volume buying power. Thus was born his small-town location strategy. In fact, in some small towns, Sahakian discovered that there was no local competition! Residents in these areas had to drive—often long distances—to the closest city just to shop for ordinary household items.

Sahakian plans to continue his location strategy. And why not? The company's revenues and profits have *quadrupled* in just the past decade! Sahakian and his family own 59 percent of Uni-Mart's stock (he took the company public in 1986), which is worth an estimated $26.3 million. Sahakian plans to expand his connection with fast-food franchises such as Arby's, Burger King, and Blimpie's. The minirestaurants he has established in Uni-Marts have increased the foot traffic in those stores while generating attractive gross profit margins as high as 72 percent. Sahakian is also completing a deal with PNC Bank to place full-service automated teller machines inside Uni-Marts.

The next time you find yourself in the middle of nowhere, needing cash, something to eat, gas for your car, and maybe even a dozen nightcrawlers, look around. You might find a Uni-Mart there ready to serve you!

---

1. What advantages does Sahakian's location strategy offer Uni-Mart? What are its disadvantages?

2. What tools and techniques should Sahakian use to identify potential sites for future Uni-Mart stores?

SOURCE: Adapted from Randall Lane, "The Sleepier, the Better," *Forbes*, November 6, 1995, pp. 84–88. ◆

---

streets should be in good repair with adequate drainage. Locating in a jurisdiction that does not provide these services will impose higher costs on a business over time.

The Location's Reputation. Like people, a city or parts of a city can have a bad reputation. In some cases, the reputation of the previous business will lower the value of the location. Sites where businesses have failed repeatedly create negative impressions in customer's minds; customers often view any business locating there as just another one that will soon be gone. They carry negative impressions based on previous experiences and simply never give the new business a try. *One restaurateur struggled early on to overcome the negative image his new location had acquired over the years, as one restaurant after another had failed there. He eventually established a base of loyal customers and succeeded, but it was a slow and trying process.*

*S*electing the Site

The final step in the location selection process is choosing the actual site for the business. Again, facts will guide the entrepreneur to the best location. Each type of business has different evaluation criteria for what makes an ideal location. A manufacturer's prime consideration may be access to raw materials, suppliers, labor, transportation, and customers. Service firms need access to customers but can generally survive in lower-rent properties. A retailer's prime consideration is customer traffic. The one element common to all three is the need to locate where customers want to do business.

Site location draws on the most precise information available on the makeup of the area. By using the published statistics mentioned earlier in this chapter, an owner can develop valuable insights regarding the characteristics of people and businesses in the immediate community. Two additional Census Bureau reports entrepreneurs find especially useful when choosing locations are *Summary Population*, which provides a broad demographic look at an area, and *Housing Characteristics*, which offers a detailed breakdown of areas as small as city blocks. The data are available on CD-ROM and on the World Wide Web at the Census Bureau's home page. Any small business owner with a properly equipped personal computer can access this incredible wealth of data with a few clicks of a mouse.

*L*ocation Criteria for Retail and Service Businesses

◆ Describe the location criteria for retail and service businesses.

Because their success depends upon a steady flow of customers, retail and service businesses must locate with their target customers' convenience and preferences in mind. The following are important considerations.

TRADE AREA SIZE

Every retail business should determine the extent of its **trading area:** the region from which a business can expect to draw customers over a reasonable time span. The primary variables that influence the scope of a trading area are the type and size of the operation. If a retailer is a specialist with a wide assortment of products, he may draw customers from a great distance. In contrast, a convenience store with a general line of merchandise may have a small trading area because it is unlikely that customers would drive across town to purchase what is available within blocks of their homes or businesses. As a rule, the larger the store and the greater its selection of merchandise, the broader its trading area.

For instance, the typical movie theater draws its customers from an area of five to seven miles; however, the AMC Grand, a collection of 24 screens under one roof in Dallas, Texas, draws customers from as far as 25 miles away. This "megaplex" has expanded the normal theater trading area and attracts an amazing 3 million moviegoers a year. AMC Grand's attendance per screen is 38 percent higher than what AMC Entertainment's traditional theaters average; its revenue per customer is 10 percent higher; and its profit margins are 12.5 percent higher.[16]

The following environmental factors influence the retail trading area size.

◆ *Retail compatibility.* Shoppers tend to be drawn to clusters of related businesses. That's one reason shopping malls and outlet shopping centers are popular destinations for shoppers and are attractive locations for retailers. The concentration of businesses pulls customers from a larger trading area than a single free-standing business does. **Retail compatibility** describes the benefits a company receives by locating near other businesses selling complementary products and services. *Not long after the AMC Grand opened, for instance, seven new restaurants popped up within easy walking distance of the theaters.* Clever business owners choose their locations with an eye on the surrounding mix of businesses. *When Vic and Suzette Brounsuzian started Meg-A-Nut Inc., a retail shop selling fine chocolates and nuts, they wanted to find just the right location. Vic spent considerable time investigating potential sites and studying their demographic* *profiles using census data and information from a local Small Business Development Center. He also analyzed each site's existing businesses to judge their retail compatibility with Meg-A-Nut. "I learned all about the kinds of people who live in the area," he says, "their salary ranges, purchasing habits, and all that—and I made sure to choose a location where other businesses were coming in to provide a solid merchant mix." Relying on the concept of retail compatibility, the Brounsuzians decided to locate their shop in a growing shopping plaza near a movie theater. "Since we're so close to the theater, we expected that people on the way to see a movie would stop in, pick up a little snack, . . . and munch on it. . . . It's working out that way," says Vic.*[17]

◆ *Degree of competition.* The size, location, and activity of competing businesses also influence the size of the trading area. If a business will be the first of its kind in a location, its trading area might be extensive. However, if the area already has eight or ten nearby stores that directly compete with a business, its trading area might be very small. How does the size of your planned operation compare with those that presently exist? Your business may be significantly larger and have more drawing power, giving it a competitive advantage.

◆ *Transportation network.* The transportation networks are the highways, roads, and public service routes that presently exist or are planned. An inconvenient location reduces the business's trading area. Entrepreneurs should check to see if the transportation system works smoothly and is free of barriers that might prevent customers from reaching their store. Is it easy for customers traveling in the opposite direction to cross traffic? Do signs and lights allow traffic to flow smoothly?

◆ *Physical, cultural, or emotional barriers.* Physical barriers may be parks, rivers, lakes, or any other obstruction that hinders customers' access to the area. Locating on one side of a large park may reduce the number of customers who will drive around it to get to the store. In urban areas, new immigrants tend to cluster together, sharing a common culture and language. These trading areas are defined by cultural barriers, where inhabitants patronize only the businesses in their neighborhoods. The Little Havana section of Miami or the Chinatown sections of San Francisco, New York, and Los Angeles are examples. One powerful emotional barrier is fear. If high-crime areas exist around a site, most of a company's potential customers will not travel through those neighborhoods to reach the business. For instance, in the heart of South Central Los Angeles, decimated by riots in 1992, only a handful of businesses have reopened to serve the local population. Deterred by the area's high crime, racial tension, and burned-out buildings, entrepreneurs prefer to do business in other areas of the city. One entrepreneur who has braved the grim environment to open a hair-and-nail-care business says, "No entrepreneur expects to turn a profit in the first year. I'm surviving."[18]

◆ *Political barriers are creations of law.* Federal, state, county, or city boundaries—and the laws within those boundaries—can influence the size of a company's trading area. For instance, in South Carolina, some counties have outlawed video poker machines while others allow them. In the counties where betting on video poker is legal, hundreds of small video parlors have sprung up, especially near the borders of the counties that no longer permit the practice. State laws also create conditions where customers cross over to the next state to save money. For instance, North Carolina imposes a very low cigarette tax, and shops located on its borders do a brisk business in the product.

CUSTOMER TRAFFIC

Perhaps the most important screening criteria for a potential retail (and often for a service) location is the number of potential customers passing by the site during business hours. To be successful, a business must be able to generate sufficient sales to surpass its break-even

Source: *Industry Week,* February 21, 1994, p. 8.

point, and doing that requires an ample volume of traffic. One of the key success factors for a convenience store, for instance, is a high-traffic location with easy accessibility. Entrepreneurs should know the traffic counts (pedestrian and auto) at the sites they are considering.

Express Shipping Centers, a network of UPS shipping centers, knows that locating in convenient, high-traffic destinations is central to its success. In just five years, the company has set up more than 4,000 locations across the United States, almost all in supermarkets. "Our whole business is making UPS convenient for consumers, and supermarkets are the best place to do that," says CEO Ken Ross. With no self-standing storefronts of its own, Express Shipping Centers' "store within a store" concept generates $11 million in annual sales.[19]

ADEQUATE PARKING

If customers cannot find convenient and safe parking, they are not likely to stop in the area. Many downtown areas have lost customers because of inadequate parking. Although shopping malls typically average five parking spaces per 1,000 square feet of shopping space, many central business districts get by with 3.5 spaces per 1,000 square feet. Customers generally will not pay to park if parking is free at shopping centers or in front of competing stores. Even when a business provides free parking, some potential customers may not feel safe on the streets, especially after dark. Many large city business districts become virtual ghost towns at the end of the business day. A location where traffic vanishes after 6 P.M. may not be as valuable as mall and shopping center locations that mark the beginning of the prime sales at 6 P.M.

ROOM FOR EXPANSION

A location should be flexible enough to provide for expansion if success warrants it. Failure to consider this factor can force a successful business to open a second store when it would have been better to expand in its original location.

VISIBILITY

No matter what a small business sells and how well it serves customers' needs, it cannot survive without visibility. Highly visible locations simply make it easy for customers to make purchases. A site lacking visibility puts a company at a major disadvantage before it even opens its doors. *Consider the story of Coffee, Etc., a small gourmet coffee store–restaurant in San Francisco. Located on the outside of a suburban mall, the store attracted shoppers and mall employees. Then mall owners remodeled the center, building a large department store over the old parking lot. Coffee, Etc. found itself literally hidden in the shadow of the new store, completely invisible to automobile traffic. Sales dropped off, and within a year the store went out of business. Several other restaurants tried the location, but all of them failed. The site remains vacant.*[20]

Some service businesses, however, can select sites with less visibility if the majority of their customer contacts are by telephone, fax, or the Internet. For example, customers usually contact plumbers by telephone; so rather than locating close to their customer bases, plumbers have flexibility in choosing their locations. Similarly, businesses that work at their customers' homes, such as swimming pool services, can operate from their homes and service vans.

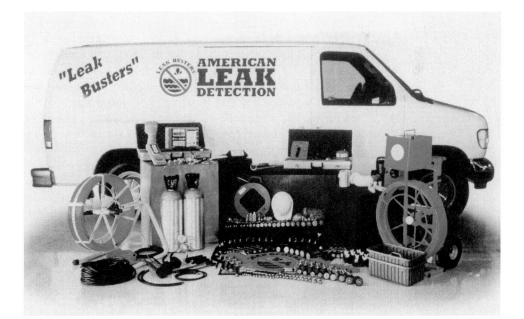

Because American Leak Detection franchisees go to their customers' homes and businesses, the location decision is a secondary one. In fact, the founders of many service businesses choose to operate out of their homes, keeping the costs low.

*L*ocation Options for Retail and Service Businesses

<aside>
3 Outline the basic location options for retail and service businesses.
</aside>

There are six basic areas where retailers and service business owners can locate: the central business district, neighborhoods, shopping centers and malls, near competitors, outlying areas, and at home. According to the International Council of Shopping Centers, the average cost to lease space in a shopping center is about $15 per square foot. At a regional mall, rental rates run from $20 to $40 per square foot, and in central business locations, the average cost is $43 per square foot (although rental rates can vary significantly in either direction of that average, depending upon the city.)[21] Of course, cost is just one factor a business owner must consider when choosing a location.

CENTRAL BUSINESS DISTRICT

The central business district (CBD) is the traditional center of town: the downtown concentration of businesses established early in the development of most towns and cities. Small business owners derive several advantages from a downtown location. Because their businesses are centrally located, they attract customers from the entire trading area of the city. Plus, they benefit from the traffic generated by the other stores clustered in the district. However, locating in a CBD does have certain disadvantages. Some CBDs are characterized by intense competition, high rental rates, traffic congestion, and inadequate parking facilities. In addition, many cities have experienced difficulty in preventing the decay of their older downtown business districts as a result of "mall withdrawal." Downtown districts withered as shoppers who preferred the convenience of modern shopping malls drifted away from the unique atmosphere of the traditional downtown. "Thirty years ago, downtowns had 85 percent of market retailing," says one location expert. "Today, a healthy downtown would have 15 percent."[22]

Recently, however, CBDs have experienced a resurgence in popularity as increasing numbers of shoppers have grown tired of the sameness of malls and shopping centers. "Out in edge-of-town USA, where nobody lives and everybody drives, chains and franchises have laid a carpet of uniformity on the landscape," laments one writer.[23] Downtown locations offer shoppers a multitude of amenities they cannot get at malls: plenty of fresh air and attractive "streetscapes" filled with beautiful flowers and trees, historic architecture, and collections of unique shops selling distinctive goods and services. "[People] want Main Street to be a place that's revitalized," says the head of a national preservation organization.[24] As shoppers have become more interested in preserving their downtown districts, retailers have returned to Main Street. Even large retailers such as Talbots, The Gap, J. Crew, Williams Sonoma, Eddie Bauer, Starbucks, and others are opening locations in traditional CBDs. "A village store might not do as much volume [as a mall store]," says the president of the women's apparel retailer Talbots, "but it doesn't need to," referring to the lower operating costs of his company's downtown stores.[25] One real estate developer experienced in Main Street locations says that his research shows that the best downtown retailing streets are located in densely populated, affluent areas, are one-way, offer on-street parking, and are shaded by mature trees.[26]

NEIGHBORHOOD LOCATIONS

Small businesses that locate near residential areas rely heavily on the local trading areas for business. For example, many grocers and convenience stores located just outside residential subdivisions count on local clients for successful operation. One study of food stores found that the majority of the typical grocer's customers live within a five-mile radius. The primary advantages of a neighborhood location include relatively low operating costs and rents and close contact with customers.

SHOPPING CENTERS AND MALLS

Shopping centers and mall have experienced explosive growth over the last three decades. Since 1960, the number of shopping center and malls in the United States has increased 1,500 percent! More than 41,000 of them now dot our nation's landscape, occupying 4.97 billion square feet of retail space.[27] Because many different types of stores exist under a single roof, shopping malls give meaning to the term "one-stop shopping." There are four types of shopping centers and malls:

♦ *Neighborhood shopping centers.* The typical neighborhood shopping center is relatively small, containing from three to twelve stores and serving a population of up to 40,000 people who live within a 10-minute drive. The anchor store in these centers is usually a supermarket or a drugstore.

♦ *Community shopping centers.* The community shopping center contains from 12 to 50 stores and serves a population ranging from 40,000 to 150,000 people. The leading tenant is a department or variety store.

♦ *Regional shopping malls.* The regional shopping mall serves a much larger trading area, usually from 10 to 15 miles or more in all directions. It contains from 50 to 100 stores and serves a population in excess of 150,000 people living within a 20- to 40-minute drive. The anchor is typically one or more major department stores.

♦ *Power centers.* A power center combines the drawing strength of a large regional mall with the convenience of a neighborhood shopping center. Anchored by large specialty retailers, these centers target older, wealthier baby boomers, who want selection and convenience. Anchor stores usually account for 80 percent of power center space, compared with 50 percent in the typical strip shopping center. Small companies must be careful in choosing power center locations to avoid being overshadowed by their larger neighbors. Spillover traffic from the anchor stores, although not guaranteed, is the primary benefit to small businesses locating in power centers.

Because the cost of locating in a shopping center or mall can be quite high, it is important for an entrepreneur to consider these questions:

♦ Is there a good fit with other products and brands sold in the mall or center?

♦ Who are the other tenants? Which stores are the "anchors" that will bring people into the mall or center?

♦ Demographically, is the center a good fit for your products or services? What are its customer demographics?

♦ How much foot traffic does the mall or center generate? How much traffic passes the specific site you are considering?

♦ How much vehicle traffic does the mall or center generate? Check its proximity to major population centers, the volume of tourists it draws, and the volume of drive-by freeway traffic. A mall or center that scores well on all three is probably a winner.

♦ What is the vacancy rate? The turnover rate?

♦ Is the mall or center successful? How many dollars in sales does it generate per square foot? Compare its record against industry averages.

Although they still account for the majority of retail sales, malls have waned in popularity within the last decade. Today, the average mall visit is 76 minutes, down from 106 minutes during the mall heyday of the 1980s.[28] Part of the problem is the bland sameness that malls exhibit in their design and in the storefronts they offer. After a while, customers begin to wonder "Why bother to go there?" Nearly half of the nation's enclosed malls are at least 20 years old and are in much need of a facelift.[29] One retail consultant says, "Regional malls clearly have a life cycle, and some are in their last throes."[30] The result is "demalling," in which developers renovate old malls by demolishing their interior common space, eliminating most of the small retailers, adding more entrances, and making them more closely resemble power centers. Malls that are too weak to support retail businesses are transformed into other uses. One experienced mall developer and owner predicts that "20 percent of all regional malls will be something else in 20 years."[31]

Mall developers are trying new formulas—often based on adding entertainment and offering a fresh mix of specialty stores catering to customers' changing tastes—to keep shoppers coming back. *Mills Corporation has built several massive regional shopping malls near major metropolitan areas around the country designed to draw hordes of value-conscious shoppers to its discount retail tenants. At these nearly 2-million-square-foot malls the opportunity to shop at more than 200 stores is just one part of the total mall experience; the entertainment and attractions are nearly as prominent. San Bernadino, California's Ontario Mall features dozens of theme restaurants, a 30-screen movie complex, a virtual reality arcade, two ice-skating rinks, and a man-made wildlife preserve! The mall also hosts a multitude of events including concerts, festivals, and book signings. The goal is to attract the entire family for an extended outing of shopping, dining, playing, and movie watching. The concept is working: The average visitor to the mall stays an average of 3.5 hours. If mall traffic holds up, Mills Corporation says that the mall will become California's biggest tourist attraction, even beating out Disneyland!*[32]

NEAR COMPETITORS

One of the most important factors in choosing a retail or service location is the compatibility of nearby stores with the retail or service customer. For example, stores selling high-priced goods such as cars or merchandise that requires comparisons such as antiques find it advantageous to locate near competitors to facilitate comparison shopping. Locating near competitors might be a key factor for success in businesses that sell goods that customers compare on the basis of price, quality, color, and other factors.

Although some small business owners seek to avoid locations near direct competitors, others want to locate near rivals. For instance, restaurateurs know that restaurants attract other restaurants, which, in turn, attract more customers. "A restaurant will be put in an area because of its demographics and good traffic flow," say one restaurant analyst. "Other restaurants recognize that, too." That's why in many cities, at least one "restaurant row" develops; each restaurant feeds the others. "I'd rather be right next to the competition," says the owner of one eatery. "When people decide to eat out, they make a choice of which restaurant they will go to when they get in the area. I know I'm going to get my fair share."[33]

There are limits to locating near competitors, however. Clustering too many businesses of a single type into a small area ultimately will erode their sales once the market reaches the saturation point. As the number of gourmet coffee shops has exploded in recent years, many have struggled to remain profitable, often competing with three or four similar shops, all within easy walking distance of one another. When an area becomes saturated with competitors, the stores cannibalize sales from one another, making it difficult for all of them to survive.

OUTLYING AREAS

In general, it is not advisable for a small business to locate in a remote area because accessibility and traffic flow are vital to retail and service success, but there are exceptions. Some small firms have turned their remote locations into trademarks. One small gun shop was able

Mall Appeal . . . or Apall?

The onslaught against the mall, that paradise of shopping pleasure, shows no sign of receding. Mail-order catalogs, television shopping channels, the World Wide Web, toll-free numbers, direct mail, and other methods offer customers the *ultimate* convenience in shopping: never having to leave home! In fact, one retail consulting firm predicts that by 2010, 55 percent of the nation's shopping will be from "nonstore ventures" such as these. Many experts predict that over the next few years as many as 300 of the more than 1,800 regional or superregional malls will either shut down or be converted into warehouse-style retail outlets. What's a mall owner to do?

Many owners across the United States are remodeling, redesigning, and repositioning their malls in an attempt to lure customers back. A common strategy is to add entertainment and attractions such as theme parks, large movie complexes, water parks, night clubs, themed museums, miniature golf courses, virtual reality centers, and casinos. "The idea is to give multiple reasons to come to your center," says one mall developer. Some 20 million customers visit Canada's West Edmonton Mall, the largest mall in the *world*, each year to shop at its more than 800 retail stores and to visit the mall's petting zoo, water parks, skating rink, amusement park, and Spanish Galleon in its own lagoon (which is patrolled by miniature submarines). Still, the Ghermazian family, who own the mall, recently decided to slash the available retail space in West Edmonton from 80 percent of the total to 60 percent and to double the amount of space dedicated to entertainment from 20 percent to 40 percent. "If the regional mall is going to survive as the dominant retail venue, amusements and entertainment are going to have to play an important role," says a representative of the International Council of Shopping Centers.

The goal is to make malls a destination for shoppers, and to keep them longer once they get there. "The more time people spend in a mall, the more money they are going to spend," says one mall manager. Entertainment features and attractions serve the same purpose that anchor stores, typically major department stores, do: generating traffic. Since the Forest Fair mall in suburban Cincinnati, Ohio, expanded and remodeled to incorporate an amusement park, a kids' play area called Gorillarama, a miniature golf course, and a laser tag game, traffic is up by 25 percent. To boost traffic, the Galleria mall in Cambridge, Massachusetts, opened a 17,000-square-foot sports museum designed to draw fans in the surrounding sports-crazed Boston area. The largest mall in the United States, the Mall of America near Minneapolis, Minnesota, tallies nearly 40 million visits a year by customers. Many of those visitors come not only to shop at the more than 400 retail stores but also to enjoy the mall's seven-acre Knott's Camp Snoopy amusement park (complete with roller coaster), movie complex, nine nightclubs, 18-hole minature golf course, and LEGO play center. Hundreds of couples also stop by the mall's wedding chapel to tie the knot!

Perhaps nowhere has the shift to entertainment become more obvious than in Las Vegas. A recent $90 million, 283,000-square-foot expansion of the Forum Shops, a group of upscale retail shops located next to the hotel–casino complex at Caesar's Palace, offers visitors a chance to stroll back into history. The mall resembles an ancient Roman Street, with polished flagstone floor and a painted-sky ceiling that changes colors in a dawn-to-dusk cycle using computer-controlled lights. An animated fountain comes to life hourly and entertains shoppers with stories about ancient Rome and mythology. Several times a day, actors dressed as Roman gladiators and citizens stroll along the promenade, engaging guests in conversation. The expansion features even more garish decor, including a 280-foot-high Great Roman Hall and an Interactive Atlantis Attraction with animatronic figures (who present the history and destruction of the lost continent of Atlantis), and a 50,000-gallon saltwater horseshoe-shaped aquarium displaying 600 colorful tropical fish from the Philippines. The shops all of these spectacular sites are designed to draw guests into include such upscale restaurants as Spago and The Palm and pricey retailers such as Gucci, Louis Vuiton, and Versace. Developers are already planning a third phase, called Caesars Maximus, which will recreate a Roman hill town. Five times a day, teams of white horses pulling chariots will parade along the Strip before veering off into a giant dome to engage in Ben Hur–like chariot races as shoppers and diners look on. Even without the chariots, the Forum Shops have set mall sales records. The average mall rings up sales of $278 per square foot, and sales of more than $400 per square foot are considered spectacular. At the Forum Shops, sales average $1,300 per square foot!

---

1. What advantages and disadvantages does a mall location offer a small business?
2. Use the World Wide Web to research the malls described here and other malls in your area. What trends are influencing shopping malls and the retailers located there?

SOURCES: Adapted from Tamsin Carlisle, "Gamble by World's Biggest Mall Pays Off," *Wall Street Journal*, March 7, 1997, pp. B1, B2; Gregory A. Patterson, "Malls Draw Shoppers with Ferris Wheels and Carousels," *Wall Street Journal*, June 22, 1994, p. B1; Kenneth Labich, "What It Will Take to Keep People Hanging Out at the Mall," *Fortune*, May 29, 1995, p. 103; Mitchell Pacelle, "Extravagant Themed Malls Enthrall Las Vegas Shoppers," *Wall Street Journal*, August 27, 1997, pp. B1, B10. ◆

to use its extremely remote location to its advantage by incorporating this into its advertising to distinguish itself from its competitors.

HOME-BASED BUSINESSES

As the nation's service economy has grown and communications and computing technology have become increasingly affordable, home-based businesses have flourished. For 27.1 million people (14 million full-time and 13.1 million part-time), home is where the business is, and their numbers continue to swell. Home-based businesses represent 25 percent of all newly created small companies.[34] For many new start-up companies, home is a natural choice to locate a business. Most often, home-based entrepreneurs set up shop in a spare bedroom or basement, avoiding the cost of renting, leasing, or buying a building. With a few basic pieces of office equipment such as a computer, a fax machine, a copier, a telephone answering system, and a scanner, a lone entrepreneur can look just like a major corporation, particularly on the World Wide Web. *Tyler Harwood, who designed missile guidance systems before being "downsized" by a defense contractor, operates two successful Web-based businesses from his home. His primary business, Final Touch Internet Systems, designs Web sites for other small companies and operates from Harwood's garage. His Web design skills also led Harwood to launch a virtual "store" on the World Wide Web as a sideline venture. From its virtual storefront, Aromatic Stogies <http://www.aromaticstogies.com> sells cigars, cigar accessories, and wine over the Internet. Harwood earns a six-figure income from his Web design business, and his sideline store generates revenues of more than $100,000—and Harwood never handles any inventory. He simply routes customers' orders to his suppliers, who ship directly to the customers.*[35]

Choosing a home location has certain disadvantages for entrepreneurs, however. Interruptions are frequent, the refrigerator is all too handy, work is always just a few steps away, and isolation can be a problem. Presenting a professional image to clients can also be a challenge for some home-based entrepreneurs. One entrepreneur who decided to move his home-based consulting and training business into a rented office, says, "Nine times out of ten, the dog would bark only when I was on the phone with a client. It made it very difficult to maintain a corporate image."[36] Another problem for some entrepreneurs running businesses from their homes involves zoning laws. As their businesses grow and become more successful, entrepreneurs' neighbors often begin to complain about the increased traffic, noise, and disruptions from deliveries, employees, and customers who drive through their residential neighborhoods to conduct business. After a dispute arose over zoning violations in a residential area, one small town in New York recently passed an ordinance outlawing home-based businesses![37] Many cities now face the challenge of passing updated zoning laws that reflect the reality of today's home-based businesses while protecting the interests of residential homeowners. Refer to Table 1.2 in chapter 1 for advice on issues to consider before setting up a home-based business.

4 Explain the site selection process for manufacturers.

7he Location Decision for Manufacturers

The criteria for the location decision for manufacturers is very different from those of retailers and service businesses; however, the decision can have just as much impact on the company's success. In some cases, a manufacturer has special needs that influence the choice of a location. In other cases the decision is influenced by municipal regulations.

Local zoning ordinances will limit a manufacturer's choice of location. If the manufacturing process creates offensive odors or noise, the business may be even further restricted in its choices. City and county planners will be able to show potential manufacturers the area of the city or county set aside for industrial development. Some cities have developed industrial parks in cooperation with private industry. These industrial parks typically are equipped with sewage and electrical power sufficient for manufacturing. Many locations are not so equipped, and it can be extremely expensive for a small manufacturer to have such utilities brought to an existing site.

Location of the plant can be dictated by the type of transportation facilities needed. Some manufacturers may need to locate on a railroad siding; others may only need reliable trucking service. If raw materials are purchased by the carload for economies of scale, the location must be convenient to a railroad siding. Bulk materials are sometimes shipped by barge and, consequently, require a facility convenient to a navigable river or lake. The added cost of using multiple shipping (e.g., rail-to-truck or barge-to-truck) can significantly increase shipping costs and make a location unfeasible for a manufacturer.

In some cases the perishability of the product dictates location. Vegetables and fruits must be canned near the fields in which they are harvested. Fish must be processed and canned at the water's edge. Location is determined by quick and easy access to the perishable products. Needed utilities, zoning, transposition, and special requirements may also work together to limit the number of locations that are suitable for a manufacturer.

FOREIGN TRADE ZONES

Foreign trade zones can be an attractive location for many small manufacturers that are engaged in global trade and are looking to lower the tariffs they pay on the materials and parts they import and on the goods they export. A **foreign trade zone** is a specially designated area that allows resident companies to import materials and components from foreign countries; assemble, process, package, or manufacture them; and then ship finished products out while incurring low tariffs and duties or, in some cases, paying no tariffs or duties at all. For instance, a bicycle maker might import parts and components from around the world and assemble them onto frames made in the United States. If located in a foreign trade zone, the manufacturer pays no duties on the parts it imports or on the finished bicycles it exports. The only duty the manufacturer would pay is on bicycles it sells in the United States (see Figure 15.2).

EMPOWERMENT ZONES

Originally created to encourage companies to locate in economically blighted areas, **empowerment zones** offer entrepreneurs tax breaks on investments they make within zone boundaries. Companies can get federal tax credits for hiring workers living in empowerment zones and for investments they make in plant and equipment in the zones. Before becoming an empowerment zone, downtown Detroit had become a virtual ghost town, littered with crum-

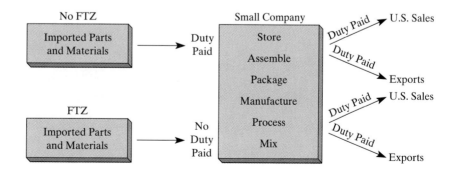

Figure 15.2 **How a Foreign Trade Zone (FTZ) Works**

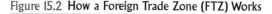

bling buildings and unsightly vacant lots. With the tax incentives available through the empowerment zone, businesses came back to the downtown, investing more than $2 billion in 80 new projects in just the first two years. Projects ranged from a Chrysler engine factory and retail stores to housing developments and an art museum.[38]

Thomas Bridgewater, CEO of Brey Corporation, a small engineering company, and James Grimes, owner of Apollo Plating, a small maker of car-polishing materials, teamed up to create a company that would supply polishing products to the Big Three automakers. Their location: an empowerment zone in Roseville, a suburb of Detroit. "Relocating to the zone lets us build a state-of-the-art facility at less cost because the land is less expensive," says Bridgewater. "Plus, the location is ideal."[39]

BUSINESS INCUBATORS

❺ Discuss the benefits of locating a start-up company in a business incubator.

For many start-up companies, a business incubator may make the ideal initial location. A **business incubator** is an organization that combines low-cost, flexible rental space with a multitude of support services for its small business residents. The overwhelming reason for establishing an incubator is to enhance economic development in an area and to diversify the local economy. Common sponsors of incubators include government agencies (49 percent); colleges or universities (13 percent); partnerships among government agencies, nonprofit agencies, and private developers (18 percent); and private investment groups (12 percent). Business and technical incubators vary to some degree as to the types of clients they attempt to attract, but most incubator residents are engaged in light manufacturing, service businesses, and technology- or research-related fields (see Figure 15.3).[40] For additional information on incubators, contact the National Business Incubator Association at their World Wide Web address <http://wnn.nbia.org/>.

The shared resources incubators typically provide their tenants include secretarial services, a telephone system, a computer and software, fax machines, meeting facilities, and, sometimes, management consulting services. An incubator will normally have entry requirements that are tied to its purpose and that detail the nature and scope of the business activities to be conducted. Incubators also have criteria that establish the conditions a business must meet to remain in the facility as well as the expectations for "graduation." One recent study found that more than 80 percent of companies become profitable within three years of entering an incubator.[41]

Donna Altieri's company, Altieri Instrument Bags, experienced a growth spurt after moving from her basement into the Enterprise Center, an incubator in Denver, Colorado. The company, which makes soft cases for musical instruments, rents a 2,000-square-foot space in the center. Since its arrival in the incubator, company sales are up, its workforce has doubled to four, and it has several new products under development. Altieri credits her

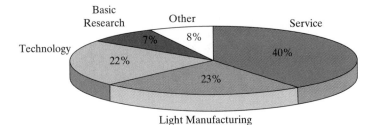

Figure 15.3 **Business Incubator Tenants by Industry** Source: National Business Incubation Association, Athens, OH, 1998.

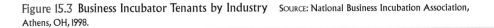

company's incubator location with much of the success. "[The incubator] has dramatically changed everything," she says. "I was stagnant for years operating from my basement. My business would have died if I hadn't moved in here." In the incubator, Altieri has discovered many other benefits. The copier she shares with other tenants has eliminated time wasted running to a copy shop. Plus, tenants are always willing to help one another. An accountant in the incubator helped her incorporate her business, and she brainstorms design ideas with engineers and designers housed there as well.[42]

In addition to shared services, incubators offer their fledgling tenants reduced rents and another valuable resource: access to the early-stage capital that young companies need to grow. A recent survey by the National Business Incubation Association found that 83 percent of incubators provide some kind of access to seed capital, ranging from help with obtaining federal grants to making connections with angel investors.[43] Some incubators also provide assistance to resident businesses interested in exporting. *The Decatur Industry and Technology Center in Decatur, Illinois, recently helped Cassie Koehne learn how to start exporting her company's odor-eliminating product.*[44]

More than 600 active incubators operate across the United States, and a new incubator opens, on average, every week. Most receive some type of financial assistance from their sponsors to continue operations. The investment that supports the incubator is generally a wise one because firms that graduate from incubators have only an 11 percent failure rate. The average incubator houses 17 ongoing businesses employing 55 people.[45]

ℒayout Considerations: Analyzing the Building

❻ Describe the criteria used to analyze the layout and design considerations of a building, including the Americans with Disabilities Act.

Once an entrepreneur finds the right location for her business, the next question deals with the physical facility and the layout of the facility. The building where the business will operate and the physical arrangement within the building both contribute to the success of the business. In planning the layout of a building, the goal is to maximize employees' and customers' safety and comfort the business's effectiveness and efficiency, and, in retail settings, sales. Wise small business owners understand that attention to detail is crucial when designing a proper layout for a business. The following layout and design factors have a significant impact on a building's influence on the business.

SIZE

A building must be large enough to accommodate a business's daily operations comfortably. If it is too small at the outset of operations, efficiency will suffer. There must be room enough for customers' movement, inventory, displays, storage, work areas, offices, and restrooms. Haphazard layouts undermine employee productivity and create organizational chaos. Too many small business owners start their operations in locations that are already overcrowded and lack room for expansion. The result is that the owner is forced to make a costly move to a new location within the first few years of operation.

If an owner plans any kind of expansion, will the building accommodate it? Will hiring new employees, purchasing new equipment, expanding production areas, or increasing service areas require a new location? How fast is the company expected to grow over the next three to five years? Inadequate room may become a limitation on the growth of the business. Most small businesses wait too long before moving into larger quarters, and they fail to plan the new space arrangements properly. Some experts recommend that, to avoid such problems, new businesses should plan their space requirements one to two years ahead and update the estimates every six months. When preparing the plan, managers should include the expected growth in the number and location of branches to be opened.

CONSTRUCTION AND EXTERNAL APPEARANCE

Is the construction of the building sound? It pays to have an expert look it over before buying or leasing the property. Beyond the soundness of construction, does the building have an attractive external and internal appearance? The physical appearance of the building provides customers with their first impression of a business and contributes significantly to establishing its identity in the customer's mind. This is especially true in retail businesses. Is the building's appearance consistent with the entrepreneur's desired image for the business? Small retailers must recognize the importance of creating the proper image for their store and how their shop's layout and physical facility influence this image. In many ways the building's appearance sets the tone for what the customer can expect in the way of quality and service. The appearance should, therefore, reflect the business's "personality." Should the building project an exclusive image or an economical one? Is the atmosphere informal and relaxed or formal and businesslike? Externally, the storefront, its architectural style and color, signs, entrances, and general appearance give important clues to customers about a business's image.

A glass front enables a retail business to display merchandise easily and to attract potential customers' attention. Passersby can look in and see attractive merchandise displays or, in some cases, employees busily working. *Krispy Kreme, a chain of doughnut shops along the Atlantic seaboard, attracts attention—and customers—by prominently displaying its doughnut-making equipment behind a glass wall. Most customers are mesmerized as they watch the machine turn out a batch of those tasty golden circles, which it then coats with molten icing. After watching the machine go through its doughnut-making cycle, viewers can hardly resist buying a doughnut. The smell of fresh-baked doughnuts wafting through the air doesn't hurt business either!*

A window display can be a powerful selling tool if used properly. Often, a store's display window is an afterthought, and many business owners change their displays too infrequently. For maximum eye-catching potential, businesses should display small merchandise such as jewelry, cosmetics, or shoes in windows with elevations of at least 36 inches. Displays of larger merchandise can start lower: just 12, 18, or 24 inches from the ground. The following tips will help business owners create window displays that will sell:

♦ *Keep displays simple.* Simple, uncluttered arrangements of merchandise will draw the most attention and will have the greatest impact on potential customers. Avoid taping posters on display windows; it cheapens a store's look.

♦ *Keep displays clean and up to date.* Dusty, dingy displays or designs that are outdated send the wrong message to customers.

♦ *Promote local events.* Small companies can show their support of the community by devoting part of the display window to promote local events. "Embracing your community can give you a real edge with customers who want to support businesses that are trying to make a difference in their neighborhood," says one design expert.[46]

♦ *Change displays frequently.* Customers don't want to see the same merchandise every time they visit a store. Experts recommend changing window displays at least quarterly. Businesses that sell fashionable items, however, should change their displays at least twice a month, if not weekly. "The best way to get passersby to come into your shop is to keep your window displays fresh and exciting," says one designer.[47]

♦ *Get expert help, if necessary.* Some business owners have no aptitude for design! In that case, their best bet is to hire a professional to design window and in-store displays. If a company cannot afford a professional designer's fees, the entrepreneur should check with the design departments at local colleges and universities. There, he might be able to locate a faculty member or a talented student willing to work on a freelance basis.

Bruce Julian, owner of Milton's Clothing Cupboard, catches customers' attention with attractive in-store displays. Successful retailers know that a well-designed layout and eye-catching display can draw customers like a magnet and boost a small store's sales.

◆ Contact the companies whose products you sell to see if they offer design props and assistance. *When Judith Mogul, owner of Violet Camera Shop in Chattanooga, Tennessee, featured Pentax cameras in her window display, she convinced the camera maker to foot half the $1,000 cost.*[48]

Bruce Julian, owner of Milton's Clothing Cupboard, uses unique window and in-store diplays to catch customers' attention and to bring a smile to their faces. In his retail clothing store stands a small statue of Yoda, clutching expensive silk neckties. Near the shoe display, a large bronze alligator appears to rise out of the carpet. On their way out, customers get a fortune cookie, but all of the fortunes are exactly the same: "You are about to get some new clothes."[49]

ENTRANCES

All entrances to a business should invite customers in. Wide entryways and attractive merchandise displays that are set back from the doorway can draw customers into a business. Retailers with heavy traffic flows such as supermarkets or drugstores often install automatic doors to ensure a smooth traffic flow into and out of their stores. Retailers should remove any barriers that interfere with customers' easy access to the storefront. Broken sidewalks, sagging steps, mud puddles, and sticking or heavy doors not only create obstacles that might discourage potential customers, but they also create legal hazards for a business if they cause customers to be injured. Entrances should be lighted to create a friendly atmosphere that invites customers to enter a business.

THE AMERICANS WITH DISABILITIES ACT

The **Americans with Disabilities Act (ADA),** passed in July 1990, requires practically all businesses to make their facilities available to physically challenged customers and employees. In addition, the law requires businesses with 15 or more employees to accommodate physically challenged candidates in their hiring practices. The rules of the ADA's Title III are designed to ensure that mentally and physically challenged customers have equal access to a firm's goods or services. For instance the act requires business owners to remove architectural and communication barriers when "readily achievable." The ADA allows flexibility in how a business achieves this equal access, however. For example, a restaurant could either provide menus in Braille or offer to have a staff member read the menu to blind customers. Or, a small dry cleaner might not be able to add a wheelchair ramp to its storefront without incurring significant expense, but the owner could comply with the ADA by offering curbside pickup and delivery services for disabled customers at no extra charge.

Although the law allows a good deal of flexibility in retrofitting existing structures, buildings that were occupied after January 25, 1993, must be designed to comply with all aspects of the law. For example, buildings with three stories or more must have elevators; anywhere the floor level changes by more than one-half inch, an access ramp must be in place. In retail stores, checkout aisles must be wide enough—at least 36 inches—to accommodate wheelchairs. Restaurants must have 5 percent of their tables accessible to wheelchair-bound patrons.

Complying with the ADA does not necessarily require businesses to spend large amounts of money. The Justice Department estimates that more than 20 percent of the cases customers have filed under Title III involved changes the business owners could have made at no cost![50] In addition, companies with $1 million or less in annual sales or with 30 or fewer full-time employees that invest in making their locations more accessible to all qualify for a tax credit. The credit is 50 percent of their expenses exceeding $250 but not more than $10,250.

The Disabilities Act also prohibits any kind of employment discrimination against anyone with a physical or mental disability. A physically challenged person is considered to be "qualified" if he can perform the essential functions of the job. The employer must make "reasonable accommodation" for a physically challenged candidate or employee without causing "undue hardship" to the business. The following are some of the specific provisions of Title III of the act:

◆ Restaurants, hotels, theaters, shopping centers and malls, retail stores, museums, libraries, parks, private schools, day-care centers, and other similar places of public accommodation may not discriminate on the basis of disability.

◆ Physical barriers in existing places of public accommodation must be removed if readily achievable (i.e., easily accomplished and able to be carried out without much difficulty or expense). If not, alternative methods of providing services must be offered, if those methods are readily achievable.

◆ New construction of places of public accommodation and commercial facilities (nonresidential facilities affecting commerce) must be accessible.

◆ Alterations to existing places of public accommodation and commercial facilities must be done in an accessible manner. When alterations affect the utility of or access to a "primary function" area of a facility, an accessible path of travel must be provided to the altered areas, and the restrooms, telephones, and drinking fountains serving the altered areas must also be accessible, to the extent that the cost of making these features accessible does not exceed 20 percent of the cost of the planned alterations. The additional accessibility requirements for alterations to primary function areas do not apply to measures taken solely to comply with readily achievable barrier removal.

◆ Elevators are not required in newly constructed or altered buildings under three stories or with less than 3,000 square feet per floor, unless the building is a shopping center; shopping mall; professional office of a health care provider; terminal, depot, or station used for public transportation; or an airport passenger terminal.

The American with Disabilities Act has affected, in a positive way, how businesses deal with this segment of their customers and employees. *For instance, restaurant owner Donna Parrish recently won an award from the National Multiple Sclerosis Society, recognizing her business, the Lazy H Chuck Wagon and Western Show, for its easy accessibility for patrons in wheelchairs. Parrish and her husband have made sure the restaurant complies with the Americans with Disabilities Act even though they were not required to; they simply see it as a good business practice!*[51]

SIGNS

One of the lowest-cost and most effective methods of communicating with customers is a business sign. Signs tell potential customers what a business does, where it is, and what it is selling. America is a very mobile society, and a well-designed, well-placed sign can be a powerful tool for reaching potential customers.

A sign should be large enough for passersby to read it from a distance, taking into consideration the location and speed of surrounding traffic arteries. To be most effective, the message should be short, simple, and clear. A sign should be legible both in daylight and at night; proper illumination is a must. Contrasting colors and simple typefaces are best. Because signs become part of the surrounding scenery over time, business owners should consider changing their features to retain their effectiveness. Animated parts and unusual shapes can attract interest.

The most common problems with business signs are that they are illegible, poorly designed, improperly located, poorly maintained, and have color schemes that are unattractive or are hard to read. Most communities have sign ordinances. Before investing in a sign, an entrepreneur should investigate the local community's ordinance. In some cities and towns, local regulations impose restrictions on the size, location, height, and construction materials used in business signs.

INTERIORS

Like exterior considerations, the functional aspects of building interiors are very important and require careful evaluation. Designing a functional, efficient interior is not easy. Technology has changed drastically the way employees, customers, and the environment interact with one another.

Piecing together an effective layout is *not* a haphazard process. **Ergonomics,** the science of adapting work and the work environment to complement employees' strengths and to suit customers' needs, is an integral part of a successful design. For example, chairs, desks, and table heights that allow people to work comfortably can help employees perform their jobs faster and more easily. Design experts claim that proper lighting, good accoustics, a comfortable climate, and properly designed equipment and work spaces benefit the company as well as employees. An ergonomically designed work space can improve workers' productivity significantly and lower days lost due to injuries and accidents. Unfortunately, not many businesses use ergonomics to design their layouts, and the result is costly. The Occupational Safety and Health Administration (OSHA) estimates that poor design in the work environment results in more than $20 billion in workers' compensation claims every year. One OSHA study found that 62 percent of all workplace injuries are musculoskeletal injuries, most of which could have been prevented by ergonomic designs.[52]

When planning store, office, or plant layouts, business owners too often focus on minimizing costs. Although staying within a budget is important, enhancing employees' productivity or maximizing sales with an effective layout should be the overriding issues. One extensive six-year study concluded that changes in office design have a direct impact on

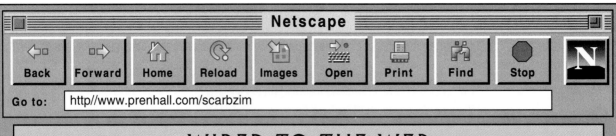

WIRED TO THE WEB

THE APPLICANT

"*H*ey Ramon, what did the guy in the wheelchair want?" said Pete Kowalsky as he strode into Ramon Hernandez's office.

"He was applying for the job we advertised in *The Dispatch* this past Sunday," said Ramon, holding up a résumé for Pete to see. Ramon was the founder and CEO of American Classic Lighting, Inc., a company that manufactures high-quality reproductions of antique and period lighting fixtures. Ramon had started the company after he and his wife had purchased an old home and had difficulty finding lighting fixtures to blend with the house's classic style. He researched the market and found that there was very little competition in a market with bright growth prospects. Located in Savannah, Georgia, Ramon knew that the large number of historic homes within 300 miles would present a large market for his company. Ramon's research had proved to be correct; the company's growth rate for the past seven years was in the double digits.

"You mean the manufacturing job? The one in assembly?" Pete, who was the company's manufacturing manager, asked.

"That's the one," said Ramon.

"But a guy in a wheelchair . . ." said Pete, his voice trailing off. "I mean, a guy in a wheelchair can't assemble lamps, can he?"

"To be honest, I've never really thought about it," Ramon said. "This fellow, Jacob Saunders, used to work for an old friend of mine on the West Coast before he moved here. He's got a lot of good experience. Looking at his résumé and his qualifications, I'd say he's very qualified to do the job."

"How'd he end up in a wheelchair?"

"An auto accident. He's paralyzed from the waist down. He doesn't let it slow him down, though. He has a specially equipped van and drives himself everywhere he goes. He's even into racing."

"Racing?" asked Pete, his voice tinged with surprise.

"Wheelchair racing. We talked about it in the interview. He's a champion and has won events at several levels."

"After looking at how powerful his arms and shoulders are, I can believe that," said Pete. "But a job in our production department? None of the other 27 people in this company are in wheelchairs. Wouldn't we have to change everything just to accommodate him?"

"We'd have to make some adjustments, I'm sure, but I don't really see that it would require a major overhaul or anything. I guess I'll have to check with some of the people in engineering. Plus, I'll need to talk with our attorney about our responsibilities under the Americans with Disabilities Act."

"The what? asked Pete.

"Never mind."

"Ramon, we've never had a situation like this come up before," said Pete. "Do you think he'd fit in with the other employees? Would they accept him?"

"Come on, Pete! He's a really nice guy. He just happens to be in a wheelchair. I want you to meet him. I told him I needed to call his references and if those checked out, I'd invite him back to interview with you and several others."

"Well, OK, but I'm a little nervous about what this means in terms of production," Pete said.

1. Use the World Wide Web to research the Americans with Disabilities Act. What obligations does American Classic Lighting have to Jacob Saunders under the act?

2. On the basis of your research, what advice would you give to Ramon Hernandez about Jacob Saunders's application for employment?

3. Is it ever ethical for businesses such as American Classic Lighting to take into consideration a job applicant's physical qualities in a hiring decision? If so, when?

workers' performance, job satisfaction, and ease of communication. The report also concluded that the savings generated by effective layouts are substantial, and conversely, that poorly planned designs involve significant costs.[53] Ergonomics experts are convinced that a properly designed work environment not only reduces accidents, injuries, and absenteeism but also increases productivity and morale. Plus, retailers know that an effective store layout can increase traffic in their shops and boost sales and profits.

When evaluating an existing building's interior, an entrepreneur must be sure to determine the integrity of its structural components. Are the building's floors strong enough to hold the business's equipment, inventory, and personnel? Strength is an especially critical factor for manufacturing firms that use heavy equipment. Are the upper floors anchored as solidly as the primary floor? Can inventory be moved safely and easily from one area of the plant to another? Is the floor space ideal for safe and efficient movement of goods and people? Consider the cost of maintaining the floors. Hardwood floors may be extremely attractive but require expensive and time-consuming maintenance. Carpeted floors may be extremely attractive in a retail business but may be totally impractical for a manufacturing firm. The small business manager must consider both the utility and durability of flooring materials as well as their maintenance requirements, attractiveness, and, if important, effectiveness in reducing noise.

Like floors, walls and ceilings must be both functional and attractive. On the functional side, walls and ceilings should be fireproof and soundproof. Are the colors of walls and ceilings compatible, and do they create an attractive atmosphere? Retail stores should have a light and bright appearance. Ceilings should therefore be done in light colors to reflect the store's lighting. Walls may range from purely functional, unpainted cement block in a factory to wallpapered showpieces in expensive restaurants and exclusive shops. Wall coverings are expensive and should be considered only when the additional cost will enhance the sale of goods or services.

For many businesses, a drive-through window adds another dimension to the concept of customer convenience and is a relatively inexpensive way to increase sales. Although drive-through windows are staples at fast-food restaurants and banks, they can add value for customers in a surprising number of businesses. *For instance, when Marshall Hoffman relocated his business, Steel Supply Company, to a building that had been used as a bank, the idea of using the drive-through window intrigued him. Looking for a way to improve customer service, Hoffman transformed the former bank lobby into his showroom floor and began advertising the convenience of buying steel at the drive-through window. Customers place their steel orders by telephone, pull up to the window and pay, and receive a ticket. The order goes by computer to a warehouse Hoffman built on the site. By the time the customer pulls up to the warehouse, the order is waiting! The window has been a hit with customers. Since moving into its new location, Steel Supply's sales have grown from $3.5 million to more than $6 million.*[54]

LIGHTS AND FIXTURES

Good lighting allows employees to work at maximum efficiency. Proper lighting is measured by what is ideal for the job being done. Proper lighting in a factory may be quite different from that required in an office or a retail shop. Retailers often use creative lighting to attract customers to a specific display. Jewelry stores provide excellent examples of how lighting can be used to display merchandise effectively.

Modern advances in lighting technology give small businesses more options for lighting their stores, factories, and offices. New lighting systems offer greater flexibility, increased efficiency, and lower energy consumption. Studies also show that by installing systems that automatically turn the lights off when people leave a room, businesses can reduce their lighting bills by as much as 75 percent![55]

Lighting is often an inexpensive investment when considering its impact on the overall appearance of the business. Few people seek out businesses that are dimly lit because they convey an image of untrustworthiness. The use of natural and artificial light in combination can give a business an open and cheerful look. Many restaurant chains have added greenhouse glass additions to accomplish this.

$\mathcal{L}$ayout: Maximizing Revenues, Increasing Efficiency, and Reducing Costs

7 Explain the principles of layouts for retailers, service businesses, and manufacturers.

Layout is the arrangement of the physical facilities in a business. The ideal layout contributes to efficient operations, increased productivity, and higher sales. What is ideal depends on the type of business and on the entrepreneur's strategy for gaining a competitive edge. Retailers design their layouts with the goal of maximizing sales revenue; manufacturers design theirs to increase efficiency and productivity and to lower costs.

LAYOUT FOR RETAILERS

Retail layout is the arrangement and method of display of merchandise in a store. A retailer's success depends, in part, on a well-designed floor display. It should pull customers into the store and make it easy for them to locate merchandise; compare price, quality, and features; and ultimately to make a purchase. In addition, the floor plan should take customers past displays of other items that they may buy on impulse. *Journeys, a retailer that sells stylish shoes aimed at the youth market, has successfully attracted customers by integrating public telephones into its store design. The company installed telephones, some pay phones and some free, and seats as a test in some of its new stores with the idea of presenting an open invitation to teenagers to "come in and hang out." Managers at Journeys credit the new layout, including the phones, for the store's 26 percent sales increase.*[56]

Retailers have always recognized that some locations within a store are superior to others. Customers' traffic patterns give the owner a clue to the best location for the items with the highest gross margin. Merchandise purchased on impulse and convenience goods should be located near the front of the store. Items people shop around for before buying and specialty goods will attract their own customers and should not be placed in prime space. Prime selling space should be restricted to products that carry the highest markups. Table 15.2 offers suggestions for locating merchandise in a small retail store.

Layout in a retail store evolves from a clear understanding of customers' buying habits. If customers come into the store for specific products and have a tendency to walk directly to those items, it will benefit retailers to place complementary products in their path. Observing customer behavior can help the owner identify the "hot spots" where merchandise sells briskly and the "cold spots" where it may sit indefinitely. By experimenting with factors such as traffic flow, lighting, aisle size, display location, sounds, signs, and colors, an owner can discover the most productive store layout.

Retailers have three basic layout patterns to choose from: the grid, the free-form layout, and the boutique. The **grid layout** arranges displays in rectangular fashion so that aisles are parallel. It is a formal layout that controls the traffic flow through the store. Most supermarkets and many discount stores use the grid layout because it is well suited to self-service stores. This layout uses the available selling space efficiently, creates a neat organized environment, and facilitates shopping by standardizing the location of items. Figure 15.4 shows a typical grid layout.

Table 15.2 Classification and Arrangement of Merchandise in a Small Retail Store

Merchandise Type	How or Why Bought	Placement in Store
Impulse goods	As result of attractive visual merchandising displays	Small store: near entrance Larger store: on main aisle
Convenience goods	With frequency in small quantities	Easily accessible feature locations along main aisle
Necessities or staple goods	Because of need	Rear of one-level stores, upper floors of multilevel stores (not a hard-and-fast rule)
Utility goods	For home use: brooms, dustpans, similar items	As impulse items, up front or along main aisle
Luxury and major expense items	After careful planning and considerable "shopping around"	Some distance from entrance

SOURCE: U.S. Small Business Administration, "Small Business Location and Layout," *Administrative Management Course Program, Topic 13* (Washington, D.C.: SBA, 1980), p. 6.

Unlike the grid layout, the **free-form layout** is informal, using displays of various shapes and sizes. Its primary advantage is the relaxed, friendly shopping atmosphere it creates, which encourages customers to shop longer and increases the number of impulse purchases they make. Still, the free-form layout is not as efficient as the grid layout in using selling space, and it can create security problems if not properly planned. Figure 15.5 on page 524 illustrates a free-form layout.

The **boutique layout** divides the store into a series of individual shopping areas, each with its own theme. It is like building a series of specialty shops into a single store. The boutique layout is informal and can create a unique shopping environment for the customer.

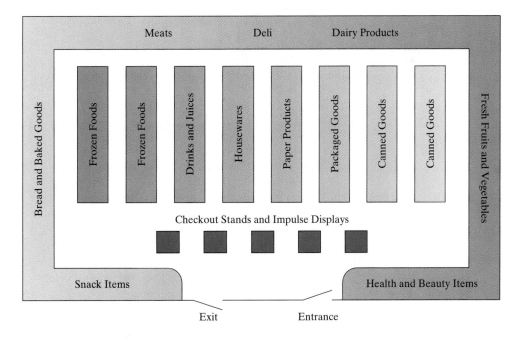

Figure 15.4 The Grid Layout

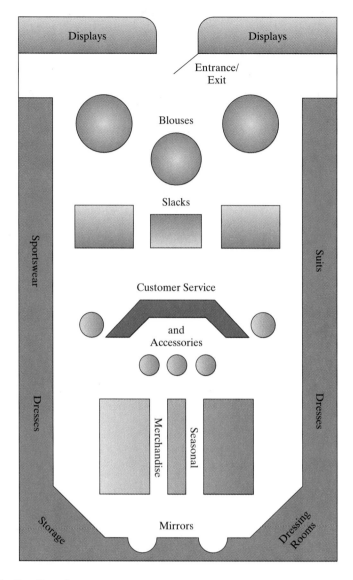

Figure 15.5 The Free-Form Layout

Small department stores sometimes use this layout to create a distinctive image. Figure 15.6 shows a boutique layout for a small department store.

Business owners should display merchandise as attractively as their budgets will allow. Customers' eyes focus on displays, which tell them the type of merchandise the business sells. It is easier for customers to relate to one display than to a rack or shelf of merchandise. Open displays of merchandise can surround the focal display, creating an attractive selling area. Retailers can boost sales by displaying together items that complement each other. For example, displaying ties near dress shirts or handbags next to shoes often leads to multiple sales.

Spacious displays provide shoppers an open view of merchandise and reduce the likelihood of shoplifting. An open, spacious image is preferable to a cluttered appearance. Display height is also important because customers won't buy what they cannot see or reach. When planning displays, retailers should remember the following:

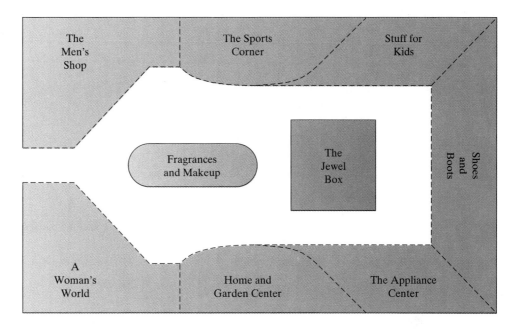

Figure 15.6 The Boutique Layout

◆ The average man is 68.8 inches tall, and the average woman is 63.6 inches tall.

◆ The average person's normal reach is 16 inches, and the extended reach is 24 inches.

◆ The average man's standing eye level is 62 inches from the floor, and the average woman's standing eye level is 57 inches from the floor.[57]

Retailers must remember to separate the selling and nonselling areas of a store. They should never waste prime selling space with nonselling functions (storage, office, dressing area, etc.). Although nonselling activities are necessary for a successful retail operation, they should not take precedence and occupy valuable selling space. Many retailers place their nonselling departments in the rear of the building, recognizing the value of each foot of space in a retail store and locating their most profitable items in the best selling areas.

Clearly, the portions of a small store's interior space are not of equal value in generating sales revenue. Certain areas contribute more to revenue than others. The value of store space depends on floor location in a multistory building, location with respect to aisles and walkways, and proximity to entrances. Space values decrease as distance from the main entry-level floor increases. Selling areas on the main level contribute a greater portion to sales than do those on other floors because they offer greater exposure to customers than either basement or higher-level locations. Therefore, main-level locations carry a greater share of rent than other levels. Figure 15.7 on page 526 offers one example of how rent and sales could be allocated by floors.

The layout of aisles in the store has a major impact on the customer exposure that merchandise receives. Items located on primary walkways should be assigned a higher share of rental costs and should contribute a greater portion to sales revenue than those displayed along secondary aisles. Figure 15.8 on page 526 shows that high-value areas are exposed to two primary aisles.

Space values also depend on the spaces' relative position to the store entrance. Typically, the farther away an area is from the entrance, the lower its value. Another considera-

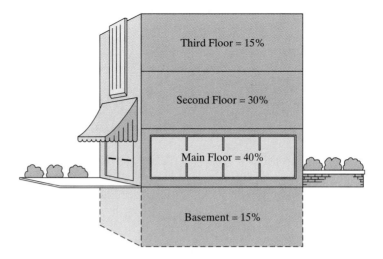

Third Floor = 15%

Second Floor = 30%

Main Floor = 40%

Basement = 15%

Figure 15.7 Rent Allocation by Floors   SOURCE: From Dale M. Lewison, *Retailing*, 4th ed. (New York: Macmillan, 1991), p. 287. Used with permission.

tion is that most shoppers turn to the right when entering a store and move around it counter-clockwise. Finally, only about one-fourth of a store's customers will go more than halfway into the store. Using these characteristics, Figure 15.9 illustrates space values for a typical small-store layout.

Understanding the value of store space ensures proper placement of merchandise. The

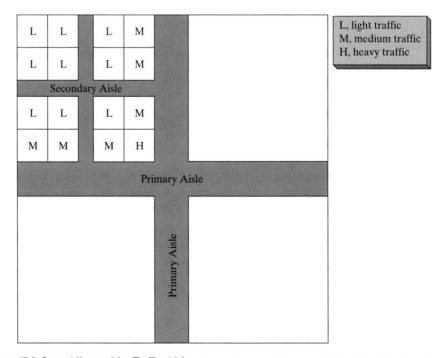

Figure 15.8 Rent Allocated by Traffic Aisle   SOURCE: From Dale M. Lewison, *Retailing*, 4th ed. (New York: Macmillan, 1991), p. 289. Used with permission.

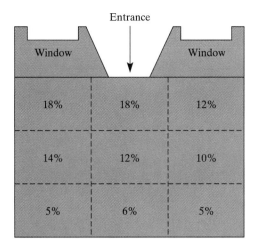

Figure 15.9 Space Values for a Small Store Source: From Dale M. Lewison, *Retailing*, 4th ed. (New York: Macmillan, 1991), p. 288. Used with permission.

items placed in the high-rent areas of the store should generate adequate sales and contribute enough profit to justify their high-value locations. The decline in value of store space from front to back of the shop is expressed in the 40-30-20-10 rule. This rule assigns 40 percent of a store's rental cost to the front quarter of the shop, 30 percent to the second quarter, 20 percent to the third quarter, and 10 percent to the final quarter. Similarly, each quarter of the store should contribute the same percentage of sales revenue.

For example, suppose that the owner of a small department store anticipates $120,000 in sales this year. Each quarter of the store should generate the following sales volume:

Front quarter	$120,000 × 0.40 = $48,000
Second quarter	$120,000 × 0.30 = $36,000
Third quarter	$120,000 × 0.20 = $24,000
Fourth quarter	$120,000 × 0.10 = $12,000
Total	$120,000

LAYOUT FOR MANUFACTURERS

Manufacturing layout decisions take into consideration the arrangement of departments, workstations, machines, and stock-holding points within a production facility. The general objective is to arrange these elements to ensure a smooth work flow (in a production area) or a particular traffic pattern (in a service area).

Manufacturing facilities have come under increased scrutiny as firms attempt to improve quality, decrease inventories, and increase productivity through facilities that are integrated, flexible, and controlled. Facility layout has a dramatic effect on product mix, product processing, materials handling, storage, control, and production volume and quality. Some manufacturers are using 3-D simulation software (based on the same technology as the 3-D video games people play) to test the layout of their factory and its impact on employees and their productivity *before* they ever build them. The highly realistic simulations tell designers how well a particular combination of people, machinery, and environment interact with one another. The software can identify potential problem areas, such as layouts that force workers into awkward positions that would cause injuries, equipment designs that cause workers to reach too far for materials, and layouts that unneccesarily add extra time to the manufacturing process by requiring extra materials handling or unneeded steps.[58]

When It Comes to Store Layout, She Keeps 'Em Guessing

*A*bout the only thing that Atchison, Kansas, is famous for is that it is the birthplace of Amelia Earhart. So what makes people drive up to three hours to this quaint little railroad town about 50 miles north of Kansas City that is surrounded by nothing but farmland? Most of the people who go to Atchison are looking to buy home furnishings from Mary Carol Garrity's unique shop named Nell Hill's (after Garrity's grandmother). Garrity's unique little shop sells an eclectic mix of European antiques and less-expensive home-decorating items ranging from baskets and pottery to dinnerware and pillows. Twenty percent of the inventory is antique; 80 percent is new. Sixteen years ago, Nell Hill's began as a gourmet shop, but, over time, the shop evolved into the unique home furnishings store it is today.

A significant part of the store's success is due to its unique layout and Garrity's effective use of her inventory and props to create a wonderfully warm and friendly environment that makes customers want to linger and shop—and buy. Housed in an old bank building, Nell Hill's gives shoppers the impression that they are in someone's tastefully decorated home rather than a retail shop. The colors are soft, warm, and inviting. Ornaments and greenery hang from the ceiling; lamps, candles, and vases are displayed on tables and desks; framed paintings cover the walls; and everywhere there is furniture, so much that customers can barely turn around without seeing something that they want to buy. Practically everything customers see is for sale.

In addition to the store's welcoming ambiance, Nell Hill's offers customers something new every time they come in. Garrity is constantly changing the store layout. Even customers whose visits are just days apart will see a layout that is completely different! For many, shopping at Nell Hill's has become a game; they can hardly wait to see what Garrity will come up with next. Because she sells merchandise straight off the shop floor, the store's merchandise is never the same. Not only is the inventory changing, but Garrity also repaints every room in the store at least once a year. The primary reason Garrity is constantly changing the layout of the store is to keep her customers interested and coming back frequently. "If they are going to drive all the way from out of town to get here," she says, "I'm going to make sure they're happy and see something they haven't seen before." Many of Nell Hill's items are one-of-a-kind pieces that Garrity picks up at auctions and estate sales. Even the new items she stocks are unique and not the run-of-the-mill items customers could find in a mall. Prices range from as little as a few dollars for candles and small "sit-around" items to $7,875 for a gorgeous French carved Walnut antique hutch.

Garrity is so busy working the floor and helping customers that she doesn't even have an office or a desk; she works from an in-basket, where all of her work goes. She says that keeping in such close contact with her customers helps her know which items to stock and how to display them in the store. "People bring in magazines, fabrics, and pictures, and we do what they want at a really good value," she says. Garrity's husband, Dan, who quit his law practice several years ago to help run the business, takes care of the company's finances and handles the furniture selection.

Garrity's recipe for Nell Hill's is a success. The company's net profit margin of 10 percent is well above that of similar shops and is growing at an amazing 20 percent a year. She recently opened a second store in Atchison: G. Dieboldt's (named after her father) that focuses on bedroom furnishings and fabrics, which had formerly occupied the top floor at Nell Hill's. Garrity's plan is to open four or five stores, all with different themes, but with the same spirit as Nell Hill's—all in Atchison. "I have no visions of expanding outside Atchinson," says Garrity. "I just want to keep it small and personal, and I want to keep the romance to it."

1. Why is layout such an important component in stores, such as Garrity's, that sell home furnishings and decorations?

2. Use the World Wide Web to develop a demographic profile of the residents of Atchinson, Kansas. On the basis of your analysis, discuss the importance of Garrity's approach to store layout and her overall sales strategy for Nell Hill's.

SOURCE: Adapted from Maria Atanasov, "Meet the Best Little Merchant in Kansas," *Your Company*, February/March 1998, pp. 54–56.   ◆

Factors in Manufacturing Layout. The ideal layout for a manufacturing operation depends on several factors, including the following:

- *Type of product.* Product design and quality standards; whether the product is produced for inventory or for order; and physical properties such as the size of materials and products, special handling requirements, susceptibility to damage, and perishability

- *Type of production process.* Technology used; types of materials handled; means of providing a service; and processing requirements in terms of number of operations involved and amount of interaction between departments and work centers

At the Bass Pro Shop store in Springfield, Missouri, the layout is designed to appeal to the company's target customer: outdoor enthusiasts in search of the right equipment.

- ◆ *Ergonomic considerations.* To ensure worker safety; to avoid unnecessary injuries and accidents; and to increase productivity
- ◆ *Economic considerations.* Volume of production; costs of materials, machines, workstations, and labor; pattern and variability of demand; and length of permissible delays
- ◆ *Space availability within the facility itself.*

Types of Manufacturing Layouts. Manufacturing layouts are categorized either by the work flow in a plant or by the production system's function. There are three basic types of layouts that manufacturers can use separately or in combination—product, process, and fixed position—and they differ in their applicability to different levels of manufacturing volume.

In a **product** (or **line**) **layout,** a manufacturer arranges workers and equipment according to the sequence of operations performed on the product (see Figure 15.10 on page 530). Conceptually, the flow is an unbroken line from raw materials input to finished goods. This type of layout is applicable to rigid-flow, high-volume, continuous or mass-production operations or when the product is highly standardized. Automobile assembly plants, paper mills, and oil refineries are examples of product layouts.

Product layouts offer the advantages of lower materials-handling costs; simplified tasks that can be done with low-cost, lower-skilled labor; reduced amounts of work-in-process inventory; and relatively simplified production control activities. All units are routed along the same fixed path, and scheduling consists primarily of setting a production rate.

Disadvantages of product layouts include their inflexibility, monotony of job tasks, high fixed investment in specialized equipment, and heavy interdependence of all operations. A breakdown in one machine or at one workstation can idle the entire line. Such a layout

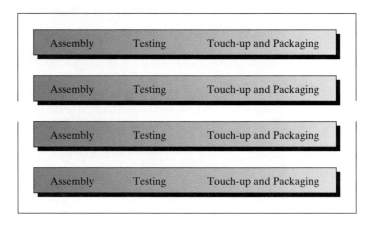

Figure 15.10 Product Layout

also requires the owner to duplicate many pieces of equipment in the manufacturing facility; duplication can be cost-prohibitive for a small firm.

In a **process layout,** a manufacturer groups workers and equipment according to the general function they perform, without regard to any particular product (see Figure 15.11). Process layouts are appropriate when production runs are short, when demand shows considerable variation and the costs of holding finished goods inventory are high, or when the product is customized.

Process layouts have the advantages of being flexible for doing customer work and promoting job satisfaction by offering employees diverse and challenging tasks. Its disadvantages are the higher costs of materials handling, more skilled labor, lower productivity, and more-complex production control. Because the work flow is intermittent, each job must be individually routed through the system and scheduled at the various work centers, and its status must be monitored individually.

In **fixed-position layouts,** materials do not move down a line as in a product layout; because of the bulk or weight of the final product, materials are assembled in one spot. In other words, workers and equipment go to the materials rather than having the materials flow down a line to them. Aircraft assembly shops and shipyards typify this kind of layout.

Designing Layouts. The starting point in layout design is determining how and in what sequence product parts or service tasks flow together. One of the most effective techniques is to create an overall picture of the manufacturing process using assembly charts and process flowcharts. Given the tasks and their sequence, plus knowledge of the volume of products to

Figure 15.11 Process Layout

be produced, an owner can analyze space and equipment needs to get an idea of the facility's demands. When a product layout is being used, these demands take precedence, and manufacturers must arrange equipment and workstations to fit the production tasks and their sequence. If a process layout is used, different products place different demands on the facility. Rather than having a single best flow, there may be one flow for each product, and compromises will be necessary. As a result, any one product may not get the ideal layout.

Analyzing Production Layouts. Although there is no general procedure for analyzing the numerous interdependent factors that enter into layout design, specific layout problems lend themselves to detailed analysis. Two important criteria for selecting and designing a layout are worker effectiveness and materials-handling costs.

Designing layouts ergonomically so that they maximize workers' strengths is especially important for manufacturers. Creating an environment that is comfortable and pleasant for workers will pay big benefits over time in the form of higher productivity, lower absenteeism and tardiness, and fewer injuries. Designers must be sure that they match the environment they create to workers' needs rather than trying to force workers to adapt to the environment.

Manufacturers can lower materials-handling costs by using layouts designed to automate product flow whenever possible and to minimize flow distances and times. The extent of automation depends on the level of technology and amount of capital available, as well as behavioral considerations of employees. Flow distances and times are usually minimized by locating sequential processing activities or interrelated departments in adjacent areas. The following features are important to a good manufacturing layout:

1. Planned materials flow pattern
2. Straight-line layout where possible
3. Straight, clearly marked aisles
4. Backtracking kept to a minimum
5. Related operations close together
6. Minimum of in-process inventory
7. Easy adjustment to changing conditions
8. Minimum materials-handling distances
9. Minimum of manual handling
10. No unnecessary rehandling of material
11. Minimum handling between operations
12. Materials delivered to production employees quickly
13. Use of gravity to move materials whenever possible
14. Materials efficiently removed from the work area
15. Material handling done by indirect labor
16. Orderly materials handling and storage
17. Good housekeeping

*B*uild, Buy, or Lease?

8 Evaluate the advantages and disadvantages of building, buying, and leasing a building.

Another important decision business owners must make involves the ownership of the building. The ability to obtain the best possible physical facilities given the cash the owner has available may depend largely on whether the entrepreneur decides to build, buy, or lease a building.

THE DECISION TO BUILD

If a business had unlimited funds, the owner could design and build a perfect facility. However, few new business owners have this luxury. Constructing a new facility can project a positive image to potential customers. The business looks new and consequently creates an image of being modern, efficient, and of top quality. A new building can incorporate the most modern features during construction, which can significantly lower operating costs. In addition, by constructing a new building, a business owner can incorporate into the layout features that meet the business's unique design needs such as loading docks, laboratories, or refrigeration units. Building a new facility can also improve a company's long-term productivity and efficiency.

In some rapidly growing areas, there are only a few or sometimes no existing buildings to buy or lease that match an entrepreneur's requirements. In these situations, a business owner must consider the cost of constructing a building as a significant factor in her initial estimates of capital needs and break-even point. Constructing a building imposes a high initial fixed cost that an owner must weigh against the facility's ability to generate revenue and to reduce operating expenses. Building a new structure also requires more time than either buying or leasing an existing one.

THE DECISION TO BUY

In many cases, there may be an ideal building in the area where an entrepreneur wants to locate. Buying the facility allows her to remodel it without seeking permission from anyone else. As can building, buying can put a drain on the business's financial resources, but the owner knows exactly what her monthly payments will be. Under a lease, rental rates can (and usually do) increase over time. If an owner believes that the property will actually appreciate in value, a decision to purchase may prove to be wise. In addition, the owner can depreciate the building each year, and both depreciation and interest are tax-deductible business expenses.

When considering the purchase of a building, the owner should use the same outline of facilities requirements developed for the building option to ensure that this property will not be excessively expensive to modify for his use. Remodeling can add a significant initial expense. The layout of the building may be suitable in many ways, but it may not be ideal for a particular business. Even if a building housed the same kind of business, its existing layout may be completely unsuitable for the way the new owner plans to operate.

Building or buying a building greatly limits an entrepreneur's mobility, however. Some business owners prefer to stay out of the real estate business to retain maximum flexibility and mobility. Plus, not all real estate appreciates in value. Surrounding property can become rundown and consequently can lower a property's value despite the owner's efforts to keep it in excellent condition. Many downtown locations have suffered from this problem.

THE DECISION TO LEASE

The major advantage of leasing is that it requires no large initial cash outlay, so the business's funds are available for purchasing inventory or for supporting current operations. Also, lease expenses are tax-deductible. Firms that are short on cash usually end up leasing their facilities. Because leasing is usually the least expensive option, most start-up businesses lease their buildings. According to one small business expert, entrepreneurs typically begin to consider buying or constructing a building when their companies are about five years old. "In the start-up stage, [entrepreneurs] need to be putting their equity contribution and loan money into growing the business," he says. "After they've leased for a while, and they're growing and need more space, they'll buy a piece of real estate and build an investment for the future rather than paying increased rent."[59]

How to Get the Best Deal on a Lease

*T*he Lion's Head, a popular Greenwich Village restaurant and bar, recently closed its doors after three decades as the favorite gathering place of writers, artists, and actors. "It was a great place to meet and talk," says Mike Reardon, who once owned the Lion's Head. The restaurant and bar had its ups and downs over the years, but its base of loyal customers kept it going. Then, a series of steep increases in the Lion's Head's lease payments put the restaurant in a precarious financial situation. A five-year lease negotiated in 1989 raised the company's monthly rent from $5,000 to $8,000. Severe cash flow problems, due in part to the higher lease payments, forced the Lion's Head into Chapter 11 bankruptcy. Reardon and two partners bought the business and reorganized it. When the lease came up for renewal in 1994, however, the monthly rent jumped to $10,000. The Lion's Head's monthly overhead costs skyrocketed to $40,000, making it extremely difficult for the company to break even. Reardon began looking for a new location, but before he could find one, fate struck another blow: The neighboring Circle Repertory Theater moved, taking with it a steady stream of theater customers. Shortly thereafter, the Lion's Head closed. "New Yorkers go to the newest, hottest areas, and right now those are the Upper East Side and Soho," says one restaurateur. "[Greenwich] Village restaurants rely more on local clientele. It's hard to make it if you have a heavy rent."

Rent or lease payments represent one of the largest expenses many business owners pay. As the Lion's Head proves, failing to negotiate a satisfactory lease can push a company's operating expenses so high that ultimately the company fails. What can a business owner do to avoid lease nightmares? The following tips will help.

◆ *Read the lease agreement before you sign it.* Amazingly, some small business owners simply sign their leases without even reading them, often because they fear losing out on a great location. One attorney specializing in leases says, "Take your time and read every word of the lease, no matter how many would-be tenants are behind you."

◆ *Ask an experienced attorney to review the lease before you sign it.* At one time, leases were relatively simple contracts. Today, however, it is not uncommon for a lease to be a "40- to 60-page document filled with very complex issues many tenants are not always equipped to deal with on their own," says a real estate broker.

◆ *Incorporate (or form an LLC) before you sign a lease.* Otherwise, if the business cannot make the lease payments, the landlord has the right to make the business owner personally responsible for them.

◆ *Try to negotiate a lease term that is as short as possible at the outset.* Many landlords ask business owners to personally guarantee lease payments. To reduce the risk of getting stuck with long-term payments, try to get a short-term lease that you can renew rather than agreeing to a 5- or 10-year term.

◆ *Get everything in writing.* Under the Statute of Frauds, courts require all contracts that transfer an interest in land (such as a lease) to be in writing to be enforceable. Those oral promises from a landlord don't mean a thing if a dispute arises! The owners of a small medical consulting firm learned this lesson the hard way when they relied on their landlord's verbal promises to renew the company's lease. Within a few months, they were looking for a new location.

◆ *Pay close attention to the details.* Make sure the lease agreement doesn't contain any unpleasant surprises. The owner of a small flower shop was amazed when his landlord told him that he would be responsible for the damage a broken pipe in his part of the building had caused in other businesses. "If you're moving into [an older] building, you could be partially liable for large future repair bills for items such as the air-conditioning system or roof if you don't structure your lease carefully," says one expert.

◆ *Make sure you have good insurance to cover any damage to the property.* Renter's insurance is usually very inexpensive and can be a company's salvation if something goes wrong.

◆ *Verify that the lease's provisions on such issues as parking spaces, improvements, operating hours, air conditioning and heating, cleaning and other services, and maintenance suit your business and its financial situation.* Too often, business owners overlook these small but important matters.

◆ *Ask for the ability to sublease (with the landlord's approval, of course).* Otherwise, if your company folds, you may be committed to making large lease payments for many years out of your own pocket.

◆ Retailers who lease spaces in shopping centers should try to *include a clause that guarantees the landlord will not lease to another competing business* (called an "exclusive"). They should also include an *occupancy clause*, which states that they do not pay rent until the center has a specific level of occupancy.

SOURCES: Adapted from Jan Norman, "How To: Negotiate a Lease," *Business Start-Ups*, March 1998, pp. 48–52; Kitty Barnes, "Rising Costs, Changing Tastes Lead to Last Call at Legendary Tavern," *Inc.*, March 1997, p. 26; Barabara Etchieson, "Shutting the Door on Lease Problems," *Nation's Business*, March 1996, pp. 24–25; Susan Hodges, "Getting a Grip on Your Lease," *Nation's Business*, December 1997, pp. 48–49. ◆

One major disadvantage of leasing is that the property owner might choose not to renew the lease. A successful business might be forced to move to a new location, and relocation can be extremely costly and could result in a significant loss of established customers. In many cases, it is almost like starting the business again. Also, if a business is successful, the property owner may ask for a significant increase in rent when the lease renewal is negotiated. The owner of the building is well aware of the costs associated with moving and has the upper hand in the negotiations. In some lease arrangements, the owner is compensated, in addition to a monthly rental fee, by a percentage of the tenant's gross sales. This practice is common in shopping centers.

Still another disadvantage to leasing is the limitation on remodeling. A building owner who believes that modifications will reduce the future rental value of the property, will likely require a long-term lease at a higher rent or might not allow the modifications to be made. In addition, all permanent modifications of the structure become the property of the building owner.

Chapter Summary

1. Explain the stages in the location decision.
   - The location decision is one of the most important decisions an entrepreneur will make, given its long-term effects on the company. An entrepreneur should look at the choice as a series of increasingly narrow decisions: Which region of the country? Which state? Which city? Which site?
   - Demographic statistics are available from a wide variety of sources, but government agencies such as the Census Bureau have a wealth of detailed data that can guide an entrepreneur in her location decision.

2. Describe the location criteria for retail and service businesses.
   - For retailers and many service businesses, the location decision is especially crucial. They must consider the size of the trade area, the volume of customer traffic, number of parking spots, availability of room for expansion, and the visibility of a site.

3. Outline the basic location options for retail and service businesses.
   - Retail and service businesses have six basic location options: central business districts (CBDs), neighborhoods, shopping centers and malls, near competitors, outlying areas, and at home.

4. Explain the site selection process for manufacturers.
   - A manufacturer's location decision is strongly influenced by local zoning ordinances. Some areas offer industrial parks designed specifically to attract manufacturers. Two crucial factors for most manufacturers are the accessibility to (and the cost of transporting) raw materials and the quality and quantity of available labor.

5. Discuss the benefits of locating a start-up company in a business incubator.
   - Business incubators are locations that offer flexible, low-cost rental space to their tenants as well as business and consulting services. Their goal is to nurture small companies until they are ready to "graduate" into the larger business community. Many government agencies and universities offer incubator locations.

6. Describe the criteria used to analyze the layout and design considerations of a building, including the Americans with Disabilities Act.
   - When evaluating the suitability of a particular building, an entrepreneur should consider several factors: size (is it large enough to accommodate the business with some room for growth?); construction and external appearance (is the building structurally sound, and does it create the right impression for the business?); entrances (are they inviting?); legal issues (does the building comply with the Americans with Disabilities Act? If not, how much will it cost to bring it up to standard?); signs (are they legible, well located, and easy to see?); interior (does the interior design contribute to our ability to make sales? Is it ergonomically designed?); lights and fixtures (is the lighting adequate for the tasks workers will be performing, and what is the estimated cost of lighting?).

7. Explain the principles of effective layouts for retailers, service businesses, and manufacturers.

- Layout for retail stores and service businesses depends on the owner's understanding of her customers' buying habits. Retailers have three basic layout options from which to choose: grid, free-form pattern, and boutique. Some areas of a retail store generate more sales per square foot and are, therefore, more valuable than others.
- The goal of a manufacturer's layout is to create a smooth, efficient work flow. Three basic options exist: product layout, process layout, and fixed-position layout. Two key considerations are worker productivity and materials-handling costs.

8 Evaluate the advantages and disadvantages of building, buying, and leasing a building.

- Building a new building gives an entrepreneur the opportunity to design exactly what he wants in a brand-new facility; however, not every small business owner can afford to tie up significant amounts of cash in fixed assets. Buying an existing building gives a business owner the freedom to renovate as needed, but this can be an expensive alternative. Leasing a location is a common choice because it is economical, but the business owner faces the uncertainty of lease renewals, rising rents, and renovation problems.

Discussion Questions

1. How do most small business owners choose a location? Is this wise?
2. What factors should a manager consider when evaluating a region in which to locate a business? Where are such data available?
3. Outline the factors entrepreneurs should consider when selecting a state in which to locate a business.
4. What factors should a seafood-processing plant, a beauty shop, and an exclusive jewelry store consider in choosing a location? List factors for each type of business.
5. What intangible factors might enter into the entrepreneur's location decision?
6. What are zoning laws? How do they affect the location decision?
7. What is the trade area? What determines a small retailer's trade area?

8. Why is it important to discover more than just the number of passersby in a traffic count?
9. What types of information can an entrepreneur collect from census data?
10. Why may a cheap location not be the best location?
11. What function does a small firm's sign serve? What are the characteristics of an effective business sign?
12. Explain the statement: "The portions of a small store's interior space are not of equal value in generating sales revenue." What areas are most valuable?
13. What are some of the major features that are important to a good manufacturing layout?
14. Summarize the advantages and disadvantages of building, buying, and leasing a building.

Step into the Real World

1. Ask your librarian to help you with a search of government documents to gain additional insight about a city or town you are familiar with. What did you learn about the area and its residents? What kind of businesses would be most successful there? Least successful?
2. Visit a successful retail store and evaluate its layout. What, if anything, struck you about the layout of the store? What suggestions can you make for improving it?
3. Locate the most recent issue of either *Entrepreneur* or *Fortune* describing the "best cities for (small) business." (For *Entrepreneur*, it is usually the October issue, and for *Fortune*, it is normally an issue in November.) Which cities are in the top 10? What factors did the magazine use to select these cities? Pick a city and explain what makes it an attractive destination for locating a business.
4. Spend some time researching the details of creating an attractive window display. On the basis of your research, develop a simple rating system to evaluate the effectiveness of window displays. Then visit an area of your town or city where there is a cluster of small retail shops. Evaluate the window displays you see using your rating scale. Which ones are most effective? Least effective? Why?

Take It to the Net

Visit the Scarborough/Zimmerer home page at
www.prenhall.com/scarbzim
for updated information, on-line resources, and Web-based exercises.

Endnotes

1. Tom Shachtman, "Neighborhood Watch," *Entrepreneur*, March 1998, pp. 116–123.
2. Erik W. Matson, "Location, Location, Location!" *Industry Week*, January 9, 1995, p. 42.
3. Srikumar S. Rao, "Corporate Treasure Maps," *FW*, June 20, 1995, p. 61.
4. Bernard Wysocki Jr., "A Staid Research Park Finds New Life As a Cultivator of High-Tech Start-Ups," *Wall Street Journal*, August 16, 1996, p. B1.
5. Janean Chun, Debra Phillips, Cynthia E. Griffin, Heather Page, and Charlotte Mulhern, "20 Best Cities for Small Business," *Entrepreneur*, October 1997, pp. 102–120.
6. Andrew Kupfer, "The Champ of Cheap Clones," *Fortune*, September 23, 1991, pp. 115–120.
7. Jan Larson, "Density Is Destiny," *American Demographics*, February 1993, pp. 38–43.
8. Ibid.
9. Marc Ballon, "Start-up Covets Spokes of Northwest's Hub," *Inc.*, February 1998, pp. 19–20.
10. Bernard J. LaLonde, "New Frontiers in Store Location," *Supermarket Merchandising*, February 1963, p. 110.
11. Suzanne Oliver, "It's the Costs, Stupid," *Forbes*, October 21, 1996, pp. 252–258.
12. Joe Charles, "The Benefits of Staying Home," *Nation's Business*, February 1997, p. 6.
13. Cynthia E. Griffin, "Tech It to the Streets," *Entrepreneur*, October 1997, p. 15.
14. Charles, "The Benefits of Staying Home."
15. James A. Schriner, "Where Will Employees Want to Live?" *Industry Week*, March 3, 1997, p. 62.
16. Kevin Helliker, "Monster Movie Theaters Invade the Cinema Landscape," *Wall Street Journal*, May 13, 1997, pp. B1, B13.
17. Kylo-Patrick Hart, "Step 7: Choosing a Location," *Business Start-Ups*, November 1996, pp. 76–80.
18. Benjamin A. Holden and John R. Emshwiller, "Selling Paint, Salsa, and Cappucino on Site of L.A. Riots," *Wall Street Journal*, April 24, 1997, pp. B1, B2.
19. Susan Greco, "Where the Shoppers Are," *Inc.*, May 1995, p. 113.
20. Michael Totty, "'Power' Centers Lure Shoppers by Mixing Elements from Big Malls and Small Plazas," *Wall Street Journal*, December 27, 1988, p. B1.
21. Roberta Maynard, "A Growing Outlet for Small Firms," *Nation's Business*, August 1996, pp. 45–48.
22. Hollis L. Engley, "Cloning in America," *Greenville News*, April 28, 1996, p. 4F.
23. Ibid., p. 1F.
24. Mitchell Pacelle, "More Stores Spurn Malls for the Village Square," *Wall Street Journal*, February 16, 1996, p. B1.
25. Ibid.
26. Ibid.
27. International Council of Shopping Centers, New York <http://www.icsc.org/>.
28. Dale D. Buss, "Malls Seek Single Store Flavor," *Nation's Business*, April 1998, p. 57.
29. Mitchell Pacelle, "The Aging Shopping Mall Must Either Adapt or Die," *Wall Street Journal*, April 16, 1996, pp. B1, B16.
30. Kenneth Labich, "What It Will Take to Keep People Hanging Out at the Mall," *Fortune*, May 29, 1995, p. 103.
31. Pacelle, "The Aging Shopping Mall Must Either Adapt or Die," p. B1.
32. Laura Bird, "Huge Mall Bets on Formula of Family Fun and Games," *Wall Street Journal*, June 11, 1997, pp. B1, B12; Labich, "What It Will Take to Keep People Hanging Out at the Mall," pp. 102–106.
33. Marsha Gilbert, "Restaurants Cluster in Prime Locations," *Upstate Business*, March 23, 1997, pp. 1, 4–5.
34. Laura Meyers, "Tough New Zoning Laws Threaten Activity of Home Businesses," *Your Company*, Fall 1995, pp. 8–9; Lynn Beresford, Janean Chun, Cynthia E. Griffin, Heather Page, and Debra Phillips, "Homeward Bound," *Entrepreneur*, September 1995, pp. 116–129.
35. Catherine Siskos, "Home Businesses Are Smokin'," *Kiplinger's Personal Finance Magazine*, March 1998, pp. 143–149.
36. Roger Rickleffs, "Home-Office Dropouts Flee Dogs, Kids for Professional Aura of Rented Suites," *Wall Street Journal*, July 23, 1996, p. B2.
37. Ellen Wojahn, "They Can't Shut Us Down," *Business@Home*, Summer 1997, pp. 16–23.
38. Veronica Byrd, "Getting into a Zone Could Be This Year's Smart Move," *Your Company*, April/May 1997, pp. 8–10; Cynthia E. Griffin, "In the Zone," *Entrepreneur*, May 1998, pp. 16–17.
39. Ibid.
40. The National Business Incubation Association, Athens, OH. <http://www.nbia.org>.
41. Dale Buss, "Bringing New Firms Out of Their Shell," *Nation's Business*, March 1997, pp. 48–50.
42. Ibid.
43. David R. Evanson, "Fertile Ground," *Entrepreneur*, August 1997, pp. 55–56.
44. Lynn Beresford, "Training Ground," *Entrepreneur*, June 1997, p. 50.
45. National Business Incubation Association, Athens, OH. <http://www.nbia.org>.
46. Jennifer Zajac, "How to Dress Your Windows for Success," *Your Company*, June/July 1997, pp. 23–24.
47. Ibid.
48. Ibid.
49. Lynn Beresford, "Funny Business," *Entrepreneur*, January 1998, p. 50.

50. Deborah L. Jacobs, "The Americans with Disabilities Act," *Your Company*, Summer 1994, pp. 10–12; "The Americans with Disabilities Act," Department of Justice <http://gopher.usdoj.gov/crt/ada.html>.

51. "How to Check on Your Firm's Accessibility," *Nation's Business*, May 1994, p. 14.

52. "Sit Up Straight—OSHA Is Watching," *Business Ethics*, May/June 1994, p. 12.

53. Mitchel Brill and Cheryl Parker, "Office Planning," *Small Business Reports*, December 1988, p. 36.

54. Heather Page, "Pedal to the Metal," *Entrepreneur*, August 1996, p. 15.

55. Robert A. Mamis, "Even the Lights Have Eyes," *Inc.*, June 1993, p. 49.

56. "Business Bulletin," *Wall Street Journal*, May 1, 1997, p. A1.

57. "The Law of Averages," *Entrepreneur*, March 1992, p. 18.

58. Tom Stevens, "Practice People," *Industry Week*, March 17, 1997, pp. 33–36.

59. "Release Me," *Entrepreneur*, January 1998, pp. 48–49.

Purchasing, Quality Control, and Vendor Analysis

Without the right goods, sales are impossible.

—Anonymous

Quality is never an accident; it is always the result of high intention, sincere effort, intelligent direction, and skillful execution; it represents the wise choice of many alternatives.

—William A. Foster

Upon completion of this chapter, you will be able to

1 Understand the components of a purchasing plan.

2 Explain the principles of total quality management (TQM) and its impact on quality.

3 Conduct economic order quantity (EOQ) analysis to determine the proper level of inventory.

4 Differentiate among the three types of purchase discounts vendors offer.

5 Calculate a company's reorder point.

6 Develop a vendor rating scale.

7 Describe the legal implications of the purchasing function.

---

*P*urchasing is not one of the most glamorous or exciting jobs an entrepreneur will undertake, but it is one of the most vital functions to a small company's ultimate success. When entrepreneurs begin producing products or providing services, they soon discover how dependent their products and services are on the quality of the components and services they purchase from their vendors, or suppliers. Selecting the right vendors and ensuring that the purchasing process operates efficiently determine a small company's ability to produce and sell quality products at a reasonable price. Entrepreneurs who neglect the purchasing function often end up overpaying for the parts and supplies their companies use, so their finished products or services are not price-competitive with those of rivals. Also, their products or services may not meet customers' expectations because of the poor quality of the raw materials from suppliers. The effects of an entrepreneur's decisions on purchasing, quality, and vendor selection ripple throughout the entire company, affecting everything it does and producing a dramatic impact on its "bottom line." Depending on the type of business involved, the amounts spent by the purchasing department range from 25 to 85 cents per one dollar of sales. The average manufacturer, for example, spends 55 cents of each dollar in sales on purchases of goods and services. By finding savings in its purchasing bill of 5 percent, the typical manufacturer can add 3 percent to its net profit![1]

Bill Blocher, owner of BBC Computers, a small computer manufacturer, knows that the purchasing function is an integral part of his company's success in an industry driven by ever-falling prices, constantly accelerating technology, and price-sensitive customers. Before making purchases, Blocher makes sure he shops the market, calling at least three regular suppliers to make sure he's getting a good deal. He also works to keep his inventory of components as lean as possible, relying on just-in-time principles whenever possible. "Why tie up our cash in inventory?" says Blocher. BBC pays as much attention to its suppliers' terms as it does to their prices. "If one supplier quotes us a slightly higher price, but at net 60 days instead of net 30, we'll do a complete cost analysis to figure out which way we're better off, making certain to factor in the cost of our money," he says. "The way we make every purchase every day will make or break us."[2]

◆ Understand the components of a purchasing plan.

*7*he Purchasing Plan

Purchasing involves the acquisition of needed materials, supplies, services, and equipment of the right quality, in the proper quantities, for reasonable prices, at the appropriate time, from the right vendor, or supplier. A major objective of purchasing is to acquire enough (but not too much!) stock to ensure smooth, uninterrupted production or sales and to see that the merchandise is delivered on time. Companies large and small are purchasing goods and supplies from all across the globe, and coordinating the pieces of the global puzzle requires a comprehensive purchasing plan. The plan must identify a company's quality requirements, its cost targets, and the criteria for determining the best supplier, considering such factors as reliability, service, delivery, and cooperation.

The purchasing plan is closely linked to the other functional areas of managing a small business: production, marketing, sales, engineering, accounting, finance, and others. A purchasing plan should recognize this interaction and help integrate the purchasing function into the total organization. A small company's purchasing plan should focus on the five key elements of purchasing: quality, quantity, price, timing, and vendor selection (see Figure 16.1).

◆ Explain the principles of total quality management (TQM) and its impact on quality.

*2*uality

Not long ago businesses saw quality products and services as luxuries for customers who could afford them. Many companies mistakenly believed that producing, and therefore purchasing, high-quality products and services was too costly. "Those were the days when people actually believed that higher quality was going to cost more money," says one quality manager.[3] The last few decades, however, have taught every businessperson that quality goods and services are absolutely *essential* to staying competitive. The benefits companies earn by pursuing quality products, services, and processes come not only in the form of fewer defects but also as lower costs, higher productivity, reduced cycle time, greater market share, increased customer satisfaction, and higher customer retention rates. W. Edwards Deming, one of the founding fathers of the modern quality movement, always claimed that

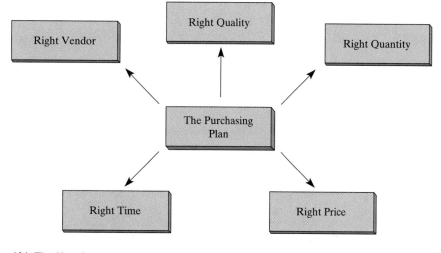

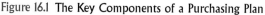

Figure 16.1 The Key Components of a Purchasing Plan

"higher quality is less expensive to produce than lower quality."[4] Internally, companies with a quality focus report significant improvements in work-related factors such as increased employee morale, lower employee turnover, and enhanced quality of work life. Benefits such as these can result in earning a significant competitive advantage over rivals of *any* size.

Total quality companies believe in and manage with the attitude of continuous improvement, a concept the Japanese call *kaizen*. The kaizen philosophy holds that small improvements made continuously over time accumulate into a radically reshaped and improved process. *The Alexander Doll Company of New York City knows the value of improving quality through continuous improvement. The company fell into such bad financial shape that it declared bankruptcy before managers decided to try to turn it around with kaizen. Managers began by setting up a cross-functional team (a team of workers from different functional areas of the business) to identify problems with the production process and to make suggestions for solving them. The first problem the team tackled was the manufacturing process itself, which was spread out over three floors, causing a high breakage rate. The team recommended moving the production process onto one floor and rearranging it to minimize handling. Alexander created more teams, which went to work on 65 projects covering all phases of its operation. The results: The distance dolls traveled during manufacturing decreased from 630 feet to just 40 feet. The inventory of unfinished doll pieces dropped from 29,000 to 34, and productivity went from eight dolls per person per day to 25! In addition, the lead time to produce a doll went from 90 days to just 90 minutes. Managers cannot credit any single change with producing such dramatic results; rather, they are the outcome of many small changes teams of creative workers came up with over time.[5]*

Despite the benefits their companies can reap from quality improvements, many managers have yet to get on the quality bandwagon. According to one recent study, 83 percent of managers at midsized companies said that quality was a top priority. However, only 31 percent had actually calculated the cost of quality: the costs associated with scrap, rework, inspections, training, technology, and other factors.[6] Other studies show that executives estimate the cost of bad quality to be just 5 percent (or less) of sales when, in reality, the actual percentage is between 20 and 30 percent of sales![7] For a quality improvement system to be successful, *everyone* in the company must understand the real cost of bad quality and make a commitment to lowering it.

TOTAL QUALITY MANAGEMENT

Under the total quality management (TQM) philosophy, companies define a quality product as one that conforms to predetermined standards that satisfy customers' demands. That means getting *everything*—from delivery and invoicing to installation and follow-up—right the first time. Although these companies know that they may never reach their targets of perfect quality, they never stop striving for perfection, recognizing that even a 99.9 percent level of quality is not good enough (see Table 16.1). The businesses, both large and small, that have effectively implemented these programs understand that the process involves a total commitment from strategy to practice from the top of the organization to the bottom.

Rather than trying to inspect quality into products and services after they are completed, TQM instills the philosophy of doing the job right the first time. Although the concept is simple, implementing such a process is a challenge that requires a very different kind of thinking and very different culture than most organizations are comfortable with. Because the changes TQM requires are so significant, patience is a must for companies adopting the philosophy. Consistent quality improvements rarely occur overnight. Yet too many small business managers think, "We'll implement TQM today and tomorrow our quality will soar." TQM is *not* a "quick-fix," short-term program that can magically push a company to world-class status overnight. Because it requires such fundamental, often drastic, changes in the way a company does business, TQM takes time both to implement and to produce results. Patience is a must. Although some small businesses that use TQM begin to see some improvements within just a matter of weeks, the *real* benefits take longer to realize. Studies show that it takes at least three or four years before TQM principles gain acceptance among employees, and that eight to ten years are necessary to fully implement TQM in a company.[8]

Table 16.1 Why 99.9% Quality Isn't Good Enough

Most companies willingly accept a certain percentage of errors and defects. Usually the range is one to five percent. In some companies, it is regarded as a routine part of daily operations.

However, quality consultants say that even 99.9 percent isn't good enough. To improve their own quality, many companies are relying on a single supplier for their raw materials and components. Partnering between suppliers and customers in such a close relationship means that those sole-source suppliers have to shoot for 100 percent quality and performance! One small maker of fabrics used in the paper industry forged such a partnership with a single supplier but made it clear that just one late or poor-quality shipment would terminate the relationship.

What would be the result if some things were done right "only 99.9 percent of the time?" Consider these facts:

◆ Two unsafe landings at Chicago's O'Hare Airport.

◆ 16,000 lost pieces of mail per hour.

◆ 20,000 incorrectly-filled drug prescriptions per year.

◆ 500 incorrect surgical procedures performed each week.

◆ 22,000 checks deducted from the wrong accounts every hour.

◆ 1,314 telephone calls misdirected every minute.

◆ 14 babies delivered to the wrong parents each day.

◆ 2,488,200 magazines published with the wrong covers every year.

If you are in the unlucky one-tenth of one percent, the error affects you 100 percent! Plus, unless a company strives for 100 percent product or service quality, there is little chance that it will ever achieve 99.9 percent quality.

SOURCES: Adapted from "On the Job Performance," (Chicago: Dartnell Corporation), p. 3; Sal Marino, "Is 'Good Enough' Good Enough?" *Industry Week*, February 3, 1997, p. 22.

To implement TQM successfully, a small business owner must rely on 10 fundamental principles:

◆ *Shift from a management-driven culture to a participative, team-based one.* Two basic tenets of TQM are employee involvement and teamwork. Business owners must be willing to push decision-making authority down the organization to where the real experts are. Teams of employees working together to identify and solve problems can be a powerful force in an organization of any size. "Brain power is the sum of all the intelligence of the people in a company, not just one person," says one TQM consultant. "If [managers] can tap into that brain power, their company will be far ahead of the competition."[9]

◆ *Modify the reward system to encourage teamwork and innovation.* Because the team, not the individual, is the building block of TQM, companies often have to modify their compensation systems to reflect team performance. Traditional compensation methods pit one employee against another, undermining any sense of cooperation. Often, they are based on seniority rather than on how much an employee contributes to the company. Compensation systems under TQM usually rely on incentives, linking pay to performance. However, rather than tying pay to individual performance, these systems focus on team-based incentives. Each person's pay depends on whether the entire team (or, sometimes, the entire company) meets a clearly defined, measurable set of performance objectives. *For instance, when Laitram Corporation, a small manufacturing company, implemented TQM, it determined employees' base pay on their "market value" using regional and local surveys. Managers also set up a profit-sharing incentive system based on overall company and team performances. Workers have input into the system because they evaluate their coworkers' performances as well as those of their managers. "Employees were skeptical of the whole system," says human resource manager James Evans, "until they started getting checks."*[10]

◆ *Train workers constantly to give them the tools they need to produce quality and to upgrade the company's knowledge base.* One of the most important factors in making long-term, constant improvements in a company's processes is teaching workers the philosophy and the tools of TQM. Admonishing employees to "produce quality" or offering them rewards for high quality is futile unless a company gives them the tools and the know-how to achieve that end. Managers must be dedicated to making their companies "learning organizations" that encourage people to upgrade their skills and give them the opportunities and incentives to do so. The most successful companies spend anywhere from 1 to 5 percent of their employees' time on training, most of it invested in workers, not managers. To give employees a sense of how the quality of their job fits into the big picture, many TQM companies engage in **cross-training,** teaching workers to do other jobs in the company.

◆ *Train employees to measure quality with the tools of statistical process control (SPC).* The only way to ensure gains in quality is to measure results objectively and to track the company's progress toward its quality objectives. That requires teaching employees how to use statistical process control techniques such as fishbone charts, Pareto charts, control charts, and measures of process capability.* Without knowledgeable workers using these quantitative tools, TQM cannot produce the intended results.

◆ *Use Pareto's Law to focus TQM efforts.* One of the toughest decisions managers face in companies embarking on TQM for the first time is "Where do we start?" The best way

---

*To learn more about the tools of statistical quality control, look in modern statistics or production management textbooks or visit the following websites: <http://deming.eng.clemson.edu/pub/tutorials/qctools/qct.htmPCHART> and <http://www.eniac.com/whitepap/project6.htm>.

to answer that fundamental question is to use Pareto's Law (also called the 80/20 Rule), which states that 80 percent of a company's quality problems arise from just 20 percent of all causes. By identifying this small percentage of causes and focusing quality improvement efforts on them, a company gets maximum returns for minimum efforts. This simple, yet powerful rule forces workers to concentrate resources on the most significant problems first, where payoffs are likely to be biggest, and helps build momentum for a successful TQM effort. *For instance, when one company's customers began complaining about product losses during shipment, a team of salespeople used Pareto analysis to identify the small percentage of shippers who were responsible for the bulk of the losses. They collected the data they needed, analyzed them, and solved the problem with a just a few telephone calls and visits.*[11]

◆ *Share information with everyone in the organization.* Asking employees to make decisions and to assume responsibility for creating quality necessitates that the owner share information with them. Employees cannot make sound decisions consistent with the company's quality initiative if managers are unwilling to give them the information they need to make those decisions. *For instance, at City Concrete Products, a small building supply company that embraces the TQM philosophy, owner Mel Chambers has created work teams and an employee council that meet regularly for the purpose of sharing key information about the company's processes and results. Chambers also makes sure that information flows both ways at employee council meetings; workers routinely offer ideas and suggestions for improvement (most of which the company implements) because they know that managers will listen and act on them.*[12]

◆ *Focus quality improvements on astonishing the customer.* The heart of TQM is customer satisfaction—better yet, customer astonishment. Unfortunately, some companies focus their quality improvement efforts on areas that never benefit the customer. Quality improvements with no customer focus (either internal or external customers) are wasted.

◆ *Don't rely on inspection to produce quality products and services.* The traditional approach to achieving quality was to create a product or service and then to rely on an army of inspectors to "weed out" all of the defectives. Not only is such a system a terrible waste of resources (consider the cost of scrap, rework, and no-value-added inspections), but it gives managers no opportunity for continuous improvement. The only way to improve a process is to discover the cause of poor quality, fix it (the sooner, the better), and learn from it so that workers can *avoid* the problem in the future. Using the statistical tools of the TQM approach allows a company to learn from its mistakes with a consistent approach to constantly improving quality.

◆ *Avoid using TQM to place blame on those who make mistakes.* In many firms, the only reason managers seek out mistakes is to find someone to blame for them. The result: a culture based on fear and an unwillingness of workers to take chances to innovate. The goal of TQM is to improve the processes in which people work, *not* to lay blame on workers. Searching out "the guilty party" is fruitless! The TQM philosophy sees each problem that arises as an opportunity for improving the company's system.

◆ *Strive for continuous improvement in processes as well as in products and services.* There is no finish line in the race for quality. A company's goal must be to improve the quality of its processes, products, and services constantly, no matter how high it currently stands!

Many of these principles are evident in quality guru W. Edwards Deming's 14 points, a capsulized version of how to build a successful TQM approach (see Table 16.2).

Table 16.2–Deming's 14 Points

Total quality management cannot succeed as a piecemeal program or without true commitment to its philosophy. W. Edwards Deming, the man most visibly connected to TQM, drove home these concepts with his 14 points, the essential elements for integrating TQM successfully into a company. Deming's message was straightforward: Companies must transform themselves into customer-oriented, quality-focused organizations where teams of employees have the training, the resources, and the freedom to pursue quality on a daily basis. The goal is to track the performance of a process, whether manufacturing a clock or serving a bank customer, and to develop ways to minimize variation in the system, eliminate defects, and spur innovation. The 14 points are:

1. *Constantly strive to improve products and services.* This requires total dedication to improving quality, productivity, and service—*continuously.*

2. *Adopt a total quality philosophy.* There are no shortcuts to quality improvement; it requires a completely new way of thinking and managing.

3. *Correct defects as they happen,* rather than relying on mass inspection of end products. Real quality comes from improving the process, not from inspecting finished products and services. At that point, it's too late. Statistical process control charts can help workers detect when a process is producing poor-quality goods and services. Then they can stop it, make corrections, and get the process back on target.

4. *Don't award business on price alone.* Rather than choosing the lowest-cost vendor, businesses should work toward establishing close relationships with the vendors who offer the highest quality.

5. *Constantly improve the system of production and service.* Managers must focus the entire company on customer satisfaction, must measure results, and must make adjustments as necessary.

6. *Institute training.* Workers cannot improve quality and lower costs without proper training to erase old ways of doing things.

7. *Institute leadership.* The supervisor's job is not to boss workers around; it is to lead. The nature of the work is more like coaching than controlling.

8. *Drive out fear.* People often are afraid to point out problems because they fear the repercussions. Managers must encourage and reward employee suggestions.

9. *Break down barriers among staff areas.* Departments within organizations often erect needless barriers to protect their own turf. Total quality requires a spirit of teamwork and cooperation across the entire organization.

10. *Eliminate superficial slogans and goals.* These only offend employees because they imply that workers could do a better job if they would only try.

11. *Eliminate standard quotas.* They emphasize quantity over quality. Not everyone can move at the same rate and still produce quality.

12. *Remove barriers to pride of workmanship.* Most workers want to do quality work. Eliminating "de-motivators" frees them to achieve quality results.

13. *Institute vigorous education and retraining.* Managers must teach employees the new methods of continuous improvement, including statistical process control techniques.

14. *Take demonstrated management action to achieve the transformation.* Although success requires involvement of all levels of the organization, the impetus for change must come from the top.

These 14 interrelated elements contribute to a chain reaction effect. As a company improves its quality, costs decline; productivity increases; the company gains additional market share due to its ability to provide high-quality products at competitive prices; and the company and its employees prosper.

SOURCE: The W. Edwards Deming Institute, <http://www.deming.org/deminghtml/wedi.html>.

Implementing a TQM program successfully begins at the top. If the owner or chief executive of a company doesn't actively and visibly support the initiative, the employees who must make it happen will never accept it. "Unless the CEO is personally involved, . . . then the TQM implementation cannot be very successful," says the head of a high-tech company.[13] TQM requires change: change in the way a company defines quality, in the way it sees its customers, in the way it treats employees, and in the way it sees itself. "To do it right, you have to change your culture as much as your processes," explains one top man-

Why Certify?

*I*t took LabChem more than nine months and cost the small specialty chemical manufacturer more than $50,000, but, according to vice president Mike Semon, it was definitely worth it. "It was like winning our Stanley Cup," says Semon. LabChem has seen costs drop, productivity rise, and more customers come on board, many of whom had never considered buying from the small, 25-employee company. What caused the transformation? LabChem earned ISO 9000 certification!

Once a concern only for major corporations, ISO 9000 certification has attracted the attention of a growing number of small businesses who see the benefits of certification. Established by the International Organization for Standards (ISO) in 1979, ISO 9000 certification established a uniform set of standards that are designed to improve a company's quality, productivity, and efficiency. Rather than certify the quality of a company's finished products or services, ISO's standards verify that it has established a functional quality control process and consistently follows it. The logic is that if a company's quality processes are appropriate and it follows them consistently, high-quality products and services will result. More than 100 countries have adopted ISO 9000 as their national quality standard.

Why are small companies such as LabChem spending thousands of dollars to become ISO 9000 certified? One-fourth of all the corporations around the globe *require* their suppliers to be ISO 9000 certified. In other words, these companies are telling their suppliers, large and small, who want to keep their business that they must prove their quality by meeting the ISO's requirements. One survey by the *Quality Systems Update* newsletter of all ISO 9000–certified companies found that 83 percent encourage their suppliers also to become certified. "The pressure for companies to become certified is . . . increasing and will continue to increase," says one ISO consultant.

Many of the companies that are discovering the benefits of becoming certified are small businesses. The *Quality Systems Update* newsletter survey found that 58 percent of all registered companies had annual sales of less than $100 million. "The growth among smaller firms seeking ISO 9000 registration [in] the past several years has been phenomenal," says the head of an ISO consulting firm.

The benefits of ISO 9000 certification are both internal and external. A quality survey of ISO 9000–certified compa-

nies found that 95 percent had derived internal benefits such as improved quality, more-efficient systems, and higher productivity. Nearly 85 percent cited higher quality awareness among workers as an advantage. Externally, ISO certification opens the door to more customers. After losing a customer because their company lacked certification, managers at Arizona Calibration and Electronics Corporation, an eight-person company that repairs and calibrates mechanical testing equipment, set gaining ISO certification as a top priority. Now that the company is certified, "We're getting a lot of new interest all of a sudden from people who didn't even know we existed before," says president Frank Havelock. At Sub-Tronics, a 25-employee manufacturer of magnetic devices, keeping a major customer, 3M Corporation, was the incentive to earn ISO 9000 certification. "3M notified us [that] it [preferred] its vendors to be ISO-certified," says Nancy Peck, the company's quality-assurance manager. "We didn't want to lose them [as a customer]."

Gaining ISO 9000 certification, like most things that are worthwhile, takes time, money, and effort. The average cost for a small business (those with less than $11 million in sales) to earn certification is $71,000: $51,000 for internal expenses and $20,000 for external expenses such as quality consultants and trainers. The average time required to pass the final ISO 9000 audit is 15 months. Despite the cost and time involved, companies see the payoff of becoming certified. Nancy Peck of Sub-Tronics says that her company now has the processes—and the credentials—to go head to head with any competitor anywhere in the world. LabChem's Mike Semon says, "There will be some firms that won't need ISO 9000 certification. But for many firms that don't have it, they need to ask themselves one question: 'Do I want my company to be in business five years from now?' "

---

1. What benefits does a small company derive from becoming ISO-certified? What are the costs?

2. Use the World Wide Web to research ISO 9000 requirements. How many levels of certification are there? What areas does each level cover?

3. Canvass the businesses in your area. Work with a team of your classmates to develop a list of companies that you believe would benefit from becoming ISO 9000 certified. Develop a second list of companies for whom ISO 9000 certification would offer only limited benefits. What characteristics define the differences between the companies on your two lists?

SOURCES: Adapted from Harvey R. Meyer, "Small Firms Flock to Quality System," *Nation's Business*, March 1998, pp. 66–68; Hugh D. Menzies, "Quality Counts When Wooing Overseas Clients," *Your Company*, June/July 1997, p. 64. ◆

ager.[14] Leadership from above and employee training are both essential to ensuring an effective transition to a new mind-set and process.

Drastic changes such as these naturally create turmoil. Planned and implemented properly, however, TQM can use the energy from that turmoil to drive the changes a company must make if it is to become truly world-class. Training employees so that they have the tools they need to achieve quality results and creating a participative environment marked by free-flowing communication and teamwork can minimize an organization's natural resistance to change. As W. Edwards Deming said, "It's easy to develop a system of precise standards for quality; the challenge is to lead your personnel effectively so they feel ownership and commitment to measures of quality."[15]

*2*uantity: The Economic Order Quantity (EOQ)

3 Conduct economic order quantity (EOQ) analysis to determine the proper level of inventory.

The typical small business has its largest investment in inventory. But an investment in inventory is not profitable because dollars spent return nothing until the inventory is sold. In a sense, the small firm's inventory is its largest non-interest-bearing "account." The owner must focus on controlling this investment and on maintaining proper inventory levels.

A primary objective of this portion of the purchasing plan is to generate an adequate turnover of merchandise by purchasing proper quantities. Tying up capital in the maintenance of extra inventory limits the firm's working capital and exerts pressure on its cash flows. Also, the firm risks the danger of being stuck with spoiled or obsolete merchandise, an extremely serious problem for many small businesses. Excess inventory also takes up valuable store or selling space that could be used for items with higher turnover rates and more profit potential. On the other hand, maintaining too little inventory can be extremely costly. An owner will be forced to reorder merchandise frequently, escalating total inventory costs. Also, inventory stockouts will occur when customer demand exceeds the firm's supply of merchandise, causing customer ill will. Persistent stockouts are inconvenient for customers, and many will eventually choose to shop elsewhere.

Clearly the small business must maintain enough inventory to meet customer orders, but not so much that storage costs and inventory investment are excessive. The analytical techniques used to determine **economic order quantities (EOQs)** will help the manager compute the amount of stock to purchase with an order or to produce with each production run to minimize total inventory costs. To compute the proper amount of stock to order or to produce, the small business owner must first determine the three principal elements of total inventory costs: the cost of the units, the holding (or carrying) cost, and the setup (or ordering) cost.

COST OF UNITS

The cost of the units is simply the number of units demanded for a particular time period multiplied by the cost per unit. Suppose that a small manufacturer of lawn mowers forecasts demand for the upcoming year to be 100,000 mowers. He needs to order enough wheels at $1.55 each to supply the production department. So he computes:

$$\text{Total annual cost of units} = D \times C$$

where:

$$D = \text{Annual demand (in units)}$$

$$C = \text{Cost of a single unit (\$)}$$

In this example,

$$D = 100,000 \text{ mowers} \times 4 \text{ wheels per mower} = 400,000 \text{ wheels}$$

$$C = \$1.55/\text{wheel}$$

Total annual cost of units $= D \times C$

$$= 400,000 \text{ wheels} \times \$1.55$$

$$= \$620,000$$

HOLDING (CARRYING) COSTS

The typical costs of holding inventory include the costs of storage, insurance, taxes, interest, depreciation, spoilage, obsolescence, and pilferage. The expense involved in physically storing the items in inventory is usually substantial, especially if the inventories are large. The owner may have to rent or build additional warehousing facilities, pushing the cost of storing the inventory even higher. The firm may also incur expenses in transferring items into and out of inventory. The cost of storage also includes the expense of operating the facility (e.g., heating, lighting, refrigeration), as well as the depreciation, taxes, and interest on the building. Most small business owners purchase insurance on their inventories to shift the risk of fire, theft, flood, and other disasters to the insurer. The premiums paid for this coverage are also included in the cost of holding inventory. In general, the larger the firm's average inventory, the greater its storage cost.

Many small business owners fail to recognize the interest expense associated with carrying large inventories. In many cases the interest expense is evident when the firm borrows money to purchase inventory. But a less obvious interest expense is the opportunity cost associated with investing in inventory. In other words, the owner could have used the money invested in inventory (a non-interest-bearing investment) for some other purpose, such as plant expansion, research and development, or reducing debt. Thus, the cost of independent financing of inventory is the cost of forgoing the opportunity to use those funds elsewhere. A substantial inventory investment ties up a large amount of money unproductively.

Depreciation costs represent the reduced value of inventory over time. Some businesses are strongly influenced by the depreciation of inventory. For example, a small auto dealer's inventory is subject to depreciation because he must sell models left over from one year at reduced prices.

Spoilage, obsolescence, and pilferage also add to the costs of holding inventory. Some small firms, especially those that deal in fad merchandise, assume an extremely high risk of obsolescence. For example, a fashion merchandiser with a large inventory of the latest styles may be left with worthless merchandise when styles suddenly change. Small companies selling perishables must always be aware of the danger of spoilage. For example, the owner of a small fish market must plan purchases carefully to ensure a fresh inventory. And unless the owner establishes sound inventory control procedures, the business will suffer losses from employee theft and shoplifting.

Let us use the lawn mower manufacturer example to illustrate the cost of holding inventory:

$$\text{Total annual holding (carrying) costs} = \frac{Q}{2} \times H$$

Table 16.3 Carrying Cost

If Q Is . . .	$Q/2$, Average Inventory, Is . . .	$Q/2 \times H$, Carrying Cost, Is . . .
500	250	$312.50
1,000	500	625.00
2,000	1,000	1,250.00
3,000	1,500	1,875.00
4,000	2,000	2,500.00
5,000	2,500	3,125.00
6,000	3,000	3,750.00
7,000	3,500	4,375.00
8,000	4,000	5,000.00
9,000	4,500	5,625.00
10,000	5,000	6,250.00

where:

$$Q = \text{Quantity of inventory ordered}$$

$$H = \text{Holding cost per unit per year}$$

The greater the quantity ordered, the greater the inventory carrying costs. This relationship is shown in Table 16.3, assuming that the cost of carrying a single unit of inventory for 1 year is $1.25.

SETUP (ORDERING) COSTS

The various expenses incurred in actually ordering materials and inventory or in setting up the production line to manufacture them determine the level of setup or ordering costs of a product. The costs of obtaining materials and inventory typically include preparing purchase orders; analyzing and choosing vendors; processing, handling, and expending orders; receiving and inspecting items; and performing all the required accounting and clerical functions. Even if the small company produces its own supply of goods, it encounters most of these same expenses. Ordering costs are usually relatively fixed, regardless of the quantity ordered.

Setup or ordering costs are found by multiplying the number of orders made in a year (or the number of production runs in a year) by the cost of placing a single order (or the cost of setting up a single production run). In the lawn mower manufacturing example, the annual requirement is 400,000 wheels per year and the cost to place an order is $9.00, so the ordering costs are as follows:

$$\text{Total annual setup (ordering) cost} = \frac{D}{Q} \times S$$

where:

$$D = \text{Annual demand}$$

$$Q = \text{Quantity of inventory ordered}$$

$$S = \text{Setup (ordering) costs for a single run (or order)}$$

Table 16.4   Setup Cost

If Q Is . . .	D/Q, Number of Orders per Year, Is . . .	$D/Q \times S$, Ordering (Setup) Cost, Is . . .
500	800	$7,200
1,000	400	3,600
5,000	80	720
10,000	40	360

The greater the quantity ordered, the smaller the number of orders placed. This relationship is shown in Table 16.4, assuming an ordering cost of $9.00 per order.

SOLVING FOR EOQ

Clearly, if carrying costs were the only expense involved in obtaining inventory, the small business manager would purchase the smallest number of units possible in each order to minimize the cost of holding the inventory. For example, if the lawn mower manufacturer purchased four wheels per order, carrying cost would be minimized:

$$\text{Carrying cost} = \frac{Q}{2} \times H$$

$$= \frac{4 \times \$1.25}{2}$$

$$= \$2.50$$

but his ordering cost would be outrageous:

$$\text{Ordering cost} = \frac{D}{Q} \times S$$

$$= \frac{100,000 \times \$9}{4}$$

$$= \$2,250,000$$

Obviously this is not the small manufacturer's ideal inventory solution!

Similarly, if ordering costs were the only expense involved in procuring inventory, the small business manager would purchase the largest number of units possible in order to minimize the ordering cost. In our example, if the lawn mower manufacturer purchased 400,000 wheels per order, ordering cost would be minimized:

$$\text{Ordering cost} = \frac{D}{Q} \times S$$

$$= \frac{400,000 \times \$9}{400,000}$$

$$= \$9$$

but his carrying cost would be tremendously high:

$$\text{Carrying cost} = \frac{Q}{2} \times H$$

$$= \frac{400,000 \times \$1.25}{2}$$

$$= \$250,000$$

A quick inspection shows that neither of those solutions minimizes the total cost of the manufacturer's inventory. Total cost is composed of the cost of the unit, carrying cost, and ordering costs:

$$\text{Total cost} = (D \times C) + (Q/2 \times H) + (D/Q \times S)$$

These cost are graphed in Figure 16.2. Notice that as the quantity ordered increases, the ordering costs decrease and the carrying costs increase.

The EOQ formula simply balances the ordering cost and the carrying cost of the small business owner's inventory so that total costs are minimized. Table 16.5 summarizes the total costs for various values of Q for our lawn mower manufacturer.

As Table 16.4 and Figure 16.2 illustrate, the EOQ formula locates the minimum point on the total cost curve, which occurs where the cost of carrying inventory ($Q/2 \times H$) equals the cost of ordering inventory ($D/Q \times S$). If the small business places the smallest number of orders possible each year, its ordering cost is minimized but its carrying cost is maximized. Conversely, if the firm orders the smallest number of units possible in each order, its carrying cost is minimized, but its ordering cost is maximized. Total inventory cost is minimized when carrying cost and ordering costs are balanced.

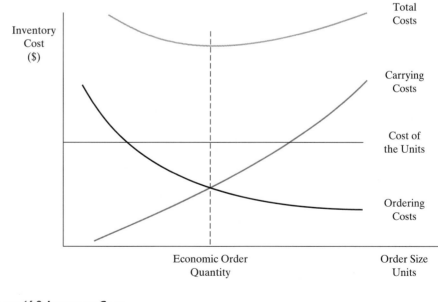

Figure 16.2 Inventory Costs

Table 16.5 Economic Order Quantity and Total Cost

If Q Is . . .	$D \times C$, Cost of Units, Is . . .	$Q/2 \times H$, Carrying Cost, Is . . .	$D/Q \times S$, Ordering Cost, Is . . .	Total Cost Is . . .
500	$ 620,000	$ 312.50	$ 7,200.00	$ 627,512.50
1,000	$ 620,000	$ 625.00	$ 3,600.00	$ 624,225.00
2,400	**$ 620,000**	**$ 1,500.00**	**$ 1,500.00**	**$623,000.00**
5,000	$ 620,000	$ 3,125.00	$ 720.00	$ 623,845.00
10,000	$ 620,000	$ 6,250.00	$ 360.00	$ 626,610.00

Let us return to our lawn mower manufacturer and compute its economic order quantity, EOQ, using the following formula:

$$S = \$9.00 \text{ per order}$$

$$C = \$1.55 \text{ per wheel}$$

$$EOQ = \sqrt{\frac{2 \times D \times S}{H}}$$

$$= \sqrt{\frac{2 \times 400,000 \times 9.00}{1.25}}$$

$$= 2,400 \text{ wheels}$$

To minimize total inventory cost, the lawn mower manufacturer should order 2,400 wheels at a time. Further,

$$\text{Number of orders per year} = \frac{D}{Q}$$

$$= \frac{400,000}{2,400}$$

$$= 166.67 \text{ orders}$$

This manufacturer will place approximately 167 orders this year at a minimum total cost of $623,000, computed as follows:

$$\text{Total cost} = (D \times C) + \left(\frac{Q}{2} \times H\right) + \left(\frac{D}{Q} \times S\right)$$

$$= (400,000 \times 1.55) + \left(\frac{2,400}{2} \times 1.25\right) + \left(\frac{400,000}{2,400} + 9.00\right)$$

$$= \$620,000 \qquad + \$1,500 \qquad + \$1,500$$

$$= \$623,000$$

ECONOMIC ORDER QUANTITY (EOQ) WITH USAGE

The preceding EOQ model assumes that orders are filled instantaneously; that is, fresh inventory arrives all at once. Because that assumption does not hold true for many small manufacturers, it is necessary to consider a variation of the basic EOQ model that allows inventory to be added over a period of time rather than instantaneously. In addition, the manufacturer is likely to be taking items from inventory for use in the assembly process over the same time period. For example, the lawn mower manufacturer may be producing blades to replenish his supply, but, at the same time, assembly workers are reducing the supply of blades to make finished mowers. The key feature of this version of the EOQ model is that inventories are used while inventories are being added.

Using the lawn mower manufacturer as an example, we can compute the EOQ for the blades. To make the calculation, we need two additional pieces of information: the usage rate for the blades, U, and the plant's capacity to manufacture the blades, P. Suppose that the maximum number of lawn mower blades the company can manufacture is 480 per day. We know from the previous illustration that annual demand for mowers is 100,000 units (therefore, 100,000 blades). If the plant operates 5 days per week for 50 weeks (250 days), its usage rate is

$$U = \frac{100,000 \text{ units per year}}{250 \text{ days}} = 400 \text{ units per day}$$

It costs $325 to set up the blade manufacturing line and $8.71 to store one blade for 1 year. The cost of producing a blade is $4.85. To compute EOQ we modify the basic formula to get:

$$EOQ = \sqrt{\frac{2 \times D \times S}{H \times \left(1 - \dfrac{U}{P}\right)}}$$

For the lawn mower manufacturer,

$$D = 100,000 \text{ blades}$$
$$S = \$325 \text{ per production run}$$
$$H = \$8.71 \text{ per blade per year}$$
$$U = 400 \text{ blades per day}$$
$$P = 480 \text{ blades per day}$$

$$EOQ = \sqrt{\frac{2 \times 100,000 \times 325}{8.71 \times \left(1 - \dfrac{400}{480}\right)}}$$

$$= 6,691.50 \text{ blades}$$
$$= 6,692 \text{ blades}$$

Therefore, to minimize total inventory cost, the lawn mower manufacturer should produce 6,692 blades per production run. Also,

$$\text{Number of production runs per year} = D/Q$$

$$= \frac{100,000 \text{ blades}}{6,692 \text{ blades/run}}$$

$$= 14.9 \approx 15 \text{ runs}$$

The manufacturer will make 15 production runs during the year at a total cost of:

$$\text{Total cost} = (D \times C) + \left(\frac{1 - \dfrac{U}{P} \times Q}{2} \times H \right) + \left(\frac{D}{Q} \times S \right)$$

$$= (100,000 \times \$4.85) + \left(\frac{1 - \dfrac{400}{480} \times 6.692}{2} \times 8.71 \right) + \left(\frac{100,000}{6,692} \times \$325 \right)$$

$$= \$485,000 + \$4,857 + \$4,857$$

$$= \$494,714$$

Small business managers must remember that the EOQ analysis is based on estimations of cost and demand. The final result is only as accurate as the input used. Thus, this analytical tool serves only as a guideline for decision making. The final answer may not be the ideal solution because of intervening factors, such as opportunity costs or seasonal fluctuations. Knowledgeable entrepreneurs use EOQ analysis as a starting point in making a decision and then will use managerial judgment to produce a final ruling.

$\mathcal{P}$rice

For the typical small business owner, price is always a substantial factor in purchasing inventory and supplies. In many cases, an entrepreneur can negotiate price with potential suppliers on large orders of frequently purchased items. In other instances, perhaps when small quantities of items are purchased infrequently, the small business owner must pay list price.

The typical small business owner shops around and then orders from the supplier offering the best price. Still, this does not mean the small business manager should always purchase inventory and supplies at the lowest price available. The best purchase price is the lowest price at which the owner can obtain goods and services *of acceptable quality*. This guideline usually yields the best value more often than simply purchasing the lowest-priced goods.

Recall that one of Deming's 14 points is "End the practice of awarding business on the basis of price tag." Without proof of quality, an item with the lowest initial price may produce the highest total cost. Deming condemned the practice of constantly switching suppliers in search of the lowest initial price because it increases the variability of a process and lowers its quality. Instead he recommended that businesses establish long-term relationships built on mutual trust and cooperation with a single supplier. *For instance, when New Pig Inc., a small manufacturer of contained absorbents (socklike bundles of absorbent materials*

A Funny Thing Happened on the Way to Your Business

*E*very year, U.S. companies spend an amount equivalent to 10.5 percent of the nation's GDP—more than $700 billion—just to package and transport goods from one place to another. With so much at stake, it is little wonder that distribution, or logistics, has become an important part of companies' competitive strategies. "You have far more opportunities to get cost out of the supply chain than you do out of manufacturing," says one CEO. Streamlining a company's ordering and distribution process can reduce delivery times and its investment in inventory as well as cut costs and avoid costly mistakes. Consider, for example, the following (true) distribution horror stories.

The shipping manager at a plant in China is struggling to ready a rush order of men's and women's athletic shoes for shipment to a retailer in the United States. He runs into a snag when trying to load the cartons containing the shoes into 40-foot shipping containers. He places a call to the retailer's logistics manager to ask how many shoes to put in each container. "As many as you can fit," comes the reply. "Please don't bother me with such silly questions."

The Chinese shipping manager complies with the customer's request. He has workers take the shoes out of the cartons, remove them from their individual shoe boxes, and put them into the shipping containers. When the shipment arrives in the United States, the retailer's warehouse manager gets an even bigger surprise: The Chinese workers didn't even tie the shoes in pairs. The containers are filled with thousands of pairs of shoes—all floating around loose! The retailer has already advertised a big sale on these shoes and quickly arranges for workers to go to the warehouse, where they match and box thousands of pairs of shoes. The company incurs thousands of dollars of unplanned labor expenses and eventually sells the shoes at close to its cost.

A dock worker is handling a shipment of margarine traveling from Denmark to Tacoma, Washington, when he notices a leak in one of the shipping containers. The cargo is loaded onto a truck headed for a warehouse, but as the driver rolls down the highway, he looks in his rearview mirror and notices yellow blobs flying from the back of his truck. At the warehouse, workers open the containers to find 2,000 cartons of margarine that has experienced a complete meltdown. "Anyone got any popcorn?" asks one worker. The shipping document from the company in Denmark failed to specify a temperature setting for the cargo.

One freight company that has contracts with two movie studios mistakenly switches their shipments. Of course, one shipment contains X-rated films, and the other contains family films. The manager at the adult video store is sorely disappointed in the mild films he receives, and the nuns at the convent expecting to watch *The Sound of Music* really get a surprise!

How can business owners avoid shipping problems such as these? Although some shipping foul-ups are inevitable, the following tips can help minimize them:

◆ Communicate clearly with vendors, suppliers, and shipping companies. Never assume that the other party will do what you expect.
◆ Specify special shipping instructions when required.
◆ Make sure all shipping labels and instructions are legible and firmly attached to the package.
◆ Use pressure-sensitive packing tape to seal packages. Masking tape and cellophane tape are not strong enough to do the job.
◆ Try to use single shipments rather than multiple shipments. Items sent at different times or in multiple containers are more likely to go astray.
◆ On international shipments, verify that the shipper is familiar with the customs regulations of the destination country and knows how to negotiate them. Otherwise, your shipment could founder indefinitely in customs.
◆ When in doubt about a shipment, contact a shipping professional for advice.

SOURCE: Adapted from Steve Bates, "The Dog Ate My Shipment," *Nation's Business*, December 1997, pp. 36–37. ◆

used to soak up industrial leaks and spills), set out to improve quality, reduce the time required to introduce new products, and innovate new product development, it turned to its suppliers for help. New Pig depends on its suppliers for some element of every one of the 3,000 items it sells, so establishing closer supplier relationships was one of management's top priorities. The company began forming strategic alliances with its 30 largest-volume suppliers, improving communication with them and involving them in product development and quality improvement efforts. One joint project resulted in changing a shipping method that produced savings of hundreds of thousands of dollars. "We've developed a synergy and are moving forward together [with our suppliers] to cut costs, be more efficient, and increase profits," says Doug Evans, New Pig's director of strategic purchasing.[16]

When evaluating a supplier's price, small business owners must consider not only the actual price of the goods and services but also the selling terms accompanying them. In some cases the selling terms can be more important than the price itself. Sometimes a vendor's terms might include some type of purchase discount. Vendors typically offer three types of discounts: trade discounts, quantity discounts, and cash discounts.

4 Differentiate among the three types of purchase discounts vendors offer.

TRADE DISCOUNTS

Trade discounts are established on a graduated scale and depend on a small firm's position in the channel of distribution. In other words, trade discounts recognize the fact that manufacturers, wholesalers, and retailers perform a variety of vital functions at various stages in the channel of distribution and compensate them for providing these needed activities. Figure 16.3 illustrates a typical trade discount structure.

QUANTITY DISCOUNTS

Quantity discounts are designed to encourage businesses to order large quantities of merchandise and supplies. Vendors are able to offer lower prices on bulk purchases because the cost per unit is lower than for handling small orders. Quantity discounts normally exist in two forms: noncumulative and cumulative. Noncumulative quantity discounts are granted only if a large enough volume of merchandise is purchased in a single order. For example, a wholesaler may offer a small retailer a 3 percent discount only if she purchases 10 gross of Halloween masks in a single order. Table 16.6 shows a typical noncumulative quantity discount structure.

Cumulative quantity discounts are offered if a firm's purchases from a particular vendor exceed a specified quantity or dollar value over a predetermined time period. The time frame varies, but a yearly basis is most common. For example, a manufacturer of appliances may offer a small firm a 3 percent discount on subsequent orders if its purchases exceed $10,000 per year.

Some small business owners who normally buy in small quantities and are unable to qualify for quantity discounts can earn such discounts by joining buying groups, purchasing pools, or buying cooperatives. *For instance, Edward Reagan, owner of Performance Audio,*

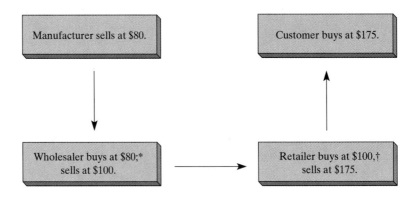

* Wholesale discount = 54% of suggested retail price.
† Retail discount = 43% of suggested retail price.

Figure 16.3 **Trade Discount Structure**

Table 16.6 Noncumulative Quantity Discount Structure

Order Size	Price
1–1,000 units	List price
1,001–5,000 units	List price – 2%
5,001–10,000 units	List price – 4%
10,001 units and above	List price – 6%

joined a purchasing pool in an attempt to cut his company's health insurance costs. By joining with more than 4,300 other small business owners in California's state-sponsored Health Insurance Plan of California, Reagan was able to cut health insurance costs for himself and his eight employees by 42 percent.[17]

CASH DISCOUNTS

Cash discounts are offered to customers as an incentive to pay for merchandise promptly. Many vendors grant cash discounts to avoid being used as an interest-free bank by customers who purchase merchandise and then neglect to pay within the invoice due date. To encourage prompt payment of invoices, many vendors allow customers to deduct a percentage of the purchase amount if payment is remitted within a specified time. Cash discount terms "2/10, net 30" are common in many industries. This notation means that the total amount of the invoice is due 30 days after its date, but if the bill is paid within 10 days, the buyer may deduct 2 percent from the total. A discount offering "2/10, EOM" (EOM means "end of month") indicates that the buyer may deduct 2 percent if the bill is paid by the tenth of the month after purchase.

In general, it is sound business practice to take advantage of cash discounts. The money saved by paying invoices promptly is freed up for use elsewhere. Conversely, there is an implicit (opportunity) cost of forgoing a cash discount. By forgoing a cash discount, the small business owner is, in effect, paying an annual interest rate to retain the use of the discounted amount for the remainder of the credit period. For example, suppose the Print Shop receives an invoice for $1,000 from a vendor offering a cash discount of 2/10, net 30. Figure 16.4 illustrates this situation and shows how to compute the cost of forgoing the cash discount.

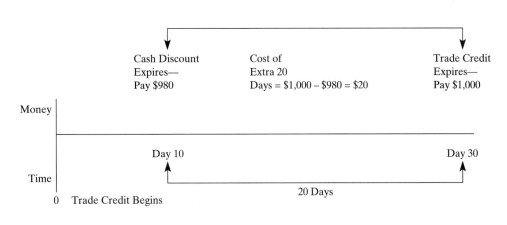

Figure 16.4 A Cash Discount

Actually, it costs the Print Shop $20 to retain the use of its $980 for an extra 20 days. Translate this into an annual interest rate:

$$I = P \times R \times T$$

where:

$$I = \text{Interest (\$)}$$
$$P = \text{Principle (\$)}$$
$$R = \text{Rate of interest (\%)}$$
$$T = \text{Time (number of days/360)}$$

So, to compute R, the annual interest rate,

$$R = \frac{I}{P \times T}$$

In our example,

$$R = \frac{\$20}{980 \times \dfrac{20}{360}}$$

$$= 36.735\%$$

When David Brent took over the Nutty Bavarian, a small company selling cinamon-glazed nuts, his straightforward approach with suppliers concerning the company's past due bills earned him their respect and continued support.

The cost to the Print Shop of forgoing the cash discount is 36.735 percent per year! If there is $980 available on day 10 of the trade credit period, the owner should pay the invoice unless he is able to earn a return greater than 36.735 percent on it. If the owner does not have $980 on day 10 but can borrow it at less than 36.735 percent, he should do so to take advantage of the cash discount. Table 16.7 summarizes the cost of forgoing cash discounts offering various terms.

Although it is a good idea for business owners to take advantage of cash discounts, it is not a wise practice to stretch accounts payable to suppliers beyond the payment terms specified on the invoice. Letting payments become past due can destroy the trusting relationship a small company has built with its vendors. *When David Brent took over the Nutty Bavarian, a small company that sells cinnamon-glazed almonds and pecans from kiosks, the company was growing rapidly and was experiencing cash flow problems. Brent soon discovered that the company owed more than $100,000 to its nut suppliers, almost all of it past due. To make matters worse, the previous managers had ignored past due notices and telephone calls from suppliers seeking payment. Brent took an honest, straightforward approach to solving the problem. "I went to my*

Table 16.7 The Cost of Forgoing Cash Discounts

Cash Discount Terms	Cost of Forgoing (Annually)
2/10, net 30	36.735%
2/30, net 60	34.490%
2/10, net 60	14.693%
3/10, net 30	55.670%
3/10, net 60	22.268%

suppliers to ask for longer credit terms and worked out a payment plan that we could meet," he says. Although it took more than a year, Brent eventually paid off all of the company's past-due bills. "Instead of lying and saying the check's in the mail, tell suppliers what's happening and what you propose to do about it," he advises. "If you have a [bill] that's due, you call them, instead of waiting for them to call you. If you owe them, suppliers are eager to find a way to work with you." Thanks to his forthright approach with the Nutty Bavarian's suppliers, Brent has maintained close partnerships with all of the company's suppliers.[18]

$\mathcal{T}$iming

5 Calculate a company's reorder point.

Timing the purchase of merchandise and supplies is also a critical element of any purchasing plan. The owner must schedule delivery dates so that the firm does not lose customer goodwill from stockouts. Also, the owner must concentrate on maintaining proper control over the firm's inventory investment without tying up an excessive amount of working capital. There is a trade-off between the cost of running out of stock and the cost of carrying additional inventory.

When planning delivery schedules for inventory and supplies, the owner must consider the **lead time** for an order, the time gap between placing an order and receiving it. In general, business owners cannot expect instantaneous delivery of merchandise. As a result, the manager must plan its reorder points for inventory items with lead time in mind.

To determine when to order merchandise for inventory, a small business manager must calculate the reorder point for key inventory items. Developing a reorder point model involves determining the lead time for an order, the usage rate for the item, the minimum level of stock allowable, and the economic order quantity (EOQ). The lead time for an order is the time gap between placing an order with a vendor and actually receiving the goods. It may be as little as a few hours or as long as several weeks to process purchase requisitions and orders, contact the supplier, receive the goods, and sort them into the inventory. Obviously, owners who purchase from local vendors encounter shorter lead times than those who rely on distant suppliers.

The usage rate for a particular product can be determined from past inventory and accounting records. The small business owner must estimate the speed at which the supply of merchandise will be depleted over a given time. The anticipated usage rate for a product determines how long the supply will last. For example, if an owner projects that she will use 900 units in the next 6 months, the usage rate is 5 units per day (900 units/180 days). The simplest reorder point model assumes that the firm experiences a linear usage rate; that is, depletion of the firm's stock continues at a constant rate over time.

The small business owner must determine the minimum level of stock allowable. If the firm runs out of a particular item (i.e., incurs stockouts), customers may lose faith in the business, and the customer ill will may develop. To avoid stockouts, many firms establish a minimum level of inventory greater than zero. In other words, they build a cushion, called **safety stock,** into their inventories in case demand runs ahead of the anticipated usage rate. In such cases the owner can dip into the safety stock to fill customer orders until the stock is replenished.

To compute the reorder point for an item, the owner must combine this inventory information with the product's EOQ. The following example will illustrate the reorder point technique:

$$L = \text{Lead time for an order} = 5 \text{ days}$$
$$U = \text{Usage rate} = 18 \text{ units/day}$$
$$S = \text{Safety stock (minimum level)} = 75 \text{ units}$$
$$EOQ = \text{Economic order quantity} = 540 \text{ units}$$

The formula for computing the reorder point is:

$$\text{Reorder point} = (L \times U) + S$$

In this example,

$$\text{Reorder point} = (5 \text{ days} \times 18 \text{ units/day}) + 75 \text{ units}$$
$$= 165 \text{ units}$$

Thus, this owner should order 540 more units when inventory drops to 165 units. Figure 16.5 illustrates the reorder point situation for this small business.

The simple reorder technique makes certain assumptions that may not be valid in particular situations. First, the model assumes that the firm's usage rate is constant, when in fact for most small businesses demand varies daily. Second, the model assumes that lead time for an order is constant, when, in fact, few vendors deliver precisely within lead time estimates. Third, in this sample model, the owner never taps safety stock; however, late deliveries or accelerated demand may force the owner to dip into this inventory reserve. More advanced models relax some of these assumptions, but the simple model can be a useful inventory guideline for making inventory decisions in a small company.

Another popular reorder point model assumes that the demand for a product during its lead time is normally distributed (see Figure 16.6). The area under the normal curve at any given point represents the probability that that particular demand level will occur. Figure 16.7 illustrates the application of this normal distribution to the reorder point model *without* safety stock. The model recognizes that three different demand patterns can occur during a product's lead time. Demand pattern 1 is an example of below-average demand during lead time; demand pattern 2 is an example of average demand during lead time; and demand pattern 3 is an example of an above-average demand during lead time.

If the reorder point for this item is the average demand for the product during lead time, 50 percent of the time, demand will be below average (note that 50 percent of the area under the normal curve lies below average). Similarly, 50 percent of the time, demand during lead time will exceed the average, and the firm will experience stockouts (note that 50 percent of the area under the normal curve lies above average).

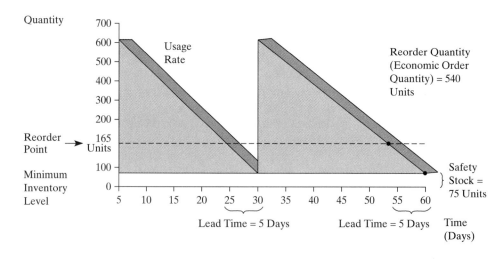

Figure 16.5 Reorder Point Model

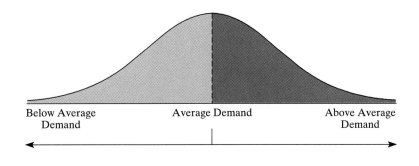

Below Average Demand   Average Demand   Above Average Demand

Figure 16.6 Demand During Lead Time

To reduce the probability of inventory shortage, the small business owner can increase the reorder point above $\bar{D}_L$ (average demand during lead time). But how much should the owner increase the reorder point? Rather than attempt to define the actual costs of carrying extra inventory versus the costs of stockouts (remember the trade-off described earlier), this model allows the small business owner to determine the appropriate reorder point by setting a desired customer service level. For example, the owner may wish to satisfy 95 percent of customer demand for a product during lead time. This service level determines the amount of increase in the reorder point. In effect, these additional items serve as a safety stock:

$$\text{Safety stock} = SLF \times SD_L$$

where:

SLF = Service level factor (the appropriate Z score)

SD_L = Standard deviation of demand during lead time

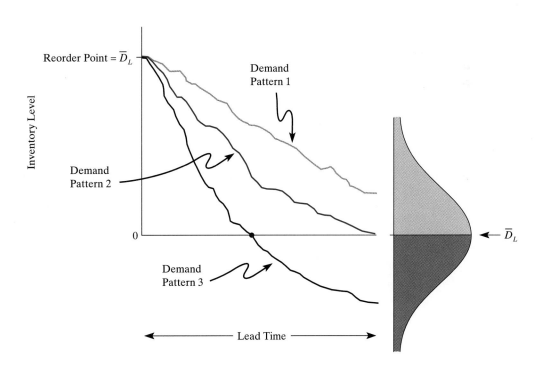

Figure 16.7 Reorder Point without Safety Stock

Table 16.8 Service Level Factors and Z Scores

Target Customer Service Level	Z Score*
99%	2.33
97.5%	1.96
95%	1.645
90%	1.275
80%	0.845
75%	0.675

* Any basic statistics book will provide a table of areas under the normal curve, which will give the appropriate Z score for *any* service level factor.

Table 16.8 shows the appropriate service level factor (Z score) for some of the most popular target customer service levels.

Figure 16.8 shows the shift to a normally distributed reorder point model with safety stock. In this case the manager has set a 95 percent customer service level; that is, the manager wants to meet 95 percent of the demand during lead time. The normal curve in the model without safety stock (from Figure 16.7) is shifted up so that 95 percent of the area under the curve lies above the zero inventory level. The result is a reorder point that is higher than the original reorder point by the amount of the safety stock:

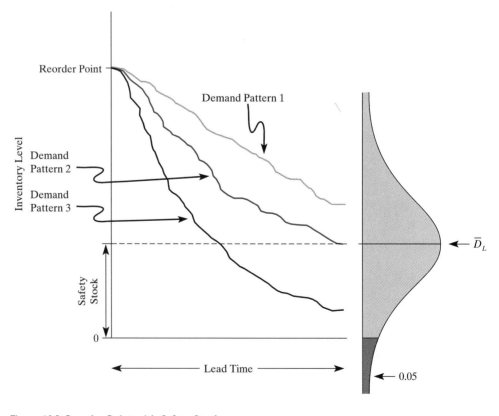

Figure 16.8 Reorder Point with Safety Stock

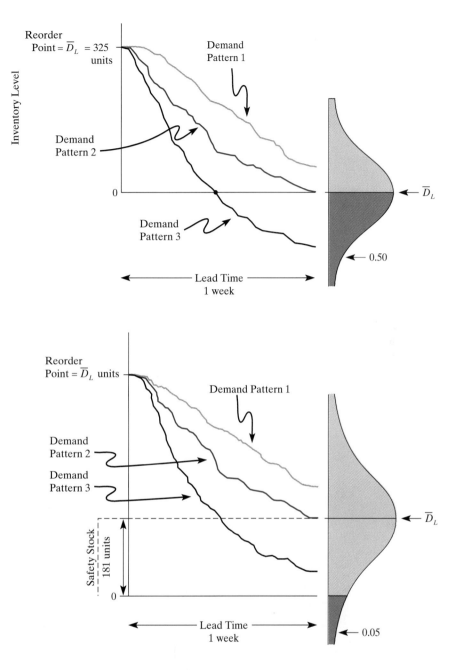

Figure 16.9 Shift from a No-Safety Stock System to a Safety Stock System

$$\text{Reorder point} = \bar{D}_L + (SLF \times SD_L)$$

where:

$\bar{D}_L$ = Average demand during lead time (original reorder point)
SLF = Service level factor (the appropriate Z score)
SD_L = Standard deviation of demand during lead time

To illustrate, suppose that the average demand for a product during its lead time (1 week) is 325 units with a standard deviation of 110 units. If the service level is 95 percent, the service level factor (from Table 16.7) would be 1.645. The reorder point would be:

$$R = 325 + (1.645 \times 110) = 325 + 181 = 506 \text{ units}$$

Figure 16.9 on page 563 illustrates the shift from a system without safety stock to one with safety stock for this example. With a recorder point of 325 units ($\bar{D}_L$), this small business owner will experience inventory shortages during lead time 50 percent of the time. With a reorder point of 506 units (i.e., a safety stock of 181 units), the business owner will experience inventory stockouts during lead time only 5 percent of the time.

$\mathscr{V}$endor Analysis

6 Develop a vendor rating scale.

Experienced business owners realize the importance of finding vendors that can supply them with quality merchandise, equipment, supplies, and services at reasonable prices in a timely manner. Selecting the right vendors or suppliers for a business can have an impact well beyond simply obtaining goods and services at the lowest costs. Although searching for the best price will always be an important factor, successful small business owners must always consider other factors in vendor selection such as reliability, reputation, quality, support services, and proximity.

VENDOR CERTIFICATION

To add some objectivity to the selection process, many firms are establishing **vendor certification programs:** agreements to give one supplier the majority of their business once that supplier meets rigorous quality and performance standards. Today, businesses of all sizes and types are establishing long-term "partnering" arrangements with vendors that meet their certification standards. When creating a vendor certification program, a business owner should remember the three Cs: commitment, communication, and control. *Commitment* to consistently meeting the quality standards of the company is paramount. No small company can afford to do business with vendors that cannot meet its quality targets. Second, a company must establish two-way *communication* with vendors. Communication implies trust, and trust creates working relationships that are long-term and mutually beneficial. Treating suppliers like partners can reveal ways to boost quality and lower costs for both parties. Finally, a company must make sure that its vendors and suppliers have in place the *controls* that enable them to produce quality results and to achieve continuous improvements in their processes. "Control must be proactive and continuous," says one quality manager.[19]

Creating a vendor certification program requires a small company to develop a vendor rating scale that allows the company to evaluate the various advantages and disadvantages of each potential vendor. The scale allows managers to score each vendor on some measure of those purchasing criteria that are most important to their companies' success. The first step in developing a scale is to determine which criteria are most important in selecting a vendor (e.g., price, quality, prompt delivery). The next step is to assign weights to each criterion to reflect its relative importance. The third step involves developing a grading scale for comparing vendors on the criteria. Developing a usable scale requires that the owner maintain proper records of past vendor performances. Finally, the owner must compute a weighted total score for each vendor and select the vendor that scores the highest on the set of criteria. Consider the following example. Bravo Bass Boats, Inc., is faced with choosing from among several suppliers of a critical raw material. The company's owner has decided to employ a vendor rating scale to select the best vendor using the following procedure.

Fewer Surprises Are a Good Thing

*T*om Thornbury, CEO of Softub, a $15 million maker of hot tubs, understands just how important the right vendors can be to a small company's success. In fact, he learned the hard way that one bad supplier can threaten the health of a growing business. Several years ago, Softub purchased from an outside supplier the motor, pump, and assembly unit that provide the jet action in its hot tubs. Thornbury met with the company's owner and heard other customers rave about its quality. "That was back when *I* was the purchasing department," says Thornbury. "That might have been the problem." Before long, defective jet assemblies turned up in Softub's factory and in customers' homes. Then the supplier went out of business. Thornbury scrambled to repair all of the faulty assemblies and to try to keep its network of distributors from defecting. He estimates the entire episode cost his company about $500,000. "If we had done a better job of surveying our suppliers," he says, "this might not have happened."

The odds of its happening again are slim. Because two-thirds of Softub's products cost is in materials—from sheet metal to nuts and bolts—that the company purchases from outside suppliers, managers saw the need to evaluate vendors more thoroughly before inviting them to become a crucial link in its production process. Under the direction of Gary Anderson, Softub's purchasing agent, cross-functional teams of 10 employees visit potential vendors on site and use a checklist Anderson developed to evaluate them. The checklist covers everything from safety devices and cleanliness to pre-ventive maintenance and quality processes. "[The checklist] forces the team to focus on specific areas so we don't forget anything when we're on a visit," says Anderson. Team visits may take as little as two hours or as long as two days, and team members delve into every aspect of the prospective supplier's business. They interview everyone from the president to the factory workers and ask lots of questions. Before going on site, every team member receives a packet of information about the company, including any articles about it from trade journals.

Back in Softub's offices, the checklist generates a great deal of discussion about critical issues such as quality and on-time delivery. Anderson also verifies the accuracy of every potential vendor's claims by contacting at least three of its customers. When all the information is in, the team makes its recommendation to the management team, who selects one vendor. "The payoff is that we're recruiting a better breed of supplier," says Thornbury. Since beginning to use the form, Softub is getting fewer defective products from its suppliers, and its vendor turnover rate has been cut in half. Plus, Softub has discovered one more unexpected benefit: closer relationships with quality suppliers. On several occasions, suppliers have given employees at Softub ideas and suggestions on how to solve production problems. "We're developing partnerships in which we have a pretty free exchange of information," says Thornbury. "Also, as we've gotten to know our vendors better, there are fewer surprises. In a manufacturing operation, surprises can be lethal."

---

1. Why is using a vendor evaluation scale important to companies such as Softub?

2. What benefits can companies that conduct vendor audits expect to gain?

SOURCE: Adapted from Stephanie Gruner, "The Smart Vendor-Audit Checklist," *Inc.*, April 1995, pp. 93–95. ◆

Step 1: Determine important criteria. The owner of Bravo has selected the following criteria:

Quality
Price
Prompt delivery
Service
Assistance

Step 2: Assign weights to each criterion to reflect its relative importance.

Criterion	Weight
Quality	35
Price	30
Prompt delivery	20
Service	10
Assistance	5
Total	100

Step 3: Develop a grading scale for each criterion.

Criterion	Grading Scale
Quality	Number of acceptable lots from vendor X
	Total number of lots from vendor X
Price	Lowest quoted price of all vendors
	Price offered by vendor X
Prompt delivery	Number of on-time deliveries from vendor X
	Total number of deliveries from vendor X
Service	A subjective evaluation of the variety of service offered by each vendor
Assistance	A subjective evaluation of the advice and assistance provided by each vendor

Step 4: Compute a weighted score for each vendor.

Criterion	Weight	Grade	Weighted Score (weight × grade)
Vendor 1			
Quality	35	9/10	31.5
Price	30	12.5/12.5	30.0
Prompt delivery	20	10/10	20.0
Service	10	8/10	8.0
Assistance	5	5/5	5.0
Total weighted score			94.5
Vendor 2			
Quality	35	8/10	28.0
Price	30	12.5/12.5	27.8
Prompt delivery	20	8/10	16.0
Service	10	8/10	8.0
Assistance	5	4.5	4.0
Total weighted score			83.8
Vendor 3			
Quality	35	7/10	24.5
Price	30	12.5/12.5	30.0
Prompt delivery	20	6/10	12.0
Service	10	7/10	7.0
Assistance	5	1/5	1.0
Total weighted score			74.5

On the basis of this analysis of the three suppliers, Bravo should purchase the majority of this raw material from Vendor 1.

This vendor analysis procedure assumes that the business owner has a detailed working knowledge of the suppliers' network. Start-up companies seldom will. Owners of start-up companies must focus on finding suppliers and then gathering data to conduct the vendor analysis. One of the best ways to do that is to ask potential vendors for references. *Anthony Dell'Aquila, co-founder of the Hoboken (NJ) Brewing Company, a small beer brewery, recognizes that his company's suppliers have a major impact on the quality of the beer he produces. When he launched Hoboken Brewery, Dell'Aquila invested the time to contact four or five references each potential supplier gave him. What he learned proved to be extremely valuable in selecting his vendors. After several years in business, he still follows the same practice when looking for vendors because it worked so well for the company.*[20]

FINDING SUPPLY SOURCES

Many new entrepreneurs have difficulty locating supplies of inventory and materials to start their businesses. One obvious way for entrepreneurs to find vendors for their products is to approach established businesses selling similar lines and interview the managers. Clearly, local competitors are not likely to be very cooperative with new competitors, but a beginning entrepreneur can get the necessary information from businesses outside the immediate trading area.

Another source for establishing vendor relationships is the industry trade association. These associations often have available to members lists of vendors and suppliers as well as other useful information. They also sponsor trade shows, where large numbers of vendors and suppliers promote their versions of the latest styles, product innovations, and technological advancements.[21] The local chamber of commerce also can provide vendor and supplier connections to entrepreneurs just starting out.

A number of publications offer the entrepreneur a great deal of assistance in locating vendors. A ready source of cheap information for any new owner is the telephone directory's Yellow Pages. Scouring the appropriate product categories should yield a good list of prospective vendors. *Before D. J. Waldow and Matt Campbell launched their on-campus dry-cleaning pickup and delivery center in a room in the student lounge at the University of Michigan, they needed to find a reliable dry-cleaner to do the actual cleaning. They began by poring over the Yellow Pages and developing a list of cleaners. "We contacted about 20 dry cleaners in Ann Arbor to find out how much they charged to clean suits and shirts," says Waldow. On the basis of what they learned, the partners set target costs they were willing to pay a dry cleaner to perform their service. Next, they generated a list of criteria their supplier would have to meet. The list included their target costs as well as delivery schedule, quality of work, and other factors. After using their vendor rating scale to narrow their list to three potential suppliers, Waldow and Campbell visited each one in person. "The first thing we noticed about the dry cleaner we selected was the state-of-the-art system he had for tracking orders, which was most impressive and efficient," says Waldow. In addition, that cleaner was the one who was most excited about working with Waldow and Campbell. Ultimately, says Waldow, "he offered us prices that were a dollar or two better than [any other cleaner], plus free pickup and delivery. We both had a feeling that he was going to be a great person to work with, and it has certainly worked out that way."*[22]

Vendor advertisements in trade publications also offer a good list of information about needed merchandise and materials. Library reference books that list national distributors and their product lines are another information source. Publications such as *MacRae's Blue Book* and the *Thomas Register of American Manufacturers* <http://www.thomasregister.com> provide lists of products and services along with names, addresses, telephone numbers, and ratings of manufacturers. The *Thomas Register* and its accompanying Web site lists more than 60,000 products from 5,500 vendors selling 124,000 brands. GE Information Services and the *Thomas Register* also operate the Trading Process Network <http://tpn.geis.com> that allows companies to transmit design and engineering specifications for their products over the Web to dozens of potential suppliers at once.[23] *The Hoboken Brewery's Anthony Dell'Aquila started his search for vendors and suppliers by using the* Thomas Register. *"Every manufacturer in the world is listed there," he says, exaggerating only slightly. "It's like the encyclopedia of vendors."*[24] The *U.S. Industrial Directory* is similar to the *Thomas Register*, although its coverage is not as broad. Business owners also should consult the U.S. Chamber of Commerce publication *Sources of State Information and State Industrial Directories*, which lists state directories of manufacturers. Entrepreneurs whose product lines have an international flair may look to *Kelly's Manufacturers and Merchants Directory, Marconi's International Register*, or *Trade Directories of the World* for information on companies throughout the world dealing in practically every type of product or service.

The World Wide Web is another rich source of information on potential suppliers. Studies show that purchasing agents in companies of all sizes are stepping up their use of the Internet as a tool for locating and buying merchandise, equipment, and supplies.[25] When they go to the Web to get supplier information or to purchase goods and services, business owners' first stop usually is one of the sites that serves as an "electronic Yellow Pages" for vendors. One of the most popular sites is Worldwide Internet Solutions' "WIZnet" site <http://www.wiznet.net>. WIZnet's site is a "virtual product-catalog library" that lists complete catalogs of manufacturers, distributors, and service providers from around the globe. Through WIZnet, Web surfers can get more than just company listings; they can also flip through the "pages" of a supplier's catalog, review product specifications, and contact the vendor through secure e-mail for more information or to place an order. "For a purchasing agent who wants a quick [look] at what models are available—or what the latest prices are— the WIZnet system can provide a basis for judging other vendors," says one purchasing manager.[26] One of the primary benefits of Web-based catalogs such as WIZnet is their ability to reduce dramatically the lead time for an order. "The fact that they have catalog data online is a substantial time saver," says one purchasing agent. "With WIZnet, you don't have to phone [a vendor] then wait for a call back or a mail or fax reply."[27] Look for the volume of Web-based purchasing activity to grow in the future as more business owners discover its power to reduce the cost of placing an order and the time required to get it delivered.

THE FINAL DECISION

Once small business owners identify potential vendors and suppliers, they must decide which one (or ones) to do business with. Entrepreneurs should consider the following factors before making the final decision about the right supplier.

Number of Suppliers. One important question the small business owner faces is "Should I buy from a single supplier or from several different sources?" Concentrating purchases at a single supplier gives the individual attention from the sole supplier, especially if orders are substantial. Second, the firm may receive quantity discounts if its orders are large enough. *For example, Duds 'n Suds, a combination bar and laundromat chain, purchases all of the equipment for its franchised outlets from a single supplier so that it can negotiate the best package of price, quality, warranties, and service.*[28] Finally, the firm is able to cultivate a closer, more cooperative relationship with the supplier. Suppliers are more willing to assist companies they consider to be their loyal customers. The result of such a partnership can be better quality goods and services.

However, using a single vendor also has disadvantages. The small firm may experience shortages of critical materials if its only supplier suffers a catastrophe, such as a fire, strike, or bankruptcy. *For instance, one small clothing maker experienced an interruption in its supply of fabric when its primary supplier's textile factory was damaged by a tornado. The textile manufacturer resumed production one month later, but the clothing maker's output suffered because it was unable to purchase material in sufficient quantities from other suppliers on such short notice.*

The advantages of developing close, cooperative relationships with a single supplier outweigh the risks of sole sourcing in most cases. A business owner must exercise great caution in choosing a supplier to make sure she picks the right one, however. Otherwise the outcome could be disastrous.

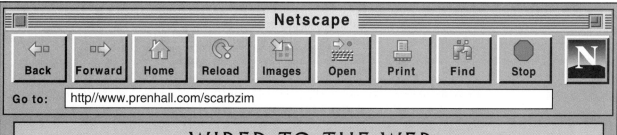

WIRED TO THE WEB

THE POWER OF THE WEB

"*P*laying with that computer again, are you, son?" asked Jack Lampeer.

His son, Miles, turned from his screen, and, ignoring the hint of disdain in his father's voice, replied, "Pop, I told you I'm not playing. Believe it or not, I'm actually *working*."

"When pigs fly . . ." muttered his father as he shuffled through a stack of papers on Miles's desk. "Computers are for playing games."

"Pop, I know you don't put much stock in computers, but that's because you don't *understand* them. This computer has already helped up track our costs more effectively, and our financial reports don't take nearly as long to prepare now that we use that accounting package to track all of our transactions. In fact, Betty is using the computer more and more now that she's comfortable with it. I think we're going to have to buy another one!"

"Just what we need," said Jack sarcastically. "*Two* of those things to tell me how to run a business I've been in for more than 20 years!"

Jack Lampeer had started Industrial Supply nearly 22 years before to supply other small companies in the area with the industrial equipment, supplies, and materials they needed. The company carried a wide assortment of industrial products—from ladders and generators to mops and cleaning supplies.

As long as Jack was at the helm, Industrial Supply had refused to enter the computer age. Miles was right about one thing: Jack didn't understand computers, nor did he want to. He didn't trust them at all. He had run Industrial Supply for more than two decades with little more than an adding machine, an accountant's pad, and his brain.

"Pop, while I was looking through one of our industry publications yesterday, I came across an article about using the World Wide Web to make purchasing inventory more efficient," he said, tossing an open magazine in his father's direction. "So I started investigating. I've already found some awesome Web sites. We don't even need a paper catalog! You can browse through a company's catalog right here on the screen. Look at this," he said, swiveling his computer monitor toward his father. "*All* of the product information, including specs, on line. Instant access; no waiting for a catalog to arrive by 'snail mail.'"

Jack glanced at the screen and pretended not to be interested. Although he didn't want to admit it, it sounded like a pretty good idea. "That's nice, son," said Jack, doing his best to sound uninterested. He had finished sorting through the stacks on Miles's desk and was now shuffling through the files in his filing cabinet.

"What are you looking for?" Miles asked.

"That catalog from Carswell. I thought I saw one the other day. We need to order some new ladders for Babb Painting Contractors, and I wanted to do a little shopping for features and prices. I also needed to check out the latest prices on some generators."

"We can do that right here, Pop," said Miles, as he pulled another chair up to the computer. "Sit down and let's see what we can find on the Web." His voice was full of enthusiasm.

As Jack pulled the chair closer to the computer, he said, "The World Wide Web, huh? Show me how it works, son. Show me how it works."

1. Use one of the search engines on the World Wide Web to help Miles find the information he is looking for. Check out some of the following sites as well:

   National Association of Purchasing Managers <http://www.napm.org>

   W.W. Grainger Company <http://www.grainger.com>

   IndustryNET <http://www.industry.net>

   Worldwide Internet Solutions <http://www.wiznet.net>

Which sites did you find most useful? Why?

2. What advantages does the Web offer purchasing agents in small businesses?

Reliability. The business owner must evaluate the potential vendor's ability to deliver adequate quantities of quality merchandise when it is needed. The most common complaint purchasing managers have against suppliers is late delivery.[29] Late deliveries or shortages cause lost sales and create customer ill will.

Proximity. The small firm's physical proximity is an important factor in choosing a vendor. Costs for transporting merchandise can substantially increase the cost of merchandise to the buyer. *For example, one East Coast glass manufacturer found that to obtain proper-quality sand for its production operation it had to make its purchases from a Midwestern supplier. The cost of transporting the sand was greater than the cost of the sand itself!* Also, some vendors offer better service to local small businesses because they know the owners. In addition, a small business owner is better able to solve coordination problems with nearby vendors than with distant vendors.

Services. The small business owner must evaluate the range of services vendors offer. Do salespeople make regular calls on the firm, and are they knowledgeable about their product line? Will the sale representatives assist in planning store layout and in creating attractive displays? Will the vendor make convenient deliveries on time? Is the supplier reasonable in making repairs on equipment after installation and in handling returned merchandise? Are sales representatives able to offer useful advice on purchasing and other managerial functions? *The Hoboken Brewery's Anthony Dell'Aquila says that service is one of the top criteria he used to judge vendors. "It's a combination of things, of course," he says, but look for service-oriented companies."*[30] Before choosing a vendor, the small business owner should answer these and other relevant questions about suppliers.

$\mathcal{L}$egal Issues Affecting Purchasing

7 Describe the legal implications of the purchasing function.

When a small business purchases goods from a supplier, ownership passes from seller to buyer. But when does title to the goods pass from one party to the other? The answer is important because any number of things could happen to the merchandise after it has been ordered but before it has been delivered. When they order merchandise and supplies from their vendors, small business owners should know when the ownership of the merchandise—and the risk associated with it—shifts from supplier to buyer.

TITLE

Before the Uniform Commercial Code (UCC) was enacted, the concept of **title**—the right to ownership of goods—determined where responsibility for merchandise fell. Today, however, the UCC has replaced the concept of title with three other concepts: identification, risk of loss, and insurable interest.

IDENTIFICATION

Identification is the first requirement that must be met. Before title can pass to the buyer, the goods must already be in existence and must be identifiable from all other similar goods. Specific goods already in existence are identified at the time the sales contract is made. For example, if Graphtech, Inc. orders a Model 477-X computer and a plotter, the goods are identified at the time the contract (oral or written) is made. Generic goods are identified when they are marked, shipped, or otherwise designated as the goods in the contract. For example, an order of fuel oil may not be identified until it is loaded into a transfer truck for shipment.

RISK OF LOSS

Risk of loss determines which party incurs the financial risk if the goods are damaged, destroyed, or lost before they are transferred. Risk of loss does *not* always pass with title. Three particular rules govern the passage of title and the transfer of risk of loss:

Rule 1: Agreement. A supplier and a small business owner can agree to the terms under which title passes. Similarly, the two parties can agree (preferably in writing) to shift the risk of loss at any time during the transaction. In other words, any explicit agreement between buyer and seller determines when title and risk of loss will pass. Without an agreement, title and risk of loss pass when the seller delivers the goods under the contract.

Rule 2: F.O.B. seller. Under a sales contract designated F.O.B. seller (free on board seller), title passes to the buyer as soon as the seller delivers the goods into the care of a carrier or shipper. Similarly, risk of loss transfers to the small business owner when the supplier delivers the goods to the carrier. In addition, an **F.O.B. seller contract** (also a **shipment contract**) requires that the buyer pay all shipping and transportation costs. For example, a North Carolina manufacturer sells 100,000 capacitors to a buyer in Ohio with terms "F.O.B. North Carolina." Under this contract the Ohio firms pays all shipping costs, and title and risk of loss pass from the manufacturer as soon as the carrier takes possession of the shipment. If the goods are lost or damaged in transit, the buyer suffers the loss. Of course, the buyer has legal recourse against the carrier.

Rule 3: F.O.B. buyer. A sales contract designated F.O.B. buyer requires that the seller deliver the goods to the buyer's place of business (or to an agent of the buyer). Title and risk of loss are transferred to the small business when the goods are delivered there or to another designated destination. Also, an **F.O.B. buyer contract** (also called a **destination contract**) requires the seller to pay all shipping and transportation costs. In the example above, if the contract were "F.O.B. Ohio," the North Carolina manufacturer would pay the cost of shipping the order, and title and risk of loss would pass to the Ohio company when the shipment was delivered to its place of business. In this case losses due to goods lost or damaged in transit are borne by the seller.

Who bears the risk of lost or damaged goods? Too often, buyers and sellers ignore such details in their sales contracts. The Uniform Commercial Code offers three rules to allocate the risk of loss: the parties' agreement, shipment contract terms, and destination contract terms.

INSURABLE INTEREST

Insurable interest ensures the right to either party to the sales contract to obtain insurance to protect against lost, damaged, or destroyed merchandise as long as that party has "sufficient interest" in the goods. In general, if goods are identified, the buyer has an insurable interest in them. The seller has a sufficient interest as long as he retains title to the goods. However, under certain circumstances both the buyer and the seller have insurable interests even after title has passed to the buyer.

RECEIVING MERCHANDISE

Once the merchandise is received, the buyer must verify its identity and condition. When the goods are delivered, the owner should check the number of cartons unloaded against the carrier's delivery receipt so that none are overlooked. It is also a good idea to examine the boxes for damage; if shipping cartons are damaged, the carrier should note this on the delivery receipt. The owner should open all cartons immediately after delivery and inspect the merchandise for quality and condition and also check it against the invoices to eliminate discrepancies. If merchandise is damaged or incorrect, the buyer should contact the supplier immediately and follow up with a written report. The owner should never destroy or dispose of tainted or unwanted merchandise unless the supplier specifically authorizes it. Proper control techniques in receiving merchandise prevent the small business owner from paying for suppliers' and shippers' mistakes.

SELLING ON CONSIGNMENT

Small business owners who lack the necessary capital to invest or are unwilling to assume the risk of investing in inventory may be able to sell the goods on consignment. Selling on **consignment** means that the small business owner does not purchase the merchandise carried from the supplier (called the consignor); instead, the owner pays the consignor only for the merchandise actually sold. For providing the supplier with a market for his goods, the small business owner normally receives a portion of the revenue on each item sold. The business owner (called the consignee) may return any unsold merchandise to the supplier without obligation. Under a consignment agreement, title and risk of loss do not pass to the consignee unless the contract specifies such terms. In other words, the supplier (consignor) bears the financial costs of lost, damaged, or stolen merchandise. The small business owner who sells merchandise on a consignment basis realizes the following advantages:

- The owner does not have to invest money in these inventory items, but the merchandise on hand is available for sale.
- The owner does not make payment to the consignor until the item is sold.
- Because the consignment relationship is founded on the law of agency, the consignee never takes title to the merchandise and does not bear the risk of loss for the goods.
- The supplier normally plans and sets up displays for the merchandise and is responsible for maintaining it.

Before selling items on consignment, the small business owner and the supplier should create a workable written contract, which should include the following items:

- A list of items to be sold and their quantities
- Prices to be charged
- Location of merchandise in store

- Duration of contract
- Commission charged by the consignee
- Policy on defective items and rejects
- Schedule for payments to consignor
- Delivery terms and merchandise storage requirements
- Responsibility for items lost to pilferage and shoplifting
- Provision for terminating consignment contract

If managed properly, selling goods on consignment can be beneficial to both the consignor and the consignee.

Chapter Summary

1. Understand the components of a purchasing plan.
   - The purchasing function is vital to every small business's success because it influences a company's ability to sell quality goods and services at reasonable prices. Purchasing is the acquisition of needed materials, supplies, services, and equipment of the right quality, in the proper quantities, for reasonable prices, at the appropriate time, and from the right suppliers.

2. Explain the principles of total quality management (TQM) and its impact on quality.
   - Under the total quality management (TQM) philosophy, companies define a quality product as one that conforms to predetermined standards that satisfy customers' demands. The goal is to get everything—from delivery and invoicing to installation and follow-up—right the first time.
   - To implement TQM successfully, a small business owner must rely on 10 fundamental principles: Shift from a management-driven culture to a participative, team-based one; modify the reward system to encourage teamwork and innovation; train workers constantly to give them the tools they need to produce quality and to upgrade the company's knowledge base; train employees to measure quality with the tools of statistical process control (SPC); use Pareto's Law to focus TQM efforts; share information with everyone in the organization; focus quality improvements on astonishing the customer; don't rely on inspection to produce quality products and services; avoid using TQM to place blame on those who make mistakes; and strive for continuous improvement in processes as well as in products and services.

3. Conduct economic order quantity (EOQ) analysis to determine the proper level of inventory.

   - A major goal of the small business is to generate adequate inventory turnover by purchasing proper quantities of merchandise. A useful device for computing the proper quantity is economic order quantity (EOQ) analysis, which yields the ideal order quantity: the amount that minimizes total inventory costs. Total inventory costs consist of the cost of the units, holding (carrying) costs, and ordering (setup) costs. The EOQ balances the costs of ordering and of carrying merchandise to yield minimum total inventory cost.

4. Differentiate among the three types of purchase discounts vendors offer.
   - Trade discounts are established on a graduated scale and depend on a small firm's position in the channel of distribution.
   - Quantity discounts are designed to encourage businesses to order large quantities of merchandise and supplies.
   - Cash discounts are offered to customers as an incentive to pay for merchandise promptly.

5. Calculate a company's reorder point.
   - There is a time gap between the placing of an order and actual receipt of the goods. The reorder point model tells the owner when to place an order to replenish the company's inventory.

6. Develop a vendor rating scale.
   - Creating a vendor analysis model involves four steps: Determine the important criteria (i.e., price, quality, prompt delivery, service, etc.); assign a weight to each criterion to reflect its relative importance; develop a grading scale for each criterion; compute a weighted score for each vendor.

7. Describe the legal implications of the purchasing function.
   - Important legal issues involving purchasing goods involve title, or ownership of the goods; identification of the goods; risk of loss and when it shifts

from seller to buyer; and insurable interests in the goods. Buyer and seller can have an insurable interest in the same goods at the same time.

Discussion Questions

1. What is purchasing? Why is it important for the small business owner to develop a purchasing plan?
2. What is TQM? How can it help small business owners achieve the quality goods and services they require?
3. One top manager claims that to implement total quality management successfully, "You have to change your [company] culture as much as your processes." Do you agree? Explain.
4. List and briefly describe the three components of total inventory costs.
5. What is the economic order quantity? How does it minimize total inventory costs?
6. Should a small business owner always purchase the products with the lowest prices? Why or why not?
7. Briefly outline the three types of purchase discounts. Under what circumstances is each the best choice?
8. What is lead time? Outline the procedure for determining a product's reorder point.
9. Explain how an entrepreneur launching a company could locate suppliers and vendors.
10. What factors are commonly used to evaluate suppliers?
11. Explain the procedure for developing a vendor rating scale.
12. Explain briefly the three concepts that have replaced the concept of title. When do title and risk of loss shift under an F.O.B. seller contract and under an F.O.B. buyer contract?
13. What should a small business owner do when merchandise is received?
14. Explain how a small business would sell goods on consignment. What should be included in a consignment contract?

Step into the Real World

1. Interview a number of small business owners and attempt to discover if they have implemented any of the following:
   a. a purchasing plan
   b. a quality management program
   c. a vendor analysis program
   On the basis of their responses, how would you rate the effectiveness of their programs?
2. Interview two or three retailers and ask about the nature and type of their purchase discounts. Do they normally take advantage of the discounts that are offered? If not, why? Do the businesses you interviewed have a formal vendor analysis program? If not, what steps should they take to create one?
3. Contact the owner of a small retail shop in your area. How does the owner determine inventory levels? How does he or she know how many items to keep in stock? Are there certain items that move much faster than others? Does the owner purchase all of a particular type of item from a single vendor or from several vendors? Why?
4. Interview the owner of a small manufacturing company. What percentage of the components in the company's finished product comes from outside vendors and suppliers? How does the owner select those vendors? What problems does he or she normally encounter when buying from vendors? Does the owner use a checklist or vendor rating scale to select vendors? How does the owner judge the quality of incoming shipments from vendors?

Take It to the Net

Visit the Scarborough/Zimmerer home page at
www.prenhall.com/scarbzim
for updated information, on-line resources, and Web-based exercises.

Endnotes

1. Shawn Tully, "Purchasing's New Muscle," *Fortune*, February 20, 1995, pp. 75–83.
2. Jill Andresky Fraser, "Controlling Supply Costs," *Inc.*, March 1993, p. 39.
3. John H. Sheridan, "Suppliers: Partners in Prosperity," *Industry Week*, March 1990, p. 14.
4. Loretta Owens and Mark Henricks, "Quality Time," *Entrepreneur*, October 1995, p. 159.
5. Roberta Maynard, "A Company Is Turned Around through Japanese Principles," *Nation's Business*, February 1996, p. 9.
6. "What Price Quality?" *Small Business Reports*, August 1990, p. 7.
7. Thomas M. Rohan, "Sermons Fall on Deaf Ears," *Industry Week*, November 20, 1989, pp. 35–36.
8. "Patience Pays Off," *Industry Week*, April 4, 1994, p. 9.
9. Owens and Henricks, "Quality Time," p. 158.
10. Michael Barrier, "Who Should Get How Much—and Why?" *Nation's Business*, November 1995, pp. 58–59.
11. Mark Henricks, "80/20 Vision," *Entrepreneur*, April 1996, pp. 68–71.
12. Owens and Henricks, "Quality Time," p. 158.
13. George Taninecz, "Mutual Learning," *Industry Week*, July 7, 1997, p. 29.
14. John Hillkirk, "Quality Down But Not Out," *USA Today*, October 25, 1993, p. 2B.
15. George W. Appenzeller and John M. Bond, "Leadership Plus Honor Equals Total Quality Success," *South Carolina Business Journal*, April 1994, p. 12.
16. Roberta Maynard, "Striking the Right Match," *Nation's Business*, May 1996, pp. 18–28.
17. Roberta Maynard, "The Power of Pooling," *Nation's Business*, March 1995, pp. 16–22.
18. "The Nuts and Bolts of Supplier Relations," *Nation's Business*, August 1997, p. 11.
19. Mark Henricks, "Quality Makes a Difference," *Small Business Reports*, December 1992, p. 29.
20. Glen Weisman, "Stocking Up," *Business Start-Ups*, December 1996, pp. 14–15.
21. Jan Norman, "How to Find Suppliers," *Business Start-Ups*, October 1998, pp. 44–47.
22. Kylo-Patrick Hart, "Get What You Need," *Business Start-Ups*, July 1997, pp. 70–75.
23. Joel Kurtzman, "These Days, Small Manufacturers Can Play on a Level Field," *Fortune*, July 20, 1998, p. 156[F].
24. Weisman, "Stocking Up," p. 14.
25. "Business Bulletin," *Wall Street Journal*, November 13, 1997, p. A1.
26. John H. Sheridan, "Buying Globally Made Easier," *Industry Week*, February 2, 1998, pp. 63–64.
27. Ibid.
28. Richard J. Maturi, "The One and Only," *Entrepreneur*, June 1993, p. 152.
29. "Rarely Just in Time," *Small Business Reports*, April 1990, p. 12.
30. Weisman, "Stocking Up," p. 14.

Managing Inventory

We've got it if we can find it.

—*Sign in hardware store*

Great American axiom: Some is good. More is better. Too much is just right.

—*Anonymous*

Upon completion of this chapter, you will be able to

1 Explain the various inventory control systems and the advantages and disadvantages of each.

2 Describe how just-in-time (JIT) and JIT II inventory control techniques work.

3 Describe some methods for reducing loss from slow-moving inventory.

4 Discuss employee theft and shoplifting and how to prevent them.

*I*n the previous chapter, we saw the impact entrepreneurs' purchasing decisions have on their company's bottom line. This chapter focuses on the procedures designed to maximize the value of a small company's inventory and to reduce both the costs and the risks of owning inventory. Businesses in the United States spend more than $700 billion a year on inventory and moving it around from place to place.[1] Indeed, the largest expenditure most small companies make is for inventory, and entrepreneurs can realize tremendous savings from managing their company's inventory effectively. The costs of failing to do so can be astronomical. Carrying too much inventory "lowers a company's profitability—and not just because of the money spent to produce all those goods sitting unsold on your shelves," says one banker. Excess inventories "also eat up additional warehouse space; boost personnel needs for security, production, and warehouse staff; necessitate the purchase of extra inventory insurance; and increase borrowing needs."[2] In addition to lowering costs, any savings better inventory control produces for a company go directly to its bottom line. The payoff can be huge. "Companies can increase their profitability 20 to 50 percent through prudent inventory management," says one expert.[3]

Managing inventory effectively involves the following interrelated steps:

1. *Develop an accurate sales forecast.* The proper inventory levels for each item are directly related to the demand for that item. A business can't sell what it does not have, and conversely, an owner does not want to carry what will not sell.

2. *Develop a plan to make inventory available when and where customers want it.* Inventory will not sell if customers have a difficult time finding it. If a company is constantly running out of items customers expect to find, its customer base will dwindle over time as shoppers look elsewhere for those items.

3. *Build relationships with your most critical suppliers to ensure that you can get the merchandise you need when you need it.* Business owners must keep suppliers and vendors aware of how their merchandise is selling and communicate their needs to them. Vendors and suppliers can be an entrepreneur's greatest allies in managing inventory. Increasingly, the word that describes the relationship between world-class companies and their suppliers is *partnership.*

4. *Set realistic inventory turnover objectives.* Keeping in touch with their customers' likes and dislikes and monitoring their inventory enables owners to estimate the most likely buying patterns for different types of merchandise. As we learned in chapter 7, one of the factors having the greatest impact on a company's sales, cash flow, and ultimate success is its inventory turnover ratio.

5. *Compute the actual cost of carrying inventory.* Holding inventory in stock is expensive! Carrying costs include such items as interest on borrowed money, insurance expenses associated with the inventory, inventory-related personnel expenses, and all other related operating costs. In the fast-paced computer business, for example, the onrush of new technology causes the value of a personal computer held in inventory to drop by about 1 percentage point each week![4] That gives computer makers big incentives to move their inventories quickly. Without an accurate cost of carrying inventory, it is impossible to determine an optimal inventory level.

6. *Use the most timely and accurate information system the business can afford to provide the facts and figures necessary to make critical inventory decisions.* Computers and modern point-of-sale terminals that are linked to a company's inventory records enable business owners to know exactly which items are selling and which ones are not. *For example, the owner of a chain of baby products stores uses a computer network to link all of his stores to the computer at central headquarters. Every night, after the stores close, the point-of-sale terminals in each store download the day's sales to the central computer, which compiles an extensive sales and inventory report. When he walks into his office every morning, the owner reviews the report and can tell exactly which items are moving fastest, which are moving slowest, and which are not selling at all. He credits the system with the company's above-average inventory turnover ratio—and much of his chain's success.*

7. *Teach employees how inventory control systems work so that they can contribute to managing the firm's inventory on a daily basis.* All too often, the employees on the floor have no idea of how the various information systems and inventory control techniques operate or interact with one another. Consequently, the people closest to the inventory contribute little to controlling it. Well-trained employees armed with

information can be one of an entrepreneur's greatest weapons in the battle to control inventory.

The goal is to find and maintain the proper balance between the cost of holding inventory and the requirements to have the merchandise when the customer demands it. Either extreme can be costly. If entrepreneurs focus solely on minimizing cost, they will undoubtedly lose sales and generate ill will because they cannot satisfy their customers' needs. On the other hand, entrepreneurs who attempt to hold inventory to meet every peak customer demand will find that inventory costs have diminished their chances of remaining profitable. Walking this inventory tightrope is never easy, but the following inventory control systems can help business owners strike a reasonable balance between the two extremes.

*I*nventory Control Systems

◆ Explain the various inventory control systems and the advantages and disadvantages of each.

Regardless of the type of inventory control system business owners choose, they must recognize the importance of Pareto's Law (or the 80/20 rule), which holds that about 80 percent of the value of the firm's sales revenue is generated by 20 percent of the items kept in stock. Some of the firm's items are high dollar volume goods, while others account for only a small portion of sales volume. Because most sales are generated by a small percentage of times, owners should focus the majority of their inventory control efforts on this 20 percent. Observing this simple principle ensures that entrepreneurs will spend time controlling only the most productive—and, therefore, most valuable—inventory items. With this technique in mind, we now examine three basic types of inventory control systems: perpetual, visual, and partial.

PERPETUAL INVENTORY SYSTEMS

Perpetual inventory systems are designed to maintain a running count of the items in inventory. Although a number of different perpetual inventory systems exist, they all have a common element: They all keep a continuous tally of each item added to or subtracted from the firm's stock of merchandise. The basic perpetual inventory system uses a perpetual inventory sheet that includes fundamental product information such as the item's name, stock number, description, economic order quantity (EOQ), and reorder point.

These perpetual inventory sheets are usually placed next to the merchandise in the warehouse or storage facility. Whenever a shipment is received from a vendor, the quantity is entered in the receipts column and added to the total. When the item is sold and taken from inventory, it is simply deducted from the total. As long as this procedure is followed consistently, the owner can quickly determine the number of each item on hand.

Although consistent use of the system yields accurate inventory counts at any moment, sporadic use creates problems. If managers or employees take items out of stock or place them in inventory without recording them, the perpetual inventory sheet will yield incorrect totals and can foul up the entire inventory control system. Another disadvantage of this system is the cost of maintaining it. Keeping such records for a large number of items and ensuring the accuracy of the system can be excessively expensive. Therefore, these systems are used most frequently and most successfully in controlling high dollar volume items that require strict monitoring. Management must watch these items closely and ensure that inventory records are accurate.

Technical advances in computerized cash registers have overcome many of the disadvantages of using the basic perpetual inventory system. Small businesses now are able to afford computerized **point-of-sale (POS) systems** that perform all of the functions of a traditional cash register and maintain an up-to-the-minute inventory count. Although POS systems are not new (major retailers have been using them for more than 25 years), their affordable prices are. Not so long ago, most systems required mini- or mainframe computers and cost $20,000 or more. Today, small business owners can set up POS systems on personal computers for less than $1,000! Combining a POS system with Universal Product Code (bar code) labels and high-speed scanners gives a small business a state-of-the-art checkout system that feeds vital information into its inventory control system. These systems rely on an inventory database; as items are rung up on the register, product information is recorded and inventory balances are adjusted. Using the system, business owners can tell how quickly each item is selling and how many items are in stock at any time. Plus, their inventory records are accurate and always current. They also can generate instantly a variety of reports to aid in making purchasing decisions. The system can be programmed to alert owners when the supply of a particular item drops below a predetermined reorder point or even to print automatically a purchase order for the EOQ indicated. Computerized systems such as these make it possible for the owner to use a basic perpetual inventory system for a large number of items—a task that, if performed manually, would be virtually impossible.[5]

A well-designed POS system gives an owner the information he needs to make sound inventory and purchasing decisions on a timely basis without spending a small fortune to do it. *For example, Steve Janus, owner of three Koala Blue clothing stores, uses a PC-based POS system to manage his company's inventory. Each store carries a variety of fashion lines, and, in the past, Janus had always struggled with the problem of deciding which lines of clothing to buy. Like many retailers, Janus recognized the essential need to stock only the merchandise that was "hot." With his new POS system, Janus gets a report showing the sales for each clothing line for each store. The system has improved his ability to keep the stores' inventory "in line with what people want," and the merchandise turns more quickly. For the first time, says Janus, his inventory buying decisions are more than just "guesstimates."[6]*

Specific Perpetual Inventory Control Systems. Perpetual inventory systems operate in a number of ways, but three basic variations are particularly common: the sales ticket method, the sales stub method, and the floor sample method.

The Sales Ticket Method. Most small businesses use sales tickets to summarize individual customers' transactions. These tickets serve two major purposes: They provide the customer with a sales receipt for the merchandise purchased, and they provide the owner with a daily record of the number of specific inventory items sold. The **sales ticket method** operates by gathering all the sales tickets at the end of each day and transcribing the data onto the appropriate perpetual inventory sheet. By posting inventory deductions to the perpetual inventory system from sales tickets, the small business manager can monitor sales patterns and keep close control on inventory. The primary disadvantage of using such a system is the time required to make it function properly. Most managers find it difficult to squeeze in the time needed to post sales tickets to the perpetual inventory system.

The Sales Stub Method. The principle behind the **sales stub method** of inventory control is the same as that underlying the sales ticket method, but its mechanics are slightly different. Retail stores often attach a ticket with two or more parts containing relevant product information to each inventory item in stock. When an employee sells an item, he removes a portion of the stub and places it in a container. At the end of the day, the owner posts the inventory deductions recorded by the stubs to the proper perpetual inventory sheet.

The Floor Sample Method. The **floor sample method** of controlling inventory is commonly used by businesses selling big-ticket items with high unit cost. In many cases, these items are somewhat bulky and are difficult to display in large numbers. For example, the owner of a small furniture store might receive a shipment of 15 roll-top desks in a particular style. A

IN THE FOOTSTEPS OF AN ENTREPRENEUR

A High-Tech Salvage Yard

*I*n 1983, Ron Sturgeon realized that his auto salvage yard, AAA Small Car World, was growing so fast that he was having difficulty maintaining control over it. The company, which salvaged parts from wrecked cars and resold them, "had an awful lot of parts in stock, with sales doubling almost every year," recalls Sturgeon. Sturgeon managed AAA's vast inventory of parts the same way all of the other businesses in the traditionally low-tech auto salvage industry did: by hand! When a wrecked car arrived, employees would evaluate its condition and then develop a list of the usable parts on a tracking sheet. Employees labeled each part by hand and filled out another label that they filed in the tiny drawers of an old pharmaceutical filing cabinet AAA had on hand. If a customer requested an alternator for an Acura Legend, a salesperson would have to rummage through the tiny labels on file in the pharmaceutical cabinet. "We had no automated way of tracking the fact that an alternator for a Honda might also fit an Acura, "' says Sturgeon. "We needed to track parts more efficiently."

That's when Sturgeon set out to solve the problem by writing his own inventory-tracking program to run on the three microcomputers the company already used. After spending a couple of years and $20,000, Sturgeon realized he was getting nowhere. The idea of using computers to track the salvage yard's inventory languished for another year or so before Sturgeon upgraded to newer, more powerful computers. By 1986, he had begun exploring the possibilities of using inventory-tracking software, but this time he decided to *buy* a software package rather than attempt to write his own. After talking with two software vendors at an industry trade show, he knew that buying a software package was the way to go.

In 1987, Sturgeon took a great leap of faith and spent $70,000 (company sales then were just $2 million!) on an automated inventory tracking system called Checkmate. The system gave AAA 20 networked PCs, various printers, modems, and other peripherals, technical assistance, two weeks of training for every employee, and the inventory-tracking software. He financed the cost over four years. (With advances in technology, a similar system today costs less than $10,000.)

The investment paid off! Sturgeon credits the inventory-control system with giving him the tools he needed to make his company one of the leaders in the industry. Today, AAA rings up sales of $8 million, processing 100 cars a week. Now, however, when a wrecked car arrives, the process is quite different. An assessor tells the computer system that, for example, a 1996 Jeep Grand Cherokee has arrived. The database spits out a parts sheet that lists all of the car's parts with a part number assigned to each one. The assessor evaluates the car using the printout, circling all of the parts that are usable, and then enters those parts into the database. The computer then prints out labels for each part. What used to take workers more than two hours to do by hand now requires just 15 minutes with the computer's help.

The system tracks every part in its database and even recognizes interchangeable parts. If, for instance, a customer needs an alternator for a 1997 Acura, the computer notifies the salesperson that the 1997 Honda alternator in stock fits the Acura as well. All 19 salespeople at AAA's six locations can use the system simultaneously. The system also handles sales transactions and invoices in one step. With the computerized tracking system, Sturgeon can determine the number of times customers request a particular part, so he knows whether AAA is missing sales on parts it should be stocking. Similarly, if he sees customers refusing to buy parts that are in stock, he knows to lower their prices. The new system prevents salespeople from missing sales because they don't have the information they need. It also gives salespeople the ability to locate parts instantly, which boosts AAA's level of customer service. "Without this system, we couldn't have tripled sales," says Sturgeon. "We'd still be pulling pieces of paper out of file cabinets to see if we had a BMW part. That kind of limits your growth."

1. What benefits do inventory-tracking systems such as the one AAA Small Car World uses give small businesses characterized by large inventories?

2. Can investing in such systems give a company a competitive advantage? How?

Source: Adapted from Phaedra Hise, "High-Tech Salvage Yard," *Inc. Technology* 4 (1995), p. 102. ◆

simple technique for maintaining control of these items is to attach a small pad to the display desk with sheets numbered in descending order from 15 to 1. Whenever an employee sells a roll-top desk, she removes a sheet from the pad. As long as the system is followed consistently, the owner is able to determine accurate inventory levels with a quick pass around the sales floor. When the supply of a particular item dwindles, the owner simply calls the vendor to replenish the inventory. The procedure is simple and serves its purpose.

VISUAL INVENTORY CONTROL SYSTEMS

The most common method of controlling inventory in a small business is the **visual control system,** in which managers simply conduct periodic visual inspections to determine the quantity of various items they should order. As mentioned earlier, manual perpetual inventory systems can be excessively costly and time-consuming. Such systems are impractical when the business stocks a large number of low-value items with low dollar volume. Therefore, many owners rely on the simplest, quickest inventory control method: the visual system. Unfortunately, this method is also the least effective for ensuring accuracy and reliability. Oversights of key items often lead to stock-outs and resulting lost sales. The biggest disadvantage of the visual control system is its inability to detect and to foresee shortages of inventory items.

In general, a visual inventory control system works best in firms where daily sales are relatively consistent, the owner is closely involved with the inventory, the variety of merchandise is small, and items can be obtained quickly from vendors. For example, small firms dealing in perishable goods use visual control systems very successfully, and rarely, if ever, rely on analytical inventory control tools. For these firms, shortages are not likely to occur under a visual system; when they do occur, they are not likely to create major problems. Still, the manager who uses a visual inventory control system should leave reminders to make regular inspections and should be alert to shifts in customer buying patterns that alter required inventory levels.

PARTIAL INVENTORY CONTROL SYSTEMS

For small business owners with limited time and money, the most viable option for inventory management is a partial inventory control system. Such a system relies on the validity of the 80/20 rule. For example, if a small business carries 5,000 different items in stock, roughly 1,000 of them account for about 80 percent of the firm's sales volume. Experienced business owners focus their control efforts on those 1,000 items. Still, many managers seek to maintain tight control over the remaining 4,000 items, a frustrating and wasteful practice. Smart small business owners design their inventory control systems with this principle in mind. One of the most popular partial inventory control systems is the ABC system.

The ABC Method of Inventory Control. Too many managers apply perpetual inventory control systems universally when a partial control system would be much more practical. Partial inventory systems minimize the expense involved in analyzing, processing, and maintaining records, a substantial cost of any inventory control system. The ABC method is one such approach, focusing control efforts on that small percentage of items that account for the majority of the firm's sales. The typical **ABC system** divides a firm's inventory into three major categories:

A items account for a high dollar usage volume.

B items account for a moderate dollar usage volume.

C items account for low dollar usage volume.

The **dollar usage volume** of an item measures the relative importance of that item in the firm's inventory. Note that value is not necessarily synonymous with high unit cost. In some instances, a high-cost item that generates only a small dollar volume can be classified as an A item. But, more frequently, A items are those that are low to moderate in cost and high-volume by nature.

The initial step in establishing an ABC classification system is to compute the annual dollar usage volume for each product (or product category). **Annual dollar usage volume** is simply the cost per unit of an item multiplied by the annual quantity used. For instance, the owner of a stereo shop may find that she sold 190 pairs of a popular brand of speaker during the previous year. If the speakers cost her $75 per unit, their annual dollar usage volume would be as follows:

$$190 \times \$75 = \$14{,}250$$

The next step is to arrange the products in descending order on the basis of the computed annual dollar usage volume. Once so arranged, they can be divided into appropriate classes by applying the following rule:

A items: roughly the top 15 percent of the items listed

B items: roughly the next 35 percent

C items: roughly the remaining 50 percent

For example, Florentina's, a small retail shop, is interested in establishing an ABC inventory control system to lower losses from stock-outs, theft, or other hazards. Florentina has computed the annual dollar usage volume for the store's merchandise inventory, as shown in Table 17.1. (For simplicity, we show only 12 inventory items.)

The ABC inventory control method divides the firm's inventory items into three classes depending on the items' value. Figure 17.1 graphically portrays the segmentation of the items listed in Table 17.1.

The purpose of classifying items according to their annual dollar usage volume is to establish the proper degree of control over each item held in inventory. Clearly, it is wasteful and inefficient to exercise the same level of control over C items and A items. Items in the A

Table 17.1 Calculating Annual Dollar Usage Volume and an ABC Inventory Analysis for Florentina's

Item	Annual Dollar Usage Volume	Percent of Annual Dollar Usage
Paragon	$374,100	42.0
Excelsior	294,805	33.1
Avery	68,580	7.7
Bardeen	54,330	6.1
Berkeley	27,610	3.1
Tara	24,940	2.8
Cattell	11,578	1.3
Faraday	9,797	1.1
Humboldt	8,016	0.9
Mandel	7,125	0.08
Sabot	5,344	0.06
Wister	4,453	0.05
Total	$890,678	100.0

Classification	Items	Annual Dollar Usage	Percent of Total
A	Paragon, Excelsior	$668,905	75.1
B	Avery, Bardeen, Berkeley, Tara	175,460	19.7
C	Cattell, Faraday, Humboldt, Mandel, Sabot, Wister	46,313	5.2
Total		$890,678	100.0

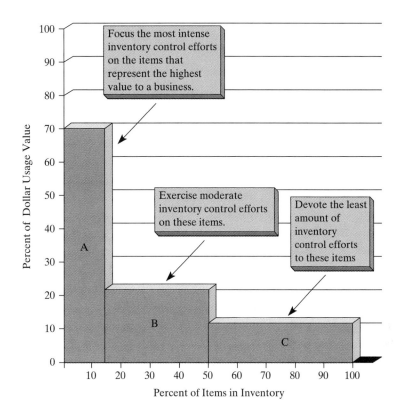

Figure 17.1 ABC Inventory Control

classification should be controlled under a perpetual inventory system with as much detail as necessary. Analytical tools and frequent counts may be required to ensure accuracy, but the extra cost of tight control for these valuable items is usually justified. Managers should not retain a large supply of reserve or safety stock because doing so ties up excessive amounts of money in inventory, but they must monitor the stock closely to avoid stock-outs and lost sales.

Control of B items should rely more on periodic control systems and basic analytical tools such as EOQ and reorder point analysis (discussed in chapter 16). Managers can maintain moderate levels of safety stock for these items to guard against shortages and can afford monthly or even bimonthly merchandise inspections. Because B items are not as valuable to the business as A items, less rigorous control systems are required.

C items typically constitute a minor proportion of the small firm's inventory value and, as a result, require the least effort and expense to control. These items are usually large in number and small in total value. The most practical way to control them is to use uncomplicated records and procedures. Large levels of safety stock for these items are acceptable because the cost of carrying them is usually minimal. Substantial order sizes often enable the business to take advantage of quantity discounts without having to place frequent orders. The cost involved in using detailed recordkeeping and inventory control procedures greatly outweighs the advantages gleaned from strict control of C items.

One practical technique for maintaining control simply is the **two-bin system,** which keeps two separate bins full of material. The first bin is used to fill customer orders, and the second bin is filled with enough safety stock to meet customer demand during the lead time. When the first bin is empty, the owner places an order with the vendor large enough to refill both bins. During the lead time for the order, the manager uses the safety stock in the second bin to fill customer demand.

When storage space or the type of item does not suit the two-bin system, the owner can use a **tag system.** Based on the same principles as the two-bin system, which is suitable for many manufacturers, the tag system applies to most retail, wholesale, and service firms. Instead of placing enough inventory to meet customer demand during lead time into a separate bin, the owner marks this inventory level with a brightly colored tag. When the supply is drawn down to the tagged level, the owner reorders the merchandise. Figure 17.2 illustrates the two-bin and tag systems of controlling C items.

In summary, business owners minimize total inventory costs when they spend time and effort controlling items that represent the greatest inventory value. Some inventory items re-

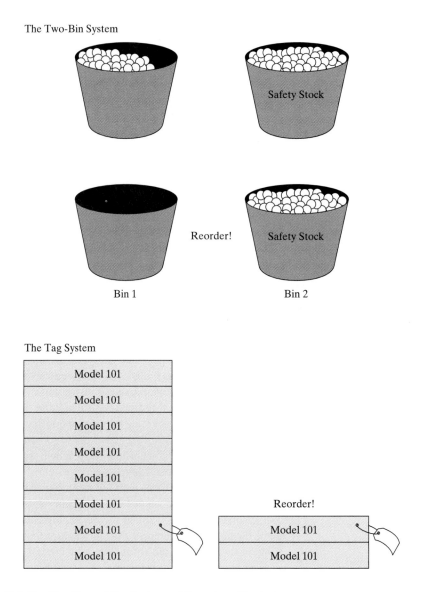

Figure 17.2 **The Two-Bin and Tag Systems of Inventory Control**

Table 17.2 ABC Inventory Control Features

Feature	A Items	B Items	C Items
Level of control	Monitor closely and maintain tight control.	Maintain moderate control.	Maintain loose control.
Reorder	Based on forecasted requirements.	Based on EOQ calculations and past experience.	When level gets low, reorder.
Record keeping	Keep detailed records of receipts and disbursements.	Use periodic inspections and control procedures.	No records required.
Safety stock	Keep low levels of safety stock.	Keep moderate levels of safety stock.	Keep high levels of safety stock.
Inspection frequency	Monitor schedule changes frequently.	Check on changes in requirements periodically.	Make few checks on requirements.

quire strict, detailed control techniques; others cannot justify the cost of such systems. Because of its practicality, the ABC inventory system is commonly used in industry. In addition, the technique is easily computerized, speeding up the analysis and lowering its cost. Table 17.2 summarizes the use of the ABC control system.

PHYSICAL INVENTORY COUNT

Regardless of the type of inventory control system used, every small business owner must conduct a periodic physical inventory count. Even when a company uses a perpetual inventory system, the owner must still count the actual number of items on hand because of the possibility of human error. A physical inventory count allows owners to reconcile the actual amount of inventory in stock with the amount reported through the inventory control system. These counts give managers a fresh start in determining the actual number of items on hand and enable them to evaluate the effectiveness and the accuracy of their inventory control systems.

The typical method of taking inventory involves two employees; one calls out the relevant information for each inventory item, and the other records the count on a tally sheet. There are two basic methods of conducting a physical inventory count. One alternative is to take inventory at regular intervals. Many businesses take inventory at the end of the year. In an attempt to minimize counting, many managers run special year-end inventory reduction sales. This periodic physical count generates the most accurate measurement of inventory. The other method of taking inventory, called **cycle counting,** involves counting a number of items on a continuous basis. Instead of waiting until year-end to tally the entire inventory of items, the manager counts a few types of items each week and checks the numbers against the inventory control system. Such a system allows for continuous correction of mistakes in inventory control systems and detects inventory problems sooner than an annual count would.

Once again, technology can make the job of taking inventory much easier for the small business owner. **Electronic data interchange (EDI)** systems enable business owners to track their inventories and to place orders with vendors quickly and with few errors by linking them to their vendors electronically. These systems often rely on hand-held computer terminals equipped with a scanning wand. An employee runs the wand across a bar-code label on the shelf that identifies the inventory item; then he counts the items on the shelf and enters that number using the number pad on the terminal. Then, by linking the hand-held ter-

HOG Heaven

*A*rmand Schaubroeck's business, the House of Guitars, caters to guitarists of all skill levels—from beginning amateurs to professionals in rock bands. A few years ago, when the rock band Metallica performed a concert in a nearby town, band members wanted to shop at "the HOG" (as its fans affectionately call it), but their only free time was *after* their concert. Schaubroeck, who normally closes at 9 P.M., reopened the shop at 11 P.M. so that band members could browse through the store's extensive collection of guitars. He and his employees were treated to a miniconcert of their own as the musicians tried out the guitars and other musical instruments the store carries. HOG's customer list includes not only Metallica but also bands such as Motley Crue, Aerosmith, and a host of lesser-known groups as well as individual performers such as Ozzy Osbourne and Matthew Sweet.

Although HOG sells everything from CDs and drums to amplifiers and keyboards, its specialty is guitars. The business occupies an old feed store, which is connected to its five cavernous warehouses by a labyrinth of passages so complex that employees sometimes get lost. Ozzy Osbourne says the House of Guitars has "a great vibey feel." Mountains of T-shirts and CDs fill one room. Autographs of famous musicians decorate a wall in another warehouse, and rock 'n' roll memorabilia, such as a pair of Elvis Presley's leather pants, are everywhere. But what sets the House of Guitars apart from other musical instrument stores is its inventory and the way it is displayed. Rather than keep his guitars locked in glass cases, Schaubroeck puts them out in the open and encourages customers to try them out. He has even built small, soundproof rooms so that customers can hook guitars up to amplifiers and play as loudly as they like.

The huge selection of guitars the HOG offers attracts many customers. The business stocks practically every make of instrument (and what the store doesn't stock, it can get), whereas most other instrument stores specialize in a single brand. Schaubroeck estimates that he has 9,000 guitars in stock. After taking a guest on a tour, however, he revises his estimate upward to 11,000 guitars. "It is total guitar heaven and the high point of any tour," says alternative musician Matthew Sweet. Sweet once missed a preconcert sound check because he couldn't tear himself away from the HOG. He bought three new guitars, spending several thousand dollars. The House of Guitars has 20 employees, all musicians, and racks up sales of $7 million a year. Andy Babiuk, a salesperson at HOG for 17 years, is a member of a local heavy-metal band called the Chesterfield Kings. Wading through a knee-deep collection of vintage amplifiers, Babiuk marvels, "You can't walk into any music store and get this," waving his hand.

Schaubroeck's accountant almost panicked when he saw the inventory level the House of Guitars maintains. On paper, it looks like a recipe for disaster. In person, at first glance, the disarray looks like a disaster. Then, the beauty of Schaubroeck's strategy begins to emerge. The HOG, says Schaubroeck's accountant, "doesn't turn its inventory as fast as it should, but they carry older things—so once they become out of stock at other places, [HOG's] prices go up." One of the store's prize pieces, for instance, is a 1947 D'Angelico New York, which Schaubroeck calls "the Stradivarius of guitars." The valuable collector's item is worth more than $50,000! Although Schauboeck's investment in inventory is what most musical instrument store owners would consider excessive, it is actually an important part of the company's success. Guitarists and musicians across the country plan their tours so they can shop there. When asked about the HOG, one rock star says simply, "All the pros know it."

---

1. What benefits does maintaining a large inventory offer the House of Guitars? What costs are associated with holding a large inventory?

2. What advice would you offer Armand Schaubroeck about controlling his company's inventory more effectively?

SOURCE: Emily Nelson, "Meet the Master of the House of Guitars," *Wall Street Journal*, June 12, 1997, pp. B1, B7. ◆

minal to a personal computer, he can download the physical inventory count into the company's inventory control software in seconds!

In the past, suppliers simply manufactured a product, shipped it, and then sent the customer an invoice. To place an order, employees or managers periodically would estimate how much of a particular item they would need and when they would need it. Today, however, in many EDI systems, the vendor is tied directly into a company's POS (point-of-sale) system, monitoring it constantly; when the company's supply of a particular item drops to a preset level, the vendor automatically sends a shipment to replenish its stock to an established level. Information that once traveled by mail (or was never shared at all), such as shipping information, invoices, inventory balances, sales, even funds, now travels instantly between businesses and their suppliers. The result is a much more efficient system of purchasing, distribution, and inventory control. *For example, when one of Ideal Supply company's top customers asked the small supplier of industrial pipes and valves to set up an EDI system in 1990, general manager Michael Fidenza decided that doing so would give his company an edge over its rivals. "Our industry is old-fashioned," says Fidenza. "We tend to lag behind the times." Ideal Supply not only forged an even closer relationship with its big customer; it also reaped benefits from its suppliers. Because Ideal Supply was one of the few companies in the industry with EDI capability, Fidenza was able to negotiate higher discounts from its suppliers because of increased efficiencies in the purchasing process. "One of our vendors offered us an extra 5 percent in discounts," he says. "Another plugs in an extra $10,000 worth of product with every $50,000 purchase—just because we're EDI." Ideal Supply has earned an impressive return on its original investment of $5,000 for EDI hardware and software. Today, 80 percent of the company's purchases and 15 percent of its sales are processed through its EDI system.*[7]

*J*ust-in-Time (JIT) Inventory Control Techniques

2 Describe how just-in-time (JIT) and JIT II inventory control techniques work.

Many U.S. manufacturers have turned to a popular inventory control technique called **just-in-time (JIT)** to reduce costly inventories and turn around their financial fortunes. Until recently these firms had accepted and practiced without question the following long-standing principles of manufacturing: Long production runs of standard items are ideal; machines should be up and running as much as possible; machines must produce a large number of items to justify long setup times and high costs; similar processes should be consolidated into single departments; tasks should be highly specialized and simplified; and inventories (raw materials, work-in-process, and finished goods) should be large enough to avoid emergencies such as supply interruptions, strikes, and breakdowns.

The just-in-time philosophy, however, views excess inventory as a blanket that masks problems and as a source of unnecessary costs that inhibit a firm's competitive position. Under a JIT system, materials and inventory should flow smoothly through the production process without stopping. They arrive at the appropriate location just in time instead of becoming part of a costly inventory stockpile. Just-in-time is a manufacturing philosophy that seeks to improve a company's efficiency. The key measure of manufacturing efficiency is the level of inventory maintained; the lower the level of inventory, the more efficient the production system.

In the past, only large companies could reap the benefits of computerized JIT and inventory control software, but now a proliferation of inexpensive programs designed for personal computers gives small companies that ability. *At Mothers Work Inc., a chain of 450-plus shops, Rebecca and Dan Mathias rely on a computerized inventory management system to tell them exactly what is selling, what isn't, and how long it will take to make or order more. Mothers Work uses the system to test market fashion ideas in its stores before committing to long production runs of goods that might not sell. With the system, if the Mathiases discover a hot-selling item, they can fill their stores' shelves with it in less than two weeks, compared with about six months at their competitors. The company also can replenish its inventory at its stores on a daily basis. The result: a lean stock of inventory that turns over quickly and is not likely to require markdowns to move off the shelf.*[8]

Almost any change that has this aim can be counted as part of the JIT philosophy. Companies adopting the JIT system look for ways to cut machine setup times, reduce the number of adjustments made during production, redesign parts so that machines involved in the same processes are closer together, and move parts to each manufacturing station only when they are needed. *For instance, at the Alexander Doll Company, a 75-year-old maker of collectible dolls, managers have adopted the JIT philosophy, scrapping the traditional assembly-line process. Employees now work in teams called "production cells." Because they are now cross-trained in a variety of jobs, workers no longer perform the same task all day. In addition to making employees' work more interesting, cross-training allows the company to improve its manufacturing flexibility. With its more skilled workforce, the company can shift its production seamlessly as customer demand for different dolls changes. "In the past, we made [dolls] in large batches and put them in inventory," says one manager. "Frequently, at the end of the season, we would have lots of leftovers." With its new system in place, inventory levels are down, sales are up, and the Alexander Doll Company is meeting customer demand better than ever before.*[9]

Today, many suppliers recognize that extremely high quality and absolutely on-time delivery are essential elements of remaining competitive. Just-in-time systems work because suppliers recognize that if they are unable to meet the demands their customers set forth, some other company surely will. *Cisco Systems, a manufacturer of computer hardware, ships thousands of sophisticated computer routers to customers in Europe each week. Cisco's customers expect to know where their shipments are at all times, which also is important information for Cisco because it may have to reroute a shipment to meet a customer's urgent request. To be able to meet these rather exacting demands, Cisco hired UPS Worldwide Logistics to design a computerized system to schedule and track all of its shipments. Before Cisco implemented its new system, deliveries to its European customers took up to three weeks; now, those same deliveries arrive in just four days. Deliveries are much faster and more reliable; customers are more satisfied; and Cisco has saved a bundle on its inventory investment. "We want to replace inventory with information," explains one manager.*[10]

Advocates claim that when JIT is successfully implemented, companies experience five positive results:

1. Lower investment in inventory
2. Reduced inventory carrying and handling costs
3. Reduced costs from obsolescence of inventory
4. Lower investment in space for inventories and production
5. Reduced total manufacturing costs from the better coordination needed between departments to operate at lower inventory levels

For JIT systems to be most productive, small business owners must consider the human component of the equation as well. The two primary human elements on which successful JIT systems are built are:

1. *Mutual trust and teamwork.* Managers and employees view each other as equals, have a commitment to the organization and its long-term effectiveness, and are willing to work as a team to find and solve problems.
2. *Empowerment.* Effective organizations provide their employees with the authority to take action to solve problems. The objective is to have the problems dealt with at the lowest level and as quickly as possible.

At a technical level, JIT is most effective in repetitive manufacturing operations where there are significant inventory levels, where production requirements can be forecast accurately, and where suppliers are an integral part of the system. Experience shows that companies with the following charcteristics have the greatest success with JIT:

◆ Reliable deliveries of all parts and supplies
◆ Short distance between client and vendors

- Consistently high quality of vendors' products
- Stable and predictable product demand that allows for accurate production schedules

JUST-IN-TIME II TECHNIQUES

In the past, some companies that adopted JIT techniques discovered an unwanted side effect: increased hostility resulting from the increased pressure they put on their suppliers to meet tight, often challenging schedules. To resolve that conflict, many businesses have turned to an extension of JIT, **just-in-time II (JIT II),** which focuses on creating a close, harmonious relationship with a company's suppliers so that both parties benefit from increased efficiency. Lance Dixon, who created the JIT II concept when he was a manager at Bose Corporation, a manufacturer of audio equipment, calls it "empowerment of the supplier within the customer's organization."[11] To work successfully, JIT II requires suppliers and their customers to share what was once closely guarded information in an environment of trust and cooperation. Under JIT II, customers and suppliers work hand in hand, acting more like partners than mere buyers and sellers. *For instance, Dell Computer Corporation uses the Internet and modern Web-based software to link its suppliers' manufacturing systems with its own. Sharing information with suppliers over the Internet has allowed Dell to reduce its inventory investment significantly and to speed its inventory turnover.*[12]

In many businesses practicing JIT II, suppliers' employees work on site at the customer's plant, factory, or warehouse almost as if they were its employees. These on-sight workers are responsible for monitoring, controlling, and ordering inventory from their own companies. While at Bose, Dixon decided to try JIT II because it offered the potential to reduce sharply the company's inventories of materials and components, to cut purchasing costs, and to generate cost-cutting design and production tips from suppliers who understood Bose's process. This new alliance between suppliers and their customers would form a new supply chain that would lower costs at every one of its links. To protect against leakage of confidential information, Dixon had all of the employees from Bose's suppliers who would work in its plant sign confidentiality agreements. Dixon also put a ceiling on the amount each supplier's employee could order without previous authorization from Bose. The JIT II system worked even better than Dixon had imagined. One purchasing manager who admits that he was skeptical in the beginning is now a believer in the system. "You can't get improvement any more simply by negotiating a better price and showing suppliers half the cards," he says. "Something has to change."[13]

Growing numbers of small companies are forging JIT II relationships with their suppliers and customers. *For instance, Northern Polymer Corporation, a seven-person plastics maker, sells plastic resin to G & F Industries, a 170-employee injection molding company in Sturbridge, Massachusetts, under a JIT II arrangement. Northern employees visit G & F's plant several times each month to check its inventory and consumption levels. Northern has set up a resin storage facility near G & F's plant so that it can restock its resin supply within just a few hours, if necessary. The arrangement "secures that piece of business [for us] for a long period," says Northern's founder, Joseph St. Martin.* As Northern Polymer's experience with G & F Industries indicates, an EDI system such as those mentioned earlier in this chapter allows many companies to operate JIT II systems without having an employee from the supplier in-house. G & F Industries, in turn, has a JIT II relationship with one of its biggest customers, Bose Corporation, and G & F does keep an employee in Bose's plant on a full-time basis.[14]

Manufacturers are not the only companies benefiting from JIT II. In a retail environment, the concept is more commonly known as **efficient consumer response (ECR),** but the principles are the same. Rather than build inventories of merchandise that might sit for months before selling (or worse, never sell at all), retailers using ECR replenish their inventories constantly on an as-needed basis. Because vendors are linked electronically to the retailer's point-of-sale system, thay can monitor the company's inventory and keep it stocked with the right merchandise mix in the right quantities. Both parties reduce the inventories they must carry and experience significant reductions in paperwork and ordering costs.

Just-in-time II works best when two companies transact a significant amount of business that involves many different parts or products. Still, trust is the biggest barrier the companies must overcome. "The hardest thing is to find two partners who really will put together a relationship based on trust, an open-door policy, and mutual benefit," says one manager experienced in JIT II.[15]

*T*urning Slow-Moving Inventory into Cash

3 Describe some methods for reducing loss from slow-moving inventory.

Managing inventory effectively requires a business owner to monitor the company's inventory turnover ratio and to compare it with that of other firms of similar size in the same industry. As you recall, the inventory turnover ratio is computed by dividing the firm's cost of goods sold by its average inventory. This ratio expresses the number of times per year the business turns over its inventory. In most cases, the higher the inventory turnover ratio, the better the small firm's financial position will be. A very low inventory turnover ratio indicates that much of the inventory may be stale and obsolete or that inventory investment is too large. One business owner says that to keep his company out of the "inventory danger zone," he uses a monthly report showing his company's inventory broken down into raw materials, work-in-process, and finished goods. He compares the current month's report with the previous month's numbers and with the numbers for the same month one year before. "When I detect significant variances in either number, I want an explanation," he says.[16]

Slow-moving items carry a good chance of loss resulting from spoilage or obsolescence. Firms dealing in trendy fashion merchandise or highly seasonal items often experience losses as a result of being stuck with unsold inventory for long periods of time. Some small business owners are reluctant to sell these slow-moving items by cutting prices, but it is much more profitable to dispose of this merchandise as quickly as possible than to hold it in stock at the regular prices. The owner who postpones marking down stale merchandise, fearing it would reduce profit and hoping that the goods will sell eventually at the regular price, is making a huge mistake. The longer the merchandise sits, the dimmer the prospects of ever selling it, much less selling it at a profit. Pricing these items below regular price or even below cost is difficult, but it is much better than having valuable working capital tied up in unproductive assets.

The most common technique for liquidating slow-moving merchandise is the markdown. Not only is the markdown effective in eliminating slow-moving goods, but it also is a successful promotional tool. Advertising special prices on such merchandise helps the small business garner a larger clientele and contributes to establishing a favorable business image. Using special sales to promote slow-moving items helps create a functional program for turning over inventory more quickly. To get rid of a large supply of out-of-style neckties, one small business offered a "one cent sale" to customers purchasing neckwear at the regular price. One retailer of stereos and sound equipment chooses an unusual holiday—George Washington's birthday—to sponsor an all-out blitz, including special sales, prices, and promotions, to reduce its inventory. Other techniques that help eliminate slow-moving merchandise include the following:

♦ Middle-of-the-aisle display islands that attract customer attention

♦ One-day-only sales

♦ Quantity discounts for volume purchases

- Bargain tables with a variety of merchandise for customers to explore
- Eye-catching lights and tickets marking sale merchandise

Protecting Inventory from Theft

3 Discuss employee theft and shoplifting and how to prevent them.

Small companies are a big target for crime. Security experts estimate that businesses lose $400 billion annually to criminals, although the actual loss may be even greater because so many business crimes go unreported. Whatever the actual loss is, its effect is staggering, especially on small companies. Studies show that small businesses are more susceptible to crime than large companies; a small firm is 35 times as likely to be a victim of employee theft, shoplifting, robbery, or burglary as a business with sales in excess of $5 million.[17] Because small companies' losses to crime represent a greater proportion of their assets, the impact on them is many times greater than on the typical large company.

Certain types of businesses are particularly vulnerable to losses from crime. For instance, the very nature of retail leaves that industry highly susceptible to criminal attacks. Research shows that retailers foot approximately one-fourth of the national crime bill. According to the Small Business Administration, a retail theft occurs every five seconds, and those thefts cost the average American household more than $200 per year.[18]

Although they may not want to admit it, small business owners are frequent victims of business crimes. Crime can assume a variety of forms, but the most serious threats to entrepreneurs are employee theft and shoplifting.

EMPLOYEE THEFT

The greatest criminal threat to small businesses, ironically, comes from inside. Employee theft accounts for the greatest proportion of the criminal losses businesses suffer. One of the problems is that small business owners simply don't want to believe that the people who work for them would steal from them! "Employee dishonesty is just like a fire, storm, or other natural disaster," says one insurance executive. "It's an unexpected disaster that can cause a company or business to collapse."[19] One U.S. Justice Department study reports that approximately 30 percent of all employees are "hard-core pilferers." The study also estimates that without preventive security measures in place, 80 percent of employees will become involved in theft.[20] These employees steal from the companies that employ them simply because the opportunity presents itself. Many thefts by employees involve "nickel-and-dime" items (nails for a home repair job, a box of pencils for personal use), but a significant number of them involve large sums of money. *For instance, when Craig Bernstein, president of a 100-employee real estate management company, hired a construction foreman, he thought he had found the ideal employee. "He worked weekends and paid for building materials out of his own checkbook," recalls Bernstein. Bernstein discovered the truth six months later, however, when a new employee who conducted warehouse inspections noticed an entire warehouse of missing supplies and tools. The foreman had stolen more than $300,000 in tools and materials from the company and had taken kickbacks from suppliers by inflating the invoices the company was paying. Bernstein, of course, fired the worker, but he did not prosecute him. "Being a small business owner, you're just so vulnerable," he says.[21]*

How can thefts such as this one go undetected? Most thefts occur when employees take advantage of the opportunities to steal that small business owners give them. Typically, small business owners are so busy building their companies that they rarely even consider the possibility of employee theft—until disaster strikes. Also, small companies are not likely to have adequate financial, audit, and security procedures in place. Add into that mix the

The Best Hardware Store in the World

*C*ustomers walking into Harvey's Hardware in Needham, Massachussetts, for the first time have a tendency to be overwhelmed by what they see: a modest-sized store loaded with wall-to-wall and floor-to-ceiling inventory. As far as the eye can see, there is hardware . . . and more hardware. Most customers are also taken aback by the squadron of salespeople stationed at the front door. All decked out in flannel and hardware aprons and ranging from age 16 to 70, these devotees of hardware stand ready to guide customers through the store's crowded aisles and multiple floors. Its devoted following of extremely loyal customers are not joking when they tell the uninitiated that Harvey's is simply the best hardware store in the world. First-time customers soon begin to understand why.

Harvey Katz started the hardware store shortly after he returned from the Korean War. In the early days, Harvey had very little money to invest in the business, and he couldn't afford much inventory. To make his store look well-stocked, he scattered his meager inventory of hardware around the shelves and then filled in the gaps with empty boxes he had taped shut. Business picked up gradually, and Harvey noticed that quite a few customers came in looking for odd items that none of the hardware stores in town—including his own—carried. He also observed that when he did happen to have a hard-to-find item, the customer seemed to be especially pleased and usually came back repeatedly to buy other items. Harvey's competitive strategy was born! Stock as much merchandise as you possibly can, and you can build a large base of loyal customers.

Today, Harvey's strategy lives on through his two sons, Gary and Jeff, who now manage the store. One customer describes the store this way: "Every square inch of shelf and wall space, and the vast majority of floor space—even a significant percentage of *ceiling space*—is crammed with a riotous mélange of wares. The lighting is on the dim side. There are no aisle placards or any other store navigational aids; nor does any logical scheme of organization suggest itself."

The cornerstone of Harvey's strategy for success led to the second factor that puts the store so far ahead of the competition. (Although competitors are scarce. Seven hardware stores have tried to outdo Harvey's, and all have failed. The last one folded in 1993.) The second pillar on which Harvey's success is built is customer service. "This is not a self-service store," explains Gary. "We have people here to help you find what you're looking for." Years ago, not long after he began stocking so much hardware, Harvey realized that he either had to move to a much larger building where he could spread his merchandise out so customers could help themselves or he had to hire workers to serve customers. He really didn't want to move, and besides that, there weren't any places in town big enough to spread that much inventory out! Soon, superior customer service became another hallmark of Harvey's. "When you get to know your customers and build a relationship with them, it creates a sense of loyalty and trust," explains Gary. (A customer once recognized Gary from a restaurant window and called to him as the hardware retailer floated down a canal in Venice, Italy!)

Gary and Jeff installed a computer system several years ago to help them maintain control over their extensive inventory, but they found that they didn't need most of the features it offered. The sales staff knows and watches the inventory so closely that they know they need to order duct tape before the computer tells them to! Stocking and displaying such a volume of merchandise provides a challenge, but the Katz brothers use the store's crowded look to their advantage as well. Harvey's packs $135 worth of inventory per square foot into its building, whereas the typical hardware store carries just $35 worth of goods per square foot. "The trick is to keep everything organized," says Harvey. "Not too neat—but organized."

Customers apparently love the overcrowded look because it seems to encourage them to buy, buy, buy. Harvey's sales are more than three times the average for hardware stores: $503 per square foot versus $129 per square foot at the average hardware store. "When someone comes in and finds what they're looking for and tells me they've been to eight other places looking for it, I say to them, 'Maybe you'll come here first next time,'" says Gary. The sheer volume of merchandise offers customers an almost subliminal invitation to engage in a hardware shopping spree. The average sale at a typical hardware store is $12; at Harvey's, it is $17.

Retail experts know that the key to success is rapid inventory turnover. With such a huge stockpile of inventory, much of it admittedly slow-moving, one would suspect that Harvey's average inventory turnover ratio would be dangerously low. Not so! Those slow-moving items in the store's stock seem to draw customers from far and wide who buy *lots* of fast-moving merchandise. The result is an inventory turnover ratio of 4.5 times per year, compared with just 3.7 times per year at the typical hardware store.

Gary and Jeff have built a highly successful hardware department for appliances and other items, and they have turned Harvey's into one of the nation's leading distributors of Weber gas grills. But, for the most part, they have kept their father's basic strategy intact. After all, why tinker with the strategy that built the best hardware store in the world?

---

1. What factors set Harvey's Hardware apart from its competitors? What role have these factors played in the company's success?

2. What dangers does the company face as a result of its unique retail strategy?

SOURCE: Adapted from David H. Freedman, "Best Hometown Business in America," *Inc.*, July 1997, pp. 57–66. ◆

high degree of trust most small business owners place in their employees, and you have a perfect recipe for employee theft. A recent study by the Association of Certified Fraud Examiners found that small companies (those with fewer than 100 employees) "were the most vulnerable to fraud and abuse." The study found that the median loss per fraud was $120,000, nearly as large as that for firms with more than 10,000 workers (median of $126,000 per fraud). Although no business can afford such large losses, crimes of that magnitude can drive a small company out of existence because they lack the financial resources to absorb such devastating losses. Survey participants estimated that their companies lose about 6 percent of their annual revenues to employee theft and fraud.[22]

What Causes Employee Theft? Employees steal from their companies for any number of reasons. Some may have a grudge against the company; others may have a drug, alcohol, or gambling addiction to support. "Employees take from the company for four reasons: need, greed, temptation, and opportunity," says one security expert. "A company can control the last two."[23] To minimize their losses to employee theft, business owners must understand how both the temptation and the opportunity to steal creep into their companies. The following are conditions that lead to major security gaps in small companies.

The Trusted Employee. The fact is that any employee could be a thief, although most are not. Studies show that younger, less devoted employees steal from their companies most often, but long-time employees can cause more damage. In many small businesses, the owner views employees, especially long-time workers, almost as partners, operating the business in a family atmosphere. Such a feeling, although not undesirable, can develop into a security breach. "Your guard is down because you know the people who work for you and would never suspect that they would steal from you," explains a security expert.[24] Many owners refuse to believe that their most trusted employees present the greatest security threat, but these workers have the greatest accessibility to keys, cash registers, records, and even safe combinations. Because of their seniority, these employees hold key positions and are quite familiar with operations, so they know where weaknesses in control and security procedures lie. *In one small company, a long-time bookkeeper stole $150,000 from the business by including checks made out to himself in stacks of legitimate business checks submitted for the owner's signature. The bookkeeper always waited until the owner was busy or distracted to get the checks signed. The owner trusted his bookkeeper and never even looked at the checks he signed.*[25]

Small business owners should also be wary of "workaholic" employees. Is this worker really dedicated to the company, or is he working so hard to cover up theft? Employee thieves are unwilling to take extended breaks from their jobs for fear of being detected. As long as the dishonest employee remains on the job, he can cover up theft. As a security precaution, business owners should require every employee to take vacations long enough so

SOURCE: *The Greenville News,* March 11, 1995. King Features Syndicate.

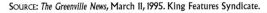

that someone else has to take over their responsibilities (at least 5 consecutive business days). Most schemes are relatively simple and require day-to-day maintenance to keep them going. Business failure records are filled with stories of firms in which the "ideal" employee turned out to be a thief. "In 90 percent of the cases in which people steal from their companies, the employer would probably have described this person, right up to the time the crime was discovered, as a trusted employee," says one expert.[26]

Disgruntled Employees. Small business managers must also monitor the performance of disgruntled employees. Employees are more likely to steal if they believe that their company treats employees unfairly, and the probability of their stealing goes even higher if they believe they themselves have been treated unfairly.[27] Employees dissatisfied with their pay or their promotions may retaliate against an employer by stealing. Dishonest employees will make up the difference between what they are paid and what they believe they are worth by stealing. Many believe pilfering is a well-deserved "perk." They defend their actions through rationalization.

Organizational Atmosphere. Many entrepreneurs unintentionally create an atmosphere that encourages employee dishonesty. Failing to establish formal controls and procedures invites theft. Nothing encourages dishonest employees to steal more than knowing they are unlikely to be caught. Four factors encourage employees theft:

1. The need or desire to steal (e.g., to support a habit or to cope with a sudden financial crisis)

2. A rationalization for the act ("They owe me this.")

3. The opportunity to steal (e.g., access to merchandise, complete control of financial functions)

4. The perception that there is a low probability of being caught ("Nobody will ever know.")

The owner must recognize that he sets the example for security and honesty in the business. Employees place more emphasis on what the owner does that on what he says. A business owner who installs a complete system of inventory control and then ignores it is telling employees that security in unimportant. No one should remove merchandise, materials, or supplies from inventory without recording them properly. There should be no exceptions to the rules, even for the boss and his relatives. "If the owner of a convenience store takes home milk and a six-pack of beer, employees will think it's OK for them to do the same thing," says one security consultant.[28] Managers should develop clear control procedures and establish penalties for violations. "The single biggest deterrent [to employee theft] is a strong, top-down policy that is well-communicated to all employees that theft will not be tolerated and that anyone caught stealing will be prosecuted—no exceptions," advises the head of a security agency.[29]

Managers must constantly emphasize the importance of security. Small business owners must use every available opportunity to lower the temptation to steal. One business owner relies on payroll inserts to emphasize to employees how theft reduces the funds available for growth, expansion, and higher wages. Another has established a written code of ethics, spelling out penalties for violations. Workers must know that security is a team effort. Security rules and procedures must be reasonable, and the owner must treat the workers equitably. Unreasonable rules are no more effective—and may even be more harmful—than poorly enforced procedures. A work environment that fosters honesty at every turn serves as an effective deterrent to employee theft.

Physical Breakdowns. Another major factor contributing to employee theft is weak physical security. The owner who pays little attention to the distribution of keys, safe combinations, and other entry devices is inviting theft. Also, owners who fail to lock doors and windows or to install reliable alarm systems are literally leaving their businesses open to thieves both inside and outside the organization.

Open windows give dishonest employees a prime opportunity to slip stolen merchandise out of the plant or store. A manufacturer of small appliances discovered that several employees were dropping crates of finished products out of an unlocked window, picking them up after work, and reselling them. By the time the perpetrators were detected, the owner had lost nearly $10,000 worth of merchandise and supplies.

Unlocked or unmonitored doors represent another security leak for many small businesses. The greater the number of doors in a plant or store, the greater the chance of employee theft. Every unnecessary door should be locked (while still conforming to fire regulations), and all regularly used doors should be monitored. Many thefts occur as workers load and unload merchandise. If the owner allows the same employee who prepares purchase orders and handles invoices to check shipments in or out, the temptation to alter documents and steal merchandise may be too great.

Many businesses find that their profits go out with the trash, literally. When collecting trash, a dishonest employee may stash valuable merchandise in with the refuse and dump it in the receptacle. After the store closes, the thief returns to collect the loot. One drugstore owner lost more than $7,000 in merchandise in just six months through trash thefts.

Improper Cash Control. May small business owners encourage employee theft by failing to implement proper cash control procedures. Without a system of logical, practical audit controls on cash, a firm will likely suffer internal theft. Dishonest employees quickly discover there is a low probability of detection and steal cash with impunity.

Cashiers clearly have the greatest accessibility to the firm's cash and, consequently, experience the greatest temptation to steal. The following scenario is all too common: A customer makes a purchase with the exact amount of cash and leaves quickly. The cashier fails to ring up the purchase and pockets the cash without anyone's knowledge. Some small business owners create a cash security problem by allowing too many employees to operate cash registers and handle customer payments. If a cash shortage develops, the manager is unable to trace responsibility.

A daily inspection of the cash register tape can point out potential employee theft problems. When tapes indicate an excessive amount of voided transactions or no-sale transactions, the owner should investigate. A no-sale transaction could mean the register was opened to give a customer change or to steal cash. A large number of incorrect register transactions also is a sign of foul play. Clerks may be camouflaging cash thefts by voiding transactions or by underringing sales amounts. Shortages and overages are also clues that alert the manager to possible theft. All small business owners are alarmed by cash shortages, but few are disturbed by cash overages. However, cash discrepancies in either direction are an indication of inept cashiering or of poor cash controls. The manager who investigates all cash discrepancies can greatly reduce the opportunity for cashiers to steal.

Preventing Employee Theft. Many incidents of employee theft go undetected, and of those employees who are caught stealing, only a small percentage are prosecuted. The burden of dealing with employee theft falls squarely on the owner's shoulders. Although business owners cannot eliminate the possibility of employee theft, they can reduce its likelihood by using some relatively simple procedures and policies that are cost-effective to implement.

Screen Employees Carefully. Perhaps a business owner's greatest weapon against crime is a thorough pre-employment screening process. The best time to weed out prospective criminals is before hiring them! Although state and federal regulations prohibit employers from invading job applicants' privacy and from using discriminatory devices in the selection process, employers have a legitimate right to determine job candidates' integrity and qualifications. A comprehensive selection process and reliable screening devices greatly reduce the chances that an entrepreneur will hire a thief. Smart entrepreneurs verify the information applicants provide on their résumés because they know that some of them will either exaggerate or misrepresent their qualifications. A thorough background check with references and previous employers also is essential. (One question that sheds light on a former employer's feelings toward a one-time employee is "Would you hire this person again?")

Some security experts recommend the use of integrity tests, paper-and-pencil tests that offer valuable insight into job applicants' level of honesty. Business owners can buy integrity tests for $20 or less that are already validated (to avoid charges of discrimination) and that they can score on their own. "These tests can help companies reduce theft-related losses up to 50 percent on average over three years," claims one experienced psychologist.[30] Because drug addictions drive many employees to steal, employers also should administer drug tests consistently to all job applicants. The most reliable drug tests cost the company from $35 to $50 each, a small price to pay given the potential losses that can result from hiring an employee with a drug habit.

Create an Environment of Honesty. Creating an environment of honesty and integrity starts at the top. That requires business owners to set an impeccable example for everyone else in the company. In addition to creating a standard of ethical behavior, business owners should strive to establish high morale among workers. A positive work environment where employees see themselves as an important part of the team is an effective deterrent to employee theft. Establishing a written code of ethics and having new employees sign "honesty clauses" offer tangible evidence of a company's commitment to honesty and integrity.

Establish a System of Internal Controls. The basis for maintaining security on the job is establishing a set of reasonable internal controls designed to prevent employee theft. An effective system of checks and balances goes a long way toward deterring internal crime; weak or inconsistently enforced controls are an open invitation for theft. "Very few losses are actually the result of an ingenious plan," claims one security consultant. "What [employees] see is a weakness they can exploit."[31] The most basic rule is to separate among several employees related duties that might cause a security breach if assigned to a single worker. For instance, owners should avoid letting the employee who issues checks reconcile the company's bank statement. Similarly, the person who orders merchandise and supplies should not be the one who also approves those invoices for payment. Spreading these tasks among a number of employees makes organizing a theft more difficult. The owner of a small retail art shop learned this lesson the hard way. After conducting an inventory audit, he discovered that more than $25,000 worth of art supplies were missing. The owner finally traced the theft to the company's bookkeeper, who was creating fictional invoices and then issuing checks to herself for the same amounts. "It was a very painful experience," says the shop owner. "Before, the business was run on trust, without safeguards; now, it's run only with safeguards."[32]

Business owners should insist that all company records be kept up to date. Sloppy recordkeeping makes theft difficult to detect. All internal documents—shipping, ordering, billing, and collecting—should be numbered. Missing numbers should arouse suspicion. One subtle way to test employees' honesty is to commit deliberate errors occasionally to see if employees detect them. If you send an extra case of merchandise to the loading dock for shipment, does the foreman catch it, or does it disappear?

Finally, business owners should demonstrate zero tolerance for theft. They must adhere strictly to company policy when dealing with employees who violate the company's trust. When business owners catch an employee thief, the best course of action is to fire the perpetrator and to prosecute. Too often, owners take the attitude: "Resign, return the money, and we'll forget it." Letting thieves off, however, only encourages then to move on to other

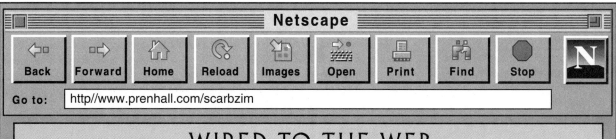

WIRED TO THE WEB

STOLEN TRUST

*O*ver the past 25 years, Powell's Books has become a landmark in Portland, Oregon. Owner Michael Powell operates a chain of seven bookstores, but the most famous store is the one in downtown Portland; it is the largest bookstore in the United States, taking up an entire city block. Customers pick up maps as they enter the store so that they can find the books they want and so that they can find their way back out!

Powell's Books is known not only for its huge selection of books but also for the authority and responsibility it gives its workers. Here, workers don't just hear about empowerment and shared decision making; they practice them. "We want to be a business that operates on trust and respect," says Powell. Unfortunately, Powell had to reexamine his commitment to those principles after he discovered that one of his most trusted employees had stolen more than $60,000 from the company. "As a result," he says, "we changed some of our security systems. Yet, in terms of what's important, we didn't change a thing."

In most major bookstores, one person, the buyer, is in charge of making all inventory decisions. At Powell's about 70 percent of the employees have a voice in the company's inventory decisions. Powell practices open-book management, sharing the company's financial statements with his employees. Plus, the business has between 30 and 40 working committees reviewing every aspect of its operation. The principle underlying it all is empowerment. "We want the people working with customers to have the authority to make decisions," he says.

Unfortunately, the employee who stole from Powell's robbed the company of more than money and books; he also tried to steal the atmosphere of trust Powell had worked so hard to create since launching the business. One day, an alert worker noticed that one worker had authorized an unusually large number of cash payouts for used books. Because the company encourages workers to rotate tasks during the day, it was possible that the employee could have authorized cash payouts and then worked the cash register. However, when confronted with the suspicious pattern, the employee confessed his guilt. Powell chose to prosecute.

"My first reaction was a kind of numbness and denial," he recalls. "Oddly, once I acknowledged what had happened, I felt angry with *myself*—angry for having such vulnerable systems. I had a momentary impulse to go out and lock everything up—to start treating everybody as a potential thief."

The theft pointed out obvious weaknesses in Powell's business system. "Our systems were based more on trust than on responsibility. So we made some immediate changes." Powell said. He also created a security committee to revise the entire chain's systems. Although the crime cost the company a significant amount of money, it has made it stronger in many ways.

Powell's business philosophy remains the same, but his method of implementing it is more cautious. "We believe that the modern demands of a business call for an empowered and fully flexible staff, and we know that such a staff will have to handle valuable commodities and money," Powell says. "We also believe that most people are not going to abuse our trust if they are put in a position with a reasonable amount of review and responsibility."

1. Evaluate Powell's response to his company's encounter with employee theft. Would the result have been the same if Powell had cracked down and imposed a strict set of controls on all employees, in effect taking back the authority and responsibility he had delegated to them?
2. Use the resources of the World Wide Web to learn more about Powell's Books and to research ways to reduce the likelihood of employee theft. What recommendations would you suggest Powell implement? Explain.

SOURCE: Adapted from Michael Powell, "Betrayal," *Inc.*, April 1996, pp. 23–24.

businesses where they will steal again. Prosecuting a former employee for theft is never easy, but it does send a clear signal about how the company views employee crime.

SHOPLIFTING

The most frequent business crime is shoplifting. Businesses lose an estimated $17 billion to $20 billion to shoplifters each year, and small businesses, especially retailers, suffer a significant share of those losses. Shoplifting takes an especially heavy toll on small businesses because they usually have the weakest lines of defense against shoplifters. Shoplifting losses, which ultimately are passed on to the consumer, account for approximately 3 percent of the average price tag.[33]

Types of Shoplifters. Anyone who takes merchandise from a store without paying for it, no matter what the justification, is a shoplifter. Shoplifters look exactly like other customers. They can be young children in search of a new toy or elderly people who are short of money. Anyone can be a shoplifter, given the opportunity, the ability, and the desire to steal.

Fortunately for small business owners, most shoplifters are amateurs who steal because the opportunity presents itself. Many steal on impulse, and the theft is the first criminal act. Many of those caught have the money to pay for their "five-finger discounts." Observant business owners supported by trained store personnel can spot potential shoplifters and deter many shoplifting incidents; however, they must understand the shoplifter's profile. Experts identify five types of shoplifters.

Juveniles. Juveniles account for approximately one-half of all shoplifters. Many juveniles steal as a result of peer pressure. Most have little fear of prosecution, assuming they can hide behind their youth. When owners detect juvenile shoplifters, they must not let sympathy stand in the way of good judgment. Many hard-core criminals began their careers as shoplifters, and small business owners who fail to prosecute the youthful offender do nothing to discourage a life of crime. Juvenile offenders should be prosecuted through proper legal procedures just as any adult shoplifter would be.

Businesses lose an estimated $17 billion to $20 billion each year to shoplifting. Anyone can be a shoplifter, given the opportunity, the ability, and the desire to steal. What can business owners do to deter shoplifters?

Impulse Shoplifters. Impulse shoplifters steal on the spur of the moment when they succumb to temptation. These shoplifters do not plan their thefts, but when a prime opportunity to shoplift arises, they take advantage of it. For example, a salesperson may be showing a customer pieces of jewelry. If the salesperson is called away, the customer might pocket an expensive ring and leave the store before the employee returns.

Many well-respected individuals are impulse shoplifters. The perpetrator might even be a regular customer. Impatient customers after a hectic shopping day might be unwilling to wait to pay for merchandise, or a disgruntled customer may be seeking revenge against a company; whatever the case, shoplifting is the result. *Bealls Inc., a chain of nearly 200 department and outlet stores, undertook a study to determine the extent of shoplifting in its stores. "We were stunned," says the vice president of loss prevention. "Some of our biggest customers were also our biggest shoplifters."*[33]

The most effective method of fighting impulse shoplifting is prevention. To minimize losses, the owner should remove the opportunity to steal by implementing proper security procedures and devices.

Alcoholics, Vagrants, and Drug Addicts. Shoplifters motivated to steal to support a drug or alcohol habit are usually easy to detect because their behavior is usually unstable and erratic. One shoplifter recently apprehended was supporting a $100-a-day heroin habit by stealing small items from local retailers and then returning the merchandise for refunds. (The stores almost never asked him for sales receipts.) Small business owners should exercise great caution in handling these shoplifters because they can easily become violent. Criminals deranged by drugs or alcohol might be armed and could endanger the lives of customers and employees if they are detained. It is best to let the police apprehend these shoplifters.

Kleptomaniacs. Kleptomaniacs have a compulsive need to steal even though they have little, if any, need for the items they shoplift. In many cases these shoplifters could afford to purchase the merchandise they steal. Kleptomaniacs account for less than 5 percent of shoplifters, but their "disease" costs business owners a great deal.[34] They need professional psychological counseling, and the owner only helps them by seeing that they are apprehended.

Professionals. Although only about 15 percent of shoplifters are professionals, they can severely damage a small business.[35] Because the professional shoplifter's business is theft, he is very difficult to detect and deter. Career shoplifters tend to focus on expensive merchandise they can sell quickly to their "fences," such as stereo equipment, appliances, guns, or jewelry. Usually the fences don't keep the stolen goods long, often selling them at a fraction of their value. Thus, apprehending and prosecuting professional shoplifters is quite difficult. Police have apprehended professional shoplifters with detailed maps of a city's shopping districts, showing target stores and the best times to make a "hit." Furthermore, many professional shoplifters are affiliated with organized crime, and they are able to rely on their associates to avoid detection and prosecution.

Detecting Shoplifters. Although shoplifters can be difficult to detect, small business owners who know what to look for can spot them in action. They must always be on the lookout for shoplifters, but merchants should be especially vigilant on Saturdays and around Christmas, when shoplifters can hide their thefts more easily in the frenzy of a busy shopping day.

Shoplifters can work alone or in groups. In general, impulse shoplifters prefer solitary thefts, whereas juveniles and professionals operate in groups. A common tactic for group shoplifters is for one member of the gang to create some type of distraction while other members steal the merchandise. Business owners should be wary of loud, disruptive gangs that enter their stores.

Solitary shoplifters are usually quite nervous. They avoid crowds and shy away from store personnel, preferring privacy to ply their trade. To make sure they avoid detection, they constantly scan the store for customers and employees. These shoplifters spend more time nervously looking around the store than examining merchandise. Also, they shop when the store is most likely to be understaffed, during early morning, lunch, or late evening hours. Shoplifters frequently linger in the same area for an extended time without purchasing anything. Customers who refuse the help of sales personnel or bring in large bags and packages (especially empty ones) also arouse suspicion. *At the Carson Pirie Scott department store, near downtown Chicago, security workers rely on a $50,000 bank of 60 electronic cameras and plainclothes agents patrolling the floor to monitor shoplifters. Chief security agent Schanise Feltus, monitoring the images from the cameras, spots a middle-aged woman in the men's cologne department looking around nervously. The woman's behavior makes Feltus suspicious, and she begins to track the woman's movements with the cameras. Using a two-way radio, she instructs the plainclothes agents on the floor to move toward the woman. The woman drops a bottle of expensive cologne in her purse, and Feltus alerts the floor agents. "We have concealment," she says. "She's moving fast." Giving the woman every chance to pay for the merchandise, the agents finally apprehend her outside the store. When they search her purse, agents find the cologne, a bottle of bath gel, and a sharp knife. Thirty minutes later, a Chicago police officer arrives to take the shoplifter away.*[36]

Shoplifters have their own arsenal of tools to assist them in plying their trade. They often shop with booster boxes, shopping bags, umbrellas, bulky jackets, baby strollers, or containers disguised as gifts. These props often have hidden compartments that can be tripped easily, allowing the shoplifter to fill them with merchandise quickly. *One 19-year-old shoplifter in Florida says that her mother taught her the nuances of shoplifting. The two work together to steal merchandise from stores, and their favorite prop is the baby stroller. "We both have infants, and we take them into the stores together," she says. "We use the strollers, the blankets, and big diaper bags [to conceal stolen goods]. Mom and I help each other. Sometimes we even get matching outfits."*[37]

Some shoplifters use specially designed coats with hidden pockets and compartments that can hold even large items. Small business owners should be suspicious of customers wearing out-of-season clothing (heavy coats in warm weather, rain gear on clear days) that could conceal stolen goods. Hooked belts also are used to enable the shoplifter to suspend items from hangers without being detected.

Another common tactic is "ticket switching"; the shoplifter exchanges price tickets on items and pays a very low price for an expensive item. An inexperienced or unobservant cashier may charge $9.95 for a $30.00 item that the shoplifter re-marked while no one was looking.

One variation of traditional shoplifting techniques is the "grab-and-run," in which a shoplifter grabs an armload of merchandise located near an exit and then dashes out the door into a waiting getaway car. The element of surprise gives these thieves an advantage, and they are often gone before anyone in the store realizes what has happened. *One San Diego shoplifter uses this technique to steal nothing but Levi's 501 jeans, which he resells for $42 a pair. "I leave my car idling, go inside, grab a stack of jeans and split. I can make $500 a day," he boasts.*[38]

Deterring Shoplifters. The problem of shoplifting is worsening. Every year, business losses due to customer theft increase, and many companies are declaring war on shoplifting. Their funds allocated for fighting shoplifting losses are best spent on *prevention*. By focusing on preventing shoplifting rather than on prosecuting violators after the fact, business owners take a stronger stand in protecting their firms' merchandise. Of course, no prevention plan is perfect. When violations occur, owners must prosecute; otherwise the business becomes known as an easy target. Merchants say that when a store gets a reputation for being tough on shoplifters, thefts drop off.

Knowing what to look for improves dramatically a small business owner's odds in combating shoplifting:

◆ *Watch the eyes.* Amateurs spend excessive time looking at the merchandise they're about to steal. Their eyes, however, are usually checking to see who (if anyone) is watching them.

◆ *Watch the hands.* Experienced shoplifters, like good magicians, rely on sleight of hand.

◆ *Watch the body.* Amateurs' body movements reflect their nervousness; they appear to be unnatural.

◆ *Watch the clothing.* Loose, bulky clothing is the uniform of the typical shoplifter.

◆ *Watch for devices.* Anything a customer carries is a potential concealing device.

◆ *Watch for loiterers.* Many amateurs must work up the nerve to steal.

◆ *Watch for switches.* Working in pairs, shoplifters will split duties; one will lift the merchandise, and, after a switch, the other will take it out of the store.

Store owners can take other steps to discourage shoplifting, including the following.

Train Employees to Spot Shoplifters. One of the best ways to prevent shoplifting is to train store personnel to be aware of shoplifters' habits and to be alert for possible theft. In fact, most security experts agree that alert employees are the best defense against shoplifters. Employees should look for nervous, unusual customers and monitor them closely. Shoplifters prefer to avoid sales personnel and other customers, and when employees approach them, shoplifters know they are being watched. Even when all salespeople are busy, an alert employee should approach the customer and mention, "I'll be with you in a moment." Honest customers appreciate the clerk's politeness, and shoplifters are put off by the implied surveillance.

All employees should watch for suspicious people, especially those carrying the props of concealment. Employees in clothing stores must keep a tally of the items being taken into and out of dressing rooms. Some clothing retailers prevent unauthorized use of dressing rooms by locking them. Customers who want to try on garments must check with a store employee first.

An alert cashier can be a tremendous boon to the store owner attempting to minimize shoplifting losses. A cashier who knows the store's general pricing policy and is familiar with the prices of many specific items is the best insurance against the ticket-switching shoplifter. A good cashier also should inspect all containers being sold; tool boxes, briefcases, and other containers could conceal stolen merchandise.

Employees should be trained to watch for group shoplifting tactics. A group of shoppers that enters the store and then disperses in all directions may be attempting to distract employees so that some gang members can steal merchandise. Sales personnel should watch closely the customer who lingers in one area for an extended time, especially one who examines a lot of merchandise but never purchases anything.

The sales staff should watch for those individuals who consistently shop during the hours when most personnel are on breaks. Managers can help eliminate this cause of shoplifting by ensuring that their stores are well staffed at all times. Coordinating work schedules to ensure adequate coverage of customers is a simple but effective method of discouraging shoplifting.

The cost of training employees to be alert to shoplifting "gimmicks" can be regained many times over in preventing losses from retail theft. The local police department or chamber of commerce may be able to conduct training seminars for local small business owners and their employees, or security consulting firms might sponsor a training course on shoplifting techniques and protective methods. Refresher courses every few months can help keep employees sharp in spotting shoplifters.

Pay Attention to the Store Layout. A well-planned store layout also can be an effective obstacle in preventing shoplifting losses. Proper lighting throughout the store makes it easier for employees to monitor shoppers, whereas dimly lit areas give dishonest customers a prime opportunity to steal without detection. Also, display cases should be kept low, no more than three or four feet high, so store personnel can have a clear view of the entire store. Display counters should have spaces between them; continuous displays create a barrier between customers and employees.

Business owners should keep small expensive items such as jewelry, silver, and pocket calculators behind display counters or in locked cases with a salesclerk nearby. Valuable or breakable items also should be kept out of customer reach and should not be displayed near exits, where shoplifters can pick them up and quickly step outside. All merchandise displays should be neat and organized so that it will be noticeable if an item is missing.

Cash registers should be located so that cashiers have an unobstructed view of the entire store. Other protective measures include prominently posting antishoplifting signs describing the penalties involved and keeping unattended doors locked (within fire regulations). Exits that cannot be locked because of fire regulations should be equipped with noise alarms to detect any attempts at unauthorized exit.

Install Mechanical Devices. Another option a small business owner has in the attempt to reduce shoplifting losses is to install mechanical devices. A complete deterrence system can be expensive, but failure to implement one is usually more expensive. Tools such as two-way mirrors allow employees at one end of the store to monitor a customer at the other end, and one-way viewing windows enable employees to watch the entire store without being seen.

Other mechanical devices, such as closed-circuit TV cameras, convex wall mirrors, and peepholes, also help the owner protect the store from shoplifters. Not every small business can afford to install a closed-circuit camera system, but one clever entrepreneur got the benefit of such a system without the high cost. He installed one "live" camera and several "dummy" cameras that did not work. The cameras worked because potential shoplifters thought they were all live. Another high-tech weapon used against shoplifters is a mannequin named Anne Droid, who is equipped with a tiny camera behind one eye and a microphone in her nose!

An owner can deter ticket-switching shoplifters by using tamper-proof price tickets: perforated gummed labels that tear away if a customer tries to remove them or price tags attached to merchandise by hard-to-break plastic strips. Some owners use multiple price tags concealed on items to deter ticket switchers. One of the most effective weapons for combating shoplifting is the electronic article surveillance system, small tags that are equipped with electronic sensors that set off sound and light alarms if customers take them past a store exit. These tags are attached to the merchandise and can be removed only by employees with special shears. Owners using these electronic tags must make sure that all cashiers are consistent in removing them from items purchased legitimately; otherwise, they may be liable for false arrest or, at the very least, may cause customers embarrassment.

Apprehending Shoplifters. Despite all of the weapons business owners use to curtail shoplifting, the sad reality is that about 98 percent of the time shoplifters are successful at plying their trade! Of the more than 60 million estimated shoplifting incidents that occur in a typical year, business owners detect only 1.2 million. Of those shoplifters who do get caught, less than half are prosecuted. The chance that any shoplifter will actually go before a judge is just one in 100![39] Building a strong case against a shoplifter is essential; therefore, small business owners must determine beforehand the procedures to follow once they detect a

An Error in Judgment?

*P*atricia Caldwell was shopping in a retail store. A store security employee became suspicious when he saw that she was carrying a large purse and was handling many small items. As she shopped, Caldwell went into several departments and bent down out of sight of the security guard. (She says she bent down to look at items displayed on low shelves.) She also removed her glasses to read labels and returned them to her purse several times. The guard, believing he had seen Caldwell put some items in her purse, followed her into the parking lot and accused her of shoplifting. He asked Caldwell to open her purse. She did, but the guard found none of the store's merchandise inside. Rather than releasing her, he told Caldwell to return to the store with him, where he escorted her back to areas where she had been shopping. They walked around the store for approximately 15 minutes, during which time the guard told her six or seven times that he had seen her conceal merchandise in her purse. No one touched Caldwell or

searched her. With no evidence of stolen merchandise, another employee told Caldwell she could leave the store.

Caldwell brought a lawsuit against the retailer for slander (making false defamatory statements about another) and false imprisonment (depriving a person of his liberty without justice). The court allowed the retailer's loss prevention manual to be introduced as evidence. The manual spelled out the company's guidelines for employees in making shoplifting arrests. For instance, the manual stated that before apprehending a suspected shoplifter, an employee "must see the shoplifter take our property." It also stated that an employee should watch the suspect continuously and should apprehend him after he has had the opportunity to pay for the merchandise and is outside the store. The manual said that apprehension should be made in the presence of a witness and that any interrogation should be done in the privacy of the Loss Prevention Office.

The jury in the case awarded Caldwell $175,000 in total damages, and the retailer appealed. The appellate court affirmed the lower court's ruling.

1. What did the retailer in this case do wrong?
2. What guidelines should store employees follow when dealing with a suspected shoplifter?

SOURCE: Caldwell v. K-Mart Corporation, No. 1171 (S.C. Ct. App. filed October 14, 1991).

◆

shoplifter. The store owner has to be certain that the shoplifter has taken or concealed the merchandise and has left the store with it. Although state laws vary, owners must do the following to make the charges stick:

1. See the person take or conceal the merchandise.
2. Identify the merchandise as the store's.
3. Testify that it was taken with the intent to steal.
4. Prove that the merchandise was not paid for.

Most security experts agree that an owner should never apprehend the shoplifter if she has lost sight of the suspect even for an instant. In that time the person may have dumped the merchandise. *At the Carson Pirie Scott department stores, security agents adhere to this rule. If they do not witness (either by a nearby plainclothes agent or a video camera) the theft, they do not make an arrest. If an employee apprehends the shoplifter and cannot find the stolen merchandise, an accusation of false arrest may follow.*[40]

Another primary consideration in apprehending shoplifters is the safety of store employees. In general, employees should never directly accuse a customer of shoplifting and should never try to apprehend the suspect. The wisest course of action when a shoplifter is detected is to alert the police or store security personnel and let them apprehend the suspect. Apprehension *outside* the store is safest. This tactic strengthens the owner's case and eliminates unpleasant in-store scenes that upset other customers or that might be dangerous. Of course, if the stolen merchandise is very valuable, or if the criminal is likely to escape once outside, the owner may have no choice but to apprehend in the store.

Once business owners detect and apprehend a shoplifter, they must decide whether to prosecute. Many small business owners fail to prosecute because they fear legal entanglements or negative publicity. However, failure to prosecute encourages shoplifters to try again and gives the business the image of being an easy target. Of course, each case is an individual matter. For example, the owner may choose not to prosecute elderly or senile shoplifters or those who are mentally incompetent. But in most cases, prosecuting the shoplifter is the best option, especially for juveniles and first-time offenders. The small business owner who prosecutes shoplifters consistently soon develops a reputation for toughness that most shoplifters hesitate to test. "Aggressive prosecution can be a real deterrent," says one security specialist.[41]

$\mathcal{C}$onclusion

Inventory control is one of those less-than-glamorous activities that business owners must perform if their businesses are to succeed. Although it doesn't offer the flash of marketing or the visibility of customer service, inventory control is no less important. In fact, business owners who invest the time and the resources to exercise the proper degree of control over their inventory soon discover that the payoff is huge!

Chapter Summary

1. Explain the various inventory control systems and the advantages and disadvantages of each.
   - Inventory represents the largest investment for the typical small business. Unless properly managed, the cost of inventory will strain the firm's budget and cut into its profitability. The goal of inventory control is to balance the cost of holding and maintaining inventory with meeting customer demand.
   - Regardless of the inventory control system selected, business owners must recognize the relevance of the 80/20 rule, which states that roughly 80 percent of the value of the firm's inventory is in about 20 percent of the items in stock. Because only a small percentage of items account for the majority of the value of the firm's inventory, managers should focus control on those items.
   - Three basic types of inventory control systems are available to the small business owner: perpetual, visual, and partial. Perpetual inventory control systems are designed to maintain a running count of the items in inventory. Although they can be expensive and cumbersome to operate by hand, affordable computerized point-of-sale (POS) terminals that deduct items sold from inventory on hand make perpetual systems feasible for small companies. The visual inventory system is the most common method of controlling merchandise in a small business. This system works best when shortages

are not likely to cause major problems. Partial inventory control systems are most effective for small businesses with limited time and money. These systems operate on the basis of the 80/20 rule.
   - The ABC system is a partial system that divides a firm's inventory into three categories depending on each item's dollar usage volume (cost per unit multiplied by quantity used per time period). The purpose of classifying items according to their value is to establish the proper degree of control over them. A items are most closely controlled by perpetual inventory control systems; B items use basic analytical tools; and C items are controlled by very simple techniques such as the two-bin system, the level control method, or the tag system.

2. Describe how just-in-time (JIT) and JIT II inventory control techniques work.
   - The just-in-time system of inventory control sees excess inventory as a blanket that masks production problems and adds unnecessary costs to the production operation. Under a JIT philosophy, the level of inventory maintained is the measure of efficiency. Materials and parts should not build up as costly inventory. They should flow through the production process without stopping, arriving at the appropriate location just in time.
   - JIT II techniques focus on creating a close, harmonious relationship with a company's suppliers so

that both parties benefit from increased efficiency. To work successfully, JIT II requires suppliers and their customers to share what was once closely guarded information in an environment of trust and cooperation. Under JIT II, customers and suppliers work hand in hand, acting more like partners than mere buyers and sellers.

3 Describe some methods for reducing loss from slow-moving inventory.

- Managing inventory requires monitoring the company's inventory turnover ratio; slow-moving items result in losses from spoilage or obsolescence.
- Slow-moving items can be liquidated by markdowns, eye-catching displays, or quantity discounts.

4 Discuss employee theft and shoplifting and how to prevent them.

- Employee theft accounts for the majority of business losses due to theft. Most small business owners are so busy managing their companies' daily affairs that they fail to develop reliable security systems. Thus, they provide their employees with prime opportunities to steal.
- The organizational atmosphere may encourage employee theft. The owner sets the organizational tone for security. A complete set of security controls, procedures, and penalties should be developed and enforced. Physical breakdowns in security invite employee theft. Open doors and windows, poor key control, and improper cash controls are major contributors to the problem of employee theft. Employers can build security into their businesses by screening and selecting employees carefully. Orientation programs also help the employee to get started in the right direction. Internal controls, such as division of responsibility, spot checks, and audit procedures, are useful in preventing employee theft.
- Shoplifting is the most common business crime. Fortunately, most shoplifters are amateurs. Juveniles often steal to impress their friends, but prosecution can halt their criminal ways early on. Impulse shoplifters steal because the opportunity suddenly arises. Simple prevention is the best defense against these shoplifters. Alcoholics, vagrants, and drug addicts steal to supply some need and are usually easiest to detect. Kleptomaniacs have a compelling need to steal. Professionals are in the business of theft and can be very difficult to detect and quite dangerous.

- Three strategies are most useful in deterring shoplifters. First, employees should be trained to look for signs of shoplifting. Second, store layout should be designed with theft deterence in mind. Finally, anti-theft devices should be installed in the store.

Discussion Questions

1. Describe some of the incidental costs of carrying and maintaining inventory for the small business owner.
2. What is a perpetual inventory system? How does it operate? What are the advantages and disadvantages of using such a system?
3. List and describe briefly the four versions of a perpetual inventory system.
4. Give examples of small businesses that would find it practical to implement the four systems described in question 3.
5. What advantages and disadvantages does a visual inventory control system have over other methods?
6. For what type of business product line is a visual control system most effective?
7. What is the 80/20 rule, and why is it important in controlling inventory?
8. Outline the ABC inventory control procedure. What is the purpose of classifying inventory items using this procedure?
9. Briefly describe the types of control techniques that should be used for A, B, and C items.
10. What is the basis for the JIT philosophy? Under what condition does a JIT system work best?
11. What is JIT II? What is its underlying philosophy? What risks does it present to businesses?
12. Outline the two methods of taking a physical inventory count. Why is it necessary for every small business manager to take inventory?
13. Why are slow-moving items dangerous to the small business? What can be done to liquidate them from inventory?
14. Why are small companies more susceptible to business crime than large companies?
15. Why is employee theft a problem for many small businesses? Briefly describe the reasons for employee theft.
16. Construct a profile of the employee most likely to steal goods or money from an employer. What four elements must be present for employee theft to occur?
17. Briefly outline a program that could help the typical small business owner minimize losses due to employee theft.

18. List and briefly describe the major types of shoplifters.
19. Outline the characteristics of a typical shoplifter that should arouse a small business manager's suspicions. What tools and tactics is a shoplifter likely to use?
20. Describe the major elements of a program designed to deter shoplifters.
21. How can proper planning of store layout reduce shoplifting losses?
22. What must an owner do to have a good case against a shoplifter? How should a suspected shoplifter be apprehended?

Step into the Real World

1. Contact a local small business owner and interview him or her to get answers to the following questions: What type of inventory control system is used? How well does it work? Does the 80/20 rule apply to the entrepreneur's inventory? Does the owner's inventory control system reflect the 80/20 rule? How does the owner liquidate slow-moving merchandise?

2. Visit a small manufacturer and ask if the company is using a JIT or JIT II system to integrate inventory and production. If it is, what the results have been? What problems has the company encountered? How did the company solve those problems? What improvements, if any, has the business experienced by using JIT?

3. Interview a local small business owner who has been a victim of shoplifting or employee theft. What security breaches contributed to the theft? How can the owner prevent a recurrence of the theft? What changes has the owner made in the business since the theft occurred?

4. Contact an attorney and interview him or her about the laws governing the apprehension of suspected shoplifters in your state. What should the small business owner who suspects someone of shoplifting do? Write a policy spelling out the proper procedure.

5. Invite a security consultant, police officer, or security agent from a local business to speak to your class about preventing employee theft and shoplifting. How extensive is the problem? What techniques does he or she recommend to prevent losses due to theft?

Take It to the Net

Visit the Scarborough/Zimmerer home page at
www.prenhall.com/scarbzim
for updated information, on-line resources, and Web-based exercises.

Endnotes

1. Scott Woolley, "Replacing Inventory with Information," *Forbes*, March 24, 1997, pp. 54–58.
2. Jill Andresky Fraser, "Know Thy Inventory," *Inc.*, June 1996, p. 120.
3. Bob Weinstein, "Taking Stock," *Entrepreneur*, January 1995, p. 50.
4. Evan Ramstead, "Compaq Stumbles as PCs Weather New Blow," *Wall Street Journal*, March 9, 1998, pp. B1, B8.
5. Tim McCollum, "A Cutting Edge for Small Stores," *Nation's Business*, February 1998, pp. 43–46.
6. Larry Stevens, "Point-of-Sale Inventory Systems: Now Ready for Small Businesses," *Nation's Business*, December 1991, p. 41.
7. Phaedra Hise, "Early Adoption Pays Off," *Inc.*, August 1996, p. 101.
8. Laura Bird, "High-Tech Inventory System Coordinates Retailer's Clothes with Customer's Tastes," *Wall Street Journal*, June 12, 1996, pp. B1, B7.
9. Paul Howell, "N.C. Firm Helps Toy Makers Meet Christmas Demand," *Greenville News*, December 25, 1996, p. 3D.
10. Woolley, "Replacing Inventory with Information."

11. Mark Henricks, "On the Spot," *Entrepreneur*, May 1997, p. 80.
12. John H. Sheridan, "Pushing the Envelope," *Industry Week*, August 17, 1998, pp. 84–90.
13. Fred R. Bleakley, "Strange Bedfellows," *Wall Street Journal*, January 13, 1995, p. A6.
14. Henricks, "On the Spot," pp. 80–82.
15. Ibid., p. 82.
16. Fraser, "Know Thy Inventory."
17. "Crime Prevention for Small Business," *Small Business Reporter* 13, no. 1 (1988), p. 1.
18. "How to Protect Your Business," Council of Better Business Bureaus with The Benjamin Company and Prentice Hall Publishers (Upper Saddle River, NJ, 1992), p. 5; William Ecenbarger, "They're Stealing You Blind," *Reader's Digest*, June 1996, pp. 97–103.
19. Robert T. Gray, "Clamping Down on Worker Crime," *Nation's Business*, April 1997, p. 44.
20. Seth Kantor, "How to Foil Employee Crime," *Nation's Business*, July 1983, p. 38.
21. Lori Ioannou, "Are Your Employees Robbing You Blind?" *Your Company*, August/September 1996, pp. 23–28.

22. Ioannou, "Are Your Employees Robbing You Blind?"; see also Heather Page, "Easy Target," *Entrepreneur*, May 1996, p. 16; John R. Emshwiller, "Small Business Is the Biggest Victim of Theft by Employees, Survey Shows," *Wall Street Journal*, October 25, 1995, p. B2.
23. Kantor, "How to Foil Employee Crime," p. 38.
24. Page, "Easy Target."
25. Emshwiller, "Small Business Is the Biggest Victim of Theft by Employees, Survey Shows."
26. Gray, "Clamping Down on Worker Crime."
27. Dale Buss, "Ways to Curtail Employee Theft," *Nation's Business*, April 1993, pp. 36–38; "Stop, Thief!" *Entrepreneur*, October 1995, pp. 66–67.
28. Ioannou, "Are Your Employees Robbing You Blind?" p. 26.
29. "Stop, Thief!" p. 66.
30. Ioannou, "Are Your Employees Robbing You Blind?"
31. Joshua Hyatt, "Employee Theft," *Inc.*, February 1988, p. 98.
32. Ioannou, "Are Your Employees Robbing You Blind?" p. 28.
33. Ecenbarger, "They're Stealing You Blind," p. 102.
34. Ibid., p. 99.
35. Ibid., p. 98.
36. Robert Berner, "Better Watch Out," *Wall Street Journal*, December 18, 1996, pp. A1, A8.
37. Ecenbarger, "They're Stealing You Blind," p. 99.
38. Ibid.
39. Ibid., p. 101.
40. Berner, "Better Watch Out."
41. Ibid., p. 102.

Using Technology to Gain a Competitive Edge

Improving technology can improve your competitiveness.

—*Chuck Stegman*

A businessman's judgment is no better than his information.

—*P. R. Lamont*

Upon completion of this chapter, you will be able to

1 Explain how technology can help small businesses gain a competitive advantage over their rivals.

2 Describe how to create a technology plan that enables business owners to get the most out of their investments in technology.

3 Explain how computers have transformed the way entrepreneurs do business and how to computerize a small business.

4 Outline the major business software applications, identify guidelines for buying computer hardware, and explain the hardware issues entrepreneurs face.

5 Discuss the peripheral equipment, such as printers, scanners, digital cameras, and personal digital assistants, that enhances the performance of the computer.

6 Discuss the role of communications technology, such as the telephone, voice mail, and e-mail, in small companies.

*T*echnology is one of the most powerful tools in an entrepreneur's arsenal of competitive weapons. It can transform the way a small company works, the way it does business, and the way it interacts with its customers. Rather than spend their time tangled in the mundane operational details of their companies, technologically savvy entrepreneurs are free to focus more on the strategic and creative sides of their businesses. The result is not only an improvement in a company's productivity and efficiency but also a major change in its basic philosophy. Technology is no longer a threat, absorbing vast amounts of capital for no apparent purpose; instead, it becomes a tool for enhancing a company's performance and for gaining an edge over rivals. Smart entrepreneurs see technology not as an expenditure on the latest gadgetry but as an investment in making their companies more competitive and more successful. They invest in technology—whether it's a digital camera, a fax machine, or a computer—only when they see it as a way to improve productivity or the ability to serve customers better, faster, or more efficiently than before. Figure 18.1 shows the results of a recent survey of the Inc. 500 fastest-growing private companies, graphing the areas of these companies that benefit most from technology.

Martha Stewart, the First Lady of Domesticity, relies on technology to manage her $2-million-a-year business, Martha Stewart Living Enterprises. Stewart, most famous for her weekly syndicated television show, also publishes a magazine, Martha Stewart Living, *writes a syndicated newspaper column, produces "askMartha" radio spots, manages a mail-order catalog,* Martha by Mail, *and keeps her Web site <http://www.marthastewart.com/Nav/> going. How does she control these far-flung ventures? "Technology allows me to do them," says Stewart. "Fax machines, computers, efficient phones, e-mail. Technology makes it possible, so it's going to get done." Stewart's home in West Port, Connecticut, from which she often works, has 10 telephone lines, a powerful personal computer, several cellular telephones, a fax machine, and a portable computer. Stewart's driver takes her to her New York City office in a specially rigged Chevrolet Suburban, equipped with extras such as a portable disk recorder for dictation, a smaller disk recorder for short messages, a cellular telephone, a television set, and mobile navigation software. Her company's office includes a conference room equipped with an audiovisual teleconferencing system that enables her to have face-to-face business meetings without having to leave the building. Stewart often writes for her television and radio shows or her newspaper column during the commute using her portable computer. "You have to be able to communicate, and I have an awful lot of communicating to do," explains Stewart. "[My portable computer] faxes from the airplane, it faxes from my car, from my home, wherever I am."*[1]

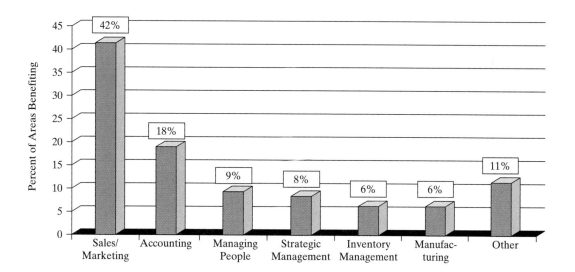

Figure 18.1 **Technology Payoff** SOURCE: "Benchmark," *Inc.,* December 1996, p. 120.

$\mathcal{I}$nformation Technology and Competitive Advantage

◆ Explain how technology can help small businesses gain a competitive advantage over their rivals.

Small businesses that learn to exploit the ability to use information and technology to serve their customers better will gain a competitive edge. Those who fail to do so run the risk of falling far behind in the battle of business. "The objectives of business, namely survival and profit, are still the same," says one management consultant. "But how we manage business to achieve these objectives has changed markedly, due in no small part to the PC."[2] Small companies that collect *and use* valuable information to manage their operations effectively will have a competitive advantage over their rivals, whatever their size. They will be able to develop new products rapidly, boost productivity, control inventory and cash flow, collect accounts promptly, produce goods and services efficiently, identify customer needs and preferences quickly, and anticipate problems and opportunities. One business owner explains how mastering the new technology will influence small firms' ability to compete:

> *Information—or the lack of it—is fast becoming the competitive edge by which the growing company wins or loses in the marketplace. The ability of small business management to use the new computer and communications technologies to access information will determine a company's future just as much as product design or marketing savvy has in the past.*[3]

SOURCE: The *Wall Street Journal*, December 10, 1997, p. A23. With permission from Cartoon Features Syndicate.

More small businesses are discovering ways to create what one expert calls a "techno-edge." "High-tech or low, big business or small, [gaining a techno-edge] means using tools in such a way as to give customers more of what they want, such as greater speed of satisfaction of their problem or need, and getting it to them in a way that is more convenient," he says.[4]

Entrepreneurs who use technology most successfully focus their efforts on their customers' needs. *For instance, Kenneth Meade, owner of Meade Group, a collection of car dealerships around Detroit with $200 million in annual sales, uses technology to revolutionize the used-car market. His goal: to improve dramatically customers' used-car buying experiences. "We wanted to figure out a new way of handling the customer to make it a more friendly atmosphere," explains Meade. Before introducing technology into his Cars & Cars dealership, however, Meade started with decidedly low-tech solutions to customers' most frequent complaints. He put the sales staff on salary, not commission, and he priced his cars below the value listed in the industry pricing guide, the* Blue Book. *Then, with his son Barron's help, Meade launched a high-tech shopping system that makes selecting, locating, and financing a car a snap for customers. "The computers are a whole new way of making a sales transaction with the least amount of anxiety and pressure," says Meade. Customers can search through the dealership's extensive inventory of cars on almost any criteria— price, make, model (sedan, sports coupe, sport utility), features—without ever having to leave the showroom floor. When customers enter Cars & Cars, a salesperson guides them through an interactive touch-screen computer program. From their computer search, customers can pick out the cars they are interested in, print out a spec sheet that includes a photo of the car, its price, mileage, and features. The program also helps them develop a payment plan that suits their budgets. Then the salesperson takes them in a golf cart to the cars they have selected so they can test drive them. Although the touch-screen displays and databases that drive the Cars & Cars system are not new (large department stores have used them for years), Meade was among the first to introduce them to the used-car business. The system has been so successful that Meade is now introducing the touch-screen displays in high-traffic areas such as shopping malls. These units give Cars & Cars valuable marketing information, recording the kiosks' busiest hours and tracking where customers come from and the most popular models.*[5]

Kenneth Meade's experience at Cars & Cars proves that it is not the technology itself that is so important to a company's success but how the entrepreneur behind the business devises creative, innovative ways to use that technology to forge lasting relationships with customers and to surpass their expectations. In the twenty-first century, the most successful companies will be those that formulate technology strategies designed not to merely support their operations but to change the fundamental ways they do business. Figure 18.2 describes the benefits small business owners say their companies earn from their investments in technology.

*D*eveloping a Technology Plan

2 Describe how to create a technology plan that enables business owners to get the most out of their investments in technology.

To get the most out of their investments in technology, entrepreneurs should develop a comprehensive technology plan. Otherwise, it is easy to get caught up in a cycle of purchasing the latest technology without a clear idea of how it will benefit the business or its customers. A recent study by Yankelovich Partners concluded that, although small companies have the greatest potential for improvements from technology, most small businesses do not use technology effectively. The primary reason? They lack a comprehensive plan for integrating technology in ways that could transform their businesses.[6] Building a workable technology plan includes the following steps.

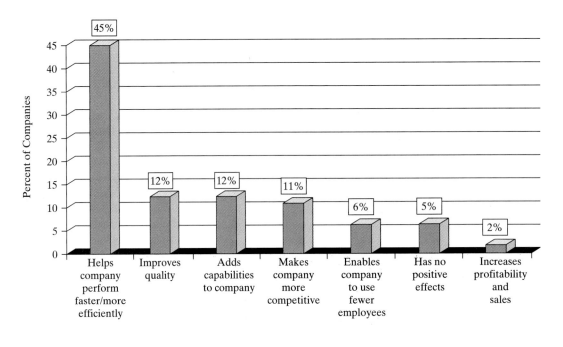

Figure 18.2 **Technology's Impact on Small Business** Source: Keycorp Survey, 1996.

DECIDE WHAT YOU WANT YOUR COMPANY TO BE ABLE TO DO FOR ITSELF AND FOR YOUR CUSTOMERS

The tasks you want to be able to perform, to a great extent, determine the level of technology you must buy. A company that wants every employee to have access to the same files and documents through standard business software such as word processing and spreadsheets may need something as simple as several basic personal computers linked together via a local area network (LAN). On the other hand, a company that wants its field sales representatives to be able to access a database in company headquarters from customers' locations will need a more powerful system with a dedicated relational database and laptop computers equipped with high-speed modems and powerful processors. The focus of this first step is not on technology; it emphasizes the tasks entrepreneurs want their companies to perform or the service they want to provide to their customers.

DETERMINE THE TECHNOLOGY AND THE EQUIPMENT YOU WILL NEED TO PERFORM THOSE TASKS

Once entrepreneurs know what they want to accomplish, they can turn their attention to finding the appropriate technology to perform those tasks and functions. The goals established in the first step will drive the technology decisions in this step. Will cellular telephones and pagers solve the problem, or is the solution a longer-term project, such as building a Web site to market products and services? It is important to view every project as part of an integrated whole because so much of today's technology can work together in a smooth system *if it is planned properly.*

Talking with other entrepreneurs at this step can be extremely helpful. It's perhaps the best way to find out what technology works best for certain functions and to get practical reviews of specific pieces of equipment. Researching technology reviews in magazines such as *Information Week* <http://techweb.cmp.com/iw/666/>, *PC Computing* <http://www.zd-net.com/pccomp/>, *Computer Shopper* <http://www5.zdnet.com/cshopper/>, *PC Magazine* <http://www8.zdnet.com/pcmag/>, *MacWEEK* <http://www8.zdnet.com/macweek/>, *Tech-Web* <http://www.techweb.com/>, *Byte* <http://www.byte.com/>, and others will help entrepreneurs make informed buying decisions. These reviews discuss important features such as benefits, performance, advantages, disadvantages, and price. All of these magazines (and many others) have Web sites as well. The World Wide Web is another useful source of up-to-the-minute information on the latest technology available. With the search engines available on the Web, entrepreneurs looking for specific technology can find hundreds of references with just a few mouse clicks. Technology-related "chat groups" on the Internet are another excellent source of information.

CONDUCT A TECHNOLOGY AUDIT

The next step in developing a technology plan is to perform an audit of the company's existing technology. This involves more than merely counting! It is important to include a thorough description of each piece of equipment. For instance, a business may have six computers, but only two of those may be capable of running the software necessary to do the task at hand. Some jobs require "hot rod" equipment; others need only "economy model" equipment. Conducting an audit allows entrepreneurs to know where they are on the road to technology.

MATCH GOALS AND RESOURCES

After completing the technology audit, the next step is to match the technology to the task. This ensures that the business will get maximum value from its existing equipment, from cellular telephones and fax machines to personal computers and digital cameras. Inevitably there will be gaps where a company lacks the technology needed to do the job, and the owner will have to purchase the equipment.

DEVELOP A TECHNOLOGY BUDGET

Entrepreneurs must determine the financial resources necessary to purchase the equipment the technology plan has identified. It is best to prepare budgets for two or three years into the future, the useful life of most of today's technology. One way to stretch a company's investment in technology is to compare the cost and resulting capability of upgrading existing equipment with that of buying new equipment. In some instances, upgrading can deliver the necessary power at a fraction of the cost of new equipment; in others, upgrades simply cannot produce the desired level of performance. *When one home-based business owner purchased a new database program to improve her ability to manage her mail-order catalog company, she was able to upgrade her existing computer by adding more memory and a second hard-disk drive at very little expense. The extra computing power enabled the entrepreneur to run the program smoothly, extending the life of her existing computer system another two years—an eternity in computer years!*

MAKE THE NECESSARY PURCHASES

Once you have identified the gaps in your company's technology, it is time to buy. Avoid the tendency to buy the fastest, most powerful (and therefore most expensive) technology *unless you really need it*. Entrepreneurs who never take the time to develop a technology plan often fall into this trap. Remember to let the demands of the tasks you want to accomplish drive the technology you buy. "Stay focused on what you need today and in the immediate future," advises one computer consultant. "It's better to stay one generation behind the [technology] curve. You'll have a better perspective and won't waste money."[7]

Shopping for the best prices on equipment can be time-consuming for busy entrepreneurs but can pay off handsomely. Common supply sources for small business owners include major retailers such as Best Buy, Office Depot, or Radio Shack, discount warehouses such as Sam's Club or Costco, direct-mail merchants such as computer makers Gateway <http://www.gw2k.com>, Dell <http://www.dell.com>, and Micron <http://www.micron.com>, and local vendors. Using the World Wide Web is an excellent way to locate the best bargains on many kinds of equipment. Smart entrepreneurs know that price is not always the primary purchase criteria, however. They recognize that sometimes it is best to pay a little more for equipment to get the benefit of fast, convenient service and support. The more complex the equipment or the more crucial it is to your operation, the more you should be willing to pay for service and support. Figure 18.3 shows that cost is the number one barrier to technological advancement that small business owners cite.

$\mathcal{P}$ersonal Computers

3 Explain how computers have transformed the way entrepreneurs do business and how to computerize a small business.

An astounding array of technological devices, all designed to make conducting business easier and more efficient, faces modern entrepreneurs. From fax machines to cellular telephones, these devices enable entrepreneurs to do business in ways never before possible, but none has had as much impact as the personal computer.

CHANGING THE FACE OF BUSINESS

Products that change the way we live and work don't come along often; but when they do, the world is never the same again. Who, for instance, could have foreseen the impact that the personal computer (PC) would have on the world when it was introduced in 1981? The ubiquitous PC has transformed the workplace: sending typewriters the way of the papyrus scroll, enabling workers scattered across the globe to communicate as if they were in the same room, giving managers the power to analyze countless financial scenarios in just seconds,

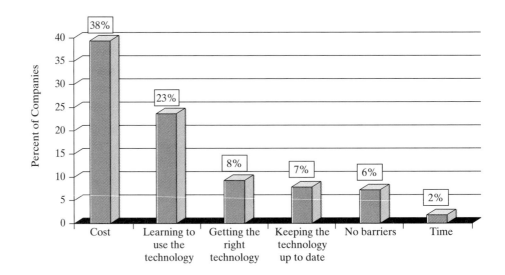

Figure 18.3 Barriers to Technological Advancement in Small Businesses   SOURCE: Keycorp Survey, 1996.

and providing small companies the opportunity to become just as "big" in the eyes of their customers as any Fortune 500 company. "The power of the modern computer offers people with a distinctive concept or a unique idea for launching a new business a vast array of tools that puts them on a par with large corporations, which means they can compete with the big guys," says the founder of a computer-based business. "In this sense, the computer . . . has become the great equalizer."[8]

Terry McGrath, co-founder with his wife, Katherine, of ValueQuest, an investment firm that manages $700 million in pension funds for such clients as Xerox and 3M, says, "Our company wouldn't be here today if it weren't for the technology." The McGraths have hired one full-time employee and several part-time workers, who use personal computers linked through a network to collect investment information and to handle the necessary accounting and record keeping. McGrath estimates that without the computers ValueQuest would require a staff of 20 to perform those tasks. "Computers allow us to compete with bigger firms," he says. Because of their investment in technology, the McGraths are not tied to their desks, despite the fact that their business demands that they know what's going on in financial markets constantly. With their well-equipped laptop PC, they often run the company while cruising the Caribbean on their boat, exchanging market reports and trade orders with the home office in Marblehead, Massachusetts.[9]

Today's personal computers rival or exceed yesterday's minicomputers and mainframes in power and flexibility. According to **Moore's Law,** the speed of microprocessors, the "brains" of a computer, doubles approximately every 18 months, but their prices remain about the same.[10] In fact, if a 1946 Rolls Royce had paralleled the price and performance record of a 1946 computer, it would sell for just 2 cents and would travel at the speed of light![11] This increase in technological capacity has been accompanied by the decline in computer prices over time. These two forces have brought a spectacular amount of processing power into the grasp of the smallest businesses.

In its brief existence, the computer has already proved to be a revolutionary tool for businesses of all sizes. The transition to computer-based operations has not been easy or smooth for many small companies, and many entrepreneurs find computers frustrating and exasperating at times. But no one can dispute the power they give small companies to compete with their larger, wealthier rivals. "Whereas all previous tools have leveraged human muscle, the computer is the first tool that leverages the human brain," says one computer expert. "That means it amplifies or substitutes for human thinking. This is the number one aspect that makes the computer revolutionary. It's the equivalent of any other great invention that has transformed the world."[12]

HOW TO COMPUTERIZE YOUR BUSINESS

The key issues facing the small business owner who decides to buy a computer are when to buy a computer, how much to spend, what functions to computerize first, which software to use, which hardware to buy, and where to buy the computer. Making these decisions is not easy, especially for the novice. But, by following a rational, step-by-step approach, the small business owner can navigate "the computer jungle" and avoid common pitfalls along the way. Blinded by dreams of increasing their business's productivity, many business owners rush into the purchase without a working plan, almost always ending up with a system that fails to meet expectations. The real key to success with any technology is making sure that it fits the company's needs, which might include everything from improving the level of customer service to increasing control over inventory. The process of choosing a personal computer must begin with what the owner knows best: the business and its needs. The key to making a wise purchase is to translate what the owner knows about the company into the criteria a computer system must meet, following the steps described next.

Step 1. Develop a List of Current Activities. What is the nature of the business? Does it move merchandise, sell ideas, process information, serve people, or crunch numbers? After defining the general scope of the business, the owner should break down current business activities into more detailed categories that can be computerized, such as accounting, record keeping, inventory control, file management, presentations, time management, financial analysis, forecasting, word processing, training, and telecommunications. This is a process that requires the involvement of employees who will be using the system or be affected by it. Their input also might identify areas the owner would have overlooked.

At this stage, the owner should separate the most important activities of the business from the least important ones. Activities in the business are not all equally important. High-priority items are those driving the decision to computerize; they are essential. Medium-priority items are desirable but not essential. Low-priority items are those that would be nice to have but the company could do without. The plan to computerize must center on high-priority items first. Focusing efforts on improving the performance of a least-important activity produces little benefit to the company.

Maxine Most and Shirley Gines, co-founders of Senshu, a contemporary lingerie shop, decided that one of the keys to success in their young business was stocking the right merchandise for their customers and controlling it properly. That would require a computerized point-of-sale (POS) system that could track every transaction. Their POS system gives them detailed information on every purchase customers make. "We know 30 percent of our sales are the higher-priced items, and 45 percent are in the lower end," says Gines. "So we know which [merchandise] to restock and at very specific quantities." Next on their computerization list: a bar code labeling system and software to create their own mail-order business.[13]

Step 2. Decide How Much and Which Areas of the Business to Computerize. Entrepreneurs just getting started with computing should not choose "a problem area" when they begin computerizing. If the source of trouble is in the manual system itself, computerizing it will generate the same faulty information, only faster. A better approach is to start with a smooth, well-functioning system. The chances for success are much greater, and success in the early stages of computerization builds confidence in the new computer system. In addition, computerizing a company strength increases the owner's understanding of exactly what a computer can do for the business. As one expert claims, "Managers should always use the personal computer to leverage what they do best. They should not use it to try and fix that part of the business which is broken, at least not at first."[14]

Finally, when deciding which functions to computerize first, a small business manager should consider these questions:

◆ Which activities are critical to success now?

◆ Which activities will become critical as the business grows?

◆ Which activities will be critical to maintaining a competitive advantage?

◆ Which activities will improve the company's ability to serve our customers?

◆ Which of these activities could benefit from the speed, accuracy, and timeliness of computerization?

Step 3. Develop a Computer Budget. Once an entrepreneur has determined which areas of her business to computerize, she can develop a computer budget to do so. An attorney may want a relatively simple system aimed at improving word-processing efficiency. But the owner of a retail shop may want an integrated multiuser system to track inventory, process receivables and payables, produce financial reports, and forecast sales and cash flow. The budget must consider the cost of the computer system as well as additional costs such as training, peripheral equipment, support, consultants (if necessary), and maintenance. In fact,

A Technological Edge = A Competitive Edge

*T*he 1950 census counted fewer than 900 computer operators in the United States. Today, the proportion of all jobs that require using computer stands at 46 percent, up from 25 percent in 1984. More than 70 percent of management jobs now demand computer literacy. In short, the computer is a fact of life in the business world. But just how much has the computer changed the way people work? Jennifer Jarratt, a manager in a Washington, D.C.–based think tank that specializes in forecasting the future, says that the computer has only begun to transform the business world. "Information technology is one of the key enabling technologies of the future," she says, "so it crops up in everything and is having a profound effect in many different fields."

Jarratt says that any new technology progresses gradually through three stages: substitution, adaptation, and revolution. Computers currently are in the last part of stage 2, adaptation, and are beginning to spill over into the revolution stage, where they will generate tremendous changes in the way entrepreneurs and others do business. In stage 1, substitution, the new technology replaces existing tools, but people are doing the same things they did before, only faster and better. Computers, for instance, make performing such mundane tasks as accounting, record keeping, and cash management much less tedious than before. Business owners once performed all of these tasks manually with the help of calculators and adding machines; now, computers take much of the drudgery out of these necessary functions and give business owners better financial information on a much more timely basis.

In stage 2, adaptation, people discover that the new technology gives them the ability to do new things they never could do before. Users begin to branch out from their traditional approaches to basic tasks and functions to explore new possibilities the technology opens up. For example, many entrepreneurs now use their computers to conduct much of their business with their banks. Others use standard software packages such as Quick Books and Money to balance their checkbooks, create budgets, and track revenues and expenses, something many of them never had the time to do before. Still others use communication and computer technology to streamline inventory control by using electronic data interchange systems.

Stage 3 involves using technology to create major shifts not only in the way things are done but also in things to be done. "People basically throw out everything they did before and start to rearrange not only the task they're doing but also the entire process that it stems from," says Jarratt. The result is a major shift in the way companies do business. "We're right on the brink of this exciting third stage," she says. "The real key will involve figuring out how to use that computer to benefit the customer so that the customer sees it as an advantage to his or her life."

An investment in technology has enabled Dominick Segrete's small architectural design company to revamp the way it designs buildings and deals with its customers. The payoff to both the company and its customers has been tremendous. Like many architectural design firms, Tucci, Segrete, and Rosen uses computer-aided design (CAD) programs such as AutoCAD to create blueprints for clients. However, Segrete's company has taken the computer-design process one step further. Using an inexpensive conference and document-sharing program called ProShare, architects establish "virtual meetings" to present and to discuss with clients (which include Saks Fifth Avenue, Eatons [Canada], and Printemps [Paris]) the plans they have created. Segrete sends the drawing to the client over the computer using ProShare and then places a telephone call. "We can both call up the same file and are literally reading off the same page," he says. "We can type text back and forth while we talk, and it's all in real time."

This communication technology has transformed the design process at Tucci, Segrete, and Rosen. The on-line discussions with clients make the design process more collaborative, and, because clients can make comments and ask questions "live," the technique actually enhances the architects' creativity. Electronic pens that allow parties at either end to sketch ideas directly onto the plans frequently turn virtual meetings into brainstorming sessions as architects incorporate new ideas into drawings on the computer screen. Even though the small company has spent more than $350,000 on technology over the last decade, Segrete is convinced that the investment has paid for itself many times over in the form of new contracts and more-satisfied customers. Using its high-tech setup, Segrete recently landed a job that generated $800,000 in earnings; before architects from a competing firm had a chance to contact the client, Segrete already had sent a set of plans to the client using ProShare. Score one for technology!

Segrete recently added 3-D and video capability to its computer system; now architects can take clients on a "virtual tour" through the spaces they design long before they are built. "It enhances the way we think," he says. "When designers think in 3-D, it opens up worlds like never before." Not only has the company's investment in technology increased productivity and sales, but, more important, it has produced more-satisfied clients who stay with the company over time.

1. How has Tucci, Segrete, and Rosen's investment in technology changed the way in which it competes in the marketplace?

2. In what ways has this technology changed the company's dealings with its clients? What are the benefits of these changes?

3. What dangers exist for companies that rely on technology such as this to gain a competitive edge?

SOURCES: Adapted from Karen Miles, "Afraid of Your Computer?" *Reader's Digest*, February 1998, pp. 181–184; Tim McCollum, "The Future Is Now," *Nation's Business*, December 1996, pp. 16–28; Kylo-Patrick Hart, "The Future of Your Business," *Business Start-Ups*, April 1997, pp. 26–32; Rivka Tadjer, "Better by Design," *Success*, October 1996, pp. 55–56; John Teresko, "The Next 50 Years," *Industry Week*, July 7, 1997, pp. 37–38. ◆

such costs usually exceed that of hardware and software, but few business owners recognize them in planning a computer budget.

Inexperienced computer buyers may spend $3,000 on a computer and software, expecting that to be all there is. WRONG! When preparing their computer budgets, entrepreneurs must consider the **total cost of ownership (TCO).** Total cost of ownership looks at more than just the cost of the equipment; it considers all of the costs—from software and technical support to training and maintenance—that owners will incur over the life of their computers. According to one recent study, the out-of-pocket costs of hardware account for just 15 percent of the total cost of owning a computer. The purchase price of the software makes up about 20 percent of total cost of ownership. Training, support, and development costs make up between 40 and 60 percent of the total cost![15] The wise business owner recognizes that the ongoing cost of a computer will be two to four times the cost of hardware and software. A study by The Gartner Group found that the average total cost of a personal computer over five years used in a business is $40,000. The study estimated that in small companies, a $5,000 personal computer's total cost of operation is even higher, lying somewhere between $15,000 and $20,000 per year.[16] The accompanying Gaining the Competitive Edge feature describes several ways a company can lower its TCO.

Step 4. Define the Informational Needs of the Functions to Be Computerized First. A company's information needs manifest themselves in a number of ways. For example, if the manager plans to computerize the inventory control system, she should begin by studying the flow of information through the manual inventory recordkeeping system. How are purchase orders and invoices routed and recorded? What is the system for recording inventory receipts and distributors? Are employees recording the same information more than once? Which employees produce and receive which reports? Identifying these and other related issues will help the owner define the nature and flow of the information the company needs. Still, the owner must define the type, the quantity, the flow, and the users of the information needed. For instance, if the system must make information available to several people in either the same or scattered locations, a business owner will need to set up a local area network. A **local area network (LAN)** is a group of computers linked together in a system that makes all of the data, programs, and resources of one computer available to all of the other computers on the network. A **peer-to-peer LAN,** which links a company's computers to one another (picture a string of Christmas tree lights), is the simplest kind of LAN and works best for small businesses with five or fewer computers. Because they are connected to one another, these computers allow workers to share files and peripheral equipment. Other companies with more sophisticated networking needs set up **client/server LANs** in which a dedicated computer, called a server, coordinates all of the network's operations such as sharing programs, documents, and peripheral devices (e.g., printers) among the other computers (clients) in the network. Networks can boost productivity in a small company because they encourage collaborative work among employees rather than individual productivity gains. Nearly half of all small companies now use local area networks.[17] "Networks connect people to people and people to data," explains one writer.[18]

Network computers can lower a company's total cost of computer ownership. Because they run applications off of the server, network computers need no local storage devices or software, which means they can be stripped-down, very basic machines. Network computers cost as little as $800 to $1,200 to purchase. Although they offer many benefits over the PC, network computers are not yet capable of completely replacing PCs in the workplace. They are best suited for workers who use information rather than for those who create it. They are also very useful for workers whose jobs involve accessing information and sharing it with others. People in jobs that require heavy use of software applications such as desktop publishing or presentation packages would be better equipped with PCs. "Don't throw away your PCs; network nirvana is not yet a reality," says one network expert.[19]

How to Lower the Total Cost of Owning (TCO) a Personal Computer

The Total Cost of Ownership for a Personal Computer

Hardware costs

The costs of software, maintenance, technical support, training, supplies, equipment, etc.

*P*ersonal computers and icebergs have a great deal in common. The majority of an iceberg's bulk lies under the surface of the water; what an observer sees *really* is "only the tip of the iceberg"! Similarly, the majority of the total cost of ownership (TCO) for a computer lies beneath the surface in factors such as software, maintenance, technical support, training, supplies, equipment, and others. When preparing their computer budgets, experienced entrepreneurs plan with these factors in mind. They also find ways to keep their TCO down. What can business owners do to minimize their companies' TCO?

Consider a network. Linking the computers in a business together into a local area network may help keep software costs to a minimum. Installing network versions of software packages enables employees throughout the company to use the programs, and the company does not have to purchase individual packages for each machine.

Buy software bundles. Software makers offer special pricing on bundles of programs. All of the major software companies produce "suites" of programs—usually a word processor, a spreadsheet, a database, a presentation program, and communications software—all in one package at significant discounts compared with purchasing each program separately.

Consider hiring freelance computer technicians. Most small business owners cannot afford to hire a computer technician, but when something goes wrong, they *really* need one! Hiring a "computer wizard" on an as-needed basis usually is the best solution. Local colleges, universities, or computer-user groups (contact the Association of Personal Computer User Groups in Dallas, Texas, at (914) 876-6678) are excellent sources of people with the necessary computer skills.

Shop for the best deals on hardware and software purchases. Even though these costs are not the greatest portion of TCO, cutting them can save vital cash. Entrepreneurs can use publications such as the *Computer Shopper* and can conduct searches on the World Wide Web to find the best bargains on hardware and software.

Standardize your hardware and software purchases. Trying to maintain and use a hodge-podge of computers increases a company's TCO significantly. Providing technical support, training, and maintenance for a mix of computers is a real challenge for most business owners. Making your computers as uniform as possible simplifies the system and keeps costs down. Although it may not be possible to have all computers exactly alike, basing purchase decisions on a standard system profile will make maintaining your company's computers much easier.

Consider ways to maximize employees' use of computers. Studies show that employees waste one hour a week on personal tasks on their computers (probably a conservative estimate). Although you want to avoid the role of the "computer police" in your company, it is probably a good idea to set clear policies on using computers for work instead of play during business hours.

Invest in training. Too many business owners invest heavily in computer technology only to shortchange the employees who will be using them by failing to invest in training. The best way to ensure that your employees will be able to get the most out of their computers is to train them. Leaving busy employees to teach themselves is most inefficient and almost guarantees unsatisfactory results. Training, whether through formal classroom sessions, informal "hands-on" instruction, or computer-based teaching, is the way to maximize employees' computer productivity.

Don't hold on to old technology forever. Although common sense would suggest that keeping computers forever is one way to lower TCO, it just isn't true! Studies show that keeping a PC too long actually *raises* your costs! Having several generations of equipment in a company complicates the system and increases TCO. Set up a timetable for replacing old equipment and stick to it.

Buy new technology for the right reasons. The best reason to purchase new technology is that it will improve your ability to do something that you already do or that it will enable you to do something you could not do before. Technology for technology's sake is not important; it's the competitive advantage that technology gives you that really matters! Remember: You don't always have to have the latest, fastest, most powerful technology to get the job done. Buy what you need when you need it.

SOURCE: Adapted from Heather Page, "What Price PC?" *Entrepreneur*, October 1997, pp. 50–53. ◆

Computers linked through a network can change the way a company does business and the way employees do their jobs. Because of a network's connective power, employees in some small companies can work together on the same project simultaneously even though they may be thousands of miles apart! Another plus is that everyone on the network can work on the same file rather than giving everyone a copy of his own and then integrating all of the changes into a single file later. *Gus Stergis, president of Stergis Aluminum Products Corporation, a 33-year-old window and door maker, knew that his company could benefit from a network. The company's old system was incredibly inefficient, requiring every customer order to be written down at least seven times. "Errors were tremendous," says Stergis. Order errors translated into wasted materials because correcting them usually involved re-cutting or scrapping entire parts. To streamline the process, Stergis set up a computer network that enabled sales representatives to send orders directly to the office. The network also gives every department access to the company's business records, letting employees see the status of every order, from sales through shipping. The new system has produced impressive results for Stergis. Bills go out much faster, which means payments come back in sooner. Production waste is down, and profitability is up.*[20]

Before purchasing a local area network, experts recommend that entrepreneurs consider the following questions:[21]

◆ *How many PCs do you have?* The number of PCs to be included in a network will determine its structure, the network hardware and software required, and the type of cable used to connect it all.

◆ *How do you plan to use your network?* The tasks you expect a network to perform will determine its design and construction. Do you want the network to store simple files and standard software applications so that users can share them? Are you looking for a more sophisticated communications device that will link your business with customers around the globe via the Internet? Do you expect it to be able to handle large databases containing information about your company's customers?

◆ *Where do you plan to buy it?* Some network kits are so easy to set up that some computer-savvy entrepreneurs install their own networks. Most business owners purchase their networks from resellers who handle the installation for them. If you choose the latter option, make sure your reseller will offer sufficient training and support to get the network up and running smoothly.

◆ *How crucial will the network be to your business?* The implication here is: What will happen to your business if your network goes down? The more dependent a business is on its network, the greater is its need to have a system of controls and a contingency plan in place. Otherwise, a network glitch may put you out of business, at least temporarily.

Step 5. Shop for Software Packages That Will Perform the Required Functions. A computer is only as good as the software it is running, whether the application is word processing, spreadsheets, accounting, computer-aided design, or others. A computer without proper software is like a car without an engine. Each year, computer users spend about $3 on software for every $1 they spend on hardware. Every year software makers introduce programs that are more powerful than before; however, that software also requires more-powerful computers to run it. Because not all computers are capable of running all software programs, the best approach is to choose the appropriate software first and then select a computer that will run it efficiently. Unfortunately, too many entrepreneurs buy hardware first and then purchase the software they need. Only then do they discover their mistake. One computer consultant advises "Constraining your software options by choosing hardware first is like deciding not to have children because your car is a two-seater."[22]

The first phase of evaluating software packages is to collect information on those that perform the functions the owner is most interested in. Practically every issue of most computer magazines contains detailed descriptions of popular programs, comparisons of similar packages, and reviews of software. Computer user groups are another valuable source of information. A user group is an informal club with members who use a similar type of computer. Most groups meet frequently (and are easy to find) to swap information on their computers as well as software and its applications.

Trade associations also may be able to offer advice on which programs companies in an industry rely on. The Institute of Management Consultants (located in New York City at [212] 697-8262) can provide information about its members who would have expertise in selecting software for particular industries. In addition, directories such as the *Datapro Directory of Microcomputer Software* provide detailed listings of thousands of different packages. Reference books, such as Donald Hockney's *Personal Computers for the Successful Small Business*, and software catalogs, such as *Business Software* (Elsevier Science Publishing Company) and the *Whole Earth Software Catalog* (Quantum Press/Doubleday) also offer valuable assistance. These sources can help the manager answer key questions about software: Is it easy to use (i.e., "user-friendly")? How does it handle errors? Does it perform the necessary functions efficiently? How good is the documentation? Will the publisher or the vendor provide service and support? How long does it take to learn to use? We will explore software in more detail later in this chapter.

Step 6. Choose the Hardware. After selecting the software that best suits their needs, entrepreneurs can focus their attention on finding the right hardware to run it. The final decision depends on many features, but the machine's processing power, expandability, compatibility, and serviceability are crucial. Small business owners must resist the temptation to shop for a computer on the basis of price alone. Sticking to a reasonable budget is important, but cost should *not* be the driving factor. Hardware options range from high-powered, desktop models to tiny, portable "notebook" or even smaller subnotebook computers. We will discuss hardware in more detail later in this chapter.

Step 7. Integrate the System into the Business. Converting a business from a manual system to a computerized one takes time and hard work. Employees who will be using the new system must have time to become familiar with it before putting it into action. In addition, the system must be tested thoroughly. Entrepreneurs must be sure that their systems are free of bugs before switching existing procedures onto the computer. The conversion process takes time, money, and a great deal of patience. Computer experts estimate that a user can expect to spend at least four hours learning to use a machine and up to 40 hours learning to use the software.

Conversion also requires a financial investment. In addition to the cost of getting the hardware and the software in place, there is the cost of training employees to use the system. Cutting corners here is dangerous because employees who are unskilled in running the computer system will render it useless. Adequate training is vital to the success of a new computer system. On-site sessions, training consultants, vendor representatives, and full-blown courses to improve employees' computing skills are well worth the price. One small business owner found that sharing the cost of computers for his employees' use at home drastically boosted their level of computer expertise on the job.

Most companies find that a gradual phasing in of the computer system works much better than an overnight change. This approach gives the company enough time to solve the nagging little problems that inevitably arise when introducing a computer system. One business owner says, "We first started working with the accounting system and installed it in sections—general ledger, accounts receivable, accounts payable, inventory, and sales orders. The last part was purchase orders."[23] Typically, with such a step-by-step process, each subsequent phase becomes easier than the last. Many business owners follow a common sequence when computerizing their business functions: financial operations, production, sales, marketing, and customer service.

Another advantage of a gradual phase-in is that the small business owner has the ability to run the new system parallel to the old one before relying solely on the new one. Computer experts highly recommend parallel operations to ensure the reliability of the new computer system. The owner should compare the results of the two systems for at least a month or two. Doing the same work twice may appear to be a waste of time, but the confidence it builds in the new system is worth the extra work.

Small business owners can make the conversion process go much more smoothly by heeding the following suggestions:

♦ Do not be intimidated by computers. Business owners must be determined to get control of the computer system and to use it productively to gain a competitive edge.

♦ Become computing-literate. The best way to avoid intimidation is to learn more about computers and how to use them.

♦ Set a good example. Business owners must take the lead in showing how the computer can boost efficiency and productivity in the company.

♦ Reward employees for becoming computing-literate. Rewards can help overcome employees' misgivings and anxieties about the new system.

♦ Be sensitive to employees' feelings. Because many people fear being replaced by a computer, emphasize their skills that the computer cannot replace.

♦ Create an appropriate environment for learning. The least effective setting is in the midst of the workplace with its constant distractions and pressures.

♦ Set up a training center. A manager should offer instruction on the new computer system and its applications *on company time*.

♦ Offer incentives for improved performance. Reward teams of employees (if possible) for increased productivity. Recognition can be as effective as money.

♦ Set up controls. A system of controls ensures that the company will get the most from its computers.

*C*hoosing Software and Hardware

SOFTWARE CONSIDERATIONS

♦ Outline the major business software applications, identify guidelines for buying computer hardware, and explain the hardware issues entrepreneurs face.

Without the right software to accomplish the tasks the owner has defined, a business owner might as well use a computer as a doorstop. Choosing the proper software: whether off-the-shelf or customized—to do the job at hand determines the ultimate success of a computer system.

Small business owners can purchase software for practically any application: from simple spreadsheets or word processors to more complex inventory control systems and 3-D design packages. Over the years, computer software has become more powerful and much easier to use. The learning curve for most programs is much less steep than before because most software makers give their programs the same look and use the same commands and keystrokes even though the software packages perform different functions. Computer users are able to transfer their knowledge from one program to another more readily, so training is faster and less expensive. We turn now to the programs small business owners use most often: word processing, accounting, database management, spreadsheets, graphics, communications, and software suites (see Figure 18.4).

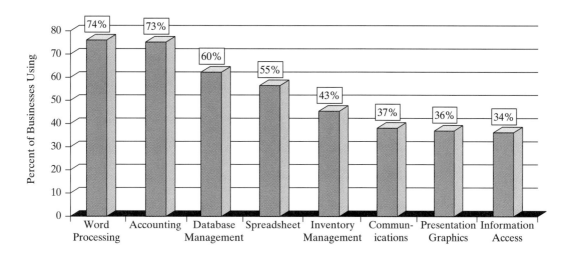

Figure 18.4 **Software Applications in Small Businesses** Source: "More Than Meets the IBM," *Business Start–Ups, August 1997, p. 6.*

Word Processing. The most popular business (and home) application for personal computers is word processing. Some experts estimate that word processing is the primary use for 75 percent of all computer systems. Modern word processors follow a "what you see is what you get" ("WYSIWYG") philosophy; the system will print out just what you see on the screen. Most come with helpful features such as spell checkers, grammar checkers, a thesaurus, and an HTML (Hypertext Markup Language) converter, which translates documents into HTML format for publication on the World Wide Web. *The owner of a small eco-retail company uses a standard word processor to publish a quarterly newsletter, which he sends to his customers. Each newsletter is filled with information of interest to the company's customers: from herbal and homeopathic remedies and organic food products to all-natural clothing and nature CDs. He also uses the HTML conversion feature to transfer the newsletter into a format ready for the World Wide Web. Within minutes, the newsletter appears on his company's Web site. Both the newsletter and the Web site have become important marketing tools for the small company.* Popular word-processing programs include Microsoft Word for Windows, Lotus Word Pro, WordPerfect, PFS: Professional Write, Displaywrite, MacWrite, and Office Writer.

Accounting. A large number of small business owners are running their accounting functions in-house on personal computers. Software packages can handle a company's general ledger, accounts payable and receivable, inventory control, purchasing, and financial statement preparation much faster and more accurately than manual systems.[24] That means entrepreneurs have more time to focus on developing their business ideas and selling their products and services. Plus, these programs save businesses money on their professional accounting fees by keeping their financial transactions and records more organized. They also are a tremendous help when tax season rolls around. Most accounting packages allow business owners to customize the software to their specific industries and offer Internet access to handle on-line banking transactions. There are two types of accounting software: modular and integrated. A **modular program** is built around a specific accounting application (such as accounts receivable) and can be used alone or combined with other modules. A complete accounting system built from modules is more expensive than an integrated system, but it usually is more flexible. In addition, owners can choose only those modules they need in their accounting systems.

An **integrated package** is a comprehensive accounting system that usually operates from the transactions entered through the general ledger. Once the owner enters transactions into the general ledger, the integrated accounting package automatically posts them to the appropriate subprogram.

A small business owner can spend as little as $50 for an accounting program that will perform the complete accounting function. More than 500 accounting programs are on the market; some of the most popular ones are 4-in-1 Basic Accounting, MYOB, The Accounting Partner, QuickBooks, Simply Accounting, Accpac Easy Accounting Series, Bedford Integrated Accounting, Business Works PC, One-Write Plus, Peachtree Complete Accounting, Profit, ACT-1, Dac Easy Accounting, MICA IV, BPI Enterprise, Back to Basics, and Interconnect Software's modular package.

Mark Kettler, office manager for Kettler Casting, a family-owned iron-products manufacturing company, relies on a high-end modular accounting system to control the company's finances. Kettler and two employees use the MICA IV accounting package to track receivables, prepare payroll, maintain the general ledger, and produce financial statements. Although more expensive than many standard off-the-shelf accounting programs, MICA IV is worth the extra money because it is better suited to Kettler Casting's business, according to Kettler. "Without the computer system, we would have to have two more people in the office to handle all the bookwork that comes through here," says Kettler. Because the company operates a local area network, any number of employees can use the accounting software simultaneously.[25]

Database Management. These programs are the equivalent of electronic file folders and file cabinets. A computer file is merely a collection of individual records, such as a customer list or a schedule of a company's inventory. Database programs enable business owners to translate large volumes of pure data into manageable, meaningful information they can use to make more-informed business decisions. They can provide entrepreneurs with the answers to questions that no manual system can begin to address. Database management programs record information into *fields*, which are accumulated into *records*, which, in turn, are compiled into *files*. Business owners can comb through large numbers of files to gather necessary information in just seconds; performing the same function by hand frequently is impossible or would require too much time to be practical. For example, with a database program, an owner could quickly search his entire list of accounts receivable to find those customers whose accounts have balances of $100 or more and are more than 30 days past due. Most database programs also permit users to transfer data from a database file to other programs (such as spreadsheets).

Maurice Badler, owner of Maurice Badler Fine Jewelry in New York City, uses database software to gain a distinct competitive advantage over other jewelers in the area. Badler's uses the software to cull important demographic information from his company's database; then he purchases large demographic mailing lists from list brokers and uses the program to sift through the lists to identify those household that could afford his fine jewelry. The result: an average order size of $1,000, more than five times the revenue an average catalog order generates. That gives Badler a $15 average profit per catalog mailed, a number that places Badler's catalog among the most profitable in the entire United States![26]

As Maurice Badler's experience indicates, database management programs are spreading quickly because of their flexibility, speed, capabilities, and ease of use. Popular packages include Microsoft Access, Lotus Approach, Act!, Q&A, dbase, Alpha Four, PFS: Professional File, R:Base 5000, Reflex, PC File, Paradox, Knowledgeman, Dayflo, Data Ease, and FileMaker Pro.

Spreadsheets. Electronic spreadsheets have remained a popular application since VisiCorp introduced the first spreadsheet, VisiCalc, in 1979. A spreadsheet is simply a grid of rows and columns, much like an accountant's pad. Entrepreneurs can enter data, text, and formulas into the cells on the spreadsheet. Once they set up the format of the spreadsheet, entrepreneurs can take advantage of its powerful "what if" capacity. They can evaluate the outcome of various scenarios and assumptions (called sensitivity analysis) merely by changing the appropriate cell value and pushing a button. For example, a business owner can determine the effects of various product prices on the company's bottom line in just a matter of seconds.

Spreadsheets allow an owner to enter data, create formulas, format cells, copy and move entries, and produce a variety of graphs. They also include routine arithmetic and statistical calculations and valuable financial functions (present value, future value, loan payments, etc.). Most spreadsheet programs also provide the ability to perform basic database operations (although these are not nearly as powerful as those in an actual database program).

Popular spreadsheet packages include Microsoft Excel for Windows, Lotus 1-2-3, Quattro Pro, SuperCalc, PFS: Professional Plan, PC-Calc, Perfect Calc, Multiplan, Wingz, Framework, and Enable. By using the "ready-made" functions and features of a spreadsheet, entrepreneurs can create customized sheets to help them manage practically every part of their business, from benefit packages in human resources and cash flow in finance to accounts payable in accounting and raw materials inventory in production. *Camelot Enterprises, a music store chain, uses Lotus 1-2-3 to manage its daily operations. "We use [the spreadsheet] for a lot of accounting-specific business tasks, from tracking sales store by store to sorting warehousing data and other types of analytical information on the retail end," says information manager Jay Chapman.*[27]

Presentation Graphics. Businesses that need basic graphics capability (bar and line graphs or pie charts) may find that a spreadsheet program meets their needs. But for more sophisticated graphs, business owners turn to specialized presentation graphics programs. These packages can transform a personal computer into a professional slide presentation that looks as though a Madison Avenue advertising agency put it together. A presentation designed with one of these programs can include special effects such as transitions between slides (fades, blinds, wipes, etc.), clip art, animated graphics, photographs, video clips, sound bites, and many others. Popular presentation graphics packages include Microsoft PowerPoint, Astound, Lotus Freelance Plus, Harvard Graphics, Windows Draw, Draw Applause, GEM Presentation, 35mm Express, PFS:Graph, Boardroom Graphics, Chart-Master, Graphease, Super Chartman, Frame-Up, and Executive Briefing.

Communications. Communications programs enable small business owners to use their computers to communicate with other computers and to send both faxes and e-mail messages. All that is necessary is a modem, which links the computer to the telephone line. With this system, owners can use computer linkups, remote computer terminals, and large databases such as CompuServe, Prodigy, or the Dow-Jones News/Retrieval service, and, of course, the World Wide Web from almost anywhere.

Telecommunications packages enable owners to tap into their own company's databases from remote locations and to exchange information with branch offices or sales representatives in the field. They also provide automatic telephone dialing and answering, electronic mailbox services, and access to an unbelievable amount of up-to-the-minute information on a wide variety of topics. Popular communications and e-mail programs include LapLink, HotOffice, Smartcom II, Eudora Pro, Pegasus Mail, Claris Em@iler, Crosstalk, Datapath, Passport, PFS: Access, Starlink, Lync, Micro Phone, and Dyna-Comm.

Kirby Knight, CEO of San Luis Sausage Company, counts many restaurants, hotels, and resorts in a 10-state area among his company's customers. Like many entrepreneurs working hard to grow their companies, Knight spends lots of time on the road trying to land

Kirby Knight, CEO of San Luis Sausage Company, relies on a multitude of technological tools to maintain control over his business. Whether he is in his office or on the road, Knight has access to the same information, thanks to his collection of high-tech equipment.

new accounts; yet, it is important that he stay in touch with his office. To accomplish that, Knight uses a laptop computer equipped with LapLink communications software. From his hotel room or anywhere else that has a telephone connection, Knight can access the personal computer on his desktop and control it as if he were sitting in front of it. Although he and his wife, Grace, who develops all of the company's recipes, may be in different cities, they can work on the same file or document at the same time. Knight routinely uses LapLink to transfer price lists, spreadsheets, presentations, and other data among his laptop, his office computer, and his home computer. "As entrepreneurs, one thing we have going for us over a large company is that we can make decisions and change gears quickly," he says. Asked if the software saves him money, Knight shakes his head and says, "No. It helps me make money."[28]

World Wide Web Browsers. The proliferation of the World Wide Web (WWW) as a business tool has led to the development of software packages designed to make exploring the Web much easier and more efficient. Two software packages dominate this market segment: Netscape Navigator and Microsoft Explorer. With these packages, entrepreneurs use the Web to conduct market research, study their competitors, learn about trends in their industries, locate sources of financing, manage their companies' cash, and perform a host of other important activities. In addition to enabling users to search the Web productively, these programs also offer extras such as real-time video conferencing, news-clipping services, built-in search engines, and secure electronic transactions.

World Wide Web Page Design. Once they have surfed the Web and have seen the tremendous marketing potential it has for their own companies, entrepreneurs quickly become interested in posting their own Web sites in cyberspace. Modern Web page design programs help them create eye-catching, innovative Web sites *without* having to invest huge blocks of time learning some arcane computer language. Although the language of the World Wide Web, HTML (Hypertext Markup Language) is not that difficult to master, most entrepreneurs have neither the time nor the inclination to do so. The good news is that these programs allow users to create documents and files for their Web sites using standard programs (such as the word processors, spreadsheets, and presentation graphics packages described earlier) and then automatically handle the HTML coding "behind the scenes."

Approximately 70,000 small business owners in the United States are doing business online, and the number is growing daily.[29] The sheer number of potential customers on the World Wide Web and the money they are spending are driving entrepreneurs' move into cyberspace. Forrester Research estimates that some 52 million people (up from 27 million in 1996) are now on the WWW, which means that the Web is fast gaining mass media status.[30] Web shoppers now spend more than $10 billion a year![31] The profile of these Web surfers is extremely attractive to businesses of all sizes; they are educated, wealthy, and young. The proportion of female Web users is climbing, now standing at 40 percent, up from just 5 percent in 1994.[32] Figure 18.5 gives a profile of those on the WWW by age. Companies are discovering that their Web shoppers are beginning to resemble closely their in-store shoppers, and those shoppers are looking for a broader range of products and services. In addition to computers, books, and music that have always sold well on the Web, products such as clothing, tools, and jewelry are now big sellers.[33] "On-line shopping is hitting the mainstream, and real, honest-to-goodness, ordinary people are shopping on-line," says Andrew Kantor, editor of *Internet Shopper*, an on-line magazine.[34]

Popular Web design programs include Microsoft FrontPage, Adobe PageMill, Claris Home Page, IBM's HomePage Creator, and NetObjects Fusion. Entrepreneurs are capitalizing on the power of this easy-to-use Web design software to give on-line customers ready ac-

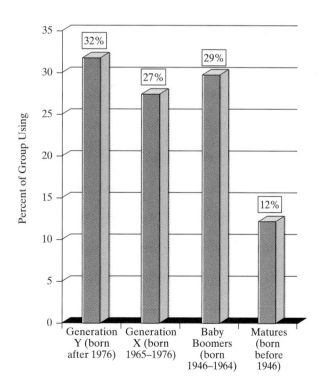

Figure 18.5 **Who's Online, by Generation** SOURCE: Yankelovich Partners/Cyber Dialogue, 1997.

cess to their products and services and to information about their companies. In the process, they are discovering the many advantages virtual stores offer. Virtual stores are open 24 hours a day, 365 days a year, so shoppers can visit at their convenience. Entrepreneurs with Web sites can make money while they sleep. In addition, the Web provides unparalleled exposure for small businesses by opening their cyberdoors to customers all across the globe. Stores in cyberspace also do not require a staff of expensive employees. In fact, cyberstores have another major cost advantage over traditional brick-and-mortar stores: no need for bricks or mortar!

The more he heard about the World Wide Web, the more Brian Bennett became convinced that his company, Culinary Software Services, was missing out on a significant marketing opportunity. Culinary Software Services sells software designed specifically for the needs of chefs, restaurant owners, and other food-service professionals. "Everything I had been reading in the computer and restaurant press told me I needed to get up on the Web," he says. Bennett's first foray onto the Web, the result of a bartering agreement with a Web site designer, was less successful than he had hoped. The trial site had only three pages of basic information and drew an average of just 24 hits a day. Bennett decided to revamp the Web site himself. "I wanted to have not only our business information up there but also value-added content like recipes, glossaries, and conversion charts," he says. "I figured I could develop a Web site where the revenue would pay for our expenses, but only if I could keep the initial outlay low."

He did. Bennett paid $100 to register his domain name <http://www.culinarysoftware. com> and pays $100 a month to the site's host. The payoff was immediate; the number of hits on the new site quickly reached 146 a day. Within four months, the site was generating more than 18,000 hits a month and accounted for 15 percent of the company's revenues. "The best part of the business we do over the Web is that it's all new revenue," says Bennett. "Fifteen percent of the business we do over the Web is international business, so now we're getting sales from customers we could never have reached without the Web site. As a new part of our marketing mix, the Web has become significant to our business. If I had known it was going to be so successful, I would have done it a lot earlier."[35]

Project Management. Project management software is designed to help small business managers plan and control the intermediate steps in completing large projects: introducing new products, entering new markets, launching businesses. Once the manager outlines the basic steps in the project and identifies their priorities, the computer programs calculate the start and finish dates for each task and for the whole project. They also track the resources required and account for total project costs. In addition, these programs highlight the project's critical path: those tasks that must be completed on time if the entire project is to remain on schedule. (These tasks are most sensitive to delays.) Finally, project management systems flag those tasks that lack sufficient resources for on-time completion. Most of them rely on graphics to present the flow of the entire project. Common project management programs include Harvard Total Project Manager, MacProject, Time Line, and Microsoft Project 4.0.

Software Suites. A **software suite** is an integrated collection of programs from a single maker that look alike; use similar commands, menus, and icons; and interact more smoothly than a set of similar programs from different software companies mixed and matched together. Software suites typically contain a word processor, a spreadsheet, a database, and a presentation graphics package: all of the standard applications a small company needs most. By purchasing a suite, entrepreneurs can save money compared with purchasing each application separately. In fact, 75 percent of word processors and 85 percent of spreadsheets are sold as part of software suites.[36] The most popular suites include Microsoft Office, Lotus Smart Suite, and Corel WordPerfect Suite.

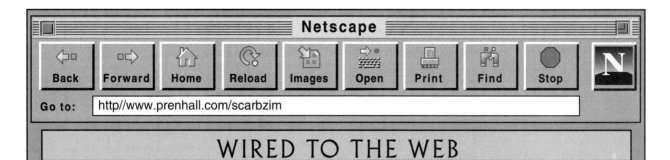

WIRED TO THE WEB

THE FRUIT OF THE VIRTUAL VINEYARD

*B*ill Knight, owner of the Wine House, a 19,000 square-foot retail wine shop in Los Angeles, has found a very inexpensive way to boost his company's sales and profits: the World Wide Web. Seeing the Web's potential as a marketing tool, Knight established his company's site in 1995 to complement the retail operation and the Wine House direct-mail catalog. Visitors to the site <http://www.winehouse.com> can browse through its 32 pages to choose from the Wine House's on-line catalog of 500 wines, read reviews of wines from experts, and get tips on the fine points of the art of wine tasting. Guests can even e-mail questions about wine selection for a particular dish, and a Wine House associate will recommend just the right vintage. Not long after the site premiered, it began winning praise from both customers and Web experts. One on-line magazine recently rated the Wine House as one of its top site picks.

To make sure his site gets noticed, Knight has forged cross-marketing relationships with other wine-related sites such as WineAccess, which includes an on-line locator visitors can use to track down almost any wine. Knight, who pays a flat annual fee for his link to WineAccess, says the connection gives the Wine House "a lot more marketing power." He has also established links with Internet commerce sites such as Giftscape, which sells Wine House gift baskets, and the Bloomberg financial information network, which lists the Wine House as its in-house wine store. Knight's Bloomberg connection is a perfect way to reach many of his company's target customers.

Knight's philosophy for attracting visitors to the company's Web site is to provide lots of information. He says, "I think most serious wine hobbyists enjoy shopping in person at local stores, so an on-line or mail-order shop has to offer something special to justify going to that alternative." To encourage customers to order over the Web, Knight has added a secure server. Still, many customers shop for wines using the Web and then place their orders by phone.

Business from the Web site is beginning to pick up. Currently, Knight estimates that the Wine House receives about 30 on-line orders each month, a number he expects to grow significantly over time. Knight believes the Web is on the cusp of skyrocketing as a sales and marketing tool, and he is reinvesting most of the revenue the site generates into its development. He is developing plans to add a part-time employee to serve as in-house Webmaster, which will enable him to expand the site, to update it weekly rather than monthly, and to forge an association with another Web site, Verdistyle, which features information on cooking, gardening, and wine.

The Wine House is reaping many benefits from its Web site, including expanding its mailing list. The company mails a newsletter to about 22,000 customers 11 times a year. Because reaching customers through the Web site is so much more cost-efficient than mailing catalogs and newsletters, Knight hopes to eventually shift his marketing efforts more toward the Web.

Although measuring the gains from the Web site is difficult, Knight has no doubt that his investment in the Web is paying off. Since the site came on-line, sales revenue has climbed from $7 million to $10 million, and profits are also up. The site now gets about 20,000 hits a month, and the flow of traffic is rising rapidly. As electronic commerce becomes more common, Knight is convinced that his decision to get on the Web early will pay off many times over.

1. What benefits does marketing on the World Wide Web offer small businesses?
2. What barriers must companies selling products such as wine overcome when they sell over the World Wide Web?
3. What advice would you offer a small retailer whose company is not yet using the WWW as a marketing tool?

Source: Adapted from Tricia Curry, "Uncorked," *Computer Shopper Extra*, February 1998, pp. 21–23.

Winning rave reviews—and sales—from its Web site, the Wine House expects more sales to come from the World Wide Web in the future. To increase the number of "hits" the site receives, owner Bill Knight has established cross-marketing relationships with other wine-related Web sites.

Richard and Pamela Rhodes, co-owners of Rhodes Masonry, a business that designs and installs fountains, monuments, walls, and statues, rely on Microsoft Office to help them manage the mundane chores of running a busy office. They use the suite of programs to track revenues and expenses, prepare estimates, create letters, schedule projects, publish promotional pieces, plan delivery routes, and perform a host of other activities. The Rhodes say that the software allows them and their employees to complete the necessary office work efficiently, freeing them up to focus their time and energy on making the business successful. "We don't have time to learn software," says Richard. "We don't want to become computer experts in order to use our software." [37]

Industry-Specific Software. A growing number of small businesses are turning to industry-specific software to solve problems unique to their particular business. Designed to handle transactions and situations in a specific business, this software has increased productivity and streamlined procedures in a variety of industries. For example, one of the trickiest elements to manage in any retail business is inventory, and many software companies have developed programs to help. *The owner of a small ladies' clothing shop installed a point-of-sale system, which updates inventory records directly from cash register transactions. She has access to up-to-the-minute readings of what items are selling (or not selling); the result has been greatly improved cash flow and minimal under- and overstocking of key inventory items. She also has improved the company's inventory turnover ratio. "I'm well above the industry average now," she claims.*

HARDWARE CONSIDERATIONS

Perhaps no machine since the automobile has spawned a more intense love–hate relationship with its human users than the personal computer. The hatred often begins when small business owners set out to perform what they assume will be a "simple" task: buying a computer.

Although it sounds simple enough—like buying a toaster—buying a computer is no easy task, especially for computer novices. The computer hardware and software choices are virtually endless, and the "language" computer salespeople speak can be as foreign—and as intimidating—as ancient Greek. One expert claims, "The personal computer industry says it is moving toward making the machines as easy to use as toasters, but purchasing one is still more like buying a jet fighter than a household appliance."[38]

The key to picking the right computer is identifying which software packages a company will need; determining their speed, power, and peripheral requirements; and then matching the hardware to those requirements. Although there are no magic formulas for selecting the right hardware, the following guidelines will be helpful.

- *Do your homework before shopping for hardware.* Take the time to learn the basic components of a computer system and what they do. You don't have to become a computer technician, but you should be able to differentiate a CPU from a CD-ROM. A basic understanding of a computer's components will make finding the right hardware much easier.

- *Buy enough power and speed.* Computer processing speed and power accelerate faster than the space shuttle during takeoff, so keeping up with the latest in computer technology is virtually impossible. Fortunately, most business owners don't have to. Most small business applications do not require extraordinarily fast or powerful hardware to run them. A good rule here is to buy more power and speed than you currently need. A common "rookie" mistake is being lured in by a really low price and buying a computer system with insufficient memory, speed, and expansion capacity.

- *Plan for expansion.* Smart business owners get extra mileage out of their computers by buying hardware with expansion capabilities. As their machines age, they simply add more memory or swap out their processors for faster ones, extending their useful life. It is also a good idea to find out what is required to convert the independent PCs you buy today into a local area network tomorrow. The right hardware can make converting to a network much easier.

- *Keep it simple.* Avoid buying too much computer. You won't need a top-of-the-line super-PC to run basic a accounting program and a software suite. Also, try to avoid buying a hodge-podge of computer hardware. Remember: It only increases your total cost of ownership (TCO).

The accompanying Gaining the Competitive Edge feature describes some of the hardware basics a small business owner should know before buying a computer.

One hardware option many business owners choose is a laptop (or notebook or portable) computer. For entrepreneurs on the go, a notebook computer is an ideal choice because it gives them the power to work as if they were sitting at their desks from practically anywhere. With notebook computers, entrepreneurs can transform wherever they may be into their workplaces. Computer manufacturers produce three levels of notebook computers: Top-of-the-line systems are desktop PC replacements; "value" notebooks perform most of the same tasks as a desktop machine and have almost as much speed and power; and ultra-portable notebooks weigh just two to four pounds but, because of their smaller screens and keyboards, are not suitable as desktop replacements. The top-of-the-line computers are just that; they offer everything a desktop PC does, including speed, memory, and power, and their price tags (typically in the $5,000 to $7,000 range) reflect their capabilities. The value notebooks offer performance a notch below a desktop, but they still provide plenty of power to do what most entrepreneurs want to accomplish on the road. Their midrange prices of $2,000 to $4,000 make them extremely popular for small business applications. Ultra-portable notebooks are designed for entrepreneurs who want enough computing power to make presentations on the road, stay in touch with the office

What to Look for When Buying Computer Hardware

*T*oday, a small business owner who wants a computer system capable of handling virtually any task should consider purchasing the following equipment:

- A Pentium II processor that runs at 300 MHz or faster with at least 96 megabytes of RAM (which should be expandable)
- A hard disk drive with a capacity of at least 8 gigabytes
- A 56.6 kb per second fax modem for communications capability
- A noninterlaced super-VGA 15-inch color monitor with a dot pitch of at least 0.24 mm (easier on the eyes)
- At least one high-density (1.44 megabyte) 3^1/$_2$-inch floppy disk drive
- A 12x CD-ROM drive or DVD-ROM drive
- A tape backup system (to back up programs and data in case of a system "crash")

- A color printer (ink-jet, laser, or dot-matrix) capable of handling both text and graphics at a speed of at least 4 pages per minute with resolution of at least 600×600 dpi (dots per inch)
- A flatbed scanner with an automatic document feeder capable of inputting a page in no more than 3 minutes (for scanning photos, text, graphics, or anything else into documents)

As with the purchase of any technical piece of equipment, the small business owner must consider a computer's serviceability. Although computer reliability is increasing, computers occasionally break down. For some companies, a computer breakdown can interrupt the entire flow of business. Still, too many owners give little, if any, consideration to a computer's serviceability. Before purchasing a computer, the wise business manager will investigate the manufacturer's after-sale support. What happens when the computer breaks down? Will the vendor repair it, or must the owner return it to the manufacturer for repair? Does the computer come with a warranty? If so, what are its terms? Will the vendor offer a loaner machine until repairs are made? If not, how long can the business operate without the computer? What backup plan does the company have during a breakdown? Finally, the owner must remember that the lowest-priced computer may not be the best deal when it comes to service and support. ◆

from the field, and use basic software applications away from the office—all without being weighed down by heavy equipment. Their small keyboards make extensive typing a challenge, and their diminutive screens can be difficult to read.

At Medtronic Inc., a maker of devices used in surgical procedures (pacemakers, heart valves, angioplasty catheters, etc.), notebook computers have become lifesaving devices. Medtronic sales representatives are in a highly technical, high-stakes situation because they actually go into the operating room with surgeons to show them how to implant or use the company's equipment properly! Because sales representatives must understand proper techniques themselves and have no room for mistakes, training is essential to their success. Medtronic's first project was an interactive CD-ROM on the features, benefits, and proper usage of a heart valve. After studying the CD themselves, a few sales representatives equipped with their personal notebook computers went into doctors' offices, where they taught physicians about the valve. The project was so successful that, within two weeks, the company had equipped every Medtronic sales representative with a notebook computer. Almost overnight, the sales force was high-tech. Soon, sales representatives saw their job tasks changing, and their customers noticed the change too. No longer were they merely salespeople; they had become consultants and problem solvers to their customers (which made them more successful at their sales jobs). The company sees a promising future for notebook computers and multimedia applications in both sales and training. "With interactive multimedia, the computer evolves from being a tool in the communication process to a partner in the learning process," says one manager.[39]

As computer technology constantly improves, notebook computers continue to grow smaller, lighter, faster, and more powerful. In many instances, other than size and portability, there is little distinction between a desktop PC and a notebook computer. Figure 18.6 describes what entrepreneurs should look for in a notebook PC.

1. Motherboard
This is a plastic or fiberglass board containing circuits, chips, and sockets that control system performance. Tips: Keep upgrade options fully open by choosing a PC with eight memory module sockets, an "overdrive" socket for a faster central processing unit (CPU), and at least three open add-in-card slots, one or more of which are so-called local bus slots.

2. Central Processing Unit (CPU)
The CPU chip, or microprocessor, is a PC's silicon brain. The clock is a timing device that plays a big role in determining how fast the brain can "think." Tip: Intel's Pentium CPU with a clock speed of 300 megahertz (MHz) is today's best value for most business users.

3. Random Access Memory (RAM)
RAM is where programs and data are stored while you work with them. In general, the more RAM, the better the PC performs. Today's RAM usually comes in 4 megabyte (MB) or 8 MB packages of chips called single in-line memory modules (SIMM). Tip: To run Windows applications, get 96 MB or more.

4. Floppy-Disk Drive
Still the most convenient way to install software or share files. Tip: Save money and space by installing only a 3½-inch, high-density (1.44 MB) floppy drive, because almost all software comes on these disks now.

5. Hard-Disk Drive
The medium on which all programs and files are stored until you retrieve them. Integrated drive electronics (IDE) type drives are easier to install and cost less per megabyte of storage than others. Tip: Programs are getting incredibly large, bargain-priced drives abound, and replacing even an IDE drive is inconvenient. Get a disk bigger than you ever imagine filling–8 GB or larger.

6. CD-ROM Drive
This increasingly popular device plays platters that look like audio CDs but hold about 600 MB of data. Most new software will be shipped on these. Insist on 12X or faster drives; slower ones can drive you crazy.

7. Tape-Backup Drive
The easiest, least expensive way to back up hard-disk programs' data. Tip: Get one. Hard disks die; don't let your business records die as well.

8. Modem
A modem is a PC-to-telephone link that allows the tapping of electronic databases, sending and receiving electronic mail, and even sending and receiving faxes. It's an especially useful tool for home offices. Tip: Today's best values are data/fax modems that operate at 56,600 bits per second (bps).

9. Monitor
This is where PC and user meet face to face, and it's the wrong place to pinch pennies. For your eyes' sake, buy a bright, clear, flicker-free model. Tip: Unless you do lots of graphics, the best value is a 15- or 17-inch multiscan, noninterlaced (ni) monitor with a dot size (called dot pitch) of 0.24 millimeters and a refresh rate of at least 70 hertz.

10. Mouse
Windows programs have made standard equipment of this rolling device for pointing to objects on the monitor.

Source: Based on "Tips from *Nation's Business* for Pulling the PC Pieces Together," *Nation's Business*, April 1994, pp. 25–26.

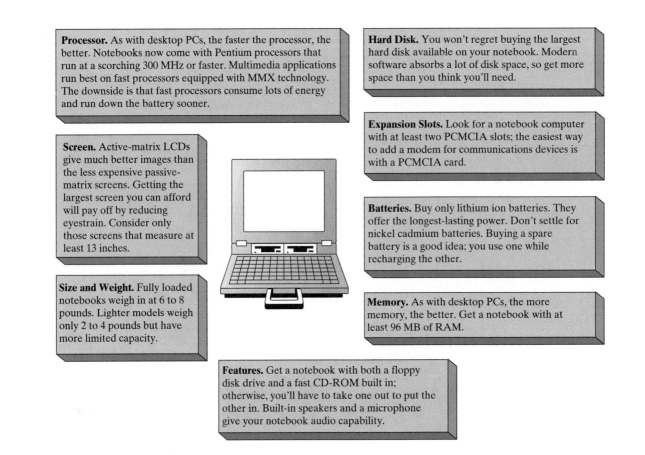

Processor. As with desktop PCs, the faster the processor, the better. Notebooks now come with Pentium processors that run at a scorching 300 MHz or faster. Multimedia applications run best on fast processors equipped with MMX technology. The downside is that fast processors consume lots of energy and run down the battery sooner.

Screen. Active-matrix LCDs give much better images than the less expensive passive-matrix screens. Getting the largest screen you can afford will pay off by reducing eyestrain. Consider only those screens that measure at least 13 inches.

Size and Weight. Fully loaded notebooks weigh in at 6 to 8 pounds. Lighter models weigh only 2 to 4 pounds but have more limited capacity.

Hard Disk. You won't regret buying the largest hard disk available on your notebook. Modern software absorbs a lot of disk space, so get more space than you think you'll need.

Expansion Slots. Look for a notebook computer with at least two PCMCIA slots; the easiest way to add a modem for communications devices is with a PCMCIA card.

Batteries. Buy only lithium ion batteries. They offer the longest-lasting power. Don't settle for nickel cadmium batteries. Buying a spare battery is a good idea; you use one while recharging the other.

Memory. As with desktop PCs, the more memory, the better. Get a notebook with at least 96 MB of RAM.

Features. Get a notebook with both a floppy disk drive and a fast CD-ROM built in; otherwise, you'll have to take one out to put the other in. Built-in speakers and a microphone give your notebook audio capability.

Figure 18.6 **The Well-Equipped Notebook Computer**   SOURCE: Adapted from "The Dream Notebook," *PC Magazine*, July 1997, p. 132; "Taking It with You," *Fortune Technology Buyer's Guide*, Winter 1998, pp. 81–86.

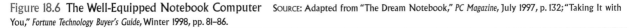

THE DARK SIDE OF COMPUTERS

Unfortunately, many small companies have discovered the dark side of computerization: electronic disasters and computer crime. Both problems have become more lethal as companies have grown more dependent on computer technology.

Electronic Disasters. Despite their dependence on technology, computer experts say most companies are ill-prepared to handle an electronic disaster. *For instance, when a fire knocked out computer telephone links at one office-products wholesaler, everything went down. Customers could not place orders, salespeople could not check inventory, and clerks couldn't even find pencils and other supplies in the company's vast warehouses.*[40]

Experts agree that the best ways to avoid becoming a victim of an electronic disaster are to always back up valuable data and to have an alternate plan in case the system crashes. Many computers include tape drives, which can back up data from floppy or hard disks quickly and easily. Most disk management programs include backup features, which *automatically* make copies (to tape or to disks) at a predetermined time. The wise business owner also will make arrangements for a backup computer system in case the computer goes down. When one retailer purchased a computer, she included a rental backup system in the deal. When her computer crashed, her business was running on the backup in less than two hours.

Computer Crime. According to Safeware, a computer-insurance firm, computer theft costs U.S. businesses about $1.5 billion each year.[41] That estimate likely is very conservative "because the victims do everything they can to hide the experience and to avoid reporting it," says one computer-crime fighter. "We are seeing only the tip of the iceberg." If only a few computer crimes are ever reported, even fewer are prosecuted; one study found that just 6 percent of those reported resulted in a criminal prosecution.[42]

Computer crime is on the rise because modern-day Bonnie and Clydes have discovered that they can steal more with a computer than with a gun. A recent study by the Computer Security Institute for the FBI revealed that 75 percent of the companies surveyed had been victims of computer-related crimes in the preceding year.[43] For years, only large corporations had to be concerned about computer crime. But, because of the rapid proliferation of personal computers and their more lax control procedures, small companies are the favorite target of electronic thieves. Computer networks and Internet access only compound the problem of computer security. The Computer Security Institute's study found that 49 percent of the companies surveyed had reported some type of unauthorized use of their computer systems within the past year. Even more alarming, more than 20 percent of the companies said that their systems provided no way of knowing if criminals had invaded their computers.[44]

Computer criminals get plenty of rewards for their illicit efforts. The FBI estimates that a computer thief nets $600,000 in the average job. According to one computer security specialist, "If you want to steal money and get away with it, use a computer and steal a lot."[45]

The computer has become the burglary tool of the electronic age. Despite the prominent media attention given to hackers (outsiders who illegally invade a company's computer system), the greatest threat to computer security comes from within. Security experts say that the most common cyberthieves are loyal employees who misuse the authority their employers' give them. Current employees have the greatest access to a company's computer systems and often know what security precautions, if any, are in place. Computer security specialists offer a profile of the potential inside computer criminal:

> *He or she is a trusted employee of long tenure, but has recently become a gambler, a boozer, or a helpless victim of love. He or she has a sick spouse, hungry kids. He or she is overwhelmed, most commonly by debt, but occasionally by an unappeasable longing for the rich life. He or she is disappointed, disgruntled, torn apart by resentment and envy. He or she is not just anyone—clerk, manager, teller, salesperson, friend, relative, or anyone in the stockroom—but anyone, under certain circumstances, could be he or she.[46]*

When MC², a network consulting company in Warren, New Jersey, was forced to abandon its building after the roof collapsed in a blizzard, it moved to a temporary, hastily outfitted location. While the company was at the unsecure location, an engineer found a way to log into MC²'s network from his home computer. Shortly afterward, he left the company but maintained the illicit computer connection. Soon he was stealing confidential documents concerning MC²'s projects and personnel matters and forwarding them to employees still at the company. He even sent sensitive customer information to a friend at one of MC²'s competitors, which used the information to win over several of MC²'s clients. Executives at MC² did not discover that the former employee had broken into their computer network for two months. By then, the stolen messages and data had cost the company more than $1 million in lost business.[47]

Sabotage is another worry for the small business owner. *Three weeks after Omega Engineering Company in Stamford, Connecticut fired a network programmer, a software bomb the former employee had planted in the company's computer system destroyed data estimated to be worth $10.4 million![48]*

The recent proliferation of viruses has alarmed many computer users. The National Computer Security Association (NCSA) estimates that 67 percent of U.S. companies have their computers infected by viruses each year.[49] Like a biological virus, a computer virus invades a system and attacks it, destroying data and wrecking programs. Viruses are to computer systems what Freddie Krueger is to Elm Street! Designed by insidious hackers, these viruses are disguised in other programs available on the World Wide Web. They invade a computer system when the unsuspecting user downloads what appears to be an innocent-looking file. One virus can disable an entire computer system in no time! At the end of 1997, the NCSA estimated that more than 16,000 computer viruses existed, and that number was growing daily![50]

To avoid virus problems, entrepreneurs should make sure that their computers are equipped with the latest virus detection programs, which should run automatically *every* time the computer boots up. Popular antivirus programs include VirusShield and NetShield (McAfee Associates), Norton Antivirus (Symantec Corporation), and Interscan VirusWall and ScanMail (Trend Micro Inc.). Because new viruses pop up every day, it is important to download the latest versions of these virus detection programs at least once a month. Many of these programs not only detect viruses but also disarm them. Entrepreneurs should download files from the Internet and the World Wide Web with caution; it is best to test downloaded files with a vaccination program before using them. Figure 18.7 shows that virus infection leads the list of problems in companies experiencing financial losses from computer-related criminal activities.

Most computer security experts agree that the key to computer security is *people*, and that requires *education*. Improperly trained people are the weakest link in any company's computer security system. A common problem is that some employees innocently give classified information to outsiders who claim to be systems analysts or consultants.

Encouraging employees to maintain security standards on a daily basis is crucial to the success of a security system. Occasionally, every small business manager should conduct a walkthrough inspection to ensure that employees are following security procedures. Another key is avoiding reliance on a single form of security. The ideal system uses two independent methods in tandem. In general, the type of security system a small business owner chooses depends on the cost of security devices, the impact of potential data losses on the company, and the way the system affects employee productivity. Although no security system is fool-

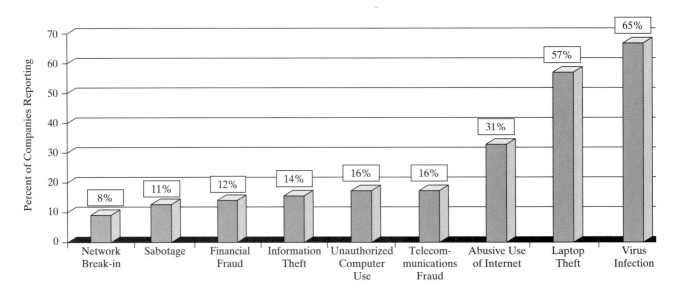

Figure 18.7 **High-Tech Criminal Activity** SOURCE: Computer Security Institute, 1997.

proof, the small business manager who uses a balanced approach will protect data adequately without alienating honest employees.

Other Technology Choices

5 Discuss the peripheral equipment, such as printers, scanners, digital cameras, and personal digital assistants, that enhances the performance of the computer.

Many other items enhance the performance of computers in small businesses. The most common pieces of peripheral equipment include printers, scanners, digital cameras, and personal digital assistants.

PRINTERS

The much-heralded "paperless office" that many experts predicted the computer era would produce has yet to materialize. Indeed, it seems that, if anything, computers generate more paper in a work environment! Printers also give small business owners much more flexibility than ever before. Today, entrepreneurs can generate documents, signs, fliers, and advertisements on their own printers that they once had to get professional print shops to design and produce. The almost endless array of fonts, point sizes, and clip art printers can give business owners the ability to create practically anything they can imagine. Printer choices range from simple monochrome inkjet printers costing little more than $100 to full-color laser printers priced at more than $6,000. Selecting the ideal printer for a business boils down to determining exactly its printing needs. Will you need to print in color? Will you have several computers linked to a single network printer? Will you be printing high-volume jobs? Will you primarily print black-and-white text documents? Answering these questions will help entrepreneurs choose among the four basic types of printers: inkjet printers, monochrome laser printers, color laser printers, and network printers.

Inkjet Printers. Business owners who need to print in color but have limited budgets should consider buying an inkjet printer. Color inkjet printers spray colored ink onto a variety of paper types, ranging from plain paper to clear transparency film. Their low prices (plain black-and-white printers start at a little more than $100, and color printers are available for less than $200) and versatility make them popular choices for small business owners. Because the ink cartridges they use are expensive ($25 to $35 for color cartridges), inkjet printers have a relatively high cost per page and are not the best choice for high-volume printing needs.

Monochrome Laser Printers. The workhorse printer in most business environments remains the monochrome laser printer, which uses a laser to "burn" images onto paper and clear transparency film. Although they are more expensive than inkjet printers (starting at about $300 and going up to $3,000), laser printers are much faster, print higher-quality text, and cost less on a per-page basis. They provide 600 to 1,200 dpi (dots per inch) resolution at speeds of up to 24 pages a minute. For business purposes, six pages a minute is the minimum speed to consider. These characteristics make laser printers ideal for text documents and for high-volume printing.

Color Laser Printers. Color laser printers produce color images with the same high resolution that monochrome laser printers do; however, their costs are significantly higher, starting at around $3,000. They also tend to run more slowly than monochrome laser printers, typically at two to six pages a minute. Companies that print large volumes of graphical images would benefit from a color laser printer. Because they are more expensive to purchase and to maintain, color laser printers have a high cost per page.

Bob Perkins, CEO of La Fonda Restaurant in Artesia, New Mexico, bought a color laser printer for $6,300 to give his company more flexibility. Before buying the printer,

Perkins relied on a professional printer to produce its brightly colored menus. Unfortunately, printing costs were so high that La Fonda could not update its menu or change its prices as often as Perkins thought necessary. Perkins also wanted the ability to experiment with different label designs on the line of jalapeños and salsa La Fonda sells to local grocery stores. Perkins designs different labels on his PC and prints them on the color laser printer so he can conduct market tests to see which labels sell the best before he commits to buying large quantities of labels from a commercial label-printing company. Perkins also uses the printer to produce colorful promotional materials and special menus for holidays, events, and groups.[51]

Network Printers. Businesses that want to have a central printer networked to multiple computers should choose a network printer. These printers usually are high-volume monochrome laser printers specially configured to handle the flow of documents channeled to them from multiple sources. Their prices normally start at around $2,000 and can go up to more than $6,000.

The key determinant of the print quality from any printer is resolution, which is measured by the number of dots per inch (dpi). The higher the resolution a printer offers, the better is its print quality. For business purposes, 600 dpi is the minimum standard. Sufficient memory is also important in selecting a printer. Printing photographs and other graphic images requires more memory than plain text. For most business applications, a printer with 512 kb to 2 MB of memory is sufficient. A network printer needs at least 2 MB of memory.

SCANNERS

Scanners, once reserved only for graphics design houses or newspapers, are now common office tools in businesses of all types. Scanners allow entrepreneurs to make a "digital copy" of an image or a document, which they can then edit, download into other files, or post on Web pages. *For instance, the owner of a small flower shop scans photographs of some of the arrangements she designs for weddings, banquets, and other special occasions and puts them into a newsletter she mails to her customers and to those she hopes to attract as customers. Her newsletter recently helped her land an account with a corporation that has a tradition of keeping unique arrangements of fresh flowers in its headquarters.*

Entrepreneurs can purchase either sheet-fed scanners or flatbed scanners. A flatbed scanner operates much like a photocopier. The user places a document or graphic image on the scanning bed; the scanner head moves down the page, reading the image and transferring it into a digital format. Because of their design, flatbed scanners can read images from single sheets, books, magazines, and a host of other media. Prices start at about $200 and go up to $2,000, depending on the features and the resolution included. Sheet-fed scanners take up much less space on a desktop than flatbed scanners, but they can accept only single-sheet documents or images. They are much cheaper, however, selling from $150 to $350, and are suitable for most small business or home office needs.

As with printers, an important feature to watch for when shopping for a scanner is its resolution. The higher the resolution, the more detail a scanner can provide. For business applications, a scanner should have a resolution of at least 300 dpi. Entrepreneurs should also pay attention to the software that is bundled with a scanner. A good scanner should include software that enables a user to scan both images and text. For text, the scanner should include optical character recognition (OCR) software that transforms the scanned text into a document that any standard word processing package can read and edit.

DIGITAL CAMERAS

On the surface, digital cameras resemble traditional cameras, but inside they are very different. Unlike traditional 35 mm cameras, digital cameras use no film; instead, they capture images in digital codes onto either standard floppy disks or removable memory cards. Most digital cameras are equipped with small color display screens that allow photographers to view their photos immediately. If a photo is not suitable, you simply delete it and try again! These cameras also connect to any computer so that photographers can download their images, view them on the monitor, and even edit them using software such as PictureIt! (Microsoft), LivePix (LivePix Software), Photo Suite (MGI Software), Kai's Photo Soap (MetaCreations), and PhotoDeluxe (Adobe). Most digital cameras include a video-out port, with which users can display their images directly on a television monitor or through a VCR. Some even have the capacity to send images directly from the camera to a printer without going through a computer. The quality of the images a digital camera can produce depends on its resolution; the minimum any entrepreneur should consider is 640 by 480 resolution. A good digital camera also should have the ability to store at least 60 images and should have a flash. An LCD viewfinder that allows photographers to see their pictures and rechargeable batteries also are helpful features. Digital cameras are in the $400 to $700 price range, but professional-quality cameras with high resolutions and lots of extra features can easily exceed $1,000.

Thomas Garrett, owner of Executive Fashions in New York City, uses a digital camera to take photographs of his customers' clothing purchases. He stores the photographs in every customer's personal profile, giving him the equivalent of a photograph of each customer's closet. With the help of a database, Garrett can call up the photographs in a customer's profile, review them, and offer suggestions for accessories and future clothing purchases. The system "allows us not only [to] sell wardrobes but to plan them," says Garrett.[52]

PERSONAL DIGITAL ASSISTANTS AND PAGERS

Small, hand-held devices such as personal digital assistants (PDAs) and pagers make it easy for entrepreneurs to keep up with their business from practically anywhere: their cars, a hotel room, the beach, wherever! Personal digital assistants are a combination of personal computer, appointment book, pager, organizer, and fax machine—all rolled into one wireless device that fits in the palm of your hand. (In fact, they are sometimes called palmtop computers.) A user can enter information into a PDA with either a stylus or a small keyboard. Entrepreneurs routinely use these devices to organize their daily schedules, to send and receive e-mail, to track appointments, and even to create simple spreadsheets (on Pocket Excel) and word-processing documents (on Pocket Word) or make presentations (on Pocket PowerPoint) while away from their offices. Personal digital assistants are compatible with either PCs or Apple computers. Those equipped to connect to PCs run Windows CE, a compact version of the desktop operating system familiar to millions of computer users. The newest versions of PDAs come with color screens, fast processors, large memories (up to 16 MB of RAM), high storage capacity, and speakers, all of which make them the most portable of portable computers. Some manufacturers now offer PDAs that incorporate cellular phones as well. Prices range from $250 to $1,000 for PDAs.

Although PDAs incorporate many of the same features as standard portable computers, they are not intended to be portable computer substitutes. Their small size limits their ability to function as full-fledged PCs. For instance, touch-typing on the Chiclet-like keys of a PDA is impossible. When choosing a PDA, entrepreneurs should decide exactly how they intend to use the devices: as a simple pocket organizer and communication tool or as a more versatile (and more costly) hand-held computer. Those who want to use a PDA as a communications device will need to buy one with a modem and must be sure that the PDA is compatible with their desktop computer. With a modem-equipped PDA, an entrepreneur can send and receive e-mail and download information from the World Wide Web.

Tony Castle, president of the Castle Group, a technology consulting firm, uses a PDA to improve his company's level of customer service. When he gets a call on his cellular phone, Castle reaches for his PDA and, using its contact management software, calls up a

WIRED TO THE WEB

POST IT, AND THEY WILL COME

*T*ia Branerd, owner of Tie One On, a small chain of retail stores selling neckties, couldn't help but wonder if Mel Gadsden, one of her part-time employees, was right.

"I'm telling you, Tia," he said. "The World Wide Web is the place you need to be. That's where the future of retailing is!"

Tia wondered how much of Mel's idea was youthful enthusiasm and how much was sound business advice. Mel was still in college, but Tia knew that he was extremely bright and had a knack for business. She was glad to have him working at Tie One On while he was in school and hoped to hire him on a full-time basis after his graduation from the local college.

Tia trusted Mel's opinions. She had spotted his business acumen early on after he had come to her with an idea for a location of another Tie One On center. He had done all of the market research as part of a project in a marketing class, and when Tia saw the results, she knew he was right. After building the new store, Tia watched it reach the break-even point faster than any of her other locations had, and it was now one of her top-grossing stores.

"I've been studying the Web for more than a year now," Mel told her. "I'm also taking a course this semester on how to develop a Web site. We're learning how to develop Web pages using both HTML and software packages such as FrontPage and Page Mill. It's not nearly as hard as it looks. In fact, it's pretty easy once you get the hang of it!" Tia could see Mel's enthusiasm for another project bubbling up again.

"Let me guess," she laughed. "You've got another assignment like that marketing project except this time you have to develop a Web site, right?"

"Well, yeah," said Mel, "but that's beside the point. With the right kind of Web site, you could sell a whole lot of ties on the Web. Imagine what a hit your line of novelty ties would be with customers on the Web. The Star Trek and Star Wars designs would be a big hit, and so would the cartoon character ties and the ones with the nature scenes."

"What makes you so sure?" said Tia. "I've heard that the Web is dominated by computer nerds, and you know those guys don't wear ties!"

"Tia, the Web is now a mainstream marketing tool," Mel said with a touch of exasperation. "E-commerce totals more than $10 billion a year, and it's growing fast. I've got some studies here to prove it. Look!" he said, shoving a fistful of reports her way.

"OK," said Tia. "I'll take your word for it. But if you design a Web site for Tie One On, how do we get it posted on the Web? How much will it cost? What kind of upkeep is required? What will we put on our site? Can people order over the Web? Even if they can, *will* they?"

Tia paused to catch her breath. "I have a few hundred more questions, but those will do for now," she said with a grin.

"Post it, and they will come," said Mel.

"They'd better, or I may have to fire you," Tia joked. "One more question, though. Just what does a good Web site look like? Or maybe I should ask: What does a *bad* Web site look like?"

1. Use the resources of the library and the World Wide Web to convince Tia that she should consider setting up a Web site and to answer Tia's question about doing business on the Web.
2. Again using your research, write a brief report describing for Tia what a good Web site looks like. Go to the Web, locate a sight that meets your criteria, and include some of its screens in your report.
3. Search the Web for a sight that you consider to be poorly designed. Prepare a short report on it and include some of its screens in your report. [Hint: Try <http://www.websitesthatsuck.com> for some leads.]

file of the customer's complete history with the company. Castle says the PDA has become his "pocket virtual office" and is a valuable business tool.[53]

For entrepreneurs for whom a PDA is more computing power than they need on the road, a pager may be the ideal solution. Pagers still provide the easiest and most timely way to communicate with the office. Pagers that handle both phone numbers and text messages are priced at less than $100. High-end pagers provide entrepreneurs with the ability to not only receive information but to transmit it as well.

Telephone, Voice Mail, and E-mail Technology

TELEPHONE TECHNOLOGY

Discuss the role of communications technology, such as the telephone, voice mail, and e-mail, in small companies.

Within the next several years, no communication device will undergo more changes than the telephone. That reliable instrument sitting on the desk is already beginning its transformation from a relatively dumb device into a computerized communications tool with video capability to enhance its current audio capacity. Screen phones (or video phones) have built-in monitors that allow entrepreneurs to conduct video conferences with customers and business associates around the world without ever leaving their offices. These phones also provide the ability to send and receive e-mail messages and to access the latest business news or sports scores. As technological advances improve the performance of screen phones, expect them to work more like digital personal assistants. Entrepreneurs shopping for a screen phone should ask about the following:

◆ Compatibility with standard e-mail services

◆ Other Internet applications that are available

◆ The phone's ability to download files

◆ The ability to attach a full-size computer keyboard

◆ Which Internet service providers the system can access[54]

Like their desktop cousins, cellular phones are undergoing an identity transformation, taking on the role of tiny portable computers that do much more than make telephone calls. The latest models of these "smart phones" come with small screens that can display e-mail and fax messages and information from the World Wide Web. Some models also double as personal digital assistants and have small keyboards that allow users to input data and infrared ports for wireless hookups with PCs to download data. More than 43 million people across the United States now use cellular phones, and that number grows by 30,000 every day![55]

VOICE MAIL

Although voice mail systems record messages just as telephone answering machines do, they offer many more features. They have the ability to take calls while an entrepreneur is on the phone with another call, preventing customers from experiencing annoying busy signals. They also offer multiple voice mailboxes, pager notification, and the ability to check messages from remote locations. These features can be especially important to small businesses because they create the impression that a company is much bigger than it really is. Entrepreneurs who operate part-time businesses or home-based businesses will find voice mail especially useful; the voice mail system can field business calls and record them until the entrepreneur is free to make return calls. Two basic types of voice mail systems are available: services purchased through local telephone companies and systems for sale. The most eco-

CHAPTER 18   USING TECHNOLOGY TO GAIN A COMPETITIVE EDGE   **641**

nomical option is to subscribe to a voice mail service through a local telephone company; fees typically range from just $6 to $25 a month, and the business owner lets the telephone company handle equipment repairs and maintenance. Plus, there is no equipment to buy. Most systems for sale work through a personal computer but require business owners to purchase and maintain equipment. Prices range from $500 up to as much as $25,000 for large, sophisticated systems. Perhaps the biggest benefit of voice mail to small business owners is that they no longer miss important business calls and the potential revenue they can generate.

E-MAIL

Electronic mail (or e-mail), the messages that people send across the Internet from one computer to another, can be a useful business communications tool. E-mail is a convenient way for employees within a business to communicate, especially if they are in different locations or if their work schedules do not coincide. It is also vital to employees who telecommute: that is, work from their homes or from some other location besides the office. Studies suggest that the average e-mail user receives 15 messages a day and that, worldwide, more than 200 million e-mail messages streak across the Internet daily.[56]

Like many small businesses, Galacticomm, a network-services software company, has discovered the benefits of using e-mail to market and to service its products. The small company cannot afford a staff large enough to offer live demonstrations of its products and on-site service for its software, but founder Yannick Tessier has found a way to do both by using the Internet. With the help of one of its own products, Worldgroup, Galacticomm has set up an on-line chat group, where customers e-mail questions about the company's software and "talk live" to a technician.[57]

CompuPets, a company that sells Web-site services to the pet industry, hosts on-line chat groups with pet breeders, veterinarians, and pet fanciers. Owner Robert Kerr has found that the chat groups increase the number of visitors to the company's Web site, which translates into higher sales. "Chat adds traffic, and higher levels of traffic promote other services on the site," says Kerr. "It [also] makes the site more lively."[58]

Chapter Summary

1. Explain how technology can help small businesses gain a competitive advantage over their rivals.
   - Technology is one of the most powerful tools in an entrepreneur's arsenal of competitive weapons. It can transform the way a small company works, the way it does business, and the way it interacts with its customers. Entrepreneurs who understand how to use technology to make their businesses more efficient and more capable and to serve their customers better and faster will have an edge in the marketplace.

2. Describe how to create a technology plan that enables business owners to get the most out of their investments in technology.
   - Building a workable technology plan includes the following steps:
     1. Decide what you want your company to be able to do for itself and for your customers.

2. Determine the technology and the equipment you will need to perform those tasks.
3. Conduct a technology audit.
4. Match goals and resources.
5. Develop a technology budget.
6. Make the necessary purchases.

3. Explain how computers have transformed the way entrepreneurs do business and how to computerize a small business.
   - Computers are the "great equalizer" in business; they give entrepreneurs the power to be as big in the eyes of their customers as competitors many times their size.
   - Computerizing a small business involves seven basic steps:
     1. Develop a list of current activities.
     2. Decide how much and which areas of the business to computerize.
     3. Develop a computer budget.

4. Define the informational needs of the functions to be computerized first.
5. Shop for software packages that will perform the required functions.
6. Choose the hardware.
7. Integrate the system into the business.

④ Outline the major business software applications, identify guidelines for buying computer hardware, and explain the hardware issues entrepreneurs face.

- The software most small business owners use includes word processing, accounting, database management, spreadsheets, graphics, communications, software suites, and industry-specific software.
- Although there are no magic formulas for selecting the right hardware, the following guidelines will be helpful:

  Do your homework before shopping for hardware.
  Buy a computer with enough power and speed.
  Plan for expansion.
  Keep it simple.
- In addition to the powerful desktop computers available, entrepreneurs can choose portable computers that have practically all of the same features. For entrepreneurs on the go, a portable computer is an ideal choice because it gives them the power to work as if they were sitting at their desks from practically anywhere.

⑤ Discuss the peripheral equipment, such as printers, scanners, digital cameras, and personal digital assistants, that enhances the performance of the computer.

- With the right printers, entrepreneurs can generate documents, signs, fliers, and advertisements on their own printers that they once had to get professional print shops to design and produce. Entrepreneurs can choose among the four basic types of printers: inkjet printers, monochrome laser printers, color laser printers, and network printers.
- Scanners, once reserved only for graphics design houses or newspapers, are now common office tools in businesses of all types. Scanners allow entrepreneurs to make a "digital copy" of an image or a document, which they can then edit, download into other files, or post on Web pages.
- On the surface, digital cameras resemble traditional cameras, but inside they are very different. Unlike traditional 35 mm cameras, digital cameras use no film; instead, they capture images in digital codes onto either standard floppy disks or removable memory cards and then download them to a computer file.

- Small, hand-held devices such as personal digital assistants (PDAs) and pagers make it easy for entrepreneurs to keep up with their business from practically anywhere. Personal digital assistants are a combination of personal computer, appointment book, pager, organizer, and fax machine.

⑥ Discuss the role of communications technology such as the telephone, voice mail, and e-mail, in small companies.

- Communications technology is undergoing major technological changes. The telephone is rapidly becoming a "smart" communications tool, incorporating many of the features of a computer into its design. Screen phones (or video phones) have built-in monitors that allow entrepreneurs to conduct video conferences with customers and business associates around the world without ever leaving their office, and they provide the ability to send and receive e-mail messages and to access the latest business news or sports scores.
- Although voice mail systems record messages just as telephone answering machines do, they offer many more features such as the ability to take calls while an entrepreneur is on the phone with another call, multiple voice mailboxes, pager notification, and the ability to check messages from remote locations. These features can be especially important to small businesses because they create the impression that a company is much bigger than it really is.
- Electronic mail (or e-mail), the messages that people send across the Internet from one computer to another, can be a useful business communications tool. E-mail is an easy way for employees within the same company but in different locations to keep in touch; it is also a useful tool for communicating with customers.

Discussion Questions

1. How can technology help a small company gain a competitive advantage over its rivals?
2. Why is it important for entrepreneurs to develop a technology plan for their companies? What issues should such a plan address?
3. Explain the statement, "More information does not necessarily mean better information."
4. "Computers have become the great equalizer, giving small companies the power to be as big in the eyes of their customers as companies many times their size."

What does this statement mean? Do you agree with it? Explain.

5. What factors should the manager consider in the decision to computerize?

6. Explain the steps involved in computerizing a small company.

7. What is a local area network (LAN)? What advantages does a LAN offer business owners?

8. What factors should a business owner consider before setting up a LAN?

9. What is software? How should the small business manager select software?

10. Describe the major types of software packages, explain what they do, and give an example of each one.

11. What is hardware? What factors should the small business manager consider when evaluating hardware?

12. What advantages does a portable computer offer? Disadvantages? In what situations would a portable computer benefit an entrepreneur?

13. Why is computer security a problem? What can the small business manager do to improve computer security?

14. Explain the differences in the four types of printers, and discuss the circumstances for which each type is best suited.

15. In what ways can entrepreneurs use the following technology? Give an example of how an entrepreneur might use each type.

    Scanners
    Digital cameras
    Personal digital assistants (PDAs)
    Screen and cellular telephones
    Voice mail
    E-mail

Step into the Real World

1. Locate a small business that does not use a computer. What reasons does the owner give for not using one? Help the owner evaluate the firm's computer needs. What business functions, if any, could benefit from computerization? Do you recommend the purchase of a computer? Why? If so, what kind of software and hardware do you recommend?

2. Contact a local small business that uses a computer. How is it used in the firm? What functions does it perform? Can you suggest an expansion of the system into other functional areas? What software does the owner use? Did the owner follow the procedure for purchasing a computer outlined in this chapter? Is the computer well suited to the firm's needs?

3. Contact a local small business that uses a computer. What steps does the owner take to ensure computer security? Do you spot any problem areas? What recommendations can you make to the owner for improving the level of security?

4. Locate a computer users' group in your area and attend a meeting. What business applications for computers do you find?

5. Select a small business in your area. Assume that the owner wants to computerize his or her company. Locate a recent issue of a computer magazine (e.g., *PC World, MacWorld, PC Computing, Computer Shopper*) and use the product reviews and ads to develop a computer budget for the owner. Which software packages and hardware configurations do you recommend? What percentage of the total budget did you allocate for hardware? For software? For training and support?

Take It to the Net

Visit the Scarborough/Zimmerer home page at
www.prenhall.com/scarbzim
for updated information, on-line resources, and Web-based exercises.

Endnotes

1. "Martha Stewart," *Forbes ASAP*, February 24, 1997, pp. 70–72.
2. Christopher O'Malley, "Business: The Power of Information Access," *Personal Computing*, October 1989, p. 74.
3. Robert B. Forest and F. Douglas DeCarlo, "Computer Information Strategies for Smaller Corporations," *Inc.*, November 1984, p. 129.
4. Robert B. Tucker, "Using Technology to Boost Productivity," *Managing the Future: 10 Driving Forces of Change*, Special Edition, p. 28.
5. Kristin Dunlap Godsey, "Road Testers," *Success*, June 1996, pp. 49–50.
6. Tim McCollum, "Computer Systems According to Plan," *Nation's Business*, August 1998, pp. 44–50.
7. Alana Joch, "Map a Two-Year Plan to Get the PC Power You Need," *Your Company* (Forecast 1998), pp. 67–68.
8. Kylo-Patrick Hart, "The Future of Your Business," *Business Start-Ups*, April 1997, p. 30.
9. Douglas Bartholomew, "Unleash Your Computing Power," *Your Company*, Fall 1994, pp. 36–40.
10. Leigh Buchanan, "Killer Apps," *Inc.*, May 1998, pp. 92–96.
11. Rich Karlgaard, "The 2¢ Rolls Royce," *Forbes ASAP*, October 7, 1996, p. 13.
12. Hart, "The Future of Your Business," p. 27.
13. Erika Kotite, "Computer Revolution," *Entrepreneur*, November 1991, pp. 77–78.
14. Richard B. Byrne, "Leveraging Productivity," *Personal Computing*, June 1985, p. 41.
15. Heather Page, "What Price PC?" *Entrepreneur*, October 1997, pp. 50–53; Michael Kolowich, "So How Much Is That PC on Your Desk Really Costing You?" *PC Computing*, September 1991, p. 72; Tim McCollum, "Choosing Software for Your Firm," *Nation's Business*, July 1996, pp. 38–41.
16. Tim McCollum, "The Future Is Now," *Nation's Business*, December 1996, pp. 16–28; Steven Cherry, "Web Access: Small Business Power Tool," *Computer Shopper Extra*, February 1998, pp. 14–20.
17. Tim McCollum, "The Net Result of Computer Links," *Nation's Business*, March 1998, pp. 55–58.
18. Thomas A. Stewart, "Managing in a Wired Company," *Fortune*, July 11, 1994, p. 44.
19. John D. Ruley and Nancy A. Lang, "PC vs. NC: The Whole Story," *Windows Magazine*, April 1997, pp. 186–204.
20. Sarah Glazer, "Before and After," *Inc./Technology Guide*, Winter 1994, pp. 72–79.
21. Heather Page, "Get It Together," *Entrepreneur*, November 1997, pp. 52–54.
22. Ellen Braun, "How to Select Software for Your Specific Needs," *The Office*, February 1990, p. 64.
23. Doni Fordyce, "The User Challenge," *Venture*, November 1985, p. 86.
24. Tim McCollum, "More Than Just Number Crunchers," *Nation's Business*, April 1998, pp. 46–48.
25. Tim McCollum, "Taking Account of Software," *Nation's Business*, January 1997, pp. 41–44.
26. David H. Freedman, "Through the Looking Glass," *Inc. Special Report: The State of Small Business 1996*, pp. 48–54.
27. Ripley Hotch and Jon Pepper, "How to Buy Business Software," *Nation's Business*, June 1994, p. 26.
28. David Carnoy, "Being There," *Success*, February 1997, pp. 63–66.
29. Sarah Roberts-Witt, "Set Up Shop on the Internet," *Biz.Excite.Com*, September 1998, pp. 21–28.
30. Linda Himelstein, Ellen Neborne, and Paul M. Eng, "Web Ads Start to Click," *Business Week*, October 6, 1997, pp. 128–138.
31. Mary J. Cronin, "Business Secrets of the Billion-Dollar Web," *Fortune*, February 2, 1998, p. 142.
32. The Graphic, Visualization, and Usability Center at Georgia Technical Institute <http://www.gvu.edu/user_surveys/>.
33. Richard Karpinski, "Web E-Mailing Mirrors In-Store Opportunities," *Internet Week* <http://techweb.cmp.com/internetwk/news/news0120-6.htm>.
34. Chris Allbritton, "Shoppers Leaving the Malls in Droves, Heading to Net," *Greenville News*, December 20, 1997, p. 10D.
35. Lynn Ginsburg, "A Recipe for Web Profits," *Windows Magazine*, April 1997, p. 214.
36. Tim McCollum, "Delivering the Whole Package," *Nation's Business*, February 1997, pp. 45–48.
37. Ibid.
38. Paul B. Carroll, "When Picking a Personal Computer, First Be Prepared to Be Overwhelmed: Then . . ." *Wall Street Journal*, September 28, 1987, p. 37.
39. Wendy Webb, "High-Tech in the Heartland," *Training*, May 1997, pp. 51–56.
40. Wendy I. Wall, "Few Firms Plan Well for Mishaps That Disable Computer Facilities," *Wall Street Journal*, May 31, 1988, p. 27.
41. Tim McCollum, "Computer Crime," *Nation's Business*, November 1997, pp. 19–28.
42. Gayle Hanson, "Computer Users Pack a Keypunch in a High-Tech World of Crime," *Insight*, April 15, 1991, p. 10.
43. McCollum, "Computer Crime" <http://www.gocsi.com/preleas2.htm>.
44. McCollum, "Computer Crime" <http://www.gocsi.com/preleas2.htm>; "Computer Crime Wave," *Journal of Business Strategy*, July/August 1996, p. 8.
45. "Labor Letter," *Wall Street Journal*, November 22, 1988, p. 1.
46. Vin McClellan, "Of Trojan Horses, Data Diddling, & Logic Bombs," *Inc.*, June 1985, p. 106.
47. McCollum, "Computer Crime."
48. Nikhil Hutheesing & Philip E. Ross, "Hackerphobia," *Forbes*, March 23, 1998, pp. 150–154.
49. McCollum, "Computer Crime."
50. Ibid.
51. Tim McCollum, "Printers Expand Creative Horizons," *Nation's Business*, January 1998, pp. 38–40.
52. Thomas Garett, "Dressed for Success," *Inc. Technology*, 1998, No. 2, pp. 29–30.
53. David Cornoy, "Office to Go," *Success*, November 1997, pp. 41–44.
54. Jill Amadio, "Phone Ahead," *Entrepreneur*, November 1997, pp. 56–59.
55. "Smart Talk," *Fortune Technology Buyer's Guide*, Winter 1998, pp. 159–162.
56. Chris Lee, "Notes from E-Mail Hell," *Training*, May 1997, p. 10.
57. Fred Hapgood, "Let Your Fingers Do the Talking," *Inc. Technology*, no. 4, 1997, pp. 119–120.
58. Ibid., p. 120.

Staffing and Leading a Growing Company

A leader knows best what to do; a manager knows merely how best to do it.

—Ken Adelman

The two things people want more than sex or money are recognition and praise.

—Mary Kay Ash

Upon completion of this chapter, you will be able to

1. Explain the challenges involved in the entrepreneur's role as leader and what it takes to be a successful leader.

2. Understand the potential barriers to effective communication and describe how to overcome them.

3. Describe the importance of hiring the right employees and how to avoid making hiring mistakes.

4. Explain how to build the kind of company culture and structure to support the entrepreneur's mission and goals and to motivate employees to achieve them.

5. Discuss the ways in which entrepreneurs can motivate their workers to higher levels of performance.

1. Explain the challenges involved in the entrepreneur's role as leader and what it takes to be a successful leader.

*T*he Entrepreneur's Role As Leader

To be successful, a small business manager must assume a wide range of roles, tasks, and responsibilities, but none is more important than the role of *leader*. Some entrepreneurs are uncomfortable in this role, but they must learn to be effective leaders if their companies are to grow and reach their potential. **Leadership** is the process of influencing and inspiring others to work to achieve a common goal and then giving them the power and the freedom to achieve it. Without leadership ability, entrepreneurs—and their companies—never rise above mediocrity. Yet, leadership is not easy to learn; the skills needed to lead well are constantly changing. In the past, many small business managers relied on

647

fear and intimidation as their primary leadership tools. But today's more knowledgeable, more skilled workforce demands a more sophisticated style of leadership.

Until recently, experts compared the leader's job to that of a symphony orchestra conductor. Like the symphony leader, a small business manager made sure that everyone was playing the same score, coordinated individual efforts to produce harmony, and directed the members as they played. The conductor (manager) retained virtually all of the power and made all of the decisions about how the orchestra would play the music without any input from the musicians themselves. Today's successful small business leader, however, is more like the leader of a jazz band, which is known for its improvisation, innovation, and creativity. Max DePree, former head of Herman Miller, Inc., a highly successful office furniture manufacturer, explains the connection this way:

Jazz band leaders must choose the music, find the right musicians, and perform—in public. But the effect of the performance depends on so many things—the environment, the volunteers playing in the band, the need for everybody to perform as individuals and as a group, the absolute dependence of the leader on the members of the band, the need for the followers to play well.... The leader of the jazz band has the beautiful opportunity to draw the best out of the other musicians. We have much to learn from jazz band leaders, for jazz, like leadership, combines the unpredictability of the future with the gifts of individuals.[1]

In short, management and leadership are not the same; yet both are essential to a small company's success. Leadership without management is unbridled; management without leadership is uninspired. Leadership gets a small business going; management keeps it going. Stephen Covey, author of *Principle-Centered Leadership*, explains the difference between management and leadership this way:

Leadership deals with people; management deals with things. You manage things; you lead people. Leadership deals with vision; management deals with logistics toward that vision. Leadership deals with doing the right things; management focuses on doing things right. Leadership deals with examining the paradigms on which you are operating; management operates within those paradigms. Leadership comes first, then management, but both are necessary.[2]

Leadership and management are intertwined; a small business that has one but not the other will go nowhere.

Effective leaders exhibit certain behaviors. They:

- *create a set of values and beliefs for employees and passionately pursue them.* Employees look to their leaders for guidance in making decisions. Leaders should be like beacons in the night, constantly shining light on the principles, values, and beliefs on which they founded their companies.

- *respect and support their employees.* To gain the respect of their employees, leaders must first respect those who work for them.

- *set the example for their employees.* A leader's words ring hollow if he fails to "practice what he preaches." Few signals are transmitted to workers faster than the hypocrisy of a leader who sells employees on one set of values and principles and then acts according to a different set. One manager explains, "You've got to walk the talk. If there is ambiguity about your message or values, people will opt out."[3]

- *focus employees' efforts on challenging goals and keep them driving toward those goals.* Effective leaders have a clear vision of where they want their companies to go, and they are able to communicate their vision to those around them. Leaders must repeatedly reinforce the goals they set for their companies.

- *provide the resources employees need to achieve their goals.* Effective leaders know that workers cannot do their jobs well unless they have the tools they need. They provide workers with not only the physical resources they need to excel but also the necessary intangible resources such as training, coaching, and mentoring.

- *communicate with their employees.* Leaders recognize that helping workers see the company's overarching goal is just one part of effective communication; encouraging employee feedback and then listening is just as vital. In other words, they know that communication is a two-way street.

- *value the diversity of their workers.* Smart business leaders recognize the value of their workers' varied skills, abilities, backgrounds, and interests. When channeled in the right direction, such diversity can be a powerful weapon in achieving innovation and maintaining a competitive edge.

- *celebrate their workers' successes.* Effective leaders recognize that workers want to be winners and do everything they can to encourage top performance among their people. The rewards they give are not always financial; in many cases, a reward may be as simple as a hand-written congratulatory note.

- *encourage creativity among their workers.* Rather than punish workers who take risks and fail, effective leaders are willing to accept failure as a natural part of innovation and creativity. They know that innovative behavior is the key to future success and do everything they can to encourage it among workers.

- *maintain a sense of humor.* One of the most important tools a leader can have is a sense of humor. Without it, work can become dull and unexciting for everyone.

- *keep their eyes on the horizon.* Effective leaders are never satisfied with what they and their employees accomplished yesterday. They know that yesterday's successes are not enough to sustain their companies indefinitely. They see the importance of building and maintaining sufficient momentum to carry their companies to the next level.

Leading an organization, whatever its size, is one of the biggest challenges any manager faces. Yet, for an entrepreneur, leadership success is one of the key determinants of the company's success. In addition to the uncertainties of dealing with people, the job of the organizational leader is constantly changing. One business writer explains, "The new leader is . . . the one who sees clearly the goal, shares repeatedly and forcefully the vision, provides the tools, trains and enables co-workers to manage and improve their processes, remains persistent in the face of adversity, and inspires others to take an ownership position in the completion of the mission—by example."[4]

Unfortunately, studies show that managers rate their own leadership skills higher than their employees rate those managers' skills. One recent study by Zenger Miller found that managers rated themselves higher than their employees rated them on every item on a leadership scale, including such important issues as defining the organization's vision and values and building personal credibility among workers. According to the researchers, the discrepancies in the ratings exist because employees rate leaders on the basis of what they do rather than on what they say.[5] The study points out the importance of managers' integrity to their companies' success. One of the most crucial requirements for being an effective leader is consistency in words and in actions. Employees know they can trust business owners who truly mean what they say. Similarly, they quickly learn *not* to trust leaders whose day-to-day actions belie the principles they preach.

True leaders know that they are not self-appointed. "Real leadership happens only when your people say you are their leader," says one expert, emphasizing the role of followers. "Leadership is an earned honor, not something that comes with the job."[6] Astute business leaders know that their success is intertwined with their employees' success. After all, it is the employees who will actually do the work, implement the strategy, and produce the results. To be effective, leaders must establish for their workers an environment in which they can achieve success. One expert identifies six conditions that leaders must create for their followers if a company is to succeed. Followers must (1) know what to do, (2) know how to do it, (3) understand why they are doing it, (4) want to do it, (5) have the right resources, and (6) believe they have the proper leadership.[7] Great leaders do everything in their power to make these conditions thrive in their companies.

To be effective, a small business leader must perform four vital tasks:

◆ Communicate the vision and the values of the company effectively and create an environment of trust among workers.

◆ Hire the right employees and constantly improve their skills.

◆ Build an organizational culture and structure that allow both workers and the company to reach their potential.

◆ Motivate workers to higher levels of performance.

*C*ommunicating Effectively

2 Understand the potential barriers to effective communication and describe how to overcome them.

Like all leaders, small business owners constantly confront dilemmas as they operate their businesses. Frequently, they must walk the fine line between the chaos involved in encouraging creativity and maintaining control over their companies. At other times, they must steer their companies around those questionable actions that might produce large short-term gains into those that are ethical. As leaders, an important and highly visible part of their jobs is to communicate the values, beliefs, and principles for which their business stands. In other words, a leader's foremost job is to be the communicator of the company's vision. It is a job that never ends. "The essence of leadership today is to make sure that the organization knows itself," says one entrepreneur when asked about his job as leader. "There are certain durable principles that underlie an organization. The leader should embody those values. They're fundamental."[8]

For example, the head of a foreign pharmaceutical company focuses his employees on five basic values: integrity, safety, innovation, partnership, and quality/customer focus. These values are "the social cement" holding his company together, and he communicates them constantly. "As a leader, I have to set the expectations for the company, energize the people around goals, and give the people the assurance that the company is behind them. I have to say it, talk about it a lot, and jawbone it, if you will."[9] As this entrepreneur's experience suggests, one of the first skills successful leaders must acquire is the ability to communicate. Nowhere is this skill more important than among entrepreneurs, whose organizations are predicated on their founders' ability to communicate a vision and a set of values that everyone in the company can embrace.

IMPROVING COMMUNICATION

Research shows that managers spend about 80 percent of their time in some form of communication: 30 percent talking, 25 percent listening, 15 percent reading, and 10 percent writing.[10] To some managers, however, communicating means only one thing: sending messages to others. Although talking to people both inside and outside the organization is an important part of an entrepreneur's job, so is the other aspect of an entrepreneur's job as chief communicator: listening.

Sending Messages. One of the most frustrating experiences for entrepreneurs occurs when they ask an employee to do something and nothing happens! Although entrepreneurs are quick to perceive the failure to respond as the employee's lack of motivation or weak work ethic, often the culprit is improper communication. One expert says that the primary reasons employees usually don't do what they are expected to do have little to do with their motivation and desire to work. Instead, workers often fail to do what they are supposed to because:

◆ They don't know what to do.

◆ They don't know how to do it.

◆ They don't have the authority to do it.

◆ They get no feedback on how well or how poorly they're doing it.

◆ They are ignored or punished for doing it right.

◆ They realize that no one ever notices even if they *are* doing it right.[11]

The common thread running through all of these causes is poor communication between business owner and employee. What barriers to effective communication must small business managers overcome?

Managers and employees don't always feel free to say what they really mean. CEOs and top managers in companies of any size seldom hear the truth about problems and negative results from employees. This less-than-honest feedback results from the hesitancy of subordinates to tell "the boss" bad news. Over time, this tendency can paralyze the upward communication in a company.

Ambiguity blocks real communication. The same words can have different meanings to different people, especially in modern companies, where the workforce is likely to be highly diverse. For instance, a business owner may tell an employee to "take care of this customer's problem as soon as you can." The owner may have meant "solve this problem by the end of the day," but the employee may think that fixing the problem by the end of the week will meet the owner's request.

Information overload causes the message to get lost. With information from mail, telephone, faxes, e-mail, face-to-face communication, and other sources, employees in modern organizations are literally bombarded with messages. With such a large volume of information washing over workers, it is easy for some messages to get lost.

Selective listening interferes with the communication process. Sometimes, people hear only what they want to hear, selectively tuning in and out on a speaker's message. The result is distorted communication.

Defense mechanisms block a message. When people are confronted with information that upsets them or conflicts with their perceptions, they immediately put up defenses. Defense mechanisms range from verbally attacking the source of the message to twisting perceptions of reality to maintain self-esteem.

Conflicting verbal and nonverbal messages confuse listeners. Nonverbal communication includes a speaker's mannerisms, gestures, posture, facial expressions, and other forms of "body language." When a speaker sends conflicting verbal and nonverbal messages, research shows that listeners will believe the nonverbal message almost every time. "When people don't know whether to believe what they're hearing or what they're seeing, they go with the body language—it tells the truth," says one management consultant.[12]

How can entrepreneurs overcome these barriers to become better communicators? The following tips will help:

Clarify your message before you attempt to communicate it. Before attempting to communicate your message, identify exactly what you want the receiver to think and do as a result of the message. Then focus on getting that point across clearly and concisely.

Use face-to-face communication whenever possible. Although not always practical, face-to-face communication reduces the likelihood of misunderstandings because it allows for immediate feedback and nonverbal clues.

Be empathetic. Try to put yourself in the place of those who will receive your message, and develop it accordingly. Be sure to tell your audience up front what's in it for them.

Match your message to your audience. A business owner would be very unlikely to use the same words, techniques, and style to communicate his company's financial position to a group of industry analysts as he would to a group of workers on the factory floor.

Be organized. Effective communicators organize their messages so that their audiences can understand them easily.

Encourage feedback. Allow listeners to ask questions and to offer feedback. Sometimes, employees are hesitant to ask the boss any questions for fear of "looking stupid." One useful technique, especially when giving instructions, is to ask workers to repeat the message to make sure they understand it correctly.

Tell the truth. The fastest way to destroy your credibility as a leader is to lie.

Don't be afraid to tell employees about the business, its performance, and the forces that affect it. Too often, entrepreneurs assume that employees don't care about such details. Research suggests that employees *are* interested in the business that employs them and want to understand where their company is headed and how it plans to get there.[13] *A few years after Michele Wong launched her software company, Synergex, the business ran into deep financial trouble. Rather than share information about the problems with her workers, Wong tried to deal with them alone. Soon, however, forced layoffs pushed the company's woes out into the open, and employees suggested that Wong hold problem-solving meetings in which employees could ask questions and offer solutions. As a result of the meetings, Wong got some great ideas from Synergex employees, and morale soared. The following year was one of the best the company had ever had. Recognizing a good idea when she sees one, Wong retained the information-sharing sessions and even expanded them. Today, Synergex focuses on sharing knowledge in a variety of ways, including employee open forums in which employees can inform, thank, and question one another; a biweekly newsletter that carries company and employee news; team meetings that focus on goal setting and problem solving; a learn-at-lunch program, in which workers from different departments share ideas; and sessions in which the financial manager reviews Synergex's monthly financial statements. Not only has the information sharing improved morale in the company, but it also has boosted its level of customer service.*[14]

Listening. Listening is the most important communication skill an entrepreneur can develop. Unfortunately, many business owners focus their efforts on telling others what they need to know, and devote little time and energy to listening. "Not many managers are good at listening to their employees," says one management consultant. "They don't see listening as part of their jobs, [or] that it's essential to managing successfully."[15] Listening is a skill that entrepreneurs must develop if they are to improve the quality of their company and achieve growth. The employees who perform the work in the company and serve its customers are the *real* experts in its day-to-day activities and are in closer contact with potential problems and opportunities at the operating level. By encouraging employees to develop creative solutions to problems and innovative ideas and then listening to and acting on them, business owners can make their companies more successful. *For instance, the manager of a plant making toothpaste found that the frequent need to wash out the steel holding tank interrupted the company's production schedule. One day the manager was talking to one of the operators, who suggested that the company put in a second tank. "That way we can use one tank while we wash the second one, and we don't have to stop production to do it." This simple, yet effective, solution that was so obvious to the worker because he dealt with the problem every day had never occurred to the plant's managers.*[16]

Such improvements depend on an owner's ability to listen. To improve listening skills, one management consultant suggests managers use the "PDCH formula": identify the speaker's *purpose*; recognize the *details* that support that purpose; see the *conclusions* they can draw from what the speaker is saying; and identify the *hidden* meanings communicated by body language and voice inflections.[17]

THAT INFORMAL COMMUNICATION NETWORK: THE "GRAPEVINE"

Despite all of the modern communication tools available, the grapevine, the informal lines of communication that exist in every company, remains an important link in a company's communication network. The grapevine carries vital information—and sometimes rumors—through every part of the organization with incredible speed. One researcher describes the grapevine this way: "With the rapidity of a burning powder trail, information flows like magic out of the woodwork, past the water fountain, past the manager's door and the janitor's mop closet. As elusive as a summer zephyr, it filters through steel walls, bulkheads, or glass partitions, from office boy to executive."[18] In one classic study, researchers found that when management made an important change in the organization, most employees would hear the news first by the grapevine. A supervisor and an official memorandum ran a poor second and third, respectively.[19] In a more recent study, 96 percent of executives said their employees routinely use the company grapevine to communicate and that their workers consider the grapevine to be a reliable source of information.[20]

*H*iring the Right Employees

3 Describe the importance of hiring the right employees and how to avoid making hiring mistakes.

The decision to hire a new employee is an important one for every business, but its impact is magnified many times in a small company. Every "new hire" a business owner makes determines the heights to which the company can climb—or the depths to which it will plunge. "Bad hires" are incredibly expensive, and no organization, especially a small one, can afford too many of them. One study concluded that an employee hired into a typical entry-level position who quits after six months costs a company about $17,000 in salary, benefits, and training. In addition, the intangible costs—time invested in the new employee, lost opportunities, reduced morale among coworkers, and business setbacks—are seven times the direct costs of a bad hire. In other words, the total price tag for this bad hire is about $136,000![21]

For many companies, attracting and retaining qualified employees remains a challenge, but the problem is especially acute for rapidly growing small businesses. According to a recent survey by National Small Business United, one-fourth of the CEOs at growing companies said that a lack of skilled workers is a major threat to their business's growth and continued survival.[22] *In 1992, after four years in business, Erler Industries, an industrial painting and finishing service, earned a large contract with Dell Computer Corporation. After working with just six employees since its founding, the company was in the awkward posi-*

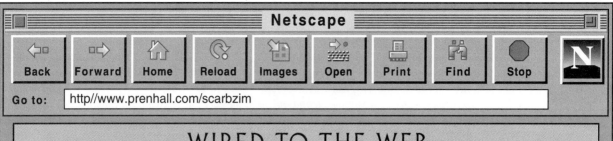

WIRED TO THE WEB

WWW.HELPWANTED.COM

The Monster Board <http://www.monster.com>
Online Career Center <http://www.occ.com>
Minorities' Job Bank <http://www.minoritiesjb.com>
The Catapult <http://www.jobweb.org/catapult>

*T*he World Wide Web is the latest tool businesses are using to recruit employees. One small business owner who recently began using the Web to attract new employees says he did so because he needed to "cast a wide net, and there is none wider than the World Wide Web." A recent survey of executives conducted by Management Recruiters International found that 37 percent said they are using the Web to recruit employees, up from just 26.5 percent 18 months before.

Jean E. West, recruiting manager at Salestar, a company making software for the telephone industry, has found the Web to be a powerful and low-cost recruiting tool. Because of the nature of its software products, Salestar prefers to hire workers with backgrounds in the telephone industry. Candidates with the right qualifications are scattered all around the country, and with 60 employees and $6 million in annual sales, Salestar doesn't have the resources to track them down through ads in traditional media. So West decided to give employment ads on the World Wide Web a try. She purchased an ad that ran for 60 days on an Internet recruiting service for only $125. A weekend ad in the local paper would have cost the company three times as much. Not only did the Web-based ad prove to be a bargain, but it also turned out to be very effective. West found just the kind of applicants she was looking for and filled the position quickly. She now uses the Web to advertise all types of job openings. Résumés have come from as far away as Saudi Arabia.

The following are some of the most popular commercial sites where companies can post their ads:

Career Magazine <http://www.careermag.com>
CareerMosaic <http://www.careermosaic.com>
CareerPath <http://www.careerpath.com>
CareerWeb <http://www.cweb.com>
JobCenter <http://www.jobcenter.com>

Although Web-based job postings remain skewed toward high-tech jobs, the mix is becoming more diverse. Jeffrey Taylor, president of the Monster Board, says that about 45 percent of the jobs listed on his company's site are for some type of technical position, 20 percent involve product development and management, and 35 percent are nontechnical positions such as marketing and retailing jobs. About one-third of the commercial Web sites do not charge companies for job listings. Those that do charge fees have prices that range from $25 to $150 for listings that run for four weeks.

Companies that expect to do extensive recruiting on the Web should consider not only placing ads on commercial sites but also creating their own Web sites. Ads are more likely to be successful if they include an on-line response form for candidates. The company can screen candidates initially using the on-line form and then invite viable candidates to submit a résumé.

1. What benefits does Web-based recruiting offer small companies?
2. Visit some of the sites mentioned above. What recommendations would you make to a small company interested in advertising a job on the Web?
3. Assume that you are the owner of a small software company that designs and develops Web pages for businesses. You need to hire a new Web designer. Write an ad describing the position and the sites on which you would list it. Visit some of the sites mentioned above and find several candidates whom you think could fill this position. Which ones would you want to interview? Why?

SOURCES: Adapted from Jeff Bennett, "WWW.HELPWANTED.COM," *Upstate Business*, February 22, 1998, pp. 1, 8–9; Roberta Maynard, "Casting the Net for Job Seekers," *Nation's Business*, March 1997, pp. 29–29; Thomas Love, "Smart Tactics for Finding Workers," *Nation's Business*, January 1998, p. 20.

tion of having to hire 175 people into entry-level positions almost overnight! Desperate for employees, Linda and Mark Erler ran a coupon in the North Vernon, Indiana, paper offering a $50 bonus to anyone they hired. The coupon enticed enough applicants so that the Erlers met their staffing goals. Unfortunately, they had to hire workers so rapidly that they could not check references, and problems quickly surfaced. "It was very risky," says Linda, recalling the night that one group of new hires came to work with "whiskey in their soda cans." Employee turnover skyrocketed. "Everyone had to be replaced five or six times before we found a person who really wanted to work," she says.[23]

As crucial as finding good employees is to a small company's future, it is no easy task. One expert estimates that of every three employees a business hires, one makes a solid contribution, one is a marginal worker, and one is a hiring mistake.[24] For instance, the owner of four franchised fast-food restaurants who deals with an annual turnover rate of 150 to 175 percent says, "Sometimes we have to hire people, knowing full well that they aren't going to work out for the long term."[25] Because employees' roles in a small company's success are magnified by the company's size, entrepreneurs can *least* afford to make hiring mistakes. Most often, entrepreneurs make mistakes because they rush into a hiring decision or they neglect to investigate thoroughly candidates' qualifications and suitability for a job. The CEO of one fast-growing technology firm says, "Most companies spend more time picking out an office copier than deciding on a $40,000 employee. And look which one can do the most damage."[26]

Even though the importance of hiring decisions is magnified in small companies, small businesses are most likely to make hiring mistakes because they lack the human resources experts and the disciplined hiring procedures large companies have. In the early days of a company, an entrepreneur rarely takes the time to create job descriptions and specifications; instead, he usually hires people because he knows or trusts them rather than for their job skills. Then, as the company grows, the business owner hires people to fit in around these existing employees, often creating a very unusual, inefficient organizational structure built around jobs that are poorly planned and designed.

The following guidelines can help small business managers avoid making costly hiring mistakes.

CREATE PRACTICAL JOB DESCRIPTIONS AND JOB SPECIFICATIONS

Small business owners must recognize that what they do *before* they ever start interviewing candidates for a position determines to a great extent how successful they will be at hiring winners. The first step is to perform a **job analysis,** the process by which a firm determines the duties and nature of the jobs to be filled and the skills and experience required of the people who are to fill them. The first objective of a job analysis is to develop a **job description,** a written statement of the duties, responsibilities, reporting relationships, working conditions, and materials and equipment used in a job. A results-oriented job description explains what a job entails and the duties the person filling it is expected to perform. One small business owner uses the following "recipe" for writing job descriptions in his company: job title, job summary, duties to be performed, nature of supervision, job's relationship to others in the company, working conditions, definitions of job-specific terms, and general comments needed to clarify any of the above.[27]

Preparing job descriptions may be one of the most important parts of the hiring process because it creates a "blueprint" for the job. One hiring consultant explains, "It's important for a small company to spend a good amount of time defining the tasks that need to be accomplished." If they do, he says, "they've gone a long way toward finding the right person."[28] Without this blueprint, a manager tends to hire the person with experience whom she likes the best. Useful sources of information for writing job descriptions include the manager's knowl-

Table 19.1 A Sample Job Description from the *Dictionary of Occupational Titles*

Worm picker: Gathers worms to be used as fish bait; walks about grassy areas, such as gardens, parks, and golf courses and picks up earthworms (commonly called dew worms and nightcrawlers). Sprinkles chlorinated water on lawn to cause worms to come to the surface, and locates worms by use of lantern or flashlight. Counts worms, sorts them, and packs them into containers for shipment.

edge of the job, the workers currently holding the job, and the *Dictionary of Occupational Titles (D.O.T)*, available at most libraries. The *Dictionary of Occupational Titles*, published by the Department of Labor, lists more than 20,000 job titles and descriptions and serves as a useful tool for getting a small business owner started when writing job descriptions. Table 19.1 provides an example of the description drawn from the *D.O.T.* for an unusual job.

The second objective of a job analysis is to create a **job specification,** a written statement of the qualifications and characteristics needed for a job stated in such terms as education, skills, and experience. A job specification shows the small business manager what kind of person to recruit and establishes the standards an applicant must meet to be hired. When writing job specifications, some managers define the traits a candidate needs to do a job well. Does the person have to be a good listener, empathetic, well-organized, decisive, a "self-starter"? A business owner about to hire a new employee who will be telecommuting from home, for instance, would look for someone with excellent communication skills, problem-solving ability, a strong work ethic, and the ability to use technology comfortably. Table 19.2 provides an example that links the tasks for a sales representative's job (drawn from a job description) to the traits or characteristics a small business owner identified as necessary to succeed in that job.

PLAN AN EFFECTIVE INTERVIEW

Once the manager knows what she must look for in a job candidate, then she can develop a plan for conducting an informative job interview. Too often, small business owners go into an interview unprepared, and, as a result, they fail to get the information they need to judge

THE WALL STREET JOURNAL

PERSONNEL

"The interview usually takes about twenty minutes, and then you go to recovery."

SOURCE: The *Wall Street Journal*, September 22, 1997, p. A22.

Table 19.2 Linking Tasks from a Job Description to the Traits Necessary to Perform the Job

Job Task	Trait or Characteristic
Generate and close new sales.	Outgoing, persuasive, friendly
Make 15 "cold calls" per week.	A self-starter, determined, optimistic, independent, confident
Analyze customers' needs and recommend proper equipment.	Good listener, patient, empathetic
Counsel customers about options and features needed.	Organized, polished speaker, other-oriented
Prepare and explain financing methods; negotiate finance contracts.	Honest, numbers-oriented, comfortable with computers
Retain existing customers.	Customer-oriented, relationship builder

the candidate's qualifications, qualities, and suitability for the job. Conducting an effective interview requires a small business owner to know what she wants to get out of the interview in the first place and to develop a series of questions to extract that information. The following guidelines will help an owner develop interview questions that will give her meaningful insight into an applicant's qualifications, personality, and character.

◆ *Develop a series of core questions and ask them of every candidate.* To give the screening process consistency, smart business owners rely on a set of relevant questions they ask in every interview. Of course, they also customize each interview using impromptu questions based on an individual's responses.

◆ *Ask open-ended questions rather than questions calling for "yes or no" answers.* Open-ended questions are most effective because they encourage candidates to talk about their work experience in a way that will disclose the presence or the absence of the traits and characteristics the business owner is seeking.

◆ *Create hypothetical situations candidates would be likely to encounter on the job and ask how they would handle them.* Building the interview around such questions gives the owner a preview of the candidate's work habits and attitudes. Rather than telling interviewers about what candidates might do, these scenarios give them an idea of what candidates would do (or have done) in a job-related situation.

◆ *Probe for specific examples in the candidate's work experience that demonstrate the necessary traits and characteristics.* A common mistake interviewers make is failing to get candidates to provide the detail they need to make an informed decision.

◆ *Ask candidates to describe a recent success and a recent failure and how they dealt with them.* Smart entrepreneurs look for candidates who describe them both with equal enthusiasm because they know that peak performers put as much into their failures as they do their successes and usually learn something valuable from their failures.

◆ *Arrange a "noninterview" setting that allows several employees to observe the candidate in an informal setting.* Taking candidates on a plant tour or setting up a coffee break gives everyone a chance to judge a candidate's interpersonal skills and personality outside the formal interview process. These informal settings can be very revealing. One business owner was ready to extend a job offer to a candidate for a managerial position until he saw how the man mistreated a waitress who had made a mistake in his lunch order.

Table 19.3 shows an example of some interview questions one manager uses to uncover the traits and characteristics he seeks in a top-performing sales representative.

Table 19.3 Interview Questions for Candidates for a Sales Representative Position

Trait or Characteristic	Question
Outgoing, persuasive, friendly, a self-starter, determined, optimistic, independent, confident	How do you persuade reluctant prospects to buy?
Good listener, patient, empathetic, organized, polished speaker, other-oriented	What would you say to a fellow salesperson who was getting more than his share of rejections and was having difficulty getting appointments?
Honest, customer-oriented, relationship builder	How do you feel when someone questions the truth of what you say? What do you do in such situations?

Other questions:

    If you owned a company, why would you hire yourself?

    If you were head of your department, what would you do differently? Why?

    How do you acknowledge the contributions of others in your department?

CONDUCT THE INTERVIEW

An effective interview contains three phases: breaking the ice, asking questions, and selling the candidate on the company.

Breaking the Ice. In the opening phase of the interview the manager's primary job is to diffuse the tension that exists because of the nervousness of both parties. Many skilled interviewers use the job description to explain the nature of the job and the company's culture to the applicant. Then, they use icebreakers—questions about a hobby or special interest—to get the candidate to relax. *For instance, to loosen up one very tense but promising candidate, one entrepreneur asked about his hobby, military history. "He launched into a description of the Battle of Midway that was so enthralling, I told him, 'Since you can come across like that, I'm going to give you a shot,'" recalls the business owner. "He went on to be a star salesman."*[29]

Asking Questions. During the second phase of the interview, the employer asks the questions from her question bank to determine the applicant's suitability for the job. Her primary job at this point is to *listen*. Effective interviewers spend about 25 percent of the interview talking and about 75 percent listening. They also take notes during the interview to help them ask follow-up questions based on a candidate's comments and to evaluate a candidate after the interview is over. Experienced interviewers also pay close attention to a candidate's nonverbal clues, or body language, during the interview. They know that candidates may be able to say exactly what they want with their words but that their body language does not lie! One interviewer refers to an applicant's body language as "music," saying, "An interviewer who listened only to the words without taking the music . . . into account would miss [much] make-or-break data about the candidate."[30]

    Increasingly, companies are moving away from traditional questions that offer little insight into candidates' psyches and toward unusual questions that test their creativity, reasoning, and logic. *At Amy's Ice Creams, owner Amy Miller hands job applicants a white paper bag and tells them to be creative. One applicant who received a job offer created a girl's head with curly paper hair. Stick an ice cream spoon in her mouth, and her eyes light up! Another applicant showed the kind of creativity Miller is looking for when he created an elaborate jack-in-the-box using his white paper bag.*[31]

    Small business owners must be careful to make sure they avoid asking candidates illegal questions. At one time, interviewers could ask wide-ranging questions covering just about every area of an applicant's background. Today, interviewing is a veritable minefield of legal liabilities, waiting to explode in the unsuspecting interviewer's face. Companies are more vulnerable to job discrimination lawsuits now than ever before. Although the Equal Employment Opportunity Commission (EEOC), the government agency responsible for enforcing employment laws, does not outlaw specific interview questions, it does recognize that some questions can result in employment discrimination. If a candidate files charges of discrimination against a company, the burden of proof shifts to the employer to prove that all preemployment questions were job-related and nondiscriminatory. In addition, many states have passed laws that forbid the use of certain questions or screening tools in interviews. To avoid trouble, a business owner should keep in mind why he is asking a particular question. The goal is to find someone who is qualified to do the job well. By steering clear of questions about subjects that are peripheral to the job itself, employers are less likely to ask questions that will land them in court. Wise business owners ask their attorneys to review their bank of questions before using them in an interview. Table 19.4 offers a quiz to help you understand which kinds of questions are most likely to create charges of discrimination, and Table 19.5 describes a simple test for determining whether an interview question might be considered discriminatory.

Table 19.4 Is It Legal?

Some interview questions can land an employer in legal hot water. Review the following interview questions and then decide whether you think each one is legal or illegal.

Legal	Illegal	
☐	☐	1. Are you currently using illegal drugs?
☐	☐	2. Have you ever been arrested?
☐	☐	3. Do you have any children or are you planning to have children?
☐	☐	4. When and where were you born?
☐	☐	5. Is there any limit on your ability to work overtime or to travel?
☐	☐	6. How tall are you? How much do you weigh?
☐	☐	7. Do you drink alcohol?
☐	☐	8. How much alcohol do you drink each week?
☐	☐	9. Would your religious beliefs interfere with your ability to do this job?
☐	☐	10. What contraceptive practices do you use?
☐	☐	11. Are you HIV-positive?
☐	☐	12. Have you ever filed a lawsuit or a workers' compensation claim against a former employer?
☐	☐	13. Do you have any physical or mental disabilities that would interfere with your doing this job?
☐	☐	14. Are you a U.S. citizen?

Answers: 1. Legal. **2.** Illegal. Employers cannot ask about an applicant's arrest record, but they can ask if a candidate has ever been *convicted* of a crime. **3.** Illegal. Employers cannot ask questions that could lead to discrimination against a particular group (e.g., women). **4.** Illegal. The Civil Rights Act of 1964 bans discrimination on the basis of race, color, sex, religion, or national origin. **5.** Legal. **6.** Illegal. Unless a person's physical characteristics are important for high job performance (e.g., lifting 100-pound sacks of flour), employers cannot ask candidates such questions. **7.** Legal. **8.** Illegal. Notice the fine line between question 7 and question 8; this is what makes interviewing a challenge! **9.** Illegal. This question would violate the Civil Rights Act of 1964. **10.** Illegal. What relevance would this have to an employee's job performance? **11.** Illegal. Under the Americans with Disabilities Act, which prohibits discrimination against people with disabilities, people with HIV or AIDS are considered "disabled." **12.** Illegal. Workers who file such suits are protected from retribution by a variety of federal and state laws. **13.** Illegal. This question also would violate the Americans with Disabilities Act. **14.** Illegal. This question violates the Civil Rights Act of 1964.

Table 19.5 A Guide for Interview Questions

Small business owners can use the "**OUCH**" test as a guide for determining whether an interview question might be considered discriminatory:

◆ Does the question **O**mit references to race, religion, color, sex, or national origin?
◆ Does the question **U**nfairly screen out a particular class of people?
◆ Can you **C**onsistently apply the question to every applicant?
◆ Does the question **H**ave job-relatedness and business necessity?

Selling the Candidate on the Company. In the final phase of the interview, the employer tries to sell her company to desirable candidates. This phase begins by allowing the candidate to ask questions about the company, the job, or other issues. Again, experienced interviewers note the nature of these questions and the insights they give into the candidate's personality. This part of the interview offers the employer a prime opportunity to explain to the candidate why her company is an attractive place to work. Remember: The best candidates will have other offers, and it's up to you to make sure they leave the interview wanting to work for your company. Finally, before closing the interview, the employer should thank the candidate and tell him what happens next (e.g., "We'll be contacting you about our decision within two weeks.").

CHECK REFERENCES

Small business owners should take the time to check *every* applicant's references. Although many business owners see checking references as a formality and pay little attention to it, others realize the need to protect themselves (and their customers) from hiring unscrupulous workers. Is a reference check really necessary? Yes! According to the American Association for Personnel Administration, approximately 25 percent of all résumés and applications contain at least one *major* fabrication.[32] One business owner who always conducts reference checks says that a candidate's résumé "is like a balance sheet without any liabilities."[33] Checking references thoroughly can help an employer uncover false or exaggerated information. Failing to do so can be costly. *One small company became the subject of an expensive lawsuit when it failed to check the references of a newly hired sales representative. While driving to a sales call, the employee, who was intoxicated, caused an accident that severely injured a person. The lawsuit came about when the injured party discovered that the sales representative had been fired from his three previous jobs for drunkeness, something a reference check would have revealed.*[34] Rather than contacting only the references listed, experienced employers call an applicant's previous employers and talk to their immediate supervisors to get a clear picture of the applicant's job performance, character, and work habits.

CONDUCT EMPLOYMENT TESTS

Although various state and federal laws have made using employment tests as screening devices more difficult in recent years, many companies find them quite useful. To avoid charges of discrimination, business owners must be able to prove that the employment tests they use are both valid and reliable. A **valid test** is one that measures what it is intended to measure: e.g., aptitude for selling, creativity, integrity. A **reliable test** is one that measures consistently over time. Employers must also be sure that the tests they use measure aptitudes and factors that are job-related. Many testing organizations offer ready-made tests that have been proved to be both valid and reliable, and business owners can use these tests safely.

GAINING THE COMPETITIVE EDGE

How to Hire and Keep Great Employees

*H*iring and retaining quality workers is always a challenge, especially for small business owners, who rarely can match the wages, salaries, and benefits their larger rivals offer employees. Rather than settle for second-rate employees, however, creative business owners are finding ways to attract top-notch workers without breaking their human resources budgets. Which techniques are most successful?

Make a commitment to hire only the best workers. Business owners who refuse to compromise the quality of their workforce have the greatest success in hiring. They go after the employees they want; they know that even though they may not be able to pay what a larger business can, they can offer employees a total package that includes much more than a big salary, such as more meaningful work and a stock ownership plan.

Search out the best and brightest young people. Small companies looking for part-time or full-time employees often establish relationships with local colleges and universities. They work with students on internships, class projects, and service programs, and, in the process, find highly motivated, talented workers.

Hire older, retired people interested in returning to work. Business owners have discovered that retirees have excellent work habits, impressive experience, and valuable skills that many small companies need. Don't overlook this valuable source of workers.

Transform help-wanted ads into marketing pieces. Traditional help-wanted ads can easily get lost in the clutter of other ho-hum ads. Smart business owners find a different angle for their ads. In the ads he runs in the search for new employees, Roger Telschow, owner of Ecoprint, a small printing company, has been more successful getting responses by using the lead-in "Enjoy coming to work!" As a small business, says Telschow, "we treat our employees as individuals, and that makes our company special in the printing industry."

Offer "psychic income." Smart employers recognize that there are ways other than money to reward employees. The opportunity to make a difference, to be more than a small cog in a large machine, and to experience job satisfaction are powerful rewards for many people. In fact, a recent Gallup survey conducted for *Inc.* magazine found that workers in small companies are more satisfied with their jobs than employees at big companies.

Create a dynamic, fun workplace that attracts quality applicants. Companies that are great places to work because of the supportive, energetic environment they create find it much easier to recruit workers than those that are not. Tara Cronbaugh and Stephen Harris, owners of two coffee houses near the University of Iowa, have no trouble finding outstanding workers because of their coffee houses' reputation as cool places to work. The word-of-mouth approach the two entrepreneurs use generates 15 to 20 applicants each week! "Our stores are attractive places for people who enjoy being surrounded by sophisticated coffee, people, and books," says Cronbaugh.

Involve staff members in interviewing prospective employees. Business owners who encourage staff members to take an active role in the interview process find that their workers offer valuable insight into candidates' qualifications. "The more people involved in the interview process, the better the chance you have to flesh out whether that person has the personality and skills to fit in," says one experienced recruiter.

"Test drive" new employees before hiring them. Companies of all sizes increasingly are using temp-to-perm hiring strategies, in which they hire temporary workers with the understanding that if the temporary's work is satisfactory for a specified period (often three months), they will hire that person full-time. According to the National Association of Temporary and Staffing Services, approximately 40 percent of all temporary workers get permanent job offers from the companies to which they are assigned.

Always be on the lookout for new employees. Smart business owners are constantly looking for people who would make great employees. Errol Smith, owner of Building Maintenance of America, a contract cleaning service, pays close attention to every salesclerk he meets. "I recently hired a salesman from Circuit City," he says. "I could tell he was a real go-getter. He's worked out very well."

Consider offering employees ownership in the company. One of the most attractive carrots entrepreneurs can offer prospective employees is a share of ownership in the company. Many executives are willing to forgo large salaries up front in exchange for an equity position in a promising small company.

SOURCES: Adapted from "Hire Learning," *Success*, December 1997, pp. 80–81; Jeffrey A. Tannenbaum, "Worker Satisfaction Found to Be Higher at Small Companies," *Wall Street Journal*, May 5, 1997, p. B2; "A Hire Authority," *Business News*, Fall 1996, p. 15; Ripley Hotch, "Break the Rules to Hire Smart," *Your Company*, February/March 1997, pp. 23–28; Mark Henricks, "Labor Pains," *Entrepreneur*, April 1998, pp. 114–121. ◆

Spirit Rent-A-Car, a small auto rental agency, uses an aptitude test for job candidates for sales and sales management positions in the company. However, Spirit took a different approach to developing and validating the test it uses. The company started testing the managers and salespeople already on staff. The test results were amazingly consistent with employees' job performances. "You could literally have put them into three piles," *says Spirit's vice president of operations.* "These tested the best, these tested average, and these tested not so well, and those would have been the performance levels of those individuals."[35] In general, unless business owners can prove that the tests they administer are valid, reliable, and job-related, they should avoid using them.

Experienced small business owners don't rely on any one element in the employee selection process. They look at the total picture painted by each part of a candidate's portfolio. They know that the hiring process provides them with one of the most valuable raw materials their companies count on for success—capable, hard-working people. They also recognize that hiring an employee is not a single event but the beginning of a long-term relationship. The accompanying Gaining the Competitive Edge feature describes how to hire and keep great employees.

*B*uilding the Right Culture and Structure

4 Explain how to build the kind of company culture and structure to support the entrepreneur's mission and goals and to motivate employees to achieve them.

CULTURE

Company culture is the distinctive, unwritten code of conduct that governs the behavior, attitudes, relationships, and style of an organization. It is the essence of "the way we do things around here." In many small companies, culture plays as important a part in gaining a competitive edge as strategy does. In others, it adds practically nothing to the business's competitive position because managers fail to give employees a sense of ownership in the company. A company's culture has a powerful impact on the way people work together in a business, how they do their jobs, and how they treat their customers. Company culture manifests itself in many ways—from how workers dress and act to the language they use. For instance, at some companies, the unspoken dress code requires workers to wear suits and ties, but at companies such as Netscape Communications, employees routinely come to work in jeans and T-shirts. Netscape CEO Marc Andreesen frequently shows up for work in shorts and a T-shirt. At rival Excite Inc., another World Wide Web company, employees use a twisty red slide rather than stairs to travel between floors.[36] The culture in these companies is *very* informal—and fun!

In many companies, the culture creates its own language. At Disney, for instance, workers are not "employees"; they are "cast members." They don't merely go to work; their jobs are "parts in a performance." Disney's customers are "guests." When a cast member treats someone to lunch, it's "on the mouse." Anything negative—such as a cigarette butt on a walkway—is "a bad Mickey," and anything positive is "a good Mickey."

Creating a culture that supports a company's strategy is not easy; the entrepreneurs who have been most successful at it "have a set of overarching beliefs that serve as powerful guides for everyday action—and that are reinforced in a hundred different ways, both symbolic and substantive," explains one business writer.[37] Culture arises from an entrepreneur's consistent and relentless pursuit of a set of core values that everyone in the company can believe in. *For instance, Amy Miller, founder of Amy's Ice Creams, a seven-store chain of gourmet ice cream shops, knows that her company's competitive edge comes not only from selling quality products and friendly service but also from selling entertainment. Miller hires employees who enjoy performing for customers. They juggle their serving spades, toss scoops of ice cream to one another behind the counter, and dance on top of the freezer. They offer free ice cream to customers who will sing, dance, or recite poetry. Walking into an Amy's Ice Cream shop, customers might see employees wearing pajamas (on Sleepover Night) or masks (on Star Wars Night); candles (on Romance Night) or strobe lights (on Disco Night) decorating the store. Because of the culture Miller has created, employees know that part of their jobs is to create fun and entertainment for their customers; that's what keeps them coming back! Amy Miller has created a culture that values creativity in her company. It allows her employees to have fun, entertains the customers, and keeps the company growing at 30 percent a year![38]*

Nurturing the right culture in a company can enhance a company's competitive position by improving its ability to attract and retain quality workers and by creating an environment in which workers can grow and develop. In fact, as a younger generation of employees enters the workforce, companies are finding that offering a "cool" culture gives them an edge in attracting the best workers. Like Amy's Ice Creams, these companies embrace nontraditional, relaxed, fun cultures that incorporate concepts such as casual dress, virtual teams, telecommuting, flexible work schedules, on-site massages, cappucinos in company cafeterias, and other cutting-edge concepts. "Cool companies are revamping the traditional notions of business," explains one expert.[39] Although creating a "cool" culture involves both art and science, the companies that have been most successful tend to rely on certain principles:[40]

Respect for work and life balance. Cool companies recognize that their employees have lives away from work. One recent study of Generation X workers found that the companies that people most wanted to work for erased the traditional barriers between home life and work life by making it easier for employees to deal with the pressures they face away from their jobs. These businesses offer flexible work schedules, part-time jobs, job sharing, telecommuting, sabbaticals, and on-site day care and dry cleaning. *At OddzOn Products, a small toy manufacturer, managers recently closed the office in the middle of the day and took all 100 employees to a movie! At the Rockwell Group, employees are free to bring their dogs to work.* In short, cool companies see that work can be fun and do everything they can to make it so.

A sense of purpose. Cool companies use a strong sense of purpose to make employees feel connected to the company's mission. At motorcycle legend Harley-Davidson, employees are so in tune with the company's mission that some of them have tatooed the company's name on their bodies!

Diversity. Cool companies not only accept cultural diversity in their workforces, they embrace it, actively seeking out workers with different backgrounds. As one researcher puts it, "Cool companies are *a part of* the world rather than *apart from* the world."[41] They recognize that a workforce that has a rich mix of cultural diversity gives their companies more talent, skills, and abilities from which to draw. The result is a stronger company. *For example, Patrick Thean, founder of Metasys, Inc., a small company producing transportation software, says that his company's culturally diverse workforce has become one of its greatest strengths. "A diverse team increases my speed of doing business," says Thean. Thean, himself an immigrant from Singapore, considers the entire globe his hiring ground. His employees hail from such places as India, Nigeria, Wales, the United States, and many other nations.[42]*

Integrity. Employees want to work for a company that stands for honesty and integrity. They do not want to check their own personal value system at the door when they report to work. Indeed, many workers take pride in the fact that they work for a company that is ethical and socially responsible. They expect their company to communicate with them openly and honestly about issues that matter to them. We will discuss the issue of integrity in more detail in chapter 21.

Companies with "cool" cultures find it much easier to attract and retain quality workers than those that lack "coolness." One characteristic that "cool" companies exhibit is a culturally diverse workforce. At Metasys, employees come from all over the globe. Their diversity strengthens the company, according to founder Patrick Thean.

Participative management. According to a recent study, one of the primary characteristics of a cool company is a participative management style. Company owners and managers trust and empower employees at all levels of the organization to make decisions and to take the actions they need to do their jobs well. "These companies realize that employees on the front lines often have the best ideas," says the study's author.[43] *For instance, at Nantucket Nectars, a small juice company, the management style is so participative that there is no established organizational hierarchy and there are no secretaries.*

Learning environment. Cool companies encourage and support lifelong learning among their employees. "These are companies in which employees leave at the end of the day knowing more than when they started," says one author.[44] That attitude is a strong magnet for the best and the brightest young workers, who know that to stay at the top of their fields, they must always be learning.

Does it really matter how cool a company is? Netcape Communication's Margie Mader, whose official title is Director of Bringing in the Cool People, believes that it is. "With all the competition in hiring, you need to give yourself an edge," she says.[45] Cool companies find it much easier to attract, retain, and motivate workers. In short, the right culture helps a small company compete more effectively.

Managing Growth and a Changing Culture. As companies grow from seedling businesses into leggy saplings and beyond (perhaps into giants in the business forest), they often experience dramatic changes in their culture. Procedures become more formal, operations grow more widespread, jobs take on more structure, communication becomes more difficult, and the company's personality begins to change. As more workers come on board, employees find it more difficult to know everyone in the company and what their jobs are. Unless an entrepreneur works hard to maintain her company's unique culture, she may wake up one day to find that she has sacrificed that culture—and the competitive edge that went with it—in the name of growth.

Ironically, growth can sometimes be a small company's biggest enemy, causing a once successful business to spiral out of control into oblivion. The problem stems from the fact that the organizational structure (or lack of it!) and the style of management that makes an entrepreneurial start-up so successful often cannot support the business as it grows into adolescence and maturity. As a company grows, not only does its culture tend to change but so does its need for a management infrastructure capable of supporting that growth. Compounding the problem is the entrepreneur's tendency to see all growth as good. After all, who wouldn't want to be the founder of a small company whose rapid growth makes it destined to become the next rising star in the industry? Yet, achieving rapid growth and *managing* it are two distinct challenges. Entrepreneurs must be aware of the challenges rapid growth brings with it; otherwise they may find their companies crumbling around them as they reach warp speed. *Looking back, one entrepreneur whose specialty-food business "crashed into the wall" sees fast, uncontrolled growth as the primary cause of his company's troubles. In just five years, James Bildner took his business from start-up to a publicly held company with 20 retail stores, 1,250 employees, and $48 million in sales. Uncontrolled growth, which magnified J. Bildner and Sons' other problems, sent the company careening into "the wall." Bildner says, "Rapid growth itself—too many locations, new products, new people; too much or too little capital; and always too little investment up front in financial systems and controls—makes everything worse." Like many entrepreneurs, Bildner never saw (or chose to ignore) the signs of trouble—diminishing cash flow, rapid turnover of good people, expanding general and administrative expenses, and increasing distance from the core of the business—until it was too late. The company survived, but, according to Bildner, it is "a shadow of its former self."*[46]

In many cases, small companies achieve impressive growth because they bypass the traditional organizational structures, forgo rigid policies and procedures, and maintain maximum flexibility. Small companies often have the edge over their larger rivals because they are naturally quick to respond; they concentrate on creating new product and service lines; and they are willing to take the risks necessary to conquer new markets.

But growth brings with it change: changes in management style, organizational strategy, and methods of operations. Growth produces organizational complexity. In this period of transition, the entrepreneur's challenge is to walk a fine line between retaining the small-company traits that are the seeds of the business's success and incorporating the elements of the infrastructure essential to supporting and sustaining the company's growth.

STRUCTURE

Entrepreneurs have traditionally relied on six different management styles to guide their companies as they grow. The first three (craftsman, classic, and coordinator) involve running a company without any management assistance and are best suited for small companies in the early stages of growth; the last three (entrepreneur-plus-employee team, small partnership, big-team venture) rely on a team approach to run the company as its growth speeds up.[47] In recent years entrepreneurs whose companies are growing have been turning more and more to a formerly, big-business strategy: team-based management.

The Craftsman. One of the earliest management styles to emerge was the craftsman. These entrepreneurs literally run a one-man (or one-woman) show; they do everything themselves because their primary concern is with the quality of the products or services they produce. Woodworkers, cabinetmakers, glassblowers, and other craftsmen rely on this style of management. The benefits of this style include minimal operating expenses (no employees to pay), very simple operations (no workers' compensation, incentive plans, or organization charts), no supervision problems, and the entrepreneur's total control over both the business and its quality.

Of course, one disadvantage of the craftsman management style is that the entrepreneur must do *everything* in the business, including those tasks that she does not enjoy. The biggest disadvantage of this style, however, is the limitations it puts on a company's ability to grow. A business can grow only so big before the craftsman has to take on other workers and delegate authority to them. Before choosing this management style, a craftsman must decide: "How large do I want my business to become?"

The Classic. As business opportunities arise, a craftsman quickly realizes that she could magnify the company's capacity to grow by hiring other people to work. The classic entrepreneur brings in other people but does not delegate any significant authority to them, choosing instead to "watch over everything" herself. She insists on tight supervision, constantly monitors employees' work, and performs all of the critical tasks herself. Classic entrepreneurs do not feel comfortable delegating the power and the authority for making decisions to anyone else; they prefer to keep a tight rein on the business and on everyone who works there.

Even though this management style gives a business more growth potential than the craftsman style, there is a limit to how much an entrepreneur can accomplish. Therefore, entrepreneurs who choose to operate this way must limit the complexity of their business if they are to grow at all. An inherent danger of this style is the entrepreneur's tendency to "micromanage" every aspect of the business rather than spend her time focusing on those tasks that are most important and most productive for the company.

The Coordinator. The coordinator style of management gives an entrepreneur the ability to create a fairly large company with very few employees. In this type of business (often called a virtual corporation because the company is actually quite "hollow"), the entrepreneur farms out a large portion of the work to other companies and then coordinates all of the activities from "headquarters." By hiring out at least some of the work (in some cases, most of the work), the entrepreneur is free to focus on pumping up sales and pushing the business to higher levels. Some coordinators hire someone to manufacture their products, pay brokers to sell them, and arrange for someone to collect their accounts receivable! With the help of just a few workers, a coordinator can build a multimillion-dollar business!

Although the coordinator style sounds like an easy way to build a business, it can be very challenging to implement. The business's success is highly dependent on its suppliers and their ability to produce quality products and services in a timely fashion. Getting suppliers to perform on time is one of the hardest tasks. Plus, if the entrepreneur hires someone else to manufacture the product, she loses control over its quality.

The Entrepreneur-plus-Employee Team. As their companies grow, many entrepreneurs see the need to shift to a team-based management style. The entrepreneur-plus-employee team gives an entrepreneur the power to grow the business beyond the scope of the manager-only styles. In this style, the entrepreneur delegates authority to key employees, but she retains the final decision-making authority in the company. Of course, the transition from a management style where the entrepreneur retains almost total authority to one based on delegation requires some adjustments for employees and especially for the entrepreneur! Employees have to learn to make decisions on their own, and the manager must learn to give workers the authority, the responsibility, and the information to make them. Delegating requires a manager to realize that there are several ways to accomplish a task and that sometimes employees will make mistakes. Still, delegation allows a manager to get the maximum benefit from each employee while freeing herself up to focus on the most important tasks in the business.

The Small Partnership. As the business world grows more complex and interrelated, many entrepreneurs find that there is strength in numbers. Rather than manage a company alone, they choose to share the managerial responsibilities with one or more partners (or shareholders). As we saw in chapter 3, the benefits are many. Perhaps the biggest advantage is the ability to share responsibility for the company with others who have a real stake in it and are willing to work hard to make it a success. Some of the most effective partnerships are those in which the owners' skills complement one another, creating natural lines for dividing responsibilities. Of course, the downside to this management style includes the necessity of giving up total control over the business and the potential for personality conflicts and disputes over the company's direction.

The Big-Team Venture. The broadest-based management style is the big-team venture, which typically emerges over time as a company grows larger. The workload demands on a small number of partners can quickly outstrip the time and energy they can devote to them, even if they are effective delegators. Once a company reaches this point, managers must expand the breadth of the management team's experience to handle the increasing level of responsibility that results from the sheer size of the company. If the company's operations have become global in scope, the need for such a big management team is even more pronounced; the big-team venture is almost a necessity.

Any of these management styles can be successful for an entrepreneur if it matches her personality and the company's goals. The key is to plan for the company's growth and to lay out a strategy for managing the changes the company will experience as it grows. "Ask yourself whether your management style is really effective for a business of this particular size, shape, and complexity," advises Ronald Merrill and Henry Sedgwick, the authors of *The New Venture Handbook*. "If the answer is no, modify your plan."[48]

Team-Based Management. Large companies have been using self-directed work teams for years to improve quality, increase productivity, raise morale, lower costs, and boost motivation; yet team-based management is just now beginning to catch on in small firms. In fact, a team approach may be best suited for small companies. Even though converting a traditional company to teams requires a major change in management style, it is usually relatively easy to implement with a small number of workers. A **self-directed work team** is a group of workers from different functional areas of a company who work together as a unit largely without supervision, making decisions and performing tasks that once belonged only to managers. Some teams may be temporary, attacking and solving a specific problem, but many are permanent components of an organization's structure. As their name implies, these teams manage themselves, performing such functions as setting work schedules, ordering raw materials, evaluating and purchasing equipment, developing budgets, hiring and firing team members, solving problems, and a host of other activities. The goal is to get people working together to serve customers better.

Managers in companies using teams don't just sit around drinking coffee, however. In fact, they work just as hard as before, but the nature of their work changes dramatically. Before teams, managers were bosses who made most of the decisions affecting their subordinates alone and hoarded information and power for themselves. In a team environment, managers take on the role of coaches who empower those around them to make decisions affecting their work and share information with workers. As facilitators, their job is to support and to serve the teams functioning in the organization and to make sure they produce re-

Table 19.6 Making the Transition from a Traditional Organization to a Team-Based One

Traditional Organization	Team-Based Organization
Management-driven	Customer-driven
Isolated specialists	Multiskilled workforce
Many job descriptions	Few job descriptions
Information limited	Information shared
Many management levels	Few management levels
Departmental focus	Whole-business focus
Management-controlled	Team-regulated
Policy- and procedure-based	Values- and principles-based
Selection-based employment	Training-based employment
Temporary changes	Ongoing changes
Seemingly organized	Seemingly chaotic
Incremental improvement	Continuous improvement
High management commitment	High worker commitment

SOURCE: Kenneth P. De Meuse and Thomas J. Bergmann, "Managers Must Relinquish Control If They Are to Establish Effective Work Teams," *Small Business Forum*, Spring 1996, p. 86.

sults. "It's not easy for an entrepreneur to take this role, but it is the way to get a productive team," says one management consultant.[49]

Companies have strong competitive reasons for using team-based management. Companies that use teams effectively report significant gains in quality, reductions in cycle time, lower costs, increased customer satisfaction, and improved employee motivation and morale. "Your competitiveness is your ability to use the skills and knowledge of people most effectively, and teams are the best way to do that," says one manager.[50] A team-based approach is not for every organization, however. Teams are *not* easy to start, and switching from a traditional organization structure to a team-based one is filled with potential pitfalls. Teams work best in environments where the work is interdependent and people must interact to accomplish their goals. Although a team approach might succeed in a small plant making gas grills, it would most likely fail miserably in a real estate office, where salespeople work independently with little interaction required to make a sale. Table 19.6 describes some of the transitions a company must make as it moves from a traditional organizational structure to a team-based style.

In some cases, teams have been a company's salvation from failure and extinction; in others, the team approach has flopped. What made the difference? What causes teams to fail? The following errors are common:

◆ *Assigning teams inappropriate tasks.* One of the biggest mistakes managers make with teams is assigning them to tasks that individuals ought to be performing.

◆ *Creating "make-nice" teams.* For a team to perform effectively it must have a clear purpose, and every team member must understand it. Unfortunately, managers sometimes create a team but fail to give it any meaningful work assignments other than to "make nice with one another."

◆ *Inadequate training for team members and team leaders.* Some organizations form teams and then expect employees, long accustomed to individual responsibilities, to magically become team players and contributors. Teams are very complex social systems influenced by pressures from within and buffeted by forces from without, and workers need training to become effective team players.

- *Sabotaging teams with underperformers.* Rather than fire poor performers (always an unpleasant task), some managers put them on teams, hoping that the members will either discipline them or get rid of them. It never works. Underperformers undermine team performance.

- *Switching to team responsibilities but keeping pay individually oriented.* One of the quickest ways to destroy a team system is to pay team members on the basis of their individual performance.[51]

To ensure teams' success, managers must:

- *Make sure that teams are appropriate for the company and the nature of its work.* A good starting point is to create a "map" of the company's work flow that shows how workers build a product or deliver a service. Is the work interdependent, complex, and interactive? Would teamwork improve the company's performance?

- *Form teams around the natural work flow and give them specific tasks to accomplish.* Teams can be effective only if managers challenge them to accomplish specific, measurable objectives. They need targets to shoot for.

- *Provide adequate support and training for team members and leaders.* Team success requires a new set of skills. Workers must learn how to communicate, resolve conflict, support one another, and solve problems as a team. Smart managers see that workers get the training they need.

- *Involve team members in determining how their performances will be measured, what will be measured, and when it will be measured.* Doing so gives team members a sense of ownership and pride about what they are accomplishing.

- *Make at least part of team members' pay dependent on team performance.* Companies that have used teams successfully still pay members individually, but they make successful team work a major part of an individual's performance review. "Teams will not work unless compensation is at least partly team-based," says one expert.[52]

Figure 19.1 on page 670 shows the four stages teams go through on their way to performing effectively and accomplishing goals.

When Michael Dettmers, co-founder of Dettmers Industries, a small company that makes seating and table products for private aircraft, decided to reorganize his company around teams, he knew that success depended on training his workers properly. Starting with just a single team of workers, Dettmers promised them 25 percent of sales on the specific products they made, and he guaranteed them that they would not earn less than they had the previous year. The team would bear the responsibility of hiring, scheduling, serving customers, maintaining quality, and managing its own cash flow. To give team members the tools they needed, Dettmers required them to attend 13 hours of training each quarter for a full year.

The experiment was a success, and soon workers were busy forming more teams. "Once people began to see that if they worked more effectively as a team, they would make more money," says Dettmers. "They had enthusiasm for working in this new way, and they made a commitment to learning." Dettmers continued training workers in team processes and also spent a lot of time on the shop floor coaching teams, "facilitating meetings and helping resolve disputes." The payoff for the company and its workers has been phenomenal. Dettmers' employees earn between $13 and $20 per hour (compared with $11 to $12 in comparable industries) and cycle time is down. One team has reduced the time required to produce a single product from 140 hours to just 80! The company's sales are up by 50 percent, and its profit margins are a healthy 20 percent—twice the industry standard. Workers are

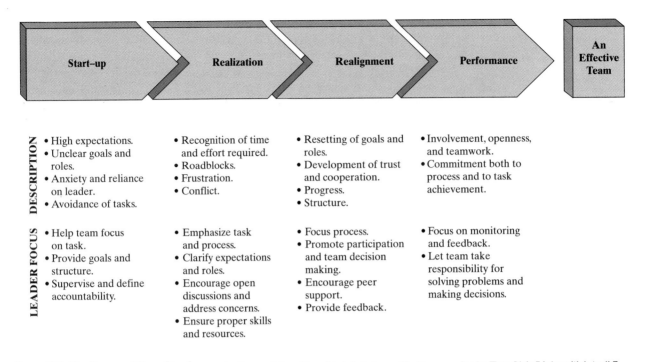

	Start-up	Realization	Realignment	Performance	An Effective Team
DESCRIPTION	• High expectations. • Unclear goals and roles. • Anxiety and reliance on leader. • Avoidance of tasks.	• Recognition of time and effort required. • Roadblocks. • Frustration. • Conflict.	• Resetting of goals and roles. • Development of trust and cooperation. • Progress. • Structure.	• Involvement, openness, and teamwork. • Commitment both to process and to task achievement.	
LEADER FOCUS	• Help team focus on task. • Provide goals and structure. • Supervise and define accountability.	• Emphasize task and process. • Clarify expectations and roles. • Encourage open discussions and address concerns. • Ensure proper skills and resources.	• Focus process. • Promote participation and team decision making. • Encourage peer support. • Provide feedback.	• Focus on monitoring and feedback. • Let team take responsibility for solving problems and making decisions.	

Figure 19.1 The Stages of Team Development   SOURCE: Adapted from Mark A. Frohman, "Do Teams . . . But Do Them Right," *Industry Week*, April 3, 1995, p. 22; "The Stages of a Group," *Communication Briefings*, October 1997, p. 6.

more satisfied as well. "[Team-based management] gives you a sense of ownership," explains one team leader.[53]

7he Challenge of Motivating Workers

5 Discuss the ways in which entrepreneurs can motivate their workers to higher levels of performance.

Motivation is the degree of effort an employee exerts to accomplish a task; it shows up as excitement about work. Motivating workers to higher levels of performance is one of the most difficult and challenging tasks facing a small business manager. Few things are more frustrating to a business owner than an employee with a tremendous amount of talent who lacks the desire to use it. This section discusses four aspects of motivation: empowerment, job design, rewards and compensation, and feedback.

EMPOWERMENT

One of the principles underlying the team-based management style is empowerment. **Empowerment** involves giving workers at every level of the organization the authority, the freedom, and the responsibility to control their own work, to make decisions, and to take action to meet the company's objectives. Competitive forces and a more demanding workforce challenge business owners and managers to share power with everyone in the organization, whether they use a team-based approach or not.

Empowering employees requires a different style of management and leadership from that of the traditional manager. Many old-style managers are unwilling to share power with anyone because they fear doing so weakens their authority and reduces their influence. In fact, exactly the *opposite* is true! Business owners who share information, responsibility, authority, and power soon discover that their success (and their company's success) is magnified many times over. Empowered workers become more successful on the job, which means the entrepreneur also becomes more successful.

Empowerment builds on what real business leaders already know: that the people in their organizations bring with them to work an amazing array of talents, skills, knowledge, and abilities. Workers are willing—even anxious—to put these to use; unfortunately, in too many small businesses, suffocating management styles and poorly designed jobs quash workers' enthusiasm and motivation. Enlightened business owners recognize their workers' abilities, develop them, and then give workers the freedom and the power to use them. "Employees work best when you give them the opportunity to use their own creativity and imagination," explains one manager.[54]

When implemented properly, empowerment can produce impressive results, not only for the small business but also for newly empowered employees. For the business, benefits typically include significant productivity gains, quality improvements, more satisfied customers, improved morale, and increased employee motivation. *When Rheacom, a supplier of parts to the aerospace industry, switched to empowered work teams, workers unleashed a torrent of new ideas aimed at improving the company's performance. One suggestion led to a reduction in the machine time required for a brake shoe the company had been making for 25 years from more than three and a half hours to less than one hour.[55]*

For workers, empowerment offers the chance to do a greater variety of work that is more interesting and challenging. Empowerment challenges workers to make the most of their creativity, imagination, knowledge, and skills. This method of management encourages them to take the initiative to identify and solve problems on their own and as part of a team. As empowered workers see how the various parts of a company's manufacturing or service systems fit together, they realize their need to acquire more skills and knowledge to do their jobs well. Entrepreneurs must realize that empowerment and training go hand in hand.

Not every worker *wants* to be empowered, however. Some will resist, wanting only to "put in their eight hours and go home." One expert estimates that companies moving to empowerment can expect to lose about 5 percent of their workforce. "Out of every 100 employees, five are diehards who will be impossible to change," he says. Another 75 percent will accept empowerment and thrive under it, if it is done properly. The remaining 20 percent will pounce eagerly on empowerment because it is something they "have been waiting to do . . . their whole [work] lives," he says.[56] Empowerment works best when a business owner:[57]

- ◆ *is confident enough to give workers all of the authority and responsibility they can handle.* Early on, this may mean giving workers the power to tackle relatively simple assignments. But, as their confidence and ability grow, most workers are eager to take on more responsibility.

- ◆ *plays the role of coach and facilitator, not the role of meddlesome boss.* One sure-fired way to make empowerment fail is to give associates the power to attack a problem and then to hover over them, criticizing every move they make. Smart owners empower their workers and then get out of the way so they can do their jobs!

- ◆ *recognizes that empowered employees will make mistakes.* The worst thing an owner can do when empowered employees make mistakes is to hunt them down and punish them. That teaches everyone in the company to avoid taking risks and to always play it safe—something no innovative small business can afford.

- ◆ *hires people who can blossom in an empowered environment.* Empowerment is not for everyone. Owners quickly learn that as costly as hiring mistakes are, such errors are even more costly in an empowered environment. Ideal candidates are high-energy, self-starters who enjoy the opportunity to grow and to enhance their skills.

◆ *trains workers continuously to upgrade their skills.* Empowerment demands more of workers than traditional work methods. Managers are asking workers to solve problems and make decisions they have never made before. To handle these problems well, workers need training, especially in effective problem-solving techniques, communication, teamwork, and technical skills.

◆ *trusts workers to do their jobs.* Once workers are trained to do their jobs, owners must learn to trust them to assume responsibility for their jobs. After all, they are the real experts; they face the problems and challenges every day. One Japanese study found that workers "in the trenches" knew 100 percent of the problems in a company; supervisors knew 74 percent; and top managers knew just 4 percent![58]

◆ *listens to workers when they have ideas, solutions, or suggestions.* Because they are the experts on the job, employees often come up with incredibly insightful, innovative ideas for improving them—*if* business owners give them the chance. Failing to acknowledge or to act on employees' ideas sends them a clear message: Your ideas really don't count. "The greatest source of motivation is giving people some input into what they do every day," explains one expert.[59]

◆ *recognizes workers' contributions.* One of the most important tasks a business owner has is to recognize jobs well done. Some businesses reward workers with monetary awards; others rely on recognition and praise; still others use a combination of money and praise. Whatever system an owner chooses, the key to keeping a steady flow of ideas, improvements, suggestions, and solutions is to recognize the people who supply them.

◆ *shares information with workers.* For empowerment to succeed, business owners must make sure workers get adequate information, the raw material for good decision making. Some companies have gone beyond sharing information to embrace **open-book management,** in which employees have access to *all* of a company's records, including its financial statements. The goal of open-book management is to enable employees to understand why they need to raise productivity, improve quality, cut costs, and improve customer service. Under open book management, employees: (1) see and learn to understand the company's financial statements and other critical numbers in measuring its performance; (2) learn that a significant part of their jobs is making sure those critical numbers move in the right direction; and (3) have a direct stake in the company's success through profit sharing, ESOPs, or performance-based bonuses. In short, open-book management establishes the link between employees' knowledge and their performance. One expert writes, "Instead of telling employees how to cut defects, [open book management] asks them to boost profits—and lets them figure out how. Instead of giving them a reengineered job, it turns them into businesspeople. They experience the challenge—and the sheer fun and excitement—of matching wits with the marketplace, toting up the score, and sharing in the proceeds. . . . There's no better motivation."[60]

    To launch his art framing company's open-book management program, Jay Goltz, CEO of Artists' Frame, used a role-playing exercise designed to show employees exactly where the company's money went. "It occurred to me that employees had no idea what workers' compensation costs or what I spend on advertising or rent," he says. Goltz gathered his 110 employees and used oversized dollar bills from a hypothetical $100 order to show what portion of each sales dollar expenses eat up. At the end of the exercise, the volunteer who started with the $100 in revenue had $5 left. "It was easy for employees to see that the difference between making money and losing money is sliver thin," says Goltz. According to Goltz, the fact that his simple demonstration got through to his employees is evident throughout the company.[61]

JOB DESIGN

Over the years, managers have learned that the job itself and the way it is designed can be a source of motivation (or demotivation!) for workers. In some companies, work is organized on the principle of **job simplification,** breaking the work down into its simplest form and standardizing each task, as in some assembly-line operations. The scope of jobs organized in such a way is extremely narrow, resulting in impersonal, monotonous, and boring work that creates little challenge or motivation for workers. Job simplification invites workers to "check their brains at the door" and offers them little opportunity for excitement, enthusiasm, or pride in their work. The result can be apathetic, unmotivated workers who don't care about quality, customers, or costs.

To break this destructive cycle, some companies have redesigned jobs so that they offer workers intrinsic rewards and motivation. Three strategies are common: job enlargement, job rotation, and job enrichment.

Job enlargement (or **horizontal job loading**) adds more tasks to a job to broaden its scope. For instance, rather than having an employee simply mount four screws in computers as they come down an assembly line, the worker might assemble, install, and test the entire motherboard (perhaps as part of a team). The idea is to make the job more varied and to allow employees to perform a more complete unit of work.

Job rotation involves cross-training employees so they can move from one job in the company to others, giving them a greater number and variety of tasks to perform. As employees learn other jobs within an organization, both their skills and their understanding of the company's purpose and processes rise. Cross-trained workers are more valuable because they give a company the flexibility to shift workers from low-demand jobs to those where they are most needed.[62] As an incentive for workers to learn to perform other jobs within an operation, some companies offer **skill-based pay,** a system under which the more skills workers acquire, the more they earn.

Job enrichment (or **vertical job loading**) involves building motivators into a job by increasing the planning, decision-making, organizing, and controlling functions— i.e., traditional managerial tasks—workers perform. The idea is to make every employee a manager—at least a manager of his own job. Notice that empowerment is based on the principle of job enrichment.

To enrich employees' jobs, a business owner must build five core characteristics into them:

◆ *Skill variety.* The degree to which a job requires a variety of different skills, talents, and activities from the worker. Does the job require the worker to perform a variety of tasks that demand a variety of skills and abilities, or does it force him to perform the same task repeatedly?

◆ *Task identity.* The degree to which a job allows the worker to complete a whole or identifiable piece of work. Does the employee build an entire piece of furniture (perhaps as part of a team), or does he merely attach four screws?

◆ *Task significance.* The degree to which a job substantially influences the lives or work of others—employees or final customers. Does the employee get to deal with customers, either internal or external? One effective way to establish task significance is to put employees in touch with customers so that they can see how customers use the product or service they make.

◆ *Autonomy.* The degree to which a job gives a worker freedom, independence, and discretion in planning and performing tasks. Does the employee make decisions affecting his work, or must he rely on someone else (e.g., the owner, a manager, or a supervisor) to "call the shots"?

◆ *Feedback.* The degree to which a job gives the worker direct, timely information about the quality of his performance. Does the job give employees feedback about the quality of their work, or does the product (and all information about it) simply disappear after it leaves the worker's station?

Tom Warner, a fourth-generation plumber who took over his father's heating, ventilation, and air conditioning (HVAC) company in 1989, has used innovative job designs to transform his employees' motivation and attitudes toward their jobs, and, in the process, to revitalize the company's sales and profits. Until 1992, Warner Corporation was a traditional HVAC business with a crew of workers waiting for the boss to tell them where to go, what to do, and when to do it. Warner Corp. was also a company headed for financial trouble. Then Warner decided to redesign the jobs in his company. The HVAC technicians, plumbers, and electricians would become "area technical directors" (ATDs), who would, in essence, manage their own businesses within Warner Corporation. ATDs got their own territories (based on Zip Codes) in which they developed customer relationships, handled their own equipment, did their own sales work, and collected their own accounts. By transforming his technicians into businesspeople who make decisions and are responsible for generating profits and keeping customers happy, Warner has instilled in them a sense of pride and ownership in their work that was missing before.

Customers couldn't be happier because they now have "personal ATDs." Describing Ron Inscoe, "her" ATD, one satisfied customer says, "Ron told me to call him if I have any problems because this is his territory. I think it's a great idea. I have somebody to relate to—not just some corporation." That satisfaction is showing up in rising profits, sales, and market share. The ATDs share in Warner's success; the more money the company makes, the more money they make. Warner credits the job redesign with his company's turnaround. "Two or three years ago, I had to think of everything, and people just waited for me," he says. "Now our people come up with their own ideas, and I'm cheering more than leading."[63]

As the nation's workforce and the companies employing them continue to change, business is changing the way people work, moving away from a legion of full-time employees in traditional 8-to-5, on-site jobs. Organizational structures, even in small companies, are flatter than ever before, as the lines between traditional "managers" and "workers" get blurrier. Rather than resembling the current pyramid, the organization of tomorrow will more closely resemble a spider's web, with a network of interconnected employee specialists working in teams and using lightning-fast communication to make decisions without having to go through three or four layers of management. One expert in organizational change says, "There is going to be a tremendous shift during the next 25 years toward independence, autonomy, and self-directedness, with people and teams accountable for their own performances. Companies [won't] be able to compete without redefining the way that work is done and how organizations are managed."[64] Many of these shifts are already taking place in the form of flextime, job sharing, flexplace, and telecommuting.

Flextime is an arrangement under which employees build their work schedules around a set of "core hours"—such as 11 A.M. to 3 P.M.—but have flexibility about when they start and stop work. For instance, one worker might choose to come in at 7 A.M. and leave at 3 P.M. to attend her son's soccer game, while another may work from 11 A.M. to 7 P.M. A recent survey by the Society for Human Resources Management found that 46 percent of companies with fewer than 500 workers offered flextime programs.[65]

Flextime not only raises worker morale, but it also makes it easier for companies to attract high-quality young workers who want rewarding careers without sacrificing their lifestyles. In addition, companies using flextime schedules often experience lower levels of tardiness and absenteeism. *Patty DeDominic, founder of PDQ Personnel Services in Los Angeles, says her company's decade-old flextime policy has played an important role in the company's ability to attract and retain quality workers. DeDominic's 30 employees can choose from several flextime options, depending on the nature of their particular jobs. De-Dominic has found that flextime suits both her company and her employees quite well. "The demands on service companies like mine are not confined to nine to five," she says.*[66]

Job sharing is a work arrangement in which two or more people share a single full-time job. For instance, two college students might share the same 40-hour-a-week job, one working mornings and the other working afternoons. Although job sharing affects a relatively small portion of the nation's workforce, it is an important job design strategy for some companies that find it difficult to recruit capable, qualified full-time workers.

Flexplace is a work arrangement in which employees work at a place other than the traditional office, such as a satellite branch closer to their homes or, in some cases, at home. Flexplace is an easy job design strategy for companies to use because of **telecommuting.** Using modern communication technology such as e-mail, fax machines, and laptop computers, employees have more flexibility in choosing where they work. Today, it is quite simple for workers to hook up electronically to their workplaces (and to all of the people and the information there) from practically anywhere on the planet! According to Link Resources, approximately 12 million workers are telecommuters, and the number is growing rapidly; by 2002, the Department of Transportation estimates that 15 percent of the U.S. workforce will be telecommuting.[67]

Telecommuting not only makes it easier for employees to strike a balance between their work and home lives, but it also leads to higher productivity. Studies show that workers say they are from 5 percent to 20 percent more productive when working at home because they encounter fewer distractions.[68] "Telecommuting lets you escape the standard office distractions—meetings, interruptions, the mad search for the missing file, the executive mood swings, the hotheaded turf battles, the corporate mating dances and posturing," explains one telecommuting employee.[69] *Richard Grove, owner of PrimeTime Publicity and Media Consulting, reaps the many benefits of telecommuting, including increased productivity, fewer sick days, the need for less office space, and, perhaps most important, the ability to recruit top-quality workers. Eight of the 15 employees at Grove's public relations firm telecommute from their homes. He sees them face to face just twice a year, but that doesn't interfere with their ability to perform their jobs well.*[70] Before shifting to telecommuting, Grove had to address some important issues:

- *Does the nature of the work fit telecommuting?* Obviously, some jobs are better-suited for telecommuting than others. Positions in which employees work independently, use computers frequently, or spend a great deal of time calling on customers and clients are good candidates for telecommuting.

- *Can you monitor compliance with federal wage and hour laws for telecommuters?* In general, employers must keep the same employment records for telecommuters that they do for traditional office workers.

- *Which workers are best-suited for telecommuting?* Those who are self-motivated, are disciplined, and have been around long enough to establish solid relationships with coworkers make the best telecommuters.

- *Can you provide the equipment and the technical support telecommuters need to be productive?* Telecommuting often requires an investment in portable computers, fax machines, extra telephone lines, and software. Workers usually need technical training as well because they often assume the role of their own technical support staff.

- *Are you adequately insured?* Employers should be sure that the telecommuting equipment employees use in their homes is covered under their insurance policies.

◆ *Can you keep in touch?* Telecommuting works well as long as long-distance employees stay in touch with headquarters. Frequent telephone conferences, regular e-mail messages, and occasional personal appearances in the office will prevent employees from losing contact with what's happening "at work."

A variation of telecommuting that is growing in popularity is **hoteling,** in which employees who spend most of their time away from the office anyway use the same office space at different times, just as travelers use the same hotel rooms on different days. Businesses that use hoteling have been able to reduce the cost of leasing office space, sometimes by as much as 50 percent. *At Tandem Computers, for example, an average of three employees use each of the company's hotel offices, greatly reducing its need for permanent offices.*[71] Workers can connect their laptops into the company's computer network and e-mail system, forward their telephone calls to their temporary offices, and even move mobile file cabinets in when they need them. Flexible office designs and furnishings allow workers to configure these "hot offices" (so called because they turn over so quickly that the seats are still hot from the previous user) to suit their individual needs.

REWARDS AND COMPENSATION

The rewards an employee gets from the job itself are intrinsic rewards, but managers have at their disposal a wide variety of extrinsic rewards to motivate workers. The key to using rewards to motivate involves tailoring them to the needs and characteristics of the workers. "The core of successful motivation is tapping into the things that are really important to people: taking the time to find out what those are, and structuring your recognition around those in the context of the job," says one motivation expert.[72] For instance, to a technician making $25,000 a year, a chance to earn a $3,000 performance bonus would most likely be a powerful motivator. To an executive earning $125,000 a year, it would not be.

One of the most popular rewards is money. Cash is an effective motivator—up to a point. Over the last 20 years, many companies have moved to **pay-for-performance compensation systems,** in which employees' pay depends upon how well they perform their job. In other words, extra productivity equals extra pay. By linking employees' compensation directly to the company's financial performance, a business owner increases the likelihood that workers will achieve performance targets that are in their best interest and in the company's best interest. One recent survey of small companies by National Small Business United found that more than half rewarded their workers with bonuses and other performance-related incentives.[73] Such systems work only when employees see a clear connection between their performance and their pay. That's where small companies actually have an advantage over large businesses. Because they work for small companies, employees can see more clearly the impact their performance has on the company's profitability and ultimate success than their counterparts at large corporations. To be successful, however, pay-for-performance systems should meet the following criteria:

◆ Employees' incentive pay must be clearly and closely linked to their performances. That's where most compensation systems based on simple annual raises lose their effectiveness.

◆ Entrepreneurs must set up the system so that employees see the connection between what they do every day on the job—selling to customers, producing a product, or anything else—and the rewards they receive under the system.

◆ The system must be simple enough so that employees understand and trust it. Complex systems that employees have difficulty understanding will not produce the desired results.

IN THE FOOTSTEPS OF AN ENTREPRENEUR

How Do You Manage Generation X?

*E*veryone has heard the stereotypes of Generation X, those born between 1965 and 1977: they are lazy, anti-authority slackers with brief attention spans and absolutely no loyalty to their employees. But are these stereotypes true? Not necessarily.

The key lies in knowing what Gen X workers expect in the workplace. Pamela Hamilton, founder of Collaborative Communications, a public relations agency with 13 employees (12 of whom are Generation Xers) says, "It is a challenge to manage them, but if you do, you'll get terrific results." Indeed, learning to manage Generation X workers is essential; they make up 34 percent of the workforce! The problem is that most managers (many of whom sit squarely in the baby boomer generation) assume that Generation X workers are just like themselves, with the same goals and aspirations. As a result, they treat their Generation X workers the way they themselves want to be treated and are befuddled when their attempts fail.

How can business owners motivate, stimulate, and reward their Generation X employees? The following suggestions will help:

Don't rely on the traditional career motivators such as fancy job titles and more pay. "What gets these folks up in the morning is very different from why baby boomers wake up," says Pamela Hamilton. "They are not interested in climbing the conventional job ladder. Offer them an additional $10,000 a year, and they won't necessarily hop jobs." Gen X workers prefer instead jobs that challenge them, require diverse skills, and contribute to the company's success. They want to have an impact on the company's overall mission.

Give them challenging assignments that allow them to learn more skills. Generation X workers value education and want to continuously upgrade their knowledge. Lee Hunt, founder of a creative design firm, has had tremendous success in attracting and retaining Generation X employees by emphasizing the educational benefits his company offers them. "When I talk to them, I say, 'You can probably make more money at a bigger company, but I'll give you a chance to try a lot of different things at once,'" he says.

Treat them as individuals. One hallmark of Generation X employees is their desire to be treated as individuals. Busi-

ness owners who set up reward systems that take into account their employees' unique tastes and preferences will be more successful than those who don't. One entrepreneur found that concert tickets and CDs were effective motivators for some of his Gen X employees. Also, Generation X employees are drawn to companies that offer flextime, telecommuting, and casual dress codes—all features that allow them to express their individuality. "Provide a degree of choice, and members of this generation flourish," says one employer.

Avoid an authoritarian approach. The surest way to alienate Gen X employees is to manage with the attitude "It's my way or the highway." These employees expect managers to explain the "whats" and the "whys"—but *not* the "hows"—of their assignments. They thrive on a participative approach coupled with plenty of two-way communication.

Trust them. Another turnoff for Generation X employees is a manager who is constantly checking up on them to make sure they are doing their job. These workers call it "parenting," and they hate it! Of course, managers must have control systems in place, but they must learn to trust employees to do their jobs without constant intervention and supervision. One expert advises, "Don't check to see if they are doing the job right—that sends the wrong parental signal—but check to see if they need any support or guidance."

Offer them varied assignments. Gen Xers thrive on multiple challenges. "They are happy doing three things at once," says one business owner. "A job with plenty of variety keeps them challenged."

Say what you mean and mean what you say. Generation X workers also value companies that have principles and stand for integrity. If they sense a streak of insincerity or hypocrisy in a business owner, they are likely to leave the company. They judge their managers not so much by what they say but by what they do.

Offer frequent rewards. Annual performance appraisals and salary adjustments don't click with Generation Xers. They want lots of feedback on their performance, and they want it frequently. Offbeat awards such as a special parking space, a day off, or a massage often have as much impact as financial rewards. The key is to recognize top performers frequently.

Small companies are ideally suited for Generation X employees because they offer workers the chance to get involved in many different aspects of the company and because workers can make a difference in the company's future, both of which rank high on Gen Xer's list of priorities. Indeed, many of those who choose not to work for small companies start their own! One-fifth of all small business owners in the United

States are Generation Xers, and this generation has the highest business start-up rate among all the others.

---

1. How would you respond to a manager who used the technique described above? Explain.

2. Write a one-page paper describing a job you have held in which your manager did *not* use effective management and motivational techniques. What impact did the manager's style

have on your level of motivation? On job performance? On morale? What suggestions would you make to improve the situation?

Sources: Adapted from Roberta Maynard, "A Less-Stressed Work Force," *Nation's Business*, November 1996, pp. 50–51; Robert McGarvey, "X Appeal," *Entrepreneur*, May 1997, pp. 87–89; "Who Is Generation X?" *Business News*, Summer 1996, pp. 31–34; Susan Caminiti, "Young and Restless," *Your Company*, February/March 1998, pp. 36–47. ◆

◆ Employees must believe the system is fair.

◆ The system should be inclusive. Entrepreneurs are finding creative ways to reward *all* employees, no matter what their jobs might be. *Caribou Coffee, a chain of coffee houses located in the Southeast and Midwest, offers incentives to its coffee servers as well as to its store managers.*[74]

◆ The company should make frequent payouts to employees. A single annual payout is the worst schedule because employees have long since forgotten what they did to earn the incentive pay. Many companies pay employees the week after they have achieved an important goal. Regular and frequent feedback is an essential ingredient in any incentive-pay program.

For example, Mark Swepston, owner of Atlas Butler Heating and Cooling, was looking for a way to increase sales and to improve his company's cash flow, so he decided to enlist the help of his sales force. Swepston switched to a pay-for-performance system under which his six full-time sales representatives receive sales commissions rather than salaries. A salesperson gets 50 percent of a job's net income, but only after the company receives the customer's payment. Since the switch, Atlas receives customer payments four times faster than before, and its bad debt losses have dropped from 2.7 percent to just 0.3 percent. In addition to improving the company's financial performance, the new compensation system is also producing better customer service. "It's made [the sales representatives] pay more attention to the customers' needs. . . . This practice brings them one step closer to customers because their pocketbooks are affected," says Swepston.[75] Money isn't the only motivator business owners have at their disposal, of course. In fact, nonfinancial incentives can be more important sources of employee motivation than money! "Money is only a short-term motivator," claims one manager.[76] After its initial motivational impact, money loses its impact; it does not have a lasting motivational effect (and for small businesses, with their limited resources, a lasting effect is a plus). Often, the most meaningful motivating factors are the simplest ones—praise, recognition, respect, feedback, job security, promotions, and others—things that any small business, no matter how limited its budget, can do. "To get the right kind of people, you have to put together a compensation package for them," says one entrepreneur, "but what people really work for is appreciation and the feeling that success brings to them."[77] *For instance, one innovative home builder rewards his employees for exceptional work by naming streets after them in his subdivisions.*[78] *David Kaufer, co-founder of Kaufer Miller Communications, a small communications agency, surprises his 27 employees by treating them to a fun event such as a Seattle Mariners baseball game or an outing to play laser tag when the company reaches an important target.*[79] Small companies find that younger workers, especially Generation Xers, respond best to intangible rewards and not to monetary rewards. Wanting more balance in their work and personal lives than their baby boomer parents, Generation X workers are looking for workplaces that offer challenging assignments coupled with a sense of fun. They respond best to constant feedback that is specific and accurate and to managers who take the time to celebrate their successes. *When Trinity Communications, a small marketing-communications company surveyed its 11 Generation X employees to find out what attracts and motivates them, managers were a bit surprised to find that employees ranked a good 401(k) retirement plan, not salary, at the top of their financial concerns. Other motivating factors the employees ranked high were opportunities to learn, access to up-to-date technology, workforce diversity, and flexibility in job design and schedules. On the basis of the results of its survey, Trinity changed its benefits package to one more consistent with its employees' desires, including a more aggressive 401(k) plan, a more generous and flexible vacation policy, and home computers with Internet access for all workers.*[80]

Praise is another simple, yet powerful, motivational tool. People enjoy getting praise, especially from a manager or business owner; it's just human nature. As Mark Twain once said, "I can live for two months on a good compliment." Praise is an easy and inexpensive reward for employees producing extraordinary work. *For instance, at Mary Kay Inc.'s annual meeting, praise is the watchword; indeed it is one of the main reasons more than 36,000 beauty consultants from around the world gather in Dallas every year. At the meeting, superstar saleswomen receive praise and recognition from their peers and from company founder Mary Kay Ash in sessions that resemble a cross between an awards banquet and a tent revival. Women come away with crowns, sashes, pins, bracelets, and, of course, those coveted pink Cadillacs—plus a fervor to go out and sell lots of makeup!*[81]

One of the surest ways to kill high performance is simply to fail to recognize it and the employees responsible for it. Failing to praise good work eventually conveys the message that the owner either doesn't care about exceptional performance or cannot distinguish between good work and poor work. In either case, through inaction, the manager destroys employees' motivation to excel.

Because they lack the financial resources of bigger companies, small business owners must be more creative when it comes to giving rewards that motivate workers. In many cases, however, using rewards other than money gives small businesses an advantage because they usually have more impact on employee performance over time. One expert on employee motivation says, "To consistently enjoy [high] levels of performance, you've got to give them more than a paycheck. What gets people to excel on a daily basis, to stay late, to work weekends in a pinch is when you regularly communicate to them that you value what they do."[82] In short, rewards do *not* have to be expensive to be effective, but they should be creative and should have a direct link to employee performance.[83] At one company, high-performing employees get a free car wash from the boss in the employee parking lot at lunchtime. Employees gather around to hear about how the worker earned such an honor—a real source of motivation![84] Other creative rewards entrepreneurs are using successfully to motivate their workers include:

◆ A $25 "pot" for the week's "poker hand." John Spomar Jr., president of Norco Cleaners, used a weekly "poker game" to solve his problem with employee tardiness and absenteeism. Every day that workers show up on time, they draw a card from a deck. (Employees who are late or absent don't get to draw.) At the end of the week, the employee with the best hand of five cards wins the $25 pot. Since Spomar started the contest, absenteeism has dropped 30 percent![85]

◆ A trip to Disney World. At Kinko's the employee who offers the best suggestion wins a trip to Disney World, not just for himself, but for everyone who works in that store![86]

◆ A facial or a massage. When employees at one of The Gap's retail outlets met a key deadline successfully, the store manager gave everyone a gift certificate for either a facial or a massage.[87]

- Company points that employees can redeem for prizes. At IdeaScope Associates, a strategic consulting firm, top-performing employees earn IdeaScope Dollars, which they cash in for more than 60 prizes ranging from art supplies to an office party to sky-diving lessons.[88]

Whatever system of rewards they use, managers will be most successful if they match rewards to employees' interests and tastes. For instance, the ideal reward for one employee might be tickets to a hockey game; to another, it might be tickets to a musical show. Once again, because they know their employees so well, this is an area in which small business owners have an advantage over large companies. "By watching how people spend their time and listening to what they talk about, you learn what turns them on," says one management consultant. "You can then tailor your rewards."[89]

In the future, managers will rely more on nonmonetary rewards—praise, recognition, car washes, pins, letters of commendation, and others—to create a work environment where employees take pride in their work, enjoy it, are challenged by it, and get excited about it: in short, act like owners of the business themselves. The goal is to let employees know that every person is important.

FEEDBACK

Business owners not only must motivate employees to excel in their jobs, but they must also focus their efforts on the right targets. Providing feedback on progress toward those targets can be a powerful motivating force in a company. To ensure that the link between her vision for the company and its operations is strong, an entrepreneur must build a series of specific performance measures that serve as periodic monitoring points. For each critical element of the organization's performance (e.g., product or service quality, financial performance, market position, productivity, employee development), the owner should develop specific measures that connect daily operational responsibilities with the company's overall strategic direction. These measures become the benchmarks for measuring employees' performance and the company's progress. The adage "what gets measured and monitored gets done" is true for most organizations. By connecting the company's long-term strategy to its daily operations and measuring performance, an entrepreneur makes it clear to everyone in the company what is most important. Jack Stack, CEO of Springfield Remanufacturing Corporation, explains the importance of focusing every employee's attention on key performance targets:

> To be successful in business, you have to be going somewhere, and everyone involved in getting you there has to know where it is. That's a basic rule, a higher law, but most companies miss . . . the fact that you have a much better chance of winning if everyone knows what it takes to win.[90]

In other words, getting or giving feedback implies that a business owner has established meaningful targets that serve as standards of performance for her, her employees, and the company as a whole. One characteristic successful people have in common is that they set goals and objectives, usually challenging ones, for themselves. Business owners are no different. Successful entrepreneurs usually set targets for performance that make them stretch to achieve, and then they encourage their employees to do the same. The result is that they keep their companies constantly moving forward. *J. J. Stupp, founder of TableTalk, a company that produces decks of cards imprinted with fascinating facts and questions designed to stimulate meaningful conversations, makes goal-setting a regular part of her business routine. "Goals are vital to the work plan of any small business," she says. "Writing down short-term and long-term goals for my business helps me stay focused."*[91]

For feedback to have impact as a motivating force in a business requires business owners to follow the procedure illustrated in Figure 19.2.

Deciding What to Measure. The first step in the feedback loop is deciding what to measure. Every business is characterized by a set of numbers that are critical to its success, and these "critical numbers" are what the entrepreneur should focus on. Obvious critical numbers include sales, profits, profit margins, cash flow, and other standard financial measures. However, running beneath these standard and somewhat universal measures of performance is an undercurrent of critical numbers that are unique to a company's operations. In most cases, these are the numbers that actually drive profits, cash flow, and other financial measures and are the company's *real* critical numbers. *For instance, in a conversation with another business owner, a hotel franchisee said that his company's critical number was profit and that the way to earn a profit was to control costs. His managerial efforts focuses on making sure that his employees knew exactly what to do, how to do it, and how much they could spend doing it. The only problem was that the hotel was losing money.*

"Tell me," said his friend, "how do you make money in this business?"

"We fill rooms," said the hotelier.

"How many rooms do you have to fill to break even?"

"Seventy-one percent," came the reply, "but we're only running at 67 percent."

"How many people know that?" asked his friend.

"Two," he said.

"Maybe that's your problem," observed his friend.

The hotel owner quickly realized that one of his company's most critical numbers was occupancy rate; that's what drove profits! His managerial focus had been misguided, and he had failed to get his employees involved in solving the problem. The hotel owner put together

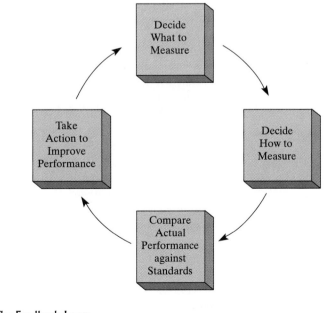

Figure 19.2 **The Feedback Loop**

an incentive plan for employees based on occupancy rate. Once the rate surpassed 71 percent, employees qualified for bonuses; the higher the occupancy rate, the bigger the bonuses. He also involved employees in identifying other critical numbers, such as customer retention rates and customer satisfaction levels, and began tracking results and posting them for everyone to see. Before long, every employee in the hotel was involved in and excited about exceeding their targets. The occupancy rate, customer retention rate, and customer satisfaction scores all shot up. The hotel owner had learned not only what his company's critical number was but how to use it to motivate employees![92]

Deciding How to Measure. Once a business owner identifies his company's critical numbers, the issue of how to best measure them arises. In some cases, identifying the critical numbers defines the measurements the owner must make—e.g., the occupancy rate at the hotel mentioned above—and measuring them simply becomes a matter of collecting and analyzing data. In other cases, the method of measurement is not as obvious—or as tangible. For instance, in some businesses, social responsibility is a key factor, but how should a manager measure his company's performance on such an intangible concept? One of the best ways to develop methods for measuring such factors is to use brainstorming sessions involving employees, customers, and even outsiders. For example, one company used this technique to develop a 'fun index," which used the results of an employee survey to measure how much fun employees had at work (and, by extension, how satisfied they were with their work, the company, and their managers).

Comparing Actual Performance against Standards. In this stage of the feedback loop, the idea is to look for deviations *in either direction* from the performance standards the company has set for itself. In other words, opportunities to improve performance arise when there is a gap between "what should be" and "what is." The most serious deviations usually are those where actual performance falls far below the standard. Managers and employees must focus their efforts on figuring out why actual performance is substandard. The goal is not to hunt down the guilty party (or parties) for punishment, but to discover the cause of the subpar performance and fix it! Managers should not ignore deviations in the other direction, however. When actual performance consistently exceeds the company's standards, it is an indication that the standards are set too low. The company should look closely at "raising the bar another notch" to spur motivation.

Taking Action to Improve Performance. When managers or employees detect a performance gap, their next challenge is to decide on a course of action that will eliminate it. Typically, several suitable alternatives to solving a performance problem exist; the key is finding an acceptable solution that solves the problem quickly, efficiently, and effectively.

John Westrum, founder of Westrum Development Company, a home-building business, was concerned about his employees' ability to maintain quality standards in the face of rapid growth. He was afraid his company was losing sight of the four principles on which the business was founded: quality construction, customer satisfaction, on-time delivery, and cost control. Westrum and his 30 employees developed an 11-point plan designed to measure the company's performance on those principles. Workers then set specific, measurable objectives in each of the four areas, including scores on a 178-point checklist for construction quality. If the company met its objectives, employees would receive incentive pay and set new objectives. Westrum tracked performance on an Excel spreadsheet and posted graphs of the company's progress for all to see. "Employees started focusing not so much on the dollars but on the results," says Westrum. The company's goal-driven incentives have worked. Employees are earning more, and the company's scores have improved dramatically. [The system] has boosted quality, financial controls, and customer satisfaction and has cultivated a team spirit that is second to none," says Westrum.[93]

Performance Appraisal. One of the most common methods of providing feedback on employee performance is through **performance appraisal,** the process of evaluating an employee's actual performance against desired performance standards. Most performance appraisal programs strive to accomplish three goals: (1) to give employees feedback about how they are doing their jobs, which can be an important source of motivation; (2) to provide a business owner and an employee the opportunity to create a plan for developing the employee's skills and abilities and for improving his performance; and (3) to establish a basis for determining promotions and salary increases. Although the primary purpose of performance appraisals is to encourage and to help employees improve their performances, too often they turn into uncomfortable confrontations that do nothing more than upset the employee, aggravate the business owner, and destroy trust and morale. Why? Because most business owners don't understand how to conduct an effective performance appraisal. Although American businesses have been conducting performance appraisals for about 75 years, most companies, their managers, and their employees are dissatisfied with the entire process. Common complaints include unclear standards and objectives; managers who lack information about employees' performances; managers who are unprepared or who lack honesty and sincerity; and managers who use general, ambiguous terms to describe employees' performances.[94]

Perhaps the biggest complaint concerning appraisals is that they happen only periodically: in most cases, just once a year. Employees do not have the opportunity to receive any ongoing feedback on a regular basis. All too often, a manager saves up all of the negative feedback to give an employee and then dumps it on him in the annual performance review. Not only does it destroy the employee's motivation, but it does *nothing* to improve the employee's performance. What good does it do to tell an employee that six months before, he botched an assignment that caused the company to lose a customer? One writer compares the lack of ongoing feedback to asking employees to bowl in the dark. They can hear some pins falling, but they have no idea which ones are left standing for the next frame. "Two pins left," comments the manager. "Which ones?" asks the employee. "Don't bother me. Just keep bowling," says the manager. "I'll be back tomorrow to tell you how you did." At the end of the next day, the manager tells the worker, "You bowled poorly yesterday." "What was my score?" asks the employee. "I don't know, but it was terrible," the manager replies.[95] How motivated would you be to keep bowling? Managers should address problems when they occur rather than wait until the performance appraisal session. Continuous feedback, both positive and negative, is a much more effective way to improve employees' performances and to increase their motivation.

If done properly, performance appraisals can be effective ways to provide employee feedback and to improve workers' performances. However, it takes some planning and preparation on the business owner's part. The following guidelines can help a business owner create a performance appraisal system that actually works:

◆ *Link the employee's performance criteria to the job description discussed earlier in this chapter.* To evaluate an employee's performance effectively, a manager must understand the job he is in very well.

◆ *Establish meaningful, job-related, observable, measurable, and fair performance criteria.* The criteria should describe behaviors and actions, not traits and characteristics. What kind of behavior constitutes a solid performance in this job?

◆ *Prepare for the appraisal session by outlining the key points you want to cover with the employee.* Important points to include are the employee's strengths and weaknesses and developing a plan for improving his performance.

◆ *Invite the employee to provide an evaluation of his own job performance based on the performance criteria.* In one small company, workers rate themselves on a one-to-five scale in categories of job-related behavior and skills as part of the performance appraisal system. Then, they meet with their supervisor to compare their evaluations with those of their supervisor and discuss them. Workers there also evaluate their bosses as part of the review process.[96]

◆ *Be specific.* One of the most common complaints employees have about the appraisal process is that managers' comments are too general to be of any value. Offer the employee specific examples of his desirable or undesirable behavior.

◆ *Keep a record of employees' critical incidents—both positive and negative.* The most productive evaluations are those based on a manager's direct observation of their employees' on-the-job performances. Such records also can be vital in case legal problems arise.

◆ *Discuss an employee's strengths and weaknesses.* An appraisal session is not the time to "unload" about everything an employee has done wrong over the past year. Use it as an opportunity to design a plan for improvement and to recognize employees' strengths, efforts, and achievements.

◆ *Incorporate employees' goals into the appraisal.* Ideally, the standard against which to measure an employee's performance is the goals he has played a role in setting. Workers are likely to be motivated to achieve goals that they have helped establish.

◆ *Keep the evaluation constructive.* Avoid the tendency to belittle employees. Do not dwell on past failures. Instead, point out specific things they should do better and help them develop meaningful goals for the future and a strategy for getting there.

◆ *Focus on behaviors, actions, and results.* Problems arise when managers move away from tangible results and actions and begin to critique employees' abilities and attitudes. Such criticism creates a negative tone for the appraisal session and undercuts its primary purpose.

◆ *Avoid surprises.* If a business owner is doing her job well, performance appraisals should contain no surprises for employees or the business owner. The ideal time to correct improper behavior or slumping performance is when it happens, not months later. Managers should provide employees with continuous feedback on their performances and use the appraisal session to keep employees on the right track.

◆ *Plan for the future.* Smart business owners use appraisal sessions as gateways to workers' future success. They spend only about 20 percent of the time discussing past performance; they use the remaining 80 percent of the time to develop goals, objectives, and a plan for the future.

Many companies are encouraging employees to evaluate each others' performance in **peer reviews** or to evaluate their boss's performance in **upward feedback,** both part of a technique called **360-degree feedback.** Studies suggest that 30 percent of U.S. companies use 360-degree evaluations as part of their performance appraisal systems.[97] Peer appraisals can be especially useful because an employee's coworkers see his on-the-job performance every day. As a result, peer evaluations tend to be more accurate and more valid than those of some managers. Plus, they may capture behavior that managers might miss. Disadvantages of peer appraisals include potential retaliation against coworkers who criticize, the possibility that appraisals will be reduced to "popularity contests," and the refusal of some workers to offer any criticism because they feel uncomfortable evaluating others. Some bosses using upward feedback report similar problems, including personal attacks and extreme evaluations by vengeful subordinates.

Chapter Summary

1. Explain the challenges involved in the entrepreneur's role as leader and what it takes to be a successful leader.

   - Leadership is the process of influencing and inspiring others to work to achieve a common goal and then giving them the power and the freedom to achieve it.

   - Management and leadership are not the same; yet both are essential to a small company's success. Leadership without management is unbridled; management without leadership is uninspired. Leadership gets a small business going; management keeps it going.

2. Understand the potential barriers to effective communication and describe how to overcome them.

   - Research shows that managers spend about 80 percent of their time in some form of communication; yet their attempts at communicating sometimes go wrong. Several barriers to effective communication include: managers and employees don't always feel free to say what they really mean; ambiguity blocks real communication; information overload causes the message to get lost; selective listening interferes with the communication process; defense mechanisms block a message; and conflicting verbal and nonverbal messages confuse listeners.

   - To become more effective communicators, business owners should: clarify their messages before attempting to communicate them; use face-to-face communication whenever possible; be empathetic; match their messages to their audiences; be organized; encourage feedback; tell the truth; not be afraid to tell employees about the business, its performance, and the forces that affect it.

3. Describe the importance of hiring the right employees and how to avoid making hiring mistakes.

   - The decision to hire a new employee is an important one for every business, but its impact is magnified many times in a small company. Every "new hire" a business owner makes determines the heights to which the company can climb or the depths to which it will plunge.

   - To avoid making hiring mistakes, entrepreneurs should: develop meaningful job descriptions and job specifications; plan and conduct an effective interview; and check references before hiring any employee.

4. Explain how to build the kind of company culture and structure to support the entrepreneur's mission and goals and to motivate employees to achieve them.

   - Company culture is the distinctive, unwritten code of conduct that governs the behavior, attitudes, relationships, and style of an organization. Culture arises from an entrepreneur's consistent and relentless pursuit of a set of core values that everyone in the company can believe in. Small companies' flexible structures can be a major competitive weapon.

   - Entrepreneurs rely on six different management styles to guide their companies as they grow. The first three (craftsman, classic, and coordinator) involve running a company without any management assistance and are best suited for small companies in the early stages of growth; the last three (entrepreneur-plus-employee team, small partnership, big-team venture) rely on a team approach to run the company as its growth speeds up.

   - Team-based management is growing in popularity among small firms. Companies that use teams effectively report significant gains in quality, reductions in cycle time, lower costs, increased customer satisfaction, and improved employee motivation and morale.

5. Discuss the ways in which entrepreneurs can motivate their workers to higher levels of performance.

   - Motivation is the degree of effort an employee exerts to accomplish a task; it shows up as excitement about work. Four important tools of motivation are empowerment, job design, rewards and compensation, and feedback.

   - Empowerment involves giving workers at every level of the organization the power, the freedom, and the responsibility to control their own work, to make decisions, and to take action to meet the company's objectives.

   - Job design techniques for enhancing employee motivation include job enlargement, job rotation, job enrichment, flextime, job sharing, and flexplace (which includes telecommuting and hoteling).

   - Money is an important motivator for many workers, but not the only one. The key to using rewards such as recognition and praise to motivate involves tailoring them to the needs and characteristics of the workers.

   - Giving employees timely, relevant feedback about their job performance through a performance appraisal system can also be a powerful motivator.

Discussion Questions

1. What is leadership? What is the difference between leadership and management?
2. What behaviors do effective leaders exhibit?
3. Why is it so important for small companies to hire the right employees? What can small business owners do to avoid making hiring mistakes?
4. What is a job description? A job specification? What functions do they serve in the hiring process?
5. Outline the procedure for conducting an effective interview.
6. What is company culture? What role does it play in a small company's success? What threats does rapid growth pose for a company's culture?
7. Explain the six different management styles entrepreneurs rely on to guide their companies as they grow (craftsman, classic, coordinator, entrepreneur-plus-employee team, small partnership, and big-team venture).
8. What mistakes do companies make when switching to team-based management? What can they do to avoid these mistakes? Explain the four phases teams typically go through.
9. What is empowerment? What benefits does it offer workers? The company? What must a small business manager do to make empowerment work in a company?
10. Explain the differences among job simplification, job enlargement, job rotation, and job enrichment. What impact do these different job designs have on workers?
11. Is money the "best" motivator? How do pay-for-performance compensation systems work? What other rewards are available to small business managers to use as motivators? How effective are they?
12. Suppose that a mail-order catalog company selling environmentally friendly products identifies its performance as a socially responsible company as a "critical number" in its success. Suggest some ways for the owner to measure this company's "social responsibility index."
13. What is performance appraisal? What are the most common mistakes managers make in performance appraisals? What should small business managers do to avoid making those mistakes?

Step into the Real World

1. One leadership development program demonstrates how leaders can overcome resistance within a work group by using the following exercise. Participants are organized into groups and are assigned to a table. At each table, one person is assigned to be the change agent, another to be a change supporter, and two others to be change resisters. On the table sits an unopened carton of buttermilk. The change agent must convince the other members of the group to taste the buttermilk. Only when the change agent opens the carton does the full challenge of the task become apparent. The buttermilk has been injected with a harmless, but GREEN food coloring. Set up your own buttermilk experiment. How would you convince other members of your group to taste the green buttermilk? What does this experiment say about your leadership style?
2. Visit a local business that has experienced rapid growth in the past three years and ask the owner about the specific problems he or she had to face that were caused by the organization's growth. How did the owner handle these problems? Looking back, what would he or she do differently?
3. Contact a local small business with at least 20 employees. Does the company have job descriptions and job specifications? What process does the owner use to hire a new employee? What questions does the owner typically ask candidates in an interview?
4. Using a search engine such as InfoSeek, Yahoo! or Excite!, conduct a search on the various employment tests that are available to companies as screening devices. The American Psychological Association's Web site <http://wwwapa.org/> may be a good place to begin. Write a one-page summary of what you learn about employment tests.
5. Ask the owner of a small manufacturing operation to give you a tour of his or her operation. During your tour, observe the way jobs are organized. To what extent does the company use the following job design concepts: job simplification? job enlargement? job rotation? job enrichment? flextime? job sharing? On the basis of your observations, what recommendations would you make to the owner about the company's job design?

Take It to the Net

Visit the Scarborough/Zimmerer home page at
www.prenhall.com/scarbzim
for updated information, on-line resources, and Web-based exercises.

Endnotes

1. Max DePree, *Leadership Jazz* (New York: Currency Doubleday, 1992), pp. 8–9.
2. Francis Huffman, "Taking the Lead," *Entrepreneur*, November 1993, p. 101.
3. Stratford Sherman, "How Tomorrow's Leaders Are Learning Their Stuff," *Fortune*, November 27, 1995, p. 102.
4. Bernard A. Nagle, "Wanted: A Leader for the 21st Century," *Industry Week*, November 20, 1995, p. 29.
5. Annie Bissett, "Legends in Their Own Minds?" *Training*, May 1997, p. 16.
6. Robert McGarvey, "Learn to Lead," *Entrepreneur*, October 1994, p. 140.
7. William H. Miller, "The Stuff of Leadership," *Industry Week*, August 18, 1997, p. 100.
8. Mort Meyerson, "Everything I Know about Leadership Is Wrong," *Fast Company's Handbook of the Business Revolution*, 1997, p. 9.
9. Michael A. Verespej, "Lead, Don't Manage" *Industry Week*, March 4, 1996, p. 58.
10. "Message Methods for Managers," *Communication Briefings*, February 1997, p. 5.
11. Robert F. Mager, *What Every Manager Should Know about Training* (Belmont, Calif.: Lake Publishing Company, 1994).
12. Dianne Hales, "The Secret Language of Success," *Reader's Digest*, January 1994, pp. 165–169.
13. "What Employees Want to Know," *Communication Briefings*, December 1993, p. 3.
14. Roberta Maynard, "Sharing the Wealth of Information," *Nation's Business*, September 1997, p. 14.
15. Robert McGarvey, "Now Hear This," *Entrepreneur*, June 1996, p. 87.
16. *Bits & Pieces*, February 1, 1996, pp. 10–11.
17. McGarvey, "Now Hear This," p. 89.
18. E. Rogers and R. Agarwala Rogers, *Communication in Organizations* (New York: Free Press, 1976), p. 82.
19. Eugene Walton, "How Efficient Is the Grapevine?" *Personnel*, March–April 1961, pp. 45–49.
20. Janean Huber, "In the Loop," *Entrepreneur*, December 1994, p. 23.
21. "Hiring Mistakes," *Practical Supervision*, October 1994, pp. 4–5.
22. Tom Stein, "Create Your Own Dream Team," *Success*, October 1996, p. 8.
23. Michael Barrier, "Hiring the Right People," *Nation's Business*, June 1996, pp. 18–27.
24. Richard J. Pinsker, "Hiring Winners," *Small Business Forum*, Fall 1994, pp. 66–84.
25. Barrier, "Hiring the Right People," p. 19.
26. Stephanie Gruner, "Once Burned," *Inc. 500* (1995), p. 65.
27. Jim Johnson, "Take It from Me: Write a Job Description," *Small Business Forum*, Fall 1994, pp. 10–11.
28. Barrier, "Hiring the Right People," p. 21.
29. "Making the Most of Job Interviews," *Your Company*, Spring 1993, p. 6.
30. Michael Mercer, "Consider These Guidelines on Conducting Interviews," *Small Business Forum*, Fall 1994, pp. 11–14.
31. Nina Munk and Suzanne Oliver, "Think Fast!" *Forbes*, March 24, 1997, pp. 146–151.
32. David K. Lindo, "Hiring Strategies," *Business Start-Ups*, November 1997, pp. 66–69; Greg Norred, "Weeding Out the Bad Apples," *Small Business Reports*, November 1993, pp. 58–61; Emma Fluker, "Checking Employee References," *Small Business Digest* (Premier Issue 1990), p. 7.
33. Gruner, "Once Burned."
34. Peter Weaver, "Ignoring a Résumé Can Prove Costly," *Nation's Business*, September 1997, pp. 32–34.
35. Barrier, "Hiring the Right People," p. 26.
36. Kara Swisher, "Oh, What a Tangled Web Silicon Valley Moguls Weave," *Wall Street Journal*, March 5, 1998, pp. B1, B6.
37. John Case, "Corporate Culture," *Inc.*, November 1996, p. 45.
38. Ibid., pp. 42–53.
39. Shari Caudron, "Be Cool!" *Workforce*, April 1998, p. 50.
40. Caudron, "Be Cool," pp. 50–61; Julie Creswell, "The Coolness Factor," *Fortune*, July 6, 1998, pp. 62–66; Melanie Warner, "Cool Companies 1998," *Fortune*, July 6, 1998, pp. 69–89.
41. Caudron, "Be Cool," p. 56.
42. "Master of Mixology," *Success*, October 1997, p. 27.
43. Caudron, "Be Cool!" p. 58.
44. Ibid.
45. Ibid., p. 61.
46. James L. Bildner, "Hitting the Wall," *Inc.*, July 1995, pp. 21–22.
47. Ronald E. Merrill and Henry D. Sedgwick, "To Thine Own Self Be True," *Inc.*, August 1994, pp. 50–56.
48. Ibid., p. 56.
49. Robert McGarvey, "Joining Forces," *Entrepreneur*, September 1996, p. 83.
50. Brian Dumaine, "The Trouble with Teams," *Fortune*, September 5, 1994, p. 86.
51. McGarvey, "Joining Forces," pp. 80–83; "Whoa, Team," *Journal of Business Strategy*, January/February 1996, p. 8; Mark Fischetti, "Team Doctors, Report to ER," *Fast Company*, February/March 1998, pp. 170–177.
52. McGarvey, "Joining Forces," p. 80.
53. Donna Fenn, "A Formula for Success," *Inc.*, May 1996, p. 111.
54. Brian S. Moskal, "Supervision (or Lack of It)," *Industry Week*, December 3, 1990, p. 56.
55. Michael Barrier, "Beyond the Suggestion Box," *Nation's Business*, July 1995, pp. 34–37.
56. Theodore B. Kinni, "The Empowered Workforce," *Industry Week*, September 19, 1994, p. 37.
57. Robert McGarvey, "More Power to Them," *Entrepreneur*, February 1995, p. 73.

58. David Maize, "Where It Pays to Have a Great Idea," *Reader's Digest*, June 1995, pp. 100–104.

59. Barrier, "Beyond the Suggestion Box," p. 37.

60. John Case, "The Open-Book Revolution," *Inc.*, June 1995, pp. 26–43.

61. Donna Fenn, "Open-Book Management 101," *Inc.*, August 1996, p. 92.

62. Thomas Love, "Keeping the Business Going When an Executive Is Absent," *Nation's Business*, March 1998, p. 10.

63. Jay Finnegan, "Pipe Dreams," *Inc.*, August 1994, pp. 64–70.

64. Michael Verespej, "A Workforce Revolution?" *Industry Week*, August 21, 1995, p. 23.

65. Laura Koss-Feder, "Motivate Your Staff with a Flextime Plan," *Your Company* (Forecast 1997), pp. 64–65.

66. Ibid.

67. "Tips for Telecommuting," *Your Company*, Spring 1995, p. 2; Alice LaPlante, "Voluntary No More," *Forbes ASAP*, October 9, 1995, pp. 133–138.

68. Melanie Warner, "Working at Home—The Right Way to Be a Star in Your Bunny Slippers," *Fortune*, March 3, 1997, pp. 165–166.

69. Marc Hequet, "Virtually Working," *Training*, August 1996, p. 31.

70. "Tips for Telecommuting."

71. "Alternative Officing Gains Favor," *Upstate Business*, May 11, 1997, p. 8.

72. Michael Barrier, "Improving Worker Performance," *Nation's Business*, September 1996, p. 30.

73. Stein, "Create Your Own Dream Team."

74. Shari Caudron, "Spreading Out the Carrots," *Industry Week*, May 19, 1997, pp. 20–24.

75. Harvey R. Meyer, "Linking Payday to Cash in Hand," *Nation's Business*, May 1996, pp. 36–38.

76. Shari Caudron, "Motivation? Money's Only No. 2," *Industry Week*, November 15, 1993, p. 33.

77. Michael Barrier, "Improving Worker Performance," *Nation's Business*, September 1996, p. 28.

78. *Bits & Pieces*, July 21, 1994, p. 19.

79. Christopher Caggiano, "Perks You Can Afford," *Inc.*, November 1997, pp. 107–108.

80. Donna Fenn, "Managing Generation X," *Inc.*, August 1996, p. 91; Roberta Maynard, "A Less-Stressed Work Force," *Nation's Business*, November 1996, pp. 50–51.

81. Alan Farnham, "Mary Kay's Lessons in Leadership," *Fortune*, September 20, 1993, pp. 68–77.

82. Robert McGarvey, "Bonus Points," *Entrepreneur*, July 1994, p. 74.

83. Jacquelyn Lynn, "Stretching Your Dollars," *Entrepreneur*, March 1998, p. 32; Richard Laliberte, "For Love, Not Money," *Success*, August 1998, pp. 63–65.

84. McGarvey, "Bonus Points," p. 74.

85. Howard Scott, "Contests Can Rev Up Employees," *Nation's Business*, July 1996, p. 37.

86. "Seven Ways to Have Fun at Work," *Business Ethics*, September/October 1997, p. 11.

87. "Seven Offbeat Employee Rewards for Tight Times," *Business Ethics*, March/April 1997, p. 11.

88. Donna Fenn, "Play Cash Pays Off," *Inc.*, February 1996, p. 97.

89. Barrier, "Improving Worker Performance," p. 30.

90. Jack Stack, "That Championship Season," *Inc.*, July 1996, p. 27.

91. Carla Goodman, "Destination Success," *Business Start-Ups*, December 1996, p. 50.

92. Jack Stack, "The Logic of Profit," *Inc.*, March 1996, p. 17.

93. Roberta Maynard, "Hammering Home Performance Incentives," *Nation's Business*, May 1996, p. 10; Donna Fenn, "Goal-Driven Incentives," *Inc.*, August 1996, p. 91.

94. Gina Imperato, "How to Give Good Feedback," *Success*, September 1998, pp. 144–156.

95. Ferdinand Fournies, "Why Performance Appraisals Don't Work," *Small Business Forum*, Winter 1993/1994, pp. 69–77.

96. Joan Delaney, "Rave Reviews," *Your Company*, Spring 1994, pp. 12–13.

97. Brian O'Reilly, "360 Feedback Can Change Your Life," *Fortune*, October 17, 1994, p. 93.

CHAPTER

20

Management Succession and Risk Management Strategies in the Family Business

There is a time for departure even when there's no place to go.

—*Tennessee Williams*

When it works right, nothing succeeds like a family firm. The roots run deep, embedded in family values. The flash of the fast buck is replaced with long-term plans. Tradition counts.

— *Eric Calonius*

> **Upon completion of this chapter, you will be able to**
>
> ❶ Explain the factors necessary for a strong family business.
>
> ❷ Understand the exit strategy options available to an entrepreneur.
>
> ❸ Discuss the stages of management succession.
>
> ❹ Explain how to develop an effective management succession plan.
>
> ❺ Understand the four risk management strategies.
>
> ❻ Discuss the basics of insurance for small businesses.

❶ Explain the factors necessary for a strong family business.

𝓕amily Businesses

More than 80 percent of all companies in the United States are family-owned. Yet family-owned businesses are often overlooked by the media, who focus most of their attention on the larger firms in our economy. In reality, family businesses generate 50 percent of the U.S. gross domestic product, employ more than 40 million people, and pay 65 percent of all wages.[1] Not all family-owned businesses are small, however; one-third of the Fortune 500 companies are family businesses.

When a family business works right, it is a thing of beauty. Family members share deeply rooted values that guide the company and give it a sense of harmony. Family members understand and support one another as they work together to achieve the company's mission. But family businesses also have a dark side, and it stems from their lack of continuity. Sibling rivalries, fights over control of the business, and personality conflicts often lead to nasty battles that can tear families apart and destroy once-thriving businesses. Unfortunately, 70 percent of first-generation businesses fail to survive into the second generation, and of those that do, only 13 percent make it to the third generation.[2]

The best way to avoid deadly turf battles and conflicts is to develop a succession plan for the company. Although business founders want their businesses to survive them, and almost 80 percent intend to pass the business on to their children, they seldom support their intentions by a plan to accomplish that goal. About 54 percent of all family business owners do *not* have a formal management succession plan![3]

Long before succession issues arise, however, they can be mitigated by strengthening the family business in its early stages. David Bork, founder of the Aspen Family Business Conference, has identified several qualities that are essential to a successful family business: shared values, shared power, tradition, a willingness to learn, family behavior, and strong family ties.[4]

SHARED VALUES

The first, and probably most overlooked, quality is a set of shared values. What family members value and believe about people, work, and money shapes their attitude toward the business. All members of a family business should talk openly to determine, in a nonjudgmental fashion, each one's values. Without shared values, it is difficult to create a future direction for a business.

Individual family members may share the values of the family but may be motivated to achieve personal goals that are different from those of their parents or siblings. This situation might be an advantage when there are many children in the family. One or two of the children may elect to work in the business while the others select alternatives careers.

To avoid the problems associated with conflicting values and goals, the family should consider taking the following actions:

◆ Make it clear to all involved that they are not required to join the business on a full-time basis. Family members' goals, ambitions, and talents should be foremost in their career decisions.

◆ Do not assume that a successor must always come from within the family. Simply being born into a family does not guarantee that a person will make a good business leader.

◆ Give family members the opportunity to work *outside* the business first to learn firsthand how others conduct business. Working for others will allow them to develop knowledge, confidence, and credibility before stepping back into the family business.

SHARED POWER

Shared power is not necessarily equal power. Rather, shared power is based on the simple idea that the skills and talents of family members may run in different directions. Shared power is based on the idea that family members should allow those with the greatest expertise, ability, and knowledge in particular areas to handle decisions in those areas. Dividing responsibilities along the lines of expertise is an important way of acknowledging respect for each family member's talents and abilities. *For instance, when Thad Garner invented a concoction of red peppers and vinegar called Texas Pete Hot Sauce during the Great Depression, he and his brothers, Harold and Ralph, built a business, T. W. Garner Food Company, around the product. Each assumed responsibilities in a different area of the company aligned with his talents and interests. Thad (known as "Mr. Texas Pete") took over the sales and marketing side of the business; Harold managed its financial and operational aspects;*

and Ralph handled production. Working together, the brothers built the company into a very successful business, selling millions of dollars' worth of Texas Pete a year.[5]

TRADITION

Tradition is necessary for a family business because it serves to bond family members and to link one generation of business leaders to the next. However, successors must hold tradition in check when it becomes a barrier to change. The key is to select those traditions that provide a solid foundation for positive behavior while taking care not to restrict the future growth of the business. *When David Langsam joined his father's personnel services franchise, he had to fight some of the traditions his father had established before he could move the company forward. When Langsam arrived, the company had no computers, no fax machines—not even a copier! His father believed in doing business the old-fashioned way, but Langsam saw that the company's antiquated business methods were stifling its growth. It took him six years and many battles with his father, but Langsam finally automated the company and expanded it. The year after he took over the company's reins from his father, revenues soared 40 percent. Today, the company is one of the top performers in the chain.*[6]

A WILLINGNESS TO LEARN

A willingness to learn and grow is the hallmark of any successful firm, and it is essential to a family business. The family business that remains open to new ideas and techniques is likely to reduce its risk of obsolescence. The current generation of leadership must set the stage for new ideas involving the next generation in today's decisions. In many cases, a formalized family council serves as a mechanism through which family members can propose new ideas. Perhaps more important than a family council is fostering an environment in which family members trust one another enough to express their ideas, thoughts, and suggestions openly and honestly. Open discussion of the merits of new ideas is a tradition that has proved valuable for many a family business's ability to sustain its competitive advantage.

FAMILY BEHAVIOR

Families that play together operate family businesses that are likely to stay together. Time spent together outside the business creates the foundation for the relationships family members have at work. Too often, life in a family business can degenerate into nothing but day after day of work and discussions of work at home. In some cases, work is the only way some parents interact with their children. But when a family adds activities outside the scope of the business, relationships develop in a different arena. A family should not force members to "play together," but instead should create an environment that welcomes every member into fun family activities. Planned activities should be broad enough in scope to involve all family members. In time, trust, respect, openness, and togetherness will lead to behavior that communicates genuine caring and concern for the well-being of each family member and that spills over into the working relationship as well.

STRONG FAMILY TIES

Strong family ties grow from one-on-one relationships. Shared time conveys the message that the family business is *more* than just a business; it is a group of people who care for one another working together toward a common goal. The bond that a family business creates among relatives can be powerful. With all the stress and tension that can tear apart a family business, behavior that demonstrates concern for one another knits together more tightly the fabric of the family.

The same emotions that hold family businesses together can also rip them apart if they run counter to the company's and the family's best interest. Emotions run deep in family businesses, and the press is filled with examples of once-successful companies that have been ruined by family feuds over who controls the company and how to run it. Conflict is a natural part of any business, but it can be especially powerful in family businesses because family relationships magnify the passions binding family members to the company. "Ignoring the passions that arise in a family business is like turning your back on a fire in your stockroom," say brothers (and business partners) Roger and Russell Allred. "You can ignore it for a while, but it will eventually destroy your business."[7] *Unfortunately, the successful business Thad Garner and his brothers built around Texas Pete Hot Sauce was not immune to a family battle. Problems began when the founding brothers handed the reins of the T. W. Garner Food Company over to the next generation of family managers. Thad Garner managed to hold the company and the family together until he developed Alzheimer's disease. Shortly afterward, several family members who worked in the business staged a coup, firing the elderly Thad as president and removing his daughter, Kathryn, from the company as well. After Thad died, lawsuits erupted among family members over who was to control the company. Only when a court-appointed arbitrator handed down a decision did the battle finally end, but by that time, the rift had split the family for good.[8]*

*E*xit Strategies

2 Understand the exit strategy options available to an entrepreneur.

Most family business founders want their companies to stay within their families, although, in some cases, maintaining family control is not practical. Sometimes, no one in the next generation of family members has an interest in managing the company or has the necessary skills and experience to handle the job. Under these circumstances, the founder must look outside the family for leadership if the company is to survive. Whatever the case, entrepreneurs must confront their mortality and plan for the future of their companies. Having a solid management succession plan in place well before retirement is absolutely critical to success. Entrepreneurs should examine their options once they decide it is time to step down from the business they have founded. Three options are available to entrepreneurs planning to retire: sell to outsiders, sell to (nonfamily) insiders, or pass the business on to the family members with the help of a management succession plan.[9]

SELLING TO OUTSIDERS

As you learned in chapter 5, selling a business to an outsider is no simple task. Done properly, it takes time, patience, and preparation to locate a suitable buyer, strike a deal, and make the transition. Advance preparation and maintaining accurate financial records are keys to a successful sale. Too often, however, business owners postpone selling their businesses until the last minute, when they reach retirement age or when they face a business crisis. Such a "fire sale" approach rarely yields the maximum value for a business.

A straight sale may be best for entrepreneurs who want to step down and turn the reins over to someone else. However, selling a business outright is not an attractive exit strategy for those who want to stay on with the company or for those who want to surrender control of the company gradually rather than all at once.

The financial terms of a sale also influence the selling price of the business and the number of potential bidders. Does the owner want "clean, cash-only, 100 percent at closing" offers, or is he willing to finance a portion of the sale? The 100 percent, cash-only requirement dramatically reduces the number of potential buyers. On the other hand, the owner can exit the business "free and clear" and does not incur the risk that the buyer may fail to operate the business in a profitable fashion and therefore not be able to complete the financial transition. In such a case, the owner may be required to return to the business only to discover that the buyer's incompetent management has destroyed its value. In some cases, the buyer may have been unethical or even illegal in his management practices. Entrepreneurs who don't look beyond the financial issues to the character and competence of the buyer accept more risk than is necessary.

SELLING TO INSIDERS

When entrepreneurs have no family members to whom they can transfer ownership or who want to assume the responsibilities of running a company, selling the business to employees is often the preferred option. In most situations, the options available to owners are (1) sale for cash plus a note, (2) a leveraged buyout, and (3) an employee stock ownership plan (ESOP).

A Sale for Cash Plus a Note. Whether entrepreneurs sell their business to insiders, outsiders, or family members, they often finance a portion of the sales price. The buyer pays the seller a lump-sum amount of cash up front and the seller holds a promissory note for the remaining portion of the selling price, which the buyer pays off in installments. Because of its many creative financial options, this method of selling a business is popular with buyers. They can buy promising businesses without having to come up with the total purchase price all at one time. Sellers also appreciate the security and the tax implications of accepting payment over time. They receive a portion of the sale up front and have the assurance of receiving a steady stream of income in the future. Plus, they can stretch their tax liabilities from the capital gains on the sale over time rather than having to pay them in a single year. The seller's risk can be even lower if he retains a seat on the board of directors to ensure that the new owners are keeping the business on track.

Leveraged Buyouts (LBOs). The **leveraged buyout (LBO)** was one of the most popular exit strategies of the 1980s. In an LBO, managers or employees, or both, borrow money from a financial institution and pay the owner the total agreed-upon price at closing; then they use the cash generated from the company's operations to pay off the debt. During the economic boom of the 1980s, financial institutions were willing to accept the risks associated with highly leveraged businesses. Because of the high levels of debt they had taken on, the new managements had very little room for error. Unfortunately, once the booming economy slowed, many highly leveraged businesses ended up in bankruptcy.

If properly structured, LBOs can be attractive to both buyers and sellers. Because they get their money up front, sellers do not incur the risk of loss if the buyers cannot keep the business operating successfully. The managers and employees who buy the company have a strong incentive to make sure the business succeeds because they own a piece of the action and some of their capital is at risk in the business. The result can be a highly motivated workforce that works hard and makes sure that the company operates efficiently. *In one of the most successful LBOs in recent years, Jack Stack and a team of managers and employees purchased an ailing subsidiary of International Harvester. The new company, Springfield Remanufacturing Corporation (SRC), which specializes in engine remanufacturing for automotive, trucking, agricultural, and construction industries, began with a debt-to-equity ratio that was astronomically high, but the team of motivated managers and employees turned the company around. Today SRC has more than 1,000 employees and $140 million in sales.*[10]

Employee Stock Ownership Plans (ESOPs). Unlike LBOs, employee stock ownership plans (ESOPs) allow employees or managers, or both, to purchase the business gradually. An ESOP frees up enough cash to finance the venture's future growth. Employees contribute a portion of their earnings over time toward purchasing shares of the company's stock from the founder. It is a long-term exit strategy that benefits everyone involved. The owner sells the business to the people he can trust the most: his managers and employees. The managers and employees buy a business they already know how to run successfully. Plus, because they own the company, the managers and employees have a huge incentive to see that it operates effectively and efficiently.

When Bob Daggs, founder of GRC, an imaging supplies manufacturer with $50 million in annual sales, decided to retire, his two sons were in management positions in the company. He considered transferring ownership to them and phasing them in as his successors. Daggs, however, did not believe his sons were quite ready to lead the fast-growing business, so he decided to use an ESOP as his exit strategy. "Our company would not be where it is today without our employees, so they represented a much larger family whose welfare I had to consider," says Daggs. GRC established an ESOP, which purchased 51 percent of the company. Dagg says he is "thrilled with the results. Sales and profits are up, the ESOP defers taxes, and I'm financially diversified." [11]

The third exit strategy available to company founders is transferring ownership to the next generation of family members with the help of a comprehensive management succession plan.

*M*anagement Succession

3 Discuss the stages of management succession.

Experts estimate that between 1993 and 2013, $4.8 trillion in wealth will be transferred from one generation to the next, much of it through family businesses. [12] Most of the family businesses in existence today were started after World War II, and their founders are ready to pass the torch of leadership on to the next generation. A recent study by Arthur Andersen and MassMutual Insurance Company found that 43 percent of family business founders expect to transfer leadership within the next five years. [13] For a smooth transition from one generation to the next, these companies need a succession plan. Without a succession plan, family businesses face an increased risk of faltering or failing in the next generation. The businesses with the greatest probability of surviving are the ones whose owners prepare a succession plan well before it is time to pass the torch to the next generation. Succession planning also allows business owners to minimize the impact of taxes on their businesses, their estates, and their successors' wealth as well. With tax rates on gifts and estates as high as 55 percent, a plan that reduces the bite taxes take out of a business transfer is no small matter.

Why, then, do so many entrepreneurs postpone succession planning until it is too late? One barrier to succession planning is that, in planning the future of the business, owners are forced to accept the painful reality of their own mortality. Also, many business founders hesitate to let go of their business because their personal identities are so wrapped up in their companies. Over time, the founder's identity becomes so intertwined in the business that, in the entrepreneur's mind, there is no distinction between the two. Plus, turning over the reins of a business they have scarificed for, fretted over, and dedicated themselves to for so many years is extremely difficult to do—even if the successor is a son or daughter! *Paul Snodgrass, son of the founder of Pella Products, a maker of apparel for work and outdoor activities, who accepted leadership of the company from his father, explains, "Dad loves you and wants you to take over the business, but he also put heart and soul into that business, and he's not going to let anybody screw it up—not even you."* [14] Finally, many family business founders believe that controlling the business also gives them a degree of control over family members and family behavior. [15]

Planning for management succession protects not only the founder's, successors', and company's financial resources, but it also preserves what matters most in a successful business: its heritage and tradition. "Real succession planning involves developing a strategy for transferring the trust, respect, and goodwill built by one generation to the next," explains Andy Bluestone, who took over as president of the financial services company his father founded.[16] Management succession planning requires, first, an attitude of trusting others. It recognizes that other family members have a stake in the business and want to participate in planning its future. Planning is an attitude that shows that decisions made with open discussion are more constructive than those without family input. Second, management succession as an evolutionary process must reconcile the entrepreneur's inevitable anguish with her successors' desire for autonomy. Owners' emotional ties to the business may be as strong as or stronger than their financial ties. On the other side are the successors, who may desire or even crave autonomy. These inherent conflicts can, and often do, result in skirmishes.

Succession planning reduces the tension and stress created by these conflicts by gradually "changing the guard." A well-developed succession plan is like the smooth, graceful exchange of a baton between runners in a relay race. The new runner still has maximum energy; the concluding runner has already spent her energy by running at maximum speed. The athletes never come to a stop to exchange the baton; instead, the handoff takes place on the move. The race is a skillful blend of the talents of all team members—an exchange of leadership so smooth and powerful that the business never falters, but accelerates, fueled by a new source of energy at each leg of the race.

Management succession involves a lengthy series of interconnected stages that begin very early in the life of the owner's children and extend to the point of final ownership transition (see Figure 20.1). If management succession is to be effective, it is necessary for the process to begin early in the successor's life (stage I). *For instance, the owner of a catering business recalls putting his son to work in the family-owned company at age 7. On weekends, the boy would arrive at dawn to baste turkeys and was paid in his favorite medium of exchange—doughnuts.*[17] In most cases, family business owners involve their children in their businesses while they are still in junior high or high school. In this phase, the tasks are routine, but the child is learning the basics of how the business operates. Young adults begin to appreciate the role the business plays in the life of the family. They learn firsthand about the values and responsibilities of running the company.[18] While in college, the successor moves

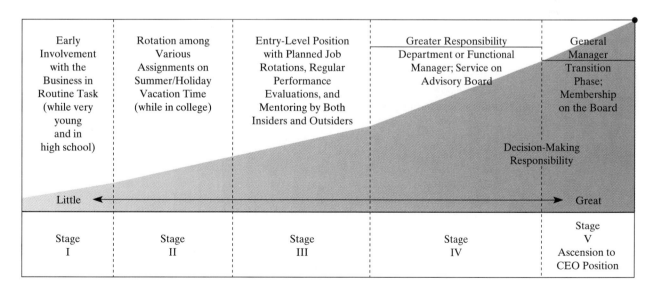

Figure 20.1 **Stages in Management Succession**

Seventy percent of first-generation businesses fail to survive into the second generation, often because owners fail to develop management succession plans. Dick Monsen (left), founder of Monsen Engineering Company, not only developed a management succession plan, but he also set up a special mentoring committee to help prepare his son, Eric (right), to take over the company's reins.

to stage II of the continuum. During this stage, the individual rotates among a variety of job functions both to broaden his base of understanding of the business and to permit the parents to evaluate his skills. Upon graduation from college, the successor enters stage III. At this point, the successor becomes a full-time worker and ideally has already earned the respect of coworkers through his behavior in the first two stages of the process. Stage III focuses on the successor's continuous development, often through a program designed to groom him using both family and nonfamily managers as mentors. *For example, at Monsen Engineering Company, an air-conditioning design, installation, and service company, president Dick Monsen formed a special mentoring committee (dubbed the Merlin Group, after the magician who, according to legend, helped Arthur become king) as part of his management succession plan. The Merlin Group's "student" was Dick's son, Eric, and their task was to groom him to take over the business when Dick retired. In addition to Dick, the committee consisted of the company's chief operating officer, its chief financial officer, and an outside executive coach.*[19]

As the successor develops his skills and performance, he moves to stage IV, in which real decision-making authority grows rapidly. Stage IV of the succession continuum is the period when the founder makes a final assessment of the individual's abilities to take full and complete control over the firm. The skills the successor will need include the following:

◆ *Financial abilities.* Understanding the financial aspects of a business, what its financial position is, and the managerial implications of that position are crucial to success.

◆ *Technical knowledge.* Every business has its own body of knowledge, from how the distribution system works to the trends shaping the industry, that an executive must master.

IN THE FOOTSTEPS OF AN ENTREPRENEUR

Is Two a Crowd?

*S*everal years ago, Marshall Paisner, founder of a highly successful car wash chain in Boston, faced a daunting decision: how to handle passing the torch of leadership in the business to the next generation. The problem he faced is a common one: He had one business and two sons, Bob and Dan, both of whom worked in the company and both of whom were highly capable of doing the job. "Choosing one child over another is certain to hurt the one who has been passed over," he told his family. Ultimately, Paisner and his two sons decided that both of the brothers would lead the company. "A recipe for disaster," said many observers. But Pasiner knew his sons better than the "experts" did, and he knew that they had been working for years in the business as an effective team.

Paisner's decision is one that business founders are making more frequently. A recent Arthur Andersen and Mass Mutual Family Business Survey found that 42 percent of family business owners expected to pass their companies on to co-CEOs, rather than to a single next-generation leader. Paisner and his sons recognized that for a co-leadership arrangement to work, they had to put in place a system to address problems that would arise such as handling disputes. "There are different risks and different dynamics that arise compared to the single, dynamic CEO," says the head of Arthur Andersen's Center for Family Business. "It can work, but it creates a significant need for developing some mechanism to resolve disagreements."

In Scrub-A-Dub's second generation, Bob and Dan operate from the "office of the presidency" model. The two receive the same compensation and own the same percentage of the company's stock. They have different titles, however. Bob is CEO; Dan is president. They will also focus on different areas of responsibility. Bob's specialties are R&D and operations, whereas Dan focuses on training, sales, and marketing. With their father's help, the brothers have worked out a system for resolving disputes and have created an agreement outlining their own children's entry into the family business.

Bob and Dan Paisner had a history of working together well on many projects during their years in the family business before assuming their roles as co-leaders. Although having two captains may not work well for some family businesses, co-CEOs can increase their odds of success by having the following factors firmly in place:

Inherent mutual trust in and respect for one another. Co-leadership is doomed to an early failure unless these elements are present.

Divided responsibilities. Siblings should base their division of labor on their areas of interests, their talents, and their skills.

A board of advisers that includes members from outside the family. It is important for co-leaders to have people they can turn to for advice, support, or a listening ear.

A way to resolve conflict. The Paisners have a third party (currently their father, but he has designated another person to assume that role after he dies) who can break stalemates should the brothers totally disagree on key issues. So far, it hasn't happened. For the most part, the brothers defer to the judgment of the brother who has expertise in a particular issue.

A formal structure for communication. Informal communication is important, but it helps if co-leaders have a time set aside specifically for communication. That way, they avoid the tendency to let their busy schedules interfere with keeping each other informed.

Business founders want to make sure that their successors are capable and competent. If they are fortunate enough to have two children who fit that description, then why not let both of them share in leading the company? With the proper safeguards in place, it can work beautifully. Scrub-A-Dub's experience is proof that co-CEOs can be as effective, if not more so, than a lone leader.

1. What pitfalls and dangers do you see with family businesses run by co-CEOs?

2. What steps can business founders and their successors do to avoid these problems? Use the resources of the World Wide Web to research the issue of the co-leaders in family businesses. What other recommendations can you find for making co-leadership work in a family business?

SOURCES: Adapted from Patricia Schiff Estess, "Two's Company," *Entrepreneur*, May 1997, pp. 90–92; Sharon Nelton, "Major Shifts in Leadership Lie Ahead," *Nation's Business*, June 1997, pp. 56–58; Sharon Nelton, "Team Playing Is on the Rise," *Nation's Business*, June 1996, pp. 53–55; Janean Chun, "Daughter Knows Best," *Entrepreneur*, October 1997, p. 58; Charlotte Mulhern, "Like Father, Like Daughter," *Entrepreneur*, February 1998, p. 42. ◆

◆ *Negotiating ability.* Much of business, whether buying supplies and inventory or selling to customers, boils down to negotiating, and a business owner must be adept at it.

◆ *Leadership qualities.* Leaders must be bold enough to stake out their company's future and then give employees the resources, the power, and the freedom to pursue it.

- *Communication skills.* Business leaders must communicate the vision they have for their business; good listening skills also are essential for success as a top manager.
- *Juggling skills.* Business owners must be able to handle multiple projects effectively. They must maintain control over several important assignments simultaneously.
- *Commitment to the business.* It helps if a successor has a genuine passion for the business. Leaders who have enthusiasm for what they do create a spark of excitement throughout the entire organization.[20]

The final stage in the management succession process involves the ultimate transition of organizational leadership. Often, the successor becomes the organization's CEO while the former CEO retains the title of chairman of the board. In other cases, it may be best for the founder to step out of the business entirely to give the successor the chance to establish his own identity within the company.

*D*eveloping a Management Succession Plan

◆ Explain how to develop an effective management succession plan.

Families that are most committed to ensuring that their business survives from one generation to the next exhibit four characteristics: (1) They believe that owning the business helps achieve their family's mission; (2) they are proud of the values their business is built on and exemplifies; (3) they believe that the business is contributing to society and makes it a better place to live; and (4) they rely on management succession plans to ensure the continuity of their company.[21] Developing a plan takes time and dedication, yet the benefits are well worth the cost. It is important to start the planning process early, well before the founder's retirement. Succession planning is not the kind of activity an entrepreneur can do in a hurry, and the sooner an entrepreneur starts, the easier it will be. Unfortunately, too many entrepreneurs put it off until it's too late. "Succession works best when parents have enough fortitude to discuss everything with their kids and resolve these issues while they're still alive," says one expert.[22] Creating a succession plan involves the following steps.

STEP 1: SELECT THE SUCCESSOR

Entrepreneurs should never assume that their children want to take control of the business. Above all, they should not be afraid to ask the question: "Do you really want to take over the family business?" Too often, children in this situation tell Mom and Dad what they want to hear out of loyalty, pressure, or guilty feelings. It is critical to remember at this juncture in the life of a business that children do not necessarily inherit their parents' entrepreneurial skills and desires. By leveling with the children about the business and their options regarding a family succession, the owner will know which heirs, if any, are willing to assume leadership of the business. In the choice of a successor, merit and desire are better standards to use than birth order.

One of the worst mistakes entrepreneurs can make is to postpone naming a successor until just before they are ready to step down. The problem is especially acute when more than one family member works for the company and is interested in assuming leadership of it. Sometimes, founders avoid naming a successor because they don't want to hurt the family members who are not chosen to succeed them. However, both the business and the family will be better off if, after observing the family members as they work in the business, the founder picks a successor on the basis of that person's skills and abilities. *For instance, Fred Jones, owner of 26 family-owned One Hour Martinizing Dry Cleaning stores, faced what could have been a difficult succession decision because all five of his children were involved in running the business. After carefully evaluating each child's strengths and weaknesses,*

Jones named his son Tom as his successor. Tom, who is not the oldest of the Jones children, was well qualified, having earned both business experience as a CPA and the trust and respect of the company's employees. None of Tom's brothers and sisters were surprised or upset at their father's decision.[23]

Involving the siblings themselves in the process of identifying the successor can alleviate some of the hard feelings that might otherwise surface. *Like Fred Jones, Mort and Marcy Ockenfels, owners of City Carton Inc., a recycling company, had five children, all working for the family business. As part of their succession planning process, the Ockenfels held family meetings in which they and their five sons discussed the issue of which of them would head the company. They ultimately decided that John, the oldest, had the most experience and was most qualified for the job. A consultant also helped each son develop a specific job description to avoid unnecessary conflicts later on. The Ockenfels sold all of their ownership in the business to their sons, who have been running the business successfully since 1990.*[24]

STEP 2: CREATE A SURVIVAL KIT FOR THE SUCCESSOR

Once he identifies a successor, the entrepreneur should prepare a survival kit and then brief the future leader on its contents, which should include all of the company's critical documents (wills, trusts, insurance policies, financial statements, bank accounts, key contracts, corporate bylaws, and so forth). The founder should be sure that the successor reads and understands all the relevant documents in the kit. Other important steps the owner should take to prepare the successor to take over leadership of the business include:

◆ Create a strategic analysis for the future. Working with the successor, the entrepreneur should identify the primary opportunities and challenges facing the company and the requirements for meeting them.

◆ On a regular basis, the entrepreneur should share with the successor his vision of the business's future direction, describing key factors that have led to its success and those that will bring future success.

◆ Be open and listen to the successor's views and concerns.

◆ Teach and learn at the same time.

◆ Explain the strategies of the business and their link to key success factors.

◆ Discuss the values and philosophy of the business and how they have inspired and influenced past actions.

◆ Discuss the people in the business and their strengths and weaknesses.

◆ Discuss the philosophy underlying the firm's compensation policy and explain why employees are paid what they are.

◆ Make a list of the firm's most important customers and its key vendors and review the history of all dealings with the parties on both lists.

◆ Discuss how to treat these key players to ensure the company's continued success and its smooth and error-free ownership transition.

◆ Develop a job analysis by taking an inventory of the activities involved in leading the company. This analysis can show successors which activities they should be spending most of their time on.

◆ Document as much process knowledge ("how we do things") as possible. After many years on the job, business owners are not even aware of their vast reservoirs of knowledge. For them, making decisions is a natural part of their business lives. They do it effortlessly because they have so much knowledge and experience. It is easy to forget that a successor will not have the benefit of those years of experience unless the founder communicates it. "Objectively documenting what it takes to run the business is probably the most difficult and least-attended-to part of the succession process," says Leslie Dashew, a family business consultant.[25]

Morry Stein, the head of Camp Echo Lake, a family-run youth camp, took the time to develop a successor's survival kit in case something happened to him. When he was killed in an airplane crash, Stein's sons, Tony and George, and his wife were able to use the written instructions to help make the difficult transition. In the kit he left behind, Stein included the names of his most trusted advisers, advice for handling different employees, where to find important company documents, and a touching pep talk for his family. The transition went smoothly not only because of the survival kit Stein had prepared but also because he had taken the time to sit down regularly with both of his sons to discuss "the state of the camp" as he called it. "About ten years ago, we started having business meetings around the dining room table at my parents' house," explains Tony. "We talked about new program ideas, the future of camping, how we could raise tuition, when we would enter the business, what our strengths were, and what we liked to do."[26]

STEP 3: GROOM THE SUCCESSOR

The discussions that set the stage for the transition of leadership are time-consuming and require openness by both parties. This is the process by which business founders transfer their knowledge to the next generation. In fact, grooming the successor is the founder's greatest teaching and development responsibility, and it takes time. To implement the succession plan, the founder must be:

◆ Patient, realizing that the transfer of power is gradual and evolutionary and that the successor should earn responsibility and authority one step at a time until the final transfer of power takes place.

◆ Willing to accept that the successor will make mistakes.

◆ Skillful at using the successor's mistakes as a teaching tool.

◆ An effective communicator and an especially tolerant listener.

◆ Capable of establishing reasonable expectations for the successor's performance.

◆ Able to articulate the keys to successor's performance.

Teaching is the art of assisting discovery. Teaching also requires letting go rather than controlling. When a problem arises in the business, the founder should consider delegating it to the successor-in-training. If he does delegate it, he must resist the temptation to wade in and fix the problem unless it proves to be beyond the successor's ability. Most great teachers are remembered more for the success of their students than for their own.

STEP 4: PROMOTE AN ENVIRONMENT OF TRUST AND RESPECT

Another priceless gift a founder can leave a successor is an environment of trust and respect. Trust and respect on the part of the founder and others fuel the successor's desire to learn and excel and build the successor's confidence in making decisions. Developing a competent successor over a period of five to ten years is realistic. Empowering the successor by gradually delegating responsibilities creates an environment in which customers, creditors, suppliers, and staff members can objectively view the successor's growth and development and gradually develop confidence in him. The final transfer of power will not be a dramatic, wrenching change but a smooth, coordinated passage.

STEP 5: COPE WITH THE FINANCIAL REALITIES OF ESTATE AND GIFT TAXES

The final step in developing a workable management succession plan is structuring the transition so as to minimize the impact of estate, gift, and inheritance taxes on family members and the business. Entrepreneurs who fail to consider the impact of these taxes may force their heirs to sell a successful business just to pay the estate's tax bill. In a recent survey of small business owners by researchers at Kennesaw State University, more than half believed that their estates would be hit with a tax bill that would limit their company's growth potential. One-third said that paying the expected estate tax would require their heirs to sell either part or all of their businesses![25] *Ella Perkins, co-owner of Perkins Flowers, and her son Gordon saw the need to develop an estate plan to minimize the impact of estate and gift taxes on the company, which Gordon was running. Each year, Ella gave Gordon $10,000 worth of stock in the company, the maximum amount the law allows without triggering gift taxes. She also transferred majority ownership in the company to Gordon using other estate planning tools so that estate taxes would be smaller on her minority share of the business. Gordon also purchased enough life insurance for his mother to pay the estimated estate tax bill. When Ella died at age 83, Gordon discovered that despite their attempts at estate planning, the amount of tax due was more than he had expected. "At the very least," he says, "it's going to repress the growth of my business for some significant amount of time." He says that he may have to sell a 43-acre tree farm the company owns to pay the full tax bill.[28]*

Although tax laws currently allow individuals to pass up to $1.3 million of assets to their heirs without incurring any estate taxes, the tax rate on transfers above that amount *starts* at 37 percent! The tax rate climbs to 55 percent for estates valued at more than $3 million. Without proper estate planning, an entrepreneur's family members will incur a painful tax bite when they inherit the business. Yet, according to the Arthur Andersen Center for Family Business, only 10 to 20 percent of all small business owners have written estate plans, even though they have 70 to 80 percent of their net worth tied up in their business![29] Entrepreneurs should be actively planning their estates by no later than age 45; those who started a business when they were very young or whose business is growing rapidly may need to begin as early as age 30. A variety of options may prove to be helpful in reducing the estate tax liability. They operate in different fashions, but their objective remains the same: to remove a portion of business owners' assets out of their estate so that, when they die, those assets will not be subject to estate taxes. Many of these estate planning tools need time to work their magic, so the key is to put them in place early on in the life of the business.

Buy/Sell Agreement. One of the most popular estate planning techniques is the buy/sell agreement. A recent survey by the Chartered Life Underwriters and the Chartered Life Financial Consultants found that 76 percent of small business owners who have estate plans have created buy/sell agreements.[30] A **buy/sell agreement** is a contract that co-owners often rely on to ensure the continuity of a business. In a typical arrangement, the co-owners create a contract stating that each agrees to buy the other out in case of the death or disability of one. That way, the heirs of the deceased or disabled owner can "cash out" of the business while leaving control of the business in the hands of the remaining owners. The buy/sell agreement specifies a formula for determining the value of the business at the time the agreement is to be executed. One problem with buy/sell agreements is that the remaining co-owners may not have the cash available to buy out the disabled or deceased owner. To resolve this issue, many businesses buy life and disability insurance for each of the owners in amounts large enough to cover the purchase price of their respective shares of the business.

Michael Stebbins and Carl Jacobs, co-owners of the 60-year-old Shiloh Nurseries Inc., have set up a buy/sell agreement as part of their management succession plan. Although the two entrepreneurs have six children between them, none of their offspring are interested in taking over the business. However, two of their most valued employees, their top salesman and their landscape architect would like to own the business some day. Under the buy/sell arrangement, the two employees will each purchase 24 percent of the company over two five-year time periods. At the end of ten years, the owners will have several options, including having the two employees purchase the remaining 52 percent of the company or setting up an ESOP to allow other employees to become owners in the business as well. Shiloh Nurseries has taken out insurance policies on each of the four owners to ensure that if any of them dies before the agreement is completed the other owners will have enough cash to purchase the deceased party's shares.[31]

Lifetime Gifting. The owners of a successful business may transfer money to their children (or other recipients) from their estate throughout their lives. Current federal tax regulations allow individuals to make gifts of $10,000 per year, per parent, per recipient, that are exempt from federal gift taxes. Each child would be required to pay income tax on the $10,000 gift, but the children are usually in lower tax brackets than the giver. For instance, husband and wife business owners could give $1.2 million worth of stock to their three children and their spouses over a period of 10 years without incurring any estate or gift taxes at all.

Setting Up a Trust. A **trust** is a contract between a grantor (the founder) and a trustee (generally a bank officer or an attorney) in which the grantor gives to the trustee legal title to assets (e.g., stock in the company), which the trustee agrees to hold for the beneficiaries (children). The beneficiaries can receive income from the trust, or they can receive the property in the trust, or both, at some specified time. Trusts can take a wide variety of forms, but two broad categories of trusts are available: revocable trusts and irrevocable trusts. A **revocable trust** is one that the grantor can change or revoke during his lifetime. Under present tax laws, however, the only trust that provides a tax benefit is an **irrevocable trust,** in which the grantor cannot require the trustee to return the assets held in trust. The value of the grantor's estate is lowered because the assets in an irrevocable trust are excluded from the value of the estate. However, an irrevocable trust places severe restrictions on the grantor's control of the property placed in the trust. Business owners use several types of irrevocable trusts to lower their estate tax liabilities:

♦ *Bypass trust.* The most basic type of trust is the bypass trust, which allows a business owner to put $600,000 into trust naming his spouse as the beneficiary upon his death. The spouse receives the income from the trust throughout her life, but the principal in the trust goes to the couple's heirs free of estate taxes upon the spouse's death.

♦ *Irrevocable life insurance trust.* This type of trust allows a business owner to keep the proceeds of a life insurance policy out of his estate and away from estate taxes, freeing up that money to pay the taxes on the remainder of the estate. To get the tax benefit, business owners must be sure that the business or the trust (rather than themselves) owns the insurance policy. The disadvantage of an irrevocable life insurance trust is that if the owner dies within three years of establishing it, the insurance proceeds do become part of his estate and are subject to estate taxes.

♦ *Irrevocable asset trust.* An irrevocable asset trust is similar to an irrevocable life insurance trust except that it is designed to pass the assets in the parents' estate on to their children. The children do not have control of the assets while the parents are still living, but they do receive the income from those assets. Upon the parents' death, the assets in the trust go to the children without being subject to the estate tax.

◆ *Grantor retained annuity trust (GRAT).* A grantor retained annuity trust (GRAT) is a special type of irrevocable trust and has become one of the most popular tools for entrepreneurs to transfer ownership of a business while maintaining control over it and minimizing estate taxes. Under a GRAT, an owner can put property into an irrevocable trust for a maximum of 10 years. While the trust is in effect, the grantor retains the voting power and receives the interest income from the property in the trust. At the end of the trust (not to exceed 10 years), the property passes to the beneficiaries (heirs). The beneficiaries are required to pay a gift tax on the value of the assets placed in the GRAT. However, the IRS taxes GRAT gifts only according to their discounted present value because the heirs did not receive use of the property while it was in trust. The primary disadvantage of using a GRAT in estate planning is that if the grantor dies during the life of the GRAT, its assets pass back into the grantor's estate. These assets then become subject to the full estate tax.

Establishing a trust requires meeting many specific legal requirements and is not something business owners should do on their own. It is much better to hire experienced attorneys, accountants, and financial advisers to assist. Although the cost of establishing a trust can be high, the tax savings they generate are well worth the expense.

Estate Freeze. An **estate freeze** attempts to minimize estate taxes by having family members create two classes of stock for the business: (1) preferred voting stock for the parents and (2) nonvoting common stock for the children. The value of the preferred stock is frozen while the common stock reflects the anticipated increased market value of the business. Any appreciation in the value of the business after the transfer is not subject to estate taxes. However, the parent must pay gift taxes on the value of the common stock given to the children. The value of the common stock is the total value of the business less the value of the voting preferred stock retained by the parent. The parents also must accept taxable dividends at the market rate on the preferred stock they own.

Family Limited Partnership. Creating a **family limited partnership (FLP)** allows business-owning parents to transfer their company to their children (thus lowering their estate taxes) while still retaining control over it for themselves. To create a family limited partnership, the parents (or parent) sets up a partnership among themselves and their children. The parents retain the general partnership interest, which can be as low as 1 percent, and the children become the limited partners. As general partners, the parents control both the limited partnership and the family business. In other words, nothing in the way the company operates has to change. Over time, the parents can transfer company stock into the limited partnership, ultimately passing ownership of the company to their children. One of the principal tax benefits of an FLP is that it allows discounts on the value of the shares of company stock the parents transfer into the limited partnership. Because a family business is closely held, shares of ownership in it, especially minority shares, are not as marketable as those of a publicly held company. As a result, company shares transferred into the limited partnership are discounted at 20 to 50 percent of their full market value, producing a large tax savings for everyone involved. The average discount is 40 percent, but that amount varies on the basis of the industry and the individual company involved. A business owner should consider an FLP as part of a succession plan "when there has been a buildup of substantial value in the business and the older generation has a substantial amount of liquidity," says one expert.[32] Because of their ability to reduce estate and gift taxes, family limited partnerships have become one of the most popular estate planning tools in recent years.

Developing a succession plan and preparing a successor requires a wide variety of skills, some of which the business founder will not have, so it is important to bring experts into the process when necessary. Entrepreneurs often call on their attorneys, accountants, in-

IN THE FOOTSTEPS OF AN ENTREPRENEUR

Pyrrhic Revenge

*M*anagement succession decisions in family businesses usually are defining moments in the life of the business and the family because they are so filled with emotion. Whenever two or more siblings are involved in a family business and more than one wants to assume the leadership role, the founder faces a tough decision. Once the owner chooses one child as successor, the remaining siblings battle feelings that they are the "losers." The results of succession turf wars can be devastating to both the business and the family, and the losers' behavior can sometimes be bizarre and destructive.

Psychologist Steven Berglas has coined the name Pyrrhic Revenge for this phenomenon, referring to the Greek general Pyrrhus, whose string of victories came at a catastrophic cost to his own men. Losers in the battle for succession in family businesses "set out to commit professional suicide," explains Berglas, "and they don't care because they're bringing down everyone else they resent too"—even their own family members. It can happen all too easily, as George Berkowitz, founder of Legal Sea Foods, a chain of Boston seafood restaurants generating $50 million in sales per year, discovered. In 1992, George announced that he would be turning the reins of the company over to the older of his two sons, Roger. That meant that younger brother Marc would be reporting to his older sibling, a situation he wasn't at all happy about. Marc decided to remain in the family business. After all, he had spend most of his life working there—just as Roger had.

From the time they were 8 and 11, Marc and Roger had spent their weekends and vacations working hard in the family's restaurants. "I watched them carefully," says George. "I observed how they took orders, how they got along with people." At work, the boys called their parents "Harriet" and "George" because it sounded more professional than "Mom" and "Dad." Unknowingly, the stage was set for a lifetime of competition between the brothers. The competition ended in 1992 when George declared Roger, whom he called "the brilliant one," the winner. With the management succession issue settled, however, another soon arose: What would Marc do?

George appointed Marc head of Legal Sea Foods' newly created "ventures" division, a job from which he was supposed to seek out new opportunities for the company such as mall and airport locations. A nice prize for the "loser" in the race for management succession that had developed? Perhaps. According to Marc, however, the new division had no funding, and he had no clear description of his new position. Marc floundered in his new job and became increasingly frustrated that neither his father nor his brother would define his role in the company. A vehement clash with his father sealed Marc's fate with the company. After a heated argument, George ordered Marc out of the business.

Once he had left the company, the Pyrrhic Revenge syndrome kicked in, and Marc decided he would launch his own seafood company, Marco Solo. After 18 months, the business folded. With no income and lots of hard feelings, Marc filed a lawsuit against his family and Legal Sea Foods, knowing that the lawsuit would cripple the restaurant chain, distract Roger from running the company, and threaten his own inheritance. News of the lawsuit splashed across local newspapers, further damaging the company's reputation. "They underestimated me," ranted Marc. "I'm not going anywhere."

After two years of legal wrangling, the Berkowitz family finally settled its differences out of court, but not before news of the family dispute cast negative attention on the restaurant chain. Unfortunately, the family itself remains divided. Marc has no contact with either his brother or his parents.

Steven Berglas offers these suggestions to avoid falling victim to Pyrrhic Revenge:

> Raise your children to know the difference between your love for them as people and your respect for them as workers and producers.
> Sensitize your children to the fact that there are multiple forms of intelligence and skill sets and not everyone possesses equal amounts of leadership potential.
> Let your children know that they are not alien beings if they don't love the business as much as you do.

1. Use the resources of your library and the World Wide Web to locate stories about family businesses and management succession. Find an example of a family business that faced the difficult issue of Pyrrhic Revenge. Summarize your findings in a one-page paper.

2. What can parents and their children do to avoid Pyrrhic Revenge syndrome?

SOURCES: Adapted from Shelly Branch, "Mom Always Liked You Best," *Your Company*, April/May 1998, pp. 26–38; Steven Berglas, "A Loser's Revenge," *Inc.*, July 1997, pp. 37–38. ◆

surance agents, and financial planners to help them build a succession plan that works best for their particular situation. "Planning business succession is not a do-it-yourself project," claims one writer.[33] Because the issues involved can be highly complex and charged with emotion, bringing in trusted advisers to help improves the quality of the process and provides an objective perspective. Table 20.1 provides an estate planning checklist for entrepreneurs.

Table 20.1 An Estate Planning Checklist

Would your estate be in order if you died unexpectedly? Would your family suffer because you hadn't planned? Would your estate be socked with high taxes? Would your business be able to continue? Answer these 10 questions to measure how well you have done your estate planning.

1. Do you have a will?
2. Has your will been updated within the past three years?
3. Do you know your net worth?
4. Do you know the value of your business?
5. Do you know who would acquire ownership of your business if you were to die tomorrow?
6. Do you know who would run your business if you were to die tomorrow?
7. Would your business be likely to survive under the ownership and leadership of the people named in questions 5 and 6?
8. Do you know how your estate would finance the applicable estate taxes if you were to die tomorrow?
9. Do you know how the new owner of your business would finance its purchase?
10. Has your estate plan been prepared or reviewed by an attorney, an accountant, and other professionals who specialize in estate planning?

Scoring: Give yourself 10 points for every question you answered "yes." If your score is:

between 80 and 100. Your estate is in secure hands. You should talk with an estate planning professional periodically to adjust your plan as your needs change.

between 50 and 70. Your estate is exposed to more risk than it should be. Your family is likely to incur unnecessary expenses and trouble with your estate. See an estate planning professional for advice soon.

between 0 and 50. Your estate is in imminent danger! You should call an estate planning professional immediately and develop a sound plan to make sure your business survives you.

SOURCE: Randy Myers, "Where There's a Will . . ." *Nation's Business,* April 1997, p. 26.

*R*isk Management Strategies

5 Understand the four risk management strategies.

Insurance is an important part of creating a management succession plan because it can help business owners minimize the taxes on the estates they pass on to their heirs and can provide much-needed cash to pay the taxes the estate does incur. However, insurance plays an important role in many other aspects of a successful business—from covering employee injuries to protecting against natural disasters that might shut a business down temporarily. When most small business owners think of risks such as these, they automatically think of insurance. However, insurance companies are the first to point out that insurance does not solve all risk problems. Instead, dealing with risk successfully requires a combination of four risk management strategies: avoiding, reducing, anticipating, and transferring (or spreading) risk.

Avoiding risk requires a business to take actions to shun risky situations. For example, you could substantially reduce the risk of an automobile accident if you sold your automobile, refused to ride with others, walked to work, and carefully looked both ways before crossing the street. Such actions would be possible, but not practical, because in our busy society people depend on transportation by car or bus. However, business people *can* avoid risk by thoughtful business practices. For instance, conducting credit checks of customers can help decrease losses from bad debts. Wise managers know that they can avoid some risks simply by taking positive management actions. Workplace safety improves when business owners implement programs designed to make all employees aware of the hazards of their jobs and how to avoid being hurt. Business owners who have active risk identification and prevention programs can reduce their potential insurance costs as well as create a safer, more

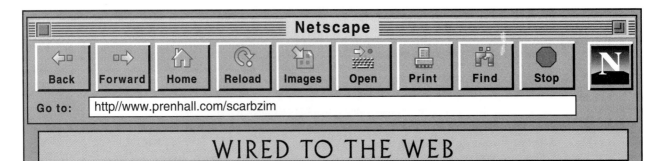

WIRED TO THE WEB

ALL IN THE FAMILY?

*M*arie and Mark Henson, both 60, were ready to sell the business they had founded more than 30 years ago with just $4,000. They had contacted a business broker friend who had told them that he thought he could help them get the price they wanted for Saltillo Tile Company. Then, the couple's oldest daughter, Lynn, made a surprise announcement. "Rather than sell the business to someone outside the family, why not sell it to me?" she asked her parents one Sunday afternoon. "I'd like to buy it." All three of the Henson's daughters, Lynn, 30, Amy, 28, and Sara, 25, had attended college, but Lynn was the only one to graduate. Amy and Sara are both married and live out of state. Neither has indicated any interest in the family business.

The thought of buying the business had occurred to Lynn only recently, but she didn't want to let this opportunity slip by. She had worked at Saltillo as a clerk in the front office while completing her MBA, so she could appreciate the long hours and sacrifices her parents had put into building the company. She also recognized their desire to be free from the company to enjoy their retirement years traveling and pursuing their hobbies. She understood that her parents needed to maintain their financial resources, most of which were tied up in the business.

Lynn had used her parents' company as a case study for several business classes during her college years and

was impressed by the potential it offered. Although surprised by their daughter's last-minute declaration, Marie and Mark were trying to be flexible so that Lynn could have the opportunity to buy them out. Their goal, however, was to be free from the company.

As much as Lynn wanted the company, she was not sure if she could really afford it. "It was recently valued at $2 million, and I don't expect my parents to sell it to me for any less." Lynn remembers studying the different ways of purchasing a business in one of her MBA classes, but that was several years ago. "Are there ways to purchase a family business that will give my parents the financial security and the freedom they deserve while minimizing their tax exposure?" she wondered. "If so, will those methods permit me to raise the money I need to buy the business without putting the company so deep in debt that its future is threatened?"

1. Use the resources of the World Wide Web and the local library to research ways that Lynn might be able to buy the family business and allow her parents to achieve their retirement goals at the same time.
2. Should Marie and Mark sell the business to Lynn or to an outsider? Explain.
3. What could the Hensons have done to avoid this last-minute proposal?

SOURCE: "Case Study: Keep the Firm in the Family?" *Nation's Business*, May 1996, p. 60.

attractive work environment for their employees. Because avoiding risk altogether usually is not practical, however, a strategy of reducing risk becomes necessary.

A risk-reducing strategy takes actions that build an extra degree of safety into a situation with an identified level of risk. Businesses can reduce risk by following common safety practices, such as installing a sprinkler system to lower the threat of damage from fire. The sprinkler system cannot guarantee that a fire will not occur, but it may minimize the damage that results. Risk reduction strategies do not eliminate the source of the risk, but they lessen the impact of its occurrence. Even with avoidance and reduction strategies, the source of the risk is still present; thus, losses can occur.

Risk anticipation strategies promote self-insurance. Knowing that some element of risk still exists, a business owner puts aside money each month to cover any losses that might occur. For example, suppose that a business owner checks each customer's credit very carefully. She takes all reasonable steps to ensure that the customer can pay the bill and has a sound history of prompt payment. Shortly after the sale, however, a fire completely destroys the customer's business and, along with it, the unpaid-for merchandise. The business owner also discovers that the customer's business was not insured and that the loss will cause him to declare bankruptcy. She may have done all she could to determine that the customer's credit was solid, but that did not prevent the financial loss caused by the fire and subsequent bankruptcy. In this case, the owner's loss would be less devastating to the company if she had put aside cash periodically to cover such losses.

Sometimes a self-insurance fund set aside may not be large enough to cover the losses from a particular situation. When this happens, the business or individual stands to lose despite the best efforts to anticipate risk, especially in the first few years, when the fund may be insufficient to cover large losses. Most individuals and businesses therefore include in their risk strategies some form of insurance to transfer risk. *For instance, Arni Cohen, owner of seven pizza and sandwich restaurants, began offering his employees health care insurance when he opened for business in 1964. In 1978, Cohen, tired of watching the cost of the coverage climb every year, decided to establish a self-insurance fund to cover his employees' health care benefits. Cohen's restaurants, named Arni's, employ 220 workers, so Cohen knew that a self-insurance strategy alone could be risky. If employees' claims were low in a given year, he would save money over what he would have paid in insurance premiums. If several workers suffered catastrophic illnesses at once, however, his company could face a cash crisis. To minimize the risk, Cohen purchased a "stop-loss" policy, which takes over payment of all claims that exceed a certain level. Since he started self-insuring, Cohen says the strategy has saved his company tens of thousands of dollars, despite two years of high*

Frustrated with the rapidly rising cost of his employee's health care insurance, Arni Cohen, owner of Arni's, a chain of pizza and sandwich restaurants, decided to establish a self-insurance fund to cover his employees' health benefits. To limit his company's exposure, Cohen also purchased a stop-loss policy, which pays all claims that exceed a certain level.

claims in the mid-1980s. Cohen has added dental and eyecare coverage to his package as well and has established a wellness program to keep claims low. Studies suggest that about 39 percent of all full-time workers are covered by self-funded health insurance programs like Cohen's.[34]

Self-insurance is not for every business owner, however. For businesses with fewer than 50 employees, self-insurance is usually not a wise choice because there is so much variation in the number of annual claims. Also, companies using self-insurance should be financially stable and should see it as a long-term strategy for savings. *At Herzog-Meier, a Beaverton, Oregon, car dealership, co-owner James Meier discovered the disadvantages of being small and trying to self-insure. Major illnesses among several employees in two consecutive years drained the company's self-insurance fund, forcing the dealership to dig into other accounts to pay employees' claims. Even with its stop-loss coverage, the dealership spent $280,000 in just one year, an amount much higher than its health insurance premiums would have been with full insurance coverage. The company is now fully insured again, and its owners are much more comfortable with their limited exposure.*[35] Table 20.2 provides a self-test for companies to take to determine whether self-insurance is the best option for them.

Risk transfer strategies depend on the use of insurance. Insurance is a risk transfer (or risk-spreading) strategy because an individual or a business transfers some of the costs of a particular risk to an insurance company, which is set up to spread out the financial burdens of risk. During a specific time period, the insured business or individual pays money (a premium) to the insurance carrier (either a private company or a government agency). In return, the carrier promises to pay the insured a certain amount of money in the event of a loss.

Table 20.2 A Self-Test for Self-Insurers

The Self-Funding Academy, a professional association in Winston-Salem, North Carolina, offers the following test for companies considering self-insuring their health-care benefits. If you can answer yes to all seven question, then your company probably is ready to self-insure.

1. Do you have at least 50 employees among whom you can spread the risk of high claims, or do you have the assets to withstand some unpredictability year to year for claims? Are you financially able to withstand an occasional year when employee health care claims may be higher than anticipated?

2. Are your top managers comfortable leaving behind the month-to-month cost stability of a fully insured plan? Are they prepared to withstand more volatility under a self-funded plan?

3. Do you want to self-fund because you are committed to the idea of being in greater control of your company's benefits and their costs? Remember: The primary motivation for self-funding should not be to gain some minimal savings over the insurance premiums your company is paying currently.

4. Do you have partners such as insurance consultants or risk brokers you can trust to help you create and administer the plan?

5. Do you have access to reasonably priced stop-loss coverage to prevent serious cash flow problems in those years when employees' claims will exceed what you expect (and those years *will* occur)? Does that plan include specific coverage (claims from any one person's illness) as well as aggregate coverage (which protects the company in case all employee's claims exceed a particular amount)?

6. Are you aware of the many options your company has under a self-insurance plan? For instance, companies can pay claims as they come in or they can set aside money in a trust fund. Self-insured businesses can limit employees to a specific group of health-care providers, or they can let them choose any provider.

7. Have you thought through any concerns that your employees have about self-funding? Are your employees comfortable with the idea?

SOURCE: Laura M. Litvan, "Are You Ready to Self-Fund?" *Nation's Business*, March 1996, p. 21.

*7*he Basics of Insurance

Insurance is the transfer of risk from one entity (an individual, a group, or a business) to an insurance company. Without insurance, many of the activities and services we take for granted would not be possible because the risk of overwhelming financial loss would be too great for a business to assume. Yet many small business owners ignore their company's insurance needs. "We estimate that 50 percent of small businesses are either not insured or are grossly underinsured," says an executive with the Insurance Information Institute. "If a disaster occurs, they're out of business."[36]

How can insurance companies assume so much risk? On the surface, it may seem that insurance companies are themselves in a risky situation. If each business that had paid $1,000 in annual premiums had a claim of $150,000, it would not take long for the insurance company to go bankrupt. But what is actually operating here is the law of large numbers. A business owner's premiums of $1,000 per year for fire insurance are pooled with those of thousands of other business owners. Out of this pool, the insurance company pays out benefits to what it hopes is only a small fraction of those paying premiums. Even if in one year the benefits paid out are greater than the premiums paid in, the law of large numbers says that in the long run, the insurance company will have a surplus of premiums.

To be insurable, a situation or hazard must meet the following requirements:

1. It must be possible to calculate the actual loss being insured. For example, it would probably not be possible to insure an entire city against fire because too many variables are involved. It is possible, however, to insure a specific building.

2. It must be possible to select the risk being insured. It is impossible to insure against everything, and it is usually not possible to insure against events that are already under way. This is the equivalent of trying to insure a boat against sinking when it is already half-submerged.

3. There must be enough potential policyholders to assume the risk. If you are a tightrope walker specializing in walking between tall downtown buildings, you probably cannot be insured because there are simply not enough people engaging in this activity to spread the risk sufficiently. Only recently have people who engaged in skydiving or scuba diving been able to obtain certain kinds of life and accident insurance.

Most insurance companies also like to be sure that the parties (individuals or businesses) are not concentrated in a single geographic area. If the only businesses or homes holding flood insurance policies were insured by a certain company and were located in one city on the Mississippi River, the company would have to charge extremely high premiums. Having flood insurance policyholders spread out across the country would reduce the risk that one natural disaster would wipe out the insurance company, and thus the premiums could be somewhat lower.

The risk management pyramid (Figure 20.2 on page 710) is designed to help business owners decide how they should allocate their risk management dollars. Begin by identifying the primary risks your company faces: for example, a fire in the manufacturing plant, a lawsuit from a customer injured by your company's product, an earthquake, and so on. Then rate each event on three factors:

1. *Severity.* How much would the event affect your company's ability to operate?

2. *Probability.* How likely is the event to occur?

3. *Cost.* How much would it cost your company if the event occurred?

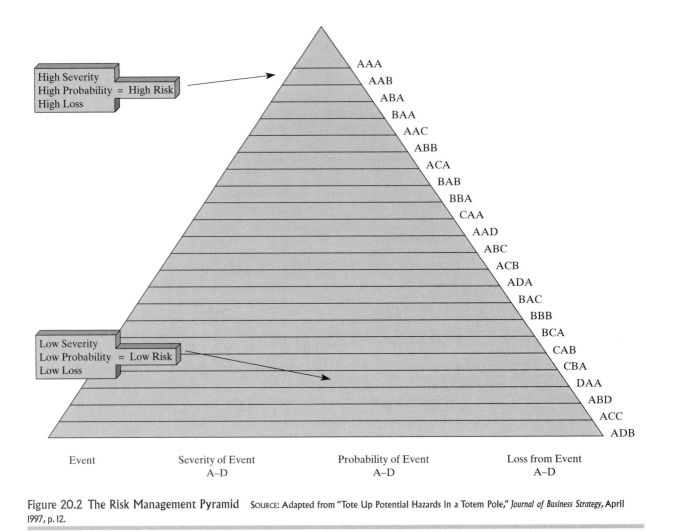

High Severity
High Probability = High Risk
High Loss

AAA
AAB
ABA
BAA
AAC
ABB
ACA
BAB
BBA
CAA
AAD
ABC
ACB
ADA
BAC
BBB
BCA
CAB
CBA
DAA
ABD
ACC
ADB

Low Severity
Low Probability = Low Risk
Low Loss

| Event | Severity of Event A–D | Probability of Event A–D | Loss from Event A–D |

Figure 20.2 The Risk Management Pyramid SOURCE: Adapted from "Tote Up Potential Hazards in a Totem Pole," *Journal of Business Strategy*, April 1997, p. 12.

Rate the event on each factor using a simple scale: A (high) to D (low). For instance, a small company might rate a fire in its manufacturing plant as ABA. On the other hand, that same company might rank a computer system crash as CBA. Using the risk management pyramid, the business owner sees that the event rated ABA is higher on the risk scale than the event rated CBA. Therefore, this company would focus more of its risk management dollars on preventing the fire in its plant than on dealing with a computer system crash.

TYPES OF INSURANCE

No longer is cost of insurance a small and inconsequential part of doing business. Now the ability to get adequate coverage and to pay the premiums is a significant factor in starting and running a small business. Sometimes just *finding* coverage for their business is a challenge for entrepreneurs. *When Anita Denunzio Wagner and her husband, Frank, moved their computer training company, Next Generation Training, from Germany to Florida, they found it very difficult to get insurance to cover the significant investment they had in computers and in the training studio they had added to their home. "Florida has hurricanes and is considered a high-risk area," explains Anita, "so many insurance companies have stopped serving this area." When insurance companies learned that their business was home-based and owned many computers, they balked at providing coverage for the Wagners. To protect their business, the Wagners knew they needed property insurance (in case their computer equipment was damaged, destroyed, or stolen), liability coverage (in case a client was injured while on their property), and other basic types of coverage. After several months of fruitless searching, the Wagners finally were able to purchase the insurance they needed through the Small Office Home Office Association (SOHOA), a trade association for home-based businesses in Reston, Virginia.*[37]

A wide range of business, individual, and group insurance is available to small business owners, and deciding which types of insurance are necessary can be difficult. Some types of insurance are essential to providing a secure future for the company; others may provide additional employee benefits. Figure 20.2 illustrates the risk management pyramid, a tool designed to help business owners decide the risks they should focus their resources on preventing, reducing, or insuring against. The four major categories of insurance are property and casualty insurance, life and disability insurance, health insurance and workers' compensation coverage, and liability insurance. Each category is divided into many specific types, each of which has many variations offered by insurance companies. Small business owners should begin by purchasing a basic **business owner's policy (BOP),** which typically includes basic property, casualty, and liability insurance coverage. Business owner's policies alone are not sufficient to meet most small business owners insurance needs, however. Entrepreneurs should start with a BOP and then customize their insurance coverage to suit their company's special needs by purchasing additional types of coverage. "Basic BOPs usually don't come close to covering all the property and casualty losses a business owner can potentially face," says one experienced insurance agent.[38]

Property and Casualty Insurance. Property and casualty insurance covers a company's tangible assets, such as buildings, equipment, inventory, machinery, signs, and others that have been damaged, destroyed, or stolen. Business owners should be sure that their policies cover the *replacement* cost of their property, not just its value at the time of the loss, even if it costs extra. *One business owner whose policy covered the replacement cost of his company's building was glad he had purchased the extra coverage when he suffered a devastating fire loss. When he began rebuilding, he discovered that the cost to comply with current building code regulations was $1 million, much higher than merely replacing the previous structure. "Without this extra coverage, he never would have made it," says his insurance agent.*[39] Specific types of property and casualty insurance include property, business interruption, surety, marine, crime, liability, and professional liability insurance.

Property insurance protects a company's tangible assets against loss from damage, theft, and destruction. It applies to automobiles, boats, homes, office buildings, stores, factories, and other items of property. Some property insurance policies are broadly written to include all of an individual's property up to some maximum amount of loss, whereas other policies are written to cover only one building or one specific piece of property, such as a company car. In some parts of the United States, business owners must buy separate insurance policies for specific causes of loss. For instance, people living in flood-prone areas usually have to buy a special insurance policy (at higher rates) for flood and water damage protection. Business owners in other areas may have to buy special coverage for earthquake, fire, wind, hail, or rain damage to property.[40] Within the past decade, business owners across the United States have suffered billions of dollars in losses from natural disasters, including floods in the Midwest, hurricanes on the East Coast, and earthquakes in California. Many businesses with inadequate insurance coverage were forced to close, and others are still struggling to recover. *Jean-Louis Wolfe, owner of Fantasy Books in Santa Monica, California, wishes she had purchased earthquake insurance for her small bookstore. Less than a year old when the Northridge earthquake hit, the science fiction and fantasy bookstore was* *forced to take out loans to cover its relocation costs and the $30,000 in inventory it lost. Wolfe had considered buying earthquake insurance but had decided not to because the premiums were so high.*[41]

Although some insurance protection is designed for both businesses and individuals, businesses often need additional types of insurance. For example, a company's BOP may insure the buildings and contents of a factory for loss from fire or natural disaster, but the owner may also buy insurance, called extra expense coverage, to cover expenses that would occur while the destroyed factory was being rebuilt. **Extra expense coverage** pays for the costs of temporarily relocating workers and machinery so that a business can continue to operate while it rebuilds or repairs its factory. A similar type of insurance, called **business interruption insurance,** covers a business owner's lost income and ongoing expenses when the company cannot operate for an extended period of time.[42] As devastating as such interruptions can be to a small company, studies show that nearly half of all business owners do not purchase business interruption coverage. *Dottie Bourgeois was glad she had purchased business interruption insurance for her small clothing and gift shop, Pierre Crawdeaux Company, Inc. When a runaway freighter slammed into the Riverwalk Mall in New Orleans where her store was located, the damage forced her company to close for six weeks. Because she had adequate property and business interruption insurance, Bourgeois was able to recover all of the losses her company sustained.*[43]

A business may also purchase **surety insurance,** which protects against losses to customers that occur when a contract is not completed on time or is completed incorrectly. Surety protection guarantees customers that they will get either the products or services they purchased or the money to cover losses from contractual failures.

Businesses also buy insurance to protect themselves from losses that occur when either finished goods or raw materials are lost or destroyed while being shipped. **Marine insurance** is designed to cover the risk associated with goods in transit. The name of this insurance goes back to the days when a ship's cargo was insured against high risks associated with ocean navigation. Today, business owners can purchase marine insurance to cover property in transit and property still under their care.

Crime insurance does not deter crime, but it can reimburse the small business owner for losses from the three Ds: dishonesty, disappearance, and destruction. Business owners should ask their insurance brokers or agents exactly what their crime insurance policies do and do not cover; after-the-fact insurance coverage surprises arc seldom pleasant. Premiums for such policies vary depending on the type of business, store location, number of employees, maximum cash value, quality of the business's security system, and the business's history of losses. Specific coverage may include fidelity bonds, which are designed to reimburse the business owner for losses due to embezzlement and employee theft. Forgery bonds reimburse the business owner for any loss sustained from the forgery of business checks.

Life and Disability Insurance. Unlike most forms of insurance, life insurance does not pertain to avoiding risk; death is a certainty for everyone. Rather, **life insurance** protects families and businesses against loss of income, security, or personal services that results from an individual's death. Life insurance policies are usually issued in a face amount payable to a beneficiary upon the death of the insured. Life insurance for business protection, though not as common as life insurance for family protection, is becoming more popular. Many businesses insure the lives of key executives to offset the costs of having to make a hurried and often unplanned replacement of important managerial personnel.

When it comes to assets that are expensive to replace, few are more costly than the key people in a business, including the owner. What would it take to replace a company's top sales representative? Its production supervisor? Clearly, money alone would not be the answer, but it would provide the business with the funds necessary to find and train their replacements and to cover the profits lost because of their death or disability. That's what key-person insurance does. It provides valuable working capital to keep a business on track while it reorganizes and searches for the right person to replace the loss of someone in a key position in the company.

Pensions and annuities are special forms of life insurance policies that combine insurance with a form of saving. With an annuity or a pension plan, the insured person's premiums go partly to provide standard insurance coverage and partly to a fund that is invested by the insurance company. The interest from the invested portion of the policy is then used to pay an income to the policyholder when she reaches a certain age. If the policyholder dies before reaching that age, either the policy converts to income for the spouse or family of the insured or the insurance proceeds (plus interest) go to the beneficiary as they would in ordinary life insurance.

Disability insurance protects against losses resulting from an unexpected, and perhaps expensive, disablement. Because a sudden disability limits a person's ability to earn a living, the insurance proceeds are designed to help make up for the loss of what that person could have expected to earn if the accident had not occurred. Sometimes called income insurance, these policies usually guarantee a stated percentage of an individual's income—usually around 60 percent—while he is recovering and is unable to run a business. Short-term disability policies cover the 90-day gap between the time a person is injured and when workers' compensation payments begin. Long-term disability policies pay for lost income after 90 days or longer. In addition to the portion of income a policy will replace, another important factor to consider when purchasing disability insurance is the waiting period, the time gap between when the disability occurs and the disability payments begin. Although many business owners understand the importance of maintaining adequate life insurance coverage, few see the relevance of maintaining proper coverage for disabilities. For most people, disability represents a greater risk than death. "Men under the age of 50 are five times as likely to be disabled as they are to die prematurely," says one insurance adviser.[44]

Health Insurance and Workers' Compensation. One of small business owners' greatest concerns in recent years has been the skyrocketing costs of health insurance. As health care costs have climbed and the average age of the workforce has risen, health insurance has become an extremely important benefit to most workers. Companies that offer thorough health coverage often find that it gives them an edge in attracting and retaining quality workers. Four basic health insurance options are available to employers:[45]

Traditional indemnity plans. Under these plans, employees choose their own health care providers, and the insurance company either pays the provider directly or reimburses employees for the covered amounts.

Managed care plans. As part of employers' attempts to put a lid on escalating health care costs, managed care plans have become increasingly popular. Two variations, the health maintenance organization (HMO) and the preferred provider organization (PPO) are most common. An HMO is a prepaid health care arrangement under which employees must use health care providers who are employed by or are under contract with the HMO their company uses. Under a PPO, an insurance company negotiates discounts for health care with certain physicians and hospitals. Employees must choose a health care provider from the approved list, but they pay only a small fee for each office visit (often just $10 to $25). The insurance company pays the remainder. PPOs are the most common type of managed care plan, accounting for 35 percent of the health care market; HMOs are the next most common plan with 30 percent of the market.[46]

Medical savings accounts (MSAs). As its name implies, a medical savings account (MSA) is a special savings account coupled with a high-deductible insurance policy.

Employees contribute pretax dollars from their paychecks into the fund and use them as they need to. Withdrawals from an MSA are not taxed as long as the money is used for approved medical expenses. Unused funds can accumulate indefinitely and earn tax-free interest. Only self-employed individuals or those who work for companies with 50 or fewer employees qualify for MSAs.

Self-insurance. As we have seen earlier in this chapter, some business owners choose to insure themselves for health coverage rather than to incur the costs of fully insured plans offered by outsiders. The benefits of self-insurance include greater control over the plan's design and the coverage it offers, fewer paperwork and reporting requirements, and, in some cases, lower costs. The primary disadvantage, of course, is the possibility of having to pay large amounts to cover treatments for several employees' major illnesses at the same time, which can strain a small company's cash flow. Many self-insured businesses limit their exposure to such losses by purchasing stop-loss insurance.

Another type of health-related coverage is **workers' compensation,** which is designed to cover employees who are injured on the job or who become sick as a result of a work environment. Before passage of workers' compensation legislation, any employee injured on the job could bring a lawsuit to prove the employer was liable for the worker's injury. Because of the red tape and expenses involved in such lawsuits, many employees were never compensated for job-related accidents and injuries. Although the details of coverage vary from state to state, workers' compensation laws require employers to provide benefits and medical and rehabilitation costs for employees injured on the job. The amount of compensation an injured employee will receive is determined by a fixed schedule of benefits based on three factors: the wages or salary that the employee was earning at the time of the accident or injury, the seriousness of the injury, and the extent of the disability to the employee. *For instance, the producers of the hit Broadway musical* The Phantom of the Opera *experienced a large workers' compensation claim when a maintenance worker was injured on the set. The worker was polishing the show's huge chandelier as it sat on the floor when another employee unknowingly hit the switch to retract the chandelier into the ceiling. The chandelier knocked the worker into the orchestra pit, seriously injuring him. That one claim ran "well into six figures," says the agent representing the insurance company.*[47]

Only three states, New Jersey, South Carolina, and Texas, do not require companies to purchase workers' compensation coverage once they reach a certain size. Usually, the state sets the rates businesses pay for workers' compensation coverage, and business owners purchase their coverage from private insurance companies. Rates vary by industry, business size, and the number of claims a company's workers make. For instance, workers' compensation premiums are higher for a typical logging business than for a retail gift store. Whatever industry they are in, business owners can reduce their worker's compensation costs by improving their employees' safety records. *For instance, Alan Layton, CEO of Layton Construction Company, set up a safety training program and a reward system to lower the number of accidents employees suffered on job sites. The company works with its workers' compensation insurance company to improve safety. "Our [insurance] carrier gives us training and shares information about new developments or techniques we can use," says Layton. Although his business is in a relatively dangerous industry with high workers' compensation costs, Layton has managed to improve his company's safety record, lower his insurance costs, and boost worker productivity.*[48]

Liability Insurance. One of the most common types of insurance coverage is **liability insurance,** which protects a business against losses resulting from accidents or injuries people suffer on the company's property or from its products or services and damage the company causes to others' property. Most BOPs include basic liability coverage; however, the limits

Fighting Workers' Compensation Fraud

*W*orkers' compensation claims cost taxpayers more than $70 billion each year, and experts estimate that about 10 percent of that total goes to fraudulent claims. Fraud is expensive. It raises companies' insurance premiums, results in higher prices for consumers, reduces employee morale and productivity, and can even drive small companies out of business. The average cost per claim for medical and disability expenses is $10,992, and the typical claimant is a 37-year-old male who is married and earns $382 per week. Although the majority of claims are legitimate, an alarming proportion are fraudulent. Why is workers' compensation fraud so prevalent? Two reasons explain it: It is easy to commit; and it is hard to detect. Fraud typically occurs in four areas of workers' compensation:

Claimant fraud. Claimant fraud occurs when workers fabricate or exaggerate an injury claim to get paid time off. Kenneth Payne, a highway maintenance worker for the California Department of Transportation filed a workers' compensation claim, saying that he could not work as a result of psychological distress caused by the 1989 Loma Prieta earthquake. Payne said that he was having nightmares from seeing so many people injured and killed from the earthquake. Psychiatrists approved his claim, and Payne was out on workers' compensation on and off for two years. Finally, someone checked Payne's employment record and discovered that he had not been hired until weeks after the earthquake had occurred! His claim cost the state of California more than $13,500. Payne was charged with grand theft and was sentenced to two years in prison.

Another form of claimant fraud is called malingering, in which an employee with a legitimate injury stretches out the recovery time to extend workers' compensation payments. Proving malingering is difficult because it is hard to determine just how long a particular injury lasts.

Insurer fraud. This type of fraud is often directed at small businesses and involves scam artists who peddle cut-rate, but nonexistent, workers' compensation policies to entrepreneurs with the promise of "saving them big money." Business owners usually end up with a certificate of insurance to file with the state that looks authentic until the business attempts to use it to file a worker's claim. Only then does the fraud become apparent.

Provider fraud. Provider fraud occurs when a doctor or other health care professional collects payment for nonexistent or unncecessary treatments. Physician Mark Kaplan was behind one of the biggest workers' compensation scams in the history of the 90-year-old program. Kaplan set up a chain of heavily advertised workers' comp clinics throughout Los Angeles. Workers at his clinics induced thousands of unemployed non-English-speaking workers to make false injury claims. The scam, perpetrated over several years, cost insurance companies more than $30 million. For his role, Kaplan was sentenced to eight years in prison and was ordered to pay fines and restitution of $7.5 million.

Premium fraud. Sometimes businesses are the perpetrators of workers' compensation fraud. In a premium fraud scam, dishonest business owners cheat insurers by understating the number of workers they have, misclassifying the nature of workers' jobs to make them sound less risky, or changing the names of their companies to mask poor safety records.

In recent years, employers' cost for workers' compensation per $100 of payroll has actually fallen because insurers, states, and employers have been cracking down on fraud. For instance, when Timothy Jans, co-owner of Cook-DuPage Transportation Company, suspected that one of its drivers was faking a back injury to collect workers' compensation, he contacted the company that provided him with coverage. The insurance company, known for its tough stance on fraudulent claims, looked at the evidence and set up a video surveillance of the "injured" worker. They discovered that, although he claimed to be disabled because of the injury to his back, he was secretly working as a tow-truck operator. The company caught the most convincing evidence of the employee's fraud on videotape. The tape showed the worker pushing a car out of a parking space to tow it away. "He goes behind the car, bends down, and physically shoves it out of the parking space—by himself!" says Jans. "It's a great video." The driver was convicted and sentenced for felony insurance fraud, and Jans's company had the claim thrown out, reducing its insurance premiums.

How can business owners help combat workers' compensation fraud?

◆ *Maintain a safe workplace.* Involve workers in identifying and removing safety risks.
◆ *Screen all job applicants carefully.* A person who lies to get a job will likely lie on the job.
◆ *Give all workers a written statement of your company's workers' compensation policies and procedures.* Teach workers about the high costs and penalties for fraud.
◆ *Be wary of insurers offering cut-rate insurance coverage.* Ask for references, and check with your state's insurance department before buying.
◆ *Work closely with your insurer.* Alert your insurance company to any suspicious claims.
◆ *Document all workers' compensation claims thoroughly.* These records will be important if fraud occurs.
◆ *Listen to your workers.* In many cases, they are aware of the fraud and are willing to talk about it.

If you suspect a worker has committed fraud, don't try to handle the case yourself. Instead, contact your insurance company and let them handle it. By working closely with their insurers, small business owners can take a bite out of workers' compensation fraud and save themselves a lot of money.

SOURCES: Adapted from Stephen Blakely, "Fighting Fraud in Workers' Comp," *Nation's Business*, April 1998, pp. 14–22; Dale Van Atta, "Disabled by a Paper Cut," *Reader's Digest*, November 1997, pp. 99–103. ◆

on the coverage are not high enough to cover the potential losses many small business owners face. For example, one "slip-and-fall" case involving a customer who is injured when he slips and falls on a wet floor could easily exceed the standard limits on a basic BOP. Claims from customers injured by a company's product or service are also covered by its liability policy. With the median jury award in product liability cases hitting $850,000, business owners who fail to purchase sufficient liability coverage may end up losing their businesses.[44] Many business owners find it necessary to purchase additional liability coverage for their companies. Most insurance experts recommend at least $1 million of liability coverage for businesses.

A typical BOP does not include liability coverage for automobiles; business owners must purchase a separate policy for auto insurance. Auto insurance policies offer liability coverage that protects against losses resulting from injuries involving the use of company vehicles.

Another important type of liability insurance for many small businesses is **professional liability insurance,** or **"errors and omissions" coverage.** This coverage protects against damage a business causes to customers or clients as a result of an employee's error or failure

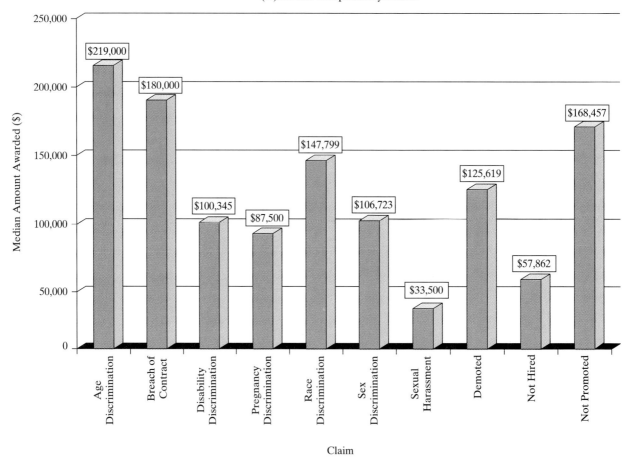

(A) Median Compensatory Awards

Figure 20.3 **Awards and Recovery Rates for Employment Law Violations, United States, 1988–1995** Source: Jury Verdict Research, Worsham, PA.

to take proper care and precautions. For instance, a land surveyor might miscalculate the location of a customer's property line. If the landowner relied on that property line to build a structure on what he thought was his land and it turned out to be on his neighbor's land, the surveyor would be liable for damages. Doctors, dentists, attorneys, and other professionals protect themselves through a similar kind of insurance, malpractice insurance, which protects them against the risk of lawsuits arising from errors in professional practice or judgment.

Employment practices liability insurance provides protection against claims arising from charges of employment discrimination, sexual harassment, and violations of the Americans with Disabilities Act, the Family and Medical Leave Act, and other employment legislation. Because awards for this type of lawsuit are quite high (see Figure 20.3A) and such suits are likely to be successful (see Figure 20.3B), this is one of the fastest-growing forms of insurance coverage. Most violations of these laws are not intentional but are the result of either carelessness or lack of knowledge, but the company that violates them is still liable. Because they often lack full-time human resources professionals, small companies are especially vulnerable to charges of improper employment practices, making this type of insurance coverage all the more important to them.

Liability insurance for some small businesses has become increasingly difficult to obtain, and at the same time, premiums have skyrocketed, pricing some businesses out of the

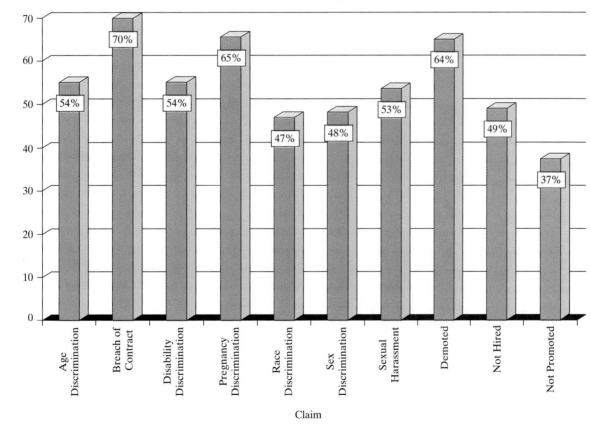

Figure 20.3 **Awards and Recovery Rates for Employment Law Violations, United States, 1988–1995** (*continued*)

"Sure, I make a decent profit, but my insurance premiums are killing me!"

SOURCE: *Industry Week*, August 21, 1995, p. 12.

market. Indeed, in recent years many small businesses have not been able to afford the insurance coverage they need and so have been forced to accept the full risk of the business or to cease operations. In addition, current court decisions have awarded high payments in many liability cases, thereby forcing the affected firms to file for bankruptcy protection.

CONTROLLING INSURANCE COSTS

Small business owners face constantly rising insurance premiums. Decades ago insurance costs were a less significant portion of the cost of the average business. Indeed, most businesses found that small increases in premiums could be passed along as a cost of doing business. In today's competitive world, however, there is little opportunity to pass along the increased cost of insurance in the form of higher prices.

Business owners must take steps to lower insurance costs. In the property and casualty insurance area, owners should take the following steps:

1. *Pursue a loss-control program*, by making risk reduction a natural part of all employees' daily routine. As discussed earlier in the chapter, risk reduction minimizes claims and eventually lowers premiums. Loss-control programs involve taking steps such as installing modern fire alarms, safety programs, and sophisticated security systems.

2. *Increase their policies' deductibles.* If a business can afford to handle minor losses, the owner can save money by raising the deductible to a level that protects the business against catastrophic events but, in effect, self-insures against minor losses. Business owners must determine the amount of financial exposure they can reasonably accept.

3. *Work with a qualified professional insurance broker or agent.* Business owners should do their homework before choosing an insurance broker or agent. This in-

cludes checking his reputation, credentials, and background by asking him to supply references.

4. *Work actively with brokers to make sure they understand the business owner's particular needs.* Brokers need to know about an entrepreneur's business and objectives for insurance coverage. They can help only if they know their client's needs and the degree of risk the client is willing to take.

5. *Work with brokers to find competitive companies* that want small companies' insurance business and have the proven resources to cover losses when they arise. The price of the premium should never be an entrepreneur's sole criterion for selecting insurance. The rating of the insurance company should always be a primary consideration. What good is it to have paid low premiums if, after a loss, the insurance company is unable to pay? Many small business owners learned costly lessons when their insurance companies, unable to meet their obligations, filed for bankruptcy protection.

When it comes to the cost of health insurance, the sky seems to be the limit for costs. The popular press and every national political candidate has debated the need to balance health services with the cost of providing them. Traditionally, businesses have been and continue to be the principal suppliers of health insurance in our society. To control the cost of health insurance, the small business owner should consider the following:

1. *Increase the dollar amount of employee contributions and the amount of the employee's deductibles.* Neither option is desirable, but rising medical costs will inevitably result in individuals' becoming, to some degree, self-insured in order to cover the high deductibles.

2. *Switch to HMOs or PPOs.* Higher premium costs have encouraged some small business owners to reevaluate health maintenance organization (HMOs) and preferred provider organizations (PPOs) as alternatives to traditional health insurance policies. Although some employees resent being told where they must go to receive treatment, the number of businesses offering the HMO and PPO options to employees is rising.

3. *Conduct a yearly utilization review.* Such a review may reveal that your employees' use of their policies is statistically low, which may provide you leverage to negotiate lower premiums or to switch to an insurer that wants a business with your track record and offers lower premiums.

4. *Create a wellness program for all employees.* We have all heard the old adage that an ounce of prevention is worth a pound of cure; when it comes to the high cost of medical expenses, this is true! Companies that have created wellness programs report cost savings of $6 for every $1 they invest. Furthermore, it makes good sense to include not only employees but their families as well. Providing a wellness program does *not* mean building a gym, however. Instead, it may be as simple as providing routine health checkups from a county nurse, incentives for quitting smoking, or lunch or after-work athletic games that involve as many employees as possible. Often a small company can begin by finding partners who want to help with the program.

5. *Conduct a safety audit.* Reviewing the workplace with a safety professional to look for ways to improve its safety has the potential for saving some businesses thousands of dollars a year in medical expenses and workers' compensation claims. The National Safety Council (1-800-621-7615) offers helpful information on creating a safer work environment.

6. *Create a safety manual and use it.* Incorporating the suggestions for improving safety into a policy manual and then using it will reduce the number of on-the-job

accidents. Training employees, even experienced ones, in proper safety procedures is also effective.

7. *Create a safety team.* Assigning the responsibility for workplace safety to workers themselves can produce amazing results. When one small manufacturer turned its safety team over to employees, the plant's lost time due to accidents plummeted to zero for three years straight! The number of accidents is well below what it was when managers ran the safety team, and managers say that's because employees now "own" safety in the plant.

The key to controlling insurance costs is aggressive prevention. Entrepreneurs who actively manage the risks that their companies are exposed to find that they can provide the insurance coverage their business needs at a reasonable cost. Finding the right insurance coverage to protect their business is no easy matter for business owners. "Just as no two companies are exactly alike," says one insurance professional, "no two business owners have the same needs or business exposure."[50] The key to dealing with those differences is to identify the risks that represent the greatest threat to a company and then to develop a plan for minimizing their risk of occurrence and insuring against them if they do.

Chapter Summary

1. Explain the factors necessary for a strong family business.
   - More than 80 percent of all companies in the United States are family-owned. Family businesses generate 50 percent of the U.S. gross domestic product, employ more than 40 million people, and pay 65 percent of all wages. Several factors are important to maintaining a strong family business, including: shared values, shared power, tradition, a willingness to learn, behaving like families, and strong family ties.

2. Understand the exit strategy options available to an entrepreneur.
   - Family business owners wanting to step down from their companies can sell to outsiders, sell to insiders, or transfer ownership to the next generation of family members. Common tools for selling to insiders (employees or managers) include sale for cash plus a note, leveraged buyouts (LBOs), and employee stock ownership plans (ESOPs).
   - Transferring ownership to the next generation of family members requires a business owner to develop a sound management succession plan.

3. Discuss the stages of management succession.
   - Unfortunately, 70 percent of first-generation businesses fail to survive into the second generation, and of those that do, only 13 percent make it to the third generation. One of the primary reasons for this lack of continuity is poor succession planning. Planning for management succession protects not only the founder's, successor's, and company's financial resources, but it also preserves what matters most in a successful business: its heritage and tradition. Management succession planning can ensure a smooth transition only if the founder begins the process early on.

4. Explain how to develop an effective management succession plan.
   - A succession plan is a crucial element in transferring a company to the next generation. Preparing a succession plan involves five steps: (1) select the successor; (2) create a survival kit for the successor; (3) groom the successor; (4) promote an environment of trust and respect; (5) cope with the financial realities of estate taxes.
   - Entrepreneurs can rely on several tools in their estate planning, including buy/sell agreements, lifetime gifting, trusts, estate freezes, and family limited partnerships.

5. Understand the four risk management strategies.
   - Four risk strategies are available to the small business: avoiding, reducing, anticipating, and transferring risk.

6. Discuss the basics of insurance for small businesses.
   - Insurance is a risk transfer strategy. Not every potential loss can be insured. Insurability requires that it be possible to estimate the amount of actual loss being insured against and to identify the specific risk and that there be enough policyholders to spread out the risk.
   - The four major types of insurance small businesses need are property and casualty insurance, life and

disability insurance, health insurance and workers compensation coverage, and liability insurance.

- Property and casualty insurance covers a company's tangible assets, such as buildings, equipment, inventory, machinery, signs, and others that have been damaged, destroyed, or stolen. Specific types of property and casualty insurance include extra expense coverage, business interruption insurance, surety insurance, marine insurance, crime insurance, fidelity insurance, and forgery insurance.
- Life and disability insurance also comes in various forms. Life insurance protects a family and a business against the loss of income and security in the event of the owner's death. Disability insurance, like life insurance, protects an individual in the event of unexpected and often very expensive disabilities.
- Health insurance is designed to provide adequate health care for business owners and their employees. Workers' compensation is designed to cover employees who are injured on the job or who become sick as a result of a work environment.
- Liability insurance protects a business against losses resulting from accidents or injuries people suffer on the company's property, from its products or services, and damage the company causes to others' property. Typical liability coverage includes professional liability insurance or "errors and omissions" coverage, which protects against damage a business causes to customers or clients as a result of an error an employee makes or an employee's failure to take proper care and precautions. Doctors, dentists, attorneys, and other professionals protect themselves through a similar kind of insurance, malpractice insurance, which protects them against the risk of lawsuits arising from errors in professional practice or judgment. Employment practices liability insurance provides protection against claims arising from charges of employment discrimination, sexual harassment, and violations of the Americans with Disabilities Act, the Family and Medical Leave Act, and other employment legislation.

Discussion Questions

1. What factors must be present for a strong family business?
2. Discuss the stages of management succession in a family business.
3. What steps are involved in building a successful management succession plan?

4. What exit strategies are available to entrepreneurs wanting to step down from their business?
5. What strategies can business owners employ to reduce estate and gift taxes?
6. Can insurance eliminate risk? Why or why not?
7. Outline the four basic risk management strategies and give an example of each.
8. What problems occur most frequently with a risk-anticipating strategy?
9. What is insurance? How can insurance companies bear such a large risk burden and still be profitable?
10. Describe the requirements for insurability.
11. Briefly describe the various types of insurance coverage available to small business owners.
12. What kinds of insurance coverage would you recommend for the following businesses? A manufacturer of steel sheets. A retail gift shop. A small accounting firm. A limited liability partnership involving three dentists.
13. What can business owners do to keep their insurance costs under control?

Step into the Real World

1. Interview two local business owners about their companies' management succession plans. Do the owners have succession plans? If so, how are they structured? Who have they designated to take over their business? What is the timetable for implementing the plan? What impact will estate and gift taxes have on the transfer of ownership? What provisions have they made to minimize the impact of those taxes? Write a two-page report on what you learned from your experience.
2. Contact an attorney and an accountant and ask them what steps they recommend small business owners take to plan for management succession. Are their small business clients well prepared to deal with management succession issues? Why or why not? What are the implications for those who are not well prepared?
3. a. Interview two small business owners in the local community and report on the types of insurance coverage each carries. Did they have difficulty finding insurance coverage?
   b. Contact an insurance agent and ask about the insurance coverage he or she would recommend for the types of businesses whose owners you interviewed. Do you see any gaps? If so, how much would the additional coverage cost? If the business owners are underinsured, what are the potential consequences of incurring losses?

Take It to the Net

Visit the Scarborough/Zimmerer home page at
www.prenhall.com/scarbzim
for updated information, on-line resources, and Web-based exercises.

Endnotes

1. MassMutual Family Business Network <http://www.massmutual.com/fbn/index.htm>.
2. "Keeping the Firm in the Family," *Upstate Business*, May 18, 1997, p. 8.
3. Sharon Nelton, "Preparing for a Loss of Leadership," *Nation's Business*, April 1997, p. 59.
4. Sharon Nelton, "Ten Keys to Success in Family Business," *Nation's Business*, April 1991, pp. 44–45.
5. "Family Members Fight Over Control of Texas Pete Hot Sauce Empire," *Greenville News*, May 17, 1997, p. 11D.
6. Carol Steinberg, "The Next Generation," *Success*, October 1996, pp. 85–87.
7. Sharon Nelton, "Some 'Hard' Lessons—Or Are They 'Soft'?" *Nation's Business*, February 1998, p. 54.
8. "Family Members Fight Over Control of Texas Pete Hot Sauce Empire."
9. Timothy Middleton, "Estate Planning—A Grave Situation," *Industry Week Growing Companies*, May 1998, p. 66.
10. Springfield Remanufacturing Corporation <http://srcreman.com/index.htm>.
11. Donna Fenn, "Should You Leave the Company to Your Kids?" *Inc.*, May 1997, p. 121.
12. Sharon Nelton, "Major Shifts in Leadership Lie Ahead," *Nation's Business*, June 1997, pp. 56–58.
13. MassMutual Family Business Network <http://www.massmutual.com/fbn/index.htm>; "Keeping the Firm in the Family."
14. TCPN Quotation Center <http://www.cyber-nation.com/victory/quotations/subjects/quotes_subjects_f_to_h.html#f>.
15. John L. Ward and Craig E. Aronoff, "Overcoming a Major Obstacle to Succession," *Nation's Business*, September 1997, p. 46.
16. Andy Bluestone, "Succession Planning Isn't Just about Money," *Nation's Business*, November 1996, p. 6.
17. Shelly Branch, "Mom Always Liked You Best," *Your Company*, April/May 1998, pp. 26–38.
18. Patricia Schiff Estess, "Freedom of Choice," *Entrepreneur*, June 1998, pp. 100–102.
19. Patricia Schiff Estess, "The Outsiders," *Entrepreneur*, November 1997, pp. 86–88.
20. Patricia Schiff Estess, "Heir Raising," *Entrepreneur*, May 1996, pp. 80–82.
21. Craig E. Aronoff and John L. Ward, "Why Continue Your Family Business," *Nation's Business*, March 1998, pp. 72–74.
22. Gordon Williams, "Passing the Torch," *Financial World*, January 21, 1997, p. 78.
23. Steinberg, "The Next Generation."
24. Fenn, "Should You Leave the Company to Your Kids?"
25. Estess, "Heir Raising," p. 80.
26. Patricia Schiff Estess, "Overnight Succession," *Entrepreneur*, February 1996, pp. 80–83.
27. Joan Pryde, "The Estate Tax Toll on Small Firms," *Nation's Business*, August 1997, pp. 20–24.
28. Ibid.
29. Amanda Walmac, "Get an Estate Plan to Protect Your Family," *Your Company*, Forecast 1997, pp. 48–54.
30. Ibid.
31. Randy Myers, "Where There's a Will . . ." *Nation's Business*, April 1997, p. 26.
32. Joan Szabo, "Spreading the Wealth," *Entrepreneur*, July 1997, pp. 62–64.
33. Williams, "Passing the Torch," p. 79.
34. Stephen Blakely, "The Backlash Against Managed Care," *Nation's Business*, July 1998, pp. 16–24.
35. Ibid.
36. Stephen Blakely, "Finding Coverage for Small Offices," *Nation's Business*, June 1997, p. 30.
37. Ibid.
38. Barbara Etchieson, "Does Your Policy Have You Covered?" *Nation's Business*, August 1996, p. 43.
39. Ibid.
40. Betty Parker Ellis, "Insurance You Never Knew Your Business Needed," *GSA Business*, July 6, 1998, p. 9B.
41. Julie Cook, "Expect the Unexpected," *Business Start-Ups*, January 1997, pp. 44–48.
42. Michael Barrier, "Planning for a Disaster," *Nation's Business*, May 1998, pp. 51–52.
43. Jacquelyn Lynn, "A Quick Guide to Insurance," *Entrepreneur*, June 1997, pp. 29–32.
44. Donald Jay Korn, "When You Can't Work," *Your Company*, Spring 1995, p. 8.
45. Lynn, "A Quick Guide to Insurance"; Stephen Blakely, "Types of Health Insurance Plans," *Nation's Business*, July 1998, p. 20.
46. Blakely, "Types of Health Insurance Plans."
47. Leslie Scism, "If Disorder Strikes This 'Titanic,' Chubb Could Lose Millions," *Wall Street Journal*, April 9, 1997, pp. A1, A4.
48. Jacquelyn Lynn, "Why Workers Comp?" *Entrepreneur*, June 1997, p. 31.
49. Susan Hodges, "Try Our Bumpless Route through the Insurance Maze," *Your Company*, April/May 1997, pp. 41–44.
50. Etchieson, "Does Your Policy Have You Covered?" p. 44.

CHAPTER 21

Ethics, Social Responsibility, and the Entrepreneur

Reputations are longer in the making than in the losing.

—*Paul Von Ringelheim*

Watch your thoughts; they become words.

Watch your words; they become actions.

Watch your actions; they become habits.

Watch your habits; they become character.

Watch your character; it becomes your destiny.

—*Frank Outlaw*

Upon completion of this chapter, you will be able to

1. Define business ethics and describe the three levels of ethical standards.

2. Determine who is responsible for ethical behavior and why ethical lapses occur.

3. Explain how to establish and maintain high ethical standards.

4. Define social responsibility.

5. Understand the nature of business's responsibility to the environment.

6. Describe business's responsibility to employees.

7. Explain business's responsibility to customers.

8. Discuss business's responsibility to investors.

9. Describe business's responsibility to the community.

*E*arning a profit is one of an entrepreneur's primary reasons for going into business, and it is an essential requirement for staying in business. Profits give owners a return on their investment, employees steady work, customers the goods and services they desire, and the government the tax dollars it requires. But does a small company's responsibility end with earning a profit? Our society says not. A recent Business Week/Harris poll found that 95 percent of adults reject the view that a company's only role is to make money.[1] Increasingly, society is imposing on firms the additional standard of considering the *ethical* and the *social* as well as the *economic* impact of their decisions.

Ethics involves the moral values and behavioral standards businesspeople draw on as they make decisions and solve problems. It originates from a commitment to do what is right. Ethical behavior—doing what is "right" and "good" as opposed to "wrong" and "bad"—is the result of such a commitment. However, an inherent difficulty exists in determining what constitutes ethical behavior. In some instances, the ethical dilemma is obvious, the implications of unethical actions are clear, and established guidelines for handling the situation exists. The owner is keenly aware of the ethical entrapment that awaits her and knows that she will be held accountable for her actions.

In most situations, however, ethical dilemmas are less obvious, cloaked in the garb of mundane decisions and everyday routine. Because they easily can catch entrepreneurs off guard and unprepared, these are the ethical challenges that are most likely to ensnare the unwary. It is these ethical "sleepers" that often catch unwary entrepreneurs, destroying their reputations as well as those of their companies. To make proper ethical choices, therefore, an entrepreneur must first be aware that a situation with ethical dimensions exists. "Awareness is the key," says one ethics consultant. "So many people get in trouble, not because they meant to be unethical, but because they lacked sensitivity and awareness."[2]

Complicating the issue even more is that, in some ethical dilemmas, no clear-cut, right (or wrong) answers exist. There is no conflict between good and evil, right and wrong, truth and falsehood; instead, there is only the issue of conflicting interests among the company's various **stakeholders,** the various groups and individuals who affect and are affected by the company. These conflicts have forced many businesses to identify their stakeholders and to consider the ways they will deal with them. For example, when the founders of a small company producing frozen foods make business decisions, they must consider how those decisions will influence, and be influenced by, its team of employees; the farmers and the companies that supply it with raw materials; the union that represents its workers in collective bargaining; the government agencies that regulate a multitude of its activities; the banks that provide it with financing; the investors who own its stock; the general public it serves; the community in which it operates; and, of course, the customers who purchase its products. Every entrepreneur must consider the roles these and other key stakeholders play in the operation of her business (see Figure 21.1).

The power these stakeholders wield determines to a great extent the degree of success a company can achieve. Relationships among a company and its multitude of stakeholders are becoming more complex, creating more ethical dilemmas. To make a decision, an entrepreneur often must balance the needs and the demands of these various stakeholders, knowing that whatever the final decision is, not every group will be satisfied.

Society is demanding a higher standard of behavior from businesses today, and businesses large and small must reevaluate their responsibilities to society as a whole. A socially responsible business considers not only what is best for the firm but also what is best for society. It is this vital link between businesses and the people of society that gives rise to the key concepts of ethics and social responsibility. No business can ignore the ethical demands of society and expect to thrive.

*A*n Ethical Perspective

◀ Define business ethics and describe the three levels of ethical standards.

Business ethics consist of the fundamental moral values and behavioral standards that form the foundation for the people of an organization as they make decisions and interact with stakeholders. Business ethics is a sensitive—and highly complex—issue, but it is not a new one. In 560 B.C., the Greek philosopher Chilon claimed that a merchant does better to take a loss than to make a dishonest profit.[3]

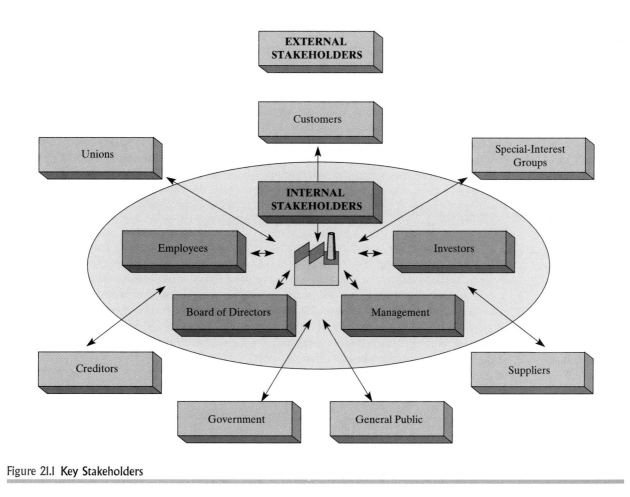

EXTERNAL STAKEHOLDERS

Customers

Unions

Special-Interest Groups

INTERNAL STAKEHOLDERS

Employees

Investors

Board of Directors

Management

Creditors

Suppliers

Government

General Public

Figure 21.1 **Key Stakeholders**

Maintaining an ethical perspective is crucial to creating and protecting a company's reputation, but it is no easy task. Ethical dilemmas abound in the decisions that entrepreneurs and managers face every day. However, these dilemmas may be severest and most apparent in entrepreneurial companies that lack the mega-budgets and -balance sheets of their larger counterparts. Although every company confronts ethically charged issues, the limited resources of small start-ups make them extremely susceptible to ethical breaches. The entrepreneurs guiding these companies may be on the verge of "making it," and putting ethics aside to gain a short-term advantage can be incredibly tempting. *For example, Ralph Warner, co-founder of Nolo Press, a successful publisher of self-help law books, faced an ethical dilemma when, on the eve of shipping out his company's new book, Congress announced a major tax overhaul. Warner had a choice: ship the books with outdated information or scrap the books and start over, which would cause the company to incur a large expense. In the end, Warner decided not to ship the books, which, he says, cost money only in the short run. He strongly believes that the long-run cost of having shipped the outdated books would have been much higher and that his company's reputation has benefited by not succumbing to the temptation to cut corners.*[4]

Succumbing to such unethical temptations ultimately will destroy a company's reputation. And reputation is one of the most precious, and most fragile, possessions a company has. Donald Perkins, former chairman and CEO of Jewel Companies, a successful chain of supermarkets, explains:

Reputation is fundamental. It represents the future of any organization, and an executive shouldn't hesitate to take the necessary steps to maintain it. Everyone understands an error. But ethical transgressions are not errors.[5]

Building a solid reputation for ethical propriety typically takes a long time; unfortunately, destroying that reputation takes practically no time at all, and the effects linger. Avon CEO James Preston likens a bad reputation to a hangover. "It takes a while to get rid of, and it makes everything else hurt," he says.[6] An entrepreneur's goal is to build a solid ethical reputation for the company and then do everything possible to maintain it. According to one ethicist, "The best way to benefit from a good reputation is to keep doing the things that earned it for you in the first place."[7]

THREE LEVELS OF ETHICAL STANDARDS

There are three levels of ethical standards:[8]

1. *The law*, which defines for society as a whole what actions are permissible and which are not. The law merely establishes the minimum standard of behavior. Actions that are legal, however, may not necessarily be ethical. Simply obeying the law is insufficient as a guide for ethical behavior; ethical behavior requires more. Few ethical issues are so uncomplicated and unidimensional that the law can serve as the acid test for making a decision.

2. *The policies and procedures of the organization*, which serve as specific guidelines for people as they make daily decisions. Many colleges and universities have established honor codes, and companies rely on policies covering everything from sexual harassment and gift giving to hiring and whistleblowing. Research suggests that some 95 percent of Fortune 500 companies and nearly half of all businesses have written codes of ethics in place.[9]

3. *The moral stance individuals take* when faced with a decision not governed by formal rules. The values people learn from an early age in the family, in church or synagogue, and in school are key ingredients at this level. A major determinant of ethical behavior is *training*. As Aristotle said thousands of years ago, you get a good adult by teaching a child to do the right thing. The culture of a company can serve to either support or to undermine its employees' concept of what constitutes ethical behavior.

Every businessperson faces at least one ethical issue every day, and some ethical choices can be tough to make. But, that's not necessarily bad! Such situations give small business people the opportunity to practice good ethics and to do what is right. One ethicist explains, "Morals are like muscles. The more we flex them, the stronger they get. Ethics is a practical skill. If we don't use them, we lose them; and the more we use them, the better we get at it."[10] No one can escape the consequences of the ethical decisions made over the course of a career.

The pressure to take shortcuts or to violate ethical standards is always present. One classic study reported that, at some point in their careers, 75 percent of managers felt a conflict between profit considerations and being ethical.[11] Another study indicated that 65 percent of managers sometimes felt pressure to compromise their personal ethical standards.[12] Without a supportive ethical structure, employees in such positions are likely to make the "wrong" ethical choices, and that can be devastating. According to one small business owner, "One employee acting unethically can give the entire company a bad reputation." Therefore, he claims, "Business ethics should be a constant priority of top management."[13]

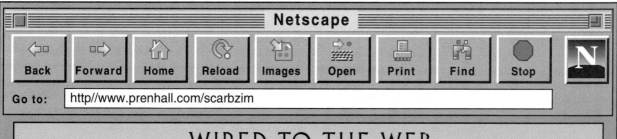

WIRED TO THE WEB

THE ETHICS OF MARKETING TO KIDS ON THE WEB

"*W*hat do you think?" Kara Hernandez, marketing director for Brauer Software asked Al Brauer. "I'm concerned about the negative publicity this group of parents and teachers is generating for the company. Who knows how much of an impact that could have on Brauer Software or for how long?"

"You're right," said Al. "And this company's reputation is one thing I am not willing to compromise or jeopardize. We've worked too hard for too long to win the trust of our customers and the community, and I don't want to risk destroying that."

Brauer Software is a small but innovative producer of educational software targeted at children aged 9 to 14. Al started the company from a spare bedroom in his home 15 years ago, and the company grew steadily over the years. Educational organizations raved about the quality of the company's software, and parents eagerly awaited the release of each package. Products covered a wide range of educational topics, from science and math to English and other languages. Brauer Software relied on a team of experienced education experts to design each program, who then worked closely with teams of programmers to implement their designs.

Recently, Brauer had seen an opportunity to use the company's excellent reputation with both children and parents to move into software that was designed strictly for entertainment, a fast-growing aspect of the software industry. The company had launched seven new games aimed specifically at children. Brauer saw the tremendous potential for marketing the new products on the World Wide Web, and he had his programmers set up a Web site separate from its educational software site. This new site was designed exclusively for kids, with lots of bright colors, funky music, and action, including demo versions of the games the company was selling. Anyone could enter the site, but those who completed periodic marketing surveys could earn "Kid's Kash," a form of virtual money they could exchange for games, discounts, and prizes. Children could earn more Kid's Kash by completing other surveys in the Web site.

"I had no idea parents and teachers would respond like this," Brauer said. "We're only trying to get the most from our marketing dollars. After all, that's a duty we owe to our shareholders. The idea was to collect demographic and other information from the kids who entered our Web site. In addition to helping us sell to them more effectively, we needed to know what they like and don't like about the site. We have to keep it updated constantly to hold their attention."

"I know," said Kara, "but just this morning I heard from several groups who say that we're using manipulative advertising techniques on the World Wide Web, and they're petitioning the Federal Trade Commission to look into the whole issue!"

"Oh, great . . ." moaned Al. "That's just what we need."

Picking up the story he clipped from yesterday's newspaper, Al read aloud the comments of one angry parent: "Companies are acting unethically when they use their Web sites as lures for young children to collect specific information from them without parental approval. No other medium has captured children's interest like the Web, and companies like Brauer Software should be ashamed for abusing it to sell to kids."

"I had no idea anything like this would ever happen when we decided to launch that Web site to promote our new entertainment products. No idea at all . . ."

1. Use the World Wide Web to research the issue of companies' using the Web to advertise to children. Find at least two sites addressing this issue, and summarize their points of view. What is your view on this issue?
2. Do you think Brauer Software has acted unethically? Explain.
3. On the basis of what you read in this chapter and on what you found on the World Wide Web, what actions would you advise Al Brauer and Kara Hernandez to take? What outcomes do you predict for Brauer Software if Brauer and Hernandez do nothing?

AN ETHICAL FRAMEWORK

To cope successfully with the myriad ethical decisions they face, entrepreneurs must develop a workable ethical framework to guide them. Although many such frameworks exist, the following four-step process can work quite well.

Step 1. Recognize the ethical dimensions involved in the dilemma or decision. Before an entrepreneur can make an informed ethical decision, she must recognize that an ethical situation exists. Only then is it possible to define the specific ethical issues involved. Too often, business owners fail to take into account the ethical impact of a particular course of action until it is too late. To avoid ethical quagmires, entrepreneurs must consider the ethical forces at work in a situation—honesty, fairness, respect for community, concern for the environment, trust, and others—to have a complete view of the decision.

Step 2. Identify the key stakeholders involved and determine how the decision will affect them. As Figure 21.1 demonstrated, every business influences, and is influenced by, a multitude of stakeholders. Frequently, the demands of these stakeholders conflict with one another, putting a business in the position of having to choose which groups to satisfy and which to alienate. Before making a decision, managers must sort out the conflicting interests of the various stakeholders by determining which ones have important stakes in the situation. Although this analysis may not resolve the conflict, it will prevent the company from inadvertently causing harm to people it may have failed to consider.

Step 3. Generate alternative choices and distinguish between ethical and unethical responses. Small business managers will find the questions in Table 21.1 to be helpful.

Step 4. Choose the "best" ethical response and implement it. At this point, there likely will be several ethical choices from which managers can pick. Comparing these choices with the "ideal" ethical outcome may help managers make the final decision. The final choice must be consistent with the company's goals, culture, and value system as well as those of the individual decision makers.

*W*ho Is Responsible for Ethical Behavior?

2 Determine who is responsible for ethical behavior and why ethical lapses occur.

Although companies may set ethical standards and offer guidelines for employees, the ultimate decision on whether to abide by ethical principles rests with the *individual*. In other words, companies really are not ethical or unethical; individuals are. Managers, however, can greatly influence individual behavior within the company. And that influence must start at the *top*. A chief executive officer who practices ethical behavior establishes the moral tone for the entire organization. "In a small company, the [ethical] standards depend almost entirely on the entrepreneur's personality, beliefs, and sense of self," says one expert.[14] Good ethics starts at the top and works its way downward through the entire organization. "If the executive suite is perceived as cutting corners," says one manager, "that attitude filters down to the lowest levels."[15] Table 21.2 on page 730 summarizes the characteristics of the three ethical styles of management: immoral, amoral, and moral management.

THE BENEFITS OF MORAL MANAGEMENT

One of the most common misconceptions about business is that there is a contradiction between ethics and profits. Andrew Warner of Nolo Press says, "I've never seen the dichotomy over the long term between running a principled business and a profitable one."[16] A recent

Table 21.1 Questions to Help Identify the Ethical Dimension of a Situation

Principles and Codes of Conduct

◆ Does this decision or action meet my standards for how people should interact?

◆ Does this decision or action agree with my religious teachings and beliefs (or with my personal principles and sense of responsibility)?

◆ How will I feel about myself if I do this?

◆ Do we (or I) have a rule or policy for cases like this?

◆ Would I want everyone to make the same decision and take the same action if faced with these same circumstances?

◆ What are my true motives for considering this action?

Moral Rights

◆ Would this action allow others freedom of choice in this matter?

◆ Would this action involve deceiving others in any way?

Justice

◆ Would I feel that this action was just (fair) if I were on the other side of the decision?

◆ How would I feel if this action were done to me or to someone close to me?

◆ Would this action or decision distribute benefits justly?

◆ Would it distribute hardships or burdens justly?

Consequences and Outcomes

◆ What will be the short- and long-term consequences of this action?

◆ Who will benefit from this course of action?

◆ Who will be hurt?

◆ How will this action create good and prevent harm?

Public Justification

◆ How would I feel (or how will I feel) if (or when) this action becomes public knowledge?

◆ Will I be able to explain adequately to others why I have taken this action?

◆ Would others feel that my action or decision is ethical or moral?

Intuition and Insight

◆ Have I searched for all alternatives? Are there other ways I could look at this situation? Have I considered all points of view?

◆ Even if there is sound rationality for this decision or action, and even if I could defend it publicly, does my inner sense tell me this is right?

◆ What does my intuition tell me is the ethical thing to do in this situation? Have I listened to my inner voice?

SOURCE: Sherry Baker, "Ethical Judgment," *Executive Excellence*, March 1992, pp. 7–8.

survey of senior managers, business school deans, and members of Congress support this view; 63 percent said that "a business enterprise actually strengthens its competitive position by maintaining high ethical standards."[17]

Although behaving ethically has value in itself, there are several other benefits to ethical companies. First, the company avoids the damaging effects of a reputation as an unethi-

Table 21.2 Approaches to Management Ethics

Organizational Characteristics	Immoral Management	Amoral Management	Moral Management
Ethical norms	Management decisions, actions, and behavior imply a positive and active opposition to what is moral (ethical).	Management is neither moral nor immoral; decisions are not based on moral judgments.	Management activity conforms to a standard of ethical, or right, behavior.
	Decisions are discordant with accepted ethical principles.	Management activity is not related to any moral code.	Management activity conforms to accepted professional standards of conduct.
	An active negation of what is moral is implicit.	A lack of ethical perception and moral awareness may be implicit.	Ethical leadership is commonplace.
Motives	Selfish. Management cares only about its or the company's gains.	Well-intentioned but selfish in the sense that the impact on others is not considered.	Good. Management wants to succeed but only within the confines of sound ethical precepts (fairness, justice, due process).
Goals	Profitability and organizational success at any price.	Profitability. Other goals are not considered.	Profitability within the confines of legal obedience and ethical standards.
Orientation toward law	Legal standards are barriers that management must overcome to accomplish what it wants.	Law is the ethical guide, preferably the letter of the law. The central question is what we can do legally.	Obedience toward letter and spirit of the law. Law is a minimal ethical behavior. Prefer to operate well above what law mandates.
Strategy	Exploit opportunities for corporate gain. Cut corners when it appears useful.	Give managers free rein. Personal ethics may apply but only if managers choose. Respond to legal mandates if caught and required to do so.	Live by sound ethical standards. Assume leadership position when ethical dilemmas arise. Enlightened self-interest.

SOURCE: Archie B. Carroll, "In Search of the Moral Manager," reprinted from *Business Horizons*, March/April. Copyright 1987 by the Foundation for the School of Business at Indiana University. Used with permission.

cal business. Unethical businesses usually gain only short-term advantages; over the long run, unethical decisions don't pay. It's simply not good business. William C. Norris, founder of Control Data Corporation, says, "It's very clear that in the long run an ethical company will outperform a company that is not."[18] Second, a solid ethical framework guides managers as they cope with an increasingly complex network of external influence, from government regulation and special interest groups to suppliers and the media. Dealing with stakeholders is much easier if a company has a solid ethical foundation on which to build.

Finally, ethical companies earn the respect of two essential groups: customers and employees. The ethics factor is intangible and virtually impossible to quantify. Yet, it is something that customers and employees clearly recognize and consider when deciding where to shop and where to work. *Lee Edelstein, CEO of TeleManagement Services, a company that coordinates telemarketing programs for pharmaceutical companies, recalls the time that a major client paid TeleManagement Services twice for a $40,000 project. Edelstein didn't hesitate; he sent the duplicate check back, although he knew that the client would be unlikely to have ever discovered the error. Later, Edelstein learned that a top manager in that company cited TeleManagement Services as the kind of company he wanted to do business with. Edelstein's decision ultimately led his company to do millions of dollars of business with the client.*[19] A company's ethical philosophy has an impact on its ability to provide value for its customers and job security for its employees. Increasingly, entrepreneurs are seeing ethical behavior as an investment in their company's future rather than as a cost of doing business.

WHY ETHICAL LAPSES OCCUR

When faced with an ethical dilemma, not every manager or employee will make the correct decision. In fact, many unethical acts are committed by normally decent people who believe in moral values. What then causes these ethical lapses to occur?[20]

The "Bad Apple." Ethical decisions are individual decisions, and some people are corrupt. Try as they might to avoid them, organizations occasionally find that they have hired a bad apple. Eliminating unethical behavior requires the elimination of these bad apples.

The "Bad Barrel." In some cases, the company culture has been poisoned with an unethical overtone; in other words, the problem is not the bad apple but the bad barrel. Pressure to prosper produces an environment that creates conditions that reward unethical behavior, and employees act accordingly.

Moral Blindness. Sometimes, fundamentally ethical people commit ethical blunders because they are blind to the ethical implications of their conduct. Moral blindness may be the result of failing to realize that an ethical dilemma exists, or it may arise from a variety of mental defense mechanisms. One of the most common mechanisms is rationalization:

- "Everybody does it."
- "If they were in my place, they'd do it too."
- "Being ethical is a luxury I cannot afford right now."
- "The impact of my decision/action on (whoever or whatever) is not my concern."
- "I don't get paid to be ethical; I get paid to produce results."

Training in ethical thinking and creating an environment that encourages employees to consider the ethical impact of their decisions can reduce the problem of moral blindness.

Competitive Pressures. If competition is so intense that a company's survival is threatened, managers may begin to view what were once unacceptable options as acceptable. Managers and employees are under such pressure to produce that they may sacrifice their ethical standards to reduce the fear of failure or the fear of losing their jobs. A study conducted by the Ethics Resource Center found that 30 percent of employees admitted to feeling pressure to compromise their company's ethical standards because of deadlines, overly aggressive objectives, concerns about the company's survival, and other factors.[21] They begin to believe that attaining objectives is their only task and what they do to reach their target is of little consequence. *For example, the high-pressure environment at Chambers Development Company, once a rising star in the solid waste disposal industry, ultimately led employees to use inappropriate accounting practices, overstating company profits. Former employees say that company founder, John Rangos Sr., pushed so hard for sales growth and for meeting his lofty profit objectives that manipulating the numbers was not only tolerated but also encouraged. "John Rangos would not tolerate the presence of someone who would not give him the answers he wanted," says one former consultant. The result was numerous violations of generally accepted accounting principles (GAAP) and grossly overstated earnings. (Although company records were reporting record profits, the company was actually losing money!) As a result, Chambers Development Company became the target of numerous lawsuits. The company survived, but has yet to recover fully from the problem stemming from its ethical violations.*[22]

Opportunity Pressures. When the opportunity to "get ahead" by taking some unethical action presents itself, some people cannot resist the temptation. The greater the reward or the smaller the penalty for unethical acts, the greater is the probability that such behavior will occur. If managers, for example, condone or even encourage unethical behavior, they can be sure it will occur. Those who succumb to opportunity pressures often make one of two mistakes: They overestimate the cost of doing the right thing, or they underestimate the cost of doing the wrong thing. Either error can lead to disaster.

Globalization of Business. The globalization of business has intertwined what once were distinct cultures. This cultural cross-pollination has brought about many positive aspects, but it has created problems as well. Companies have discovered that there is no single standard of ethical behavior applying to all business decisions in the international arena. Practices that are illegal in one country may be perfectly acceptable, even expected, in another. Actions that would send a businessperson to jail in Western nations are common ways of working around the system in others. *For example, as part of Russia's move to privatize formerly government-owned businesses, government officials decided to sell the 1,777-room Cosmos Hotel, originally built for the 1980 Olympics. The hotel generates revenues of $100 million a year (in hard currency) and produces profits of $10 million each year. Although such a business would sell for at least $100 million in the United States or in Western Europe, Mikhail Kharshan bought a 25 percent interest in the Cosmos for a mere $2.5 million! Getting the property at just 10 percent of its value was no easy task. As an insider, Kharshan knew the hotel would be put up for sale before most people did, and he used the extra time to scare off rival bidders for the popular hotel. He bribed journalists from two influential business papers to publish negative financial reports about the Cosmos. Then he arranged to be interviewed on Russian television, where he talked about the poor state of the Russian hotel industry. He bribed government officials to limit the Cosmos auction to just two locations and then bribed two other likely bidders not to participate in the auction. The result: Kharshan was the only serious bidder at the auction; that's how he managed to get the hotel at such a bargain. Kharshan says that his actions, although unethical by U.S. business standards, "are normal business practices in Russia. We didn't shoot anyone and we didn't violate any laws."*[23]

THE WALL STREET JOURNAL

MIKE SHAPIRO

"I really wish you guys would knock that off."

SOURCE: The *Wall Street Journal*, July 1, 1997, p. A14.

Establishing Ethical Standards

Although there is no single standard for ethical behavior, managers must encourage employees to become familiar with the various ethical tests for judging behavior.

The utilitarian principle. Choose the option that offers the greatest good for the greatest number of people.

Kant's categorical imperative. Act in such a way that the action taken under the circumstances could be a universal law or rule of behavior.

The professional ethic. Take only those actions that a disinterested panel of professional colleagues would view as proper.

The Golden Rule. Treat other people the way you would like them to treat you.

The television test. Would you and your colleagues feel comfortable explaining your actions to a national television audience?

The family test. Would you be comfortable explaining to your children, your spouse, and your parents why you took this action?[24]

Although these tests do not offer universal solutions to ethical dilemmas, they do help employees identify the moral implications of the decisions they face. People must be able to understand the ethical impact of their actions before they can make responsible decisions.

Table 21.3 on page 734 describes ten ethical principles that differentiate between right and wrong, thereby offering a guideline for ethical behavior.

IMPLEMENTING AND MAINTAINING ETHICAL STANDARDS

A workable ethics program recognizes that a company has a greater responsibility to society than just earning a profit. One executive claims:

> *Ethics in business means more than just conforming to prevailing standards or laws. It means approaching business in the spirit of service rather than self-enrichment. It means always viewing your enterprise as contributing to rather than extracting from society. It means running your company as if it were accountable not just to investors but to workers, customers, the community, and ultimately the planet, which sustains us all.*[25]

Establishing ethical standards is only the first step in an ethics-enhancing program; implementing and maintaining those standards is the real challenge facing management. What can managers do to integrate ethical principles into their companies?

Create a Company Credo. A **company credo** defines the values underlying the entire company and its ethical responsibilities to its stakeholders. It offers general guidance in ethical issues. The most effective credos capture the elusive essence of a company—what it stands for and why it's important—and can be an important ingredient in the company's competitive edge. A company credo is especially important for a small company, where the entrepreneur's values become the values driving the business. A credo is an excellent way to transform those values into employees' ethical behavior. *John Oertel, president of ME International, a manufacturer of metal-grinding balls, discovered the importance of having a company credo as his company grew rapidly. "When you've got people sharing the same values, you've got what amounts to a built-in quality inspector," he says. "It used to be that our workers picked up ME's values at the company picnic or on the bowling team. Not now. We're growing. Half our people are new. . . . We decided we needed a statement."*[26]

Table 21.3 Ten Ethical Principles to Guide Behavior

The study of history, philosophy, and religion reveals a strong consensus about certain universal and timeless values that are central to leading an ethical life.

1. **Honesty.** Be truthful, sincere, forthright, straightforward, frank, candid; do not cheat, lie, steal, deceive, or act deviously.

2. **Integrity.** Be principled, honorable, upright, and courageous, and act on convictions; do not be two-faced or unscrupulous or adopt an ends-justifies-the-means philosophy that ignores principle.

3. **Promise-keeping.** Be worthy of trust, keep promises, fulfill commitments, and abide by the spirit as well as the letter of an agreement; do not interpret agreements in a technical or legalistic manner in order to rationalize noncompliance or to create excuses for breaking commitments.

4. **Fidelity.** Be faithful and loyal to family, friends, employers, and country; do not use or disclose information earned in confidence; in a professional context, safeguard the ability to make independent professional judgments by scrupulously avoiding undue influences and conflicts of interest.

5. **Fairness.** Be fair and open-minded, be willing to admit error, and, when appropriate, change positions and beliefs and demonstrate a commitment to justice, the equal treatment of individuals, and tolerance for diversity; do not overreach or take undue advantage of another's mistakes or adversities.

6. **Caring for others.** Be caring, kind, and compassionate; share, be giving, serve others; help those in need and avoid harming others.

7. **Respect for others.** Demonstrate respect for human dignity, privacy, and the right to self-determination for all people; be courteous, prompt, and decent; provide others with the information they need to make informed decisions about their own lives; do not patronize, embarrass, or demean.

8. **Responsible citizenship.** Obey just laws (if a law is unjust, openly protest it); exercise all democratic rights and privileges responsibly by participation (voting and expressing informed views), social consciousness, and public service; when in a position of leadership or authority, openly respect and honor democratic processes of decision making, avoid secrecy or concealment of information, and ensure that others have the information needed to make intelligent choices and exercise their rights.

9. **Pursuit of excellence.** Pursue excellence in all matters; in meeting personal and professional responsibilities, be diligent, reliable, industrious, and committed; perform all tasks to the best of your ability, develop and maintain a high degree of competence, and be well informed and well prepared; do not be content with mediocrity, but do not seek to win "at any cost."

10. **Accountability.** Be accountable; accept responsibility for decisions, for the foreseeable consequences of actions and inactions, and for setting an example for others. Parents, teachers, employers, many professionals, and public officials have a special obligation to lead by example and to safeguard and advance the integrity and reputation of their families, companies, professions, and the government; avoid even the appearance of impropriety and take whatever actions are necessary to correct or prevent inappropriate conduct of others.

SOURCE: Michael Josephson, "Teaching Ethical Decision Making and Principled Reasoning," *Ethics: Easier Said Than Done*, Winter 1988, pp. 28–29.

Develop a Code of Ethics. A **code of ethics** is a written statement of the standards of behavior and ethical principles a company expects from its employees. Codes of ethics do not ensure ethical behavior, but they do establish minimum standards of behavior throughout the organization. Much like the Ten Commandments, a code of ethics spells out what kind of behavior is expected (and what kind will not be tolerated) and offers everyone in the company concrete guidelines for dealing with ethics every day on the job. Although creating a code of ethics does not guarantee 100 percent compliance with ethical standards, it does tend to foster an ethical atmosphere in a company.[27] Workers who will be directly affected by the code should have a hand in developing it.

Enforce the Code Fairly and Consistently. Managers must take action when they discover ethical violations. If employees learn that ethical breaches go unpunished, the code of ethics becomes meaningless. "The code is the easy part," says one ethics consultant. "The hard part is getting down in the mud and wrestling with the moral choices that arise every day."[28]

Conduct Ethics Training. Instilling ethics in an organization's culture requires more than creating a code of ethics and enforcing it. Managers must show employees that the organization truly is committed to practicing ethical behavior. One of the most effective ways to display that commitment is through ethical training designed to raise employees' consciousness of potential ethical dilemmas. Ethics training programs not only raise employees' awareness of ethical issues, but they also communicate to them the core of the company's value system.

Hire the Right People. Ultimately, the decision in any ethical situation belongs to the individual. Hiring people with strong moral principles and values is the best insurance against ethical violations. To make ethical decisions, people must have: (1) *ethical commitment*—the personal resolve to act ethically and do the right thing; (2) *ethical consciousness*—the ability to perceive the ethical implications of a situation; and (3) *ethical competency*—the ability to engage in sound moral reasoning and develop practical problem-solving strategies.[29]

Perform Periodic Ethical Audits. One of the best ways to evaluate the effectiveness of an ethics system is to perform periodic audits. These reviews send a signal to employees that ethics is not just a passing fad.

Establish High Standards of Behavior, Not Just Rules. No one can legislate ethics and morality, but managers can let people know the level of performance they expect. It is crucial to emphasize to *everyone* in the organization the importance of ethics. All employees must understand that ethics is *not* negotiable. The role that the entrepreneur plays in establishing high ethical standards is critical; no one has more influence over the ethical character of a company than its founder. One entrepreneur offers this advice to business owners: "Stick to your principles. Hire people who want to live by them, teach them thoroughly, and insist on total commitment."[30]

Set an Impeccable Ethical Example at All Times. Remember that ethics starts at the top. Far more important than credos and codes are the examples the company's leaders set. If managers talk about the importance of ethics and then act in an unethical manner, they send mixed signals to employees. The values gap between the real and the ideal is "the largest single source of cynicism and skepticism in the workplace today," says one former company president.[31] Workers believe managers' *actions* more than their words.

Create a Culture That Emphasizes Two-Way Communication. A thriving ethical environment requires two-way communication. Employees must have the opportunity to report any ethical violations they observe. Such a two-way system is integral to a whistleblowing program, in which employees anonymously report breaches of ethical behavior through proper channels.

Involve Employees in Establishing Ethical Standards. Encourage employees to offer feedback on how standards should be established. "A boss cannot write a code [of ethics], give it to employees, and think that handles it," says one ethics consultant. "Knowing a code isn't enough, any more than knowing the Ten Commandments is."[32] Involving employees improves the quality of a firm's ethical standards and increases the likelihood of employee compliance.

The Issue of Social Responsibility

4 Define social responsibility.

Since the 1980s, society has imposed a higher standard on businesses: Companies must go beyond "doing well"—simply earning a profit—to "doing good"—living up to their social responsibilities. In the past, businesses paid little attention to fulfilling their social responsibilities, and no one expected them to. Today, however, companies must fulfill their roles of social stewardship if they are to compete effectively.

In a free enterprise system, companies that fail to respond to their customers' needs and demands soon go out of business. Today, customers are increasingly demanding the companies they buy goods and services from to be socially responsible. When customers shop for "value," they no longer consider only the price-performance relationship of the product or service; they also consider the company's stance on social responsibility. In a recent survey by the Walker Group, nearly 90 percent of consumers said that when price, service, and quality are equal among competitors, they will buy from the company that has the best reputation for social responsibility. The survey also revealed that 70 percent of consumers would not buy, at any price, from a company that was not socially responsible.[33] Businesses that add the arrow of a socially responsible strategy to their quiver of competitive weapons will outperform those who fail to do so in the twenty-first century.

PUTTING SOCIAL RESPONSIBILITY INTO PRACTICE

One problem facing businesses is defining just what social responsibility is. Is it manufacturing environmentally friendly products? Is it donating a portion of profits to charitable organizations? Is it creating jobs in inner cities plagued by high unemployment levels? The specific nature of a company's social responsibility efforts will depend on how its owners, employees, and other stakeholders define what it means to be socially responsible. Typically, businesses have responsibilities to several key stakeholders, including the environment, employees, customers, investors, and the community. **Social responsibility** is the awareness by a company's managers of the social, environmental, political, human, and financial consequences their actions produce.

*B*usiness's Responsibility to the Environment

5 Understand the nature of business's responsibility to the environment.

Driven by their customers' interest in protecting the environment, companies have become more sensitive to the impact their products, processes, and packaging have on the planet. Environmentalism has become and will continue to be one of the dominant issues for companies worldwide because consumers have added another item to their list of buying criteria: environmental safety. Companies have discovered that sound environmental practices make for good business. In addition to lowering their operating costs, environmentally safe products attract environmentally conscious customers and can give a company a competitive edge in the marketplace. Socially responsible business owners focus on the three Rs: reduce, reuse, recycle.

◆ *Reduce* the amount of materials used in your company, from the factory floor to the copier room.

◆ *Reuse* whatever you can.

◆ *Recycle* the materials that you must dispose of.

Adolph Coors Company, the Golden, Colorado, brewery, has been reaping the benefits of a recycling and waste-reduction strategy since the 1950s. By using 100 percent recycled paperboard to ship its products, Coors saves 1,695 acres of forest annually. The company also recycles wood, oil, spent grains, and just about anything else it uses in production. Coors also has discovered ways to avoid creating waste and pollution. Since 1987, Coors has reduced the amount of hazardous wastes it produces by more than 90 percent. Its recycling and waste-reduction efforts are not only good for the environment; they are also good for business. The company benefits from the hundreds of thousands of dollars its actions save each year.[34]

Table 21.4 Environmentally Responsible Questions

Industry Week challenged Jonathan Schorsch, environmental research director at the Council on Economic Priorities, to describe what companies can do to be environmentally responsible. Schorsch came up with the following questions for managers to ask themselves.

◆ Are we trying to reduce the volume of our packaging?

◆ How do we deal with disposal?

◆ Are we recycling in the office?

◆ Can we get beyond the concept of volume sales to build products that last?

◆ Are we reducing waste and substituting toxic substances with nontoxic ones?

◆ Are we reformulating waste for resale?

◆ Do we have a formal environmental policy?

◆ Do we go beyond compliance?

◆ Are we uniformly stringent environmentally in operations outside, as well as inside, the United States?

◆ Do we educate employees about the hazards of working with toxic materials?

◆ Do we encourage employees to submit proposals on how to reduce waste?

◆ Do we conserve energy?

◆ Are we avoiding paying taxes, when those tax dollars might go to support environmental programs?

◆ How do our operations affect the communities they're in, including indigenous people in other countries?

SOURCE: Therese R. Welter, "A Farewell to Arms," *Industry Week*, August 20, 1990, p. 42. Copyright Penton Publishing Company, Inc., reprinted with permission from *Industry Week*.

Like Coors, truly progressive companies are taking their environmental policies a step further, creating redesigned, "clean" manufacturing systems that focus on *avoiding* waste and pollution. That requires a different manufacturing philosophy. These companies design their products, packaging, and processes from the start with the environment in mind, working to eliminate hazardous materials and by-products and looking for ways to turn what had been scrap into salable products. According to the product development manager of one small company, managers must "start looking beyond the immediate product and get involved in the entire product cycle—from the resources that are used in the product, to the resources that are used in the transition of the product from manufacture through consumer use, to the resources left in the product *after* the consumer has used it."[35] Such an approach requires an ecological evaluation of every part of the process—from the raw materials put into the product to the disposal or reuse of the packaging that surrounds it.

Table 21.4 offers a list of questions environmentally responsible entrepreneurs should ask themselves.

*B*usiness's Responsibility to Employees

◆ **6** Describe business's responsibility to employees.

Few other stakeholders are as important to a business as its employees. It is common for managers to *say* their employees are their most valuable resource, but the truly excellent ones *treat* them that way. "People—and productivity growth *through* people—are increasingly the winning edge determining the competitiveness both of companies and countries," says one top manager.[36] How can business owners prove to employees that they really are the company's number one asset?

Following Nature's Example

*R*ay Anderson had spent most of his career working for major textile companies. Then, in the early 1970s, he traveled to Europe, where he saw computer rooms furnished in square "tiles" of carpeting. Upon his return to the United States, he launched his own company, Interface, Inc., which soon became the leading manufacturer of modular carpeting in the country. Twenty years later, however, Interface was struggling as its cost had gotten out of control and its customers began to question the company's impact on the environment. An employee gave Anderson a copy of Paul Hawken's *The Ecology of Commerce,* which chronicles a thoughtful plan for business success without sacrificing the environment. Based on the model of nature itself, Hawken's book calls for controlling the creation of harmful wastes rather than focusing on their disposal. Hawken's book envisions a business system that copies nature, where everything's waste is food for something else. Nothing is wasted. Anderson says that, after reading the book, he thought about his grandchildren's future, and he wept. "It was like a spear in my chest," he recalls. Anderson decided to launch his company on a new mission: to create zero pollution and to consume zero oil without sacrificing the interests of investors, employees, or customers. Anderson took the concepts in *The Ecology of Commerce* to heart and used nature itself as the model for conducting business. He hired environmental consultants and created teams of employees to study every process in the company to find ways to "ecologize" them. Winning ideas earn employees bonuses. A new yarn tufting method reduced the use of nylon by 10 percent. Interface now combines carpet yarns with natural fibers from hemp and flax to create carpeting that is both "harvestable" and "compostable." Water from the plant is treated and recycled to irrigate a local golf course. Massive electric motors are jump-started with gravity-fed systems rather than with huge jolts of

electricity. "Looking at waste really forces you to look at how your systems are designed," says one top Interface manager. The changes not only have helped the environment, but they also have saved the company more than $75 million in just three years!

Still, some of the biggest benefits of Interface's new method of doing business come in its marketing efforts. Doing business with a "green" vendor, especially a low-cost green vendor, is an attractive feature to many companies. Interface has attracted the attention of other companies with an interest in the environment as potential customers. The Gap Inc. ordered carpet for its new headquarters because they were the low bidder; however, Gap invited Interface to bid only because of its impressive environmental record. Managers say that Interface has landed several contracts because of its ecological approach to business that it otherwise would not have.

Employees benefit from the company's natural approach as well. The typical carpet mill is a noisy, dusty place, where lint particles can be seen floating in malodorous air. Not so at Interface. The factory is not dusty, and the air is free of both odors and lint particles. Sunlight bathes the entire factory through three-story windows. Rather than a manicured and chemical-filled lawn, the plant is landscaped naturally, with wild grasses and wildflowers. Joyce LaValle, plant manager, takes about 1,000 potential customers through the plant each year. "If they come into this building, I've got them hands down," she says, "especially if they've been to other plants."

Although Interface has a long way to go to reach its environmental goals, the company has come a long way. It is once again the world leader in its market segment, and more importantly, Interface has discovered that it is possible to create business success and a renewable future at the same time by following nature's example.

---

1. What benefits does conducting business according to nature's model offer companies such as Interface? What is the impact on a company's stakeholders?

2. What future do you predict for this management philosophy? Explain.

SOURCE: Adapted from Thomas Petzinger Jr., "Business Achieves Greatest Efficiencies When at Its Greenest," *Wall Street Journal,* July 11, 1997, p. B1. ◆

♦ Listen to employees and respect their opinions.

♦ Ask for their input; involve them in the decision-making process.

♦ Provide regular feedback—positive and negative—to employees.

♦ Tell them the truth—always.

♦ Let them know exactly what's expected of them.

♦ Reward employees for performing their jobs well.

♦ Trust them; create an environment of respect and teamwork.

Successful small businesses recognize their employees as their most valuable resource and treat them that way. At Starbucks, employees are such an integral part of the company's success that they are called "partners" rather than "employees."

Starbucks Coffee Company, the successful Seattle-based specialty coffee retailer, recognizes the special role its employees (partners) play in keeping customers coming back to its retail locations, and it shows employees that it appreciates their contribution. Reflecting on the importance of having satisfied partners interacting with customers in the retail business, CEO Howard Schultz explains, "We recognized [from the outset that] we had to build trust and confidence with customers and shareholders. But first and foremost, we had to build this trust with employees." At Starbucks, employee-partners come first. Great benefits, constant training, respect, and a team approach keep costs low and employee turnover down: just one-eighth of the industry average.[37]

Several important issues face small business managers trying to meet their social responsibility to employees.

CULTURAL DIVERSITY IN THE WORKPLACE

The United States has always been a nation of astonishing cultural diversity, a trait that has imbued it with an incredible richness of ideas and creativity. Indeed, this diversity is one of the driving forces behind the greatest entrepreneurial effort in all the world, and it continues to grow. The United States, in short, is moving toward a "minority majority," and significant demographic shifts will affect virtually every aspect of business. Nowhere will the changes be more visible than in the makeup of our nation's workforce. White, non-Hispanic males, who constituted the majority of the workforce until about the 1970s, now make up just 43 percent of all employees. Women and minorities will make up 62 percent of the workforce by 2005.[38]

This rich mix of cultures within the workforce presents both opportunities and challenges to employers (see the diversity wheel in Figure 21.2 on page 740). One of the chief benefits of a diverse workforce is the rich blend of perspectives, skills, talents, and ideas em-

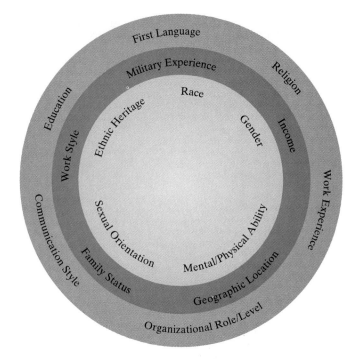

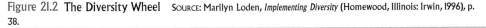

Figure 21.2 **The Diversity Wheel** Source: Marilyn Loden, *Implementing Diversity* (Homewood, Illinois: Irwin, 1996), p. 38.

ployees have to offer. Also, the changing composition of the nation will change the customer base. What better way is there for an entrepreneur to deal with culturally diverse customers than to have a culturally diverse workforce? One small business owner who has implemented a cultural diversity program in his own company says, "Don't I want greater diversity inside my organization to help attract more diversity, just like I want it to help sell to my diverse market? And don't I want my management to be more diverse so that I can manage diverse people better?"[39]

Managing a culturally diverse workforce presents a real challenge for employers, however. Molding workers with highly varied beliefs, backgrounds, and biases into a unified team takes time and commitment. Stereotypes, biases, and prejudices will present barriers that workers and managers must constantly overcome. Communication may require more effort because of language differences. In many cases, dealing with diversity causes a degree of discomfort for entrepreneurs because of the natural tendency to associate with people who are similar to ourselves. These reasons and others cause some entrepreneurs to resist the move to a more diverse workforce, a move that threatens their ability to create a competitive edge.

How can entrepreneurs achieve unity through diversity? The only way is by *managing* diversity in the workforce: That is, entrepreneurs must create an environment in which all types of workers—men, women, Hispanic, African American, white, disabled, homosexual, elderly, and others—can flourish and can give top performance to their companies. Managing a culturally diverse workforce requires a different way of thinking, however, and that requires training. One diversity expert explains, "On the job, employees interact with an eclectic mix of people who differ in race, gender, and age, as well as in work style, education, and other attributes. That means employers must create an environment that accepts, even values, those differences, provides equal opportunity, and fosters positive working relationships among all employees."[40] In essence, diversity training will help make everyone aware of the dangers of bias, prejudice, and discrimination, however subtle or unintentional they may be. Managing a culturally diverse workforce successfully requires a business owner to:

Assess your company's diversity needs. The starting point for an effective diversity management program is an assessment of the company's needs and problems. Surveys, interviews, and informal conversations with employees can be valuable tools. Several organizations offer more formal assessment tools—"cultural audits," questionnaires, and diagnostic forms—that also might be useful.

Learn to recognize and correct your own biases and stereotypes. One of the best ways to identify your own cultural biases is to get exposure to people who are not like you! By spending time with those who are different from you, you will learn quickly that stereotypes simply don't hold up.

Avoid making invalid assumptions. Decisions based on faulty assumptions are bound to be flawed. Potential employers' false assumptions made on the basis of inaccurate perceptions has kept many qualified women and minorities from getting jobs and promotions.

Push for diversity in your management team. To get maximum benefit from a culturally diverse workforce, a company must promote nontraditional workers into top management. A culturally diverse top management team that can serve as mentors and role models provides visible evidence that nontraditional workers can succeed.

Concentrate on communication. Any organization, especially a culturally diverse one, will stumble if lines of communication break down. Frequent training sessions and regular opportunities for employees to talk with one another in a nonthreatening environment can be extremely helpful.

Make diversity a core value in the organization. For a cultural diversity program to work, top managers must "champion" the program and take active steps to integrate diversity throughout the entire organization.

Continue to adjust your company to your workers. Rather than pressure workers to conform to the company, those entrepreneurs with the most successful cultural diversity programs are constantly looking for ways to adjust their businesses to their workers. Flexibility is the key.

Table 21.5 compares the traditional management assumptions that companies must change and the diversity management assumptions needed to replace them.

When an affirmative action audit at BRW, an architectural and engineering firm in Minneapolis, revealed that the promotion rate for women and minorities was questionable, CEO Don Hunt and his partners decided to take a hard look at their commitment to cultural diversity. What they discovered was that 96 percent of the company's managers were white males, but the clients they were serving were a highly culturally diverse group. "There was a feeling that we would be less competitive if we continued to be a white-male-dominated firm," says Hunt. An employee-driven diversity team began evaluating BRW's human resources policies and practices and made suggestions ranging from instituting diversity training to modifying hiring practices. Just five years later, women and minorities made up 19 percent of BRW's managers, nearly a four-fold improvement.[41] Managers at BRW are committed to a culturally diverse workplace because they do business in a culturally diverse world.

Table 21.5 The Traditional Paradigm vs. the Valuing Diversity Paradigm

Traditional Paradigm	Valuing Diversity Paradigm
Expectations, standards, and explicit and implicit rules shaped by the needs of those at the top.	Expectations, standards, and explicit and implicit rules shaped by diverse customers and employees.
Success linked to assimilation.	Success linked to unique contribution.
Limited range of appropriate communication, work, and leadership styles.	Expanded range of styles.
No strategic business linkage.	Diversity is a competitive business strategy.
Diversity equals a potential liability.	Diversity equals a unique asset.
No human resources system alignment.	Human resources system in alignment.
Token gender and/or racial diversity at middle management level.	Visible diversity at all management levels.
Uncommitted and uninformed leadership.	Aware and committed leadership.
Underlying assumption: Change the people and preserve the culture.	Underlying assumption: Modify the culture to support the people.

Source: Marilyn Loden, *Implementing Diversity* (Homewood, Illinois: Irwin, 1996), p. 28.

DRUG TESTING

Much to employers' dismay, illegal substances have infiltrated the workplace. In fact, a recent study of managers concluded that substance abuse (drug and alcohol) is the number one workplace issue across the nation. In addition to the lives it ruins, substance abuse takes a heavy financial toll on business and society, costing U.S. companies more than $1 billion each year because of reduced productivity, increased medical payments, higher accident rates, and absenteeism.[42] Unfortunately, small companies bear a disproportionate share of this burden. The majority—74 percent—of all substance abusers are employed.[43] Experts estimate that 23 percent of all American workers use illegal drugs *on the job*; yet, only 3 percent of small businesses have drug-testing programs, and only 12 percent have a formal policy on drug use.[44] Because drug testing programs and antidrug policies are much more prevalent in large companies, drug-using employees are most likely to work for small businesses. Too many small business owners refuse to face these facts, however. One survey of small business employers found that, although they agree that substance abuse is a serious national problem, only 32 percent believe it is a problem among their own workers! The report concluded, "It is clear that a significant proportion of the small-employer workforce uses drugs."[45]

What can an entrepreneur do to win the battle against drugs? Frequently, the initial response of an employer dealing with a drug problem is to fire the drug abuser. But this approach only gives temporary relief from a much bigger problem. "Firing an offender is one way to get rid of the problem but not necessarily the best way," says Susan Berger, an executive at the Corporation Against Drug Abuse. "When you fire that person, you may rid yourself of an employee who is otherwise valuable and in whom you have invested time and training. Replacing him or her could cost from $7,000 to $13,000 in recruitment, not to mention the training costs."[46]

Another instinctive action some small business owners take is instituting a drug testing program. Drug testing, although becoming increasingly more common, remains a controversial issue. If not planned and implemented properly, drug tests can lead to a variety of legal, ethical, and moral problems for the small business owner, including invasion of privacy, discrimination, slander, or defamation of character. *For instance, at one company, managers forced an employee to submit to a random drug test in front of his co-workers and then fired* *him after the results came back positive. He sued his former employer for invasion of privacy and won $125,000. Another small company lost a legal battle for defamation of character when the supervisor explained to the work team that their teammate (who had been fired on the basis of drug test results), was fired "because he was a drug addict."*[47]

To avoid these and other problems, employers should develop an effective drug program that includes four key elements:

1. *A written substance abuse policy.* The first step in the war against drugs is creating a written policy that spells out the company's position on drugs. The policy should state its purpose, prohibit the use of drugs on the job (or off the job if it affects job performance), specify the consequences of violating the policy, explain any drug testing procedures to be used, and describe the resources available to help troubled employees.

2. *Training for supervisors to detect drug-using workers.* Supervisors are in the best position to identify employees with drug problems and to encourage them to get help. The supervisor's job, however, is not to play "cop" or "therapist." The supervisor should identify problem employees early and encourage them to seek help. The focal point of the supervisor's role is to track employees' performances against their objectives to identify the employees with performance problems.

3. *A drug testing program, when necessary.* Experts recommend that business owners seek the advice of an experienced attorney before establishing a drug testing program. Preemployment testing of job applicants generally is a safe strategy to follow, as long as it is followed consistently. Testing current employees is a more complex issue.

4. *An employee assistance program (EAP).* No drug-battling program is complete without a way to help addicted employees. An **employee assistance program (EAP)** is a company-provided benefit designed to help reduce workplace problems such as alcoholism, drug addiction, a gambling habit, and other conflicts and to deal with them when they arise. Although some troubled employees may balk at enrolling in an EAP, the company controls the most powerful weapon in motivating them to seek and accept help: *their job.* The greatest fear that substance-abusing employees have is losing their jobs, and the company can use that fear to help workers recover.

AIDS

One of the most serious health problems to strike the world recently is AIDS (acquired immune deficiency syndrome). This deadly disease, for which no cure yet exists, poses an array of ethical dilemmas for business, ranging from privacy to discrimination. The disease costs the nation more than $75 billion annually in medical care and lost productivity and is the leading cause of death for Americans aged 25 to 44.[48] For most business owners, the issue is not *if* one of their employees will contract AIDS but *when.*

Coping with AIDS in the workplace is not like managing normal health care issues because of the fear and the misunderstanding the disease creates among workers. When faced with the disease, employers and employees often operate on the basis of misconceptions and fear. Many small business owners know very little about their obligations to employees with AIDS. One study found that many of the actions employers said they would take with an employee who had AIDS (including firing and telling coworkers) were illegal.[49] In fact, AIDS is considered a disability and is covered by the Americans with Disabilities Act (ADA), which applies to companies with 15 or more employees. (Small business owners with fewer than 15 employees may be covered by state and local laws.) The ADA prohibits discrimination against any person with a disability, including AIDS, in hiring, promoting,

IN THE FOOTSTEPS OF AN ENTREPRENEUR

When AIDS Attacks Your Company

"*A*IDS in *my* company? No way! I'm just a small business owner. It's the large companies that need policies and procedures to deal with AIDS-stricken employees." That's the response many small business owners offer when questioned about their readiness to cope with AIDS. Unfortunately, *it's just not true*. Small companies are not exempt from this devastating problem, and it won't just go away if owners close their eyes or turn their backs. In a small business, the impact of AIDS can be incredibly destructive. One writer explains:

> The AIDS virus itself presents a perfect metaphor for its effect on relationships and institutions. People with AIDS do not die from the virus itself, which destroys the body's immune system, but from the petty ubiquitous infections the body can no longer fight.
>
> Likewise, AIDS attacks the immune system of personal relationships and organizations like businesses, making them even more vulnerable to weaknesses already there, turning commonplace threats into legal toxins. By the same token, AIDS can bring out the strengths of people and organizations. . . . A company that already treats its employees well will respond compassionately when one of its own has AIDS; a company that doesn't, won't.

Here's a story of one company's response to an AIDS-stricken employee: After returning from another extended bout with illness, Paul asked to meet privately with the managers of Circle Solutions, Inc., a small research and consulting firm. He told them that he was HIV-positive. Paul's revelation prompted a host of questions about HIV, and managers needed answers *fast*. Were Paul's coworkers in danger of infection? What were the company's legal responsibilities to Paul? What would happen if Paul could no longer perform his duties?

Managers saw an immediate need for an AIDS education program and called in a local expert to counsel managers first and then to conduct a half-day AIDS education program for all Circle Solutions' employees. Managers also hired this expert to provide counseling to Paul, who decided to tell his coworkers about his disease.

Managers met with employees in small groups to tell them about Paul's illness. AIDS education sessions quickly followed, and management gave employees the chance to meet privately with the doctor directing the employee assistance program (EAP). "Amazingly, the response was overwhelmingly one of concern, sympathy, and support for Paul," says the company's human resources manager. "Not one person came forward to object, resign, or ask to be moved from Paul's work area." Explaining that positive response, one employee cited management's concern and Paul's openness. "We wanted to return Paul's trust by doing whatever we could for him," he said.

Circle Solution's managers also brought in an attorney specializing in AIDS discrimination cases to avoid legal problems. The attorney's advice: Keep Paul's medical information private, provide him with the same benefit as those with any life-threatening illness, allow him to work as long as he is able, and ensure that the company did not discriminate against him in any way. Managers made a commitment to living up to their legal and ethical obligations to Paul. That commitment soon was put to the test as Paul's health began to deteriorate and he missed work frequently. Managers first modified his job duties to accommodate his condition. As Paul grew weaker, managers allowed him to work whenever he could, filling in the gaps with vacation and sick leave to keep regular paychecks coming. Several of Paul's coworkers picked up the slack caused by his condition. When Paul's leave was depleted, Circle Solutions' president sent employees a memo announcing the creation of a "leave bank," to which any employee could donate a vacation day and a sick day. The memo created an outpouring of support from coworkers, who donated a total of six months' paid time. The company also arranged for a pharmacist to provide Paul's costly medications and then picked up the tab and completed the necessary paperwork. When Paul could no longer report to work, his coworkers arranged for someone in the company to contact him at least once a week to boost his morale and to keep him in touch with workplace activities.

Paul died one year after he was diagnosed. The staff held a memorial service, and several employees created a square for an AIDS quilt in his honor. What managers learned about AIDS through Paul's experience proved to be valuable when two other Circle Solutions employees contracted the HIV virus. The company is well prepared for this unfortunate reality.

1. What steps should a small company take to deal effectively with AIDS?

2. Evaluate Circle Solutions' reponse to AIDS.

SOURCES: Adapted from Tom Ehrenfield, "The Business Lesson of AIDS," *Inc.*, April 1994, pp. 29–30; Marilyn B. Ayres, "When AIDS Hits Home," *Small Business Reports,* July 1994, pp. 14–19. ◆

discharging, or compensating. In addition, employers must make "reasonable accommodations" to allow an AIDS-stricken employee to continue working. That could mean job sharing, flexible work schedules, job reassignment, sick leave, and part-time work.

Despite the fact that AIDS is becoming more common in the workplace, few businesses are prepared adequately to deal with it. Yet coping with AIDS in a socially responsible manner requires a written policy and an educational program, ideally implemented *before* the need arises. Decisions on dealing with AIDS must be based on facts rather than on emotions, so owners must be well informed.

As with drug testing, it is important to ensure that a company's AIDS policies are legal. In general, a company's AIDS policy should include the following:

Employment. Companies must allow employees with AIDS to continue working as long as they can perform the job.

Discrimination. Because AIDS is a disability, employers cannot discriminate against qualified people with the disease who can meet job requirements.

Employee benefits. Employees with AIDS have the right to the same benefits as those with any other life-threatening illness.

Confidentiality. Employers must keep employees' medical records strictly confidential.

Education. An AIDS education program should be a part of every company's AIDS policy. The time to create and implement one is before the problem arises. As part of its AIDS program, one small company conducted informational seminars, distributed brochures and booklets, established a print and video library, and even set up individual counseling for employees.

"Reasonable accommodations." Under the ADA, employers must make reasonable accommodations for employees with AIDS. These may include extended leaves of absence, flexible work schedules, restructuring a job to require less-strenuous duties, purchasing special equipment to assist affected workers, and other modifications.

SEXUAL HARASSMENT

As the number of women entering the workforce has increased, so has the number of sexual harassment charges filed (see Figure 21.3 on page 746). Estimates of the percentage of working women who have experienced sexual harassment on the job range from 40 to 60 percent.[50] Sexual harassment is a violation of Title VII of the Civil Rights Act of 1964 and is considered to be a form of sex discrimination. Studies indicate that sexual harassment and discrimination are pervasive in businesses of all sizes, but small businesses are especially vulnerable because they usually lack specific policies, procedures, and training programs. Even cartoon strips are not immune to sexual harassment charges. In Mort Walker's long-running "Beetle Bailey" comic strip, Miss Buxley filed charges against General Halftrack because of his leering stares and sexual and untoward comments.[51]

Sexual harassment is any unwelcome sexual advance, request for sexual favors, and other verbal or physical sexual conduct made explicitly or implicitly as a condition of employment. Women bring about 90 percent of all sexual harassment charges. Jury verdicts reaching into the millions of dollars are not uncommon. *For instance, a jury awarded a woman who had been a secretary in a law firm for three months $7.1 million (later reduced to $3.5 million) because, among other things, one attorney touched her inappropriately while pouring M&Ms into her shirt pocket. The jury concluded that the law firm knew about the harassment and had not done enough to prevent it.*[52] Several types of behavior may result in charges of sexual harassment.

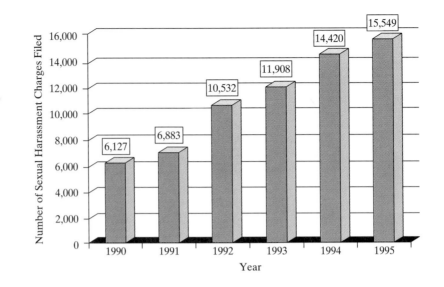

Figure 21.3 **Number of Sexual Harassment Charges Filed**   SOURCE: Equal Employment Opportunity Commission.

Quid Pro Quo Harassment. The most blatant, and most potentially damaging, form of sexual harassment is *quid pro quo* ("something for something"), in which a superior conditions the granting of a benefit (promotion, raise, etc.) upon the receipt of sexual favors from a subordinate. Only managers and supervisors, not coworkers, can engage in *quid pro quo* harassment. Unfortunately, this form of harassment is all too common. One study found that two-thirds of sexual harassment complaints were made against immediate supervisors and upper management.[53]

Hostile Environment. Behavior that creates an abusive, intimidating, offensive, or hostile work environment also constitutes sexual harassment. A hostile environment usually requires a *pattern* of offensive sexual behavior rather than a single, isolated remark or display. In judging whether a hostile environment exists, courts base their decisions on how a "reasonable woman" would perceive the situation. (The previous standard was that of a "reasonable person.") Although not easily defined, a hostile work environment is one in which continuing unwelcome sexual conduct in the workplace interferes with an employee's work performance. Most sexual harassment charges arise from claims of a hostile environment.

Harassment by Nonemployees. An employer can be held liable for third parties (customers, sales representatives, and others) who engage in sexual harassment if the employer has the ability to stop the improper behavior. *For example, one company required a female elevator operator to wear an extremely skimpy, revealing uniform. She complained to her boss that the uniform encouraged members of the public to direct offensive comments and physical contact toward her. The manager ignored her complaints, and later she refused to wear the uniform, resulting in her dismissal. The court held the company accountable for the employee's sexual harassment by nonemployees because it required her to wear the uniform after she complained of the harassment.*[54]

No business wants to incur the cost of defending itself against charges of sexual harassment, but those costs can be devastating for a small business. Multimillion-dollar jury

How Much Do You Know about Sexual Harassment?

Do you know sexual harassment when you see it? Consider the following true case:

Catherine was exposed to nude photographs posted in various areas of the plant in which she worked. She eventually complained about the pictures to the plant manager, who (1) made inappropriate personal and sexual remarks to her, (2) addressed her as "honey" and "dear," and (3) insinuated that she was a troublemaker. Thereafter, some, but not all, of the pictures were removed, despite the employer's policy to remove sexually explicit materials upon discovery.

When Catherine's immediate supervisor heard of her complaint, he indicated that he disapproved of "women's liberation" and recited a story to Catherine about employees who had quit their jobs after the jobs were made intolerable. Other employees (including another supervisor) also expressed to Catherine their annoyance over her complaint, and she was subjected to cat calls and harassing whistles. These instances of harassment were also reported by Catherine to her immediate supervisor and the plant manager, who indicated to her that she was somehow encouraging the harassment. Management failed to put an end to the whistling and cat calls.

In its defense, the company cited the fact that it had instituted a policy of using gender-neutral terms in its job titles.

Did Catherine have a legitimate sexual harassment complaint? Explain.

Yes. Although the company had a mechanism for employees to complain about sexual harassment, managers failed to take any action to stop the harassment. Indeed, the managers to whom she complained participated in the harassment. Catherine prevailed in court.

One of the primary causes of sexual harassment in the workplace is the lack of education concerning what constitutes harassment. The following quiz asks you to assume the roles of an employee and of a manager when answering the questions. Perhaps these statements can help you avoid problems with sexual harassment on the job.

A Test for Employees

Answer each question as true or false.

1. If I just ignore unwanted sexual attention, it will usually stop.
2. If I don't mean to sexually harass another employee, there's no way my behavior can be perceived by him or her as sexually harassing.
3. Some employees don't complain about unwanted sexual attention from another worker because they don't want to get that person in trouble.
4. If I make sexual comments to someone and that person doesn't ask me to stop, then I guess my behavior is welcome.
5. To avoid sexually harassing a woman who comes to work in a traditionally male workplace, the men simply should not haze her.
6. A sexual harasser may be told by a court to pay part of a judgment to the employee he or she harassed.
7. A sexually harassed man does not have the same legal rights as a woman who is sexually harassed.
8. About 90 percent of all sexual harassment in today's workplace is done by males to females.
9. Sexually suggestive pictures or objects in a workplace don't create a liability unless someone complains.
10. Displaying "girlie" pictures can constitute a hostile work environment even though most workers in the workplace think they are harmless.
11. Telling someone to stop his or her unwanted sexual behavior usually doesn't do any good.

Answers: (1) False, (2) False, (3) True, (4) False, (5) False, (6) True, (7) False, (8) True, (9) False, (10) True, (11) False.

A Test for Managers

Answer each question as true or false.

1. Men in male-dominated workplaces usually have to change their behavior when a woman begins working there.
2. Employers are not liable for the sexual harassment of one of their employees unless that employee loses specific job benefits or is fired.
3. Supervisors can be liable for sexual harassment committed by one of their employees against another.
4. Employers can be liable for the sexually harassing behavior of management personnel even if they are unaware of that behavior and have a policy forbidding it.
5. It is appropriate for a supervisor, when initially receiving a sexual harassment complaint, to determine if the alleged recipient overreacted or misunderstood the alleged harasser.
6. When a supervisor is telling an employee that an allegation of sexual harassment has been made against the employee, it is best to ease into the allegation instead of being direct.
7. Sexually suggestive visuals or objects in a workplace don't create a liability unless an employee complains about them and management allows them to remain.
8. The lack of sexual harassment complaints is a good indication that sexual harassment is not occurring.
9. It is appropriate for supervisors to tell an employee to handle unwelcome sexual behavior if they think that the employee is misunderstanding the behavior.
10. The *intent* behind employee A's sexual behavior is more important than the *impact* of that behavior on employee B when determining if sexual harassment has occurred.

11. If a sexual harassment problem is common knowledge in a workplace, the courts assume that the employer has knowledge of it.

SOURCES: Reprinted with permission from *Industry Week*, November 18, 1991, p. 40. Copyright Penton Publishing, Cleveland, Ohio; *Sexual Harassment Manual for Managers and Supervisors* (Chicago: Commerce Clearing House), 1992, p. 22; Andrea P. Brandon and David R. Eyler, *Working Together* (New York: McGraw-Hill), 1994. ◆

Answers: (1) False, (2) False, (3) True, (4) True, (5) False, (6) False, (7) False, (8) False, (9) False, (10) False, (11) True.

awards in such cases are becoming increasingly common because the Civil Rights Act of 1991 allows victims to collect punitive damages and emotional distress awards.

In recent rulings, the United States Supreme Court changed the nature of an employer's liability for sexual harassment, rejecting the previous standard that the employer had to be negligent somehow to be liable for a supervisor's improper behavior toward employees. In *Burlington Industries vs. Ellerth*, the court ruled that an employer can be held liable *automatically* if a supervisor takes a "tangible employment action" such as failing to promote or firing an employee whom he has been sexually harassing. The employer is liable even if he was not aware of the supervisor's conduct. If a supervisor takes no tangible employment action against an employee but engages in sexually harassing behavior such as offensive remarks, inappropriate touching, or sexual advances, the employer is not *automatically* liable for the supervisor's conduct. An employer would be liable for such conduct if, for example, he knew (or should have known) about the supervisor's behavior and failed to stop it.[55]

A company's best weapons against sexual harassment are education, policy, and procedures:

Education. Preventing sexual harassment is the best solution, and the key to prevention is educating employees about what constitutes sexual harassment. Training programs are designed to raise employees' awareness of what might be offensive to other workers and how to avoid sexual harassment altogether. Table 21.6 offers guidelines for battling sexual harassment in the workplace.

Policy. Another essential ingredient is a meaningful policy against sexual harassment that management can enforce. The policy should:

◆ Clearly define what behaviors constitute sexual harassment.

◆ State in clear language that harassment will not be tolerated in the workplace.

Table 21.6 Guidelines for Battling Sexual Harassment

Before you speak or act, ask yourself . . .	To keep the workplace harassment-free . . .
◆ Would you say it or do it in front of your spouse, parent, or child?	◆ Have a clear, written policy prohibiting sexual harassment.
◆ Would you say it or do it if your remark or action were going to be quoted on the front page of the newspaper or televised?	◆ Have mandatory training programs.
◆ Would you say it or do it to a member of your same sex?	◆ Ensure that your workplace is free of offensive materials.
◆ Would you behave the same way with a member of your same sex?	◆ Establish a program outlining the steps to take to file a complaint.
◆ Does it need to be said or done at all?	◆ Keep informed of all complaints and their resolution.

SOURCE: Ann Meyer, "Getting to the Heart of Sexual Harassment," *HRMagazine*, July 1992, p. 82; Jan Bohren, "Six Myths of Sexual Harassment," *Management Review*, May 1993, p. 62.

- Identify the responsibilities of supervisors and employees in preventing harassment.
- Define the sanctions and penalties for engaging in harassment.
- Spell out the steps to take in reporting an incident of sexual harassment.

In another case, the United States Supreme Court ruled that an employer was liable for a supervisor's sexually harassing behavior even though the employee never reported it. The company's liability stemmed from its failure to communicate its sexual harassment policy throughout the organization. This ruling makes employers' policies and procedures on sexual harassment the focal point of their defense.[56]

Procedure. Socially responsible companies provide a channel for all employees to express their complaints. Choosing a person inside the company (perhaps someone in the human resources area) and one outside the company (a close adviser or attorney) is a good strategy. At least one of these should be a woman. When a complaint arises, managers should:

- Listen to the complaint carefully without judging. Taking notes is a good idea. Tell the complainant what the process involves. Never treat the complaint as a joke.
- Investigate the complaint *promptly*, preferably within 24 hours. Failure to act quickly is irresponsible and illegal.
- Interview the accused party and any witnesses who may be aware of a pattern of harassing behavior *privately* and separately.
- Keep findings confidential.
- Decide what action to take, relying on company policy as a guideline.
- Inform both the complaining person and the alleged harasser of the action taken.
- Document the entire investigation.[57]

PRIVACY

Modern technology has given business owners the ability to monitor workers' performances as they never could before, but where is the line between monitoring productivity and invasion of privacy? "At the touch of a button, it's possible to view e-mail messages employees send to one another, listen to voice-mail or telephone conversations, and actually see what's on their monitors while they're sitting at their computer terminals," says the head of one ethics institute.[58] Experts estimate that 20 million workers in the United States are subject to computer monitoring.[59] Managers use electronic monitoring to track customer service representatives, word-processing clerks, data entry technicians, and other workers for speed, accuracy, and productivity. Even truck drivers, long the lone rangers of the road, are not immune to electronic tracking. Almost two-thirds of the major trucking companies now have communications devices in their trucks. Companies use these devices to monitor drivers' exact locations at all times, to regulate their speed, to make sure they stop only at approved fueling points, and to ensure that they take the legally required hours of rest. Although many drivers support the use of such devices, others worry about their ability to avoid George Orwell's "Big Brother" syndrome.[60]

Electronic communication technology also poses ethical problems for employers. Increasingly, workers are using voice-mail and electronic-mail systems to communicate with others; however, few know just what the rules governing their use and their privacy are. A study by the Society for Human Resource Management found that, although 80 percent of all organizations communicate via e-mail, only 34 percent have written policies governing the privacy of e-mail messages.[61] Most employees simply do not know that their bosses can legally monitor their e-mail and voice-mail messages, often without notification. To avoid ethical problems, a business owner should establish a clear policy for monitoring employees' communications and establish guidelines for the proper use of the company's communication technology. The policies should be reasonable and should reflect employees' reasonable expectations of privacy.

*B*usiness's Responsibility to Customers

7 Explain business's responsibility to customers.

One of the most important groups of stakeholders that a business must satisfy is its *customers*. Building and maintaining a base of loyal customers is no easy task, however. It requires more than just selling buyers a product or a service; the key is to build relationships with customers. Socially responsible companies recognize their duty to abide by the Consumer Bill of Rights, first put forth by President John Kennedy. This document gives consumers the following rights.

RIGHT TO SAFETY

The right to safety is the most basic consumer right. Companies have the responsibility to provide their customers with safe, quality products and services. The greatest breach of trust occurs when businesses produce products that, when properly used, injure customers. *For example, William Greenman was injured while using a shop tool made by Yuba Power Products. Because of defective design or construction, the set screws that held part of the machine together came loose as a result of normal vibrations during machine operation. When the screws loosened, a piece of wood Greenman was working on flew off the machine and injured him. Greenman won a $65,000 judgment from Yuba in a ruling that stated, "The purpose of such liability is to ensure that the costs of injuries resulting from defective products are borne by the manufacturers that put such products on the market."*[62]

RIGHT TO KNOW

Consumers have the right to honest communication about the products and services they buy and the companies they buy them from. In a free market economy, information is one of the most valuable commodities available. Customers often depend on companies for the information they need to make decisions about price, quality, features, and other factors. As a result, companies have a responsibility to customers to be truthful in their advertising.

Unfortunately, not every business recognizes its social responsibility to be truthful in advertising. Consider the following examples of unethical ads from small businesses.[63]

◆ A "universal coat hanger" for just $3.99. The product: a 10-penny nail.

◆ A "solid-state compact food server" for $39.95. The product: a spoon.

◆ A new "vision dieter." The product: a pair of glasses with one red lens and one blue lens; the lenses were supposed to make food look unappetizing (or at least purple).

◆ "Hide-A-Swat," guaranteed to kill flies and pests, for $9.95. The product: a rolled-up newspaper.

Businesses that rely on such unscrupulous tactics may profit in the short-term, but they will not last in the long-run!

RIGHT TO BE HEARD

The right to be heard suggests that the channels of communication between companies and their customers run in both directions. Socially responsible businesses provide customers with a mechanism for resolving complaints about products and services. Some companies have established a consumer ombudsman to address customer questions and complaints. Others have created customer hotlines, toll-free numbers designed to serve customers more effectively. One floor-covering maker dramatically reduced customer complaints by installing a toll-free customer hotline to answer questions about the proper care and maintenance of their floors.[64]

Another effective technique for encouraging two-way communication between customers and companies is the customer report card. *The Granite Rock Company* (see the In the Footsteps of an Entrepreneur feature in chapter 6) *relies on an annual report card from its customers to learn how to serve them better.* Although the knowledge a small business owner gets from customer feedback is immeasurable for making improvements, only one in 12 small companies regularly schedules customer satisfaction surveys such as Granite Rock's.[65] It's a tool that can boost a company's profitability significantly.

RIGHT TO EDUCATION

Socially responsible companies give customers access to educational programs about their products and services and how to use them properly. The goal is to give customers enough information to make informed purchase decisions. *For example, M. F. Foley, Inc., an 80-year-old family-owned fish processor, branched its business into selling to supermarkets. The company had always been obsessed with quality: it bought only the freshest fish; processed it in refrigerated plants; and paid close attention to sanitation. But Foley's efforts to ensure quality could easily be spoiled by improper handling in the supermarket. So the company created the Foley School of Fish. Student-customers learn "everything from hook to skillet," says Linda Foley, including display techniques, merchandising, perishability, and cooking tips. Foley also offers one-day crash courses for seafood department managers and employees. The educational program has paid off; in just 10 years, sales have climbed to $13 million. "Our education program is the key to our success," says Foley.*[66]

RIGHT TO CHOICE

Inherent in the free enterprise system is the consumer's right to choose among competing products and services. Socially responsible companies do not restrict competition, and they abide by the United States' antitrust policy, which promotes free trade and competition in the market. The foundation of this policy is the Sherman Antitrust Act of 1890, which forbids agreements among sellers that restrain trade or commerce and outlaws any attempts to monopolize a market.

*B*usiness's Responsibility to Investors

8▸ Discuss business's responsibility to investors.

Companies have the responsibility to provide investors with an attractive return on their investment. Although earning a profit may be a company's *first* responsibility, it is not its *only* responsibility; meeting its ethical and social responsibility goals is also a key to success. One business owner claims:

> My own company sees itself as having two bottom lines. One measures the extent to which revenues exceed expenses. The other measures our social and political impact. If we do well on the former and poorly on the latter, we're not succeeding.[67]

Many businesspeople echo these thoughts; they believe that managing a firm in an ethical, socially responsible manner is the only way to generate profits. For them, maintaining high social and ethical standards translates into profits for investors. One study of international companies supports this conclusion. The study found that firms practicing ethics on a daily basis had a distinct advantage over their rivals: Problems that once seemed muddled become clear in the ethical spotlight. The report also found that companies can reduce labor problems and increase productivity by maintaining ethical standards. Similarly, small companies tend to integrate ethics into their strategies for growth.[68]

Companies also have the responsibility to report their financial performances in an accurate and timely fashion to their investors. Firms that misrepresent or falsify their financial and operating records are guilty of violating the fiduciary relationship with their investors. *For example, investors in Bre-X Minerals, a tiny mineral exploration company in Calgary, Canada, saw the value of their stock skyrocket when the company announced that it had made the richest gold find of the century in its Busang mine in Borneo, Indonesia. Within two years, however, the value of the company's stock collapsed when an independent consulting firm discovered that drilling samples from the mine had been doctored with gold dust from other sources. Angry investors saw billions of dollars of their wealth evaporate when it became apparent that Bre-X's mine contained only planted gold. That none of the 268 holes that Bre-X had drilled over three years contained any gold amounts to what experts say is a scam "without precedent in the history of mining." Investors immediately filed several class-action lawsuits against the company, claiming that Bre-X executives had committed fraud and had misled shareholders about the Busang mine's potential. Within three months of the discovery, Bre-X was in bankruptcy.*[69]

$\mathcal{B}$usiness's Responsibility to the Community

❾ Describe business's responsibility to the community.

As corporate citizens, businesses have a responsibility to the communities in which they operate. In addition to providing jobs and creating wealth, companies contribute to the local community in many different ways. Socially responsible businesses are aware of their duty to put back into the community some of what they take out as they generate profits; their goal is to become a neighbor of choice. These companies are the ones who donate money, time, and personnel to schools, civic clubs, and volunteer organizations such as the Red Cross, the United Way, literacy programs, and a host of other groups. *For example, Terry Ehrich, owner of a highly successful automobile magazine,* Hemmings Motor News, *believes his company's social mission is as important as its economic mission. To Ehrich, his company's external stakeholders are just as important as its internal ones. Hemmings gives every employee two days of paid leave to spend working with local schools, and every May, employees take a half-day (also with pay) to pick up litter along a 30-mile stretch of road leading to their hometown of Bennington, Vermont. Every worker at Hemmings, including part-timers, receives full benefits, which includes five bushels of apples from the company orchard! The company also uses the proceeds from its popcorn wagon, a fully restored 1928 Ford pickup truck, to plant trees in local parks and to support a variety of local charities and volunteer fire departments. The company recently established the American Automotive Heritage Foundation, dedicated to educating the public about historic vehicles and promoting the collector car hobby.*[70]

Not only are community projects such as those sponsored by *Hemmings Motor News* the right thing to do, but research suggests that they may actually improve a company's financial performance. One study concluded that "companies that increased their community involvement were more likely to show an improved financial picture than those that did not increase their community involvement."[71] Other research shows that small businesses give more to their communities per employee than large ones. The majority of their donations were in the form of in-kind products and services and in volunteer time.[72]

As companies develop, making choices and setting directions, their mission statements serve as maps and navigational tools to the future. The Blue Fish Mission Spiral is full of movement, change and growth and is a blooming flower that unfolds the ever changing Blue Fish journey.

The BLUE FISH mission Spiral

The earth in all of us • limitless possibilities

evolution • understanding • connection

balance • health • clarity

truth

energy • willingness

belief

we came to live out loud • spirit

Go beyond

Express the balance and the beauty of the ever expanding circle

Live out loud in harmonious purpose, strength, integrity + compassion

Many small businesses recognize that they have a responsibility that includes more than just earning a profit. Jennifer Barclay, founder of Blue Fish Clothing, expresses her company's mission statement as a spiral. One of the results of the company's mission is BlueFishgarten, an outreach program in which Blue Fish employees leads hands-on art workshops for schools and community groups.

$\mathcal{C}$onclusion

Businesses must do more than merely earn profits; they must act ethically and in a socially responsible manner. Establishing and maintaining high ethical and socially responsible standards must be a top concern of every business owner. Managing ethics and social responsibility presents a tremendous challenge, however. There is no universal definition of ethical behavior, and what is considered ethical may change over time or may be different in other cultures. Many companies are tackling the problem with education. "Ethics education may not make people act ethically who want to act unethically," says one writer. "However, ethics education can help people act ethically who want to do so."[73]

Finally, business owners and managers must recognize the key role they play in influencing their employees' ethical and socially responsible behavior. What owners and managers *say* is important, but what they *do* is even more vital! Employees throughout a small company look to the owner and managers as models; therefore, these owners and managers must commit themselves to following the highest ethical standards if they expect their organizations to do so.

Chapter Summary

1. Define business ethics and describe the three levels of ethical standards.
   - Business ethics involves the fundamental moral values and behavioral standards that form the foundation for the people of an organization as they make decisions and interact with organizational stakeholders. Small business managers must consider the ethical and social as well as the economic implications of their decisions.
   - The three levels of ethical standards are (1) the law, (2) the policies and procedures of the company, and (3) the moral stance of the individual.

2. Determine who is responsible for ethical behavior and why ethical lapses occur.
   - Managers set the moral tone of the organization. There are three ethical styles of management: immoral, amoral, and moral. Although moral management has value in itself, companies that operate with this philosophy discover other benefits, including a positive reputation among customers and employees.
   - Ethical lapses occur for a variety of reasons:
     Some people are corrupt ("the bad apple").
     The company culture has been poisoned ("the bad barrel").
     Competitive pressures push managers to compromise.
     Managers are tempted by an opportunity to "get ahead."
     Managers in different cultures have different views of what is ethical.

3. Explain how to establish and maintain high ethical standards.
   - Philosophers throughout history have developed various tests of ethical behavior: the utilitarian principle, Kant's categorical imperative, the professional ethic, the Golden Rule, the television test, and the family test.
   - A small business manager can maintain high ethical standards in the following ways:
     Create a company credo.
     Develop a code of ethics.
     Enforce the code fairly and consistently.
     Hire the right people.
     Conduct ethical training.
     Perform periodic ethical audits.
     Establish high standards of behavior, not just rules.
     Set an impeccable ethical example at all times.

   Create a culture emphasizing two-way communication.
   Involve employees in establishing ethical standards.

4. Define social responsibility.
   - Social responsibility is the awareness of a company's managers of the social, environmental, political, human, and financial consequences of their actions.

5. Understand the nature of business's responsibility to the environment.
   - Environmentally responsible business owners focus on the three Rs: reduce, reuse, recycle: *reduce* the amount of materials used in the company from the factory floor to the copier room; *reuse* whatever you can; and *recycle* the materials that you must dispose of.

6. Describe business's responsibility to employees.
   - Companies have a duty to act responsibly toward one of their most important stakeholders: their employees. Businesses must recognize and manage the cultural diversity that exists in the workplace; establish a responsible strategy for combating substance abuse in the workplace (including drug testing) and dealing with AIDS; prevent sexual harassment; and respect employees' right to privacy.

7. Explain business's responsibility to customers.
   - Every company's customers have a right to safe products and services; to honest, accurate information; to be heard; to education about products and services; and to choices in the marketplace.

8. Discuss business's responsibility to investors.
   - Companies have the responsibility to provide investors with an attractive return on their investments and to report their financial performances in an accurate and timely fashion to their investors.

9. Describe business's responsibility to the community.
   - Increasingly, companies are seeing a need to go beyond "doing well" to "doing good"—being socially responsible community citizens. In addition to providing jobs and creating wealth, companies contribute to the local community in many different ways.

Discussion Questions

1. What is ethics? Discuss the three levels of ethical standards.
2. In any organization, who determines ethical behavior? Briefly describe the three ethical styles of man-

agement. What are the benefits of moral management?

3. Why do ethical lapses occur in businesses?

4. Describe the various methods for establishing ethical standards. Which is most meaningful to you? Why?

5. What can business owners do to maintain high ethical standards in their companies?

6. What is social responsibility?

7. Describe business's social responsibility to each of the following areas:
   The environment
   Employees
   Customers
   Investors
   The community

8. What can businesses do to improve the quality of our environment?

9. Should companies be allowed to test employees for drugs? Explain. How should a socially responsible drug testing program operate?

10. Many owners of trucking companies use electronic communications equipment to monitor their drivers on the road. They say that the devices allow them to remain competitive and to serve their customers better by delivering shipments of vital materials exactly when their customers need them. They also point out that the equipment can improve road safety by ensuring that drivers get the hours of rest the law requires. Opponents argue that the surveillance devices work against safety. "The drivers know they're being watched," says one trucker. "There's an obvious temptation to push." What do you think? What ethical issues does the use of such equipment create? How should a small trucking company considering the use of such equipment handle these issues?

11. What rights do customers have under the Consumer Bill of Rights? How can businesses ensure those rights?

Step into the Real World

1. Search the current literature (e.g., periodicals such as *Business Ethics, Inc., Entrepreneur, Fortune, Forbes,* the *Wall Street Journal,* and other business publications) to find examples of companies using each of the three ethical styles of management: immoral, amoral, and moral. Prepare a brief report summarizing each and explaining the consequences of management's behavior.

2. Obtain copies of codes of ethics from several companies or associations and compare them. What are the similarities and differences among them? Do you think these codes would be useful to an employee facing an ethical dilemma? Explain.

3. Contact several local business owners. How do they view their responsibility to society? Have they altered their management styles and their companies to reflect society's changing demands for responsible companies? What methods do they use to meet their responsibility to the stakeholders discussed in this chapter?

4. "Job safety and performance are more important than the slight invasion of privacy caused by drug testing," says one plant manager. Another, who refuses to test employees, claims, "Drug testing is an outright invasion of employee privacy." Conduct a debate in your class on these two positions.

5. Working in a team with another student, interview the owners of two small businesses with at least 10 employees about their experience with employee substance abuse in the workplace. Do the owners use drug tests? If so, what is their policy? If not, why not? Do the owners have formal drug policies? Why? Write a two-page report on your findings and include at least five specific recommendations you would make to these business owners about preventing substance abuse in their workplaces.

6. Consider the following actual case. Working with teammates, decide how you would handle the situation. What ethical and socially responsible principles guided you?

> David is a former drug user who has spent time in jail. For the past three years he has been straight, and he now operates a forklift at a small construction company. Lately, however, he's begun having seizures, or "flashbacks," as a result of his earlier use of the drug PCP. He has been carefully evaluated by EAP professionals and found to be clean of current drug use; indeed, they say flashbacks of this nature are quite common in ex-addicts. Mishandling of David's machine could be dangerous to him and his coworkers. However, he has already had flashbacks while at the controls, and in each case the seizure caused him to release a handle, which simply stopped the machine. It is the only work he is qualified to do within this company.*

*Source: Minda Zetlin, "Combating Drugs in the Workplace," *Management Review,* August 1991, pp. 17–24.

Take It to the Net

Visit the Scarborough/Zimmerer home page at
www.prenhall.com/scarbzim
for updated information, on-line resources, and Web-based exercises.

Endnotes

1. "Does It Pay to Be Ethical?" *Business Ethics*, March/April 1997, pp. 14–16.
2. Robert McGarvey, "To Pose a Question of Ethics," *Kiwanis Magazine*, February 1993, p. 32.
3. Vernon R. Loucks Jr., "A CEO Looks at Ethics," *Business Horizons*, March/April 1987, p. 2.
4. Janean Chun, "Code of Honor," *Entrepreneur*, August 1996, pp. 113–118.
5. Andrew W. Singer, "The Ultimate Ethics Test," *Across the Board*, March 1992, p. 22.
6. Susan Caminiti, "The Payoff from a Good Reputation," *Fortune*, February 10, 1992, p. 74.
7. Ibid., p. 77.
8. Thomas G. Labrecque, "Good Ethics Is Good Business," *USA Today Magazine*, May 1990, pp. 20–21.
9. Alan Farnham, "State Your Values, Hold the Hot Air," *Fortune*, April 19, 1993, p. 117.
10. McGarvey, "To Pose a Question of Ethics."
11. Raymond C. Baumhart, "How Ethical Are Businessmen?" *Harvard Business Review*, July–August, 1961, p. 6.
12. Archie B. Carroll, "A Survey of Managerial Ethics: Is Business Morality Watergate Morality?" *Business & Society Review*, Spring 1976, pp. 39–43.
13. "Promoting Ethical Business Practices," *Small Business Reports*, June 1987, p. 26.
14. Chun, "Code of Honor," p. 114.
15. Robert McGarvey, "Do the Right Thing," *Entrepreneur*, October 1992, p. 140.
16. Chun, "Code of Honor," p. 116.
17. David Vogel, "Ethics and Profits Don't Always Go Hand in Hand," *Los Angeles Times*, December 28, 1988, p. 7.
18. "Do Good Ethics Make Good Profits? The Prisoner's Dilemma," *Ethikos*, January/February 1992, p. 6.
19. Michael Barrier, "Doing the Right Thing," *Nation's Business*, March 1998, pp. 32–38.
20. O. C. Ferrell and John Fraedrich, "Understanding Pressures That Cause Unethical Behavior in Business," *Business Insights*, Spring/Summer 1990, pp. 1–4.
21. Lori A. Tansey, "Right vs. Wrong," *Managing Your Career*, Spring/Summer 1994, pp. 11–12.
22. Gabriella Stern, "Polluted Numbers," *Wall Street Journal*, October 21, 1992, pp. Al, A7.
23. Paul Klebnikov, "Russia—The Ultimate Emerging Market," *Forbes*, February 14, 1994, pp. 88–94.
24. Gene Laczniak, "Business Ethics: A Manager's Primer," *Business*, January–March, 1983, pp. 23–29.
25. Peter Barnes, "When Is Enough?" *Business & Society Review*, Fall 1989, p. 4.
26. Farnham, "State Your Values, Hold the Hot Air," p. 119.
27. Michael Barrier, "Should You Put It in Writing?" *Nation's Business*, March 1998, p. 37.
28. McGarvey, "Do The Right Thing."
29. Michael Josephson, "Teaching Ethical Decision Making and Principled Reasoning," *Ethics: Easier Said Than Done*, Winter 1988, p. 28.
30. John Rutledge, "The Portrait on My Office Wall," *Forbes*, December 30, 1996, p. 78.
31. Quotation attributed to Edward L. Hennessey Jr., *Leadership*, vol. F, no. 5 (19XX) p. 1.
32. McGarvey, "Do The Right Thing."
33. Gayle Sato Stodder, "Goodwill Hunting," *Entrepreneur*, July 1998, pp. 118–125.
34. Michael A. Verespej, "Trash to Cash," *Industry Week*, December 5, 1994, pp. 53–56.
35. Therese R. Welter, "Beyond the Dumpster," *Industry Week*, May 21, 1990, p. 54.
36. John S. McClenahen, "People (Still) the Competitive Advantage," *Industry Week*, May 6, 1991, p. 55.
37. Mary Scott, "Howard Schultz," *Business Ethics*, November/December 1995, pp. 26–29.
38. Sharon Nelton, "Nurturing Diversity," *Nation's Business*, June 1995, pp. 25–27.
39. Sharon Nelton, "Winning with Diversity," *Nation's Business*, September 1992, p. 20.
40. Genevieve Capowski, "Managing Diversity," *Management Review*, June 1996, p. 14.
41. Nelton, "Winning with Diversity."
42. "Emphasis on Recovery," *South Carolina Business Journal*, July 1997, p. 9.
43. Charles Carroll, "Five Point Plan Is a Blueprint for a Drug-Free Workplace," *South Carolina Business Journal*, April 1996, p. 10.
44. David Warner, "The War on Drugs Wants You," *Nation's Business*, February 1996, pp. 54–55.
45. "Small Employers Lack Drug Policies," *Small Business Reports*, November 1991, p. 24.
46. Doreen Mangan, "An Rx for Drug Abuse," *Small Business Reports*, May 1992, p. 30.
47. Steven K. Like, "Employee Drug Testing," *Small Business Reports*, December 1990, p. 47.
48. Cynthia E. Griffin, "Crisis Control," *Entrepreneur*, August 1995, pp. 128–135.
49. Philip Rutsohn and Donald Law, "Acquired Immune Deficiency Syndrome: A Small Business Dilemma," *Journal of Small Business Management*, January 1991, pp. 62–71.
50. Ann Scott Tyson, "U.S. Companies Move to Curb Sexual Harassment on Job," *Christian Science Monitor*, May 30, 1996, pp. 1, 18.
51. Amy Wilson, "Inappropriate Behavior Lands Beetle Bailey's General in Hot Water," *Greenville News*, November 22, 1992, p. 20D.

52. Alexandra Alger and William G. Flanagan, "Sexual Politics," *Forbes*, May 6, 1996, pp. 106–110; Gary Schweikhart, "Sexual Harassment," *Business News*, Fall 1995, pp. 30–36.

53. Brian S. Moskal, "Sexual Harassment: An Update," *Industry Week*, November 18, 1991, p. 38.

54. *Sexual Harassment Manual for Managers and Supervisors* (Chicago: Commerce Clearing House, 1992), pp. 25–26.

55. Burlington Industries vs. Ellerth (97-569) 123 F.3d 490; William H. Floyd III and Eric C. Schweitzer, "Sexual Harassment Rules Change," *South Carolina Business Journal*, August 1998, pp. 1, 8.

56. Floyd & Schweitzer, "Sexual Harassment Rules Change."

57. Nicole P. Cantey, "High Cost Rules Same Sex Harassment Is Against the Law," *South Carolina Business Journal*, April 1998, p. 3; Jack Corcoron, "Of Nice and Men," *Success*, June 1998, pp. 64–67.

58. Samuel Greengard, "Privacy: Entitlement or Illusion?" *Personnel Journal*, May 1996, p. 74.

59. Ibid., pp. 74–76.

60. Anna Wilde Matthews, "New Gadgets Trace Truckers' Every Move," *Wall Street Journal*," July 14, 1997, pp. B1, B10.

61. Samuel Greengard, "Policy Matters," *Personnel Journal*, May 1996, p. 75.

62. Greenman v. Yuba Power Products Inc., 377 P.2d 897 (1962).

63. Dennis G. Bates, "Fraud by Mail," *Modern Maturity*, April–May, 1991, p. 33.

64. Amanda Bennett, "Making the Grade with the Customer," *Wall Street Journal*, June 17, 1990, pp. Bl, B2.

65. Elyse Mall, "Make Sure That Your Customers Love You," *Your Company* (Forecast 1997), pp. 23–29.

66. Jay Finegan, "Reach Out and Teach Someone," *Inc.*, October 1990, pp. 112–124.

67. "Do Good Ethics Ensure Good Profits?" *Business & Society Review*, Fall 1990, p. 4.

68. Mark Pastin, "Ethics and Excellence," *New Management*, Spring 1987, pp. 40–43.

69. Peter Waldman and Jay Solomon, "Gold-Fraud Recipe? Bre-X Workers Saw Mine Samples Mixed," *Wall Street Journal*, May 6, 1997, pp. A1, A12; "All That Glitters Now Is the Whodunit," *Atlanta Journal/Constitution*, May 6, 1997, p. F2; Suzanne McGee and Mark Heinzl, "How Bre-X Holders Passed Warnings, Got Lost in Glitter," *Wall Street Journal*, May 16, 1997, pp. C1, C13; Rachard Behar, "Jungle Fever," *Fortune*, June 9, 1997, pp. 116–128.

70. Jeff Zygmont, "Drivers' Ed," *Sky*, November 1995, pp. 41–46.

71. "Not Business As Usual," *Business Ethics*, October 1992, p. 14.

72. "Giving Back, Big Time," *Inc.*, March 1993, p. 10.

73. William G. Shenkir, "A Perspective from Education: Business Ethics," *Management Accounting*, June 1990, p. 32.

CHAPTER 222

The Legal Environment: Business Law and Government Regulation

A verbal contract isn't worth the paper it's written on.

—Samuel Goldwyn

Most problems don't exist until a government agency is created to solve them.

—Kirk Kirkpatrick

Upon completion of this chapter, you will be able to

1 Explain the basic elements required to create a valid, enforceable contract.

2 Outline the major components of the Uniform Commercial Code governing sales contracts.

3 Discuss the protection of intellectual property rights involving patents, trademarks, and copyrights.

4 Explain the basic workings of the law of agency.

5 Explain the basics of bankruptcy law.

6 Explain some of the government regulations affecting small businesses, including those governing trade practices, consumer protection, consumer credit, and the environment.

The legal environment in which small businesses operate is becoming more complex, and entrepreneurs must understand the basics of business law if they are to avoid legal entanglements. Particularly in the United States, situations that present potential legal problems arise every day in most businesses (see Figure 22.1), although most small business owners never recognize them. Routine transactions with customers, suppliers, employees, government agencies, and others can develop into costly legal battles. For example, a manufacturer of lawnmowers might face a lawsuit if a customer injures himself while using the product. Or a customer who slips on a wet floor while shopping could sue the retailer

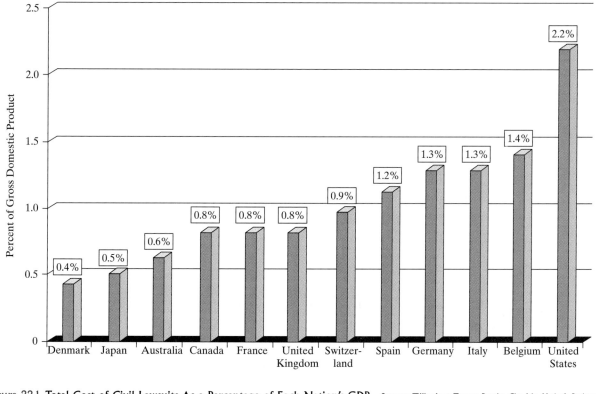

Figure 22.1 Total Cost of Civil Lawsuits As a Percentage of Each Nation's GDP SOURCE: Tillinghast-Towers Perrin. Cited in *Nation's Business,* February 1998, p. 14.

for negligence. A small manufacturer who reneges on a contract for a needed raw material when he finds a better price elsewhere may be open to a breach of contract suit. One big judgment against a small company in a legal case could force it out of business. Even when a small business wins a lawsuit, it might lose in the long run because the costs of defending itself can run quickly into tens or even hundreds of thousands of dollars. Plus, lawsuits are bothersome distractions that prevent entrepreneurs from focusing their energy on running their business. *Bruce Hoegger, owner of Remanco Hydraulics, understands the distractions lawsuits create. Recently, his company, which manufactures components for hydraulic equipment, was the target of a product liability suit. In just one three-month period, Hoegger spent 50 hours in depositions and legal meetings with attorneys. The emotional strain was more punishing than the time demands the case required, however. Throughout the case, Remanco Hydraulics faced the possibility of a large award in the plaintiff's favor, which would bankrupt both the company and Hoegger himself. After months of legal tangles, Hoegger finally settled the case for $25,000.*[1] The best way for business owners to avoid legal problems that can threaten their companies is to equip themselves with a basic understanding of the principles of business law.

This chapter is *not* designed to make you an expert in the business law or the regulations that govern business but to make you aware of the fundamental legal issues of which every business owner should be aware. Business owners should consult their attorneys for advice on legal questions involving specific situations.

The Law of Contracts

Contract law governs the rights and obligations among the parties to an agreement (contract). It is a body of laws that affects virtually every business relationship. A **contract** is simply a legally binding agreement. It is a promise or a set of promises for the breach of which the law gives a remedy and that the performance of which the law in some way recognizes as a duty. A contract arises from an agreement, and it creates an obligation among the parties involved. It is a promise to be fulfilled. Although almost everyone has the capacity to enter into a contractual agreement (freedom of contract), not every contract is valid and enforceable. A valid contract has four separate elements:

◆ *Agreement.* A valid offer by one party that is accepted by the other.

◆ *Consideration.* Something of legal value that the parties exchange as part of a bargain.

◆ *Contractual capacity.* The parties must be adults capable of understanding the consequences of their agreement.

◆ *Legality.* The parties' contract must be for a legal purpose.

In addition, a contract must meet two supplemental requirements: genuineness of assent and form. *Genuineness of assent* is a test to make sure that the parties' agreement is genuine and not subject to problems such as fraud, misrepresentation, or mistakes. *Form* involves the writing requirement for certain types of contracts. Although not every contract must be in writing to be enforceable, the law does require *some* contracts to be evidenced by a writing.

AGREEMENT

Agreement requires a "meeting of the minds" and is established by an offer and an acceptance. One party must make an offer to another party, who must accept that offer. Agreement is governed by the objective theory of contracts, which states that a party's intention to create a contract is measured by outward facts—words, conduct, and circumstances—rather than by subjective, personal intentions. In settling contract disputes, courts interpret the objective facts surrounding the contract from the perspective of an imaginary reasonable person. *For instance, Klick-Lewis, a car dealership, offered a new Chevrolet Beretta as a prize to any person who hit a hole in one on the ninth hole of a golf tournament. It displayed the car at the tee box of the ninth hole with a sign saying, "HOLE-IN-ONE Wins This 1988 Chevrolet Beretta GI Courtesy of Klick-Lewis Buick-Chevrolet-Pontiac $49.00 OVER FACTORY INVOICE in Palmyra." Amos Carbaugh was playing in the East End Open Golf Tournament and scored a hole-in-one on the ninth hole, but when he attempted to claim the prize, Klick-Lewis refused to sell him the car at $49.00 over invoice. The dealer said that it had offered the car as a prize in another golf tournament that had taken place two days earlier and that it had simply neglected to remove the car and the sign before the tournament Carbaugh was playing in. Carbaugh filed a lawsuit against Klick-Lewis and won the right to buy the car at $49.00 over invoice. The court said that, on the basis of the objective theory of contracts, an imaginary reasonable person in Carbaugh's position would have believed that the dealership was making an offer, citing the presence of the sign, the car, and no mention of a specific golf tournament. Klick-Lewis's subjective intent was irrelevant.*[2] Agreement requires that one of the parties to a contract make an offer and the other an acceptance.

Offer. An **offer** is a promise or commitment to do or refrain from doing some specified thing in the future. For an offer to stand, there must be an intention to be bound by it, reasonably certain terms, and communication of the offer. The party making the offer must genuinely intend to make an offer, and the offer's terms must be definite, not vague. The following terms must either be expressed or be capable of being implied in an offer: the parties involved, the identity of the subject matter (which goods or services), and the quantity. Other terms offerors should specify include price, delivery terms, payment terms, timing, and shipping terms. Although these elements are not required, the more terms a party specifies, the more likely it is that an offer exists.

Courts often supply missing terms in a contract when there is a reliable basis for doing so. For instance, the court usually supplies a time term that is reasonable for the circumstances. It supplies a price term (a reasonable price at the time of delivery) if a readily ascertainable market price exists; otherwise, a missing price term defeats the contract. On rare occasions, the court supplies a quantity term, but a missing quantity term usually defeats a contract. For example, the small retailer who mails an advertising circular to a large number of customers is not making an offer because one major term—quantity—is missing. Similarly, price lists and catalogs sent to potential customers are not offers.

An offer must always be communicated to the other party because one cannot agree to a contract unless she knows it exists. The offeror may communicate an offer by verbal expression, written word, or implied action.

Acceptance. Only the person to whom the offer is made (the offeree) can accept an offer and create a contract. The offeree must accept voluntarily, agreeing to the terms exactly as the offeror presents them. When the offeree suggests alternative terms or conditions, he is implicitly rejecting the original offer and making a counteroffer. Common law requires that the offeree's acceptance exactly match the offer. This is called the **mirror image rule,** which says that an offeree's acceptance must be the mirror image of the offeror's offer.

In general, silence by the offeree cannot constitute acceptance, even if the offer contains statements to the contrary. For instance, when an offeror claims, "If you do not respond to this offer by Friday at noon, I conclude your silence to be your acceptance," no acceptance exists even if the offeree does remain silent. The law requires an offeree to act affirmatively to accept an offer in most cases.

An offeree must accept an offer by the means of communication authorized by and within the time limits specified by the offeror. In general, offers accepted by alternative media or after specified deadlines are ineffective. If the offeror specifies no means of communication, the offeree must use the same medium used to extend the offer (or a faster method). According to the "mailbox rule," if an offeree accepts by mail, the acceptance is effective when the letter is dropped in the mailbox, even if it never reaches the offeror. Also, all acceptances must be properly dispatched; that is, they must be properly addressed, noted, and stamped.

CONSIDERATION

Contracts are based on promises, and because it is often difficult to distinguish between promises that are serious and those that are not, courts require that consideration be present in virtually every contract. **Consideration** is something of legal value (not necessarily economic value) that the parties to a contract bargain for and exchange as the "price" for the promise given. Consideration can be money, but parties most often swap promises for promises. For example, when a buyer promises to buy an item and a seller promises to sell it, valuable consideration exists. The buyer's promise to buy and the seller's promise to sell constitute the consideration for their contract. To constitute valuable consideration, a promise must impose a liability or create a duty.

For a contract to be binding, the two parties involved must exchange valuable consideration. The absence of consideration makes a promise not binding. A promise to perform something one is already legally obligated to do is *not* valuable consideration. Also, because consideration is what the promisor requires in exchange for his promise, it must be given after the promisor states what is required. In other words, past consideration is not valid. Also, under the common law, new promises require new consideration. For instance, if two businesspeople have an existing contract for performance of a service, any modifications to that contract must be supported by new consideration. Also, promises made in exchange for "love and affection" are not enforceable because this does not constitute valuable consideration.

One important exception to the requirement for valuable consideration is **promissory estoppel.** Under this rule, a promise that induces another party to act can be enforceable without consideration if the promisee substantially and justifiably relies on the promise. Suppose, for example, that Singleton promises to sell a franchise to Barlow if Barlow purchases a tract of land in a nearby town. Barlow sells some of her personal assets to purchase the land, but Singleton refuses to grant her the franchise. If Barlow sues Singleton on the basis of promissory estoppel, she will be awarded damages even though she gave Singleton no consideration. Thus, promissory estoppel is a substitute for consideration.

In most cases, courts do not evaluate the adequacy of consideration given for a promise. In other words, there is no legal requirement that the consideration the parties exchange be of approximately equal value. Even if the value of the consideration one party gives is small compared with the value of the bargain to the other party, the bargain stands. Why? The law recognizes that people have the freedom to contract and that they are just as free to enter into "bad" bargains as they are to enter into "good" ones. Only in extreme cases (e.g., cases affected by mistakes, misrepresentation, fraud, duress, undue influence) will the court examine the value of the consideration provided in a trade.

CONTRACTUAL CAPACITY

The third element of a valid contract requires that the parties involved in it must have contractual **capacity** for it to be enforceable. Not every individual who enters into a contract has the capacity to do so. Under the common law, minors, intoxicated people, and insane people lack contractual capacity. As a result, contracts these people enter into are considered to be voidable; that is, the party can annul or disaffirm the contract at his option.

Minors. Minors constitute the largest group of individuals without contractual capacity. In most states, anyone under age 18 is a minor, although a few states establish 19 as the age of majority. With a few exceptions, any contract make by a minor is voidable at the minor's option. In addition, a minor can void a contract during minority and for "a reasonable time" afterward. The adult involved in the contract cannot avoid it simply because he is dealing with a minor.

If a minor receives the benefit of a completed contract and then disaffirms that contract, she must fulfill her duty of restoration by returning the benefit. In other words, the minor must return any consideration she has received under the contract to the adult, and she is entitled to receive any consideration she gave the adult under the contract. The minor must return the benefit of the contract no matter what form or condition it is in. For instance, suppose that Brighton, a 16-year-old purchases a mountain bike for $415 from Cycle Time, a small bicycle shop. After riding the bike for a little more than a year, Brighton decides to disaffirm the contract. Under the law, all he must do is return the bike, whatever its condition, to Cycle Time, and he is entitled to get all of his money back. In most states, he does not have to pay Cycle Time for the use of the bike or the damage done to it. Adults enter into contracts with minors at their own risk.

Parents are usually not liable for any contracts made by their children, although a cosigner is bound equally with the minor. Small business owners can protect themselves in dealing with minors by requiring an adult to cosign. If the minor disaffirms the contract, the adult cosigner remains bound by it.

Intoxicated People. A contract entered into by an intoxicated person can be either voidable or valid, depending on the person's condition when entering into the contract. If reason and judgment are impaired so that the person does not realize a contract is being made, the contract is voidable (even if the intoxication was voluntary) and the benefit must be returned. However, if the intoxicated person understands that he is forming a contract, although it may be foolish, the contract is valid and enforceable.

Insane People. A contract entered into by an insane person can be void, voidable, or valid, depending on the mental state of the person. Those who have been judged to be so mentally incompetent that a guardian is appointed for them cannot enter into a valid contract. If such a person does make a contract, it is *void* (i.e., it does not exist). An insane person who has not been legally declared insane (e.g., someone suffering from Alzheimer's disease) or appointed a guardian is bound by a contract if he was lucid enough at the time of the contract to comprehend its consequences. On the other hand, if at the time of entering the contract, that same person was so mentally incompetent that he could not realize what was happening or could not understand the terms, the contract is voidable. Like a minor, he must return any benefit received under the contract.

LEGALITY

The final element required for a valid contract is **legality.** The purpose of the parties' contract must be legal. Because society imposes certain standards of conduct on its members, contracts that are illegal (criminal or tortious) or against public policy are void. *For instance, Valerie Coolidge, owner of Gourmet Gifts, a home-based business selling gift cakes, came up with a new idea for her product line: liqueur-flavored cakes. "I had a great recipe for rum pecan cake and thought I could sell liqueur cakes," she says. She test marketed five different kinds of liqueur cakes, which generated $1,500 in sales in just one week! With a bonfide hit product, Coolidge began making plans to make her new cakes a permanent part of*

Valerie Coolidge, owner of Gourmet Gifts, was faced with a challenge when she discovered that it was illegal in Ohio to sell liqueur cakes, one of her small company's hottest products. Today, Coolidge is still selling her cakes, but they contain only liqueur flavorings, not real liqueur.

her product line. Then she ran into a serious stumbling block: an attorney at a small business development center informed her that creating contracts to sell her cakes was illegal! In Ohio, Coolidge learned, the law prohibits adding any intoxicating substance to solids and confectionary goods and then selling them. (In fact, it's illegal to do that in all but 11 states.) Coolidge considered fighting to have the law repealed, but when she discovered that her hometown of Westerville was the home of the temperance movement of the 1800s, she figured that the odds were not in her favor. Today, Coolidge is selling cakes, but they contain only liqueur flavorings, not real liqueuer.[3]

If a contract contains both legal and illegal elements, the courts will enforce the legal parts as long as they can separate the legal portion from the illegal portion. However, in some contracts, certain clauses are so unconscionable that the courts will not enforce them. Usually, the courts do not concern themselves with the fairness and equity of a contract between parties because individuals are supposed to be intelligent. But in the case of unconscionable contracts, the terms are so harsh and oppressive to one party that the courts often rule the clause to be void. These clauses, called exculpatory clauses, frequently attempt to free one party of all responsibility and liability for an injury or damage that might occur. For instance, suppose that Miguel Sancho signs an exculpatory clause when he leaves his new BMW with the attendant at a downtown parking garage. The clause states that the garage is "not responsible for theft, loss, or damage to cars or articles left in cars due to fire, theft, or other causes." The attendant leaves Miguel's car unattended with the keys in the ignition, and a thief steals the car. A court would declare the exculpatory clause void because the garage owes a duty to its customers to exercise reasonable care to protect their property, a duty it breached because of gross negligence.

GENUINENESS OF ASSENT AND THE FORM OF CONTRACTS

A contract that contains the four elements just discussed—agreement, consideration, capacity, and legality—is *valid*, but a valid contract may still be *unenforceable* because of two possible defenses against it: genuineness of assent and form. **Genuineness of assent** serves as a check on the parties' agreement, verifying that it is genuine and not subject to mistakes, misrepresentation, fraud, duress, or undue influence. The existence of a contract can be affected by mistakes that one or both parties to the contract make. Different types of mistakes exist, but only mistakes of *fact* permit a party to avoid a contract. Suppose that a small contractor submits a bid on the construction of a bridge, but the bidder mistakenly omits the cost of some materials. The client accepts the contractor's bid because it is $12,000 below all others. If the client knew or should have known of the mistake, the contractor can avoid the contract; otherwise, he must build the bridge at the bid price.

Fraud also voids a contract because no genuineness of assent exists. **Fraud** is the intentional misrepresentation of a material fact, justifiably relied on, that results in injury to the innocent party. The misrepresentation with the intent to deceive can result from words or conduct. Suppose a small retailer purchases a new security system from a dealer who promises it will provide 20 years of reliable service and lower the cost of operation by 40 percent. The dealer knowingly installs a used, unreliable system. In this case, the dealer has committed fraud, and the retailer can either rescind the contract with his original position restored or enforce it and seek damages for injuries.

Duress, forcing an individual into a contract by fear or threat, eliminates genuineness of assent. The innocent party can choose to carry out the contract or to avoid it. For example, if a supplier forces the owner of a small video arcade to enter a contract to lease his machines by threat of personal injury, the supplier is guilty of duress. Blackmail and extortion used to induce another party to enter a contract also constitute duress.

In general, the law does not require contracts to follow a prescribed form; a contract is valid whether it is written or oral. Most contracts do *not* have to be in writing to be enforceable, but for convenience and protection, a small business owner should insist that every contract be in writing. If a contract is oral, the party attempting to enforce it must first prove its existence and then establish its actual terms. Although each state has its own set of statutes, the law generally requires the following contracts to be in writing:

- Contracts for the sale of land
- Contracts involving lesser interests in land (e.g., rights-of-way or leases lasting more than one year)
- Contracts that cannot by their terms be performed within one year
- Collateral contracts such as promises to answer for the debt or duty of another
- Promises by the administrator or executor of an estate to pay a debt of the estate personally
- Contracts for the sale of goods (as opposed to services) priced above $500

BREACH OF CONTRACT

The majority of contracts are discharged by both parties' fully performing the terms of their agreement. Occasionally, however, one party fails to perform as agreed. This failure is called **breach of contract,** and the injured party has certain remedies available. *For instance, Ronald Leek, owner of a dragstrip, entered into a contract with Randy Folk to resurface the 25-year-old raceway and to build several retaining walls required by Leek's insurance company. After Folk had completed the job, Leek refused to pay for the work, claiming that it was of poor quality and would have to be redone. At trial, several experts testified that the surface was uneven, that it contained large dips, and that it was unsafe. One race official attended a race at which the track's poor condition caused several race cars to lose control and one to crash. The court ruled that Folk had failed to perform his obligations under the contract and ruled in Leek's favor.*[4]

In general, the nonbreaching party is entitled to sue for **compensatory damages,** the monetary damages that will place him in the same position he would have been in had the contract been performed. In addition to compensatory damages, the nonbreaching party may also be awarded **consequential damages** (also called special damages) that arise as a consequence of the breach. For the nonbreaching party to recover consequential damages, the breaching party must have known the consequences of the breach. Suppose a fireworks manufacturer fails to deliver a shipment of merchandise by June 30 in anticipation of the busy July 4 holiday celebration. The retailer can sue for the profits lost because of the late delivery because the manufacturer could have foreseen the damages late delivery would cause. The injured, or nonbreaching, party does, however, have a duty to make a reasonable effort to minimize (to mitigate) the damages incurred by the breach.

In some cases, monetary damages are inadequate to compensate the injured party for the breach of contract. The only remedy that would compensate the nonbreaching party might be specific performance of the act promised in the contract. *Specific performance* is usually the remedy for breached contracts dealing with unique items (antiques, land, animals). For example, if an antique auto dealer enters a contract to purchase a Dusenberg and the other party breaches the contract, the dealer may sue for specific performance. That is, she may ask the court to order the breaching party to sell the antique car. Courts rarely invoke the remedy of specific performance. Contracts for performance of personal services generally are not subject to specific performance.

*7*he Uniform Commercial Code (UCC)

For many years, sales contracts relating to the exchange of goods were governed by a loosely defined system of rules and customs called the *Lex Mercatoria* (Merchant Law). Many of these principles were assimilated into the U.S. common law through court opinions, but they varied widely from state to state and made interstate commerce difficult and confusing for businesses. In the 1940s, a group of legal scholars compiled the **Uniform Commercial Code** (or the **UCC** or the **Code**) to replace the hodge-podge collection of confusing, often conflicting state laws that govern basic commercial transactions with a document designed to provide uniformity and consistency. The UCC <http://www.law.cornell.edu/ucc/table.html> replaced numerous statutes governing trade when 49 states, the District of Columbia, and the Virgin Islands adopted it. (Louisiana has adopted only Articles 1, 3, 4, and 5.) The Code does not alter the basic tenets of business law established by the common law; instead, it unites and modernizes them into a single body of law. In some cases, however, the Code changes some of the specific rules under the common law. The Code consists of 10 articles:

1. General Provisions
2. Sales
2A. Leases
3. Negotiable Instruments
4. Bank Deposits and Collections
5. Letters of Credit
6. Bulk Transfers
7. Documents of Title, Warehouse Receipts, Bills of Lading, and Others
8. Investment Securities
9. Secured Transactions
10. Effective Date and Repealer

This section covers some of the general principles relating to sales (UCC Article 2), but small business owners should also become familiar with the basics of the other parts of the Code. The UCC creates a "caste system" of merchants and nonmerchants and requires merchants to have a higher degree of knowledge and understanding of the Code.

SALES AND SALES CONTRACTS

Every sales contract is subject to the basic principles of law that govern all contracts: agreement, consideration, capacity, and legality. But when a contract involves the sale of goods, the UCC imposes rules that may vary slightly or substantially from basic contract law. Article 2 governs *only* contracts for the sale of goods. To be considered "goods," an item must be personal property that is tangible and movable (e.g., not real estate), and a "sale" is "the passing of title from the seller to the buyer for a price" (UCC Sec. 2-106[1]). The UCC does not cover the sale of services, although certain "mixed transactions," such as the sale by a garage of car parts (goods) and repairs (a service) will fall under the Code's jurisdiction if the goods are the dominant element of the contract.

In addition to the rules it applies to the sale of goods in general, the Code imposes special standards of conduct in certain instances when merchants sell goods to one another. Usually, a person is considered a professional **merchant** if he "deals in goods of the kind" involved in the contract and has special knowledge of the business or of the goods; employs a merchant agent to conduct a transaction for him; or holds himself out to be a merchant.

Although the UCC requires that the same elements outlined in common law be present in forming a sales contract, it relaxes many of the specific restrictions. For example, the UCC states that a contract exists even if the parties omit one or more terms (price, delivery date, place of delivery, quantity), as long as they intended to make a contract and there is a reasonably certain method for the court to supply the missing terms. For example, suppose a manufacturer orders a shipment of needed raw materials from her usual supplier without asking the price. When the order arrives, the price is substantially higher than she expected, and she attempts to disaffirm the contract. The Code verifies the existence of a contract and assigns to the shipment a price that was reasonable at the time of delivery.

Common law requires that acceptance of an offer to be exactly the same as the offer; an acceptance that adds some slight modification is no acceptance at all, and no contract exists. Any modification constitutes a counteroffer. But the UCC states that as long as an offeree's response (words, writing, or actions) indicates a sincere willingness to accept the offer, it is judged as a legitimate acceptance even though varying terms are added. In dealings between buyers and sellers, these added terms become "proposals for addition." Between merchants, however, these additional proposals *automatically* become part of the contract unless they materially alter the original contract, the offer expressly states that no terms other than those in the offer will be accepted, or the offeror has already objected to the particular terms. Unless the offeror objects to the added terms, they *will* become part of the contract. For example, suppose an appliance wholesaler offers to sell a retailer a shipment of appliances for $5,000 plus freight. The retailer responds with acceptance but adds "Price is $5,100 including freight." A contract exists, and the addition will become part of the contract unless the wholesaler objects within a reasonable time. If the wholesaler objects, a contract still exists, but it is formed on the wholesaler's original terms of $5,000 plus freight.

The UCC significantly changes the common law requirement that any contract modification requires new consideration. Under the Code, modifications to contract terms are binding without new consideration if they are made in good faith. For example, suppose a small building contractor forms a contract to purchase a supply of lumber for $1,200. After the agreement but before the lumber is delivered, a hurricane forces the price of the lumber to double, and the supplier notifies the contractor that he must raise the price of the lumber shipment to $2,400. The contractor reluctantly agrees to the additional cost but later refuses to pay. According to UCC, the contractor is bound by the modification because no new consideration is required.

The Code also has its own Statute of Frauds provision relating to the form of contracts for the sale of goods. If the price of the goods is $500 or more, the contract must be written to be enforceable. Of course, the parties can agree orally and then follow it with a written memorandum. The Code does not require both parties to sign the written agreement, but it must be signed by the party against whom enforcement is sought (which is impossible to tell before a dispute arises, so it's a good idea for both parties to sign the agreement).

The UCC includes a special provision involving the writing requirement in contracts between merchants. If merchants form a verbal contract for the sale of goods priced at more than $500 and one of them sends a written confirmation of the deal to the other, the merchant receiving the confirmation must object to it *in writing* within 10 days. Otherwise, the contract is enforceable against *both* merchants, even though the merchant receiving the confirmation has not actually signed anything.

Once the parties create a sales contract, they are bound to perform according to its terms. Both the buyer and the seller have certain duties and obligations under the contract. In general, the Code assigns the obligations of "good faith" (defined as "honesty in fact in the conduct or transaction concerned") and "commercial reasonableness" (commercial standards of fair dealing) to both parties.

The seller must make delivery of the items involved in the contract, but "delivery" is not necessarily physical delivery. The seller simply must make the goods available to the buyer. The contract normally outlines the specific details of the delivery, but occasionally the parties omit this provision. In this instance, the place of delivery will be the seller's place of business, if one exists; otherwise, it is the seller's residence. If both parties know the usual location of the identified goods, that is the place of delivery (e.g., a warehouse). In addition, the seller must make the goods available to the buyer at a reasonable time and in a reasonable manner, and the buyer must give the seller proper notice of the goods' availability. Unless otherwise noted, all goods covered in the contract must be tendered in one delivery.

The buyer must accept the delivery of conforming goods from the seller. Of course, the buyer has the right to inspect the goods in a reasonable manner and at any reasonable time or place to ensure that they are conforming goods before making payment. However, C.O.D. terms prohibit the right to advance inspection unless the contract specifies otherwise. Under the perfect tender rule in Section 2-601 of the Code, "if goods or tender of delivery fail, in any respect, to conform to the contract," the buyer is not required to accept them.

The buyer can indicate his acceptance of the goods in several ways. Usually the buyer indicates acceptance by an express statement that the goods are suitable. This expression can be by words or by conduct. For example, suppose a small electrical contractor orders a truck to use in the business. When she receives it, she equips it to suit her trade, including a company decal on each door. Later the contractor attempts to reject the truck and return it. Clearly, the buyer has acted inconsistently with continued ownership by the seller, and this constitutes acceptance of the truck. Also, the Code assumes acceptance if the buyer has a reasonable opportunity to inspect the goods and has failed to reject them within a reasonable time.

The buyer has the duty to pay for the goods on the terms stated in the contract when they are received. The seller cannot require payment before the buyer receives the goods. Unless otherwise stated in the contract, payment must be in cash.

BREACH OF SALES CONTRACTS

As we have seen, when a party to the sales contract fails to perform according to its terms, that party is said to have breached the contract. The law provides the innocent (nonbreaching) party numerous remedies, including payment of damages and the right to retain possession of the goods. The object of these remedies is to place the innocent party in the same position as if the contract had been carried out. The parties to the contract may specify their own damages in case of breach. These provisions, called **liquidated damages,** must be reasonable and cannot be in the nature of a penalty. For example, suppose that Alana Mitchell contracts with a local carpenter to build a booth from which she plans to sell crafts. The parties agree that if the booth is not completed by September 1, Mitchell will receive $500. If the liquidated damages had been $50,000, they would be unenforceable because such a large amount of money is clearly a penalty.

An unpaid seller has certain remedies available under the terms of the Code. Under a seller's lien, every seller has the right to maintain possession of the goods until the buyer pays for them. In addition, if the buyer uses a fraudulent payment to obtain the goods, the seller has the right to recover them. If the seller discovers the buyer is insolvent, the seller can withhold delivery of the goods until the buyer pays in cash. If goods are shipped to an insolvent buyer, the seller can require their return within 10 days after receipt. In some cases, the buyer breaches a contract while the goods are still unfinished in the production process. When this occurs, the seller must use "reasonable commercial judgment" in deciding whether to sell them for scrap or complete them and resell them elsewhere. In either case, the buyer is liable for any loss the seller incurs. Of course, the seller has the right to withhold performance when the buyer breaches the sales contract.

When the seller breaches a contract, the buyer also has specific remedies available. For instance, if the goods do not conform to the contract's terms, the buyer has the right to reject them. Or, if the seller fails to deliver the goods, the buyer can sue for the difference between the contract price and the market price at the time the breach became known. When the buyer accepts goods and then discovers they are defective or nonconforming, he must notify the seller of the breach. In this instance, damages amount to the difference between the value of the goods delivered and their value if they had been delivered as promised. If a buyer pays for goods that the seller retains, he can take possession of the goods if the seller becomes insolvent within 10 days after receiving the first payment. If the seller unlawfully withholds the goods from the buyer, the buyer can recover them. Under certain circumstances, a buyer can obtain specific performance of a sales contract; that is, the court orders the seller to perform according to the contract's terms. As mentioned earlier, specific performance is a remedy only when the goods involved are unique or unavailable on the market. Finally, if the seller breaches the contract, the buyer has the right to rescind the contract; if the buyer has paid any part of the purchase price, it must be refunded.

Whenever a party breaches a sales contract, the innocent party must bring suit within a specified period of time. The Code sets the statute of limitations at four years. In other words, any action for a breach of a sales contract must begin within four years after the breach occurred.

SALES WARRANTIES AND PRODUCT LIABILITY

The U.S. economy once promulgated the philosophy of caveat emptor, "let the buyer beware," but today the marketplace enforces a policy of caveat venditor, "let the seller beware." Small business owners must be aware of two general categories involving the quality and reliability of the products sold: sale warranties and product liability.

Sales Warranties. Simply stated, a **sales warranty** is a promise or a statement of fact by the seller that a product will meet certain standards. Because a breach of warranty is a breach of promise, the buyer has the right to recover damages from the seller. Several types of warranties can arise in a sale. A seller creates an **express warranty** by making statements about the condition, quality, and performance of the good that the buyer substantially relies on. Express warranties can be created by words or actions. For example, a vendor selling a shipment of cloth to a customer with the promise that "it will not shrink" clearly is creating an express warranty. Similarly, the jeweler who displays a watch in a glass of water for promotional purposes creates an express warranty that "this watch is waterproof" even though no such promise is ever spoken. An express warranty generally arises if the seller indicates that the goods conform to any promises of fact the seller makes, to any description of them (e.g., printed on the package or statements of fact made by salespersons), or to any display model or sample (e.g., a floor model used as a demonstrator).

Whenever someone sells goods, the UCC automatically infers certain types of warranties unless the seller specifically excludes them. These **implied warranties** take several forms. Every seller, simply by offering goods for sale, implies a **warranty of title,** which promises that his title to the goods is valid (i.e., no liens or claims exist) and that transfer of title is legitimate. A seller can disclaim a warranty of title only by using very specific language in a sales contract.

An implied warranty of merchantability applies to every merchant seller, and the only way to disclaim it is by mentioning the term "warranty of merchantability" in a conspicuous manner. An **implied warranty of merchantability** assures the buyer that the product will be of average quality—not the best and not the worst. In other words, merchantable goods are "fit for the ordinary purposes for which such goods are used" (UCC Sec. 2-314[1-C]). For example, a refrigeration unit that a small food store purchases should keep food cold.

Webster, a long-time New England resident, ordered a bowl of fish chowder at the Blue Ship Tea Room, a Boston restaurant that overlooked the ocean. After eating three or four spoonfuls, Webster felt something caught in her throat. It turned out to be a fish bone that was in the bowl of chowder she had ordered. Webster had to undergo two surgical procedures to remove the bone from her throat, and she filed a lawsuit against the restaurant, claiming that it had breached the implied warranty of merchantability. The Supreme Court of Massachusetts ruled in favor of the Blue Ship Tea Room, stating that "the occasional presence of [fish bones] in chowders is . . . to be anticipated and . . . [does] not impair their fitness or merchantability." Because the fish bone in the fish chowder was not a foreign object, but one that a person could reasonably expect to find in chowders on occasion, the court decided that the restaurant had not breached a warranty of merchantability.[5]

An **implied warranty of fitness for a particular purpose** arises when a seller knows the particular reason for which a buyer is purchasing a product and knows that the buyer is depending on the seller's judgment to select the proper item. For example, suppose a customer enters a small hardware store requesting a chemical to kill poison ivy. The owner hands over a gallon of chemical, but it fails to kill the weed; the owner has violated the warranty of fitness for a particular purpose.

The Code also states that the only way a merchant can disclaim an implied warranty is to include the words "sold as is" or "with all faults," stating that the buyer purchases the product as it is, without any guarantees. The following statement is usually sufficient to disclaim most warranties, both express and implied: "Seller hereby disclaims all warranties, express and implied, including all warranties of merchantability and all warranties of fitness for a particular purpose." Such statements must be printed in bold letters and placed in a conspicuous place on the product or its package.

Product Liability. At one time, only the parties directly involved in the execution of a contract were bound by the law of sales warranties. Today, the UCC and the states have expanded the scope of warranties to include any person (including bystanders) incurring personal or property damages caused by a faulty product. In addition, most states allow an injured party to sue any seller in the chain of distribution for breach of warranty. A company that might shoulder just a small percentage of the responsibility for a person's injury may end up bearing the majority of the damage award in the case. Courts have awarded billions of dollars to consumers who incurred loss or injury from products that broke, were improperly designed, were improperly inspected, were incorrectly labeled, contained faulty instructions, or had other dangerous faults. The average size of jury verdicts in product liability cases is $773,500.[6]

Although 70 percent of the products made and sold in the United States cross state lines, each of the 50 states has its own version of product liability laws, complicating matters for businesses.[7] Fortunately for businesses, less than 5 percent of product-related injuries result in some type of claim for compensation.[8] A common basis of recovery for those who do file claims is **negligence,** when a manufacturer or distributor fails to do something that a "reasonable" person would do. Typically, negligence claims arise from one or more of the following charges.[9]

Negligent design. In claims based on negligent design, a buyer claims an injury occurred because the manufacturer designed the product improperly. To avoid liability charges, a company does not have to design products that are 100 percent safe, but it must design products that are free of "unreasonable" risks.

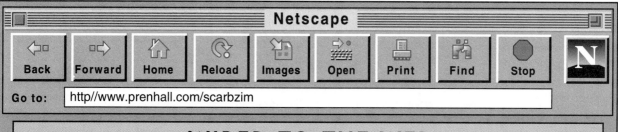

WIRED TO THE WEB

HE BIT OFF MORE THAN HE COULD CHEW

*O*n October 28, 1983, Fred Goodman and a friend stopped to get lunch at a Wendy's restaurant in Hillsborough, North Carolina. Goodman purchased a double hamburger sandwich with "everything" on it. According to his testimony, after eating about half of the sandwich, he bit into a hard substance and immediately felt a sharp pain shoot through his lower jaw. He took from his mouth a triangular bone, one and a half inches long, one-sixteenth to one-quarter inch thick, and one-quarter inch wide. Goodman also discovered that biting into the bone had caused him to break three of his teeth. Over the next several months, he had to spend a large amount of money for root canal surgery, temporary and permanent crowns, and tooth extraction.

The restaurant purchased its beef from Greensboro Meat Supply Company (GMSC). Wendy's policy manuals require its beef to be chopped and "free from bone or cartilage in excess of one-eighth of an inch in any dimension." The U.S. Department of Agriculture (USDA) had certified GMSC's processing plant, which was also inspected regularly by state inspectors. The USDA considered any bone fragment less than three-quarters of an inch long to be "insignificant."

Goodman sued Wendy's, claiming breach of an implied warranty of merchantability. Wendy's argued that it should not be held liable because the object that injured Goodman was not a foreign object but was "natural" to the food.

Use the resources of the World Wide Web* and your local library to answer the following questions:

1. Did the hamburger Goodman ate violate the implied warranty of merchantability under the Uniform Commercial Code? Explain.
2. What standards do the courts use to determine whether food complies with the requirements of an implied warranty of fitness for a particular purpose?
3. Is it reasonable to expect that every hamburger served will be "perfect"? What implications does your answer have on the outcome of this case?

* Try these Web sites to gather information about this case:
http://www.phlip.marist.edu/contemcheese/index.htm
http://www.nolo.com/dictionary/Dictionary_alpha.cfm?wordnumber=211&Alpha=I
http://www.lectlaw.com/files/cos53

SOURCE: Goodman v. Wenco Foods, Inc., 1423 S.E.2d 444 (1992).

Negligent Manufacturing. In cases claiming negligent manufacturing, a buyer claims that a company's failure to follow proper manufacturing, assembly, or inspection procedures allowed a defective product to get into the customer's hands and cause injury. A company must exercise "due care" (including design, assembly, and inspection) to make its products safe when they are used for their intended purpose.

Failure to Warn. Although manufacturers do not have to warn customers about obvious dangers of using their products, they must warn them about the dangers of normal use and of foreseeable misuse of the product. (Have you ever read the warning label on a stepladder?) Many businesses hire attorneys to write the warning labels they attach to their products and include in their instructions.

Another common basis for product liability claims against businesses is **strict liability,** which states that a manufacturer is accountable for its actions no matter what its intentions or the extent of its negligence. Unlike negligence, a claim of strict liability does not require the injured party to prove that the company's actions were unreasonable. The injured person must prove only that the company manufactured or sold a product that was defective and that it caused the injury. For instance, suppose the head of an axe flies off its handle, injuring the user. To sue the manufacturer under strict liability, the customer must prove that the defendant sold the axes, the axe was unreasonably dangerous to the customer because it was defective, the customer incurred physical harm to person or to property, and the defective axe was the proximate cause of the injury or damage. If these allegations are true, the axe manufacturer's liability is virtually unlimited.[10]

Business owners also have a duty to warn customers of physical dangers on their property under the doctrine of premises liability.[11] This duty to warn encompasses hazards such as wet floors, icy sidewalks, and broken pavement that might cause physical injuries to customers. Business owners have a duty to protect the public from harm while people are on their property; failing to do so imposes a potentially damaging liability on the business. For instance, a customer who slipped and fell on a wet floor in a retail store won an award of several thousand dollars because the store owner knew about the leaky roof that led to her fall but had failed to repair it or to warn customers of the hazard. Entrepreneurs can minimize potential problems under premises liability by maintaining their property and by notifying customers of potential dangers.

$\mathcal{P}$rotection of Intellectual Property

3 Discuss the protection of intellectual property involving patents, trademarks, and copyrights.

Entrepreneurs excel at coming up with innovative ideas for products and services. Many entrepreneurs build businesses around **intellectual property,** products and services that are the result of the creative process and have commercial value. New methods of teaching foreign languages at an accelerated pace, hit songs, books that bring a smile, and new drugs that fight diseases are just some of the ways intellectual property makes our lives better or more enjoyable. Entrepreneurs can protect their intellectual property from unauthorized use with the help of three important tools: patents, trademarks, and copyrights.

PATENTS

A **patent** is a grant from the federal government's Patent and Trademark Office (PTO) to the inventor of a product, giving the exclusive right to make, use, or sell the invention in this country for 20 years from the date of filing the patent application. The purpose of giving an inventor a 20-year monopoly over a product is to stimulate creativity and innovation. After 20 years, the patent expires and cannot be renewed. Most patents are granted for new product inventions, but design patents, extending for 14 years beyond the date the patent is issued, are given to inventors who make new, original, and ornamental changes in the design of existing products that enhance their sales. Inventors who develop a new plant can obtain a **plant patent,** provided they can reproduce the plant asexually (e.g., by grafting or cross-breeding rather than planting seeds). To be patented, a device must be new (but not necessarily better!), not obvious to a person of ordinary skill or knowledge in the related field, and useful. A device *cannot* be patented if it has been publicized in print anywhere in the world or if it has been used or offered for sale in this country before the date of the patent application. A U.S. patent is granted only to the true inventor, not to a person who discovers another's invention. No one can copy or sell a patented invention without getting a license from its creator. A patent does not give one the right to make, use, or sell an invention but the right to exclude others from making, using, or selling it.

Although inventors are never assured of getting a patent, they can enhance their chances considerably by following the basic steps suggested by the PTO. Before beginning the often lengthy and involved procedure, inventors should obtain professional assistance from a patent practitioner—a patent attorney or a patent agent—who is registered with the PTO. Only those attorneys and agents who are officially registered may represent an inventor seeking a patent. Approximately 98 percent of all inventors rely on these patent experts to steer them through the convoluted process.[12] A list of PTO-approved patent attorneys and agents is available at the U.S. Patent and Trademark Office's web site <http://www.uspto.gov/web/offices/dcom/olia/oed/roster/>.

The Patent Process. Since George Washington signed the first patent law in 1790, the U.S. Patent and Trademark Office has issued patents on everything imaginable (and some unimaginable items, too), including mouse traps (of course!), animals (genetically engineered mice), games, and various fishing devices. To date the PTO has issued more than 60 million patents, and it receives more than 230,000 new applications each year![13] To receive a patent, an inventor must follow these steps:

Establish the invention's novelty. An invention is not patentable if it is known or has been used in the United States or has been described in a printed publication in this or a foreign country.

Document the device. To protect his patent claim, the inventor should be able to verify the date on which he first conceived the idea for the invention. Inventors can document a device by keeping dated records (including drawings) of their progress on the invention and by having knowledgeable friends witness these records. Inventors also can file a disclosure document with the PTO: a process that includes writing a letter describing the invention and sending a check for $10 to the PTO.

Search existing patents. To verify that the invention truly is new, nonobvious, and useful, inventors must conduct a search of existing patents on similar products. The purpose of the search is to determine whether the inventor has a chance of getting a patent. Most inventors hire professionals trained in conducting patent searches to perform the research. Entrepreneurs can conduct an on-line search of all patents granted by the U.S. Patent and Trademark Office since 1976 from the PTO's Web site at <http://www.uspto.gov/>. An on-line search of those patents does not include sketches; however, inventors can access patents as far back as 1971, including sketches, at the IBM Patent Server web site <http://www.ibm.com/patent>.[14]

Study search results. Once the patent search is finished, inventors must study the results to determine their chances of getting a patent. To be patentable, a device must be sufficiently different from what has been used or described before and must not be obvious to a person having ordinary skill in the area of technology related to the invention.

Submit the patent application. If an inventor decides to seek a patent, he must file an application describing the invention with the PTO. Most inventors hire patent attorneys or agents to help them complete their patent applications. Two useful resources available from the Superintendent of Documents in Washington, D.C., are the *Official Gazette of the United States Patent and Trademark Office* and the *Directory of Registered Patent Attorneys and Agents.*

Prosecute the patent application. Before the PTO will issue a patent, one of its examiners studies the application to determine whether the invention warrants a patent. Approval of a patent normally takes about two years from the date of the filing.[15] If the PTO rejects the application, the inventor can amend his application so that the PTO can accept it.

IN THE FOOTSTEPS OF AN ENTREPRENEUR

A Worthwhile Patent Battle

*R*obert Kearns is an inventor with determination—*real* determination. What else could possibly explain his decision to sue *all* of the world's major car manufacturers? In his lawsuit, Kearns claimed that the automakers owed him millions of dollars in royalties for using his invention on millions of cars without his permission.

Kearns invented the intermittent windshield wiper, the stop-and-go system ideally suited for those damp, slightly misty days. His claim was that Ford Motor Company and then other car makers infringed on his patent. The idea for intermittent wipers had its origins in a most unusual place: Kearns's honeymoon suite on his wedding night. As he opened a bottle of champagne, the cork popped out, striking him in the eye and causing permanent damage. Several years later, while searching for a dissertation topic, Kearns, because of his injury, focused his attention on how his eyes worked: specifically, how his eyes were cleaned whenever he blinked. Why not develop windshield wipers that "blink"? he thought.

Kearns began to tinker. He had a working knowledge of transistors and an experimental car: his family's 1962 Ford Galaxy convertible. He had access to a supply of windshield wiper motors through his brother, who worked in Ford's research labs. By October 1963, Kearns had a working prototype of his blinking wipers mounted on his Galaxy. The device suffered a few bugs, however. When the box housing the circuits got hot, for example, the wipers would switch themselves on, rain or not. While he worked to perfect his invention, he contacted two engineers at Ford to see if they were interested. They were, and thus began a six-year relationship between Kearns and Ford. The engineers at Ford were trying to develop a similar product, but they quickly recognized that Kearn's electronically based system was far superior to the mechanical one they had been working on. As soon as he had his wipers working smoothly, Kearns took out the first of several patents on his product.

From 1966 to 1969, Kearns worked closely with engineers at Ford, teaching them how his system worked. In 1969, Ford introduced its own intermittent wiper system that incorporated many of Kearns's ideas and designs. Kearns was stunned. When he questioned Ford officials, however, they contended that the design was their own and that Kearns's patents were not valid because they were based on common knowledge. Kearns soon saw every major automaker develop intermittent wiper systems that used his ideas.

In 1978, Kearns began filing patent infringement lawsuits against every major automaker in the world, starting with Ford. Finally, in 1990, a court ruled that Kearns's patent was valid and that Ford had infringed on it. Kearns and Ford settled out of court for $10.2 million. Shortly afterward, he won $11.3 million from Chrysler in a similar suit. After decades of legal battles, Kearns has collected more than $30 million from automakers for infringing on his patent.

Use the information in this chapter and on the U.S. Patent and Trademark Office's Web site at <http://www.uspto.gov/> to answer the following questions:

1. What is a patent? What purpose does a patent serve?
2. What did Kearns have to prove to the U.S. Patent and Trademark Office to receive a patent for his intermittent wiper system?
3. Is it ethical for an inventor to be able to receive a patent—and therefore a monopoly—on an invention? Explain.

SOURCES: Adapted from Mike Hofman, "Patent Pending," *Inc.*, December 1997, pp. 97–114; Joseph B. White, "Patent Injustice," *Wall Street Journal*, April 6, 1990, pp. A1, A14; "Intermittent Wiper Inventor Wins Suit," *Greenville News*, June 12, 1992, p. 10D. ◆

Defending a patent against "copycat producers" can be expensive and time-consuming but often is necessary to protect an entrepreneur's interest. The average cost of a patent infringement lawsuit is about $600,000 if the case goes to trial (about half that if the parties settle before going to trial), but the odds of winning are in the patent holder's favor. More than 60 percent of those holding patents win their infringement suits.[16] *Knockoffs of its famous "Big Bertha" golf club have kept Callaway Golf Company busy defending its patents against counterfeiters. The company recently discovered a company making a look-alike driver called the "Big Bursa." Experts estimate that in some cases, the knockoffs, with their steeply discounted prices, actually outsell the original clubs!*[17]

TRADEMARKS

A **trademark** is any distinctive word, phrase, symbol, design, name, logo, slogan, or trade dress that a company uses to identify the origin of a product or to distinguish it from other goods on the market. (A **service mark** is the same as a trademark except that it identifies and distinguishes the source of a service rather than a product.) A trademark serves as a company's "signature" in the marketplace. A trademark can be more than just a company's logo, slogan, or brand name; it can also include symbols, shapes, colors, smells, or sounds. For instance, CocaCola holds a trademark on the shape of its bottle, and NBC owns a trademark on its three-toned chime. Motorcycle maker Harley-Davidson has applied for trademark protection for the shape of its oil tanks and the throaty rumbling sound its engines make![18] Components of a product's identity such as these are part of its **trade dress,** the unique combination of elements that a company uses to create a product's image and to promote it. For instance, a Mexican restaurant chain's particular decor, color schemes, design, and overall "look and feel" would be its trade dress. To be eligible for trademark protection, trade dress must be inherently unique and distinctive to a company, and another company's use of that trade dress must be likely to confuse customers. *Entrepreneur Sandy Lerner, co-founder of Urban Decay, a small cosmetics company, is locked in a battle with cosmetic industry giant Revlon over trade dress issues. Fledgling Urban Decay, launched in late 1995, introduced a hot-selling line of cosmetics with names such as "Rust," "Shattered," "Frostbite," "Pallor," and "Roach." Less than a year later, Revlon came out with its own line of similar products using the name "Street Wear." Lerner contends that Revlon's Street Wear name, its packaging, silver-and-black lettering, and design infringe upon Urban Decay's trade dress. Lerner and Urban Decay filed a lawsuit asking for damages because she says the similarities will confuse her customers and harm her company's sales.*[19]

There are 1.5 million trademarks registered in the United States, 900,000 of which are in actual use. Federal law permits a manufacturer to register a trademark, which prevents other companies from employing a similar mark to identify their goods. Before 1989, a business could not reserve a trademark in advance of use. Today, the first party who either uses a trademark in commerce or files an application with the PTO has the ultimate right to register that trademark. Unlike patents and copyrights, which are issued for limited amounts of time, trademarks last indefinitely as long as the holder continues to use it. However, a trademark cannot keep competitors from producing the same product and selling it under a different name. It merely prevents others from using the same or a confusingly similar trademark for the same or similar products.

Many business owners are confused by the use of the symbols ™ and ®. Anyone who claims the right to a particular trademark (or servicemark) can use the ™ (or SM) symbols without having to register the mark with the PTO. The claim to that trademark or servicemark may or may not be valid, however. Only those businesses that have registered their marks with the PTO can use the ® symbol. Entrepreneurs do not have to register trademarks or servicemarks to establish their rights to those marks; however, registering a mark with the PTO does give entrepreneurs greater power in protecting their marks. Filing an application to register a trademark or servicemark is relatively easy, but it does require a search of existing names. *Nancy Ganz, founder of Bodyslimmers® By Nancy Ganz,™ registered the name she gave her hip-shaping undergarment, Hipslip®, with the PTO as soon as she coined the name. With her company's sales now exceeding $10 million, Ganz has successfully defended her trademark against several competitors who unlawfully sold similar products using the Hipslip name. "Shielding your trademarks isn't hard," she says. "If you let things slide long enough, you could learn the hard way how much it costs to have your name taken in vain."*[20]

An owner may lose the exclusive right to a trademark if it loses its unique character and becomes a generic name. Aspirin, escalator, thermos, brassiere, super glue, yo-yo, and cellophane all were once enforceable trademarks that have become common words in the English language. Such generic terms can no longer be licensed as a company's trademark.

Nancy Ganz, founder of Bodyslimmers® Nancy Ganz™, registered her product name with the U.S. Patent and Trademark Office as soon as she coined it. She has used that protection to defend her trademark successfully.

COPYRIGHTS

A **copyright** is an exclusive right that protects the creators of original works of authorship such as literary, dramatic, musical, and artistic works (e.g., paintings, sculptures, literature, software, music, videos, video games, choreography, motion pictures, recordings, and others). The internationally recognized symbol © denotes a copyrighted work. A copyright protects only the form in which an idea is expressed, not the idea itself. A copyright on a creative work comes into existence the moment its creator puts that work into a tangible form. Just as with a trademark, obtaining basic copyright protection does not require registering the creative work with the U.S. Copyright Office <http://lcweb.loc.gov/copyright>.

Registering a copyright does give creators greater protection over their work, however. Copyright applications must be filed with the Copyright Office in the Library of Congress for a fee of $10 per application. A valid copyright on a work lasts for the life of the creator plus 50 years after her death. (A copyright lasts 75 to 100 years if the copyright holder is a business.) When a copyright expires, the work becomes public property and can be used by anyone free of charge.

Because they are so easy to duplicate, computer software programs and videotapes are among the most-often pirated items by copyright infringers. Experts estimate that the U.S. software industry loses $15 billion each year to pirates who illegally copy programs and that Hollywood loses $2 billion to those who forge videotapes and sell them. *Autodesk Inc, the maker of the popular computer-aided-design program AutoCad, recently received a call at its help desk from a group of engineers who couldn't get the software to run on their computers. When asked for a registration number, the engineers couldn't provide one because they had purchased a pirated version of the $3,750 software package "on the street" for $150. Yet, they presumed they were still entitled to software support from Autodesk! The company estimates that for every legitimate version of its program in use, there is a pirated copy working on someone's computer. Movie makers fare no better. In one New York City raid of a video warehouse, police confiscated $500,000 worth of tapes, including many titles that had not yet been released in movie theaters, on their way to dishonest rental stores.*[21]

PROTECTING INTELLECTUAL PROPERTY

Acquiring the protection of patents, trademarks, and copyrights is useless unless an entrepreneur takes action to protect those rights in the marketplace. Unfortunately, not every businessperson respects others' rights of ownership to products, processes, names, and works. Some businesspeople deliberately infringe on those rights; in other cases, the infringing behavior simply is the result of a lack of knowledge about others' rights of ownership. The primary weapon an entrepreneur has to protect patents, trademarks, and copyrights is the legal system. The major problem with relying on the legal system to enforce ownership rights is the cost of infringement lawsuits, which can quickly exceed the budget of most small businesses.

If an entrepreneur has a valid patent, trademark, or copyright, stopping an infringer often requires nothing more than a stern letter from an attorney threatening a lawsuit. Often, offenders don't want to get into expensive legal battles and agree to stop their illegal behavior. If that tactic fails, the entrepreneur may have no choice but to bring an infringement lawsuit.

Legal battles always involve costs. Before bringing a lawsuit, an entrepreneur must consider the following issues:

◆ Can the opponent afford to pay if you win?

◆ Do you expect to get enough from the suit to cover the costs of hiring an attorney and preparing a case?

◆ Can you afford the loss of time, money, and privacy from the ensuing lawsuit?

The Law of Agency

An **agent** is one who stands in the place of and represents another (the principal) in business dealings. Although he has the power to act for the principal, an agent remains subject to the principal's control. Many small business managers do not realize that their employees are agents while performing job-related tasks, but the employer is liable only for those acts that employees perform within the scope of employment. For example, if an employee loses control of a flower shop's delivery truck while making a delivery and crashes into several parked cars, the owner of the flower shop (the principal) and the employee (the agent) are liable for any damages caused by the crash. Even if the accident occurred while the employee was on a small detour of his own (e.g., to stop by his house), the owner is still liable for damages as long as the employee is "within the scope of his employment." Normally, an employee is considered to be within the scope of his employment if he is motivated in part by the principal's action and if the place and time for performing the act is not significantly different from what is authorized.

Any person, even those lacking contractual capacity, can serve as an agent, but a principal must have the legal capacity to create contracts. Both the principal and the agent are bound by the requirements of a fiduciary relationship, one characterized by trust and good faith. In addition, each party has specific duties to the other. An agent's duties include the following:

◆ *Loyalty.* Every agent must be faithful to the principal in all business dealings.

◆ *Performance.* An agent must perform his duties according to the principal's instructions.

◆ *Notification.* The agent must notify the principal of all facts and information concerning the subject matter of the agency.

◆ *Duty of care.* An agent must act with reasonable care when performing duties for the principal.

◆ *Accounting.* An agent is responsible for accounting for all profits and property received or distributed on the principal's behalf.

A principal's duties include the following:

◆ *Compensation.* Unless a free agency is created, the principal must pay the agent for her services.

◆ *Reimbursement.* The principal must reimburse the agent for all payments made for the principal or any expenses incurred in the administration of the agency.

◆ *Cooperation.* Every principal has the duty to indemnify the agent for any authorized payments or any loss or damages incurred by the agency, unless the liability is the result of the agent's mistake.

◆ *Safe working conditions.* The law requires a principal to provide a safe working environment for all agents. Workers' compensation laws cover an employer's liability for injuries agents receive on the job.

As agents, employees can bind a company to agreements, even if the owner did not intend for them to do so. An employee can create a binding obligation, for instance, if the business owner represents her as authorized to perform such transactions. As an example, the owner of a flower shop who routinely permits a clerk to place orders with suppliers has given that employee *apparent authority* for purchasing. Similarly, employees have *implied authority* to create agreements when performing the normal duties of their jobs. For example, the chief financial officer of a company has the authority to create binding agreements when dealing with the company's bank.

When an agent achieves the specific purpose of the agency, the agency ends, and the principal no longer binds the agent. For example, if the agent's task is to purchase a supply of pork bellies, the agency terminates when the agent completes the transaction. In addition, the two parties can limit the existence of the agency, or they can cancel the agency by mutual agreement. If either the principal or the agent dies or becomes mentally incompetent, the agency terminates immediately. Only when the two parties have terminated the agency themselves must the principal notify any third parties who might know of the agency relationship.

*B*ankruptcy

5 Explain the basics of bankruptcy law.

Bankruptcy occurs when a business is unable to pay its debts as they come due. Early bankruptcy laws were aimed at forcing debtors into court, where they were required to give their property to their creditors. Taking debtors to court prevented them from hiding assets from creditors and escaping repayment of debts. But in 1978 Congress passed the Bankruptcy Reform Act, drastically changing the nature of bankruptcy law. The law has removed much of the stigma from being bankrupt; in fact, a bankrupt person is now called a debtor.

Filing for bankruptcy, which was once akin to contracting a social disease, is becoming an accepted business strategy. Many of those filing for bankruptcy are small business owners seeking protection from creditors under one of the eight chapters of the Bankruptcy Reform Act of 1978. Under the act, three chapters (7, 11, and 13) govern the majority of bankruptcies related to small business ownership.[22] Usually, small business owners in danger of failing can choose from two types of bankruptcies: **liquidation** (once the owner files for bankruptcy, the business ceases to exist) and **reorganization** (after filing for bankruptcy, the owner formulates a reorganization plan under which the business continues to operate).

CHAPTER 7: LIQUIDATIONS

The most common type of bankruptcy is filed under Chapter 7 (called **straight bankruptcy**), which accounts for 70 percent of all filings. Under Chapter 7, a debtor simply declares all of his firm's debts; he must then turn over all assets to a trustee, who is elected by the creditors or appointed by the court. The trustee sells the assets and distributes all proceeds first to secured creditors and then to unsecured creditors (which include stockholders). Depending on the outcome of the asset sale, creditors can receive anywhere between 0 and 100 percent of their claims against the bankrupt company. Once the bankruptcy proceeding is complete, any remaining debts are discharged and the company disappears.

Straight bankruptcy proceedings can be started by filing either a voluntary or an involuntary petition. A voluntary case starts when the debtor files a petition with a bankruptcy court, stating the names and addresses of all creditors, the debtor's financial position, and all property the debtor owns. On the other hand, creditors start an involuntary petition by filing with the bankruptcy court. If there are 12 or more creditors, at least three of them whose unsecured claims total $10,000 or more must file the involuntary petition. If a debtor has fewer than 12 creditors, only one of them having a claim of $10,000 or more is required to file. As soon as a petition (voluntary or involuntary) is filed in a bankruptcy court, all creditors' claims against the debtor are suspended. Called an automatic stay, this provision prevents creditors from collecting any of the debts the debtor owed them before the petition was filed. In other words, no creditor can begin or continue to pursue debt collection once the petition is filed.

Not every piece of property the individual bankrupt debtor owns is subject to court attachment. According to the Bankruptcy Reform Act certain assets are exempt, although each state establishes its own exemptions. Most states make an allowance for equity in a home, interest in an automobile, interest in a large number of personal items and other personal assets. Federal law allows a $15,000 exemption for ownership of a home, a $4,000 exemption for household items and clothing, and a $400 exemption for other property.

The law does not allow a debtor to transfer the ownership of property to others to avoid its seizure in a bankruptcy. If a debtor transfers property within one year of the filing of a bankruptcy petition, the trustee can ignore the transfer and claim the assets. In addition, any transfer of property made for the express purpose of avoiding repayment of debts (called fraudulent conveyance) will be overturned. The law also enables a judge to dismiss a Chapter 7 bankruptcy petition if it is a "substantial abuse" of the bankruptcy code.

CHAPTER 11: REORGANIZATION

For the small business weakened by a faltering economy or management mistakes, Chapter 11 provides a second chance for success. The philosophy behind this form of bankruptcy is that ailing companies can prosper again if given a fresh start with less debt. Under Chapter 11, a company is protected from creditors' legal actions while it formulates a plan for reorganization and debt repayment or settlement. In most cases, the small firm and its creditors negotiate a settlement in which the company repays its debts and is freed of the remainder. The business continues to operate under the court's direction, but creditors cannot foreclose on it, nor can they collect any prebankruptcy debts the company owes. *Comic book publisher Marvel Entertainment Group filed for Chapter 11 bankruptcy in an attempt to restructure its business and recover. The company, which publishes comic books featuring such well-known animated heroes as Spider-Man, Captain America, and the X-Men, cited a steep drop in sales to comic book collectors as the cause of its financial woes. The company chose a Chapter 11 filing because its owners saw the potential to revive the flagging company. "The Marvel brand has a lot of intangible value," says one financial analyst. "It's going to survive one way or the other."*[23]

A Chapter 11 bankruptcy filing can be either voluntary or involuntary. Once the petition is filed, an automatic stay goes into effect and the debtor has 120 days to file a reorganizational plan with the court. Usually, the court does not replace management with an appointed trustee; instead, the bankrupt party, called the debtor in possession, serves as trustee. If the debtor fails to file a plan within the 120-day limit, any party involved in the bankruptcy, including creditors, may propose a plan. The plan must identify the various classes of creditors and their claims, outline how each class will be treated, and establish a method to implement the plan. It also must spell out which debts cannot be paid, which can be paid, and what methods the debtor will use to repay them.

Once the plan is filed, the court must decide whether to approve it. A court will approve a plan if a majority of each of the three classes of creditors—secured, priority, and unsecured—votes in favor of it. The court will confirm the plan if it is reasonable and is submitted in good faith, if it is "in the best interest of the creditors." If the court rejects the plan, the creditors must submit a new one for court approval.

Filing under Chapter 11 offers the weakened small business a number of advantages, the greatest of which is a chance to survive (although most of the companies that file under Chapter 11 ultimately are liquidated). In addition, employees keep their jobs, and customers get an uninterrupted supply of goods and services. But there are costs involved in bankruptcy proceedings. Customers, suppliers, creditors, and often employees lose confidence in the firm's ability to succeed. Creditors frequently incur substantial losses in Chapter 11 bankruptcies.

CHAPTER 13: INDIVIDUAL REPAYMENT PLANS

Individual debtors (not businesses) with a regular income who owe unsecured debts of less than $250,000 or secured debts under $750,000 may file for bankruptcy under Chapter 13. Many proprietors who have the choice of filing under Chapter 11 or 13 find that Chapter 13 is less complicated and less expensive. Chapter 13 proceedings must begin voluntarily. Once the debtor files the petition, creditors cannot start or continue legal action to collect payment. Under Chapter 13, only the debtor can file a repayment plan, whose terms cannot exceed five years. If the court approves the plan, the debtor may pay off the obligations, either in full or partially, on an installment basis. The plan is designed with the debtor's future income in mind, and when the debtor completes the payments under the plan, all debts are discharged.

*G*overnment Regulation

Explain some of the government regulations affecting small businesses, including those governing trade practices, consumer protection, consumer credit, and the environment.

Although most entrepreneurs recognize the need for some government regulation of business, they also think that the process is overwhelming and out of control. Government regulation of business is far from new; in fact Congress created the Interstate Commerce Commission in 1887. The Great Depression of the 1930s triggered a great deal of regulation of business. From the 1930s forward, laws regulating business practices and government agencies to enforce the regulations have expanded continuously. Not to be outdone by the federal regulators, most states have created their own regulatory agencies to create and enforce a separate set of rules and regulations. In many instances, small business owners are overwhelmed by the paperwork required to respond to all the government agencies trying to regulate and protect them.

The major complaint small business owners have concerning government regulation revolves around the cost of compliance. For small companies, the cost of regulatory compliance is significantly higher for each employee than it is for large businesses with whom they must compete. In a competitive market, small companies cannot simply pass these additional costs on to their customers; consequently, small businesses experience a squeeze on their profit margins. A 1996 law, the Small Business Regulatory Enforcement Fairness Act, offers business owners some hope. Its purposes are to require government agencies to consider the impact of their regulations on small companies and to give business owners more input into the regulatory process.

Most business owners agree that some governmental regulation is necessary. There must be laws governing work safety, environmental protection, package labeling, consumer credit, and other relevant issues because some managers will abuse the opportunity to serve the public's interest. It is not the regulations that protect workers and consumers and achieve social objectives that businesses object to but those that produce only marginal benefits relative to their costs. Owners of small firms, especially, seek relief from wasteful and meaningless governmental regulations, charging that the cost of compliance exceeds the benefits gained. Figure 22.2 shows the annual cost of federal regulation since 1978.

TRADE PRACTICES

Sherman Antitrust Act. Contemporary society places great value on free competition in the marketplace, and antitrust laws reflect this attitude. The notion of laissez-faire—that government should not interfere with the operation of the economy—that once dominated U.S. markets no longer prevails. One of the earliest trade laws was the Sherman Antitrust Act, which was passed in 1890 to promote competition in the U.S. economy. This act is the foundation on which antitrust policy in the United States is built and was aimed at breaking up the most powerful monopoly of the late nineteenth century, John D. Rockefeller's Standard Oil Trust. Although its language is very general, the Sherman Antitrust Act contains two primary provisions affecting growth and trade among businesses.[24]

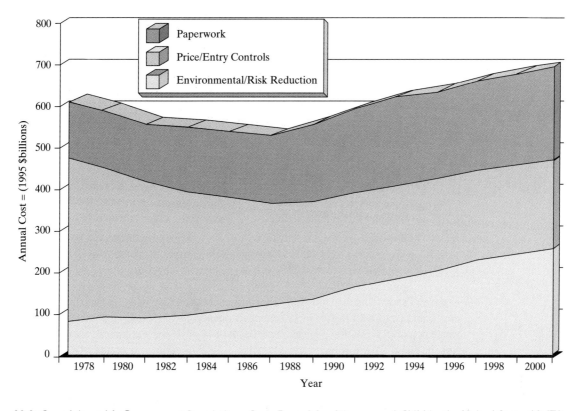

Figure 22.2 **Complying with Government Regulations Costs Every Man, Woman, and Child in the United States $2,670 per Year** SOURCE: Thomas D. Hopkins, Center for the Study of American Business.

Section I forbids "every contract, combination in the form of trust or otherwise, or conspiracy in restraint of trade or commerce among the several states, or with foreign nations." This section outlaws any agreement among sellers that might create an unreasonable restraint on free trade in the marketplace. For example, a group of small and medium-sized regional supermarkets formed a cooperative association to purchase products to resell under private labels only in restricted geographic regions. The U.S. Supreme Court ruled that this was an attempt to restrict competition by allocating territories. Such concerted activity was an example of "horizontal territorial limitations," which "are naked restraints of trade with no purpose except stifling of competition."[25]

Section II of the Sherman Antitrust Act makes it illegal for any person to "monopolize or attempt to monopolize any part of the trade or commerce among the several states, or with foreign nations." The primary focus of Section II is on preventing the undesirable effects of monopoly power in the marketplace.

Clayton Act. Congress passed the Clayton Act in 1914 to strengthen federal antitrust laws by spelling out specific monopolistic activities. The major provisions of the Clayton Act forbid the following activities:

1. *Price discrimination.* A firm cannot charge different customers different prices for the same product, unless the price discrimination is based on an actual cost savings, is made to meet a lower price from competitors, or is justified by a difference in grade, quality, or quantity sold.

2. *Exclusive dealing and tying contracts.* A seller cannot require a buyer to purchase only her product to the exclusion of other competitive sellers' products (an exclusive dealing agreement). Also, the act forbids sellers to sell a product on the condition that the buyer agrees to purchase another product the seller offers (a tying agreement). For example, a computer manufacturer could not sell a computer to a business and, as a condition of the sale, require the firm to purchase software as well.

3. *Purchasing stock in competing corporations.* A business cannot purchase the stock or assets of another business when the effect may be to substantially lessen competition. This does not mean that a corporation cannot hold stock in a competing company; the rule is designed to prevent horizontal mergers that would reduce competition. The Federal Trade Commission and the Antitrust Division of the Justice Department enforce this section (Section 7), evaluating the market shares of the companies involved and the potential effects of a horizontal merger before ruling on its legality.

4. *Interlocking directorates.* The act forbids interlocking directorates—a person serving on the board of directors of two or more competing companies. The act establishes specific provisions for the interlocking directorate requirement.

Federal Trade Commission Act. To supplement the Clayton Act, Congress passed the Federal Trade Commission Act in 1914, which created its namesake agency and gave it a broad range of powers. Section 5 gives the FTC the power to prevent "unfair methods of competition in commerce and unfair or deceptive acts or practices in commerce." Recent amendments have expanded the FTC's powers. The FTC's primary targets are those businesses that engage in unfair trade practices, often brought to the surface by consumer complaints. In addition, the agency has issued a number of trade regulation rules defining acceptable and unacceptable trade practices in various industries. Its major weapon is a "cease and desist order," commanding the violator to stop its unfair trade practices.

The FTC Act and the Lanham Trademark Act of 1988 (plus state laws) govern the illegal practice of deceptive advertising. In general, the FTC can review any advertisement that might mislead people into buying a product or service they would not buy if they knew the truth.[26] For instance, if a small business advertised a "huge year-end inventory reduction sale" but kept its prices the same as its regular prices, it would be violating the law.

In one case, the FTC challenged Pantron I Corporation's advertisements for a shampoo and conditioner (the "Helsinki Formula") that the company claimed would promote the growth of new hair on bald men. At trial, the company cited "scientific studies" proving its product's effectiveness. However, scientists testifying for the FTC stated that the studies that Pantron cited did not meet scientific standards. Instead, they attributed the fact that more than half of the company's sales came from repeat customers to the placebo effect, which is particularly strong in hair-growth products. In other words, some men may actually have experienced some hair growth simply because they believed they would. Referring to the powerful placebo effect in the case, the judge said that "massaging vegetable oil on one's head would likely produce the same results as using the Helsinki Formula" and went on to rule that the FTC had "shown that Pantron's claims were false." The company was forced to change its advertising.[27]

Robinson-Patman Act. Although the Clayton Act addressed price discrimination and the Federal Trade Commission forbade the practice, Congress found the need to strengthen the law because many businesses circumvented original rules. In 1936 Congress passed the Robinson-Patman Act, which further restricted price discrimination in the marketplace. The act forbids any seller "to discriminate in price between different purchases of commodities of like grade and quality" unless there are differences in the cost of manufacture, sale, or delivery of the goods. Even if a price-discriminating firm escaped guilt under the Clayton

Act, it violated the Robinson-Patman Act. Traditionally, the FTC has had the primary responsibility of enforcing the Robinson-Patman Act.

Other Legislation. The Celler-Kefauver Act of 1950 gave the FTC the power to review certain proposals for mergers so it could prevent too much concentration of power in any particular industry.

Congress created the Miller-Tydings Act in 1937 to introduce an exception to the Sherman Antitrust Act. This act made it legal for manufacturers to use fair-trade agreements that prohibit sellers of the manufacturer's product from selling it below a predetermined fair trade price. This form of price fixing was outlawed when Congress repealed the Miller-Tydings Act in 1976. Manufacturers can no longer mandate minimum or maximum prices on their products to sellers.

CONSUMER PROTECTION

Since the early 1960s, legislators have created many laws aimed at protecting consumers from unscrupulous sellers, unreasonable credit terms, and mislabeled or unsafe products. Early laws focused on ensuring that food and drugs sold in the marketplace were safe and of proper quality. The first law, the Pure Food and Drug Act, passed in 1906, regulated the labeling of various food and drug products. Later amendments empowered government agencies to establish safe levels of food additives and to outlaw carcinogenic (cancer-causing) additives. In 1938, Congress passed the Food, Drug, and Cosmetics Act, which created the Food and Drug Administration (FDA). The FDA is responsible for establishing standards of safe over-the-counter drugs; inspecting food and drug manufacturing operations; performing research on food, additives, and drugs; regulating drug labeling; and other related tasks. Other acts regulating the food industry include the Agricultural Marketing Act of 1946, the Poultry Products Inspection Act of 1957, the Wholesale Meat Act of 1967, and the Egg Products Inspection Act of 1970.

Congress has also created a number of laws to establish standards pertaining to product labeling for consumer protection. Since 1976, manufacturers have been required to print accurate information about the quantity and content of their products in a conspicuous place on the package. In general, labels must identify the raw materials used in the product, the manufacturer, the distributor (and its place of business), the net quantity of the contents, and the quantity of each serving if the package states the number of servings. The law also requires labels to be truthful. For example, a candy bar labeled "new, bigger size" must actually be bigger. These requirements, created by the Fair Packaging and Labeling Act of 1966, were designed to improve the customers' ability to comparison shop. A 1970 amendment to the Fair Packaging and Labeling Act, the Poison Prevention Packaging Act, required manufacturers to install child-proof caps on all products that are toxic.

With the passage of the Consumer Products Safety Act in 1972, Congress created the CPSC to control potentially dangerous products sold to consumers, and it has broad powers over manufacturers and sellers of consumer products. For instance, the CPSC can set safety requirements for consumer products, and it has the power to ban the production of any product it considers hazardous to consumers. It can also order vendors to remove unsafe products from their shelves. In addition to enforcing the Consumer Product Safety Act, the CPSC is also charged with enforcing the Refrigerator Safety Act, the Federal Hazardous Substance Act, the Child Protection and Toy Safety Act, the Poison Prevention Packaging Act, and the Flammable Fabrics Act. The Consumer Product Safety Act was created to do the following:

◆ Protect the public against unreasonable risk of injury from consumer products.

◆ Help customers compare products on the basis of safety.

- Create safety standards for products and consolidate inconsistent state regulations.
- Research the causes and possible prevention of injuries and illness from consumer products.

The Magnuson-Moss Warranty Act, passed in 1975, regulates written warranties that companies offer on the consumer goods they sell. The act does not require companies to offer warranties; it only regulates the warranties companies choose to offer. It also requires businesses to state warranties in easy-to-understand language and defines the conditions warranties must meet before they can be designated as "full warranties."

CONSUMER CREDIT

Another area subject to intense government regulation is consumer credit. This section of the law has grown in importance since credit has become a major vehicle for consumer purchases. The primary law regulating consumer credit is the Consumer Credit Protection Act (CCPA), passed in 1968. More commonly known as the Truth-in-Lending Act, this law requires sellers who extend credit and lenders to fully disclose the terms and conditions of credit arrangements. The Federal Trade Commission is responsible for enforcing the Truth-in-Lending Act. The law outlines specific requirements that any firm that offers, arranges, or extends credit to customers must meet. The two most important terms of the credit arrangement that lenders must disclose are the finance charge and the annual percentage rate. The finance charge represents the total cost—direct and indirect—of the credit, and the annual percentage rate (APR) is the relative cost of credit stated in annual percentage terms. Because computing the annual percentage rate can be quite tedious, the Federal Reserve Board publishes a booklet, *Annual Percentage Rate Tables*, Volume 1, to assist business owners in complying with the law.

The Truth-in-Lending Act applies to any consumer loan for less than $25,000 (or loans of any amount secured by mortgages on real estate) that includes more than four installments. Merchants extending credit to customers must state clearly the following information, using specific terminology:

- The price of the product.
- The down payment and any trade-in allowance made.
- The unpaid balance owed after the down payment.
- Total dollar amount of the finance charge.
- Any prepaid finance charges or required deposit balances, such as points, service charges, or lenders' fees.
- Any other charges not included in the finance charge.
- The total amount to be financed.
- The unpaid balance.
- The deferred payment price, including the total cash price and finance and incidental charges.
- The date on which the finance charge begins to accrue.
- The annual percentage rate of the finance charge.
- The number, amounts, and due dates of payments.
- The penalties imposed in case of delinquent payments.
- A description of any security interest the creditor holds.
- A description of any penalties imposed for early repayment of principal.

Another provision of the Truth-in-Lending Act limits the credit-card holder's liability in case the holder's card is lost or stolen. As long as the holder notifies the company of the missing card, she is liable for only $50 of any amount that an unauthorized user might charge on the card (or zero if the holder notifies the company before any unauthorized use of the card).

In 1974 Congress passed the Fair Credit Billing Act, an amendment to the Truth-in-Lending Act. Under this law, a credit card holder may withhold payment on a faulty product, providing she has made a good faith effort to settle the dispute first. A credit-card holder can also withhold payment to the issuing company if she believes her bill is in error. The card holder must notify the issuer within 60 days but is not required to pay the bill until the dispute is settled. The creditor cannot collect any finance charge during this period unless there was no error.

Another credit law designed to protect consumers is the Equal Credit Opportunity Act of 1974, which prohibits discrimination in granting credit on the basis of race, religion, national origin, color, sex, marital status, or whether the individual receives public welfare payment.

In 1971, Congress created the Fair Credit Reporting Act to protect consumers against the circulation of inaccurate or obsolete information pertaining to credit applications. Under this act, the consumer can request the nature of any credit investigation, the type of information assembled, and the identity of those persons receiving the report. The law requires that any obsolete or misleading information contained in the file be updated, deleted, or corrected.

Congress enacted the Fair Debt Collection Practices Act in 1977 to protect consumers from abusive debt collection practices. The law does not apply to business owners collecting their own debts, but only to debt collectors working for other businesses. The act prevents debt collectors from doing the following:

♦ Contacting the debtor at his workplace if the employer objects.

♦ Using intimidation, harassment, or abusive language to pester the debtor.

♦ Calling on the debtor at inconvenient times (before 8 A.M. or after 9 P.M.).

♦ Contacting third parties (except parents, spouses, and financial advisers) about the debt.

♦ Contacting the consumer after receiving notice of refusal to pay the debt (except to inform the debtor of the involvement of a collection agency).

♦ Making false threats against the debtor.

ENVIRONMENTAL LAW

In 1970, Congress created the Environmental Protection Agency (EPA) and gave it the authority to create laws that would protect the environment from pollution and contamination. Although the EPA administers a number of federal environmental statutes, three in particular stand out: the Clean Air Act, the Clean Water Act, and the Resource Conservation and Recovery Act.

The Clean Air Act. To reduce the problems associated with acid rain, the greenhouse effect, and airborne pollution, Congress passed the Clean Air Act in 1970 (and several amendments since then). The act targets everything from coal-burning power plants to automobiles. The Clean Air Act assigned the EPA the task of developing a national air-quality standard, and the agency works with state and local governments to enforce compliance with these standards.

Occasionally, small business owners accuse the EPA of going too far. *For instance, managers at Mrs. Baird's Bakeries, Inc., a family-owned bread bakery, were shocked to learn that the smell of baking bread is a form of air pollution under the Clean Air Act! Because it contains yeast, baking bread gives off a nontoxic substance called ethanol, which the EPA classifies as a "volatile organic compound." The "yeast police," as bakers call the EPA, want the nation's bakers to spend millions of dollars to install emission controls, which will reduce not only the ethanol but also that wonderful smell of fresh-baked bread! "When you think of the smell of baking bread, you don't think about polluting the atmosphere," says the head of Mrs. Baird's Bakeries.*[28]

The Clean Water Act. The Clean Water Act, passed in 1972, set out to make all navigable waters in the United States suitable for fishing and swimming by 1983 and to eliminate the discharge of pollutants into those waters by 1985. Although the EPA has made progress in cleaning up many bodies of water, it has yet to achieve those goals. The Clean Water Act requires that states establish water-quality standards and develop plans to reach them. The act also prohibits the draining, dredging, or filling of wetlands without a permit. The Clean Water Act also addresses the issues of providing safe drinking water and cleaning up oil spills in navigable waters.

The Resource Conservation and Recovery Act. Congress passed the Resource Conservation and Recovery Act (RCRA) in 1976 to deal with solid waste disposal. The RCRA sets guidelines by which solid waste landfills must operate, and it establishes rules governing the disposal of hazardous wastes. The RCRA's goal is to prevent solid waste from contaminating the environment. But what about those waste disposal sites that are already contaminating the environment? In 1980, Congress passed the Comprehensive Environmental Repsonse, Compensation, and Liability Act (CERCLA) to deal with those sites. The act created the Superfund, a special federal fund set up to finance and regulate the cleanup of solid waste disposal sites that are polluting the environment.

Chapter Summary

1. Explain the basic elements required to create a valid, enforceable contract.

   A valid contract must contain these elements: agreement (offer and acceptance), consideration, capacity, and legality. A contract can be valid and yet unenforceable because it fails to meet two other conditions: genuineness of assent and proper form.

   ◆ Most contracts are fulfilled by both parties' performing their promised actions; occasionally, however, one party fails to perform as agreed, thereby breaching the contract. Usually, the non-breaching party is allowed to sue for monetary damages that would place her in the same position she would have been in had the contract been performed. In cases where money is an insufficient remedy, the injured party may sue for specific performance of the contract's terms.

2. Outline the major components of the Uniform Commercial Code governing sales contracts.

   ◆ The Uniform Commercial Code (UCC) was an attempt to create a unified body of law governing routine business transactions. Of the 10 articles in the UCC, Article 2 on the sale of goods affects many business transactions.

   ◆ Contracts for the sale of goods must contain the same four elements of a valid contract, but the UCC relaxes many of the specific restrictions the common law imposes on contracts. Under the UCC, once the parties create a contract, they must perform their duties in good faith.

   ◆ The UCC also covers sales warranties. A seller creates an express warranty when he makes a statement about the performance of a product or indicates by example certain characteristics of the product. Sellers automatically create other warranties—warranties of title, implied warranties of merchantability, and, in certain cases, implied warranties of fitness for a particular purpose—when they sell a product.

3. Discuss the protection of intellectual property rights involving patents, trademarks, and copyrights.

   ◆ A patent is a grant from the federal government that gives an inventor exclusive rights to an invention for 20 years. To submit a patent, an inventor must: establish novelty, document the device, search existing patents, study the search results, submit a patent application to the U.S. Patent and Trademark Office, and prosecute the application.

- A trademark is any distinctive word, symbol, or trade dress that a company uses to identify its product or to distinguish it from other goods. It serves as the company's "signature" in the marketplace.
- A copyright protects original works of authorship. It covers only the form in which an idea is expressed and not the idea itself and lasts for 50 years beyond the creator's death.

4 Explain the basic workings of the law of agency.

- In an agency relationship, one party (the agent) agrees to represent another (the principal). The agent has the power to act for the principal but remains subject to the principal's control. While performing job-related tasks, employees play an agent's role.
- An agent has the following duties to a principal: loyalty, performance, notification, duty of care, and accounting. The principal has certain duties to the agent: compensation, reimbursement, cooperation, indemnification, and safe working conditions.

5 Explain the basics of bankruptcy law.

- Entrepreneurs whose businesses fail often have no other choice but to declare bankruptcy under one of three provisions: Chapter 7 liquidations, where the business sells its assets, pays what debts it can, and disappears; Chapter 11 reorganizations, where the business asks that its debts be forgiven or restructured and then reemerges; and Chapter 13, straight bankruptcy, which is for individuals only.

6 Explain some of the government regulations affecting small businesses, including those governing trade practices, consumer protection, consumer credit, and the environment.

- Businesses operate under a multitude of government regulations governing many areas, including trade practices, where laws forbid restraint of trade, price discrimination, exclusive dealing and tying contracts, purchasing controlling interests in competitors, and interlocking directorates.
- Other areas subject to government regulations include consumer protection (the Food, Drug, and Cosmetics Act and the Consumer Product Safety Act), consumer credit (the Consumer Credit Protection Act, the Fair Debt Collection Practices Act, and the Fair Credit Reporting Act), and the environment (the Clean Air Act, the Clean Water Act, and the Resource Conservation and Recovery Act.

Discussion Questions

1. What is a contract? List and describe the four elements required for a valid contract. Must a contract be in writing to be valid?
2. What constitutes an agreement?
3. What groups of people lack contractual capacity? How do the courts view contracts created by minors? By intoxicated people? By insane people?
4. What circumstances eliminate genuineness of assent in the parties' agreement?
5. What is breach of contract? What remedies are available to a party injured by a breach?
6. What is the Uniform Commercial Code? To which kinds of contracts does the UCC apply? How do its requirements for a sale contract differ from the common law requirements?
7. Under the UCC, what remedies does a seller have when a buyer breaches a sales contract? What remedies does a buyer have when a seller breaches a contract?
8. What is a sales warranty? Explain the different kinds of warranties sellers offer.
9. Explain the different kinds of implied warranties the UCC imposes on sellers of goods. Can sellers disclaim these implied warranties? If so, how?
10. What is product liability? Explain the charges that most often form the basis for product liability claims. What must a customer prove under these charges?
11. What is intellectual property? What tools do entrepreneurs have to protect their intellectual property?
12. Explain the differences among patents, trademarks, and copyrights. What does each protect? How long does each last?
13. What must an inventor prove to receive a patent?
14. Briefly explain the patent application process.
15. What is an agent? What duties does an agent have to a principal? What duties does a principal have to an agent?
16. Explain the differences among the three major forms of bankruptcy: Chapter 7, Chapter 11, and Chapter 13.
17. Explain the statement "For each benefit gained by regulation, there is a cost."

Step into the Real World

1. Interview a local attorney about contract law. What is the difference between a valid contract, a void contract, a voidable contract, and an enforceable contract? What

elements must be present for a valid contract to exist? What are the most common mistakes business owners make when creating contracts? What advice does the attorney offer to avoid making those mistakes?

2. Go to the U.S. Patent and Trademark Office's Web site at <http://www.uspto.gov/>. Select a product that interests you and search through some of the patents the office has granted for that product. Write a one-page summary of your search results. Do you see any ways to improve upon existing patents?

3. Contact the Small Business Development Center in your area or a local attorney and ask about the "real world" problems of obtaining a patent and enforcing your rights once it has been granted.

4. Visit a small manufacturing company in your area and interview the owner or manager about the federal and state regulations with which the company must comply. Ask to see some of the paperwork required to comply with federal and state regulations. Which government agencies regulate the company's activities? How much does it cost the company to comply with these regulations? Which regulations make the most sense to the owner? The least? Why? Write a two-page summary of your interview.

Take It to the Net

Visit the Scarborough/Zimmerer home page at
www.prenhall.com/scarbzim
for updated information, on-line resources, and Web-based exercises.

Endnotes

1. Michael Selz and Jeffrey A. Tannenbaum, "Scared of Lawsuits, Small Businesses Applaud Reform," *Wall Street Journal*, March 13, 1995, pp. B1, B2.
2. Carbaugh v. Klick-Lewis, 561 A.2d 1248 (Pa. 1989).
3. Cynthia E. Griffin, "Loony Laws," *Entrepreneur*, April 1995, p. 17.
4. Folk v. Central National Bank and Trust Co., 210 Ill. App. (1991).
5. Webster v. Blue Ship Tea Room, 198 N.E.2d 309 (Mass. 1964).
6. "Product Liability Awards Increased 44% Last Year," *Wall Street Journal*, June 27, 1997, p. B9.
7. "Reasonable Product Liability Reform," *Nation's Business*, September 1997, p. 88.
8. Paula Nergerhagan, "Product Liability," *American Demographics*, June, 1995, pp. 26–34.
9. Jeffrey F. Beatty and Susan S. Samuelson, *Business Law for the New Century* (Boston, Little, Brown and Company, 1996), p. 482.
10. Restatement (Second) of Torts §402A(1)
11. Steven C. Bahls and Jane Easter Bahls, "Damage Control," *Entrepreneur*, August 1998, pp. 74–76.
12. Tomima Edmark, "Finders Keepers," *Entrepreneur*, July 1998, pp. 100–103.
13. *General Information Concerning Patents* (Washington, D.C.: U.S. Patent and Trademark Office, 1997), p. 15; Tomima Edmark, "Bright Ideas," *Entrepreneur*, April 1997, p. 98.
14. Tomima Edmark, "How Much Is Too Much?" *Entrepreneur*, February 1998, pp. 93–95.
15. Edmark, "How Much Is Too Much?" pp. 93–95.
16. Tomima Edmark, "On Guard," *Entrepreneur*, August 1997, pp. 92–94; Tomima Edmark, "On Guard," *Entrepreneur*, February 1997, pp. 109–111.
17. Michael J. McCarthy, "Fake King Cobras Tee Off Makers of High-End Clubs," *Wall Street Journal*, February 11, 1997, pp. A1, A8.
18. Nina Munk, "The Smell of This Magazine Is a Registered Trademark," *Forbes*, May 5, 1997, pp. 39–40.
19. Ron Harris, "Nail Wars Rage over Modern Shades," *Upstate Business*, April 20, 1997, p. 2; Tara Parker-Pope, "How about a Nail Polish Called 'Bare-Knuckle Trademark Battle'?" *Wall Street Journal*, March 18, 1997, p. B1; Dana Wechsler Linden, "Does Pink Make You Puke?" *Forbes*, August 25, 1997, p. 108.
20. Nancy Ganz, "Protecting Your Good Name," *Nation's Business*, September 1995, p. 6.
21. Philip E. Ross, "Cops versus Robbers in Cyberspace," *Forbes*, September 9, 1996, pp. 134–139.
22. David Warner, "Bills Seek to Slow Bankruptcy Filings," *Nation's Business*, March 1998, p. 6.
23. Farrell Kramer, "Comic Purveyor Marvel Files for Bankruptcy," *Greenville News*, December 28, 1996, p. 16B.
24. John Steele Gordon, "Read Your History, Janet," *Forbes*, February 23, 1998, pp. 92–95.
25. United States v. Topco Associates, Inc., 405 U.S. 596 (1972).
26. Steven C. Bahls and Jane Easter Bahls, "Bragging Rights," *Entrepreneur*, April 1998, pp. 82–84.
27. FTC v. Pantron Corp., 33 F.3d 1088 (9th Cir. 1994).
28. Bridget O'Brian, "An Illegal Pleasure: The Smell in the Air of Bread Being Baked," *Wall Street Journal*, April 13, 1994, pp. A1, A6.

APPENDIX

Nature's Oven

1305 Westminster Place • Birmingham, AL 35235
205-856-0296 • 800-705-1805

Business Plan

Prepared by:
Melissa Boyett
Owner & President

Table of Contents

Executive Summary

New! Different! Made with only the finest ingredients! High quality! How many times have those exclamations appeared on a product in the grocery store, mall, or on the pages of a catalog? And how many times have you been disappointed by those claims upon purchase of the product? Read on to see why these phrases fit *Nature's Oven* and why you won't be disappointed by our claims.

Nature's Oven is a home-based sole proprietorship, and we are in business to sell the highest quality and widest variety of bread mixes by mail. We will strive to offer the utmost in convenience and customer service as we provide our product to our customers.

The Owner and President is Melissa Boyett. She will soon graduate from Presbyterian College with a degree in Accounting and Business Administration. The classes she has taken have given her background and training in preparing and implementing a business plan, budgeting, maintaining accounting records, managing a business's resources—both financial and human—marketing a business' product, and more. Melissa also has gained invaluable experience in small business management through a summer job at Synovus Mortgage in which she planned and implemented a company reorganization.

Bill Boyett, Melissa's father, will serve as a consultant to the business. Bill is an entrepreneur by profession and brings a wealth of experience, creativity, and success to the venture. He has experience with start-ups and small businesses in the specialty food industry. He has experience in stationery and form design, home business operation, and market research. In addition, his contacts throughout the small business industry in the Southeast will prove invaluable.

Our target market is generally upscale, educated men and women. Our potential customers are those with small children in the home, as well as those who enjoy baking as a hobby. Our market also includes: those who have purchased from mail order catalogs previously, the health conscious, and those who own bread machines.

Nature's Oven will focus on the above-described market, focusing on that segment within the Southeastern market, although we sell to all areas of the United States. We will seek to introduce our product by ads in *Southern Living* and *Cooking Light*, establishing a kiosk in a large and very popular mall in Birmingham, Alabama, appearing on local news and talk shows in Birmingham, Executive Summary and pursuing a corporate gift-giving partnership with a successful gift basket company in the Birmingham area.

A key component of our strategy to offer convenience to our customer is our service that allows customers to specify their favorite mixes and have them shipped automatically at an established time each month.

All financing will be provided by the Owner. She has accumulated a significant sum of money from summer jobs and inheritances in anticipation of one day being able to open her own business. Also, a company credit card will be used judiciously to make the wisest use of our cash possible.

Nature's Oven is the product of a dynamic and promising marriage between the already popular and successful niche-oriented mail order industry and the increasingly popular interest in baking and specialty breads.

Purpose of Business

MISSION STATEMENT

Nature's Oven is a home-based sole proprietorship located at 1305 Westminster Place, Birmingham, Alabama. This plan marks the inception of the business.

At *Nature's Oven* we aim to offer the widest variety of quality, nutritious, all-natural bread mixes via mail order, focusing especially on the southeastern market. In providing this product, we aim to continually delight our customers by providing them with the very best product and customer service possible.

DESCRIPTION OF BUSINESS

Nature's Oven is in the start-up phase of organization and seeks to fill a demand for a variety of all-natural, healthy bread mixes and the demand for convenience. The business positions itself at the crossroads of the already successful and dynamic bread-making and mail order industries.

Although we are in the business of selling bread mixes by mail, we will also initially utilize distribution methods other than mail order to gain name recognition and a customer base and to take advantage of less costly means of obtaining sales. These methods include operation of a kiosk in a Birmingham mall, corporate gift-giving "partnerships," and doing demonstrations of preparing our mixes on local television shows in the Birmingham area. As regards the corporate gift-giving "partnerships," we will supply bread mixes to an established, successful gift basket company to be included in their baskets under their existing corporate gift-giving contracts. We have such a contract arranged for the Thanksgiving and Christmas seasons during our first year in business.

We are proud to have an existing private labeling arrangement that will enable us to offer 15 varieties of mixes, plus seasonal varieties, all of which are all-natural and/or organic, "healthy," and require minimum addition of ingredients. The costs of the mixes to us will be the supplier's cost of ingredients, discounted at a 10% rate, plus the cost of the packaging and freight costs.

This private labeling arrangement requires bulk orders (minimum of 6 dozen per flavor): orders to be placed three weeks in advance. More than adequate storage facilities for bulk shipments of the mixes exist in the Owner's home and will be available at no charge to the business.

Nature's Oven will be required to provide packaging to the supplier. We are confident that our packaging will become a trademark of *Nature's Oven*, as it will entice both the experienced and novice baker and will come as close as possible to ensuring a successful baking experience. It will include very detailed and illustrated instructions, plus serving suggestions and recipe variations. The packaging will be produced by the printer of our supplier's packages. This printer is near the supplier and has prepared templates for bread mix packages. These factors will minimize costs and will reduce chances for production delays, as the packaging will not have far to travel to the supplier.

We will hire a service to take our orders. Outsourcing order taking will enable *Nature's Oven* to minimize costs; this service costs much less than paying salaries and benefits and installing additional lines and such; also, this arrangement will maximize convenience and professional service for our customers by providing 24-hour, 7-day-a-week service—something we could not afford to do initially.

We are sure that our dynamic marketing strategy will propel our company to success. Please see the marketing section for detailed information.

In summarizing the essence of our plan and the most distinguishing aspects of our company, we offer our goals and objectives.

GOALS AND OBJECTIVES

- To continually delight our customer and distinguish *Nature's Oven* from the competition by best serving the needs and desires of bread makers—both experienced and novice bakers—through the products we offer and customer service we provide.
  - Establish and maintain private labeling contracts with only those suppliers who share *Nature Oven's* standards of high quality, all-natural, healthy ingredients.
  - Package each mix with detailed, illustrated instructions on how to make the bread and achieve the best results; serving suggestions and recipe variations will be included as well.
  - Provide each customer service representative with thorough product information to ensure that they are able to answer the customers' questions and aid them in making purchase decisions.
  - Give customer service representatives the freedom to research a customer's question and return that customer's call if the customer service representative is unable to initially answer the customer's question.
  - Send a customer service/product survey to all first-time customers and periodically to repeat customers to ensure that we are offering the products and features they desire and that we are going beyond the level of service required by the customer; adjustments will be made as necessary.
- To capitalize on the opening in the bread business in the southeastern market that has been left by other bread product/baking companies.
  - Advertise in *Southern Living* magazine.
  - Capitalize upon holiday baking and holiday gift giving by introducing our product line at the end of the summer.
  - Educate our market by providing preparation demonstrations and taste tests at mall kiosks and on local newscasts and talk shows.
  - Negotiate corporate gift-giving contracts throughout the Southeast.
- Achieve 50 percent annual increases in sales during each of our first three years in business.
  - Build upon and expand on our own base of customers upon completion of our first year of business by purchasing a mailing list.
  - Seek corporate gift-giving partnerships for contracts throughout the year, as opposed to just at the holiday season.
  - Secure our own corporate gift-giving contracts in addition to the partnership arrangement.
  - Buy space in other baking/cooking oriented mail-order catalogs.

Industry Profile

CURRENT TRENDS IN THE INDUSTRY

As Americans' lives become more complex and hurried, convenience is becoming increasingly important. As a result, mail order is becoming an ever more popular method of shopping. Also on the rise in popularity throughout the United States is baking, especially bread making. The rapid increase in bread machine owners and the interest in fresh, natural, healthy foods has contributed to the popularity of cooking as a hobby.

In the mail order industry, success is no longer found in the Sear's catalog approach of offering every imaginable product to the customer from one source. Instead, the successful companies are segmenting the market and are offering a specialized product. Customers are willing to pay a premium for convenience, quality, and uniqueness.

In the baking industry, gone are the days when bread—a loaf of bleached white or wheat bread bought from the grocery store—is used only for making the kids' sandwiches. Specialty bread stores are popping up rapidly across the United States and are offering a wide variety of breads, from unbleached white to sun-dried tomato focaccia. As a result, breads are being served as appetizers and main accompaniments to a meal and are used to create delicious bread-based desserts, such as bread pudding. The wide selection of breads are giving rise to specialty delis and pizza parlors as specialty breads are used to create flavorful and unique sandwiches and pizzas; also, bread making is becoming a more popular hobby as more people buy bread machines.

Currently, what a customer will find on grocery store shelves or on the pages of mail-order cooking catalogs is a very limited selection of "flavors" of bread mixes. Although there may be four or five brands of mixes, each brand will most likely offer a wheat, white, cinnamon raisin, and sourdough. Admittedly, in specialty mail-order cooking catalogs, there are some more unusual flavors; however, the selection is still quite limited—usually they offer five varieties or so, which are the same five offered since the company included specialty bread mixes in its product line.

INDUSTRY DATA

Market size and growth trends: This information will be included in the Marketing section.

Ease of market entry/exit: As the market for bread mixes is an infant, yet rapidly growing industry, other companies producing bread mixes are quite young (even if the company is established, the product line of bread mixes is new); so now is an opportune time to enter the market while entry is still quite easy. As mail order becomes more and more niche-oriented, demand for new mail-order services will grow. Since demand for more specialized bread mixes is growing, a mail-order company providing such goods is in order. As mentioned above, catalog production and mailing costs are the main obstacles for start-up mail order companies. Exiting this industry would be complicated only by any outstanding contracts.

Ability to achieve economies of scale: Negotiating a private labeling contract, as opposed to the company doing its own production, will facilitate our achieving an economy of scale more expeditiously.

Seasonal economies: According to many caterers and specialty bakeries in the Southeast, in general, bread making is not seasonal throughout the area. However, this assessment of the market does not take into account holiday baking. It is undeniable that baking, and therefore, our sales will increase during the holiday season as entertaining increases. Also, gift giving increases mail orders during the holidays. The corporate gift-giving contract forces a seasonal component into our sales projections since it will be executed during the holidays.

Potential threats: Bad weather is a potential threat for commodity prices for wheat and flour, thereby causing uncertainty in the forecast of costs of supplies for the mixes. Research shows, however, that these increases in prices may be passed along to the customer without much incident; for, according to industry research, bread is considered "a staple or an affordable treat." Research also indicates that consumers are willing to pay more for healthy choices among bakery goods.

Sales tax: Sales tax issues are of special concern to mail order companies. It must be collected on purchases from states in which the company is actually located or in which it has an actual retail location.

Business Strategy

KEY SUCCESS FACTORS AND HOW WE INTEND TO CAPITALIZE ON THEM

In mail order:

◆ **Specialization:** According to one small business consultant, "specialization is a must [for mail-order businesses] . . . don't try to be all things to all people." Unlike many companies that offer many types of products, including a limited line of bread mixes, *Nature's Oven* focuses solely on bread mixes and offers a wide variety of flavors.

◆ **Quality:** One entrepreneur couple explains that gaining consumers' confidence in the quality of your product is key. *Nature's Oven* insists on using only the highest quality ingredients in our bread mixes so that we can produce the highest quality end product. Quality of ingredients will be strongly emphasized in our advertising and our catalog.

◆ **Convenience:** The same couple is confident that this is the perfect time to launch a mail-order business because "people don't have time to shop anymore." Convenience is a real attraction to mail order. Customers may order from us either by mail or by calling our 800 number 24 hours a day. Additionally, credit card sales will be accepted. As mentioned below, some start-ups are unable to accept credit card sales initially; however, the Owner's connection with a local bank for whom she worked last summer, has enabled the company to offer this added convenience to our customers. Also, we will offer customers a unique service for added convenience: they may specify their favorite mixes to be shipped automatically at a set time each month, with their credit card automatically being billed for the purchase.

◆ **Catalog quality:** Small business consultants indicate that a key hurdle for small business owners in the mail-order industry is to produce a professional-looking, high-quality catalog that presents the product in an enticing way. As catalog production is a large component of expenses facing mail-order entrepreneurs, this key to success often proves to be very tricky. *Nature's Oven* will produce a small catalog of the highest quality possible, given our budget. Also, we will not rely entirely upon our catalog to sell our product; please see the marketing section to learn how we will enhance our marketing strategy.

◆ **Customer service/satisfaction:** According to an article in *Entrepreneur*, the keys to providing the level of customer service that results in customer satisfaction are a toll-free telephone number, the ability to use credit cards when placing an order, quick delivery of orders, and having someone to assist customers with purchase decisions when necessary. Also according to this article, start-ups are often not able to offer this level of customer service because banks will not extend credit card acceptance services until the business has been in operation for some time. As mentioned above, a toll-free line will be available and credit card sales will be accepted. We will ship by U.P.S. to provide speedy delivery for our customers. Also, *Nature's Oven* will employ a service to take our orders, thereby enabling us to utilize a greater number of thoroughly trained personnel than we would otherwise be able to, considering the part-time nature of the business and cost considerations.

◆ **Reaching the proper market:** Precisely defining one's target market and then reaching that market with the catalog is absolutely crucial to obtaining sales and achieving profitability. Please see the marketing section to learn how *Nature's Oven* will meet this success factor.

◆ **Minimizing mailing costs:** Mailing costs are one of the largest expenses faced by mail-order business. Thus, minimizing these costs is key to achieving profitability. As the company grows and we begin mailing out more catalogs, we will minimize our mailing costs by employing a mailing house that will presort our mail, encode the pieces with bar codes, and pool our mail with other small businesses so that we can enjoy discounts offered for bulk mail.

In bread mixes:

◆ **Variety:** According to professionals in the bread-making industry, sales increase as variety does. The more flavors and the more uses for the mixes (e.g., mixes for focaccia, loaves, and pizza crust), the more often customers will make purchases and the more they will spend per sales transaction. In contrast to other companies selling bread mixes, we are committed to providing a wide selection to our customers. *Nature's Oven* will offer fifteen varieties, plus seasonal flavors.

◆ **All-natural/organic products:** All natural/organic products are enjoying an increase in popularity.

Business Strategy (continued)

Many hobbyist cooks initially gain their interest in cooking because of their desire for food that is prepared from all-natural and organic products. *Nature's Oven* is committed to only using all-natural and/or organic ingredients in our mixes.

♦ **"Healthy":** This term translates into low-fat or no-fat products. Busy consumers are drawn toward fat-laden fast food simply because of the convenience. However, healthy food that requires minimal preparation wins hands-down over the fatty fast food among the majority of consumers. *Nature's Oven* is committed to selling only mixes that require minimum, if any, addition of oils and eggs.

♦ **Ease of use:** Customers want mixes that require minimal additional ingredients and that come with clear instructions. Unlike other bread mixes, ours will come packaged with detailed and illustrated instructions that will help the consumer make the best loaf possible. Serving suggestions and recipe variations will also be included.

PLANNING FOR GROWTH

On the basis of the experiences of other companies selling bread mixes by mail and the sales of specialty bread stores throughout the Southeast, we can realistically expect sales to increase by 50% each year during our initial years in business. As we begin to build our own base of customers and are financially able to purchase mailing lists, our sales have the potential to increase dramatically. We intend to achieve this growth as indicated in the Goals and Objectives section above.

The private labeling contract, the contract with the order-taking service, and the contract with the packaging producer do not limit the amount of business we can sustain, so no alterations to these agreements would be necessary to accommodate a higher level of sales. In terms of the 800 number, *Nature's Oven* may easily sustain an increase in sales by adding additional lines. These additional lines may be rented from the order-taking service or ordered from AT&T. Additional part-time workers from the local high school co-op program could be hired to assist in packing and shipping duties if needed.

In the printing and mailing categories, our unit costs for catalogs will be lowered as we grow. As indicated previously, we will contract with a mailing house to sort our catalogs to minimize costs in this area. Such discounts for "bulk" rates are achievable only upon reaching a minimum threshold of mailing activity. Printing actually becomes cheaper per piece as quantity increases.

Organization and Management

LEGAL STRUCTURE: SOLE PROPRIETORSHIP

Nature's Oven is a part-time endeavor for its Owner; and the financial requirements of starting and running it do not necessitate a large pool of start-up capital or large infusions of cash investments during the early years of the business. The ability to start a sole proprietorship with minimum cost and legal requirements, as compared with other forms of ownership, is a perfect match to such a business.

MANAGEMENT

Melissa Boyett will serve as the Owner and President of *Nature's Oven* and will perform the majority of administrative and operational duties. By the time the business begins operation, I will have an Accounting and Business Administration degree from Presbyterian College, the course work for which included classes in marketing, business law, and small business management, all of which have prepared me to successfully run this business.

In addition, the Owner's father, Bill Boyett, is a successful entrepreneur and has been since the inception of his career. His entrepreneurial ventures include specialty food shops and bookstores. He has agreed to serve as a consultant and to perform administrative and operational duties as needed.

Education

Expected graduation date: May, 1997 from Presbyterian College
Study abroad: In the Spring of 1996, I studied at the London School of Economics and Political
Science and interned with the Honorable Michael Stephen, a Member of Parliament
Majors: Accounting/Business Administration
            Key course work included classes in Small Business Management, Applied
            Management Information Systems, Cost Accounting, Management, Statistics, and
            Intermediate Accounting
G.P.A.:   4.0
GMAT: 610

Honors

Quattlebaum Honors Scholar
Taylor Stukes Merit Scholarship recipient
Dean's Freshman Honors Seminar member
Sigma Kappa Alpha member
Pi Gamma Mu member
President's List, 6 consecutive semesters
Dean's List, 6 consecutive semesters

Extracurricular Activities

Accounting Club, President
Society for the Advancement of Management
Judicial Council:
            Member
            Prosecutor
Student Government Association:
            Women's Council Delegate
            Dorm President
            Food Committee member
            Student Union Board
Student Volunteer Services:
            Joanna Tutors
            Clinton Child Outreach, coordinator
            Good Shepherd Free Clinic, coordinator
Pre-Law Society:
            Founding member
            Treasurer
            President
Campus Publications:
            Yearbook Section Editor
            Russell Subcommittee on Campus Communications
Wellness Committee
Leadership Presbyterian College

Work Experiences

Summer clerk in the Accounting Department of First Commercial Bank and at Synovus Mortgage Corp.,
an affiliate of First Commercial Bank, May–August 1996
◆ Organized and implemented a company restructuring.
◆ Served as corporate secretary on a temporary basis.
◆ Processed and distributed all incoming payments, invoices.

Intern for the Honorable Michael Stephen, Member of Parliament, Spring 1996
◆ Researched and responded to constituent mail and requests.
◆ Participated in an Environment Standing Committee inquiry into housing.
◆ Researched and wrote two speeches on economic issues and a paper regarding the relationship between Parliament and the judiciary for
  Mr. Stephen.

Figure A.1 A Baker's Profile: Melissa Boyett

Intern for the City Attorney's office, Birmingham, Alabama, May–August 1995

◆ Designed and implemented a filing system.
◆ Prepared trial notebooks by assembling key information and indexing it in preparation for a trial.
◆ Executed an enforcement phase of a newly instituted ordinance passed by the Mayor and City Council.

Intern for Mr. Claude Howe III, Public Defender for Laurens County, South Carolina, Fall 1994

◆ Interviewed clients and compiled the resulting pertinent information for use in court.
◆ Assembled needed information from the files in preparation for trials.

Intern for Congressman Glen Browder, Washington, D.C., May 1994

◆ Researched constituent requests and responded to them.
◆ Gave tours of the Capitol.
◆ Redesigned and updated the filing system.
◆ Performed key research for a welfare bill and for an Armed Service Committee bill.

Summer teller at First Commercial Bank, Birmingham, Alabama, June–August 1993

◆ In the process of performing the various teller duties, gained valuable experience in customer relations and customer service.
◆ Assisted head tellers in balancing the vault and in preparing shipments of money to the Federal Reserve.

References

Mr. Bill Pate
Assistant City Attorney
600 City Hall
Birmingham, AL 35203
205-254-2369

Dr. J. William Moncrief, Senior
Vice-President for Academic Affairs
Presbyterian College
403 South Adair Street
Clinton, SC 29325
864-833-8233/
800-476-7272, ext. 8233

Mrs. Beverly Harris
1301 Westminster Place
Birmingham, AL 35235
205-854-9273

Dr. Suzanne J. Smith
Assoc. Professor of Business
Presbyterian College
403 South Adair Street
Clinton, SC 29325
864-833-8454
800-476-7272, ext. 8454

Figure A.1 **A Baker's Profile: Melissa Boyett** (*continued*)

Location

Nature's Oven is based at the Owner's home at 1305 Westminster Place, Birmingham, Alabama. This location best suits the business for the following reasons:

◆ It is convenient for the Owner, which facilitates her devoting as much time as possible to the business outside of school and work.

◆ Due to the part-time nature of the business, costs associated with leasing office space are prohibitive. This location would incur no expense for the business.

◆ *Nature's Oven* would have access to an 800 number and computer at no expense to the company. Both the toll-free number and the computer are used by the Owner's father in his home-based business and can realistically be used by this business as well.

A home-based business of this nature is permissible under laws governing sole proprietorships in the City of Birmingham.

Marketing

MARKETPLACE INTEREST, MARKET SIZE, AND TRENDS

Franchisers for specialty bread stores, professionals within the bread mix industry, and professionals within the mail-order business indicate that marketplace interest in specialized mail-order products and in bread mixes is keen and growing.

Professionals within the bread-making industry also express that, although bread making has traditionally not been as popular in the Southeast as it has in other areas of the country, recent trends indicate that its popularity is growing nationwide, and especially within the southern states. Its growing popularity is evidenced by specialty bread chains and bread mix companies easing into the southern market. These companies are not keeping pace with the demand, for at many locations, orders must be placed in advance if customers hope to get the bread products they want. Mail order is also especially popular in the Southeast as compared with other regions of the country

As numerical evidence of these trends, we offer the following:

◆ According to industry professionals, approximately 12 million households own a bread machine, providing a lucrative potential market for sales of bread mixes. But the market is even more expansive, as untold numbers of households use bread mixes to make bread in the so-called conventional method.

◆ According to *American Demographics*, surveys in recent years indicate that approximately 65% of women and approximately 60% of men used a baking mix of some kind within a six-month time frame. These surveys also indicate a rise in consumption of breads.

◆ Approximately 25% of those who shop by mail order are Southerners. The significance of this figure is enhanced by learning that the South accounts for just over 34% of the U.S. population, thereby indicating that a significant portion of Southerners shop by mail order (according to *Southern Living* research).

◆ *Southern Living* research also indicates that the South accounts for more retail sales than any other U.S. region in all sales categories.

As indicated above, the base of bread machine makers is a large and existing opportunity for retailers marketing bread mixes. Recent stock market news indicates that Sunbeam, a major manufacturer of bread machine makers, is cutting prices of their appliances. This event could increase sales of bread machines even more quickly than expected, thereby increasing the most visible and lucrative target market for bread mix sales.

According to *Bakery Production and Marketing* and those in the industry, healthy (low/no fat), all natural and/or organic specialty products, especially bread-related products, are enjoying great popularity; and their popularity is projected to continue to rise. In fact, this magazine indicates that, as better-tasting, healthy baking products emerge, people who do not normally buy bakery goods will begin to do so. Baking healthy, good-for-you foods is also on the rise in popularity. Witness the birth and success of such healthy cooking magazines as *Cooking Light* and *Eating Well*, both of which indicate that their subscriber base has grown substantially in recent years, as has the number of subscribers who bake healthy foods.

Bakery Production and Marketing also indicates that our fast-paced society, filled with two-career couples has increased the demand for food that is easy and convenient to obtain and prepare. Those within the mail-order business also indicate that a rise in the demand for convenience has increased mail-order sales in recent years. Such trends in both industries are projected to rise.

PRICING

Industry magazines and the success of current mixes on the market indicate that specialized products that offer convenience and food products that are all-natural and/or organic and healthy will command a premium price. Currently bread mixes sold in grocery stores are priced in a range of approximately $3.50 to $4.50. Mixes of a more specialized nature that are sold via mail order range from $3.50 to $8.50, depending upon the specialty of the mix.

Nature's Oven will not attempt to compete on the basis of offering the lowest price on the market, but our prices will be comparable to our competitors.

As indicated above, the spirit of buying bread products is not dampened by a moderate price increase, as consumers of specialty bread products view bread as a relatively affordable treat.

Nature's Oven will offer a sampler pack, by which customers receive a discount for volume orders. Please see the attached order form for a detailed price list.

Marketing *(continued)*

TARGET MARKET

Data from *Home World, American Demographics*, and those within the industry suggest the following target market:

Age: Early 30's to late 50's

Income: Generally annual income is $40,000 or higher

Gender: Male and female

Education: College-educated

Lifestyle: Have children under the age of 11; upscale homemakers with free time; two-career couples; those with little free time; and nutrition-conscious individuals (this encompasses the younger generations especially)

Cooking habits/preferences: Own and use a bread machine; utilize prepared mixes in food preparation; enjoy cooking as a hobby; prepare healthy food

Shopping habits/preferences: Have previously shopped by mail order

Additional data about the southern market:

The South is the nation's number one region in total retail sales.

The South accounts for 42.6% of U.S. population growth (in the period 1984–1994).

The South ranks number 1 in number of adults who order by mail.

Additional data about the Birmingham market:

The City of Birmingham is located in a four-county Metropolitan Statistical Area, with a population of 881,761.

Within this MSA is Shelby County, the sixth wealthiest and sixteenth fastest growing county in the nation!

Twenty-five percent of the population is composed of children under 18.

Average household incomes in Birmingham suburbs: $100,000 in Mountain Brook, $78,955 in Inverness, $71,033 in Hoover, and $66,451 in Vestavia Hills.

Education levels of area residents are high, as the health care industry is the largest employer and there are seven four-year college or universities in the area.

THE WORLD WIDE WEB

The World Wide Web is highly regarded as the marketplace of the future, and the typical WWW user shares many characteristics with our target customer; however, as we are entering a young industry, our sales and costs are going to be difficult enough to project as is. The need to ship internationally, prepare for a potential growth explosion, and other issues related to marketing on the Web make it an unattractive selling tool at this time. We intend to reevaluate this decision in the future.

ADVERTISING

As mentioned above, catalog production and mailing costs are two of the most substantial costs facing start-ups in this industry. In an effort to minimize unnecessary initial cost outlays, we will take cues from other specialized mail-order companies' success; we will seek to initially publicize our name and product and obtain sales by means other than large mailings of catalogs to customers who match our target customer profile.

Our marketing strategy includes running ads in *Southern Living* and *Cooking Light* magazines; operating a kiosk at the Galleria, which is the largest mall in Birmingham, Alabama; soliciting corporate gift contracts; and appearing on local news and talk shows in Birmingham.

The focus on Birmingham is threefold: First, because the business will be based in Birmingham, operating our initial kiosk in Birmingham minimizes costs (no travel necessary, the Owner and her family members will be able to man the kiosk, etc.). Second, Birmingham's market has been determined by many national chains to be a prime target for growth in the specialty bread area. Several franchises have already established a presence in town, and many others have plans to begin business in the future. Finally, this strategy is in keeping with our focus on the southeastern market.

Regarding *Nature's Oven*'s particular emphasis on garnering sales in the South: we hope to take advantage of the opportunity identified in this market by those within the specialty bread and mail-order industries. Although the opportunity has been identified, established companies have not yet made the change in their marketing plans, so the Southeast is not being heavily targeted by those companies.

What Southern Living has to offer us as an advertising medium:

Southern Living's subscribers' annual incomes range, on average, from $61,470 to $73,594.

Thirty-one percent of their readers responded that they show "considerable interest" in the magazine's advertising. (See Figure A.2.)

Southern Living is an effective advertising tool because the magazine is ranked high in the category of reader involvement: 30.8% of adult readers say the magazine is "one of my favorites"; 50.1% "read 4 of 4 issues"; and, as noted above, a considerable number show a great deal of interest in the advertising. (See Figure A.3.)

32.9% of *Southern Living* subscribers lend or give away issues of the magazine.

Approximately 65% of the magazine's subscribers have a college-level education or higher.

The median age of a *Southern Living* subscriber is 46.5, with the majority of readers in the 35–54 age range.

121,874 readers attended the *Southern Living* Cooking School in 1995.

68.7% of subscribers have purchased a *Southern Living* cookbook.

18.7% of *Southern Living* readers order by mail; this is the second highest percentage among comparable magazines.

What *Cooking Light* has to offer us as an advertising medium:

74% of *Cooking Light* readers are female homemakers.

The median age of the typical reader is 44.8.

Approximately 83% of readers have received a college degree or higher.

The median household income is $44,941, with 65% of readers having a household income of $35,000 or greater.

Cooking Light is the rate base leader among "food magazines" (e.g., *Bon Appetit, Gourmet, Eating Well, Food & Wine*). (See Figure A.4.)

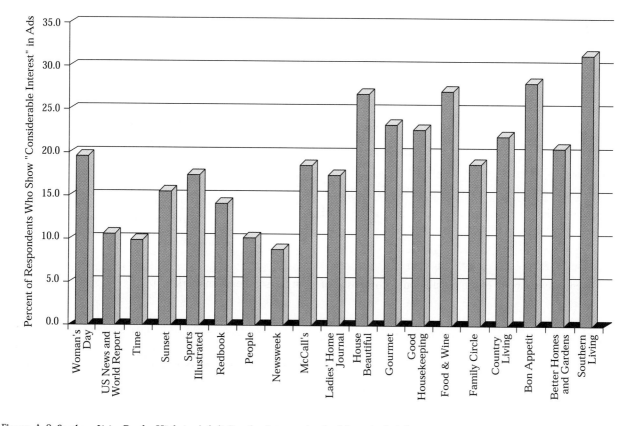

Figure A.2 *Southern Living* Ranks High in Adult Reader Interest in the Magazine's Advertising

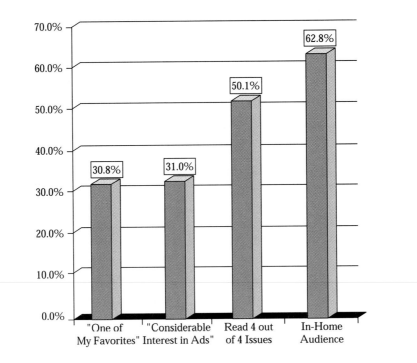

Figure A.3 *Southern Living* Adult Readers Are Highly Involved

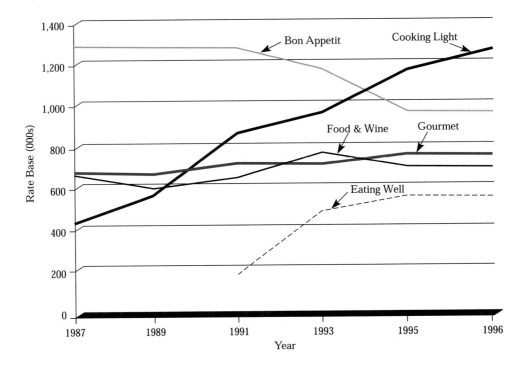

Figure A.4 *Cooking Light* Strengthens Its Position As the Rate Base Leader among Food Magazines

The magazine ranks number 2 in rate base among "health magazines" (e.g., *Prevention, Health, American Health*) and is gaining on the number 1 magazine in this area.

Cooking Light's readers rank number 1 in reader involvement: 47.4% cut out or used recipes; 52.7% "took any action"; 53.8% "read 4 of 4 issues"; and 32.9% indicated a considerable interest in advertising. (See Figure A.5.)

Research demonstrates that the typical reader enjoys cooking and owns time-saving kitchen appliances such as bread machines.

97.5% of readers ordered by mail in the previous year. Almost 100% of the readers placed a mail order for some kind of food/cooking product.

A start-up company, similar to *Nature's Oven* that sells cake and muffin mixes has experienced great success (500 calls a week) with their advertising in this magazine.

What the kiosk location at the Galleria has to offer us as an advertising medium:

The Galleria is visited by more than 11 million shoppers each year.

The average household income of the area in which the mall is located is $65,000.

The Galleria is flanked by the only Four Star, Four Diamond Preferred Hotel in Alabama and a 17-story "Class A" office tower.

Rental (including payment plans) terms are flexible to cater to entrepreneurs.

Merchandising consultants create a merchandise layout so that the best possible visual presentation is made, thereby offering opportunities for increased sales.

Merchandise is secured after hours in such a way that it is not necessary to remerchandise each day.

DISTRIBUTION

Orders will be shipped by U.P.S. This method offers the most economical and speedy service for the customer. Also, a large U.P.S. shipping center is located near the business location.

PACKAGING

Our packaging is:
- informative from a nutritional and standpoint
- informative and detailed as regards how to prepare, serve, and vary the recipe

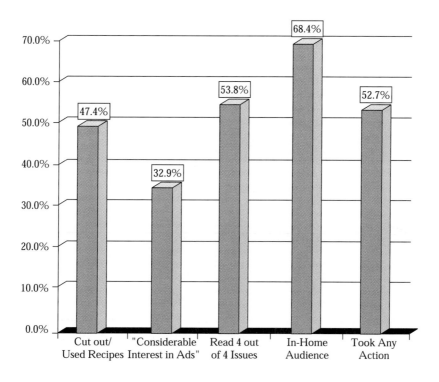

Figure A.5 *Cooking Light* Female Adult Readers Are Highly Involved

Marketing *(continued)*

- key to promoting a belief in the quality of the product, and it inspires confidence in the truth of our claims regarding nutrition, quality, and the ease of preparation

- a vehicle for sharing a little about *Nature's Oven* with the consumer
- attractive

Competitor Analysis

EXISTING COMPETITORS

Walnut Acres, Williams-Sonoma, King Arthur Flour, Wanda's Breads, and The Gluten Free Pantry are the main mail-order sources for bread mixes of the sort *Nature's Oven* will be selling. Grocery stores and cooking stores sell bread mixes as well.

Our potential customers buy from grocery and cooking stores for convenience. Also, when purchasing other items from a mail-order catalog, it is convenient to purchase a few bread mixes. *Nature's Oven* will offer convenience to our customers as indicated in the business strategy section. A key component of our strategy is our service to automatically ship on a monthly basis those mixes designated by our customers. Such service is matched only by Walnut Acres. Yet, Walnut Acres does not match our variety; and their mixes do not come with the detailed preparation instructions as ours do, which is a turn-off to novice bakers. Also, their target customer base is largely restricted to those interested in organic foods. Although we do offer organic mixes, our target market is more wide-ranging than theirs.

In addition to the convenience factor mentioned above, Williams-Sonoma has the benefit of a top-notch reputation, as does King Arthur Flour. Also, they offer more specialty mixes than other sources do. We will certainly meet and surpass their offering of specialty mixes.

Although we desire a reputation for quality, as Williams-Sonoma and King Arthur already enjoy, we realize that we cannot initially compete with their established reputation. We will begin to build our reputation by advertising in only reputable magazines of the highest quality such as *Southern Living* and *Cooking Light*.

Only Wanda's has the level of variety we will offer. Yet their provision for convenience is lacking: they require a minimum purchase of a dozen mixes. We have no such requirement and offer the same level of variety. Wanda's does not focus on the mail-order component of their business; the majority of their business is wholesaling mixes to grocery stores.

In the case of The Gluten Free Pantry, customers buy from them due to special needs for gluten-free products. We will not attempt to offer such products and, therefore, do not seek to compete on this basis.

POTENTIAL COMPETITORS

The main potential for competition is if Wanda's or King Arthur Flour chooses to focus more on the Southeastern market. Their marketing strategy, according to industry research, does not suggest their entering that market in the near future. Even if they do, we are prepared to compete with them as indicated above.

Financials

Assets

Cash	$1,500.00
Inventory	3,387.60
Prepaid Expenses	
(P.O. Box)	120.00
Total Assets	**$5,007.60**

Liabilities and Owner's Equity Liabilities

Accounts Payable	$3,866.40
Total Liabilities	**$3,866.40**

Owner's Equity

Melissa Boyett, Capital	$1,141.20
Total Liabilities and Stockholder's Equity	**$5,007.60**

Figure A.6 Nature's Oven Balance Sheet, December, XXXX

Inventory
Initial order

Quantity	Price	Total
504	$2.15	$1,083.60
576	$2.50	$1,440.00
288	$3.00	$864.00

Accounts Receivable
No orders have yet been taken.

Prepaid Expenses
P.O. box costs $10 per month. The contract is for 1 year, payable at the beginning of the contract.

Accounts Payable

Inventory (as computed above):	$3,387.60
Freight ($105 per 300 lbs):	1,386 mixes @ 1 lb. ea/300 lbs
	= 4.56 × $105 = $487.80
Total	$3,866.40

Figure A.7 Supporting Computations for the Balance Sheet

Net Sales Revenue	$109,890.11
Cost of Goods Sold	57,802.20
Gross Profit Margin	52,087.91
Operating Expenses	41,318.68
Net Profit	$10,000.00

Supporting Figures and Computations

Net Sales Revenue

Desired Net Profit:	$10,000/
RMA % = 9.1%	0.091
	$109,890.11

Gross Profit Margin

Net Sales Revenue	$109,890.11
RMA % = 47.4%	× 0.474
	$52,087.91

Operating Expenses

Net Sales Revenue	$109,890.11
RMA % = 37.6%	× 0.376
	$41,318.68

Figure A.8 Nature's Oven Projected Income Statement (for year ended December 31, XXXX)

ASSUMPTIONS

Desired minimum cash balance $1,000.00

   Credit sales:

Only the corporate gift-giving sales are made on credit. It is reasonable to estimate that, as specified under the terms in the contract, 60% of the bill will be collected within the month the contract is executed. The remaining 40% will be collected in the following month.

SALES FORECAST:

	Pessimistic (45% less)	Most Likely	Optimistic (35% higher)
Jan–Sept.	3,000.00	$5,555.00	$7,500.00
October	5,225.00	9,500.00	12,800.00
November	7,150.00	13,000.00	17,550.00
December	15,125.00	27,500.00	37,125.00

Orders (at min. level) from supplier each month:
Avg. cost (to customer) of one mix is approx $5.
The required min. order from the supplier is 1,386 mixes.

	Monthly Sales	Avg cost	Units sold	Min. order	No. of orders each month
Jan–Sept	$5,555.00	$5.00	1,111	1,368	1
Oct	$9,500.00	$5.00	1,900	1,368	2
Nov	$13,000.00	$5.00	2,600	1,368	2
Dec	$27,500.00	$5.00	5,500	1,368	4

Approximate cost of one minimum level order:

Quantity	Cost	No. of flavors @ this cost	Total
72	$2.15	7	$1,083.60
72	$2.50	8	1,440.00
72	$3.00	4	864.00
			$3,387.60

We estimate that 500 orders will be shipped by mail per month.
This number was adjusted down by 45% for the pessimistic forecast and up by 50% for the optimistic.

This is based on the experience of other similar businesses that placed an ad in *Southern Living* and *Cooking Light*. Their experience suggests that we can expect 1000 inquiries per week as a result of these ads. We estimate that, of those inquiries, 10%–15% will result in sales. Traditionally, a 2% response rate on a direct mail solicitation is considered good. However, it is reasonable, based on research on mail-order response rates, that this percentage will be much higher in this case since the customers are the ones actually initiating the request for the direct mail piece.

We estimate that 12,000 catalogs will be needed each month.
This estimate was adjusted down by 45% for the pessimistic forecast and up by 50% for the optimistic.

This is based on the estimate of 1000 inquiries per week resulting from the ads in *Southern Living* and *Cooking Light*. The remaining 8000 catalogs will be made available at the kiosk. We made this estimate high in case of a higher-than-expected interest from the magazine ads.

Our mailing costs are based on mailing 2500 catalogs per month.
This estimate was adjusted down by 45% for the pessimistic forecast and up by 50% for the optimistic.

Experience of other businesses similar to ours indicates that approximately 20% of those responding to the magazine ads will request a catalog be sent to them. The other 80% will simply request information over the phone and choose to purchase (or to not purchase) based on that. Since mailing costs are so high, we are adding a generous cushion onto this estimate so as to avoid a cash crisis.

Figure A.9 Nature's Oven Cash Budget

ASSUMPTIONS

Nature's Oven pays all accounts payable within 30 days, in accordance with our suppliers' terms

Expenses are as follows:		
Business license		$55 monthly fee
P.O. Box		$120
(annual fee payable at beg. of yr.)		
Catalog	(12,000/mo.)	$.02 per piece
Mailing	(2500 mailed p/mo.)	$.32 per piece
Kiosk	Annual fee	$900, payable in equal monthly install.
	Variable fee	2% of net sales revenue
Order-taking service		
	Initial fee:	$750
	Monthly fee:	$75
	Cost per phone call:	$.35 (4500 calls/month)
Advertising	Cooking Light ad:	$185 per issue } 10% discount for reprints
	South. Living ad:	$185 per issue }
Credit Card equip.		$15 per month
Salaries	Part-time worker	$450 per month
	(Owner and Consultant will take a salary as allowed by the growing success of the business.)	
Average cost of product (includes cost of pkg.)		
	mixes in $4.25 category	$2.15/mix
	mixes in $5.00 category	$2.50/mix
	mixes in $6.00 category	$3.00/mix
Freight		$95 per 300 lbs
(paid by supplier)		(1 box of mix = 1 lb)
Avg S/H cost		$4.25 per order

It is assumed the increase in sales in October, November, and December are due to corporate gift giving and an increase in kiosk sales. We expect mail-order sales to remain relatively constant.

Figure A.9 Nature's Oven Cash Budget (*continued*)

Table A.1 Nature's Oven Cash Budget Based on Most Likely Sales Forecast

	January	February	March	April	May	June	July	August	September	October	November	December
Sales	$ 5,555.00	$ 5,555.00	$ 5,555.00	$ 5,555.00	$ 5,555.00	$ 5,555.00	$ 5,555.00	$ 5,555.00	$ 5,555.00	$ 9,500.00	$ 13,000.00	$ 27,500.00
Credit sales	0	0	0	0	0	0	0	0	0	0	4,550.00	17,875.00
Cash Receipts												
Cash sales	$ 5,555.00	$ 5,555.00	$ 5,555.00	$ 5,555.00	$ 5,555.00	$ 5,555.00	$ 5,555.00	$ 5,555.00	$ 5,555.00	$ 9,500.00	$ 8,450.00	$ 9,625.00
Shipping & handling	$ 3,475.00	$ 3,475.00	$ 3,475.00	$ 3,475.00	$ 3,475.00	$ 3,475.00	$ 3,475.00	$ 3,475.00	$ 3,475.00	$ 3,475.00	$ 3,475.00	$ 3,475.00
Credit sales:												
60% within month of sale	0	0	0	0	0	0	0	0	0	0	2,730.00	10,725.00
40% in following month	0	0	0	0	0	0	0	0	0	0	0	1,820.00
Total Cash Receipts	$9,030.00	$9,030.00	$9,030.00	$9,030.00	$9,030.00	$9,030.00	$9,030.00	$9,030.00	$9,030.00	$12,975.00	$14,655.00	$25,645.00
Cash Disbursements												
Business license	$ 55.00	$ 55.00	$ 55.00	$ 55.00	$ 55.00	$ 55.00	$ 55.00	$ 55.00	$ 55.00	$ 55.00	$ 55.00	$ 55.00
P.O. Box	120.00											
Catalogs	240.00	240.00	240.00	240.00	240.00	240.00	240.00	240.00	240.00	240.00	240.00	240.00
Mailing	800.00	800.00	800.00	800.00	800.00	800.00	800.00	800.00	800.00	800.00	800.00	800.00
Shipping & handling	2,125.00	2,125.00	2,125.00	2,125.00	2,125.00	2,125.00	2,125.00	2,125.00	2,125.00	2,125.00	2,125.00	2,125.00
Kiosk annual fee	75.00	75.00	75.00	75.00	75.00	75.00	75.00	75.00	75.00	75.00	75.00	75.00
Kiosk variable fee	111.10	111.10	111.10	111.10	111.10	111.10	111.10	111.10	111.10	190.00	260.00	550.00
Order-taking service:												
Initial fee	550.00											
Monthly fee	75.00	75.00	75.00	75.00	75.00	75.00	75.00	75.00	75.00	75.00	75.00	75.00
Variable costs of calls	1,575.00	1,575.00	1,575.00	1,575.00	1,575.00	1,575.00	1,575.00	1,575.00	1,575.00	1,575.00	1,575.00	1,575.00
Advertising:												
Cooking Light	185.00	166.50		166.50		166.50		166.50	166.50	166.50	166.50	166.50
Southern Living	185.00	166.50		166.50		166.50		166.50	166.50	166.50	166.50	
Credit card equip.	15.00	15.00	15.00	15.00	15.00	15.00	15.00	15.00	15.00	15.00	15.00	15.00
Salaries	450.00	450.00	450.00	450.00	450.00	450.00	450.00	450.00	450.00	450.00	450.00	450.00
Purchases	3,387.60	3,387.60	3,387.60	3,387.60	3,387.60	3,387.60	3,387.60	3,387.60	3,387.60	6,775.20	6,775.20	13,550.40
Total Cash Disb:	$9,948.70	$9,241.70	$8,908.70	$9,241.70	$8,908.70	$9,241.70	$8,908.70	$9,241.70	$9,241.70	$12,708.20	$12,778.20	$19,676.90
End-of-Month Balance												
Beginning Cash	$ 1,500.00	$ 1,000.00	$ 1,000.00	$ 1,121.30	$ 1,000.00	$ 1,121.30	$ 1,000.00	$ 1,121.30	$ 1,000.00	$ 1,000.00	$ 1,266.80	$ 3,143.60
Cash Receipts	$ 9,030.00	$ 9,030.00	$ 9,030.00	$ 9,030.00	$ 9,030.00	$ 9,030.00	$ 9,030.00	$ 9,030.00	$ 9,030.00	$ 12,975.00	$ 14,655.00	$ 25,645.00
Cash Disbursements	9,948.70	9,241.70	8,908.70	9,241.70	8,908.70	9,241.70	8,908.70	9,241.70	9,241.70	12,708.20	12,778.20	19,676.90
Ending Cash	$ 581.30	$ 788.30	$ 1,121.30	$ 909.60	$ 1,121.30	$ 909.60	$ 1,121.30	$ 909.60	$ 788.30	$ 1,266.80	$ 3,143.60	$ 9,111.70
Addt'l Cash	418.70	211.70	0	90.40	0	90.40	0	90.40	211.70	0	0	0
Cash After Borrowing	$1,000.00	$1,000.00	$1,121.30	$1,000.00	$1,121.30	$1,000.00	$1,121.30	$1,000.00	$1,000.00	$ 1,266.80	$ 3,143.60	$ 9,111.70

Table A.2 Nature's Oven Cash Budget, Based on Optimistic Sales Forecast

	January	February	March	April	May	June	July	August	September	October	November	December
Sales	$ 7,500.00	$ 7,500.00	$ 7,500.00	$ 7,500.00	$ 7,500.00	$ 7,500.00	$ 7,500.00	$ 7,500.00	$ 7,500.00	$ 13,500.00	$ 15,500.00	$ 35,500.00
Credit sales	0	0	0	0	0	0	0	0	0	0	5,425.00	23,075.00
Cash Receipts												
Cash sales	$ 7,500.00	$ 7,500.00	$ 7,500.00	$ 7,500.00	$ 7,500.00	$ 7,500.00	$ 7,500.00	$ 7,500.00	$ 7,500.00	$ 13,500.00	$ 10,075.00	$ 12,425.00
Shipping & handling	$ 5,212.50	$ 5,212.50	$ 5,212.50	$ 5,212.50	$ 5,212.50	$ 5,212.50	$ 5,212.50	$ 5,212.50	$ 5,212.50	$ 5,212.50	$ 5,212.50	$ 5,212.50
Credit sales:												
60% within month of sale	0	0	0	0	0	0	0	0	0	0	3255	13845
40% in following month	0	0	0	0	0	0	0	0	0	0	0	2170
Total Cash Receipts	$12,712.50	$12,712.50	$12,712.50	$12,712.50	$12,712.50	$12,712.50	$12,712.50	$12,712.50	$12,712.50	$18,712.50	$18,542.50	$33,652.50
Cash Disbursements												
Business license	$ 55.00	55.00	55.00	55.00	55.00	$ 55.00	55.00	55.00	55.00	55.00	55.00	$ 55.00
P.O. Box	120.00											
Catalogs	360.00	360.00	360.00	360.00	360.00	360.00	360.00	360.00	360.00	360.00	360.00	360.00
Mailing	1,080.00	1,080.00	1,080.00	1,080.00	1,080.00	1,080.00	1,080.00	1,080.00	1,080.00	1,080.00	1,080.00	1,080.00
Shipping & handling	3,187.50	3,187.50	3,187.50	3,187.50	3,187.50	3,187.50	3,187.50	3,187.50	3,187.50	3,187.50	3,187.50	3,187.50
Kiosk annual fee	75.00	75.00	75.00	75.00	75.00	75.00	75.00	75.00	75.00	75.00	75.00	75.00
Kiosk variable fee	150.00	150.00	150.00	150.00	150.00	150.00	150.00	150.00	150.00	270.00	310.00	710.00
Order-taking service:												
Initial fee	550.00											
Monthly fee	75.00	75.00	75.00	75.00	75.00	75.00	75.00	75.00	75.00	75.00	75.00	75.00
Variable cost of calls	2,362.50	2,362.50	2,362.50	2,362.50	2,362.50	2,362.50	2,362.50	2,362.50	2,362.50	2,362.50	2,362.50	2,362.50
Advertising:												
Cooking Light	185.00	166.50	166.50	166.50	166.50	166.50		166.50	166.50	166.50	166.50	166.50
Southern Living	185.00	166.50	166.50	166.50	166.50	166.50	166.50	166.50	166.50	166.50	166.50	166.50
Credit card equip.	15.00	15.00	15.00	15.00	15.00	15.00	15.00	15.00	15.00	15.00	15.00	15.00
Salaries	450.00	450.00	450.00	450.00	450.00	450.00	450.00	450.00	450.00	450.00	450.00	450.00
Purchases	6,775.20	3,387.60	6,775.20	3,387.60	6,775.20	3,387.60	6,775.20	3,387.60	3,387.60	6,775.20	6,775.20	13,550.40
Total Cash Disb:	$15,625.20	$11,530.60	$14,585.20	$11,530.60	$14,585.20	$11,530.60	$14,585.20	$11,530.60	$11,530.60	$15,038.20	$15,078.20	$22,086.90
End-of-Month Balance												
Beginning Cash	$ 1,500.00	$ 1000.00	$ 2,181.90	$ 1,000.00	$ 2,181.90	$ 1,000.00	$ 2,181.90	$ 1,000.00	$ 2,181.90	$ 3,363.80	$ 7,038.10	$ 10,502.40
Cash Receipts	$12,712.50	$12,712.50	$12,712.50	$12,712.50	$12,712.50	$12,712.50	$12,712.50	$12,712.50	$12,712.50	$18,712.50	$18,542.50	$33,652.50
Cash Disbursements	15,625.20	11,530.60	14,585.20	11,530.60	14,585.20	11,530.60	14,585.20	11,530.60	11,530.60	15,038.20	15,078.20	22,086.90
Ending Cash	$ (1,412.70)	$ 2,181.90	$ 309.20	$ 2,181.90	$ 309.20	$ 2,181.90	$ 309.20	$ 2,181.90	$ 3,363.80	$ 7,038.10	$ 10,502.40	$ 22,068.00
Borrowing	2,412.7	0	691	0	691	0	691	0	0	0	0	0
Cash After Borrowing	$ 1,000	$ 2,182	$ 1,000	$ 2,182	$ 1,000	$ 2,182	$ 1,000	$ 2,182	$ 3,364	$ 7,038	$ 10,502	$ 22,068

Table A.3 Nature's Oven Cash Budget, Based on Pessimistic Sales Forecast

	January	February	March	April	May	June	July	August	September	October	November	December
Sales	$ 3,000.00	$ 3,000.00	$ 3,000.00	$ 3,000.00	$ 3,000.00	$ 3,000.00	$ 3,000.00	$ 3,000.00	$ 3,000.00	$ 3,000.00	$ 3,000.00	$ 3,000.00
Credit sales	0	0	0	0	0	0	0	0	0	0	1,050.00	1,950.00
Cash Receipts												
Cash sales	$ 3,000.00	$ 3,000.00	$ 3,000.00	$ 3,000.00	$ 3,000.00	$ 3,000.00	$ 3,000.00	$ 3,000.00	$ 3,000.00	$ 3,000.00	$ 1,950.00	$ 1,050.00
Shipping & handling	$ 1,911.25	$ 1,911.25	$ 1,911.25	$ 1,911.25	$ 1,911.25	$ 1,911.25	$ 1,911.25	$ 1,911.25	$ 1,911.25	$ 1,911.25	$ 1,911.25	$ 1,911.25
Credit sales:												
60% within month of sale	0	0	0	0	0	0	0	0	0	0	630	1170
40% in following month	0	0	0	0	0	0	0	0	0	0	0	420
Total Cash Receipts	$ 4,911.25	$ 4,911.25	$ 4,911.25	$ 4,911.25	$ 4,911.25	$ 4,911.25	$ 4,911.25	$ 4,911.25	$ 4,911.25	$ 4,911.25	$ 4,491.25	$ 4,551.25
Cash Disbursements												
Business license	$ 55.00	55.00	55.00	55.00	55.00	55.00	55.00	55.00	55.00	55.00	55.00	55.00
P.O. Box	120.00											
Catalogs	132.00	132.00	132.00	132.00	132.00	132.00	132.00	132.00	132.00	132.00	132.00	132.00
Mailing	440.00	440.00	440.00	440.00	440.00	440.00	440.00	440.00	440.00	440.00	440.00	440.00
Shipping & handling	1,168.75	1,168.75	1,168.75	1,168.75	1,168.75	1,168.75	1,168.75	1,168.75	1,168.75	1,168.75	1,168.75	1,168.75
Kiosk annual fee	75.00	75.00	75.00	75.00	75.00	75.00	75.00	75.00	75.00	75.00	75.00	75.00
Kiosk variable fee	60.00	60.00	60.00	60.00	60.00	60.00	60.00	60.00	60.00	60.00	60.00	60.00
Order-taking service:												
Initial fee	550.00											
Monthly fee	75.00	75.00	75.00	75.00	75.00	75.00	75.00	75.00	75.00	75.00	75.00	75.00
Variable cost of calls	866.25	866.25	866.25	866.25	866.25	866.25	866.25	866.25	866.25	866.25	866.25	866.25
Advertising:												
Cooking Light	185.00	166.50		166.50		166.50		166.50	166.50	166.50	166.50	166.50
Southern Living	185.00	166.50		166.50		166.50		166.50	166.50	166.50	166.50	
Credit card equip.	15.00	15.00	15.00	15.00	15.00	15.00	15.00	15.00	15.00	15.00	15.00	15.00
Salaries	450.00	450.00	450.00	450.00	450.00	450.00	450.00	450.00	450.00	450.00	450.00	450.00
Purchases	3,387.60	0.00	3,387.60	0.00	3,387.60	0.00	3,387.60	0.00	3,387.60	0.00	3,387.60	6,775.20
Total Cash Disb:	$ 7,764.60	$ 3,670.00	$ 6,724.60	$ 3,670.00	$ 6,724.60	$ 3,670.00	$ 6,724.60	$ 3,670.00	$ 7,057.60	$ 3,670.00	$ 7,057.60	$ 10,278.70
End-of-Month Balance												
Beginning Cash	$ 1,500.00	$ 1,000.00	$ 2,241.25	$ 1,000.00	$ 2,241.25	$ 1,000.00	$ 2,241.25	$ 1,000.00	$ 2,241.25	$ 1,000.00	$ 2,241.25	$ 1,000.00
Cash Receipts	$ 4,911.25	$ 4,911.25	$ 4,911.25	$ 4,911.25	$ 4,911.25	$ 4,911.25	$ 4,911.25	$ 4,911.25	$ 4,911.25	$ 4,911.25	$ 4,491.25	$ 4,551.25
Cash Disbursements	7,764.60	3,670.00	6,724.60	3,670.00	6,724.60	3,670.00	6,724.60	3,670.00	7,057.60	3,670.00	7,057.60	10,278.70
Ending Cash	$ (1,353.35)	$ 2,241.25	$ 427.90	$ 2,241.25	$ 427.90	$ 2,241.25	$ 427.90	$ 2,241.25	$ 94.90	$ 2,241.25	$ (325.10)	$ (4,727.45)
Borrowing	2,353.35	0.00	572.10	0.00	572.10	0.00	572.10	0.00	905.10	0.00	1,325.10	5,727.45
Cash After Borrowing	$ 1,000	$ 2,241	$ 1,000	$ 2,241	$ 1,000	$ 2,241	$ 1,000	$ 2,241	$ 1,000	$ 2,241	$ 1,000	$ 1,000

Table A.4 Nature's Oven Cash Budget, Year 2 (based on 50% increase in sales from most likely forecast in year 1)

	January	February	March	April	May	June	July	August	September	October	November	December
Sales	$ 7,500.00	$ 7,500.00	$ 7,500.00	$ 7,500.00	$ 7,500.00	$ 7,500.00	$ 7,500.00	$ 7,500.00	$ 7,500.00	$ 13,500.00	$ 15,500.00	$ 35,500.00
Credit sales	0	0	0	0	0	0	0	0	0	0	5,425.00	23,075.00
Cash Receipts												
Cash sales	$ 7,500.00	$ 7,500.00	$ 7,500.00	$ 7,500.00	$ 7,500.00	$ 7,500.00	$ 7,500.00	$ 7,500.00	$ 7,500.00	$ 13,500.00	$ 10,075.00	$ 12,425.00
Shipping & handling	$ 5,212.50	$ 5,212.50	$ 5,212.50	$ 5,212.50	$ 5,212.50	$ 5,212.50	$ 5,212.50	$ 5,212.50	$ 5,212.50	$ 5,212.50	$ 5,212.50	$ 5,212.50
Credit sales:												
60% within month of sale	0	0	0	0	0	0	0	0	0	0	3255	13845
40% in following month	0	0	0	0	0	0	0	0	0	0	0	2170
Total Cash Receipts	$12,712.50	$12,712.50	$12,712.50	$12,712.50	$12,712.50	$12,712.50	$12,712.50	$12,712.50	$12,712.50	$18,712.50	$18,542.50	$33,652.50
Cash Disbursements												
Business license	$ 55.00	55.00	55.00	55.00	55.00	55.00	55.00	55.00	55.00	55.00	55.00	$ 55.00
P.O. Box	120.00											
Catalogs	360.00	360.00	360.00	360.00	360.00	360.00	360.00	360.00	360.00	360.00	360.00	360.00
Mailing	1,080.00	1,080.00	1,080.00	1,080.00	1,080.00	1,080.00	1,080.00	1,080.00	1,080.00	1,080.00	1,080.00	1,080.00
Shipping & Handling	3,187.50	3,187.50	3,187.50	3,187.50	3,187.50	3,187.50	3,187.50	3,187.50	3,187.50	3,187.50	3,187.50	3,187.50
Kiosk annual fee	75.00	75.00	75.00	75.00	75.00	75.00	75.00	75.00	75.00	75.00	75.00	75.00
Kiosk variable fee	150.00	150.00	150.00	150.00	150.00	150.00	150.00	150.00	150.00	270.00	310.00	710.00
Order-taking service:												
Initial fee	550.00											
Monthly fee	75.00	75.00	75.00	75.00	75.00	75.00	75.00	75.00	75.00	75.00	75.00	75.00
Variable cost of calls	2,362.50	2,362.50	2,362.50	2,362.50	2,362.50	2,362.50	2,362.50	2,362.50	2,362.50	2,362.50	2,362.50	2,362.50
Advertising:												
Cooking Light	185.00	166.50		166.50		166.50		166.50	166.50	166.50	166.50	
Southern Living	185.00	166.50		166.50		166.50		166.50	166.50	166.50	166.50	166.50
Credit card equip.	15.00	15.00	15.00	15.00	15.00	15.00	15.00	15.00	15.00	15.00	15.00	15.00
Salaries	450.00	450.00	450.00	450.00	450.00	450.00	450.00	450.00	450.00	450.00	450.00	450.00
Purchases	6,775.20	3,387.60	6,775.20	3,387.60	6,775.20	3,387.60	6,775.20	3,387.60	3,387.60	6,775.20	6,775.20	13,550.40
Total Cash Disb:	$15,625.20	$11,530.60	$14,585.20	$11,530.60	$14,585.20	$11,530.60	$14,585.20	$11,530.60	$11,530.60	$15,038.20	$15,078.20	$22,086.90
End-of-Month Balance												
Beginning Cash	$ 1,500.00	$ 1,000.00	$ 2,181.90	$ 1,000.00	$ 2,181.90	$ 1,000.00	$ 2,181.90	$ 1,000.00	$ 2,181.90	$ 3,363.80	$ 7,038.10	$ 10,502.40
Cash Receipts	$ 12,712.50	$ 12,712.50	$ 12,712.50	$ 12,712.50	$ 12,712.50	$ 12,712.50	$ 12,712.50	$ 12,712.50	$ 12,712.50	$ 18,712.50	$ 18,542.50	$ 33,652.50
Cash Disbursements	15,625.20	11,530.60	14,585.20	11,530.60	14,585.20	11,530.60	14,585.20	11,530.60	11,530.60	15,038.20	15,087.20	22,086.90
Ending Cash	$ (1,412.70)	$ 2,181.90	$ 309.20	$ 2,181.90	$ 309.20	$ 2,181.90	$ 309.20	$ 2,181.90	$ 3,363.80	$ 7,038.10	$ 10,502.40	$ 22,068.00
Borrowing	2412.7	0	691	0	691	0	691	0	0	0	0	0
Cash After Borrowing	$ 1,000	$ 2,182	$ 1,000	$ 2,182	$ 1,000	$ 2,182	$ 1,000	$ 2,182	$ 3,364	$ 7,038	$ 10,502	$ 22,068

Table A.5 Nature's Oven Cash Budget, Year 3 (based on 50% increase in sales from most likely forecast in year 2)

	January	February	March	April	May	June	July	August	September	October	November	December
Sales	$ 11,250.00	$ 11,250.00	$ 11,250.00	$ 11,250.00	$ 11,250.00	$ 11,250.00	$ 11,250.00	$ 11,250.00	$ 11,250.00	$ 20,250.00	$ 23,250.00	$ 53,250.00
Credit sales	0	0	0	0	0	0	0	0	0	0	8,137.50	34,612.50
Cash Receipts												
Cash sales	$ 11,250.00	$ 11,250.00	$ 11,250.00	$ 11,250.00	$ 11,250.00	$ 11,250.00	$ 11,250.00	$ 11,250.00	$ 11,250.00	$ 20,250.00	$ 15,112.50	$ 18,637.50
Shipping & handling	$ 7,818.75	$ 7,818.75	$ 7,818.75	$ 7,818.75	$ 7,818.75	$ 7,818.75	$ 7,818.75	$ 7,818.75	$ 7,818.75	$ 7,818.75	$ 7,818.75	$ 7,818.75
Credit sales:												
60% within month of sale	0	0	0	0	0	0	0	0	0	0	4882.5	20767.5
40% in following month	0	0	0	0	0	0	0	0	0	0	0	3255
Total Cash Receipts	$19,068.75	$19,068.75	$19,068.75	$19,068.75	$19,068.75	$19,068.75	$19,068.75	$19,068.75	$19,068.75	$28,068.75	$27,813.75	$50,478.75
Cash Disbursements												
Business license	$ 55.00	55.00	55.00	55.00	55.00	55.00	55.00	55.00	55.00	55.00	55.00	55.00
P.O. Box	120.00											
Catalogs	540.00	540.00	540.00	540.00	540.00	540.00	540.00	540.00	540.00	540.00	540.00	540.00
Mailing	1,620.16	1,620.16	1,620.16	1,620.16	1,620.16	1,620.16	1,620.16	1,620.16	1,620.16	1,620.16	1,620.16	1,620.16
Shipping & handling	4,781.25	4,781.25	4,781.25	4,781.25	4,781.25	4,781.25	4,781.25	4,781.25	4,781.25	4,781.25	4,781.25	4,781.25
Kiosk annual fee	75.00	75.00	75.00	75.00	75.00	75.00	75.00	75.00	75.00	75.00	75.00	75.00
Kiosk variable fee	225.00	225.00	225.00	225.00	225.00	225.00	225.00	225.00	225.00	405.00	465.00	1,065.00
Order-taking service:												
Initial fee	550.00											
Monthly fee	75.00	75.00	75.00	75.00	75.00	75.00	75.00	75.00	75.00	75.00	75.00	75.00
Variable cost of calls	3,543.75	3,543.75	3,543.75	3,543.75	3,543.75	3,543.75	3,543.75	3,543.75	3,543.75	3,543.75	3,543.75	3,543.75
Advertising:												
Cooking Light	185.00	166.50		166.50		166.50		166.50	166.50	166.50	166.50	
Southern Living	185.00	166.50		166.50		166.50		166.50	166.50	166.50	166.50	166.50
Credit card equip.	15.00	15.00	15.00	15.00	15.00	15.00	15.00	15.00	15.00	15.00	15.00	15.00
Salaries	450.00	450.00	450.00	450.00	450.00	450.00	450.00	450.00	450.00	450.00	450.00	450.00
Purchases	10,162.80	6,775.20	6,775.20	6,775.20	6,775.20	6,775.20	6,775.20	6,775.20	6,775.20	6,775.20	6,775.20	16,938.00
Total Cash Disb:	$22,582.96	$18,488.36	$18,155.36	$18,488.36	$18,188.36	$18,488.36	$18,155.36	$18,488.36	$18,488.36	$18,668.36	$18,728.36	$29,324.66
End-of-Month Balance												
Beginning Cash	$ 1,500.00	$ 1,000.00	$ 1,580.39	$ 1,000.00	$ 1,580.39	$ 1,000.00	$ 1,580.39	$ 1,000.00	$ 1,580.39	$ 2,160.78	$ 2,160.78	$ 1,000.00
Cash Receipts	$ 19,068.75	$ 19,068.75	19,068.75	$ 19,068.75	$ 19,068.75	$ 19,068.75	$ 19,068.75	$ 19,068.75	$ 19,068.75	$ 28,068.75	$ 27,813.75	$ 50,478.75
Cash Disbursements	22,582.96	18,488.36	18,155.36	18,488.36	18,155.36	18,488.36	18,155.36	18,488.36	18,488.36	18,668.36	18,728.36	29,324.66
Ending Cash	$ (2,014.21)	$ 1,580.39	$ 2,493.78	$ 1,580.39	$ 2,493.78	$ 1,580.39	$ 2,493.78	$ 1,580.39	$ 2,160.78	$ 11,561.17	$ 20,646.56	$ 41,800.65
Borrowing	3,014.21	0.00	3,493.78	0.00	3,493.78	0.00	3,493.78	0.00	0.00	0.00	0.00	0.00
Cash After Borrowing	$ 1,000	$ 1,580	$ 1,000	$ 1,580	$ 1,000	$ 1,580	$ 1,000	$ 1,580	$ 2,161	$ 11,561	$ 20,647	$ 41,801

Fixed Expenses:

Business license	$ 660.00
P.O. Box	120.00
Kiosk annual fee	900.00
Order service monthly fee	900.00
Advertising	4,440.00
Credit Card equipment	180.00
Salaries	5,400.00
Purchases	54,589.20
Total	$67,189.20

Variable Expenses:

Direct mail pieces	$ 2,880.00
Mailing	9,600.00
Shipping & Handling	25,500.00
Kiosk variable fee	1,333.20
Cost of calls	18,900.00
Total	$58,213.20

Contribution Margin: 42%
Break-Even Sales: $160,801.69

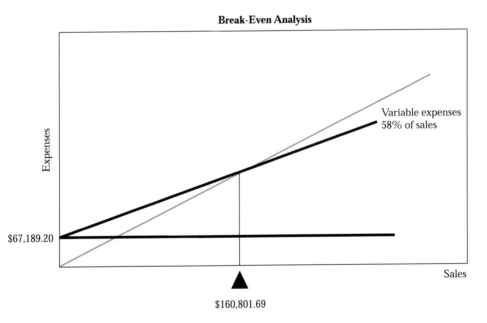

Figure A.10 Break-Even Analysis (based on most likely sales forecast for year 1)

Nature's Oven

To order:
Call us toll free at 1–800–000–0000
or complete this form and return it to
Nature's Oven
P.O. Box xxxx
Birmingham, AL 35235

☐ Gourmet Sampler (choose any 8 flavors & get 10% off the total price of the mixes)
Desired flavors:

1) _____   5) _____
2) _____   6) _____
3) _____   7) _____
4) _____   8) _____

☐ Bread of the Month (have 12 mixes sent to a friend every month of the year) A *gift card* and information on flavors to come is included with the first shipment. Plus, shipping and handling is charged for only one shipment!

Please indicate the month in which you would like your gift to begin: _____

Please indicate the message you would like to appear on your gift card: _____

_____

Quantity	Flavors: $4.25 each	Quantity	Flavors: $5.00 each	Quantity	Seasonal Flavors: $6.00 each
☐	Sourdough	☐	Pesto	☐	Pumpkin spice
☐	Whole wheat	☐	Rye	☐	Cranberry–orange
☐	White	☐	Rosemary-basil	☐	Pumpkin seed
☐	Orange-cinnamon	☐	Dried tomato cheddar	☐	Chocolate cherry
☐	Oatmeal-cinnamon	☐	Onion		
☐	Oatmeal	☐	Ten-grain		
☐	European–style white	☐	Oregano-garlic		
		☐	Cinnamon-raisin		

We are proud that our mixes are
LOW FAT and contain
NO PRESERVATIVES
NO ARTIFICIAL FLAVORS
NO HYDROGENATED OILS
and are made from only
ORGANICALLY PRODUCED GRAINS

Ship to: _____
Address: _____
City: _____ State: _____ Zip: _____
Day phone: _____
Bill to: _____
____ Check/Money Order
____ MasterCard
____ VISA
Card No. _____ Exp. date: _____
Address: _____
City: _____ State: _____ Zip: _____
Signature: _____

Shipping & handling:
6 or fewer mixes: $ 6.95
6–12 mixes: $ 8.30
13–24 mixes: $10.85
more than 24 mixes: $12.85

Order Summary:
___mixes × $4.25=_____
___mixes × $5.00=_____
___mixes × $6.00=_____
Shipping & handling=_____
6% sales tax (for AL residents only)=_____
Total=_____

Figure A.11 Sample Order Form

Index

Beater Wear, 382
Benefit and product or service feature, 286, 287t
Benefits of owning a small business, 8–10
Ben & Jerry's Homemade Inc., 369–70, 401
Bennett, Brian, 628
Benususan, Danny, 389
Ben-Yaacov, Yaacov, 428
Berger, Susan, 742
Berglas, Steven, 704
Berkowitz, George, 704
Berkowitz, Marc, 704
Berkowitz, Roger, 704
Bernhard, Lannie, 411
Bernstein, Craig, 591
Berthold, John, 71
Best-efforts agreement, 435, 437
Better Business Bureau, 141
Bezos, Jeff, 15
BFW, 392
Bicknell Manufacturing Company, 376
Big Brother syndrome, 749
Big Onion Walking Tours, 26
Big-team venture management style, 667
Bildner, James, 665
Birch, David, 24–25
Bitelman, Leon, 370
Bizzell, Robert, 16
Black, Bob, 288–89
Black Cat Computer Wholesale, 91
Black Enterprise, 183
Black Tie Affair, Inc., 471
Blame, avoid laying, 544
Blimpies, 127
Blocher, Bill, 540
Bloom, Shelly, 330
Bloom, Steve, 330
Blue Fish Clothing, 443–44, 753
Blue Note jazz club, 389
Bluestone, Andy, 695
Body language, 651
Bodyslimmers, 775
Bonds, 466–67
Book market, 60–62
Bootstrap financing
    credit cards, 482–84
    factoring accounts receivable, 481–82
    leasing, 482
Bose Corporation, 589
Bottlers, soda, 52
Boutique layout, 523–24, 525f
Boyett, Melissa, A6–A8
Bracken, Josh, 52
Bracken, Michael, 52
Brady, Sheila, 375
Brady Associates, Inc., 375
Brand name appeal, 107
Brannon, Bart, 75
Brauer, Al, 727
Brauer Software, 727
Braun, Tom, 60
Brazil, 377, 392, 399
Breach of contract, 765, 768–69
Break-even analysis
    calculations, 237, 239
    chart, constructing a break-even, 240–42, 241f
    Nature's Oven, A23
    pricing, 322–26
    profit, adding in a, 239
    units, break-even point in, 239–40
    using, 242
Brent, David, 558
Brey Corporation, 514
Bridgewater, Thomas, 514
Bromby's Sport & Ski, Inc., 368
Brooker, Robert, 398
Brophy, Greg, 9
Brounsuzian, Suzette, 90, 335, 504

Brounsuzian, Vic, 90, 335, 504
BRW, 741
Buckle, The, 438
Budget, the cash
    advertising, 366–71
    computerizing your business, 616, 618
    construction and external appearance, 516–17
    defining, 249
    department store, small, 252t–55t
    end-of-month cash balance, 259–60
    forecasting cash disbursements, 259
    minimum cash balance, determining an
        adequate, 256
    Nature's Oven, A18–A23
    preparing, 251, 256–60
    receivables, account, 257–58
    sales forecast, 256, 257t
    technology, 613
Buildings and layout considerations
    Americans with Disabilities Act of 1990 (ADA),
        517–19
    entrances, 517
    interiors, 519, 521
    lights and fixtures, 521–22
    ownership, choosing a form of, 531–32, 534
    signs, 519
    size, 515
Bulk transfers, 148
Bundling, 314–15
Burnham, Thomas, 447–48
Business barriers to international trade, 401
Business format franchising, 103
Business Lenders Inc., 453
Business owner's policy (BOP), 711
Business Software, 621
Business Start-Ups, 119
Butler, Ted, 186
Buybacks/transfers and franchising, 124–25
Buying power, centralized, 109
Buy/sell agreement, 701–2
Bypass trust, 702

C

C. E. Niehoff Company, 465–66
Cahaba Cycles, 368
Caldwell, Patricia, 603
Callaway, Ely, 192
Callaway Golf Company, 192, 774
Camelot Enterprises, 625
Cameras, digital, 638–39
Campbell, Matt, 567
Camp Echo Lake, 700
Canada
    franchising, 125, 389
    malls, 511
    Vancouver Stock Exchange, 449
Candidates, identifying potential acquisition, 140
Candlertown Chairworks, Inc., 479
Capacity and loan applications, 298
Capital, start-up
    chemistry between companies and their funding
        sources, 412
    corporations, 86, 87
    existing business, buying an, 136, 142
    franchising, 112
    importance of, 412–13
    international business, 394, 396
    loan, bank, 298
    ownership, choosing a form of, 71
    partnerships, 79, 80
    plans, business, 292–94
    sole proprietorship, 75
    successful business financing, four secrets for,
        411–12
    types of, 413–15, 415t
    See also Debt financing; Equity financing;
        Financial resources, managing

Capital, working, 230–31, 411
Capitalized earnings approach, 157–58
Capital Sanitary Supply Company, 480
CAPline Program, 477
Capweld, Inc., 189
Carolee Designs, 17–18
Carpenter, Larry, 459
Carpenter Outdoor Advertising, 459
Carrying costs, 548–49, 549t
Cars & Cars, 611
Carson Pirie Scott, 600
Caruso, Vincent, 436
Cash flows, 150, 245
    avoiding the cash crunch, 271–75
    bank loans, 455–56, 455f
    budget, the cash, 249–51, 252t–55t, 256–60,
        257t–58t, 258f
    conclusions, 275
    crisis, cash, 250, 454
    discounts, 454, 557–59, 557f, 558t
    discussion questions, 276
    inventories, 590–91
    managing, 246, 247f–48f, 247t, 248
    payable, accounts, 267–71, 270t
    profits and, differences between, 248–49, 249f
    receivables, account, 260–65, 266t, 267
    statement of, 213–14
    summary, chapter, 276
    theft, employee, 595
    See also Capital, start-up; Financial resources,
        managing
Cashing out, 177t
Cassell, Warren, 172
Castelluccio, Vincent, 482–84
Castle, Tony, 639
Castle Group, 639, 641
Casto, Maryles, 28
Casto Travel, 28–29
Catalog exhibition program, multi-state, 387t
Catamount Pellet Fuel Corporation, 481
Cause marketing, 370–71
Cavallarin, Robert, 396
C corporations. *See* Corporations
CDuctive, 44–45
Census Bureau, U.S., 494, 495, 504
Center for Community Self-Help, 481
Central business district (CBD), 508
Centralized buying power, 109
Centralized management, 94
Certificate of incorporation, 85
Certificate of limited partnership, 83
Certification programs, 546, 564–67
Certified development company (CDC), 477–78
Certified lender program (CLP), 473
Chamber of Commerce, U.S., 567
Chambers, Mel, 544
Champfleury, Pierre de, 441
Change and buying an existing business, 137
Channel of distribution, 203–4, 203f
Chapman, Jay, 625
Character and loan applications, 298, 300, 459
Charles, Joe, 501, 502
Charles Industries, 501, 502
Chartered Life Financial Consultants, 701
Chartered Life Underwriters, 701
Check fraud, 274
Chef's Companion, 365
Chelsea and Scott, 175
Childers, John, 462
Chilon, 724
China
    culture, business, 404
    entrepreneurial growth, 3, 392
    GP66 Chemical Corporation, 394
Chocolates á la Carte, 193
Choice, right to, 751
Chong, Anna, 384

Photo Credits